GROLIER

ENCYCLOPEDIA OF KNOWLEDGE

Grolier Incorporated
Danbury, Connecticut

ISBN 0-7172-5300-7 (complete set)
ISBN 0-7172-5304-X (volume 4)

Printed and manufactured in the United States of America.

This publication is an abridged version of the *Academic American Encyclopedia.*

10 9 8 7 6 5 4 3

Cc

C *C/c,* the 3d letter of the English and other Western alphabets, is derived from the Semitic letter *gimel* and from the Greek *gamma.* In both systems, the letter represented a hard *g,* as in *get,* a voiced palatal stop. In Etruscan, the sign was used for the voiceless stop, *k.* In late Latin, *c* had only the sound of *k.* As different pronunciations developed in languages derived from Latin or that were influenced by it, *c* was given different sounds. In English, it still has the sound of *k* before *a, o,* or *u,* as in *cat*; before a consonant (except *h*), as in *clip*; or when it is in final position, as in *drastic.* Before *e, i,* or *y,* however, it has the sound of *s (cell, cede, cite, cycle).* When *e* or *i* is followed by another vowel, *c* becomes *sh (ocean).* After *n,* especially with a preceding *i* or *e,* it is pronounced *ts* with a weak *t (patience).* Combined with another consonant, *c* follows the same rules, with some exceptions: *cc* is pronounced *k (occult)* or *ks (accident); xc* is *ksk (exclude)* or *ks (excess); ck* has the *k* sound *(rocky). C* followed by *h* is usually recognized as one sound, *ch* (č), as in *chart,* which is also expressed as *tsh,* as in *bench.* In words derived from Greek, however, *ch* becomes *k (chrome)*; the combination *sch* is pronounced *sk (school).* Numerous variations occur in other Latinate languages. In French, Portuguese, and Spanish, for example, a small stroke called a cedilla is added to the *c* (ç); this indicates the pronunciation of *c* as *s* (façade).

Caballé, Montserrat [kah-bahl-yay', mohn-sair-aht'] The Spanish soprano Montserrat Caballé, b. Apr. 12, 1933, is admired for her appearances in the bel canto operas of Donizetti, Bellini, and Rossini. She studied voice in Barcelona and made her opera debut in Basel in 1956 as Mimi in *La Bohème.* Her wide repertoire includes the title roles in *Aïda, Der Rosenkavalier, Norma, Manon Lescaut, Adriana Lecouvreur,* and *Lucrezia Borgia,* in which she made her New York debut in 1965. Caballé is noted for her floating high notes and brilliant coloratura passages. She occasionally performs with her husband, the tenor Bernabé Martí, and frequently sings at the Metropolitan Opera.

cabaret [cab-uh-ray'] Although the exact derivation of the term *cabaret* is obscure, it is generally recognized to be from the French, meaning a tavern or wine cellar where informal entertainment took place. The beginnings of the modern cabaret date from the establishment in Paris in 1881 of the most famous cabaret of all, Le Chat Noir ("The Black Cat").

Originally, the cabaret was a meeting place for artists who could perform for their own entertainment and experiment freely without the pressures of public exposure or critical scrutiny. Le Chat Noir became especially identified with the art of the CHANSON, then experiencing a revival. The first German cabaret was founded in Berlin in January 1901 by Baron Ernst von Wolzogen and named Überbrettl ("Super-plank"), but the most famous pre-Weimar German cabaret was Die Elf Scharfrichter ("Eleven Executioners"), which opened the next year in the Inn of the Golden Hare on Munich's Türkenstrasse. Cabaret was also a prominent feature of East European cultural life in this period. In Polish Kraków (then part of Austria), the Zielony Balonik ("Little Green Balloon") opened in 1905. It was primarily a painters' club, but it won renown for its annual *szopka,* an elaborate puppet show on topical subjects. The first and most famous of all Russian cabarets, the Letuchaya Mysh ("Bat"), was established in Moscow in 1908. The last great European artists' cabaret

Otto Dix's Grosstadt *(1928) captures the underground spirit of the German cabaret, a forum for entertainment, satire, and radical thought. (Galerie de Stadt, Stuttgart.)*

founded before the 1920s was the Cabaret Voltaire in Zürich. It opened in 1916, and under the guidance of its principal contributor, the poet Hugo Ball, became the birthplace of the DADA movement.

cabbage The vegetable cabbage, *Brassica oleracea* var. *capitata*, is grown for its large, dense terminal bud, or head, which consists of many enfolded leaves closely spaced on a short stem. Cabbage and cabbagelike vegetables are grouped as cole crops in the Cruciferae family. The cole crops were derived from wild cabbage that is indigenous to the coastal areas of western Europe and Great Britain. In the United States, most of the commercial cabbage crop originates in Florida, Texas, California, New York, and Wisconsin. It is consumed fresh, cooked, and as a fermented product, sauerkraut.

Cabbage types are grouped according to time required for maturity (early, midseason, or late); head shape (conical, round, or flat); leaf form (smooth or savoyed); or leaf color (predominantly green or red).

Among the many cultivated varieties of cabbage are the common cabbage (left) *and the red cabbage* (right), *a cross-section of which reveals a white, thick core.*

Cabell, James Branch [kab'-uhl] James Branch Cabell, b. Richmond, Va., Apr. 14, 1879, d. May 5, 1958, was an American novelist known for his series of antiromantic romances set in the mythical kingdom of Poictesme. Cabell used these novels to attack modern orthodoxies. His best-known work, *Jurgen* (1919), whose symbolism was persistently sexual, earned him a popularity that faded when the arch, sophisticated style he used passed from fashion. Among the best of his novels are *The Cream of the Jest* (1917), *Figures of Earth* (1921), and *The High Place* (1923).

Cabet, Étienne [kah-bay', ay-tee-en'] Étienne Cabet, b. Jan. 1, 1788, d. Nov. 8, 1856, was a French socialist who founded a utopian community in the United States (see UTOPIAS). In 1834, Cabet was forced to leave France because of his radical politics. In London he was influenced by the utopian ideas of Robert OWEN. Returning to France in 1839, Cabet published *Voyage en Icarie* (1840), a novel depicting an ideal community in which the instruments of production were owned in common. In 1848 he and his followers sailed for America, where they founded a utopian community called Icaria in Illinois. In 1856 a schism arose, and he left with some followers to found a new settlement in St. Louis, Mo., where he died.

Cabeza de Vaca, Álvar Núñez [kah-bay'-thah day vah'-kah, ahl'-var noon-yayth] The Spanish explorer Álvar Núñez Cabeza de Vaca, *c.*1490–*c.*1557, sailed to Florida in 1527–28 with the expedition led by Pánfilo de NARVÁEZ. The expedition struggled through Florida and was later shipwrecked off the coast of present-day Texas. Most of the remaining Spaniards died—either of exposure or at the hands of the Indians. Eventually, however, Cabeza de Vaca and three companions escaped and wandered about the American Southwest, finally encountering Spaniards again in 1536. They told exaggerated stories of their odyssey, from which arose the fable of the Seven Golden Cities of CIBOLA. Cabeza de Vaca's 1542 account of his travels includes the earliest written description of the Great Plains.

cabinet A cabinet is a body of official advisors to a head of state. Cabinet members usually control some executive or administrative operations of the government. The term was originally used to describe a committee of the English Privy Council that gave secret counsel to the king in his cabinet, or study.

The cabinet form of government, also called the parliamentary form, is used by Great Britain, by most Commonwealth members, and by most Western European countries. Executive power is wielded by a group of legislators who are selected to head the various government ministries, or departments, and who form a collective body, or cabinet, under the prime minister. The cabinet is responsible to the legislature.

In the presidential system of government found in the United States and many Third World countries, the cabinet is an executive body separate from the legislature. The president of the United States, with the consent of the Senate, appoints the heads, or secretaries, of the major departments —(in order of establishment) state; treasury; interior; agriculture; justice; commerce; labor; defense; housing and urban development; transportation; energy; education; health and human services; and veterans affairs. These secretaries, together with the vice-president or any other officials the president may designate, form the president's cabinet. They are responsible to the president and, except for the vice-president, subject to removal at the president's will.

The cabinet has been an accepted institution in the United States since the 1790s. Since the time of Andrew Jackson, some presidents have also created, in addition to the formal cabinet, bodies of personal advisors, variously called the KITCHEN CABINET or Brain Trust.

cable A cable is a cord or rope made from strands of fiber or wire, of great tensile strength, used to support a bridge or cable car; to secure a ship at anchor; for towing, hauling, and construction work; or for similar purposes. Transmission cables carry electric power or communications signals.

Supporting and Construction Cable

Supporting or towing cable is called wire rope, because it is made in the same manner as fiber rope and is often used for similar purposes. To make wire rope, a stranding machine unwinds wire from spools and twists together up to 37 separate wires to form a strand. A standard wire rope usually consists of 6 wire strands twisted around a core, which may be another wire strand or, more commonly, a strand of vegetable fiber, such as hemp or jute. Increased flexibility is provided by using strands made of thinner wire or by twisting strands that are themselves composed of thinner strands.

Major wire-rope types include the hoisting ropes used on cranes, dredges, and drilling rigs, which are made of 6 strands of 19 wires each (6 × 19), wound around a fiber core; flattened-strand rope, where the flat-edged strands provide greater flexibility and longer wear; galvanized wire rope, used for rigging and stays aboard ship and in bridge construction; and steel-clad rope, a 6-strand rope with each strand housed in a winding of flat steel strips. Steel-clad rope is used in dredging and other heavy construction work.

Two common ways of twisting, or laying, wire rope are the Lang lay, in which the strands and the wire in each strand are laid in the same direction (A), *and the regular lay, in which the twists are in opposite directions* (B). *Cable construction varies, depending on use, as the cross sections* (C) *show: fiber cores for hauling* (1), *wire cores for bridges* (2), *strands with triangular fiber cores for earth-moving machinery* (3), *and wire-locked coils for cable-car supports* (4).

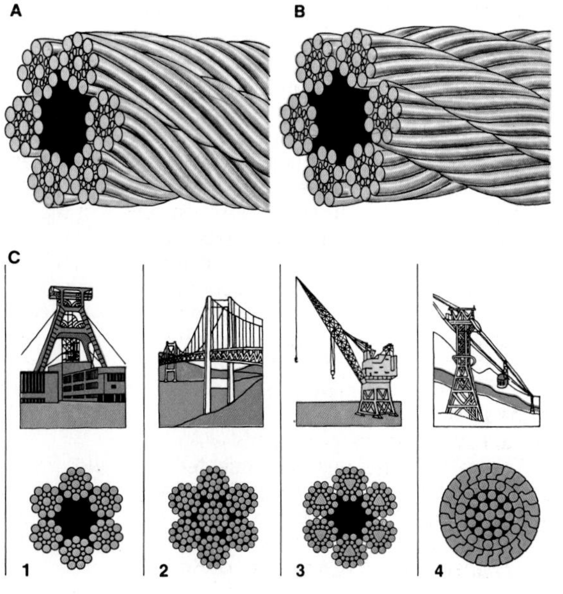

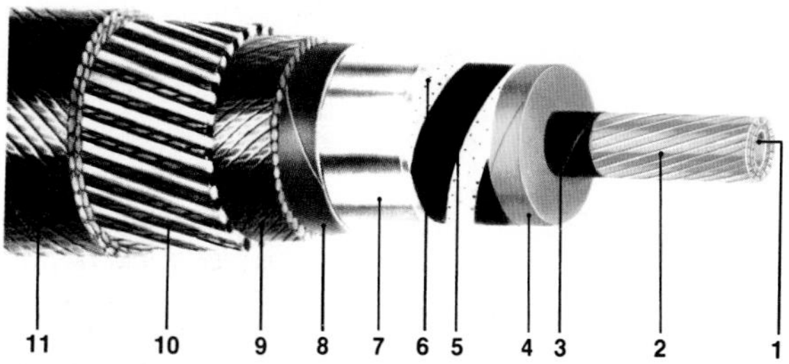

A typical 150,000-volt cable for underground transmission of electricity consists of heat-dissipating oil (1) *filling a hollow core of spirally stranded copper wires* (2); *weakly conductive carbon-impregnated paper tape* (3); *oil-impregnated paper insulation layers* (4); *carbon-impregnated paper tape* (5); *metal tape* (6); *lead sheath* (7); *paper layers* (8), *and jute layers* (9) *impregnated with asphalt; steel wire armor* (10); *and a jute outer covering* (11).

Transmission Cable

Electric Power Transmission. In the insulated cable that transmits electric power, metal wire is used, since metal is an excellent conductor of electricity. Copper alloy is frequently used. Weight is an important factor, because the large amounts of power generated and transmitted by modern power plants necessitate the use of thick cables. Maximum overhead line voltages have been increased from 345,000 volts in the 1950s to 765,000 volts at present. Even higher voltages can be attained, although it is contended that ultrahigh-voltage (UHV) lines are already emitting dangerous radiation.

It is possible that for high-capacity, long-distance lines, direct-current (DC), rather than alternating-current (AC), power will be used in the future. Direct-current lines emit less radiation over long distances, are less expensive, and are more easily brought up to high voltages; however, they require conversion facilities at sending and receiving ends, since both generating plants and receiving devices are designed for alternating current. (See POWER, GENERATION AND TRANSMISSION OF.)

Communications Cable. Communications cable operates at lower voltages and higher frequencies than electric-power cable. An ordinary telephone wire can easily carry signals of limited frequency, and trunk lines are capable of handling thousands of simultaneous conversations. While modern electronics permits multiple conversations to be carried on a single wire, great numbers of wires are often needed because of the high volume of calls. Interference (cross talk) between the circuits then becomes a problem. Other types of information are now also carried over the communications network, including television signals that require higher frequencies than the ordinary telephone wire can carry.

The modern coaxial cable can carry both multiple signals and extremely high frequencies. A single cable consists of a thin copper wire accurately centered by nonconducting plastic spacers inside a copper tube about 7 mm (0.28 in) in diameter. The signal travels in the space formed between the two copper conductors—an arrangement that reduces the resistance of the cable to the passage of high-frequency signals.

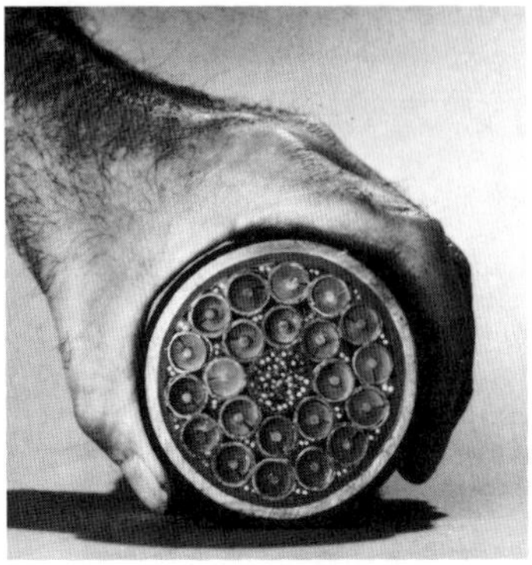

The coaxial cable can handle 1,100 telephone conversations at one time. It consists of a core of standard wire conductors surrounded by 12 coaxial units. Each unit is composed of a single hollow copper tube about 7 mm (0.28 in) in diameter and a thin copper wire surrounded by nonconducting plastic disks.

A typical telephone coaxial cable consists of 8 to 22 coaxial tubes sheathed in metal and plastic. In order to obtain many different voice channels for separate telephone conversations within a tube, a carrier wave (a broadband signal of several megahertz) is divided into separate sections; each of the conversations is funneled into a different section of the carrier wave by a device called a MULTIPLEXER.

The development of FIBER OPTICS has led to the use of fiber cables that carry digital signals instead of the analog signals of copper cables. The hair-thin glass fibers transmit encoded laser light and can handle huge numbers of messages simultaneously. Telephone systems in particular have made broad use of fiber-optic cables.

See also: Atlantic cable; CABLE TV; TELEGRAPH; TELEPHONE.

Cable, George Washington George Washington Cable, b. New Orleans, La., Oct. 12, 1844, d. Jan. 31, 1925, an exponent of the local-color movement in American literature, is best known for his works depicting 19th-century New Orleans and Louisiana society. After appearing in periodicals, his sketches were collected under the title *Old Creole Days* (1879). His most important novels are *The Grandissimes* (1880) and *Dr. Sevier* (1885). Both in his fiction and in such nonfiction as *The Silent South* (1885) and *The Negro Question* (1888), Cable showed his concern with the position of the Southern black following Reconstruction.

cable car A cable car is, simply, a vehicle pulled by a cable. Cable cars are used when the grade is steep or when there are obstructions to be traversed such as canyons or rivers.

Aerial cable cars are suspended from overhead cables supported by towers; the system is called a cableway or aerial tramway. A rail cable car runs on supporting rails and is pulled by a cable. Any cable railroad that traverses a steep grade may be called a funicular (railroad); more specifically, a funicular has two cars connected to opposite ends of a cable, with the cable looped around and powered by a pulley system at the top of the grade.

cable TV Cable TV is a system for delivering television signals by means of coaxial cable. For an installation charge and a monthly fee, cable TV viewers receive a clear picture of the conventional channels and can watch up to several dozen additional channels. By 1990 the cable audience comprised more than half of all television-receiving households.

Originating in 1949 as a way of providing good reception to areas where the conventional TV signal was weak, cable spread quickly among rural municipalities, each negotiating a franchise agreement with a cable operator. Operators usually pay a small amount per subscriber to each of the pay-cable channels they carry. Industry growth burgeoned when the Cable Act of 1984 removed local control over cable rates and made it difficult for municipal franchises to be revoked. Today, most cable companies have no competition within their areas and function as monopolies.

The use of COMMUNICATIONS SATELLITES to transmit TV signals has greatly increased the range of cable offerings. Several specialized channels transmit programs via satellite, including the all-news Cable News Network (CNN); Music Television (MTV), which shows rock-music videos; and the Sports Programming Network (ESPN), an all-sports channel. Pay-cable program suppliers such as Home Box Office (HBO) and Showtime also transmit via satellite, offering recent movies and other entertainments. HBO is a power in the field of cable TV. One of the first cable programmers, it produces many of the programs it shows, runs a videotape distributing firm, and owns Cinemax, another movie channel.

The success of cable TV has transformed the television industry, once almost entirely in the hands of the major broadcasting networks (see RADIO AND TELEVISION BROADCASTING).

See also: TELEVISION TRANSMISSION.

Cabot, John John Cabot, b. Giovanni Caboto, *c.*1451, was a navigator and explorer who crossed the Atlantic in

John Cabot, among the first European explorers after Columbus to reach the North American coast, is thought to have landed on the shores of Newfoundland in 1497.

the service of HENRY VII of England, making possible later English claims to North America. Probably born in Genoa, he became a citizen of Venice before moving to England with his family, including his son Sebastian Cabot. With backing from Bristol merchants, John Cabot sailed from Bristol in May 1497 with 18 or 20 men on the *Matthew*. He landed in North America, probably Newfoundland, on June 24 and may have sailed as far south as Maine or as far north as Labrador.

Returning to England, Cabot, who seems to have thought he had reached the northeast corner of Asia, prepared a second voyage to sail beyond his earlier landing point to Japan. He set out in May 1498 with 5 ships and about 200 men. Cabot was lost at sea in 1498, but no clear records of this second voyage have survived.

Cabot, Sebastian Sebastian Cabot, b. Venice, Italy, *c.*1482, d. 1557, was a cartographer, navigator, and explorer. He was the son of John Cabot, with whom he may have sailed in 1497. About 1508 he apparently sailed west—possibly reaching Hudson Bay—for HENRY VII of England. He was the English king's cartographer but in 1512 transferred his allegiance to Spain. In 1526 he led an expedition that intended to follow Ferdinand MAGELLAN's route, but it reached only the Rio de la Plata region. When he returned to Spain in 1530, he was prosecuted. In 1548, Cabot again went to England, where he joined the Muscovy Company as governor in 1553 and aided Sir Hugh Willoughby and Richard CHANCELLOR in their unsuccessful search for the NORTHEAST PASSAGE. Cabot died in London.

Cabral, Pedro Álvares [kuh-brahl', ped-ru uhl-vah-ruhsh] Pedro Álvares Cabral, b. *c.*1468, d. 1520, was a Portuguese explorer who claimed Brazil for Portugal. In 1500, King MANUEL I of Portugal gave him command of a large fleet and instructed him to duplicate the feat of Vasco da GAMA, who had sailed around the Cape of Good Hope to India. Cabral, however, sailed too far west and landed on the coast of Brazil on Apr. 22, 1500. He took possession of the area in the name of the king of Portugal and called it the Land of the True Cross.

From Brazil, Cabral resumed his journey east. He rounded the Cape of Good Hope, reaching Madagascar, Mozambique, and eventually India. After establishing a trading factory at Cochin, on the Indian coast, he returned to Lisbon.

Cabrillo, Juan Rodríguez [kah-breel'-yoh, hwahn rohd-ree'-gayth] Juan Cabrillo, d. Jan. 3, 1543, was a Portuguese explorer employed by Spain. He took part in the Spanish conquest of Mexico and Guatemala and in 1540 joined the exploring voyage of Pedro de ALVARADO up the west coast of Mexico. Assuming command when Alvarado died, he sailed north from Navidad in 1542 and discovered San Diego Bay, Santa Catalina Island, Point Reyes, and Monterey Bay.

Frances Xavier Cabrini was named a saint in 1946, thus becoming the first U.S. citizen to be canonized. Born in Italy, she moved to the United States in 1889 to work among poverty-stricken immigrants. She is known as "the saint of the immigrants" for her service to the poor and uprooted.

Cabrini, Saint Frances Xavier Frances Xavier Cabrini, b. Sant' Angelo Lodigiano, Italy, July 15, 1850, d. Dec. 22, 1917, was the first citizen of the United States to be canonized. After founding (1880) the Missionary Sisters of the Sacred Heart, she and a small group of sisters left Italy to work among Italian immigrants in America.

In 1909, Mother Cabrini, as she was called, became a naturalized American citizen. She also established strong bases in Chile and Argentina and founded more than 60 convents. She was canonized in 1946. Feast day: Nov. 13.

cacao [kah-kah'-oh] Cacao, *Theobroma cacao*, is a tropical evergreen tree in the family Byttneriaceae. It is

The cacao tree is unusual in bearing its pink-and-yellow flowers and its reddish fruits directly on the branches and trunk.

native to Central and South America and is cultivated extensively for its seed, which is the source of COCOA, CHOCOLATE, and cocoa butter. Cacao is a wide-branched evergreen that grows up to 7.5 m (25 ft) tall and bears seedpods up to 30 cm (1 ft) long and 10 cm (4 in) thick, with a hard leathery shell. Pods contain as many as 40 seeds, or beans, some up to 2.5 cm (1 in) wide.

Several species of *Theobroma* are cultivated in tropical America. *T. cacao*, the principal species used for cocoa, is grown throughout the wet, lowland tropics, especially in Southeast Asia, South America, and West Africa, where the trees are planted under the shade of taller trees. They usually bear fruit 4 years after they have been planted. Workers harvest cacao beans with knives. After extraction from the fruit, the beans are placed in piles, covered with banana leaves, and allowed to ferment; afterward, they are dried to prevent molding. They are then sacked and shipped to chocolate or cocoa manufacturers. Cacao beans were once used as money by the people of Mexico and Central America.

cacomistle [kak'-oh-mis-uhl] Cacomistles, or ring-tailed cats, are two species of night-hunting carnivores that belong to the RACCOON family, in the order Procyonidae. *Bassariscus astutus* lives in the western United States and south to southern Mexico; *B. sumichrasti* is found in tropical forests from southern Mexico to Peru. Cacomistles are 50 to 100 cm (20 to 40 in) in length, half of which consists of a bushy, black-and-white-ringed tail, and weigh up to 1.3 kg (3 lb). Their faces are small, with large, staring eyes and pointed muzzles. They feed on rodents, birds, insects, and fruit.

The North American cacomistle, or ring-tailed cat, is a member of the raccoon family. It prowls for food at night.

cacti and other succulents The cacti are a family of spiny plants (Cactaceae) that have large, leafless, long-living stems of widely varying shapes and sizes, on which are usually borne clusters of spines. The stems of most cacti are succulent, having fleshy tissues that are enlarged because they are filled with water.

The cacti are one of several groups including succulent flowering plants. Succulents other than cacti occur in several families: the spurge family (Euphorbiaceae), the lily family (Liliaceae), and the orpine family (Crussulaceae), among others. Most succulents lack spines, exceptions being the cacti; African spurges, genus *Euphorbia*; and carrion flowers, genus *Stapelia*. Some are stem succulents, like the cacti, African spurges, and carrion flowers. Others have succulent leaves—for instance, the AGAVES, ALOES, and YUCCAS of the Americas; the jade plant, *Crassula argentea*, the ice plant, *Mesembryanthemum crystallinum*, and the kalanchoes of Africa; and the STONECROPS, genus *Sedum*, of worldwide distribution.

Succulence is a characteristic usually found in plants that inhabit dry regions. These plants can survive by storing enough water during rainy times to continue to function during dry periods. They cannot continue to live indefinitely without water, however; once the reservoir within the fleshy stem is empty, the plant will die. The enlarged stem or leaves are filled with water-storage cells and are covered with a wax- or cutin-covered epidermis to reduce water loss by evaporation. Even the roots are able to withstand long exposure to dryness. The root system usually is fibrous, very shallow, and wide-spreading to enable the plant to absorb the small amounts of water that penetrate the soil.

Classification and Occurrence of Cacti

About 90 genera and approximately 2,000 species of cacti exist, 10 percent of which occur within the United States. The family Cactaceae is divided into three subfamilies: the Pereskioideae, the Opuntioideae, and the Cactoideae. The Pereskioideae have persistent large leaves, areoles, or specialized lateral buds, without glochids (barbed bristles), and terminal or stalked flowers. This subfamily, particularly the nonsucculent, leafy genus *Pereskia*, is perhaps the least specialized of the cacti. Because they have remained in the relatively benign tropical climates, these interesting bushes or small trees hardly appear to be cacti and retain many ancestral characteristics. The Opuntioideae have small and short-lived leaves, areoles with glochids, and flowers with floral tubes not extending beyond the ovaries. This group is best represented by the prickly pear and cholla cacti, both of the genus *Opuntia*. The Cactoideae have microscopic leaves, areoles without glochids, and flowers with definite floral tubes or cups extending beyond the ovaries. The greatest variety and number of species are in this group.

Cacti probably originated in the tropics of Central America, but no fossils have been discovered to aid in studying their early history. They migrated northward and southward, undergoing evolutionary adjustments to the ever-increasing dry periods caused by the slow uplift of the Andes in South America and the Rocky Mountain complex in North America. Some small groups became isolated and underwent separate evolutionary changes, resulting in a family of great structural diversity capable of tolerating extensive dry periods. Cacti occur primarily in the Western Hemisphere, from the Peace River in Canada south to Patagonia. Most cacti live in the hot deserts. The genus *Rhipsalis*, one of several cacti that hang from forest trees, grows in tropical America but also is found in equatorial Africa, Madagascar, and Sri Lanka.

Characteristics

One of the distinct characteristics of a cactus is the are-

(Above) *Barrel cacti are ovoid to cylindrical and often grow in dense clumps. Flowers range from yellow to red.*

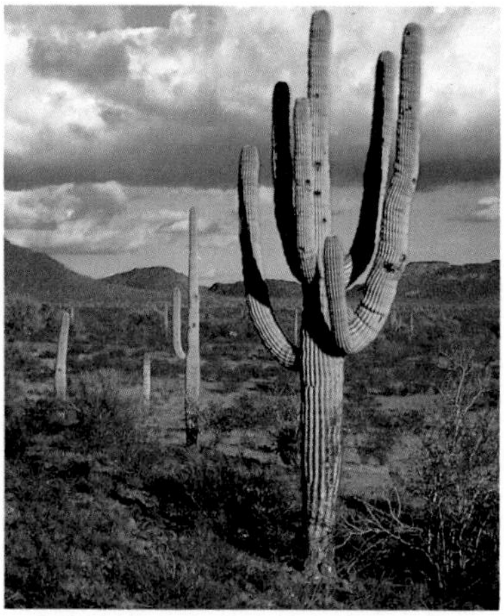

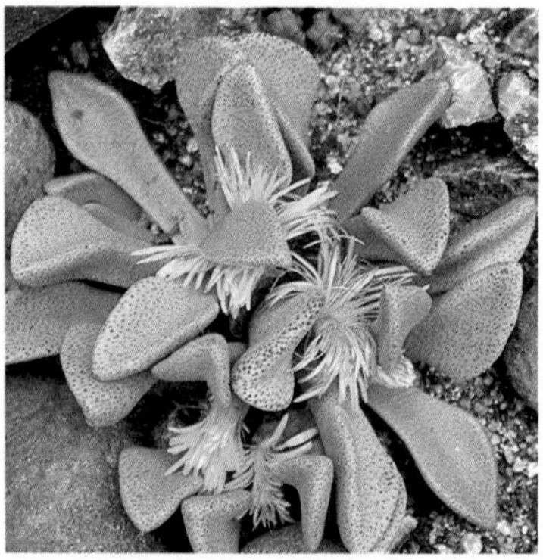

(Above) *One of several stone-mimicry plants is a perennial leaf succulent native to South Africa. The thick leaves are rounded on the underside.*

(Above) *The branched columns of the saguaro cactus characterize many regions of Arizona and northwestern Mexican deserts. The stems, having woody ribs, are used for fuel or building material.*

(Right) *The rattail cactus, native to Mexico and South America, has pink flowers that bloom for several days. It is vinelike and often hangs from trees and even walls.*

(Left) *The strawberry, or hedgehog, cactus grows in dense tufts and is found in northern Mexico, Texas, and New Mexico. It bears scarlet or bright pink flowers and edible fruit.*

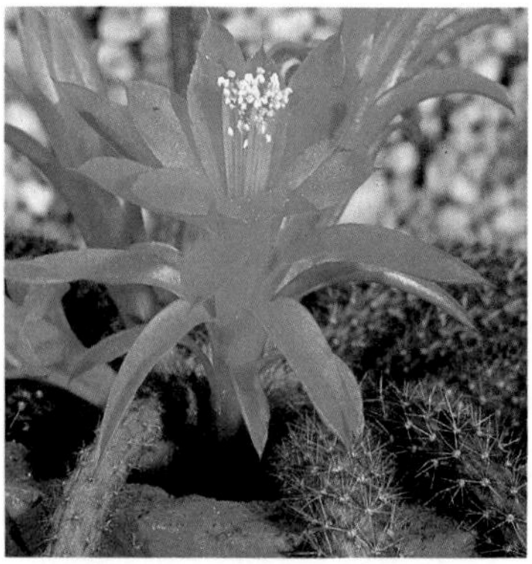

ole from which the spines, leaves, hairs, and flowers arise. The areole is a lateral bud or dwarf shoot growing on a persistent leaf base. Spines and glochids are equivalents of leaves and have been evolutionarily derived from them. Cactus flowers are usually large, single, and with numerous stamens. The flower color varies from white through yellow and red to purple. The sepals and petals are united at their bases to form a floral tube. The ovary is inferior and may be either naked or covered by scales or hairs, or both. Once a cactus has matured, it usually flowers each year. The fruits are either fleshy or dry at maturity, but all contain numerous seeds.

Cacti vary widely in size and shape. Some species are less than 1.5 cm (0.6 in) in diameter and do not rise above ground level. Others, such as the saguaro, *Carnegiea gigantea,* of Arizona, may reach a height of about 18 m (60 ft) and weigh many tons. The trunks or stems of some cacti have a maximum diameter of more than 1 m (3.3 ft). The fleshy stem may be spherical or columnar and either simple or many-branched. In the subfamily Opuntioideae, the stems are typically jointed. The stems in some species may be nearly smooth, whereas in others they have distinct ribs or tubercles formed from the persistent leaf bases. The areoles are located along the ribs or at the ends of the tubercles. Spines vary greatly in length, color, and texture; a few species lack spines. The spines of some species point downward and act as tips to concentrate the light rain or heavy dew into droplets of water, which then fall to the ground as effective moisture. The shallow root system quickly absorbs the available water and conducts it to the stem.

The circumference of a columnar cactus, such as the saguaro, may increase by as much as 20 percent during the rainy season, and a plant 6 m (20 ft) high may store more than 378.5 l (100 gal) of water in a 4-month period. Unlike most plants, cacti do not need to open their stomata (pores) during the hot daylight hours, when there would be high rates of water loss, because they carry on a method of food manufacture called CAM (crassulacean acid metabolism) PHOTOSYNTHESIS. This process occurs in the green outer cells of the succulent stem. The stomata open during the cool night hours to permit the entry of carbon dioxide, which is immediately converted into organic acids that accumulate within the plant and are then converted back to carbon dioxide to be used in photosynthesis the following day.

Variety of Cacti

Some of the world's most spectacular cacti are found on the Galápagos Islands, where the genus *Opuntia*—the most widespread of all cactus genera—produces giants more than 10 m (33 ft) high, with trunks more than 1 m (3.3 ft) in diameter. Various columnar cacti, including the organ-pipe cactus, *Lemairocereus marginata*—are commonly planted closely in rows around fields in Mexico as living fences.

Several cacti are sources of food, the most common being the fleshy fruits of various species of prickly pear, genus *Opuntia.* In the drier regions of Texas the flattened stems of the prickly pear cactus are fed to cattle. Another cactus that yields edible fruits is a leaf cactus, the Barbados gooseberry, *Pereskia aculeata.* The sweet fruits of various cacti may also be allowed to ferment, to produce alcoholic drinks.

Travelers to the deserts of North America encounter the infamous jumping chollas, several species of the genus *Opuntia*, whose fragile stem joints covered with barbed spines seem literally to jump out to fasten themselves to one's boots or clothes. It is difficult and painful to remove these spines from flesh because of their barbs. The barrel cacti, genera *Echinocactus* and *Ferocactus*, are a source of fresh water in the desert. Considerable moisture can be squeezed from the fleshy pulp within these giant plants, some of which attain a height of 2 m (6.6 ft) and a diameter of more than 1 m (3.3 ft).

Although cacti are generally thought of as desert dwellers, the American tropical forests and woodlands have many species of cacti, most of which are either vines or epiphytes—plants that live attached to the branches of trees but not as parasites on the trees. The Christmas cactus, *Schlumbergera bridgesii*, and the orchid cacti, genus *Epiphyllum*, are also tropical and produce spectacular flowers, some of which open only at night.

Some species of the prickly pear cactus, as well as the cochineal plant, *Nopalea cochenillifera*, host the small cochineal insect, *Dactylopius coccus*, that is the source of a crimson dye that was commercially important before the synthesis of aniline dyes.

Indians believe that some cacti have important medicinal properties. The most famous is PEYOTE (*Lophophora williamsii*), a small, spineless, globular cactus of Texas and northern Mexico. Indians have long considered this plant divine and a means of communicating with the spirits.

caddis fly A caddis fly is any mothlike insect of the order Trichoptera. Most caddis flies measure 5–25 mm (0.2–1 in) in length. They are dull-colored, and their larvae are aquatic. Most larvae construct portable cases of twigs or pebbles that are fastened together with silk. Stream-living larvae construct tiny silk nets and feed on the materials caught in them. When a larva is fully grown, it fastens its case to an object in the water and pupates in the case.

Caddo The Caddo are a group of linguistically related North American Indian tribes whose aboriginal homeland was the Red River valley of present-day northeastern Texas and adjacent areas of Arkansas, Oklahoma, and Louisiana. The Caddo lived in dispersed communities loosely united into three confederacies. Their population in the late 17th century was an estimated 8,000.

The traditional Caddo way of life was based on the cultivation of maize, beans, and squash, supplemented by the hunting of deer, buffalo, and bear. They lived in conical, grassthatched dwellings. Political and religious authority was intertwined with ranked matrilineal clans and included hereditary chiefs who were carried about on tribesmen's shoulders.

First noted by the Spanish explorer Hernando de Soto, the Caddo did not have intensive contact with Europeans until the French founded Natchitoches in 1699. The effects of trade and a sharp decline in population during the 18th century resulted in an early breakdown of traditional culture. The Civil War divided the Caddo, with those supporting the Union fleeing to Kansas.

Highly acculturated, the Caddo today are engaged principally in farming and ranching. They are governed by a constitutionally organized tribal council. There were about 900 members of the Caddo tribe on or near the Wichita reservation in Oklahoma in 1987.

cadenza [kuh-den'-zuh] In music, a cadenza was originally an improvised vocal or instrumental passage in-

An adult caddis fly (A) *has long antennae and large wings. As a larva* (B), *it lives underwater and weaves a case of silk with an embedded spiral of leaf fragments. Other species build cases out of grains of sand* (C) *and pebbles* (D).

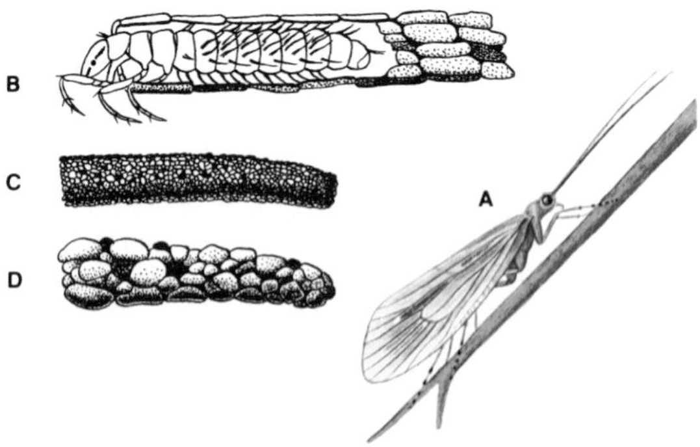

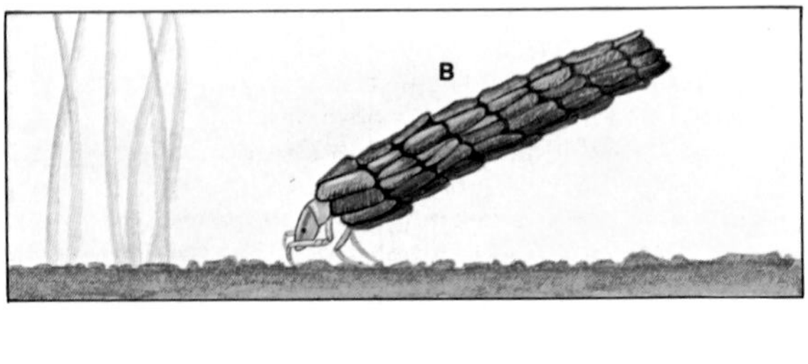

serted by a solo performer in the final cadence of a movement or piece. (A musical cadence is the phrase that brings a section of music to an end, usually by supplying a harmonic resolution.) By the time of Mozart and Beethoven, however, composers had begun to write musical passages called cadenzas into their compositions, so that the original charm of the cadenza—that it was a more or less spontaneous outpouring of the soloist's technical ability—was lost.

Cadillac, Antoine Laumet de la Mothe, Sieur de [kah-dee-yahk', loh'-may duh lah mawt'] Antoine Laumet de la Mothe Cadillac, b. Mar. 5, 1658, d. Oct. 15, 1730, was the founder of Detroit, Mich. As a lieutenant in the French army, Cadillac went to Canada in 1683, where from 1694 to 1697 he commanded the strategic western fort at Michilimackinac. In 1699 he returned to France and urged the establishment of a post on the Detroit River to protect the fur trade from the English. Receiving a land grant and trade monopoly, he founded Fort Pontchartrain du Détroit in 1701, serving as its commandant from 1704 until his appointment as governor of Louisiana in 1711. There he quarreled fiercely with the colonists and was recalled (1716) to France.

Cádiz [kah'-deeth] Cádiz is the chief port of southwestern Spain and the capital of Cádiz province; it has a population of 157,766 (1981). It occupies a narrow, rocky peninsula that partially encloses the Gulf of Cádiz, forming a protected harbor.

The city is elegantly built, with many large buildings of Moorish origin. Shipbuilding and food processing, as well as shipping, are the mainstays of the economy. The seat of a diocese, Cádiz has a medical school affiliated with the University of Seville. Its archaeological museum contains relics of its Carthaginian and Roman past.

According to ancient sources, Cádiz was founded by Phoenicians about 1100 BC. It later became a center of Carthaginian trade with Atlantic Europe. Thereafter, it became a Roman city, was subsequently plundered and occupied by the Visigoths, and was eventually captured by the Moors. In 1262 it fell to Christian Spaniards. As the chief port of the Spanish treasure fleets, it was burned by Sir Francis DRAKE in 1587, but was rebuilt and enjoyed great prosperity for two centuries as Spain's principal port for traffic to the New World.

cadmium The chemical element cadmium is a relatively rare, soft, silver-white metal closely related to ZINC. Its chemical symbol is Cd, its atomic number is 48, and its atomic weight is 112.40. Cadmium was discovered in 1817 by the German chemist Friedrich Strohmeyer and named *cadmia fornacum*, meaning "furnace zinc."

Cadmium is a TRANSITION ELEMENT. Its place in the periodic table is in Group IIB, below zinc and above mercury, and it has many properties in common with these elements. Cadmium compounds are almost always found together with zinc compounds. The two metals are always mined together, and most cadmium is obtained as a by-product in the preparation of zinc.

About 75% of all cadmium produced is used for cadmium plating of easily corroded metals such as iron and steel. The advantage of cadmium plating over zinc plating is that the treated objects can be soldered and are not attacked by corrosive bases.

Because of its low melting point (320° C), cadmium is used in aluminum solder (40% cadmium, 50% lead, 10% tin), Wood's metal (50% bismuth, 25% lead, 15% cadmium, 10% tin), and related alloys that are used, for example, in sprinkler installations and other fire-protection systems. Cadmium is also used to absorb neutrons in the control rods and shielding of nuclear reactors, and in the manufacture of artists' pigments, automobile enamels, vinyl plastics, and phosphors for color television tubes. Nickel-cadmium (Ni-cad) rechargeable batteries operate by a reversible reaction between cadmium and hydrated nickel oxide and are used in such portable devices as radios and hearing aids.

Cadmium ions are extremely poisonous; their action is similar to that of mercury ions. The metal itself is not dangerous except at high temperatures. Cadmium forms only bivalent compounds, which do, however, form COORDINATION COMPOUNDS with other ions and molecules.

Cadmus In Greek legend Cadmus was the founder of THEBES. He had been sent by his father, King Agenor of Phoenicia, to find his abducted sister, EUROPA. Unable to find her, Cadmus consulted the Delphic oracle who directed him to establish a new city. Armed warriors sprang up from the sown teeth of a serpent, fighting each other until all but five were slain. These five were regarded as ancestors by Thebes' noble families.

caduceus [kuh-doo'-see-uhs] The caduceus was the wand of the Greek god HERMES. The wand, made of olive wood and gold, was entwined with serpents and surmounted by wings. It possessed magical powers over dreams, waking, and sleep. Hermes placed the wand gently upon the eyes of those who were being summoned to the hereafter, and he carried it as his staff in conducting the dead to the netherworld.

The caduceus has become a widely accepted symbol for the medical profession, together with the staff of ASCLEPIUS, the Greek god of healing, which is entwined by a single snake.

Cædmon [kad'-muhn] According to BEDE's *Historia Ecclesiastica*, Cædmon, fl. 670, was an uneducated herdsman who, being unable to improvise verse, was divinely inspired to compose his 9-line "Cædmon's hymn" in praise of God the Creator. The other Old English religious verse once ascribed to him is now assigned to others.

Caen [kahn] Caen is the capital of Calvados department in Normandy in northern France and has a population of 144,000 (1982). It is a major port and trade center for the surrounding agricultural region and is connected to the English Channel by canal. The development of nearby iron mines has enhanced its economy. Other industries include steel, textiles, and electronic equipment. A university, founded in 1432 by Henry VI of England, is located there. Historical landmarks include the 11th-century Abbaye-Aux-Hommes and Abbaye-Aux-Dames and the Church of Saint-Pierre.

Caen served as the capital of Normandy under William the Conqueror. It was captured by the English in 1346 and was ruled by them from 1417 to 1450. During the French Revolution, Caen was an anti-Republican stronghold. The city was severely damaged in June and July of 1944 during the Allied invasion of France, but it has since been largely rebuilt.

Caernarvon [kar-nar'-vuhn] Caernarvon (1981 pop., 9,506), the county town of Gwynedd in northwestern Wales, is a seaport on the Menai Strait. Slate from nearby quarries is exported, and tourism is important. The well-preserved castle was the site of the investiture of the Prince of Wales in 1911 and 1969. The Romans built a fort there about AD 75, as did the Normans in the 11th century. The present structure was begun (1283) by King Edward I, whose son, later Edward II, was born (1284) there. Until the redistricting of Welsh counties in 1974, Caernarvon was the county town of Caernarvonshire.

caesar [see'-zur] Caesar, the family name of the Roman leader Gaius Julius Caesar, was used as a title by the Roman emperors from AUGUSTUS, who was actually an adopted member of the family, to HADRIAN. Hadrian (r. AD 117–38) initiated a practice whereby the title caesar was given to the heir apparent to the imperial throne. The German imperial title *kaiser* and the Russian *tsar* are both derived from *caesar.*

Caesar, Gaius Julius [see'-zur, gy'-uhs joo'-lee-uhs] Julius Caesar rose from relative obscurity to supreme power in the late Roman republic. A brilliant general and formidable politician, he defeated all rivals to become dictator of Rome. Fear that he would make himself king prompted his assassination in 44 BC.

Early Life. Gaius Julius Caesar was born on July 13, 100 BC, the son of Gaius Julius Caesar, who was Gaius MARIUS's brother-in-law. In 84 BC young Caesar married Cornelia, daughter of Marius's old partner Lucius Cornelius CINNA, and rejected the order of Lucius Cornelius SULLA to divorce her.

Caesar first distinguished himself by collecting a fleet from the Roman ally Nicomedes IV of Bithynia and by his conspicuous bravery at the siege of Mytilene (80 BC). He returned home after Sulla's death (78 BC). Again leaving Rome for studies in Rhodes, he was captured en route by pirates. After obtaining ransom, he recruited private troops, captured the pirates, and had them executed in 75–74 BC. His studies in Rhodes were interrupted by the outbreak of war with MITHRADATES VI of Pontus, against whom he hastily gathered a force in 74.

Julius Caesar, a military genius and major figure in Roman history, conquered Gaul and defeated his archrival, Pompey the Great. He was appointed dictator for life in 44 BC but was assassinated the same year. (Museo Nazionale, Milan.)

Political Rise and Military Success. Caesar was made a pontiff at Rome in 73 BC, and after his military tribunate and possible service against SPARTACUS (72 or 71), he sided with those seeking power from outside the circle of nobles who dominated the Senate. He supported restoration of tribunician powers and the recall from exile of those who had supported Marcus Aemilius LEPIDUS in his revolt of 77 BC. Caesar also advertised his Marian connections.

After a quaestorship in Spain (69 BC), Caesar earned popularity among the Transpadane Gauls by supporting (68) their agitation for Roman citizenship. Following the death of Cornelia he married (68) Pompeia, granddaughter of Sulla and relative of POMPEY THE GREAT, and supported important military assignments for Pompey in 67 and 66. As aedile in 65 BC, Caesar achieved great popularity by financing splendid games. He also probably cooperated (65) with Marcus Licinius CRASSUS in an attempt to annex Egypt, in supporting (64, 63) CATILINE for the consulship, and in promoting the land-distribution bill of Publius Servilius Rullus.

In 64 BC, Caesar presided over the trials of those who had committed murder during Sulla's proscriptions. The following year he attacked the legality of the Senate's decree of a state of emergency. In the elections of that year, massive bribery helped him become Pontifex Maximus. Caesar took no part in Catiline's conspiracy, but he courted popularity by opposing the execution of Catiline's accomplices and, as praetor in 62, by supporting measures favorable to Pompey. Soon after, however, he divorced Pompeia on suspicion of infidelity with Publius CLODIUS. Caesar later married (58) Calpurnia.

In 61 BC Caesar became governor of Further Spain, where military action restored his finances, and in 60 he outwitted his political enemies by forgoing a triumph (the traditional victor's procession in Rome) in order to win election to the consulate with the support of Crassus and Pompey. Faced with increased opposition from conservatives such as CATO the Younger, Caesar, Crassus, and Pompey formed the so-called First TRIUMVIRATE to further their ambitions in 60–59. Caesar received the governorships of Illyricum, Cisalpine Gaul, and Transalpine Gaul. He was also given control of a large army, which he used to subjugate GAUL. He gained enormous political strength from the GALLIC WARS, which lasted from 58 to 51 BC.

War with Pompey. The "Triumvirate" was renegotiated at Luca in 56 BC, but the death of Caesar's daughter, who had married Pompey, in 54 and of Crassus in 53 and the phenomenal success of Caesar in Gaul eventually destroyed Caesar's relationship with Pompey. In 50 BC Pompey joined opponents of Caesar's bid for a second consulate. Caesar's offers of compromise were rejected by the Senate, and on Jan. 10, 49 BC, Caesar precipitated civil war by leading his army across the RUBICON into Italy proper. Caesar's veteran army soon overran Italy, forcing the unprepared Pompey to withdraw to Greece. In August 49 BC a lightning campaign secured Spain, and Caesar then crossed to Greece, where he totally defeated Pompey's superior numbers at Pharsalus on Aug. 9, 48. Pompey fled to Egypt, where he was murdered. Following him there, Caesar became involved in the civil war between CLEOPATRA and her brother PTOLEMY XIII. He made Cleopatra his mistress as well as queen of Egypt.

In 47 BC, Caesar went to Anatolia, where he defeated Pompey's ally Pharnaces, king of Bosporus, at Zela; this victory occasioned Caesar's famous boast *Veni, vidi, vici* ("I came, I saw, I conquered"). He returned to Rome, but in December 47 BC he crossed to North Africa to meet a new threat from the Pompeian forces. After victory at Thapsus, he returned home to an unprecedented quadruple triumph in 46 BC. And in 45 he defeated Pompey's sons at Munda, in Spain.

Dictator of Rome. Caesar, now showered with political powers and honors, was appointed dictator (49, 48 BC), then dictator for ten years (46), and finally dictator for life (44). He was also elected consul (48, 46–44), appointed prefect of morals (46), awarded tribunician sacrosanctity (44), and honored by portrayal on coins and by the erection of a temple to his clemency (45). Caesar introduced numerous reforms, such as limiting the distribution of free grain, founding citizen colonies, introducing (Jan. 1, 45) the Julian CALENDAR, and enlarging the Senate. At the same time he reduced debts, revised the tax structure, and extended Roman citizenship to non-Italians. While meeting genuine needs, these popular reforms also strengthened Caesar's control of the state at the expense of his opponents, whom he tried to placate with ostentatious clemency.

In 44 BC, Caesar, likening himself to Alexander the Great, began planning the conquest of Parthia. Fearing that he would become an absolute king, many whom he had earlier pardoned conspired to murder him. The con-

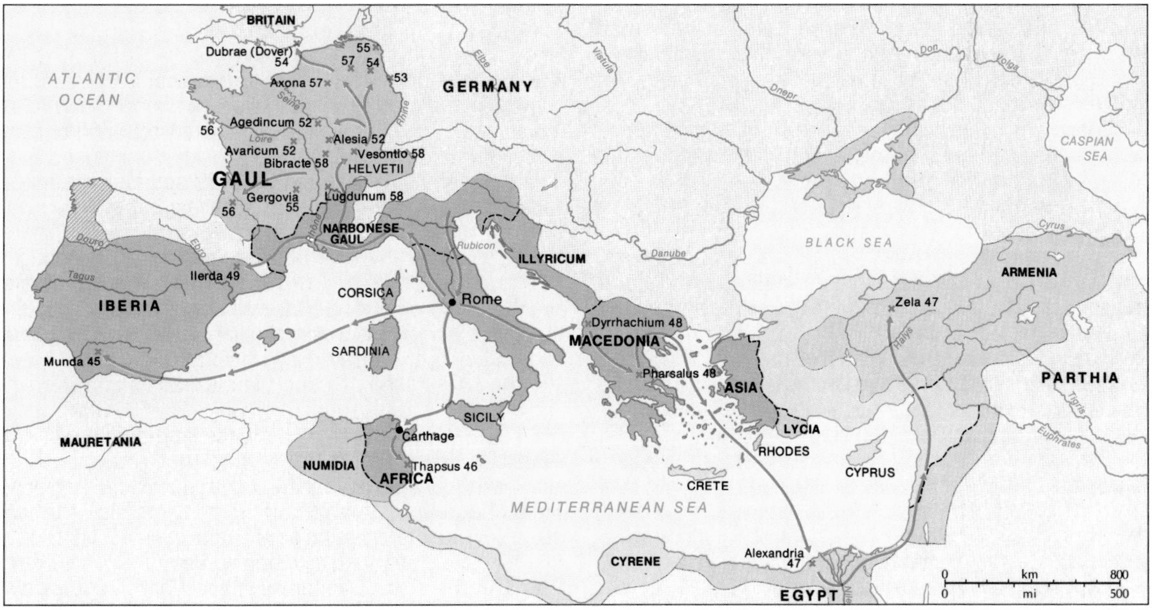

CONQUESTS OF JULIUS CAESAR

Roman Republic, 63 B.C. | Acquisitions by Pompey and others up to 58 B.C. | Acquisitions by Julius Caesar up to 44 B.C. | Client kingdoms and dependencies | Caesar's campaigns | Battle sites

Cartographic Production by Lothar Roth & Associates

spirators, led by Marcus Junius BRUTUS and Gaius CASSIUS LONGINUS, stabbed him at a meeting of the Senate in Pompey's theater on Mar. 15 (the Ides of March), 44 BC. Falling at the foot of Pompey's statue, Caesar addressed Brutus in Greek: "Even you, lad?"

Caesar was an accomplished orator and writer. His two surviving works, *On the Gallic War* and *On the Civil War*, introduced the genre of personal war commentaries. Subtle propaganda for Caesar, they are also lucid narratives that hold the reader.

Dynamic, witty, urbane, and highly intelligent, Caesar aroused loyalty and admiration among both contemporaries and later generations. Nevertheless, his immense ambition and the contempt he displayed for the republican traditions of his opponents drove them to desperate measures against him. He therefore left Rome's great problems for his adopted son and heir Octavian, the future AUGUSTUS.

Caesar, Sid [see'-zur] Sid Caesar, b. Yonkers, N.Y., Sept. 8, 1922, is an American comedian and actor who, with his comedy partner, Imogene Coca, became famous starring in the highly acclaimed television series "Your Show of Shows" (1950–54). He later starred in "Caesar's Hour" (1954–57) and appeared in such films as *It's a Mad Mad Mad Mad World* (1963), *Silent Movie* (1976), *The Cheap Detective* (1978), *Grease* (1978), *Grease 2* (1984), and the TV movie *Side by Side* (1988).

Caesarea (site in Israel) [see-zuh-ree'-uh] Caesarea Maritima (Qisarya), 55 km (34 mi) north of Tel Aviv, Israel, was an ancient city of Palestine. Originally a small Phoenician town, it was rebuilt between 22 and 10 BC by Herod the Great, who renamed the site for the Roman emperor and made it a major port.

Caesarea became the seat of the Roman governor of Judea in AD 6. Pontius Pilate resided there, and in the Book of Acts the work of Philip, Peter, and Paul at Caesarea is described. After the destruction of Jerusalem in AD 70, Caesarea became the most important city in Palestine; by the 6th century its population may have reached 100,000. Last occupied during the period of the Crusades, it was abandoned after its destruction by the Mamelukes in 1265.

Archaeological excavations between 1950 and 1961 revealed the main features of the city as described by the 1st-century historian Josephus. An aqueduct and a theater from Herod's time are still standing today.

caesura see VERSIFICATION

caffeine Caffeine is an odorless, slightly bitter, ALKALOID chemical found in COFFEE beans, KOLA NUTS, and TEA leaves. It can be manufactured synthetically in the laboratory. In small amounts caffeine acts as a mild stimulant and is harmless to most people. In large amounts, however, it may result in insomnia, restlessness, and anxiety. Caffeine also raises urination and heart rates and can cause heart irregularities; some researchers maintain that heavy coffee drinkers are more prone to develop coronary heart disease. Caffeine decreases blood flow to the brain, however, and has been used in treating migraine headaches. It is also used in treating cases of poisoning by depressants such as alcohol and morphine, and studies suggest that it somewhat increases the effectiveness of common analgesics such as aspirin. By widening bronchial airways, caffeine can help to relieve asthma attacks. In plants, the drug apparently functions as a natural insect repellant.

Cage, John The composer John Cage, b. Los Angeles, Sept. 5, 1912, has rejected the compositional practices of the past to explore a new world of musical sound and structure. His influence on many contemporaries has been profound.

Cage has experimented widely with extramusical sounds and noises in musical compositions (*Second Construction, Third Construction*). He drew unorthodox sonorities from the piano by preparing it, that is, by inserting bolts, screws, wood, felt, spoons, clothespins, and other materials between the strings or on the soundboard (*Sounds and Interludes*). At the other extreme, probably his most provocative piece is *4'33"*, in which the performer, seated in front of the piano, plays nothing for 4 minutes and 33 seconds.

Cage has composed using chance methods such as tossing coins (see ALEATORY MUSIC), (*Variations I, Variations II, Renga*). Cage's many writings include *Silence* (1961), *Empty Words* (1979), and *X* (1983).

Cagliari [kahl-yar'-ee] Cagliari (ancient Caralis) is the capital of the Mediterranean island of Sardinia. The island's largest city and main port, with a population of 232,785 (1981), Cagliari exports lead and zinc and produces cement and ceramics. First controlled by Carthage and later by Rome (from the 3d century BC), it was independent through the early Middle Ages, falling to Pisa in the 13th century, to the Spanish kingdom of Aragon in 1327, and to Savoy in 1720. Important Axis submarine and air bases were located there during World War II. In the old city are the Romanesque-Gothic Cathedral of Santa Cecilia, the 5th-century Basilica di San Saturnino, and the 14th-century Pisan Tower of San Pancrazio.

Cagney, James A fast-talking Irish-American film actor who danced brilliantly and frequently on screen, James Cagney, b. New York City, July 17, 1899, d. Mar. 30, 1986, achieved fame as a cocky gangster in *Public Enemy* (1931) and became stereotyped for several years thereafter. His best roles, which reflect his punchy, cheerful personality, were in *Footlight Parade* (1933), *Lady Killer* (1933), *G-Men* (1935), *A Midsummer Night's Dream* (1935), *Boy Meets Girl* (1938), *Angels with Dirty Faces* (1938), *The Roaring Twenties* (1939), *Yankee*

James Cagney administers the famous "grapefruit massage" to the face of Mae Clarke in the 1931 film Public Enemy. *Although Cagney rose to stardom on the strength of his roles in gangster films, it was his performance as George M. Cohan in the musical* Yankee Doodle Dandy *(1942) that earned him an Academy Award.*

Doodle Dandy (1942), *White Heat* (1949), *Love Me or Leave Me* (1955), *Man of a Thousand Faces* (as Lon Chaney, 1957), *One Two Three* (1961), and *Ragtime* (1981).

Cahokia Mounds [kuh-hoh'-kee-uh] The Cahokia Mounds are a group of Indian earthworks clustered over several square kilometers in the Mississippi River valley east of St. Louis, Mo. Some 200 mounds in all were built between about 700 and 1500, making this the largest mound complex north of Mexico. Archaeologists apply the term *Mississippian* to the ancient mound-building culture of this region, which had the largest concentration of Indian farming communities in the eastern United States. The pyramidal mounds probably served as bases for important public and ceremonial buildings; the largest in the Cahokia complex measures 32 m (100 ft) high and covers about 6.5 ha (16 acres).

Caicos Islands see TURKS AND CAICOS ISLANDS

Caillaux, Joseph Marie Auguste [kah-yoh'] Joseph Marie Auguste Caillaux, b. Mar. 30, 1863, d. Nov. 22, 1944, was a French politician who advocated a peaceful policy toward Germany before World War I. He served as finance minister in 1899–1902 and 1906–09. As premier (1911–12), Caillaux tried to avert war during the MOROCCAN CRISIS of 1911 by establishing a French protectorate in Morocco and ceding parts of French Equatorial Africa to Germany. This concession came under public attack, and he was forced to resign.

Caillaux was briefly (1913–14) finance minister again, but his antimilitarism led to charges of treason against him and his arrest after the outbreak of World War I. After 1924, Caillaux again headed the finance ministry and reduced the war debt to England. In 1938 he advocated negotiation with Nazi Germany, but he refused to support the VICHY GOVERNMENT in 1940.

caiman [kay'-muhn] Caimans are any of several large tropical New World amphibious reptiles that are related to the alligators and crocodiles. Caimans belong to the family Alligatoridae, order Crocodylia, and the three genera are: *Caiman* (two species), spectacled and broad-nosed caimans; *Melanosuchus* (one species), black caiman; and *Paleosuchus* (two species), armored caimans. Broad-snouted carnivores, they live in rivers, lakes, and streams from coastal Mexico to Argentina. The spectacled caiman, 1.8–2.7 m (6–9 ft) long, is the most widespread and best known. The black caiman of the lower Orinoco and Amazon rivers is the longest, reaching 4.5 m (15 ft) or more, and the mountain stream-dwelling armored caimans are the smallest, seldom reaching 2.1 m (7 ft). Like most crocodilians, female caimans bury their hard-shelled eggs in sandbanks or masses of rotting vegetation and guard them until they hatch. All caimans are endangered, either from habitat destruction or from hide hunters. The black caiman, because of its large size and the high quality of its skin, is virtually extinct.

The black caiman represents one species of alligatorlike reptiles of Central and South America. This species can measure 4.5 m (15 ft) long.

Cain According to Genesis 4, Cain was the first son of Adam and Eve. When he slew his brother ABEL, God condemned him to wander the Earth but placed a mark of protection on him lest anyone seek revenge for Abel.

Cain, James M. The novelist and journalist James Mallahan Cain, b. Annapolis, Md., July 1, 1892, d. Oct. 27, 1977, set a standard for tough psychological thrillers with *The Postman Always Rings Twice* (1934; play, 1936; films, 1946, 1981), *Mildred Pierce* (1941; film, 1945), *Double Indemnity* (1943; film, 1944), and *Serenade* (1937; film, 1956). The typical plot portrays obsessive lovers driven to crime. Cain's *The Baby in the Icebox and Other Short Fiction* (1981) was published posthumously.

cairn terrier The cairn terrier is a working dog native to the Isle of Skye, whence the ancestors of today's breed

The cairn terrier, a working dog native to Scotland, was bred to drive small game and vermin from their hiding places.

were brought to the Scottish mainland. A highly prized member of landowners' and tenants' households, it was bred to go to ground after small game and vermin. The cairn is a strong but not heavily built, short-legged breed. Its coat is the typical, protective, double jacket of several terrier breeds; the undercoat is short, soft, and furry, whereas the outercoat is profuse and harsh. Although cairns may be any color except white, they are usually red, tan, black, brindle, or a shade of gray. Typically, a cairn, whatever its color, has a dark muzzle, tail tip, and ears. Minimal grooming is needed. Its size, ideally 25 cm (10 in) high at the shoulder and a weight of 6.4 kg (14 lb), combined with its alertness, makes the breed a popular pet.

Cairo (Egypt) [ky'-roh] Cairo (Arabic: al-Qahirah), the capital of Egypt and the largest city in Africa, is located on the eastern bank of the Nile River. Cairo's population is 6,052,836 (1986), with more than 14 million in the metropolitan area.

The Citadel, a 12th-century walled fortress, has served as the administrative center of Egypt's rulers and as a military base. In 1983 it underwent a major renovation as the first venture in a project to restore Cairo's Islamic landmarks.

Contemporary City. The Nile is Cairo's traditional focus. Eleven bridges link the banks with Cairo's islands, Zamalik and Rodah. The medieval city contains narrow, winding streets, open bazaars, and historic mosques. The modern city, whose main street is the Corniche, is characterized by broad boulevards and high-rise buildings; Africa's first subway opened there in 1987. Cairo is extremely overcrowded, and its aging infrastructure is inadequate to meet the needs of its rapidly increasing population.

Cairo is the largest industrial, business, commercial, and transportation center in Egypt. Its industries, centered in the suburbs of Helwan and Shubra al-Khaymah, produce iron and steel, automobiles, cement, appliances, and other metallurgical products, textiles, tires, and plastics. The Middle Eastern publishing and filmmaking industries are centered in Cairo, and tourism is an important part of the city's economy.

Cairo is one of the leading educational centers of Africa and the Arab world. Its universities include Al-Azhar (970), Cairo (1908), Ain Shams (1950), and the American University (1919). Among Cairo's many museums is the famous Egyptian Museum, housing one of the world's finest archaeological collections. A new opera house opened in 1988.

Cairo's historic landmarks reflect Egypt's long history. The pyramids and sphinx are at nearby GIZA. The gigantic statue of Ramses II, brought from nearby Memphis, stands in front of the railroad station. The many mosques include al-Azhar (built 970) and Muhammed Ali mosque (built 1824–57), which is located inside the 12th-century citadel built by Saladin.

History. About 2,000 years ago the Romans built a fortress called Babylon on the site of present-day Cairo, and in 640 Arabs established a military camp called al-Fustat there. Real growth began after 969, when the FATIMID dynasty made Cairo its capital. The city continued to expand and prosper under SALADIN (r. 1169–93) and later the MAMELUKES (13th to the 15th century). In the 15th century the city began a long decline, the result of plagues, Mongol attack (*c.*1400), and, finally, Turkish conquest (1517). It did not recover until the 19th century, when, under MUHAMMAD ALI PASHA (r. 1805–49), Egypt became virtually independent of Ottoman Turkey. Modern Cairo dates from the mid-19th century, when the Egyptian ruler ISMAIL PASHA began European-style construction projects. From 1882 to 1922, Egypt was under British control.

Cairo (Illinois) [kay'-roh] Cairo (1990 pop., 4,846) is the seat of Alexander County and the southernmost city in Illinois. Its location at the confluence of the Mississippi and Ohio rivers makes it a natural trade and shipping center for local manufacture of lumber, cottonseed, and soybean products. Permanent settlement began in 1837, when a levee was built.

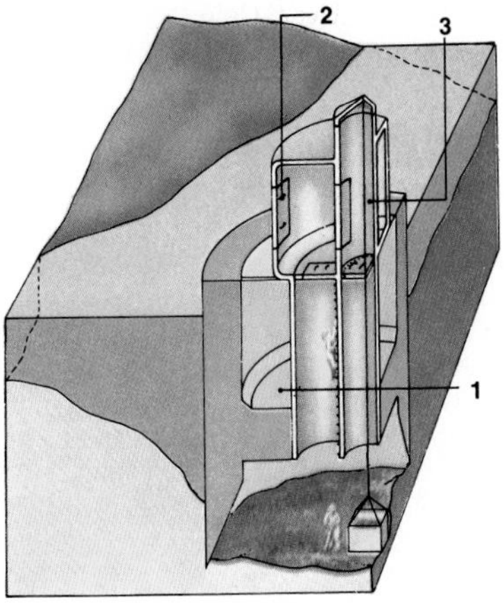

The pneumatic caisson, an open-ended boxlike or cylindrical structure, is employed in underwater construction and excavation. Once the caisson is lowered into position, air is pumped into a chamber (1) below the deck, to prevent water from seeping in. Access for the work crew is through an air lock (2). Debris accumulated during construction is removed through a larger air lock (3).

caisson [kay-sahn] A caisson is a boxlike or cylindrical shell used in constructing a foundation, either underwater, below the groundwater level, or in unstable soils. It permits excavation to proceed inside while protecting the workers.

Open caissons, used on dry ground or in shallow water, are open at both bottom and top and are fitted with a cutting edge that facilitates sinking of the structure while the inside is excavated. As the caisson sinks, sections are added on above. When excavation is complete, the interior is filled with concrete. Used for bridge abutments and other deep foundations, open caissons are usually made of reinforced concrete.

Floating, or box, caissons, open at the top and closed at the bottom, are built on shore and floated to the site, where they are sunk in place onto a previously prepared foundation. Built of reinforced concrete, steel, or wood, they serve as shells for piers, seawalls, or breakwaters and for bridge foundations underwater.

Pneumatic caissons are similar to open caissons, but they have a sealed-off working chamber at the bottom. Used to excavate deep foundations, pneumatic caissons are made of reinforced concrete, sometimes faced with steel plates.

Open caissons were used by the Chinese as early as 1500 BC. The floating caisson was developed in 1738 during the building of London's Westminster Bridge. The pneumatic caisson was made possible by the invention (1830) of the air lock by the British admiral Thomas Cochrane. It was pioneered (1850s) in England by John Wright and Isambard Kingdom Brunel (see BRUNEL family).

See also: BRIDGE (engineering); FOUNDATION, BUILDING; LIGHTHOUSE.

Caithness [kayth'-nes] Caithness, a former county in the extreme northeast of Scotland, became part of the new HIGHLAND region in 1975. Wick was the county town.

The region is bordered by the Atlantic Ocean on the west and by the North Sea on the east. Most of the land is a plateau that gradually descends to the coast, where it forms cliffs about 120 m (400 ft) high. The western portion of the area is covered with peat bogs. Agriculture (oats, turnips, fodder crops), fishing, sheep raising, and dairying are the primary economic activities.

Caithness was invaded by the Norse during the 10th century, and the remains of many structures built during their occupation still stand. During the 13th century, Caithness came under Scottish jurisdiction.

Cajuns [kay'-juhns] Cajuns are the descendants of exiles from the French colony of ACADIA (present-day Nova Scotia and adjacent areas) who left their homeland in 1755 and found refuge in southern Louisiana a decade later. By 1790 about 4,000 Acadians occupied the wetlands along Bayou Lafourche and Bayou Teche; they later settled the Louisiana prairies. In the fertile bayous they fished, trapped the fur-bearing animals, gathered moss, and raised sugarcane, cotton, and corn; on the prairies they established cattle ranches and planted rice. Their traditional domestic architecture consisted of daubed or half-timbered houses with gable roofs, mud chimneys, and outside stairways leading to attics. The landholdings were often surrounded by the characteristic *pieux*, a rail-and-post fence.

The French-speaking, Roman Catholic Cajuns, today estimated to number about 500,000, maintain many cultural and occupational traditions of their ancestors. Their speech is an archaic form of French into which are incorporated words taken from English, German, Spanish, and various Indian languages. With the decline of the muskrat in the wetlands, the nutria, an import from Argentina, became the Cajun trapper's staple. Oystering and shrimping are increasingly important industries. Recently, the exploratory drilling for oil in the wetlands and adjacent offshore areas has provided the Cajuns with another source of employment.

cake and pastry Cakes and pastries are foods that have a flour batter base and contain a substantial amount of sweetening. Cakes, cookies, doughnuts, and pies are familiar types. Cakes and cookies are made from batters that contain varying proportions of eggs, shortening, water or milk, and sugar, and that are flavored with spices, extracts, cocoa, fruit juices, and purees. Baked pies and fried batters are made by combining different crusts, fillings, and toppings. Yeast-leavened pastries include Danish pastries, sweet rolls, coffee cakes, and numerous ethnic specialties.

Ingredients. Each ingredient has one or more specific effects on the product. FLOUR forms the basic structure of the dough or batter and affects the appearance, flavor, texture, and nutritional properties of the finished product.

The amount of liquid influences the physical properties of the batter and many characteristics of the baked

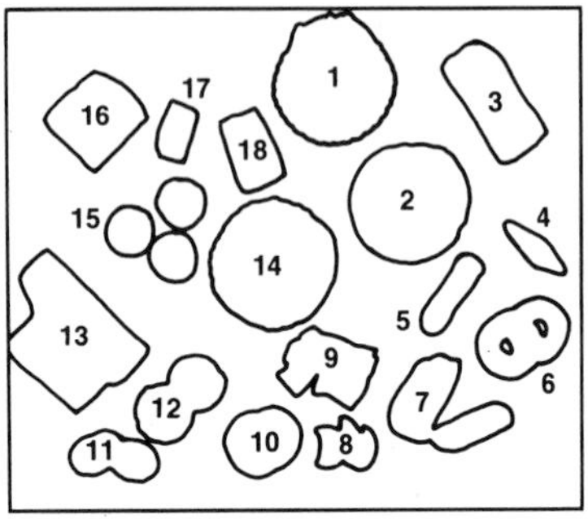

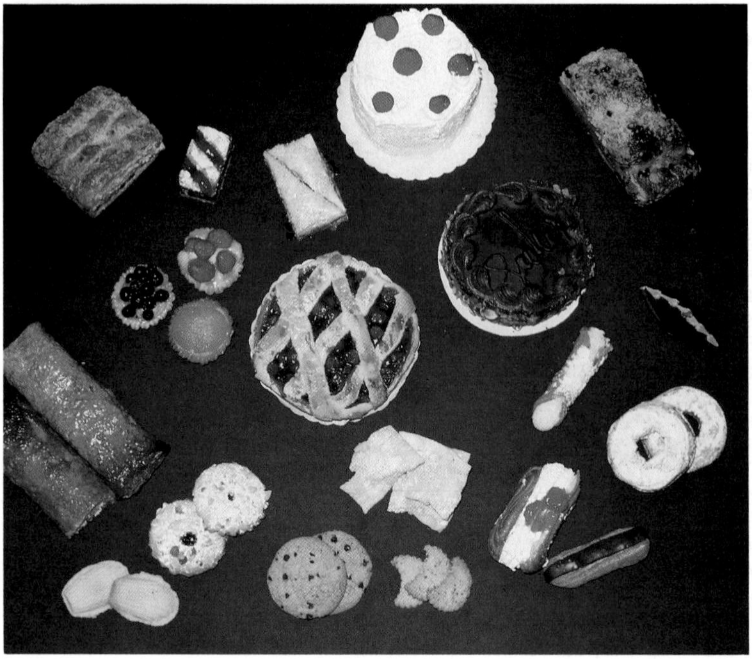

This selection of cakes and pastries includes: strawberry whipped cream cake (1); *chocolate layer cake* (2); *nut cake* (3); *almond crisp* (4); *Italian cannoli, a crisp pastry shell filled with sweetened ricotta cheese and candied fruit and nuts* (5); *sugared doughnuts* (6); *iced eclairs* (7); *almond crescents* (8); *crischiki, deep-fried sweet dough* (9); *chocolate chip cookies* (10); *madeleines, French butter cookies* (11); *Linzer nut cookies filled with raspberry jam* (12); *apple and nut strudels* (13); *latticed cherry pie* (14); *fruit tarts* (15); *yeast cake* (16); *Napoleon, puff pastry filled with pastry cream* (17); *and baklava, made of layers consisting of paper-thin phyllo pastry, ground nuts, and honey* (18).

pastry. Hard water tends to toughen dough; very alkaline water may soften it. Baking time must be increased for a recipe with high water content. Milk generally darkens the crust color and yellows the interior. Skim milk may toughen a product.

Whipped egg whites or whole eggs yield an air-retaining foam that is the basis for the leavening effect in sponge cakes and meringues. When unbeaten eggs are added to an already leavened batter, they tend to entrap gas and generally lead to a higher rise in the finished product. Yolks have a tenderizing effect because they contain fats and emulsifiers.

Fats and oils also tenderize the product. They generally reduce the volume if the leavening effect comes principally from beaten eggs: pound cakes are denser than angel food cakes, which contain no fat.

Sugar, the most common sweetener, tends to weaken batter structure and produce a more tender product. Corn syrup tenderizes, but it also darkens the crust. Honey darkens the crust and sometimes the interior, and flavors the product.

Because it absorbs water, COCOA tends to toughen dough. High-fat cocoa has a shortening effect. Natural cocoa is somewhat acidic, but Dutch process or alkalized cocoa is practically neutral; this should be considered when adding soda. The hue of pastries containing cocoa is affected by the degree of acidity of the dough.

Products such as ordinary pie crusts are unleavened: volume is not significantly increased because of internal gas expansion. Puff-pastry doughs and cakes based on whipped eggs are leavened during baking primarily by expansion of water vapor and entrapped air. Sweet-dough pastries are YEAST-leavened. Sheet cakes, cupcakes, and many cookies are leavened by chemical systems such as BAKING POWDER.

Processing. The order in which ingredients are added to the mixture affects the product's quality. The extent of mixing also varies. Yeast-leavened doughs must be kneaded like BREAD doughs; layer-cake batters need only to be thoroughly blended. Altitude can influence results, because the lower barometric pressure at higher altitudes affects the boiling point of water, reducing the highest temperature reached inside the cake, which in turn affects the leavening system.

cakewalk The cakewalk was a competitive dance characterized by a high, strutting step and a backward-tilted body position. A cake was awarded to the dancer who did the most intricate steps. Cakewalk contests were a popular part of late 19th-century variety shows, and around the turn of the century such contests proliferated in the United States.

calabash [kal'-uh-bash] The calabash, *Crescentia cujete*, is a tropical American tree in the bignonia family, Bignoniaceae. The trees grow up to 1.2 m (40 ft) high, and their flowers are yellow with red or purple veins. Their hard-shelled fruits are made into water vessels, pipes, and other utensils. The calabash gourd is the common name for hard-shelled fruits of the vine *Lagenaria siceraria* in the cucumber family, Cucurbitaceae. Its fruits are used for dippers and bowls.

Calabria [kah-lah'-bree-uh] Calabria is a region of southern Italy with a population of 2,146,724 (1988 est.). The toe of the Italian boot, Calabria is a peninsula covering 15,080 km^2 (5,822 mi^2), lying between the Tyrrhenian and Ionian seas. It is separated from Sicily by the Strait of MESSINA. Calabria comprises three provinces—Catanzaro, Cosenza, and Reggio di Calabria—and its capital is Catanzaro. The region is generally mountainous, a condition that has hindered economic development. On its narrow coastal strip, olives, grapes, wheat, and citrus fruits are grown. Fishing and the manufacture of foodstuffs, forest products, and chemicals are among the minor industries. Several hydroelectric plants also contribute to the local economy.

Called Ager Bruttius in ancient times and later Southern Apulia, Calabria was so named in the early Middle Ages. It was taken by the Norman rulers of Sicily in the 11th century and became part of the Kingdom of Naples after 1282. It was taken by Garibaldi in 1860.

Calais [kah-lay'] Calais is a city in Pas-de-Calais department in northern France on the Strait of Dover. It has a population of 76,587 (1982). Only 34 km (21 mi) from Dover, England, Calais is a major point for crossing the English Channel. It is situated on an island that is surrounded by canals and harbors. Calais is a popular tourist resort as well as an agricultural distribution center. The city has some light industry, and the manufacture of fine lace and embroidery is important. Notable points of interest are the city museum and *The Burghers of Calais*, a sculpture by Auguste Rodin that stands in front of the town hall. The statue commemorates a famous event during the Hundred Years' War when, after Calais had withstood an English siege (1346) for almost a year, six burghers surrendered themselves to the English to avoid a massacre.

Originally a fishing village, Calais was a prospering seaport when captured by the English in 1347. In 1558 the duc de Guise recovered the city for France. Occupied (1940–44) by the Germans during World War II, Calais was used as a launching base for the bombing of Britain. Much of the city was razed during retaliatory bombing but has been largely rebuilt since the war.

Calamity Jane Calamity Jane, b. Princeton, Mo., May 1?, 1852, d. Aug. 1, 1903, was a wandering American frontierswoman who dressed like a man and frequented bars, telling stories of her adventures. Originally named Martha Jane Canary, she was orphaned by 1867 and began roaming the mining districts of the west. In the late 1870s she was a familiar sight in Deadwood, Dakota Territory, where she became the companion of Wild Bill HICKOK. In 1891 she married Clinton Burke, a cabdriver, but he soon deserted her. She toured in Wild West shows and claimed to have been a pony express rider and a scout. She was buried in Deadwood (S. Dak.), beside Hickok.

Iceland spar, originally found in basalt cavities in Iceland, is an optically clear, rhombohedral crystalline form of pure calcite. It shows strong double refraction and has been used for making polarizing prisms.

calcite [kal'-site] Calcite, $CaCO_3$, is the most common of the CARBONATE MINERALS and one of the most common and widely distributed of all minerals. It is the only form of calcium carbonate that is fully stable at Earth-surface conditions. Calcite occurs in virtually all geologic settings: as a primary igneous mineral in carbonatite and KIMBERLITE; in metamorphic form as MARBLE; as a common mineral in hydrothermal ORE DEPOSITS; and as a common secondary mineral, filling fractures and cavities. The pure, optically clear variety named Iceland spar, found in cavities in BASALT, displays an extreme form of birefringence known as double refraction. The most abundant and important occurrences, however, are in SEDIMENTARY ROCKS, where biogenic calcite, derived from the remains of calcareous marine organisms, is the principal constituent of LIMESTONE. Calcite is deposited as travertine in springs and CAVES.

Natural and precipitated calcite is an ingredient of such commodities as toothpaste, antacids, chewing gum,

How Calamity Jane, the American folk heroine, received her nickname is uncertain, like much else about her legendary life. "Calamity" may have referred to her hard-luck times, to her willingness to help those in trouble, or to the fate of her enemies (because of her skills with a pistol).

rubber, food fillers, glue, and soap, and is also the main source of calcium for the chemical industry.

Calcite forms soft (hardness, 2.5–3.0) hexagonal crystals with cleavage perfect in three directions, specific gravity 2.72, and vitreous-to-earthy luster. Color is white or variously tinted.

calcitonin see HORMONE, ANIMAL; THYROID GLAND

calcium The chemical element calcium is a malleable, light, silver-white metal, an ALKALINE EARTH METAL of Group IIA in the periodic table. Its symbol is Ca, its atomic number is 20, and its atomic weight is 40.08.

Calcium was first prepared by Sir Humphrey DAVY in 1808. Following the method of J. J. Berzelius and M. M. Pontin, Davy electrolyzed a mixture of lime, CaO, and mercury to produce an amalgam (a mercury alloy). By heating the amalgam to distill off mercury, he obtained a sample of calcium. The name is derived from the mineral calcite, a form of calcium carbonate ($CaCo_3$).

Occurrence. In cosmic abundance calcium is 13th among the elements; on Earth it ranks 5th and forms 3.2% of the Earth's crust, being less prevalent than aluminum (7.3%) or iron (4.1%). It is not found free in nature but is common as the carbonate rock limestone, $CaCO_3$. It is also well distributed as the minerals calcium phosphate, silicate, fluoride, and sulfate. As calcium magnesium carbonate it is one of the principal components of dolomite minerals and is found in pearls, coral, natural chalk, calcite, onyx, and marble.

Chemical Properties. Calcium almost always has an oxidation number of +2. It reacts readily as a reducing agent with most nonmetals, reacting with all halogens (X_2) as follows:

$$Ca + X_2 \rightarrow CaX_2$$

When heated with nitrogen it forms calcium nitride, Ca_3N_2, and when heated with oxygen it burns with a brilliant light to give the oxide, CaO. Calcium reacts spontaneously with water and acids to liberate hydrogen gas.

Biological Functions. Besides being a major mineral in such hard biological structures as shells, bones, and teeth, calcium plays other important roles in the biochemistry of most organisms. In the human body, which is about 2% calcium by weight, about 99% of this calcium occurs in the bones and teeth and the remainder in body cells and fluids. This remainder, however, is essential to muscle contraction and hence to cardiac function. Calcium ions are also essential in the transmission of nerve impulses and in blood coagulation, and their roles in processes such as vision are the subject of ongoing research.

Parathyroid and thyroid hormones help to maintain proper calcium balance in tissues. A lack of calcium can impair growth and lead to such conditions as RICKETS and tetany. Milk, milk products, leafy green vegetables, and shellfish are sources of dietary calcium (see NUTRITION, HUMAN).

Production. An important method of producing pure calcium is by the reduction of calcium chloride using metallic aluminum, according to the reaction

$$3CaCl_2 + 2Al \rightarrow 3Ca + 2AlCl_3$$

It is also produced by the electrolysis of fused calcium chloride at 800° C. As it forms, the light molten calcium metal floats to the surface, where it is continuously withdrawn.

Important Compounds. Because limestone—calcium carbonate, $CaCO_3$—is so abundant in nature and so readily converted to other compounds, it is the most important calcium compound. The reaction of calcium with hydrochloric acid

$$CaCO_3 + 2HCl \rightarrow CaCl_2 + CO_2 + H_2O$$

is typical of reactions with acids that produce calcium compounds containing such anions as phosphate (PO_4^{3-}), acetate ($C_2H_3O_2^-$), nitrate (NO_3^-), or oxalate ($C_2O_4^{2-}$).

Decomposition of limestone by heating is an inexpensive method for the production of lime, CaO.

$$CaCO_3 \rightarrow CaO + CO_2$$

Lime has been used since ancient times in making mortar. When lime reacts with water in the process called "slaking," 15.96 kcal (66.78 kJ) of heat is liberated for each mole, and calcium hydroxide, $Ca(OH)_2$, is formed. Ordinary mortar and some plasters are mixtures of calcium hydroxide, sand, and water. Exposure to air causes evaporation of the water; the mortar hardens, and in the course of time reaction with the carbon dioxide of the atmosphere reforms calcium carbonate, the starting material.

Calcium fluoride, CaF_2, as fluorspar, is the raw material from which fluorine is derived; calcium chloride, $CaCl_2$, found in salt brines and as a by-product in the Solvay process of production of sodium carbonate, is well known as a dehydrating agent and ice-melting chemical. Calcium sulfate dihydrate, $CaSO_4{\cdot}2H_2O$, is known as gypsum, and the hemihydrate, $CaSO_4{\cdot}\frac{1}{2}H_2O$, is plaster of paris. Calcium phosphate, $Ca_3(PO_4)_2$, is converted to superphosphate by the reaction with sulfuric acid and used extensively as a fertilizer.

calcium carbonate Calcium carbonate, $CaCO_3$, is one of the most widespread minerals. It exists in two distinctly different crystal forms, CALCITE and aragonite. It is the chief constituent of LIMESTONE and MARBLE, and is a component of other metamorphic and sedimentary rock. Blackboard CHALK is a form of calcium carbonate mixed with a claylike binder.

Calcium carbonate is practically insoluble in water but soluble in dilute acid. It reacts with acid to evolve carbon dioxide gas, a property that is the basis for a simple test for its presence in minerals.

calculator, electronic

calculator, electronic Electronic calculators are the modern counterparts of the ADDING MACHINE but are able to perform many more functions.

Principles. Calculators are a direct outgrowth of DIGITAL TECHNOLOGY. In some calculators, commands are permanently built into the system. The commands are programmed—that is, planned so that one command follows another—in groups called microprogrammed routines. Such programming provides a way of drastically reducing the cost of the INTEGRATED CIRCUITS that constitute a calculator's main circuitry. The programs, however, cannot be changed by an operator.

By contrast, in calculators that can be programmed by an operator, some or all of the stored commands can be changed. Thus a so-called programmable calculator is actually a simple MICROCOMPUTER, one that is programmed from a special keyboard rather than by using a symbolic computer language.

Components. In a hand-held programmable calculator, the principles of programmed digital systems are applied in a way similar to that of a COMPUTER. Four main functions are involved: input, storage, processing, and output. Input involves taking information from switches operated by the keyboard and translating it into digital code. Storage, or memory, involves holding information for use. Processing is the creation of new information based on the old, and output is the display of this information by means of light-emitting diodes. The magnetic card system used in such calculators corresponds to a computer's magnetic tape unit, but it can store only instructions, not numbers.

The memory consists of four different units: the program memory, the microprogram memory, the so-called "constant" memory, and the number memory. The processing parts consist of two sections: the controller and the arithmetic and logic unit (ALU).

calculus

calculus Calculus is a branch of mathematics designed to find lengths, areas, and volumes and to study the rate of change of variable quantities called FUNCTIONS. INTEGRAL CALCULUS uses the integral of a function to measure lengths, areas, and volumes, and DIFFERENTIAL CALCULUS uses the derivative of a function to study rates of change. Both are fundamental for any physical or social science dealing with changing quantities, such as the velocity of a satellite (as a function of time) or the profits of a corporation (as a function of sales); questions about such quantities can often be phrased in terms of finding areas or rates of change (see MATHEMATICS, HISTORY OF).

More than 4,000 years ago the Babylonians investigated areas and volumes, and more than 2,000 years ago the Greek scientists Archimedes and Apollonius found areas and tangents for many curved figures. In 1637 the French mathematician René DESCARTES combined the algebra inherited from medieval Muslim civilization with the geometry of the Greeks to produce ANALYTIC GEOMETRY, a method of solving geometric problems by using algebra and COORDINATE SYSTEMS. In 1665–66 the English scientist Isaac NEWTON, while still a student, discovered the fundamental theorem of calculus, which shows the close connection between finding areas under curves and finding tangents to curves. He also invented a general method that used this theorem and his discovery of the BINOMIAL THEOREM to solve many problems involving areas and tangents. With these discoveries, calculus was born.

Ten years later the German mathematician Gottfried LEIBNIZ independently made the same discoveries, and over the next 125 years mathematicians extended the theory of calculus to deal with quantities depending on many variables. One important step was the introduction in 1734, by the Swiss mathematician Leonhard EULER, of partial derivatives of functions of several variables. Euler and other mathematicians, such as Jacques, Johann, and Daniel Bernoulli of Switzerland (see BERNOULLI, DANIEL; BERNOULLI, JACQUES) and Pierre LAPLACE of France, applied calculus to problems in mechanics and probability. Early in the 19th century the French mathematician A. L. CAUCHY put calculus on a logically rigorous basis, and it became part of a general theory of real and complex variables.

Calcutta

Calcutta Calcutta, a city and port in eastern India and capital of West Bengal state, is India's largest metropolis and one of the largest cities in the world. It lies opposite HOWRAH on the Hooghly River 128 km (80 mi) north of the Bay of Bengal. The city has an area of about 100 km^2 (40 mi^2) and a population of 3,291,655 (1981). It is the largest of the approximately 75 local governing bodies

Calcutta, the capital of British India from 1773 to 1911, has many elegant structures of both European and Indian design. The Jain temple (left), an Indian shrine noted for its lavish interior, is a major tourist attraction.

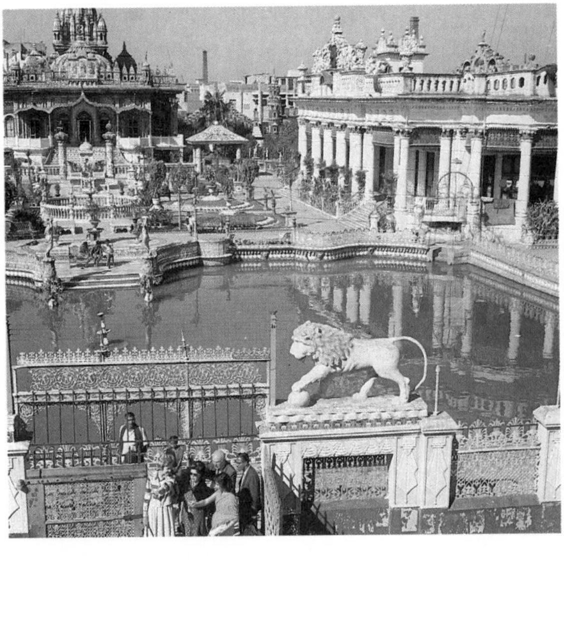

that make up the Calcutta Metropolitan District (CMD), which has a total area of 1,425 km^2 (550 mi^2) and a population of 9,165,650 (1981).

Contemporary City. The city is one of the most crowded in the world. The housing shortage and overcrowding are openly apparent in many parts of the city, especially to the north. An estimated 200,000 people live in the streets or in temporary sheds.

Calcutta is a major banking and commercial center, and the CMD is one of India's leading industrial areas. Significant industries include jute milling, engineering, metallurgy, paper, pharmaceuticals, glass, and synthetic fabrics. Calcutta's busy port serves the adjacent interior and handles much of India's import-export cargo. High labor costs and a long-neglected infrastructure have hampered economic growth.

An intellectual center, Calcutta is the seat of the University of Calcutta (1857), one of the largest universities in the world. Landmarks include the Botanical Gardens in Howrah, the Zoological Gardens in Alipur, the Jain temple, the Dakshineswar temple, the Victoria Memorial, the Indian Museum, and the cantilever Howrah Bridge.

History. Calcutta was founded by the British East India Company, which purchased the villages of Sutanati, Kalikata, and Govindapur in 1698. The name *Calcutta* is possibly derived from Kalikata, which was the mythological landing place for the goddess KALI. In 1756 the nawab of Bengal captured Calcutta and killed most of the British defenders by shutting them up in a tiny airless room—the infamous Black Hole of Calcutta. In 1757, Robert CLIVE retook the city. Calcutta served as the capital of British India from 1773 to 1911. In 1912 the capital was moved to Delhi.

In 1942 and 1945–47 the independence movement sparked bloody riots in Calcutta. After independence millions of impoverished peasants and Hindu refugees flocked to the city; rapid growth caused much social unrest. The revolutionary Naxalite movement was crushed in the early 1970s, but Calcutta remains a leftist stronghold.

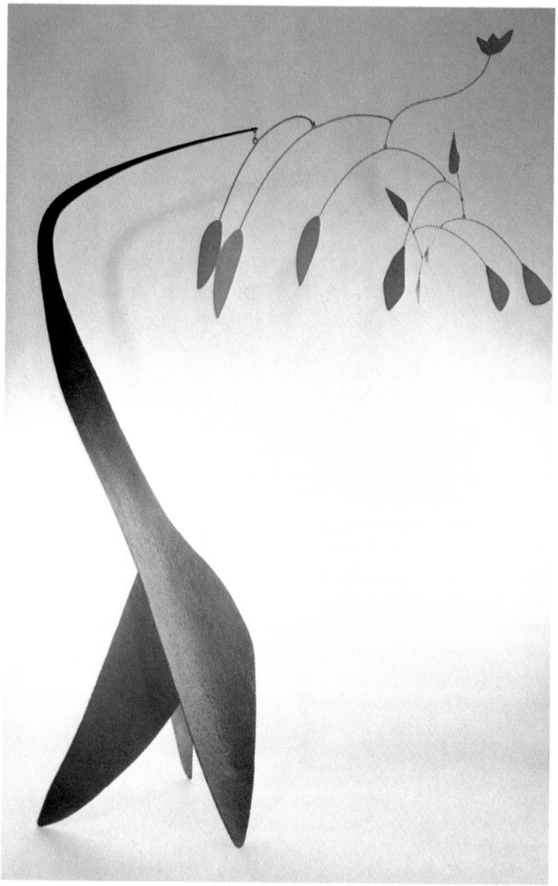

Red Petals *(1942), one of many mobiles constructed by Alexander Calder beginning in the 1930s, is made of sheet steel, steel wire, and sheet aluminum. This kinetic sculpture stands 2.8 m (9.2 ft) high. (Arts Club of Chicago.)*

Caldecott Medal [kawl'-duh-kuht] The Caldecott Medal, named for the 19th-century English illustrator Randolph J. Caldecott, is presented annually by the American Library Association for the best American illustrated children's book. Winners have included artist Ludwig Bemelmans, cartoonist William Steig, and illustrator Maurice Sendak.

Calder, Alexander [kawl'-dur] Alexander Calder, b. Philadelphia, July 22, 1898, d. Nov. 11, 1976, one of the most innovative sculptors of the 20th century, is best known for bringing motion to sculpture through the ingenious mobiles he created from the early 1930s through the 1970s. In Paris from the late 1920s, Calder was influenced by ABSTRACT ART. He first attracted European attention with his novel wood and wire creations, especially the *Circus* group of 1927 (Whitney Museum, New York City).

In 1930, after a visit to Piet MONDRIAN's Paris studio, Calder began experimenting with abstraction. Direct contact with painter Joan MIRÓ; and sculptor Jean ARP also stimulated Calder's move to free forms and kidney shapes. In 1931 he sought to create a dynamic sculpture through freestanding, mechanically driven structures. By 1932, Calder had abandoned representational wire sculpture. Synthesizing surrealist, organic form with constructivist kineticism and structure, he began making the delicately balanced, wind-propelled constructions of painted sheet-aluminum, brass, or steel wired together (called "mobiles" by Marcel DUCHAMP) with which his name has since become synonymous. During the 1950s and 1960s Calder turned to monumental stationary pieces, a variation on his earlier, smaller stabiles.

Calderón de la Barca, Pedro [kahl-day-rohn' day lah bahr'-kah] Pedro Calderón de la Barca, b. Jan. 17, 1600, d. May 25, 1681, was a Spanish playwright who dominated the Spanish stage for much of the 17th century. His philosophical play *Life Is a Dream* (1635; Eng. trans., 1959) is a masterpiece of world literature. In his own time, however, Calderón was known mainly for his *autos sacramentales*—one-act allegorical plays concerning the mystery of the Eucharist—and for his *comedias de capa y espada*, cloak-and-dagger comedies with elaborate plots. He is also credited with having started the ZARZUELA, a Spanish opera genre.

Among Calderón's more than 100 *comedias* are *The Constant Prince* (1629; Eng. trans., 1960) and *The Mayor of Zalamea* (*c.*1640; Eng. trans., 1958). Notable among the *autos sacramentales* are *Balshazzar's Feast* (*c.*1630; Eng. trans., 1960) and *The Great Theatre of the World* (*c.*1635; Eng. trans., 1856).

Caldwell, Billy Billy Caldwell, 1780–1841, known in the folklore of early Chicago as a great POTAWATOMI Indian chief, was actually the son of an Irish immigrant to America, Capt. William Caldwell, Sr., and a Mohawk Indian woman. Raised in his father's home in Ontario as a loyal Briton, he served as a captain in the British Indian Service during the War of 1812. He later migrated to Chicago, where American officials appointed him as a chief of the Illinois Potawatomi Indian bands, hoping to use him to obtain Indian lands. The Potawatomi chiefs, however, sought and obtained Caldwell's loyalty, and he served their interests until his death. He was also called the Sagaunash, meaning "English-speaking Canadian."

Caldwell, Erskine [ur'-skin] Erskine Caldwell, b. Moreland, Ga., Dec. 17, 1903, d. Apr. 11, 1987, was an American author best known for his novel TOBACCO ROAD (1932; film, 1941). The 1933 stage version set Broadway records with its 7-year run. Caldwell's other novels include *God's Little Acre* (1933; film, 1958) and *Georgia Boy* (1943). With his second wife, photographer Margaret BOURKE-WHITE, Caldwell produced a word-and-picture study of the rural South, *You Have Seen Their Faces* (1937).

Erskine Caldwell, an American author, chronicled rural Southern life and values in his major works. His best-known novel, Tobacco Road *(1932), was adapted for the stage and became one of the longest-running plays on Broadway.*

Caldwell, Sarah Sarah Caldwell, b. Maryville, Mo., Mar. 6, 1924, is an opera conductor, director, and producer. Caldwell headed the Opera Workshop at Boston University from 1952 to 1960, and in 1957 she founded the Boston Opera Group (the Boston Opera Company since 1965). Caldwell was named artistic director of the New Opera Company of Israel in 1983.

Caldwell, Taylor Janet Taylor Caldwell, b. England, Sept. 7, 1900, d. Aug. 30, 1985, was a popular and prolific American novelist. Her first novel, *Dynasty of Death* (1938), traced the lives of two powerful families over a 60-year period. Many of her other novels followed this generational pattern, including *The Captain and the Kings* (1972; film, 1976) and *Glory and the Lightning* (1974). Caldwell, who sometimes used the pseudonym Max Reiner, also wrote *The Devil's Advocate* (1952), *Dear and Glorious Physician* (1959), and *Answer Like a Man* (1981).

Caledonia [kal-uh-dohn'-yuh] Caledonia is the ancient Roman name for the northern part of Great Britain north of the Firth of Forth, approximating Highland Scotland. Although the Romans made repeated attempts from the 1st to the 3d century to subdue the indigenous tribes they called the Caledones, they never succeeded.

calendar A calendar is a system, defined by rules, for designating the year, dividing it into smaller units, and assigning days to those units; it is also used for determining the dates of civil and religious holidays. The rudiments of a calendric system may have been constructed as long ago as 2000 BC, when STONE ALIGNMENTS were used, it is believed, to determine the length of the solar year by marking the progress of the Sun along the horizon.

Modern international society requires that the same civil calendar be used worldwide. The civil calendar so used is the Gregorian calendar, which was introduced in 1582. The average length of a Gregorian YEAR is close to that of the solar year, or tropical year, about 365.2422 mean solar days, so that the seasons begin on about the same dates each year. The Gregorian calendar, which is derived from ancient calendars, is a determinate calendar; that is, it is defined solely by numerical rules and can be formed for any year in advance. This was not generally true for ancient calendars, which depended on observational rules.

Ancient Calendars. The earliest complete calendars were probably based on lunar observations. The Moon's phases occur over an easily observed interval, the month; religious authorities declared a month to have begun when they first saw the new crescent Moon. During cloudy weather, when it was impossible to see the Moon, the beginning of the month was determined by calculation. The interval from new moon to new moon, called a synodic month, is about 29.53 days. Hence, calendar months contained either 29 or 30 days. Twelve lunar months, which total 354.36 days, form a lunar year, almost 11 days shorter than a tropical year.

A lunar year is not suitable for agricultural purposes. To keep in step with the Sun, lunar-solar calendars were formed by adding an additional (leap) month when the observation of crops made it seem necessary. Hundreds of such calendars, with variations, were formed at various times in such different areas as Mesopotamia, Greece, Rome, India, and China. The month was not always based on the phases of the Moon; the Mayan calendar divided the year into 18 20-day months, with a 5-day period at the end.

The Roman calendar was in error by several months during the reign of Julius Caesar, who recognized the need for a stable, predictable calendar and formed one with the help of an astronomer, Sosigenes. The year 46 BC was given 445 days, to compensate for past errors, and every common year thereafter was to have 365 days. Every fourth year, starting with 45 BC, was to be designated a leap year of 366 days, during which February, which commonly had 28 days, was extended by one day. The rule was not correctly applied, but the calendar was corrected by Augustus Caesar by AD 8.

Gregorian Calendar. The Julian leap-year rule created three leap years too many in every period of 385 years. As a result, the actual occurrence of the equinoxes and solstices drifted away from their assigned calendar dates. Because the date of the spring equinox determines that of Easter, the church was concerned, and Pope Gregory XIII, with the help of an astronomer, Christopher Clavius, introduced what is now called the Gregorian calendar. Wednesday, Oct. 4, 1582 (Julian), was followed by Thursday, Oct. 15, 1582 (Gregorian); leap years occurred in years exactly divisible by four, except that years ending in 00 had to be divisible by 400. Thus, 1600, 1984, and 2000 were leap years, but 1800 and 1900 were not.

The Gregorian calendar is a solar calendar, calculated without reference to the Moon. The methods it uses to determine the dates of Easter and other Christian holidays, however, are based on both solar and lunar calculations. The calendar was quickly adopted by Roman Catholic countries and, eventually, by every Western country, as well as by Japan, Egypt, and China.

Year Beginning. The Roman year began in March; December, whose name is derived from the Latin word for "ten," was the tenth month of the year. In 153 BC, Roman consuls began taking office on January 1, which became the beginning of the year. This practice was retained in the Julian and Gregorian calendars, although other starting dates continued to be used. England and its colonies, for example, used March 25 and the Julian reckoning until 1752. Thus, George Washington was officially born on Feb. 11, 1731, Old Style (O.S.); this is Feb. 22, 1732, Gregorian, or New Style (N.S.).

The Months. In every Western European language, the names of the months retain their Roman origin. English names are January, for Janus, god of beginning and endings; February, derived from *Februalia*, a time for religious atonement; March, for Mars, the god of war; April, from *aperire*, Latin for "to open" (as, spring flowers); May, for Maia, the goddess of plant growth; June, from *juvenis*, "youth"; July, for Julius Caesar; August, for Augustus, first Roman emperor; September, from *septem*, "seven"; October, November, and December, from *octo, novem,* and *decem*, "eight," "nine," and "ten." (Note that the earliest Latin calendar had only 10 months, with September as the 7th month and December the 10th.)

Week. The Babylonians used a nonastronomical, 7-day interval, the week, which was adopted by the Jews. The seventh day, the Sabbath, was given a religious significance. Independently, the Romans associated a cycle of 7 days with the Sun, the Moon, and the five known planets. Their names became attached to the days of the

By 1582 the Julian calendar no longer corresponded to the astronomical dates for the seasons and religious holidays. At a meeting called by Pope Gregory XIII, a new calendar was devised that combined more accurately the lunar dating of religious feasts and the solar dating of the seasons. The Gregorian calendar has come to be observed in most Christian nations. (Archivo di Stato, Siena.)

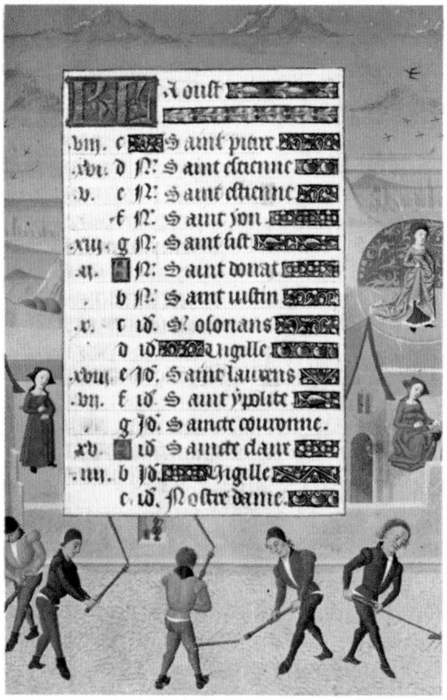

This saints' calendar for half the month of August, from the Breviary of the Duchess of Burgundy (c. 1450), is based in part on the Roman calendar.

week: Sunday (*dies solis*, "Sun's day"), Monday (*dies lunae*, "Moon's day"), and Saturday (*dies Saturni*, "Saturn's day") retain names derived directly from the Roman culture, and Tuesday ("Tiw's day"), Wednesday ("Woden's day"), Thursday ("Thor's day"), and Friday ("Frigg's day") are derived from the Germanic equivalents of Mars, Mercury, Jupiter, and Venus, respectively.

Year. In ancient calendars, years were generally numbered according to the year of a ruler's reign. About AD 525, a monk named Dionysius Exiguus suggested that years be counted from the birth of Christ, which was designated AD (*anno Domini*, "the year of the Lord") 1. This proposal came to be adopted throughout Christendom during the next 500 years. The year before AD 1 is designated 1 BC (before Christ). The 1st century of the Christian Era began in AD 1, the 2d in AD 101; the 21st will begin in 2001.

The Hebrew Calendar. The Hebrew calendar in use today begins at the Creation, which is calculated to have occurred 3,760 years before the Christian era. The week consists of 7 days, beginning with Saturday, the Sabbath; the year consists of 12 lunar months—Tishri, Heshvan, Kislav, Tebet, Shebat, Adar, Nisan, Iyar, Sivan, Tammuz, Ab, and Elul—which are alternately 29 and 30 days long. Because a year is some 11 days longer than 12 lunar months, a 13th month, ve-Adar, is added seven times during every 19-year cycle.

The Islamic Calendar. Muslims begin their calendar at the day and year (July 16, 622, by the Gregorian calendar) when Muhammad fled from Mecca to Medina. There are 12 lunar months of alternate 30 and 29 days, making the year 354 days long. Because of the shortness of the year, the months move backward through all the seasons, completing a cycle every 32½ years. The months are Muharram, Safar, Rabi I, Rabi II, Jumada I, Jumada II, Rajab, Shaban, Ramadan, Shawwal, Zulkadah, and Zulhijjah.

Calendar Reform. Although many proposals have been made for improving the calendar, the basic difficulty lies primarily with the incommensurability of week, month, and year. In addition, correcting some problems invariably causes others, especially those connected with religious holidays.

calendula [kuh-len'-juh-luh] The calendula is a herbaceous annual or perennial in the daisy family, Compositae. To most gardeners the name refers to pot marigold, *Calendula officinalis*. This annual plant is native to southern Europe but will grow and bloom well in cooler areas. Plants grow up to 60 cm (2 ft) high and bear yellow or orange heads of ray and disk flowers. The flower petals are used sometimes to give color to stews or puddings, and medicinally as tincture in treating cuts, burns, and sprains.

Calgary [kal'-guh-ree] Calgary is a city in southern Alberta, Canada, at the confluence of the Bow and Elbow rivers. It has a population of 636,104 (1986). Served by the Trans-Canada Highway, two transcontinental railroads, and an airport, it is a major distribution center of industrial and agricultural products. The University of Calgary, Mount Royal Community College, and the Southern Alberta Institute of Technology are located there. The annual Calgary Stampede, a rodeo and fair, is held in July. The city was also the site of the 1988 Winter Olympic Games.

Established in 1875 as a North-West Mounted Police post named Fort Brisebois, it was soon renamed Fort Calgary by J. F. MacLeod, first commissioner of the Mounties. The arrival of the Canadian Pacific Railway in 1883 increased Calgary's importance as the center of a wheat-farming and cattle-raising area. The implementation of the Western Irrigation District Projects in 1904 contributed to the agricultural prosperity. The discovery (1914) of oil and natural gas in the Turner Valley fields led to considerable economic growth. Today, many oil companies are based in Calgary.

Calhoun, John C. John Caldwell Calhoun, b. near Abbeville, S.C., on Mar. 18, 1782, d. Mar. 31, 1850, statesman and political philosopher, was vice-president (1825–32) of the United States and a leading champion of Southern rights. He was educated at Yale University and studied law under Tapping Reeve in Litchfield, Conn. Admitted to the South Carolina bar in 1807, Calhoun served in the state legislature from 1809 to 1811 and in Congress from 1811. Appointed (1817) secretary of war in the cabinet of James MONROE, Calhoun supported the American System, which called for federal power to nurture American commerce and industry through a protective tariff, a federally chartered BANK OF THE UNITED STATES, and federally financed road, canal, and harbor construction.

In 1824, Calhoun was elected vice-president under

John Calhoun, a South Carolina politician who was twice elected vice-president of the United States, developed a philosophy of sectional rights that ultimately fostered secessionist thought in the South.

John Quincy ADAMS. At that time he was not identified with the STATE RIGHTS position advocated by Southern conservatives. His views on federal power, however, were undergoing a transformation inspired in part by the expansion of cotton cultivation, dependent upon slavery, into South Carolina. Believing the South could no longer be served by an active federal government fostering commerce and industry, Calhoun repudiated the American System and broke with the Adams administration. In 1828, he secretly authored the *South Carolina Exposition and Protest*, which asserted that a state had the power of NULLIFICATION over any federal law it deemed unconstitutional.

Supporting Andrew JACKSON's presidential candidacy in 1828, Calhoun was reelected to the vice-presidency. His efforts to dominate the Jackson administration were frustrated by Jackson's refusal to endorse an extreme state rights position. Calhoun's role in the ostracization of Peggy Eaton, wife of Secretary of War John H. EATON, further weakened his position. After Jackson opposed South Carolina's efforts to nullify the tariff of 1832, Calhoun resigned from the vice-presidency.

Serving (1842–43, 1845–50) in the Senate, Calhoun was a powerful spokesman for slavery and Southern rights. He secured passage of the GAG RULES that forbade discussion of slavery on the floor of Congress. Serving briefly as secretary of state (1844–45), he engineered the controversial annexation of Texas. He spent the rest of his career defending the right of slavery to expand into federal territories and predicting disunion and civil war if that right were not respected.

Cali [kah'-lee] Cali, a city on the Cali River in western Colombia, has a population of 1,397,433 (1985). It is a center of trade, industry, and transportation for a rich agricultural region. Its manufactures include tires, textiles, tobacco products, paper, chemicals, and construction materials. The University of Valle (1945) and Santiago University of Cali (1958) are located there. Although the town was founded in 1536, its development as an economically important city is recent. Colombia's third largest city after Bogotá and Medellín, Cali also became a center of the violent international drug trade in the 1980s.

calico One of the oldest cotton fabrics, calico was originally made in Calicut, India. It was highly valued for its fine texture and the beauty of its block-printed colors. The term later was used to indicate most plain-woven cottons. Today, it often means lightweight, narrow-width cottons that are made into such items as aprons, curtains, and blouses.

California California, a state of the far-western United States, is widely known for its great natural beauty, its highly productive farms and factories, and its innovative social and political ideas. Its many cities include LOS ANGELES, a major center of the entertainment and aerospace industries, and SAN FRANCISCO, a sophisticated financial center. The state has lured millions of migrants since the mid-19th century, when gold was discovered there, and by the late 1970s it was the nation's most populous state. California is bordered by Oregon on the north, by Nevada and Arizona on the east, by Mexico on the south, and by the Pacific Ocean on the west. The state is named for a fictional island of great wealth described in a novel (published about 1500) by the Spanish writer Garcí Ordóñez de Montalvo.

Land and Resources

California is a state of great scenic beauty, and it is well endowed with natural resources. Its highest point is Mount WHITNEY (4,418 m/14,494 ft), the loftiest point in the conterminous United States; and its lowest point, in DEATH VALLEY (86 m/282 ft below sea level), is the lowest point in the Western Hemisphere.

Physiographic Regions. California has a varied topography, the main features of which are the large and fertile Central Valley and the mountain ranges that enclose it. The Central, or Great, Valley, about 805 km (500 mi) long and 80 km (50 mi) wide, includes two major drainage basins: the SACRAMENTO RIVER system, in the north, and the SAN JOAQUIN RIVER system, in the south. Both ultimately empty into the Pacific Ocean. The Central Valley generally is very flat, with elevations of less than 150 m (492 ft). It is bounded on the northwest by the Klamath Mountains, a rugged, forested range. The southern portion of the CASCADE RANGE borders the Central Valley on the northeast. The Cascades include isolated lofty volcanic peaks, the highest of which is Mount SHASTA (4,317 m/14,162 ft), as well as cinder cones, lava flows, and beds of ash, pumice, and tuff. LASSEN PEAK (3,187 m/10,457 ft) is one of the two active volcanoes in the conterminous United States.

To the east of the Central Valley is the great SIERRA NEVADA, a north-south mountain barrier with many peaks rising more than 4,267 m (14,000 ft); the highest point is Mount Whitney. The western slopes are cut by deep

AT A GLANCE

CALIFORNIA

Land: Area: 411,047 km^2 (158,706 mi^2); rank: 3d. Capital: Sacramento (1990 pop., 369,365). Largest city: Los Angeles (1990 pop., 3,485,398). Counties: 58. Elevations: highest—4,418 m (14,494 ft), at Mount Whitney; lowest— -86m (-282 ft) at Death Valley.

People: Population (1990): 29,839,250; rank: 1st; density: 72.6 persons per km^2 (188.0 per mi^2). Distribution (1988): 95.7% metropolitan, 4.3% nonmetropolitan. Average annual change (1980-90): +2.6%.

Government (1991): Governor: Pete Wilson, Republican. U.S. Congress: Senate—1 Democrat, 1 Republican; House—26 Democrats, 19 Republicans. Electoral college votes: 47. State legislature: 40 senators, 80 representatives.

Economy: State personal income (1988): $531 billion; rank: 1st. Median family income (1979): $21,537; rank: 10th. Agriculture: income (1988)—$16.6 billion. Fishing: value (1988)—$199 million. Forestry: sawtimber volume (1987)—312 billion board feet. Mining: value (1986)—$8.3 billion. Manufacturing: value added (1987)—$134 billion. Services: value (1987)—$157.9 billion.

Miscellany: Statehood: Sept. 9, 1850; the 31st state. Nickname: Golden State; tree: California redwood; motto: *Eureka* ("I have found it") ; song: "I Love You, California."

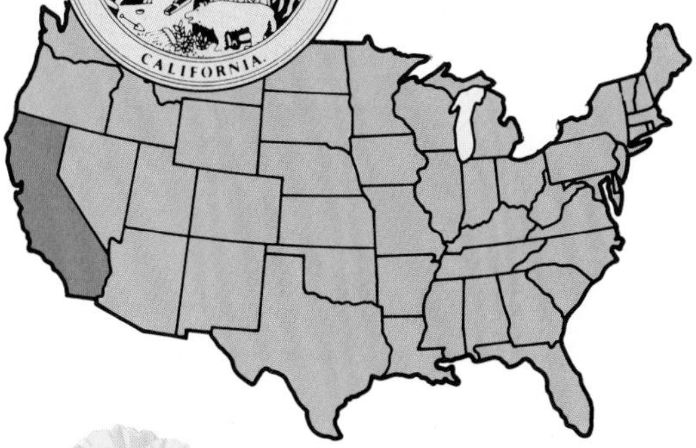

Golden poppy

California valley quail

river canyons, such as the Yosemite Valley, that were formed in part by glacial action. DONNER PASS (2,161 m/7,089 ft high) is part of an important route across the Sierra Nevada.

The Central Valley is bounded on the west and south by the COAST RANGES, which extend parallel to the Pacific. The northern parts of the Coast Ranges are forested and have fertile valleys (such as the Napa Valley), whereas the drier southern portion is covered with chaparral, a dense brush, or with oak-grass woodlands. The SAN ANDREAS FAULT, a fracture in the Earth's crust, cuts through the Coast Ranges; movements along the fault cause periodic earthquakes.

Southeast of the Coast Ranges are the Transverse Ranges, a group of east-west trending mountains. The highest point is Mount San Gorgonio (3,506 m/11,502 ft). The Transverse Ranges enclose many valleys and lowlands, but the only large expanse of flatland is the Los Angeles Lowland, the site of the city of Los Angeles. South of the Los Angeles Ranges are the Peninsular Ranges.

To the east of California's major mountain systems are extensive regions of arid basins and valleys, with several other mountain ranges. In the northeast and east-center are parts of the GREAT BASIN; the latter area includes Death Valley as well as the Panamint range. In southeastern California is the large MOJAVE DESERT and the Salton Trough, which includes the SALTON SEA and the IMPERIAL VALLEY.

The state has about 1,348 km (838 mi) of coastline along the Pacific Ocean. Much of it is rocky and rugged, but southern California has numerous large sand beaches. The Channel Islands (see SANTA BARBARA ISLANDS), which include Santa Catalina Island, are located in the Pacific near Los Angeles.

Rivers and Lakes. The principal rivers of California are the Sacramento and San Joaquin, which merge shortly before emptying into the Pacific Ocean via San Francisco Bay. Most of the state's other large rivers flow into either the Sacramento or the San Joaquin. Additional important rivers not part of these systems include the Colorado, Kern, and Klamath.

California has many large natural lakes. These include Lake TAHOE, astride the border with Nevada; Goose Lake, straddling the boundary with Oregon; Honey Lake, in the northeast; and the shallow Salton Sea, in the south. The state also has numerous artificial lakes, created by dams on rivers.

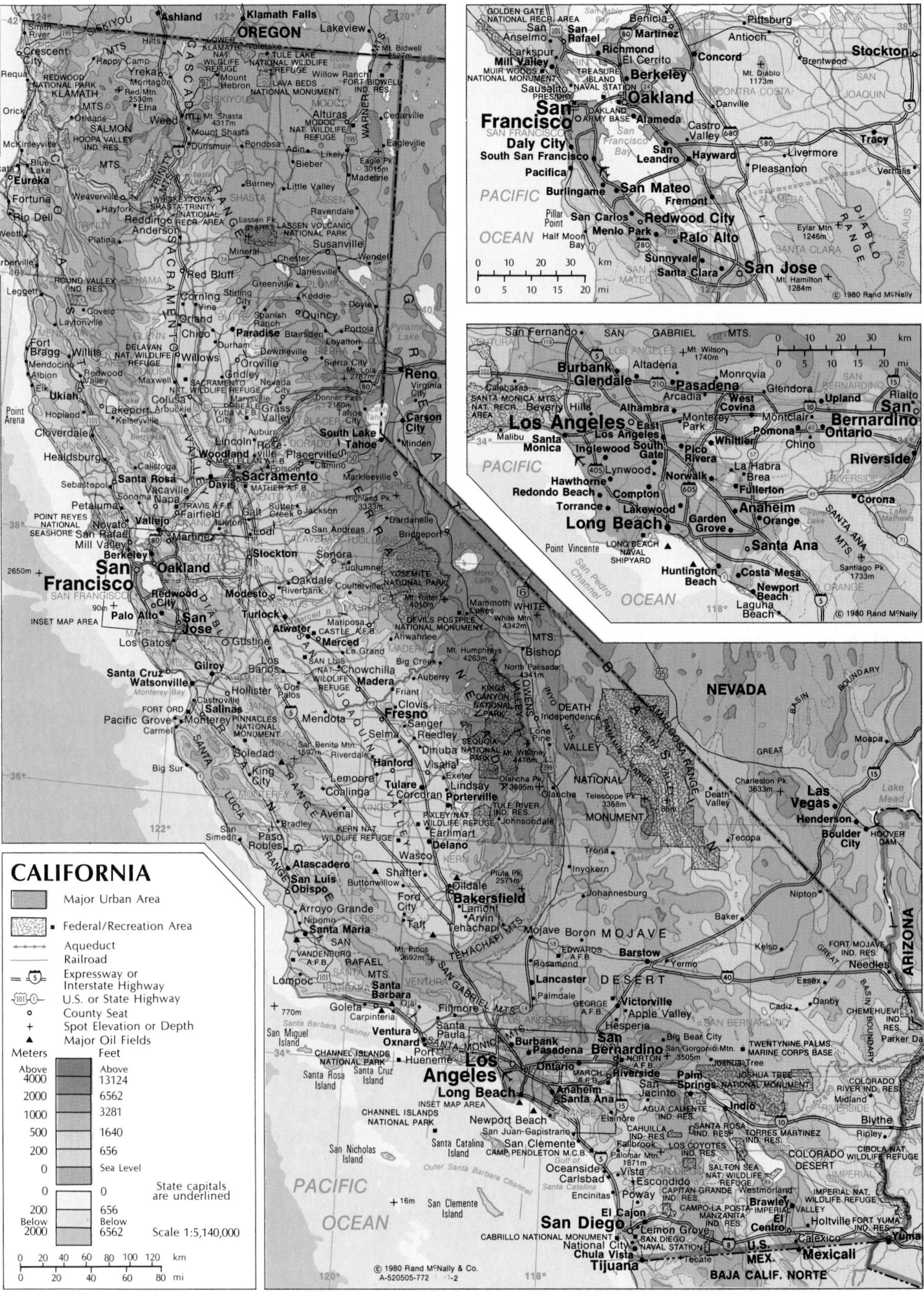
CALIFORNIA
Major Urban Area
Federal/Recreation Area
Aqueduct
Railroad
Expressway or Interstate Highway
U.S. or State Highway
County Seat
Spot Elevation or Depth
Major Oil Fields
Meters
Feet
Above 4000
Above 13124
2000
6562
1000
3281
500
1640
200
656
0
Sea Level
0
0
200
656
Below 2000
Below 6562
State capitals are underlined
Scale 1:5,140,000
OREGON
NEVADA
ARIZONA
BAJA CALIF. NORTE
MEX.
U.S.
PACIFIC OCEAN
Sacramento
San Francisco
Oakland
San Jose
Fresno
Stockton
Modesto
Bakersfield
Los Angeles
Long Beach
San Diego
Santa Barbara
Eureka
Redding
Reno
Las Vegas
San Bernardino
Riverside
Tijuana
Mexicali
Yuma
MOJAVE DESERT
DEATH VALLEY NATIONAL MONUMENT
YOSEMITE NATIONAL PARK
SIERRA NEVADA
SAN JOAQUIN VALLEY
SACRAMENTO VALLEY
INSET MAP AREA
© 1980 Rand McNally & Co.
A-520505-772

Water Distribution. Natural water supplies in California are distributed unevenly and do not parallel the need. The northern third of the state receives about 70% of California's total annual precipitation, but the southern two-thirds (with large population centers, huge tracts of farmland needing irrigation, and numerous industrial establishments) requires about 80% of the water. As a consequence, several great projects have been constructed to transfer water to the south. These include the immense California Water Project, the Central Valley Project, the All-American Canal, and the Owens Valley and Colorado River aqueducts.

Climate. California has a varied climate pattern, the result of its complex topography and wide latitudinal range. Most of the state has only two distinguishable seasons—a rainy period (October to April) and a dry period (May to September). Annual precipitation is greatest in the north, especially near the coast, which receives about 2,032 mm (80 in) of moisture yearly. The south gets much less precipitation; Los Angeles receives only about 381 mm (15 in), and San Diego just 254 mm (10 in). Desert areas receive even less moisture.

Temperatures are mild along the coast, with relatively small variations between the warmest and coolest months; the southern coast is somewhat warmer than the central and northern coasts. The average recorded January temperature in Los Angeles is 13° C (56° F), and in San Francisco it is 10° C (50° F); the mean recorded July temperature in Los Angeles is 22° C (72° F), and in San Francisco it is 15° C (59° F). The Central Valley often has a mild climate, but other parts of the interior are either markedly hotter (Death Valley and the Mojave Desert, for example) or colder (the lofty peaks of the Sierra Nevada).

Vegetation and Animal Life. Forests cover about 42% of California; almost half the forestland is in the state's 22 national forests. The humid northwest has dense coniferous forests, which include numerous tall trees, especially the redwood (ranging to about 113 m/371 ft high). The forests thin toward the east, and much of the Coast Ranges is covered with chaparral. The Sierra Nevada foothills and coastal southern California also have much chaparral. Higher parts of the Sierra Nevada and some sections of the Transverse and Peninsular ranges are covered by woodlands of conifers. The Sierra Nevada is noted for its massive sequoia trees. California's deserts have a sparse cover of xerophytes (drought-resistant plants), including many types of cactus in the Mojave Desert.

Large mammals, such as deer, bears, and cougars, are found in the northwest and in the Sierra Nevada. Chaparral areas have deer, rabbits, coyotes, rattlesnakes, tortoises, and many rodents. Desert wildlife, surprisingly rich, includes bighorn sheep, wild burros, coyotes, hares, sidewinders (a variety of rattlesnake), and numerous lizards. The extremely rare California condor, the largest bird of North America, is found in the Transverse ranges. The state's rivers and lakes contain salmon, bass, and trout; coastal marine waters are noted for their shellfish and grunion.

Mineral Resources. California has economically important deposits of many minerals. Among the more important are crude petroleum and natural gas, found in the southern Central Valley and in coastal southern California (both onshore and offshore); boron and tungsten, located in the deserts of the southeast; and sand and gravel, found in most parts of the state. Other minerals include asbestos, copper, feldspar, gold, iron ore, mercury, potash, soda ash, sulfur, uranium, and zinc.

People

California, the nation's most populous state, has a population of 29,839,250 (1990) and an average population density of 72 persons per km^2 (188 per mi^2). The total population increased by 25.7% during 1980–90 (national rate, 9.8%). Since it became a state in 1850, California has had a high population growth rate, the result, in part, of the large number of persons migrating into the

As space becomes scarcer in downtown Los Angeles, more high-rise buildings appear on the city's skyline. Until the development of earthquake-resistant structures, city laws forbade construction of buildings taller than 150 ft (45.7 m).

state. Net in-migration during 1970–79 was 1,248,000 (46% of the total population growth).

The great majority of California's inhabitants are white, but there are significant communities of minority groups. Blacks (7.6% of the total population in 1980) make up an important minority group; they live mainly in the Los Angeles and Oakland metropolitan areas. Many persons (about 45%) of Hispanic background, known as Chicanos, live in Los Angeles County, which also has many Japanese Americans. San Francisco has a well-known community of Chinese Americans. Substantial numbers of Filipinos and East Indians live, primarily, in the Imperial Valley. California has about 201,311 American Indians, who live on reservations or in the cities. The largest religious community in California is made up of Roman Catholics; large Protestant bodies include Baptists, Episcopalians, Methodists, and Presbyterians. California has a sizable Jewish community.

More than 91% of California's population is classified as urban, and in 1990 the state had 44 cities with 100,000 or more inhabitants. The largest city, by far, is Los Angeles, followed by, in order of decreasing population within the city proper, SAN DIEGO, SAN JOSE, San Francisco, LONG BEACH, OAKLAND, SACRAMENTO (the capital), FRESNO, SANTA ANA, ANAHEIM, RIVERSIDE, Stockton, HUNTINGTON BEACH, and Glendale, all of which have populations greater than 180,000.

Education and Cultural Activity

California is widely known for its excellent educational institutions and for its rich cultural life.

Education. The 1849 California constitution called for a statewide system of free public education. The school system grew rapidly in the 20th century. Private schools proliferated too; they are now about one-third as numerous as public elementary and secondary schools. Many of California's colleges and universities are supported with public funds. The state's system of public higher education has two major branches, the University of California (see CALIFORNIA, UNIVERSITY OF) and the California State Universities. There are 17 universities and 2 technical universities in the California State Universities system, including San Jose (established 1857), San Diego (1897), San Francisco (1899), Fresno (1911), Sacramento (1947), Los Angeles (1947), Long Beach (1949), and Northridge (1958). The state also has an extensive community college system. The nation's first tax-supported junior college was established at Fresno in 1910.

San Diego's rapid growth during the 20th century is due partly to the city's fine natural harbor.

The Golden Gate Bridge, which spans the channel separating Marin County from San Francisco, was the longest suspension bridge in the world when completed in 1937.

Among the state's better-known private institutions of higher education are the California Institute of Technology (1891), at Pasadena; the Claremont Colleges; Mills College (1852), at Oakland; Pepperdine University (1937), at Los Angeles; Stanford University (1885), at Stanford; the University of the Pacific (1851), at Stockton; the University of San Diego (1952); the University of San Francisco (1855); the University of Santa Clara (1851); the University of Southern California (1880), at Los Angeles; and Whittier College (1901), at Whittier.

Cultural Institutions. All of California's larger cities support institutions devoted to learning and the arts. Notable museums include the M. H. de Young Memorial Museum, with exhibitions of American Indian, European, and Oriental art, and the California Palace of the Legion of Honor, featuring displays of French painting, both in San Francisco; the Los Angeles County Museum of Art, expanded in 1986 with its Robert O. Anderson wing devoted to 20th-century works, the Los Angeles Museum of Contemporary Art, opened in 1986, the Los Angeles County Museum of Natural History, with Ice Age fossils from the LA BREA asphalt pits in Los Angeles, and the Southwest Museum, with displays of American Indian artifacts, all in Los Angeles; the Crocker Art Gallery, in Sacramento; the Henry E. Huntington Library, Art Gallery, and Botanical Gardens, in San Marino; the J. Paul GETTY MUSEUM, with noteworthy holdings of ancient Greek and

(Above) *Salt washing down from the Panamint and Amargosa mountains has accumulated over the centuries, forming vast flats in Death Valley. This desert basin contains the lowest point in the Western Hemisphere, 86 m (282 ft) below sea level.*

(Left) *Heavenly Valley, in the Sierra Nevada Mountains of eastern California, is one of the state's many popular ski resorts.*

Roman art, in Malibu; and the San Diego Society of Natural History Museum. Several important research libraries are located in the state. These include the Los Angeles Public Library (about 5.4 million volumes, many destroyed or damaged by fire in 1986); the Stanford University libraries (5.1 million volumes, including the library of the Hoover Institution on War, Revolution, and Peace), at Stanford; the University of California at Berkeley library (6.3 million volumes); and the University of California at Los Angeles library (5.2 million volumes).

Both Los Angeles and San Francisco have respected symphony orchestras, and San Francisco has a noted opera company. Included among the numerous theaters in the state are the Mark Taper Forum in Los Angeles and the American Conservatory Theater in San Francisco.

Historic Sites. Among California's places of historic interest are Cabrillo National Monument, at San Diego, commemorating the voyage of the Spanish explorer Juan Rodríguez Cabrillo in 1542 (see *History* below); John Muir National Historic Site, at Martinez, including the home of the famous naturalist; and several 18th-century Franciscan missions, at or near San Diego, San Juan Capistrano, Santa Barbara, San Luis Obispo, Carmel, and other places.

Recreation and Sports. Ample opportunities for outdoor recreation are found in California—camping, backpacking, and skiing in the mountains; and fishing and water sports along the coast. The state's 6 national parks, numerous public forests, and Lake Tahoe are recreation and vacation centers. Major-league professional sports teams are located in San Diego, Anaheim, Los Angeles, San Francisco, and Oakland.

Communications. California is well supplied with radio and television stations and also daily newspapers. Among the more influential dailies are the *Los Angeles Times*, the *Oakland Tribune*, the *Sacramento Bee*, the *San Diego Union*, the *San Francisco Chronicle*, and the *San Jose Mercury News*. The state's first newspaper, the *Californian*, was initially published in 1846 in Monterey.

Government and Politics

California is governed under a constitution of 1879, as amended; a previous constitution had been adopted in 1849. The chief executive of the state is a governor, elected to a 4-year term; a governor may serve an unlimited number of terms. California has a bicameral legislature, made up of a 40-member Senate and an 80-member Assembly; senators are elected to 4-year terms, and assemblymen are elected to 2-year terms. State laws can be passed directly by voters through an initiative, and laws approved by the legislature can be challenged by voters in a REFERENDUM. The highest tribunal in California is the supreme court, composed of 7 justices appointed by the governor to 12-year terms (and subject to subsequent voter approval). The state has 58 counties, most of them with a government headed by a 5-member board of supervisors plus several countywide elected officials.

Politics at the state and local levels have a fluid quality, with neither party holding a decisive advantage. On some issues, such as water diversion, divisions are more pronounced between northern and southern Californians than between Democrats and Republicans. The Republicans, however, have dominated the governorship for most of the period since 1900. In contests for the U.S. presidency the Democrats carried the state from 1932 through 1948, but since then the Republican candidate has usually won in California.

Cypress Point, a rocky promontory overlooking Monterey Bay, is one of many tourist attractions along the Monterey Peninsula's 17 Mile Drive.

Economy

California has the most productive economy of any U.S. state. Its modern economic growth began in the second half of the 19th century, and the greatest spurt came after 1940.

Agriculture. California's annual cash receipts from farming are consistently far greater than those of any other state. More than two-thirds of the cropland is irrigated. A wide variety of farm goods is produced in the state, and California is the nation's leading, or only, producer of many commodities. Cattle, milk, cotton, and grapes are among the state's chief sources of farm income. Other major products of California are grain, vegetables, fruit, and nuts.

Important farming regions in California include the Imperial Valley, in which highly mechanized farms produce great amounts of vegetables, cotton, alfalfa, and fattened cattle; the Coachella Valley (north of the Salton Sea), noted for its carrots, table grapes, grapefruit, and dates; the coastal southern California area, with a large output of citrus fruit, dairy goods, and vegetables; the Central Valley, producing huge amounts of vegetables, fruit, grain, dairy goods, nuts, and livestock; the Salinas Valley, producing much lettuce, poultry, and almonds; the Santa Clara Valley, growing great quantities of apricots, pears, cherries, and plums; and the Napa Valley, noted for its wine grapes. Many of these regions are important suppliers of winter fruits and vegetables to the entire nation.

Forestry and Fishing. California has large forest-products industries, producing lumber, pulp, and paper. The Sierra Nevada and the northwest part of the state are the chief sources of timber; the principal trees cut are Douglas fir, redwood, and yellow and sugar pine.

Fishing also is a major industry in California, along with fish canning. San Pedro (a district of Los Angeles) is one of the nation's leading fishing ports and also has canneries and processing plants. Other important fishing centers include San Diego and San Francisco. Marine fish make up almost all of the commercial catch; the chief species caught are tuna, mackerel, and anchovies.

Mining. Identified with mining since the 1848 gold rush, California usually ranks among the top three or four states in the annual value of its mineral output. Of the many minerals produced, the most valuable are petroleum, cement, natural gas, and sand and gravel. California leads the nation in the production of asbestos, boron, portland cement, diatomite, gypsum, sand and gravel, natural sodium sulfate, and tungsten. The mineral output of the state also includes much borax, iron ore, mercury, salt, and talc. Gold, largely responsible for the state's growth in the mid-19th century, was mined in relatively small quantities in the late 20th century.

Manufacturing. California ranks first among the states in manufacturing. The leading categories of fabricated goods produced in the state are transportation equipment, processed food, and electrical and electronic goods. The transportation equipment includes aerospace products (notably airplanes), made principally in the Los Angeles area and in San Diego; motor vehicles, assembled in Oakland and in the San Jose and Los Angeles areas; and ships, constructed at Long Beach, San Diego, and San Francisco. The state's food products include canned and frozen fruits and vegetables, processed meat, canned fish, and beverages (wine, fruit juices). Major centers of fruit and vegetable processing include the Los Angeles and San Francisco areas, Bakersfield, Fresno, Sacramento, San Jose, and Stockton. Electrical and electronic goods made in California include communications equipment, household appliances, and motors. The Santa Clara (or "Silicon") Valley, Sacramento, and the Los Angeles area have numerous firms producing and developing electronic equipment. Other goods manufactured in California include steel; textiles and clothing; refined

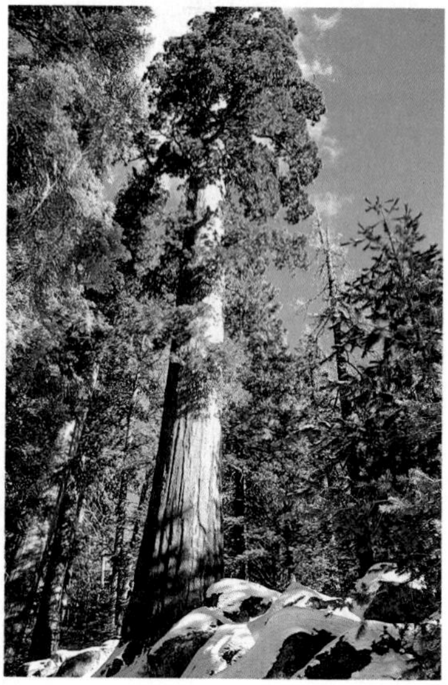

California's towering sequoias, many of which may live to an age of 2,000–3,500 years, grow along the western slopes of the Sierra Nevada. The largest of these trees in Sequoia National Park measures 83 m (272 ft) in height.

petroleum; metal, wood, and plastic products; chemicals; and printed materials. The Los Angeles area (particularly the Hollywood district, Burbank, and Culver City) is the nation's chief center for producing motion pictures and television programs.

Tourism. California each year attracts millions of tourists, lured by the state's equable climate and beautiful scenery, its outdoor recreation opportunities, and the cultural offerings. Popular urban tourist spots include the motion-picture and television studios of the Los Angeles area; DISNEYLAND, a large amusement park at Anaheim; the San Diego zoo and Sea World; and Fishermen's Wharf, Chinatown, and other parts of San Francisco. Many persons visit the state's six national parks (Channel Islands National Park, Kings Canyon National Park, Lassen Volcanic National Park, REDWOOD NATIONAL PARK, SEQUOIA NATIONAL PARK, YOSEMITE NATIONAL PARK) and such national monuments as Death Valley National Monument and Muir Woods National Monument.

Transportation. California is well supplied with land, air, and sea transport facilities, but it has few inland waterways. Motor-vehicle transport is especially important, and in the late 1980s California had more than 21 million registered motor vehicles, far more than any other state. The extensive system of all-weather roads and highways includes many heavily used limited-access roadways (mainly in southern California). San Francisco is a terminus of two famous vehicular bridges, the Golden Gate Bridge and the San Francisco–Oakland Bay Bridge.

(Left) *Yosemite Falls, the highest waterfall on the North American continent, cascades 732 m (2,400 ft) to the valley floor. One of California's six national parks, Yosemite is situated in the Sierra Nevada Range.*

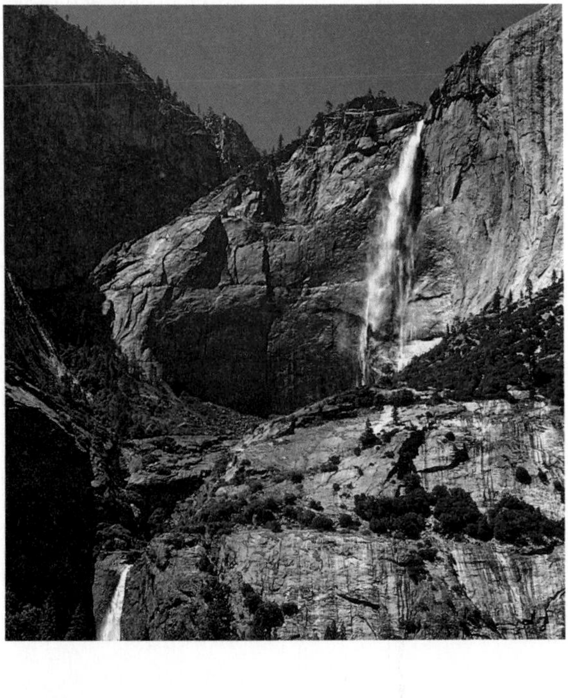

Some railroads continue to operate but are less important than other transportation.

The state's busiest airports are the Los Angeles and San Francisco international airports and the airport at Santa Ana. California's several major seaports include Oakland, San Francisco, and Richmond, on San Francisco Bay; Eureka, on Humboldt Bay; Los Angeles-Long Beach; and San Diego. The state's inland commercial waterways include the lower Sacramento and San Joaquin rivers, and the Stockton Ship Canal.

Energy. In the late 1980s California's installed electric generating capacity was about 45,400,000 kW, and the annual production was about 130.3 billion kW h. About two-thirds of the electricity is generated in thermoelectric plants, mainly burning refined petroleum or natural gas; several nuclear-power facilities operate in the state. About one-third of the state's electricity is produced by hydroelectric installations.

History

When the first Europeans arrived, in the early 16th century, the region of California was inhabited by a relatively sparse Indian population. Among the Indian groups were the HUPA, POMO, Wishosk, and Yuki, in the north; the Costano, Miwok, Salinan, and Yokut, in the center; the Mono and Panamint, in the east; and the Chumash, Serrano, and Diegueño, in the south.

Juan Rodríguez CABRILLO, a Portuguese navigator exploring for Spain, was probably the first European to see California. Sailing north from present-day Mexico, he visited San Diego Bay in September 1542. The next major voyage along the coast was made by the English navigator Sir Francis DRAKE, in 1579. He discovered San Francisco Bay and claimed the region of northern California for England. Fearing English intrusion, the Spanish sent several coastal expeditions, including that of Sebastián VIZCAÍNO to Monterey Bay in 1602–03. No European settlements were established until Capt. Gaspar de PORTOLÁ;, the Spanish governor of Baja California, led an expedition north in 1769–70, partly in order to offset Russian activity. During the journey, forts were established at San Diego and Monterey, thus asserting a minimum of Spanish control. Father Junípero SERRA went along on the expedi-

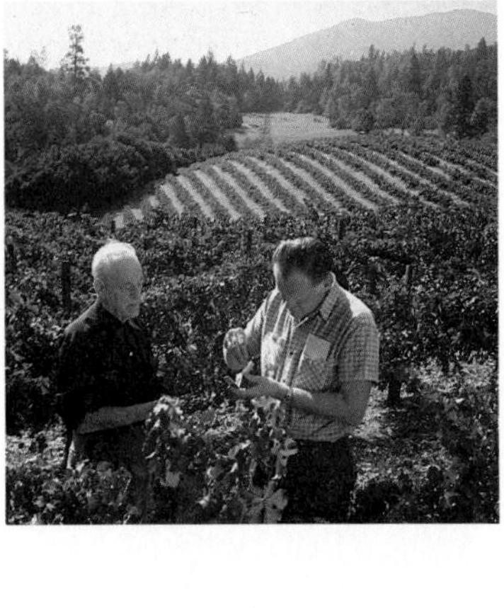

Vintners check the sugar content of grapes near their winery in the Napa Valley, a region noted for its premium table wines.

(Left) *California's fertile Imperial Valley is irrigated by a canal system that draws water from the Colorado River, nearly 129 km (80 mi) away.* (Right) *This aerial photograph of a freeway interchange near Los Angeles indicates the dominant role of automobiles in California's transportation system. With the most extensive network of multilane highways in the United States, California also has the greatest number of registered motor vehicles of any state.*

tion, and in 1769 he founded a Franciscan mission, San Diego de Alcalá, near modern San Diego. This was the first of a string of 21 missions, ranging to Sonoma (north of present-day San Francisco), founded by the Franciscans during the next 54 years. The missions controlled much land, and, using Indian labor, they produced large quantities of cattle hides and tallow (the area's chief exports at the time) and fruit and vegetables.

California was little affected by the political upheavals in Mexico during 1808–11. In 1812 the Russians established Fort Ross along the northern coast (near the mouth of the Russian River) as a trading and fur-trapping center, which they maintained until 1841. In 1821 Mexico gained independence from Spain, and in 1822 California (known as Alta California) became a province of the new nation. For a time, about 1825–35, the Mexicans sought to exert control over California, but they had little success, and the region generally was neglected thereafter.

During the 1840s a few hundred U.S. citizens moved into California to farm, hunt, and trade. They were aided by John A. SUTTER, a Swiss who held a vast tract of land at present-day Sacramento. In 1843–46, Captain John C. FRÉMONT led two U.S. government surveying expeditions into California. In May 1846 the United States went to war with Mexico over Texas (see MEXICAN WAR). The following month, before news of the outbreak of war had reached California, a group of U.S. citizens under the influence of Frémont captured the Mexican presidio at Sonoma. This short-lived event is known as the Bear Flag Revolt. On July 7, 1846, Commodore John D. Sloat claimed California for the United States by raising the U.S. flag over Monterey. This episode was followed by the easy conquest of California by Commodore Robert F. STOCKTON, Gen. Stephen Watts KEARNY, and other U.S. soldiers. California was officially transferred to the United States by the Treaty of GUADALUPE HIDALGO, signed Feb. 2, 1848.

On Jan. 24, 1848, a few days before the treaty was signed, gold had been found at a sawmill (owned by Sutter) on the South Fork of the American River, at Coloma. News of the discovery spread rapidly, and a gold rush was soon under way, bringing thousands of "forty-niners" to stake claims in northern California. San Francisco grew as a gateway to the area. From 1848 to 1850 the state's white population more than tripled, to 93,000 inhabitants. After heated discussions in the U.S. Congress concerning the spread of slavery, California was admitted to the Union as a nonslavery state on Sept. 9, 1850 (see COMPROMISE OF 1850); it was the country's 31st state. California's first capital was San Jose; the capital was moved later to Vallejo and then to Benicia before Sacramento became the permanent capital in 1854. Although proslavery sentiment was considerable in southern California, the entire state remained in the Union during the Civil War, a war that had little direct effect on Californians.

Gold production had peaked in 1852 and thereafter declined rapidly. During the 1860s agriculture grew in importance. Economic growth was furthered by the completion, in 1869, of the first transcontinental railroad, which linked Sacramento with the rest of the nation. Four Californians—Charles Crocker, Mark Hopkins, Collis P. Huntington, and Leland STANFORD—helped finance the railroad, and their Southern Pacific Company exerted great influence over the economy and the political life of the state in the late 19th century. About 30,000 Chinese laborers were brought to California to help build the railroad, and they remained in the state after its completion.

When poor economic conditions in the 1870s led to a high rate of unemployment, the white settlers were bitter toward the Chinese, who were willing to work for low wages. Anti-Chinese riots occurred in San Francisco in 1877. In 1882 the federal government enacted a law prohibiting further Chinese immigration.

The economy of California improved in the 1880s, and southern California, especially the Los Angeles area, began a period of rapid growth. Citrus groves around Los Angeles started to produce large quantities of fruit in the late 1880s, major petroleum fields were discovered in the same region beginning in the early 1890s, and the first motion picture produced in southern California was completed in 1907. In 1906 San Francisco was devastated by a great earthquake and fire.

California politics, dominated for many years by the Southern Pacific Company, underwent major reforms in the early 20th century, especially during the governorship (1911–17) of Hiram W. Johnson, a founder of the Progressive party. During Johnson's administration, the political power of the Southern Pacific was greatly reduced, and many reforms were passed to make the state government more responsive to popular needs. California's economy benefited from the opening (1914) of the Panama Canal (which greatly shortened the sea route between the east and west coasts) and from the many factories established in the state to help meet the requirements of the U.S. effort in World War I. The state's population grew rapidly in the 1920s, increasing from 3,427,000 in 1920 to 5,677,000 in 1930, as farming and industry were developed. California was deeply affected by the Great Depression of the 1930s. The state's high unemployment rate was exacerbated by the influx of many impoverished farmers from the Dust Bowl region of the American West. California's economy improved greatly during World War II, as the state became a major center for building aircraft and ships. During the war, persons of Japanese descent living in California were placed in detention camps outside the state, and much of their property was confiscated.

Prosperity continued into the postwar period, and the population increased at an amazing pace, jumping from 10,586,000 in 1950 to 15,717,000 in 1960. Able governors like Earl WARREN (in office, 1943–53) and Edmund G. "Pat" Brown (1959–67) helped Californians meet some of the social and economic problems that accompanied the rapid growth, but California was the scene of several major social protests in the 1960s, including organized campaigns by blacks to end racial discrimination in housing, education, and employment. In 1965 rioting occurred in the predominantly black Watts district of Los Angeles, and similar violent outbursts by blacks occurred in several other California cities in the mid-1960s. At the same time Cesar CHAVEZ attempted to organize migrant farm laborers, most of whom were of Mexican descent, but in the face of stiff opposition by farm owners he made little progress until the mid-1970s. The Free Speech Movement (which began in late 1964) at the University of California at Berkeley set a pattern for many other campaigns in the country to increase student influence over the management of institutions of higher education. Several major protest demonstrations against U.S. military involvement in Southeast Asia took place in California, mainly during 1965–71.

In the 1970s, under governors Ronald REAGAN (in office, 1967–75) and Jerry BROWN (1975–83), the son of Edmund "Pat" Brown, California tried to meet such pressing environmental problems as air and water pollution and threats to the natural beauty of the coastline from development. In 1978, California voters overwhelmingly passed an initiative (called Proposition 13) that mandated a major reduction in property taxes. Under Gov. George Deukmejian in the 1980s the state's economy grew in most sectors; the most striking demographic development was the fast growth of the Asian segment of the population. A major problem facing Gov. Pete Wilson, who took office in 1991, was California's worsening drought.

California, Gulf of The Gulf of California is an arm of the Pacific Ocean on the northwest coast of Mexico, separating the peninsula of Baja California from the mainland. It is more than 1,100 km (700 mi) long and from 65 to 240 km (40 to 150 mi) wide and has an area of 160,000 km^2 (62,000 mi^2). Depths of up to 3,700 m (12,100 ft) have been found.

The Colorado River enters the gulf at the north end. Its huge volume is one cause of the tidal bore that makes navigation dangerous. The largest islands are Tiburón and Angel de la Guarda, in the north. La Paz in Baja California and Guaymas on the mainland are the principal ports. Sport and commercial fishing is carried on, and sponges and pearls are harvested. The first exploration (1539) of the gulf was by Francisco de Ulloa, at the direction of Hernán Cortés, the conqueror of Mexico. The gulf has also been called the Sea of Cortés.

California, University of The University of California is a system of higher education consisting of nine campuses, the first of which was established in 1868 in Oakland. This moved in 1873 to Berkeley. Other campuses are at Davis, Irvine, Los Angeles, Riverside, San Diego (at La Jolla), San Francisco, Santa Barbara, and Santa Cruz. Unique aspects of their individual locations have attracted special research and professional programs, for instance, a theater arts program in Los Angeles, the Scripps Institution of Oceanography at San Diego, and a research center for the desert and another for citrus fruits at Riverside. The San Diego and Santa Cruz campuses are divided into separate smaller component colleges in a system modeled on that of Oxford and Cambridge. A high minimum eligiblity standard applies to all campuses within the system.

The University of California system is governed by a board of regents appointed by the governor of the state. They in turn appoint a president for the system and, with his or her advice, chancellors for each of the branch campuses.

California Institute of Technology Established in 1891, the California Institute of Technology (Caltech) is a private coeducational university in Pasadena, Calif. The curriculum stresses astronomy, biology, chemistry, engineering, physics, and seismology. Caltech operates the Jet Propulsion Laboratory for the National Aeronautics and Space Administration; Palomar Observatory, formerly part of the Hale Observatories; and Big Bear Solar Observatory.

californium Californium is a chemical element, a radioactive metal of the actinide series. Its symbol is Cf, its atomic number is 98, and its atomic weight is 251 for the stablest isotope. Californium does not occur naturally. The element was first synthesized in 1950 by S. G. Thompson, K. Street, Jr., A. Ghiorso, and Glenn T. SEABORG, who bombarded a few micrograms of curium-242 with helium ions to form the mass-245 isotope of the new element. Named for the University of California and for the state, californium has been used extensively in the study of fission.

Caligula, Roman Emperor [kuh-lig'-yoo-luh] Caligula, b. Aug. 31, AD 12, d. Jan. 24, AD 41, Roman emperor from 37 to 41, was the son of GERMANICUS CAESAR and Agrippina I. He grew up in a military camp, where his father's soldiers nicknamed him Caligula ("Little baby boots"), but his official name as emperor was Gaius Julius Caesar Germanicus. His father died in 19, and his mother and two elder brothers perished in the purge organized by TIBERIUS. Caligula succeeded, however, in gaining the confidence of Tiberius, and from 32 he lived with the recluse emperor on Capri.

Upon the death of Tiberius, Caligula was proclaimed emperor to the exclusion of Tiberius's own grandson, whom he later executed. He pledged cooperation with the Senate, but he soon began to rule in an autocratic manner. Senatorial propaganda asserted that after an illness in October 37 he became mentally unbalanced. To denigrate the senators, he bestowed the consulship on his horse. His military operations on the Rhine in 39–40 were totally ineffective. He was murdered in a plot conceived by an officer of the Praetorian Guard and was succeeded by his uncle CLAUDIUS I.

caliper [kal'-i-pur] The caliper is a centuries-old mechanical instrument for manual MEASUREMENT of small lengths. Once constructed of wood and now made of tool steel, a caliper is configured like a drawing compass, with a specially shaped tip on each leg for contacting points or edges of surfaces to determine inside or outside dimensions. A fixed caliper compares measurements against a standard. An adjustable caliper uses a calibrated screw for direct reading and, when equipped with a vernier scale, achieves an accuracy of .025 mm (.001 in). Electronic and pneumatic calipers improve speed and accuracy and are widely used for automatic gauging of metal and plastic parts.

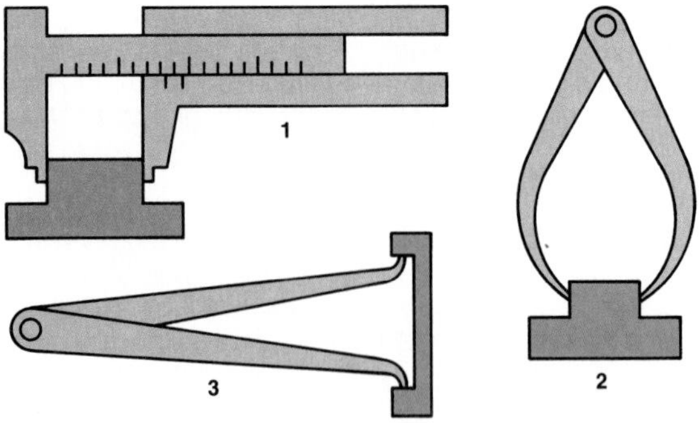

Calipers are used to measure the distance between two surfaces. A slide caliper (1) consists of a jaw fixed on one end of a measuring rule along which a second jaw slides. Simple firm-joint outside calipers (2) and inside measuring calipers (3) have two legs, which pivot about a rivet and are used in conjunction with a separate measuring scale.

caliphate [kal'-if-ayt] The caliphate was the office of the successors to MUHAMMAD in the leadership of the Muslims after the death of the Prophet in 632. Muhammad did not create the office or designate its authority. The Muslim community at first elected the successor and pledged its allegiance, but this practice was replaced by hereditary succession. The title implied the assumption by Muhammad's successor of his functions as judge and temporal leader of the community.

The caliph's powers grew immensely with the expansion of the Islamic empire. The UMAYYADS developed the idea that unconditional obedience was owed to the reigning caliph, and the ABBASIDS claimed that the office must be held by a descendant of the Prophet's family.

By the end of the 9th century the political control of the caliph was increasingly eroded. In the mid-10th century political power was taken over by military commanders (called emirs or sultans), although the caliphate reserved some influence in dogmatic and judicial matters. There was a brief revival of the caliphate under al-Nasir from 1180 to 1225, before the MONGOLS put an end to the Abbasid caliphate in 1258.

Aside from this, the main line of caliphs in Baghdad, there also existed in Spain the Umayyad caliphate (928–1031), which was followed by the Almohad caliphs; in Egypt and Syria the FATIMIDS established a rival SHIITE caliphate (909–1171). From 1258 to 1517 the Abbasid caliphate survived in Cairo under the MAMELUKES. In the 18th century the Turkish sultans of the OTTOMAN EMPIRE presented themselves to the West as caliphs. In 1924 the caliphate was abolished by the Turkish Republic; attempts to revive the institution since that time have been unsuccessful.

Calixtus see CALLISTUS

Call of the Wild, The In *The Call of the Wild* (1903), Jack LONDON tells the story of a pet dog named Buck, who is kidnapped from his California home and turned by the brutality of humans into a sled dog in the Klondike, and finally into a leader of wolves.

calla Calla is the common name of several different plant genera of the arum family, Araceae, and in particular of *Calla palustris*, native to the United States. Species of *Zantedeschia*, native to South Africa, are planted in the United States as the calla lily. Water arum, or wild calla, *C. palustris*, which grows in cold bogs, has a spathe (flowerlike bract) that is green outside and white inside. *Zantedeschia aethiopica*, the familiar calla sold by American florists and grown in gardens, is a sturdy plant with large, arrow-shaped leaves and a creamy white spathe.

Callaghan, James, Baron Callaghan of Cardiff Leonard James Callaghan, b. Mar. 27, 1912, was leader of the British Labour party from 1976 to 1980 and prime minister of the United Kingdom from 1976 to 1979. Elected to the House of Commons in 1945, he remained a member for the constituency of South Cardiff until he gave up his seat in 1985.

In Harold WILSON's first cabinet, which took power in 1964, Callaghan was chancellor of the exchequer and, later, home secretary. As a member of the shadow cabinet, following Labour's defeat in the 1970 election, Callaghan opposed British entry into the European Economic Community (EEC). When the Labour party returned to office in 1974, Wilson appointed Callaghan secretary of state for foreign and commonwealth affairs.

On Apr. 5, 1976, after Wilson's retirement, Callaghan was chosen as Labour party leader and prime minister. Facing a stagnating economic situation in the country, the Labour party was able to reach initial agreement with the unions over wage restraint. But in March 1979, following a series of strikes, Callaghan's Labour government lost a vote of confidence in the House of Commons, the first government to do so since 1924. In the elections that followed in May the Conservatives, led by Margaret Thatcher, won a majority. Callaghan led Labour in opposition until October 1980, when he was succeeded by Michael Foot. In 1987 he was created a life peer, Baron Callaghan of Cardiff.

Callaghan, Morley Morley Edward Callaghan, b. Toronto, Feb. 22, 1903, d. Aug. 25, 1990, was one of Canada's foremost fiction writers. From *Strange Fugitive* (1928), the first of many novels, to *A Time for Judas* (1983), Callaghan revealed society's abuses of its less fortunate members. His memoir of the 1920s, *That Summer in Paris* (1963), describes his friendship with Hemingway and Fitzgerald. His last novel was *A Wild Old Man on the Road* (1988).

Callao [kah-yah'-oh] Callao, a commercial city on Callao Bay, an arm of the Pacific Ocean, is the port of Lima and the major seaport of Peru, handling three-fourths of the nation's imports. Callao has a population of 560,000 (1988 est.). Its fine natural harbor is one of the best equipped on South America's Pacific coast. The city is also a fishing center, and it contains shipyards and a great variety of heavy and light manufactures. Founded (1537) by Francisco Pizarro, Callao was frequently attacked by English and Dutch pirates. A tidal wave demolished the city in 1746. Its fortress, built in the 18th century and still used as a military post, was the last stronghold of Spanish royalist forces in South America; they capitulated in 1826.

Callas, Maria For well over a decade, soprano Maria Callas, b. Maria Kalogeropoulos to Greek parents in New York City, Dec. 2, 1923, d. Sept. 16, 1977, dominated the opera stage with her powerful voice, vivid acting, and musical intelligence. She sang an astounding range of

James Callaghan, later Baron Callaghan of Cardiff, became Britain's 50th prime minister in 1976. Plagued by Britain's economic stagnation, Callaghan was replaced by the Conservative party's Margaret Thatcher in 1979 national elections.

Maria Callas, a coloratura soprano, epitomized the prima donna temperament. She made headlines for her volatile personality and her personal life almost as frequently as for her dazzling operatic ability.

roles—from Wagner's Isolde and Brünnhilde to Gluck and Haydn operas and more standard works by Verdi and Rossini. Callas revived the extraordinarily difficult bel canto operas by Donizetti and Bellini, and sang the role of Norma in her debuts at London's Covent Garden (1952), the Chicago Lyric Opera (1954), and the Metropolitan Opera House in New York City (1956). Her early retirement, in 1965, was probably due to the strain of celebrity and increasing vocal deficiencies.

Calles, Plutarco Elías (kah-yays) Plutarco Elías Calles, b. Sept. 25, 1877, d. Oct. 19, 1945, was a leader in the Mexican Revolution and president (1924–28) of Mexico. He joined Francisco MADERO against Porfirio DÍAZ, fought against Victoriano HUERTA, and in 1917 became governor of his native province, Sonora. In 1919 he became secretary of commerce, labor, and industry under Venustiano CARRANZA, but the next year he joined with Álvaro OBREGÓN to overthrow Carranza.

Calles served as minister of interior during Obregón's presidency and was elected president in 1924. His enforcement of legislation (1926) against the Roman Catholic church led to a three-year suspension of religious services and a bloody popular rebellion of Catholics. During 1928–34, Calles ruled behind the scenes through a series of appointed presidents, guiding the revolution to the right. He established the National Revolutionary party in 1929. Agrarian reform almost ceased, government corruption was rampant, and the government favored the goals of the country's business.

For the 1934–40 presidential term Calles picked Lázaro CÁRDENAS, but the latter assembled a leftist coalition that overthrew Calles and drove him into exile in 1936. Calles lived in California until 1941, when he returned to Mexico. His major accomplishment was the formation of the Mexican one-party system.

Callias [kal'-ee-uhs] Callias was a 5th-century BC Athenian leader. He fought at the Battle of Marathon (490), and later went as ambassador to Persia, where he supposedly negotiated (*c.*449) the "Peace of Callias" between Persia and Athens. Although the existence of such a treaty has been called into doubt, the Persians did at this time recognize the Athenian sphere of influence. Callias was probably a negotiator of the 30-year peace between Athens and Sparta that began in 446 BC.

calligraphy [kuh-lig'-ruh-fee] Calligraphy (from a Greek word meaning "beautiful writing") is the art of fine handwriting. The term may refer to letters, words, pages, or even whole documents to which aesthetic principles and skilled penmanship have been applied. Calligraphy differs from INSCRIPTION in referring only to scripts written on perishable materials such as PAPYRUS, PARCHMENT, textiles, or paper (see WRITING SYSTEMS, EVOLUTION OF). In the Far East, calligraphy is produced by means of a pointed brush held vertically. In Western and Islamic cultures,

A simplified form of hieroglyphics, known as hieratic script, appears on this fragment from the Egyptian Book of the Dead, a collection of funerary spells and formulas intended for guidance in the afterlife.

calligraphic writing is accomplished by using a broad-edged reed, quill, or nib pen held at a slant.

Development in the West

Egyptian papyri dating from the 5th dynasty (*c.*2494–2345 BC) are the earliest known examples of calligraphy. The hieratic script, created to facilitate speed in writing, derived from a simplified type of pictorial or HIEROGLYPHIC lettering. In Greece two styles of writing emerged concurrently: a formal script used for literary works and a more utilitarian cursive hand used to keep accounts. Rounded, more easily inscribed uncial letters eventually became the characteristic Greek script for literary works. A celebrated example is the *Codex Sinaiticus* (British Museum, London), a biblical manuscript of the 4th century AD. In Italy, Latin scripts were developed out of Greek and native Etruscan traditions.

The art of calligraphy flourished in medieval monasteries. This 14th-century miniature portrays a monk transcribing a manuscript from an exemplar. (Bibliothèque Nationale, Paris.)

The richly illustrated manuscript of the Book of Kells (c.800), written in an insular script, is the acme of Celtic calligraphy and illumination. It features full-page initials of intricate design, such as this Christ monogram combining the Greek letters chi and rho. (Trinity College, Dublin.)

Middle Ages. After the fall of the Roman Empire, a bewildering variety of styles flourished in Europe because of regional preferences and the rise of specialized schools of writers. From the 6th to the 9th century AD, manuscripts were characterized by an abundance of intricate designs and letters often so elaborate as to be illegible. Notable examples of the insular scripts of Britain are the *Lindisfarne Gospels* (*c.*700; British Museum, London) and the Book of Kells (*c.*800; Trinity College, Dublin), in which capitals are ornamented with lively animal motifs and bits of color inserted in the voids of the letters. When Irish monks began to establish monasteries in Switzerland and Italy, their complicated, often flamboyant scripts soon spread throughout the continent.

The unifying policy of Charlemagne increased the need in his domain for a more uniform and simplified script. Under the direction of the Anglo-Saxon scholar Alcuin, a distinctive script evolved at Charlemagne's court at Aachen. This script, distinguished by the Caroline minuscule, was based on the small-letter alphabet and made generous use of white space.

By about 1100, writing began to be more condensed laterally, and the space between lines was reduced. This development led to a general decline in the quality of calligraphy throughout Europe in the late Middle Ages. In northern Europe a script of small, highly condensed letters emerged. Named Black Letter because a page of it looked black, this script served as the basis for the types developed (*c.*1450) for the Gutenberg Bible.

Renaissance Italy. During the Renaissance, the Italian humanists revived the simpler forms of the Caroline minuscule and adapted the letters of the old Roman geometric inscriptions. Feliciano of Verona wrote (1463) one of the earliest known treatises on calligraphy, with instructions and diagrams for the geometric execution of Roman capitals. He contributed a round bookletter that is the basis for modern so-called roman printing. Similarly, the modern italic script is derived from that of the 15th-century scriveners of the papal chanceries.

The fashion of writing private letters as a demonstration of the writer's erudition spurred interest in calligraphy. In 1522, Lodovico degli Arrighi of Vicenza, a Vatican scribe,

Lodovico degli Arrighi's elegant chancery script was prescribed in his Operina di scrivere littera cancellaresca *(1522), the first writing manual.*

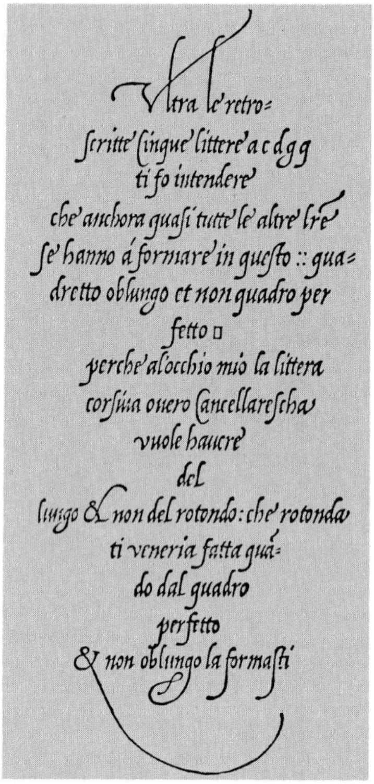

published *Operina*, the first writing manual, based on the chancery italic. The later script of the 16th century was influenced strongly by the technique of engraving. The first calligraphy manual printed in copperplate, *Lo scrittor' utile* (The Useful Writer) by Hercolani, a notary of Bologna, was published in 1571. By these and other publications, Italian scripts were disseminated through Europe.

Spanish and French Scripts. In Spain, the national hand was devised by the 16th-century Spanish writing-master Francisco Lucas, who created a characteristic Spanish upright roundhand accompanied by an inclined minuscule. With almost no variations, this style prevailed for 200 years, until the general triumph of the English system.

In France, the *cursive francoyse*, a Gothic hand, appears in early books. From this, the *civilité* style emerged that later produced the elegant *ronde* (round) script, in which letters are continuously connected through sweeping strokes. This style may be designated as the French national hand; most of its Gothic traits disappeared in the 17th century.

British and American Scripts. The first English manual of calligraphy, written by Jean de Beauchesne and John Baildon, appeared in 1571. The Dutch style also influenced the English, and the calligraphic works of the draftsman Jan van de Velde I (1568–1623) were in great demand. By the 18th century, the English had developed a characteristic hand used extensively in their business documents. Admiration for England's mercantile success also won admiration for England's mercantile script, which was based on efficiency and the necessity for speed. Transported to the continent, it became known as *anglaise* in France, *letra inglesa* in Spain, and by the end of the 19th century, *lettere inglese* were preferred even in Italy.

The first American copybook, published (1791) by the writing master John Jenkins, followed the mid-18th-century English mercantile script. In the early 19th century a writing technique was devised in England by which movement of the forearm, and not the fingers, formed the script. Introduced in the United States in 1830, it became known erroneously as the American System. However, the American national hand did emerge from a combination of this method with the earlier British running hand. Platt R. Spencer (1800–64) disseminated the new style in a chain of business colleges he established in 44 American cities during the mid-1800s; it became known as the Spencerian System.

Twentieth-Century Revival. With the development of the steel pen, the typewriter, and related technologies of modern life, the art of calligraphy declined. Changes in print typeface, originally derived from popular styles of handwriting, grew increasingly remote from calligraphic traditions (see also PRINTING). In 1890 the Englishman William MORRIS attempted a revival and founded the Kelmscott Press in order to experiment with new calligraphic type styles. *Writing and Illuminating and Lettering*, published (1906) in London by Morris's friend the educator Edward Johnston (1872–1944), stimulated a renewed interest in calligraphy among wealthy connoisseurs and collectors.

By the late 1920s Germany had its own school of calligraphers. The Old Gothic hands were also championed, and the Bund für Deutsche Schrift was established to encourage their revival. The impetus given to calligraphy by Morris, Johnston, and their followers continues. Today calligraphy is taught in art academies and schools of arts and crafts.

Far Eastern Traditions

Calligraphy in China, termed *shufa* when practiced as a fine art, has an ancient and venerated history. Painting and

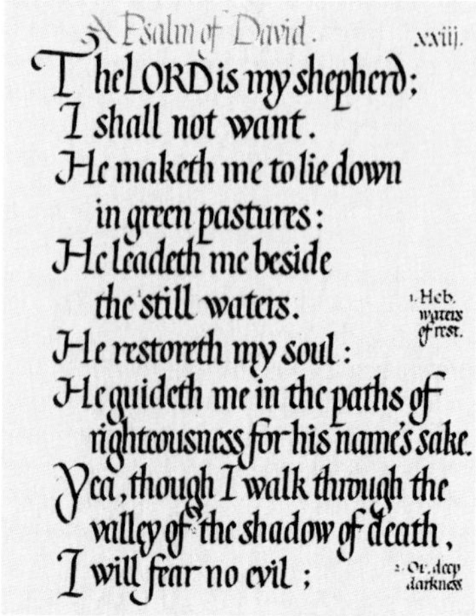

A Psalm of David. xxiij.
The LORD is my shepherd;
I shall not want.
He maketh me to lie down
in green pastures:
He leadeth me beside
the still waters.
1. Heb. waters of rest.
He restoreth my soul:
He guideth me in the paths of
righteousness for his name's sake.
Yea, though I walk through the
valley of the shadow of death,
I will fear no evil;
2. Or, deep darkness

The graceful calligraphy of Edward Johnston, based on classical designs, is a blend of styles. The script of the 23d Psalm shows the influence of early book type and of Anglo-Saxon calligraphers.

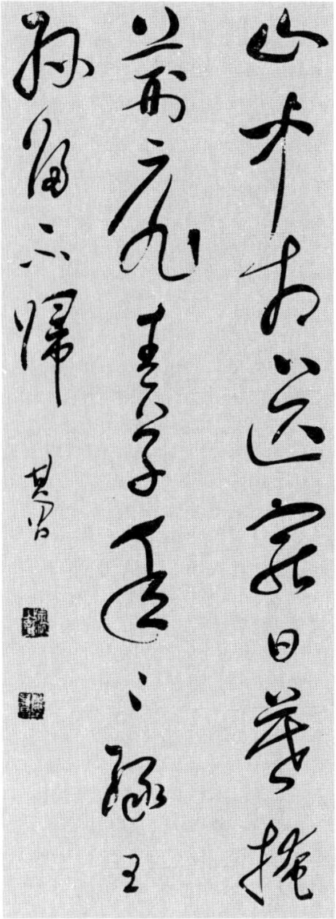

This 17th-century cursive script emulates classical forms, yet it is filled with calligraphic inventiveness. (John M. Crawford, Jr. Collection, New York City.)

calligraphy are considered interrelated arts and employ similar methods and materials. Not until the 5th century AD, however, was the painter accorded status comparable to that of the calligrapher; until that time, painters were considered as mere artisans, while calligraphers had been long esteemed as cultured, erudite scholars.

Chinese script dates from as early as the latter half of the 2d millennium BC. Its origins, traced through inscriptions on ORACLE BONES and shells and on the bronzes of the Shang (*c.*1600–1027 BC) and Zhou (1027–256 BC) dynasties, indicate that the script evolved from a system of symbols drawn to represent the object denoted. These symbols, called pictographs, eventually developed into abstract characters, the basic word-unit of the language.

Chinese Scripts. The oldest calligraphic script, referred to as archaic or seal script (*juanshu*), was linear in appearance, of even thickness, and distinctly inscribed. By the time of the Han dynasty (202 BC–AD 220), a simplified version of *juanshu* was in use. Referred to as *lishu*, or clerical script, it became the basis for modern Chinese. With its strokes of various widths that end broadly or in rough, uneven flourishes, it reveals the characteristic suppleness of the implement of its execution, the brush.

Lishu remained the dominant calligraphic style until the 4th century AD. From this script emerged the three modern modes of Chinese writing. The first, designated *kaishu*, or regular script, is a formal hand analogous to western print script; it became the model for printed characters. *Xingshu*, or running script, is a semicursive form of *kaishu*. *Caoshu*, or grass script, is abbreviated and highly expressive.

The two golden ages of the calligrapher's art are the Tang dynasty (618–906) and the Song dynasty (960–

The characters of this 14th-century manuscript epitomize Kaishu, *the regular script of China. This highly legible hand is still in use today. (Wango H. C. Weng Collection, New York City.)*

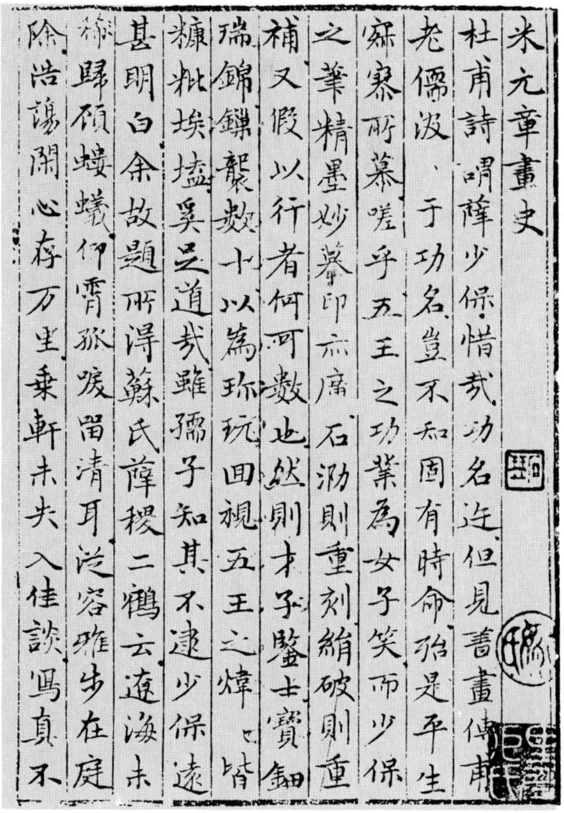

Japanese calligraphy is based on that of China and is held in similar cultural esteem. An unwavering hand is crucial for the prescribed rapid execution of Japanese characters.

In Islamic countries, Kufic script had been largely replaced by the rounder, more fluent Naskhi script by the 11th century. The text of this 12th-century Arabic manuscript of the Bagdhad school features a Naskhi hand.

1279). The Tang emperor Ming Huang (r. 713–755), renowned as a calligrapher, stimulated the art by his enthusiastic patronage. In the Song period, the relationship between painting and calligraphy was extremely close, and Song artists such as Su Dongbo and Mi Fei formulated the literati theory of painting that stressed this interdependence.

Japanese Scripts. Chinese script was introduced into Japan in the 7th century and was initially used to copy Buddhist texts. The Japanese monk Kukai (774–835) developed the *hiragana* script, which was produced by simplifying and abbreviating Chinese characters. This style was used for the early courtly literature. Two types of calligraphy are in common use today: *wa-yo,* related to the original Japanese script and used especially by Shintoists, and *kara-yo,* a Chinese style used in court circles. Under the influence of close contacts with China during the 17th and 18th centuries, interest in Chinese calligraphy grew. Today the art of writing is still held in high regard.

Islamic Calligraphy

The copying of the Koran is considered a religious act, and Islamic calligraphy is much esteemed because of its religious associations. Two major styles of script developed: Kufic, a formal style with an angular character, was in evidence by the 7th century AD; Naskhi, a cursive flowing script, appeared in the 10th century.

Arabic Scripts. Kufic was first developed in the Arab city of Kufa in Iraq. The earliest extant Koran (*c.*785; Egyptian Library, Cairo) was written in this style. By the 12th century, Kufic was almost entirely displaced by Naskhi, although chapter headings continued to be rendered in the former style. The Korans of the Mameluke period (1252–1517) were written in Thuluth or Tumar script, both variations of Naskhi. These ornamental manuscripts were frequently embellished with gold letters and delicate arabesques drawn on a rich blue ground. Maghribi, also referred to as Andalusian or Cordovan, was the distinctive script of Korans written during the 12th century in Spain and North Africa.

Persian Scripts. Islamic Persian calligraphers of the Abbasid dynasty (750–1258) early adapted the Kufic script, stressing the vertical aspect of the characters. By the 11th and 12th centuries, Persian Kufic had fully evolved. Seljuk Korans of this period are typically written on illuminated pages rich with arabesques, interlaceries, and palmettes.

During the 13th century, a variation of Naskhi appeared in Persia. Designated Talik, this script inclined downward from right to left and was much used in ceramic decoration. Naskhi, however, continued to be used for religious texts. By the 14th and 15th centuries, under the Timurids, Persian calligraphy was considered a fine art. A master calligrapher of the 15th century, Mir Ali from Tabriz, is believed to have created the Nastalik script, used especially for poetry.

The calligraphers of the Safavid period (16th–18th century) continued in the sumptuous tradition established by the Timurid artists. Among the renowned calligraphers of the period was Sultan Muhammad, whose style is seen in a magnificent manuscript of poems by Nizami (1524–25; Metropolitan Museum of Art, New York City). A famous 17th-century calligrapher, Mir Imad, one of the most admired of Persian artists, copied many fine manuscripts for Abbas I.

Tughras, or the bold calligraphic emblems that prefaced edicts issued by the sultans, are well-known examples of Turkish script. Often they were intricately combined with floral motifs created in a multicolored scheme

calliope [kuh-ly'-uh-pee] The calliope, a set of tuned brass whistles powered by steam, was invented in 1855 by J. C. Stoddard of Worcester, Mass., in imitation of a locomotive whistle. Operated by a keyboard or a pin-barrel mechanism (see BARREL ORGAN), it was used in circus parades, at fairs, and on river steamers. Its sound carries up to 19 km (12 mi). The instrument is named for the traditional Greek muse of eloquence.

Callisto [kuh-lis'-toh] Callisto is a satellite of the planet JUPITER. It lies 1,880,000 km (1,168,000 mi) from the planet's center and is 4,820 km (2,995 mi) in diameter. Callisto is the outermost and least geologically active of the four moons of Jupiter discovered by Galileo in 1610. Its density, 1.8 times that of water, indicates a core of rock and a thick mantle of ices. The surface, quite dark, is probably dirty ice or a thin rock layer. It is heavily cratered, exposing brighter ice. The general shallowness of the craters is probably due to flattening of their rims by the flow of ice.

Callistus I, Pope [kuh-lis'-tuhs] Saint Callistus I, d. 222, was pope from *c.*217 to 222. A Roman by birth, Callistus was originally a slave. According to Saint HIPPOLYTUS, he was sent to the mines after a brawl in a synagogue. As pope Callistus helped to codify church doctrine by condemning Sabellius, a priest who taught that the persons of the Trinity were merely modes of divine activity (see SABELLIANISM). He also favored a policy of readmitting adulterers, apostates, and murderers to communion. In this, as in other matters, he was opposed by Hippolytus, who established himself as the first antipope. Callistus died a martyr. Feast day: Oct. 14.

Callistus II, Pope Callistus II, b. *c.*1050, d. Dec. 13 or 14, 1124, was pope from 1119 to 1124. He was a Burgundian of noble birth named Guido di Borgogne. He became (1088) archbishop of Vienne, where he convened (1112) a synod that excommunicated Holy Roman Emperor HENRY V for his stand during the INVESTITURE CONTROVERSY. Henry eventually set up an antipope, Gregory VIII, whom Callistus imprisoned when he became pope. Callistus was responsible for ending the investiture controversy with the Concordat of Worms in 1122. In 1123 he convoked the First Lateran Council, which confirmed the concordat and issued decrees against the marriage of priests and the buying or selling of church offices or spiritual benefits.

Callistus III, Pope Callistus III, b. Dec. 31, 1378, d. Aug. 6, 1458, was pope from 1455 to 1458. He was a Spaniard named Alfonso de Borja (part of the BORGIA family). Much of his pontificate was dedicated to organizing a crusade to recover Constantinople from the Turks, but his plans met with little success. In 1456 an appellate court appointed by Callistus annulled the trial of Joan of Arc and declared her innocent of heresy. The reign of Callistus reflected the papacy's increased involvement in the style of life and the politics of Renaissance Italy. His nephew Rodrigo, whom he named cardinal, became the more famous Borgia pope, ALEXANDER VI.

Callot, Jacques [kah-loh'] Jacques Callot, b. *c.*1592, d. Mar. 24, 1635, was a French engraver and etcher best known for his masterful representations of court ceremonies, festivities, and the military campaigns of his patrons. The aristocracy, *commedia dell'arte* actors, beggars, gypsies, grotesques, saints and sinners, and the *Miseries of War* (a series) appear as subjects among the more than 1,400 prints and more than 2,000 drawings he created during his short lifetime. Callot's preferred medium was ETCHING. He liked to work on an extremely small scale, many of his works measuring less than 39 cm^2 (6 in^2). While in Florence, he developed the technique that permitted him to turn his small etched compositions into richly detailed microcosms of the human scene. Abandoning the traditional soft ground used in etching, he adopted a hard varnish and achieved greater precision in small details and a wider range of tone.

Calloway, Cab The bandleader Cabell "Cab" Calloway, b. Rochester, N.Y., Dec. 24, 1907, won the hearts of Depression-ridden America with his song "Minnie the Moocher" (1931), which made him famous as the scat-singing "hi-de-ho" man. Calloway led a big band until 1948. He has appeared in many movies, in the Broadway production of George Gershwin's folk opera, *Porgy and Bess* (1952), in which he played Sportin' Life, and in the all-black *Hello Dolly!* (1967).

callus see FOOT DISORDERS

Calonne, Charles Alexandre de [kah-luhn'] Charles Alexandre de Calonne, b. Jan. 20, 1734, d. Oct. 29, 1802, was a French statesman whose reforms as controller general of finance (1783–87) led to the government bankruptcy that initiated the FRENCH REVOLUTION. His tenure began with massive borrowing and ended when a royally appointed Assembly of Notables rejected his tax on nobles and clergy. Dismissed by LOUIS XVI, he advised and financed French counterrevolutionaries from exile in Turin and England.

calorie A calorie is a unit of heat energy, originally defined as the amount of energy, as heat (*calor* in Latin means heat), required to raise the temperature of 1 g of liquid water from 14.5° to 15.5° C. Today a calorie is defined in mechanical rather than thermal terms. In this system, 1 calorie (cal) equals 4.184000 watt-seconds (W-s), or joules (J). A calorimeter is one laboratory instrument often used to measure heat energy.

The energy required to melt 1 g of ice is 80 cal, and to boil 1 g of water, 540 cal. The Earth receives from the Sun approximately 2 cal/min/cm^2 of surface area. One horsepower (hp) is equal to 550 ft lbs/s (second), which is equal to 10,700 cal/min.

The combustion of 1 g of carbon liberates 7,830 cal, or 7.830 kcal (kilocalorie—nutritionists write Cal for kcal). Metabolism of carbohydrates liberates about 4 kcal/g. Fats yield about 9 kcal/g. The caloric requirement of an average adult is about 2,000 kcal/d (day).

calotype [kal'-oh-tipe] Calotype was the name given a negative-positive photo process patented in 1841 by William Henry Fox Talbot, an Englishman. Paper impregnated with light-sensitive chemicals was exposed in a camera; then the negative image was fixed through chemical development. The negative was used with more photo paper in a glass frame to make a positive contact-print by sunlight. The calotype print could be reproduced many times, but the paper negative's fibrous opaqueness reduced image quality. (See also PHOTOGRAPHY.)

calumet [kal'-yoo-met] Calumet is the name French missionaries gave the peace pipe that was common among Indians of central and eastern North America. These large, ornately decorated tobacco pipes had bowls made of clay or stone and long stems of reed or wood. They were of great symbolic value to their users. Smoke itself was regarded as a vehicle for sending messages to the spirit world. The pipes functioned as flags of truce and were ceremonially smoked for purposes of binding or renewing alliances and friendships. Traditionally, each person present at a council meeting smoked the pipe.

Calvary Calvary was the place of Jesus Christ's crucifixion, just outside the walls of Jerusalem. The name, from the Latin word for skull, may derive from its use as an execution site, or perhaps from its appearance or proximity to a cemetery. Recent excavations support the traditional location of Calvary at the Church of the Holy Sepulchre.

Calvert (family) The Calvert family was principally responsible for the planning and settlement of the province of Maryland. **George Calvert, 1st Baron Baltimore**, b. 1580, d. Apr. 15, 1632, was an early investor in colonization efforts. He attempted to settle a colony in Newfoundland in 1623, but his principal effort as a colonizer was in Maryland, where he received a land grant in 1632. George died before that charter became official, but his eldest son, **Cecil Calvert, 2d Baron Baltimore**, b. *c.*1605, d. Nov. 30, 1675, carried out his plans.

The Calvert family had converted to Roman Catholicism about 1624, and the Maryland colony, first settled in 1634 under Cecil Calvert's direction, was intended as a haven for persecuted Catholics. Cecil's younger brother, **Leonard Calvert**, b. 1606, d. June 9, 1647, was the first governor of Maryland, serving from November 1633, when he sailed from England, until his death. **Charles Calvert, 3d Baron Baltimore**, b. Aug. 27, 1637, d. Feb. 21, 1715, was appointed governor of Maryland by his father, Cecil, in 1661. Charles was energetic in his attempts to defend the proprietary rights of his family, but in 1689 his charter was revoked, and by 1692 the colony reverted to royal control.

John Calvin, a leader of the Protestant Reformation, developed a comprehensive theology, which he detailed in successive editions of Institutes of the Christian Religion *(1536–59). Calvin's teachings have been a major influence on Presbyterian and Reformed church beliefs. (Bibliothèque du Protestantisme, Paris.)*

Calvin, John French theologian John Calvin, b. July 10, 1509, d. May 27, 1564, was, after Martin Luther, the guiding spirit of the Protestant REFORMATION. After studying and writing in Paris, Calvin was forced to flee in 1535 to Basel, Switzerland. There he produced the first edition of *Institutes of the Christian Religion* (1536) about his new reformed beliefs. It was designed to offer a brief summary of essential Christian belief and to defend French Protestants, who were then undergoing serious persecution, as true heirs of the early church. By the last edition (1559), it presented with unmatched clarity a vision of God in his majesty, of Christ as prophet, priest, and king, of the Holy Spirit as the giver of faith, of the Bible as the final authority, and of the church as the holy people of God. Its doctrine of PREDESTINATION is Calvin's deduction from his belief in human sinfulness and God's sovereign mercy in Christ.

After the publication of the *Institutes*, Calvin fully intended to devote his life to further study. On a trip to Strasbourg in July 1536, however, he was forced to detour through Geneva where he hoped to stay only one night. The fiery Guillaume FAREL, who had labored long for the reform of that city, had other plans. Threatening Calvin with a curse from God, Farel persuaded him to remain. In 1538, Calvin and Farel were expelled from the city. Calvin proceeded to Strasbourg where he spent the most enjoyable years of his life as pastor of the city's French congregation. While in Strasbourg, Calvin produced an influential commentary on the Book of Romans, oversaw the preparation of a liturgy and a psalm book that he would use later in Geneva, and married the widow Idelette de Bure. When friends of Calvin gained control of the Geneva council in 1541, they asked him to return, and he reluctantly agreed. During the next 14 years his reforms met stiff resistance. Some Genevans considered Calvin's morality absurdly severe, with its banning of plays and its attempt to introduce religious pamphlets and psalm singing into Geneva's taverns. Finally, his opponents blundered in 1553 by offering backhanded support to the antitrinitarian Michael SERVETUS. Servetus was condemned to death by burning for heresy, and by 1555 the city belonged to Calvin. The Presbyterian church order that he instituted established a principle of lay involvement that had great impact throughout Europe.

During Calvin's last years, Geneva was home to many religious refugees who carried away the desire to implement a Genevan reform in their own countries. His influence was felt especially in Scotland through the work of John KNOX.

Calvin, Melvin The American chemist Melvin Calvin, b. Saint Paul, Minn., Apr. 8, 1911, was awarded the 1961 Nobel Prize for chemistry for his study of the biological process of PHOTOSYNTHESIS in plants. After early work on the structure of organic compounds, Calvin began using radioactive carbon-14 in the 1940s to trace the various steps of photosynthesis. By 1957 he and his associate, James A. Bassham, had made a detailed analysis of the many reactions that take place. Calvin then turned his attention to formulating theories on the chemical evolution of life. He also conducted solar energy research, including studies of the possibilities of artificial photosynthesis.

Calvinism Calvinism, the Protestant religious perspective associated with the work of John CALVIN, includes both the teachings of Calvin and the later developments of his world view. Calvin's doctrine was catholic in its acceptance of the Trinity, human sinfulness, and the saving work of Jesus Christ. It was Protestant in its commitment to the final authority of the Bible, justification by grace through faith alone, and the bondage of the will for salvation. It was distinctly reformed in its stress on the omnipotent sovereignty of God, the need for discipline in the church, and the ethical seriousness of life.

The so-called Five Points of Calvinism were formulated by Dutch Reformed theologians at the Synod of Dort (1618–19) in response to the teachings of ARMINIANISM. The five points teach that (1) humankind is spiritually incapacitated by sin; (2) God chooses (elects) unconditionally those who will be saved; (3) the saving work of Christ is limited to those elected ones; (4) God's grace cannot be turned aside; (5) those whom God elects in Christ are saved forever (see PREDESTINATION).

Early in the 20th century the German sociologist Max WEBER and the English economist R. H. TAWNEY put forth the thesis that Calvinism promoted the rise of capitalism (see PROTESTANT ETHIC). PURITANISM in England and America is a product, to one degree or another, of the Calvinistic spirit, and Calvinism provides the basic doctrinal orientation of the REFORMED CHURCHES and PRESBYTERIANISM.

Calvino, Italo [kahl-vee'-noh, ee'-tah-loh] The Italian writer Italo Calvino, b. Oct. 15, 1923, d. Sept. 19, 1985, achieved international fame for a body of work that, beginning with the novel *The Path to the Nest of Spiders* (1947; Eng. trans., 1956), spanned four decades. His collections of short stories include *Cosmicomics* (1965; Eng. trans., 1968) and *Marcovaldo* (1963; Eng. trans., 1983). Among other works are *Italian Fables* (1956; Eng. trans., 1959), *The Non-Existent Knight* (1959; Eng. trans., 1962), and the experimental *If on a Winter's Night a Traveler* (1979; Eng. trans., 1981) and *Mr. Palomar* (1983; Eng. trans., 1985). *Six Memos for the Next Millennium*, on the art of writing, was published posthumously in 1988.

Calypso In Greek mythology, Calypso was a nymph, on whose island ODYSSEUS spent seven years on his way home from Troy. Calypso so loved Odysseus that she offered him immortality if he would remain with her. Odysseus, however, longed for his home. At the command of Zeus, Calypso helped Odysseus build a raft to continue his journey.

calypso A form of music and dance of the Caribbean, calypso had its primary development in Trinidad, where it is associated particularly with the pre-Lenten carnival. Before the carnival begins musicians try out their songs nightly before audiences in Port of Spain. The most popular are used during the carnival.

The words of calypso songs are witty and humorous and convey popular attitudes on social, political, or economic problems. The music is set in *duple metre* (2 beats to the bar) and is based on about 50 standard calypso melodies. For the form of carnival street dance called "jump dancing," rhythms are provided most often by STEEL BAND percussion instruments, made from the tops of oil drums. As a type of ballroom dance, calypso resembles the rumba, and the music often is performed with conventional dance-band instruments.

Camagüey [kah-mah-gway'] Camagüey (1988 est. pop., 274,974) is one of Cuba's largest cities and the capital of Camagüey province. The city's economy is based on the processing and shipping of sugarcane, pineapple, and cattle. Diego Velázquez de Cuéllar founded the city in 1514, and in 1528 it was moved inland to its present location. Spanish fleets depended on the salted beef they procured there, and English and Dutch colonists carried on an illegal trade with the city.

Cambacérès, Jean Jacques Régis de [kahm-bah-say-res'] Jean Jacques Régis de Cambacérès, b. Oct. 18, 1753, d. Mar. 8, 1824, French revolutionary and jurist, helped to draft the NAPOLEONIC CODE. A member of the National Convention, the Committee of Public Safety, and the Council of Five Hundred, he aided the 1799 coup of Bonaparte (later NAPOLEON I) and became second consul (1799–1804) and then archchancellor of

AT A GLANCE

CAMBODIA

Land: Area: 181,035 km^2 (69,898 mi^2). Capital and largest city: Phnom Penh (1987 est. pop., 750,000).

People: Population (1990 est.): 6,991,107. Density: 38.6 persons per km^2 (100.0 per mi^2). Distribution (1989): 11% urban, 89% rural. Official language: Khmer. Major religion: Buddhism

Government: Type: republic (State of Cambodia); coalition government in exile (Democratic Kampuchea). Legislature: National Assembly. Political subdivisions: 20 provinces, 1 autonomous municipality.

Economy: GDP (1989 est.): $890 million; $130 per capita. Labor distribution (1989): agriculture and fishing—80%; manufacturing—3%; commerce and services—17%. Foreign trade (1988): imports—$147 million; exports—$32 million; Currency: 1 new riel = 100 sen.

Education and Health: Literacy (1983): 48% of adult population. Universities (1990): 1. Hospital beds (1985): 17,856. Physicians (1985): 506. Life expectancy (1990): women—50; men—47. Infant mortality (1990): 128 per 1,000 live births.

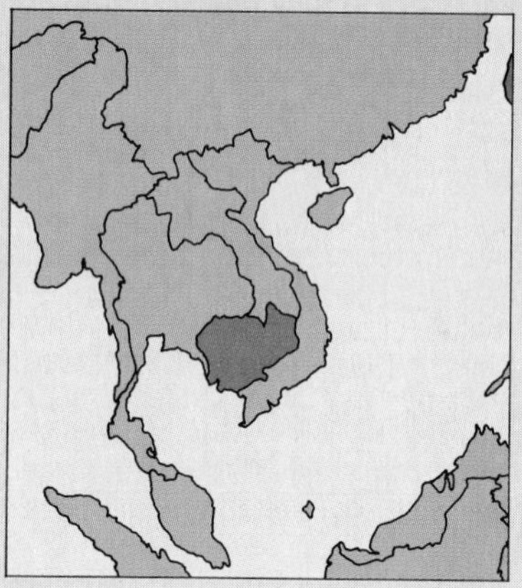

the empire. Exiled after Napoleon's first defeat (1814), he returned for the Hundred Days as minister of justice and was exiled again from 1815 to 1818.

Cambodia [kahm-boo-dyah'] Cambodia, also known as Kampuchea, is located in mainland Southeast Asia between Vietnam, Laos, Thailand, and the Gulf of Thailand. From the 9th to the 15th century, the mighty KHMER EMPIRE extended its sway far beyond the present boundaries of Cambodia. This period produced the glorious temple complex and royal palace that lie crumbling at ANGKOR. The Khmer kingdom gradually declined; it accepted French protection in 1863 and was later incorporated into French INDOCHINA. Cambodia was granted independence by France in 1953, but it was soon entangled in the VIETNAM WAR. In April 1975, Cambodian Communists known as the KHMER ROUGE took control of the country, instituting radically agrarian and xenophobic policies that led to the deaths of at least 1,000,000 people. The Khmer Rouge were driven out in 1979 by the Vietnamese army and Cambodian exiles. The Vietnamese-backed State of Cambodia was opposed by the Chinese-backed Coalition Government of Kampuchea (in exile), which included the Khmer Rouge and two non-Communist factions. In August 1990, the UN Security Council approved a comprehensive peace plan calling for internationally supervised elections for a new government.

Land and Resources

Cambodia is heavily forested; only a small portion (16%) of the land is cultivated. Most of the country is low-lying. The Dangrek Mountains provide a watershed escarpment boundary with Thailand in the north. The Cardamom Range dominates the southwest, rising to 1,771 m (5,810 ft) at Phnom Aral, the highest point in the country. Adjacent to the coast is the Elephant Range, and highlands adjoin Laos and Vietnam east of the Mekong River in northern Cambodia. Two types of soil predominate in Cambodia: alluvium deposited by riverine flooding and soil resulting from rock decay.

Monsoon rains prevail from mid-April to October, followed by drier and cooler air until March. Average annual rainfall in the central lowlands is 1,400 mm (55 in) and may be three or more times greater in the southwestern mountains. Temperatures range from 20° to 36° C (68° to 97° F).

The MEKONG RIVER bisects and irrigates the eastern lowlands of Cambodia. Close to the center of the country is the largest lake in Southeast Asia, the Tonle Sap ("great lake"), which acts as a natural reservoir for the Mekong. Only a few of Cambodia's rivers, in the southwest, lie outside the drainage system of the Mekong and the Tonle Sap.

Dense tropical rain forests cover the uplands, while mangroves predominate along the coast. The natural vegetation of the central plains is prairie grass. Larger species of wildlife, including buffalo, elephants, rhinoceroses, bears, tigers, and panthers, are found at higher elevations. Exotic birds and reptiles are common.

Hardwood forests have long been exploited for timber. Phosphate, salt, and gems (rubies, sapphires, and zircons) have been exported, and there are iron ore deposits. The Mekong has great hydroelectric and irrigation potential.

People

Cambodia's population is unusually homogenous, with the Khmer constituting more than 85%. The Khmer are thought to have migrated from southern China prior to 200 BC. The chief minority groups are the Chinese and the Vietnamese. Although most Vietnamese were driven out or killed under Khmer Rouge rule, several hundred thousand Vietnamese have settled in Cambodia since 1979. It is unclear how various upland minorities, such as the Oham-Malays and Khmer Loeus, fared under the Khmer Rouge.

Theravada Buddhism has been the religion of almost all Khmer since the 13th century, when it replaced animism and ancestor worship among the peasants and Brahmanic beliefs at the royal court. The Khmer Rouge banned all religions, disrobed and punished thousands of monks, and desecrated hundreds of temples and monasteries. Since 1979 the practice of Buddhism has been permitted, and monasteries are being restored with government support.

Cambodia is overwhelmingly agricultural and rural. The largest cities are Phnom Penh, the capital, Battambang, and Kompong Cham. The Khmer Rouge evacuated the refugee-swollen cities and towns in 1975 with great loss of life. Massive population shifts again took place after 1979 as the new government allowed people to rejoin their families and return home. The population of Phnom Penh (1975 est., 3,000,000) increased from less than 200,000 in 1979 to nearly 800,000 in 1990.

Formal education was abandoned during the Khmer Rouge period in favor of basic task training and political indoctrination in agricultural communes. Since 1979, with Vietnamese assistance, public schools have been reopened and adult literacy courses have been widely promoted.

Health care was very limited under French rule, and many physicians did not survive the Khmer Rouge revolution. Hospitals in the major towns have since been reopened.

The greatest monuments of Khmer culture are the ruins of Angkor Wat and Angkor Thom. The Vietnamese-backed government prides itself on having started to restore some of Cambodia's lesser architectural monuments and temples. It has also organized classical- and folk-dance performances, song troupes, and shadow plays.

Economy

Cambodia's myriad small plots, primitively cultivated once a year, traditionally produced an exportable surplus of rice. During the Vietnam War, dikes were destroyed and rubber plantations and processing plants were crippled by military damage; corn, groundnut, sugar, and livestock production also suffered. A large refugee population became dependent on imported rice. The Khmer Rouge, who emphasized economic self-sufficiency, abolished money and personal property and forcibly collectivized agriculture. By 1978, renewed civil war caused further economic disruption. After the Khmer Rouge were driven out in 1979, a massive international relief effort provided Cambodia with food and other aid. The Vietnamese-

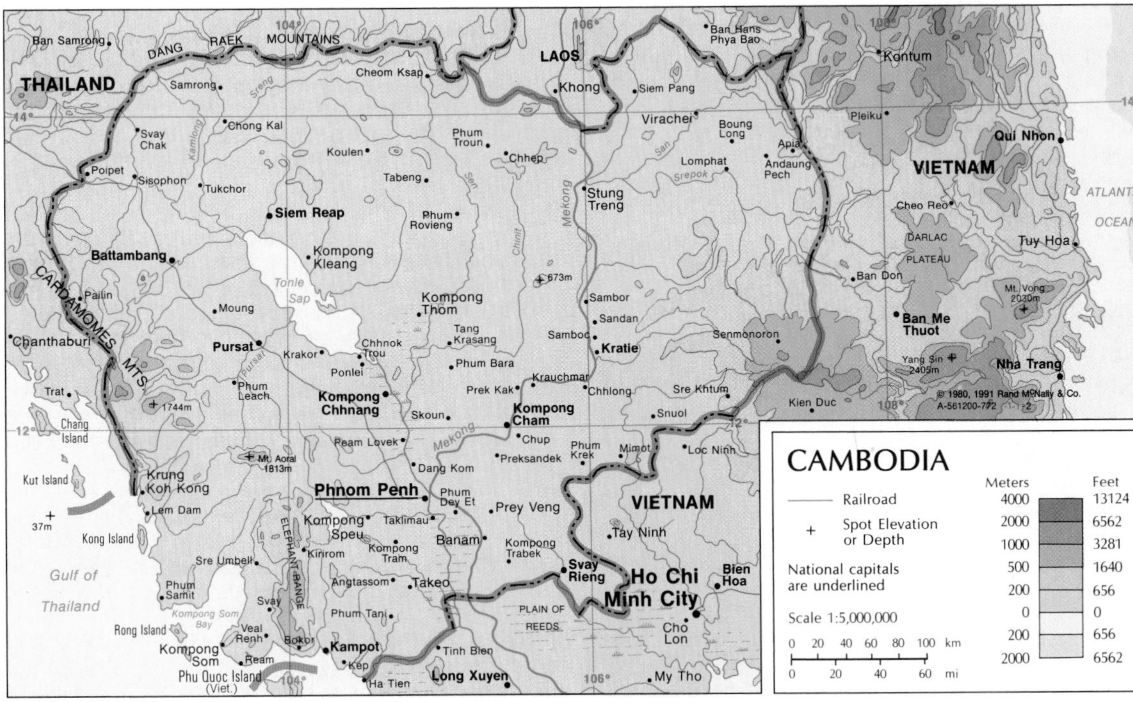

Homes in this village along the Mekong River, like many throughout Cambodia, are supported on stilts several feet above the water. These villages permit farmers to maximize cultivable land for rice, the nation's staple food crop, on fertile riverbank property.

backed government abandoned its efforts to collectivize agriculture in 1989, and much small enterprise is in private hands. Fish harvesting has increased dramatically, although the country is still not self-sufficient in rice.

Manufacturing facilities are also being rehabilitated. The surviving industries process agricultural and forest products and produce consumer goods. Transportation lines are slowly being restored. The road from Phnom Penh to Kompong Som is a vital link in the economy.

Under the Khmer Rouge, foreign trade was almost nonexistent. The Vietnamese-backed government depended almost exclusively on aid from Vietnam, the USSR, and its allies, but this aid declined after the breakup of Communism in Eastern Europe. Khmer Rouge attacks on economic targets further hampered recovery, driving up to 130,000 people from their homes by mid-1989 and increasing pressures for a negotiated settlement.

Phnom Penh, the capital and largest city of Cambodia, is located in the south central portion of the country on the Mekong River. The city has become a major port as well as a processing and distributing center serving the surrounding provinces

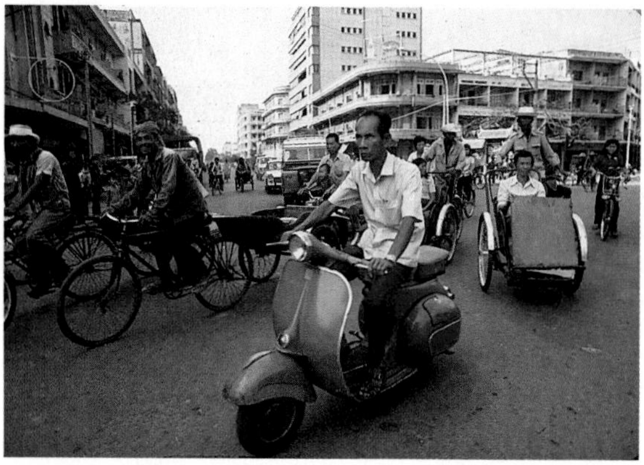

Government

On Jan. 8, 1979, Vietnamese-backed opponents of the Khmer Rouge proclaimed the foundation of the People's Republic of Kampuchea (renamed State of Cambodia in 1989), headed by a People's Revolutionary Council. In 1981 the newly elected National Assembly, whose members serve 5-year terms, ratified a constitution providing for a council of state and a council of ministers. The sole political party is the Cambodian People's Revolutionary party, an offshoot of the Indochina Communist party dating from 1951.

The Coalition Government of Democratic Kampuchea (in exile) was formed in 1982, with Prince NORODOM SIHANOUK as president, Khieu Samphan (Khmer Rouge) as vice-president in charge of foreign affairs, and former premier Son Sann as prime minister. These leaders meet infrequently, and the armed forces of each faction operate independently.

History

Five significant periods can be discerned in the history of Cambodia. From the 1st century AD, the kingdoms of Funan organized life in support of royal courts that adopted the Indian Brahmanic cult of the god-king; Indic culture spread into the legal code and an alphabet. During the 6th and 7th centuries, kingdoms of Khmer origin known as Chenla kept the institutions of Funan while conquering neighboring kingdoms in present-day Laos, Vietnam, and Thailand. Chenla was succeeded by the classical (Angkor) period of Khmer history, which lasted from the 9th to the mid-15th century. During this period, Cambodian artistic, architectural, and military achievements reached their zenith. A gradual decline in the coercive authority of the Khmer Empire was followed by losses of territory to the Vietnamese and the Thais.

The French protectorate began by treaty in 1863 and became a colonial relationship with Cambodia's incorporation into the Union of Indochina in 1887. Indochina fell to the Japanese during World War II, but France reclaimed it in 1945 as part of the newly conceived French Union. King Norodom Sihanouk (installed by France in 1941) was pressed by new nationalist parties to gain full independence, which was granted in 1953.

After independence, opposition groups continued to demand further political and social reforms, although the Cambodian offshoot of Ho Chi Minh's Indochina Communist party withdrew its cadres to North Vietnam in 1954 following the Geneva cease-fire agreements for Indochina. Sihanouk gave up the throne to his father in 1955, but he remained a prince, premier, leader of the dominant political movement (the *Sangkum*), and, after 1960, elected head of state. He tried to minimize the risk of involvement in the Vietnam conflict by rejecting membership in the SOUTHEAST ASIA TREATY ORGANIZATION (SEATO), accepting military aid from China, breaking relations with South Vietnam and the United States, and allowing the North Vietnamese use of his seaport to support their forces in South Vietnam. A new Communist group under Soloth Sar (POL POT) sprouted secretly in 1960. This group, later named the Communist party of Kampuchea (Khmer Rouge), moved away from their North Vietnamese mentors, launching an armed struggle to topple the government in 1968.

The United States began secretly bombing North Vietnamese sanctuaries in Cambodia in 1969, and in April 1970, U.S. and South Vietnamese forces launched a limited incursion to wipe them out. By this time Sihanouk had been overthrown by one of his top generals, LON NOL. The new Khmer Republic's government became increasingly authoritarian and corrupt, and it fought a losing battle against the North Vietnamese on its territory and the Khmer Rouge guerrilla forces.

The Paris Peace Accords for Vietnam in January 1973 failed to halt the fighting in Cambodia, and in April 1975 the Khmer Rouge took Phnom Penh. Without hesitation they drove the entire urban population out among the poor peasants of the countryside, in whose name a revolutionary leveling was to take place. For the next three and a half years the population was conscripted into agricultural communes by zonal and local Khmer Rouge commanders, referred to only as *Angkar* ("Organization"). A few light industries were maintained in the otherwise empty cities and towns. Hundreds of thousands of people died of exhaustion, malnutrition, revolutionary and disciplinary executions, and paranoid purges within the movement itself. Conservative estimates have put the toll at about 1,000,000 persons; it may have been much higher. The Khmer Rouge almost totally isolated Cambodia from the outside world. China was its chief ally.

In January 1979, following violent disputes with Vietnam over boundaries and revolutionary leadership, Phnom Penh was overrun by the Vietnamese army. Khmer Rouge defectors headed by HENG SAMRIN established a Vietnamese-style people's republic backed by the authority of up to 180,000 Vietnamese troops and myriad advisors. The Khmer Rouge forces staggered to the western boundary with Thailand, where the United Nations eventually organized camps for further waves of Cambodians variously seeking food, haven, or resettlement. The Khmer Rouge launched guerrilla resistance with arms supplied by the Chinese. In 1982, Prince Sihanouk and Son Sann formed a coalition government with the Khmer Rouge. The Association of Southeast Asian Nations (ASEAN), opposed to the growing Soviet and Vietnamese influence in the region, helped to arm this more acceptable resistance group, which held Cambodia's seat in the United Nations. In May 1989, constitutional revisions restored the right to private property and reinstated Buddhism as the official religion. The Vietnamese withdrew almost all of their forces from Cambodia by September 1989 despite the collapse of multinational peace talks on the future of the country. In July 1990, as the Khmer Rouge intensified their guerrilla war, the United States withdrew diplomatic recognition from the government in exile, but it still aided the non-Communist rebel factions; China continued to aid the Khmer Rouge. Although many obstacles to peace remained, the four factions were pressed by their allies into forming an interim national council as part of a peace plan approved in August by the UN Security Council. The plan called for disarming the warring groups and holding UN-supervised elections, with international guarantees of Cambodian neutrality.

Cambodian languages see SOUTHEAST ASIAN LANGUAGES

Cambodians see CAMBODIA; KHMER EMPIRE

Cambrai Cambrai is a town in the Nord department in northern France on the Escaut River. It has a population of 35,272 (1982). Cambrai is the center of an agricultural area that produces sugar beets, grain, cattle, and dairy products. Originally settled by the Romans, it was an episcopal see by the 4th century. From the 10th to the 16th century the area was ruled by the Holy Roman Empire. The League of Cambrai against Venice was formed (1508) there, and in 1529 the Treaty of Cambrai between Emperor Charles V and Francis I of France was signed there. Its possession disputed by several claimants, the town finally went to France in 1677. Cambrai gives its name to cambric, a woven fabric first made there, and until 1914 Cambrai's textile-based economy flourished. Occupied by the Germans in both world wars, the town was severely damaged.

Cambrian Period see EARTH, GEOLOGIC HISTORY OF; GEOLOGIC TIME

Cambridge (England) The site of one of the world's great universities, Cambridge (derived from the Latin *Cantabrigia*) is located in southeast central England on the River Cam. The city is also the county seat of Cambridgeshire and has a population of 99,800 (1986 est.). Although light industry has developed on the city's outskirts, it is essentially a university community, and its life revolves around the many great colleges. Cambridge retains a charming medieval atmosphere, with old turreted houses, narrow winding lanes, and a multitude of spired churches. Landscaped lawns and gardens extend behind the magnificent old college buildings to the meandering, tree-shaded river.

The site of a Roman fort, Cambridge grew as a river crossing (hence its name) and was an early Anglo-Saxon trade center. The city was chartered in the 12th century. During that century two monasteries were established there, and from their schools eventually developed CAMBRIDGE UNIVERSITY.

Cambridge (Massachusetts) Cambridge, a city in eastern Massachusetts, is the seat of Middlesex County and has a population of 95,802 (1990). Separated by the Charles River from Boston, it is best known as the home of HARVARD UNIVERSITY (1636) and the MASSACHUSETTS INSTITUTE OF TECHNOLOGY (located in Cambridge since 1916). It is also a major industrial center. The city houses companies specializing in scientific equipment, research, and publishing, as well as considerable diversified manufacturing.

Cambridge was settled in 1630, and the first bridge linking the city to Boston was built in 1793. A subway connection was constructed in 1912. Such intellectual leaders as Henry Wadsworth Longfellow, Oliver Wendell Holmes, and James Russell Lowell lived in Cambridge.

Cambridge University Cambridge University, in Cambridge, England, was founded at the beginning of the 13th century. Originally, scholars were assigned to masters, who saw to their lodging and instruction; this practice soon led to the establishment of residential colleges, of which there are now 31, more than one-third constituted as colleges since 1949. Women students were first admitted in 1869, but only in 1948 did they gain full membership and all the privileges of degrees; their numbers were limited because only two colleges provided for them. Since the 1960s most colleges have become coresidential (coeducational).

All students of the university must be members of the largely autonomous colleges. Admission of undergraduates, numbering about 9,900, is controlled entirely by the colleges, but acceptance of graduate students is decided primarily by university bodies. The colleges, which have their own incomes and property, are responsible for the accommodation and general welfare of their students; they provide tutorial teaching to undergraduates either individually or in small groups. The university provides formal teaching through lectures, seminars, classes, and practical work in laboratories. Homerton College is restricted to students of education, but in the other colleges, students of all subjects are mixed.

The university's main governing body is, as in medieval times, the Regent House, made up of resident university officers and college fellows (tutors and researchers). The chief executive body is the Council of the Senate. The ceremonial and nominal head of the university is the chancellor, who is elected for life.

Almost all undergraduates seek the 3-year bachelor of arts degree. The honors examination is called a tripos, the name originating in the three-legged stool on which a 15th-century examiner sat to dispute formally with the senior undergraduate. A tripos is usually divided into two or more parts, and the possibility of combining parts of more than one tripos allows flexibility of study. Graduate students work generally for the 3-year Ph.D. degree or for the 1-year or 2-year M.Phil. degree. Their studies consist of research for a thesis, preparation for written examinations, or a combination of the two.

Special features of the university include the university library (more than 4 million volumes), the colleges' libraries, the Fitzwilliam Museum and other specialized museums, and the Cavendish Laboratories, for the study of physics. Cambridge University Press was founded in 1521.

The university consists of the following colleges (the founding date being given in parentheses): **Christ's College** (1448); **Churchill College** (1960); **Clare College** (1326); **Clare Hall** (1966, for graduate men and women); **Corpus Christi College** (1352); **Darwin College** (1964, for graduate men and women); **Downing College** (1800); **Emmanuel College** (1584); **Fitzwilliam College** (1869); **Girton College** (1869); **Gonville and Caius College** (1348); **Homerton College** (1824); **Hughes Hall** (1885); **Jesus College** (1496); **King's College** (1441); **Lucy Cavendish College** (1964, for women); **Magdalene College** (1542; for men); **New Hall** (1954, for women); **Newnham College** (1871, for women); **Pembroke College** (1347); **Peterhouse** (1284); **Queen's College** (1448); **Robinson College** (1977); **St. Catharine's College** (1473); **St. Edmund's College** (1896); **St. John's College** (1511); **Selwyn College** (1882); **Sidney Sussex College** (1596); **Trinity College** (1546); **Trinity Hall** (1350); **Wolfson College** (1965, graduate men and women).

Cambridgeshire Cambridgeshire (also called Cambridge) is a county in southeastern England. It covers 3,409 km^2 (1,316 mi^2), and the population is 651,600 (1988 est.). The county seat is at CAMBRIDGE, the site of Cambridge University. The southern part of the county is an area of low hills and chalk downs drained by branches of the River Ouse. In the north, The FENS, formerly a swamp that was drained, is a flatland of rich soils where grains, potatoes, and vegetables are grown. Food processing and light manufacturing take place in the main towns, Cambridge, Peterborough, and Wisbech.

Romans, Saxons, Danes, and Normans invaded Cambridgeshire, the Normans beginning the famous cathedral in Ely during the 11th century. In 1974 the counties were redistricted, and Cambridgeshire was greatly expanded.

Camden Camden, the seat of Camden County, is an industrial city and port in southwestern New Jersey with a population of 87,492 (1990). The city lies opposite Philadelphia, with a long waterfront on the Delaware River. The economy is maintained by shipbuilding and highly diversified industry. The Esterbrook Pen Company (1858) and the Campbell Soup Company (1869) both originated in Camden.

Settled in 1681 by William Cooper, the area was originally named Pyne Poynte. In 1773, Jacob Cooper, a descendant of William, laid out the present site and named it for Charles Pratt, 1st earl of Camden. After the Revolutionary War, the introduction of ferry service to Philadelphia and the coming of the railroad promoted growth in the area. The poet Walt WHITMAN lived there from 1873 until his death in 1892.

camel The camel is a cud-chewing mammal of the family Camelidae, order Artiodactyla (see ARTIODACTYL). It is distinguished from other camelids—the ALPACA, GUANACO, LLAMA, and VICUÑA—by the one or two fat-filled humps on its back. The family arose in North America and, about 10 million years ago, began spreading to other continents. It became extinct in North America itself about 2 million years ago.

Two species of camel now exist: the one-humped dromedary, *Camelus dromedarius*, and the two-humped Bactrian, *C. bactrianus*. The dromedary was domesticated more than 5,000 years ago in the Middle East, serving as a means of transport and as a source of milk, meat, wool, hides, and dried manure for fuel. The more docile Bactrian of Central Asia was domesticated about 2,500 years ago.

Adult male dromedaries stand about 2 m (7 ft) at the shoulder and weigh up to 680 kg (1,500 lb). Bactrians are shorter because of shorter legs. The gray to brown coat is short and fine in dromedaries, longer in Bactrians. Both species are well adapted to desert life and temperature extremes. Their two-toed feet have spreading, padded toes for walking on sand. When camels move quickly, both legs on the same side of the body advance together, producing a rolling gait.

Camels can obtain enough water from desert vegetation to survive for many months without another water supply. The animals can tolerate water losses equal to 25 percent of their body weight, and they excrete a concentrated urine. Other internal modifications enable them to maintain a steady water level in the blood and to drink amounts of water at a single time that would kill other animals. By having fat localized in a hump, the body is able to lose heat more rapidly. When these fat reserves are called upon, the hump shrinks and tends to sag.

camellia About 80 species of flowering evergreen shrubs and trees constitute the genus *Camellia* of the family Theaceae, including the TEA plant, *C. sinensis*. The genus is native to Asia, but several species called camellias are now grown worldwide in mild climates. The common camellia, *C. japonica*, reaches a height of about 14 m (45 ft). Its glossy, deep green, elliptical leaves are about 10 cm (4 in) long, and the red to pink or white flowers are about 13 cm (5 in) wide. Several thousand cultivars have been developed.

(Above) *The dromedary, or one-humped camel, can be trained to carry heavy loads on long journeys. Adapted to life in the desert, the camel has horny pads on the knees, thigh joints, and chest—the areas on which it rests—and long eyelashes, hair-covered ear openings, and slitlike nostrils for protection from sand and wind.*

(Below) *The Bactrian, or two-humped, camel has shorter legs than the dromedary and is not able to move as swiftly at its fastest pace. A few wild bands still roam the Gobi.*

Camelot In the Arthurian legends of ancient Britain, Camelot was the site of King Arthur's court and the Knights of the Round Table. It has been identified with the cathedral city of Winchester in England and with Caerleon, a town in Monmouthshire, Wales. Some versions, however, name both Camelot and Caerleon as sites of Arthur's court.

See also: ARTHUR AND ARTHURIAN LEGEND.

cameo The technique of cutting away one or more outer layers of glass, precious gems, hardstones, ceramics, or shells, or any work of art produced by this process, is known as cameo. Since the Hellenistic age (late 4th to 1st century BC), artisans have used small cutting tools, grinding wheels, and abrasives to fashion JEWELRY and other ornaments that feature figures, geometric and organic patterns, or portraits. These stand out in bold relief against the background, which has been cut away. Cameos may be bicolored, as seen in the familiar pink and white carvings made from seashells, or multicolored, as in jewelry made from agates, sardonyx, or specially prepared glass gems. Some Victorian cameo brooches and rings are of only one color, elaborately carved from gray, beige, or black lava stone; they are frequently set in gold.

Cameo glass is made by a process popular during the 19th century: undecorated vessels called "blanks," composed of as many as five layers of glass of different colors, were either carefully cut back layer by layer by grinding wheels or etched with hydrofluoric acid to produce multicolored cameo patterns.

This cameo pendant, dating from the Greco-Roman period, shows the snake-coiffed head of Medusa carved in semiprecious stone. The art of cameo design flourished in the classical world, and mythological themes were common designs. (Archaeological Museum, Florence.)

camera A camera is a device that directs an image focused by a lens or other optical system onto a photosensitive surface housed in a light-tight enclosure. In this very basic sense, these components perform the same function today that they did when photography was invented nearly 150 years ago. In simple cameras the lens is generally of the fixed-focus variety: no provision is made to focus on objects at varying distances from the camera. More complicated cameras have a system to achieve good focus that is manually or automatically actuated, in order to vary the lens-to-focal-plane distance. (The focal plane is the point behind the lens where the image comes into focus.)

The photographic surface used in modern cameras is almost exclusively light-sensitive film (see PHOTOGRAPHY). Flexible roll film may be housed in a cassette or on a paper-backed spool. A gear mechanism built into the camera advances the film between exposures. On professional, large-format cameras the film is a fairly stiff sheet that is carried in a holder to be inserted into the focal-plane area after the image has been focused.

Cameras are manufactured in a variety of types and sizes. Miniature instruments producing incredibly small images are used in medical research. Commercial portrait studios may use large-format view cameras that produce a film image as large as 11×14 in.

Camera Development

Centuries before the invention of the first practical photographic process, artists had been using a device called a CAMERA OBSCURA, literally a dark chamber, as an aid in rendering proper perspective or tracing a scene. Originally, in fact, it was a dark room, with a small opening in an outside wall. An image of an illuminated object outside the room passed through the hole and was reproduced, upside down and in small scale, on an opposite wall. Later, a light-tight box replaced the room, and a simple lens was inserted in the hole. In 1839 the pioneer inventor Louis J. M. DAGUERRE developed the light-sensitive DAGUERREOTYPE, a photographic plate on which a camera obscura image could be held and fixed permanently. That same year, a French firm began production of the world's first commercial camera. In basic design, this instrument was remarkably like a camera obscura. The surface on which an artist sketched the projected image became a removable piece of ground glass, onto which the image could be brought into focus. After the photographer focused the image, the ground glass was replaced by a special wooden frame, which held the light-sensitive plate. Moving a simple, manually operated slide, or just removing the lens cap for a time, made the exposure (see PHOTOGRAPHY, HISTORY AND ART OF). The development of the gelatine dry plate in the 1870s began a revolution in camera design that was accelerated by the invention of flexible film. The dry, sensitized new materials allowed designers to make very compact instruments that were much more convenient to operate.

The Kodak camera was introduced in 1888. It was preloaded at the factory with sufficient film for 100 exposures. When the roll was finished, the entire camera was returned to the factory in Rochester, N.Y., where the film was developed and printed and the camera reloaded. In 1900 the marketing of Eastman's Kodak Brownie #1 popularized photography even further. At a cost of $1.00 for the camera and 10 cents per roll for the film, the Brownie put a basic photographic system within reach of virtually everyone.

The continuing improvements of sensitized film prod-

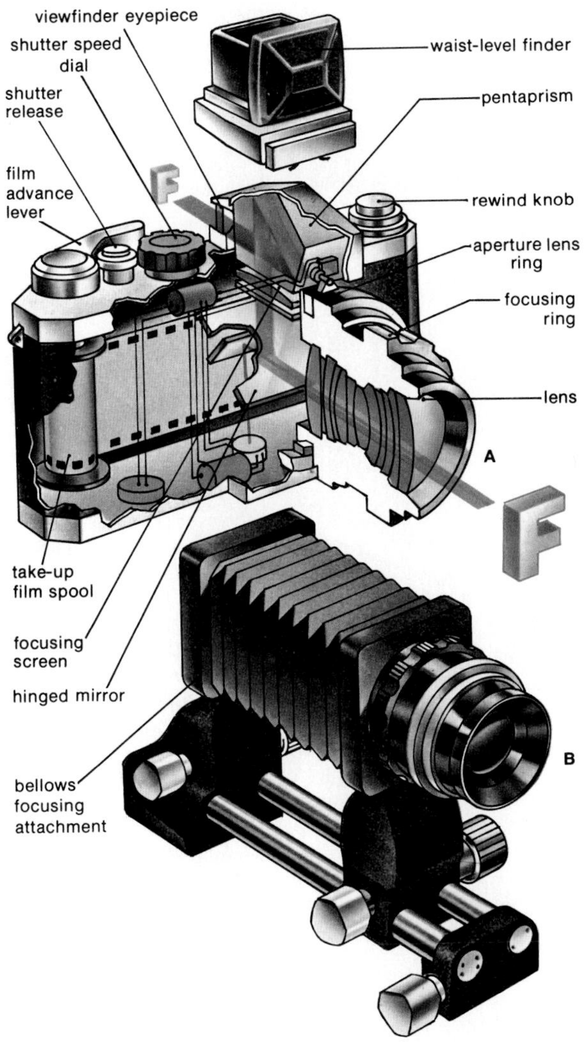

This 35-mm single-lense reflex camera (A) *is equipped with a hinged mirror and an eye-level pentaprism, which enable the photographer to see exactly the same scene as the one that will be recorded on film. For waist-level viewing, the pentaprism can be replaced with a folding waist-level viewfinder. Depressing the shutter-release button causes the hinged mirror to swing up against the underside of the focusing screen, allowing light from the lens to fall on the film. When the exposure has been made, the mirror automatically returns to its original position, thus blocking the path of the light to the film and redirecting the light to the viewfinder. The camera's accessories include a variable focusing attachment for close-up work* (B).

ucts were paralleled by the development of more sophisticated cameras. The first optical rangefinder became available in 1916, and a very high-speed lens, the Ernostar, which had an effective aperture of f/2.0, appeared on a compact camera in 1924, marking the beginning of the era of natural-light candid photography.

After World War II the availability of miniaturized electronic components made automatic exposure systems commonplace on even the most inexpensive cameras. The process of automating most camera functions was completed in the late 1970s, when the first of what have come to be known as "point and shoot" cameras appeared on the market.

The Parts of a Camera

Lens. The LENS is the image-forming device on a camera. It may be composed of from 1 to as many as 10 or 12 elements. The first cameras were fitted with a single-element meniscus lens, but on improved cameras it was soon replaced with greatly improved, more complicated designs. The single-element lens remained in use on inexpensive cameras, however.

The three basic types of lenses are normal, wide angle, and telephoto. The lens's focal length—the point at which light rays converge, or focus, through the lens—determines the size of the image that will be produced on the film. With a normal lens, the viewing field is approximately 50 degrees. The objects photographed appear normal in size and shape, relative to the picture's background. A camera that uses a 35-mm film will usually have a 50-mm lens for normal coverage; on a medium-format 6 × 6-cm camera, the same coverage is obtained with an 80-mm lens.

In a wide-angle lens, the field of view is much wider: about 90 degrees. Telephoto, or long-focus lenses, have a smaller field of view than a normal lens and show an enlarged detail of the image over the same film area. Interchangeable-lens cameras offer the photographer the opportunity to select a focal length that is optimum for any given situation. In recent years, variable-focal-length, or "zoom," lenses, have become very popular.

The speed, or light-gathering power, of a lens is indicated by the f number, called the aperture. The lower the f number, the faster the lens—that is, the more light it lets through. A fast lens has an aperture of at least f/2.0. As the speed increases, the cost of the lens tends to increase, since it is more costly to maintain high standards of optical correction at very high apertures.

Diaphragm. One of the two factors that determines correct film exposure is the amount of light allowed to pass through the lens. Mechanically reducing the aperture improves optical performance, particularly toward the edge of the picture, and increases the DEPTH OF FIELD, which is the zone of good focus. Most cameras use an iris-type diaphragm, which consists of a number of very thin metal blades. They are so mounted that by rotating a ring or moving a lever, the size of the lens opening can be varied. On automatic cameras the diaphragm is adjusted by a built-in mechanism.

The various openings of the diaphragm—called f-stops—are stamped on the lens mounting. Each change of diaphragm opening changes the amount of light passing through the lens by a factor of 2. For example, the amount of light allowed through the lens at a setting of 2 is twice the amount allowed at a setting of 2.8. The standard diaphragm settings found on most lenses are 2, 2.8, 4, 5.6, 8, 11, 16, 22, and so on. The smallest lens opening on a lens whose f-stops end in 22 is, in fact, 22.

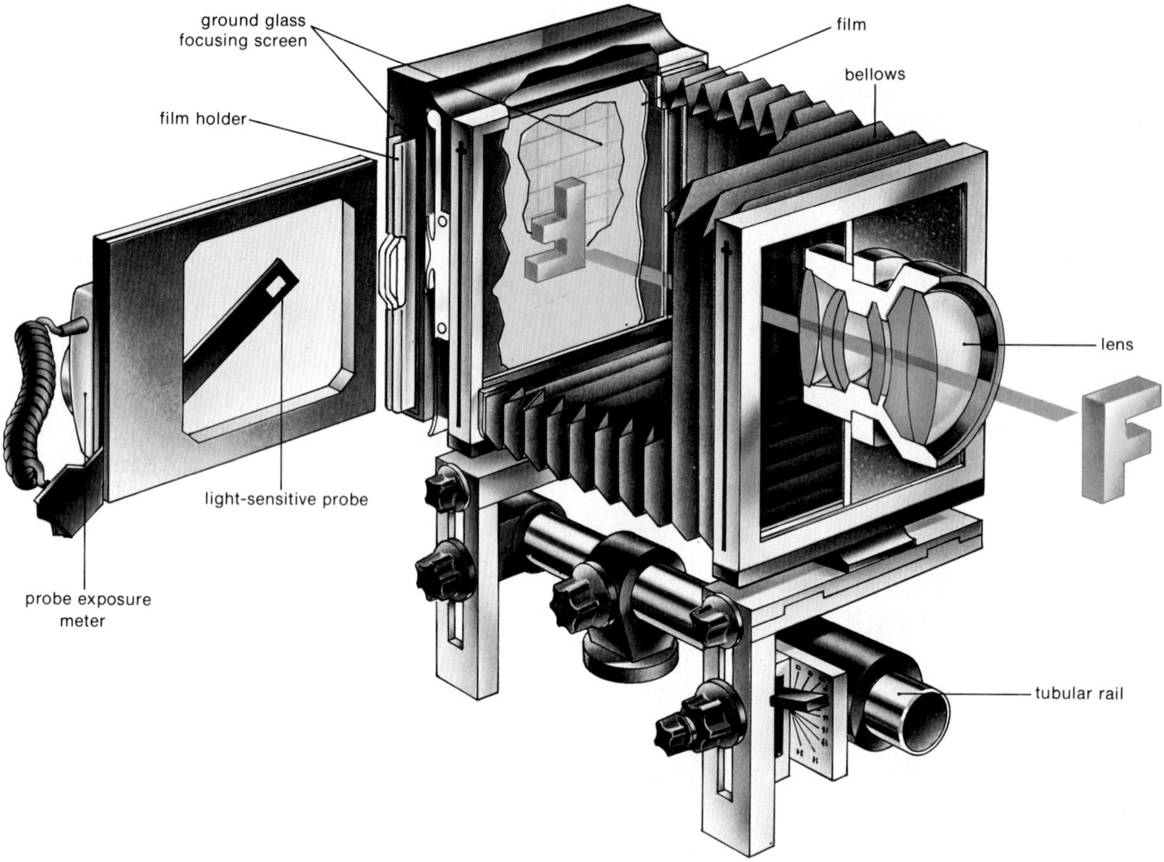

A view camera consists of a lens and a ground-glass focusing screen linked by a flexible bellows and mounted on a tripod-supported tubular rail. Various lenses may be used, and either the lens or the screen, or both, may be moved for focusing. The screen can be moved backward and replaced with a reversible holder containing sheet film on each side, under sliding panels. Removal of a panel exposes the film. A movable, light-sensitive probe, shaped like a film holder, may be inserted in front of the screen to measure lighting conditions.

Shutter. The second exposure control factor is the shutter, a mechanical device that acts as a gate, controlling the duration of time that light is allowed to pass through the lens and fall on the film. Two types of shutters are in general use. The leaf type, like the diaphragm, is made up of a number of thin metal blades that are opened and closed. Shutters of this type usually have a maximum speed of 1/500th of a second.

The focal-plane shutter in modern cameras usually consists of two pieces of rubberized fabric that move across the focal plane. The spacing between the fabric edges and the speed of transit determine the effective shutter speed. Shutters of this type are capable of very high speeds, in some cases 1/4,000th of a second.

Exposure Control. Many professional photographers still use exposure meters, which are instruments that measure light intensity, indicating what aperture and shutter speed are appropriate to the film type used, under prevailing light conditions. Completely automatic exposure control, however, is now virtually standard on all snapshot cameras.

On nonreflex instruments (see the section Types of Cameras) a selenium cell mounted adjacent to the lens measures the incoming light and selects a combination of lens aperture and shutter speed that will produce a negative of good quality. Single-lens reflex cameras are fitted with through-the-lens metering systems (TTLs) that automate the control of exposure. A light-sensing cell is located in the optical path inside the camera and gives an extremely accurate reading of the prevailing light conditions, which is used to set the aperture and shutter speeds accordingly.

The Viewfinder. For the photographer, the viewfinder defines the area covered by whatever lens is in use on the camera. The most primitive type is a simple wire frame mounted just over the lens. Proper eye position is determined by a vertical post mounted at the rear of the camera. The view seen through the frame with the post in the center is equal to the area covered by the lens.

The type of viewfinder in most frequent use today is actually a reversed telescope found on all cameras except single- and twin-lens reflex instruments. On a typical high-grade 35-mm camera with interchangeable lenses, a bright line in the viewfinder outlines the area covered by the lens in use and changes size automatically to correspond with lenses of different focal lengths. In a single-lens reflex camera the image focused by the camera lens is reflected by a mirror onto a ground-glass screen, usually through a special prism arrangement. Twin-lens reflex cameras have two coupled lenses; one of them acts as a viewfinder and, like the single-lens reflex, reflects the image it sees on a ground-glass screen.

Focusing Methods. On adjustable-lens cameras, a sharp picture requires accurate positioning of the lens system. Although its use has declined sharply, the optical-coupled rangefinder is one of the best methods of achieving good focus quickly. If the camera is out of focus, the user sees a double image in a portion of the viewfinder field. Focusing the lens brings the two images together, until—as the lens moves into focus—they are perfectly aligned.

In the single- and twin-lens reflex cameras, the image is visually focused on the ground glass in the viewfinder. Ground glass is used, whether or not the camera is fitted with a prism system for eye-level viewing. Because of the very slight distance between the picture-taking lens and the viewfinder lens in a twin-lens reflex camera, in close-ups the view seen by the photographer does not precisely match the view focused on the film. This very slight difference is called "parallax," and there are various devices available to correct for it.

Many modern cameras used by the casual snapshotter are fitted with an automatic focusing system. There are two general types, active and passive. In the active system, a circuit so elaborate that it is actually a complete miniature computer sends out an infrared beam. This beam bounces off the photographic subject and is reflected back to the camera. By electronically measuring the angle of the beam, the distance to the subject can be determined. A servomotor then adjusts the lens appropriately. The passive system works on the principle that an in-focus subject will show more contrast than an out-of-focus subject. A CCD light sensor (see CHARGE-COUPLED DEVICE) mounted behind the lens will search out the point

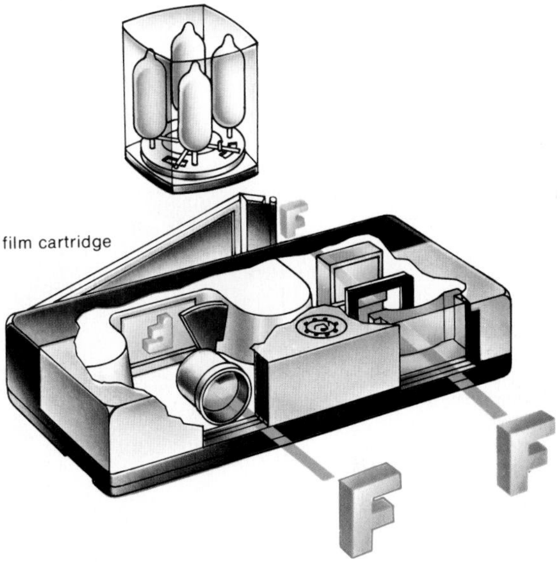

Thin, pocket-sized cameras, such as the Instamatic 100, were designed for easy carrying, as well as easy film loading with drop-in cartridges.

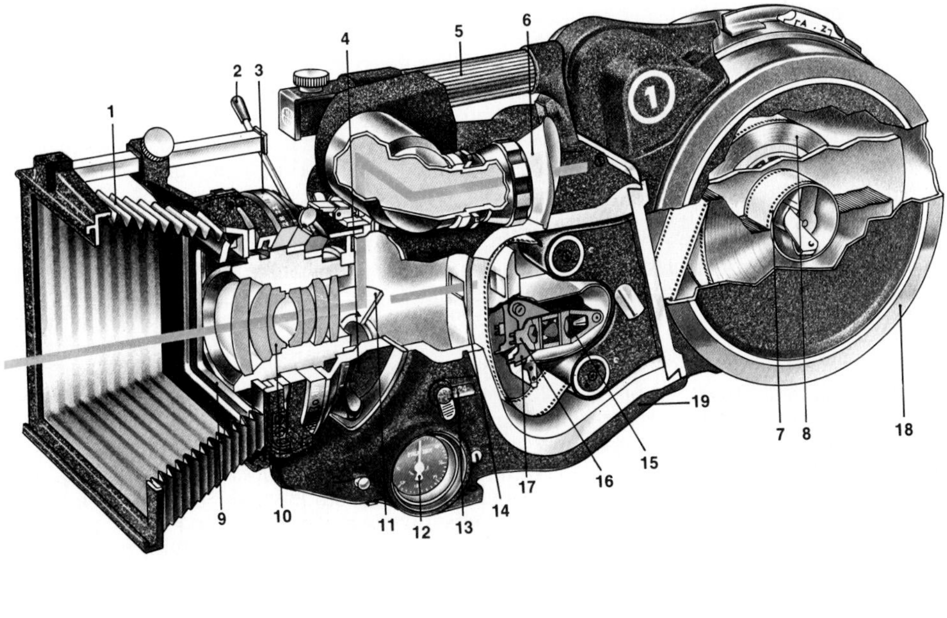

The cutaway reveals internal parts of a 35-mm movie camera. (Left) *The crystal-controlled, motor-driven camera features a matte box* (1)*; focus control* (2)*; aperture control* (3)*; soundproof housing, or blimp* (4)*; reflex viewer* (5)*; diopter-correctable, swivel eyepiece* (6)*; take-up reel* (7)*; feed reel* (8)*; optical flat seal for mounting the blimp* (9)*; compound lens* (10)*; revolving, two-bladed mirror shutter* (11)*; footage indicator* (12)*; film-speed tachometer* (13)*; film gate* (14)*; sprocket drive* (15)*; registration pins* (16)*; pull-down claw* (17)*; film magazine* (18)*; and camera case* (19).

The new (1986) Polaroid Spectra uses the same basic technology as Polaroid's earlier SX-70, but adds new electronics and an entirely innovative optical system. Film size is rectangular, and about 10% larger than the SX-70's. New film chemistry provides improved color. The sonar autofocus system and a dual photodiode that measures both visible and infrared light control an unusual, 3-element lens system. The viewfinder features digital readouts of exposure conditions and camera status. All controls are in the back of the camera.

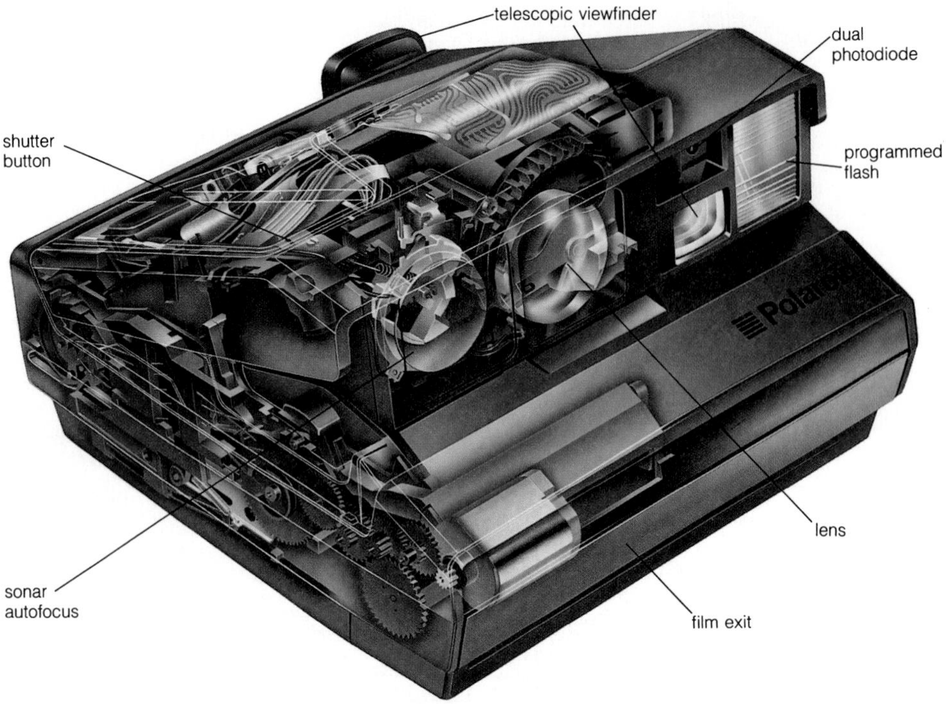

of greatest contrast and set the lens. Single-lens reflex cameras often use this type of automatic focusing.

Types of Cameras

For more than seven decades the box camera was the instrument of choice for the casual amateur photographer. Inexpensive and simple, it was, nevertheless, capable of excellent results under many conditions. Box cameras were normally fitted with a single-element lens, a limited range of aperture control, and a single-speed leaf shutter.

The Folding-Roll Film Camera. Second in popularity only to the box camera, the folding camera was manufactured in a variety of formats. Basically, though, it was a box camera whose lens was incorporated into a movable bellows that could slide back and forth on a rail, allowing the lens to change focus. Lenses and shutters were often one-piece units. More-elaborate models were first-rate instruments with high-quality optical systems and precision shutters. Many were fitted with coupled rangefinders. The most significant advantage they had over the box camera, however, was their compact design when folded, which made them easier to pack and transport.

There has been something of a minor renaissance in folding-roll film cameras in recent years, with the appearance of several new professional instruments. They are appreciated for their large negative size and compact design.

Twin-Lens Reflex Cameras. A medium-format camera—one that uses film larger than 35 mm—the twin-lens reflex was immensely popular after World War II. It is fitted with two lenses of identical focal length, one mounted atop the other. The lower, or taking, lens focuses its image directly on the film, while the image produced by the upper viewing lens is reflected through 90 degrees by a mirror, and brought to focus on a horizontal ground-glass focusing screen. The light paths to the film plane and the focusing screen are exactly equal so that if the photographer brings the scene on the focusing screen to sharp focus, the image on the film plane will be equally sharp.

Single-Lens Reflex Cameras. One of the most popular designs available today, the single-lens reflex (SLR) both views and photographs through one lens. Light passing through the lens is reflected by a mirror and brought to focus on a ground glass. The mirror causes a reversal of the image seen on the ground glass, but the addition of a pentaprism mounted over the ground glass allows the camera to be used at eye level, with the image seen upright and in proper left/right orientation. An instant before the exposure is made, the mirror swings upward, and the shutter is activated. A single control cocks the shutter for the next exposure, advances the film, and returns the mirror to focusing position.

View Cameras and Technical Cameras. Cameras in this category are used almost exclusively by professional photographers. The most common film formats are 4 × 5 or 8 × 10 in, the latter often used in the very large view cameras found in portrait studios. Film for these cameras is loaded in the darkroom into two-sided holders, which are inserted at the back of the camera. Both the camera's back and front can be tilted in various positions to permit the photographer to make certain types of corrections in the image. By raising the lens in relation to the film plane, when photographing a tall building, for example, the tendency for parallel lines to look as if they converge is eliminated.

Instant Cameras. An instant camera will produce a finished print in from 20 seconds to about 4 minutes. The film, after exposure, is passed between two stainless steel rollers inside the camera. These rollers rupture a chemical pod on the film and spread developing agent evenly over the film's surface. In the original Polaroid system it was necessary for the user to peel the finished print from the base material. Professional Polaroid films, both color and black and white, are still developed in this manner.

Beginning in 1972 with the all new model, the SX-70, Polaroid Instant Cameras eject the developing picture from the camera, and the film reaches its final development in full daylight. The process is completed in about 4 minutes. The Spectra, introduced in 1986, employs this type of technology and a more advanced type of electronic exposure control and automatic focusing system. Like the SX-70 models, it employs an ultra-high-frequency sound emitter. An electronic circuit in the camera measures the time required for the sound to be reflected back from the object being photographed. This time measurement is converted into a measurement of distance, and an electrical mechanism coupled to the focusing circuit sets the lens for the proper exposure.

Disc Cameras. Since its introduction in the 1880s, flexible film has usually been rolled onto a spool or loaded into a cassette. In 1980 the Eastman Kodak Company introduced a new format for mass-market cameras. Fifteen images, each 5⁄16 × 3⁄8 in, can be photographed on a piece of circular film about 2½ in in diameter, which is housed in a thin, light-tight film disc. Disc cameras are exceptionally compact, and most are fitted with an electronic flash and a motor that advances the disc after each exposure.

Electronic Imaging. The world's first electronic still camera, the Japanese Canon, uses a cluster of light-sensitive electronic charge-coupled devices, instead of film, at the focal plane. Each light sensor on a CCD is called a pixel. The pixel converts light into an electrical signal, which is recorded on a magnetic disc in the camera. The more dense the grouping of pixels, the sharper the resulting picture, which is recorded in full color. Once recorded, the image can be "played" on a television set by inserting the magnetic disc in a still video recorder, or a paper print can be made using a new three-color electrostatic process. The quality of the image, while not as fine as that on photographic film, is still very good and certainly will be improved during the coming years. At the present time the system will be used primarily by photojournalists, who will be able to transmit the information on the magnetic disc over ordinary telephone lines by using a Canon analog transceiver. A picture taken in Los Angeles can be viewed in full color a few minutes later in New York City.

Massive research efforts and increased production can be expected eventually to lower the cost of all-electronic still systems. Traditional film, however, will dominate the market for the foreseeable future.

camera obscura The camera obscura ("dark chamber"), forerunner of the photographic camera, was a darkened room or box with a single small opening. Light coming through the opening projected an inverted image of a brightly lit exterior object onto the opposite wall. The ancients used the camera obscura to view eclipses; by the 19th century, lenses and mirrors had been added to correct the inversion and to project the image onto paper, where it could be easily traced. In 1826, J. N. NIEPCE used a camera obscura to project an image onto light-sensitive paper, creating in effect the first photographic camera.

Cameron, Charles Charles Cameron, 1740–1812, was a Scottish architect who worked in Russia for Catherine II and her successors. Neoclassical in the manner of Robert Adam, Cameron redesigned and redecorated (1780–84) a number of rooms in the Summer Palace near St. Petersburg (now Leningrad), where he also built the Agate Pavilion (1780–83) and the Cameron Gallery (1783–85). One of his grandest projects was Pavlovsk, Grand Duke Paul's country palace (1782–86).

Cameron, Julia Margaret Julia Margaret Cameron, b. June 11, 1815, d. Jan. 26, 1879, was a controversial English photographer best known for her searching portraits of eminent Victorians and for her romantic depictions of women and children. "Annie, My First Success" (1864) was followed by "Sir John Herschel" (1867), "Mrs. Herbert Duckworth" (1867), and "Thomas Carlyle" (1867). Cameron's pioneering use of the close-up format and of dramatic lighting made her portraits unusually expressive, but her lack of technical skill, evidenced in blurring and smudges, sparked a hostile reaction from some critics. Influenced by Pre-Raphaelite painting, she illustrated literary and religious subjects such as *Idylls of the King* (1874).

Cameron, Simon Simon Cameron, b. Maytown, Pa., Mar. 8, 1799, d. June 26, 1889, is regarded by many historians as the first state boss in U.S. politics. He served (1845–49) as a Democratic senator from Pennsylvania and was reelected as a Republican in 1856. A candidate for the Republican presidential nomination in 1860, he threw his support to Abraham Lincoln in return for promises—by Lincoln's associates—of a cabinet post. As secretary of war (1861–62), he was accused of tolerating corruption. Returning to the Senate in 1867, he retired in 1877 after securing the seat for his son. The political machine that Cameron built in Pennsylvania enabled the Republicans to carry the state in every presidential election until 1936.

AT A GLANCE

REPUBLIC OF CAMEROON

Land: Area: 475,442 km^2 (181, 569 mi^2). Capital: Yaoundé (1985 est. pop., 583,000). Largest city: Douala (1985 est. pop., 852,700).

People: Population (1990 est.): 11,092,470. Density: 23.3 persons per km^2 (61.1 per mi^2). Distribution (1987): 58% rural, 42% urban. Official languages: English, French. Major religions: traditional religions, Roman Catholicism, Islam.

Government: Type: one-party state. Legislature: National Assembly. Political subdivisions: 10 provinces.

Economy: GDP (1988 est.): $12.9 billion; $995 per capita. Labor distribution (1985): agriculture—74.4%; industry and transport—11.4%; other services—9.7%. Foreign trade (1988): imports—$2.3 billion; exports—$2.0 billion. Currency: 1 C. F. A. franc = 100 centimes.

Education and Health: Literacy (1985): 66% of adult population. Universities (1990): 1. Hospital beds (1984–85): 26,382. Physicians (1985–86): 833. Life expectancy (1990): women—53; men—49. Infant mortality (1990): 120 per 1,000 live births.

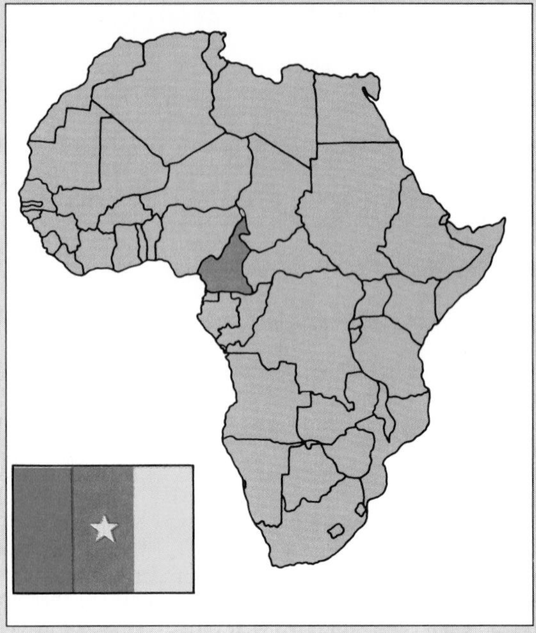

Cameroon The Republic of Cameroon is an independent state in western Africa bordered by Nigeria to the northwest; Chad to the northeast; the Central African Republic to the east; the Congo, Equatorial Guinea, and Gabon to the south; and the Atlantic Ocean to the southwest. Most of Cameroon was once ruled by France; the remainder was under British control. French influence remains strong, especially in YAOUNDÉ, the capital.

Rural villages in northeastern Cameroon feature the cylindrical earthen dwellings with conical, thatched roofs that are common throughout much of equatorial West Africa.

The Land

The country has a diverse topography. In the south, a densely forested plateau extends from the Sanaga River to the Gabon border; a coastal plain separates these highlands from the Atlantic. The central region rises gradually, culminating in the Adamawa Plateau, and in the far north the land drops toward Lake Chad. The western part of Cameroon is mountainous. Here Cameroon Mountain, the highest point in the country, rises to 4,070 m (13,354 ft). The climate is tropical. Average temperatures range between 21° and 28° C (70° and 82° F). In the south, rains fall between April and November and are rare the rest of the year. The central zone has two dry seasons and two wet periods; in the north, rain falls only between May and October. Average annual rainfall ranges from 10,160 mm (400 in) in the west to 386 mm (15.2 in) in the north.

People and Economy

Cameroonians belong to more than 150 ethnic groups that fall into two broad divisions. The northern savanna is home to cattle keepers and semipastoralist grain growers, most of whom are Muslims; the south shelters settled agricultural peoples. Although many southerners are Christians, most adhere to traditional African religions.

Languages can be divided into five groups. In the southeast, peoples such as the Douala and FANG speak Bantu languages. The highlands are home to Bantoid

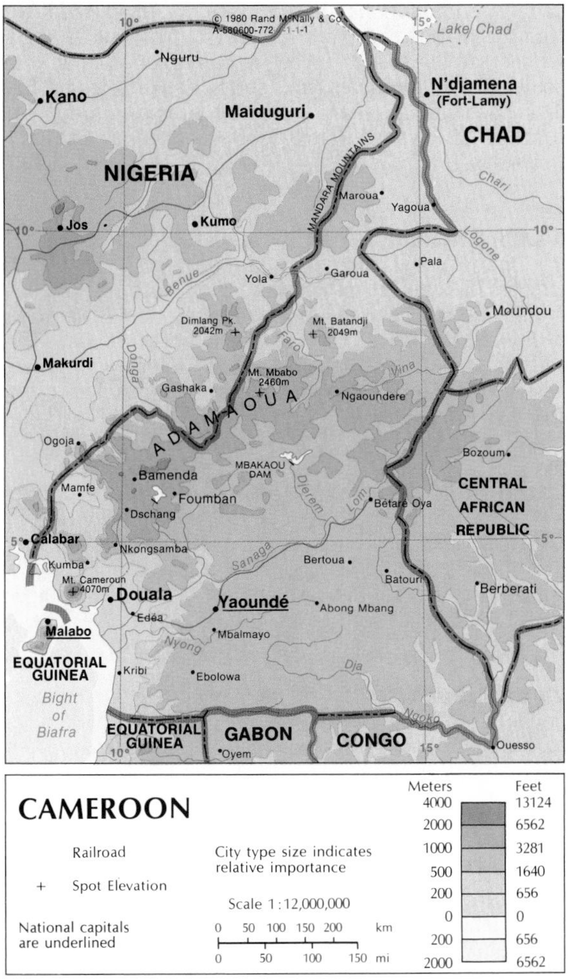

speakers, notably the Bamileke. Speakers of Sudanic languages—such as the HAUSA, Margi, and Kapsigi—inhabit the north, along with FULANI immigrants from West Africa. In the east central region live the Gbaya and Mbum, who speak Adamawa Eastern languages. Hausa, Fulani, Pidgin English, and Douala serve as trade languages; French and English are used in government.

Cameroon is mainly rural. Population distribution is uneven, and the central and southeastern parts of the country are sparsely populated. Since independence, educational and health services have greatly expanded.

Although Cameroon remains predominantly agricultural, the economy is being transformed by mining and industrial development. Staple foodstuffs include yams, plantains, cassava, and millet; peanuts, palm oil, timber, cacao, coffee, bananas, and cotton are the major commercial crops. Exports of petroleum from offshore fields began in 1977. The country has a variety of other mineral resources, including bauxite and iron ore, but few are commercially exploited. Possessing both heavy industry and light manufacturing, Cameroon is rapidly becoming one of the major industrial centers of Francophone Africa. Hydroelectric power from the Sanaga River, a network of roads, railroads, and airports, and an excellent port have encouraged progress in this sector.

History and Government

Little is known about the country's early history, but the population probably included migrants from the north who had abandoned the increasingly arid Sahara. In addition, it appears that the Bantu languages, now found throughout Africa to the southeast, spread from the Cameroon region. Later the Fulani filtered into northern Cameroon, where they founded Muslim states with economies based on cattle keeping and slave raiding among neighboring non-Muslim peoples.

Germany proclaimed Cameroon a protectorate in 1884. It remained a German colony until World War I, when it was divided into French- and British-administered zones under the League of Nations mandate system and later the United Nations trusteeship system. The French zone become a sovereign state in 1960, and a year later the southern half of the British zone federated with it. The federal system ended in 1972 under a new constitution. Alhaji Ahmadou Ahidjo governed the country through the Union Nationale Camerounaise, the sole political party, from 1960 until his resignation in 1982. His successor, Paul Biya, was reelected president in 1984 after suppressing an Ahidjo-led coup. The name of the country was then changed from United Republic of Cameroon to Republic of Cameroon, and the post of prime minister was abolished. On Aug. 21, 1986, in a rare natural disaster, toxic gases erupted from a volcanic lake in northwestern Cameroon, killing about 1,500 people. Biya, who was again reelected in 1988, confronted growing demands to legalize opposition parties.

Camino Real [kah-mee'-noh ray-ahl'] *Camino Real,* a Spanish term meaning "king's road," was the name of several highways in Spain and in Spain's New World dominions. In Mexico the land route extending from the port city of Veracruz to Santa Fe, N.Mex., was known as the Camino Real. The most famous of these royal roads, however, was the one in the present state of California. It began at San Diego in the south, generally followed the coastline, and ended at Sonoma, north of San Francisco. Along this route Father Junípero SERRA established a series of 21 Spanish missions in the second half of the 18th century.

Camisards The Camisards, HUGUENOTS (Protestants) of the Cévennes Mountains in France, rebelled (1702–10) after King Louis XIV revoked (1685) the Edict of Nantes and banned Huguenot worship. Persecuted by Roman Catholic clergy and the intendant of Languedoc, poor Camisard peasants and artisans began guerrilla activities and outmaneuvered royal troops diverted from the War of the SPANISH SUCCESSION. The duc de VILLARS negotiated (1704) a settlement with the Camisard leader Jean

Cavalier, but another leader, Pierre Laporte (called Roland), was killed. Despite an amnesty in 1705, sporadic resistance continued until 1710. After 1715 the clandestine Camisard Church of the Desert held synods.

Camões, Luis Vaz de [kay-moynzh', lu-eezh' vahzh dih] Luis Vaz de Camões (or Camoëns), b. 1524?, d. 1580, the national poet of Portugal, is the author, among many hundreds of poems, of the epic *The Lusiads* (1572), widely regarded as the greatest literary work in Portuguese. A member of the minor nobility, Camões was probably raised and educated in the university town of Coimbra before embarking on military maneuvers in North Africa, where he lost an eye. Subsequent involvement in Lisbon's palace intrigues led to a short prison sentence followed by 17 years (1553–70) of service to the crown in India, China, and Africa. With the publication of *The Lusiads*, the repatriated veteran received a modest pension, but his final years were spent in relative penury as both he and Portugal slipped into eclipse.

The classical example permeates *The Lusiads*, from its title, which suggests a Portuguese geneology with roots in Greco-Roman mythology (*Lusitania* was the Roman name for Portugal), to the poem's opening verses and a ten-canto structure patterned on Vergil's *Aeneid*. With the discovery of a maritime route to India as the basis of his narrative, Camões describes the feat of Vasco da Gama and his contemporaries as the culmination of a national history equal to all the glories of the ancient world.

camouflage Camouflage is the art of disguising the presence of troops, equipment, and other objects in order to gain military advantage. Modern camouflage was first used in the 19th century in India by British troops, who dyed their white tropical uniforms to blend with the dry earth. This produced a color called khaki, which was used for many years and has been adopted by many nations.

Camouflage changed dramatically during World War I, when aerial scouts and photography made concealment difficult. The French called upon a number of artists to devise methods of concealing guns from air surveillance. They came up with a pattern of colors to which they gave the name camouflage, from the French *camouflet* ("smoke puff"). Stunning patterns known as dazzle camouflage were devised to break up the outlines of ships at sea, making it difficult for German U-boats to spot them. Between the wars, camouflage became an accepted art. Vehicles, guns, tanks, and buildings were disguised beneath nets garnished with scrim, still the principal method used today.

Camp, Walter Walter Chauncey Camp, b. New Britain, Conn., Apr.7, 1859, d. Mar.14, 1925, was an American football player and coach who is often described as the father of American football. He was responsible for a number of innovations that distinguished American football from its immediate predecessor, rugby. As a member of the game's rules committee from 1879 until his death, Camp's contributions to the rules included reducing teams from 15 to 11 players, the system of downs, and a revised scoring system (allowing points for touchdowns, points after, field goals, and safeties). He selected the first All-American team in 1889. Camp played and coached at Yale University and coached at Stanford University.

Camp David The official retreat of the president of the United States, Camp David is located in Maryland, about 115 km (70 mi) northwest of Washington, D.C. Administered by the military, the camp was established by President Franklin D. Roosevelt. Camp David was the site of peace talks (1978) between Egypt and Israel, hosted by President Jimmy Carter, which resulted in the so-called Camp David Accords.

Camp Fire Camp Fire is a U.S. organization for girls and (since 1975) boys, founded as the Camp Fire Girls in 1910. In 300 local groups, about 450,000 members, from kindergarten through high school, participate in activities emphasizing the development of individual potential and character.

camp meetings Camp meetings are intercongregational, often transdenominational, Protestant gatherings for the purpose of giving extended time to intense, often revivalistic, preaching, Bible study, and prayer. They originated in the outdoor convocations of the American frontier during the early 19th century. At that time, those attending traveled to the appointed place and pitched camp; hence, the name *camp meeting*.

The immense success of these meetings led to their permanent establishment. Originally, Baptists, Methodists, and Presbyterians held joint camp meetings, but by the mid-1800s, both the Presbyterians and the Baptists had divided deeply over their value and generally ceased to support them officially. Thus, they became an essentially Methodist institution. With the liberalizing of Methodism, camp meetings had, by 1900, become the preserve of critics of liberal trends. Some conservative groups continue to maintain them, especially the Holiness movement.

campaign, political see POLITICAL CAMPAIGN

Campanella, Roy Roy Campanella, b. Nov. 19, 1921, an American baseball player, was a brilliant catcher for the Brooklyn Dodgers. His baseball career was curtailed in 1958, when he was nearly killed in an automobile accident that has since confined him to a wheelchair. Campanella, who was named Most Valuable Player in the National League three times, hit 242 home runs and batted in 856 runs from 1948 through 1957. Partially paralyzed, Campanella has stayed close to the sport. In 1959 the Yankees and Dodgers held an exhibition game in his honor at Los Angeles; the crowd of 93,103 remains a baseball record. Campanella was elected to baseball's Hall of Fame in 1969.

Campania [kahm-pahn'-yah] Campania is an administrative region in southern Italy on the Tyrrhenian Sea. It covers 13,595 km^2 (5,250 mi^2), and its population is 5,731,426 (1988 est.). The capital and largest city is NAPLES. The APENNINES cover Campania except for the fertile coastal plains, one of Italy's most productive agricultural areas. The port cities of Naples and SALERNO are industrial centers. Tourism is important because of the many coastal resorts and important archaeological sites, including HERCULANEUM and POMPEII. Settled by Greek colonists and Etruscans, the region was called Campania before the Roman period. After the fall of Rome, it was held by Goths, Byzantines, Lombards, and Normans before incorporation into the kingdoms of Sicily (12th century) and Naples (from the 13th century); it became part of unified Italy in 1860.

campanile [kam-puh-nee'-lee] The campanile, or bell tower (from *campana*, the Italian for "bell"), was an Italian architectural form developed during the Middle Ages. One type of campanile, the church belfry, was erected as an independent structure next to a basilica. Perhaps the best-known is the Leaning Tower of Pisa (1173–1274). The bells of the civic campanile, attached to the town hall (such as the Palazzo Vecchio, Florence, 1298–1340), were the official means of summoning citizens and of giving warning.

Campbell, Alexander Alexander Campbell, b. Sept. 12, 1788, d. Mar. 4, 1866, an Irish-born American clergyman, was one of the founders of the DISCIPLES OF CHRIST. The son of Thomas Campbell (1763–1854), a Scottish Presbyterian minister, he studied at the University of Glasgow and followed his father to the United States in 1809. Campbell and his father broke with Presbyterianism, maintaining that individuals—not the church—had the right to determine their fitness to take part in the Lord's Supper. In 1809 they formed the Christian Association of Washington, Pa., and Alexander became minister of its church at Brush Run in 1812. The group was affiliated with the Baptists until 1826, when Alexander Campbell broke that connection and formed the independent Disciples of Christ, or Reformers. The Disciples of Christ, nicknamed "Campbellites," united with Barton W. STONE's "Christians" in Kentucky in 1832, and Campbell assumed leadership of a movement that spread rapidly. In 1840 he founded Bethany College, now in West Virginia.

Alexander Campbell, an American religious reformer, cofounded the Disciples of Christ church early in the 19th century.

Campbell, Clarence Clarence Sutherland Campbell, b. Fleming, Saskatchewan, July 9, 1905, d. June 24, 1984, was a Canadian lawyer who served as president of the National Hockey League from 1946 to 1977. He served during difficult times, including the expansion of the league from 6 to 12 teams in 1967 (which he opposed) and eventually to 18 teams. Affable and approachable, Campbell possessed leadership qualities that were honed by his experience in labor negotiations. Campbell was a Rhodes scholar and a war-crimes prosecutor at Nuremberg at the end of his service (1940–46) in the Canadian army.

Campbell, Colen Colen Campbell, b. *c.*1676, d. Sept. 13, 1729, a Scottish architect, was largely responsible for the introduction and early propagation of the Palladian style (see PALLADIO, ANDREA) that dominated 18th-century English architecture. In 1715 he published the first volume of *Vitruvius Britannicus* (2d vol., 1717; supplement, 1725), a folio of 100 engravings of classical buildings in Britain that concluded with his own designs for Wanstead (1715–20; demolished 1822), Essex. It established Campbell's style as the purest, most classicizing of the time and inspired the building of Palladian country houses.

Campbell, John John Campbell, b. Scotland, 1653, d. Mar. 4, 1727 or 1728, was the founder of the *Boston News-Letter*, the first successful newspaper in Britain's American colonies. As Boston postmaster (1702–18), Campbell had ready access to newsworthy information; he used his position to produce newsletters and a *Weekly Intelligencer* before founding the weekly *News-Letter* on Apr. 24, 1704. Covering foreign news mainly, the paper lasted until 1776, although Campbell himself retired in 1722.

Campbell, Joseph Joseph Campbell, b. New York City, Mar. 26, 1904, d. Oct. 31, 1987, is the author of *The Masks of God* (1959–67), an influential four-volume study of comparative mythology. A professor of literature at Sarah Lawrence College from 1934 to 1972, Campbell was a distinguished scholar known for his Jungian interpretations of folklore, dreams, and the role of myth in the human imagination. His other books include *The Hero with a Thousand Faces* (1949), *Myths to Live By* (1972), *The Inner Reaches of Outer Space* (1986), and *An Open Life* (1988).

Campbell, Mrs. Patrick Mrs. Patrick Campbell, b. Feb. 9, 1865, d. Apr. 19, 1940, a leading English actress, specialized in such serious roles as Juliet, Ophelia, Lady Macbeth, and Hedda Gabler, but originated the comic role of Eliza Doolittle in George Bernard Shaw's *Pygmalion*, (1914).

Campbell, Robert Robert Campbell, b. Feb. 21, 1808, d. May 9, 1894, was a Scottish-born Canadian fur trader employed (1830–71) by the Hudson's Bay Company. While exploring many of the waterways of the Yukon and Northwest territories, he discovered and named the Pelly River and established posts at Francis Lake (1842), Pelly Banks (1846), and Fort Selkirk (1848).

Campbell-Bannerman, Sir Henry Sir Henry Campbell-Bannerman, b. Sept. 7, 1836, d. Apr. 22, 1908, was prime minister of Britain from 1905 to 1908. He twice served as secretary of war (1886, 1892–95) and became leader of the Liberal party in 1899; he was a moderate in the debates that split the party during the South African War (1899–1902). As prime minister, Campbell-Bannerman granted self-government to the defeated Transvaal (1906) and Orange River Colony (1907). Much of his reform legislation was vetoed by the House of Lords, which led to the curtailment of the Lords' powers under his successor, Herbert ASQUITH.

Campeche (city) [kam-pay'-chay] Campeche (1982 est. pop., 151,805) is a port city and the capital of the state of Campeche in southeastern Mexico, lying on the Bay of Campeche on the western coast of the Yucatán Peninsula. The city is active in commercial fishing and serves as a regional transportation and processing center.

Founded by the Spanish in 1540 at a Mayan site, it grew to prominence as one of the three ports in the area permitted to trade with Spain. In 1867, Campeche became the state capital. In 1936 the entire city was declared an architectural monument because of its many colonial buildings.

Campeche (state) Campeche is a state in southeastern Mexico on the Yucatán Peninsula. It covers 50,812 km^2 (19,619 mi^2), and the population is 617,133 (1989 est.). The city of Campeche is the state capital. Forestry is important in the humid, tropical rain forests in the south; in the arid north, stock raising and agriculture are important.

Campeche was part of the Maya civilization, and many of its ruins still remain. In 1517 the Spanish landed in Campeche, one of their first visits to Mexico. Campeche became a state in 1867 after seceding from Yucatán state.

camphor Camphor ($C_{10}H_{16}O$) is a TERPENE compound obtained from the Asian camphor tree, *Cinnamonum camphora*, of the laurel family. Slightly soluble in water and very soluble in organic solvents, camphor forms translucent crystals that melt at 179° C (355° F) and readily sublime. It has the familiar odor of mothballs. Camphor is used in liniment, embalming fluid, and anti-itching medication; as a preservative in cosmetics and pharmaceuticals; and in various industrial processes.

Campin, Robert Robert Campin, b. *c.*1378, d. Apr. 26, 1444, was a Flemish artist usually considered to be the anonymous Master of Flémalle and one of the founders of the 15th-century Netherlandish school of painting. The *Salting Madonna* (*c.*1428; National Gallery, London) and the *Mérode Triptych* (*c.*1426; Metropolitan Museum of Art: The Cloisters, New York) show sculpturesque figures in meticulously detailed bourgeois surroundings. Campin's combination of realism and symbolism marks an important stage in the stylistic evolution leading to the art of Hubert and Jan van EYCK.

Campion, Saint Edmund Saint Edmund Campion, b. Jan. 25, 1540, d. Dec. 1, 1581, was an English Jesuit martyr. He served as a deacon in the Church of England before joining (1571) the Roman Catholic church in France. After studying at Douai, he became a Jesuit and returned to England in disguise in 1580; he was soon arrested, however. Charged with treason, Campion was tortured on the rack and then hanged at Tyburn. He was canonized in 1970. Feast day: Dec. 1.

Campion, Thomas Thomas Campion, b. Feb. 12, 1567, d. Mar. 1, 1620, was an English physician best known as a poet and composer of songs. His more than 100 songs, for which he wrote both text and music, are known for their poetry and simple, yet sensitive, melodies. In addition to four masques, Campion wrote *Observations on the Art of English Poesie* (1602), a treatise on poetry, and *A New Way of Making Fowre Parts in Counterpoint* (1613), a treatise on music theory.

Campobello Island Campobello Island, once the summer home of President Franklin D. Roosevelt, is located in southwestern New Brunswick, Canada. It is linked by a highway bridge to Lubec, Maine, .4 km (1/4 mi) away. The island, 14 km (9 mi) long and 5 km (3 mi) wide, is the site of the Roosevelt Campobello International Park.

Camus, Albert [ka'-mue] Albert Camus, b. Mondovi, Algeria, Nov. 7, 1913, d. Jan. 4, 1960, earned a world-

Albert Camus, a French essayist and playwright, won the 1957 Nobel Prize for literature largely on the basis of philosophical tracts such as The Rebel *(1951). In his writing, he was concerned with the dilemma of individuals who believe that values are relative but who cannot live without moral commitment.*

wide reputation as a novelist and essayist and won the Nobel Prize for literature in 1957. He became the leading moral voice of his generation during the 1950s. At the height of his fame, Camus died in an automobile accident near Sens, France.

Life in Algeria. Although born in extreme poverty, Camus attended the *lycée* and university in Algiers. His university career was cut short by a severe attack of tuberculosis, from which he suffered throughout his life. The themes of poverty and the horror of human mortality figure prominently in his volumes of so-called Algerian essays: *L'Envers et l'endroit* (The Wrong Side and the Right Side, 1937), *Noces* (Nuptials, 1938), and *L'Été* (Summer, 1954). In 1938 he became a journalist with *Alger-Républicain*, an anticolonialist newspaper, writing detailed reports on the condition of poor Arabs in the Kabyles region. These reports were later published in abridged form in *Actuelles III* (1958).

The War Years. Camus went to France during World War II to work for the Combat resistance network and edited the clandestine Parisian daily *Combat.* During the war Camus published the main works associated with his doctrine of ABSURDISM—the view that human life is rendered ultimately meaningless by the fact of death and that the individual cannot make rational sense of his or her experience. These works include the novel The STRANGER (1942; Eng. trans., 1946); a long essay on the absurd, *The Myth of Sisyphus* (1942; Eng. trans., 1955); and two plays published in 1944, *Cross Purpose* (Eng. trans., 1948) and *Caligula* (Eng. trans., 1948). In these works Camus explored NIHILISM with considerable sympathy, but his own attitude toward the "absurd" remained ambivalent. Camus found that neither his own temperament nor his experiences in occupied France allowed him moral neutrality. The growth of his ideas on moral responsibility is partly sketched in the four *Letters to a German Friend* (1945) included in *Resistance, Rebellion, and Death* (1960).

Rebellion. From this point on, Camus explored avenues of rebellion against the absurd as he strove to create a humane stoicism. In the symbolic novel *The Plague* (1947; Eng. trans., 1948), the important achievement of those who fight bubonic plague in Oran lies not in their little success but in their human dignity. In the controversial essay *The Rebel* (1951; Eng. trans., 1954), he criticized what he regarded as the deceptive doctrines of "absolutist" philosophies.

Camus wrote two overtly political plays, the satirical *State of Siege* (1948; Eng. trans., 1958) and *The Just Assassins* (1950; Eng. trans., 1958), as well as stage adaptions of William Faulkner's *Requiem for a Nun* (1956) and Dostoyevsky's *The Possessed* (1959). He also published a third novel, *The Fall* (1956; Eng. trans., 1957) and a collection of short stories *Exile and the Kingdom* (1957; Eng. trans., 1958). Posthumous publications include two sets of *Notebooks* covering 1935–51, an early novel, *A Happy Death* (1971; Eng. trans., 1972), and a collection of essays, *Youthful Writings* (1973; Eng. trans., 1976 and 1977).

Canaanite civilization [kay'-nuhn-yt] Canaanite civilization flourished in what is now Israel, Syria, Lebanon, and Jordan during the Bronze Age (*c.*3000–*c.*1200 BC). The name "Canaanite" comes from the Bible, where it designates the peoples that occupied Syria-Palestine (Canaan) before the coming of the Israelites. The Canaanites spoke a Semitic language that later developed into Hebrew and Phoenician. When the Israelites, Philistines, and Aramaeans invaded the region after 1200 BC, most of the Canaanites were conquered and assimilated; a remnant survived for many centuries in PHOENICIA, along the Mediterranean Sea.

Canaanite culture was shaped by geography and the dominance of its powerful Egyptian and Mesopotamian neighbors. Canaan comprised an arable land bridge between the desert and the sea that served as a route for conquering armies and commercial caravans, bringing in a continual flow of external influences. The mountainous areas separated by deep valleys and the limited sources of water in the semiarid region contributed to the development of small city-states—among them BYBLOS, EBLA, HAZOR, JERICHO, LACHISH, MEGIDDO, and UGARIT—and an economy usually based on herding and subsistence farming.

The Canaanite city-states were ruled by local kings who also dominated the nearby villages and population. Conflicts between neighboring city-states were frequent, and the cities were fortified with strong walls and gates. Inside were residential, commercial, and monumental buildings. The latter normally consisted of a palace-temple complex. Priests officiated in the temples, which were dedicated to one or more gods, including El, the supreme deity; BAAL (Haddad), the storm god; Anat, consort of El; and ASTARTE. Anat and Astarte were fertility goddesses, and the Canaanite religion focused on the forces of nature that controlled the essentials of life. Various deities were revered by common folk in the open country at high plac-

AT A GLANCE

CANADA

Land: Area: 9,970,610 km^2 (3,849,672 mi^2). Capital: Ottawa (1986 pop., 300,763). Largest city: Montreal (1986 pop., 1,015,420).

People: Population (1990 est.): 26,600,000. Density: 2.9 persons per km^2 (7.5 per mi^2). Distribution (1990): 77% urban, 23% rural. Official languages: English, French. Major religions: Roman Catholicism, Protestantism.

Government: Type: federal state. Legislature: Parliament. Political subdivisions: 10 provinces, 2 territories.

Economy: GNP (1988): $471.5 billion; $18,070 per capita. Labor distribution (1988): agriculture—4%; services—75%; manufacturing—14%; construction—3%; other—4%. Foreign trade (1989): imports—$114 billion; exports—$116 billion. Currency: 1 Canadian dollar = 100 cents.

Education and Health: Literacy (1987): 99% of adult population. Universities (1989): 68. Hospital beds (1987, excludes federal and private hospitals): 170,721. Physicians (1987): 51,275. Life expectancy (1989): women—81; men—73. Infant mortality (1989): 7 per 1,000 live births.

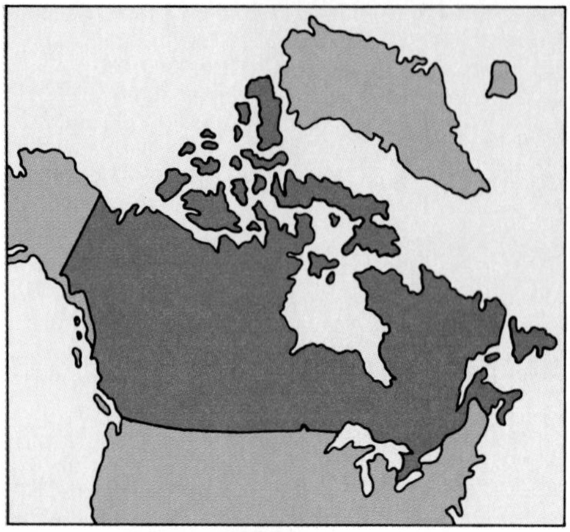

es on hilltops, beneath sacred trees, and at natural springs. (See also Canaanite Mythology under MYTHOLOGY.)

Canaanites were expert builders, using native stone and mudbrick. They developed plaster for waterproofing rock-cut cisterns and coating stone and mud-brick walls. Their artisans produced small statuettes of deities, pottery, engraved gemstones, and carved ivory.

The greatest Canaanite legacy to modern civilization was a simplified system of writing—the alphabet. Developed by 1500 BC, the Canaanite alphabet was transmitted by the Phoenicians to the Greeks, and ultimately became the basis for all modern alphabets. Similarly, because the Canaanite language was adopted by the Israelites, the Hebrew Bible is part of the written and linguistic legacy of Canaan.

Canada Canada, the world's second largest country (after the USSR), is the largest country in the Western Hemisphere and comprises all the North American continent north of the United States, with the exclusion of Alaska, Greenland, and the tiny French islands of St. Pierre and Miquelon. Its most easterly point is Cape Spear, Newfoundland, and its western limit is Mount St. Elias in the Yukon Territory, near the Alaskan border. Its east-west extent is 5,187 km (3,223 mi) and is so wide that seven time zones lie within its borders. The southernmost point is Middle Island, in Lake Erie; the northern tip of land is Cape Columbia, on ELLESMERE ISLAND, 1,850 km (1,150 mi) north of the Arctic Circle.

Canada is bounded on the north by the Arctic Ocean, on the west by the Pacific Ocean, and on the east by the Atlantic Ocean and its associated bodies of water, including Baffin Bay and the Labrador Sea. Its only international land boundary is with the United States—on the northwest, between Canada and the state of Alaska, and on the south, where the U.S.–Canada border is 6,416 km (3,987 mi) long.

Canada has a population of about 26 million, or approximately one-tenth that of the United States. About 80% of this number live within 160 km (100 mi) of the U.S. border on the south; approximately 89% of the country is virtually unsettled.

Canada is rich in natural resources. It is a world leader in value of mineral exports and produces and exports many of the minerals needed for modern industrial economies. Its soils, which are especially rich in the three prairie provinces of Alberta, Saskatchewan, and Manitoba, are intensively utilized and make Canada one of the world's largest exporters of agricultural products. Forests cover much of the land, and Canada is the world's largest exporter of newsprint and a leading supplier of lumber, pulp, paper, and wood products.

Canada has a dual cultural heritage that stems from the British conquest (1763) of the French colony of New France. Today both French and English are official languages. The threat of separatism by the largely French-speaking province of Quebec was an issue through the 1980s, although a 1980 referendum mandating the sovereignty of Quebec was defeated by Quebec's electorate. The 1987 Meech Lake accord, an addition to the 1982 constitution (see CONSTITUTION ACT) that acknowledged Quebec's distinctness, failed in 1990 when two provinces refused to finalize it.

The name *Canada* is thought to be derived from *Kanata*, the Huron-Iroquois word meaning "village" or "community."

Land and Resources

Physical Regions. Canada has six major physical, or physiographic, regions: the CANADIAN SHIELD, the Arctic Islands, the Great Lakes–St. Lawrence Lowlands, the Appalachian Region, the Interior Plains, and the Cordilleran Region.

Canadian Shield. In simple terms, Canada can be considered a vast, saucer-shaped basin, bordered by mountainous lands on the west, east, and northeast. HUDSON BAY and the lowlands along its southern shore form the central depression of this "saucer." Surrounding this depression, including BAFFIN ISLAND, is the Canadian Shield (also known as the Laurentian Plateau or Laurentian Upland), a region of ancient, mostly Precambrian rocks that covers nearly half of Canada. The Canadian Shield includes all of Labrador and large areas of Quebec, Ontario, Manitoba, and the Northwest Territories. As a result of glacial action during the Pleistocene Ice Age, much of the region is covered with lakes and marshy areas.

Arctic Islands. The Arctic Islands lie to the northwest of the central depression and constitute about 8.3% of Canada's land area. They are mostly covered by permanent snow and ice fields. The northern sections of the region include the United States Range, which reaches 2,926 m (9,600 ft) in northern Ellesmere Island. The southern sections are lower in altitude and are sometimes referred to collectively as the Arctic Lowlands and Plateaus.

Great Lakes–St. Lawrence Lowlands. The Great Lakes–St. Lawrence Lowlands region constitutes only 1.3% of Canada but is the area where most people live. It is a flat to gently rolling region that extends southwest from Quebec City to Lake Huron and includes all of the St. Lawrence River valley and the Ontario Peninsula, a triangular, densely populated area of southern Ontario that is bordered by the shores of Lakes Huron, Erie, and Ontario.

Appalachian Region. The Appalachian Region occupies approximately 3.4% of Canada and is the northward continuation into Canada of the Appalachian Mountain system of the eastern United States. It includes all of New Brunswick, Nova Scotia, Prince Edward Island, and the island of Newfoundland and forms most of Quebec's GASPÉ PENINSULA. It is a region of geologically old, worn-down uplands, with summits ranging from 150 m (500 ft) to more than 1,270 m (4,160 ft). The highest and most rugged mountains are in the Shickshock Mountains of the Gaspé Peninsula, where Mount Jacques Cartier rises to 1,270 m (4,160 ft).

Interior Plains. The Interior Plains lie between the Canadian Shield and the Rocky Mountains and are a continuation of the Great Plains of the United States. The region occupies 18.3% of Canada; it extends to the Arctic coast and includes northeastern BRITISH COLUMBIA and

Toronto, a major port on the northern shore of Lake Ontario, is the capital of Ontario. Known for its hotels, shops, and new plazas, the city is a lively cultural center.

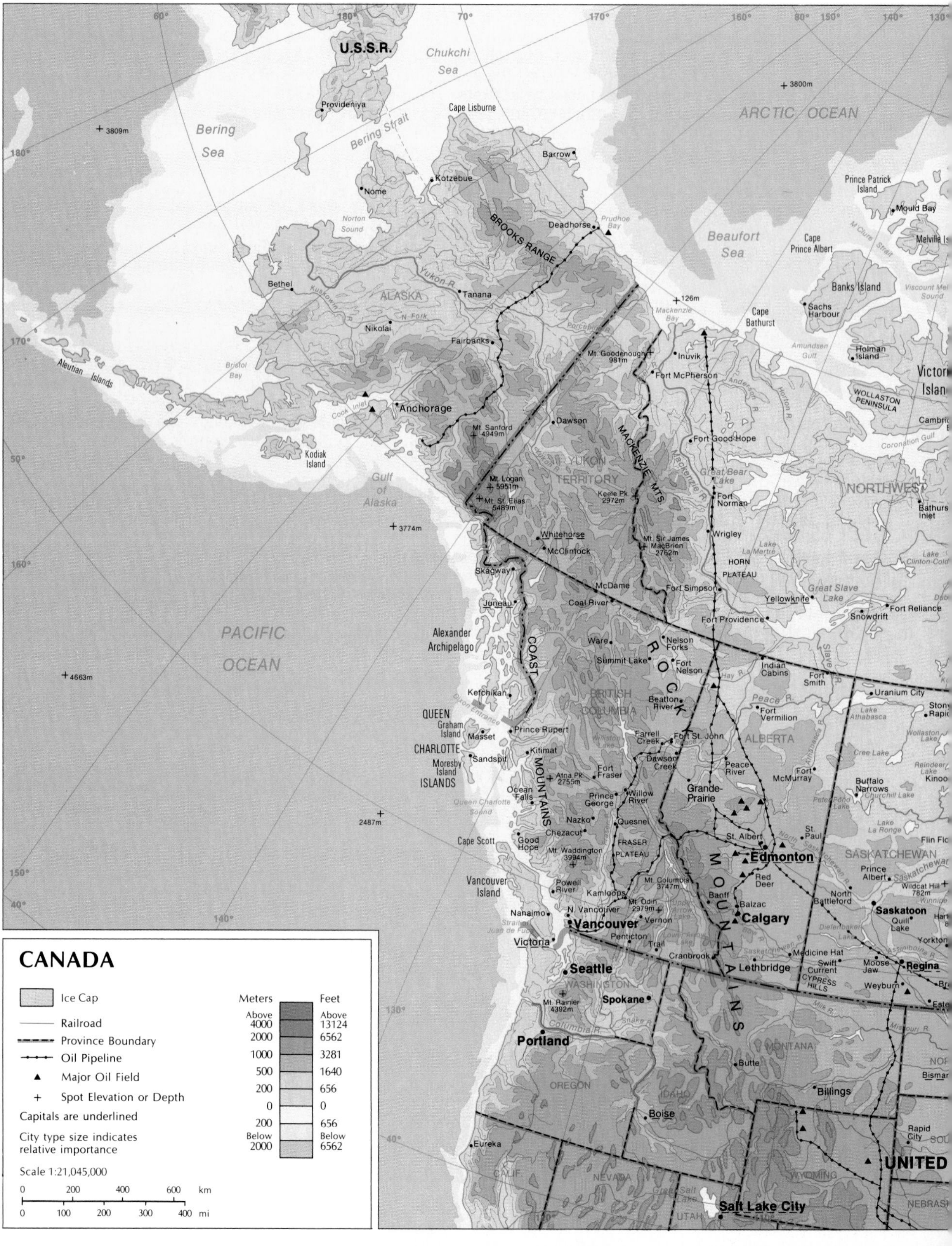
U.S.S.R.
Chukchi Sea
Provideniya
Cape Lisburne
Bering Sea
Bering Strait
ARCTIC OCEAN
Barrow
Kotzebue
Nome
Norton Sound
BROOKS RANGE
Deadhorse
Prudhoe Bay
Beaufort Sea
Prince Patrick Island
Mould Bay
Cape Prince Albert
Banks Island
Sachs Harbour
Cape Bathurst
Mackenzie Bay
Bethel
ALASKA
Yukon R.
Tanana
Nikolai
Fairbanks
Mt. Goodenough 981m
Inuvik
Fort McPherson
Holman Island
WOLLASTON PENINSULA
Aleutian Islands
Bristol Bay
Cook Inlet
Anchorage
Mt. Sanford 4949m
Dawson
MACKENZIE MTS
Fort Good Hope
Kodiak Island
Gulf of Alaska
YUKON TERRITORY
Mt. Logan 5951m
Mt. St. Elias 5489m
Keele Pk 2972m
Great Bear Lake
Fort Norman
NORTHWEST
Whitehorse
McClintock
Mt. Sir James MacBrien 2762m
Wrigley
HORN PLATEAU
Skagway
McDame
Fort Simpson
Yellowknife
Great Slave Lake
Fort Reliance
Snowdrift
Juneau
Coal River
Fort Providence
PACIFIC OCEAN
Alexander Archipelago
COAST
Ware
ROCK
Nelson Forks
Summit Lake
Fort Nelson
Indian Cabins
Fort Smith
Uranium City
Ketchikan
BRITISH COLUMBIA
Beatton River
Fort Vermilion
Lake Athabasca
QUEEN Graham Island
CHARLOTTE
Moresby Island
ISLANDS
Masset
Sandspit
Prince Rupert
Farrell Creek
Fort St. John
ALBERTA
Kitimat
MOUNTAINS
Dawson Creek
Peace River
Fort McMurray
Fort Fraser
Atna Pk 2755m
Buffalo Narrows
Ocean Falls
Prince George
Willow River
Grande-Prairie
Queen Charlotte Sound
Nazko
Quesnel
Chezacut
Cape Scott
Good Hope
FRASER PLATEAU
Mt. Waddington 3994m
St. Albert
Edmonton
St. Paul
SASKATCHEWAN
Vancouver Island
Powell River
Kamloops
Mt. Columbia 3747m
Red Deer
Prince Albert
Banff
North Battleford
Saskatoon
Nanaimo
N. Vancouver
Mt. Odin 2979m
Vernon
Balzac
Calgary
Vancouver
Victoria
Penticton
Trail
Cranbrook
Medicine Hat
Swift Current
Moose Jaw
Regina
Seattle
Lethbridge
CYPRESS HILLS
Weyburn
WASHINGTON
Spokane
Mt. Rainier 4392m
Portland
MONTANA
Butte
OREGON
IDAHO
Billings
Boise
Eureka
Rapid City
UNITED
NEVADA
WYOMING
Salt Lake City
UTAH
CALIF.
CANADA
Ice Cap
Railroad
Province Boundary
Oil Pipeline
Major Oil Field
Spot Elevation or Depth
Capitals are underlined
City type size indicates relative importance
Scale 1:21,045,000
0 200 400 600 km
0 100 200 300 400 mi
Meters
Feet
Above 4000 / Above 13124
2000 / 6562
1000 / 3281
500 / 1640
200 / 656
0 / 0
200 / 656
Below 2000 / Below 6562

GREENLAND
(Den.)
ICE
CAP
ICELAND
Reykjavik
Húsavik
Blá Mtn. 1204m
Denmark Strait
Cape Tobin
Angmagssaliq
Godhavn
Disko Bay
Godthåb
Julianehåb
Cape Farvel
Thule
Melville Bay
Baffin Bay
Davis Strait
Labrador Sea
ATLANTIC
OCEAN
Alert
Fort Conger
Cape Stallworthy
Eureka
Axel Heiberg Island
Ellesmere Island
Grise Fiord
Jones Sound
Devon Island
Resolute
Lancaster Sound
Somerset Island
Prince of Wales Island
BRODEUR PENINSULA
Arctic Bay
Mt. Thule 2133m
Clyde
Baffin Island
Home Bay
Gulf of Boothia
BOOTHIA PENINSULA
Maneetkalig Mtn 610m
Gjoa Haven
Prince Charles Island
MELVILLE PENINSULA
Pangnirtung
Cumberland Sound
Foxe Basin
TERRITORIES
Arctic Circle
Fort Hope
Wager Bay
Amadjuak Lake
Iqaluit
Frobisher Bay
Lake Harbour
Cape Dorset
Resolution Island
Southampton Island
Baker Lake
Hudson Strait
Chesterfield Inlet
Coats Island
Mansel Island
Ivujivik
Killiniq Island
Kangirsuk
Ungava Bay
UNGAVA PENINSULA
TORNGAT MTS.
Hebron
Povungnituk
Arviat
Ottawa Islands
Hudson Bay
Kuujjuak
Nain
Inukjuak
NEWFOUNDLAND
Rigolet
Cartwright
Michikamau Lake
LABRADOR
Schefferville
Happy Valley-Goose Bay
Cape Bauld
St. Anthony
Churchill
Lamprey
Cape Tatnam
York Factory
Belcher Islands
Lake Eau-Claire
Lake Bienville
Churchill Falls
Labrador City
Strait of Belle Isle
White Bay
Port Saunders
Fort Severn
Nitchequon
Springdale
St. John's
Newfoundland
Shamattawa
Thompson
Winisk
Lake River
James Bay
Kanaaupscow
La Grande R.
Otish Mtn. 1128m
Havre-St.-Pierre
Natashquan
Anticosti Island
Corner Brook
St. Brides
Cape Race
MANITOBA
Island Lake
Trout Lake
Chisasibi
Akimiski Island
Eastmain
QUEBEC
Sheldrake
Sept-Îles
Fox Bay
Gulf of St. Lawrence
Lourdes
St. Davids
Cape Ray
Lake Winnipeg
Bearskin Lake
ONTARIO
Fort Albany
Waskaganish
Lake Mistassini
Mistassini
Baie Comeau
Matane
Gaspé
GASPÉ PENINSULA
Berens River
Moosonee
Ogoki
PRINCE EDWARD ISLAND
Charlottetown
Glace Bay
Sydney
Bathurst
Anama Bay
Cat Lake
Chapais
Chicoutimi
Jonquière
La Baie
Rivière-du-Loup
LAURENTIAN MTS.
Chatham
NEW BRUNSWICK
Fredericton
NOVA SCOTIA
Sable Island (N.S.)
Oak Point
Root Portage
Ear Falls
Dryden
Lake Nipigon
Kapuskasing
Cochrane
Rouyn-Noranda
Parent
La Tuque
Quebec
Saint John
Dartmouth
Halifax
Portage la Prairie
Winnipeg
St. James
Assiniboia
Sprague
Lake of the Woods
Fort Frances
Nipigon
Marathon
Thunder Bay
International Falls
Timmins
Kirkland Lake
Val d'Or
Trois-Rivières
MAINE
Bangor
Bay of Fundy
Yarmouth
Cape Sable
Isle Royale
Wawa
Lake Superior
Sudbury
Montreal
Hull
Ottawa
Cornwall
Sault Ste. Marie
North Bay
Hancock
Duluth
Portland
MINNESOTA
Manitoulin Island
Georgian Bay
Owen Sound
Barrie
Trenton
Kingston
Lake Huron
VT.
N.H.
Boston
Minneapolis
WISCONSIN
Green Bay
Lake Michigan
MICHIGAN
Toronto
Hamilton
Lake Ontario
Niagara Falls
NEW YORK
MASS.
CONN.
R.I.
Bay City
London
Buffalo
STATES
Milwaukee
Detroit
Windsor
New York
Sioux City
IOWA
ILLINOIS
Chicago
IND.
OHIO
Cleveland
PENNSYLVANIA
N.J.
Philadelphia
Mississippi R.
Missouri R.
2136m
2750m
3809m
590m
181m
225m
365m
265m
614m
5767m
© 1980 Rand McNally & Co.
A-520200-772

Percé Rock juts from Quebec's Gaspé Peninsula into the Gulf of St. Lawrence. Much of the Gaspé is forested, with the peninsula's main highway following the scenic coast.

Lake Louise mirrors the glaciated peaks of Banff National Park, in southwestern Alberta. Set aside in 1885 as Canada's first national park, the park now covers 6,640 km² (2,564 mi²).

parts of the prairie provinces of Alberta, Saskatchewan, and Manitoba. The southern sections are principal grain-growing areas. The northern sections are generally too cold for commercial agriculture.

Cordilleran Region. The Cordilleran Region occupies 15.9% of all Canada and includes most of British Columbia and the Yukon Territory and the southwestern corner of Alberta. It is a complex mountain system, approximately 800 km (500 mi) wide, that extends along the Pacific coast. The three main subsections of the region are the eastern ranges, the western ranges, and an intermontane area between the two.

The eastern ranges include the ROCKY MOUNTAINS in the south and the Mackenzie and Richardson mountains in the north. They include such scenic areas as Banff and Jasper national parks and rise to 3,954 m (12,972 ft) in Mount Robson; at least 20 other peaks are higher than 3,000 m (10,000 ft). The western ranges of the region include the St. Elias Mountains, which reach 6,050 m (19,850 ft) in Mount LOGAN, the highest point in Canada; the scenic Coast Mountains, along the mainland shores, which rise abruptly from the sea to heights of more than 3,000 m; and a partially submerged range that appears offshore VANCOUVER ISLAND and the QUEEN CHARLOTTE ISLANDS separated from the mainland by a structural depression known as the Coastal Trough. The intermontane section of the Cordilleran Region, located between the eastern and western ranges, is a series of wide, rolling tablelands, such as the Fraser and Kamloops plateaus, and short mountain ranges, such as the Cascade, Cariboo, Selkirk, Monashee, Purcell, Stikine, Skeena, and Hazelton mountains.

Soils. Tundra and subarctic soils cover 31% of Canada, mostly in the north, with ice and stone deserts found over large areas. The subsoil in much of this area is permanently frozen, and the soils are unsuitable for agriculture.

Podzol soils, which are soils of low natural fertility found in forested regions, cover 26% of Canada. They are most extensive in the Appalachian Region and in most of the Canadian Shield north of a line through Quebec and Sudbury. Brown and gray brown soils, which are naturally fertile, cover most of the Great Lakes–St. Lawrence Lowlands and the southern fringes of the Canadian Shield in Quebec and Ontario.

Of the western soils, the three chernozemic, or black earth, soils are the most important. Although they cover only about 7% of Canada, mainly in the southern part of the interior plains, they account for nearly all of Canada's wheat production. The true chernozem, or black earth, is extremely productive and is found in an arc passing through Winnipeg, Edmonton, and Calgary; grain crops and mixed farming are the principal activities on these rich soils. To the south, forming a more southerly arc passing through Regina, Saskatoon, and Lethbridge, are the dark-brown soils, most of which are used for wheat production. Brown soils, on which agriculture is risky, predominate in the southern, semiarid parts of the interior plains.

The soils of the Cordilleran Region follow altitudinal and climatic zones and, where topography and climate are suitable, support a variety of agricultural activity, especially along the coast and in the valleys of British Columbia.

Climate. The populated southern areas of Canada have a wide variety of temperate climates. The Pacific coastal areas have a temperate marine west-coast type of climate, with cool summers in the 16°–18° C (60°–65° F) range and mild winters in the 0°–4° C (32°–39° F) range. The interior plains have a middle-latitude steppe-type climate in the drier southern sections and a more humid and extreme continental type of climate elsewhere. Temperatures average about -20° to -15° C (-5° to +5° F) in long winters and 18°–20° C (65°–68° F) in short summers.

The Great Lakes–St. Lawrence Lowlands and the Appalachian Region have a more humid version of a continental type of climate. Both areas have a long, cold winter, with January averages about -10° C (14° F) in the eastern sections and -4° C (25° F) in the Ontario Peninsula, and short, warm summers with average temperatures of near 20° C (68° F).

Precipitation is heaviest in the west, where moisture-laden winds from the Pacific Ocean are forced to rise over the mountainous coastal regions and bring more than 5,000 mm (195 in) of rain a year to some areas, although average annual precipitation is 1,525 to 2,540 mm (60 to 100 in). Precipitation is least in the Interior Plains, where many areas receive fewer than 500 mm (20 in) a year. Except for the low-lying Pacific-coast areas, winter precipitation throughout Canada is usually in the form of snow, and thick blankets of accumulated snow cover most of Canada east of the Rockies for 3 to 6 months of the year.

The sparsely settled northern areas have an arctic, or tundra, type of climate on the islands and northern coastal areas and a subarctic type of climate in the vast transitional area between the frozen north and the settled south. The arctic type of climate is characterized by long, very cold winters, with average temperatures far below freezing and no summer month with an average temperature higher than 10° C (50° F). In the subarctic areas, winters are similarly long and bitterly cold, but summers are warm enough (more than 10° C/50° F) to support vegetation. Precipitation is generally light in the western areas of the arctic and subarctic regions and heavier in northern Quebec and Labrador. Despite the low precipitation, snow covers the ground permanently for more than 6 months of every year.

Drainage. Fresh water covers an estimated 756,276 km^2 (292,000 mi^2), or 7.6% of Canada. The many rivers and lakes supply ample fresh water to meet the nation's needs for its communities and for irrigation, agriculture, industries, transportation, and hydroelectric-power generation. Large quantities of groundwater supply about 10% of municipal needs.

Canada has four principal drainage basins. By far the most important economically is the Atlantic Basin, which is the third largest of the four with a total area of 1,756,012 km^2 (678,000 mi^2) and drains to the Atlantic Ocean by way of the GREAT LAKES, the ST. LAWRENCE RIVER, and their tributaries. This great drainage system forms a waterway that reaches inland into the heart of the continent for 3,670 km (2,280 mi).

Larger but less important because of the sparsely populated area it includes is the Hudson Bay Basin, with a total area of 4,010,000 km^2 (1,548,000 mi^2). The Hudson Bay Basin drains northward into Hudson Bay via the CHURCHILL, NELSON, and SASKATCHEWAN rivers and their tributaries.

The Arctic Basin, covering an area of 1,812,992 km^2 (700,000 mi^2), is drained by the 4,241-km-long (2,635-mi) MACKENZIE RIVER, Canada's longest river, and its principal tributary, the PEACE RIVER.

The Pacific Basin covers an area of 1,095,000 km^2

Canada is one of the world's leading wheat producers and is second only to the United States in wheat exports. Canadian agriculture is highly mechanized; fewer than 5% of Canadians earn their living by farming.

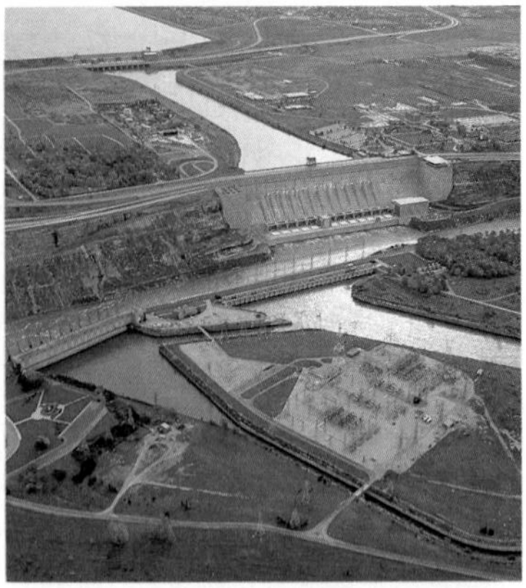

(Above) *Waterpower is Canada's chief source of electricity, supplying approximately 60% of the country's total output. Hydroelectric plants have been built on numerous rivers in Quebec, Ontario, and British Columbia.* (Left) *An aerial photograph of Hudson Bay shows an icy wilderness navigable only from July to October. Located in east central Canada, the bay is surrounded by sparsely populated tundra regions.*

(422,000 mi^2) and carries the waters of the FRASER RIVER and the headwaters of the COLUMBIA and YUKON rivers to the Pacific Ocean. In addition to these four major drainage basins, a few minor areas of inland drainage have no outlet to the sea; and a small area of the southern prairies, totaling 29,500 km^2 (11,400 mi^2), drains into the headwaters of the Mississippi River system and thus is part of the great Gulf of Mexico Basin that lies mostly in the United States.

Canada's largest lakes are the four Great Lakes—Superior, Huron, Erie, and Ontario—that lie partly on the Canadian side of the U.S.–Canada boundary. Other large lakes are GREAT BEAR LAKE, GREAT SLAVE LAKE, and Lake WINNIPEG.

Vegetation and Animal Life. Canada has three major natural vegetation zones: forests, grasslands, and tundras. The natural forests occupy the largest area and are classified into three main types. The eastern forests native to the Great Lakes–St. Lawrence Lowlands and the Appalachian Region comprise both deciduous trees such as sugar maple and beech and coniferous trees such as yellow pine, white and red pine, and hemlock. The fauna include white-tailed deer, squirrels, mink, and skunks.

The boreal, or northern, coniferous forest, sometimes also referred to as the taiga, stretches across the continent from Newfoundland to the Alaska border and accounts for 82% of all Canadian forestland. It includes white and black spruces and white birches, extensive areas of balsam poplar and tamarack, and balsam fir, jack pine, and trembling aspen in local concentrations. This northern forest supports nearly all the fauna recognized as distinctly Canadian, including the moose, beaver, Canada lynx, black bear, and Canada jay.

The third great forest zone is found along the humid Pacific coast; it is a dense, tall-timber forest, where Douglas fir, western hemlock, and western red cedar are the dominant trees.

Natural grasslands, or prairies, once extended across the southern part of the interior plains. These natural grasslands have been largely plowed under and replaced by field crops. Animals characteristic of the interior plains include gophers, badgers, jackrabbits, and elk.

Tundra vegetation covers the northern quarter of the country, where low temperatures and permanently frozen subsoil inhibit the growth of most plants except the hardy mosses and lichens. Various grasses and flowers are also found. Trees are absent, but dwarf shrubs survive in sheltered locations. Distinctive animals of the tundra include the polar bear, seal, musk-ox, caribou, lemming, Arctic wolf, and white fox.

Natural Resources. Canada has an abundance of mineral, forest, and water-power resources. The principal minerals are petroleum, nickel, copper, zinc, iron ore, natural gas, asbestos, molybdenum, sulfur, gold, and platinum.

Forests cover about 48% of Canada and are the basis for the important lumbering, pulp and paper, and wood-products industries. More than half of the forestland is capable of producing a regular harvest of commercial timber, and one-third is currently accessible.

Water is a major natural resource and hydroelectric power a leading source of energy. Major hydroelectric installations are located on the Niagara, St. Lawrence, Ottawa, St. Maurice, Saguenay, Bersimis, Manicouagan, Churchill, Peace, and Columbia rivers, and great potential exists for further development on the northern rivers.

The principal monuments of Ottawa, the capital of Canada since 1857, include the new National Gallery (1988; center right*) and the Parliament buildings* (upper right). *The city, situated on the Ottawa River in southeastern Ontario, was founded by the British in 1827.*

People

The great majority of Canadians were born in Canada, and most are of European descent. The ethnic composition of the population today is the result of successive waves of immigration by various European national groups in the past.

Composition of the Population. The French, the first to settle in large numbers, established numerous communities along the St. Lawrence River during the 17th and early 18th centuries, and they have retained their language and culture. French Canadians account for about 27% of the total population and are concentrated in the province of Quebec, where they are about 80% of the population, and in New Brunswick, where they constitute about a third of the population.

People of British origin settled mainly after the British conquest of the French territory in 1763. Also, after 1783 many Loyalists moved north from the newly independent United States. The British settled primarily in the Atlantic provinces and in Ontario and later in British Columbia. They remain a major element in the population of these regions today, although the proportion of the British ethnic group in Canada as a whole has declined steadily from 57% in 1901 to about 40% in 1986.

Continental European groups (other than French), however, have risen steadily in importance from 8.5% of the total population in 1901 to more than 20% in 1981. The principal continental European groups are Germans, Italians, Ukrainians, Scandinavians, Dutch, and Poles. The ethnic composition continued to change in the 1970s and '80s with the arrival in the large cities of many immigrants from Asia and the West Indies. Indigenous Indians and Eskimo (Inuit) account for a small percentage of the total population, but they account for the majority of the population in the Northwest Territories and are a significant population in the Yukon.

Language. Canada has two official languages, English and French, which have equal status in affairs of the federal and provincial governments and federal courts. Of the total population, more than 60% speak English and significant minorities speak French or are bilingual. About 1% speak neither language. The majority of new immigrants prefer to learn English rather than French.

Religion. The largest religious denomination in Canada is the Roman Catholic church, with about 46% of the population adhering to that faith. Second is the United Church of Canada, followed by the Anglican Church (see CANADA, ANGLICAN CHURCH OF; CANADA, UNITED CHURCH OF). In addition, the Presbyterian, Lutheran, and Baptist denominations have substantial memberships. Jews make up about 1% of the population.

Demography. Most of Canada's people live in the southern part of the country, in an elongated, discontinuous belt of settlement parallel to the U.S.–Canada border. The most populous provinces are Ontario, with 36% of the population in 1986; Quebec, with 26%; and British Columbia, with 11%.

About three-quarters of Canada's population are classified as urban. Ontario is the most urbanized of the provinces, with about 80% of its population living in urban areas. Prince Edward Island is the least urbanized, with less than 40% of the population in urban areas.

Canada's largest metropolitan areas (1986 census) are TORONTO (3,427,168) and MONTREAL (2,921,357). VANCOUVER ranks third (1,380,729), followed by metropolitan OTTAWA (including Hull), EDMONTON, CALGARY, WINNIPEG, QUEBEC, and HAMILTON, each with more than 500,000 residents. Farm dwellers accounted for only 4.3% of the nation's total population in the 1981 census.

Since the first census was taken, Canada's population has increased more than tenfold, from 2.44 million in 1851 to 25.35 million in 1986. Despite continuing immigration in every decade since 1851, the dominant components of this growth have been natural increase and a falling death rate. The peak growth decades were 1851–61, 1900–11, and 1951–61, when the annual growth rate was close to 3%. The growth rate for the period 1981–86 was less than 1% per year. Alberta grew by 6.1% between 1981 and 1986, the highest rate among the provinces.

Canada is one of the world's most sparsely populated nations, with an average population density of 2.75 persons per km^2 (7.13 per mi^2). This overall figure is misleading, however, and obscures the fact that nine-tenths of the country is virtually uninhabited and the population is concentrated in the other one-tenth. The most densely populated province is Prince Edward Island, with 22 persons per km^2 (58 per mi^2).

Education and Health. Each of the provinces and territories administers its own educational system. Schools are operated by local education authorities and generally offer 6 to 8 years of elementary and 3 to 5 years of secondary schooling. Schools for Roman Catholic students, known as separate schools, are publicly maintained by the provinces of Ontario, Saskatchewan, and Alberta. Dual public-school boards for both Protestants and Roman Catholics are maintained by the provinces of Quebec and Newfoundland.

The Charter of Rights and Freedoms (1982) guarantees the rights of Anglophone and Francophone parents to have their children educated in either of the two official languages, although each province may apply this policy as it sees fit. Ontario provides French-language schools for Francophone children in areas where they are a substantial minority. The most controversial issue today is the place of the French language in contemporary Quebec education. In 1977 the separatist Parti Québécois government passed legislation requiring the children of French origin and those of immigrants to obtain their elementary and secondary education in French-language schools. This policy has caused great resentment in Anglophone and immigrant communities and conflicts with the federal government's declared intention of providing bilingual services throughout Canada, while simultaneously promoting the concept of Canada as a multicultural nation.

Canada has community colleges and related institutions that offer technical and vocational training, and a number of universities and four-year colleges. Among the largest universities are the University of Toronto (Toronto), University of British Columbia (Vancouver), University of Alberta (Edmonton), McGill University (Montreal), and the University of Manitoba (Winnipeg), in all of which the language of instruction is English. Prominent French-language universities are the Université de Montréal, Laval Université, and the Université du Québec.

Health services are the concern of the provincial governments, conforming to certain national standards. All

(Left) *Vancouver, the third largest city in Canada, is situated on a peninsula in the southwestern corner of British Columbia. Vancouver has emerged as one of the busiest Pacific ports in North America.* (Right) *Notre Dame de Bonsecours, Montreal's oldest standing church, is part of Old Montreal, or "le Quartier." A possession of France during the 17th and 18th centuries, Montreal is today the world's second largest French-speaking city.*

Canada's agricultural production is evident in this aerial photograph, showing crops under cultivation in a relatively confined area. Canada has achieved a favorable balance of trade largely by becoming the world's fourth largest exporter of agricultural products.

participate in the national insurance program, which supplies comprehensive coverage of all required services rendered by a physician or surgeon. Hospital insurance programs operated by the provinces cover 99% of the population. The Canadian Health Act of 1984 consolidated original federal health-insurance laws and clarified the national standards that the provinces must uphold in order to be eligible for federal health contributions. In 1985 the leading cause of death in Canada was heart disease, followed by cancer, respiratory disease, cerebrovascular disease, and accidents.

The Arts. Of the visual arts, painting has been the most successful in expressing a Canadian national identity. Famous 19th-century painters include Paul KANE and Cornelius Krieghoff. The GROUP OF SEVEN developed a distinctly Canadian style in the 1920s. Other noted 20th-century painters include Emily Carr, Alfred Pellan, and Paul-Émile Borduas.

Noted Canadian sculptors include Frances Loring and Emanuel Hahn. Canada is also famous for its indigenous Eskimo sculpture. (See CANADIAN ART AND ARCHITECTURE.)

Reflecting the dual cultural heritage, Canada has developed a strong literary tradition in both French and English. Among the noted French-Canadian poets are Octave CRÉMAZIE, Louis Honoré FRÉCHETTE, and Émile Nelligan. Bliss Carman is the most famous of the English-Canadian poets, and others include E. J. Pratt, Sir Charles G. D. Roberts, Duncan Campbell SCOTT, Robert W. SERVICE, and John McCrae. Famous novelists and short-story writers include Louis Hémon, Gabrielle ROY, and Roger Lemelin for the French Canadians and Morley CALLAGHAN, Frederick Philip Grove, T. C. HALIBURTON, Stephen Leacock, Hugh MACLENNAN, Mordecai RICHLER, and Mazo de la Roche, in English. (See CANADIAN LITERATURE.)

Music is the most widespread of the performing arts in Canada. Four leading orchestras of Canada are the Montreal Symphony, Toronto Symphony, Vancouver Symphony, and the National Arts Centre Orchestra, in Ottawa. Other large orchestras include the Calgary Philharmonic, Winnipeg Symphony, Edmonton Symphony, Hamilton Philharmonic, and Quebec Symphony. Professional opera companies include the Canadian Opera Company (Toronto), the Montreal Opera, the Vancouver Opera Association, and the Edmonton Opera Association; opera is also featured at both the Stratford and Vancouver summer festivals. The three professional ballet companies of Canada are the internationally famous Royal Winnipeg Ballet, the National Ballet of Canada (formerly the National Ballet Company of Toronto), and the Grands Ballets Canadiens, in Montreal.

Professional theater flourishes in both English- and French-speaking communities. The Stratford Shakespearean Festival is held every summer at Stratford, Ontario. Other influential theaters are the National Arts Centre, in Ottawa; Theatre Toronto (formerly Toronto's Crest Theatre); the Shaw Festival Theatre, in Niagara-on-the-Lake, Ontario; and the French-language Théâtre du Nouveau Monde, in Montreal.

Canada's most important cultural institution is the Canada Council, which supports study and innovations in the arts, humanities, and social sciences. Other coveted awards are the Governor-General's Literary Award for excellence in Canadian writing and the Molson Prizes awarded by the Canada Council for special contributions to the arts, social sciences, humanities, or national unity. The National Museum (Ottawa), Royal Ontario Museum (Toronto), National Gallery of Canada (Ottawa), and the National Library (Ottawa) are other major cultural institutions.

Economic Activity

During the last 75 years, the Canadian economy has been transformed from one based primarily on agricultural production and the export of agricultural products and raw materials to one based primarily on manufacturing and the processing of raw materials. The economy remains, however, still largely resource-oriented rather than market-oriented because of the small size of the Canadian market and traditional ties with the United States and the United Kingdom.

Manufacturing and Mining. Manufacturing employs 19% of Canada's total labor force and accounts for slightly more of the gross domestic product. The 10 leading industries, by value of shipments of goods of own manufacture, are motor vehicles, pulp and paper, slaughtering and meat processing, oil refining, sawmill and planing-mill products, iron and steel, motor-vehicle parts and accessories, dairy products, miscellaneous machinery and equipment, and smelting and refining. Two-thirds of all manufacturing plants are located in the provinces of Ontario and Quebec.

Manufacturing in Ontario is diversified, with an emphasis on the manufacture of automobiles and automobile parts and accessories at Brampton, Hamilton, Oakville, Oshawa, Talbotville, and Windsor and in lesser concentrations elsewhere. Other major manufacturing activities include nickel smelting in the SUDBURY area, pulp and paper production along the St. Lawrence and Ottawa rivers, machinery production concentrated in the Toronto area, and oil refining and the manufacture of chemicals at Sarnia. The manufacturing activities of Quebec include the resource-oriented industries of pulp and paper and newsprint manufacture; power-oriented industries, such as the aluminum refineries at Arvida and Baie-Comeau; market-oriented industries, such as the huge oil refining and petrochemical complex at Montreal East; and such labor-intensive industries as the clothing and textile industries concentrated in Montreal and the Eastern Townships, an area east of Montreal and south of the St. Lawrence River.

Fishing is one of Canada's primary industries. Lobsters, scallops, and oysters are specialties of Prince Edward Island, where the size of the catch is indicated by the large piles of traps that appear along the wharf.

Of the minerals produced in Canada, the mineral fuels, which include mostly oil, some natural gas, and lesser amounts of coal, account for 56% by value. Oil and natural gas are produced mainly in Alberta and, to a lesser extent, in Saskatchewan. Metals account for 31% of production by value. The leading metals are nickel (of which Canada is the world's major producer), copper, and iron ore (produced mainly in Labrador and Quebec). The principal nonmetals, which account for 13% of production by value, include limestone and asbestos. Canada ranks third (behind the United States and the USSR) in total mineral output and leads the world in mineral exports (82% of its production).

Agriculture. Although restricted by climate and topography to the southern third of the country, agriculture remains an important segment of Canada's economy. Because the large production exceeds the needs of the small population, much agricultural produce is exported. Half of all farm income is derived from field crops and half from livestock. The principal field crops are wheat (of which Canada is the world's second largest exporter, after the United States), barley, and oats. Most of the grain crops are grown in the three prairie provinces. Other important western crops are rye, flaxseed, and rapeseed. In other parts of Canada, mixed farming predominates, with the output of field crops tied to the dairy and livestock economy and more land devoted to hay, pasture, and feed grains. Prince Edward Island and New Brunswick grow large quantities of potatoes, and soybeans are produced mainly in southwestern Ontario.

About 75% of the farms in Canada raise livestock. Generally, beef cattle are raised in Alberta and the Cordilleran Region, and dairy cattle in the Great Lakes–St. Lawrence Lowlands. Hogs, the fourth largest agricultural product by value (after wheat, cattle, and dairy products), are raised in southern Ontario, Quebec, and Alberta.

Since the 1920s the number of farms and farm workers has declined as farms have become more commercialized, more mechanized, and larger. The acreage devoted to farmland has also declined.

Forestry and Fishing. Canada is a major world producer and exporter of lumber, wood products, wood pulp, paper, and newsprint. British Columbia, Ontario, and Quebec are the leading timber-producing provinces. British Columbia leads in production of lumber and soft plywood; and Ontario and Quebec produce most of the groundwood pulp and hardwood plywood. About 90% of the annual tree crop is coniferous, and the remaining 10% is deciduous.

Since World War II, mining activities have greatly expanded in Canada, and Canada is among the world's leading exporters of minerals.

Canada is a leading producer of fish and fish-related products. The waters off the Atlantic coast, including the famous "banks" off Newfoundland (see GRAND BANKS) and the coastal waters, yield large quantities of cod, herring, and haddock and valuable amounts of lobster and scallops. The Pacific-coast catch includes mainly salmon and halibut. On both coasts, a large portion of the fish catch is frozen or canned in fish-packing plants for export. In 1977, Canada extended jurisdiction over coastal waters to 370 km (230 mi) in order to conserve and manage the fish resources. Freshwater fishing is of minor importance.

Power. In the early 1980s hydroelectric stations produced 69% of all electricity (down from 90% during the 1950s), and thermal stations (including those fueled by oil, coal, and natural gas, and nuclear-power plants) produced the remainder. Nuclear-power plants produced only about 9%, mostly in Ontario, and, to a lesser extent, in Quebec. Quebec is the leading producer of hydroelectric power, followed by Ontario, Newfoundland, and British Columbia. Ontario is also the leading producer of thermal electricity and accounts for more than half of all production. Some Canadian-generated electricity is sold to the United States.

Transportation. Canada's network of roads, totaling 884,273 km (549,462 mi), of which 712,938 km (442,999 mi) are surfaced, covers the southern populated areas and the southern fringes of the Northlands. Water transportation is dominated by traffic on the Great Lakes–ST. LAWRENCE SEAWAY system, although the seaway is closed to navigation by ice from December to April. Using this route, oceangoing vessels can reach the interior of the continent. Air transportation services are supplied primarily by Air Canada and Canadian Airlines International. Air transport is the chief means of travel in the less-developed Northlands.

Pipelines are important for the transport of oil and natural gas from the prairie provinces to the principal oil markets in the east and on the west coast. Major oil pipelines include the Interprovincial, which extends from Edmonton to Montreal, and the Trans-Mountain, from Edmonton to Vancouver. Pipelines also deliver Canadian crude to the Atlantic provinces and to the United States. In 1985 the construction of an oil pipeline linking Alberta with the northern Mackenzie valley was completed. The principal gas pipelines are TransCanada and Westcoast Transmission.

Trade. In 1988 the leading exports by value were transportation equipment and other machinery and equipment, wood and wood products (including paper), ferrous and nonferrous ores, crude petroleum, and grain. Over three-quarters of all exports (1987) went to the United States, 6% to Japan, and under 3% to the United Kingdom.

The leading imports by value in 1988 were transportation equipment, machinery, crude petroleum, food and beverages, chemicals, durable consumer goods, and electronic computers. Nearly 70% of all imports (1987) came from the United States, nearly 7% from Japan, and over 3% from the United Kingdom. Canada's principal ports are Montreal, Vancouver, and Sept-Îles-Pointe Noire, and large tonnages are also handled by the ports of Thunder Bay, Port Cartier, Hamilton, Quebec, Halifax, Saint John, and Prince Rupert.

Government

Canada is a self-governing federal union of ten provinces (Alberta, British Columbia, Manitoba, New Brunswick, Newfoundland, Nova Scotia, Ontario, Prince Edward Island, Quebec, and Saskatchewan) and two territories (Northwest Territories and Yukon Territory) within the Commonwealth of Nations. The core of the constitution is derived, with modifications, from the BRITISH NORTH AMERICA ACT of 1867, which was patriated (brought under direct Canadian control) and renamed the Constitution Act in 1982. Queen Elizabeth II is head of state and is represented in the federal government by the governor-general and in the provinces by lieutenant governors.

Legislative power is vested in Parliament, which comprises the queen; the Senate, with 104 members appointed to age 75 (or for life before 1965); and the House of Commons, with 295 elected members (as of the 1988 election). National elections are held at least once every 5 years or whenever the majority party is voted down or calls an election. The leader of the political party with the largest number of seats in the House of Commons usually serves as prime minister.

Provincial legislative power, which extends to education, municipal affairs, direct taxation, and civil law, is vested in unicameral, elected legislatures known as legislative assemblies except in Newfoundland, where it is the House of Assembly, and Quebec, where it is the National Assembly. The legislatures of the provinces are headed by premiers, who are usually the leaders of the majority party. The provincial legislatures are elected every 5 years or less.

The principal political parties are the Liberal party, whose long-time leader, Pierre Elliott TRUDEAU, served as prime minister in 1968–79 and 1980–84 and was succeeded by John N. TURNER (1984–90), prime minister briefly in 1984 and succeeded by Jean Chrétien; Progressive Conservatives, led by Brian MULRONEY, who became prime minister in 1984 and was reelected in 1988; and the New Democratic party, led by John Edward Broadbent from 1975 until 1989, when Audrey McLaughlin was elected. Major regional parties include the British Columbia Social Credit party and the Parti Québécois, important mainly in Quebec.

Canada, history of Canadian history begins at the end of the last ice age, *c.*25,000 BC, when the glaciers retreated. It was then that the first human beings made their way to Canada by walking across the land connection that then existed between Asia and North America. The history of the great Indian, and later Eskimo, migrations is a complex and still unclear story. A bone scraper found in the Yukon Territory has been dated back to 25,000 BC. Some Indian remains in the Skeena River valley in British Columbia show a site continually occupied for 5,000 years.

European Discovery

Norse sagas written in the 13th century tell the story of ERIC THE RED, who reached Greenland AD *c.*985, and of his son who founded a short-lived settlement on the northern tip of Newfoundland, at what is now called L'Anse aux Meadows. The VIKINGS apparently made numerous voyages across the Atlantic, as did later Europeans, mostly fishermen of whom no record remains. Jacques CARTIER, on his first voyage in 1534, found a French ship lost in the Gulf of St. Lawrence. Cartier—like John CABOT, who preceded him on voyages in 1497 and 1498—was seeking things of value. Cabot found fish so thick on the Grand Banks that he said they slowed his ship—fish that had been known of in western ports of England and France for years. Cartier found furs as well as fish.

Canadian history thus began as a search—for food and for riches. Granted the explorers' bravery and curiosity, and in some cases true missionary zeal, still, the driving force for Cabot in 1497, Cartier in 1534, Samuel de CHAMPLAIN in 1603, and many others after them—to say nothing of the backers of all these expeditions—was financial.

New France

Many of the early enterprises of the French regime took their character from these conditions. The fur companies of New France, on whom early colonization depended, fought in the court of LOUIS XIII (r. 1610–43) for monopoly privileges, made their money as rapidly as possible, and avoided—when they could—fulfilling conditions of settlement laid down by the crown. Such early settlements as were founded—at Port Royal (1605) by the sieur de MONTS and at Quebec (1608) by Champlain—were entirely based on the fur trade.

The staple of the fur trade was beaver, a fur especially suited to the felting process of the 17th century. The Indians were the essential middlemen of the trade. Indian wars were made more serious by the arms provided them by the Europeans and were further aggravated because the Indians now had needs they had not had before: knives, axes, guns, iron pots, and worst of all, brandy or rum.

The wars in North America, however, were also caused by European conflicts, notably during the great Franco-British rivalry that began in 1689. The ensuing series of conflicts in North America are sometimes called the FRENCH AND INDIAN WARS. In 1710 the peninsula of Nova Scotia fell into English hands, while the French retained Île Royale (Cape Breton). The French built LOUISBOURG there, to defend the St. Lawrence approaches and to act as entrepôt between New France and the West Indies.

Louisbourg fell to the English in 1745 but was restored to France in 1748; the British then built Halifax to flank it. The struggle known in Europe as the Seven Years' War (1756–63) began in 1754 with an undeclared war between Britain and France over control of the Ohio Valley. News of the defeat of General Braddock's army before FORT DUQUESNE in July 1755 helped persuade the governor of Nova Scotia, Charles Lawrence, to expel 10,000 French inhabitants of ACADIA, an element he believed dangerous. Baron AMHERST captured Louisbourg

This detail from an illustrated map depicts the landing of Jacques Cartier's group of French explorers at Stadacona (present-day Quebec) in 1542.

again in 1758, and James WOLFE followed up this victory with the seizure (1759) of Quebec. The fall of Montreal came in September 1760.

British Reorganization

British acquisition of New France was confirmed in the Peace of Paris of 1763. Approximately 60,000 French Canadians (and 1,500 Acadians who had drifted back) now faced a North America that was British from the Gulf of Mexico to Hudson Bay. For the French, this meant adjustment to an utterly alien way of life, despite the fact that subsequent British rule was, on the whole, benevolent. English criminal law was adopted, but it soon proved essential that French civil law be retained. Both were rec-

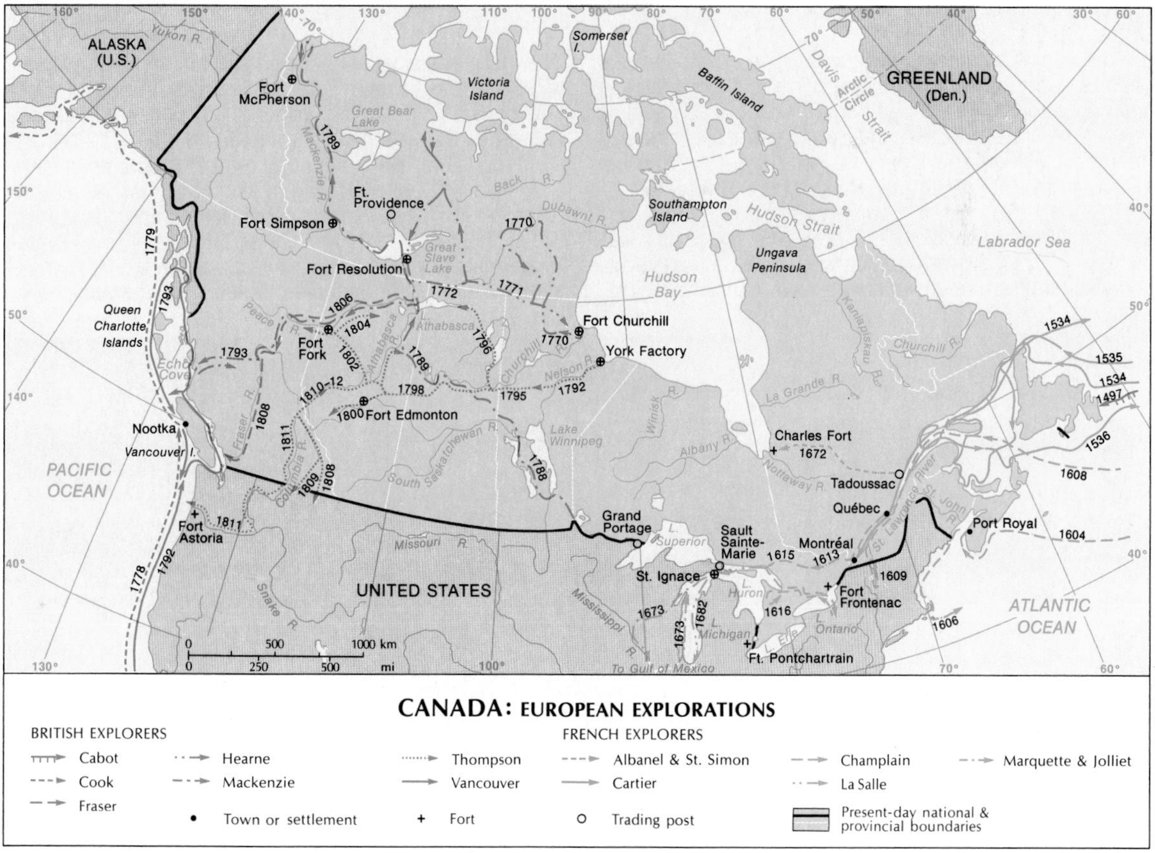

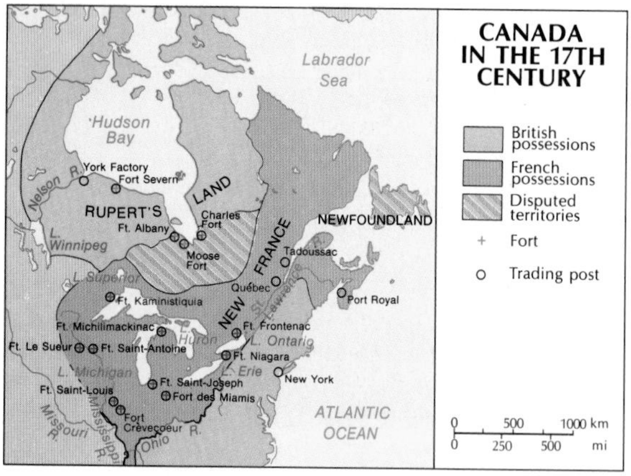

This map of 17th-century Canada indicates the territories claimed by France and England. Lured by the fur trade, France established outposts in the Canadian interior. England founded settlements along the coast.

ognized by the QUEBEC ACT of 1774. After the American Revolution, immigration to Canada rapidly increased as the LOYALISTS—both gentry and farmers—fled the new United States. The arrival of these people posed formidable problems of adjustment between two quite different peoples and their legal, religious, and social systems.

These problems were partly solved in 1791 by dividing the old province of Quebec into two parts, Lower Canada (modern Quebec) and Upper Canada (modern Ontario), each with its own legislature. The province of Nova Scotia was also divided: Prince Edward Island had been established as a separate colony in 1769; New Brunswick was created in 1784. Newfoundland was still a fishing station and was not given representative government until 1832.

Northwest Exploration

North and west of the Canadas lay the chartered territory of the HUDSON'S BAY COMPANY (founded in 1670), comprising the huge watershed of all the rivers flowing into Hudson Bay. Across the Rockies lay territory largely unknown until the voyages of Capt. James COOK in 1776–79. By the time George VANCOUVER made his survey (1792–94) of the northwest coastline, the NORTH WEST COMPANY, a fur company based in Montreal, was already exploring the interior of the Canadian Northwest. Sir Alexander MACKENZIE crossed the entire continent in 1793, and Simon FRASER, with great effort, made his way down the Fraser River in 1808. David THOMPSON spent the years 1798 to 1812 working out the geography of the Columbia River. During the War of 1812 the North West Company took over the American John Jacob Astor's (see ASTOR family) Fort Astoria at the mouth of the Columbia.

War of 1812 and Rebellions of 1837–38

The WAR OF 1812 was a conflict both the Americans and the Canadians believed they had won, whereas the British, who did no small share of the fighting, largely forgot it. Canada was defended, with difficulty, by British troops, Canadian local militia regiments, and Indians. By the end of the war (in December 1814 with the Treaty of Ghent), Britain held Maine as far south as Penobscot Bay. The main issues were left to be settled by the convention of 1818. Altogether, the settlement kept Canada and the United States relatively peaceful until the disruptions caused by the REBELLIONS OF 1837–38.

During the 1830s serious political problems arose in Lower Canada. Although not dissimilar to issues in other colonies (in Upper Canada, Nova Scotia, and New Brunswick), in Lower Canada such problems were aggravated by an assembly with a French-Canadian majority trying to acquire—under the magnetic leadership of Louis Joseph

The Death of General Wolfe *(1770), by Benjamin West, eulogizes the victorious British commander who was killed on Sept. 13, 1759, during the Battle of the Plains of Abraham, and fought for control of the city of Quebec. (National Gallery of Canada, Ottawa.)*

The French-Canadian fur trapper depicted in this print is a coureur de bois *("runner of the woods"), meaning that he operated in the wilderness without a license from the French crown.*

PAPINEAU—control over an executive council composed mainly of Englishmen. A deep-seated problem in Lower Canada was the agricultural crisis caused by declining yields of wheat on old, seigneurial lands, the result of generations of improper farming. On top of this came the commercial crisis of 1837, which affected both the United States and Canada.

Rebellion broke out in Lower Canada in November 1837. However, Papineau's followers, the Patriotes, were no match militarily for the British troops and the more ruthless British-Canadian militia. In Upper Canada a smaller rebellion took place under the volatile leadership of William Lyon MACKENZIE. It too was put down. Mackenzie and Papineau both escaped to the United States, where the former succeeded, with American help, in fomenting border troubles for another year.

Responsible Government

In May 1838 there arrived in Canada a liberal, but strong-minded and able English aristocrat, John George Lambton, 1st Earl of DURHAM, commissioned by the British government to inquire into the Canadian troubles and recommend changes. Durham recommended that the French Canadians be assimilated with the English, and to further this, urged that the colonies of Lower Canada and Upper Canada be joined. This was done in 1840 with the creation of the new Province of Canada.

Durham also recommended that the ministerial government be made responsible to the elected assembly rather than to the crown-appointed governor. The Conservative government in London believed that this system of responsible government would be impossible to implement. However, a change of ministry in London and a great deal of local agitation (in Nova Scotia and in the Province of Canada, where the the movement was spearheaded by Robert BALDWIN and Louis Hippolyte LAFONTAINE) effectively achieved responsible government by

The map indicates the network of trade routes, forts, and trading posts established to maintain the fur trade in western Canada. Until 1821 the North West Company challenged the dominance of the Hudson's Bay Company, but the two companies merged that year.

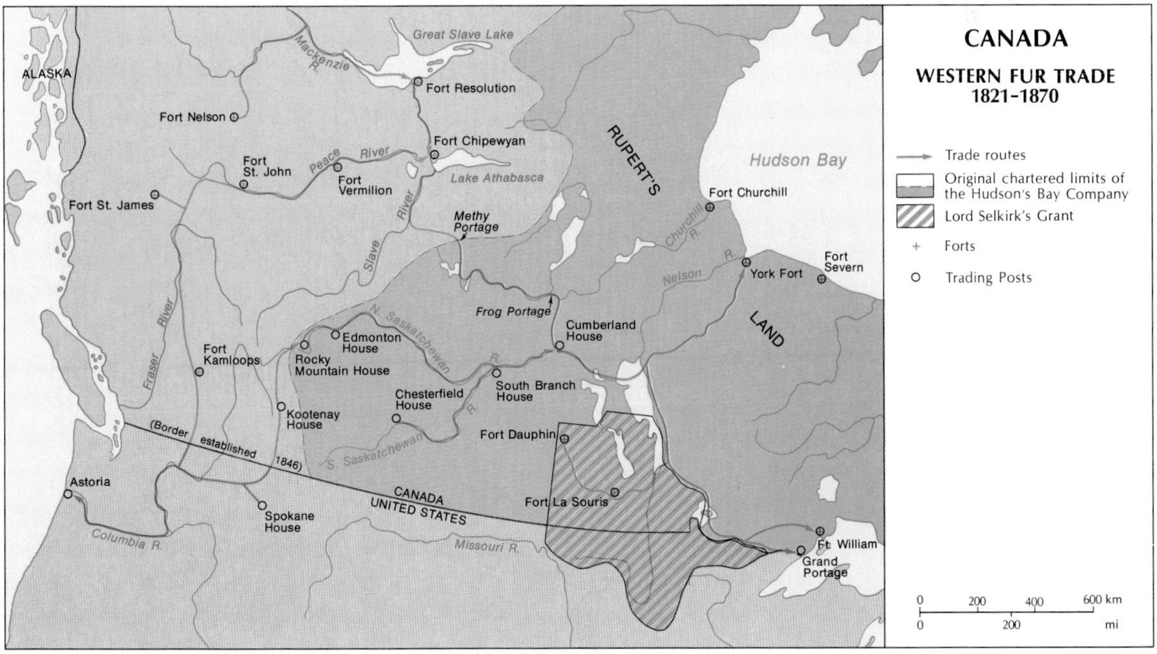

This lithograph (1824), by Peter Rindisbacher, portrays the governor of the Red River Colony (wearing top hat) *and his entourage. To take advantage of Canada's shallow waterways, British settlers adapted the canoe as their primary vehicle for transportation.*

1848. Other colonies—Newfoundland, Prince Edward Island, and New Brunswick—worked out their own approaches to the same question by 1855.

Railroads and Political Union

Railroads changed all of British North America during the 1850s. The building of the Grand Trunk Railway from Montreal to Toronto (and eventually from Portland, Maine, through Montreal and Toronto to Chicago) and other railroads produced permanent changes in Canadian society. The railroads made possible the development of cities; by breaking down isolation, they made possible the concepts that led to the union movement of the 1860s.

Of course, other forces were necessary. The American Civil War caused a climate of tension between the United States and British North America. This became increasingly noticeable after the TRENT AFFAIR in November 1861. Great Britain itself was going through a phase of profound disillusionment with its colonies. These conditions made radical political changes justifiable to some and essential to others in British North America.

Internally, the driving force for change came from Canada West (the former Upper Canada). Increasingly dissatisfied with the union of 1840, this section wanted the political power its numbers warranted. It now had half again as large a population as Canada East (Lower Canada), yet by the union of 1840 it had equal representation. The Conservative party, under John A. MACDONALD and George Étienne CARTIER, resisted these demands as long as possible, but by 1864 it was clear that no government

The map shows British North America from 1792, after the former province of Quebec had been divided into Upper (British) and Lower (French) Canada, to 1840, when the two colonies were reunited. Key battles of the War of 1812 are also shown.

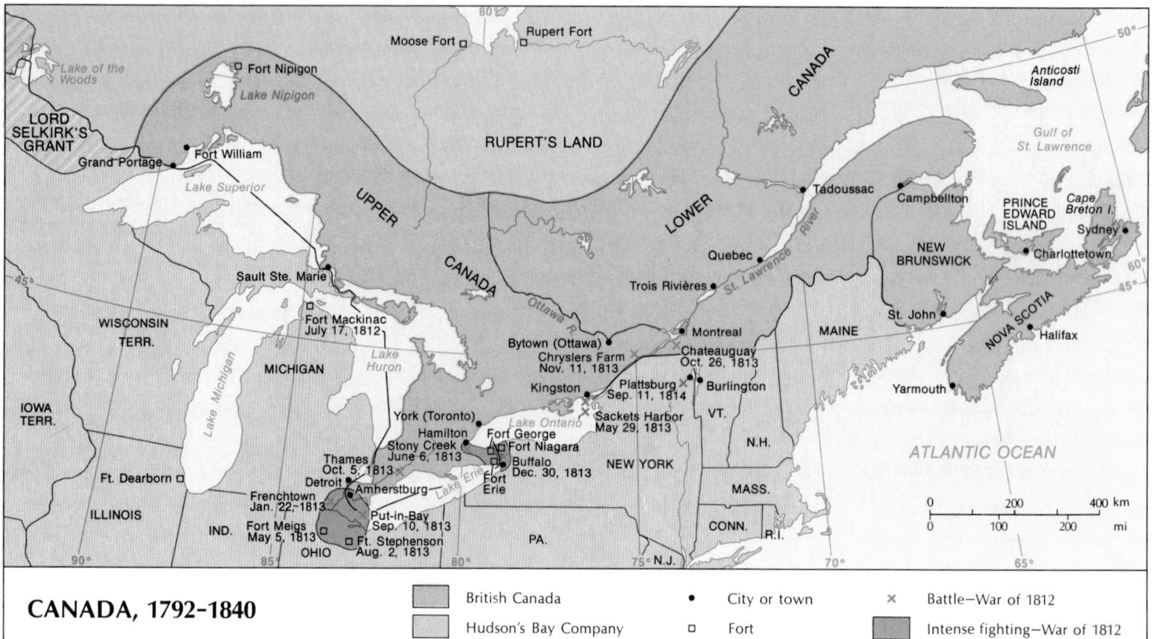

Delegates to the Quebec Conference of 1864, convened to debate forming a union of Britain's North American colonies, are pictured in Rex Wood's The Fathers of Confederation *(1916). The resolutions adopted at the conference became the basis for the founding of the Dominion of Canada in 1867.*

could long survive unless some changes were made. In June 1864 a strong coalition government was formed by Conservatives and the Reform party, with the affirmed goal of achieving a British North American federation.

The Atlantic colonies were separated from the Province of Canada by miles of forest, the hills of the Appalachian range, and the huge salient of Maine. Each colony had its own history and orientation, and Prince Edward Island and Newfoundland were both distant from mainland concerns. Nova Scotia and New Brunswick, however, evinced interest in a union with Prince Edward Island, and a conference was called on the subject at Charlottetown, Prince Edward Island, on Sept. 1, 1864. Representatives from the Province of Canada were invited, and their proposal for a union of all British North America swept everything else aside.

The proposal for British North American union, "Confederation" as it was called, was elaborated more formally in a conference at Quebec in October 1864. It was accepted enthusiastically by the British government.

The proposal also had to be ratified by the legislatures of the five colonies. The Province of Canada approved it in March 1865. New Brunswick, however, had an election in which the proposal was defeated. Prince Edward Island and Newfoundland also said no. Nova Scotia could move only when New Brunswick did.

In 1866 strong pressure from the British government, combined with threatening gestures from the United States (exemplified in raids by the FENIANS in April and June 1866), swung New Brunswick around. Nova Scotia then passed the Confederation. The BRITISH NORTH AMERICA ACT, uniting the provinces of Canada, New Brunswick, and Nova Scotia, was passed by the British Parliament early in 1867, to go into effect on July 1, 1867. The name of the new union was the Dominion of Canada.

Confederation to 1914

The union was federal and created four provinces out of the old three by splitting the Province of Canada into two—Ontario and Quebec. It provided for the future admission of Prince Edward Island, Newfoundland, the Hudson's Bay Company territory in the west, and the Pacific colony of British Columbia. The federal union was strongly weighted at the center; the federal government was given the right of veto over provincial legislation, and an aggrieved religious minority in any province could, in special circumstances, appeal educational rights to the federal government. The British system of cabinet government, responsible to an elected legislature, prevailed everywhere.

The first prime minister of the new Canada was Sir John A. Macdonald. Except for the years 1873–78, he was to remain in power until he died in 1891. By 1873 he had put together the rest of the dominion. Manitoba and the Northwest Territories were included in 1870, British Columbia in 1871, and Prince Edward Island in 1873. The problems of governing the vast new western territories were formidable, and the Canadian government had as yet very little experience or understanding. The province of Manitoba was created in 1870 only because French and English métis (half-breeds) under the leadership of Louis RIEL forced the issue by the Red River Rebellion.

When British Columbia joined in 1871, the Macdonald government rashly committed itself to start a railroad to the Pacific within 2 years and finish it by 1881. The task was impossible; routes and surveys were needed over difficult terrain of about 4,800 km (3,000 mi). Private interests were involved that wanted to build such a railroad, but the whole project—and the Conservative government of Macdonald—collapsed amid charges of corruption in the PACIFIC SCANDAL of 1873.

Alexander Mackenzie, the new Liberal prime minister, tried to pursue the project, using government surveys and construction as resources allowed. Again, it was hard going. The Conservative government could do little more when it returned to power in 1878. Only in 1880 was a private group found that was strong enough to undertake the enormous task. The Canadian Pacific Railway Company then went to work, and within 5 years the last spike was hammered in place, thanks to a driving general manager, William van Horne (1843–1915), some feats of finance, and strong support from the Macdonald government.

It was the Canadian Pacific Railway too that enabled the government to send in Canadian troops to defeat

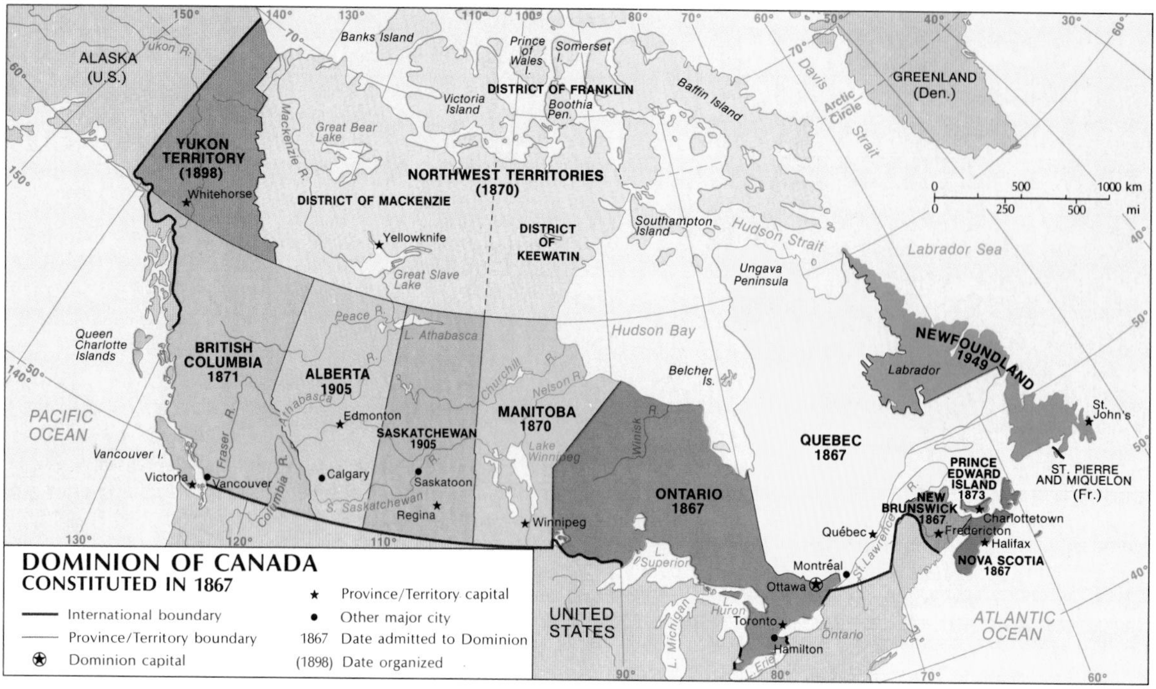

combined métis and Indian forces, again led by Louis Riel, in the Saskatchewan rebellion of 1884–85. The North-West Mounted Police had done a remarkable job of policing the west from 1873 onward, but it could not handle the political problems that caused this rebellion, foremost of which was the administration's shortsighted policy toward the west. The execution of Riel created much controversy, even more in the east than in the west. Although the Roman Catholic church condemned him as an apostate, his fate engaged the sympathies of French Canadians and served to weaken the Conservative party in Quebec for a long time to come.

The death of Macdonald in 1891 also weakened the Conservative party, although his tough-minded and capable successor, Sir John S. D. THOMPSON, did much to keep it in power. Thompson's sudden death in 1894 was a disaster, and the complicated and difficult Manitoba Schools Question finally brought the Conservatives down in 1896. Manitoba had abolished denominational schools and the official use of French in 1890, but the Conservative government avoided the controversial issue until 1895, when the courts impelled it to introduce a bill restoring Catholic schools in the province. The Liberals blocked the bill and won the ensuing election.

For the next 15 years the prime minister was the Liberal French-Canadian leader Sir Wilfrid LAURIER. Laurier,

(Left) *Louis Riel led Indians and métis, descendants of French trappers and Indian women, in two rebellions (1869–70, 1884–85) against the government. Riel was hanged in 1885.* (Right) *Lord Strathcona drove a ceremonial spike into place in 1885 to complete the Canadian Pacific Railway, stretching from Montreal to Vancouver.*

GOVERNORS OF CANADA

Appointed	Governors of New France
1612 1633	Samuel de Champlain
1636	Charles Jacques Huault de Montmagny
1648	Louis d'Ailleboust de Coulonge
1651	Jean de Lauzon
1658	Pierre de Voyer, Vicomte d'Argenson
1661	Pierre Dubois, Baron d'Avaugour
1663	Augustin de Saffray de Mézy
1665	Daniel de Rémy, Sieur de Courcelle
1672	Louis de Buade, Comte de Palluau et de Frontenac
1682	Joseph Antoine Lefebvre de la Barre
1685	Jacques René de Brisay, Marquis de Denonville
1689	Louis de Buade, Comte de Palluau et de Frontenac
1699	Louis Hector de Callière
1705	Philippe de Rigaud, Marquis de Vaudreuil
1726	Charles de Beauharnois de la Boische, Marquis de Beauharnois
1749	Jacques Pierre de Taffanel, Marquis de la Jonquière
1752	Ange Duquesne, Marquis de Menneville
1755	Pierre de Rigaud, Marquis de Vaudreuil-Cavagnal
	Governors of British Canada
1764	James Murray
1768	Guy Carleton
1778	Sir Frederick Haldimand
1786	Guy Carleton, Baron Dorchester
1797	Robert Prescott
1807	Sir James H. Craig
1812	Sir George Prevost
1816	Sir John C. Sherbrooke
1818	Charles Lennox, Duke of Richmond and Lennox
1820	George Ramsay, Earl of Dalhousie
1831	Matthew Aylmer, Baron Aylmer
1835	William Pitt Amherst, Earl Amherst of Arracan
1835	Archibald Acheson, Earl of Gosford
1838	John George Lambton, Earl of Durham
1839	Sir John Colborne

Appointed	Governors of British Canada
1839	Charles Poulett Thomson (later Baron Sydenham)
1842	Sir Charles Bagot
1843	Charles T. Metcalfe, Baron Metcalfe
1846	Charles Murray Cathcart, Earl Cathcart
1847	James Bruce, Earl of Elgin
1854	Sir Edmund W. Head
1861	Charles Stanley Monck, Viscount Monck
	Governors General of Canada
1867	Charles Stanley Monck, Viscount Monck
1868	John Young, Baron Lisgar (assumed office 1869)
1872	Frederick Temple Blackwood, Marquess of Dufferin and Ava
1878	John Douglas Sutherland Campbell, Marquess of Lorne
1883	Henry Charles Keith Petty-Fitzmaurice, Marquess of Lansdowne
1888	Frederick Arthur Stanley, Baron Stanley of Preston (later Earl of Derby)
1893	John Campbell Hamilton Gordon, Earl of Aberdeen
1898	Gilbert John Elliot, Earl of Minto
1904	Albert Henry George Grey, Earl Grey
1911	H. R. H. Arthur William Patrick Albert, Duke of Connaught
1916	Victor Christian William Cavendish, Duke of Devonshire
1921	Julian Hedworth George Byng, Viscount Byng of Vimy
1926	Freeman Freeman-Thomas, Viscount Willingdon of Ratton
1931	Vere Brabazon Ponsonby, Earl of Bessborough
1935	John Buchan, Baron Tweedsmuir
1940	Alexander Augustus Frederick William Alfred George Cambridge, Earl of Athlone
1945	Harold Rupert Leofric George Alexander, Viscount Alexander of Tunis (assumed office 1946)
1952	Vincent Massey
1959	Georges Philias Vanier
1967	Roland Michener
1973	Jules Léger (assumed office 1974)
1978	Edward Richard Schreyer (assumed office 1979)
1983	Jeanne Sauvé (assumed office 1984)
1989	Ramon Hnatyshyn

a tall, graceful, charming politician, had some genuine liberal convictions. His regime was a period of tremendous expansion in Canada. Two more transcontinental railroads were added during the years before 1914; Canada's population increased more than 30 percent in the decade from 1901 to 1911.

In 1911, Laurier's government was defeated at the polls by a strong nationalist reaction against a reciprocity treaty that the United States had proposed and the Liberals espoused. The Conservative party under Robert L. BORDEN took full advantage of their opportunity. The Borden government garnered its basic strength from a persuasive mixture of Canadian economic nationalism with the upholding of imperial ties.

The World Wars

World War I tested the implications of Borden's imperial policies. In October 1914, 33,000 Canadian troops sailed for Europe, many of them never to return. Other divisions followed. Canadians soon became the Allied shock troops on the western front, where the casualties were staggering. The losses were so heavy that Borden returned to Canada from Europe in May 1917 convinced that Canada would have to have conscription. Others at home were not yet convinced, among them many French Canadians. Borden tried to avoid a cleavage by inviting Laurier to join a coalition government. Laurier refused, however, and although a coalition government was formed that included proconscription Liberals, the French Canadians were largely alienated by the issue.

Borden insisted on Canada's voice in imperial war policy, and he procured Canada's signing of the Treaty of Versailles (1919) in its own right. A major step in the development of full autonomy was thus taken. This autonomy was confirmed by the Statute of Westminster (1931), by which Canada and the other self-governing units of the British Empire were recognized as dominions with status equal to that of Britain. The war caused inflation and maladjustment within Canada, reflected in the Winnipeg general strike of May 1919 and the great diver-

PRIME MINISTERS OF CANADA SINCE CONFEDERATION

July 1, 1867–Nov. 5, 1873	Sir John A. Macdonald (Conservative)
Nov. 7, 1873–Oct. 16, 1878	Alexander Mackenzie (Liberal)
Oct. 17, 1878–June 6, 1891	Sir John A. Macdonald (Conservative)
June 16, 1891–Nov. 24, 1892	Sir John J. Abbott (Conservative)
Dec. 5, 1892–Dec. 12, 1894	Sir John S. D. Thompson (Conservative)
Dec. 21, 1894–Apr. 27, 1896	Sir Mackenzie Bowell (Conservative)
May 1, 1896–July 8, 1896	Sir Charles Tupper (Conservative)
July 11, 1896–Oct. 6, 1911	Sir Wilfrid Laurier (Liberal)
Oct. 10, 1911–Oct. 12, 1917	Sir Robert L. Borden (Conservative)
Oct. 12, 1917–July 10, 1920	Sir Robert L. Borden (Unionist)
July 10, 1920–Dec. 29, 1921	Arthur Meighen (Unionist)
Dec. 29, 1921–June 28, 1926	William Lyon Mackenzie King (Liberal)
June 29, 1926–Sept. 25, 1926	Arthur Meighen (Conservative)
Sept. 25, 1926–Aug. 6, 1930	William Lyon Mackenzie King (Liberal)
Aug. 7, 1930–Oct. 23, 1935	Richard Bedford Bennett (Conservative)
Oct. 23, 1935–Nov. 15, 1948	William Lyon Mackenzie King (Liberal)
Nov. 15, 1948–June 21, 1957	Louis Stephen St. Laurent (Liberal)
June 21, 1957–Apr. 22, 1963	John G. Diefenbaker (Conservative)
Apr. 22, 1963–Apr. 20, 1968	Lester Bowles Pearson (Liberal)
Apr. 20, 1968–June 4, 1979	Pierre Elliott Trudeau (Liberal)
June 4, 1979–Feb. 18, 1980	Joseph Clark (Conservative)
Feb. 18, 1980–June 30, 1984	Pierre Elliott Trudeau (Liberal)
June 30, 1984–Sept. 17, 1984	John N. Turner (Liberal)
Sept. 17, 1984–	Brian Mulroney (Conservative)

sity of regional interests and parties that emerged in the general election of 1921. The prime minister was now W. L. Mackenzie KING, a prosy, clever, rotund bachelor who had become leader of the Liberal party following the death of Laurier in 1919.

Canada in the 1920s had traveled a considerable distance from the decade before. Automobiles were now commonplace; women had won (1918) the vote; and the movement for prohibition of alcoholic beverages had gained strength. Canada, however, did not adopt peacetime prohibition, as the United States did; although banned in all provinces by the end of the war, the sale of beer, wine, and liquor was gradually resumed after 1920 under provincial government control.

The stock market had a great impact during the late 1920s. Canadians were caught in its rise and, disastrously, in its crash in October 1929. Savings disappeared, and so did Mackenzie King's government in 1930. Prime Minister Richard Bedford BENNETT and his new Conservative government urged Canadians to tighten their belts. Government budgets were cut, as were private ones. Wheat and other primary exports became unsellable. The price of wheat dropped from $1.60 a bushel to 60 cents. Even at that price the farmers might have squeezed by, but what devastated the Canadian west was that the farmers could not grow wheat. A series of severe droughts in the summer of 1931 and afterward ruined thousands of western farmers, turning their farms into dust bowls.

Canadians, disillusioned with the frightening vagaries of the free-enterprise system, turned to other economic philosophies and political parties. The Co-operative Commonwealth Federation (CCF), a socialist party, was founded in 1933; the SOCIAL CREDIT PARTY won the Alberta election of 1935; the Union Nationale under Maurice DUPLESSIS came to power in Quebec in 1936; even Richard Bennett, conservative though he was, launched, early in 1935, his own desperate version of Franklin Roosevelt's New Deal in the United States. It did not save Bennett or his party, which was defeated decisively by Mackenzie King in the 1935 general election.

King was to remain in power, through World War II, until he retired in 1948. Beneath a vague and woolly manner, he had the toughness of a ward politician. He was no wartime leader, and he knew it. He could pick good men, however, and his cabinet was a remarkable aggregation.

King had long disliked European and British commitments, and the Canadian government entered the war on Sept. 10, 1939 (7 days after Britain did), with his conception of a limited commitment abroad. By June 1940, however, the war was vastly different. Between Nazi Germany and mastery of Europe stood only Britain, Canada, and the other Commonwealth countries. Canada's war effort now became total. The Canadian navy took on most of the convoy duty in the northwest Atlantic. Divisions of troops crossed to England.

The Dieppe raid of 1942, a disastrous test of the German defenses on the coast of France, the Normandy Invasion of 1944, and the Italian campaign produced heavy casualties in the Canadian army, and by the autumn of 1944 reinforcements were badly needed. King's government had promised in 1939 that there would be no conscription for overseas service. Now, however, powerful elements in the army and throughout the country felt that sending conscripts overseas was vital. The argument nearly broke the King government, but he survived the resignation of ministers on both sides. Conscripted troops were sent overseas in November 1944.

Postwar Canada

King survived the elections of 1945, too, and he retired undefeated in 1948, to be succeeded by Louis ST. LAURENT, who presided over the entrance of Newfoundland into the Confederation in 1949. He had qualities that King lacked—good sense, an enjoyment of common folk and common pleasures, and a charming, avuncular manner that people trusted.

During St. Laurent's period in power, Canada underwent remarkable postwar development. The gross national product rose from $12 billion in 1946 to $61 billion in 1966. Oil and gas were discovered in quantity in Alberta in 1947, and by 1956 oil led all other mineral resources in value. An enormous iron-ore complex in Labrador-Ungava began to be developed in 1954, and this spurred the development of the St. Lawrence Seaway, a joint Canadian-U.S. project finished in 1959. One project—a natural-gas pipeline planned to run 3,500 km (2,170 mi) from Alberta to Montreal—dealt the St. Laurent government a fatal blow. The financing was complicated, and in Parliament it had such a stormy passage that it led to the defeat of the government in the 1957 election.

That surprising upset brought the Conservative party back to power under John G. DIEFENBAKER. Diefenbaker was a Saskatchewan criminal lawyer and a dynamic political leader. In the 1958 elections he received the largest majority of any government in Canadian history to that time—208 Conservatives as against 49 Liberals and 8 CCF. Diefenbaker looked invincible, and for a time he was. A period of economic recession took its toll, however, and in the 1962 elections the Conservative majority vanished. Diefenbaker held on with a minority government until 1963, when the Liberal party took over under Lester B. PEARSON. Leader of the Liberals since the retirement of St. Laurent in 1958, Pearson was a genial former civil servant. The highlight of his premiership was Canada's celebration of its achievements in the centennial year of 1967. Expo '67 in Montreal was Canada's first world's fair. It showed what French-Canadian flair and logistical talent, buttressed by English-Canadian expertise in construction, could do.

Pearson retired in 1968 and was succeeded by Pierre Elliott TRUDEAU, the third French-Canadian prime minister since 1867. An intellectual with considerable experience of the world, Trudeau had to contend with an external problem—massive importations of U.S. capital and its consequences—and a major internal one—French Canada's desire for greater power. "*Maîtres chez nous*" ("masters of our own house") was the slogan of the Quebec government (1960–66) of Jean Lesage. It meant control by the province over Quebec's way of life as well as its economy. Ten years later, in 1976, Quebec's provincial elections were won by the Parti Québécois, a party committed to making Quebec into an independent republic. Amid the crisis caused by this separatist threat and economic difficulties, the Liberals were defeated in the national elections of May 1979. A minority Conservative government headed by Joseph CLARK, however, lasted only until February 1980, when new elections returned Trudeau and the Liberals to power. In May 1980 a referendum in Quebec turned down the proposal for political independence. In 1981 the federal and provincial governments (except Quebec) reached agreement on constitutional reforms, which were enacted in the CONSTITUTION ACT of 1982.

When Trudeau retired, resigning on June 30, 1984, he was succeeded by John TURNER, but elections in September 1984 brought the Conservatives, led by Brian MULRONEY, to power. In 1987, Mulroney reached an agreement with Quebec regarding the signing of the 1982 Constitution Act by providing an amendment recognizing Quebec as a "distinct society." By the 1990 deadline, however, he had not gained the required unanimous provincial approval to the amendment, and the so-called Meech Lake agreement failed. A 1988 free-trade agreement with the United States precipitated a general election in November 1988, which the Conservatives won comfortably.

The Canadian prime minister W. L. Mackenzie King (left), *the U.S. president Franklin Delano Roosevelt* (center), *and the British prime minister Winston Churchill* (right) *met at Quebec in August 1943 to discuss the Allied invasions of Italy and France.*

Canada, Anglican Church of The Anglican Church of Canada is a national, independent, Christian church within the worldwide Anglican Communion. The church is divided into 30 dioceses, each with its own bishop, and one Episcopal district. Its highest legislative authority is the General Synod, composed of bishops, clergy, and laity from each diocese. The church was formally established by the Church of England in 1787 with the consecration of Charles Inglis as bishop of Nova Scotia. The first General Synod of the Church of England in Canada was held in 1893. In 1955 the church was constituted as the Anglican Church of Canada.

Canada, United Church of The United Church of Canada is a Protestant denomination formed in 1925 by the union of the Congregational, Methodist, and Presbyterian churches of Canada. Negotiations for union had begun as early as 1904. Even after the formal merger, a large number of Presbyterian congregations continued as the Presbyterian Church in Canada. The Evangelical United Brethren Church joined the merger in 1968. Characterized by the spirit of unity, it nevertheless allows diversity consistent with basic Christian doctrine among the different participating denominations. At the time of the merger the presbyterian system of church government was adopted.

Canada Company The Canada Company was founded as a result of a proposal by John Galt (1779–1839) that the British government sell crown lands in Upper Canada to a colonization company in order to meet some of the compensation claims for losses in the War of 1812. The company was chartered for that purpose on Aug. 19, 1826, and acquired 560,000 ha (1,384,000 acres) of crown land and an additional 445,000 ha (1,100,000 acres) known as the Huron Tract. Galt became secretary and later (1827) superintendent of the company. The company founded the towns of Galt and Goderich and drew many settlers to western Upper Canada (Ontario). It continued in existence until the 1950s.

The British army topographer Thomas Davies is noted for vivid watercolors depicting life in Quebec, including View of the Bridge on the River La Puce *(1790). (The National Gallery of Canada, Ottawa.)*

Canadian art and architecture The history of the arts in Canada began in 1663, the year in which Quebec gained the official status of a French province.

French Colonial Period (1663–1760). The first painters of Quebec were French-born clerics who specialized in religious subjects. Of these, Frère Luc (1614–85) is best known, particularly for his influential altarpiece *L'Assomption* (1671; Hôpital-Général, Quebec).

In 1684 the École des Arts et Métiers was founded at Saint-Joachim, near Quebec, to train native-born masons, carpenters, cabinetmakers, painters, and sculptors. Their primary task was the construction and decoration of Quebec's numerous baroque churches and monastic houses. Religious wood sculpture, in particular, became an important art form in 18th-century Quebec, which is evident in the many works of the Baillargé family inspired by the ROCOCO STYLE.

The Château Frontenac, a hotel built in Quebec City by the Canadian Pacific Railway (1892) in the manner of a French château, is named for Louis de Frontenac, who served as the French governor of New France during the late 17th century.

Oxen Drinking *(1899), by Horatio Walter, was influenced by J. F. Millet and by the Barbizon school. Walker used rich color and dramatic lighting to convey the charm of Canadian farm life. (The National Gallery of Canada, Ottawa.)*

British Colonial Period (1760–1867). After the British conquest of New France in 1760, several officers attached to the garrison at Quebec, who had been trained as topographers, began to paint Canadian scenes. Their carefully rendered watercolors in the English picturesque manner constitute valuable historical documents. The most imaginative of the officer-artists was Thomas Davies (*c.*1737–1812).

Working in the same tradition in the next century was the Irish-born Paul KANE, who traveled to the Rockies, depicting the life of the western Indians. His contemporary, Cornelius Krieghoff, did much the same for the *habitants*, or settlers, of Quebec. The eclectic Joseph Legaré (1795–1855), Canada's first native-born landscape painter, is best known for his series of paintings depicting local disasters.

The buildings of the period were strongly influenced by the GEORGIAN STYLE of architecture brought to Canada by the United Empire Loyalists. After the War of 1812 this style was supplanted by a more delicate NEOCLASSICISM based on the work of Robert ADAM. Many elegantly porticoed brick and stone mansions survive from this time.

Confederation Period (1867–1910). After the confederation of British North America in 1867, most Canadian artists went to Paris to study. Only a few—for example, Homer Watson (1855–1936), the "Canadian Constable"; Lucius O'Brien (1832–99), who became president of the Royal Canadian Academy on its founding in 1880; and Horatio WALKER, the most popular North American artist working in the style of Jean François MILLET—were content to stay at home. The English Canadians William Brymner (1855–1925), George Reid (1860–1947), and Robert Harris (1849–1919) infused Canadian landscape and figure painting with an understanding of 19th-century French artistic trends, especially those of the BARBIZON SCHOOL and the *juste milieu*, a compromise between academic art and IMPRESSIONISM. The French Canadian Ozias Leduc (1864–1955) worked within the tradition of SYMBOLISM.

By 1900, impressionism had become a major force in Canadian painting, particularly in the works of Marc-Aurèle de Foy Suzor-Coté (1869–1937) and Maurice Cullen (1866–1934). Influenced by FAUVISM, James W. MORRICE created a unique style with which he captured life in France, Quebec, and later in North Africa and the Caribbean.

In architecture, despite a mid-19th century trend toward the Italianate, it was the GOTHIC REVIVAL that influenced Canadian building most strongly into the 20th century. The Second Empire style, the Romanesque revival of Henry Hobson RICHARDSON, and the Beaux-Arts tradition were also important, especially in domestic and civic buildings. The large hotels of the era, such as the Chateau Frontenac (1892) in Quebec City, were designed in the chateau style.

1910 to the Present. Shortly before World War I, several Canadian artists reacted against European-imposed subject matter and techniques by taking northern Ontario—and later, all of Canada, including the Arctic—as their terrain, painting the rugged splendor of the landscape in a vibrant and expressive manner. This "cult of the North" led to the formation of Canada's first nationalist school, the GROUP OF SEVEN, which included Lawren HARRIS, Frederick VARLEY, and J. E. H. MACDONALD. Although Tom THOMSON, a major force in the movement, tragically drowned before the group was founded, his rich, boldly colored paintings of Algonquin Park have made him a legendary figure in Canadian painting.

In Maligne Lake, Jasper Park *(1924), Lawren Harris combined dark, somber color with a bold simplicity to create a mood of solitude in a cold landscape. (The National Gallery of Canada, Ottawa).*

The bright colors and flat decorative design of Tom Thomson's The Pool *(c.1915) reveal the influences of Art Nouveau and post-impressionism. (The National Gallery of Canada, Ottawa.)*

The Group of Seven's major contemporaries were less nationalistic in outlook. Emily Carr, a Victoria-born painter, immortalized the West Coast Indians. Lionel LeMoine Fitzgerald rendered subtly colored still lifes and views of his native prairies. The most original was David MILNE, whose delicate dry-brush watercolors captured carefully composed flower arrangements, quiet interiors, and winter scenes.

The Canadian Group of Painters was founded in 1933 in opposition to the exclusivity of the Group of Seven. Carl Schaefer continued to paint landscapes in a nationalistic vein, Charles Comfort painted portraits, and Edwin H. Holgate rendered large-scale nudes in outdoor settings. Primarily through the influence of Wassily KANDINSKY, Bertram Brooker introduced pure geometric abstraction in 1926.

In Montreal, John Lyman formed the Contemporary Art Society, which displayed a strong affinity to the school of Paris. Paul-Émile Borduas and Alfred Pellan were inspired mainly by SURREALISM; the renowned nonobjectivist Jean Paul RIOPELLE developed his own distinct, abstract vocabulary.

During the 1950s, the major focus of the Toronto-based Painters Eleven, which included Jack Bush, Harold Town, and William Ronald, was ABSTRACT EXPRESSIONISM.

Constructed in 1965, Toronto's city hall was designed by Viljo Rewell, a leader of the rationalist school of Finnish architecture. The structure consists of two office buildings surrounding a lower complex of offices and council chambers.

Ronald's numerous New York exhibitions profoundly influenced the direction of Canadian painting. Another member, Michael Snow, has received international acclaim for his innovative work in a variety of media, including sculpture, video art, and film.

Elsewhere in Canada, Alex Colville's provocative figure studies and Christopher Pratt's Newfoundland subjects are exceptional examples of magic realism.

Sculpture has played a less important role in contemporary Canadian art, although the works of Robert Murray and the minimalist David Rabinovitch are known internationally. Increasing interest is being shown in the carvings of the ESKIMO and Indians of northern, central, and western Canada.

Prominent among Canada's multimedia artists of the 1970s and 1980s are Iain and Ingrid Baxter, Gathie Falk, and Edward Poitras. Rita McKeough has established herself as a front-rank mixed-media/performance artist; Krzystof Wodiczko's "public projections" interact with the environment.

Contemporary architecture in Canada has been progressive and diverse. Arthur Erickson on the West Coast is noted for his eclectic designs and sympathetic use of native materials. In Toronto the firm of Diamond and Myers designs small-scale projects with existing structures in mind, while Zeidler Partnership works in a high-technology style. Other notable architects include Ron Thom, John C. Parkin Associates, and Raymond Moriyama.

Canadian literature Canadian literature, written in Canada's two official languages, French and English, began as a colonial literature, and since most Canadians live close to the United States, their literature inevitably is influenced by that neighbor. Canadian literature—especially earlier works—also often focuses on the landscape.

Early History. Most Canadian literature has been written since 1867, when the British colonies of Canada (now Ontario and Quebec), New Brunswick, and Nova Scotia confederated to form the new nation. Some literature, however, was written by the explorers, traders, priests, and farmers who opened up New France; the mil-

(Right) *Alfred Pellan's* Végétaux Marins *(1964) combines complex design with glowing color in a surrealistic display of sea vegetation. (Art Collection Society of Kingston, Ontario.)*
(Below) *The abstract expressionist Jean Paul Riopelle painted the large triptych* Pavane *(1954), a complex mosaic of radiant color. (The National Gallery of Canada, Ottawa.)*

The motif of self-definition in Canadian literature reflects Canada's struggle to assert a national identity. Hugh MacLennan (left) *searched for a Canadian character in* The Watch That Ends the Night *(1959); Robertson Davies* (center) *explored provincial sensibilities in such novels as* Tempest-Tost *(1951); Marie Claire Blais* (right) *began her chronicles of adolescent identity with* La Belle Bête *(1959).*

itary personnel who occupied Quebec after it surrendered to the British; and the United Empire Loyalists who abandoned the newly created United States to continue to live under British rule. In 1606, Marc Lescarbot, who was wintering with Samuel de Champlain at Port Royal in Acadia (now Annapolis Royal, Nova Scotia), produced a masque, *Le Théâtre de Neptune* (The Theater of Neptune, 1606), the first French drama of the New World. Frances Brooke, whose husband was chaplain to the British garrison in Quebec City during the 1760s, wrote there at least part of the four-volume *History of Emily Montague* (1769), considered the first Canadian novel.

Descendants of these early authors wrote some British North American best-sellers. John Richardson's *Wacousta* (1832), a novel about the Pontiac conspiracy, was typical of the historical fiction that dominated early Canadian literature. T. C. HALIBURTON, whose family emigrated from New England to Nova Scotia, created in *The Clockmaker, or The Sayings and Doings of Samuel Slick of Slickville* (1835–36) Sam Slick, the Connecticut Yankee clockmaker whose "sayings and doings" were recorded in various books published from the 1830s on. F. X. Garneau composed a history of Canada (1845–48), inspiring a whole generation of writers, including Octave CRÉMAZIE, to remember their French heritage.

1867 through World War I. The Confederation of 1867 and the later addition of the British possessions of Rupert's Land (1870), British Columbia (1871), and Prince Edward Island (1873) encouraged the first genuine development of a national Canadian literature. One phase of this was a conscious attempt to make Canadians aware of their past. Louis Honoré FRÉCHETTE composed his poem "La Découverte du Mississippi" (1873) to celebrate the 200th anniversary of the discovery of the Mississippi by Louis Jolliet and Jacques Marquette and to state his faith in Canada's "destins nouveaux." William Kirby wrote *The Golden Dog* (1877), a novel set in New France just before its fall to the British, partly to help incorporate into English-Canadian history and mythology the treasures of Canada's French heritage.

Another phase of the coming of age was fostered by a loosely knit group of Canadian authors writing during the decades before World War I. This group, popularly called the "poets of the Confederation," began to write poetry and fiction in a style that blended realism with regionalism. Representative authors are Duncan Campbell SCOTT, Wilfred Campbell, Bliss Carman, and Charles G. D. Roberts.

L. M. Montgomery's *Anne of Green Gables* (1908), the delightful, bittersweet evocation of the life of an orphan growing up on Prince Edward Island, is still an international best-seller. The fame that novels such as Montgomery's brought to Canada encouraged writers of other nationalities to produce literature about Canada. A remarkable example is Louis Hémon's novel, *Maria Chapdelaine* (1916), which provided an image of Canada for many Europeans and helped encourage more realistic Canadian fiction.

Modern Times. Modern Canadian literature has continued in paths laid out by the writers of the Confederation. Thomas Raddall's novel *His Majesty's Yankees* (1942) examines the problems faced by Nova Scotians during the American Revolution. In *Towards the Last Spike* (1952), an epic poem telling the story of building the Canadian-Pacific Railway, E. J. Pratt explores Canadian-American relations and the problem of communications in a huge but sparsely populated country. Hugh MACLENNAN's *Two Solitudes* (1945) and *Return of the Sphinx* (1967), and Gabrielle ROY's *Bonheur d'occasion* (1945), go far to explain Quebec's separatist movement.

Although few modern Canadian writers have left Canada permanently, many spend considerable periods abroad. Both Morley CALLAGHAN and Paul Morin have lived in Paris, and Mavis Gallant now lives there. Mordecai RICHLER recently returned to Canada from London; the son of Jewish immigrant parents, he is representative of a group that has helped change Canada into a multicultural, multilingual society. Leonard Cohen, like Richler, is a Jewish writer from Montreal who occasionally lives in the United States.

French Canada's desire to establish its own identity has brought into prominence a number of talented novelists, poets, and journalists. The novelist Marie Claire BLAIS is perhaps the best known. Poet and novelist Jacques Godbout's *Têtes a Papineau* (1982) is a novel about the political tensions in French Quebec. Antonine MAILLET won the French Prix Goncourt in 1979 for her novel of Acadia, *Pélagie's Return to the Homeland* (Eng. trans., 1982). Its sequel, *Cent ans dans le bois*, was published in 1982. Michel Tremblay, whose first play, *Les belles-soeurs*, was written in the French dialect of the Québécois, is perhaps the most influential of the French-Canadian playwrights. The last volume of the trilogy comprising his fictionalized autobiography, *La duchesse et la roturier*, was published in 1982.

Of the English-Canadian writers whose works are read internationally, the best known range from the Irish-born Canadian novelist Brian MOORE (*I Am Mary Dunne*, 1968) to the venerable literary critic Northrop FRYE. Poet and novelist Margaret ATWOOD offers her singular feminist versions of life in such books as *The Handmaid's Tale* (1986) and *Cat's Eye* (1988). Short-story writer Alice Munro's widely praised collection *The Progress of Love* was published in 1986. Robertson DAVIES, essayist, dramatist, and novelist (*The Deptford Trilogy*, 1970–75), is one of Canada's most renowned writers. Prize-winning poet Michael Ondaatje, of Sri Lankan origin, published his novel *In the Skin of the Lion* in 1987. Josef Śkvoreck , a Czech emigré, has written a number of important books in Canada, including the critically praised novel *Dvorak in Love* (1986). Elizabeth Spencer, U.S.-born but a long-time resident of Canada, published a collection of memorable short stories, *The Light in the Piazza*, in 1986. Among eminent poets, Dorothy Livesay collected her favorites from a lengthy poetic career in *The Self-Completing Tree* (1986).

Canadian Pacific Railway The Canadian Pacific Railway is the major privately owned railroad in Canada. In 1880, George Stephen and several business associates were awarded a land grant of 25 million acres (10.1 million ha) and considerable government financial aid to build a transcontinental railroad that, when finished in 1885, linked Halifax on the Atlantic with Vancouver on the Pacific. The Canadian Pacific continued to grow, and the total system now has more than 25,000 km (15,500 mi) of track. The railroad also operates steamboat lines, hotels, and an airline—although it is no longer responsible for passenger traffic, which is now managed by the government-sponsored corporation VIA Rail Canada.

Canadian River The Canadian River, 1,459 km (905 mi) long, rises in northern New Mexico, flows east through Texas, and crosses Oklahoma to enter the Arkansas River. Its chief tributary is the North Canadian River. Dams have created Conchas Reservoir (New Mexico) and Eufaula Reservoir (Oklahoma), which are used for irrigation, flood control, and electric power.

Canadian Shield The Canadian Shield (Laurentian Shield) is a triangular base of Precambrian rock located in the eastern half of Canada and the northeastern United States. It extends from the Mackenzie Basin east to the Davis Strait and south to southern Ontario, Quebec, and northern Minnesota, Wisconsin, Michigan, and New York. It has an area of about 4,828,000 km^2 (1,864,000 mi^2). Although the mountains of the shield were once high, glaciation has worn them down and left numerous lakes and marshes. Most elevations in the shield area are from 183 m (600 ft) to 367 m (1,200 ft). The eastern edge is tilted up, and some mountains in this area are as high as 1,500 m (5,000 ft) or more. One of the 11 CONTINENTAL SHIELDS on the Earth, the Canadian Shield is the nucleus of the North American continent. During the Cambrian Period (570 million to 500 million years ago), the Canadian Shield was the most important of the four ancient provinces of North America. It includes some of the Earth's oldest rock formations, mainly Precambrian igneous rocks 2 to 4 billion years old.

canal A canal is an artificial waterway built either for navigation or for the transport of water. Water may be transported to remove excess surface water, for irrigation or water supply, or for the generation of power. In this article the main emphasis is on canals used for commercial navigation.

History

Many canals used for navigation are constructed to bypass hazards on otherwise navigable river courses; these link different water levels above and below falls or rapids. Canals of this sort have been important for commercial navigation for a long time; for instance, the GRAND CANAL of the Chang Jiang (Yangtze) basin in China dates from the 7th century. It was not until the 12th century, however, that canals similar to those used today were built in western Europe. In the Rhine delta of the Low Countries, canals were concurrently developed for the purposes of drainage improvement and navigation.

The perfection of the flash lock—actually a movable weir, or barrage, across a river or drainage cut—made it possible to dam and then release suddenly a mass of water, thus allowing a shallow-draft BARGE to float over a minor obstruction. It was not until the development of the pound lock (probably near Utrecht around 1370) that commercial canal transport by barge evolved on a major scale. Crude by modern standards, the first pound locks did, however, incorporate the basic principle of a basin enclosed between inner and outer (upper and lower) gates, within which the water level could be controlled by raising or lowering the gates.

The primitive pound lock with portcullis gates was gradually improved, and by the beginning of the 16th

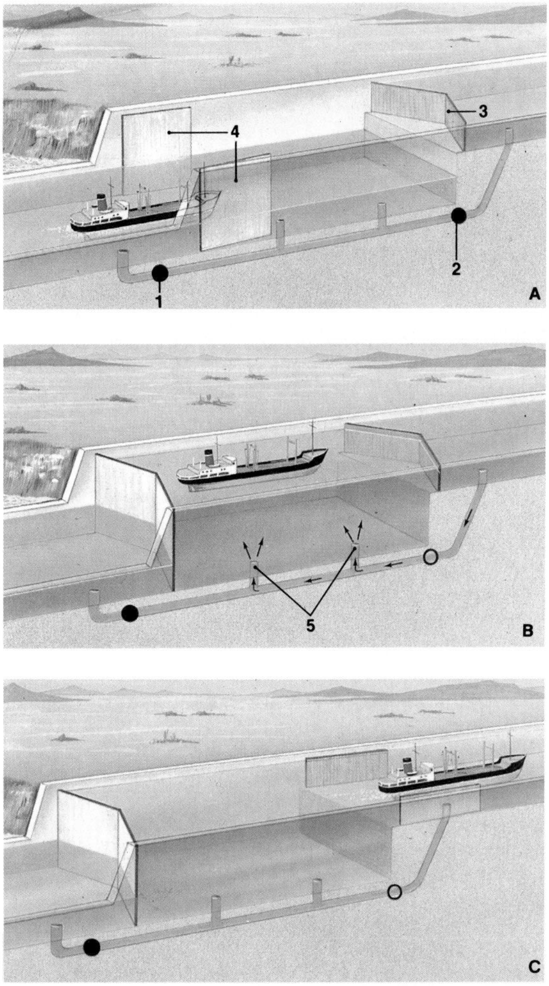

A canal lock is a water-filled chamber used to raise or lower ships, barges, or boats from one elevation to another along part of a canal. It consists of artificial sidewalls; movable, watertight gates at both ends, which can be opened or closed as needed; and a water conduit with inlet and outlet valves for letting water in and out of the lock by gravity flow. When a ship is to be raised, the water height in a lock is first brought to the same level as that in the lower portion of the canal. (A) *When the levels are equalized, the drain valve* (1), *the inlet valve* (2), *and the upper gate* (3) *are kept closed, and the lower gate* (4) *is opened to allow the ship to enter.* (B) *When the ship is in the lock, the lower gate is closed and the inlet valve is opened, so that water may enter through the conduit openings* (5), *filling the lock and raising the ship.* (C) *When the water levels of the lock and the upper canal portion are equal, the upper gate is opened and the ship proceeds. To lower a ship from an upper to a lower elevation, the process is reversed: the ship enters a lock filled to its level; the water is drained to the lower level; and the lower gate is opened, allowing the ship to proceed. Many canals have two locks side by side, which allows two ships to move in opposite directions at once.*

century the pound lock had been flanked by pairs of mitre, or double-leaf, gates pointing upstream. This marked the beginning of the modern era of canal construction.

The level of technological sophistication involved in canal construction and operation rose steadily. Bigger locks were built, and large differences in water level were overcome by constructing great lock staircases. Sometimes abrupt changes in level were overcome by the canal lift. In this procedure, canal barges were floated onto a metal box filled with water; the box was then raised or lowered vertically within a lift framework or lifted and lowered by the direct application of electrical power.

The most common types of navigable canals are those that handle barges—special flat-bottomed, shallow-draft vessels designed originally to move along the tortuous watercourses and through the narrow lock chambers of the early contoured canals. These first inland WATERWAYS usually adhered closely to the natural topography of the countryside through which they ran, winding around natural obstructions and making full use of navigable stretches of river. Drawn by horses walking along towpaths, the barges carried bulk cargo.

As the railroads began to compete effectively with canals in the mid-19th century, canal engineers built great aqueducts, tunnels, and embankments to provide the most direct route between any two points. Steam and then diesel power replaced the slow and uneconomical horse-drawn barges.

As inland canals were modernized, a new type of waterway—the ship, or sea, canal—was built. When completed, the ship canal linked many of the world's great ports to the open sea, thus enabling them to handle directly a wide variety of cargo for transportation by large oceangoing vessels. Such canals were built at New Orleans; Manchester, England; Amsterdam, Holland; and Newry, Ireland. Some of these canals are considered great engineering masterpieces of the Victorian era. They were constructed across strategic isthmuses, through lake-studded countryside, or around major obstacles separating large areas of navigable water: for example, the SUEZ CANAL, the PANAMA CANAL, the WELLAND SHIP CANAL in Canada, the Göta Canal in Sweden, and the Caledonian Canal in Scotland.

Greece's Corinth Canal (1893) is a short (6.3 km/4 mi) but spectacular canal linking the Aegean and Ionian seas through the Isthmus of Corinth. The Kiel Canal (1895–1914) runs 98 km (61 mi) across a narrow isthmus in northern Germany to connect the Baltic and North seas. The Kiel today carries a greater annual tonnage than the Suez and Panama canals combined (see SHIPPING).

Along the eastern coast of the United States, the Allegheny Mountains formed a barrier to the construction of canals leading inland from the early settlements. The first major canal to be constructed was the Erie Canal, which linked the important Hudson–Mohawk Valley and New York City with the Great Lakes and the Midwest. A continuous water transportation route was soon established from the Erie Canal to the St. Lawrence, and with the opening (1829) of the Welland Canal and the improvement of river navigation between Kingston and Montreal, it became possible to go from Montreal and New York to Lake Michigan and Chicago via canals.

Other important U.S. canals built during the 19th

At the formal opening of the Suez Canal on Nov. 17, 1869, a convoy of 68 vessels from various countries passed through the canal. This engraving from the period depicts some of the ships that made the journey from Port Said on the Mediterranean Sea to Port Suez on the Red Sea, about 170 km (106 mi) away.

century were the Susquehanna–Ohio Canal, which ran from Philadelphia to Pittsburgh around the southern end of the Allegheny Mountains; and the Illinois–Michigan Canal, which connected the two great water systems of the subcontinent, the Mississippi River and the Great Lakes.

In Europe, canal construction began in the 17th century, although it was not until the 1770s that the accelerating momentum of the Industrial Revolution created a demand for an efficient, economical system of inland waterways throughout many countries.

Canals and Inland Waterways

The canal-building era of the 19th century produced networks of inland waterways that, particularly in Europe, are still vital and growing today. In Western Europe the major waterways are based on the great rivers, linked by canals wherever possible to form an integrated network that crosses national boundaries. Most of the Western European system has been enlarged since World War II to carry craft of a minimum 1,225 metric tons (1,350 U.S. tons). The systems are administered by the governments of the countries through which the waterways pass and by multinational regulatory commissions for such major rivers as the Rhine and the Danube.

Central to the European waterways system are the networks that originate in Germany. The Rhine, with its tributaries, carries more traffic than any other river in Western Europe. The complex of rivers and canals that constitute the still-incomplete Rhine-Main-Danube waterway may connect the Rhine with the Black Sea by the early 1990s. France utilizes 8,600 km (5,350 mi) of waterway and is linked to the Rhine and the central European system via several large canals. The 4,850 km (3,000 mi) of inland waterway in the Netherlands are central to the economy of that small country. Over half the nation's freight is carried by barge over this system. Some Dutch canals are large enough to be navigated by oceangoing

Electric locomotives tow a ship into the Miraflores lock on the Panama Canal. The locomotives, which run on rails along each side of the ship, reduce the danger of collision.

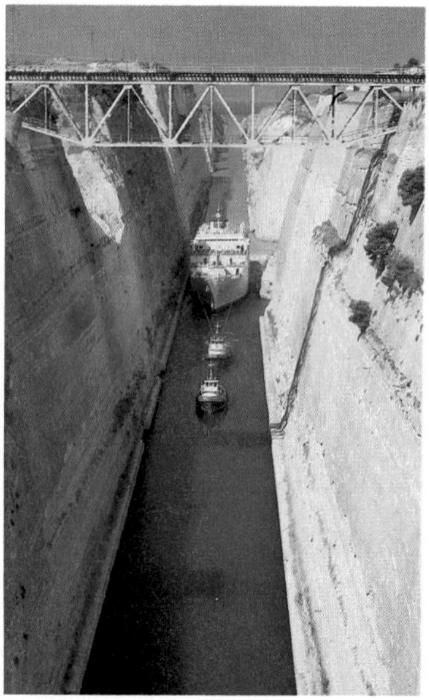

The Greek Corinth Canal through which this ship is being towed connects the Corinthian and Saronic gulfs. Although the canal is only 6.3 km (4 mi) long, it eliminates a 325-km (202-mi) journey around the Peloponnese peninsula from the Aegean Sea to Athens.

ships: the North Sea Canal, linking the port of Amsterdam with the North Sea, is the deepest and widest in the world (15 m/49 ft deep; 160 m/525 ft wide).

Canals in the USSR link the White Sea with the Baltic through the Volga River, and the Moscow and Don rivers with the Caspian, Azov, and Black seas.

In much of Asia, Africa, and Latin America, geographic and economic conditions have combined to prevent the exploitation of inland waterways beyond the use of those rivers which are naturally navigable. The exception is China, which since 1949 has almost doubled the length of its waterways system. In 1985 inland waterways in China totaled 109,075 km (68,000 mi). The Chang Jiang and its tributaries is central to the system. Portions of the ancient Grand Canal, China's primary north-south water route, have been rebuilt, and eventually the entire canal will be renovated.

The total inland waterways system in the United States equals about 41,000 km (25,000 mi). The INTRACOASTAL WATERWAY is a 4,800-km (3,000-mi) passage made up of natural waterways and canals. The vast Mississippi waterway system involves the river (navigable from Minneapolis to New Orleans) and its tributaries. The system connects with the Atlantic coast via the NEW YORK STATE BARGE CANAL and the Hudson River, and with the ST. LAWRENCE SEAWAY and the Great Lakes via the Illinois River and the canals and rivers that link the Illinois, through Chicago, to Lake Michigan.

Inland waterways in the western part of the United States do not connect with the major networks, and transport by waterway is not extensive. In recent years, however, two important waterways projects have been undertaken: the Sacramento Deepwater Ship Canal, connecting Sacramento's harbor with San Francisco Bay; and canal development on the Columbia and Snake rivers, allowing barge passage from the Pacific to Lewiston, Idaho.

Canaletto [kah-nah-let'-toh] Giovanni Antonio Canal, called Canaletto, b. Oct. 28, 1697, d. Apr. 19, 1768, was an Italian painter whose spectacular views of his native Venice set the standards by which topographical view painting was judged in the 18th century. Although his cityscapes are rendered with almost photographic accuracy, Canaletto was not an uncritical observer. His sensitivity to the placement and effect of each minute detail

Antonio Canaletto's architecturally precise and visually luminous vedutisti *(cityscapes) of Venice made him extremely popular with tourists visiting Italy during the 1700s. With works such as* Ascension Day at Venice, *characterized by correct perspective and faithfulness to detail, Canaletto ranks among the foremost landscape artists of his time. (The Crespi Collection, Milan.)*

enabled him to capture both the actual physiognomy of the city and its ephemeral atmosphere and movement. Canaletto remains one of the great recorders of Venetian life and a major practitioner of the new cityscape genre.

Canaletto's subject matter was not special events but urban space as shaped by architecture, light reflected off sun-washed squares and glistening water, and ordinary people going about their everyday business, as in his *Stonemason's Yard* (*c.*1730; National Gallery, London).

Pictures of the poorer districts of the city, however splendid as paintings, were not the images of Venice that tourists wanted to take home. Thus, because most of his patrons were foreign visitors, principally English, Canaletto began to concentrate on the city's greatest vistas, such as that portrayed in the realistic *Basin of San Marco* (*c.*1730; Museum of Fine Arts, Boston), and on colorful local customs, such as that depicted in *The Doge Visiting the Church of San Rocco* (*c.*1735; National Gallery, London). His style became increasingly brighter, lighter, and smoother. This change of emphasis from the atmospheric to the descriptive was not a happy one, and the pictures of English scenes Canaletto produced during the late 1740s and early '50s frequently appear dry and dull. Only the *capricci*, or imaginary views—which combine memories of Rome, actual Venetian monuments, and pure invention—retain the delicacy of touch evident in the artist's earlier portraits of Venice.

The common canary, native to the Canary, Azore, and Madeira islands, is among the most popular of all pet cage birds.

canary Long a popular cage bird, the domestic canary was developed from a wild ancestor, *Serinus canaria*, of the Canary Islands, Madeira, and the Azores. It belongs to the family Fringillidae, order Passeriformes, suborder Passeres. The wild bird is about 12 cm (5 in) long and mainly a streaky olive green. The brightly colored domestic varieties were developed by selective breeding to enhance chance variations in color as well as for unusual size or for the sweetness of the song.

Canaries do well in captivity if kept in cages with perches and with clean sand on the bottom. They are fed a mixture of small seeds augmented by fresh green plant material. Larger cages are required for breeding. Pairs will breed readily during early spring if provided with a nest container, nesting material, and food supplements. The female builds the nest and incubates the eggs, while the male feeds her. The chicks hatch after about 13 days, are fed by both parents, and leave the nest after about 3 weeks.

Canary Islands The Canary Islands are volcanic peaks rising above the Atlantic Ocean some 113 km (70 mi) from the coast of northwest Africa and about 1,100 km (680 mi) from Spain, to which they have belonged since 1479. The name *Canary* is derived from the name of a wild dog once found there. The name was later given to the small greenish-yellow bird still found there. Seven islands—Gran Canaria, Tenerife (the most populous), Gomera, Ferro, La Palma, Fuerteventura, and Lanzarote, together with a few, mostly uninhabited islets—make up the group. About 7,273 km^2 (2,808 mi^2) in area, the Canaries are mountainous; Tenerife rises in the Pico de Teide to 3,706 m (12,156 ft). The most recent volcanic eruption occurred in 1909.

The islands are situated at about 28° north latitude, in the belt of the northern trade winds. Their climate is tropical. Rainfall, generally less than 508 mm (20 in) a year, comes mainly in the winter, when snow falls at high elevations. Flora is varied, with only the aridity of some parts of the islands restricting growth. At lower altitudes the terrain is semidesert.

Most of the people are Spanish-speaking and of Spanish descent, but they distrust mainland Spain. Vineyards, which formerly covered much of the fertile volcanic soil, have yielded to banana plantations. Sugarcane, tomatoes, and early vegetables are also grown for export. The largest towns, SANTA CRUZ DE TENERIFE and Las Palmas de Gran Canaria, have lucrative tourist industries.

Known to the Romans as the "Fortunate Isles," the Canaries were later forgotten and then rediscovered by the Arabs. In 1927 the island group was divided into two provinces: Las Palmas (1988 est. pop., 753,116) in the east and Santa Cruz de Tenerife (1988 est. pop., 700,214) in the west.

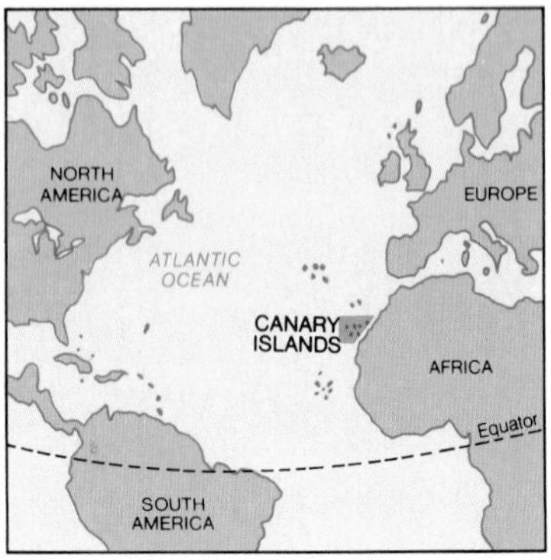

The locator map indicates the position of the Canary Islands, a Spanish archipelago off the western coast of Morocco. During the 16th century these islands became important as supply bases serving ships bound for Spanish colonies in the West Indies and South America.

canasta Canasta is a card game related to RUMMY. In its most popular form, it is a four-person game for two sets of partners played with two regular 52-card decks, plus four jokers. The dealer distributes 11 cards clockwise, one at a time and face down, to each player. For each card drawn thereafter, one from that player's hand must be placed in the discard pile.

The object of the game is for a partnership to meld, or lay down, groups of cards that are all alike in face value, such as 3 (or more) queens, 3 (or more) eights, and so on. These group melds are formed and added to by drawing from the deck or when picking up the discard pile.

All jokers and deuces are wild, jokers counting 50 points each, deuces 20 points each. The point value of each of the remaining cards is: ace, 20; eight through king, 10; four through seven and black three, 5. Red threes (treys) are bonus cards at scoring time, each worth 100 points to the side holding them; all four are worth 800 points. The first side to reach a total of 5,000 points or more wins the game.

Canberra [kan'-buh'-ruh] Canberra, the national capital of Australia, is located in the Australian Capital Territory (1988 est. pop., 273,300; area, 2,400 km^2/900 mi^2), an enclave in New South Wales. It is 250 km (155 mi) southwest of Sydney in southeast Australia. Canberra is small compared with most state capitals, but it is Australia's largest inland city and has a population of 267,600 (1987 est.). It has long had a high growth rate, having mushroomed from less than 25,000 in the early 1950s. Government is the leading employer; the city has little industry.

Canberra is a model of city planning and rigid zoning. Its focal point is the large artificial lake, Burley Griffin. Another distinguishing characteristic is Canberra's landscaping; the many trees and shrubs have been carefully selected to provide variety in color and texture. Other visual attractions are the official buildings—especially the embassies—the Australian War Memorial, the National Library, and the new Parliament House.

Construction of Canberra began in 1913, based on a design by Walter Burley GRIFFIN, a Chicago architect. Although Griffin was discharged in 1920, the city developed in basic accord with his plan. The first Parliament House opened in 1927; a new, largely subterranean Parliament House on Capital Hill opened for Australia's 1988 bicentennial.

cancan The cancan, or chahut, is a rowdy dance in fast 2/4 time, a flurry of nose-high kicks and daringly lifted petticoats, that burst into the public ballrooms of Paris around 1830 as a social dance for women. Starting in the 1840s, it became a showpiece in French revues, music halls, and tourist shows. Henri de Toulouse-Lautrec's paintings and Jacques Offenbach's effervescent melodies immortalize its Parisian sauciness.

Cancer Cancer, the Crab, is a constellation of the zodiac. Most prominent during spring in the Northern Hemisphere, it is shaped like an inverted Y. The constellation contains the famous open star cluster Praesepe, also known as M 44 and the Beehive. The TROPIC OF CANCER (lat. 23°30' N) was named for the constellation about 2,000 years ago because at that time the Sun was in the constellation during the summer solstice on June 22; because of PRECESSION OF THE EQUINOXES, the solstice now occurs in Gemini. In astrology, however, Cancer still governs the period from June 22 to July 22.

cancer In modern society cancer is the disease most feared by the majority of people throughout the world, supplanting the "white death," or tuberculosis, of the last century; the "black death," or bubonic plague, of the Middle Ages; and the leprosy of biblical times. Cancer has been known and described throughout history, although its greater prevalence today is undoubtedly due to the conquest by medical science of most infectious diseases and to the increased life span of humans. The study of cancer is known as the field of ONCOLOGY.

In the mid-1980s nearly 6 million new cancer cases and more than 4 million deaths from cancer were being reported worldwide each year. The most common fatal form was stomach cancer (prevalent in Asia), but lung cancer has risen rapidly, because of the spread of cigarette smoking in developing countries, to become the leading fatal cancer in the world today. Also on the increase is the third-greatest killer, breast cancer, particularly in China and Japan. Fourth on the list is colon or rectum cancer, which mainly strikes the elderly.

In the United States in the mid-1980s, more than one-fifth of all deaths were caused by cancer; only the cardiovascular diseases accounted for a higher percentage. In 1990 the American Cancer Society predicted that about 30 percent of Americans will eventually develop some form of the disease. In the United States skin cancer is the most prevalent cancer in both men and women, followed by prostate cancer in men and breast cancer in women. Lung cancer, however, causes the most deaths in both men and women. LEUKEMIA, or cancer of the blood, is the most common type seen in children. An increasing incidence of cancer has been clearly observable over the past few decades, due in part to improved cancer screening programs, to the increasing number of older persons in the population, and also to the large number of tobacco smokers.

The U.S. government and private organizations spent about $1.2 billion annually for cancer research in the early 1980s, and more than $20 billion annually on the care and treatment of cancer patients. Because of the marked improvement in the types of drugs available and in the methods by which drug therapy is given, the number of deaths among cancer patients under 30 years of age is decreasing, even though the number of deaths from cancer is increasing in the population as a whole.

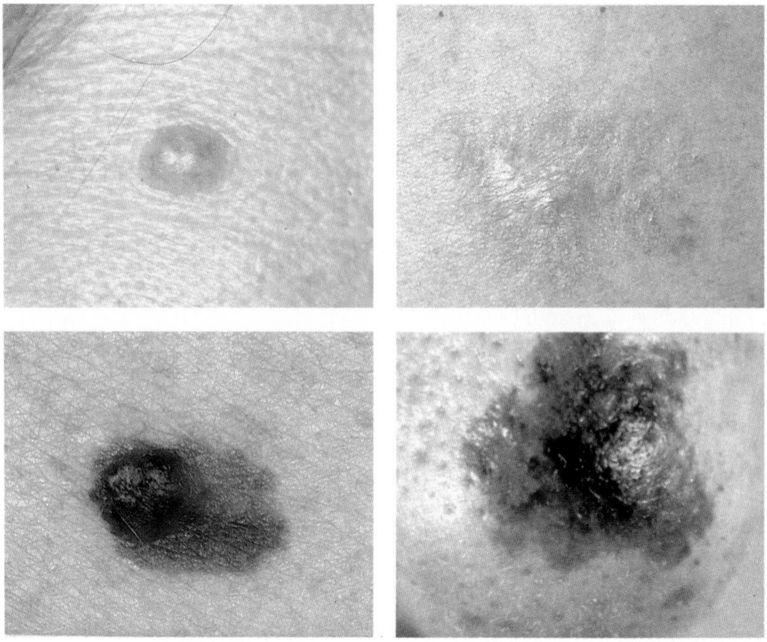

A common skin cancer that often results from exposure to the Sun's ultraviolet rays is known as squamous-cell carcinoma. It begins with the transformation of certain normal cells of the epithelial tissue into cancerous cells, which invade underlying tissue. Normal cells of skin tissue (left, magnified 400 ×) *are organized into well-defined epidermis* (dark area at top) *and dermis* (bottom) *layers. In comparison, the cancerous cells* (right) *lack this regional organization and divide more rapidly; such cells will penetrate adjacent tissue until noticeable lesions and eventual destruction of normal tissue results. Three classes of squamous-cell carcinoma, for which the incidence of metastasis varies, have recently been identified.*

Types

Cancer is the common term for aggressive and usually fatal forms of a larger class of diseases known as neoplasms. A neoplasm is described as being relatively autonomous because it does not fully obey the biological mechanisms that govern the growth and metabolism of individual cells and the overall cell interactions of the living organism. Some neoplasms grow more rapidly than the tissues from which they arise; others grow at a normal pace but because of other factors eventually become recognizable as abnormal growths. The changes seen in a neoplasm are heritable in that these characteristics are passed on from each cell to its progeny, or daughter cells.

Classification of neoplasms as either benign or malignant relates to their behavior. A benign neoplasm, for instance, is encapsulated; malignant neoplasms are not. Malignancies grow more rapidly than do benign forms and invade adjacent, normal tissue. Tissue of a benign tumor is structured similarly to the tissue from which it is derived; malignant tissue has an abnormal and unstructured appearance. Most malignant tumors, in fact, show abnormalities in chromosome structure—that is, the structure of the DNA molecules that constitute the genetic materials duplicated and passed on to later generations of cells (see GENETIC CODE). Most important, benign neoplasms do not metastasize—that is, begin to grow at sites other than the point of origin—whereas malignant tumors do. The term *cancer* always denotes a malignant neoplasm, whereas the term TUMOR indicates a readily defined mass of tissue distinguishable from normal living tissue.

Causes

A cancer-causing agent—chemical, biological, or physical—is termed a carcinogen. Substances are labeled carcinogens if, when administered to a population of previously untreated organisms, they cause a statistically significant increase in the incidence of neoplasms compared with the incidence in subjects that are left untreated.

Chemical Agents. Chemicals that cause cancer include complex hydrocarbons; aromatic amines; and certain metals, drugs, hormones, and naturally occurring chemicals in molds and plants. Many nitrosamines—simple organic oxides of nitrogen—are carcinogenic and may be produced within the human body. Hydrocarbons and nitrosamines are components of cigarette smoke and may be carcinogenic agents contributing to lung cancer in smokers. Certain aromatic amines, especially 2-naphthylamine, were originally used in the dye industry. After it became apparent that this chemical caused a high incidence of bladder cancer in workers (see DISEASES, OCCUPATIONAL), it was no longer used industrially.

Several drugs, including certain alkylating agents used to treat cancer, are also carcinogenic; although these chemicals are used to break DNA strands of cancer cells, thereby killing the cells, this same property causes the agent to induce cancer in normal cells. High levels of estrogens—a group of female hormones—administered to women after menopause result in an increased incidence of cancer of the uterus. To counteract this problem, today menopausal women are given estrogen in combination with progesterone. Aflatoxin B, a complex molecule produced by strains of the mold ASPERGILLUS, causes various cancers, particularly liver cancer. Certain salts containing arsenic are probably causally related to cancer of the skin and liver.

Biological Agents. Various forms of parasites have been associated with many animal and plant cancers, although

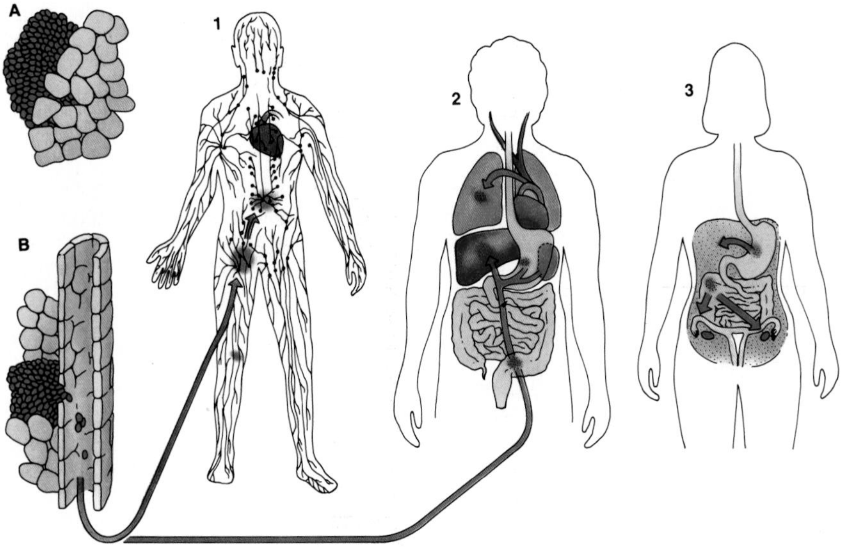

Cancer may spread by direct extension (A), *the direct invasion of adjacent tissue. Bone, soft connective tissue, and the walls of veins and lymphatic vessels are easily penetrated by cancer cells* (green), *but cartilage, artery walls, tendons, and ligaments resist invasion. Metastasis* (B) *may occur when one or more cancer cells separate from the main tumor, penetrate a vessel wall, and travel to another part of the body, resulting in secondary growths. The lymphatic system* (1) *is the most common route of metastasis, with tumors frequently developing at regional nodes. Cancers of the connective tissues and of the gastrointestinal and urogenital tracts may spread to other organs through veins* (2). *Cancer cells may also travel across body cavities* (3), *from the stomach or colon, for example, into the abdominal cavity and perhaps to other organs.*

the actual linking mechanisms remain unknown or unproved. For example, the blood flukes that cause SCHISTOSOMIASIS frequently seem, further, to cause bladder cancer, a cancer particularly prevalent in Egypt. The most clearly established biological agents, however, are the oncogenic (cancer-causing) viruses that commonly induce the formation of neoplasms in lower animals. A very few of these viruses are now strongly linked with some human cancers, and at least one has definitely been proven to cause a form of leukemia.

Among the viruses strongly linked with human cancers are a number of PAPILLOMA viruses and a HERPES virus, called the Epstein-Barr virus, that causes the disease known as infectious mononucleosis. This latter virus is also suspected of causing the malignancy called Burkitt's lymphoma, prevalent in Africa, and a cancer of the nose and throat that commonly occurs in China. Another human cancer related to a viral infection is a liver carcinoma that sometimes follows a HEPATITIS-B infection. Another link established between a human cancer and a virus is that between T-cell leukemia and a form of RETROVIRUS called HTLV-1; the cancer appears to be endemic in certain parts of Japan, the West Indies, and the U.S. Southeast.

Oncogenic viruses can be divided into DNA and RNA viruses, depending on their genome structure (see VIRUS). The DNA viruses mainly insert their genetic information directly into the cells of their hosts. The RNA viruses such as the HTLV-1 virus, on the other hand, require first that their genetic information be transcribed into DNA by an enzyme, called reverse transcriptase, supplied by the virus.

All forms of oncogenic viruses contain one or more genes that are essential for the transformation of the infected cell into a neoplastic cell. Such genes, termed oncogenes, are best characterized in the genomes of oncogenic RNA viruses. It is now apparent that many oncogenes have closely related counterparts in the normal cellular genome of the cells they infect. The viral form of the oncogene, however, has a different structure and appears to be activated and expressed abnormally by one mechanism or another, leading to neoplastic transformation of the cell. Some oncogenic viruses may activate the normal cellular counterparts of oncogenes, called c-oncogenes, by one of several mechanisms, thus causing the neoplastic transformation to occur. Possibly similar mechanisms may result from the action of chemicals or radiation, or both, resulting in the activation of c-oncogenes.

Physical Agents. Ultraviolet and high-energy radiation are also causative agents for human and animal cancers (see RADIATION INJURY). A correlation exists between exposure to the Sun's ultraviolet rays and the occurrence of skin cancer in humans. Cancers caused by radiation include leukemia as well as cancer of the thyroid, breast, stomach, uterus, and bone. Thus, such routine diagnostic tools as the X ray are used with care so that a person is not overexposed; physicians also caution people using sunlamps, which employ ultraviolet rays, against excessive exposure.

ASBESTOS is an inorganic crystal that irritates the lining of the lungs, inducing mesotheliomas in people and animals. A definite crystalline structure of this inorganic compound is required for its carcinogenic properties, and destruction of this crystalline form results in no tumor formation.

Inherited Cancer. While it is unclear why cancer develops in some individuals and not in others, heredity appears to play a role in certain cancers. For this reason, the family history—a record of diseases and the cause and age of death of family members—may be important in predicting and diagnosing cancer. Some hereditary cancers include familial polyposis of the colon, which comprises small benign tumors of the large intestine that invariably develop into colon cancer; retinoblastoma, which is a tumor of the retina occurring in children; and a type of breast cancer that arises before the age of 40. While these types of cancer exhibit a dominant mode of inheritance at the cellular level, they are recessive, requiring the alteration of both copies of the affected gene in order for a cell to become malignant. This means that the affected gene acts to suppress the neoplastic phenotype, since those cells with at least one normal copy of the critical gene do not express neoplastic properties. In contrast, activation of c-oncogenes acts in a truly dominant manner at the cellular level to cause the neoplastic phenotype.

Recessive disorders include xeroderma pigmentosum, a severely disfiguring skin disorder that results from abnormalities in the organism's ability to repair damage to DNA and is invariably associated with several different types of human cancer, including skin cancer. Ataxia telangiectasia is another recessive disorder, characterized by nervous-system disorders and abnormal dilation of small blood vessels; Hodgkin's disease, leukemia, and certain cancers of the brain are among the neoplasms associated with this disease. Other forms of cancers, such as chronic mylogenous leukemia, are associated with specific structural abnormalities in the chromosomes of the neoplastic cells. Certain chromosomal structural abnormalities characteristically seen in specific leukemias and other malignant neoplasms have been related to the activation of c-oncogenes in those neoplastic cells exhibiting such structural abnormalities.

Stages

Cancer may develop suddenly and result in rapid deterioration of the victim, or it may grow slowly for years. A person may be unaware of a developing cancer and receive treatment only in the late stages. The American Cancer Society has over the years promoted public awareness of the seven warning signals of cancer: (1) a change in bowel or bladder function; (2) a sore that does not heal; (3) unusual bleeding or discharge; (4) a thickening or lump in the breast or elsewhere; (5) indigestion or difficulty in swallowing; (6) an obvious change in a wart or a mole; and (7) a nagging cough or hoarseness. With one or more of these symptoms, a person is urged to see a physician immediately.

Initiation and Promotion. One of the general characteristics of the development of cancer is the extended period of time between the initial exposure to a carcinogen and the appearance of a neoplasm. This latency phenomenon, known as tumor induction time, occurs with virtually every type of carcinogen. Beginning in the late 1940s, a number of investigators defined the early stages in the development, or natural history, of cancer. In a classical experiment performed on the skin of mice, a single application of an agent induced no neoplasms, but when it was followed by several applications of a second agent, termed the *promoter*, neoplasms developed. Initiation by the first agent is irreversible and, once imprinted in a cell, may be followed by promotion months or even years later. Promoting agents themselves do not induce neoplasms, and unlike initiation, promotion is reversible: if the applications of the promoting agent are repeated at long, rather than short, intervals, no neoplasms result even though the total dose of the promoting agent in the two cases is the same. Further, promotion of neoplasms may be modulated by such factors as diet, hormones, environmental agents, and cell aging.

Some promoting agents exhibit tissue specificity, such as phenobarbital, which promotes only liver cancer, and saccharin, which appears to be specific for bladder neoplasia. In humans, alcoholic beverages, dietary fat, and many components in cigarette smoke are promoting agents.

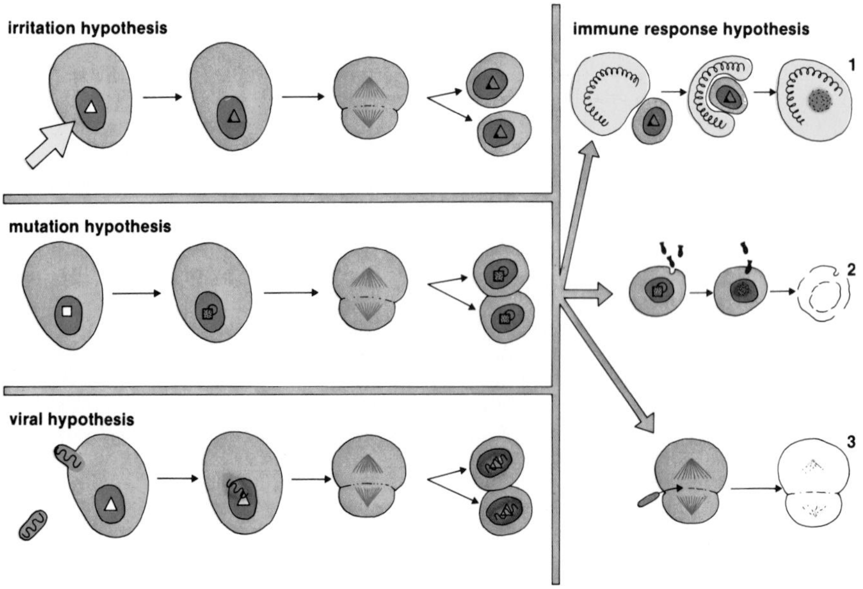

Although the mechanisms that trigger malignant cell growth are not completely understood, research has led to several explanations. According to the irritation hypothesis, a carcinogen irritates a cell, changes the genetic material (triangle), *and disturbs the control mechanism; the cell then divides and the new cells retain the altered genetic structure and continue to multiply. The mutation hypothesis suggests that the same process occurs when the genetic material* (square) *of a normel cell undergoes a mutation* (circle). *According to the viral hypothesis, a similar pattern occurs when a cancer-causing virus penetrates a cell and releases genetic material that alters the cell's genetic structure. If cancer develops, a healthy person's immune-response mechanisms, including white blood cells* (1), *antibodies* (2), *and antiviral proteins* (3), *may be capable of destroying its cells.*

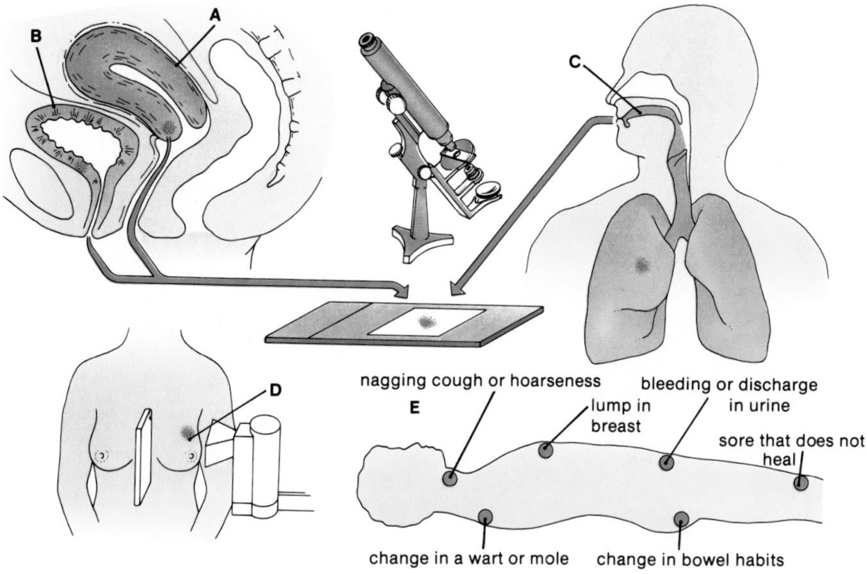

The likelihood of curing cancer is greatest when the disease is diagnosed at an early stage. Several screening methods are used including the Papanicolaou, or Pap, test, most commonly used to detect cervical cancer. Cells are scraped from the uterine cervix (A), *and a slide is prepared and examined microscopically for indications of cancer or precancerous states. This technique is also used to examine body secretions for cells shed from malignant tumors. Cells found in the urinary tract* (B) *may indicate cancer of the kidney, ureter, or bladder. Suspected lung cancer may be identified in early stages by examination of sputum samples* (C). *Mammography, an X-ray technique, is used to diagnose breast cancer* (D). *Early warning signals* (E) *can aid in the detection and successful treatment of cancer.*

Progression. Once a tumor has resulted from initiation and promotion, it may progress from a benign to a malignant form or from a low-grade malignancy to a rapidly growing, highly malignant cancer. Progression of a neoplasm occurs when a cell develops one or more significant abnormalities in one or more chromosomes and then grows and multiplies excessively. It is in the stage of progression that the activation of c-oncogenes may be most readily demonstrated. In addition, it is in this stage that the elimination or inactivation, or both, of tumor suppressor genes can be demonstrated either by the specific loss or alteration of chromosomes or segments of chromosomes, or through the study of genetic polymorphisms by recombinant-DNA technology.

A major component of tumor progression is metastasis, by which cells originating in the primary neoplasm can spread in a number of ways—through the bloodstream or lymphatic system, by direct implantation, or by surgical intervention—thereby establishing secondary growths. These metastatic growths, virtually without exception, exhibit chromosomal abnormalities and usually lead to the death of the host. Although millions of cells metastasize from a primary neoplasm, only a few—probably those with certain as yet undeciphered genetic capabilities—establish metastatic lesions in various sites of the body.

Some neoplasms may "pause" and remain latent for years before continuing their progression to malignancy. Other neoplasms, even after they are well into the stage of progression and exhibit metastases, may stop growing, differentiate, and remain quiescent for the remaining life span of the host. An example of a neoplasm that may do this in humans is the neuroblastoma of the adrenal gland, a tumor that commonly arises during childhood.

Prevention

The prevention of cancer, as of any disease, depends on the knowledge available about its causes and natural history. The majority of human cancers, perhaps 80 or even 90 percent, are related to the environment, and thus identification and elimination or control of these environmental factors would seem to be the most logical approach to cancer prevention.

Two widely used methods are employed for discovering cancer-causing agents. The Ames test, which rapidly measures the ability of a test agent to cause mutations in bacteria, is more than 90 percent effective and is widely used to identify potential carcinogens, which then may be tested in animals. The identification of carcinogenic chemicals by animal testing is tedious and expensive, but it is the only way to be certain that a particular agent is a carcinogen.

The prevention of human cancers associated with viral infections—especially those cancers associated with the Epstein-Barr and hepatitis-B viruses—by means of vaccination is theoretically possible but has not yet been developed on any significant scale. Sunlight is likely to be the greatest single cause of skin cancer, but because of the high rate of cure of this type of cancer, serious preventive efforts have been made only relatively recently. Such efforts have been directed particularly toward treating malignant melanoma, a rare form of sunlight-induced skin cancer that is difficult to cure. Human cancer related to exposure to X rays, gamma rays, and other high-energy radiation is much less common, largely as a result of federal controls.

Cancer-causing environmental factors are probably related most closely to the promotion stage of the natural history of cancer. Breast cancer in women, for instance, is clearly related to dietary fat intake, and lung cancer is caused by continued, prolonged exposure to cigarette smoke. Although cigarette smoke contains many initiating agents, the cessation of smoking results in a negligible risk of lung cancer after a year or so. The incidence of the disease is directly related to the continued exposure to cigarette smoke, because of the continued action of its promoting agents. Cancer prevention can thus come about by such measures as the cessation of cigarette smoking and the reduction of dietary fat and calories.

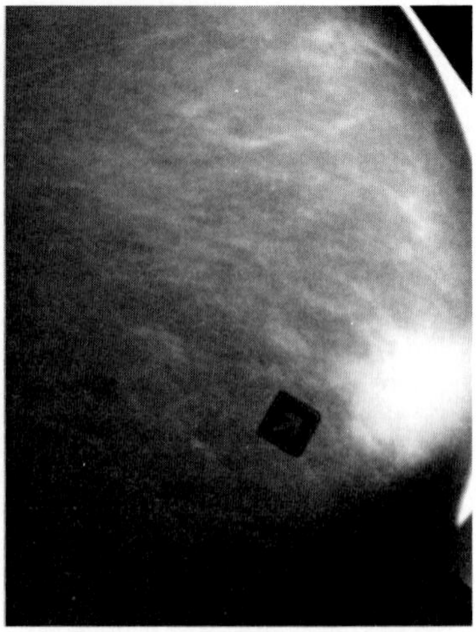

One woman in 10 will eventually develop breast cancer. Although there is no cure or way to prevent breast cancer, a mammogram, a specialized X ray of the breast, can pick up tiny, highly curable cancers that cannot be detected by touch (right). The cure rate for the earliest cancers detectable by mammogram exceeds 90 percent.

Diagnosis and Treatment

If treatment of cancer is to be successful, in most cases diagnosis must be made at an early stage in the natural history of the disease, preferably before progression of the neoplasm to metastatic growth. Although no known single test exists that can uniformly detect all early human cancers, a number of methods for early detection have been developed. Paramount among these is diagnostic cytology, especially the PAP TEST, developed for determining cancer of the uterine cervix.

Early diagnosis of bladder, breast, lung, stomach, and esophageal cancer by various cytological procedures is also possible. Cancer "markers"—biochemical factors easily determined by laboratory methods from samples of serum, urine, or other body material—have also been used. Some enzyme activities, such as acid phosphatase in prostate cancer, have also permitted early diagnosis. Radiographic screening methods (see RADIOLOGY) have included the chest X RAY in the past and, more recently, MAMMOGRAPHY as a screen for early breast cancer in women. Tests for blood in the stool are rapidly becoming accepted for screening for early colon cancer.

Surgery and Radiation. In all screening techniques a positive result must be confirmed by accepted diagnostic criteria, the most commonly used being the microscopic recognition of cancer by the pathologist. To obtain a specimen for diagnosis, surgical intervention is usually required. The removal of a suspected neoplasm or a portion of it for diagnostic purposes is termed a biopsy. If a biopsy is positive for malignancy, definitive therapy can be instituted immediately.

Surgical removal of cancer is the oldest and most classical method of treatment. Curative surgery is performed on a primary neoplastic lesion, either benign or malignant, when no evidence of metastases is present. If metastatic lesions are present, surgery may be performed to remove the primary tumor or even some metastatic tumors in order to reduce the total amount of cancerous tissue in the body. This type of surgery is preparative to other types of therapy or is performed to alleviate such specific abnormalities as blockage of blood circulation, obstruction of the bowel, or severe pain from invasion of nerve trunks.

The success of RADIATION THERAPY, such as using gamma rays emitted by cobalt-60 or using X rays, depends on the source of the radiation as well as on the susceptibility of the neoplasm to killing by radiation. Malignant lymphomas, leukemias, and most carcinomas are relatively sensitive to radiation, at least during the first such treatments. Sarcomas are classically more resistant to radiation therapy. A major problem with radiation therapy is delivering the radiation in the most efficient manner, with minimal damage to healthy tissue.

Chemotherapy. Once metastasis of most malignant neoplasms has occurred, surgical and, for the most part, radiation therapy is not curative. Although complete cure is uncommon for many of these neoplasms, chemotherapy, or treatment by chemical agents, has been instrumental in increasing the useful lifetime of many patients. A dozen or more advanced cancers that respond to drugs include acute lymphocytic leukemia in children; HODGKIN'S DISEASE, a form of malignant lymphoma; Burkitt's lymphoma; Ewing's sarcoma of bone; and Wilm's tumor of the kidney.

Compounds that have been effective in the chemotherapy of human cancers include certain hormones; antibiotics produced by a variety of microorganisms; plant alkaloids, including vinblastine and vincristine; alkylating agents—chemicals that react directly with DNA; and antimetabolites, which resemble normal metabolites (metabolic compounds) in structure and compete with them for some metabolic function, thus preventing further utilization of normal metabolic pathways.

Different drugs act by various mechanisms and affect cells in different ways at different times; furthermore, some of these agents act synergistically, producing even better effects when used in combination. For this reason, modern treatment of cancer by chemotherapy, for the most part, employs multiple drug therapies simultaneously. An added advantage is the relatively slow rate at which a tumor becomes resistant to combination drug therapy; such resistance commonly occurs when single drugs are used to treat a specific cancer.

Immunotherapy. While drug therapy seeks to kill all the cancer cells in the host by a direct toxic action on the cancer cell, stimulation of the host's immune defenses, treatment with antibodies specific for the neoplasm, and direct stimulation of lymphocytes that are effective in destroying cancer cells have been used as immunotherapy for cancers in humans and animals. Although as yet this type of treatment has been successful only in selected cases, the increasing availability of specifically "engineered" antibodies and monoclonal antibodies, and the use of growth factors (lymphokines) to stimulate the activity and replication of tumor-specific killer lymphocytes, offer promise for the future.

Recent Trends. Recently, therapies combining less radical forms of surgery with radiation, chemotherapy, or "preventive" therapy, or all three, have been employed. Such therapy has been especially useful in the treatment of breast cancer where the traditional radical MASTECTOMY involving removal of the breast, lymph nodes, and parts of the arm and chest muscles is becoming less common. It is being replaced by relatively simple surgery involving removal of only the lump itself or the breast, followed by chemotherapy or the use of preventive drugs. An example of the latter is tamoxifen, an antiestrogen that prevents the growth of breast cancer cells with little or no toxicity to the host and remaining normal cells.

Rehabilitation. The success of cancer treatment is usually measured by the number of surviving patients. Equally important, but more difficult to analyze, is the quality of life of such patients. Rehabilitation of the cancer patient after definitive therapy is critical for the patient's complete care. Restoration of function that had been altered by surgical, radiation, or drug treatment is most important wherever possible. When a permanent deformity or dysfunction results from therapy, rehabilitation must play a supportive role in returning the patient to self-supporting status. Finally, for those patients whose therapy has not been curative, palliative rehabilitation is important in order for the patient to maintain some degree of independence in reasonable comfort.

Remission. For most patients, rehabilitation is a continuous process after therapy. Most cancers are considered cured if the patient exhibits no recurrence within 5 years. Some tumors require 10 years or more without further clinical signs before a cure is considered definitive. Although many patients, especially those suffering from leukemia, may show a remission of all symptoms and signs of the disease following therapy, such remission may not be permanent even though it may last for several years. A relapse after remission is usually more difficult to treat than the initial occurrence.

Present and Future Research

Knowledge of the causes and control of cancer has increased dramatically in recent years. Also, because the means to identify most of the carcinogenic agents in the environment are now available, a major program of cancer prevention is within reach. Vaccination against the few known viruses causing human cancer is realistically possible.

Therapy in the future may be directed toward the chemical induction of differentiation of cancer cells into stable, nondividing cell populations. Evidence from animal experiments that some malignant cells can develop into perfectly normal cells when placed in the early embryo suggests that the neoplastic transformation is not always irreversible.

Patient Psychology

Numerous psychological reactions and problems affect the cancer patient. The delay in seeking medical help for a health problem that the patient fears might be cancer is a tragic example, because in many instances delay may mean the difference between effecting a cure or not. In the 1980s the cure rate was one in three cases, and the potential cure rate is one in two cases.

Patients with cancer have various psychological reactions related to their sociocultural backgrounds, the site of the tumor, their knowledge of and experience with cancer, and their personal evaluation of the clinical situation and the medical care they receive. The psychological problems become more serious with recurrent tumors because of greater fear of the outcome or doubt on the part of the patient as to the physician's expertise; the patient's relations with relatives, friends, and business associates are also factors. Cancer is a frightening but not a desperate disease. Education, reassurance, and love, as well as psychiatric therapy where indicated, are all necessary for the complete care of the cancer patient.

candela see UNITS, PHYSICAL

Candela, Félix [kahn-day'-lah] Outeriño Félix Candela, b. Madrid, Jan. 27, 1910, is a Mexican architect renowned for his dynamic use of vaulted space in reinforced concrete industrial buildings and churches. His major works include the Cosmic Rays Laboratory of the University of Mexico (1954) and the Church of the Miraculous Virgin (1954), both in Mexico City; Los Manantiales (1957; Xochimilco); the Chapel of Saint Vincent de Paul (1959–60; Coyoacán); and the Bacardi Rum Company (1963; Cuatitlán).

Candide [kan-deed'] *Candide* (1759), Voltaire's famous philosophical tale, is a biting satire of 18th-century life and thought. VOLTAIRE singles out religious fanaticism and the injustices of class distinction and war; the belief in providence and the reliance on the optimism that ensues bear the full weight of his attack. Pangloss, Candide's mentor and a disciple of the German philosopher Leibniz, accepts all forms of suffering and evil, be they earthquakes, shipwrecks, the Spanish Inquisition, or crime. His motto is "All is for the best in this best of all possible worlds." The young hero Candide, however, after countless perils and adventures, becomes disillusioned; he becomes wiser but also becomes a pessimist. His conclusion is that the safest reaction to an incoherent world is "cultivating his own garden."

candidiasis [kan-duh-dy'-uh-sis] Candidiasis, or moniliasis, is an infection by a yeastlike *Candida* fungus, known commonly as *C. albicans*. The people most often infected are those with natural defenses depressed by excessive use of antibiotics and steroids or by certain diseases or operative procedures. Symptoms depend on the organs or tissues involved, and vary from a redness of the skin to MENINGITIS, SEPTICEMIA, or endocarditis. The antibiotics nystatin and amphotericin B are used in the treatment of the disease. Oral candidiasis is called thrush.

candle A candle is a source of illumination made of a slow-burning solid material such as WAX or tallow (animal fat), usually cylindrical in shape and enclosing a fiber wick. Beeswax candles were used in Egypt and Crete as early as 3000 BC. In medieval Europe, both cheap tallow candles and more expensive wax candles were produced. An important advance in chandlering (candlemaking) was the discovery of other candle materials, such as STEARIN, spermaceti, paraffin wax, microcrystalline wax, and ceresin. A candle-molding machine invented in 1834 formed candles in rows of molds threaded with spools of wicking and ejected the finished candles by pistons.

These machine-made candles are hand-dipped to give them a color coat. Candles have been manufactured since ancient times by dipping wick material in wax or by filling molds with the hot liquid.

candlefish The candlefish, *Thaleichthys pacificus*, is an elongate, silvery marine fish in the smelt family, Osmeridae. Native to the Pacific northwest, from Alaska to northern California, candlefish reach lengths of about 25 cm (10 in) and live in deep coastal waters. Candlefish spawn at the lower depths of rivers. Food for humans and many animals, they are so oily that dried candlefish were once made into candles by running wicks through them.

candlenut Candlenut, *Aleurites moluccana*, is a small to large tree, up to 18 m (60 ft) high, in the family Euphorbiaceae. It is native to the Asiatic tropics and is grown chiefly for its nuts, which contain a large proportion (up to 70 percent) of an oil used in paints and varnishes. Species of *Aleurites* are grown in plantations in the Gulf states of the United States.

candy Candy is the generic term for confections with a boiled and crystallized sugar base. Indeed, the term candy is derived from the Persian word *qand,* meaning sugar. From its ancient origin in the Far East, the use of cane sugar gradually spread west, until by 1600 sugar confectionery was an established art in Europe. The products included molded hard candies, stick candies, dragees (nuts in a sugar shell), and sugar paste (a sugar dough confection).

Today more than 2,000 different kinds of candy are made in the United States, including all-sugar types such as hard candy, stick candy, and creams; types made with 95 percent sugar, such as pectin jellies, marshmallows, and nougats; and types made with less than 50 percent sugar, such as fudge, caramel, starch jellies, gums, and licorice. These candies can include every kind of nut, fruit, dairy, or egg product and are frequently chocolate-covered. Per capita candy consumption in the United States hovers around 8 kg (18 lb) annually.

Today's highly mechanized plants are equipped with continuous cookers, crystallizers, forming machines, chocolate enrobers, and cooling tunnels, but the basic candymaking process is simply the boiling of sugar.

A mixture of 80 parts sugar and 20 parts corn syrup is dissolved in a slight excess of water and boiled. When boiling, the composition of sugar and water is fixed, and the hot solution contains more sugar than it can hold at a lower temperature; on cooling, the excess sugar crystallizes. By choice of temperature, from 113.3° C (236° F) for fondant creams to over 148° C (300° F) for toffees, and the manner in which the sugar mixture is crystallized (or, in some products, kept from crystallizing by the addition of acid or invert sugars), the confectioner can make the whole spectrum of all-sugar candies.

To the basic sugar fondant recipe, the confectioner adds other ingredients: whipped egg whites to make marshmallows and nougat; fat and milk solids to make fudges, toffees, and caramels; cooked starches or gums for jellies; and chocolate to flavor and cover the delicate centers.

candytuft Candytuft, genus *Iberis*, is any of several small perennial and annual herbs, native to Europe, that belong to the mustard family, Cruciferae. The perennial species are typically evergreen and somewhat woody near the base. Many species have white flowers, but a number of varieties and hybrids have been developed with purple or crimson flowers. Candytufts are commonly used in rock gardens or as edging plants.

Canetti, Elias Elias Canetti, b. Ruse, Bulgaria, July 25, 1905, a novelist and playwright of Jewish descent who writes in German, was awarded the Nobel Prize for literature in 1981. He spent most of his early life in Vienna, where he received a doctorate in chemistry. Canetti wrote three plays during the 1930s and in 1960 published *Crowds and Power* (Eng. trans., 1962), a study of mass behavior and totalitarianism. He is best known for his symbolic novel *Auto da Fé*; (1935; Eng. trans., 1946), about a scholarly recluse destroyed by contact with the everyday world. Canetti, who has lived in England since 1939, has written three volumes of memoirs (1979, 1982, 1986).

Canis Major and Canis Minor [kay'-nis] Canis Major, the Larger Dog, and Canis Minor, the Smaller Dog, are winter constellations located near the celestial equator. Canis Major contains Sirius, the brightest star in the sky in terms of apparent magnitude—actually a binary star with a white dwarf component. Directly below Sirius is the open star cluster M41, in which a central red star is visible through binoculars. Canis Minor contains Procyon, the eighth brightest star, also accompanied by a white dwarf. In mythology, Canis Major and Canis Minor are the two dogs of ORION the Hunter, a nearby constellation containing the star Betelgeuse, with which Sirius and Procyon form an equilateral triangle.

Canisius, Saint Peter [kuh-nish'-uhs] Saint Peter Canisius, b. May 8, 1521, d. Dec. 21, 1597, was a Dutch Jesuit who played a leading part in the reestablishment of Roman Catholicism in South Germany after the Reformation. An indefatigable preacher and writer who compiled a number of catechisms, he was canonized and created a doctor of the church in 1925. Feast day: Dec. 21.

canker (plant) Canker is a plant disease in which lesions caused by a wide range of fungi and bacteria appear on the stem, branches, leaves, or fruits of the plant. The infected tissues die and the lesions may then crack and split open, exposing underlying tissue to further infection. The lesions also tend to spread, interfering with water transport in the plant; if they girdle a trunk or a stem, the parts of the plant above the affected area wither and die. Natural chemicals in a plant can resist some infecting agents, and woody plants may form wound tissues around a canker that halts its spread. Growers of crop plants can deal with some cankers by developing resistant varieties and by the use of fungicides, antibiotics, and treated soils. For many cankers, however, no known cures exist.

cannabis see MARIJUANA

Cannes [kan] Cannes (1982 pop., 72,259) a city in the Alpes-Maritime department of southern France, is a fashionable resort on the French Riviera. Tourism is the main industry. In the 12th century the monks of Lérin, protectors of the city since the 4th century, fortified Cannes against Muslim sea raiders. Napoleon landed near Cannes on his return from Elba in 1815. Cannes is known for palm-lined streets and subtropical vegetation, and its harbor is a favorite port of call for cruise ships and private yachts. The Cannes Film Festival, the most famous of international film festivals, has been held in Cannes each spring since 1946.

cannibalism Cannibalism, the eating of human flesh by humans, has been practiced in a wide variety of cultural settings, some dating from Paleolithic times. The term is derived from the Spanish word *caníbal*, referring to the Carib Indians of the West Indies, whom Christopher Columbus and others reported as eaters of human flesh.

Where cannibalism has been socially sanctioned, the reasons for its practice have ranged from a belief in its magico-ritual significance to its necessity as a means of survival. In the cannibalism traditionally practiced in Sierra Leone, Africa, by the leopard society, members of this secret society claimed they turned into leopards, after which they disemboweled their enemies and ate portions of the corpses. In certain religious festivals of the ancient Aztec people of Mesoamerica, the meat of sacrificial victims was distributed among the crowds congregated around the temples. In North America in the past, among the Kwakiutl Indians of western Canada, human flesh was eaten ritually by secret-society members. The Shoshoni Indians of the Great Basin and the Eskimo of the Far North ate human flesh in cases of near starvation, although both of these peoples feared and hated cannibals. In Fiji in the early 19th century, the introduction of firearms and European interference resulted in expanded war making, including cannibalism on a larger scale than was customary.

The Australian Aborigines traditionally did not kill others for the purpose of eating them, but burial cannibalism was widespread. Usually, this involved cooking and eating parts of a corpse to gain strength. In some areas a mother

The cut marks on this 6,000-year-old human bone—the collarbone of a young child—are seen by some experts as evidence of butchering for eating in the Neolithic Period. Others claim that the marks are the result of secondary burial practices.

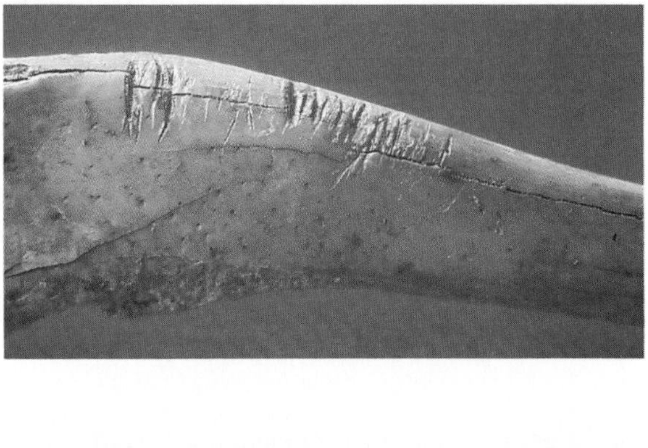

A sacrificial victim is secured by attendants as an Aztec priest cuts out his heart. The ritual may have included eating the remains. Some authorities, however, have questioned the accounts of cannibalism among the Aztecs.

would eat her stillborn child to reabsorb its spirit and later, it was believed, give birth to it again. Normally only certain relatives were permitted to eat a dead person's flesh. The few cases of ritual cannibalism among the Aborigines were mostly totemic: only persons of the same totem as the deceased could eat his or her flesh to make sure it returned to its rightful totemic source. Aboriginal doctors are supposed to eat a victim's caul, or kidney fat, for purposes related to the performance of MAGIC. Human flesh was also eaten in order to absorb some of the dead person's qualities or to identify publicly with the deceased and so ward off accusations of sorcery.

In Papua New Guinea, cannibalism, like HEAD-HUNTING, was formerly widespread, but was not necessarily linked to the latter. Although the Kuni Papuans ate only their enemies, the Kiwai Papuans ate only their own dead: they believed that to eat others would spoil their crops. Papuans living in the Purari Delta viewed human meat as a food source. In the eastern highlands, the ritual eating and garden burial of dead kin and lineage members were considered significant for fertility, but only enemy dead could be regarded as food. Some of these people exhumed the body of a dead relative in order to eat it when partially decomposed.

Interdistrict fighting in the eastern highlands of New Guinea involved aggressive and violent behavior toward victims. It was also often accompanied by dancing and singing. In this context cannibalism could be a formal affair, but the situation sometimes exploded into uncontrolled action, including the assault of a corpse and fights over the best portions of meat. By the early 1950s, through administration and mission pressures, open cannibalism in Papua New Guinea had almost entirely ceased.

Recently, some scholars have questioned the existence of cannibalistic societies altogether. They claim that an overwhelming majority of historical and anthropological accounts are based upon hearsay and false accusations. This argument is countered by 20th-century anthropologists who claim to have witnessed cannibalistic acts.

canning Canning is the technique of preserving food in airtight containers through the use of heat. This process of FOOD PRESERVATION is possible because the heat treatment inactivates enzymes and kills microorganisms that would cause food to spoil during storage. The airtight packaging protects the food from recontamination follow-

Beverage cans are manufactured from broad sheets of aluminum (1), from which small circular discs (2) are stamped. These are die stamped in cylindrical molds (3) to form vessels (4) approximately half the height and twice the thickness of the finished can. Further stamping (5, 6, 7) produces deeper, thinner cans while maintaining the original thick, sturdy base. When cans have attained their final shape, the insides are sprayed with a lacquer to prevent contamination of the drink (8), and the outsides are printed (9). Cans are filled with beverage (10), carbon dioxide is introduced into soft drinks (11), and aluminum lids with ring tops are stamped on and sealed (12).

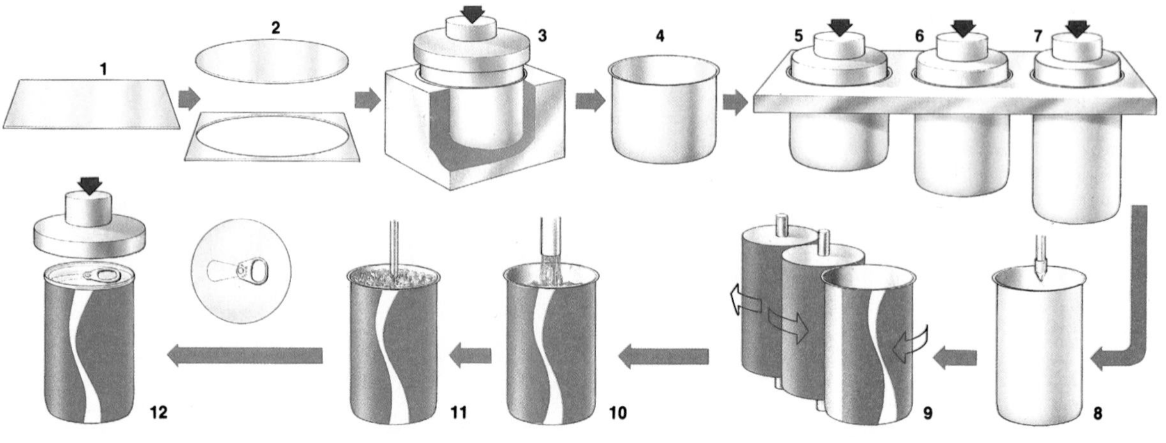

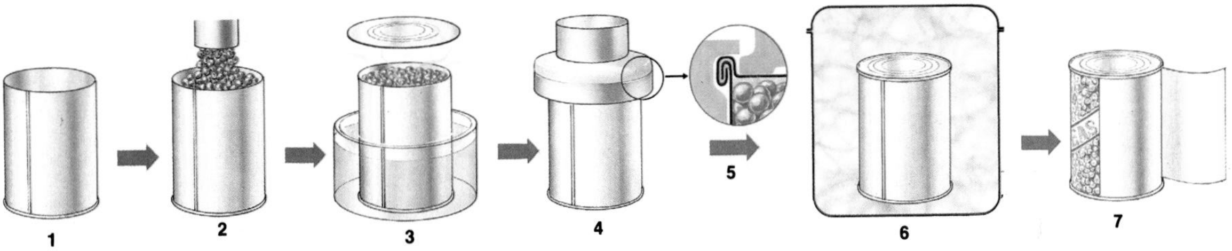

Industrial canning techniques use heat to kill the microorganisms that cause food spoilage. Sterile cans (1) *are filled with fresh food that has been cleaned, sorted, and blanched* (2), *and liquid is added. Cans are heated briefly in a hot water bath to drive out remaining air* (3) *before they are sealed* (4, 5). *The air-tight cans are then heated in a steam-pressure container until their contents are sterile* (6). *Food type determines the temperature and duration of the heat. Finally, inspected cans are labeled for marketing* (7).

ing sterilization, thus permitting storage at room temperature for many months without spoilage.

History. In 1795 a prize was offered by the French for the invention of a method of keeping food safe for military troops. Nicolas Appert, a chef in Paris, won the prize when he developed the canning process. At about the same time, the tin-coated metal can was patented in England.

Techniques. The canning process is basically the same for home or for industrial canning. High-quality fresh produce is washed, sorted, and prepared promptly for canning. After it has been peeled and seeds and other waste have been removed, the product is placed in the canning container (a glass jar or a metal can) in pieces of the desired size and shape. Water or syrup is sometimes added, leaving headspace in the container. The remaining air is driven out by heating the filled container for a few minutes. Then the container is closed in preparation for the heat processing.

The food must be heated to a high enough temperature and for a long enough time to ensure that microorganisms that are present have been killed. Many fruits are high in acid, and the microorganisms present in them will be killed if the jars or cans are processed in boiling water for periods of slightly less than half an hour, depending on the food. Meats, fish, poultry, and vegetables, however, are low in acid and must be heated to at least 115.5° C (240° F) for periods of half an hour or longer, again depending on the food. This temperature can be reached only by processing under pressure; commercially, a retort (a large, steam-pressured vessel) is used, and in the home a pressure canner must be used. Water-bath canning—processing for appropriate periods of time in closed jars covered with boiling water—although adequate for processing some fruits, is dangerous because spores of the organism *Clostridium botulinum* are not killed in vegetables, meat products, and certain fruits. Even when canned under pressure, home-canned meats and vegetables should be boiled actively for 20 minutes before they are even tasted, to prevent the possibility of BOTULISM, an often fatal type of food poisoning.

Canning, George George Canning, b. Apr. 11, 1770, d. Aug. 8, 1827, was a British liberal Tory statesman, who was twice foreign minister (1807–09, 1822–27) and briefly prime minister (1827).

Canning's arrogance, his middle-class connections, and his personal feud with Lord CASTLEREAGH (with whom he fought a duel in 1809) prevented him from holding office steadily in the long-lived Tory government. He was destined to be governor-general of India when Castlereagh's suicide (1822) gave him the foreign office. In defending the independence of Latin America he was perhaps the true author of the MONROE DOCTRINE. In 1827, when George IV was compelled to make Canning prime minister, the ultra-Tory half of the cabinet refused to serve under him and forced him to rely on Whig support. After his death the Canningite Tories became Whigs.

Cannizzaro, Stanislao [kah-nit-tsah'-roh, stah-nees-lah'-oh] The Italian scientist Stanislao Cannizzaro, b. July 13, 1826, d. May 10, 1910, laid the foundations of modern CHEMISTRY with his experimental ATOMIC WEIGHT determinations. He showed that the application of AVOGADRO'S LAW (1811) could yield a comprehensible system of atomic weights. At the First International Congress of Chemists at Karlsruhe in 1860, Cannizzaro presented his ideas with little effect. Fortunately, a paper of his was distributed to those in attendance, and Lothar Meyer included its ideas in his influential text of 1864, which developed theoretical chemistry on the basis of Cannizzaro's propositions.

cannon The essential ARTILLERY weapon, the cannon is a large gun composed of a barrel or hollow tube closed at one end by a breech, with a mechanism designed for firing projectiles. In modern usage, certain large guns, HOWITZERS and MORTARS, are classed as cannon, as distinguished from small firearms such as muskets, pistols, and rifles.

The cannon was the first European firearm and predated by many decades the development of small arms, which themselves were originally miniature cannon. The first crude cannon date from the 12th century, when European armies used gunpowder to hurl metal balls,

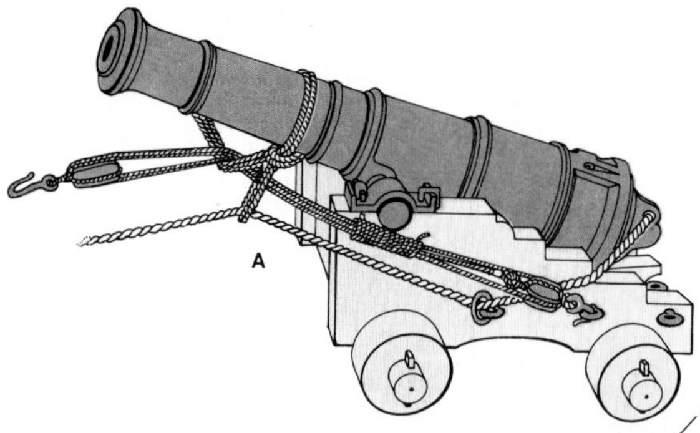

(Left) A cannon used in the Napoleonic Wars is illustrated in full view (A) and in cross section (B). To load it, a powder cartridge (1) was placed at the rear of the barrel. Wadding (2) held the shot (3), or projectile, in place. To ignite the charge, a torch was applied to the touchhole (4). (Below left) Chain shot (1), bar shot (2), and elongating bar shot (3) were used at sea against enemy ships. Grapeshot (4) and cannister shot (5) burst open upon firing, scattering fragments widely. (Below) Muzzle-loading cannon required a sponge (1) for dousing sparks in the bore, a rammer (2) for pushing the shot into place, and a worm (3) for withdrawing unfired charges. Cartridges were kept in a protective box (4). Once the cannon was loaded, a priming wire (5) was thrust through the touchhole, piercing the cartridge and exposing the powder.

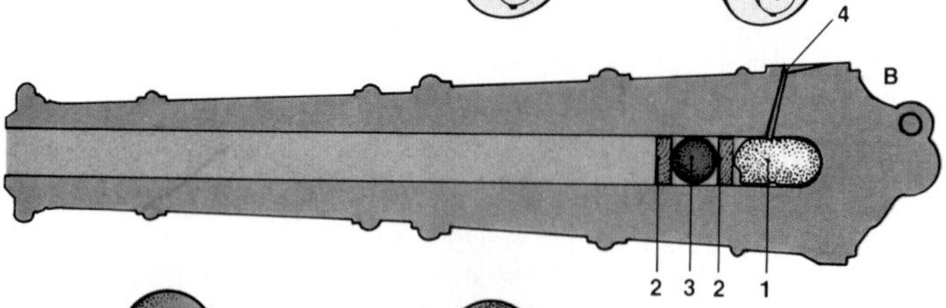

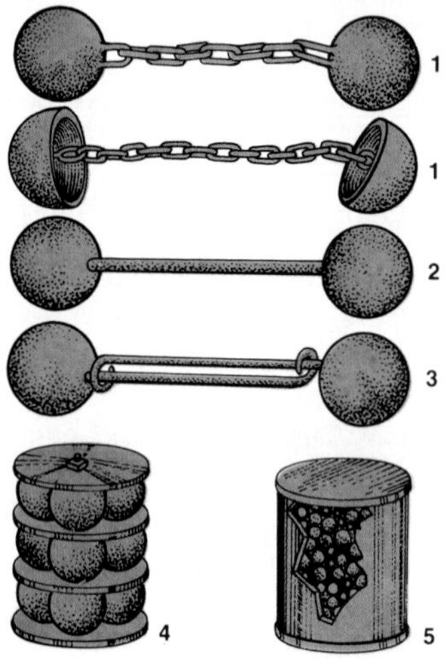

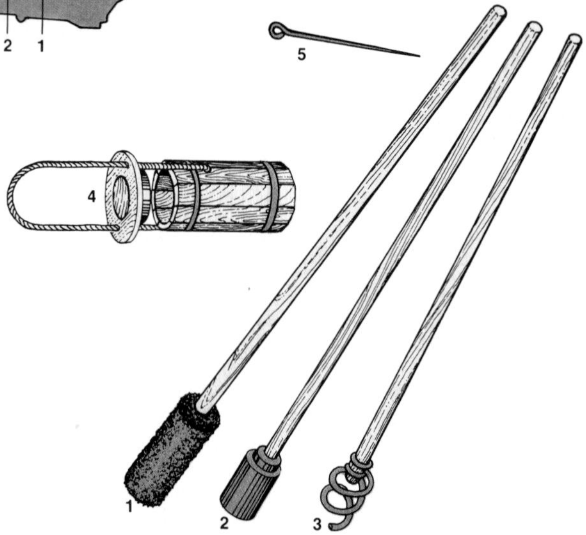

stones, or other projectiles from tubes made of wood or metal. The tubes were constructed of wooden or iron strips, or staves, bound together with iron hoops in much the same way a barrel was made—hence, the name "barrel" for the hollow cannon tube. All early cannon were fired from ground level with their muzzles, or open ends, elevated on a mound of earth.

Most cannon were loaded from the muzzle. Powder was poured into the barrel and rammed into a tight mass with a ramrod; a wad of cloth was pushed in to hold the powder, and the ball, or shot, was rammed in over the wad. The powder was ignited through an opening in the breech, and between rounds the barrel was swabbed with a sponge to remove leftover bits of burning wad.

During the centuries following their introduction, the varieties of cannon shapes and sizes multiplied. During the first third of the 17th century, the Swedish king Gustav II Adolf introduced mobile field cannon that fired lightweight 0.7-kg (1.5-lb) projectiles. The term *cannon* came to be applied to any gun that was fired from a carriage or fixed mount and had a bore larger than 2.5 cm (1 in). With increased mobility, cannon began to be used more effectively as field weapons; and the use of shot (clusters of small, iron balls fired at short range) proved deadly in battle against men and horses.

Although new devices for improving mobility were developed, cannon design remained fundamentally unchanged for almost three centuries. Breech-loading mechanisms, recoil-absorbing systems, and the rifled barrel (a grooved bore that imparted spin to the projectile, giving it a more accurate trajectory) were inventions of the 1800s. Explosive shells replaced cannonballs. By World

War I the varieties of cannon included howitzers and mortars; during World War II the use of tank-mounted cannon increased; and postwar developments have resulted in a self-propelled cannon and new varieties of special-use guns, such as the cannon designed to launch rockets.

See also: AMMUNITION; NAVAL VESSELS.

Cannon, Annie Jump Recognized by many as the dean of women astronomers, Annie Jump Cannon, b. Dover, Del., Dec. 11, 1863, d. Apr. 13, 1941, is best known for her work on stellar spectra. A graduate of Wellesley College, Cannon joined the staff at Harvard in 1896, and developed the Harvard classification system of spectra. Her compilation of *The Henry Draper Catalogue* (1924) and *The Henry Draper Extension* (1925–36) classified some 272,000 stars according to spectral type.

Cannon, Joseph Gurney Joseph G. "Uncle Joe" Cannon, b. New Garden, N.C., May 7, 1836, d. Nov. 12, 1926, was a U.S. politician whose term (1903–11) as Speaker of the House of Representatives was so imperious that it resulted in reform of the House rules. Cannon practiced law in Danville, Ill., before beginning his long career (1873–91, 1893–1913, 1915–23) in the House. A leader of the reactionary Republicans, Cannon used his powers as Speaker to appoint political allies to the leadership of key committees and thus blocked much reform legislation on issues such as child labor, tariffs, and railroad regulation. Finally, in March 1910 a coalition of Democrats and progressive Republicans led by George W. NORRIS put through reforms that severely cut back the power of the Speaker.

canoe A canoe is a small, open boat whose beam, or width, is narrow relative to its length. Most canoes are designed to be poled or paddled on inland waterways or lakes. Today, the term refers to several types of thin, elongated small craft, but originally it meant a type of Caribbean Indian log dugout, the *canaoa*, which the Spanish called the *canoa*.

In many parts of the world, early people used fire and crude tools to hollow out large tree trunks. In the case of the log dugout canoe, with only stone tools and glowing coals available, they were forced to use a long length of tree trunk for the boat hull. A portion of one side was chopped flat, coals were applied, and a hollow was carefully burned in the log. The heat of the coals drove the moist sap into the unburned portions of the log, thus swelling the wood and preventing it from shrinking and cracking.

Even when people wandered to areas where no large trees were available, they found that nature supplied other materials. They began to build boats with the same materials they used for portable shelters. Making a framework of wood or animal bones, they wrapped and fastened hides around it. If only a tiny boat was needed, an oval frame was covered with a single hide. Larger craft required several hides and, to assure a minimum of joints, the builder chose long, narrow frames. Canoelike craft such as the Eskimo kayak and umiak and the Celtic curragh were the result. Such canoes were more seaworthy than log dugouts because they flexed with waves instead of resisting them.

The North American Indians were probably the first to make all-wood canoes that were not simply log dugouts. These Indians switched from the use of hides to birch bark, a stiffer, but still flexible, covering. Moreover, birch bark was available in larger pieces, so the bark from a single tree could completely cover a long, narrow canoe frame. They built long, narrow-beam craft that, even with heavy loads aboard, were easily propelled.

European explorers and settlers opened up North America's wilderness with such canoes, and even today modern versions serve as workboats. But the canoe, like its close relative the decked kayak, has become mainly a sporting craft.

Canoes are among the oldest known forms of river transportation. The first canoes, developed in prehistoric times, were crude dugouts (A), *laboriously hewn from logs. Peoples of the South Pacific adapted the dugout for ocean travel by adding a sail for speed and by developing an outrigger* (B), *a buoyant framework extending beyond the canoe's railing, to prevent the craft from tipping over. To protect themselves from icy Arctic waters, the Eskimo of North America and Asia developed the kayak* (C) *for use in hunting. This one-person craft was covered with animal skins and sealed so tightly that it could be tipped over without taking on water. Because the North American Indians required a lighter craft* (D) *that could be portaged through forests, they built canoes with sturdy frames covered with birchbark.*

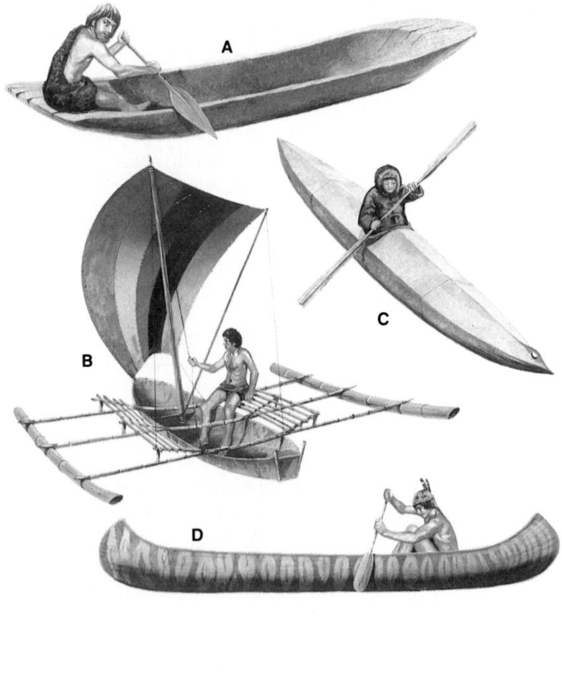

A team of canoeists negotiates a gate in the Canadian pairs competition of a white-water slalom race. Competitors cover a rapid river course, passing through a series of gates in a predetermined sequence while trying to avoid natural and artificial hazards.

canoeing and kayaking Canoeing and the related sport of kayaking have been pastimes for many centuries. Their roots go back to the North American Indian canoe and the Eskimo kayak. The origins of the competitive and organized sport, however, can be more formally traced to the founding (1866) of the Royal Canoe Club in England. Although the vessels used were developed in North America, much of the sport's growth took place in England and Europe. A German firm founded in 1907 developed some of the finest canoes and kayaks. The Germans also introduced the sport to the Olympic Games in 1936. In Great Britain and some other countries, the term *canoe* is often used to describe either a canoe or a kayak, although differences exist. A canoeist kneels and uses a single-blade paddle, whereas a kayakist sits and uses a double-blade paddle. A canoe is open at the top, whereas a kayak is enclosed.

International Competition

The International Canoe Federation has about 40 member nations from 6 continents, many of whom compete at the Olympic level. Competitive canoes and kayaks are classified by a *C* for Canadian canoe or by a *K* for kayak, followed by a number that designates the number of persons in the craft. Three basic events are held: slalom, in which racers travel a course of rough rivers having steep falls and treacherous turns around gates, as in skiing; wild water, in which they race straight forward in rough waters; and sprint or distance, in which the course is relatively calm. In international races, the number of competitors in a craft ranges from 1 to 7.

Recreational

Paddling a canoe, or more rarely a kayak, has long been a popular pastime. Newer versions of the sport include white-water canoeing and canoe sailing.

canon A canon, in vocal or instrumental music, is a contrapuntal form (see COUNTERPOINT) in which a melody first heard in one voice is strictly imitated by one or more additional voices. A phrase heard in the leading voice, called the *dux*, is thus soon heard again in the following voice or voices, called the *comes*, which may seem to "chase" the *dux*. Special forms include the "crab canon," in which the *comes* is the *dux* played backward, and the circle, or perpetual, canon, the end of which leads back to the beginning. Popular ROUNDS, such as "Row, row, row your boat," are vocal circle canons with imitation at the unison, that is, the *comes* begins on the same pitch as the *dux*. Canonic writing is found in numerous works of the medieval and Renaissance composers, the Viennese classical masters, and in the music of Béla Bartók, Arnold Schoenberg, and other 20th-century composers.

canon law Canon law is the body of legislation that regulates the discipline of the Roman Catholic, Orthodox, and Anglican churches, as enacted by their respective ecclesiastical authorities. From the 3d century, at first on a regional and then on a church-wide basis, assemblies of bishops approved canons, or norms, for Christian communities. Eventually, other ecclesiastical rulings were deemed on a par with conciliar enactments (see DECRETALS).

After the Second Council of NICAEA in 787, the last ecumenical council to be accepted in both East and West, the history of canon law diverges sharply. The recensions of ecclesiastical law made at the time of the patriarch PHOTIUS (*c.*880) proved to be the last for the Orthodox church and were transmitted to all the churches derived from Constantinople, most notably the Russian. In the West the classical period extends to 1348. Up to the Reformation the six collections eventually known as the *Corpus Iuris Canonici* (*Body of Canon Law*) constituted the universal church law for all of Western Christendom.

In 1917 the first *Code of Canon Law* was promulgated for the Latin rite of the Roman Catholic church. Four parts of a code for the Eastern Rite Catholic churches were adopted between 1949 and 1957. During the Second VATICAN COUNCIL (1962–65), a commission was set up to revise the 1917 code. After two decades of work it produced a revision that was approved by Pope John Paul II in 1983.

The new code differs from the old in two notable respects. First, authority has been somewhat decentralized so that in many instances the law is to be determined at the regional or local level. Second, for the first time the rights and obligations of all church members have been specified in law. The new code consists of 1,752 canons arranged in seven books: I, "General Norms" (203 canons), concerning the interpretation of law, custom, administrative acts, and ecclesiastical offices; II, "On the People of God" (543 canons), about the rights and obligations of the laity, the clergy, and religious communities; III, "On the Teaching Role of the Church" (87 canons), treating mission activity, preaching the word of God, Catholic educational institutions, and the communications media, particularly books; IV, "On the Sanctifying Role of the Church" (420 canons), respecting the seven sacraments, funerals, veneration of the saints, vows, church buildings, cemeteries, holy days, and fasting; V, "On Ecclesiastical Property" (57 canons), regulating its acquisition, administration, alienation, and accountability; VI, "On Ecclesiastical Sanctions" (89 canons), about violations of church law, excommunication, suspension, and interdict; VII, "On Judicial Procedures" (353 canons), about church courts, trials, matrimonial cases, recourse against administrative decrees, and the removal of pastors. A commission was organized in 1971 to prepare a codification for the Eastern Rite Catholic churches, and drafts for that code have been published.

In 1976 representatives from 14 Orthodox churches agreed on an agenda for the first Great Synod of Orthodoxy since the 8th century. Among the topics proposed for further study was the codification of the Holy Canons.

canonization Canonization is the final step of the process by which a deceased person's name is inscribed in the catalog of SAINTS in the Roman Catholic church. Originally the process took place locally and the bishop proclaimed someone a saint. Gradually it was reserved to the pope, and the process used since 1918 is described in detail in the *Code of Canon Law*.

An exhaustive investigation is made of the person's life to determine extraordinary holiness. The steps of investigation involve an initiation of the process by a competent person or group; the advancement of the investigation by the advocate of the cause, called the postulator; objections to the evidence by the promotor of the faith, popularly called the devil's advocate; the initial judgment of the validity of the process in terms of veracity and authenticity; the declaration and celebration of beatification, by which the person is called blessed; and celebration of canonization, by which the person is called saint.

Besides the investigation into the life of the person, which documents her or his holiness, canon law demands a confirmation of holiness in the form of MIRACLES. It is believed that the miracles constitute an irrefutable proof of God's approval of the person's life.

Canova, Antonio [kah-noh'-vah] Antonio Canova, b. Nov. 1, 1757, d. Oct. 13, 1822, was a prolific Italian sculptor and a leading exponent of NEOCLASSICISM in the second half of the 18th century. Canova, who achieved world renown in his lifetime, produced a polished and often sensual sculptural style based on close study and understanding of ancient Roman sculpture.

By 1774, Canova had his own studio in Venice and a reputation as a portraitist. His early works, such as *Daedalus and Icarus* (1778; Museo Correr, Venice), show a degree of naturalism that he later lost. He established himself in Rome in 1779, and one of his first major productions was *Theseus and the Minotaur* (1783; Victoria and Albert Museum, London). It is transitional between the early and mature styles, with the dead minotaur depicted naturalistically. Canova was also commissioned to carve monuments to two popes, Clement XIV (completed 1787; Santi Apostoli, Rome) and Clement XIII (completed 1792; Saint Peter's Basilica, Rome), that brought him a long series of tomb commissions.

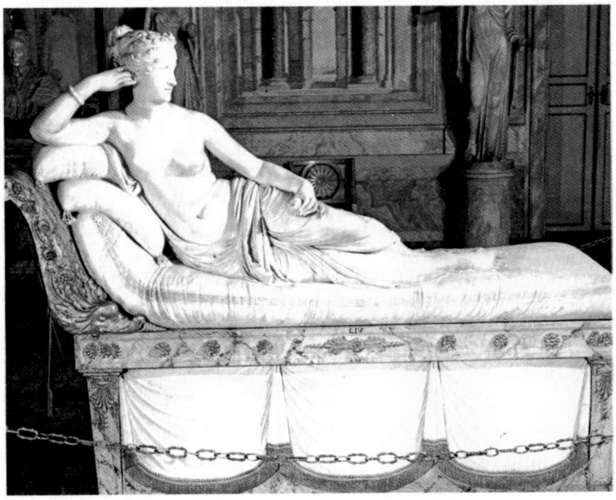

The sculptor Antonio Canova carved Pauline Borghese as Venus victrix, *a life-size marble statue of Napoleon's sister, in 1808. (Borghese Gallery, Rome.)*

Canova lived abstemiously and never married; works such as *Cupid and Psyche* (1787–93; Louvre, Paris) and *Perseus* (1801; 2d version, Metropolitan Museum of Art, New York City) are charged with the sexuality he repressed in life. One of his best-known works portrays Napoleon's sister, Pauline Borghese, as a seminude *Venus victrix* (1808; Borghese Gallery, Rome); the sensuous curve of the body establishes the main design.

cantata Vocal compositions with instrumental accompaniment, consisting of several movements based on related text segments, are called cantatas. Two types flourished between about 1600 and 1750. The secular, Italian solo cantata, originally a simple strophic piece with varied stanzas, by about 1650 had become two or three RECITATIVES and ARIAS in alternation, usually for soprano voice and continuo accompaniment (see FIGURED BASS). The German religious cantata, usually for soloists, chorus, and orchestra, was used as part of the principal Lutheran worship service. Johann Sebastian BACH and Georg Philipp TELEMANN were prolific in the genre, writing nearly 300 and 700 cantatas respectively. English and, later, American church composers adopted the cantata form, generally imitating the German type but substituting the organ for the orchestra.

Canterbury A historic city on the Stour River in Kent, southeastern England, Canterbury is the country's ecclesiastical capital, seat of the primate of the Church of England, and a major tourist attraction. The city's population is 34,404 (1987); that of the district is 127,700 (1986 est.).

Canterbury is dominated by its magnificent cathedral, scene of the murder of Saint Thomas BECKET in 1170. Becket's tomb there (destroyed by Henry VIII in 1538) was a great Christian shrine, attracting pilgrims from all over Europe. A fictional group of such pilgrims was portrayed in Geoffrey Chaucer's CANTERBURY TALES. The cathedral, built on the site of Saint Augustine's basilica, is the third on the site. The first was destroyed by fire in 1067; the second, a Norman building that was the scene of Becket's murder, was severely damaged by fire in 1174. The rebuilding of the choir under master mason WILLIAM OF SENS in Gothic style adapted to the Norman remains was completed in 1179. The remainder of the huge sanctuary was completed in a similar style in the next few years. The STAINED GLASS of the choir and sanctuary, installed in the early 13th century, is the finest in England.

Canterbury, inhabited since pre-Roman days, was the capital of Æthelbert, king of Kent. Æthelbert was converted to Christianity by AUGUSTINE OF CANTERBURY, who arrived from Rome in 597, founded an abbey, and became the first archbishop. In the 16th century Canterbury was a haven for French Huguenots. The city was severely bombed during World War II, but the cathedral escaped with minor damage.

Canterbury, archbishop of The archbishop of Canterbury is primate of all England with metropolitan jurisdiction over 29 dioceses of the Church of England (see ENGLAND, CHURCH OF). The Lambeth Conference of the bishops of the ANGLICAN COMMUNION meets every ten years at his invitation, and he is its presiding officer. He is also president of the Anglican Consultative Council. The archbishopric began in AD 597 when Saint AUGUSTINE OF CANTERBURY was sent to England by Pope Gregory I. The see has been occupied by a succession of outstanding men, including Saint ANSELM, Saint Thomas BECKET, Thomas CRANMER, William LAUD, and William TEMPLE. In 1991, George Leonard CAREY succeeded Robert RUNCIE to become the 103d archbishop in an unbroken succession. During the Middle Ages the archbishops exercised considerable power in affairs of state. In recent times their power has been largely restricted to church matters, although they continue to exercise such influence in national affairs as comes to them by custom. Appointment to the office is made by the crown.

Canterbury Tales, The *The Canterbury Tales*, a masterpiece of ENGLISH LITERATURE written by Geoffrey CHAUCER, is a collection, with frequent dramatic links, of 24 tales told to pass the time during a spring pilgrimage to the shrine of Saint Thomas Becket in Canterbury. The *General Prologue* introduces the pilgrims, 29 "sondry folk" gathered at the Tabard Inn in Southwark (outside London). Some are described by the narrator with subtle irony: the Prioress, Monk, and Friar, among others. The tales, some of them probably composed as early as the 1370s, are a virtual anthology of medieval literary genres and verse forms. The work concludes with a curious Retraction, in which Chaucer asks forgiveness for most of his literary output.

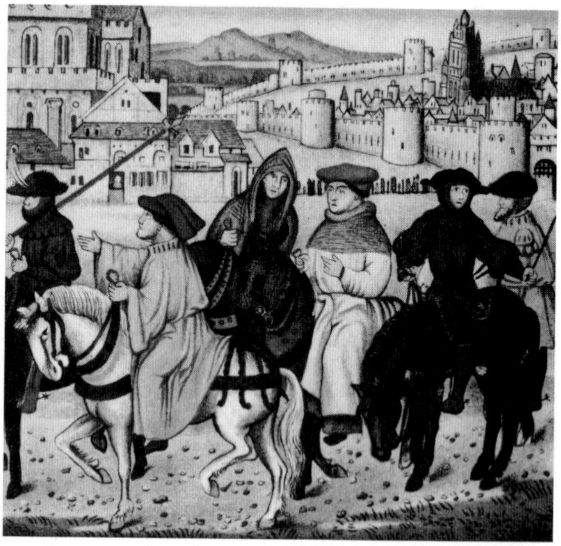

This illustration from a 15th-century manuscript edition of Chaucer's Canterbury Tales, *one of the most brilliant works of English literature, shows six of the pilgrims at the outset of their journey to Canterbury. (British Museum, London.)*

cantilever [kan'-ti-lee-vur] In architecture, a cantilever refers either to the section of a building that, without vertical supports, overhangs the part with a foundation (for example, a balcony that is attached to a high-rise apartment), or to the beam-and-weight arrangement that itself supports the projecting member, the beam acting as a fulcrum. In classically styled buildings, cantilevers are the bracketlike motifs of wood, stone, or metal that support eaves, cornices, or balconies. The use of cantilever construction became widespread after the invention of reinforced concrete in the 20th century.

Cantinflas [kahn-teen'-flahs] Cantinflas is the stage name of Mario-Moreno, b. Mexico City, Aug. 12, 1911, one of the most famous comic stars of the Latin American cinema. Humorously garbled speech is his trademark. Cantinflas made his feature film debut in *Ahi está el detalle!* (Here's the Point!, 1941). His portrayal of the valet Passepartout in *Around the World in Eighty Days* (1956) made him well known outside the Spanish-speaking world. Cantinflas helped organize the Mexican Cinema Production Workers Union in 1944.

Canton (China) see GUANGZHOU

Canton (Ohio) [kan'-tuhn] Canton is a city in Ohio and the seat of Stark County. Incorporated in 1822, it is located in the northeastern part of the state about 93 km (58 mi) south of Cleveland. It has a population of 84,161 (1990). Manufactures of steel, machinery, and other metal products, with coal mines, limestone quarries, and gas wells nearby, have helped make the city prosperous.

Canton is the site of the national Pro Football Hall of Fame and the monumental tomb of President William McKinley.

cantor A cantor is a singer who leads the liturgical music of a religious service. The office originated in Judaism but is also used by Anglicans, Lutherans, and Roman Catholics. Jewish practice gives the name *cantor* to the leading singer, who is entrusted with singing the prayers and psalms in the sacred service of the synagogue. In Lutheran practice, the name *cantor* is given to the head of a parochial school's music program, as it was to J. S. Bach in Leipzig. In Roman Catholic practice, the cantor was traditionally responsible for the musical life of a large church.

Cantor, Eddie Eddie Cantor was the stage name of Edward Israel Iskowitz, b. Jan. 31, 1892, d. Oct. 10, 1964, an American entertainer noted for his light songs and comedy routines. After appearing in vaudeville, he starred in the Ziegfeld Follies from 1917 to 1919 and in the musicals *Kid Boots* (1923; film, 1926) and *Whoopee* (1928). During the 1930s, Cantor appeared in films and hosted a popular radio show; in the early 1950s he appeared on television's "Colgate Comedy Hour."

Cantor, Georg Georg Ferdinand Ludwig Philipp Cantor, b. Mar. 3, 1845, d. Jan. 6, 1918, was a Russian-born German mathematician best known as the creator of SET THEORY and for his discovery of the transfinite numbers, which are related to the concept of INFINITY. He also advanced the study of trigonometric series, was the first to prove the nondenumerability of the real numbers, and made significant contributions to dimension theory. Cantor taught at the University of Halle beginning in 1869.

Cantos, The Ezra POUND's epic poem *The Cantos*, begun in 1915, was 800 pages long when laid aside about 1960. Published in ten volumes from 1925 to 1969, and collected in 1970, it is Pound's attempt to explain history, economics, and culture. The poet leaps from ancient Greece to 19th-century America to Renaissance Italy, interweaving occult meanings with private events. Because of Pound's wartime collaboration with the Italian Fascist regime, controversy ensued when the finest portion of the work, *The Pisan Cantos* (1948), was awarded the 1949 Bollingen Prize.

cantus firmus see COUNTERPOINT

Canute, King of England, Denmark, and Norway [kuh-noot' or kan'-yoot] Canute, b. *c.*995, d. Nov. 12, 1035, son of King SWEYN Forkbeard of Denmark, was king of England (1016–35), of Denmark (1019–35), and of Norway (1028–35), as well as lord of the Orkney and Shetland Islands and of Scotland. He became ruler of England as a result of military victory over ÆTHELRED II. After the death (1016) of Æthelred's son, Edmund Ironside, he won acceptance by the English nobility. He regarded himself as a successor to previous English kings and married Æthelred's widow, Emma.

Canute was the first VIKING chieftain welcomed as an equal to Christian kings by the church; indeed, he became a Christian and was a founder and patron of monasteries. On his death a succession dispute occurred between his sons, Harold Harefoot and Harthacanute. The latter was succeeded (1042) by Edward the Confessor, marking the restoration of the house of Wessex.

canvas Canvas is a closely woven, firm fabric, made of cotton, linen, hemp, or synthetic fibers. It is manufactured in a number of weights for a variety of uses: as a sailcloth, for awnings and outdoor furniture, as a tarpaulin when it is waterproofed, and as the ground for NEEDLEWORK when it is woven as an open mesh. Artists' canvas is treated to retain paint. Lightweight canvas, often used for clothing, is sometimes called duck.

Canyon de Chelly National Monument Canyon de Chelly National Monument, in northeastern Arizona within the Navajo Indian Reservaton, covers 339 km^2 (131 mi^2). The ANASAZI, ancestors of the modern Pueblo Indians, built villages in the canyon between 350 and 1300 (when they deserted it), inhabiting it longer than any other site. Among the many ruins, some with pictographs on the walls, are White House, Antelope House, and Mummy Cave. The Navajo Indians migrated to Canyon de Chelly about 1700, and the monument includes the sites of battles they fought against the Spanish (1805) and, later, the U.S. Cavalry under Kit CARSON (1864). Canyon de Chelly became a national monument in 1931.

Cao Xueqin (Ts'ao Hsüeh-Ch'in) Cao Xueqin, b. c.1717, d. Feb. 12, 1763, is best remembered as the author of *Honglu meng* (1791; trans. as *The Dream of the Red Chamber*, 1929), one of the greatest Chinese novels. Born into a wealthy and powerful family, Cao died in poverty, the wrongdoings of a relative having led to the family's downfall in 1728. His novel—said to be inspired by the vicissitudes of his own life—first appeared in 80 chapters, but in later editions 40 more were added by the editor Gao O, who claimed to have found them among the author's papers.

Cap-Haïtien [kahp-ah-ees-yan'] Cap-Haïtien, (1987 est. pop., 72,161) a seaport on the Atlantic northern coast of Haiti, is Haiti's second largest city after Port-au-Prince. As the French colonial capital, the city was called Cap Français (founded in 1670) and was the site of the beginning of the 1791 slave revolt that resulted in independence for Haiti. Just to the south of the city are the ruins of Henri CHRISTOPHE's baroque Sans-Souci palace (built 1813) and his citadel, a huge mountaintop fortress. Burned in 1802, Cap-Haïtien was rebuilt, only to be partially destroyed by an earthquake in 1842 and a hurricane in 1928.

Capa, Robert Robert Capa, was the pseudonym of André Friedman, b. Oct. 22, 1913, a Hungarian-American photojournalist who first gained recognition in the 1936 Spanish Civil War with his "Moment of Death (of a Loyalist Soldier)." During World War II he photographed the fighting in Africa, Sicily, and Italy for *Life* magazine and landed at Normandy with the D-Day troops. He became cofounder of Magnum Photos, an international cooperative photographic agency, in 1947. While covering French troops in the Indochina War, he was killed (May 25, 1954) by a landmine in Vietnam.

Capablanca, José Raúl José Raúl Capablanca, b. Nov. 19, 1888, d. Mar. 8, 1942, was a Cuban-born chess genius. In 1911 he won his first international tournament. From 1916 to 1924, Capablanca did not lose a game. In 1921 he defeated Emanuel Lasker, who had been world champion since 1894. Capablanca was world champion on and off until 1927, when he lost the title to Alexander Alekhine. In 1931 he defeated Max Euwe, who had succeeded Alekhine as world champion.

capacitance see CAPACITOR

capacitor A capacitor is an electrical component that consists of two conductors separated by an insulator; it has the property of electrical capacitance, or capacity, and opposes any change in the voltage across its terminals. Formerly known as a condenser, the capacitor is the only device other than a BATTERY that can store electric charge (see CHARGE, ELECTRIC) or electrical energy, and it is this stored energy that enables the capacitor to resist changes of voltage.

The earliest form of capacitor was the LEYDEN JAR. The simplest capacitor consists of two metal plates separated by an insulator, or DIELECTRIC. When equal but opposite charges, q and $-q$, are deposited on the two plates (for example, by connecting the two conductors to opposite poles of a battery), a voltage, or potential difference, V, is set up between the two plates. The capacitance C is defined as the ratio of the charge on one of the plates to the voltage between them: $C = q/V$. The value of C depends only on the geometry of the system and on the nature of the dielectric and is independent of the charge q. If the charge is given in coulombs and the voltage in volts, the capacitance will be in farads. Fractions used include microfarads (μF) and picofarads (pF). The characteristics and applications of capacitors also depend on the dielectric used.

Capacitors can be described in terms of their capacitance, their maximum DC (direct current) working voltage (DCWV), the type of dielectric, and whether the value of the capacitance is fixed or variable.

Because the dielectric is an insulator, a capacitor will not permit a direct current to flow through it, but its continuous charging and discharging action will allow ALTERNATING CURRENT (AC) to pass. Thus, one of the important applications of capacitors is to block DC, but pass, or couple, AC from one amplifier to another; such capacitors are known as blocking, or coupling, capacitors. Capacitors used for this purpose can have dielectrics of paper, ceramic, mica, or polystyrene; they are known, respectively, as paper, ceramic, mica, or plastic-film capacitors.

Many applications in electronics require electrolytic capacitors, which are relatively small in size but have very high values of capacitance because of the very thin dielectric used to separate the plates. A disadvantage of an electrolytic capacitor is its high leakage current (the current that flows across the plates). Electrolytic capacitors are used as electronic filters (see FILTER, ELECTRONIC) in power supplies that rectify AC (convert AC to DC). The rectified output still contains some AC, so a large capacitor is often connected across the output. Energy stored by the capacitor when the voltage is increasing is released to the load when the voltage is decreasing, which helps to smooth out the flow of energy. Electrolytic capacitors are also used in electronic photographic flash units.

Capacitors are also used in conventional ignition systems to reduce arcing across the points. Variable capacitors consist of two interleaved sets of metal plates, one set fixed and one movable; the air surrounding the plates serves as the dielectric. Such capacitors are used in radio tuners.

Cape Breton Island Cape Breton Island is the northeastern segment of Nova Scotia, Canada. The Strait of Canso, 3 km (2 mi) wide, separates it from the mainland and is spanned by a road and rail causeway. The Atlantic Ocean lies to the east, and the Gulf of St. Lawrence to the west. The island is about 177 km (110 mi) long from north to south; its greatest width is 129 km (80 mi). The area is about 10,282 km^2 (3,970 mi^2). The coastline is jagged with many inlets. BRAS D'OR LAKE, a large body of tidal saltwater in the center of the island, is a recreational area. The island's terrain is hilly, with the highest point being 532 m (1,747 ft).

Fishing is rich along the coast of Cape Breton Island. Coal and iron are mined in the east, and steel is manufactured in SYDNEY and Glace Bay. Farming is concentrated in the west. Cape Breton Highlands National Park is in the north, and tourism is an important industry. Bretons from France fished off the coast in the 16th century, and the island belonged to France until 1763, when it passed to Great Britain after the French and Indian War. The island was a separate province from 1784 to 1820.

Cape Canaveral A promontory on a barrier island off the Atlantic coast in east central Florida, Cape Canaveral is famous as the site of the KENNEDY SPACE CENTER. Formerly consisting of uninhabited sand moors, it has since 1947 been the main launching site for all American space exploration. Today the center is a vast complex extending across the Banana River onto Merritt Island to the west and 24 km (15 mi) south to Patrick Air Force Base. The first rocket was launched in 1950, the first satellite in 1958, the first manned spaceflight in 1961, and the first manned lunar exploration in 1969. The name was changed to Cape Kennedy in 1963 after the assassination of John F. Kennedy, but the original Spanish name of Canaveral was applied to it again in 1973.

Cape Cod Cape Cod is a narrow, 105-km-long (65-mi) sandy peninsula extending east and north like a bent arm into the Atlantic Ocean from southeastern Massachusetts. It is bounded on the west by Cape Cod Bay, on the south by Nantucket Sound, and on the east by the Atlantic Ocean. With its beautiful beaches and charming old towns, it is one of the country's most popular summer vacation spots. It has become a favored year-round retirement area as well, since its climate is tempered by the Gulf Stream.

Cape Cod was discovered in 1602 by the English navigator Bartholomew GOSNOLD, who named it for the teeming codfish off its shores. The first landing of the PILGRIMS was at the site of Provincetown at the northern end of the Cape, in November 1620. Early settlers engaged in fishing and whaling. Tourism developed in the late 1800s and is today the major industry, although the area's economic activity also includes fishing and cranberry growing. Much of the northern extension of the Cape is part of Cape Cod National Seashore.

Cape Coloureds see SOUTH AFRICA

Cape Denbigh [den'-bee] Cape Denbigh, along Norton Sound on the west coast of Alaska, has lent its name to the Cape Denbigh Flint Complex, a prehistoric tool industry that initiated the development of the earliest ESKIMO cultures in Alaska. This tool industry was first identified (1948) at Iyatayet, on Cape Denbigh, but has since been discovered at many other Alaskan sites. Dating from 3000 to 2500 BC, the Denbigh Flint Complex is considered a late offshoot of pre-Eskimo tool industries brought from Siberia to Alaska during the last period of the BERING LAND BRIDGE. It is characterized by small, well-made flint implements, including tiny blades, or microliths. Some of the artifacts, in particular the burins (engraving tools), show affinities with late PALEOLITHIC and MESOLITHIC industries of the Old World. Others are more typical of flint-working techniques of North American Paleo-Indian groups and reflect the adaptation to coastal life.

Cape Girardeau [jir-ar'-doh] Cape Girardeau (1990 pop., 34,438) is a city in Missouri on the Mississippi River, 50 km (30 mi) northwest of its confluence with the Ohio River. It is an interstate traffic crossroad. Industrial products include cement, furniture, and shoes.

Cape Krusenstern Cape Krusenstern, north of Kotzebue in northwest Alaska, is the site of a lengthy archaeological sequence of ESKIMO and pre-Eskimo cultures. The American archaeologist J. Louis Giddings discovered a 10-km-long (6.2-mi) and 3.2-km-wide (2-mi) area of 114 ancient beach ridges formed 5,000 to 6,000 years ago. On the innermost and therefore oldest ridges, he found traces of the Denbigh Flint Complex (3000–2500 BC), a cultural phase that shows a transition from inland hunting to coastal life (see CAPE DENBIGH). Remains of the Old Whaling culture (2000–1500 BC), in which whale hunting is clearly evident, were also found. Succeeding those phases were early Eskimo cultures—Choris (1500–500 BC), Norton (second half of the 1st millennium BC), IPIUTAK (first half of the 1st millennium BC), and Western Thule (AD 500–1000)—and more recent Eskimo cultures. The site is named for Adm. A. J. KRUSENSTERN, who explored the area in 1803–04.

Cape May Cape May (1990 pop., 4,668) is a coastal town at the southernmost tip of New Jersey. Cape May was settled in 1664 and is one of the oldest ocean resorts in the United States. The streets are lined with well-preserved Victorian houses. A Coast Guard air station is located there.

Cape of Good Hope see GOOD HOPE, CAPE OF

Cape Province Cape Province, also called Cape of Good Hope Province, is the largest of the four provinces of the Republic of South Africa. It has an area of 641,379 km^2 (247,638 mi^2) and a population of 5,041,137 (1985), and it occupies the southern and western parts of the country. Its capital is Cape Town, with a metropolitan area population of 1,911,521 (1985).

Agriculture and the raising of livestock were the basis of the province's economy until the discovery of diamonds in 1867. The current economy is based on mining, farming, sheep and cattle raising, dairy farming, and fishing. Factories produce textiles, clothing, chemicals, and tires.

The Cape of Good Hope, named by Portuguese sailors in 1488, specifically applies to the promontory 48 km

(30 mi) south of Cape Town but has been extended to refer to the entire province. The Dutch settlement (1652) at Table Bay was the first European town in southern Africa. In 1806 the British seized the area and established the Cape Colony. In 1910, with the establishment of the Union of South Africa, Cape Colony became a province.

Cape Town Cape Town (Afrikaans: Kaapstad) is the legislative capital and largest city of South Africa and the capital of Cape Province. It has a population of 776,617 (1985) in the city proper and 1,911,521 in the metropolitan area. It is situated on Table Bay at the foot of TABLE MOUNTAIN at the northern end of the Cape Peninsula. Cape Town's industries today include food processing, wine production, fishing, clothing, publishing, and engineering.

The city center focuses on the Public Gardens, a remnant of the original settlement, and on the Houses of Parliament. The Castle, constructed from 1666 to 1677, was a seat of government in the 17th century and is now a museum. Cape Town has theaters, museums, an orchestra, and two universities: the University of the Western Cape and the University of Cape Town. The latter is on the grounds of Groote Schuur, the estate of Cecil John RHODES, which he bequeathed to South Africa.

Cape Town was founded in 1652 by Jan van Riebeeck as a supply station for the Dutch East India Company. In 1795 it was captured by a British force but was returned to the Dutch by the Treaty of Amiens in 1803. In 1806 it again came under British control. Following the discovery of diamonds (1867) and gold (1886) in the interior, Cape Town became one of the country's largest ports and rail terminals.

The downtown business district of Cape Town, the Republic of South Africa's oldest European settlement, has been expanded through a series of land reclamation projects.

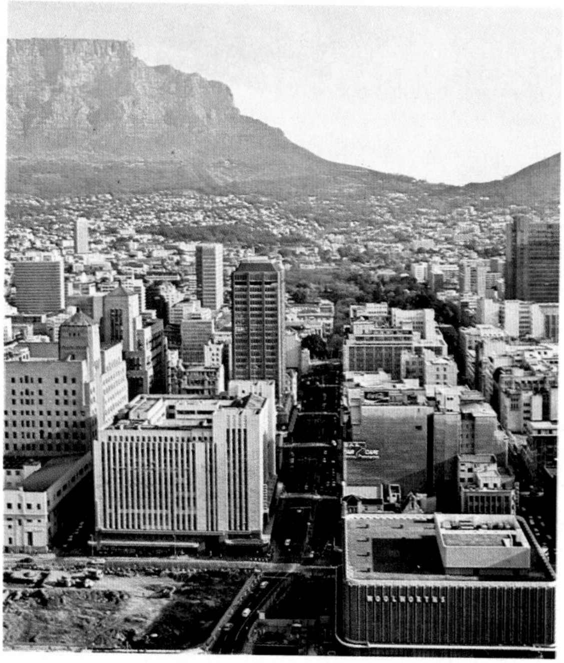

Cape Verde [vur'-dee] Cape Verde is an African country consisting of 15 islands located in the Atlantic Ocean about 600 km (375 mi) west of their namesake, Cape Verde, the western tip of Africa. The islands are volcanic in origin and mountainous, with relatively little level land. The highest point, Cano Peak, rises to 2,829 m (9,281 ft). The largest towns are Praia, the capital, and Mindêlo, the largest port. The islands suffer from an arid climate (average annual rainfall is only 260 mm/10 in) and are subject to cyclical droughts. Temperatures are moderate and equable, with an annual average of 24° C (75° F).

About 70% of the population are Creole (mulatto); most of the remainder are black. Crioulo, a Creole form of Portuguese, is spoken. Prolonged drought (since 1968) has contributed to severe soil erosion in this predominantly agricultural country; government irrigation and reforestation projects are a major source of employment. Maize, cassava, sweet potatoes, and bananas are the chief crops, and fish is the leading export. About 90% of all foodstuffs and 95% of all consumer goods are imported. Cape Verde is a refueling station for both sea and air traffic. Although it is a poor country, foreign aid and remittances from nearly one million Cape Verdeans working abroad have given it one of the highest rates of economic growth in Africa.

The archipelago had no permanent inhabitants when discovered in 1456. Portuguese settlers arrived in 1492, establishing plantations worked by slaves and creating a commercial center for the slave trade. The country received independence from Portugal on July 5, 1975. A one-party state from 1975 to 1990, it has held periodic unification talks with neighboring Guinea-Bissau.

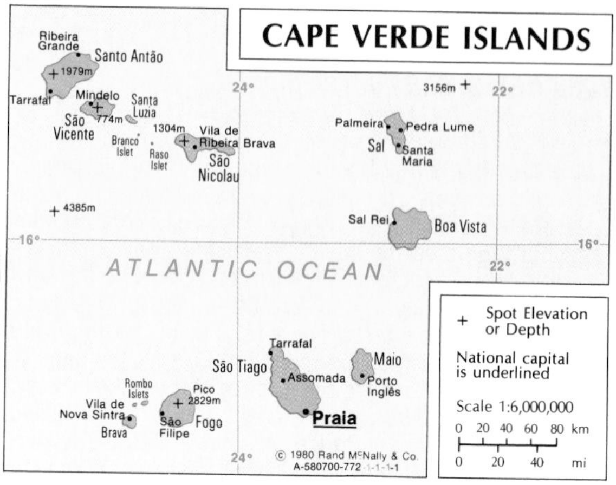

AT A GLANCE

REPUBLIC OF CAPE VERDE

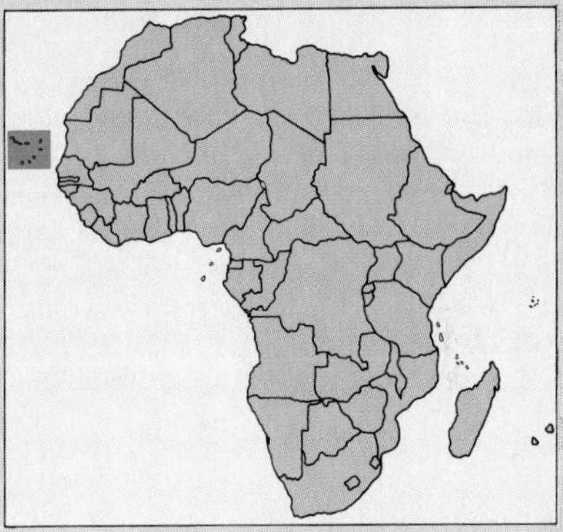

Land: Area: 4,033 km^2 (1,557 mi^2). Capital and largest city: Praia (1985 est. pop., 49,500).

People: Population (1990 est.): 374,984. Density: 93.0 persons per km^2 (240.8 per mi^2). Distribution (1980): 35% urban, 65% rural. Official language: Portuguese. Major religions: Roman Catholicism, traditional religions.

Government: Type: republic. Legislature: People's National Assembly. Political subdivisions: 14 districts.

Economy: GDP (1987): $181 million; $500 per capita. Labor distribution (1981): agriculture—57%; services—29%; industry—14%. Foreign trade (1987): imports—$82 million; exports—$5.6 million. Currency: 1 Cape Verde escudo = 100 centavos.

Education and Health: Literacy (1986): 48% of adult population. Universities (1990): none. Hospital beds (1980): 632. Physicians (1984): 60. Life expectancy (1990): women—63; men—59. Infant mortality (1990): 65 per 1,000 live births.

Cape York Peninsula Cape York Peninsula is the northernmost extension of Australia. It is 645 km (400 mi) wide at its base and 280 km (450 mi) long. It juts into TORRES STRAIT, which connects the Gulf of Carpentaria on the west and the Coral Sea on the east. The low, granite ridge along its eastern shore is the beginning of the Continental Divide. Mostly covered by tropical rain forest, it is sparsely populated. Discoveries of bauxite have stimulated development in the area.

Čapek, Karel [chah'-pek] Karel Čapek, b. Jan. 9, 1890, d. Dec. 25, 1938, first made his mark in the Czech literary world by collaborating with his brother Josef on a number of works, notably two plays, *The Insect Play* (1921; Eng. trans., 1923) and *Adam the Creator* (1927). Josef was primarily a painter, but Karel earned an international reputation with his widely successful play *R.U.R.* (1921; Eng. trans., 1923), an indictment of industrialized society, in which he coined the word *robot.* He developed his utopian themes further in novels such as *The Absolute at Large* (1922; Eng. trans., 1944) and *Krakatit* (1924; Eng. trans., 1948), and his play *The Makropoulas Secret* (1923; Eng. trans., 1925; opera, 1925). His belief that positing an absolute truth is sheer vanity forms the basis for his prose trilogy, *Hordubal* (1933; Eng. trans., 1934), *An Ordinary Life* (1934; Eng. trans., 1936), and *The Meteor* (1934; Eng. trans., 1935), and for several collections of short stories, detective and fantasy fiction, travel essays, children's pieces, and feuilletons. His finest novel, *The War with the Newts* (1936; Eng. trans., 1937), is a science fiction satire on the rise of totalitarianism.

caper [kay'-pur] Caper, *Capparis spinosa*, is a spiny deciduous shrub in the caper family, Capparaceae, which has about 300 species, also called capers. It is grown for

The caper bush produces large blossoms having numerous stamens, giving the effect of a fireworks display.

its flower buds, which are picked, pickled, and sold as a pungent condiment. Native to the Mediterranean region, it is grown as a greenhouse plant in the northern United States and outdoors in warmer areas. The leaves are round, and the white flowers have purple-tipped stamens. The flowers of other species, usually white or shades of yellow, are borne in flat-topped groups or are solitary, with four petals. The Jamaica caper tree, *C. cynophallophora*, found in the Caribbean and in southern Florida, has a bronze scale covering.

Capernaum [kuh-pur'-nay-uhm] Capernaum (Kefar Nahum, Israel) was a city of ancient Palestine located on the northwestern shore of the Sea of Galilee. During New Testament times it was a prominent city as well as a center for administrative and customs offices. Capernaum was also closely associated with Jesus' Galilean ministry (Mark 2:1–13; Matt. 4:13, 8:5–17, 9:1,9, 11:23; John 4:46–54). Today, the site of Capernaum is identified as Tell Hum. A 2d- or 3d-century synagogue has been excavated there.

Capetians (dynasty) [kuh-pee'-shuhnz] The Capetians were a family of French royalty whose ancestors, dating back to the 9th century, were known as the "third race" of French kings. The founder of the family, Robert the Strong, governed the lower Loire region and died fighting the Vikings in 866. His warrior son Eudes (d. 898) was elected king of France in 887. Eudes's brother later usurped the throne and ruled briefly (922–23) as Robert I. Robert's son, Hugh the Great (d. 956), was never king, but he ruled as duke over a large area of the Île-de-France and Loire valley. His son, HUGH CAPET, from whom the dynasty was to take its name, lost control of Anjou and Blois—key sections of the family domain—to subordinate counts, but in 987 he was elected king of France in preference to the CAROLINGIAN claimant, Charles, duke of Lorraine. Soon after, Hugh's son, Robert II, was associated with him as king designate.

Thereafter the French throne became hereditary in the Capetian family, and the descendants of Robert II's younger son were dukes of Burgundy from 1032 to 1361. The male line of the Capetian kings died with CHARLES IV in 1328, and the throne passed to a closely related younger branch, the VALOIS, who were followed in 1589 by the BOURBONS. In all, the family produced 38 French kings by 1848.

capillarity [kap-ih-lair'-it-ee] Capillarity is the rise or fall of a liquid between solid walls due to the equilibration of SURFACE TENSION forces and the weight of the raised fluid. The forces acting on a fluid particle at the top of the meniscus (surface) are the surface tension between the atmosphere and the wall, the surface tension between the liquid and the atmosphere, and the surface tension between the liquid and the wall. When the liquid wets the solid, there is also a force of ADHESION between the liquid and solid that is greater than the cohesion of the liquid. Thus, the liquid between the walls rises or falls to a height required to balance all forces; for nonwetting liquids such as mercury, the meniscus is depressed. The height to which a liquid is raised in a capillary tube is inversely proportional to the radius of the tube. Capillarity is responsible for the rapid wetting and retention of liquids by absorbent paper and fabrics.

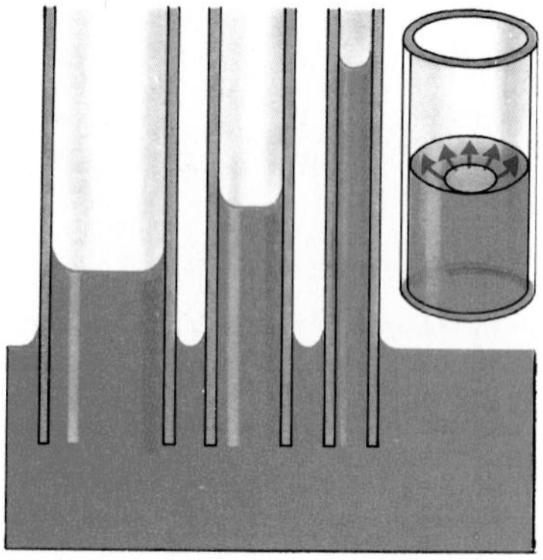

Water rises in a capillary tube because adhesion between the water and the solid causes the fluid particles to cling to the wall of the tube; thus the surface of the water curves upward against the glass, and the cohesion of the water particles along the surfacelifts the liquid. The narrower the tube, the greater the lifting force.

capillary see CIRCULATORY SYSTEM

capital (architecture) A capital is the topmost section of a column, pier, shaft, or pilaster (see ARCHITECTURE). Its function is to transmit the load borne by the column to its shaft and base. Classical capitals were divided into three sections: the narrow neck immediately atop the shaft; the echinus, wider at the top than at the bottom and bearing whatever decorative elements were involved; and the abacus, or flat block, connecting the capital to the architrave, the lowest section of the entablature above. Greek temple columns were adorned by Doric, Ionic, or Corinthian capitals; Egyptian columns by capitals with lotus, papyrus, or palm leaf motifs; and medieval European columns by capitals incorporating plants, animals, or grotesques.

The Ionic capital is the distinguishing feature of the Ionic order, one of the three Greek architectural orders. The capital ornamentation, with its characteristic volute, or scroll, above a delicate border, originated in Anatolia.

capital (economics) Capital, in economics, generally refers to all productive assets, or the stock of goods and moneys from which further goods and money are produced. The classical economists—David RICARDO, Adam SMITH, and others—defined capital as the "produced means of production" and distinguished it from land and labor, the two other major factors of production. In modern theory, however, capital refers to land and labor (including such intangibles as skills and education, called human capital), as well as buildings, machinery and tools, stores of raw materials and unsold finished merchandise, and means of transportation.

In financial terms, capital is money invested in productive assets and therefore yielding income. In accounting, capital is the part of a business enterprise's net worth that represents claims on assets. Capital gain, as used by the income-tax authorities, is an increase in the value of one's assets over time.

See also: CAPITALISM.

capital punishment Capital punishment is the lawful infliction of the death penalty, and since ancient times it has been used to punish a wide variety of offenses. The Bible prescribes death for murder and many other crimes, including kidnapping and witchcraft. By 1500 in England, only major felonies carried the death penalty: treason, murder, larceny, burglary, rape, and arson. By 1800, however, Parliament had enacted many new capital offenses, and hundreds of persons were being sentenced to death each year.

Reform of the death penalty began in Europe by the 1750s and was championed by such thinkers as the Italian jurist Cesare Beccaria, the French philosopher Voltaire, and the English law reformer Jeremy Bentham. These philosophers of the Enlightenment argued that the death penalty was needlessly cruel, overrated as a deterrent, and occasionally imposed in fatal error. Along with Quaker leaders and other social reformers, they defended life imprisonment as a more rational alternative.

By the 1850s these reform efforts bore fruit. In the United States the death penalty for murder was first abolished in Michigan (1847); Venezuela (1853) and Portugal (1867) were the first nations to abolish it altogether. Today, it is abolished de facto or de jure in all of Western Europe and most of Latin America. Elsewhere—in Eastern Europe, Asia, Africa, and the Middle East (except Israel)—most countries still authorize capital punishment for many crimes and use it with varying frequency.

Methods of inflicting the death penalty have ranged from stoning in biblical times, crucifixion under the Romans, beheading in France, to those used in the United States today: ELECTROCUTION, GAS CHAMBER, HANGING, LETHAL INJECTION, and firing squad.

In the United States, beginning in 1967, executions were suspended to allow the federal appellate courts to decide whether the death penalty was unconstitutional. In 1972 the Supreme Court ruled in *Furman* v. *Georgia* that the death penalty violated the prohibition against "cruel and unusual punishment" because it was meted out with "freakish" irregularity and so its use was "arbitrary" and "cruel." Most state legislatures enacted new death-penalty statutes, however, and in 1976 the Supreme Court in *Gregg* v. *Georgia* held that these were not per se unconstitutional, allowing executions to resume in 1977. These statutes typically authorized the trial court to impose sentence (death or life) only after a postconviction hearing, at which evidence is submitted to establish which "aggravating" or "mitigating" factors were present in the crime. If the "aggravating" factors prevail and the sentence is death, then the case is automatically reviewed by a state appellate court. In 1977, however, the Supreme Court also ruled that death for rape was "grossly disproportionate and excessive" (*Coker* v. *Georgia*). Thus, apart from certain crimes against the state (notably, treason, espionage, sabotage) on which the Supreme Court has not ruled, the only capital crime in the United States today is murder.

capitalism Capitalism is an economic system in which the means of production are owned privately. Business organizations produce goods for a market dominated by the forces of SUPPLY AND DEMAND. Capitalism requires a financial system that enables business firms to borrow large sums of money, or CAPITAL, to maintain and expand production. Underlying capitalism is the presumption that private enterprise is the most efficient way to organize economic activity. Adam SMITH expressed this idea in his *Wealth of Nations* (1776), extolling the free market in which the businessman is "led by an invisible hand to promote an end which was no part of his intention."

The marketplace is the center of the capitalist system. It determines what will be produced, who will produce it, and how the rewards of the economic process will be distributed. From a political standpoint, the market system has two distinct advantages over other ways of organizing the economy: (1) no person or combination of persons can control the marketplace, which means that power is diffuse and cannot be monopolized by a party or a clique; (2) the market system tends to reward efficiency with profits and to punish inefficiency with losses. Economists often speak of capitalism as a free-market system ruled by competition. Capitalism in this ideal sense, however, cannot be found anywhere in the world. The economic systems operating in Western countries today are mixtures of free competition and governmental control.

Historical Development

Many of the institutions of capitalism existed in ancient times. Trade, moneylending, and insurance were well known to the Greeks and Romans. But the growth of state power under the Roman empire prevented any further development of a private business class. Modern capitalism evolved in the late Middle Ages out of the social order of medieval Europe. The medieval economy was based on MANORIALISM, a system in which peasants cultivated large estates and had rights to what they produced, in return for services and dues paid to their lords. The land remained under the lord's ownership, but the tillers inherited the right to cultivate it. Some peasants were free, while others were bound to the manor where they worked.

Little commerce and little incentive to develop productive resources existed.

With the rise of centralized monarchies, kings competed with the local autonomy of the manor lords. In the towns a merchant class grew, and the development of commerce began to create a regional and international economy. From the 14th to the 18th century, a merchant capitalism developed; this period saw the expansion of international trade, the growth of banking, and the emergence of a new class of businessman who accumulated huge sums of capital. Through the JOINT-STOCK COMPANY, the forerunner of the modern CORPORATION, these businessmen were able to finance large ventures for exploring and developing distant lands. Their activities were controlled by rising national governments that sought to make commerce serve the state through policies known as MERCANTILISM. The influx of gold and silver from overseas colonies caused inflation, which gradually impoverished the aristocracy.

From the 16th to the 18th century, great rural-to-urban migrations created an abundance of capitalist labor. The REFORMATION encouraged a view of life that was more favorable to commerce than the medieval Roman Catholic outlook had been. The rise of science, with its emphasis on observation and inductive reasoning, tended to undermine the authority of the old order. The rising commercial and industrial classes, called by the French the *bourgeoisie*, sought a new political order corresponding to their economic interests.

Indeed, the concept of interest became a new political idea. The 17th-century English political theorists Thomas HOBBES and John LOCKE thought of society as created by a compact among people, in which the state's primary obligation was to protect the interests of its citizens. A central interest was the right of property. This current in political thought culminated in the work of Adam Smith, who argued that the commercial classes, if allowed enough freedom, could best achieve prosperity for the country. The crux of Smith's argument was that the economic order should be as independent as possible from the political order. Smith's *Wealth of Nations* was a critique of the existing system of state controls that he called mercantilism. He argued that state intervention not only diminished human freedom but was also economically inefficient. The state's proper role should be to protect private property and enforce contracts; production and distribution should be regulated by the market.

The 19th century was an era of unprecedented economic growth, especially in Britain and the United States. It was the age of LAISSEZ-FAIRE economic liberalism and FREE TRADE, when politics and economics were thought of as separate spheres of human endeavor. The INDUSTRIAL REVOLUTION transformed society, first in Britain, then in France and Germany, and later in the United States. By the end of the century, most people worked in the factory and the office. Large industrial cities developed, and with them trade unions and working-class political parties that regarded employers and capitalists as their enemies and the capitalist system itself as something to be modified or even eliminated. The most far-reaching attack on capitalism was that of Karl MARX and Friedrich ENGELS, whose writings became the intellectual basis of European SOCIALISM and COMMUNISM (see also MARXISM).

Another development that the early theorists of capitalism had not foreseen was the tendency of the business enterprise to grow larger and larger. This occurred in several ways: the industrial plant grew larger in order to gain the advantage of lower unit costs from mass production; the business firm grew from the artisan's small shop to a corporation operating a number of mills, factories, and transportation lines; and corporations in turn merged with one another to form combines or trusts. Thus a large segment of industry came to be controlled by a relatively few firms (see MONOPOLY AND COMPETITION).

The modern firm was characterized by several innovations. The sale of stocks and bonds gave it access to the savings of the public. The corporate form of organization gave it independence from its owners—in the eyes of the law, the corporation was a "person" and could sue as a legal entity, independently of its stockholders. The stockholders, concerned primarily with the return on their investment, tended to cede their powers to salaried managers who were in a position to make the critical business decisions.

Modern Conceptions of Capitalism

The rise of the corporation and the domination of many industries by a few firms led to new ideas about capitalism. Many liberals and populists favored breaking up large corporations and requiring them to refrain from practices that were monopolistic or injurious to competition. For this they turned to the state, pressing for ANTITRUST LAWS to guarantee a competitive economy. Others held that large firms were not necessarily less competitive than small ones. The Austrian-American economist Joseph SCHUMPETER, arguing in defense of large firms, held that the prime mover in capitalist progress was not the small businessperson but the entrepreneur who introduced new technologies and developed them.

Schumpeter evolved his ideas during the DEPRESSION OF THE 1930S, at a time when laissez-faire capitalism seemed to many people to have outlived its day. The British economist John Maynard KEYNES held that the capitalist slump might continue indefinitely unless the state took measures to raise aggregate demand for goods and services (see ECONOMY, NATIONAL). Keynes and his followers argued that an unregulated economy was not necessarily progressive and that intelligent FISCAL POLICY and MONETARY POLICY were required to stabilize the economy and keep it growing. The government should spend more money in times of slump, and also reduce taxes, in order to increase aggregate demand. In boom times, according to Keynes, the policies should be reversed in order to hold down inflation. In the decades after World War II, the Western industrial countries gradually adopted Keynesian policies of managing demand.

Modern capitalism thus differs from the capitalism of the 19th century in its dependence on the state. The government is expected to take measures to combat both mass unemployment and inflation. The government is also charged with other economic responsibilities, from regulating business practices and defending the environment to enforcing minimum wages and ensuring equal opportunity (see GOVERNMENT REGULATION). Modern capitalism may be thought of as a hybrid, combining private enterprise and state control.

Capitol of the United States The Capitol of the United States crowns Capitol Hill in Washington, D.C., and houses the legislative branch of government, comprising the House of Representatives and the Senate. The 1792 competition for its design was won by Dr. William Thornton, a gifted amateur architect, with a Palladian-inspired scheme featuring a central shallow-domed rotunda flanked by the Senate (north) and House (south) wings. President George Washington laid the cornerstone in 1793, but construction proceeded slowly under a succession of architects, including Stephen Hallet (1793), George Hadfield (1795–98) and James HOBAN (1798–1802). Benjamin LATROBE took over in 1803; by 1811 he had completed the wings. The Capitol was burned by British troops in 1814; in the following year Latrobe began its reconstruction and redesign. Charles BULFINCH, who succeeded him in 1818, completed the building in 1830.

By 1850 it had become necessary to enlarge the building, and the Philadelphian Thomas U. WALTER was commissioned to design and build the enormous (214-m/702-ft by 107-m/350-ft) present Capitol. Grandiose new House and Senate wings of white marble in Greek Revival style were added by 1859. Walter's cast-iron dome (82 m/270 ft), topped with Thomas Crawford's statue *Armed Freedom* (1855–62), was completed in 1863.

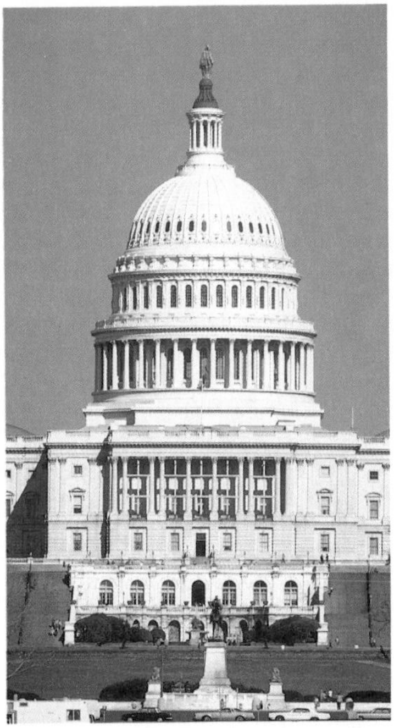

The Capitol building's imposing cast-iron dome in the Greek Revival style, added (1855–65) by Thomas U. Walter to the original designs by Thornton and Latrobe, surmounts the building's central rotunda. The dome is in turn crowned by Thomas Crawford's bronze, Armed Freedom *(1855–62).*

Capitoline Hill [kap'-it-uh-lyn] The Capitoline Hill, one of the Seven Hills of Rome, was the site of the Capitoline Temple and a center of the state religion in the ancient city. The least inhabited of the Roman hills, it was a fortified citadel (the Arx) and religious sanctuary. From the Tarpeian Rock, a cliff on the southwest side, criminals were hurled to their deaths. The Capitoline

The diagram identifies the major rooms and chambers of the U.S. Capitol: (1) Committee on Appropriations (2) House Minority Whip (3) House Chamber (4) Speaker's Offices (5) Statuary Hall (6) House Minority Leader (7) Rotunda (8) East Front (site of presidential inaugurations) (9) Senate Minority Leader (10) Senate Chamber (11) Senate Majority Leader (12) President's Room (13) Vice-President's Room

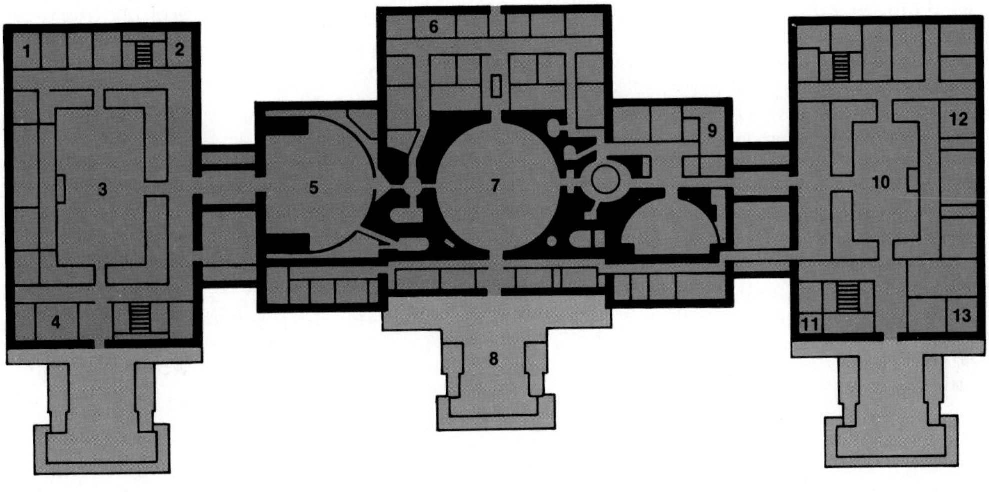

Temple, one of the earliest and grandest of Rome's temples, was begun by TARQUINIUS PRISCUS, fifth king of Rome, and was dedicated in 509 BC to the gods Jupiter, Juno, and Minerva. In 390 BC, according to legend, the sacred geese of Juno saved the hill by alerting the Romans to a sneak attack by the Gauls.

The temple was destroyed three times—in 83 BC, AD 69, and AD 80—and was rebuilt each time. It reached its final form under the emperor DOMITIAN, who added gilded tiles and gold-plated doors to a richly decorated marble structure. The temple was plundered by the Vandals under GAISERIC in AD 455. Today the Capitoline Hill is occupied by the Piazza del Campidoglio, which was designed by Michelangelo.

Capo d'Istria, Giovanni Antonio, Count [kah-poh dees-tree-ah] Count Capo d'Istria (or Kapodistrias), b. Feb. 11, 1776, d. Oct. 9, 1831, was a Greek statesman who spent a major portion of his career in Russian service before becoming the first president of independent Greece. In Russian employ from 1809, he represented Tsar ALEXANDER I at the Congress of Vienna and, with Count NESSELRODE, shared the conduct of Russian foreign policy. The outbreak of the Greek revolt against Turkish rule caused his resignation in 1822. In April 1827, Capo d'Istria was elected president of Greece by the Greek assembly. Landing at Nauplia in January 1828, he attempted to deal with the interests of the three protective powers (Russia, Britain, and France) as well as rivalries among the local Greek leaders. He was assassinated by dissident Greeks.

Capone, Al [kuh-pohn'] Alphonse "Al" Capone, b. Brooklyn, N.Y., Jan. 17, 1899, d. Jan. 25, 1947, was perhaps the most famous of all American mobsters. He grew up in Brooklyn, acquiring an education in petty crime and the name "Scarface Al" because of a razor slash across his face. He moved to Chicago and worked his way upward in the crime syndicates. His domination of the bootleg liquor traffic brought him an income of more than $20 million a year by the end of the 1920s. Capone survived the Chicago gang wars of the 1920s by killing his rivals; in the St. Valentine's Day Massacre (1929) his gunmen, dressed as policemen, executed seven members of the "Bugs" Moran gang. The federal authorities finally succeeded where the Chicago police could not: in October 1931, Capone was fined $80,000 and sentenced to 11 years in prison for income-tax evasion. Capone was released in November 1939, terminally ill with syphilis, and died seven years later at his Florida estate.

Capote, Truman [kuh-poh'-tee] Truman Capote, b. New Orleans, La., Sept. 30, 1924, d. Aug. 25, 1984, was a Southern Gothic novelist, journalist, and celebrated man-about-town. His earliest writings include his novel of alienated youth, *Other Voices, Other Rooms* (1948), the Gothic short stories in *A Tree of Night* (1949), and the lighter novel *The Grass Harp* (1951; play, 1952). The novella *Breakfast at Tiffany's* (1958; film, 1961) introduced the charming, hedonistic Holly Golightly. Childhood reflections formed the basis of two short stories adapted for television: "A Christmas Memory" (1956) and "The Thanksgiving Visitor" (1968). Capote's sensational so-called nonfiction novel *In Cold Blood* (1966; film, 1967) was based on a 6-year study of the murder of a rural Kansas family by two young drifters. *Answered Prayers*, an unfinished novel, was published posthumously in 1987.

The American writer Truman Capote's sense of the bizarre is evident in all of his work—from the Gothic fiction of A Tree of Night *(1949) to the almost surreal journalism of* In Cold Blood *(1966).*

Photo Jill Krementz © 1973

Capp, Al Al Capp, b. Alfred Gerald Caplin in New Haven, Conn., Sept. 28, 1909, d. Nov. 5, 1979, was a popular American cartoonist known for his comic strip "Li'l Abner" (1934–77). Capp worked with Ham Fisher on "Joe Palooka" before launching "Li'l Abner" in the *New York Mirror* and seven other papers. In early strips Capp attacked conservatives, but he later pursued liberals and radicals; the inhabitants of the hillbilly world of Dogpatch U.S.A. became familiar caricatures. Capp later introduced a second strip, "Fearless Fosdick," a parody of "Dick Tracy."

Al Capp, an American cartoonist, created the popular "Li'l Abner," a comic strip set in the fictional backwoods community of Dogpatch. The characters featured in this syndicated strip—Li'l Abner, Daisy Mae, Mammy Yokum, and others—have entertained generations of readers.

Cappadocia [kap-uh-doh'-shuh] Cappadocia is the ancient name of a region of the central Anatolian plateau, in what is now Turkey. It is sometimes considered to have extended from Cilicia to the Black Sea in the north and from the Halys River eastward to the Euphrates. More specifically, the name alludes throughout history to the central and southern part of this territory (Greater Cappadocia). Although the region is well watered, its harsh climate limits agricultural pursuits to cereal and fruit growing. Its vast grassland was ideal for raising horses as well as sheep and other small stock. Silver, copper, and salt have been mined there as well. During the 19th century BC, Old Assyrian trading colonies were established among the numerous native city-states of Cappadocia. Between *c.*1750 and 1200 BC, Cappadocia formed the "Lower Land" of the HITTITE kingdom. From the 9th century BC on, the Late Assyrians penetrated the area, and SARGON II (r. 721–705 BC) carved out an Assyrian province there. Subsequently the Persians made Cappadocia a satrapy (province), through which passed the famous Persian Royal Road from Sardis to Susa.

Under the satrap Ariarathes (*c.*404–322 BC), Cappadocia avoided submitting to Alexander the Great. Ariarathes established a dynasty of Iranian origin that preserved the region's independence, at least nominally, throughout the entire Hellenistic period. After 190 BC the Cappadocian rulers became friendly to Rome. Following invasions by Mithradates VI of Pontus and by the Armenian ruler Tigranes I during the Mithradatic Wars (88–63 BC), Rome restored the Cappadocian kingdom. In AD 17, Cappadocia was annexed outright by Rome as a procuratorial province. Under Vespasian, Cappadocia was joined (AD 72) with the provinces of Galatia and Lesser Armenia to form a large new Roman administrative unit. Soon after, under Trajan, it was united with Pontus.

Capra, Frank The Sicilian-born American film director Frank Capra, b. May 18, 1897, d. Sept. 3, 1991, virtually created a genre with his 1930s film comedies in which an idealistic innocent is pitted against the forces of corruption. Capra won Academy Awards for best direction with *It Happened One Night* (1934), *Mr. Deeds Goes to Town* (1936), and *You Can't Take It with You* (1938). His other films include *Lost Horizon* (1937), *Mr. Smith Goes to Washington* (1939), *Meet John Doe* (1941), *Arsenic and Old Lace* (1942), and *It's a Wonderful Life* (1946). Capra was in charge of the U.S. government's war documentary series *Why We Fight* (1942–45).

Frank Capra, an American filmmaker, won three Academy Awards for directing during the 1930s. A former gag writer for the slapstick films of Mack Sennett, Capra changed the public's taste in comedy with such witty situation comedies as It Happened One Night.

Capri Capri is an island near the southern entrance of the Bay of Naples off the southwest coast of Italy. A single block of limestone, the island has an area of 10 km^2 (4 mi^2). It rises to 589 m (1,932 ft) at Monte Solaro in the west and has a population of 7,489 (1981).

Inhabited in prehistoric times, it was colonized by the Greeks. Capri served as a vacation retreat for several Roman emperors, including Augustus and Tiberius, who built villas there. The island is mostly cliff-lined, and the main towns are Capri in the east and Anacapri in the west. The climate is mild, and vegetation is abundant and varied, although water is scarce. Hotels dot the island, and tourism is the major economic resource. Fishing and viticulture are also important. Many caves line the shore, the most famous of which is the shimmering Blue Grotto.

Capricornus Capricornus the Sea Goat is a constellation of the zodiac most prominent during autumn in the Northern Hemisphere. It contains no bright stars, but it does have several BINARY STARS and the globular cluster M 30. The TROPIC OF CAPRICORN, at 23°5' south latitude, was named for the constellation because at that time (about 2,000 years ago) the Sun was in the constellation during the winter solstice on December 22. Because of the PRECESSION OF THE EQUINOXES, it is no longer in this position during the solstice, having been replaced by Sagittarius. In astrology Capricorn still governs the period December 22–January 19.

Caprivi, Georg Leo, Graf von [kah-pree'-vee, gay'-awrg lay'-oh, grahf fuhn] Graf von Caprivi, b. Feb. 24, 1831, d. Feb. 6, 1899, succeeded Otto von BISMARCK as chancellor of Germany in 1890. Trying to liberalize the policies of the government, he abrogated Bismarck's antisocialist legislation, attempted to conciliate the Polish minority of Prussia, reduced the length of army service, and reached an agreement (1890) with Great Britain on the countries' respective spheres of influence in Africa. He also abandoned Bismarck's treaty with Russia. Caprivi's policies angered the powerful JUNKERS, who helped force his resignation in 1894. The Caprivi Strip, a region of Namibia, is named for him.

Caprivi Strip [kah-pree'-vee] The Caprivi Strip is a long, narrow territory of northeastern Namibia (South West Africa), in southern Africa. About 450 km (280 mi) long and from 32 to 105 km (20 to 65 mi) wide, it runs from northeast Namibia to the Zambezi River and has an area of 17,410 km^2 (6,722 mi^2). It was ceded in 1893 to Germany by Great Britain so that German Southwest Africa would have access to the Zambezi River.

Captain Jack see KINTPUASH

Captains Courageous *Captains Courageous* (1897; film, 1937), by Rudyard KIPLING, is a novel about the coming of age of Harvey Cheyne, a spoiled, wealthy American adolescent washed overboard from an ocean liner and rescued by the crew of a fishing trawler. Once aboard, the boy is forced to work for his keep and slowly develops the skills and self-reliance of a mariner. He has grown to sturdy manhood by the time he is reunited with his family. Through the medium of his narrative, Kipling expresses his admiration for capitalism and the spirit of adventure that drives people to risk all in pursuit of wealth, power, and self-fulfillment.

capuchin [kap'-yoo-chin] Capuchin monkeys, genus *Cebus*, of the family Cebidae, are so named because their crown hair resembles the cowl, or capuche, of Franciscan friars. Among the most intelligent of New World monkeys, capuchins are 38 to 53 cm (15 to 21 in) long, with a tail 38 to 60 cm (15 to 24 in) long; they weigh 1.6 to 3.6 kg (3.5 to 8 lb). They are called ring-tailed because they often carry their slightly prehensile tails coiled at the tip. Capuchins live in the tops of large trees, rarely descending to the ground. They eat fruits, leaves, insects, young birds, and eggs. Popular as pets, they are the monkeys that traditionally pass the hat for organ grinders. The brown capuchin, *C. apella*, has tufts of hair on the forehead. On the head is a dark brown cap with a border. This species is common in South American forests. The untufted group includes three species. The white-throated capuchin, *C. capucinus*, has a coat of black with white in the pale areas and is found in Central America, in western Colombia, and along the Pacific coast of Ecuador. The white-fronted capuchin, *C. albifrons*, is yellowish to brown in color and is found in northwestern South America. The weeper capuchin, *C. nigrivittatus*, has a coarser brownish coat with some white and a smaller cap; it is found in northern South America.

The white-throated capuchin, native to Central America, is named for its black cap of fur that resembles the cowl of a Capuchin monk. It is one of the most intelligent monkeys.

Capuchins see FRANCISCANS

capybara [kap-i-buhr'-uh] The capybara, *Hydrochoerus hydrochaeris*, the world's largest rodent, lives in South America and Panama. It is the only species in its genus, which belongs to the family Hydrochoeridae, order Rodentia. The capybara—also called carpincho and water hog—has a massive body, a large head with a blunt snout, short legs, and a very small tail. It may weigh as much as 50 kg (110 lb) and have a shoulder height of 50 cm (20 in) and a body length of 130 cm (51 in). Its hair is coarse, reddish brown above and yellowish below. The feet are webbed and armed with strong claws. Capybaras eat only plants. They are fast runners and swim well, even under water.

The docile capybara, which may grow to the size of a sheep, is the largest rodent in the world.

Caracalla, Roman Emperor Caracalla, b. Apr. 4, AD 188, d. April 217, whose real name was Marcus Aurelius Antoninus, was Roman emperor from 211 to 217. He was the elder son and successor of Septimius SEVERUS. At first Caracalla ruled with his brother Geta, but he murdered Geta in 212 and massacred his followers. To meet rising military expenditures and the costs of his elaborate building program (of which his Baths in Rome are a splendid relic), Caracalla depreciated the currency, increased taxes, and in the process plunged the Roman Empire into a grave economic crisis. By an edict of 212, he granted Roman citizenship to all free inhabitants of the empire. The reason was probably financial, for only Roman citizens paid the inheritance tax.

During his reign, the Germanic tribes resumed their attacks, and in 213, Caracalla conducted a successful campaign against the Alamanni on the Upper Rhine, where he received his nickname Caracalla from the Gallic tunic he wore. He fancied himself to be a new Alexander the Great and dreamed of the conquest of the Parthian empire in Mesopotamia and Iran. He invaded Parthia, but after initial successes he was assassinated by Macrinus, commander of the Praetorians, who succeeded him as emperor.

caracara see FALCON

Caracas [kah-rah'-kahs] The capital and chief city of Venezuela, Caracas is situated in a narrow valley surrounded by mountains and lies only 11 km (7 mi) from the Caribbean Sea. The city's population is 1,246,677 (1987 est.) and that of the metropolitan area is 3,247,000. Caracas lies within a federal district, which is administered by a governor with a cabinet-level rank.

Caracas is a distribution center for Venezuela, handling both foreign and domestic trade. Its diversified industries include food processing, tobacco, textiles, chemicals, rubber goods, and pharmaceuticals.

The city is the location of the Central University of Venezuela (1725), the University of Simón Bolívar (1970), and the Catholic University of Andrés Bello. Museums include the Criollan Museum of Raul Santana, the Bolívar Museum, and the Museum of Colonial Art.

Caracas was established (1567) by Diego de Losada, who named it Santiago de León de Caracas, Caracas being the name of a local Indian tribe. In the colonial period, Caracas surpassed older cities because of its central location, proximity to the ocean, and the richness of nearby soils. It was the birthplace of Simón BOLÍVAR and site of the proclamation of Venezuelan independence in 1811. In 1812 a massive earthquake destroyed the city, killing an estimated 12,000 people. In the ensuing century, however, Caracas developed as the Venezuelan transshipment center for expanding coffee and cacao exports and for European imports. Caracas experienced phenomenal population growth during the 1960s and '70s, at the height of Venezuela's oil boom. Many of these new arrivals were migrants from depressed rural areas. They were hit particularly hard by the decline in national living standards in the 1980s, which sparked riots in Caracas in 1989.

Caracas, the capital of Venezuela, is one of the most modern cities in Latin America. The extensive programs of metropolitan development in the 1970s were financed primarily through revenues from Venezuela's petroleum industry.

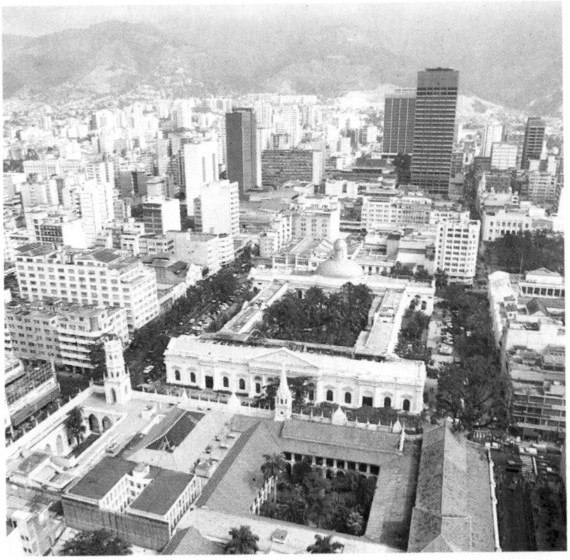

carat The carat is the unit of weight for DIAMONDS and other precious stones. Once based on the weight of grains or seeds and thus of variable weight, the carat was standardized in 1913 at 0.2 g (0.007 oz). The standard metric carat and the point, 0.01 carat, replaced the weight system previously in use.

Caravaggio, Michelangelo Merisi da [kah-rah-vahj'-joh, mee-kel-ahn'-jay-loh may-ree'-zee dah] Michelangelo Merisi da Caravaggio, b. October 1571, d. July 18, 1610, known as Caravaggio, was one of the most innovative baroque painters in Rome (see BAROQUE ART AND

In his Entombment of Christ *(1602–04), Michelangelo Caravaggio achieves the effects of realism and emotional intensity with such characteristic devices as assymetrical composition and dramatic lighting. (Vatican Museums, Rome.)*

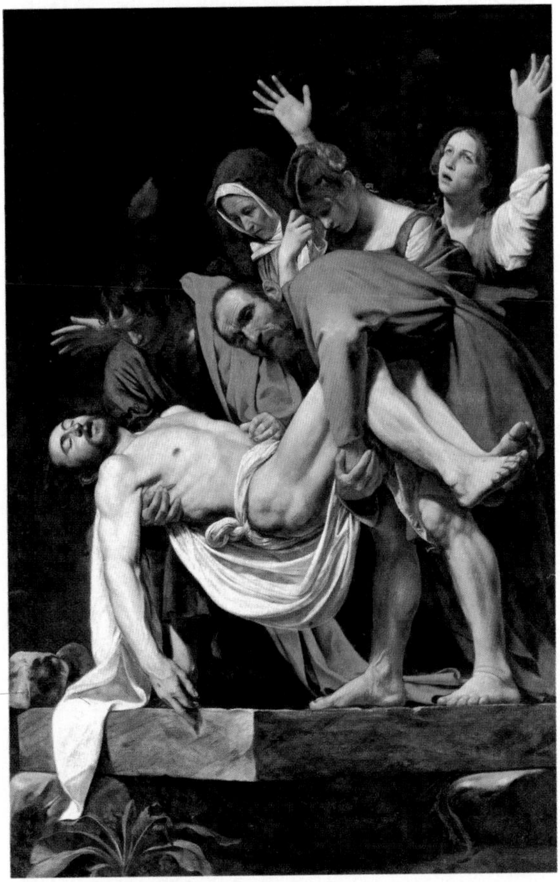

ARCHITECTURE). Although his first independent paintings were unsuccessful, his career changed significantly when Cardinal Francesco del Monte purchased several genre scenes, among them *The Fortune Teller* (*c.*1595; Louvre, Paris) and *The Musical Party* (*c.*1597; Metropolitan Museum of Art, New York City). More importantly, del Monte obtained (*c.*1597) for the artist his first commission, the monumental paintings in the Contarelli Chapel of San Luigi dei Francesi.

From 1597 on, Caravaggio turned almost exclusively to religious subjects and, with the St. Matthew cycle (1599–1600) in the Contarelli Chapel, he displayed a far more complex and mature style. In the *Martyrdom of St. Matthew*, Caravaggio introduced violent gestures and physical movement to intensify the emotionalism of a spiritual event. In the foreground, radically foreshortened figures project out from the picture plane, compelling the spectator to become a participant. The sculpturesque solidity of the figures is further emphasized by Caravaggio's unique use of a light that, in a break with tradition, strikes upon but never dissolves forms. In the *Calling of St. Matthew*, Christ, entering at the right, summons St. Matthew, who is seated with friends at the left. From the upper right a beam of brilliant light rakes diagonally across the composition, highlighting and following Christ's gesture, becoming an iconographic symbol of Christ's command. Thus Caravaggio united physical and pictorial light, a procedure he repeated in the St. Paul cycle (1600–01) in the Cerasi Chapel of Santa Maria del Popolo.

In constant revolt against all forms of authority, Caravaggio's life was filled with controversy and violence. In 1606 he committed murder. Forced to flee Rome, he spent the remaining years of his life wandering through Naples, Malta, Syracuse, and Messina. The paintings produced in these years exhibit a marked stylistic change. In *Nativity* (1609; Museo Nazionale, Messina) the explosive activity of his earlier paintings has been replaced by a compact, friezelike arrangement across the center of the composition, creating a sad, contemplative atmosphere.

caravel see SHIP; SHIPBUILDING

Caraway, Hattie Wyatt [kair'-uh-way] Hattie Wyatt Caraway, b. near Bakerville, Tenn., Feb. 1, 1878, d. Dec. 21, 1950, was the first woman ever elected to the U.S. Senate. An Arkansas Democrat, she was appointed (1931) to complete her husband's Senate term and then won election in 1932. Serving until 1945, she sponsored an early version of the Equal Rights Amendment.

carbohydrate Carbohydrates, which are classified as MONOSACCHARIDES, disaccharides, and POLYSACCHARIDES, include CELLULOSE, STARCHES, SUGARS, and many other compounds. They are the most abundant single class of organic substances found in nature. They are formed in green plants and certain bacteria by a process known as PHOTOSYNTHESIS, in which energy derived from sunlight is used for the assimilation of carbon dioxide (CO_2) from the air. If CO_2, water, minerals, and an appropriate inorganic source of nitrogen are available, these organisms, with the aid of solar energy, can synthesize all the different carbohydrates, proteins, and lipids they need for their existence. Other organisms cannot do this. It follows that life on Earth ultimately depends on this process of CO_2 assimilation in which carbohydrates are the first intermediates.

Chemists in the 19th century found that carbohydrates contain the elements of carbon, hydrogen, and oxygen in the proportion represented by $C_x(H_2O)_y$. Hence they referred to them as carbon hydrates, the contracted form of which is still used today, even though it is now known that deviations from the required hydrogen-to-oxygen ratio of H_2O do occur.

Carbohydrates function as the main structural elements in plants, in two forms: cellulose, a polymer of GLUCOSE, and hemicelluloses, which are polymers of 5-carbon sugars and other compounds. The exoskeleton of crustacea and insects is composed of CHITIN, a polymer of the amino sugar N-acetyl-D-glucosamine. In animal tissues, acid carbohydrates occur in the cell coats of cartilage, bone, and other tissues and form the ground substance between connective tissue cells. The cell wall of bacteria consists of a rigid framework of sugar-polymer chains linked to peptide chains. The glycoproteins, which contain covalently attached carbohydrate groups, are widely distributed in cell membranes. In red blood corpuscles, the carbohydrate side chains determine the blood group specificity.

Carbohydrates also serve as storage products of energy. The principal forms are starch in plants and GLYCOGEN in animal tissues. These are polymers of glucose; they are deposited in cells when a surplus of glucose is available. In times of metabolic need, the polymers are broken down by enzymatic action and become fuel (see METABOLISM).

Plants store starch in roots, tubers, and leafy parts, mainly during photosynthetic activity; some plants, such as sugar beets and sugarcane, also store sucrose. A large part of the human diet consists of carbohydrates in the form of starch and sucrose. Both must first be broken down to their component sugars by digestive enzymes before absorption into the blood can take place. (See also DIET, HUMAN; NUTRITION, HUMAN.)

carbolic acid see PHENOL

carbon The chemical element carbon is a nonmetal of Group IVA in the periodic table and is found widely in nature. Its symbol is C, its atomic number is 6, and its atomic weight is 12.011. The sixth most abundant element in the universe, carbon plays an essential role in the thermonuclear "burning" of hydrogen in the hotter stars (see CARBON CYCLE, ASTRONOMY). On Earth, carbon is found both in native form and in compounds with other elements, making up about 0.2% by weight of the Earth's crust. The element is found in its purest form as diamond

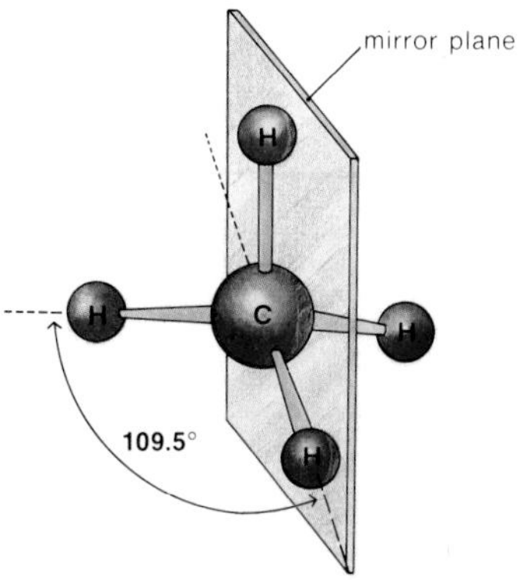

When a carbon atom forms single bonds to four identical atoms, such as hydrogen, the three-dimensional structure of the molecule is tetrahedral. Four axes exist, each of which extends in a different direction. Six planes, each of which involves two hydrogen atoms and the carbon atom, divide the molecule into two mirror images.

and graphite and in less pure form as a constituent of natural coal (see COAL AND COAL MINING), COKE, and CHARCOAL. Its most abundant compounds are carbon dioxide, which constitutes about 0.05% of the atmosphere and is found dissolved in all natural waters; the CARBONATE MINERALS, such as limestone and marble; and the hydrocarbons, which are principal constituents of coal, PETROLEUM, and NATURAL GAS.

Carbon is the most versatile element known. Only carbon is capable of combining with other elements in arrangements of sufficient variety and complexity to fulfill the essential functions on which life depends. Carbon compounds are continually replenished by PHOTOSYNTHESIS in green plants. The exchange of carbon with the environment ceases when an organism dies, and the amount of the radioactive isotope carbon-14 remaining can be used to determine the age of materials of biological origin (see RADIOMETRIC AGE-DATING).

Carbon and its compounds have assumed a position of major influence on the economy, especially in the more industrialized nations. SYNTHETIC FIBERS and PLASTICS, which are ultimately derived from petroleum-based chemicals (PETROCHEMICALS), have largely supplanted natural substances. These materials serve as the basis for numerous technological advances, including those in such fields as the electronics and transportation industries. The development of synthetic DRUGS has radically affected the practice of medicine. Carbon-based fuels have provided most of the world's energy needs since 1900.

Characteristics of the Carbon Atom

Carbon, a member of Group IVA of the periodic table along with SILICON, GERMANIUM, TIN, and LEAD, is the lightest and least metallic of these elements. Unlike many other groups in the periodic table, the Group IVA elements differ greatly from each other in their chemistry, with carbon being the least representative in its behavior.

Its most abundant ISOTOPE is carbon-12, which makes up 98.89% of naturally occurring carbon. Five radioactive isotopes are known, of which carbon-14 (half-life 5,730 years) is the most stable and useful.

Bonds. The free carbon atom has two electrons in the 1s shell and four valence electrons in the 2s and 2p shells that are available for bonding (see ELECTRON CONFIGURATION). Unlike the metals and many of the nonmetals, the bonding in carbon is generally covalent rather than ionic (see CHEMICAL BOND).

In covalent bonding, each carbon atom mutually shares its valence electrons with other atoms. In most carbon compounds an adjacent atom will contribute one to three electrons, which are matched by an equal number from carbon to form a single, double, or triple bond, respectively. The total number of bonds to a carbon atom—that is, its VALENCE—is normally four. These four bonds may be single or multiple bonds. Carbon forms strong single bonds to itself and to most other elements. It forms very strong double and triple bonds to itself and to nitrogen and oxygen (double bonds only). The endless structural variation and complexity characteristic of the chemistry of carbon ultimately depend on the ability of carbon atoms to bond to each other.

Structure. Most of the bonding situations for carbon are described spatially in terms of three geometries: tetrahedral, trigonal, and linear. Carbon compounds having four single bonds take on the approximate form of a tetrahedron, having 109.5° angles between bonds. A carbon atom bearing one double and two single bonds may be described as trigonal—the three groups bonded to carbon take on a symmetrical planar arrangement, with angles of about 120° between bonds. A carbon atom with one single and one triple bond is held in linear arrangement with the two groups on opposite sides of the carbon atom.

Basic Elemental Forms

Pure carbon exists as any of three ALLOTROPES, which are different crystal forms of the same element. These allotropes are DIAMOND, graphite, and amorphous carbon.

Graphite. Graphite is a black, lustrous substance that easily crumbles or flakes. It has a slippery feel because of its tendency to cleave from the crystal in thin layers. It is chemically inert, although less so than diamond, and is an excellent conductor of both heat and electricity. It occurs as a mineral and can be produced artificially from amorphous carbon. Graphite is composed entirely of planes of trigonal carbon atoms joined in a honeycomb pattern. Each carbon molecule is bonded to three others at 120° angles. These planes are arranged in sheets to form three-dimensional crystals. The layers are separated at a distance that represents a nonbonding situation. Because each atom is formally bonded to only three neighboring atoms, the remaining valence electron (one in each atom) contributes to partial double bonding and is free to circulate within each plane of atoms, contributing to graphite's ability to conduct electricity.

One of the main uses for graphite—as a lubricant—results from the characteristic sliding of one layer over another within the crystal. The "lead" in pencils is actually graphite. Graphite is also used as a heat-resistant material; as an electrical conductor and electrode material (in dry cells, for instance); and in nuclear reactors as a neutron moderator.

Amorphous Carbon. Less well defined in structure than diamond or graphite, amorphous carbon has physical and

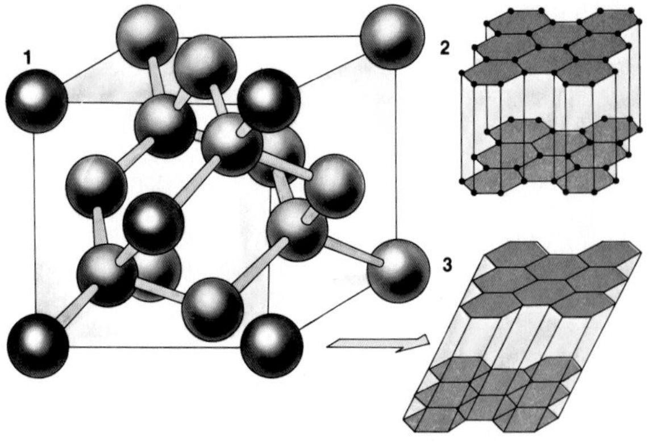

The arrangement of carbon atoms in a diamond (1) differs from that of graphite (2). In a diamond the atoms are bonded as closely as possible to each other, which accounts for a diamond's hardness. In graphite the carbon atoms are arranged in sheets. Within each sheet the atoms are fairly well bonded to each other, but bonds between sheets are weak, causing layers to slide (3), which accounts for graphite's softness.

chemical properties that may vary depending on its method of manufacture and conditions to which it is later subjected. It is a deep black powder that occurs in nature as a component of coal and lignite. It may be obtained artificially by heating almost any organic substance to very high temperatures in the absence of air. In this way coke is produced from coal, and charcoal from wood. Burning organic vapors with insufficient oxygen produces such forms as carbon black and lampblack. The most important uses for carbon black are as a stabilizing filler for rubber and plastics and as a black pigment in inks and paints. Charcoal and coke are used as clean-burning fuels. Certain types of "activated" charcoal are useful as absorbents of gases and of impurities from solutions.

Spherical Molecules. Theoretical studies have suggested that carbon atoms can form naturally in molecular spheres, if the spheres are large enough to put little stress on the bonds between atoms. Spheres of 60 or 80 atoms are considered particularly stable possibilities that may be common in space. By vaporizing graphite with a laser, scientists in 1985 apparently produced a 60-carbon molecule with 32 sides. Because of its shape they named it buckminsterfullerine, after the geodesic domes of American inventor R. Buckminster FULLER. Spherical carbon molecules in general are now called fullerines.

Important Carbon Compounds

Carbon compounds traditionally have been classified as either inorganic or organic. Inorganic carbon compounds include binary compounds of carbon that do not contain carbon-carbon bonds and salts or complexes that contain simple carbon species. Organic compounds generally contain covalent carbon-carbon and carbon-hydrogen bonds.

Inorganic Compounds. Binary compounds (containing two elements) of carbon with metals or semimetals are known as carbides. They have properties ranging from saltlike to inert and very hard as in boron carbide, which is used as an abrasive. Binary compounds of carbon with nonmetals are usually gases or low-boiling liquids. Carbon monoxide (CO) is a colorless, odorless, toxic, and flammable gas that forms during the incomplete combustion of carbon. Carbon dioxide (CO_2) is a colorless, odorless gas that results from the complete combustion of carbon. It is a product of respiration in most living organisms. In water solution carbon dioxide is partly converted to carbonate (CO_3^{2-}) and hydrogen carbonate (HCO_3^-) ions.

Of the halides, CARBON TETRACHLORIDE (CCl_4) is best known. It is a colorless, fairly inert and toxic liquid often used as a solvent. Fluorochlorocarbons, such as FREON 12 (CF_2Cl_2), are used as refrigerants.

Organic Compounds. The simplest organic compounds, the hydrocarbons, consist only of carbon and hydrogen. Those containing only single bonds are called saturated hydrocarbons or ALKANES and are composed of chains, rings, or three-dimensional frameworks of carbon atoms. Those containing up to 4 carbons are gases, and those containing up to about 20 carbons are liquids. Alkanes having higher molecular weights are solids. Unsaturated hydrocarbons are those containing double bonds (ALKENES) and triple bonds (ALKYNES). They are more reactive than saturated hydrocarbons but have similar physical properties. Hydrocarbons that are based on a stable six-membered ring of carbons with three double bonds are called AROMATIC COMPOUNDS (this has no relation to odor). BENZENE (C_6H_6) is the simplest molecule of this class.

More complex organic molecules are derived from the hydrocarbons by replacing one or more hydrogens with other atoms or functional groups. One major class is the halides, such as RCl and RBr, in which R refers to a hydrocarbon fragment having an unoccupied bonding site. Other classes are alcohols (ROH), ethers (ROR), ketones (RCOR), aldehydes (RCHO), carboxylic acids (RCO_2H), amines (RNH_2, R_2NH, R_3N), nitriles (RCN), and such organometals as RLi and RM_2Cl.

Biochemical Substances. Living systems contain many complex molecules that have specific functions. They may be classified as seven major structural types. The acetogenins include many useful pigments and antibiotics. Nitrogen-containing ALKALOIDS include many major types of drugs. CARBOHYDRATES include sugars, starches, and cellulose and are primary products of photosynthesis. LIPIDS or fats are used for energy storage and as components of cell membranes. Nucleic acids (see GENE) store and transmit genetic information. Peptides and proteins (see PROTEIN; PROTEIN SYNTHESIS) serve as enzymes, hormones, sense receptors, structural and mechanical components, transport proteins, energy-transfer proteins, and gene regulators. TERPENES and STEROIDS include many hormones and pheromones and often serve as flavor and odor components.

carbon cycle (environment) The carbon cycle is the complex of biological and chemical processes that make carbon available to living things for use in tissue building and energy release.

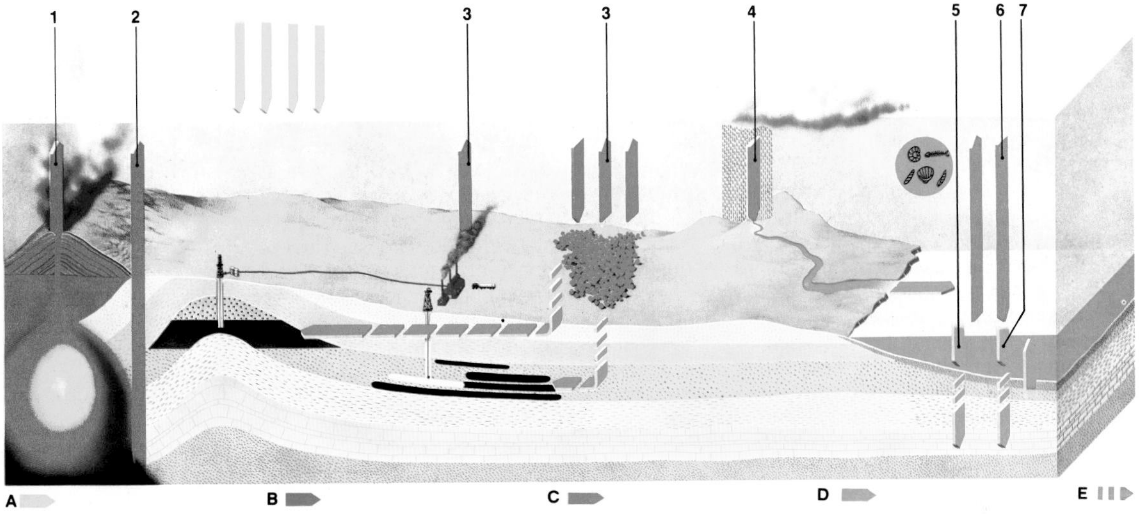

Carbon, in such forms as carbon dioxide (C) *and carbonates* (D), *continuously cycles, or circulates, through the biosphere, atmosphere, and hydrosphere. Utilizing sunlight* (A), *by the process of photosynthesis* (B), *green plants convert atmospheric carbon dioxide into living matter. Petroleum, coal, and natural gas are formed through the partial decay of plants and their subsequent burial and compaction* (E). *Atmospheric carbon dioxide is replenished from the Earth's interior during volcanic activity* (1), *by decomposition of uplifted carbonate rocks* (2), *by the burning of petroleum* (3) *and other organic matter, and by animal respiration. Dissolved carbon dioxide is present in rainwater* (4) *and seawater* (6). *Most of the carbon dioxide in seawater is deposited as carbonate sediments by marine organisms* (5) *or through chemical reactions* (7).

All living cells are basically composed of PROTEINS consisting of carbon, hydrogen, oxygen, and nitrogen in various chemical combinations, and each living organism puts these elements together according to its own genetic code. To do this the organism must have these available in special compounds built around carbon. These special compounds are produced only by green plants, by the process of PHOTOSYNTHESIS, in which CHLOROPHYLL, serving as a CATALYST, traps and uses solar energy in the form of light. Six molecules of carbon dioxide combine with six molecules of water to form one molecule of glucose (sugar). Six oxygen molecules are also produced and are discharged into the atmosphere unless the plant needs energy for its life processes. In that case, the oxygen combines with the glucose immediately, releasing carbon dioxide and water and completing the cycle.

The above process is described by the formula $6CO_2 + 6H_2O \rightleftharpoons C_6H_{12}O_6 + 6O_2$, with the double arrows indicating a reversible process, or cycle. The length of time required to complete the cycle varies. In plants without an immediate need for energy, the chemical processes continue in a variety of ways.

By reducing the hydrogen and oxygen content of most of the sugar molecules by one water molecule and combining them to form large molecules, plants produce substances such as starch, inulin, and fats and store them for future use. Regardless of whether the stored food is used later by the plant or consumed by some other organism, the molecules will ultimately be digested (broken into smaller molecules) and oxidized, and carbon dioxide and water will be discharged.

Other molecules of sugar undergo a series of chemical changes and are finally combined with nitrogen compounds to form protein substances called amino acids, which are then used to build tissues. Although these substances may pass from organism to organism, eventually they too are oxidized and form carbon dioxide and water as cells wear out and are broken down and excreted, or as the organisms die. A new set of organisms then uses the waste products or tissues for food, digesting and oxidizing the substances for energy release.

At various times in the Earth's history, plant and animal remains have become buried by EROSION AND SEDIMENTATION and converted into fossil fuels such as PETROLEUM and coal (see COAL AND COAL MINING). The carbon cycle, temporarily interrupted in this manner, is completed as the fuels are burned, and carbon dioxide and water are again added to the ATMOSPHERE for reuse by living things.

See also: ECOLOGY; METABOLISM; NUTRIENT CYCLES.

carbon dioxide see CARBON; GREENHOUSE EFFECT

carbon monoxide see CARBON; POLLUTION, ENVIRONMENTAL

carbon star Some STARS have spectra that do not fit into the normal stellar spectral classification. Carbon stars, also known as stars of spectral types R and N, are one such type. Their spectra show features caused by combinations of carbon with itself and with elements such as nitrogen and hydrogen, whereas ordinary M-type stars show titanium-oxide features instead. Carbon stars are thought to have higher carbon-to-oxygen ratios than do ordinary stars. They are rare and all are red giants, indicating an advanced stage of evolution.

carbon tetrachloride Carbon tetrachloride, CCl_4, is a clear, colorless, nonflammable, volatile liquid with a characteristic odor. It boils at 76.7° C and solidifies at -23° C. Practically insoluble in water, carbon tetrachloride forms an organic phase more dense than the aqueous phase. Because of this it has laboratory use in chemical separations. It has various applications in industry and serves as a starting material in the manufacture of some organic compounds. It was once widely employed in commercial dry cleaning, but it is poisonous and must be handled carefully. It is no longer permitted in products for home use. Inhalation of vapors or absorption through the skin can lead to accumulations in the body that cause kidney and liver damage and can be fatal.

carbon-14 dating see RADIOMETRIC AGE-DATING

carbonate minerals Carbonate minerals are those having the carbonate ion CO_3^{2-} as a major component. This ion reacts readily with acid to produce carbon dioxide and water. The carbonate minerals are thus generally characterized by solubility in acids.

The more common carbonates are anhydrous minerals forming three structural groups: (1) the CALCITE ($CaCO_3$) group, which includes magnesite ($MgCO_3$), SIDERITE ($FeCO_3$), rhodochrosite ($MnCO_3$), and smithsonite ($ZnCO_3$); (2) the DOLOMITE ($CaMg(CO_3)_2$) group, comprising dolomite and ankerite ($Ca(Mg,Fe)(CO_3)_2$); and (3) the aragonite group, comprising aragonite (a less stable form of $CaCO_3$ than calcite), strontianite ($SrCO_3$), CERUSSITE ($PbCO_3$), and witherite ($BaCO_3$). Calcite and dolomite are the commonest carbonate minerals, being the chief constituents of vast deposits of LIMESTONE and dolomite rock. Aragonite is common in modern marine SEDIMENTS. The other carbonates, found in EVAPORITES, hydrothermal ORE DEPOSITS, and SEDIMENTARY ROCKS, are often important sources of the metals they contain, as are the hydrous copper carbonates, AZURITE and MALACHITE.

Carboniferous Period see EARTH, GEOLOGIC HISTORY OF; GEOLOGIC TIME

carbonyl group [kahr'-buh-nul] The carbonyl group, which is composed of a carbon atom that is doubly bonded to an oxygen atom and singly bonded to two other combining groups, is the distinguishing structural feature of the molecules of ALDEHYDES and KETONES, which are commonly called carbonyl compounds.

Carborundum see ABRASIVE

carboxylic acid [kahr-bahk-sil'-ik] The carboxylic acids are a class of organic compounds containing one or more carboxyl groups, COOH. Examples commonly encountered are the sour constituents of vinegar, acetic acid; of cream of tartar, the monopotassium salt of tartaric acid; of sour apples, rhubarb, and other fruits, malic acid; and of citrus fruits, citric acid. Carboxylic acids as such are not widespread in nature, despite the occurrence of derivatives such as AMIDES and ESTERS in all living organisms.

Acidic Properties. An acid, by one definition, is a substance that is able to donate a proton to another substance, called a base. Thus acetic acid, to a small extent, donates protons to water to form hydronium ions, H_3O^+. The carboxylic acids vary greatly in this ability, depending on their structure and substitution, and they range from strong to extremely weak acids. All carboxylic acids react with strong bases such as sodium hydroxide to form SALTS, which, except for the simplest acids, are more soluble in water than are the acids themselves. Soaps, in general, are sodium salts of long-chain carboxylic acids, calcium and magnesium salts being relatively insoluble.

Most of the straight-chain carboxylic acids are known by trivial names that stem from the original natural source. The first four members of the series are commonly known as FORMIC ACID, HCO_2H; ACETIC ACID, CH_3CO_2H; propionic acid, $CH_3CH_2CO_2H$; and *n*-butyric acid, $CH_3CH_2CH_2CO_2H$. Systematic naming is based on the number of carbon atoms in the molecule. Thus, caproic acid, from goat-milk fat, has the systematic name hexanoic acid.

Natural Esters. FATS AND OILS are esters of FATTY ACIDS (carboxylic acids with long straight chains) combined with glycerol, a trihydroxy alcohol. If such a glyceryl ester is liquid at room temperature, the substance is an oil; if a solid at room temperature, the substance is a fat. The longer the chains in the acid groups, the higher the melting point of the fat. Carbon-carbon double bonds in the chains decrease the melting point. Strong mineral acids or bases can split an ester into the component acid and alcohol, and a fat or oil into the component fatty acids and glycerol. Then the mixture of acids may be separated and identified. Such analysis shows that most natural fats and oils give sizable amounts of palmitic acid, $CH_3(CH_2)_{14}CO_2H$, a typical fatty acid, and also stearic and oleic acids. Vegetable oils (peanut, corn, sesame, cottonseed, soybean, safflower) have large percentages of the polyunsaturated linolenic acid. Acetic acid is a precursor in the synthesis of cholesterol and fatty acids in the body.

Aromatic Carboxylic Acids. If the carboxyl group is attached to a benzene ring, as is the case with benzoic acid, $C_6H_5CO_2H$, certain physical properties result, such as higher melting points. These compounds are called aromatic acids. Salicylic acid has a hydroxyl group adjacent to a carboxyl group on the ring. The acetate ester of the hydroxyl group is aspirin, and the methyl ester of salicylic acid is present in oil of wintergreen. Ascorbic acid (vitamin C) is a LACTONE, a ring created by ester formation between carboxyl and hydroxyl groups on the same chain. The bile acids, complex structures related to the steroids, occur as bile salts in the stomach and intestines and serve as emulsifiers.

See also: ACIDS AND BASES; SOAP AND DETERGENT.

carburetor [kahr'-bur-ay-tur] A carburetor is a device that vaporizes a liquid fuel such as gasoline and mixes it with air in the proper ratio for combustion in an INTERNAL-COMBUSTION ENGINE, such as the gasoline engine that powers most AUTOMOBILES. Under ordinary conditions the ratio of gasoline to air should be about 1:15 by weight. A higher ratio of gasoline is called a richer mixture, and a lower ratio is called leaner.

A simple form of carburetor consists of a float chamber, a jet nozzle, and an air chamber that is narrowed at one point. Such a narrowing in a chamber or tube is called a venturi. A float valve keeps the gasoline at a constant level in the float chamber. When the engine is running, air is drawn into the air chamber, where it is accelerated by the venturi. In accordance with BERNOULLI'S LAW, this high-velocity air creates a low-pressure region, and the jet nozzle, which is attached in this region, draws a fine spray of gasoline from the float chamber into the venturi. Here it mixes with the air, and the mixture is then fed to the engine cylinders, where it is ignited. A choke valve at the entrance to the carburetor is used to reduce the amount of air entering the chamber when the engine is cold, producing a richer mixture.

In practice, carburetors use various means to ensure an optimal mixture of gasoline and air under differing conditions, including idling and rapid acceleration. Instead of having a carburetor, an engine can have a system of fuel injection, which delivers a metered quantity of gasoline directly to each cylinder. Fuel injection has always been used with diesel engines; it has also been gaining in use with gasoline engines.

An automotive fuel system consists of the carburetor or fuel injector, the fuel tank, the fuel pump, and the fuel filter, along with tubing connecting the parts.

Carchemish [kahr'-kem-ish] Carchemish was an ancient settlement on the upper Euphrates at the Syrian border in Turkey, near present-day Jerablus. The site was occupied from the late 6th millennium BC. Pre-1st millennium BC remains include a nearby cemetery and a

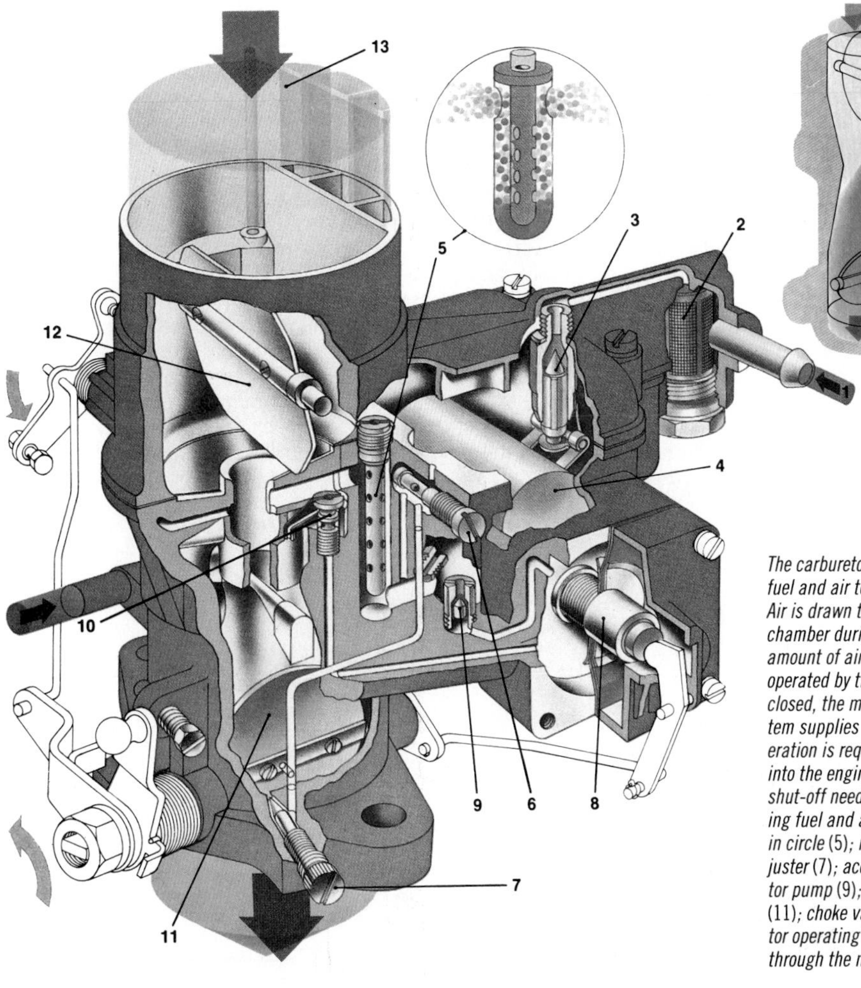

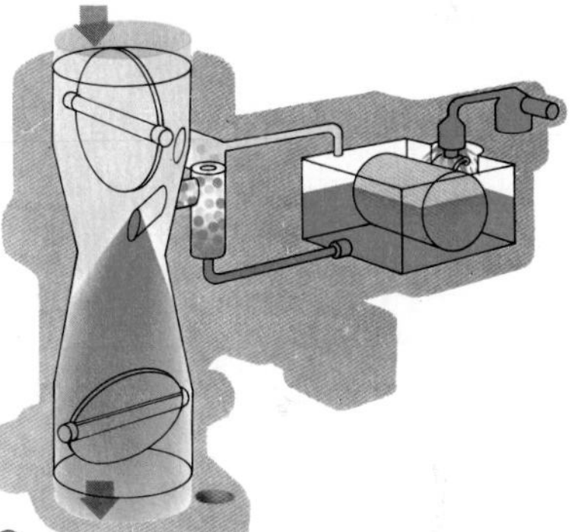

The carburetor supplies the appropriate mixture of fuel and air to the combustion chambers of the engine. Air is drawn through the carburetor into the combustion chamber during the intake stroke of the piston. The amount of air is controlled by the throttle valve, operated by the accelerator pedal. When the throttle is closed, the main system is bypassed, and an idling system supplies fuel to keep the engine idling. When acceleration is required, the accelerator pump jet forces fuel into the engine. Shown are fuel intake (1); *filter* (2); *shut-off needle valve* (3); *float* (4); *main jet incorporating fuel and air mixture and air corrector jet, also shown in circle* (5); *idling mixture adjuster* (6); *idling speed adjuster* (7); *accelerator pump* (8); *feed valve to accelerator pump* (9); *accelerator pump jet* (10); *throttle valve* (11); *choke valve* (12); *and air intake* (13). *The carburetor operating at cruising speed* (above right) *sucks fuel through the main jet into the incoming air stream.*

unique HITTITE-period jewelry assemblage preserved in a later tomb. The important Late Hittite center of the early 1st millennium BC comprised a large citadel and an inner and an outer town. Impressive sculptural reliefs representing historical figures and mythic, cultic, and war scenes, some with Hittite hieroglyphic inscriptions, date to this period. Carchemish was conquered by ASSYRIA in 717 BC.

carcinoma see CANCER; TUMOR

card games Recorded evidence of the existence of playing cards—usually in the form of ordinances prohibiting their use—does not appear in Europe until the 14th century. (The many varieties of Chinese and Indian cards are far older.) TAROT cards were the first type to appear in the Western world. Neither the origin of the tarot deck, nor its original purpose, is known with certainty. The popular belief that the deck was devised for fortune-telling is denied by many scholars.

Designed in the Middle Ages, the tarot deck reflected medieval society, where kings ruled a world that was divided into four broad classes: the church, the military, merchants, and farmers. Thus, in addition to the cards of the major arcana—the symbolic picture cards for which the tarot deck is still famous—the deck included 56 cards divided into four suits: cups (the church); swords (the military); pentacles, or 5-pointed stars (merchants); and batons (farmers).

These first decks were made by hand, and only the wealthy could afford them. When the printing press was invented in the 15th century, cards were reproduced by means of hand-colored woodcuts and, later, engravings. Their popularity spread rapidly across the continent. The old tarot cups soon became hearts, the swords became spades, the pentacles became diamonds, and the batons, clubs. In Germany, however, hearts, leaves, acorns, and bells illustrated the four suits.

The French had the greatest influence on the creation of the modern deck. They eliminated the major arcana and combined the knight and page, reducing the size of the deck to 52 cards and simplifying the suit symbols to plain red hearts and diamonds, black spades and trefoils (clover leaves). This simplification allowed the deck to be more easily printed and lowered its cost. The French also began to identify the court cards. The king of hearts was Charlemagne, for example; of diamonds, Julius Caesar; of spades, King David; and of clubs, Alexander the Great.

Card designs remained basically the same until the mid-19th century. Double-headed court cards, and indices—the small suit-number identification in the card corners—were both innovations of the 1800s. Card backs were usually plain until the 1850s, when the English artist Owen Jones designed a number of ornate backs. Complex back designs then began to be printed on most decks. The first joker appeared in 1865 in an American deck.

Although early card makers often signed their products, the inventors of card games remain anonymous. From the 17th century on, innumerable books on "gaming" accompanied the card-playing fever that had developed with the increasing availability of cards. The first accurate compendiums of rules, however, were those of the English writer Edmond HOYLE, in his treatise on whist (1742) and his later works on other games. His books became immensely popular, and the expression "according to Hoyle" still means to play strictly by the rules.

Most card games can be classified according to their basic structure. Games of rank include the various tarot games and the many games based on the old game of triomphe (triumph in England), a trump-card game that evolved into the German skat, as well as WHIST, EUCHRE, ecarte, and BRIDGE. These games are usually played with three or four players, each bidding for the opportunity to play out their hand by specifying the number of tricks (one trick being the cards played in one round) the hand may be able to take. Tricks are taken by the cards of highest rank. The trump suit outranks all other suits.

Games of combination can be divided into two types. The first are those which require combinations of sets (3 or 4 cards of a kind) or groups (3 or more cards in se-

When cards were introduced in Europe, Italian suits were widely used and taken to represent the church (cup), military (sword), merchant class (money), and peasantry (club). By the 15th century the French had replaced the old suits with the heart (church), pike (knight), tile (or arrowhead, for archer), and trefoil (peasantry). Early German card suits differed from both.

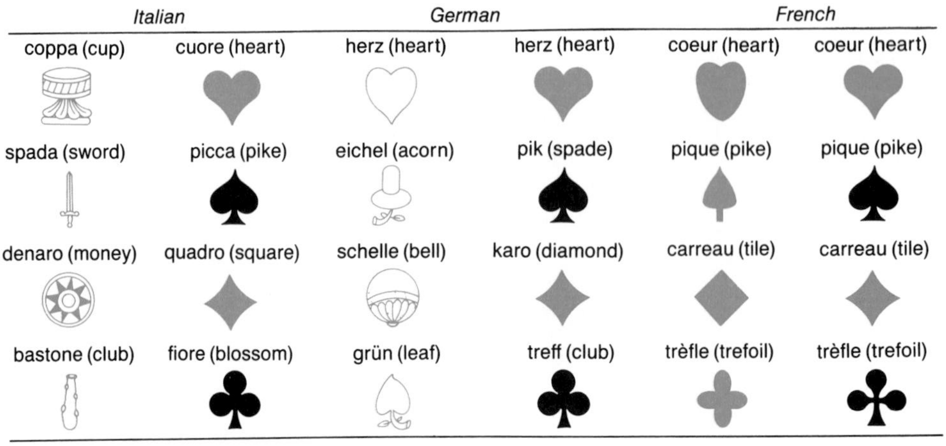

This late-19th-century lithograph pictures a popular pastime of the era: fortune-telling, using the chance lay of the cards to predict the future.

quence). The second are those which require groups of cards that add up to a predetermined score. POKER and all RUMMY games fall into the first group. The second group includes CRIBBAGE and games such as CASINO and BLACKJACK.

In some games, where both combination and rank are important, the object is to score combinations and also to win points by rank. BEZIQUE, a 19th-century French game, was the forerunner of PINOCHLE, several versions of which are widely played in the United States. The primary object of such games is to "meld"—to declare certain cards or combinations that are each worth points—and then to take tricks using both cards of ranked value and trump cards.

In SOLITAIRES, games played by one person, all the cards in the deck must be brought into a predetermined order according to certain rules. There are at least 350 solitaire versions; some can be played with two or more players.

The most popular card games in gambling casinos are blackjack and its variants. These are also known as banking games, because the casino's dealer opposes all other players and controls the deal and the "bank." Blackjack (vingt-et-un) is the generic casino game. It requires players to ask for cards one at a time until they reach a total of 21 or a number as close as possible to but less than 21. BACCARAT and CHEMIN DE FER are similar, except that only two or three cards are dealt, and the winning number is 9.

Another large category of card games are those played by children. Many involve simply collecting combinations ("Have you any threes?" "Go Fish"—whereupon the first player takes a card from the pile of undealt cards) or being quicker to slap or cover a card (Slapjack, Spit). Some children's games, however, are fairly complex (Concentration, Cuckoo, Frogs in the Pond). Special decks of cards designed to teach (for example, Authors, which features pictures of famous writers; or Geography, with maps of continents and countries) have also been popular.

Cardano, Gerolamo [kahr-dah'-noh, jay-roh'-lah-moh] Gerolamo Cardano, b. Sept. 20, 1501, d. Sept. 21, 1576, was a great Italian mathematician of the Renaissance. He lectured and wrote on mathematics, medicine, astronomy, astrology, alchemy, and physics. His *Ars magna* (The Great Art, 1545), was the first great Latin treatise on algebra. His *Liber de ludo aleae* (The Book on Games of Chance, 1663) was the first study of the theory of probability. *De vita propria liber* (*Book of My Life*, 1575; Eng. trans., 1930), Cardano's autobiography, is one of the first modern psychological autobiographies.

Cárdenas, Lázaro [kahr'-day-nahs, lah'-sah-roh] Lázaro Cárdenas, b. May 21, 1895, d. Oct. 19, 1970, was a Mexican revolutionary leader and president who carried out sweeping social and economic reforms during the 1930s. Coming from a poor family, he received little education. At age 18, Cárdenas joined the revolutionary movement and rose quickly to the rank of general. By 1920 he was governor of Michoacán, and in 1930 he became chairman of the National Revolutionary party.

Chosen by Plutarco CALLES to be president for the term 1934–40, Cárdenas went to the people for support and assembled a leftist coalition that forced Calles into exile in 1936. He then carried out agrarian reforms that included massive land distribution to the peasants. He encouraged the development of the labor movement and in 1938 nationalized the foreign-owned petroleum industry, thereby incurring the wrath of U.S. business interests. Cárdenas retired from the presidency in 1940, but his ruling coalition, although extensively modified, has dominated Mexico since then. He himself remained an important influence in Mexico until his death.

Cardiff Cardiff is the capital and largest city of Wales. Formerly the county town of Glamorgan, it became part of South Glamorgan in 1974. It has a population of 283,900 (1988 est.). An international seaport, it is situated in southern Wales on the Taff River at its mouth in the Bristol Channel. Once the world's greatest coal-exporting port, Cardiff is now the commercial, financial, industrial, and distribution center for southern Wales. It has a well-planned central city and many open park spaces. University College, Cardiff, founded in 1883, is there. Points of interest include Cardiff Castle, dating from 1090; early 12th-century Llandaff cathedral; and the important National Museum of Wales, established in 1927. Although the site was established in Roman times, the present city developed around Cardiff Castle, a Norman fortress. After 1800 the city grew rapidly. Cardiff was chartered as a city in 1905 and became the official capital of Wales in 1955.

The Cardigan Welsh corgi, a working dog, was used by farmers of Wales to drive cattle. The name means "dwarf dog" in Welsh.

Cardigan Welsh corgi The Cardigan is one of the oldest breeds in the British Isles. A working dog of the Welsh farmer, it was used to drive cattle into unfenced common (crown-owned) land. The breed, however, began to be seen at dog shows in England only in the 1920s. In 1934 the English Kennel Club separated the Cardigan and PEMBROKE WELSH CORGI into two distinct breeds. The Cardigan is short-legged and long-bodied, with erect ears and a foxlike head; the word *corgi*, in Welsh, means "dwarf dog." It stands about 30 cm (12 in) at the shoulders, weighs about 11 kg (25 lb), and measures about 1 m (3 ft) from nose to tip of tail. The dense, medium-length coat may range from reddish to blue gray to black, usually with white markings; pure white is a disqualification for show dogs.

Cardiganshire see DYFED

cardinal The common cardinal, *Cardinalis cardinalis*, a member of the finch family, Fringillidae, is a bird found in the eastern United States and parts of Mexico and southern California. It is named for the red of the robes of Roman Catholic cardinals. The male is bright red with a black throat; the female is buffy brown with red on its crest, wings, and tail. Both sexes have stout, conical bills for feeding on seeds, fruits, and insects. The song is clear and cheerful. The cardinal is the official bird of several U.S. states.

The cardinal is native to North America. The male (foreground) *is recognized by its red color, crest, and black face; the female, by its brown plumage and red-tipped crest, wings, and tail.*

Cardinals, College of The College of Cardinals is the body of Roman Catholic churchmen that elects a new pope. The precise origin of the term *cardinal* is uncertain, but it began to achieve acceptance by the 6th century. At that time cardinals were those bishops whose dioceses had been overtaken by the barbarians and who were then assigned by the pope to vacant dioceses. Later the term was applied to the senior priests of certain parish churches in Rome. By the 11th century, the organization of these Roman pastors had developed into the sacred college of cardinals. At first the cardinals functioned as assistants and counselors to the popes, but after 1059 they became the papal electors as well. By the late 11th century, prelates outside of Rome were elected cardinals, a practice that continues to this day.

cardiopulmonary resuscitation Cardiopulmonary resuscitation is an emergency FIRST AID procedure combining external cardiac, or HEART, massage, which keeps blood flowing through the circulatory system, with artificial respiration, which keeps air flowing in and out of the LUNGS. The procedure can save victims of cardiac arrest (cessation of the heartbeat) and respiratory arrest. The two are closely related. Although cardiopulmonary resuscitation can be performed successfully by lay people, health authorities recommend special training to recognize the signs of cardiac arrest and perform the resuscitation correctly.

cardiovascular diseases Cardiovascular diseases include the wide range of disorders that afflict the HEART and the blood vessels, the parts of the CIRCULATORY SYSTEM that pump BLOOD and convey it throughout the body. Such diseases are the leading cause of death worldwide. They are the product of many influences, ranging from hereditary and nutritional to environmental in nature.

The circulatory system consists of two interconnected systems, both originating in the heart: systemic circulation and pulmonary circulation. In systemic, or greater, circulation, blood is pumped from the left ventricle of the heart into the AORTA. It is then distributed by a series of increasingly smaller arteries (see ARTERY) into the tiny capillaries in which the blood circulates through the body tissues. From the capillaries in the tissues the blood is then collected in VEINS of increasing diameter, finally entering the right atrium of the heart.

In pulmonary, or lesser, circulation, blood is pumped from the right ventricle into the pulmonary arteries and courses through the LUNG capillaries; there it is reoxygenated and collected again in veins to enter the left atrium. Because capillaries are where oxygen and foodstuffs enter body cells and waste products are removed by the bloodstream, any peripheral vascular disease affects the function of the tissues supplied by the capillaries; in fact, cardiovascular diseases can cause diseases in all other tissues and organs of the body. For a discussion of diseases of the heart itself, see HEART DISEASES.

Artery Diseases. Many diseases affect the arteries, but the single major cause of disease is the thickening and hardening of artery walls by deposits of fatty materials, known as ARTERIOSCLEROSIS. In major vessels such as the aorta, this process is called ATHEROSCLEROSIS. Several conditions are thought to contribute to the development of such deposits, including excessive fats in the diet (see NUTRITION, HUMAN), high BLOOD PRESSURE (see HYPERTENSION), and genetic factors.

Other major diseases of the aorta include true ANEURYSMS and so-called dissecting aneurysms. The former are balloonlike swellings that result from weakening of the aorta wall, most commonly because of atherosclerosis or syphilis. Dissecting aneurysms are usually the result of an inherited degeneration of the middle layer of the aorta wall, leading to a separation of the layers by blood, under high pressure, pouring through a tear in the inner layer.

A danger in any aneurysm is rupture and sudden death. True aneurysms, in particular, may cause severe pressure symptoms on nearby structures. These aneurysms may so dilate the aortic valves of the heart as to render them incompetent, and heart failure and death result. Aneurysms are often repaired by replacement.

Atherosclerosis may result in occlusion, or blockage, of an artery. In many cases the proximate cause of the blockage is clot formation in a narrowed atherosclerotic area. In the coronary arteries this is the major cause of myocardial infarctions, or heart attacks. In peripheral arteries such as those of the legs, untreated narrowing may result in gangrene and require amputation. (Since the condition appears to be accelerated in patients with DIABETES mellitus, gangrene of the lower extremities is a significant danger for such persons.) Bypass surgery is used for arterial narrowing in coronary arteries; elsewhere, replacement of the narrowed segment is the usual procedure. Alternative therapies include dilating the narrowed segment with a tiny balloon delivered by catheter (see ANGIOPLASTY). Catheters may also be used to deliver materials that convert plasminogen, a normal constituent of the blood, into plasmin, which is a dissolver of clots. This procedure is effective if done within three hours. Arteriosclerotic changes in smaller arteries are not amenable to the therapies that are used in larger arteries.

A disorder of the small arteries in the extremities, known as RAYNAUD'S DISEASE, leads to numbness of the fingers and toes. The disorder is often of unknown origin but may also be secondary to some known disorder, and it is usually not serious. In some cases, however, the disease may grow progressively worse and lead to blood clots and the onset of gangrene.

Vein Diseases. The most important peripheral vascular disease of the veins is thrombophlebitis (see PHLEBITIS). This disorder involves the formation of a blood clot (or clots) in large veins, usually in the leg or pelvis. Any or all of three major factors can cause such clots: slowing of the bloodstream (or even stoppage for a short period of time), increase of coagulability of the blood, and injury to the lining of the vein. The disorder can cause local inflammation, redness, and swelling, but it may also be entirely free of local symptoms. In either case, but particularly in the latter one, the clot may break off and travel to the right side of the heart. From there it is pumped to the lung, to be trapped as the pulmonary artery branches and narrows, blocking the blood supply to a portion of the lung, a process called pulmonary infarction. The immediate SHOCK may be fatal and is a major cause of sudden death in postoperative hospitalized patients. To prevent such an occurrence postoperative patients are constantly monitored and are encouraged to walk as soon as possible.

A distressing but usually minor disorder of the veins, known as VARICOSE VEIN, results from a failure of valves in the veins to keep blood flowing back toward the heart. In some cases, however, the condition can lead to varicose ulcers or the inflammation of vein walls, with resulting development of clots and of thrombophlebitis.

Hypertension. High blood pressure affects up to 20 percent of the adult population in the United States. By far the most common type is essential hypertension, the causes of which are unknown. The remaining cases are secondary to at least 30 different conditions. Untreated hypertension can cause severe kidney damage, precipitate a cerebral hemorrhage (see STROKE), or result in heart failure. A number of drugs for treating essential hypertension have been introduced over the past few decades; they vary in effectiveness.

Another form of hypertension, called pulmonary hypertension (see COR PULMONALE), is caused by various conditions that result in lung scarring and consequent obstruction of branches of the pulmonary artery.

Historical Background. Physicians of ancient Egypt and China had already recognized the PULSE and were using it as a diagnostic tool, but the true nature of the circulatory system was not understood until the Renaissance and the anatomical discoveries of such scientists as Michael SERVETUS and Hieronymus Fabricius ab Aquapendente. Their work culminated in the experimental demonstration of blood circulation by the English physician William HARVEY in the 17th century, and Harvey's work in turn led directly to such developments as French physician Raymond Vieussen's correlation of abnormalities of the heart valves with types of heart failure.

Modern drug therapy of cardiac illnesses began with the discovery of DIGITALIS in a folk-medicine herbal mixture in the 18th century. In the early 19th century the invention of the STETHOSCOPE and the refinement of methods of physical examination created the specialty of cardiology.

In the late 19th and the early 20th century, the study and treatment of cardiovascular disease was advanced by developments such as the X ray, the ELECTROCARDIOGRAPH, and the cardiac catheter. Remarkable advances were also made in SURGERY, such as the repair of congenital deformities of the heart and the large blood vessels. More recently, advances in RADIOLOGY imaging techniques allow medical specialists not only to define defects but also to position catheters through which procedures can be performed and drugs administered.

Cardozo, Benjamin N. [kahr-doh'-zoh] Benjamin Nathan Cardozo, b. New York City, May 24, 1870, d. July 9, 1938, was an American judge who was particularly successful in applying existing law to changing social needs. His influential opinions and writings stress the original purpose of a given legal rule rather than the form in which it was cast. Cardozo practiced law from 1891 to 1913, when he was elected a New York state judge. He served (1914–32) on the state court of appeals, becoming chief judge in 1927. His opinions won him wide attention and helped make that court one of the best known in the United States. Appointed to the U.S. Supreme Court by President Hoover in 1932, Cardozo often sided with liberals Louis BRANDEIS and Harlan STONE in voting for NEW DEAL social legislation opposed by the majority of the court. In a key case, Cardozo wrote the majority opinion upholding federal social security legislation.

cards, playing see CARD GAMES

Carducci, Giosuè [kahr-doot'-chee, joh-zoo-ay'] An influential poet and critic known for his pastoral and historical poems, Giosuè Carducci, b. July 27, 1835, d. Feb. 16, 1907, was the first Italian to receive (1906) the Nobel Prize for literature. A representative early work, modeled on the classical canzone and sonnet, is *Rime* (1857). Carducci's anti-Catholic, republican views are reflected in *Inno a Satana* (Hymn to Satan, 1865). In his later poems, collected in *Odi barbare* (1877–87) and *Rime nuove* (1887), he returned to patriotic and sentimental themes.

CARE CARE (Cooperative for American Relief Everywhere) is a U.S.-based international agency founded in 1945 to help needy people in war-torn or developing countries. Funded primarily by private contributions, it distributes food, tools, and building materials and provides medical care in recipient countries, many of which share some of the costs.

career education Career education as a movement emphasizes a "careers" orientation throughout the school curriculum and also stresses the links between school and community. Career education officially became a concern of the U.S. Office of Education in 1971, following years of social unrest that exposed the inadequacy of traditional educational content as a means of dealing with current social realities.

Among the social and occupational problems that a career-education approach is targeted to solve or ameliorate are the high rates of youth unemployment, particularly among minorities; the lack of marketable employment skills or clear personal goals of many students on leaving high school; and the excess of students choosing college-preparatory programs rather than vocational or technical training over the number likely to complete a college degree or for whom jobs requiring a college preparation may be available in the future. Career education is also concerned with worker alienation and mid-career occupational dislocation due to changing technological processes and occupational opportunities, and with sex bias that restricts the opportunities and mobility of women.

Broadly, career education is expected to solve the problems it addresses by reducing the separation of academic education from VOCATIONAL EDUCATION and TECHNICAL EDUCATION by making all subject matter practically applicable insofar as possible. It must also provide opportunities for career awareness, exploration, and prepartion through career guidance for all students throughout the educational process. In 1977, Congress passed the Career Education Incentive Act, which in 1979 provided funds to implement career education from kindergarten through grade 12 and to demonstrate its efficacy in postsecondary education. From 1973 to 1982 the federal government, through its Comprehensive Employment Training Act (CETA) programs, provided many types of on-the-job training opportunities in local communities. The Job Training Partnership Act of 1982, which replaced CETA, is aimed mainly at training disadvantaged youths.

Carew, Rod [kuh-roo'] The Panamanian-born American baseball star Rodney Cline Carew, b. Oct. 1, 1945, had the highest lifetime batting average (.328) of any player whose entire, completed career was in the postwar era. During a long American League (AL) career with the Minnesota Twins (1967–78) and the California Angels (1979–85), Carew accumulated 3,053 hits, only the 16th man to achieve the 3,000-hit plateau. The left-handed hitting second, then first, baseman was Rookie of the Year in 1967 and was an all-star selection every year except one through 1978. From 1969 to 1978 he won 7 league batting championships—only Ty Cobb, with 12, and Honus Wagner, with 8, ever won more. In 1977, when he won the AL Most Valuable Player award, Carew hit .388, an average surpassed only once since Ted Williams hit .406 in 1941. In 1991, Carew was inducted into the Baseball Hall of Fame.

Carew, Thomas [kair'-ee] Thomas Carew, 1595–1640, was one of the first English CAVALIER POETS. A friend and admirer of Ben Jonson, he also praised John Donne for discarding "servile imitation" and opening "a mine of rich and pregnant fancy." Carew's love lyrics, collected in *Poems* (1640), combine brilliant imagery, intelligent craftsmanship, and refined wit. His masque, *Coelum Britannicum*, was performed in 1634. He was a favorite of King Charles I and led the life of a courtier.

Carey, George Leonard The English churchman George Leonard Carey, b. Nov. 13, 1935, became archbishop of Canterbury in January 1991. The son of a hospital porter, Carey was educated at the University of London (graduated 1962), served (1982–87) as principal of Trinity Theological College, Bristol, and was bishop of Bath and Wells from 1987 to 1991.

Carey, William William Carey, b. Aug. 17, 1761, d. June 9, 1834, was an English Baptist missionary and linguist. He joined the Baptists in 1783 and began to preach. A part-time pastor, he supported himself by working as a shoemaker and taught himself several languages. Carey sailed (1793) with his family to India and settled near Calcutta. He translated the New Testament into Bengali in 1801, the Old Testament in 1809, and parts of the Bible into more than 20 Indian dialects. He also wrote grammars and dictionaries in Sanskrit, Marathi, Punjabi, and Telugu. His efforts led to the abolition (1829) of the SUTTEE, the Hindu custom of having widows cremated at their husband's funerals.

cargo cults Cargo cults are usually revivalist, and in some cases messianic and millenarian, movements found among certain peoples indigenous to Oceania. The word *cargo* refers to foreign goods possessed by Europeans; cult adherents believe that such goods belong to themselves and that, with the help of ancestral spirits, the goods can be returned to them through magico-religious means.

This imitation airstrip was constructed by members of cargo cults in Melanesia. These cults are often centered on the belief that such efforts facilitate the return of ancestors bearing a wealth of material goods.

Such movements represent the efforts of local inhabitants to cope with problems arising from contact with foreign cultures. They first appeared during the late 19th century among Papua New Guinea and other Oceanic peoples impressed by the abundance of material wealth they saw. The movements received new impetus during World War II. In a West Irian (western New Guinea) cult of 1942, entire villages were organized into an imitation army with dummy equipment, in the hope that this would be transformed into real equipment. Followers of John Frum on Tanna (New Hebrides) built landing strips and warehouses in anticipation of the arrival of air cargo. All such movements draw on traditional custom, experience, and ideology. Cargo cults, some of them politically oriented, demonstrate a people's resilience and imagination in coping with new and difficult problems.

Carib The Carib are an Indian people found principally in northern Honduras, Belize, and the Guiana region of South America. Former inhabitants of the Lesser Antilles, they were traditionally known for their CANNIBALISM (from the Spanish *caníbal*, the name by which the Carib were also known). A fiercely aggressive people, the Island Carib drove the ARAWAK from the Lesser Antilles and captured their women; as a result, many Carib wives spoke Arawakan as their native language.

Essentially a maritime people, both Guiana and Island Carib were excellent navigators. They crossed much of the Caribbean in huge canoes, fitted with woven cloth sails, that held as many as 50 people. With the arrival of European colonizers in the 17th century, the Island Carib were all but eradicated. A small surviving group was brought (1795) by the British to Roatán island off Honduras, from which the Carib gradually migrated along the north coast of Central America. Today, as in the past, the Carib live in small communities composed of several matrilineal kin groups. Their diet is based on tropical forest horticulture, the main crops being maize, beans, and manioc, supplemented by hunting and fishing.

Caribbean Sea The Caribbean Sea is a partially enclosed body of water in the Western Hemisphere, a western extension of the Atlantic Ocean. It is bordered by South America (Venezuela, Colombia) on the south, Central America (Panama, Costa Rica, Nicaragua, Honduras, Guatemala, Belize, Mexico) on the west, and the islands of the WEST INDIES on the north and east. The Yucatán Channel between Cuba and Yucatán connects the Caribbean Sea with the Gulf of Mexico, numerous passages between the islands join it to the Atlantic, and the Panama Canal furnishes access to the Pacific Ocean.

The West Indies, which form the nucleus of the Caribbean region, consist of two main groups: the Greater Antilles (Cuba, Jamaica, Hispaniola, and Puerto Rico) to the north and the Lesser Antilles, which again are subdivided into the Windward and Leeward islands, to the east. The major channels separating the islands are Windward Passage, between Cuba and Hispaniola; Mona Passage, be-

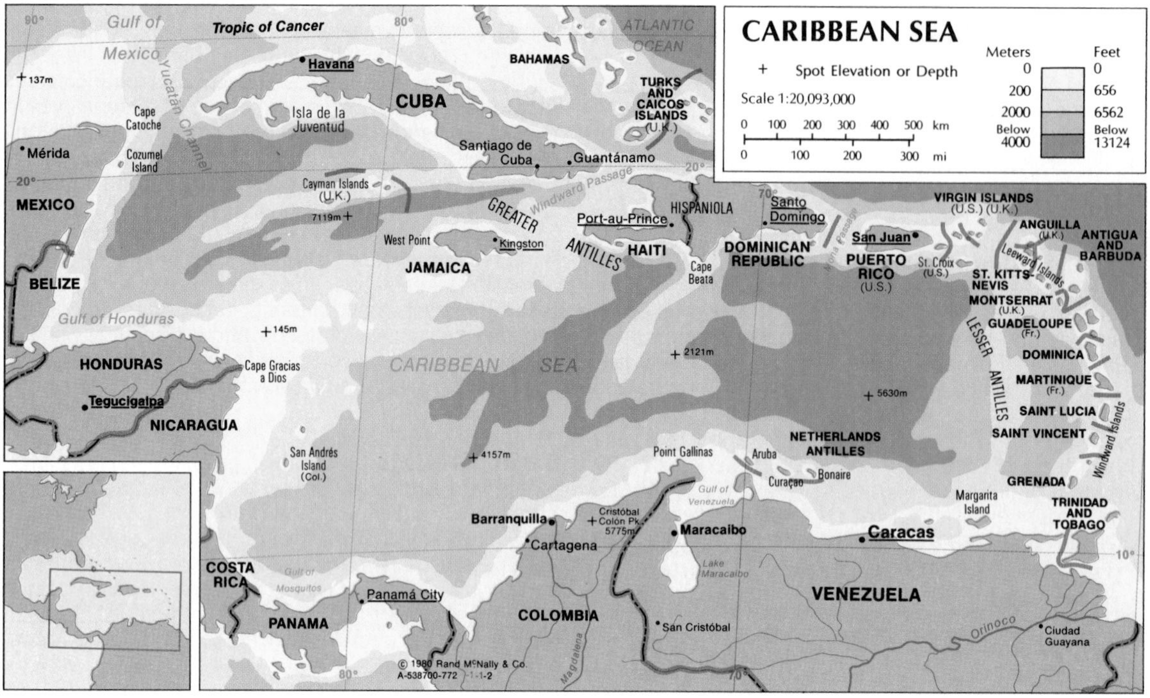

tween Hispaniola and Puerto Rico; and Anegada Passage, between the British and U.S. Virgin Islands.

The total area of the Caribbean Sea is about 2,500,000 km^2 (965,000 mi^2). First explored by Christopher COLUMBUS, the Caribbean was named after the CARIB, a warlike tribe of cannibalistic Indians that inhabited some of the Lesser Antilles at the time of the European conquest. The sea is of major importance for international shipping to and from the Panama Canal and for its natural resources, including oil. It is also a major tourist and recreation area.

Environment

The fringes of the Caribbean are characterized by many small volcanic islands, coral reefs, and irregular shorelines. The floor consists of a complex structure of ocean ridges, trenches, and basins. The Jamaica Ridge, one of the major ocean ridges, runs from Honduras through Jamaica to Hispaniola and divides the sea into two major basins, western and eastern. The former is, in turn, divided by the Cayman Ridge into the Yucatán Basin and the Cayman Trough, the deepest part of the sea, more than 7,000 m (22,960 ft) deep. The Beata Ridge divides the eastern basin into the Colombian and Venezuelan basins. The Aves Ridge separates the easternmost part of the sea, the Grenada Trough, from the Venezuelan Basin. The average depth of the basin floors is about 4,400 m (14,430 ft). The bottom is composed of sedimentary rocks overlaid with carbonate marine sediments that consist mostly of tan to brown muds containing varying amounts of coarse organic and inorganic particles.

The Caribbean is known for its long periods of fair weather; during the warmer months, however, the moist, tropical air becomes unstable and produces a variety of tropical disturbances. Afternoon thunderstorms, which are sometimes intense, are common over both land and sea. From late July through October, hurricanes also develop and frequently cause great damage to adjacent land areas. (See HURRICANE AND TYPHOON.)

Surface-water temperatures range from 23° C (73° F) to 29° C (84° F); air temperatures above it are similar. A well-developed THERMOCLINE exists at a depth of about 300 m (1,000 ft), below which temperatures are relatively uniform. At depths of 1,500 m (5,000 ft) or more, the water temperature remains at about 4° C (39° F) year-round.

The salinity of surface water varies from 34.93 to more than 36 parts per 1,000, depending on the amount of evaporation, precipitation, and surface runoff. It is generally lowest in the northern parts of the sea and highest in the southern parts.

Caribbean waters are composed of four water masses: surface water, subtropical subsurface water, subantarctic intermediate water, and North Atlantic deep water. Most of the channels between the sea and the open Atlantic are so shallow that only surface waters intermix. Thus the movement of water at depths greater than 1,200 m (3,900 ft) is sluggish; the waters at these depths contain little dissolved oxygen and, as a result, little marine life. Some of the deeper channels play a major role in the Caribbean circulation. The Guiana Current flows northwest along the South American coast and enters the Caribbean Sea between the Windward Islands. The water follows the deepest path through the Caribbean and exits through the Yucatán Channel. Some oceanic UPWELLING also occurs along the coast of Colombia and Venezuela.

History and Economy

The Spanish were the first Europeans to explore the Caribbean. They eventually settled the Greater Antilles and either killed or absorbed the ARAWAK Indians native to the larger islands. The Antilles held a favored position because of their proximity to gold deposits, supply of Indian labor, easy access, fertile soil, and favorable climate. The region became known for its production of sugar, coffee, spices, and tropical fruits. The importance of the Antilles declined as the Spanish advanced into the New World through Mexico and Peru, and the islands mostly became supply bases. For centuries the Caribbean was a war zone fought over by European powers—England, France, Spain, and Holland—as well as pirates. Now the Windward Passage is a major shipping route between the eastern United States and the Panama Canal.

Many former island colonies in the Caribbean have gained independence since the early 1960s. Despite high standards of literacy, modernization and expansion of the fishing industry, and development of an oil industry (especially along the coast of Venezuela near Lake Maracaibo), most Caribbean nations remain overly reliant on tourism and a few exports (such as bauxite, sugar, and bananas) and depend heavily on imported food and fuel.

caribou Caribou are the great travelers of the deer family, Cervidae. Herds roam constantly in search of food, consisting generally of ground lichens, sedges, and bark from small trees. They are found in Arctic and sub-Arctic regions. North American caribou are classified with the European REINDEER in one species, *Rangifer tarandus*. Reindeer have been introduced into North America and have interbred with caribou. A bull caribou may weigh up to 300 kg (660 lb), stand 1.5 m (5 ft) high at the shoulder, and measure 2 m (7 ft) long. Caribou are the only deer in which both male and female have antlers. Calves develop tiny "spike horns" at 3 or 4 months of age. Broad hooves with sharp edges give the caribou stability on boggy land or snow and help it move across frozen surfaces and dig down to lichen. Because of efforts of environmentalists, the Alaska oil and gas pipelines were redesigned to allow the barren-ground caribou group unimpeded passage to feeding grounds. These caribou migrate from Alaskan and Canadian Arctic tundra in summer, far southward to Canadian forests in winter. The woodland caribou group lives in bogs and forests of the northwestern United States and southwestern Canada.

Both female and male caribou use visual signals to communicate danger. To show alarm, the male raises its tail; as a sign of caution, it thrusts one of its hind legs out to the side.

caricature In art, caricature is a pictorial representation in which the physical features of a person or object have been grossly exaggerated for comic effect. Caricature is distinguished from mere fantasy and from the GROTESQUE by its intent: it is a process of unmasking the subject to reveal the inner character by drawing on his or her external features. Because caricature tends to emphasize the peculiarities of a subject, it is often an effective vehicle for pictorial SATIRE.

Early Caricature. The term *caricature* (from the Italian *caricate*, "overloaded") was first used in Italy in the mid-17th century. Although intentional distortions and exag-

(Left) *His victory in the election of 1864 made "Long Abraham Lincoln a Little Longer" according to a caricature in* Harper's Weekly. (Below) *A caricature of Leo Tolstoi by David Levine exaggerates his craggy features and long, distinctive beard.*

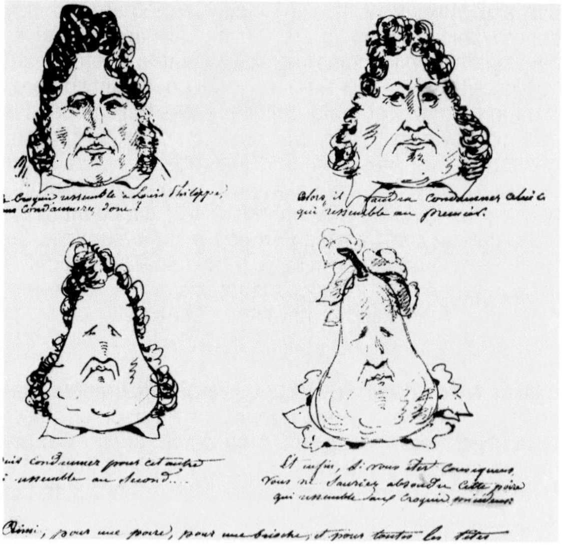

This famous caricature by Charles Philipon likened the head of the king of France, Louis Philippe, to a pear. The king, incensed over the satirical drawing, had the artist charged with libel.

gerations of human anatomy date from ancient times, caricature as a companion to realism originated during the Renaissance. Unusual early caricatures are those of the 16th-century Italian artist Giuseppe ARCIMBOLDO, who created recognizable human portraits from a collage of animals, vegetables, fish, and household articles. The tradition of caricature as a satirical portrait of an individual was developed in its present form during the 17th century by two Italian painters, Giovanni BERNINI and Agostino CARRACCI. The earliest known satirical portrait, however, appears in MICHELANGELO's *The Last Judgment* (1536–41; Sistine Chapel, Rome). In it, the papal master of ceremonies, Biagio da Cesena, is represented as King Minos, the Prince of Hell.

Social and Political Caricature. The moral undertone of caricature soon stimulated its application to social and political comment. During the Reformation, Lucas CRANACH created woodcuts attacking the papacy, such as *The Pope in Hell* (1521). The revolutionary political movements at the end of the 18th century, coupled with improvements in the wood-engraving technique and the invention of lithography—which provided a cheap method of reproduction—further encouraged the development of caricature.

The greatest proliferation and the highest quality of the art form were realized during the 19th century. England produced an exemplary group of caricaturists, notably Thomas ROWLANDSON, James GILLRAY, and George CRUIKSHANK. In France, Charles Philipon began (1830) the first comic weekly, *La Caricature.* A talented caricaturist in his own right, Philipon also discovered and published the best French caricaturists of the 19th century: Honoré DAUMIER, Gustave DORÉ, and Paul GAVARNI. By expressing his political convictions with a sense of moral urgency, Daumier developed caricature into a serious art form.

The 19th-century caricature began to lose its distinction as a genre when it became a staple newspaper feature. The political caricature became the CARTOON; caricatures rendered as narratives eventually grew into a new form, the COMIC STRIP. A notable early example was the late-19th-century series *Max und Moritz*, a feature of Germany's satirical magazine *Die Fliegende Blätter* and the creation of the great caricaturist Wilhelm BUSCH.

Today the caricature is most often in evidence in the work of political cartoonists. Pure caricature—usually a pen-and-ink sketch that conveys its message without words—is produced in the United States by only a few: the most notable are David Levine and the theatrical caricaturist Al Hirschfeld.

carillon see BELL

Carissimi, Giacomo [kah-ris'-see-mee, jah'-koh-moh] Giacomo Carissimi, baptized Apr. 18, 1605, d. Jan. 12, 1674, was the leading master in the early development of the sacred ORATORIO and also the secular CANTATA. From the late 1620s until his death, he was director of music at the church of Sant' Apollinare in Rome. In his oratorios, such as *Jephtha*, *Judgment of Solomon*, *Jonas*, and *Baltazar* (all with Latin texts), Carissimi wrote tighter recitatives, freer melodies for the arias, more dramatic choruses, and more varied instrumental accompaniments than the genre had seen up to that time.

Carl XVI Gustaf see CHARLES XVI GUSTAV, KING OF SWEDEN

Carleton, Guy, 1st Baron Dorchester Guy Carleton, b. Sept. 3, 1724, d. Nov. 10, 1808, was a British commander during the American Revolution and governor of Quebec. Commissioned an ensign, Carleton served in the SEVEN YEARS' WAR in Canada, Europe, and Cuba. He was appointed lieutenant governor of Quebec in 1766 and governor in 1768 and was responsible for Canada's military defense when the revolution started in 1775.

Canada remained in the British Empire largely through Carleton's efforts. He instituted a policy of conciliation toward the French Roman Catholic inhabitants with the QUEBEC ACT of 1774. When American forces invaded Canada in 1775 under Gen. Richard Montgomery and Col. Benedict Arnold, Carleton repelled an attack on Quebec and drove the enemy back to Lake Champlain. He was superseded (1777) as military commander by Gen. John Burgoyne, but in 1782 he returned to command the royal forces in New York, evacuating the British troops and loyalists from the city.

From 1786 to 1796, Carleton was governor of Quebec again. In that position he proposed the federation of all British North America—an idea ahead of his time. He was created Baron Dorchester in 1786 and promoted to general in 1793.

Carleton College Established in 1866 by the Congregational Church, Carleton College is an independent 4-year liberal arts school for men and women in Northfield, Minn. It has a cooperative engineering program with Columbia University and Washington University.

Carlisle (England) [kahr-lile'] Carlisle (1981 pop., 100,692) is the seat of the county of Cumbria, England. Located on the River Eden, 14 km (9 mi) south of the Scottish border, it was an important Roman fortification. From the Middle Ages, Carlisle was a border outpost frequently attacked by the Scots. Carlisle Castle (built 1092) was the site of a brief imprisonment of Mary, Queen of Scots. The Newcastle-Carlisle Railway (1835) was England's first east-west line, and Carlisle remains a transportation hub.

Carlisle (Pennsylvania) [kahr'-lile] Carlisle is a quiet college and light-manufacturing borough in the Cumberland Valley of southern Pennsylvania. With a population of 18,419 (1990), it is the seat of Cumberland County. Carlisle is known for Dickinson College, founded by Thomas Penn in 1773, and for the U.S. Army War College—originally Carlisle Barracks, one of the oldest military posts in the country and from 1879 to 1918 the site of the famous Carlisle Indian School. The attractive tree-shaded borough, with its numerous authentic colonial homes, was settled in 1720. Three signers of the Declaration of Independence lived here.

Carlists The Carlists constituted a regionalist and reactionary political movement in 19th-century Spain. King FERDINAND VII had named his infant daughter ISABELLA II as his successor. When he died in 1833, however, antiliberal aristocrats and clergy proclaimed his brother Don Carlos (1788–1855) King Charles V. Supported by Basque and Catalan mountaineers, Carlists fought the government until their defeat in 1839. They rose again in 1846–48 and 1872–76 in the name of Don Carlos's son and grandson.

Although the leaders had dynastic and ultraconservative goals, most Carlists fought for the local privileges of their provinces against the encroaching power of the central government. Toward the end of the 19th century, the movement was weakened by defeat and by the rise of Basque nationalism and liberal Roman Catholicism. Carlism survived as the Traditionalist party until 1937, when it merged with the Falange to form the sole legal party of the Franco regime (see FRANCO, FRANCISCO).

Carlota Carlota, b. June 7, 1840, d. Jan. 19, 1927, the daughter of Leopold I of Belgium, became empress of Mexico in 1864 when her husband MAXIMILIAN, archduke of Austria, accepted the throne from Mexican conservatives backed by the troops of Napoleon III of France. When Maximilian's support eroded two years later, Carlota returned to Europe to seek the aid of the French emperor and the pope. Her efforts were unsuccessful, and Maximilian was executed in 1867. Showing symptoms of madness, Carlota spent the rest of her life in isolation in a chateau near Brussels.

Carlow Carlow (Irish: Ceatharlach) is a county in LEINSTER province, southeastern Ireland. It covers 896 km^2 (346 m^2) and has a population of 40,988 (1986). The town of Carlow is the county seat. Except in the southeast, where the Blackstairs Range and Mount Leinster (796 m/2,610 ft) dominate the landscape, the county is mostly fertile, level flatland. Agriculture is the primary economic activity, with barley, wheat, and sugar beets the principal crops, although dairying and fishing are also important. Food processing is the major industry in the towns.

The Anglo-Normans invaded Carlow in the late 12th century, and portions of the 13th-century Castle Carlow remain today.

Carlsbad Caverns see NATIONAL PARKS

Carlson, Chester Floyd Chester Floyd Carlson, b. Feb. 8, 1906, d. Sept. 19, 1968, invented (1938) xerography, the first successful electrostatic dry-copying process. In 1934, while pursuing a career as a patent lawyer, he began looking for a fast, inexpensive way of making copies of line drawings and text, since he often needed copies of patent records. He conducted experiments in ELECTROSTATIC PRINTING and after four years succeeded in producing the first xerographic copy. In 1940 he was issued his first patent, but it took another four years to find a company to develop his invention. In 1944, Carlson reached an agreement with Batelle Memorial Institute, and developmental work on his process began. The Haloid Company obtained (1947) the rights to commercial development of xerography; later the company became the Xerox Corporation. By 1958, the Xerox office copier had become a reality, and Carlson became a multimillionaire.

Carlsson, Ingvar Ingvar Gösta Carlsson, b. Nov. 9, 1934, became prime minister of Sweden following the assassination of Olof Palme in 1986. His government was endorsed by the voters in 1988. Born into a working-class family, Carlsson was graduated (1958) from the University of Lund with a degree in political science and was elected to parliament as a Social Democrat in 1964. He served as minister of education (1969–73), minister of housing (1973–76), and deputy premier (1982–86).

Carlton, Steve The professional baseball player Steven Norman Carlton, b. Miami, Fla., Dec. 22, 1944, was the only pitcher ever to win four Cy Young Awards (1972, 1977, 1980, 1982). Carlton pitched for the St. Louis Cardinals (1965–71), Philadelphia Phillies (1972–86), San Francisco Giants (1986), Chicago White Sox (1986), Cleveland Indians (1987), and Minnesota Twins (1987). In his career he accumulated 4,136 strikeouts—2d in major league history to Nolan Ryan—and a won-lost record of 329–243.

Carlyle, Thomas The Scottish essayist, social critic, and historian Thomas Carlyle, b. Dec. 4, 1795, d. Feb. 5, 1881, was among the first of the Victorian social critics. His influence on the shape of Victorian thought, through such works as *Sartor Resartus* (1833), *The French Revolution* (1837), *Heroes and Hero-Worship* (1841), and *Past and Present* (1843), was pervasive. Charles Dickens dedicated *Hard Times* to him; John Ruskin addressed him as "Papa"; Karl Marx and Friedrich Engels found in his early works the most insightful critiques of English society. Carlyle met Ralph Waldo EMERSON in 1832; their subsequent correspondence influenced them both.

Early Life and Works. Carlyle was born in Ecclefechan, Scotland, to a sternly Calvinist peasant family whose values and attitudes he carried with him throughout his life. The skeptical, empiricist thought that he absorbed at the University of Edinburgh decided him against joining the ministry, and for years afterward he struggled to find a vocation—in mathematics, law, teaching, and journalism. In 1821 he met his future wife, Jane Baillie Welsh (1801–66), and they married five years later. In 1821 he also underwent a spiritual crisis, later attributed to the character Diogenes Teufelsdröckh in the central chapters of *Sartor Resartus.*

In *Past and Present*, Carlyle describes a medieval monastery and its Abbot Samson as a model of the ideal community missing from contemporary life. *The French Revolution* lifted Carlyle from poverty. Therin, he views the destruction of the French aristocracy as a warning to England to shake off its dead institutional structures to meet the new needs of society.

Thomas Carlyle was a Scottish essayist, historian, and social critic. His critiques of industrialization and materialism are penetrating analyses of the social upheavals occurring during the 19th century. (Sir John Everett Millais, National Portrait Gallery, London.)

Later Life and Works. The massive *Cromwell* (1845) and *Frederick the Great* (1858–65) study the possibilities of the great man in history. By 1848, however, Carlyle was lapsing into despair over English society. *Latter Day Pamphlets* (1850) is a series of tirades against modern quackery, corruption, and greed. In *Shooting Niagra—and After?* (1867), Carlyle sees society as being destroyed by the forces of democracy. His *Reminiscences* (published posthumously in 1881) contains some of his loveliest and quietest prose.

Carmarthen [kuhr-mahr'-then] Carmarthen (Welsh: Caerfyrddin) is a seaport (1981 pop., 12,302) in DYFED County in southern Wales. Formerly the county town of Carmathenshire, (now incorporated into Dyfed), it is located on the River Towy near its mouth on Bristol Channel. Carmarthen's main industry is dairy processing, and it is an important cattle market and transportation center. The 14th-century Church of Saint Peter is a well-known monument.

Carmarthen was a Roman and later a Norman stronghold; Welsh princes made the Norman castle, now in ruins, their headquarters. During the Middle Ages, Carmarthen was the only town in Wales chartered as a wool market.

Carmel The city of Carmel (also called Carmel-by-the-Sea) is a town of 4,239 (1990) located on the California coast, south of Monterey Bay, on the Carmel River. It was founded in 1904 as an artists' refuge and is now a tourist attraction. The nearby mission of San Carlos Borroméo (1771) is the burial place of the early California pioneer Junípero Serra.

Carmel, Mount Mount Carmel is a short, rocky mountain ridge on the Bay of Haifa, in northwestern Israel. It is 549 m (1,800 ft) high and extends 26 km (16 mi) along the south bank of the Oishon River. Covered with gardens and villas, the mountain is important in biblical history and is considered sacred to Christians, Jews, Muslims, and Bahai. Christians have made pilgrimages to Mount Carmel since the 4th century, and it has been the site of monasteries since the 6th century. Paleolithic remains were found in caves on the western slopes of Mount Carmel in 1931–32.

Carmelites Carmelites are members of a Roman Catholic religious order founded during the 12th century by a group of hermits on Mount Carmel (in present-day Israel). They were apparently inspired by the prophets Elijah and Elisha, who had lived there, but much of their early history is unknown. In the 13th century, the Carmelites migrated to Europe, where they became friars. Because their habit was a brown tunic and scapular with an ample white cape and hood, they became known as "white friars."

During the 16th century the mystics Saint TERESA OF ÁVILA and Saint JOHN OF THE CROSS helped establish a reformed branch of the order known as the Discalced Carmelites. Today both branches engage in preaching, retreat work, and education. The Carmelite nuns live cloistered lives of prayer. Other famous Carmelites include Saint Thérèse and the Renaissance artist Fra Filippo Lippi.

The popular Roman Catholic devotion of Our Lady of Mount Carmel is based on the revelations of Simon Stock, an English Carmelite said to have lived in the 13th century.

Carmen Georges BIZET's opera *Carmen* was first performed at the Paris Opéra-Comique on Mar. 3, 1875. The libretto is by Henri Meilhac and Ludovic HALÉVY, based on Prosper MÉRIMÉE's novella, a tragic tale of jealousy and murder in 19th-century Seville.

Bizet composed *Carmen* in the form of musical numbers linked by spoken dialogue. After Bizet's death, Ernest Guiraud set the dialogue as sung recitative; this version is still in general use.

Carmichael, Frank Franklin Carmichael, b. Orillia, Ontario, 1890, d. 1945, belonged to a group of Canadian artists, called the GROUP OF SEVEN, who attempted to create a truly national art, inspired by the Canadian landscape rather than by foreign models. Carmichael's most distinctive works date from the early 1930s. Notably spare and organized in parallel planes, they capture the austere beauty of the north.

Carmichael, Hoagy Hoagland Howard "Hoagy" Carmichael, b. Bloomington, Ind., Nov. 22, 1899, d. Dec. 27, 1981, is the composer of "Stardust," "Lazy River," "I Get Along without You Very Well," "Georgia on My Mind," and many other popular American songs. Carmichael, who was also a piano player, became a film and television personality and in 1946 published his autobiography, *The Stardust Road.*

Carnac Carnac, a small French town in southern Brittany, lies at the center of the main concentration of MEGALITHS in Western Europe. The chief remains are those of six ancient STONE ALIGNMENTS, mostly oriented east-west. The largest of these comprises 11 parallel rows of some 1,100 standing stones running for more than 2 km (more than 1 mi). At least two alignments have stone circles at their ends. They probably date from about 2000 BC and may have been built by the people of the BEAKER CULTURE, possibly for astronomical purposes. In the vicinity is a dense concentration of megalithic chamber tombs, mostly on the tops of low hills.

Carnap, Rudolf Rudolf Carnap, b. May 18, 1891, d. Sept. 14, 1970, was a German-American philosopher who was one of the members of the Vienna Circle, a group associated with LOGICAL POSITIVISM.

In many of Carnap's works, he constructed model languages that employed the notation of symbolic LOGIC. He claimed that these languages "explicate" various philosophical concepts. He viewed certain philosophical problems essentially as problems of the structure of language—syntax and semantics. The metaphysician was seen as a poet who strives to clothe his poetry in the language of reason. In one of his most influential books, *The Logical Syntax of Language* (1934; Eng. trans., 1937), he characterized philosophy as a branch of logic.

Carnarvon, George Edward, 5th Earl of [kahr-nar'-vuhn] George Edward Stanhope Molyneux Herbert, 5th earl of Carnarvon, b. June 26, 1866, d. Apr. 6, 1923, was an English Egyptologist and collector of antiquities who, from 1906 to 1922, sponsored excavations around THEBES that culminated in the discovery of the tomb of King TUTANKHAMEN. His earlier discoveries with Howard CARTER of 12th- and 18th-dynasty tombs were published in *Five Years' Explorations at Thebes* (1912). In November 1922 the entrance to Tutankhamen's tomb was located, but before the royal sarcophagus was opened (1924), Lord Carnarvon died of blood poisoning and pneumonia. This gave rise to the legend of Tutankhamen's curse on those who disturbed his tomb.

carnation Carnations, *Dianthus caryophyllus*, are flowering herbaceous plants of the PINK family, Caryophyllaceae, which also includes SWEET WILLIAM and other popular, usually fragrant ornamentals. The carnation is native to Eurasia and has been cultivated for more than 20 centuries. Some carnation varieties are grown outdoors, but many are greenhouse plants.

The carnation, as it is known in North America, is 0.6 to 1 m (2 to 3.5 ft) tall and has a brittle, slightly branching stem, narrow opposite leaves, and large terminal double flowers, usually ruffled or toothed. Predominant colors are red, white, and pink; occasionally yellow or purple varieties are seen.

The carnation, a member of the pink family, is prized for its showy blooms, color, and fragrance. Chiefly grown in greenhouses for cut flowers in North America, it has been hybridized to produce many varieties.

Carnations can be propagated by planting young flowering shoots taken from the stems of mature plants or by planting terminal shoots after the flower is cut. The stem can also be bent into the ground to root. The plants need sun and well-drained soil. A rich loamy soil with some sand and a small amount of manure and leaf mold works well.

Carné, Marcel [kahr-nay'] French film director Marcel Carné, b. Aug. 18, 1909, made his name in the late 1930s when he worked with poet Jacques Prévert to produce several dark-toned, poetic films, among them *Port of Shadows* (1938) and *Daybreak* (1939). *The Devil's Envoys* (1942) and the romantic epic of the theater, *Children of Paradise* (1945), were made under German censorship during World War II. Carné continued to make films well into the 1970s, but only *The Adulteress* (1953) and *The Cheaters* (1958) carried the impact of his early work.

Carnegie, Andrew [kahr'-nuh-gee] Andrew Carnegie, b. Dunfermline, Scotland, Nov. 25, 1835, d. Aug. 11, 1919, was a dominant figure in the U.S. steel industry. Poor and with little formal education, he came to the United States with his family from Scotland in 1848 and settled in Allegheny, Pa. He worked in a cotton factory, then in a telegraph office, and subsequently for the Pennsylvania Railroad, introducing the first Pullman sleeping cars and becoming (1859) head of the western division. Carnegie recognized the growing importance of iron and steel, and resigned in 1865 to form the Keystone Bridge Company. He built a steel-rail mill, bought out the Homestead Steel Works, and by 1888 controlled a large plant.

In 1899, Carnegie consolidated his various holdings into the Carnegie Steel Company. He sold (1901) his company to J. P. Morgan's United States Steel Company and until his death devoted himself to philanthropy, donating more than $350 million to various causes. Carnegie established more than 2,500 libraries and founded (1901–11) the Carnegie Institute of Pittsburgh, the Carnegie Institution at Washington, the Carnegie Foundation for the Advancement of Teaching, the Carnegie Endowment for International Peace, and the Carnegie Corporation of New York.

The American industrialist and philanthropist Andrew Carnegie was a prime mover in creating the U.S. steel industry. Through his business acumen, Carnegie amassed a huge personal fortune, which he subsequently redistributed in endowments for the promotion of education, research, and world peace.

Carnegie Hall The New York City "music hall" built by philanthropist Andrew Carnegie is a complex that houses four halls along with studios, offices, and shops. The main hall opened on May 5, 1891, with a concert conducted in part by the composer Peter Ilich Tchaikovsky. A favorite of many of the world's great musicians, the hall was scheduled for demolition in 1962, when the New York Philharmonic moved to the new LINCOLN CENTER, but instead it was purchased by the city of New York. Extensive renovations in 1986 restored the building to its original elegance, with controversial effects on the main hall's much-admired acoustics.

Carnegie-Mellon University Formed in 1967 by the merger of the Carnegie Institute of Technology and the Mellon Institute, Carnegie-Mellon is a private university in Pittsburgh, Pa. It emphasizes the sciences and computer studies, fine arts, and urban and public affairs.

carnelian see CHALCEDONY

Carner, JoAnne Hall of Fame member JoAnne Gunderson Carner, b. Kirkland, Wash., Mar. 4, 1939, is one of the leading money winners in Ladies' Professional Golfers Association (LPGA) history, with over $2 million in career prize money. Carner was U.S. Women's Amateur champion five times during the period 1957–68 before turning (1970) professional. She won the U.S. Women's Open twice (1971, 1976), was LPGA Player of the Year three times (1974, 1981–82), and has won over 40 tournaments.

carnivals and fairs A carnival is a celebration combining parades, pageantry, folk drama, and feasting that is usually held in Catholic countries during the weeks before Lent. Carnival, probably from the Latin *carnelevarium* ("to remove meat"), typically begins early in the new year, often on the Epiphany, January 6, and ends in Feburary with MARDI GRAS on Shrove Tuesday.

Probably originating in pagan spring fertility rites, the first recorded carnival was the Egyptian feast of Osiris, an event marking the receding of the Nile's flood water. Carnivals reached a peak of riotous dissipation with the Roman Bacchanalia and Saturnalia. During the Middle Ages the church attempted to control the celebrations. Popes sometimes served as patrons, the worst excesses were gradually eliminated, and carnival was assimilated as a last festival before the asceticism of Lent. The carnival tradition still flourishes in Belgium, Italy, France, and Germany. In the Western Hemisphere, the principal carnivals are those in Rio de Janeiro (begun *c.*1840) and the Mardi Gras in New Orleans (begun in 1857).

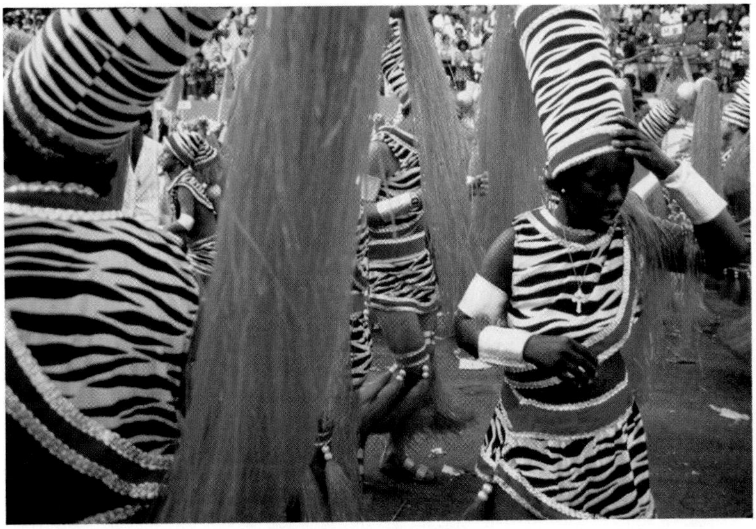

(Above) *Rio de Janeiro's annual carnival exhibits the traditional merrymaking and masquerading that characterize the boisterous pre-Lenten festivals in Roman Catholic countries.*

(Below) *Livestock are the central attraction at a judging event at the Iowa State Fair. Since the first permanent U.S. fair was initiated in Pittsfield, Mass., in 1810, county and state agricultural exhibitions have spread across the country.*

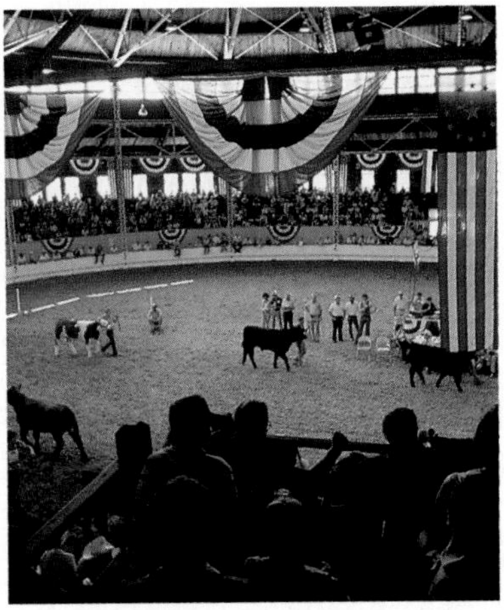

Pre-Christian, medieval, and modern carnivals share important thematic features. They celebrate the death of winter and the rebirth of nature, ultimately recommitting the individual to the spiritual and social codes of the culture. Ancient fertility rites, with their sacrifices to the gods, exemplify this commitment, as do the Christian Shrovetide plays. On the other hand, carnivals allow parody of, and offer temporary release from, social and religious constraints. For example, slaves were the equals of their masters during the Roman Saturnalia; the medieval feast of fools included a blasphemous mass; and during carnival masquerades sexual and social taboos are sometimes temporarily suspended.

In North America the term *carnival* often means a traveling show that includes rides, games of skill, and sideshows. There are hundreds of these roaming carnivals. They appear as part of state and county fairs or independently at resorts or in the parking lots of shopping malls.

Fairs are exhibition markets held at regular intervals, which often include entertainment. They serve important social, political, and economic functions. Fairs in ancient Rome included the reading of public announcements. Those at Champagne in France, Aix-la-Chapelle in Germany, and Stourbridge in England helped to break down medieval insularity by stimulating the exchange of ideas and skills as well as international commerce. By the 15th century, as shipping developed and feudalism declined, fairs had become less important to trade, although they continued as centers for entertainment. There are, nonetheless, some modern fairs that function as important trade exhibitions and markets, a notable example being the annual international book fair held in Frankfurt, Germany. The great fairs of modern times are the international expositions and WORLD'S FAIRS.

Fairs and carnivals in North America have been combined. More than 2,000 state and county fairs, which initially promoted agricultural education and trade, are now well known for their brightly lit carnival midways. Most recently, theme parks such as DISNEYLAND AND WALT DISNEY WORLD (with Epcot Center), have combined carnival rides and thrills with the educational entertainment of fairs, portraying both the serious and playful sides of American culture.

carnivore [kahr'-nih-vor] Although the term *carnivore* can be applied to any animal that subsists chiefly on a diet of other animals, biologists limit carnivores to those mammals classified in the order Carnivora, a group that includes cats, dogs, bears, and otters. The name is de-

THE CARNIVORES

Class:	Mammalia
Order:	Carnivora
Families:	Canidae—dogs, wolves, jackals, foxes
	Ursidae—bears, pandas
	Procyonidae—raccoons, lesser pandas
	Mustelidae—skunks, weasels, mink, badgers, otters, ferrets, martens, fishers, wolverines
	Viverridae—civets, mongooses
	Hyaenidae—hyenas, aardwolves
	Filidae—cats
	Otariidae*—eared seals
	Phocidae*—earless seals
	Obobenidae*—walruses

*Some authorities place these families in a separate order, Pinnipedia, or "fin-footed," or in a suborder of that name within the Carnivora, the other carnivores being grouped in the suborder Fissipedia, or "separate-toed."

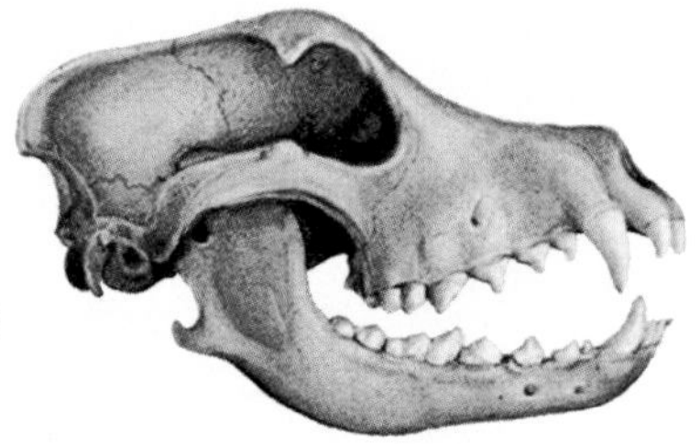

The jaws of carnivores such as the dog are specially adapted for eating flesh. The lower jaw is controlled by powerful muscles. Long, pointed canine teeth tear flesh, and premolars and molars slice meat.

rived from the Latin words *carnis*, meaning "flesh," and *vorare*, meaning "to eat"; thus, carnivores are meat eaters.

Few carnivores live exclusively on meat, and some, notably the bears and procyonids, consume vast quantities of plant material. In addition, there are other groups of animals, such as the INSECTIVORES, that are predominantly carnivorous. Nevertheless, the classification is appropriate, because all carnivores share anatomical characteristics and special adaptations to a predatory life, as well as a common ancestry.

The largest carnivores are the 3,400-kg (7,500-lb) elephant seal and the 770-kg (1,700-lb) brown bear of Alaska. The smallest, the North American least weasel, weighs no more than 56 g (2 oz). Land-dwelling carnivores are native everywhere except on oceanic islands and Antarctica but have been introduced on the islands for various purposes.

Carnivores have a high degree of intelligence, and their brains are large in relation to the size of the animal. Hinging of the lower jaw allows the jaw to move vertically but not laterally; jaw muscles are strong. Clavicles (collarbones) are either absent or disconnected from the other bones; this results in great flexibility, which allows the carnivore to spring upon its prey.

Most carnivores have carnassial, or shearing, teeth, which work much like scissors to cut sinews and slice meat. The carnassials are formed by the first lower molar and the fourth upper premolar. Nearly all carnivores have large, strong canine teeth. Bears and raccoons have as many as 42 teeth, but a walrus may have as few as 18.

Carnivores evolved in the Cenozoic Era, which began about 65 million years ago. Most early carnivores were doglike and catlike. Several later, but now extinct, species were formidable contemporaries of early humans. The saber-toothed cat, which survived until about 12,000 years ago, was no bigger than a modern tiger but had 23-cm (9-in) canine teeth. This cat probably ate large, slow-moving prey. The giant cave bear, so called because its fossil remains are found in many caves in Europe, evolved about 2,500,000 years ago and became extinct 10,000 years ago. It was about the size of a modern Alaska brown bear.

carnivorous plants [kahr-niv'-ur-uhs] Carnivorous plants are various types of flowering plants and fungi that capture and digest prey animals. Photosynthetic carnivorous plants live in habitats poor in minerals, and they benefit primarily from the mineral nutrients gained from the prey. Since the animals they capture are chiefly insects, carnivorous plants are sometimes called insectivorous plants. Some species, however, capture mollusks such as slugs, or even vertebrates such as small frogs and birds.

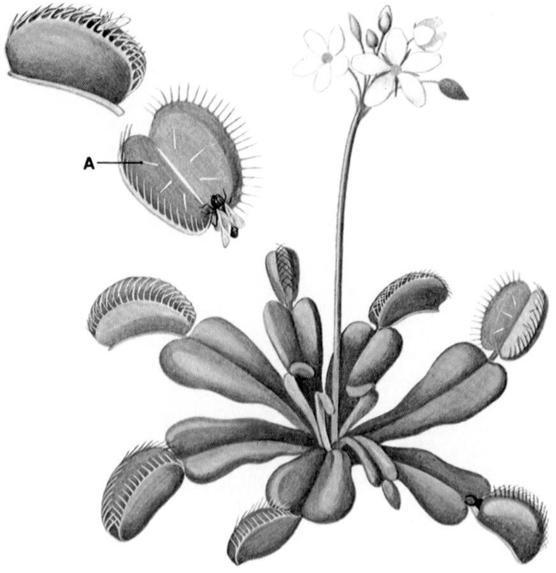

Venus's-flytrap, a carnivorous plant found only near the North Carolina–South Carolina border, has leaves that trap spiders, ants, and beetles that blunder into the hairs on the upper surface of the leaf lobes. The hairs (A) generate action potentials similar to nerve impulses in animals, closing the trap. Struggles by the prey further stimulate the plant to secrete digestive fluids.

Methods of Capture. Trap types observed in carnivorous plants include pitfalls and "lobster traps," adhesive traps, and various kinds of mechanical traps.

Pitfalls consist of tubular leaves, or arrays of leaves, that are filled with water. Insects are captured when they fall into the fluid, which often contains wetting agents and digestive enzymes. So-called lobster pots also consist of tubular leaves. In this type of trap, however, the tube is often horizontal and is lined with hairs that guide the prey along a path leading to the digestive part of the trap. Some BROMELIADS have leaf bases that form definite cups in which water accumulates. Such plants do not trap insects, however, so much as simply make use of nutrients provided by dead vegetation and animal remains that fall into the cups.

Adhesive traps involve sticky surfaces. Sticky-haired adhesive traps exist in several plant families. Typically, flying insects are captured when they adhere to slime secreted by hairs covering the leaf. In some genera, such as *Drosera*, the leaf actively moves the prey to the center and wraps around it. Sticky-seeded adhesive traps have only recently been observed but may be widespread. The seed of the shepherd's purse, *Capsera*, a common lawn weed, attracts, captures, and utilizes nutrients from prey; soil bacteria do the digesting.

Mechanical traps include so-called snap traps, such as those of Venus's-flytrap. In these plants the prey is trapped by rapid closure of a set of lobes around the animal when it touches sensory hairs that trigger the closure. The action results from acid growth in the lobes within

TYPES OF TRAPS IN CARNIVOROUS PLANTS

Pitfalls and Lobster Pots	***Adhesive Traps***	***Mechanical Traps***
PITFALLS	STICKY HAIRS	SNAP TRAPS
Nepenthaceae	Droseraceae	Droseraceae
Nepenthes	*Drosera* (sundew)	*Aldrovanda*
(pitcher plant)	*Drosophyllum*	*Dionaea* (Venus's-flytrap)
Sarraceniaceae	Lentibulariaceae	
Sarracenia	*Pinguicula*	
(pitcher plant)	(butterwort)	SUCTION TRAPS
Darlingtonia	Byblidaceae	Lentibulariaceae
(cobra lily)	*Byblis*	*Utricularia*
Cephalotaceae		(bladderwort)
Cephalotus	STICKY SEEDS	
	Cruciferae	SNARE TRAPS
LOBSTER POTS	*Capsella* (shepherd's purse)	Fungi
Lentibulariaceae		*Arthrobotrys*
Genlisea		

less than a second. Suction traps, found in the aquatic BLADDERWORT *Ultricularia*, are similar to the style of mouse trap in which a door allows the mouse to enter but not to exit. The prey trips a lever on the plant "door," which allows water and the prey to be sucked into the trap when the plant's concave side puffs outward. Snare traps are found in carnivorous fungi. One type, in the genus *Arthrobotrys*, has a trap that looks like a small lasso with three segments around the loop. When triggered by a nematode, the segments bulge out to capture the worm. The fungus then grows into the prey and digests it.

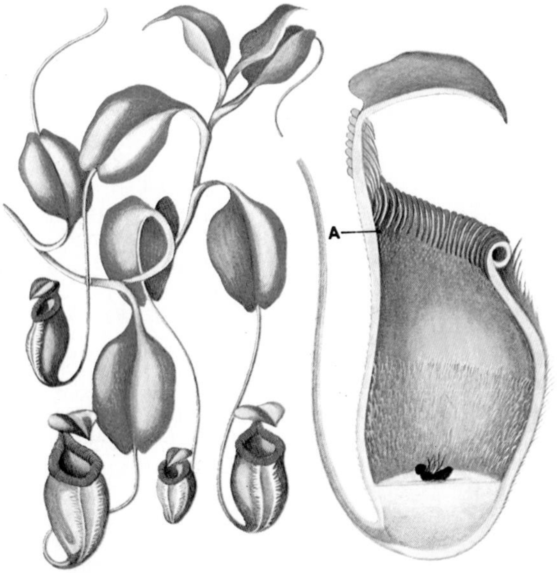

The carnivorous pitcher plant Nepenthes villosa *of Borneo has modified tendrils on the tips of its leaves that form pitcherlike traps. Prey animals are attracted to glands* (A) *on the rim. Their feet become clogged with wax from the cuticle, causing them to lose their grip and fall into the digestive fluid secreted by the trap.*

Ecology. Flowering carnivorous plants occur in freshwater, in swampy areas, on trees and old logs, and on hardened soils that are seasonally very wet. Features common to nearly all habitats of carnivorous plants include low levels of mineral nutrients, at least a periodic abundance of water, and bright sunlight. Trapping mechanisms often involve loss of water from the leaf and are likely to decrease photosynthetic efficiency. In a mineral-poor environment, these tradeoffs are apparently worth the supplementary nutrients gained.

Carnot (family) [kahr-noh'] The Carnots were a distinguished French family in the late 18th and 19th centuries. **Lazare Nicolas Marguerite Carnot**, b. May 13, 1752, d. Aug. 2, 1823, was known as the "organizer of victory" during the FRENCH REVOLUTION. Commissioned as a military engineer, he specialized in fortifications. He was elected to the Legislative Assembly (1791) and National Convention (1792) and served as a commissioner to the Army of the North. As the military strategist and logistical expert on the Committee of Public Safety, Carnot organized both defensive and offensive operations in the FRENCH REVOLUTIONARY WARS. He supported Maximilien ROBESPIERRE's overthrow in 1794 and was elected to the DIRECTORY, organizing the new ministry of war. As a moderate, Carnot was ousted in the coup d'état of 18 Fructidor (Sept. 4, 1797), but he was recalled by Napoléon Bonaparte (later NAPOLEON I) to become minister of war (1800) and a member of the Tribunate (1802). He later served (1814) as military governor of Antwerp. After Napoleon's final defeat (1815) he went into exile.

Lazare's oldest son, **Nicolas Léonard Sadi Carnot**, b. June 1, 1796, d. Aug. 24, 1832, was a physicist, best known for his related studies of the operation of both steam and internal combustion engines and of heat as a form of energy. In his book *Reflections on the Motive Power of Fire* (1824), in which he analyzed an ideal engine (the "Carnot engine"), he laid the foundations of the second law of thermodynamics.

Hippolyte Carnot, b. Apr. 6, 1801, d. Mar. 16, 1888, the second son of Lazare, was a writer and editor who was a member of the liberal opposition to both LOUIS-PHILIPPE and Louis Napoléon (later NAPOLEON III). Briefly in office (1848) as minister of public education, he initiated significant reforms.

Hippolyte's son, **Sadi Carnot**, b. Aug. 11, 1837, was the fourth president (1887–94) of the Third Republic. Elected to the National Assembly in 1871 and 1876, he served on the Committee of Public Works and became its minister in 1880. With poise and integrity, Carnot weathered the crisis caused by Gen. Georges BOULANGER and the Panama Canal scandal that tainted the government. He was assassinated by an anarchist on June 24, 1894.

Carnot cycle [kahr-noh'] The Carnot cycle is the ideal reversible operating cycle of a thermodynamic HEAT ENGINE. It was proposed in 1824 by the French engineer Sadi Carnot. Real heat engines do not operate on the

Carnot cycle, for practical reasons. Nonetheless, Carnot's ideal cycle is important in that it sets a standard for the maximum useful work a heat engine can perform.

The Carnot cycle is most easily understood by considering a volume of an ideal gas trapped in a closed, perfectly insulated container. One wall of the container is formed by a movable piston, while another wall may be either insulated or exposed to one of two infinite heat reservoirs at temperatures T_1 and T_2. The cycle begins with the isothermal (constant-temperature) expansion of the gas upon accepting heat energy at temperature T_1 from the hotter of the two reservoirs. The container is then insulated from the surroundings, allowing the gas to further expand adiabatically (with no heat transfer) by drawing upon its own internal energy. Both expansion phases of the cycle cause an outward motion of the piston, which may be harnessed to do useful work. The third phase of the cycle involves the isothermal compression of the gas and the rejection of heat energy to the colder reservoir at temperature T_2. Finally, the container is once again insulated and the gas is compressed adiabatically, returning the piston to its original position and completing the cycle. Thus, the Carnot cycle accepts heat energy from its surroundings and converts a portion of that energy to useful work.

See also: THERMODYNAMICS.

carnotite see URANIUM

Caro, Anthony [kahr'-oh] Anthony Caro, b. Mar. 8, 1924, is a British sculptor best known for the abstract welded steel sculptures he has been making since 1960. His earlier work was related to that of Henry MOORE, for whom he worked as an assistant in 1951–53. His most famous sculptures are groupings of geometric, horizontally oriented shapes painted in one color. In later works, Caro has employed bent sheets and bars of rusty, rough-textured steel that are scraped, cut, and welded together.

Pompadour *(1963), by the British sculptor Anthony Caro, is an abstract assemblage of interconnected, geometric, metal shapes. (Kröller-Müller Museum, Otterlo, The Netherlands.)*

Caro, Joseph ben Ephraim Joseph Caro, 1488–1575, compiled the *Shulhan Arukh*, the most authoritative code of Jewish law. This was a digest of his *Bet Yosef*, but it was more important because it reviewed, with commentary, all the major medieval codifications of Jewish law. Caro was also a student of the KABBALAH tradition; his mystical diary was published posthumously as *Maggid mesharim*.

carob [kair'-uhb] The carob is an eastern Mediterranean tree of the pea family, Fabaceae, and the source of carob or locust bean GUM, which is used as a stabilizer, thickener, and emulsifier in foods, cosmetics, pharmaceuticals, paints, and textile sizing and finishes. From 5 to 15 hard, brown seeds are produced in long, flat, leathery pods. The pods, containing a pulp consisting of about 50 percent sugar, are used mainly to feed livestock and as a chocolate substitute in human food. The carob tree, *Ceratonia siliqua*, is sometimes known as locust or St. John's bread, from a theory that the "locusts" that John the Baptist ate in the wilderness were really carob pods.

carol The term *carol* is currently applied to a SONG or HYMN about Christmas. Probably derived from the carole, a round dance accompanied by unison singing, the carol emerged in England during the 14th and 15th centuries as a strophic song with refrain. The carol was tied more strictly to the Christmas season in the 19th century, and Christmas songs from other countries also began to be included in the category of carols.

Carol I, King of Romania Carol I, b. Apr. 20, 1839, d. Oct. 10, 1914, the first king of Romania, was a German prince of the house of Hohenzollern-Sigmaringen. Elected (1866) prince of Romania by a plebiscite, he proclaimed himself king in 1881, after Romania had won full independence from Turkey as a result of the Russo-Turkish War of 1877–78. Carol married (1869) Elizabeth of Wied (1843–1916), better known as the poet Carmen Sylva.

Carol II, King of Romania Carol II, b. Oct. 15, 1893, d. Apr. 4, 1953, king of Romania, was the son of King Ferdinand and Queen Marie. After his morganatic marriage, soon dissolved, to Zizi Lambrino, he married (1921) Princess Helen of Greece. In 1925, because of his liaison with Magda Lupescu (1896?–1977), Carol was forced to abdicate his rights to the throne. Returning from exile, he was proclaimed king on June 8, 1930, and in February 1938 he set up a personal dictatorship. After the outbreak of World War II, powerless to resist the territorial claims on Romania by Hungary, Bulgaria, and the

Carol II, king of Romania from 1930 to 1940, had a political career plagued by turmoil and scandal. Having established (1938) a royal dictatorship, he promulgated a corporatist constitution and attempted to suppress the fascist Iron Guard. He was deposed in 1940 and fled abroad with his mistress, Madga Lupescu.

USSR, Carol was forced to abdicate on Sept. 6, 1940. In 1947 he married Magda in Brazil.

Caroline affair The *Caroline* was a small U.S. steamer based at Buffalo, N.Y., which was used during the Canadian REBELLIONS OF 1837 to take men and supplies to William Lyon MACKENZIE's camp on Navy Island in the Niagara River. On the night of Dec. 29, 1837, a small party of loyal Canadian militia crossed the Niagara River to the U.S. side, seized the *Caroline*, removed its crew, and set it on fire. It sank in the river above Niagara Falls, and one American life was lost. The incident was much exaggerated by Mackenzie in order to build up American support for his rebellion. The American press clamored for revenge, and U.S. troops were sent to the border. Relations between the United States and Britain remained tense until the WEBSTER-ASHBURTON TREATY of 1842.

Caroline Islands The Caroline Islands, largest archipelago of the northwest Pacific, have a total area of about 1,165 km^2 (450 mi^2) and a population of 100,200 (1988 est.). The people, mostly Micronesians, grow cassava, yams, bananas, and sugarcane. Exports include tapioca, copra, and dried fish. Deposits of iron ore, bauxite, and phosphates exist, and tourism is on the rise.

Spain took control of the Carolines in 1886 but sold them to Germany in 1899. Occupied by Japan during both world wars, they were heavily bombarded during World War II. Japan administered the islands between the wars as a League of Nations mandate; they became part of a United Nations trust territory administered by the United States in 1947 (see PACIFIC ISLANDS, TRUST TERRITORY OF THE). The Carolines have been divided into the Federated States of MICRONESIA (eastern Carolines) and the Republic of PALAU (Belau). Both entities are internally self-governing and have gained limited independence in "free association" with the United States.

Carolingian art and architecture [kar-ohlin'-jee-uhn] During the late 8th and early 9th centuries a major renascence took place in Western art, due in large part to the efforts of CHARLEMAGNE. Crowned emperor by Pope Leo III on Christmas Day, 800, this Frankish ruler of the Carolingian dynasty was determined to restore the Roman Empire in the West. In architecture, manuscript painting, and the crafts there was a conscious attempt to emulate the achievements of Early Christian Rome and the Byzantine Empire.

The monastery church of Saint Riquier (dedicated 799; replaced 13th–16th centuries), at Centula in northern France, was built under Abbot Angilbert. As shown in the reconstruction below, the church was particularly noted for its imposing westwork (1), *which led to a vaulted narthex* (2) *crowned by a tower* (3) *over the crossing* (4) *and flanked by two stair turrets* (5). *The towered structure was repeated over the eastern transept* (6). *Saint Riquier also introduced the choir* (7), *separating the nave* (8) *and aisles* (9) *from the apse* (10).

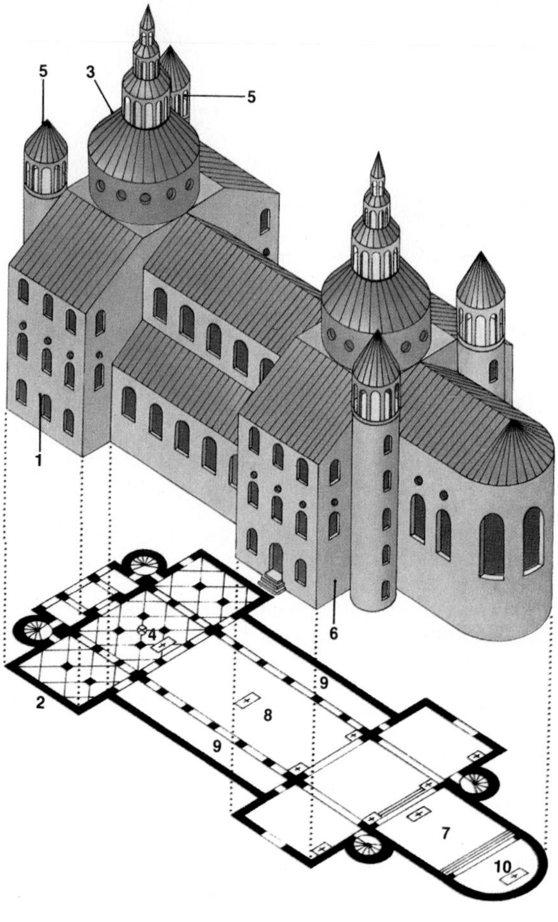

Christ in Majesty, *from the* Godescalc Gospels *(c.781–83), is believed to have been commissioned by Charlemagne to commemorate the baptism of his son Pepin. (Bibliothèque Nationale, Paris.)*

Charlemagne's own palace chapel at AACHEN (Aix-la-Chapelle), constructed between 792 and 805 by the architect Odo of Metz, is an example of the way in which he used older models. Its design, though northern in its massiveness, is based on octagonal Byzantine churches such as the 6th-century church of SAN VITALE in Ravenna. Charlemagne thus symbolically linked his empire to that of Justinian.

Many Carolingian monuments were modeled after Roman buildings. The designs of monastic churches were often based on Early Christian precedents. The 9th-century monastery church (now destroyed) at Fulda, a copy of the 4th-century SAINT PETER'S BASILICA in Rome, was one of the most ambitious examples of an attempt to imitate the art of the Roman Empire.

Carolingian architects created much that was new and innovative. For example, Early Christian churches like St. Peter's had very plain exteriors, but entrances and towers became important in the Carolingian period. Many churches, Charlemagne's palace chapel at Aachen among them, had westworks, two-story entrance complexes flanked by towers. Westworks were the forerunners of the elaborate facades of later Romanesque and Gothic cathedrals.

Carolingian monasteries were important centers for the revival of learning, for it was in their scriptoria that ancient manuscripts were copied. One of the most significant contributions of the period—Carolingian minuscule, which reformed handwriting—was accomplished under ALCUIN of York at the scriptorium of the Abbey of Saint Martin at Tours. The lowercase letters used today are based on the script developed there in the late 8th–early 9th centuries.

As in the other arts, the illuminations in Carolingian manuscripts include many references to classical art. Charlemagne's Gospel Book (*c.*795–810; Kunsthistorisches Museum, Vienna) contains Evangelist portraits that appear to have been copied directly from Roman manuscripts. In other manuscripts, such as the famous vellum Gospel Book of Archbishop Ebbo of Reims (early 9th century; Bibliothèque Municipale, Epernay), the miniatures, while having classical elements, are characterized by a restless energy. The most famous of all Carolingian books, the Utrecht Psalter (*c.*820–832; Bibliothek der Rijksuniversiteit, Utrecht), contains pen-and-ink drawings so full of emotional excitement they seem to leap from the pages.

Although there was probably no monumental stone sculpture in this period, the arts of IVORY CARVING and metalwork were highly developed. The gold- and jewel-encrusted cover of the Lindau Gospels (*c.*870; Pierpont Morgan Library, New York) is a sumptuous example. The same expressive qualities are found in ivory carvings such as those on the covers of the Lorsch Gospels (early 9th century; Biblioteca Apostolica, Vatican City, and Victoria and Albert Museum, London). Far from being merely imitative, Carolingian art was imbued with a lively, imaginative spirit. The artists of this period created much that influenced later medieval art.

See also: BYZANTINE ART AND ARCHITECTURE; EARLY CHRISTIAN ART AND ARCHITECTURE; FRENCH ART AND ARCHITECTURE; GERMAN ART AND ARCHITECTURE.

Carolingians [kair-oh-lin'-jee-uhnz] The Carolingians, a family of Ripuarian FRANKS that took its name from CHARLES MARTEL, the grandfather of CHARLEMAGNE, were the most important dynasty in early medieval Europe. They had their origins in the union of the family of Arnulf, bishop of Metz, with that of Pepin of Landen (d. *c.*640), hereditary mayor of the palace in Austrasia, during the early 7th century.

As mayors of the palace, the Carolingians were de facto rulers of the Frankish territories under the later MEROVINGIAN kings. An attempt to seize the kingship in the mid-7th century failed, but in the next 100 years Pepin of Heristal (d. 714) and his illegitimate son, Charles Martel (d. 742), restored the family's fortunes. Charles's son PEPIN THE SHORT deposed Childeric III, the last of the Merovingian monarchs; with papal support, he became king of the Franks in 751.

Charles II, called Charles the Bald, became king of the West Franks after the division of the Carolingian empire (843) and was briefly (875–77) emperor. His coronation is shown here in the Sacramentorium of Metz (late 9th century).

Pepin's sons, Carloman and Charles (Charlemagne), succeeded him jointly in 768. The former died in 771, leaving Charlemagne in control of the entire realm. He more than doubled its size and became king of the Lombards (774) and emperor (800). Charlemagne's sole surviving son, LOUIS I, inherited (814) his lands and titles but also his problems—Viking invasions, Muslim raids, and greedy nobles. The situation worsened because Louis had three heirs: LOTHAIR I, LOUIS THE GERMAN, and CHARLES II (Charles the Bald).

When Louis died in 840, the civil wars that had begun during his reign continued, resulting in the division of the empire into three kingdoms by the Treaty of Verdun (843; see VERDUN, TREATY OF). The kingdoms were redivided by the Treaty of Mersen (870). After interruptions, Carolingian rule in what is now France came to an end in 987; in what is now Germany, it ended in 911.

Carondelet, Héctor, Baron de [kah-rohn-duh-lay', ayk-tor'] Francisco Luis Héctor de Carondelet, b. July 29, 1747, d. Aug. 10, 1807, was the Spanish governor-general of Louisiana and West Florida in the period following the American Revolution. In 1791, he was posted to New Orleans. By military reorganization, the construction of forts, and an alliance (1793) with the Southern Indian tribes, Carondelet kept the American frontiersmen from advancing westward for a decade. He also quelled attempts to overthrow the government in Louisiana and West Florida and made notable economic improvements in these Spanish provinces, particularly in New Orleans and its environs.

carotenoid [kuh-raht'-in-oyd] Carotenoids are natural pigments that range in color from yellow to orange, red, and purple. They are chemically related to TERPENES. Some carotenoids, such as carotenes and xanthophylls, are synthesized in the chloroplasts of higher plants and of algae. Carotenoids also occur in some fruits, flowers, and roots of higher plants—for example, carrots and tomatoes—and also in other bacteria and in fungi. The pigments, masked by the green of chlorophyll in plant leaves, produce the bright colors of trees in autumn. In most higher animals, including humans, carotenoids are involved in the synthesis of vitamin A in the liver and are important elements in the diet. Beta carotene apparently may offer some protection against cancer, as well. Commercially, carotenes are used in food coloration.

Carothers, W.H. An organic chemist, Wallace Hume Carothers, b. Burlington, Iowa, Apr. 27, 1896, d. Apr. 29, 1937, was the inventor of NYLON, the first successful synthetic fiber. After earning his doctorate, Carothers joined the duPont Company in 1928 as head of their innovative program of basic research. In 1931, while studying the long-chain molecules known as polymers, Carothers developed a silklike fiber, nylon. His research team also developed neoprene, a synthetic rubber.

carp Carp is the general term for freshwater fishes in the large teleost family Cyprinidae, which includes barbels, GOBIES, MINNOWS, danios, and GOLDFISH, as well as the common carp, *Cyprinus carpio*. The common carp probably originated in the rivers and estuaries of eastern India

The common carp is of worldwide economic importance. The wild form (top) *is a lean, long-bodied gamefish. Two forms of cultivated carp are the fully scaled* (bottom left) *and the partially scaled mirror, or king, carp* (bottom right).

and southern China. It is now found throughout Europe, Asia, and the United States. It has been cultivated for food for many centuries in Asia and is still bred today in Southeast Asia, Europe, and, on a smaller scale, the United States and southern Africa.

Carp may be distinguished from most cyprinids by a large dorsal fin with 15 fin rays and the presence of a stiff spine at the beginning of the dorsal fin. They are often confused with the goldfish, *Carassius auratus.* Carp have longer dorsal fins, two pairs of fleshy barbels, and three rows of throat teeth. Goldfish lack the barbels and have a single row of throat teeth. All fish in the carp family lack teeth in the jaw and other mouth bones. Carp include the regular scaled carp and the nearly scaleless form, called leather carp. Carp average 1.4 to 2.3 kg (3 to 5 lb) in weight, although catches of more than 36 kg (80 lb) have been recorded.

Carp are prolific breeders. A female carp weighing less than 8 kg (17 lb) may contain as many as 2 million eggs. The eggs are scattered over vegetation in shallow water, and the young hatch in 2 to 3 days. They reach maturity in 4 to 5 years.

Carp are hardy fishes capable of flourishing in muddy, stagnant, or polluted water, even surviving for several weeks by burrowing into the mud when the water dries up. They feed on tiny plants and invertebrates by grubbing on the bottom in the mud. This muddies the water, uproots the vegetation, and drives out other fish, but conservationists point out that carp naturally inhabit waters unfavorable for most other fish.

carpal tunnel syndrome Carpal tunnel syndrome (CTS) is a disorder that causes a prickling sensation or numbness in the hand. If left untreated it can cause burning pain, decreased hand dexterity, and, in some cases, paralysis. The problem is caused by compression of the median nerve, which runs through a braceletlike bone structure in the wrist—the carpal tunnel—and branches to the thumb and first three fingers. Tendons in the carpal tunnel may swell, pinching this nerve.

CTS may be caused by arthritis, pregnancy, or drugs that cause the body to retain fluids. Persons in occupations that require repetitious or prolonged flexing or extending of the wrist, such as musicians, data processors, and players of sports, are also often subject to CTS. In mild cases, treatment of the condition may consist simply of resting the hand or varying its movements more often during the day. Patients may also be given antiinflammatory drugs or injections of cortisone to reduce swelling. If these conservative treatments are ineffective, however, surgery may become necessary.

Carpathian Mountains [kahr-payth'ee-uhn] The Carpathian Mountains are a crescent-shaped chain of mountains extending about 1,450 km (900 mi) from Bratislava, Czechoslovakia, to Orsova, Romania, crossing portions of Poland and the USSR. The highest elevation is the Gerlach Peak, in eastern Czechoslovakia, which is

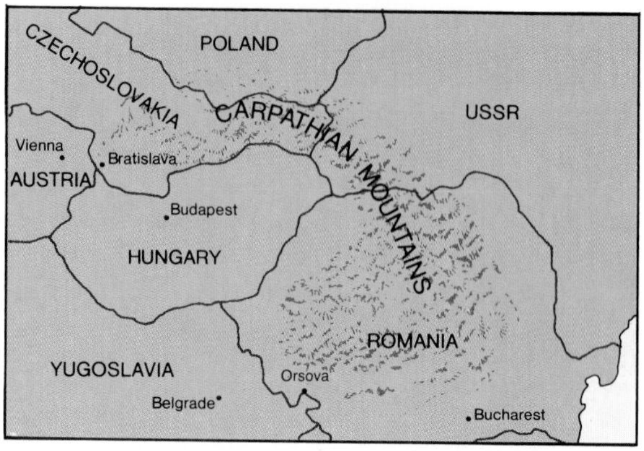

2,663 m (8,737 ft). The southernmost portion of the range is sometimes called the Transylvanian Alps.

Mostly covered by forest—predominantly beech and oak, which give way to conifers at higher elevations—the Carpathians are the source of some of Europe's major rivers, including the VISTULA, the ODER, the San, the TISZA, the DNESTR, and the Prut. The mountains are cut by many low passes, through which railroads and highways have been built.

The greatest population density is in the western end of the range. There, lumbering, farming, and mining are the main industries, followed by tourism, especially in the High Tatra.

Carpeaux, Jean Baptiste [kar-poh'] Jean Baptiste Carpeaux, b. May 11, 1827, d. Oct. 12, 1875, was a versatile French sculptor and painter who is known for revitalizing academic approaches to art. Carpeaux's artisan approach and love of surface textures may derive from his preference for modeling in clay and plaster.

As the favorite sculptor of Napoleon III and the Empress Eugénie, Carpeaux earned such notable commissions as the architectural decoration of the Pavillon de Flore of the Louvre (1863–66) and his best-known work, *The Dance* (1865–69; Louvre, Paris), for Charles Garnier's Paris Opéra. The strong movement and erotic abandon of the latter were strongly criticized, but it suited the taste of the Second Empire. Carpeaux's lively plaster sketches have a gestural feeling comparable to sculptures by Edgar Degas and Auguste Rodin. His most complex work is the bronze group *Ugolino and His Sons* (1857–63; Louvre, Paris) whose pose, modeling, and even Dantesque theme profoundly influenced Rodin's *Thinker.*

Carpenter, Scott The American astronaut Malcolm Scott Carpenter, b. Boulder, Colo., May 1, 1925, was one of the original seven astronauts and the second American to orbit the Earth. He joined the U.S. Navy in 1949 and was a test pilot (1954–59) when he was selected as an astronaut. Carpenter served as the backup pilot for John Glenn, the first American to orbit the Earth, and flew *Aurora* 7 on May 24, 1962, as part of the MERCURY PROGRAM. This three-orbit flight ended with a landing 402 km (250 mi) downrange from the intended landing spot. In 1965, Carpenter was temporarily assigned to Sealab, the navy's underwater habitability project, and spent 30 days at a depth of 62.5 m (205 ft). He resigned from NASA in 1967 and retired from the navy in 1969 to enter private business.

carpentry Carpentry is the craft and trade of working, joining, and finishing lumber and allied products, such as plywood. It has evolved as a trade since the practice of indenturing apprentices to master craftsmen began in the Middle Ages. In recent times, the apprenticeship system of training carpenters has been augmented by programs that combine on-the-job training with structured courses of study given in technical schools. Carpenters in the United States and Canada are represented by the United Brotherhood of Carpenters and Joiners of America, founded in 1881.

The three major areas of carpentry specialization are rough carpentry, framing, and finish carpentry. Rough carpentry is the kind of work performed in the building of temporary structures—for example, forms for concrete—or structures in which strength and stability are the primary concerns. Framing entails the layout and erection of the structural skeletons of buildings involving a wooden framework. Finish carpentry includes fitting doors and windows, applying wood trim, laying of wood floors, and fabricating built-in cabinets and staircases. (See also HOUSE.)

The tools used in the carpentry trade are divided into two categories—hand tools and power tools. The hand tools may be classified into a number of groups, based on the kind of work done with them: assembling, boring (see DRILLING), cutting (see SAW), holding, layout and marking, leveling and plumbing, measuring, sharpening, and wrecking.

Power tools (see MACHINE TOOLS)—tools operated by electricity or compressed air—include hand electric saws, radial-arm saws, orbital and belt sanders, electric drills, bench grinders, routers, electric planes, and pneumatic nailers and staplers.

carpetbaggers Carpetbagger was an epithet used by conservative Southern whites after the Civil War to describe Northerners who settled in the South and entered politics as Republicans during RECONSTRUCTION. Southern conservatives believed that these men had come to the South with no more belongings than could fit into a carpetbag (a small traveling bag), intending to gain political power with ex-slaves' votes and then to use their influence to get rich through economic concessions from the state, fraud, and corruption. By repeating this charge and publicizing the occasions on which it proved true, Southern conservatives fomented hatred that often led to violence against Northern-born Southern Republicans and

In "The Man with the (Carpet) Bags" the noted American political cartoonist Thomas Nast vilified the Northerners who settled in the South after the Civil War. Conservative Southerners called these individuals "carpetbaggers," charging that they were political and financial adventurers.

turned even Northern Republicans against them. Faced with such attacks and with social ostracism, many of these immigrants left the South, and others abandoned politics entirely, depriving Southern Republicans of much of their leadership.

Although there were important instances of carpetbagger corruption, historians now feel that the charges were exaggerated and politically motivated. They note that carpetbaggers provided some of the most progressive Southern political leadership of the 19th century and that many combined idealism with their political ambition.

carpet beetle Carpet beetles are members of the family Dermestidae of the order Coleoptera. The larvae feed on wool, silk, fur, feathers, hair, leather—nearly anything of animal origin. They cause extensive damage to carpets, furniture, and clothing, as well as to preserved animal specimens in museums and private collections. The dark or brightly spotted adults emerge in spring and feed on pollen, laying their eggs on or near appropriate food supplies.

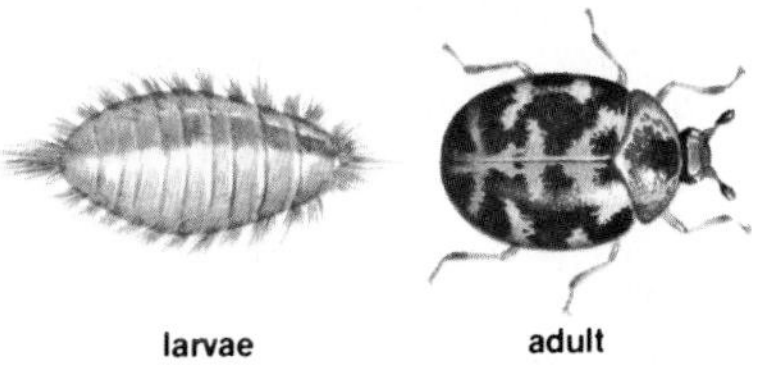

Carpet beetles, such as the buffalo carpet beetle, are common household pests, consuming even synthetic materials having food residues.

carpets see RUGS AND CARPETS

Carpini, Giovanni da Pian del [kar-pee'-nee, joh-vahn'-nee dah pyahn' del] Giovanni da Pian del Carpini, b. *c.*1180, d. Aug. 1, 1252, was an Italian Franciscan friar sent (1245–47) as a missionary to the MONGOLS by

Pope INNOCENT IV. He reached the Mongol court near Karakorum, and his observations recorded in *Historia Mongalorum* are among the comparatively small number of firsthand Western accounts of the kingdoms of the khans. Returning to Europe, Carpini advised Christian war against the Mongols.

Carr, John Dickson John Dickson Carr, b. Uniontown, Pa., Nov. 30, 1906, d. Mar. 1, 1977, was master of the locked-room murder mystery, producing over 100 novels under his own name and as Carter Dickson and Carr Dickson. His two favorite detective characters were Dr. Gideon Fell (resembling G. K. Chesterton) and Sir Henry Merrivale. His novels depend on the exercise of pure reason to solve horrific crimes. Two such classic tales are *The Arabian Nights Murder* (1936) and *The Burning Court* (1937).

Carrà, Carlo [kah-rah'] Carlo Carrà, b. Feb. 11, 1881, d. Apr. 13, 1966, was one of the founders of FUTURISM, an Italian school of painters and sculptors that began in 1909. The futurists sought to capture the incessant movement of modern urban life with a stylistic vocabulary derived from CUBISM. Carrà's *Funeral of the Anarchist Galli* (1910–11; Museum of Modern Art, New York City) is a notable example. Carrà abandoned futurism when he met the painter Giorgio de CHIRICO, with whom he founded the school of "metaphysical" painting—a style akin to surrealism but using private symbols and commonplace objects to elicit a sense of the extraordinary and sinister in everyday life.

Carracci (family) [kah-raht'-chee] The three Carracci, a family of Bolognese painters, were Agostino, b. 1557, d. Feb. 23, 1602, his brother Annibale, b. Nov. 3, 1560, d. July 15, 1609, and their cousin Ludovico, b. Apr. 21, 1555, d. Nov. 13, 1619. They are credited with leading a reform of Mannerist painting during the last years of the 16th century that led to the baroque style (see BAROQUE ART AND ARCHITECTURE; MANNERISM). During the 1580s,

Carlo Carrà's The Metaphysical Muse *(1917) was influenced by the school of metaphysical painting, which used strange perspectives, unusual objects, and mannequin figures to create oddly disturbing visions. (Emilio Jesi Collection, Milan.)*

Annibale Carracci's ceiling frescoes (1597–1604) in the Gallery of the Farnese Palace in Rome, an early example of baroque illusionism, feature scenes from Greek mythology set in an elaborate painted and sculptural framework.

their workshop in Bologna became the most active center of artistic production and discussion in Italy. The Carracci replaced the lifeless refined forms preferred by the late Mannerist artists with a style of painting marked by clarity, naturalness, and comprehensibility.

The earliest works of **Ludovico**, such as *Jason Battling the Men Born of Dragon Teeth* (*c.*1583; Palazzo Fava, Bologna), were painted in collaboration with his cousins. His own style displays his predisposition for tall, elegant figures, sensuous linear contours, and two-dimensional, friezelike compositions. In the *Bargellini Madonna* (1588; Pinacoteca Nazionale, Bologna) the forms have gained in substance, but the warmth and tenderness of expression beguile the viewer.

Agostino was known as the intellectual of the three and was probably responsible for the theoretical inclination of their academy. The strong classicizing tendency in Agostino's work is exemplified by the *Last Communion of St. Jerome* (1592; Pinacoteca Nazionale, Bologna), with its balanced, ordered composition of robust forms.

Annibale was the most influential member of the family, establishing an art based on the classical principles of the Roman High Renaissance. His passion for recording simple scenes of daily life is found in such works as *Bean Eater* (*c.*1584; Galleria Colonna, Rome) and *Butcher Shop* (*c.*1583; Christ Church, Oxford). His frescoes in the Farnese Palace gallery are masterpieces of *trompe l'oeil* (illusionistic) painting. In the scenes on the ceiling, Annibale created a race of perfectly idealized beings. In his later work, such as *Assumption of the Virgin* (1600–01; Santa Maria del Popolo, Rome), he continued to refine his vision of the ideal until it became an unnatural distillation of the human form.

Carranza, Venustiano [kah-rahn'-sah, vay-noos-tyah'-noh] Venustiano Carranza, b. Dec. 29, 1859, d. May 21, 1920, was a Mexican revolutionary and president. He came from a wealthy family in Cuatro Ciénegas, Coahuila. When President Porfirio DÍAZ prevented his election as governor of Coahuila, he joined the revolution that overthrew Díaz in 1911. He later (1913) headed the forces opposing Victoriano HUERTA.

After their triumph, and after a power struggle with Pancho VILLA and Emiliano ZAPATA, Carranza became president, first (1915) provisionally and later (1917) by election. His presidency was marked by disagreements with the United States over the invasion led by General PERSHING and over U.S. property rights. Although he favored political reforms, Carranza opposed the labor movement, agrarian reform, and the progressive constitution of 1917. He was overthrown (1920) by the reform-minded coalition led by Álvaro OBREGÓN and was killed in Tlaxcalantongo while trying to escape.

Carrera, José Rafael [kah-ray'-rah, hoh-say' rah-fay-el'] José Rafael Carrera, b. Oct. 24, 1814, d. Apr. 4, 1865, was dictator and president of Guatemala. Working with other conservative insurgents, he helped destroy (1839) the CENTRAL AMERICAN FEDERATION and declared Guatemala independent. He held the presidency from 1844 to 1848, was briefly exiled in 1848, but regained (1850) the presidency and held it until his death. He made himself president for life in 1854. A strong supporter of the Roman Catholic church, Carrera dominated Guatemalan politics for a quarter of a century and extended his influence to other countries of Central America as well. He twice fought (1850–53, 1863) against El Salvador. He was probably illiterate throughout his life.

Carreras, José [kah-ray'-rahs, hoh-say'] José Carreras, b. 1948, is a popular Spanish operatic tenor. He made his debut (1970) in Barcelona in Donizetti's *Lucrezia Borgia* and was introduced (1972) to U.S. audiences as Pinkerton in Puccini's *Madama Butterfly* at the New York City Opera. Since then, he has sung at most of the world's major opera houses.

Carrère and Hastings [kuh-rair'] At the turn of the 20th century Carrère and Hastings was one of two New York firms—the other was MCKIM, MEAD, AND WHITE—that dominated monumental architectural design in the United States. John Merven Carrère, b. 1858, d. Mar. 1, 1911, and Thomas Hastings, b. Mar. 1, 1860, d. Oct. 23, 1929, founded their firm in 1886; their first successes were hotels and mansions (1887–88) in St. Augustine, Fla., in a Spanish Renaissance style suited to the locale. The firm's major commissions were in the Beaux-Arts French neoclassical style, as in their opulent New York Public Library (1897–1911) and the first House (1906) and Senate (1905) Office Buildings in Washington, D.C. Among their many palatial residences for magnates is the Henry Clay Frick mansion, New York City (1912–14), now the Frick Collection.

carriage see COACH AND CARRIAGE

Carrier Indians The Carrier Indians, or *Takulli* ("people who go upon the waters"), are an Athapaskan-speaking Indian tribe of North America that aboriginally inhabited the Stuart Lake and upper Fraser River region of present-day British Columbia. The most populous of the Northern Athapaskan tribes, they numbered about 8,500 in 1780. The name *Carrier* was given to them because a widow, before she could remarry, was required to carry the ashes of her dead husband in a basket for 3 years while serving his family.

Traditionally, the Carriers were a semisedentary people. They had permanent homes in villages but would leave them for seasonal hunting and fishing. The Carriers borrowed many cultural traits from their coastal neighbors, especially the TSIMSHIAN. Their society was composed of an aristocratic landowning class whose members inherited property and titles through the female line, and a lower class of commoners that hunted for or with the upper class. No head chiefs existed; each clan had a leader, along with its own well-defined hunting territory. In 1987 about 6,800 Carrier Indians still resided in the upper Fraser area.

Carriera, Rosalba [kah-ree-ay'-rah roh-zahl'-bah] Rosalba Carriera, b. Oct. 7, 1675, d. Apr. 15, 1757, was a Venetian painter known for her portraits and miniatures. She worked first as a miniaturist, but from 1703 she developed the genre of pastel portraiture. The immediacy and delicacy of the images she produced influenced an entire generation of portraitists. Immensely popular in her day among the aristocracy of Europe, Carriera painted many royal and ducal figures. Her most eminent subjects were Louis XV of France, whom she painted during a triumphal trip to Paris in 1720–21, and Holy Roman Emperor Charles VI, who sat for her in Vienna in 1730. Her most avid admirer was Augustus III, elector of Saxony, whose Dresden collection contained more than 150 of her pastels and miniatures. Her portraits display a technical virtuosity and masterly handling of color, as in *Portrait of a Lady* (n.d.; Museum of Fine Arts, Boston).

Carroll, Charles Charles Carroll of Carrollton, Md., b. Sept. 19, 1737, d. Nov. 14, 1832, was an early U.S. Roman Catholic leader and a signer of the Declaration of Independence. A wealthy Maryland planter, Carroll was a strong supporter of independence from Britain and represented Maryland in the Continental Congress from 1776 to 1779. In 1776 he accompanied Benjamin Franklin on a mission to Canada, where they tried unsuccessfully to persuade the French Canadians to join the American Revolution. A U.S. senator from 1789 to 1792, Carroll enjoyed great influence among American Catholics.

Lewis Carroll, an English clergyman, mathematician, and author, composed his most famous novel, Alice's Adventures in Wonderland *(1865), as a gift for Alice Liddell, a daughter of the dean of Christ Church College.*

Carroll, Lewis Lewis Carroll is the pseudonym of the English writer and mathematician Charles Lutwidge Dodgson, b. Jan. 27, 1832, d. Jan. 14, 1898, known especially for ALICE'S ADVENTURES IN WONDERLAND (1865) and THROUGH THE LOOKING-GLASS (1872), children's books that are also distinguished as satire and as examples of verbal wit. Carroll invented his pen name by translating his first two names into the Latin "Carolus Lodovicus" and then anglicizing it into "Lewis Carroll."

The son of a clergyman and the firstborn of 11 children, Carroll attended Rugby School and graduated from Christ Church College, Oxford, in 1854. Carroll remained there, lecturing on mathematics and writing treatises and guides for students. Although he took deacon's orders in 1861, Carroll was never ordained a priest, partly because he was afflicted with a stammer that made preaching difficult. Among Carroll's avocations was photography, at which he excelled, especially at photographing children. Alice Liddell, one of the three daughters of Henry George Liddell, the dean of Christ Church, was one of his photographic subjects and the model for the fictional Alice.

Carroll's comic and children's works also include *The Hunting of the Snark* (1876), two collections of humorous verse, and the two parts of *Sylvie and Bruno* (1889, 1893), attempts to re-create the Alice fantasies. As a mathematician, Carroll was conservative and derivative; as a logician, more interested in logic as a game than as an instrument for testing reason.

carrot A member of the Umbelliferae family, which also includes celery and parsnip, the carrot, *Daucus carota*, is a widely grown vegetable. It is naturally a biennial, but it is grown as an annual for its sweet, orange-colored root. Carrots are indigenous to the Near East and

The carrot is a cool-to-moderate-weather root vegetable with long, lacy leaves reaching about 0.3 m (1 ft) in height. Long carrot varieties require loose or sandy soil, but short or medium-length varieties are required in soils laden with clay or rock.

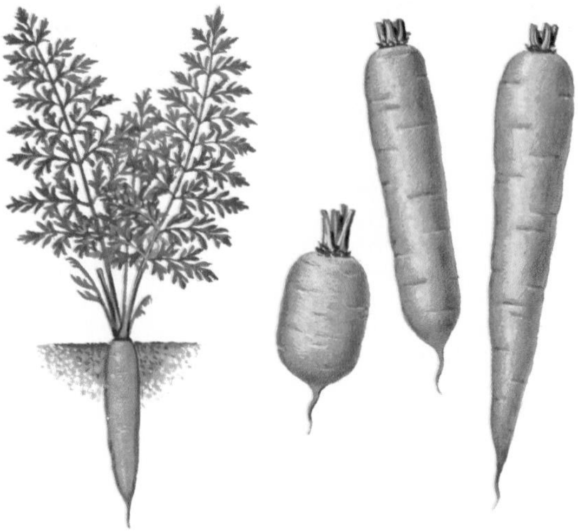

central Asia. They were first used as medicinal herbs rather than as vegetables. The root was poorly developed, woody in structure, and yellow or purple in color. Orange roots were not noted until the mid-18th century. Propagation is by seeds sown in rows on raised beds. The raised beds provide a deep, loose soil, which encourages long, straight roots. Marketable size is attained in 75 to 90 days. The sweetest, most tender carrots are harvested before the roots reach their mature size. Highest yields and quality develop with cool, moderate temperatures.

Most carrots are harvested by machines that lift and top the roots. The roots are washed, graded, and bagged. Some carrots are harvested by hand, bunched, and sold with the tops. Carrots are also grown for canning, freezing, or use in soups and prepared products. They are consumed raw or cooked and are an important source of vitamin A in the human diet.

Carson, Sir Edward Sir Edward Carson, b. Feb. 9, 1854, d. Oct. 22, 1935, an Irish statesman, led the Protestant Irish opposition to home rule for Ireland before World War I. The militancy of this opposition finally forced the British government to agree (1914) to exclude the Protestant north from the Irish home rule settlement. (See HOME RULE BILLS.)

A distinguished trial lawyer, Carson was solicitor general of Britain (1900–05), attorney general (1915), first lord of the admiralty (1917), and a member of the war cabinet (1917–18). He later served as a lord of appeal (1921–29).

Carson, Johnny Johnny Carson, b. Corning, Iowa, Oct. 23, 1925, an American comedian noted for his sly, suave humor, is best known as the host of NBC's "Tonight Show." He grew up in Nebraska where he began his show business career. He performed magic tricks as a child under the name "The Great Carsoni." Carson, whose television career began at station WOW in Omaha, Nebr., later went to Hollywood, where he took a job as a gag writer for "The Red Skelton Show" (1953). His first network series was "Earn Your Vacation" (1954). Several additional shows followed, including "Who Do You Trust?," but he acquired fame in 1962 when he replaced Jack Paar as host of "The Tonight Show."

Carson, Kit Christopher Carson, b. Madison Co., Ky., Dec. 24, 1809, d. May 23, 1868, known as Kit, was an American frontiersman famous in the annals of the West. He grew up in Missouri, but at the age of 16 he joined a caravan bound for Santa Fe and spent the rest of his life in the far West. From 1827 to 1842, Carson roamed the Rocky Mountains as a fur trapper and mountain man. In 1842 he became the guide for the explorations of John C. FRÉMONT in Oregon and California, and during the Mexican War he carried the dispatches from Frémont proclaiming the conquest of California. Afterward he settled in Taos, N.Mex., serving (1853–61) as Indian agent to the Utes despite his inability to read or write.

Kit Carson was an important figure in the westward expansion of the United States. This former trapper and mountain man distinguished himself as a trail guide for the explorations (1842–46) of John C. Frémont and by leading American troops into California during the Mexican War.

During the Civil War, Carson served as colonel of the New Mexico volunteers, distinguishing himself in repelling a Confederate invasion and in the pacification of the Mescalero Apache and Navajo Indians.

Carson, Rachel Rachel Louise Carson, b. Springdale, Pa., May 27, 1907, d. Apr. 14, 1964, was the author of several scientific and popular articles and books concerning ecology and the environment. She graduated (1929) from the Pennsylvania College for Women (now Chatham College) and received an M.A. degree from Johns Hopkins University in 1932. One of her best-known books, *The Sea Around Us* (1951), was on the U.S. nonfiction best-seller list for 39 weeks and won the National Book Award. In *Silent Spring* (1962), Carson strongly criticized the indiscriminate use of pesticides. The book has become a classic of the environmental-protection movement and has stimulated widespread public action in the decades since its publication.

Carson City Carson City (1990 pop., 40,443) is the capital of Nevada. Located 23 km (14 mi) east of Lake Tahoe in the westernmost part of the state, it also served as the county seat of Ormsby County. In 1969, Ormsby County and Carson City were consolidated to form one community. It has a semiarid climate, with annual rainfall averaging 125 to 500 mm (5 to 20 in). Although mining and the livestock industry are important, the economic mainstay is legalized gambling.

Founded in 1851 as Eagle Station, a stop for wagons and stagecoaches passing over the nearby Sierra Nevada, Carson City was renamed (1858) for the frontiersman Kit Carson. The discovery (1859) of silver (known as the COMSTOCK LODE) in the nearby Virginia City area stimulated the development of Carson City. It was named the territorial capital in 1861 and the state capital in 1864. Because of its proximity to the silver mines, the city became the site of a U.S. mint (1870–93) that now serves as the Nevada State Museum.

Cartagena (Colombia) [kar-tah-hay'-nah] Cartagena, a city and port in northern Colombia, lies on the Bay of Cartagena in the Caribbean Sea. It has a population of 491,368 (1985 est.). Its port facilities handle much of Colombia's export cargo, and its industries manufacture sugar, textiles, leather goods, cosmetics, and tobacco and petrochemical products. Tourism is important to the economy. Notable sites include the 17th-century fortress of San Felipe de Barajas, the Church of San Pedro Claver (built 1603), an ornate cathedral, the Palace of the Inquisition (1706), and the University of Cartagena (1824). Founded in 1533, Cartagena became the heavily fortified transshipment point between the New World and Spain for gold and precious stones. Later it was a center of the Inquisition and had a large slave market. In the 17th century it was, after Mexico City, the most important city in the New World. Although it declared independence from Spain in 1811, years of fighting followed. Nationalist forces prevailed in 1821, and Cartagena was incorporated into Colombia.

Cartagena (Spain) Cartagena, a city of 169,036 (1987 est.) on the southeastern coast of Spain, is a major seaport, naval base, and shipbuilding center. Other industries include oil refining, metal processing, and the production of glass, fabrics, and insecticide. Founded by Carthaginians from North Africa *c.*225 BC, the city was captured by the Romans in 209 BC and renamed Carthago Nova. In 1269, King James I of Aragon captured it from the Moors, who had held the port since 711. During the Spanish Civil War, Cartagena served as the Loyalist naval base. Of interest are an archaeological museum and the medieval Castillo de la Concepción.

cartel [kar-tel'] A cartel is an organized group of producers formed to obtain higher prices, restrict production, or divide the market. To achieve its ends, the cartel must usually control production and thus limit the market supply. As long as the members of the cartel maintain discipline, their price objectives are likely to be met. The history of cartels shows, however, that they tend to break down; each member has an incentive to cheat by selling more than its allocated share. Moreover, the uncompetitively high price stimulates production of the same commodity by nonmembers and opens the way for substitute products. In the United States cartels have been illegal except for purposes of export, but some U.S. firms have had arrangements with foreign cartels. The ORGANIZATION OF PETROLEUM EXPORTING COUNTRIES (OPEC), a famous contemporary cartel, was originally successful but in recent years has experienced the same power loss sustained by cartels of the past.

See also: MONOPOLY AND COMPETITION.

Carter, Don Donald James Carter, b. St. Louis, Mo., July 29, 1926, is an American bowler who dominated the professional ranks in the 1950s and 1960s. The Bowling Writers Asssociation of America named him "the greatest of them all" in a 1964 tribute after Carter won six Professional Bowlers Association titles and five World Invitational titles during his first 14 years in bowling. He was named Bowler of the Year six times and was selected (1962) Hickok Award winner as the outstanding U.S. professional athlete. In 1970 he was named to the Bowling Hall of Fame, though not yet retired. Carter bowled 23 perfect games during his career.

Carter, Elliott Elliott Cook Carter, Jr., b. New York City, Dec. 11, 1908, is an eminent composer of chamber music. After studying with Nadia Boulanger in Paris, he developed a challenging style, characterized by complex rhythms and metrical patterns and frequent tempo changes. This distinctive linear style of composition is evident in the String Quartet no. 1 (1951) and is further developed in his next two string quartets (1959, 1973), for which he received the Pulitzer Prize.

Carter has also written important works for orchestra, including Variations for Orchestra (1955–56), Double Concerto (1961), which won the New York Critics Circle Award, and A Symphony of Three Orchestras (1977). Despite its cerebral qualities, Carter's writing is distinguished by its intensity of expression.

Carter, Howard Howard Carter, b. May 9, 1873, d. Mar. 2, 1939, was the English Egyptologist responsible for the discovery of the tomb of King TUTANKHAMEN. In 1891 he joined the Egypt Exploration Fund as a draftsman. He became inspector general of the antiquities department of the Egyptian government in 1899 and supervised (1902–03) a number of tomb excavations in the Valley of the Kings. From 1907 he worked there with Lord Carnarvon and in November 1922 located the entrance to Tutankhamen's tomb.

Carter, Jimmy James Earl Carter served from 1977 to 1981 as the 39th president of the United States. Born on Oct. 1, 1924, in Plains, Ga., he attended Georgia Tech and the U.S. Naval Academy, from which he graduated in 1946. He married Rosalynn Smith on July 7, 1946, and they had four children. Carter served in the navy as an engineer working with nuclear-powered submarines. After the death of his father, however, he resigned (1953) his commission to manage the family's peanut-farming business. He was a state senator (1962–66) and ran unsuccessfully for governor in 1966. In his second attempt (1970), Carter was elected governor and served one term (1971–75).

Presidential Campaign. In 1972, Carter began a 4-year campaign for the Democratic presidential nomination. In 1976 he established a commanding lead over other candidates by winning the Iowa caucuses and the New Hampshire primary. He established a solid base in the South and among black voters and went on to win the

AT A GLANCE

JAMES EARL CARTER, JR.
39th President of the United States (1977–1981)

Nickname: "Jimmy"
Born: Oct. 1, 1924, Plains, Ga.
Education: U.S. Naval Academy, Annapolis, Md. (graduated 1946)
Profession: Farmer, Public Official
Religious Affiliation: Baptist
Marriage: July 7, 1946, to Rosalynn Smith (1927–)
Children: John William "Jack" (1947–); James Earl "Chip" III (1950–); Donnel Jeffrey "Jeff" (1952–); Amy Lynn (1967–)
Political Affiliation: Democrat
Vice President: Walter F. Mondale

Democratic nomination. For his running mate he chose a liberal, Sen. Walter F. MONDALE.

The presidential campaign of 1976 turned chiefly upon the state of the national economy, the personalities of the two candidates, and the desirability of change in the White House. Carter won the election narrowly with 48 percent of the total vote. Although he swept the South, the border states, and some northeastern states, he won only Hawaii in the West. Ford won 27 states against Carter's 23 (plus the District of Columbia), but only 240 electoral votes to Carter's 297.

Carter arrived in Washington as a virtually unknown political quantity without experience or familiarity with Washington. A Baptist fundamentalist who had been "born again" in the faith, Carter was a deeply and openly religious man. He had focused his campaign on government failures rather than on programs and policies. Carter was unusual in two respects. No governor since Franklin Roosevelt had gone on to become president, and no Southerner (except the Texan Lyndon Johnson) had held the office since Andrew Johnson (1865–69). Running in the wake of the Watergate scandals and the Vietnam War, Carter appeared to be an outsider, a non-Washington politician; indeed, his emphasis on morality rather than on political issues gave him an advantage.

Early Administration. During his first months as president, Carter stressed a commitment to HUMAN RIGHTS and an open foreign policy, discussing issues usually reserved for private diplomatic sessions. Many applauded the change, but his openness sometimes created diplomatic problems abroad. His human rights policy annoyed the leaders of the USSR and was subsequently given less emphasis; he also shocked Moscow by proposing drastic reductions in strategic arms. This policy was also abandoned in order to achieve a more limited but workable ARMS CONTROL treaty.

Carter's most serious problems were with Congress. He had little political credit with senators and representatives, having in effect run against them during his campaign. His inexperienced assistants on Capitol Hill failed to confer adequately with congressional leaders. Carter's attempt to establish new national energy policies languished through two congressional sessions and ended in compromise legislation that satisfied nobody. An ambitious plan to overhaul the income-tax system was shunted aside in favor of more-popular tax reductions. A plan to reform the welfare system was also pushed aside by Congress.

Foreign Policies. Public confidence in Carter began to wane during his second year in office, but he was able to secure ratification of treaties to transfer control of the Panama Canal to Panama. The Iranian revolution that toppled the shah early in 1979 surprised the U.S. government and sent Carter's popularity downward. Carter's personal diplomacy led to the signing of a peace treaty between Israel and Egypt on Mar. 26, 1979, and he signed the second Strategic Arms Limitation Treaty (SALT II) with the USSR on June 18, 1979. SALT II, however, never achieved ratification by the U.S. Senate.

Foreign policy in 1980 was dominated by Carter's efforts to secure the release of the U.S. citizens taken hostage by Iranian militants on Nov. 4, 1979 (see IRANIAN HOSTAGE CRISIS), and by the Soviet occupation of Afghanistan the following month. Carter responded to the Soviet invasion of Afghanistan with a limited trade embargo and a U.S. boycott of the 1980 Olympic Games in Moscow. The failure (Apr. 24, 1980) of a mission to rescue the hostages in Iran intensified worries that U.S. military efficacy had been eroded. The mission led to the resignation of Cyrus R. VANCE, who was succeeded as secretary of state by Edmund S. MUSKIE.

Domestic Setbacks. Although Carter's prestige suffered from allegations of impropriety in the past financial dealings of his friend and budget director Bert Lance and in his brother Billy's relations with Libya, the main source of difficulty for the Carter administration was the economy. Unemployment decreased during the first half of Carter's term, but inflation rose sharply and was a serious political liability during his second two years. Inflation was reined in somewhat in mid-1980, but at the cost of recession and rising unemployment. The Carter administration created new departments of education and energy. Its energy policy was criticized, however, especially after severe gasoline shortages developed in 1979.

Carter faced serious opposition within his own party, especially when, during his third year, he began to stress military preparedness at the expense of social programs. Sen. Edward M. KENNEDY challenged Carter for the 1980 Democratic presidential nomination, but Democratic voters gave Carter a series of primary-election victories, and the party renominated him. The Republican nominee, Ronald REAGAN, successfully built inflation and the fear of U.S. military weakness into the major campaign issues, and he easily defeated President Carter in the Nov. 4, 1980, presidential election. In the last month of Carter's administration indirect negotiations with Iran finally produced freedom for the hostages in Tehran. They were released on Jan. 20, 1981, minutes after the inauguration of Reagan.

Postpresidential Years. Carter later devoted himself to writing, teaching at Emory University, and building housing for the poor. He established the Carter Center (1986) at Emory, a research and advocacy center. His continuing interest in foreign affairs was exemplified by his monitoring of the controversial Panamanian election in May 1989.

Carteret, Philip [kart'-ur-et] Philip Carteret, b. 1639, d. 1682, was the first governor (1665–73) of colonial New Jersey. A brother (or cousin) of Sir George Carteret (*c.*1610–1680), one of the colony's proprietors, he founded Elizabethtown (modern Elizabeth) and made it the seat of the legislature. He put down a rebellion in 1668, but was ousted by the Dutch in 1673. Later, as governor (1676–82) of the smaller territory of East Jersey, he was involved in continual disputes with New York's governor Sir Edmund ANDROS.

Carthage [kar'-thij] Carthage, a city on the Tunisian coast of North Africa, was a major Mediterranean power in ancient times. It was settled by Phoenicians from TYRE as a way station and trading post for merchants exchanging eastern manufactures for gold, silver, and tin in Africa and Spain. The traditional foundation date is 814 BC, but archaeology confirms no date before *c.*750 BC. The name was Kart-Hadasht in Phoenician, rendered as Karchedon in Greek and Carthago in Latin.

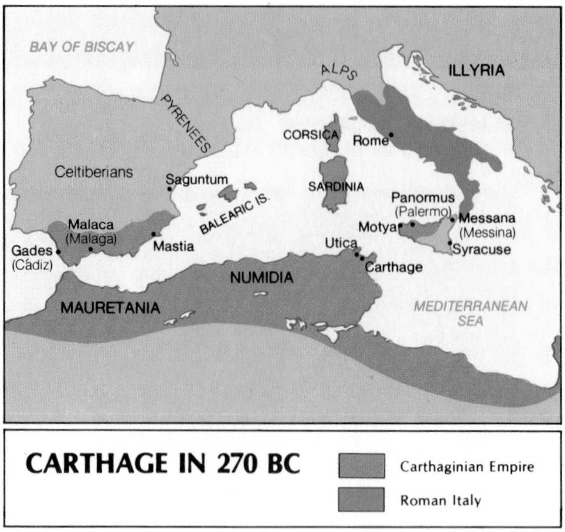

Because of its fine harbor and central location for western trade, Carthage became the Phoenicians' largest western colony when Tyre was weakened by Babylonia and Persia during the 6th century BC. After 580 BC, Carthage led Phoenician settlements in SICILY in resisting Greek aggression and sought to consolidate control of SARDINIA. Carthage then allied with the ETRUSCANS (*c.*540 BC) against the Phocaean Greeks, whom they confined to Massilia (Marseilles) and the surrounding coast. Simultaneously, under King Mago (fl. 550–520 BC), Carthage abandoned a purely citizen army and began to rely heavily on mercenaries, a move forced by its small population base.

The ruins of Carthage overlook the modern port of Tunis. Commercial expansion of this city, originally established by the Phoenicians, led to a series of conflicts with Rome known as the Punic Wars (264–146 BC), which culminated in the total destruction of the city.

An artist's reconstruction depicts Carthage as the city may have appeared at the height of its power (c.300 BC). Enclosed by a wall, the harbor offered docking facilities for as many as 200 vessels.

In Sicily, Carthaginian expansion was halted by Gelon, tyrant of SYRACUSE, who defeated the general Hamilcar at Himera in 480 BC. Shifting its attention to North Africa, Carthage established control over the Phoenician colonies from west of CYRENE to Gibraltar. In 410 and 409 BC, Hannibal, grandson of Hamilcar, reasserted Carthaginian power against the Sicilian Greeks by destroying Selinus and Himera. The resultant series of wars with Syracuse saw Cathaginian control restricted to the western third of Sicily after the tyrant Agathocles nearly captured Carthage itself in 310 BC.

During this period, relations with Rome were cordial. The historian POLYBIUS cites a treaty of 508 BC. Another treaty between Rome and Carthage was concluded in 348 BC, and Carthage aided Rome against PYRRHUS in 280 BC. By 264 BC, however, Roman expansion to the Straits of Messana (Messina), and Carthaginian occupation of Messana itself, triggered the first of the three PUNIC WARS. This war, in which the Carthaginians were driven out of Sicily, was followed by a massive revolt (240–237 BC) of the mercenaries in Carthage's army. This was suppressed by the general HAMILCAR BARCA, who then launched a campaign of conquest in Spain. Roman antagonism was again aroused, and the Second Punic War ensued (218 BC). Despite the brilliant generalship of HANNIBAL, this war ended in the expulsion (201 BC) of the Carthaginians from Spain. Carthage was no longer a great power, but it recovered economically and was still regarded as a threat by Rome. In 149 BC, therefore, Rome launched a third war and this time totally destroyed the city of Carthage in 146 BC.

Carthage's early constitution provided for a king, aristocratic senate, and popular assembly. Perhaps originally hereditary, the kingship was generally elective but was held for life. In the 3d century BC the king was replaced by two chief magistrates, shophets (Latin, *suffetes*), elected annually from the aristocracy, and by elected generals who held long-term commands and were often highly professional and successful. Membership in the senate, which was several hundred strong and discussed all important business, was for life. The assembly voted only on great issues such as war and peace or on issues that the other branches of government failed to resolve. In the mid-5th or early 4th century BC, a body of 104 senatorial judges had been created to oversee the king. They later oversaw the magistrates and generals, but a reform by Hannibal, as shophet (*c.*196 BC), mandated their annual election and forbade consecutive terms.

The Carthaginians worshiped such deities as Baal-Hammon, Tanit, and Melkart. Human sacrifice, especially of the firstborn and by self-immolation, was practiced. Carthaginian art was highly derivative, mainly from Egypt and Greece. Exports included carpets, tapestries, purple dye, jewelry, pottery, and hides. Prosperous, scientific agriculture flourished on the phosphate-rich Tunisian plain.

Resettled as a Roman colony under Julius CAESAR and AUGUSTUS, Carthage became second only to Rome in the west during the 2d century AD. As a major center of learning and Christianity, it produced many famous orators, lawyers, and churchmen such as Saint AUGUSTINE of Hippo, Saint CYPRIAN, and TERTULLIAN. In AD 439, GAISERIC made Carthage the capital of the VANDAL kingdom in North Africa. Later captured (533) by the Byzantine general BELISARIUS, Carthage remained a Christian, Byzantine stronghold until it was permanently destroyed by Muslim conquerors in AD 697–98.

See also: PHOENICIA.

Carthusians The Order of Carthusians is a Roman Catholic RELIGIOUS ORDER of monks, lay brothers, and nuns founded (1084) by Saint Bruno in the Chartreuse mountains near Grenoble, France. The order grew slowly and reached its greatest strength in the early 16th century, when it numbered nearly 200 houses (called *Charterhouses* in English). By the 20th century, however, the number had decreased to about 30. Carthusians are contemplatives who live solitary lives in hermitages and come together only for certain religious ceremonies. Their house in Chartreuse manufactures a well-known liqueur.

Cartier, Sir George Étienne [kar-teeay'] Sir George Cartier, b. Sept. 6, 1814, d. May 20, 1873, was a French-Canadian political leader, one of the founders of the Conservative party, and a father of Canadian federation. A native of Quebec, Cartier fought on the Patriote (rebel) side in the Rebellions of 1837–38. After a brief exile in Vermont he returned to Montreal and became a successful lawyer connected with railway interests. He entered the Legislative Assembly of Canada in 1848 and held a number of posts, including that of joint premier, in Conservative administrations from 1855 to 1862.

As the leader of the French-speaking Conservatives, Cartier joined (1864) the coalition that brought about (1867) the Confederation of British North America. He was instrumental in persuading French Canadians to enter the wider union. He served as minister of militia and defense in the first dominion cabinet.

Cartier, Jacques French navigator Jacques Cartier, b. 1491, d. Sept. 1, 1557, is recognized as the European discoverer of the St. Lawrence River. Born in St. Malo, Brittany, Cartier made three voyages to North America between 1534 and 1542. On the first (1534), he thoroughly explored the Gulf of St. Lawrence, claimed the Gaspé Peninsula for France, and took two Laurentian Iroquois home with him to learn French.

On the second voyage (1535–36), he used the two Indian interpreter-guides to pilot him up the St. Lawrence River to Stadacona (the site of modern Quebec). He continued to Hochelaga (Montreal) without them but was discouraged from continuing farther west by the rapids and cold weather. Wintering in Stadacona, 25 members of his crew died from scurvy before the discovery of a brew of white cedar saved the rest. He arrived back at St. Malo in July 1536.

On his third voyage (1541–42), Cartier was obliged to serve under the nominal command of Jean François de la Rocque de Roberval, although the latter did not sail with him. Cartier founded a settlement near Stadacona, discovered quartz he thought to be diamonds and iron pyrites he thought to be gold, and again traveled as far as Hochelaga. He wintered near Stadacona, where at least 35 members of his crew were apparently killed by Iroquois. He died at St. Malo. His account of his three voyages, variously published in French, English, and Italian between 1545 and 1600, stimulated later voyages of discovery.

Jacques Cartier explored the St. Lawrence River as far inland as present-day Montreal. France's claim to Canada was based on Cartier's explorations, which were originally intended as part of the search for the Northwest Passage to the Orient.

Cartier-Bresson, Henri [kar-teeay'-breh-sawn'] The French photojournalist Henri Cartier-Bresson, b. Aug. 22, 1908, is known as the master of the expressive documentary photograph. His technique is based on previsualizing the finished print, waiting until the "decisive moment," then, with a single exposure, creating a photo that is both spontaneous and carefully composed. Beginning his photographic career in 1930, Cartier-Bresson had several major exhibits before entering cinematography as assistant to Jean RENOIR in 1936. One of the founders, in 1947, of the cooperative agency Magnum, he photographed in India, China, the USSR, the United States, Canada, and Japan for the next two decades.

Cartier-Bresson's study (1948) of Kashmiri women is in his usual black-and-white. He felt that color is capable of capturing only the surface of a scene, while black-and-white often reveals the deeper meaning of a photographed moment.

cartilage [kar'-ti-lij] Cartilage is a rubbery, fibrous connective tissue that, along with bone, supports the vertebrate body. The main constituent of cartilage fibers is a protein, COLLAGEN. It is the temporary skeleton of the vertebrate embryo and the template for the development of most BONE. Cartilage persists in adults, however, as in the joints of long bones, where it acts as a cushion and provides a smooth surface; at the end of the ribs; and in the throat, ears, and nose. It is the sole supporting tissue of such vertebrate forms as lampreys and sharks.

Since most cartilage is poorly supplied with blood vessels, it receives its nourishment either from the fluid in joint cavities or through its external membrane, the perichondrium. Cartilage at the end of bones (epiphysis) plays an essential part in skeletal growth (see SKELETAL SYSTEM). Within the firm matrix lie maturing cells, the chondrocytes, that form new matrix and are continually being displaced.

Cartland, Barbara Barbara Cartland, b. July 9, 1901, is the English author of countless romance novels, almost all of them featuring spirited and virginal heroines who "educate themselves..., mind about the poor and sick..., and pray." Most of her fiction takes place in the 19th century; sales have run to the hundreds of millions.

cartography see MAPS AND MAPMAKING

cartoon, animated see ANIMATION

cartoon (art) In art the term *cartoon* (from the Italian *cartone*, or "cardboard") refers to the full-scale preparatory drawing used to transfer the outlines of a pictorial conception to the surface on which the work is to be executed. Cartoons have been used in the preparation of paintings, tapestries, stained-glass windows, and mosaics. They are especially important in the technique of FRESCO PAINTING, in which the execution of the painting must be entirely completed before the surface of damp plaster has dried.

Before the 15th century in Italy, preliminary contours were drawn directly on the fresco surface. During the High Renaissance, fresco cartoons were usually executed on either light cardboard or heavy sheets of paper and then transferred onto the plaster ground.

Because cartoons are essentially work drawings, often damaged during the transferring process, few have survived from the time of the Renaissance. Notable exceptions are Raphael's remarkably complete cartoons, executed in watercolor on paper, for the Sistine Chapel tapestries (*c.*1515; Victoria and Albert Museum, London) and a rare Michelangelo cartoon (1545–50; Museo Nazionale di Capodimonte, Naples) of the soldiers in his *Crucifixion of Saint Peter* (1545–50; Pauline Chapel, the Vatican). Today cartoons are rarely used in painting, although the prominent Mexican artist Diego RIVERA frequently sketched cartoons directly on the wall for his monumental series of frescoes.

cartoon (editorial and political) The term *cartoon* originally described an artist's preliminary sketch for a painting, fresco, or tapestry. It later came to designate the rough and unconventional sketches a comic artist produces. Today it means a drawing or painting used for amusement, editorial, or advertising purposes. A cartoon used to entertain is called a COMIC STRIP or gag cartoon; one used to explain or illustrate a story, article, or book, or to form part of an advertisement, is called a cartoon illustration; one used to sway public opinion or dramatize the news is called an editorial or political cartoon.

A cartoon by Thomas Nast warned readers that, although "Boss" Tweed's Tammany Hall cronies had been defeated in the 1871 elections, Tweed himself remained in office. Nast's cartoons were instrumental in smashing the Tweed Ring.

Homer Davenport left readers of the Hearst newspapers with little doubt concerning "Mr. Hanna's Stand on the Labor Question." The cartoon refers to Mark Hanna, a powerful industrialist whose financial support was vital to William McKinley's 1896 presidential campaign.

"Mr. Dry," a character created in the cartoons of Rollin Kirby, came to symbolize the prohibition against alcoholic beverages imposed by the Volstead Act (18th Amendment).

Editorial cartoons usually appear on the editorial pages of newspapers, although in 18th- and 19th-century Europe such cartoons, called CARICATURES, were sold as single sheets. Today *caricature* has come to refer to a drawing of an individual that exaggerates personal appearance to the point of ridicule.

The first editorial cartoons in the United States appeared in the second half of the 19th century, mainly in magazines. Thomas NAST, America's first important editorial cartoonist, did most of his work for *Harper's Weekly*. When PHOTOENGRAVING made possible quick and economical reproduction of drawings and photographs, editorial cartoons began to appear regularly in daily newspapers.

Daily Working Procedures. Typically, an editorial cartoonist meets with the editors each day to discuss the news and the editorial positions the paper is to take. The cartoonist returns to the drawing board to execute several rough sketches, and the editorial-page editor picks one for finishing. Cartoons are drawn larger than they are to appear in print and then reduced photographically.

Pompous or hypocritical politicians make the best subjects for editorial cartoons. "I start with the premise that there's not a good one in the bunch," says Patrick OLIPHANT of the Washington *Star*; "they're all guilty until proven innocent." Tony Auth of the *Philadelphia Inquirer* adds that an editorial cartoonist needs a sense of outrage: "You have to be capable of reading something and saying, 'I don't believe that!' and then translate that into a drawing."

Cartoons occasioned by the death of a public figure (obit cartoons) are the hardest to draw. One of the most memorable is Bill MAULDIN's drawing of a bowed statue of Lincoln after the assassination of President John Kennedy. One cartoonist, J. N. "Ding" Darling (1876–1962) of the *Des Moines Register*, drew his own obit cartoon.

Most well-known syndicated cartoonists tend to be politically liberal. A few, however, such as Don Hesse of the St. Louis *Globe-Democrat*, Karl Hubenthal of the Los Angeles *Herald-Examiner*, and Jeff MacNelly of the Richmond *News-Leader*, are strongly conservative. But MacNelly, a winner of the Pulitzer Prize for editorial cartoons while in his early twenties, is unique in seeming to be as interested in amusing his readers as in influencing them.

Styles. Styles of cartoon drawing generally fall into the ashcan school, the crosshatch school, and the built-in-texture school. The ashcan school was inspired by the work of the French caricaturist Honoré DAUMIER and other 19th-century lithographic artists. This style evolved in newspapers around the time of World War I, when it was used mostly by liberal or radical cartoonists concerned with poverty, among other problems. Daniel Fitzpatrick (1891–1969), for many years with the St. Louis *Post-Dispatch*, was an early practitioner of this style; his bold, stark drawings spawned many imitators. HERBLOCK of the Washington *Post* belongs to this school, as does Mauldin.

The crosshatch school, characterized by many fine crisscross lines drawn to impart roundness to figures and props, originated with Thomas Nast and Homer Davenport, who followed him. Davenport (1867–1912) worked mostly for the newspapers of William Randolph HEARST.

Many Midwestern cartoonists, including John T. McCutcheon (1870–1949) of the *Chicago Tribune* and "Ding" Darling, also used it. The crosshatch style has fallen from favor on today's newspaper pages, but it is still used by David Levine, the caricaturist for *The New York Review of Books*, and his many imitators.

The built-in-texture school includes several newer editorial cartoonists, led by Patrick Oliphant. Oliphant introduced a horizontal rather than a vertical format for cartoons and a grotesquely comic, rather than realistic, style. Cartoons in this style are drawn on paper with a built-in texture that is brought out by applying a chemical solution. MacNelly belongs to the built-in-texture school, as does Draper Hill of the *Detroit News.*

Cartoonists often experiment with other styles. Paul Conrad of the *Los Angeles Times*, who mainly works in the Ashcan style, sometimes uses a scratchboard technique for his drawings. He scratches through a coating of black ink with a knife or razor blade to expose the white of the paper.

Labels, Captions, and Visual Shorthand. To help readers recognize certain characters and better understand cartoon ideas, some editorial cartoonists include boxes, or

Bill Mauldin's cartoon from Up Front *(1944), satirizing overenthusiastic reportage of World War II events for home consumption, won him a Pulitzer Prize for cartoon in 1945. Mauldin's cartoon characters, Willie and Joe, an irreverent pair of American infantrymen, became a favorite feature of the military newspaper* Stars and Stripes.

This cartoon drawn by Paul Conrad shortly after the Arab oil embargo of 1973 alludes to suspicions held by Americans, concerning the oil industry.

labels, with words inside them. Most editorial cartoons, however, have only captions, often simply a comment made by the cartoonist.

Cartoonists have developed a kind of visual shorthand, a set of symbols to stand for organizations and concepts. The most familiar symbols are Uncle Sam for the United States, the donkey for the Democratic party, and the elephant for the Republican party. In the 1920s, Rollin Kirby of the *New York World* invented "Mr. Dry," a tall, cranky man dressed in black and carrying an umbrella, to stand for Prohibition.

cartridge, stereo see SOUND RECORDING AND REPRODUCTION

Cartwright, Edmund English inventor Edmund Cartwright, b. Apr. 24, 1743, d. Oct. 30, 1823, was one of the founders of the modern textile industry. His principal inventions—a power loom and a machine for combing wool fibers in preparation for spinning them into yarn—were both financial failures during his lifetime, but they provided the models on which later machines were based.

Cartwright attended Oxford University and then became a rector in Leicestershire. Impressed by a visit to Richard ARKWRIGHT's spinning factories, he built (1786) a steam-powered LOOM that seemed to have the potential to power the WEAVING industry. In fact, the machine posed such a threat to the livelihood of English handweavers that, when a Manchester cotton mill installed it, their building was burned down, and Cartwright went into bankruptcy. His wool-combing machine, the first of its kind, was patented in 1789.

Cartwright, Peter Peter Cartwright, b. Amherst County, Va., Sept. 1, 1785, d. Sept. 25, 1872, was an American Methodist preacher, the most famous of the itinerant preachers called the CIRCUIT RIDERS. Cartwright served for 16 years in the Illinois state legislature and was defeated by Abraham Lincoln in a race for the U.S. Congress in 1846.

Cartwright, Sir Richard John Sir Richard John Cartwright, b. Kingston, Ontario, Dec. 4, 1835, d. Sept. 24, 1912, was a Canadian political leader. A banker, he was first elected (1863) to the Legislative Assembly as a Conservative, but he later quarreled with the Conservatives over fiscal policy and joined the Liberal party. Cartwright sat for over 40 years in the Canadian House of Commons and Senate, serving as minister of finance (1873–78) under Alexander MACKENZIE and minister of trade and commerce (1896–1911) under Sir Wilfred LAURIER.

Caruso, Enrico Enrico Caruso, b. Naples, Italy, Feb. 25, 1873, is considered one of the greatest operatic tenors of all time. He made his debut in Naples in 1894. He appeared at Covent Garden in 1902 and at the Metropolitan Opera (1903–20), where he sang over 600 performances in nearly 40 operas.

Caruso possessed a sumptuously beautiful voice, which he refined until he was equally at home in both verismo and bel canto repertory. Despite his stocky figure, he was considered a good actor, especially as Eleazar in Halévy's *La Juive*.

Caruso began to record (1902) during the infancy of the phonograph and continued until his death, earning enormous royalties. His last performance, sung while mortally ill, was in *La Juive* at the Metropolitan on Christmas Eve, 1920. After an operation, Caruso returned to Naples, where he died on Aug. 2, 1921. He was mourned throughout the world.

Carver, George Washington George Washington Carver, b. near Diamond Grove, Mo., July 1861, d. June

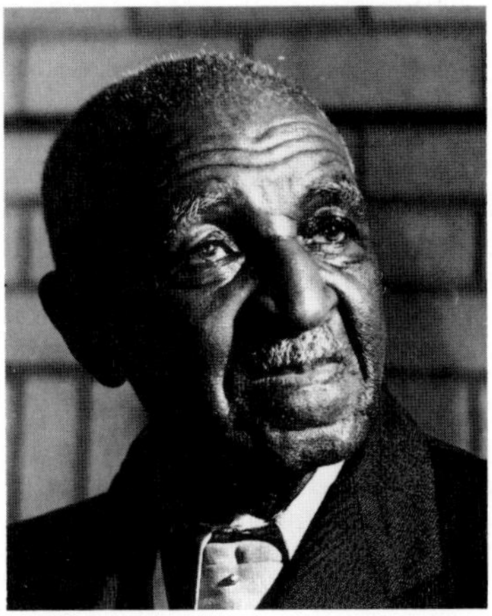

George Washington Carver, an American educator and horticulturist, developed useful by-products from peanuts, sweet potatoes, and soybeans. Carver became head of Tuskegee Institute's agricultural school, where he achieved distinction for his experimental work and teaching.

5, 1943, was a black American botanist and chemist who helped bring prosperity to large areas of the impoverished southern United States. Born a slave on a Missouri farm, he was orphaned as an infant and freed at the end of the Civil War. He spent his early years in the household of his former owner, Moses Carver, whose name he adopted. Carver began his education in a school for black children 14.5 km (9 mi) from his home. In 1889 he enrolled at Simpson College in Iowa and earned the $12 yearly tuition by working as a cook. Although Carver's ambition was to be an artist—he had considerable talent as a painter—he decided to study horticulture, and he earned (1896) a master's degree at Iowa State Agricultural College.

That same year he accepted an invitation from Booker T. WASHINGTON to head the newly formed department of agriculture at TUSKEGEE INSTITUTE in Alabama. He spent the rest of his life at Tuskegee, slowly creating a laboratory, rebuilding the exhausted land around the Institute, and pursuing research. Much of the farming land of the South had been depleted as a result of the intensive cultivation of cotton and tobacco. Carver experimented with nitrogen-producing legumes and found that peanuts and sweet potatoes both improved the soil and grew abundantly in the South. To find new uses for these crops, he developed more than 300 by-products: cereals, oils, dyes, soaps, and food substitutes. In addition, he began his notable "school on wheels," a traveling classroom that taught Alabama farmers the basics of soil enrichment. His fame as a scientist and educator grew throughout the world, and when he died at Tuskegee in 1943 he was one of America's most honored scientists.

Carver, John John Carver, b. *c.*1576, d. Apr. 5, 1621, one of the Pilgrim Fathers, was the first governor of PLYMOUTH COLONY. A wealthy merchant, he helped arrange the Pilgrims' emigration to America in 1620, chartering the *Mayflower.* He was governor for less than a year before his death.

Carver, Raymond Writer Raymond Carver, b. Clatskanie, Oreg., May 25, 1938, d. Aug. 2, 1988, is considered a master of the short story with a unique feeling for the lives of the working poor. The son of a laborer, Carver worked at a number of odd jobs while he began his writing career. His first short-story collection, *Will You Please Be Quiet, Please?* (1976), won a National Book Award. Other collections and prizes followed, both for his stories and for his poems, published in *Where the Water Comes Together with Other Water* (1985) and additional volumes.

Cary, Joyce Arthur Joyce Lunel Cary, b. Dec. 7, 1888, d. Mar. 29, 1957, was a prolific Anglo-Irish writer whose work is notable for its richly comic qualities and underlying seriousness. After studying art he served (1913–20) in the colonial service in Nigeria. His experiences there formed the basis for his early novel *Mister Johnson* (1939). Cary's first fictional trilogy includes *Herself Surprised* (1941), *To Be a Pilgrim* (1942), and *The Horse's Mouth* (1944), followed by *A Fearful Joy* (1949) and a second trilogy on politics, *Prisoner of Grace* (1952), *Except the Lord* (1953), and *Not Honour More* (1955).

Casablanca Casablanca (Arabic: Dar al-Baida) is the leading commercial, industrial, and port city of Morocco, located on the Atlantic coast. With a population of 2,600,000 (1984 est.), it is the largest Moroccan city and the second-largest city in Africa.

Casablanca's principal exports are phosphate and fertilizers, citrus fruit, vegetables, canned fish, and leather products. The city accounts for more than half of the nation's industrial output and employment. Its modern business district is arranged in a semicircle around the crowded, narrow streets of the *medina* (old city).

Casablanca was founded by the Portuguese in 1468 on the site of the ancient city of Anfa. Largely destroyed by an earthquake in 1755, it was subsequently rebuilt, and was occupied by the French in 1907. The Casablanca Conference, a meeting between U.S. president Franklin D. Roosevelt and British leader Winston Churchill to decide the future strategy of the Allies in World War II, was held in the city Jan. 14–23, 1943.

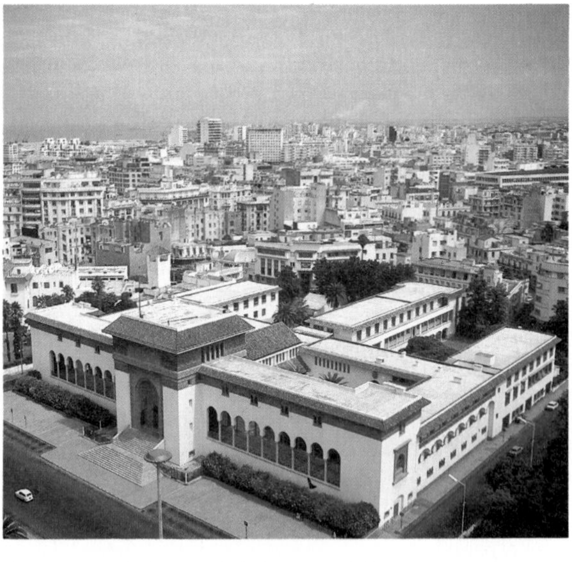

Casablanca, the largest city in Morocco, is home to more than 10% of the nation's total population. The city's artificial harbor, one of the busiest in North Africa, was constructed in 1916, during the period of French colonial rule.

Casals, Pablo [kah-sahls'] Pau (or Pablo) Casals, b. Dec. 29, 1876, d. Oct. 22, 1973, was a Spanish cellist, conductor, composer, and public figure. By age 21 he had modified the technique of the cello and was hailed as a master. He formed an acclaimed trio with the violinist Jacques Thibaud and the pianist Alfred Cortot.

Casals began conducting in 1908 and in 1919 founded and subsidized the Orquestra Pau Casals in Barcelona. An ardent opponent of fascism, he exiled himself from Spain in protest against the regime of Francisco Franco, and for a time stopped performing. After organizing music festivals in France and Puerto Rico during the 1950s, he began a fruitful association in 1960 with the Marlboro festival in Vermont.

Casanova de Seingalt, Giovanni Giacomo [kah-zah-noh'-vah day sayn-gahlt'] Giovanni Giacomo Casanova de Seingalt, b. Venice, Italy Apr. 2, 1725, d. June 4, 1798, the adventurer, soldier, spy, and famous libertine, is remembered for his autobiography, *History of My Life* (12 vols., 1826; Eng. trans., 1966–71). Containing exceedingly ripe and possibly untrue accounts of his sexual exploits, the work gives as well a fascinating picture of 18th-century European society.

Born to actor parents, Casanova received little formal education and was involved in scurrilous escapades from an early age. He served briefly in the Venetian army, played the violin at the theater of St. Samuel, and was adopted (1745) by the Venetian senator Bragadin.

From 1750, Casanova traveled throughout Europe, going first to France, where he became associated with the Freemasons, then to Dresden, Prague, and Vienna. In 1755 he was arrested in Venice for witchcraft and imprisoned. Having escaped, Casanova reappeared in Paris in 1757 as head of the French royal lottery and dispatcher of diplomatic missions, assuming in this period the title Chevalier de Seingalt and amassing a large fortune that he promptly lost. In 1782 he was expelled from Venice because of a satirical pamphlet. In 1785 the Graf von Waldstein appointed Casanova personal secretary and librarian at his castle in Dux, Bohemia, where he died.

casbah In North African cities, the casbah (from the Arabic *qasaba:* fortress, citadel) is the oldest city area, usually built on the steep sides of a hill and walled. In smaller cities, casbahs were often abandoned when their adobe structures crumbled from age. The casbahs in such larger cities as Algiers are built of brick and concrete and still house many inhabitants, as well as extensive bazaars and red-light districts.

Cascade Range The Cascade Range of mountains extends 1,120 km (700 mi) from LASSEN PEAK, in northern California, and continues northward through Oregon and Washington to the Fraser River in British Columbia, Canada. Paralleling the Pacific coast about 160 km (100 mi) inland, it contains many snowcapped volcanic cones. Eight of these have erupted in the past 200 years, two of them in the 20th century. Lassen Peak, which erupted in 1914, remained active for the next 7 years. A major eruption of Mount St. Helens in southwestern Washington, on May 18, 1980, was followed by an extended period of activity. The Cascade's volcanism has made the range a center of geologic study (see VOLCANO). The highest peak in the range, Mount Rainier (see RAINIER, MOUNT) in Washington, rises to 4,392 m (14,410 ft). Glaciation created many lakes, and glaciers mark the highest peaks. The Klamath and Columbia rivers cut the range from east to west. The Lewis and Clark expedition traversed the Columbia River gorge in 1806.

case *Case* is a grammatical term used to indicate the different forms taken by a noun, pronoun, or adjective based on its function in a sentence. The use of cases is called inflection, and languages in which they are used are called inflected languages. Modern English has only two cases for most words: the common case (for example, *woman*) and the possessive (*woman's*). Old English also had a distinct accusative case (direct object), dative (indirect object), and instrumental (to express means or agency). The dative/accusative case survives in English for certain pronouns—for example, *them*.

Latin has six cases: nominative, genitive (possessive), dative, accusative, ablative, and vocative. The ablative case would be expressed in English by prepositions such as *from, with, in,* and *by*; the vocative is used in direct address. Among modern European languages, German and the Slavic are highly inflected; the Romance and the Scandinavian languages (except for Icelandic) are not. Case inflection is rare outside the Indo-European family of languages. One notable exception is the Finno-Ugric group, which includes Finnish and Hungarian. Finnish has between 15 and 20 cases, and Hungarian between 25 and 30.

Casement, Sir Roger Sir Roger David Casement, b. Sept. 1, 1864, d. Aug. 3, 1916, was an Irish revolutionary who was executed for treason by the British. Earlier, as a British consular official, he exposed atrocities against plantation workers in the Belgian Congo (1904) and Peru (1912). Joining the Irish nationalist movement, Casement went (1914) to Germany after the outbreak of World War I to secure aid for an Irish rebellion. Ironically, he was returning empty-handed when arrested by the British. His trial and execution caused great controversy, exacerbated by the British attempt to discredit him as a homosexual.

Cash, Johnny Johnny Cash, b. Kingsland, Ark., Feb. 26, 1932, a famous country singer and guitarist, has been a success since his first songs were recorded—notably "I Walk the Line" in 1956. He regularly performs in prisons, and prison songs are an important part of his repertoire. Cash has been featured in films, on television, and at the Grand Ole Opry and has won three Grammy Awards. He wrote many of his songs in collaboration with his wife, country singer June Carter Cash.

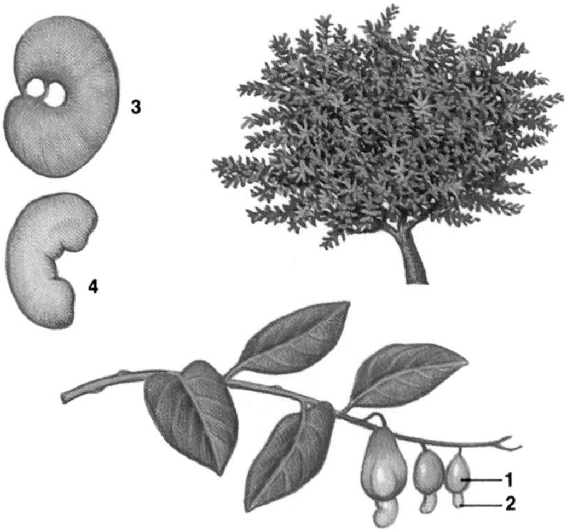

The cashew tree (top right), *a tropical American evergreen, produces a fleshy fruit, the cashew apple* (1). *The seed* (2) *is encased in an outer shell* (3) *that must be burned off and an inner shell that is removed by boiling to produce the edible nut* (4).

cashew The cashew, an edible nut, is the seed of the tropical American cashew tree, *Anacardium occidentale*, which is a member of a large family, Anacardiaceae, of which only a few species (sumac, poison ivy, the smoke tree) are found in the temperate zone. The cashew is a large evergreen tree that reaches heights of 9–12 m (29–39 ft). The leaves are oval and leathery; the rosy-tinted, fragrant flowers grow in clusters at the ends of young branches. The nut is kidney shaped, the size of a large bean, and borne beneath a yellow or orange fruit called a cashew apple. The apple is edible and can be fermented to make wine. The outer covering of the fruit contains an extremely caustic oil that must be burned off before the nut can be touched. The kernels are then boiled or roasted again, and a second shell is removed.

The cashew tree is indigenous to the West Indies, Central America, Peru, and Brazil. The Portuguese transplanted it to the East Indies as early as the 16th century, and it was later established on the eastern coast of Africa.

cashmere Cashmere is the wool from the soft undercoat, or down, of the Kashmir goat, found in Tibet, China, Iran, Iraq, Soviet Central Asia, and Outer Mongolia, as well as in the province of Kashmir. The term *cashmere* also refers to knit and woven fabrics made of cashmere, usually blended with wool and other fibers, used for sweaters, coatings, and suitings. Cashmere fabrics are soft to the touch and provide warmth without weight.

Casimir III, King of Poland (Casimir the Great) Casimir III, b. Apr. 30, 1310, d. Nov. 5, 1370, was the last PIAST king of Poland (r. 1333–70). Succeeding his father, Władysław I (or IV), he induced John of Luxemburg, king of Bohemia, to relinquish his claim to the Polish crown by granting him Silesia (Treaty of Visegrád, 1335). In 1343 he also made a territorial settlement with the TEUTONIC KNIGHTS. By the acquisition (1349) of the duchy of Galich-Vladimir (later known as GALICIA), however, Casimir began Poland's eastward expansion. Known as the "king of peasants," he curbed the power of the nobility, codified the law, founded (1364) the University of Kraków, and built towns and frontier castles. He was succeeded by his nephew, LOUIS I of Hungary.

Casimir IV, King of Poland Casimir IV, b. Nov. 30, 1427, d. June 7, 1492, king of Poland (r. 1447–92) and grand duke of Lithuania (r. 1440–92), succeeded his brother Władysław III to the Polish throne. He reinforced royal power at the expense of the magnates, preserved the Polish-Lithuanian Union, and after a 13-year war subjugated the TEUTONIC KNIGHTS. By the Peace of Toruń (Thorn) of Oct. 19, 1466, the order returned the western part of Eastern Pomerania (with Gdańsk) to Poland, while the eastern part (later called East Prussia) became a fief of the Polish crown.

casino Casino is a game of skill and some luck played with a standard deck of 52 playing cards. It is both a gambling game and one played for amusement. Four cards are dealt face down to each of the two to four players, and four cards are dealt face up on the table. To play, a player may: (1) take from the table one or any combination of cards whose sum matches a card in his or her hand; (2) add a card from his or her hand to one on the table ("building"), the sum being equal to a card still in his or her hand; or (3) simply place a card from his or her hand on the table. After the players have played their four cards, four more are dealt to each one.

Cards from ace through 10 are worth their face value, and picture cards have no numerical value. Points are allotted for winning the 10 of diamonds (2 points), the 2 of spades (1 point), aces (1 point each), and for having the most cards (3 points) and most spades (1 point). The first player to accumulate 21 points is the winner.

Caslon, William William Caslon, b. 1692, d. Jan. 23, 1766, an engraver of locks and barrels for guns, became England's first important punch-cutter and typefounder, developing the first large-scale business in this field. After commencing typefounding (the design and production of printing type) in London in 1720, Caslon was commissioned to cut an Arabic type font. His first specimen sheet in 1734 displayed 38 of his own type fonts and eventually led to the virtual cessation of importing Dutch types, on which English printers had formerly relied. His typefaces (see TYPE AND TYPESETTING), noted for their legibility, are among the best faces ever produced.

Casper Casper (1990 pop., 46,742) is a city in east central Wyoming. The seat of Natrona County, Casper is located on the North Platte River. Established as a fort on the Oregon Trail, it was named for Lt. Caspar Collins, who was killed by Indians. The city's economy is based on oil and natural-gas production, as well as sheep and cattle raising.

Casper, Billy The American William Earl Casper, Jr., b. San Diego, Calif., June 24, 1931, was one of golf's great stars in the 1950s and '60s. Among Casper's more than 50 tournament victories are three major titles: the U.S. Open twice (1959, 1966) and the Masters (1970). He won the Vardon Trophy, awarded annually to the player with the best average score per round, five times (1960, 1963, 1965–66, 1968) and was Player of the Year in 1966. Casper, then golf's finest putter, set a record by finishing in the money in 100 consecutive tournaments.

Caspian Sea The Caspian Sea is the world's largest inland body of water. It lies on the border between Europe and Asia, bounded on the west, north, and east by four Soviet republics and on the south by Iran. Approximately 1,210 km (750 mi) long and 320 km (200 mi) wide, it has an area of about 370,300 km^2 (143,000 mi^2) and lies 28 m (94 ft) below sea level. Its depth reaches 1,024 m (3,360 ft). The sea is shallow in the north but averages 305 m (1,000 ft) in the deeper southern section. The Caspian is a saltwater sea and has no outlet. It is fed by the Volga, Ural, Terek, Kuma, Safid Rud, and Atrek rivers. The Volga alone contributes about three-quarters of the sea's water. The average water salinity (1.3%) is about one-third that of the oceans. The sea is important for fishing, most notably for sturgeon, and carries between one-third and one-half of all Soviet maritime trade. The Caucasian oil fields extend into the sea.

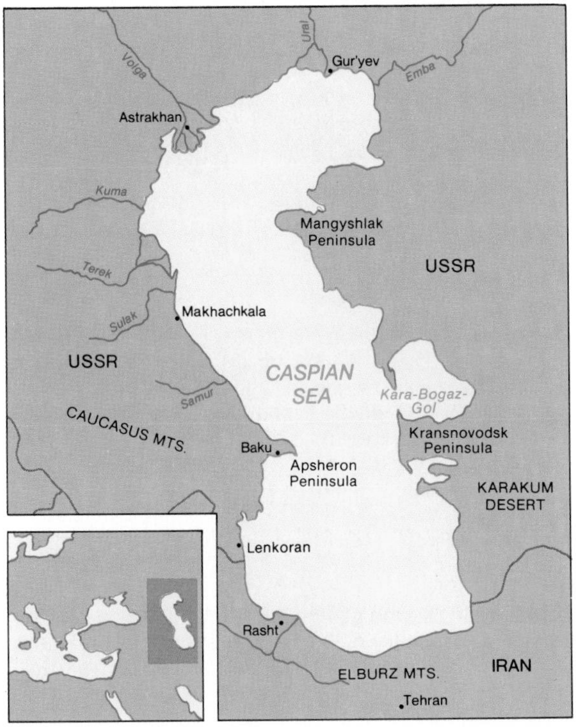

The Caspian occupies an enormous depression and at one time was linked with the Aral and Black seas. Much of the surrounding region is covered with a thick layer of yellowish-green clay that was deposited by this great inland sea. The sea's shoreline was repeatedly changed by tectonic activity, and, during the Quaternary Period, by glaciations. Fluctuations in size have been common. In the shallow north, the sea is frozen about four months a year. The lake's major ports are Baku, Makhachkala, and Astrakhan in the USSR and Bandar-e Anzali and Bandar-e Torkeman in Iran.

Cass, Lewis Lewis Cass, b. Exeter, N.H., Oct. 9, 1782, d. June 17, 1866, was an American political leader and the Democratic presidential nominee in 1848. He attended the local academy in Exeter before moving (1799) to Ohio. After a brief residence in Marietta, he began to practice law in Zanesville. He was elected (1806) to the Ohio legislature and served as U.S. marshal from 1807 to 1812. He distinguished himself in the War of 1812 and rose to the rank of brigadier general.

In 1813, President James Madison appointed Cass governor of Michigan Territory, a position he held until 1831, when President Andrew Jackson named him secretary of war. He resigned (1836) to become minister to France, where he remained until 1842. He served as U.S. senator from Michigan from 1845 to 1857 and was a strong supporter of territorial expansion. He narrowly lost the presidential election of 1848 to his Whig opponent, Zachary Taylor. President James Buchanan named Cass secretary of state in 1857. Although he generally advocated a conciliatory stand in the sectional controversy, he resigned in December 1860 when Buchanan rejected his advice to reinforce the Charleston forts during the secession crisis.

Cassandra [kuh-san'-druh] In Greek mythology Cassandra was the daughter of PRIAM, king of Troy, and HECUBA. APOLLO loved her and gave her the gift of prophecy. When Cassandra spurned Apollo's advances, however, he cursed her so that no one would believe her predictions. She warned the Trojans against the wooden horse, but they would not believe her. Taken captive by AGAMEMNON, she returned with him to Greece where both were murdered by CLYTEMNESTRA, the wife of Agamemnon, and her lover.

Cassatt, Mary [kuh-sat'] Mary Cassatt, b. Allegheny City, Pa., May 22, 1847, d. June 14, 1926, was the first

Young Woman Sewing in the Garden *(1886) by the American expatriate impressionist Mary Cassatt reveals the influence of Edgar Degas and Édouard Manet. (Musée d'Orsay, Paris.)*

American artist to associate with the impressionists and the only American ever to exhibit with them (1877, 1879, 1880, 1881, 1886). She promoted the impressionists in the United States and is responsible for the appearance of many impressionist paintings in U.S. collections (see IMPRESSIONISM).

In 1877 Cassatt met and began a close association with Edgar DEGAS, who invited her to join the impressionist group. When she exhibited *A Woman in Black at the Opera* (Museum of Fine Arts, Boston) in the impressionist show of 1880, the influence of Degas and of their mutual study of Japanese prints was clearly evident. She continued to paint many subjects for which Degas is famous, but her mature impressionist paintings, typified by *Morning Toilette* (1886; National Gallery of Art, Washington, D.C.), have an unmistakably American quality in their solidity and clarity of contours and details. Other familiar paintings are *The Blue Room* (1878; Mellon Collection, Upperville, Va.), remarkable for its form and color, and *The Boating Party* (1893; National Gallery, Washington, D.C.), noted for its radical composition.

Cassatt was primarily a figure painter; from the late 1880s on, she increasingly devoted herself to the theme of mother and child in oil, pastel, etchings, and engravings. She was commissioned to paint a mural for the Woman's Building of Chicago's World's Columbian Exposition of 1893.

cassava see MANIOC

Cassegrainian telescope [kas-uh-grayn'-ee-uhn] The Cassegrainian telescope is a type of astronomical reflecting TELESCOPE attributed to Cassegrain (fl. 1672), a Frenchman of uncertain identity. Starlight first falls on a primary concave parabolic mirror, is reflected upward to a convex hyperboloid mirror, and is finally reflected downward through a hole in the primary mirror to a focus outside the telescope tube.

Access to the Cassegrainian focus in order to make observations is easier than to other telescope focal systems, such as the Newtonian, which may be found on the same telescope. Moreover, instruments of considerable weight can be mounted at the focus. The tube length is much shorter than the focal length. Although the Cassegrainian telescope is subject to the optical aberration known as coma to the same degree as a Newtonian telescope of the same focal ratio, the spherical aberrations are partially canceled. These features make the Cassegrain one of the most popular astronomical telescope configurations.

The Cassegrainian telescope consists of a tube (1), a concave primary mirror (2), and a small convex secondary mirror (3). Incoming light rays (4) are directed by the primary mirror to the small mirror, which reflects the light back through a hole in the center of the primary mirror to a focus at the eyepiece (5).

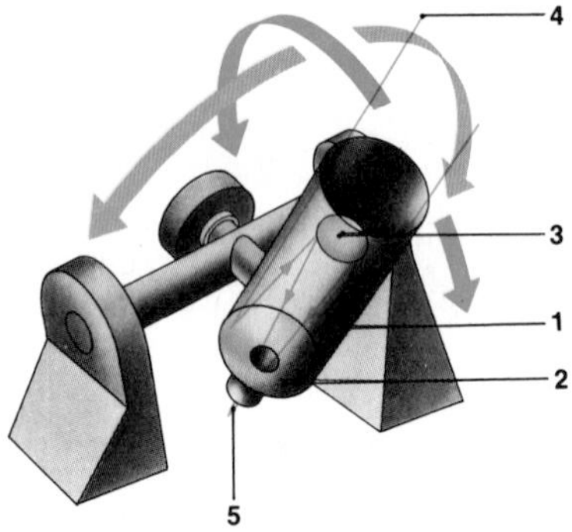

Cassian, Saint John [kash'-uhn] A Christian monk, John Cassian, *c.*360–435, is important for his writings on monasticism. He founded two monasteries in Marseilles and wrote *The Institutes* and *The Conferences*. The former deals with the structures of monasticism; the latter discusses the theory of monastic spirituality. The Eastern Church honors him as a saint. Feast day: Feb. 29.

Cassini, Oleg see FASHION DESIGN

Cassino Cassino (1981 pop., 31,139) is a town in Frosinone province in the Lazio region of central Italy. Originally a town of the ancient Volsci people, it was taken by the Romans in 312 BC and was largely razed by early medieval Germanic invasions. It was gradually rebuilt from the 9th century. In 1944, as a key German defense point blocking the route to Rome, it was leveled by the Allies. One of the first Benedictine monasteries was established in 529 at nearby MONTE CASSINO by Saint Benedict of Nursia, founder of the Benedictine order.

Cassiopeia (astronomy) [kas-ee-oh-pee'-uh] Cassiopeia is an autumn constellation of the Northern Hemisphere. It lies in the Milky Way on the opposite side of the north celestial pole from the Big Dipper. The constellation's five main stars form an M or W in the sky, depending on the time of observation. On its side, the constellation somewhat resembles a chair and is sometimes called Cassiopeia's Chair, after the mythological Queen Cassiopeia. Intense radio sources lie in the constellation, which also contains many star clusters.

Cassirer, Ernst [kahs-eer'-ur] Ernst Cassirer, b. July 28, 1874, d. Apr. 13, 1945, was a German philosopher. Cassirer's work deals mainly with how the object of human knowledge and belief comes to be known (transcendental problems) and with the theory of scientific knowledge. Influenced primarily by Kant and to a lesser extent by HEGEL and HUSSERL, Cassirer extended Kantian philosophy into new areas. He maintained in *The Philosophy of Symbolic Forms* (1923–29; Eng. trans., 1953–57) that there are concepts that determine the way humans experience the natural world for every manifestation of culture—forms of mythical, historical, and practical thought that can be discovered by examining the forms of language. Other works include *Essay on Man: Introduction to the Philosophy of Human Culture* (1944) and *Language and Myth* (1925; Eng. trans., 1946).

cassiterite see TIN

Cassius Longinus, Gaius [kas'-ee-uhs lawn-jy'-nuhs, gy'-uhs] Gaius Cassius Longinus, b. *c.*85 BC, an instigator of the assassination of Julius CAESAR, was a more ruthless and violent partisan than his associate Marcus Junius BRUTUS. A quaestor under Marcus Licinius CRASSUS during the invasion of Parthia (53 BC), he escaped after the Roman defeat at Carrhae and went to Syria. After quelling (52) an uprising in Judea, he repulsed (51) a Parthian invasion of Syria. As a tribune at Rome in 49 BC, he supported POMPEY THE GREAT and was the latter's naval commander off Sicily in the civil war with Caesar (48).

After Pompey's defeat at Pharsalus, Caesar pardoned Cassius, who became a legate in 47 and a praetor in 44 BC. After masterminding the assassination (March 44) of Caesar, Cassius, who feared for his safety, left Rome. He broke completely with Mark ANTONY and began recruiting troops in the east. In mid-October 42 BC, he and Brutus met the forces of Antony and Octavian (later Emperor AUGUSTUS) at Philippi. Antony captured Cassius's camp. Not realizing that Brutus had defeated Octavian's forces, Cassius committed suicide.

The large, flightless Australian cassowary weighs about 100 kg (220 lb) and stands more than 1.5 m (5 ft) tall. It can run through dense jungle at more than 48 km/h (30 mph), swim with astounding facility, and quickly disembowel a full-grown human with the 10-cm (4-in) claw of its innermost toe.

cassowary [kas'-oh-wair-ee] Cassowaries are any of three species (genus *Casuarius*) of large, flightless birds belonging to the family Casuariidae and the order Casuariiformes. They are found in dense forests of New Guinea and northern Australia. Females are larger than males and may attain a height of about 2 m (6 ft). The black plumage is coarse, and each feather is doubled. The naked neck and head are surmounted by a bony casque that deflects obstacles when the bird runs through the forest. The cassowary is monogamous; the male incubates the three to eight green eggs and cares for the striped young. Their main food is fallen fruit. Adults are armed with a long, sharp claw on the inner toe and are able to kill humans with their powerful kick.

cast-iron architecture Cast iron was introduced into building as a primary structural material in the late 18th century. Several textile mills with interior columns and floor beams of iron were built in England before 1800, and other kinds of buildings supported by iron frames appeared in London and Paris within the next decade. Because of the high cost of producing iron and the limited capacity of mills and foundries, ferrous metals were not used in building in the United States until the 1820s. Iron columns were used to support the balcony of a theater built in Philadelphia in 1822, but the first complete iron frame appeared in 1837, in the supporting structure of a large gas-storage tank erected in that city. During the following decade, however, construction with cast- and wrought-iron members progressed rapidly in England, France, and the United States.

The term *cast-iron architecture* was eventually applied to buildings in which one or more of the exterior walls and the interior frame were of cast iron. The American James Bogardus deserves chief credit for the invention of this form of construction. The first of his buildings with self-supporting street walls of cast-iron columns and panels was the Edward Laing Store in New York (1848; destroyed). Cast-iron architecture, or iron-front buildings, as

The Halle des Machines was designed by the engineer Victor Contamin and the architect C. L. F. Dutert for the Exposition Universelle of 1889, an exhibition in Paris devoted to advancements in science and industry. Constructed of braced steel arches and covered with glass, the hall was filled with machinery in operation.

they were sometimes called, quickly became popular because of their low cost, their fire-resistant character, and the ease with which any style of ornament could be reproduced in metal. Construction of iron buildings spread rapidly in the major U.S. and British cities after the middle of the 19th century; much of the impetus was caused by Sir Joseph PAXTON's spectacular CRYSTAL PALACE for the London Exhibition in 1851. Daniel Badger, Bogardus's chief competitor, erected structures throughout the eastern and middle western United States and had one building put up in Havana, Cuba.

Architects in New York expertly adapted Renaissance architectural styles to the new iron-and-glass construction to produce a number of remarkably open, clearly articulated, and elegantly proportioned buildings that are now regarded as masterpieces of the technique. The best of these were the Haughwout building (1857) by John P. Gaynor, A. T. Stewart's department store (1859–68; destroyed 1956), designed by John Kellum, and the Lord and Taylor Dry Goods Store (1869–70) by James H. Giles, all in New York. After 1880 the popularity of cast iron declined before newer techniques and fashions, but cast-iron architecture represented an important step toward the steel-framed, curtain-walled SKYSCRAPER.

Castaneda, Carlos [kas-tuh-nay'-da] Carlos Castaneda, b. Cajamarca, Peru, Dec. 25, 1925, an American anthropologist, is noted for a series of best-selling books that report the nonrational wisdom of a Mexican *brujo* called Don Juan, under whom Castaneda claims to have studied. The accuracy of his works has been questioned, but his skill in presenting what novelist Joyce Carol Oates calls "another way of reality" has not.

Castaneda's first book, *The Teachings of Don Juan: A Yaqui Way of Knowledge* (1968), was a master's thesis at UCLA. It relates his introduction to the visionary reality of Don Juan by means of hallucinogens. In his later works—*A Separate Reality* (1971), *Journey to Ixtlan* (1972), *Tales of Power* (1974), *The Second Ring of Power* (1978), *The Eagle's Gift* (1982), *The Fire from Within* (1984), and *The Power of Silence* (1987)—Castaneda has continued to develop his mystical themes.

castanets [kas-tuh-nets'] Castanets are percussion instruments consisting of two shallow, cup-shaped clappers that accompany dancing or give a Spanish color to music. The clappers are traditionally made of chestnut wood (castaña). They are held together by a cord and are shaken or rhythmically clicked together by the fingers. Orchestral castanets are fastened to a small stick, which is shaken. Spanish manuscripts of the 13th century show instruments of this type.

caste [kast] The term *caste* refers to an extreme form of social differentiation in which the groups that constitute society are ranked in a rigid hierarchical scale. In all true caste systems, society as a whole is divided into a series of groups determined by birth. Marriage is generally restricted to members of the same caste, castes are as-

Laborers are traditionally numbered among the lower castes of Indian society. Although Indian law prohibits caste restrictions, taboos intended to maintain purity are still widely observed.

sociated with occupational specializations, and the order of castes is linked to a moral order that dictates codes of appropriate behavior for each caste. The most elaborate form of caste is found in Hindu India; simpler systems exist in other parts of South Asia, including Sri Lanka, Pakistan, Bangladesh, and Nepal.

Castes in India

The Indian caste system appears to have evolved out of the *varna* system, which developed about 1000–800 BC. Four *varnas*—Brahmin, Kshatriya, Vaishya, and Shudra—are recognized, each associated with specific societal functions: the Brahmins served as priests, the Kshatriya were warriors or political rulers, the Vaishya were traders and cultivators, and the Shudra were artisans. About 2,000 years ago the four *varnas* became elaborated into numerous *jati*, which more or less became the castes known today. Further elaborations gave rise to the additional category of UNTOUCHABLE castes.

The structure of the Indian caste system closely reflects the central preoccupations of HINDUISM with problems of purity and pollution. Higher castes depend on the lower castes to remove their impurities, and lower castes depend upon their superiors to transmit purity down the hierarchy to them.

The caste system is also a social division of labor. For example, since gold is ranked as more pure than wood, goldsmiths as a caste rank above carpenters. The extent to which castes still perform their traditional roles varies greatly. The changing circumstances of modern times have made the traditional callings of some castes obsolete or impracticable. Thus, few if any Jats today are soldiers. The actual occupations of other castes today resemble traditional roles more closely, however, particularly those castes directly involved in the manipulation of purity and pollution.

Castes vary greatly in size. Some, such as the Maratha and the Jats, number many millions of people and are found over large areas of India. Others are small, numbering only a few thousand members. In recent years, economic and political forces and events have affected but not destroyed the Indian caste system. Most marriages are still made within castes, and castes are still ranked in terms of purity and pollution. But caste is no longer part of the legal order of Indian society and is not a legal barrier to education or occupation. After India won its independence in 1947, legislation was passed abolishing untouchability and giving the lowest castes certain political and educational advantages. But caste remains an important factor in Indian politics.

Politicians rely on the "caste vote," and castes still frequently act as economic and political pressure groups. Intercaste violence has also continued in recent years, and the superior (and richer) castes frequently use physical force to maintain their privileges.

Castes Elsewhere

Systems of social differentiation similar to those of Hindu India are found in several countries adjacent to it. In Buddhist Sri Lanka, the SINHALESE are organized in terms of castes that are related to one another partly in terms of purity and pollution. Marriages generally take place within the caste, and castes are related to traditional occupational specializations. In Sri Lanka, however, as well as in Pakistan and Bangladesh, caste is not as rigid as it is in India.

Emigrants from India to other countries have taken a form of caste with them. A highly simplified form of caste still exists in Bali, the last of the Hindu areas of Southeast Asia. More recent emigrants to East Africa, the West Indies, Mauritius, Fiji, and Britain have also retained some forms of caste, but without the elaborate social differentiation found in India.

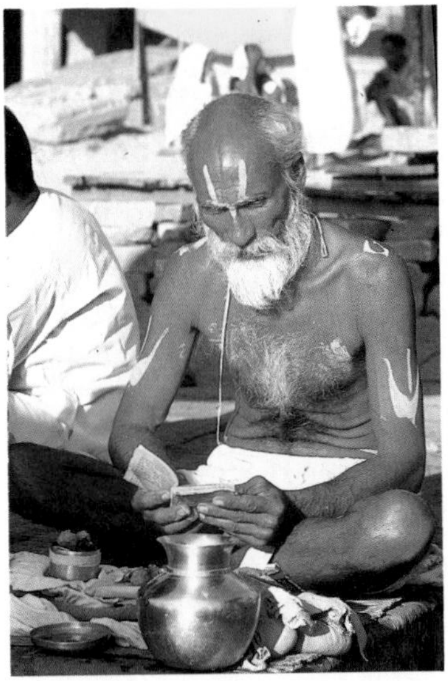

This Hindu holy man belongs to the Brahmin caste, which traditionally includes priests, scholars, and other high-ranking members of society. Brahmins still enjoy great occupational freedom and social prestige.

Castiglione, Baldassare, Conte [kahs-teel-yoh'-nay, bahl-dahs-sah'-ray] Baldassare Castiglione, b. Dec. 6, 1478, d. Feb. 2, 1529, was an Italian writer and courtier. In the service and at the court of the dukes of Urbino, he came in contact with many famous men of letters of Renaissance Italy. He carried out official missions to Henry VII of England and to Louis XII of France, and was sent (1525) by Pope Clement VII as apostolic nuncio to the court of Charles V in Spain, where he died.

His main work (*The Book of the Courtier*; Eng. trans., 1976) is an ideal picture of Renaissance court society, in which famous contemporaries such as Pietro Bembo, Bernardo Bibiena, and Giuliano de'Medici discuss the manners and virtues of the perfect courtier.

Castile Castile is a historic region of Spain, deriving from the medieval kingdom of Castile. The region occupies much of the interior of Spain and covers about 138,500 km^2 (53,500 mi^2). It extends from the Pyrenees in the north to the Sierra Morena in the south. Most of it is an undulating plateau, lying 455–1,065 m (1,500–3,500 ft) above sea level. It is, however, crossed from east to west by chains of mountains that include the Sierra de Guadarrama and Montes de Toledo.

Drainage is entirely westward to the Atlantic Ocean, by the Douro in the north and the Tagus and Guadiana in the south. The climate is marked by hot, dry, dusty summers and cool, sometimes cold, winters. Rainfall is low, except in the mountains. Much of Castile is thinly populated. The major cities are Madrid, Cuenca, Guadalajara, Ciudad Real, and Toledo. Agriculture remains the chief occupation, and irrigation is much used. Castile was once famous for its wool. Light industries are increasingly expanding in the towns.

Castile developed as a Christian state fighting to resist conquest by the Moors. Its nucleus was Old Castile, lying north of the Guadarrama Mountains, with its capital at Burgos. In the 11th century the Castilians pushed across the Sierra de Guadarrama and occupied New Castile. In 1479, Queen Isabella I of Castile married King Ferdinand II of Aragon, and the two provinces were soon merged to create the kingdom of Spain.

See also: Spain, history of.

Castilla, Ramón [kahs-tee'-yah] Ramón Castilla, b. Aug. 27, 1797, in Tarapcá, Chile, d. May 25, 1867, was twice president (1845–51, 1855–62) of Peru. He fought under Antonio José de Sucre in the war of independence and won power as a result of the civil war of 1842–45. During his first administration Castilla improved the economy by stimulating the export of guano and nitrate and by building a railroad from Lima to Callao. Seizing power again in 1855, he abolished black slavery and the traditional Indian head tax and enacted other reforms. The liberal constitution that he promulgated in 1860 became the foundation stone of subsequent Peruvian governments.

casting Casting is a process for producing a shaped object by pouring a fluid substance into a mold and allowing the substance to solidify. Although most materials that have a fluid state can be cast, and such substances as glass, clay, and metal have been cast since ancient times, modern industrial casting processes involve primarily metals and plastics.

The mold is a matrix made from an impressionable material such as sand. A pattern of the object to be molded is pressed into the sand, and the impression left is filled by the casting material, which hardens into the shape of the pattern. Of the many types of molds employed in casting, most use sand as the mold material. Other types can be made using metal, cement, or ceramic.

Sand Casting. The most common molding material used in sand casting is green sand, which is a mixture of sand—usually ordinary silica sand—clay, water, and oth-

In sand casting, a wood pattern (1) *made according to a design* (A), *wood runners* (2, 3), *and a riser* (4) *are packed with moist sand in clamped steel boxes* (B, C) *to form a cavity mold. A sand core for forming the internal casting cavities is made in a separate mold* (D) *and positioned in the cavity mold after the pattern, runners, and riser* (E) *are removed. The mold is assembled, and molten metal is poured in* (F). *The cooled castings is removed* (G); *then the runner, riser, and sand core are cut out* (H), *leaving the finished casting* (1).

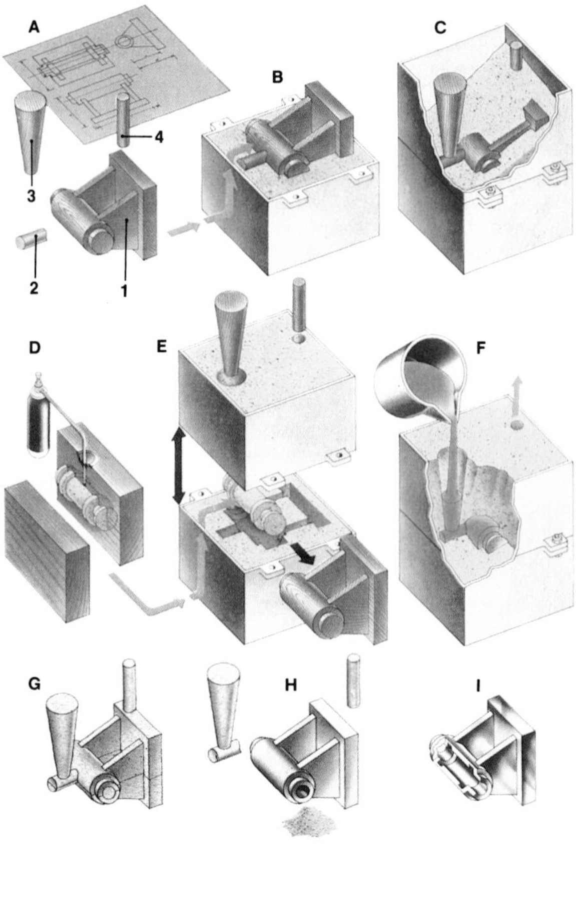

er binding materials. The molding sand is placed in a two-part form and is packed around the pattern. When the sand is compacted sufficiently, the two parts are separated and the pattern is removed.

Openings in the mold, called gates and risers, are added to allow for the escape of air and gases as the metal is poured into the mold. Large castings may be made with a central core of sand that forms an internal cavity in the finished casting. For metal alloys that react negatively with moisture, dry sand molds are used.

Investment Casting. Investment casting is an adaptation of the *cire perdue*, or LOST-WAX PROCESS. It is used industrially to produce highly detailed precision parts. The pattern is melted out by heating the mold or vaporizes as the molten metal is poured in. The pattern may be made of wax coated with fine silica, or of foamed plastic.

Shell Molding. In this casting process, the pattern is made of metal heated to a high temperature (177°–371° C/350°–700° F). The molding material is a mixture of sand and heat-setting resin. When packed around the heated pattern, the resin sets, binding the sand into a thin shell that reproduces the pattern exactly.

Centrifugal Casting. By spinning the mold while pouring the molten metal, cylindrical castings with hollow cores can be produced.

See also: METALLURGY; POWDER METALLURGY; TOOL AND DIE MAKING.

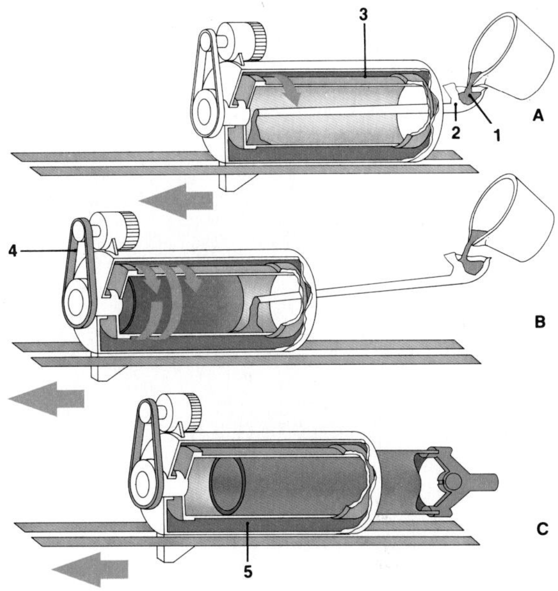

The cutaway diagrams show stages in the process by which large-diameter iron pipe is cast. (A) *Molten iron* (1) *is poured into a trough* (2) *leading into a mold* (3), *which is mounted inside the centrifugal caster.* (B) *A motor-driven belt* (4) *causes the entire assembly to revolve. The centrifugal force thus generated forces the molten iron to conform to the mold. To ensure that the iron flows along the entire length of the mold, the casting assembly is moved away from the trough.* (C) *The molten metal is quickly cooled by a water-filled jacket* (5) *surrounding the mold.*

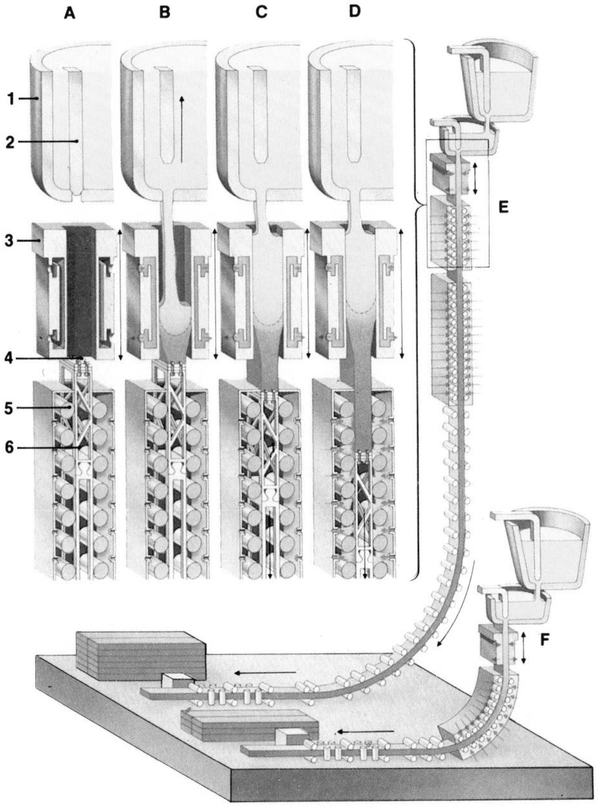

Equipment for continuous casting of steel bars (A) *consists of a reservoir for molten steel* (1), *a stopper* (2), *a reciprocating water-cooled copper mold* (3), *a movable plug* (4), *cooling water sprays* (5), *and metal rollers* (6). *After filling the mold with molten steel by opening the stoppered hold* (B), *the plug is withdrawn, causing the steel to be drawn into a bar between the rollers* (C, D). *An old machine's long, straight cooling section* (E) *is compared with a new machine's short, curved cooling section* (F), *showing the space saved.*

castle

castle Although the term *castle* is often restricted in meaning to the fortified residences of the European Middle Ages, structures with the same dual function were also built in the ancient world and form a major part of the architectural heritage of Japan's Momoyama Period.

The early royal palaces of Egypt were fortified, as was the palace of the Assyrian king Sargon II of KHORSABAD, among many ancient examples. In general, however, the practice in the ancient Near East and Egypt and in the classical world was to fortify entire cities (see FORTIFICATION). In the chaotic conditions accompanying and following the collapse of the Roman Empire in the West this pattern changed. The Germanic and other peoples who overran the empire had no urban traditions and settled across the countryside, where the more powerful individuals constructed fortified dwellings.

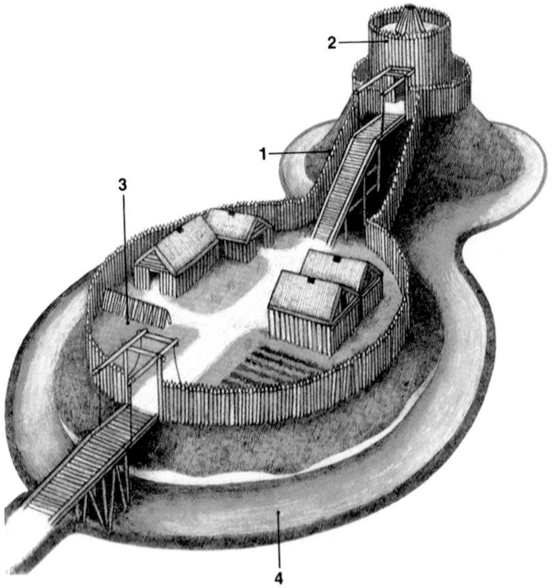

(Left) *Motte-and-bailey fortifications, forerunners of the stone castles of the Middle Ages, were built in western Europe from the 10th to the 12th century. The dominant feature of these earthworks was the motte* (1), *a mount on which a wooden citadel* (2) *was erected. During times of war, noncombatants from the surrounding area were sheltered in a lower enclosure, or bailey* (3). *The entire compound was surrounded by a moat* (4), *and a narrow gate provided the only entrance to the fortifications.*

The motte and bailey castle, dating from about the 9th century, was the earliest European castle form. Built on a natural or artificial mound (motte) and protected by one or more circular walls and often by a moat, the castle consisted of the keep, a wood or stone tower, and what ever accessory buildings were necessary for the housing of the castle retainers. These were situated in the bailey, the open area within the castle walls. In later castles the walls were topped by a parapet that could be manned during an attack. The Tower of London (*c.*1074–97) is an extant example of the motte and bailey castle. Its White Tower is the original Norman keep.

From the 12th century, castle design was influenced by the Crusaders, who introduced improvements copied from Byzantine fortifications. European castles became larger, and their fortified areas increasingly complex. A

(Below) *The inner ward of Dover Castle is shown as it might have appeared when constructed by King Henry II late in the 12th century. One of the most notable medieval fortifications still in existence, the castle stands on the cliffs of Dover overlooking the English Channel. The inner ward, or bailey* (1), *was protected by a surrounding wall and a series of mural towers* (2) *linked by a continuous walkway* (3). *The fortifications could be entered at two points, the King's Gate* (4) *and the Palace Gate* (5). *The walls of the central citadel, or keep* (6), *were reinforced with pilasters* (7) *and were guarded by an outer structure, or forebuilding* (8). *The keep's basement* (9) *and main floors* (10) *were connected by a spiral staircase* (11). *The twin-ridged roof* (12) *of the keep was protected by high walls and a walkway* (13) *for defensive fire.*

fortified wall might have separated the keep from the bailey. The keep itself was often a rectangular rather than a circular tower, with buttressed, parapeted walls and its own system of defense. Such large castles were often built on a height or into the side of a mountain. The largest could support town-sized populations and, with an assured water supply and adequate provisions, were virtually impregnable.

With the invention of gunpowder the castle lost its impregnability. Attacking artillery, out of range of the archers on the castle walls, could pour cannon shot into the heart of the castle and take it without even breaching the walls. Thus, by the 16th century, the medieval castle could no longer fulfill a defensive function, and fortified buildings were now erected only for military purposes. The architectural style of the castle, however, continued to be used for its imposing and often beautiful effects (see CHÂTEAU).

In Japan the great era of castle construction occurred in the late 1500s under the rule of the warlords Nobunaga and Hideyoshi (the Momoyama period, 1573–1615). Built primarily for defense during a period of feudal wars, and as a visual symbol of the great power of the builders, the Momoyama castles also stimulated a new era in JAPANESE ART AND ARCHITECTURE.

Castle, The *The Castle* (1926; Eng. trans., 1930; film, 1969), Franz KAFKA's longest and most complex novel, blending realistic narrative technique with surrealistic episodes, is an ambiguous parable of modern life. Kafka began and abandoned the work in 1922. The main character, a land surveyor known only as "K," is inexplicably summoned to and then desperately tries to enter a castle overlooking a seemingly normal mountain village. The novel concerns the difficulty of communication and the futility of aspiration.

Castle, Vernon and Irene Vernon and Irene Castle were exhibition ballroom dancers and teachers just before World War I. Their casual, graceful style transformed American interest in social dancing into a nationwide craze. Vernon Blythe, b. Norwich, England, May 2, 1887, d. Feb. 15, 1918, came to the United States in 1906 as an actor-dancer and married Irene Foote, b. New Rochelle, N.Y., Apr. 7, 1893, d. Jan. 25, 1969. A chance engagement at the Café de Paris led to fame. Between national tours in America, the Castles opened several dance schools and nightclubs. Their versions of the TANGO, WALTZ, and maxixe made old dances fresh and new ones respectable.

Castlereagh, Robert Stewart, Viscount [kas-ul-ray] Robert Stewart, Viscount Castlereagh, b. June 18, 1769, d. Aug. 12, 1822, was an influential British statesman, leader of the House of Commons, and foreign secretary (1812–22). As acting chief secretary in Ireland during the rebellion of 1798, he secured passage (1801)

The British statesman Lord Castlereagh is remembered primarily for his achievements as a formulator of Britain's foreign policy during the Napoleonic era.

of the Act of Union (unifying England and Ireland) as a defense measure. He then served (1805–06, 1807–09) as secretary of war and shared credit with George CANNING, a bitter personal rival, for sending British troops to the Iberian Peninsula in 1809. As foreign secretary, Castlereagh coordinated the final coalition (1814) against Napoleon and exerted major influence at the Congress of Vienna (1814–15; see VIENNA, CONGRESS OF), where he promoted establishment of the so-called *congress system* of periodic meetings of the great powers.

Castlereagh sought peace abroad and at home, where—in view of the postwar unrest—the line between repression and the maintenance of law and order was a fine one. He succeeded to the title marquis of Londonderry in 1821 but committed suicide the following year.

Castor and Pollux In Greek mythology, Castor and Pollux (or Polydeuces) were called the Dioscuri (Sons of Zeus) because Zeus, in the form of a swan, fathered them by LEDA. Identified with the city of Sparta, Castor was renowned as a horseman and Pollux as a boxer. They sailed with the Argonauts, participated in the Calydonian boar hunt, and later helped to rescue their sister HELEN OF TROY. Finally, in a fight over the intended brides of Idas and Lynceus, Pollux killed Lynceus, but Idas killed Castor. Pollux, being immortal, was allowed to share his immortality with Castor, thus permitting them to spend alternate days in heaven and in the underworld, Pollux as the Morning Star and Castor as the Evening Star. Another version held that Zeus put both in the heavens as the constellation Gemini.

castor oil Castor oil is pressed from the poisonous seeds of the castor-oil plant, *Ricinus communis*, family Euphorbiaceae. The poisonous alkaloid ricin is removed and used in insecticides. Besides its use as a laxative, the fatty oil is used in the production of synthetic resins, fibers, industrial lubricants, dyes, soaps, and cosmetics. Probably native to Africa, the herb now is cultivated not only throughout the tropics but also in temperate regions.

castration Castration is the surgical removal of one or both testicles of a male person or animal in order to suppress the development or function of the sexual glands. Male farm animals are castrated, or gelded, to improve the breed or to make the animals more docile; house pets may be castrated to keep them from wandering or from producing unwanted offspring. Castration of female animals by removal of the ovaries is called spaying.

In imperial China and other Oriental empires castrated men known as eunuchs occupied important court positions. In Europe in the 16th to the 18th century male singers were sometimes castrated before puberty so that they would retain a soprano or alto vocal range. Today the operation may be performed on men with cancer of the prostate or certain diseases of the testicles. If the operation is done after puberty, it produces sterility but has little or no effect on secondary sex characteristics.

castrato [kah-strah'-toh] A castrato was a male soprano or contralto singer whose unbroken voice had been preserved by castration performed before puberty so that the larynx would not develop. As a result his voice retained its high range, but because his lungs and chest matured he was able to produce sounds of great power. Castrati were in great demand as leading singers during the 17th and 18th centuries in opera houses throughout Europe. They were also employed in Italian church choirs, particularly in Rome. Some famous castrati were Francesco Bernardi (known as Senesino, 1680–1750), Carlo Broschi (known as FARINELLI, 1705–82), Gaetano Majorano (known as Caffarelli, 1710–83), and Giovanni Battista Velluti (1780–1861).

Castro, Cipriano Cipriano Castro, b. Oct. 14, 1858, d. Dec. 4, 1924, was president of Venezuela (1901–08) during one of the country's stormiest periods. An Andean countryman, Castro led a successful revolt against President Ignacio Andrade in 1899. He governed as supreme military leader for two years and then became president. Castro's administration, noted for its corruption, was plagued by revolts and foreign financial claims. In 1902 the country's debts became so large that European creditor nations blockaded Venezuela; the United States intervened to obtain arbitration of the dispute. Castro's departure for Europe in 1908 opened the way for his deputy, Juan Vicente Gómez, to seize power. Castro died in exile.

Castro, Fidel Fidel Castro Ruz, b. Aug. 13, 1926, is president of Cuba (since 1976; formerly prime minister), first secretary of the Cuban Communist party, and commander of the armed forces. As the country's enduring "maximum leader," he has held power since 1959.

Born on a farm in Mayarí municipality in the province of Oriente, Castro graduated from the University of Havana in 1950 with a law degree. He married Mirta Díaz-Balart in 1948, but they were divorced in 1954. Their son, Fidel Castro Díaz-Balart, born in 1949, has served as head of Cuba's atomic energy commission.

A member of the social-democratic Ortodoxo party in the late 1940s and early 1950s, Castro was an early and vocal opponent of the dictatorship of Fulgencio BATISTA. On July 26, 1953, Castro led an attack on the Moncada army barracks that failed but brought him national prominence. At the time, his political ideas were nationalist, antiimperialist, and reformist; he was not a member of the Communist party.

Following the attack on Moncada, Castro was tried and sentenced to 15 years in prison but was amnestied in 1955. He then went into exile in Mexico, where he founded the 26th of July Movement. In December 1956, he and 81 others, including Che GUEVARA, returned to Cuba and made their way to the Sierra Maestra mountains, from which they launched a successful guerrilla war. Castro proved himself a strong leader; he also demonstrated shrewd political skills, convinced that he had a historic duty to change the character of Cuban society. Seeing his army collapse, and unable to count on the support of the United States, Batista fled on Jan. 1, 1959, paving the way for Castro's rise to power.

In its early phase, Castro's revolutionary regime included moderate politicians and democrats; gradually, however, its policies became radical and confrontational. The masses—whose living conditions he improved—rallied behind him. Foreign-owned properties were confiscated, and opponents of the regime killed or driven into exile. Thousands of middle-class and professional Cubans left the island once it became clear that a Communist revolution was under way.

The U.S.-supported BAY OF PIGS INVASION failed (1961), and Castro was able to consolidate his power. In December 1961 he publicly declared that "I have been a Marxist-Leninist all along, and will remain one until I die." Cuba aligned itself with the Soviet Union, which granted Cuba massive economic, technical, and military assistance. In 1962 the CUBAN MISSILE CRISIS dramatized the Cuban-Soviet alliance. Castro believes that he has a revolutionary duty to fight imperialism in the developing world; he dispatched troops to assist Marxist regimes in Angola and Ethiopia. He remains a caustic critic of U.S. foreign policy.

Castro, who has no rivals for power, has been less than successful as an economic policymaker: Cuba remains a poor country in debt, whose livelihood depends on sugar production and Soviet aid, although the latter has diminished considerably as Soviet economic problems have mounted. He nonetheless holds the system in place. His greatest achievement is the consolidation of a Communist regime in the Caribbean, so close to Cuba's main antagonist.

Casuarina [kahs-wah-ree'-nuh] *Casuarina* is a genus of 30 to 45 species of deciduous tropical trees and shrubs belonging to the family Casuarinaceae. Commonly called Australian pines, beefwood, or she-oaks, these plants are native to Australia, the islands of the South Pacific, and Southeast Asia. They have been planted extensively along streets in Florida and California. Casuarinas have slender, often drooping branches that are covered with small, scalelike leaves. Male flowers blossom at the branches' tip, and female flowers at the base. Seeds are borne in cones. Several species of Australia are valued for their hard wood.

cat All cats, from large jungle cats to small house cats, belong to the CAT FAMILY, Felidae, order Carnivora. This article discusses the domestic cat, *Felis catus catus*, a species indigenous to the Old World that includes such related forms as the European wildcat, *F. catus sylvestris*, the African wildcat, *F. catus lybica*, and perhaps some other distinct groups. The domestic cat is apparently not a separate species: there is evidence of hybridization and interfertility between it and the wild races.

Ancient Egyptians prized cats highly, as evidenced by this statue (c.600 BC) of a cat as well as by many other carvings and wall paintings. Cats were considered sacred and often were mummified after they died.

Cats in History

The domestic cat has evolved as an urban scavenger and may have originated about 8000 BC, when nomadic humans settled into village life. From archaeological and anatomical evidence, however, it is impossible to distinguish wild from domestic types until New Kingdom times (1570–1085 BC) in Egypt. The cat was then bred by a religious cult and worshiped as a sacred animal, but this episode of cultism has perhaps been exaggerated; it was not critical in bringing about the domestication of the species. The Egyptians domesticated many species, and the cat may simply have been bred to protect granaries from rodents. Because cat mummies are so numerous, in fact, it has been suggested that the animals may sometimes have been killed for votive offerings.

The spread of domestic cats appears to have followed the pattern of progressive urbanization. Domestic cats now inhabit every continent except Antarctica and most of the world's oceanic islands. Cats have reverted to a wild state in many habitats where they were not originally found.

Distribution of Cats

Cat populations range from sparse to more than 775 per km^2 (2,000 per mi^2), depending on several factors. The largest populations exist in urban areas, especially in so-called Mediterranean climates, where opportunities abound for year-round food and shelter. Only in certain regions such as Western Europe and North America are cats kept as pets in numbers sufficient to support such large, subsidiary industries as veterinary services, pet foods, welfare societies, and publications. Elsewhere, cats are tolerated but not regarded as pets.

The Cat as Scavenger

Apart from a decrease in body size, the most notable anatomical contrast between domesticated and wild cats is the increased intestinal length in the former. This may correlate with the domesticated cat's turning from chiefly predatory to chiefly scavenging habits, and the resulting reliance on a low-protein diet; theoretically, increased small-intestinal length would maximize absorption of amino acids. One study of the stomach contents of stray city cats revealed that only 3 percent of their diet comprised rodents; the balance was garbage. Many studies have been devoted to the question of the depredations of cats on birds. Cats would seem to have only a modest effect, and generalizations are risky.

Breeding Habits

The breeding cycle is controlled by sensitivity to light. At equatorial latitudes, cats may breed throughout the year and have three or four litters. In temperate latitudes, they normally have one litter in the early spring and another in late summer. Domestic cats living under artificial light may breed at any time. Reproductive life begins at 7½ months and continues until an advanced age—15 years or more. The gestation period is usually 63 days, and the average litter is four kittens.

Health

A cat's normal temperature is about 38.6° C (101.5° F). The critical environmental temperature is about 36° C (97° F), at which point a cat begins to pant to cool itself. Sweat glands exist in the pads of the feet and scattered over the body, but sweating is not a temperature-regulating mechanism in cats.

One leading cause of death in domestic cats is feline leukemia, a cat-specific viral disease. The virus can cause fatal tumors in almost all tissues and organs of the body. It also impairs the animal's immune system, leaving it prone to other serious infections and conditions. The virus (FeLV), a RETROVIRUS, is transmitted by contact with infected cats and excrement. A vaccine against feline leukemia is available.

Another retrovirus that causes disease in cats is feline T-lymphotropic lentivirus (FTLV). Identified in 1987, the disease also attacks the immune system; infected cats exhibit numerous infections, lose weight, and waste away.

Feline distemper is a highly contagious viral disease, also transmitted by raccoons and weasels. The virus, a PARVOVIRUS, is transmitted by even brief contact with con-

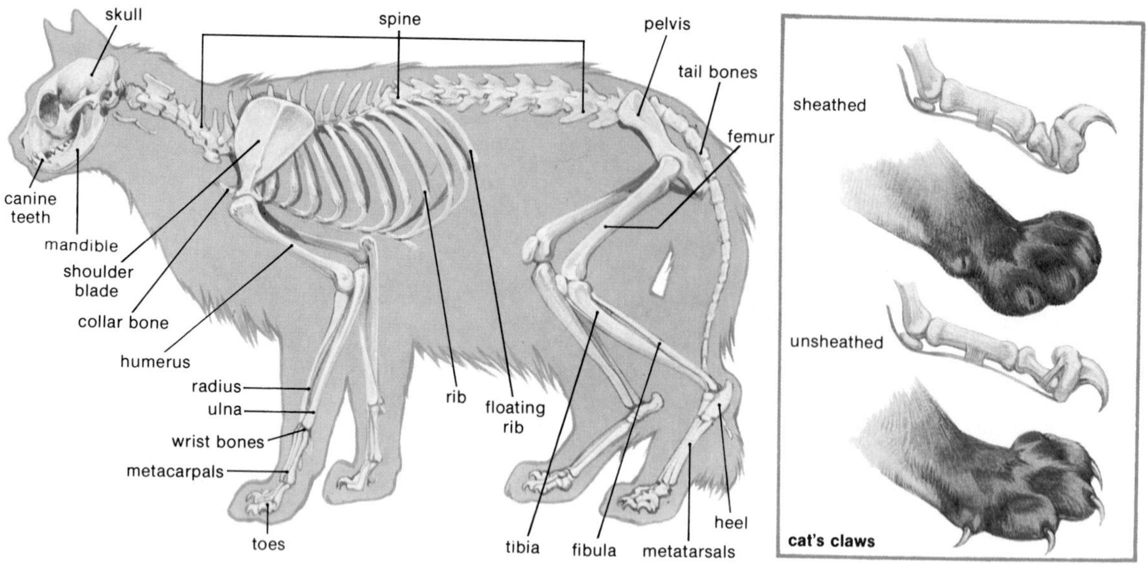

Three distinctive physical characteristics of a cat are its teeth, spine, and legs. A cat has specialized teeth for stabbing prey and cutting food. The vertebrae of the cat's spine, from the neck to the tail's tip, are connected by muscles that allow the cat to arch its back, twitch its tail, crouch, and make other movements that readily communicate its state of mind to an observer. When hurrying, a cat may pace, simultaneously moving the front and hind legs of one side and then the legs of the other side. A cat's paws are sheathed when the muscle is relaxed; when the muscle contracts, the end toe bone is pulled forward, unsheathing the claw. Most wild cats are crepuscular (twilight-active) or nocturnal, with highly sensitive eyes. The pupil's ability to contract to a vertical slit is believed to be an adaptation for shielding the eyes from intense light.

taminated material, and death may occur as soon as eight hours after the first signs of illness appear. A vaccine is available.

Feline viral rhinotracheitis, or cat flu, is not contagious to humans or other animals. An infected cat develops a fever, begins sneezing and drooling, and becomes lethargic. This is followed by a heavy discharge from the eyes and nose. Treatment consists of antibiotics, cleansing the eyes and nose, and administering fluids.

Cats are also susceptible to flea and roundworm infestations. Treatments exist for both problems.

Cats that roam outside the house can bring in parasites and transfer them and the diseases they may carry to humans. A few appear serious; cases of BRUCELLOSIS and, extremely rarely, of plague have been reported. Pregnant women are cautioned about handling cats and their litter boxes because of the possibility of transmitting TOXOPLASMOSIS to their fetuses. Some people exhibit a severe allergic reaction to cats—most likely, it has been suggested, to dried spittle on their fur.

Senses and Intelligence

Like all felids, domestic cats have senses evolved to facilitate twilight predation. Thus, they are especially well equipped to detect slight movements in semidarkness. The field of visual overlap approximates that found in primates and gives cats full depth perception. Cats are also extremely sensitive to sounds, including frequencies beyond the range of human hearing. Sense of smell is not greatly elaborated in felids.

Domestic cats may be more versatile than their wild relatives because of adaptations to urban life, but, originating from basically solitary ancestors, they are not as tractable or malleable as other domesticated species. Many of the apparent differences between cat and dog behavior, for example, stem from motivation rather than innate ability. Under controlled experiments, cats perform highly complex tasks.

Breeds of Cats

The cat differs strikingly from other domesticated animals in that it has not, until recently, been bred selectively. Hence, most of the observed genetic changes and variations in cats probably result from inherent adaptations to domesticity or to the perpetuation of novel anomalies. Most of the better-understood genetic variations in cats relate to differences in color, pattern, and texture of the coat, and to such minor skeletal peculiarities as taillessness or supernumerary digits.

The so-called breeds of cats are normal variants in free-ranging populations that do not transmit their traits as pure strains do. The Manx cat did indeed originate from the Isle of Man as the result of a local 17th-century mutation, but it does not breed true. There is no evidence that Abyssinian cats are of Ethiopian origin, and Persian cats are actually more common in the Soviet Union than in Iran. The origin of most of the older so-called breeds appears to be late 19th-century and early 20th-century England, despite the fanciful histories that are frequently proffered.

(Above) *From left to right, starting at the top, are some of the most popular breeds of cat in the United States: Maltese, Siamese, Maine coon cat, American shorthair, Japanese bobtail, Abyssinian, Angora, Russian blue, Burmese, Balinese, Havana brown, Manx, Himalayan, colorpoint shorthair, Persian, Korat, and exotic shorthair. Selective breeding techniques have resulted in the creation and perpetuation of a wide variety of domestic cat breeds. Professional breeders, known as cat fanciers, have organized into seven associations in the United States; these associations regulate the purity and quality of the breeds by requiring certain physical standards for each.*

cat family The cat family, Felidae, order Carnivora, contains about 36 species that are usually grouped into two to four genera, depending on the classification system used. According to one common system, four genera exist: *Panthera* (JAGUAR, LEOPARD, LION, TIGER), *Neofelis* (clouded leopard), *Acinomyx* (CHEETAH), and *Felis* (LYNX, PUMA, and smaller cats such as the domestic CAT, PALLAS'S CAT, and the WILDCAT). Cats are native to all continents except Australia and Antarctica.

Cats have short, rounded heads, erect ears, and large eyes with vertical-slit pupils. There are 28 to 30 teeth, depending on the species. The canines, or fangs, are large and strong and used for stabbing prey. The carnassials, a pair of teeth on each side of the jaw—the last upper premolar and the first lower molar—are formed into large, cross-shearing blades for cutting meat. The tongue is covered with sharp, curved projections (papillae) used for rasping meat off bones, cleaning the fur, and drinking. The neck is thick and heavy to withstand the shocks of the violent actions of the head and teeth.

Cats have five toes on each front foot and four toes on each hind foot and are known as digitigrade, that is, they walk on the anatomical equivalent of human fingertips and toetips; the fifth digit, or thumb (dewclaw), is carried high on the leg. All cats except the cheetah have large, curved, sharp claws that can be retracted into sheaths on the toes to prevent them from becoming blunted. The cheetah has less-developed, only partially retractile claws. Many cats walk by placing the hind feet in the tracks of the forefeet.

Most cats are crepuscular (active at twilight) or nocturnal and hunt by stealth, either lying in wait or silently stalking the prey until close enough to catch it with a short burst of great speed. The cheetah, the fastest four-legged animal in short spurts, runs down its prey in an overland chase.

Cats range from 50 cm to 3.75 m (20 in to 12.3 ft) in combined head and body length, excluding the tail, and from 2.5 to 275 kg (5.5 to about 600 lb) in weight. Most cats have one or two litters a year, but some of the larger cats may breed only once in 2 or 3 years. Litters average one to six young, which are usually born blind but covered with hair. Cats may be solitary, live in pairs, or associate in family groups.

Cat on a Hot Tin Roof *Cat on a Hot Tin Roof* (1955; Pulitzer Prize for drama; film, 1958) is typical of the work of Tennessee WILLIAMS in its Southern setting, emphasis on sex and violence, and concern with illusions. The play's heroine, the "cat," is the high-strung Maggie, frustrated by her husband, Brick, who drinks to drown feelings of guilt induced by his best friend's death and his own potential homosexuality. Maggie defeats her in-laws' attempts to wrest the inheritance of the plantation from her by announcing to Brick's wealthy father, the Rabelaisian Big Daddy dying of cancer, that she is pregnant—counting on Brick to make her announcement come true.

CAT scan see RADIOLOGY

catacombs Catacomb (from the Greek *kata kumbas*, meaning "near the low place or ravine"), originally the name of a particular district in Rome, later referred to the subterranean BURIAL places for Christians in the Roman Empire. Catacombs have been found in Anatolia, Malta, and North Africa, and in the cities of Naples, Paris, Syracuse, and Trier, Germany. However, the principal catacombs, about 40 in number, are in Rome. Found mainly along the Via Appia, the Via Ostiensis, the Via Labicana, the Via Tiburtina, and the Via Nomentana, they bear 4th-century names that identify the martyrs believed to have been buried in them.

Unlike the Romans, the Christians did not practice CREMATION because of their belief in the resurrection of the dead. In keeping with the Roman proscription against burial within the city limits, the early Christians in Rome used pagan burial places outside the city walls as cemeteries (from a Greek word meaning "place of rest"). Early burial was either in simple graves marked to preserve the memory of Christian martyrs or in the vaults of noble families sympathetic to the Christians. The construction of catacombs began in the 2d century; they were initially used both for interment of the dead and for memorial services. By the 5th century, they were used exclusively for religious services commemorating the death of a martyr. Catacombs subsequently fell into disuse.

No evidence exists that the practice of underground burial was an invention of the Christians, nor that the catacombs were used primarily as places of refuge. The orderly, reverential manner of Christian interment in catacombs is reminiscent of the earlier ETRUSCAN practice of burial in underground tomb chambers, and the celebration of memorial services was in keeping with the customs of Roman society. The move from ground-level burial sites to subterranean burial places was caused by the need for more space. The Christians excavated a vast system of galleries and linking passages, one beneath the other, joined by narrow, steep steps frequently descending as many as four stories. These passages measured about 2.5 m (8 ft) high and less than 1 m (3 ft) wide. Niches 40 to 60 cm (16 to 24 in) high and 120 to 150 cm (47 to 59 in) long were cut in the walls of soft tufa rock. The bodies were placed in these niches or in stone SARCOPHAGI, fully clothed and bound in fine linen. Lime or spiced ointments were used to offset putrefaction. Individual graves were sealed with a slab bearing the name and age of the deceased, the date of death, and a religious inscription or symbol.

These inscriptions and symbols, along with decorations on walls, arches, and sarcophagi in the catacombs, provide a rich source of information about Early Christian art and prayer. The decorative motifs were frequently adopted from Roman art. Subjects for Christian paintings were usually taken from the Bible, though occasionally they came from secular sources. Christ is generally depicted either as the Good Shepherd or as the Greek myth-

The cubiculum, or sepulchral chamber of saints Felix and Adauctus in the Catacomb of Commodilla, Rome, dates from the mid-4th century. It commemorates two Christians martyred under Diocletian.

ological character ORPHEUS. New Testament miracles are also portrayed, but not the Crucifixion or the Resurrection.

After AD 313, when Christianity was established as an official religion, the practice of subterranean burial declined. The catacombs seem to have been completely abandoned by the 9th century. Many of the relics of martyrs were transferred to churches and basilicas. The existence of the catacombs remained unknown throughout the Middle Ages; they were not rediscovered until 1578.

See also: EARLY CHRISTIAN ART AND ARCHITECTURE.

Çatal Hüyük [chah-tahl' hue-yuek'] Çatal Hüyük, a major site in south central Turkey, about 50 km (31 mi) southeast of Konya, is one of the earliest NEOLITHIC settlements. The site is a double mound of which only the eastern component has been extensively excavated (1961–63), by the British archaeologist James Mellaart. Çatal East dates from the second half of the 7th millennium to the first half of the 6th millennium BC. It is the largest Neolithic mound in southwest Asia.

Mud-brick structures feature wall paintings and reliefs of geometric elements, humans, and animals; many demonstrate an apparently cultic preoccupation with hunting and fertility.

Catalan art see SPANISH ART AND ARCHITECTURE

Catalan language see ROMANCE LANGUAGES

Catalan literature [kat'-uh-lan] Catalan literature is the body of work in the language that evolved in and around Catalonia, in Spain, during the 12th century. Its classical period was the 13th to 15th centuries, when Catalan was the language of the kingdom of Aragon. After Aragon was united with Castile in 1479, Catalan declined and was broken into local dialects, and its literature died. It was revived in the mid-19th century as part of the regional cultural revival (*Renaixença*) centering on Barcelona.

The major figures of early Catalan literature were the Christian philosopher Raymond LULL, from Majorca, and the chroniclers Bernat Desclot and Ramón Muntaner. Italian Renaissance themes were introduced after 1400 in the prose of Bernat Metge and the verse of Auziàs March. A significant mid-15th-century work was Johanot Martorell's *Tirant lo Blanch* (Eng. trans., 1984), which foreshadowed *Don Quixote*.

Catalonia [kat-uh-lohn'-yuh] Catalonia (Spanish: Cataluña) is a historic region in the northeastern corner of Spain, bounded by France on the north and the Mediterranean Sea on the east. The port city of BARCELONA is the traditional capital. The regional language, Catalan, is more closely related to Provençal than Castilian Spanish.

Most of Catalonia is covered with forested hills. On the fertile coastal plains, grains, olives, and grapes are grown. Tourism is important along the Costa Brava, and it is Spain's most industrialized region.

Beginning in the 9th century, Catalonia was ruled by the counts of Barcelona. In 1137, Catalonia was united with the kingdom of ARAGON, but it preserved considerable autonomy. During the 13th and 14th centuries, Catalonia dominated Mediterranean trade and Catalan art and literature flourished. Prosperity declined under Castilian domination in the 16th and 17th centuries. From 1640 to 1659, Catalonia allied itself with France against Philip IV of Spain, and in 1714 its autonomy was abolished. A Catalan Republic was recognized in 1932, but an attempt to secure total independence was suppressed in 1934. Catalonia was heavily Loyalist during the SPANISH CIVIL WAR. After the Nationalist victory (1939), it again lost its autonomy, which was regained in Spain's 1978 Constitution. In 1980 Catalonia's voters elected their first legislative assembly.

catalpa [kuh-tal'-puh] Trees of the genus *Catalpa* grow in North America, the West Indies, and eastern Asia.

The western catalpa, an ornamental tree of the United States, has clusters of showy, frilled flowers.

Catalpas have large, often heart-shaped leaves; showy clusters of bell-shaped white or yellow flowers; and long, narrow pods bearing seeds with tufts of white hair. The common catalpa, or Indian bean, *C. bignonioides*, is native to the southeastern United States; the western, or northern, catalpa, *C. speciosa*, native to the Mississippi Valley, has durable wood that is used for fence posts.

catalyst A catalyst is a substance that changes the velocity of a chemical reaction while not being changed itself. The change is usually positive, increasing the reaction rate. Negative catalysts are called inhibitors.

It should be emphasized that a catalyst only speeds up the rate of a reaction that is allowed thermodynamically. No catalyst will facilitate a reaction that is not so allowed.

Homogeneous catalysts are compounds that are soluble in the liquid medium in which the reaction takes place. They are often coordination compounds of transition metals. An example is the Wilkinson catalyst, tris (triphenylphosphine) rhodium chloride, which catalyzes the addition of hydrogen to ethylene in the formation of ethane.

Biological ENZYMES are nature's most active catalysts. Enzymes are complex organic compounds that contain a protein entity. They catalyze many intricate chemical reactions that, taken as a whole, represent the living process. Through GENETIC ENGINEERING, some enzymes are now being produced for industrial and medical purposes.

Heterogeneous catalysts are finely divided solids that catalyze reactions in gas and liquid media. Most industrial chemical processes take advantage of catalysts to make them cost-effective. Heterogeneous catalysts can be subdivided into the following classes: metals, metal oxides and sulfides, and acidic oxides. Metal catalysts are usually transition metals such as iron, which catalyzes the synthesis of ammonia; platinum, which catalyzes the oxidation of ammonia to nitric acid; and platinum on alumina, which catalyzes the reforming of petroleum to high-octane gasoline. Oxides and sulfides of transition metals are also used as catalysts in many industrial processes. Thus chromium oxide is used in the production of polythene, molybdenum oxide in the synthesis of acrylone, and molybdenum sulfide in the removal of sulfur from crude petroleum. A final group of catalysts is represented by the oxides of aluminum and silicon. A proper combination of these oxides gives their surface highly acidic properties that are useful in catalyzing the production of high-octane gasoline. All of the gasoline used in the United States is processed by a catalytic reaction carried out over an alumina silicate called zeolite.

catalytic converter A catalytic converter is a device in the EXHAUST SYSTEM of an automotive engine that converts environmentally harmful exhaust gases into harmless gases by promoting a chemical reaction between a catalyst and the pollutants. The catalytic converter decreases the emission of hydrocarbons, carbon monoxide, nitrogen oxide, or of all three.

In the most common type of catalytic converter, the exhaust gases are passed through a bed, or honeycomb, of small beads coated with the catalysts platinum and palladium. The catalyst in the nitrogen oxide converter splits the nitrogen from the oxygen so that nitrogen gas, carbon dioxide, and water are formed. In an automobile equipped with a catalytic converter, lead-free gasoline must be used in order to prevent coating the catalyst with lead.

One type of automobile catalytic converter consists of a porous, heat-resistant, inert material coated with a catalyst. It is supported by a wire screen and enclosed by a metal shell. The end cone of the device is connected to an engine's exhaust manifold, and the opposite end is sealed to the muffler. As hydrocarbons (HC), carbon monoxide (CO), and oxygen (O_2) in the exhaust gases pass through the system, they are converted into water (H_2O) and carbon dioxide (CO_2).

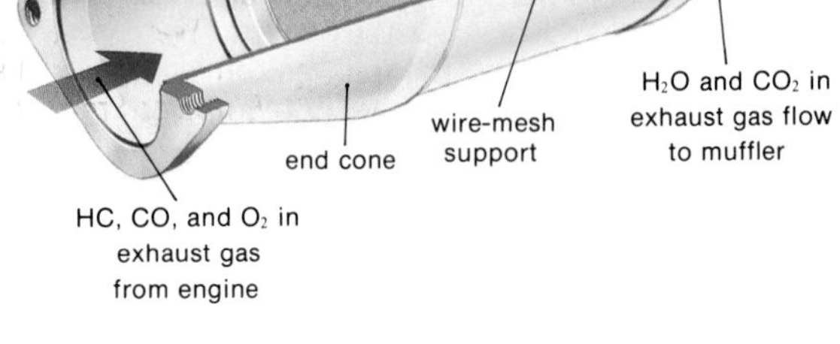

The catamaran, a twin-hulled sailboat, consists of a central cabin area resting on a pair of streamlined pontoons. These pleasure craft, among the fastest of sailing vessels, were developed from designs of dugout canoes used by peoples of the Pacific and Indian oceans.

catamaran [kat-uh-muh-ran'] *Catamaran* is a general term for various sailing rafts of Sri Lanka, India, and Polynesia; the term, however, also refers to a modern double-hulled boat used in Europe and the United States for sport sailing, which is adapted from these native rafts. A similar three-hulled craft is known as a trimaran. The native sailing rafts are made of bamboo, balsa, or mahogany logs lashed together and are used chiefly for fishing near the shore. During the 1950s in England, modern catamarans and trimarans, constructed of pontoons tied together with diagonal braces and beams, were developed for racing.

Catania [kah-tahn'-yuh] Catania is the second largest city of Sicily (1988 est. pop., 372,212) and an important commercial and fishing port located at the foot of Mount ETNA on the Gulf of Catania. It is also an important industrial center for the manufacture of chemicals and textiles. Catania was founded in the late 8th century BC by Greek colonists from Naxos and fell to Rome in 263 BC. At the crossroads of the Mediterranean, Catania was conquered successively by the Byzantines, Arabs, Normans, Germans, Aragonese, and Bourbons. In 1862, Giuseppe Garibaldi organized in Catania his unsuccessful expedition to capture Rome. The city is built on lava left by eruptions of Mount Etna and was rebuilt after the earthquakes of 1169 and 1693 and the heavy volcanic eruption of 1669. Seriously damaged in World War II, the old city still contains an 11th-century cathedral and the 13th-century Ursino Castle (built for Emperor Frederick II). Sicily's oldest university was founded there in 1434.

catapult Catapults were siege machines that could shoot arrows or hurl heavy rocks with great force and for considerable distances. Used by the ancient Greeks, catapults changed little in basic principle or design through the conquests of the Roman Empire and the battles of medieval Europe. Two major types of catapults were built: a double-armed machine (for example, the Roman ballista) that was essentially a large, mounted crossbow whose cord of twisted sinew or hair was pulled back by a winch; and a single-armed hurling lever, often with a sling attached to its end, that was cocked by a heavy, winch-pulled cord. The Roman onager, mounted on a massive, wheeled platform, was an example of the latter type. The projectiles most often used for catapults were darts or arrows about 1 m (3 ft) long or stones weighing perhaps 5 kg (11 lb). Few catapults had a range of more than 450 m (1,475 ft).

See also: ARTILLERY; FORTIFICATION.

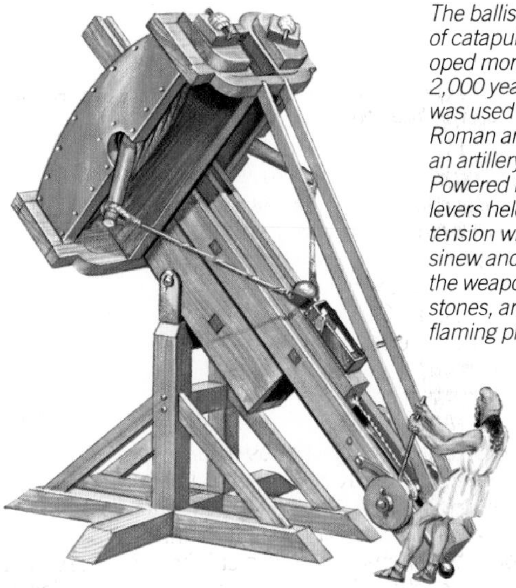

The ballista, a type of catapult developed more than 2,000 years ago, was used by Roman armies as an artillery piece. Powered by twin levers held under tension with animal sinew and ropes, the weapon hurled stones, arrows, or flaming projectiles.

cataract A cataract is a loss of transparency of the crystalline lens of the EYE. A lens that is opaque to any degree is, by definition, cataractous. A cataract may or may not be significant, however, depending on how much light it scatters or blocks from entering the eye. Small lens opacities are common, many being present from birth. The term *cataract* is generally used only to designate those opacities which impair vision. Severe cataracts are a major cause of treatable blindness.

Cataracts have many causes. Some are congenital, others develop after trauma to the eye, and some that occur in the outer layer of the lens have been linked with excessive ultraviolet radiation, as from the Sun. Still others are associated with a system-wide medical problem such as DIABETES. Most cataracts, however, occur as a consequence of AGING. As the lens ages, it may gradually become cloudy. Spectacle changes can usually correct the vision during the early stages, but surgery may become necessary. A recent development in cataract sur-

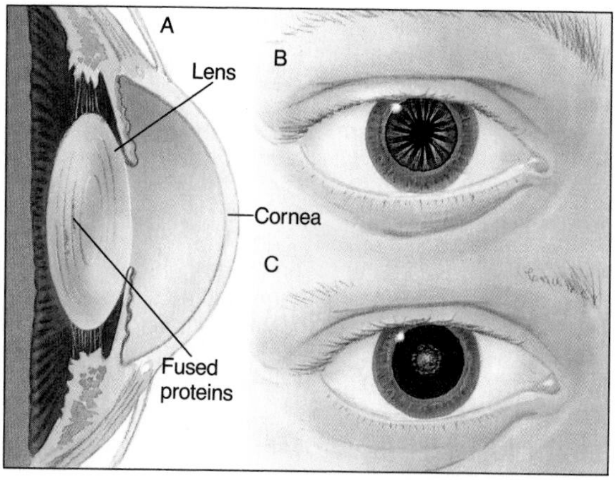

Cataracts arise from a number of causes and occur more frequently as people get older. (A) The fusion of proteins within cells of the lens causes that portion of the lens to become opaque. (B) Peripheral cataracts are characterized by wedge-shaped opacities. (C) Central opacities are called nuclear cataracts.

gery is a tiny ultrasonic probe with a tip that oscillates thousands of times a second. Placed within the eye, it can break the cataract into small pieces, which are rinsed from the eye. Another development is the use of plastic artificial lenses that can be implanted within the eye. Currently, however, these devices are not satisfactory for all patients.

catastrophe theory In mathematics, catastrophe theory seeks to describe the structure of phenomena in which sharply discontinuous results follow from continuous processes. The theory was first developed by French mathematician René Thom in a paper published in 1968, but it has roots in such fields as topology and dynamical system theory. While its subjects would include actual catastrophes such as a girder suddenly buckling, it is intended to apply to an abrupt change in any process.

When catastrophe theory first appeared, controversy was created by some of the claims being made for its possible applications to real-life situations in such diverse fields as sociology and the behavioral sciences. In the following years, however, the theory has become an established area of mathematical research and has demonstrated its usefulness in the study of many problems in physics; its wider relevance continues to be explored.

catastrophism Catastrophism was the geological doctrine, prevalent well into the 18th century, that the physical features of the face of the Earth were formed by violent cataclysms. This idea had its roots in the common supposition that features such as mountains and canyons must be the work of fast-acting and almost certainly supernatural forces.

The leading proponent of catastrophism was the French naturalist Baron Georges CUVIER. His writings lent considerable prestige to catastrophist doctrine, which held that the Earth is only a few thousand years old (see GEOLOGY). The doctrine's heyday was short-lived, however, as geologists began to grasp the true immensity of GEOLOGIC TIME. Over such vast stretches of time, they realized, long-acting geological processes could accomplish great changes, even if such processes seemed weak in the short term. A new, gradualist view of Earth history called UNIFORMITARIANISM gained acceptance, and by the later 19th century catastrophism had largely been discredited. The triumph of uniformitarianism—first introduced by James HUTTON and then championed by Sir Charles LYELL—was so nearly complete that geologists came to greet with skepticism any theory proposing sudden changes or pulsed events in the long history of Earth. Although they recognized that many natural events such as earthquakes and volcanic eruptions are truly catastrophic, they regarded these events as having only local influences, unlike the worldwide floods and other cataclysms that had been theorized by proponents of catastrophism.

Despite such skepticism, the catastrophic view of Earth history has not entirely vanished from geologic thought. According to some theories, EVOLUTION is characterized by sudden transitions, or leaps, as well as by gradual change. More strikingly, scientists have proposed the controversial idea that several of the past mass EXTINCTIONS revealed by the FOSSIL RECORD are the result of great catastrophes, such as meteor or asteroid collisions with the Earth.

The French naturalist Georges Cuvier was a chief promulgator of the theory of catastrophism. His paleontological studies led him to believe that the Earth had been successively repopulated with higher life forms after periodic upheavals and floods.

catatonia see SCHIZOPHRENIA

Catawba [kuh-taw'-buh] The Catawba are a North American Indian tribe whose aboriginal homeland was in the Carolinas. Their language belongs to the Siouan branch of the Hokan-Siouan linguistic family. The Catawba numbered an estimated 5,000 in 1600. Women farmed the land along the Catawba River; men hunted game and fought the CHEROKEE and other enemy tribes. By 1728 intermittent warfare and disease had reduced their population to 1,400. Struck by smallpox in 1738 and 1759, their tribe was again reduced by nearly half. They moved (1762) onto a small reservation on the Catawba River, but by 1841 all but one square mile of their land had been sold to the state of South Carolina. Some members of the nearly extinct tribe joined the Cherokee in western North Carolina or went to Indian Territory in Oklahoma. The majority eventually stayed in South Carolina on a 255-ha (630-acre) reservation set aside for them in 1842.

In 1959 the Catawba petitioned Congress to terminate their tribal status. They distributed (1962) their land holdings among the 631 remaining members, but in 1973 they reconstituted a tribal council.

catbird Catbird is the common name for birds that belong to several Old and New World families and have mewing calls. The gray catbird, *Dumetella carolinensis*, family Mimidae, is common over most of North America from central Canada south (except on the U.S. West Coast), wintering south to Central America. Slightly smaller (23 cm/9 in) than the American robin, it is slim and dark gray, with a black cap and chestnut red under-tail coverts. Although it is not as gifted a mimic as the related MOCKINGBIRD, the catbird has a large repertoire of notes, which it strings together in a long and variable song.

The gray catbird, named for its strident, catlike whine, can be found in dense thickets in suburbs and parks.

Catch-22 Joseph HELLER's famous first novel, *Catch-22* (1961; film 1970), is a dark but humorous portrait of a U.S. Air Force unit during World War II and a telling satire of military bureaucracy. Yossarian, the ANTI-HERO, is, like all of the characters, caught up in the maddening regulation Catch-22: he must fly more missions unless he can prove himself insane, but he cannot prove this because, by his unwillingness to fly, he proves that he is sane. In this way, Heller ironically hypothesizes that those who believe themselves insane are actually the sanest, whereas the supposedly sane people are the real madmen.

Catcher in the Rye, The Written as the autobiographical account of a fictional teenage prep school student named Holden Caulfield, *The Catcher in the Rye* (1951) established J. D. SALINGER as a thematically innovative American novelist unafraid to deal with socially scandalous material. Intelligent, inquisitive, and painfully sensitive, Holden puts his world to the test: the sexual mores of his peers and elders, the principles of his education, and his own emerging sense of self. Salinger's control of Holden's easy, conversational manner makes the introduction of these large themes appear natural and believable.

catechism In religious education, a catechism is a manual of Christian doctrine. Originally the term was applied to the oral instruction on Christian doctrine; gradually the name passed to the book containing such instructions. Traditionally, catechisms have taken the form of questions and answers and have been considered important instruments of instruction, especially for children. The content generally covers fundamental Christian doctrine; the texts and explanations of the CREED, the LORD'S PRAYER, and the TEN COMMANDMENTS are given. Some catechisms include sections on church laws, practices, and rites.

Martin Luther's Small Catechism (1529) remains the standard manual of Lutheran churches. The Heidelberg Catechism (1563; rev. ed. 1619) is the fundamental Calvinist profession of faith now used by the Reformed churches. Presbyterians generally follow the Westminister Longer and Shorter Catechisms of 1647 and 1648. The Baltimore Catechism (1885) is still widely used by Roman Catholics in the United States. The catechism of the Anglican Communion is contained in the BOOK OF COMMON PRAYER.

caterpillar A caterpillar is an elongate, wormlike larva of an insect, particularly of BUTTERFLIES AND MOTHS. Typically long and slender, a caterpillar consists of three regions: head, thorax, and abdomen. The mandibles, or jaws, are effective in chewing plant matter. The thorax bears three pairs of short legs, and the abdomen usually bears a pair of fleshy prolegs on each of the third to sixth segments and on the tenth, or last, segment. Caterpillars of small moths rarely exceed 5 mm (0.2 in) in length; those of the largest may measure up to 155 mm (6 in). They are often brightly colored and patterned, and many have hairs or spines, which are sometimes poisonous. Caterpillars are essentially the nutritive and growth stage of the insects' life span. Ecologically, they are enormous-

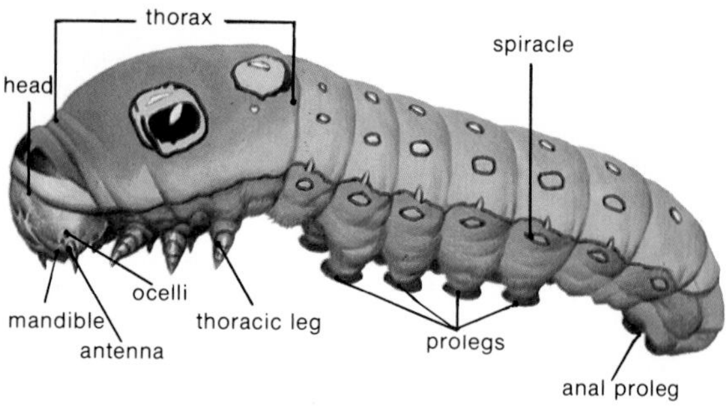

The caterpillar's anatomy is divided into the head, usually with six ocelli, or eyes, on each side; the thorax, with three pairs of legs; and the abdomen, whose fleshy prolegs have tiny hooks for clinging.

ly important, transforming large amounts of plant matter into animal matter and wastes, as well as serving as food for other animals. Many caterpillars, however, are destructive to crops and shade trees.

catfish Catfish comprise about 2,000 species of mostly freshwater fishes in the order Siluriformes. Distributed worldwide, they are most diverse in South America. Catfish are distinguished by the presence of barbels, or "whiskers"; the lack of true scales; strong spines at the front of the dorsal and pectoral fins; and, in most cases, an adipose fin on top of the body, in front of the caudal fin. The body is usually partly to completely armored. Most catfish have small eyes; they rely on taste, smell, and hearing. The barbels and much of the skin are often covered with taste buds. Many catfish are inactive during the day, coming out to feed at night. Freshwater catfish usually spend much of their time (and lay their eggs) in hollow logs, undercut banks, and other hiding places. One or both parents guard the eggs until they hatch.

Many species of freshwater catfish are used for human food. North American catfish of the genus *Ictalurus* are important commercially and are popular with anglers. Catfish farming involves raising and marketing such species as the channel catfish, *I. punctatus*.

Some catfish are quite distinctive in appearance or behavior. A parasitic catfish, the candiru, *Vandellis cirrhosa*, a minute South American catfish with strong, recurved spines, has been known to enter the urinary tract of persons wading in the water. The electric catfish, *Malapterurus electricus*, native to Africa, can produce a charge of up to 350 volts, enough to stun a human. The predatory walking catfish, *Clarias batrachus*, has lunglike organs that allow it to breathe air, enabling it to move over land from one body of water to another. A European catfish, the wels, *Silurus glanis*, is one of the largest freshwater fishes, reaching 4.5 m (15 ft) in length and 300 kg (660 lb) in weight.

cathartic A cathartic, or laxative, is a drug that stimulates the passage and elimination of feces. Stimulant laxatives such as cascara, sagrada phenolphthalein, senna, castor oil, and bisacodyl increase the propulsive activity of the intestine by local irritation of the mucous membranes. Bulk-forming agents such as psyllium seed and tragacanth dissolve or swell in the intestinal fluid and stimulate the bowels. A saline agent such as a solution of magnesium causes the retention of water in the intestine

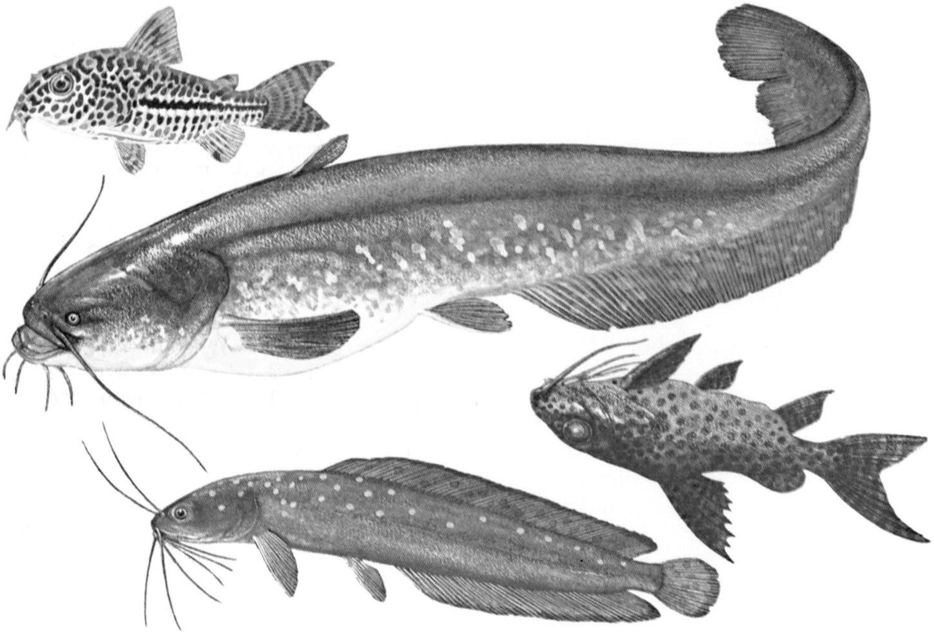

Catfish are bottom-dwelling fish marked by the presence around the mouth of sensitive tactile organs (barbels) that look like a cat's whiskers. Shown are (top to bottom): *leopard catfish, of the lower Amazon, a favorite aquarium fish; European catfish (or wels), the largest catfish; upside-down catfish, of the Congo; and walking catfish, which can live for hours out of water, commonly hunting on land.*

and thus also acts as a bulk-forming laxative, as does a water enema. Lubricant laxatives, which promote softening of the fecal mass, include mineral oil and dioctyl sodium sulfosuccinate. Stimulant laxatives or enemas are often used before surgery or X-ray examination, and saline agents in purgative doses are used in cases of food and drug poisoning.

Cathay [kath-ay'] Cathay, the ancient name for China, is derived from Khitan or Khitai, the name of a Mongol people who ruled China from 907 to 1125. Coined by the early travelers from the Middle East, the name was popularized in Europe by Marco Polo.

cathedrals and churches Understanding the development of church architecture involves considering the requirements of religious ritual, the symbolism of architectural forms, and the demands of the society served by the church building. The word *church* (from the Greek *kyriakon doma*, "the Lord's House") first described the building that housed the worshipers and later referred to the entire Christian community.

Early Christian Churches. The earliest Christians developed no ecclesiastical architecture. They usually met in private homes, frequently in a dining room, because the earliest Christian service involved a ritual meal. As the Christian community expanded and the liturgy developed, the assembly rooms became larger. By the 3d century, they were furnished with a special table, or *mensa*, for the Eucharist. The officiating bishop sat near this altar in an armchair, or *cathedra*; this chair eventually gave its name to the cathedral, which, in contrast to a parish church, is one over which a bishop presides.

From AD 313, when Emperor Constantine I granted Christianity official status throughout the Roman Empire, Christian liturgy became increasingly imperial in tone. A new and more dignified architectural setting was required for the liturgy, and Constantine's architects turned for inspiration to the Roman BASILICA, a type of large public meeting hall. The Early Christian basilica (see EARLY CHRISTIAN ART AND ARCHITECTURE) was a longitudinal structure with a central nave flanked by two or more side aisles of lower height. The clergy sat in the apse, separated from the laity by a railing or screen. In Byzantine churches the clergy were isolated even more from the laity by an iconostasis, a screen wall covered with holy pictures, or ICONS. Behind the closed doors of the iconostasis the priests performed the rite of the Eucharist.

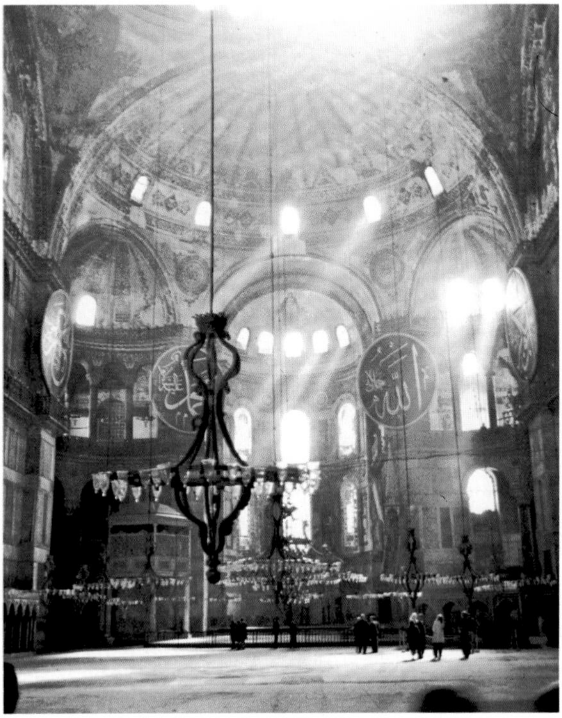

The interior of the vast Byzantine Church of Hagia Sophia (Holy Wisdom), in Istanbul, built between 532 and 537, uses the play of light to create an aura of mystery and weightlessness.

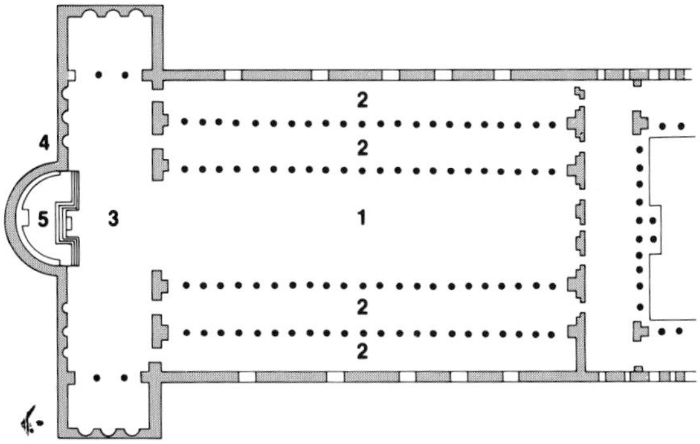

Floor plan of Old Saint Peter's Basilica, Rome, shows the longitudinal axis of the Early Christian basilica, with a long nave (1) and side aisles (2) leading to a transept (3), an apse (4), and an altar (5).

Early Christian architects also developed the centralized plan, based on the circle, the square, the polygon, and the Greek cross (arms of equal length). In a centralized plan the center of the structure becomes the liturgical focus of the church. The DOME was universally understood from Roman imperial times to symbolize the dome of heaven. The centralized domed plan, embodying the concept of Christ as the heavenly ruler, and the basilican plan, stressing the public and processional character of the mass, were merged in the great church of HAGIA SOPHIA (532–537), built by the Emperor Justinian I in Constantinople (now Istanbul), capital of the Byzantine Empire (see BYZANTINE ART AND ARCHITECTURE).

Early Medieval Churches. In his desire to revive the glories of the imperial past, Charlemagne abandoned the simple Merovingian church prototypes (see MEROVINGIAN ART AND ARCHITECTURE) and based the plan of his Palace Chapel (*c.*800) at Aachen, Germany, on a centralized

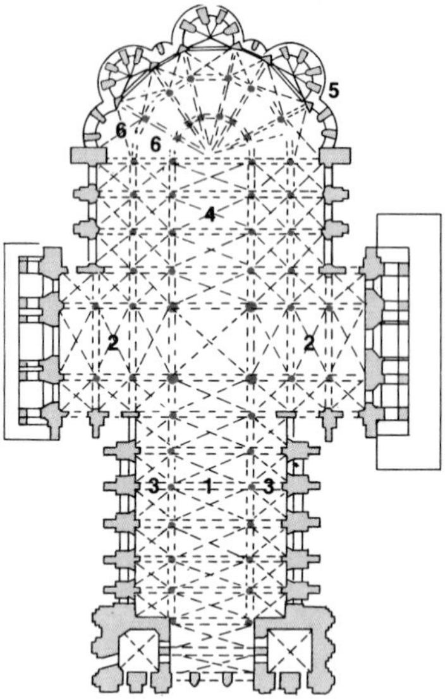

(Left) *At the Cathedral of Notre Dame de Paris (begun 1163), one of the major devices of French Gothic architecture, the flying buttress, was invented. An arched bridge construction, it transfers the thrust of the exterior church wall to a solid pier. This permitted high vaults, thin walls, and enormous windows filled with stained glass.* (Right) *The plan of Chartres Cathedral (begun 1194), a typical High Gothic church, has a wide nave* (1) *and transept* (2) *flanked by single aisles* (3) *and a deep choir* (4) *and chevet* (5) *with double aisles* (6).

Byzantine model, Justinian's octagonal Church of SAN VITALE (526–547) in Ravenna, Italy. The basilican plan, however, which was deliberately revived during the Carolingian renaissance (see CAROLINGIAN ART AND ARCHITECTURE), dominated Western ecclesiastical architecture of the Middle Ages. The abbey church of Saint Riquier (*c.*800; destroyed) at Centula in northeast France was a three-aisled basilica with transept arms; it exhibits features that had considerable impact on church architecture in the later Middle Ages: the entrance structure known as the westwork and multiple towers integrated into the structure on the exterior. The spiky silhouette of this building influenced the later Ottonian churches (see OTTONIAN ART AND ARCHITECTURE) of German.

Romanesque Cathedrals and Churches. The Romanesque (see ROMANESQUE ART AND ARCHITECTURE), an age devoted to travel in many forms, from the Crusades to pilgrimages, saw the development of such pilgrim churches as Saint Sernin (begun *c.*1080) in Toulouse, on one of the routes through southern France to the shrine of Santiago de Compostela in northwestern Spain. Saint Sernin's round arches and heavy masonry walls recall Roman architecture, which gave the Romanesque style its name. The vaulted masonry ceiling of the church reflected the desire for a more fire-resistant roof than the wooden ceilings of earlier medieval churches. The church forms a large Latin cross; the four side aisles and extended nave were created to accommodate the hordes of pilgrims. Circulation through the church was facilitated by extending the side aisles around the apse to form an ambulatory. The small radial chapels opening off the ambulatory and transept arms provided a setting for the subsidiary altars needed to serve the numerous worshipers; the radial chapels were also used to display the holy relics brought back to western Europe in quantity by the Crusaders.

The most progressive Romanesque architecture was practiced by the Normans (see NORMAN ARCHITECTURE). Durham Cathedral in England (begun 1093) exhibits two forward-looking aspects of Norman architecture: the use of pointed arches and ribbed groin vaults. These features allow the use of windows that admit light directly into the nave.

The plan of the new Saint Peter's Basilica (1506–1626) in Rome combines the original Greek-cross design of Donato Bramante and Michelangelo (in gray) *with the longitudinal Latin-cross plan* (in outline) *added by Carlo Maderno early in the 17th century. Built on the traditional site of the tomb of Saint Peter, this church replaced the 4th-century Early Christian basilica.*

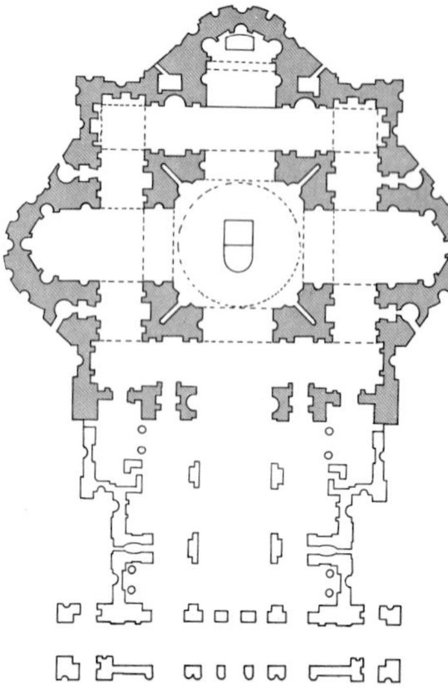

Gothic Cathedrals and Churches. For the builders of Gothic cathedrals (see GOTHIC ART AND ARCHITECTURE), bringing light into the nave by using the ribbed groin vault was not only a practical matter, but also involved theological considerations, for the sunlight entering these buildings through their enormous stained-glass windows, a light from heaven, was equated with the divine radiance. The pointed arch, a characteristic device of Gothic architecture that permits the construction of taller cathedrals, draws the eye upward, toward God. Another technical device that allowed Gothic builders to produce their soaring, light-filled structures is the flying BUTTRESS, which rises up on the exterior of the building and supports its thin upper walls. Flying buttresses allow the removal of almost all supporting elements of the building to the exterior. This results in the luminosity and seeming weightlessness of such French High Gothic interiors as that of Amiens Cathedral (begun 1220); the intricate "skeleton" of the building is visible only on the exterior.

The facades and doorways of the Gothic cathedrals, which faced the newly prosperous cities in which they were built, were covered with elaborate scriptural programs of sculptural decoration that were "read" by the townspeople as they entered the church.

Renaissance Cathedrals and Churches. For much of the 15th century, Italian Renaissance (see RENAISSANCE ART AND ARCHITECTURE) churches were intended to reflect the divine order of the universe in the mathematical proportioning of all the parts of the church to one another. Filippo BRUNELLESCHI's Church of San Lorenzo (begun in 1421) in Florence, for example, is a three-aisled, Latin cross plan with transept; the unifying elements in it are the square module on which all of the church was designed and the consistent application of the classical orders.

Learning from Brunelleschi, the great 15th-century architect and theoretician Leon Battista ALBERTI voiced the Renaissance view in calling a church (or "temple," in Renaissance parlance) the greatest and noblest ornament of a city. Thus he demanded a prominent site for a church—its location in a square and its elevation above the surrounding buildings—so that all of its parts could be admired. Moreover, geometrical proportions must govern the structure in every detail.

The ideal Renaissance church type was based on the centralized plan, exemplified by Brunelleschi's remarkable design for Santa Maria degli Angeli (1434–37) in

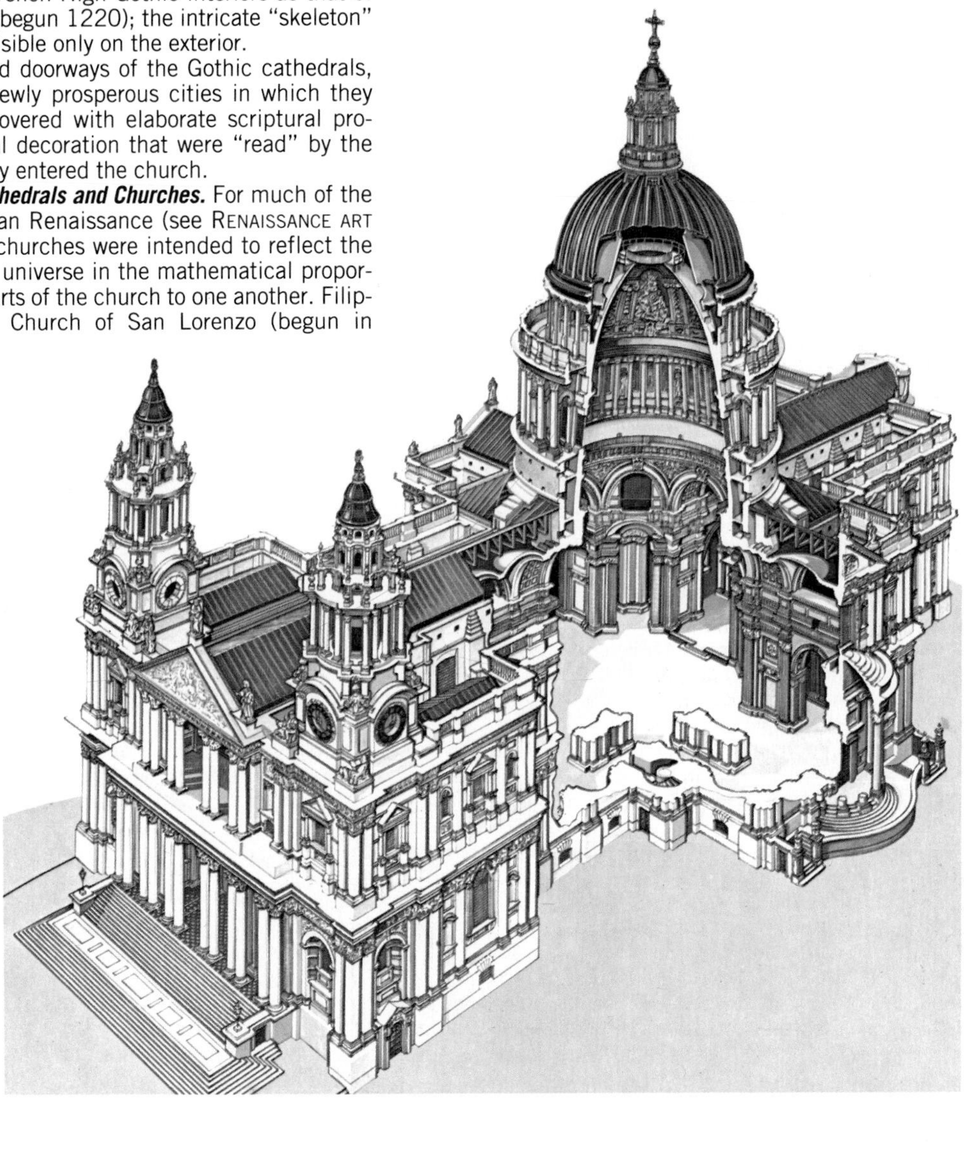

Sir Christopher Wren's masterpiece, Saint Paul's Cathedral (1675–1711), in London, is built in the form of a Latin cross. The great dome over the crossing rises 111.5 m (366 ft) above the pavement. The gabled western facade consists of a two-storied portico of coupled Corinthian and composite columns flanked by two bell towers. Built after the Great Fire of 1666, the cathedral houses the tombs of Wren, Sir Joshua Reynolds, J. M. W. Turner, and Lord Nelson, among others.

Le Corbusier's church of Notre Dame du Haut (1950–55), in Ronchamp, France, has a dark, concrete roof with curled eaves and massive, curved walls of white concrete pierced by stained-glass windows of various sizes and shapes.

Florence, an entirely centralized church formed by a ring of eight piers. Architects and theoreticians admired the centralized plan for its geometrical purity and clarity. The first such church to be built almost to completion, however, Guiliano da Sangallo's Madonna delle Carceri (begun 1484) at Prato, shows the inherent difficulties imposed by a centralized plan (here the Greek cross): geometrical focus is at the center of the plan, whereas the religious or liturgical focus, the altar, is set for practical purposes in the arm of the church opposite the main entrance. Thus there is a conflict between the geometry of the plan and the implied longitudinal axis.

Nevertheless, centralized plans were popular during the brief period of the High Renaissance (*c.*1500–20), and in 1506 Donato BRAMANTE proposed a central plan for the new Saint Peter's Basilica, when Pope Julius II (1503–13) decided to replace the old Constantinian basilica. The historical details are complex, but after the deaths of Julius II, Bramante, and, in 1514, MICHELANGELO, who was Bramante's successor as architect, religious conservatism had apparently run out and a longitudinal nave for the new basilica was tacked on the partially completed centralized domed church.

Baroque and Rococo Churches. After the sack of Rome in 1527, longitudinal churches returned to favor. Antonio Sangallo the Younger's Church of Santo Spirito (1538–44) in Sassia illustrates the new thought: a single-aisle church flanked by shallow chapels leads to a large high-altar chapel in the wide apse. In the 1530s the Jesuits had already instituted year-round preaching instead of preaching only at Lent, and in Santo Spirito the nave, with a flat wooden ceiling, serves the double purpose of providing an audience hall for preaching and congregational space for mass. Giacomo VIGNOLA's Church of Il Gesù, begun in Rome for the Jesuits in 1568, shows the full development of a new style, the baroque (see BAROQUE ART AND ARCHITECTURE). It is a large, single-aisled church, with truncated transept arms and a large dome over the crossing, all leading to the altar set in a deep, wide apse.

Subsequent church building for the Roman Catholic rite followed previous examples, but the number of regions and changes of style produced enormous variety within the rules laid down in the enactment of the Council of Trent in 1564. In the north, especially in Austria and Germany, the baroque and ROCOCO STYLE found exuberant expression, as in Johann Balthasar NEUMANN's Vierzehnheiligen (Fourteen Saints) Church (1743–72) near Bamberg. In the Roman Catholic countries of northern Europe, church plans developed much as they did in Italy, but the Gothic style endured more steadily in the north until gradually replaced by Italianate forms, and steeples continued to be dominant architectural elements.

In the Protestant north, particularly in Holland, congregations took over the Gothic churches that survived the religious wars, stripping them of most of their decoration. Stylistically, the Dutch remained attached to the familiar Gothic idiom and to the bell towers that denote the presence of churches in a city. The most pronounced changes were in the mode of worship: Roman Catholic ritual was replaced by a new emphasis on preaching, which required good lighting and pulpits. In the Zuidekerk (begun 1606) in Amsterdam, Hendrik de Keyser designed a simple pseudobasilica, without a choir but with large windows and a large wooden pulpit around a central column-pier.

Neoclassical Cathedrals and Churches. After the Great Fire of 1666 in London, Sir Christopher WREN, one of the greatest of English architects, gave the city a new skyline with the dozens of steepled churches he and his brilliant pupil Nicholas HAWKSMOOR created. Dominating them all with its massive dome on a high, pillared drum is SAINT PAUL'S CATHEDRAL (1675–1711), a vast Latin cross basilica rivaling Saint Peter's in size and splendor. Wren's parish churches are exemplified by the elegant Church of Saint Clement Danes (begun 1680), a galleried church with shallow vaults over the nave and aisles. In the United States NEOCLASSICISM found late but impressive expression in Benjamin LATROBE's Roman Catholic Cathedral of Baltimore (1804–18), a shallow-domed Latin cross plan with segmental barrel vaulting of the nave and side aisles.

Churches in the 19th and 20th Centuries. Church architecture in the 19th and early 20th centuries was dominated by a succession of revival styles, the major ones being GREEK REVIVAL, GOTHIC REVIVAL, and Romanesque Revival. The resultant buildings range from tawdry pastiches to splendid eclectic creations, many of which in the latter category are now considered national treasures. Such is the case with H. H. RICHARDSON's Byzantine-Romanesque Trinity Church (1872–77) on Boston's Copley Square, and with James RENWICK's Grace Church (completed 1846), a sensitive interpretation of English Gothic in New York City.

Contemporary church architecture is not noted for its distinction, with very few exceptions. LE CORBUSIER's stunningly original pilgrim church of Notre Dame du Haut (1950–55) in Ronchamp, France, Eliel SAARINEN's serene First Christian Church (1942) in Columbus, Ind., and Sir Basil Spence's controversial new Coventry Cathedral (1954–62) in England stand out in an uncrowded field.

See also: ARCH AND VAULT; MONASTIC ART AND ARCHITECTURE.

Willa Cather, a Pulitzer Prize–winning novelist, gained recognition for her books concerning the American frontier. Drawing on experiences from her childhood in Nebraska, she wrote with admiration about the spirit of the Great Plains pioneers.

Cather, Willa [kath'-ur] Willa Sibert Cather, b. Back Creek Valley, Va., Dec. 7, 1873, d. Apr. 24, 1947, one of the most important American novelists of the first half of the 20th century, grew up in pioneer Nebraska, and then in the East followed a distinguished career as journalist, editor, and fiction writer. Cather is often thought of as a chronicler of the pioneer American West, but her themes are intertwined with the universal story of the rise of civilizations, the drama of the immigrant in a new world, and views of personal involvements with art. Cather's fiction is characterized by a strong sense of place, the subtle presentation of human relationships, an often unconventional narrative structure, and a style of clarity and beauty.

Early Life and Works. In 1895, Cather graduated from the University of Nebraska. As a student, and then in Pittsburgh, she worked as a journalist, copy editor, critic, and fiction writer; from 1901 to 1906 she taught in the Pittsburgh and Allegheny high schools. Her first books were collections of poetry (*April Twilights*, 1903) and short stories (*The Troll Garden*, 1905). From 1906 to 1912 she worked in New York for *McClure's Magazine*, becoming managing editor.

Major Works. Beginning with *Alexander's Bridge* (1912), Cather devoted herself to writing. Many of her books drew on her memories of Nebraska. *O Pioneers!* (1913), *My Ántonia* (1918), and *A Lost Lady* (1923) develop historically the theme of the pioneer experience. *The Song of the Lark* (1915) tells of the development and success of a young singer. *One of Ours* (1922), which received the Pulitzer Prize, concerns a repressed young man of the plains and his need for freedom. *The Professor's House* (1925) and *My Mortal Enemy* (1926) explore personal crises, and *Death Comes for the Archbishop* (1927) and *Shadows on the Rock* (1931) are historical novels set in the Southwest and Quebec, respectively. The short stories in *Obscure Destinies* (1932) and the novel *Lucy Gayheart* (1935) return to Nebraska, and *Sapphira and the Slave Girl* (1940) treats life in Virginia before and after the Civil War.

Catherine of Aragon Catherine of Aragon, b. Dec. 16, 1485, d. Jan. 7, 1536, youngest daughter of Ferdinand and Isabella of Spain, was the first wife of HENRY VIII of England. They were married (1509) by papal dispensation because of Catherine's previous marriage to Henry's brother, Arthur (d. 1502). Only one of Catherine's children, the future Queen MARY I, survived infancy. Desiring a male heir, Henry sought in 1527 to have his marriage annulled, but pope Clement VII procrastinated over the annulment, thus precipitating the English Reformation. Henry married Anne BOLEYN in 1533, having had Archbishop Thomas CRANMER pronounce the annulment without reference to the pope. Catherine was then forced into retirement.

Catherine of Siena, Saint Catherine of Siena, b. Mar. 25, 1347, d. Apr. 29, 1380, was an Italian mystic. She is especially remembered for the part she played in bringing about the return (1377) of Pope GREGORY XI from the papal residence in Avignon, France, to Rome, ending the 68-year absence of the popes from Rome, Catherine traveled (1376) to Avignon to present her case personally and persuade the pope to leave France.

St. Catherine is also known for her unusual mystical revelations, the holiness of her life, and her spiritual writings. She was canonized in 1461. In 1970, she was declared a doctor of the church. Feast day: Apr. 29 (formerly Apr. 30).

Catherine de Médicis [may-dee-sees'] Catherine de Médicis, b. Florence, Apr. 13, 1519, d. Jan. 5, 1589, was the mother of the last VALOIS kings of France and guardian of the royal authority in the Wars of Religion. She was brought up by her MEDICI relatives during a period when their rule in Florence was marked by violence and intrigue. In 1533 she went to France as the bride of the future king HENRY II, who became heir apparent in 1536 and king in 1547. Until her husband's death in 1559 she endured the domination of his mistress, DIANE DE POITIERS. Seven of Catherine's children survived infancy, and three of her sons were successively kings of France as FRANCIS II, Charles IX, and HENRY III.

As queen mother, Catherine played a major part in French government and on two occasions ruled officially as regent. She relied on an inner group of experienced bureaucrats and tried to balance the noble factions against each other to preserve the authority of the crown in the civil wars. Despite her penchant for astrology, she was a political realist who sought compromise between the Roman Catholics and the Huguenots (Protestants). The SAINT BARTHOLOMEW'S DAY MASSACRE (1572) of the Huguenots was caused in part by her political miscalculation. Catherine's critics accused her of following Italian practices, especially the doctrines of Nicolò Machiavelli.

Catherine de Médicis, wife of Henry II of France, played a major role during the reigns of her sons Francis II, Charles IX, and Henry III. She is portrayed here by Jacopo da Empoli at her wedding. (Palazzo Medici-Riccardi, Florence.)

After the accession (1574) of Henry III, her favorite son, Catherine frequently negotiated with the Catholic League, which sought to control the crown. Appalled by the king's murder in December 1588 of the league leaders, she died at Blois two weeks later.

See also: RELIGION, WARS OF.

Catherine I, Empress of Russia Catherine I, b. Apr. 5, 1684, d. May 17, 1727, empress of Russia (1725–27), was a Lithuanian peasant woman originally named Marta Skowronska, who was captured by the Russians in the Great Northern War and became the mistress and then in 1712 the second wife of Emperor PETER I. Illiterate but resolute and intelligent, she was Peter's constant companion and was crowned empress consort in 1724. On Peter's death, Catherine was proclaimed empress and ruled through a new organ, the Supreme Privy Council, headed by her favorite, Aleksandr Danilovich, Prince MENSHIKOV.

Catherine II, Empress of Russia (Catherine the Great) Catherine II, or Catherine the Great, b. Stettin (now Szczecin, Poland), May 2, 1729, empress of Russia (1762–96), did much to transform Russia into a modern country. The daughter of the German prince of Anhalt-Zerbst, she went to Russia at the age of 15 to become the wife of Peter, nephew and heir of Empress ELIZABETH.

PETER III made himself unpopular soon after his succession in 1761, especially with certain army officers. In a coup in June 1762, he was deposed (and subsequently murdered), and Catherine became absolute ruler of the largest European empire, whose language she never learned to speak correctly.

At the age of 33, Catherine was not only a handsome woman (whose numerous love affairs dominate the popular accounts of her life) but also unusually well read and cultured. She knew how to select capable assistants—for example, Aleksandr SUVOROV in the military and Grigory POTEMKIN in administration. Imbued with the ideas of the Enlightenment, Catherine aimed at completing the job started by Peter I—westernizing Russia—by encouraging individual initiative. She succeeded to a degree with the upper classes but did nothing for the enserfed peasantry.

The Cossack revolt of 1773–75, led by Yemelian PUGACHEV, alerted Catherine to the necessity for reform. She reorganized the local administration, integrated the Cossacks into the regular army, and put the serfs belonging to the Russian Orthodox church under state administration. In 1785 she issued two charters—to the towns and to the nobility—to involve the educated classes in local administration.

Catherine promoted trade and the development of underpopulated regions by inviting foreign settlers such as the Volga Germans, and she founded new towns (ODESSA, for example) and enterprises on the Black Sea. She patronized arts and letters and relaxed censorship rules. Under her guidance the University of Moscow and the Academy of Sciences became internationally recognized centers of learning; she also increased the number of state and private schools. The outbreak of the French Revolution (1789) and the publication of Aleksandr Rad-

Catherine the Great, a strong ruler and patron of the arts, extended Russia's political power and advanced the country culturally during the late 18th century. (Musée des Beaux Arts, Chartres.)

ishchev's *Journey from St. Petersburg to Moscow* (1790), in which the author denounced the evils of serfdom, the immorality of society, and the abuses of government, prompted Catherine to impose repressive measures, which alienated many of her educated supporters.

Finally, Catherine vastly expanded the Russian empire. Following two successful wars against Turkey (the RUSSO-TURKISH WARS of 1768–74 and 1787–92), Russia secured the Crimea on the north shore of the Black Sea. The fertile lands of the Ukraine became the granary of Europe. Catherine also participated in the partitions of Poland (1772, 1792, and 1795), bringing a large part of that country under Russian rule.

By the time of Catherine's death on Nov. 17, 1796, modern Russian society was organized and Russia was also playing a determining role in world affairs.

Catherwood, Frederick [kath'-ur-wud] Frederick Catherwood, b. London, Feb. 27, 1799, d. Sept. 27, 1854, was an Anglo-American architect, artist, and engraver best known for his meticulously executed illustrations of ancient Mayan monuments in Central America. He accompanied archaeological field trips to Greece, Egypt, and the Levant, making sketches of numerous ruins. In 1839–40 he joined the exploration party of John Lloyd Stephens on its trip to Mexico and Guatemala. Two popular books resulted from this venture, both written by Stephens and illustrated by Catherwood. In 1844, Catherwood published his most famous volume of drawings and engravings, *Views of Ancient Monuments of Central America, Chiapas, and Yucatán*, notable for the remarkable accuracy of the illustrations.

cathode [kath'-ohd] A cathode is the terminal, or ELECTRODE, through which a positive electrical current exits (or a negative current enters) an electrical device. (The other electrode is the anode.) In ELECTROLYSIS, the negatively charged electrode immersed in a cell containing an electrolyte (a chemical mixture or compound that conducts electricity) is called the cathode. In an ELECTRON TUBE, the cathode is the electrode from which a stream of ELECTRONS is emitted.

cathode-ray tube The cathode-ray tube, often abbreviated CRT, is an ELECTRON TUBE that provides a visual display of information. The tube's glass envelope is shaped like a funnel. In operation, a thermionic CATHODE at the tube's narrow end generates a stream of ELECTRONS. (Before the discovery of the electron, such a stream was known as a cathode ray.) As they pass through one or more cylindrical electrodes, the electrons are focused into a pencil-shaped beam. The electron beam then passes through a deflection section where it is shifted either vertically or horizontally in response to an external signal. The deflection may be caused by passing a current through electromagnetic deflection coils that encircle the tube, or, in some tubes, by applying a voltage to one or more of four deflection electrodes arranged around the beam's path. After the electron beam has been deflected, it strikes a light-emitting layer of phosphor on the inside wall of the tube's face. The electrons cause the phosphor to fluoresce, and the resulting glow becomes a point of light on the face of the screen. Various phosphors or combinations of phosphors can be used to produce all the colors of the visible spectrum.

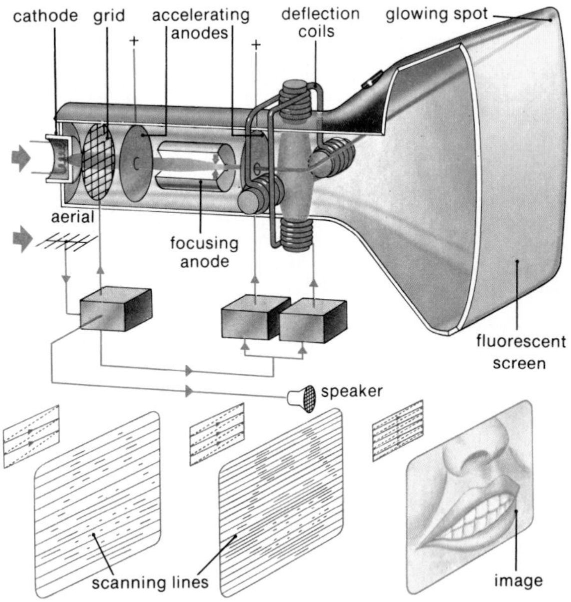

The cathode-ray tube of a black-and-white television receiver contains a coated screen that fluoresces, or glows, when struck by electrons emitted by a cathode and accelerated and focused into a beam by anodes. The electron velocity is controlled by a grid synchronized with a signal transmitted from a camera. Signals also regulate two sets of coils that move the beam across and down the screen, creating a picture of closely spaced horizontal lines.

The cathode-ray tube is by far the most important electronic visual display used today. Its best-known application is in TELEVISION. The circuitry in a television receiver causes the electron beam in the CRT to continuously sweep across the screen in a pattern of hundreds of closely spaced horizontal lines at a rapid rate. A similar SCANNING pattern is used in the TV camera. By synchronizing the camera's signals with the receiver's sweep circuits, the electron beam can be activated and deactivated in step with the signals. The result is an image on the face of the cathode-ray tube that reproduces the image picked up by the camera. Other uses for the CRT include the visual display for an OSCILLOSCOPE and the video display unit for a COMPUTER.

See also: VIDEO TECHNOLOGY.

catholic The word *catholic* comes from the Greek word *Katholikos*, meaning "universal." It was first used by IGNATIUS OF ANTIOCH (d. about AD 107) to distinguish the entire body of Christians from individual congregations.

Subsequently, the word distinguished true believers from false believers. After the break (1054) between the Western church and the Eastern church, it was used to identify the Western church; the Eastern church was called orthodox. At the time of the Reformation in the 16th century, the Church of Rome claimed the word *catholic* as its title over the Protestant or Reformed churches. In England, *catholic* was retained to describe the reformed, national church, although a distinction was made between "Roman" Catholics and members of the Church of England. The term *Anglo-Catholic* was coined at the time of the OXFORD MOVEMENT in the 19th century. In popular usage, Catholic commonly designates a member of the ROMAN CATHOLIC CHURCH.

Catholic Emancipation The Catholic Emancipation movement of the late 18th and early 19th centuries removed limitations on the political and civil rights of Roman Catholics in Britain and Ireland. Following the Reformation, a series of restrictions known as the Penal Laws had been imposed on Roman Catholics and nonconforming Protestants. These regulations restricted Catholics in the practice of their religion, barred them from voting and from political offices, and contained other limitations. During the 18th century, such penalties were gradually lifted, especially by the Roman Catholic Relief Act of 1791. In 1828, Irish agitation led by Daniel O'CONNELL succeeded in getting Parliament to repeal the TEST ACTS, which had excluded Catholics from public office. Fears of a revolution in predominantly Catholic Ireland prevailed over anti-Catholic biases, and in 1829 the government of the duke of WELLINGTON passed the Catholic Emancipation Act sponsored by Sir Robert PEEL. Thereafter, only the crown, certain judicial offices, and places in the established church remained barred to Catholics.

Catholic Worker Movement see DAY, DOROTHY

Catiline [kat'-il-line] Catiline (Lucius Sergius Catilina), *c.*108–62 BC, was a Roman soldier and politician notorious for his abortive conspiracy against the state in 63 BC. A supporter of SULLA in the civil war of 88–82 BC, Catiline became prominent during the proscriptions following Sulla's victory. He was praetor (68) and governor (67–66) of Africa. Charged with abuses of power on his return, he was acquitted, but defeated for the consulship in 64 and 63. Frustrated in his ambitions, Catiline turned to demagoguery to build popular support. At the same time, he plotted to seize control by force. Informed by his spies of what was afoot, the consul CICERO denounced Catiline in the Senate in four famous orations. Catiline fled to Etruria, where he died in battle near Pistoia.

cation see ION AND IONIZATION

catkin A catkin, or ament, is a specialized flower cluster found on certain trees and shrubs, most commonly willows, poplars, or birches. Generally, the catkin is a soft, scaly, drooping spike that bears dozens of tiny flowers. These flowers lack petals and consist only of the reproductive parts (stamens or pistils) and possibly sepals, which, if present, are modified as small, scalelike structures. Leaves, called bracts and resembling scales, may also occur.

Two types of catkins are produced: staminate, having flowers with male parts only; and pistillate, having flowers with female parts only. In some species, such as willows and poplars, individual trees bear only male or only female catkins; in others, such as birches, both kinds appear on the same tree. Variations may occur, however. In walnuts, for example, only the male flowers are in catkins, and both male catkins and female flowers are borne on the same tree.

George Catlin's portrait of an American Indian chief, The Surrounder *(1833), is one of the nearly 500 paintings of North American Indians by the 19th-century American painter. (Smithsonian Institution, Washington, D.C.)*

Catlin, George [kat'-lin] The American painter and author George Catlin, b. Wilkes-Barre, Pa., July 26, 1796, d. Dec. 28, 1872, was the foremost artist-chronicler of the American Indian in the 19th century. After working as a miniaturist in Philadelphia and New York from 1820 to 1824, Catlin spent much of the next decade living among Indians of the Southeast, Great Lakes, and Great Plains. The hundreds of paintings surviving from this period are valuable both as art and as ethnographical documents of a lost culture. His paintings and sketches also served as the basis for the engravings in his books, the best known of which is *Letters and Notes on the Manners, Customs, and Condition of the North American Indians* (1841).

In the late 1830s, Catlin established his Indian Gallery, a traveling exhibition of paintings, costumes, and artifacts that toured the United States, England, and France with great success between 1837 and 1848.

catnip Catnip, *Nepeta cataria*, in the mint family, Labiatae or Lamiaceae, is a pungent herb native to Europe and Asia. In the United States it grows as a roadside weed. The leaves emit an odor that is often stimulating to cats, which respond to catnip by licking it, chewing it, and rolling in it. It grows 50 to 100 cm (20 to 40 in) high, and has spikes with small, pink-splotched whitish flowers. Brewed as a tea, catnip leaves were once used as a sedative or as a remedy for colds.

Cato, Marcus Porcius (Cato the Elder) [kay'-toh, mar'-cuhs por'-shuhs] Marcus Porcius Cato, or Cato the Elder, was a famous censor of ancient Rome. Born at Tusculum in 234 BC, he became a military tribune in 214 during the Second PUNIC WAR and thereafter advanced rapidly. As consul with Lucius Valerius Flaccus in 195, he fought in Spain and organized its provincial administration. He later fought in the east (191) against ANTIOCHUS III. Finally, having established a reputation as a critic of many prominent Romans, especially SCIPIO AFRICANUS MAJOR, Cato became censor with Flaccus in 184 BC.

By supporting traditional Roman ways, Cato established a reputation as a stern moralist at home; abroad, he advocated limited eastern involvement but was an implacable foe of CARTHAGE. He constantly reiterated in the Senate, "Further, I think that Carthage must be destroyed," and thus helped precipitate the Third Punic War shortly before his death, in 149 BC.

Although opposed to Greek influences, Cato contributed much to Roman culture. He patronized the poet Quintus ENNIUS and stimulated Roman rhetoric by publishing his own speeches. Cato's *Origins*, the first history of Rome in Latin, set the pattern for Latin prose. Unfortunately, only his *On Farming* survives.

Cato, Marcus Porcius (Cato the Younger) Marcus Porcius Cato, b. 95 BC, called Cato the Younger and Cato of Utica to distinguish him from his great-grandfather Cato the Elder, was a leading Roman conservative in the last years of the Roman republic. Cato the Younger served against SPARTACUS (72) and became quaestor in *c.*64 BC. In 63 he helped condemn CATILINE's accomplices. Becoming tribune (62), he increased distribution of subsidized grain to blunt popular criticism, but otherwise resisted all change.

By 59 BC, Cato's inflexible opposition had forced Marcus Licinius CRASSUS, POMPEY THE GREAT, and Julius CAESAR to form the first TRIUMVIRATE. In 58 he was sent to oversee the annexation of Cyprus. When he returned, however, he continued his opposition, supporting his brother-in-law for consul and himself for praetor, offices they won in 54. Then, in a sudden political realignment in 52, Cato supported Pompey for the consulate.

During the civil war between Pompey and Caesar, Cato fled to Africa upon Pompey's defeat at Pharsalus (48 BC) and governed Utica until Caesar's victory at Thapsus. Cato then committed suicide in April of the year 46 BC. Although his belief in the republican constitution and traditional Roman virtues was supported by sincere Stoic principles, Cato's inflexibility helped precipitate the republic's downfall. His uncritical devotion to the selfish oligarchy that governed Rome showed a failure to understand the forces leading to the tyranny he most feared.

cat's-eye A cat's-eye is a GEM that, when rounded and polished, displays chatoyancy, a luminous band of reflected light similar to the slit pupil of a cat. Precious, or oriental, cat's-eye is cymophane, a greenish gem consisting of the mineral CHRYSOBERYL with minute, parallel channels that reflect light. In the common, or occidental, cat's-eye, light reflects from parallel, pale-yellowish or greenish ASBESTOS fibers contained in quartz. Cat's-eyes are also sometimes found in BERYL, TOURMALINE, diopside, and scapolite.

Catskill Mountains The Catskill Mountains, located in southeastern New York immediately west of the Hudson River, form a range 48 to 64 km (30 to 40 mi) wide, with rounded, forested summits and deep valleys. The highest peak is Slide Mountain (1,281 m/4,202 ft). Dams on the numerous streams have created artificial lakes that supply water to New York City. Close to large population centers, the Catskills are a year-round recreation area, and tourism is important to the region's economy. Catskill State Park is situated in the mountains.

The Catskills were discovered by Henry HUDSON, who sailed (1609) up the river that now bears his name. The name *catskill* is derived from the Dutch *kaaterskill*, meaning "wildcat creek." The area was the setting for Washington IRVING's story, "Rip Van Winkle."

Catt, Carrie Chapman Carrie Clinton Lane Chapman Catt, b. Ripon, Wis., Jan. 9, 1859, d. Mar. 9, 1947, a U.S. women's SUFFRAGE and peace advocate, played a major role in the 1920 ratification of the 19th Amendment giving women the vote. She joined the Iowa women's suffrage movement in 1887. As president of the National American Woman Suffrage Association (1900–04, 1915–47), she shifted the movement's emphasis from propaganda to political action and displayed outstanding organizational ability. Catt was also president of the International Woman Suffrage Alliance (1904–23). She founded the LEAGUE OF WOMEN VOTERS in 1920 and in 1925 established the National Conference on the Cause and Cure of War.

cattail Cattails, genus *Typha*, are perennial reeds found in marshy areas throughout the temperate regions of the world. The common cattail, *T. latifolia*, of North America has long, straplike leaves and stalks with thickly flowered cylindrical spikes that become dark brown at maturity. Pollinated from male flowers on the upper end of the spike, the female flowers on the lower end may produce a million or more small, downy seeds, the "cat's tail."

Cattail leaves are used for weaving rush chairseats, mats, and baskets. The young shoots and partly devel-

The cattail is a handsome, reedy plant that lines swamps of North America, Europe, and Asia. It makes a striking addition to dried-flower arrangements.

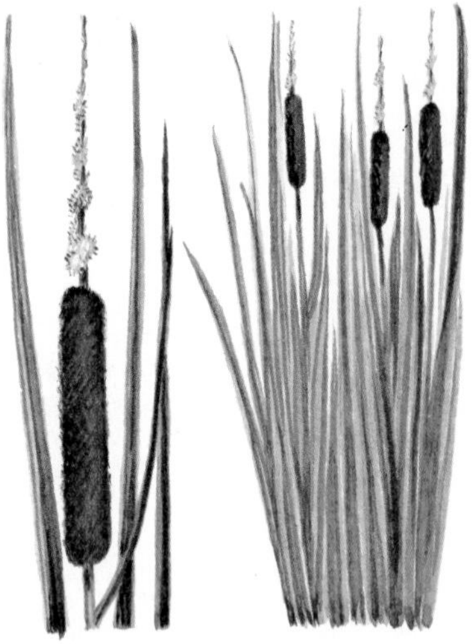

oped pollen spike may be cooked and eaten, and the starchy roots may be cooked as a vegetable or ground into a flour.

Cattell, James McKeen James Cattell, b. Easton, Pa., May 24, 1860, d. Jan. 20, 1944, was among the first to introduce the methods of German experimental psychology into the United States. He was Wilhelm WUNDT's assistant in Leipzig, when the field of experimental psychology was beginning to develop there. He founded psychological laboratories at the University of Pennsylvania and (1891–1917) at Columbia University.

Cattell was founding editor of the *Psychological Review, Popular Science, Scientific Monthly*, and *American Men of Science* (6 editions). He also edited *Science* and *School and Society* and founded the Psychological Corporation. Cattell helped develop methods of EDUCATIONAL MEASUREMENT, as well.

cattle and cattle raising Cattle are domesticated mammals of the family Bovidae. The two most important species are *Bos taurus*, which includes most of the varieties in the Western world, and *Bos indicus*, which includes the ZEBU, or Brahman cattle, of India, Africa, and the Orient. Raised for their meat and milk, for their skins, and in some countries for their strength as draft animals, cattle are ruminants whose origins, as domestic species, are uncertain. They are believed to be descended from the wild auroch, *Bos primigenius*, of Eurasia and North Africa, a species that became extinct in the 17th century.

Domestication and Breeding

Domestication probably began during the Neolithic Period and was certainly well under way 5,000 to 6,000 years ago; however, few attempts were made to improve cattle breeds through selection and breeding until the 18th century in Europe. Robert Bakewell (1725–95) of Dishley, England, is considered the founder of animal breeding and the person responsible for the development of many modern breeds.

In the United States today, the Brahman breed is an amalgam of several zebu breeds or strains introduced from India. Still other new breeds are being formed by crossing two or more established breeds and then selecting for a uniform type from among the resulting crossbred populations. ARTIFICIAL INSEMINATION is a widespread practice, particularly in dairy herds. As in earlier days, a prime objective of breeding programs is to produce cattle that are adapted to a particular environment, in order to best utilize available feed resources. Meat quality is also regarded as an important trait in developing new breeds.

History of the U.S. Cattle Industry

Cattle are not native to the Western Hemisphere; they were first brought to the West Indies in 1493 by Christopher Columbus. Hernán CORTÉS took descendants of these cattle to Mexico, and they were eventually raised throughout the Southwest. They were a hardy, all-purpose cattle. Today's pure Texas Longhorns are direct descendants of these early cattle.

In the early 17th century, English Shorthorn cattle were imported by colonists on the East Coast. These were dual- and triple-purpose cattle for producing meat, milk, and the tallow and hides that were important colonial export items. Settlers who moved westward took their cattle with them, especially oxen, which pulled wagons and later supplied the power to break the tough prairie sod. By 1860 the cattle industry of the Corn Belt was highly developed; that of the Great Plains and Mountain states was stocked by the 1880s.

During the Texas cattle drives after the Civil War, millions of Texas Longhorns were driven from overstocked ranges in the southern part of the state to railheads in Kansas, for shipment to midwestern feedlots and packing plants. Some cows from this breeding were driven to the Northwest, where they became foundation stock for present-day herds. Although Shorthorns were the dominant breed used to improve herds, Herefords and Angus quickly replaced them, especially in the range states. The disastrous droughts of 1886–88 resulted in the bankruptcy of most of the large cattle ranches, but a new era was launched with the introduction of barbed wire fences and windmills that pumped up underground water. A once-hazardous industry has been stabilized by the use of irrigation, controlled grazing, and supplemental feeds.

The Cattle Industry Today

Leading cattle-raising countries, in order of number of head of cattle, are India, Brazil, the USSR, the United States, China, and Argentina. In almost half the U.S. states, the cattle industry is a primary source of farm income. The number of cattle raised and the prices they command vary widely from year to year, depending on supply, cost of feed and fertilizers, cost of grazing land, and export demand.

The cattle on U.S. farms and ranches vary widely in type or conformation, origin, and purpose for which they are grown. The breeding segment consists of males and females in a ratio of about 1:20. Great numbers of castrated males, or steers—about one-fourth of the total population—are destined for slaughter, along with about half of the female calves, or heifers, dropped each year. In addition, an average of one-fourth of the adult cow population, both beef and dairy, is culled for a variety of reasons and is also utilized as beef. Ultimately, all cattle are sold as beef, and—along with beef imports from Australia and Latin America—supplied each U.S. consumer with almost 50 kg (110 lb) of beef annually in the mid-1980s.

Most cattle in the United States are bred for beef, meaning that their only function is profitably to convert the grasses growing on the pastures and ranges of the country into a calf crop. Eventually they are fattened in feedlots on high-grain rations to yield high-quality carcass beef. Beef cows outnumber dairy cows by about 4 to 1. The British breeds such as Angus, Hereford, and Shorthorn make up a large part of the beef-cattle population. It is now common, however, to deliberately cross bulls and cows among these breeds, as well as other types of cattle, and thereby produce large numbers of hybrid, or crossbred, beef cattle.

Dual-purpose cattle breeds, such as the British Red Poll and Milking Shorthorn, and the continental European breeds—the Charolais, Simmental, Chianina, and Limousin—are increasing in importance in the United States. Developed to produce both meat and milk, they once also served as draft animals. They are large cattle noted for rapid gain and for producing lean, muscular carcasses. Bulls of these breeds are used for crossbreeding in strictly beef cows. The resulting calves are excellent feedlot cattle. The Brahman, also a dual-purpose breed, was developed in India for draft and milk, although, because cattle are sacred in India, they are seldom slaughtered for beef. In the United States this breed is a favorite in the hot, humid regions where it is especially adapted.

Strictly dairy cattle, such as the Holstein, Jersey, Guernsey, and Ayrshire breeds, are bred mainly for milk production. The average cow of these breeds produces three to four times as much milk as the conventional beef cow. The male calves and the cows that are culled when they are no longer productive contribute perhaps 20 percent of the U.S. beef supply.

Texas, with its 14 million head, is by far the largest cattle-producing state, followed by Nebraska, Kansas, and Iowa. Wisconsin is first in rearing dairy cattle, followed by California, New York, and Pennsylvania. (See also DAIRYING; MEAT AND MEAT PACKING.)

The Process of Raising Beef Cattle

In its simplest form, production of beef cattle for slaughter consists of three steps, resulting in fattened cattle ready for market at 18 to 24 months of age. During the first 6 to 8 months, beef cows nurse their calves on a farm or ranch devoted exclusively to a commercial cow-calf program. Little feed is used, other than pasture or range in summer and possibly some protein concentrate and extra roughage in winter. At weaning time the calves, each weighing about 205 kg (450 lb), are sold to another farmer, a rancher, or a feedlot operator who, during the next 6 to 12 months, raises the calves from the weanling to the feeder stage. Feed consists mostly of high-quality roughage or excellent pasture. At this time the calves, now called yearlings, each weigh about 295 kg (650 lb) and are ready for fattening in a feeder program, where high-concentrate or high-energy rations—balanced with added protein, vitamins, and minerals—are fed in a confinement feedlot for 3 to 5 months. For a calf to reach a slaughter weight of about 500 kg (1,100 lb) at the age of 18 to 24 months, average daily gains of about 1 kg (2 lb) must be achieved.

To prevent the spread of infection and to stimulate growth, feedlot operators add antibiotics to feed, along

(Left) *Beef calves are often sent to feedlots, such as this modern one in California, after they have reached sufficient size. There the calves are confined in enclosed areas and fed specially prepared feed so that they will gain weight quickly and efficiently.* (Below) *Dairy cattle, unlike beef breeds, are usually raised on a single farm. Heifers are slaughtered for veal, and most male calves and nonproducing females are slaughtered without having been fattened in a feedlot.*

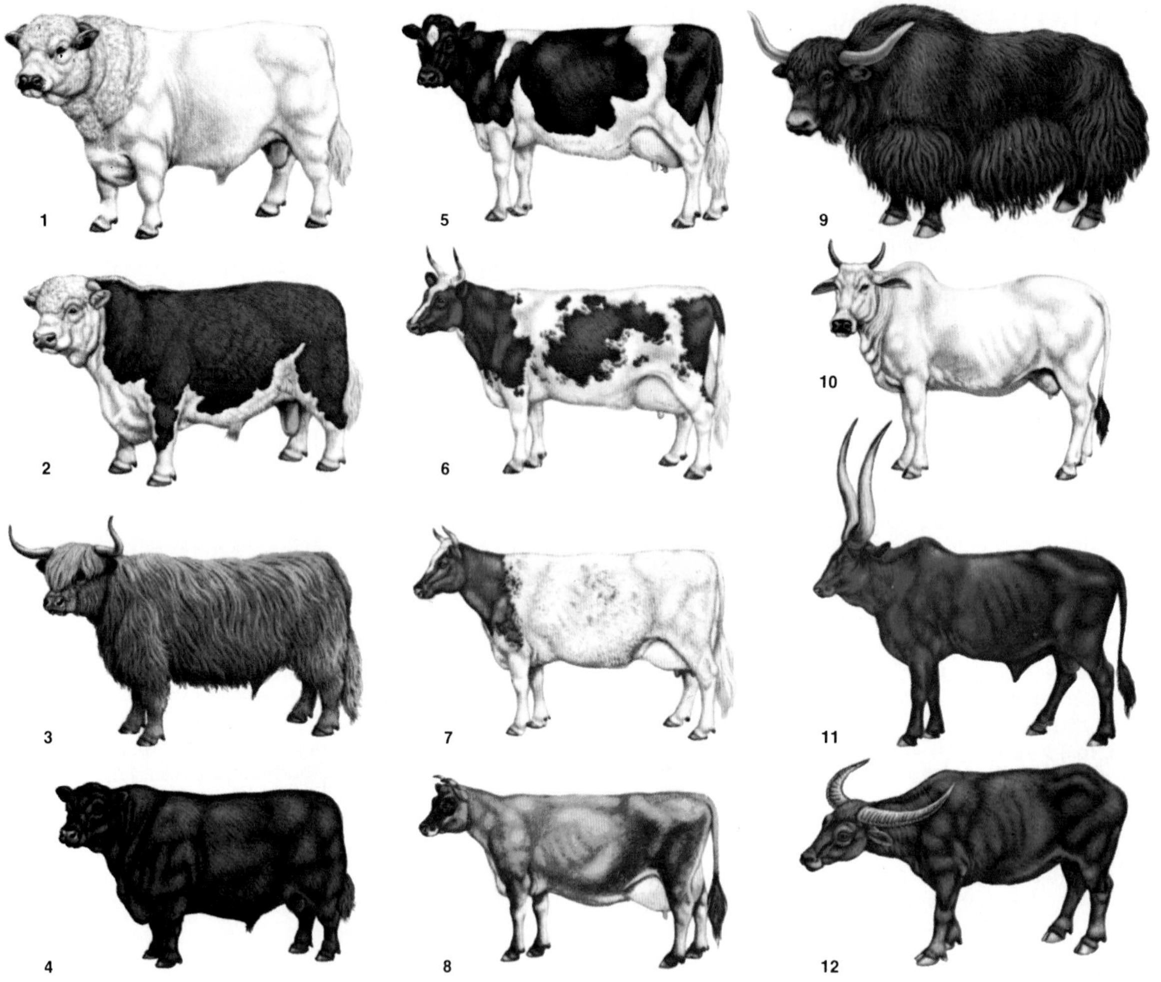

The physical characteristics of domestic cattle vary greatly and depend partly on the purposes for which they have been bred. Beef breeds include the Charolais (1), *Hereford* (2), *Highland* (3), *Angus* (4), *Shorthorn* (7), *and Brahman* (10); *dairy breeds include the Holstein-Friesian* (5), *Ayrshire* (6), *and Jersey* (8). *The Ankole* (11), *a long-horned, dual-purpose breed native to Africa, is a source of beef and dairy products. The yak* (9) *and the water buffalo* (12) *are used primarily in Asia as meat, dairy, and draft animals.*

with growth hormones and vitamin and mineral supplements. Since this practice began, many scientists have warned about the potential for creating drug-resistant bacteria, which could also infect humans. The first direct proof of the existence of such bacteria occurred in 1984, when a salmonella outbreak was traced to contaminated meat. Hormone supplements are also controversial. The European Community has banned the use of hormone implants in its own cattle and in 1988 refused to import U.S. beef because of concerns that hormone residues in the meat would have deleterious health effects.

Catton, Bruce [kat'-uhn] Charles Bruce Catton, b. Petoskey, Mich., Oct. 9, 1899, d. Aug. 28, 1978, was a popular American historian of the Civil War. A former journalist, he became an editor (1954; senior editor from 1959) of *American Heritage* magazine. *A Stillness at Appomattox* (1953), the last of his trilogy on the Army of the Potomac, won a Pulitzer Prize and a National Book Award. His other works include *Centennial History of the Civil War* (3 vols., 1961–65) and a biographical series on Ulysses S. Grant: *Grant Moves South* (1960) and *Grant Takes Command* (1969).

Catullus [kuh-tuhl'-uhs] The Latin poet Gaius Valerius Catullus, *c.*84–54 BC, is known chiefly for his poems to his mistress Lesbia, which since the 16th century have been widely imitated. They include poems of infatuation, despair, and obscene vituperation.

Little is known about the life of Catullus except what

can be learned from his poems. Only one copy of his works survived the Middle Ages, discovered in his birthplace, Verona, in the 14th century. His verse includes longer poems in the learned Greek style, erotic verse to a boy named Juventius, and occasional poems ranging from the bad manners of dinner companions to the sexual excesses of Julius Caesar.

Catullus virtually made a religion of his love for Lesbia—in reality, Clodia, sister of Cicero's archenemy, Clodius Pulcher. In this respect, Catullus was the precursor of the love poets of the next generation—OVID, PROPERTIUS, and Tibullus—as well as of the medieval tradition of COURTLY LOVE. His poetry is widely considered the epitome of lyricism, of direct and impassioned sincerity; yet his verse is also learned and allusive.

Caucasian see RACE

Caucasian languages [kaw-kay'-zhuhn] Caucasian languages are those spoken by about 5.5 million inhabitants of the Caucasus Mountains in the southern USSR. They are remarkable not merely because of their great number and diversity—about 40 languages and 150 dialects in an area the size of France—but also because their linguistic structures differ markedly from those of other languages in Eurasia.

The Caucasian languages fall into three linguistic families—the southern, with about 3.5 million speakers; the northwestern, with about 1 million; and the northeastern, with about 1 million. The southern family is subdivided into Georgian—with 2.7 million speakers—Mingrelo-Laz, and Svan. The northwestern family comprises Abkhaz-Abaza, Circassian, and Ubykh; the northeastern family, Nakh, Avaro-Andi-Dido, Lakk-Dargwa, and Lezghian. Though many of these langauges are spoken by just a few thousand people, only Ubykh, confined to Turkey, seems to be dying out. To date, no convincing relationship has been established between the Caucasian languages and any others.

Caucasus Mountains [kaw'-kuh-suhs] The Caucasus Mountains extend approximately 1,200 km (750 mi) from the Taman Peninsula on the Black Sea to the Apsheron Peninsula on the Caspian Sea in the USSR. Forming a natural boundary between Europe and Asia, they cover 440,000 km^2 (170,000 mi^2) and rise to a maximum elevation of 5,642 m (18,510 ft) in Mount ELBRUS.

The mountain system was formed near the edge of the Alpine Geosyncline, about 25 million years ago. Its more than 2,000 glaciers cover a total area of 2,000 km^2 (772 mi^2). The Greater Caucasus, the main range, separates temperate and subtropical climate zones. The cold slopes facing the Black Sea receive heavy rainfall; the Kura-Araks Lowland on the Caspian Sea is semidesert. The Kura, Sulak, Terek, and Kuma rivers rise in the Caucasus Mountains and flow into the Caspian Sea; the Rioni and Inguri rivers rise in the Caucasus and flow into the Black Sea; and the Kuban River rises in the Caucasus and flows into the Sea of Azov. Mineral resources include petroleum, natural gas, manganese, copper, tungsten, and molybdenum. Livestock is raised on the heavily forested slopes. Wheat is grown in the northern piedmont and citrus fruits, cotton, and tea in the warmer valleys.

The mountains dominate the region known as Cauca-

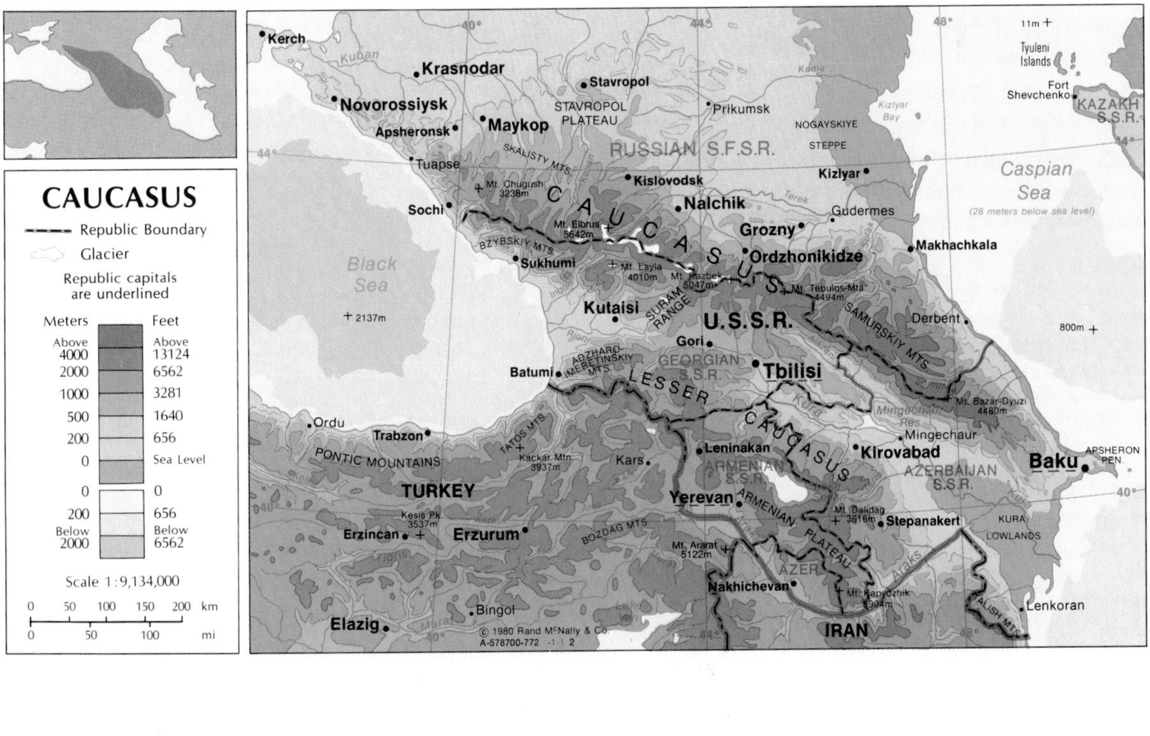

sia, which has apparently long served as a center of human settlement and gave its name to the white race of humankind. The region includes the three Soviet republics of Armenia, Azerbaijan, and Georgia and part of the Russian republic.

Cauchy, Augustin Louis [koh-shee'] Augustin Louis Cauchy, b. Aug. 21, 1789, d. May 23, 1857, was a French mathematician and mathematical physicist who proved (1811) that the angles of a convex POLYHEDRON are determined by its faces (the plane surfaces that bound a geometric solid). Numerous terms in mathematics bear his name, for example, the Cauchy integral theorem, in the theory of complex functions, and the Cauchy-Kovalevskaya existence theorem for the solution of partial DIFFERENTIAL EQUATIONS. Cauchy was the first to make a careful study of the conditions for CONVERGENCE of infinite SERIES; he also gave a rigorous definition of an integral independent of the process of differentiation and developed the mathematical theory of elasticity.

caucus [kaw'-kuhs] A caucus is a meeting of a political group to make decisions about policies or candidates. The caucus was used in the early years of the United States to choose candidates for high office. Today, caucuses are often held at political conventions, as when delegates from a particular state meet to discuss their choice of candidates, sometimes in the proverbial "smoke-filled room." In Congress the members of one party form a caucus to select their leaders and establish policy. Congressional caucuses also choose committees that make important appointments to the standing committees. Caucuses operate similarly in state legislatures, though with less independence.

caudillo [kaw-dee'-yoh] Caudillo ("military leader") was a name given to 19th-century Latin-American dictators. Caudillos arose during times of political instability. They were men of military ability and personal charisma who frequently rose to power by championing the rights of the masses. When Gen. Francisco Franco took power in Spain, he assumed the title *el caudillo.*

cauliflower Cauliflower is a cole crop of the Cruciferae, or CABBAGE, family. It is grown for its white, enlarged flower-head, called a curd. The head develops in the center of a rosette of elongated, blue green leaves and gradually becomes branched and thickened. If it is not harvested, the flower stalks comprising the head elongate and functional flowers develop.

Cauliflower seed is seeded directly or planted in greenhouses or field nurseries to obtain transplants. The highest yields and quality occur when the temperature is between 10° and 20° C (50° and 68° F). Marketable cauliflower is produced in 50 to 70 days after transplanting. Curds are sometimes blanched to produce a snowy white head. This is done by enclosing the curd inside its leaves 5 to 10 days before harvesting.

The head, or curd, of the cauliflower plant, an edible flower cluster up to 0.3 m (1 ft) in diameter, flourishes when the plant is grown under cool and moist conditions.

causality Causality refers to that quality, power, or agency by which one event causes another. The study of causality has centered, in part, on trying to discover and define the connection between cause and effect.

In the 4th century BC, ARISTOTLE offered an analysis of the kinds of causes needed to explain any kind of change. He contended that to account for any alteration, four questions need to be answered, involving four types of causes: (1) the material cause, what the entity is made of; (2) the formal cause, the shape or pattern that the changing entity acquires; (3) the efficient cause, what makes the change occur; and (4) the final cause, the goal toward which the change aims.

Aristotle's doctrine provided a basis for explaining the changes in nature. It also provided a proof used during the Middle Ages for the existence of God—namely, that there must be a first cause of any series of causes, and that is God.

With the advent of modern science in the 17th century, thinkers such as René DESCARTES and GALILEO GALILEI rejected some of Aristotle's explanatory principles and made the efficient cause the central concern of scientific reasoning. Descartes believed that the efficient cause had to contain either the features of the effect or have the power to produce them. In the 18th century, David HUME claimed that no deductive relation exists between cause and effect and that no necessary connection between them is observable. One infers effects from causes and causes from effects because they have been constantly conjoined in one's experience, and one expects (although one cannot prove it) that the future will be like the past. Thus, Hume said, causal reasoning is merely the expectation that constantly conjoined events will remain so in the future. People have no way of telling why events are so conjoined. Immanuel KANT was influenced by Hume and claimed that causality is one of the categories used to classify experience, but that people do not find it in experience.

caustic chemicals Caustic chemicals are those which burn or damage flesh on contact or, more broadly, any corrosive chemicals. The name is derived from the

Greek *kaustos* ("burning"). Some inorganic caustic chemicals are the strong ACIDS AND BASES, such as NITRIC ACID and lye (sodium hydroxide); others—particularly the weak acid hydrofluoric acid, which is used to etch glass—may cause painful, long-lasting burns of the skin. Some organic caustic chemicals are glacial ACETIC ACID, trichloracetic acid, and PHENOL (which is sometimes used as a disinfectant).

In chemistry, the term *caustic* usually refers to one of two compounds, caustic SODA or caustic potash. Caustic soda (lye, NaOH) is a widely used industrial chemical that is also used in the home as a commercial drain cleaner and an oven cleaner. Caustic potash (potassium hydroxide, KOH) is a similar compound used industrially in making soft soap.

In medicine, warts and other undesirable skin growths may be removed by burning them off with lunar caustic (caustic pencil), which is crystallized silver nitrate ($AgNO_3$).

See also: ALKALI.

Cauthen, Steve [kaw'-thuhn] Steve Cauthen, b. Covington, Ky., May 1, 1960, is an American jockey who achieved fame in 1977 when, at the age of 17, he won the greatest number of purses in horse racing. That year he rode a record 487 winners at America's top tracks, becoming the first rider to exceed $6 million in earnings. The Associated Press, the *Sporting News*, and *Sports Illustrated* named him athlete of the year. In 1978, Cauthen rode Affirmed to win the Triple Crown. Paradoxically, he had a 110-race losing streak in 1979, after which he went to England to ride. Except for brief excursions back to the United States, Cauthen remained in Europe, where he enjoyed great success.

Cavafy, C. P. [kah-vah'-fee] Constantine Peter Cavafy, b. Apr. 17, 1863, d. Apr. 29, 1933, was a renowned modern Greek poet. After living in England and Istanbul, Cavafy returned to his native Alexandria, where he remained. Except for 21 privately printed poems, he published no verse during his life, although E. M. Forster's *Pharos and Pharillon* (1923) contained an essay on his poetry. His *Poems* (Eng. trans., 1951), a collection of 154 short poems, appeared in 1935. Out of the ancient Hellenistic world Cavafy created his own universe inhabited by both historical and fictional characters. His sensual poems, set in modern Alexandria, explore homosexual love.

Cavalier poets The Cavaliers were a group of 17th-century gentlemen poets loyal to Charles I during the English Civil War, and to his son Charles following the king's execution. Their love lyrics display the urbanity and graceful wit associated with the life of the Renaissance court. At its best, Cavalier poetry delicately evokes the pathos of fleeting love. Chief among the Cavalier poets were Thomas CAREW, Robert HERRICK, Richard LOVELACE, and Sir John SUCKLING.

Cavaliers The Cavaliers were the royalist supporters of King CHARLES I during the ENGLISH CIVIL WAR (1642–48). Their opponents, the parliamentarians, were known as ROUNDHEADS. After the RESTORATION (1660), the term *cavalier* continued to be used to signify a royalist and staunch Anglican; it was eventually replaced by the term *tory* (see also TORY PARTY).

cavalry The term *cavalry* originally referred to that branch of an army in which soldiers were mounted and fought on horseback. In modern times, however, horses have been largely replaced by motor-powered vehicles.

Both the Assyrian and the Persian armies used mounted soldiers as early as the 8th century BC, but the Macedonians Philip II and his son Alexander the Great were probably the first to use cavalry as a principal attack force (4th century BC). The Carthaginian general HANNIBAL used both horse- and elephant-mounted cavalry against the Romans in the Second PUNIC WAR (218–01 BC), but the Romans finally deployed superior cavalry against him in the Battle of Zama (202 BC). In China cavalry was used extensively from the 3d century BC up to the 19th century AD.

Perhaps the most successful use of cavalry was by the MONGOLS who invaded Europe in the 13th century. Their armies, composed entirely of mounted horsemen, were divided into heavy cavalry units whose fighters wore leather armor and carried the lance as their principal weapon, and light cavalry archers who wore no armor and whose function it was to screen and support the heavy cavalry, the main attack force. Moving swiftly in precise formation, these mounted armies established an empire that extended from Germany to the Sea of Japan.

The Mongols demonstrated the value of a highly mobile cavalry, but in medieval Europe, as both horse and rider became more heavily armored, the great advantage of maneuverability was gradually lost. Mounted KNIGHTS were the shock troops of the feudal armies, but with the development of the crossbow and longbow, both capable of piercing armor, the clumsy, slow-moving knight on horseback became a vulnerable target.

The introduction of firearms in the 16th and 17th centuries changed the nature of warfare, as did the development of large standing armies. The cavalry resumed its function as a mobile, maneuverable striking force and was classified as one of the three permanent units of the army—with light-armed infantry and heavy artillery. Cavalry forces attained their final pinnacle of effectiveness as used by NAPOLEON I at the beginning of the 19th century. He divided his cavalry into a screening force of light cavalry that covered the army's advance, and a reserve of heavy cavalry that led the attack.

Cavalry was used extensively in the United States during the wars against the Indians and the Civil War. Increasingly, however, it was assigned the tasks of scouting and raiding, and the old-fashioned cavalry charge was found to be less and less effective against defenses such as repeating rifles, machine guns, trenches, and barbed

The battlefield mobility of the mounted soldier, or cavalryman, has been a decisive element in warfare throughout the ages. Depicted in the top row (left to right) *are a Roman cavalryman, a medieval English knight in battle armor, and, from the English Civil War of the 17th century, a cavalryman from Oliver Cromwell's "Ironsides" regiment. In the bottom row* (left to right) *are a French* hussar *from the Napoleonic Wars, a German* uhlan *from the 1870s, and, from the Spanish-American War, a "Rough Rider" from the 1st U.S. Volunteer Cavalry.*

wire. Cavalry continued to be used, however, in rough terrain and under other special circumstances. During World War I, cavalry was effectively used only in Palestine and, to a limited extent, in eastern Europe. Horse cavalry was still used during World War II by some countries, although only the Russians had any success with it against mechanized forces. The Chinese employed cavalry during the Korean War (1950–53) and maintained several divisions of horse cavalry as late as 1976.

Between the world wars the horse was supplanted in most armies by tanks, armored cars, and other mechanized equipment. In today's armies mechanized forces have taken over all the functions of the cavalry. Helicopters, however, were used in both the Korean and Vietnam wars in a way that was reminiscent of classic cavalry tactics; the U.S. Army even named one helicopter unit the First Cavalry Division (Airmobile).

Cavan [kav'-uhn] Cavan is a sparsely populated county in north central Ireland, immediately south of the border with Northern Ireland. The population is 53,965 (1986), and it covers 1,891 km^2 (730 mi^2). The town of Cavan is the county seat. The county is a hilly area with many lakes, some of which are linked to the River Erne. Dairy farming and hog raising are the principal economic activities, although some agriculture, mostly potato growing, takes place. Cavan became part of the province of Ulster early in the 17th century; it was subsequently colonized by English and Scottish settlers. In 1921, Cavan was one of three Ulster counties that became part of the Irish Free State.

cave Caves and caverns (large caves) are natural cavities in rock. They range from a few meters to many kilometers in length; the MAMMOTH CAVE–Flint Ridge System in Kentucky, the longest known cave in the world, contains more than 300 km (186 mi) of mapped passages. Although caves are traditionally defined as including a zone of total darkness, archaeologists use the word *cave* to mean any area sheltered by an overhanging ledge. Most caves develop in LIMESTONE that is permeable to water, although some (perhaps 10 percent) are formed as LAVA tubes in volcanic terrain.

Limestone caves are created by slightly acidic water that slowly dissolves the rock along fractures or cracks. Surface water absorbs carbon dioxide from the atmosphere and soil to produce diluted carbonic acid, which

Illustrated in this cutaway view of a limestone cave are: a swallow hole, where a stream enters underground (1); a "moon-milk" gel, or soft paste, deposit of calcium carbonate (2); carbonate terraced structures formed by pools of water overflowing from one block of stone to another (3); carrot-shaped stalactites hanging from the ceiling (4), strawlike stalactites (5), and platelike stalagmites—all built up as parallel layers of disks (6); vertical potholes, where streams formerly entered underground (7); rubble of blocks or slabs of rock from a collapsed roof (8); columns resulting from the joining of a stalactite and a stalagmite (9); blind animals with unpigmented skin that have adapted to the subterranean dark (10); and a drip-curtain stalactite deposited from a long crack in the ceiling (11). Other features depicted inlcude: a "siphon," or part of an underground stream with the cave roof below its surface (12); a balcony structure of stalactite groups formed along a ledge (13); a stalagmite with balconies and stalactites attached (14); a gallery, or horizontal passage carved out by a former stream (15); a fir-cone stalagmite (16); a chamber, which is a larger and higher opening than a gallery (17); eccentric stalactites with contorted shapes caused by water evaporation with carbonate deposition in turbulent air (18); wall paintings and other remains left by prehistoric humans (19); a resurgence, or opening in the ground, from which a subterranean stream reappears (20); and a fossil resurgence, corresponding to a former water-table level (21).

percolates down to the WATER TABLE, or saturated zone, where it slowly circulates and dissolves the limestone. In time, large rooms and long passages may be formed. If the water table drops or the land rises, the water in these rooms and passages drains away, leaving the chambers dry. If the water table rises or falls more than once, passages develop on several levels.

If the surface above the cave collapses, sinkholes develop. Areas where these collapse features are particularly numerous are said to display karst topography. Sinkholes provide vertical access for surface streams and animals. Where caves are intersected by streams cutting downward from the surface, entrances are formed that provide horizontal access.

Although cave interiors are usually dark, caverns such as the LURAY CAVERNS in Virginia and Carlsbad Caverns in New Mexico are famous for their varied and majestic rock formations. Columns rising 15 m (50 ft) from the floor, called stalagmites, and iciclelike stalactites may develop if water continues to seep into the cave after it has been formed (see STALACTITES AND STALAGMITES). These formations are all secondary mineral deposits, mainly travertine. If the water carries other minerals into the cave, the formations may be multicolored. In addition, caves may contain beds of silt or mud; calcite veins etched into relief when the walls of the cave were dissolved; columns resulting from the connection of a stalactite and a stalagmite; and thin, translucent sheets of calcite, called drapery, hanging down from the ceiling 3 m (10 ft) or more.

The interior of a cave is divided into three zones. The environment of the entrance zone is similar to that of the surface, and may serve as a place of shelter for many animals. Humans have used entrance zones as shelters and burial grounds since prehistoric times. Such zones are therefore of interest to archaeologists. Alabama's Russell Cave, for example, has yielded a sequence of human habitation dating back almost 9,000 years.

Next is the twilight zone, which is sheltered from direct sunlight and normally has a more moderate environment than above ground. This zone is host to a large, diverse population of animals such as salamanders, bats, and, during severe winters, bears. Some animals hibernate in the twilight zone; others find the cave a convenient shelter, although they usually leave it to feed.

The dark zone, which is the true cave environment, is a generally stable region. Perpetually dark, it has only slight seasonal changes in temperature, few if any air currents, and a constant relative humidity of nearly 100 percent. The dark zone is inhabited by animals that have adapted to the world of darkness, including hundreds of species of small shrimp, crayfish, millipedes, beetles, spiders, fish, and salamanders. These animals, collectively known as troglodytes, are usually blind (some lack eyes altogether). They have little or no skin pigmentation and thin cuticles (outer coverings). Many have long antennae or feelers to compensate for the lack of eyes, and all seem to require much less food than do their surface relatives. Since no green plants grow in caves, these animals are dependent either on food that is washed in by streams or mud or on bat droppings (GUANO). In good weather, bats leave the cave daily to feed on insects or, in some cases, plants. Caves in the southwestern United States and in Mexico have colonies of bats as large as 10 million. Guano accumulates on the floors of these caves, sometimes many meters deep, and becomes food for dozens of troglodytic species. It is sometimes mined as a source of nitrate for fertilizer or for SALTPETER, which was used to manufacture gunpowder in the 19th century.

Early humans created art in the dark zones of caves such as those at ALTAMIRA in Spain. These CAVE DWELLERS may also have worshiped in them. Dozens of caves containing paintings, pictographs, and statues up to 20,000 years old have been found in the Dordogne Valley of France, site of the famous Grotte de LASCAUX. In addition, animal bones thousands of years old are commonly found in dark zones. Entire skeletons have been preserved intact because of the absence of WEATHERING.

Some caves are open to the public. These so-called show caves have walkways, lights, and often elevators. Otherwise, cave exploration is a dangerous and exacting task that requires long periods of arduous work with self-contained sources of light. Cave explorers, called spelunkers or speleologists, must be familiar with map reading, climbing techniques, and underwater diving. Because cave animals and minerals are relatively rare, they should not be collected without professional guidance.

cave dwellers Caves have been the sites of human occupation for hundreds of thousands of years. Living in caves, even with the benefit of fire, may not have been very safe in prehistoric times. Most cave dwellers probably did not occupy the deeper recesses, but rather lived near openings and in the area of overhangs.

Earliest Examples. Present evidence suggests that the first definite cave occupation coincided with the controlled use of fire. This may have happened first in colder climates, as is indicated by the earliest evidence of cave-dwelling HOMO ERECTUS. Hearths that may be 750,000 years old have been found in southeastern France in the cave of l'Escale. The best evidence for early cave occupation is from the Chinese site of Zhoukoudian, near Beijing. Excavations in this 500,000-year-old cave have yielded numerous fossilized remains of *Homo erectus.* The presence of charred animal bone suggests that these protohumans cooked their food and used fire to harden antler tips and wooden-tipped spears.

The 200,000-year-old French site of Tautavel has yielded a fossilized prehuman face that represents a transitional form between *Homo erectus* and more advanced species of early humans. Although no human remains have been found in the Lazaret cave in southern France, dating to about 150,000 years ago, much has been learned about the life-styles of its ancient game-hunting occupants. The remains of tents, probably made of animal hides stretched over a wooden framework, were found in the cave, with the tent entrances facing away from the cave opening. A wolf skull was situated inside the doorway of each tent, perhaps placed there to guard the dwelling or to bring good luck in the hunt.

Neanderthal Caves. The traditional idea of the prehistoric "caveman" comes from sites yielding bones of NEANDERTHALERS, who lived some 75,000 to 45,000 years ago. The classic Neanderthal cave sites were found in the early 1900s in the Dordogne of France and include La Chapelle-aux-Saints, La Ferrassie, Le Moustier, and others. Much is known about these people and their lifeways. The Neanderthalers probably occupied the caves on a seasonal basis, taking advantage of their protection from the cold and wild animals in the winter. It is likely that the cave entrances were covered with skins, while inside, inhabitants made clothing and tools, butchered game, prepared food, and engaged in other activities.

The Neanderthalers' appreciation for art, symbolism, and religion is reflected in cave burials, in which animal bones and stone tools were placed with the body, perhaps to equip the deceased for the afterlife. The now extinct cave bear, *Ursus spelaeus*, was a favored game animal and may also have been invested with magical powers. At the cave site of Drachenloch in the Swiss Alps, several cave bear skulls were discovered buried together. Red or yellow ocher and other pigments have been found in excavations of Neanderthal cave sites, suggesting that Neanderthalers may have painted themselves for rituals or before a hunt. At the cave site of Shanidar in Iraq, pollen grains of eight different types of flowers were found in the burial site of a 40-year-old man.

Cro-Magnon Caves. A dramatic change in cave occupation occurred about 30,000 to 40,000 years ago with the advent of CRO-MAGNON MAN. The appearance of this anatomically modern human coincides with elaborate cave decoration (see PREHISTORIC ART). Wall paintings and engravings of animals have often been found in long galleries deep inside caves. These deep recesses, which in some cases could only be entered with light from lamps or torches, may have been sites for places of religious activities. In such famous caves as ALTAMIRA, LASCAUX, NIAUX, and others, ivory, stone, and bone carvings of horses, mammoths, and even humans, such as the VENUS OF WILLENDORF, have also been found.

More Recent Cave Sites. In the New World, evidence of cave-dwelling people dating to around 10,000 years ago has been found at Ventana Cave in Arizona and elsewhere. The most remarkable North American cave sites are those of the prehistoric CLIFF DWELLERS of the southwestern United States, who occupied the famous Mesa Verde site in about AD 1000. In some remote places in the world, caves and rock shelters are believed to be in use much the same way they were used in prehistoric times. A group of cave-dwellers, the TASADAY, were discovered in the Philippines in 1971, but some investigators have labeled the find a hoax.

See also: PREHISTORIC HUMANS.

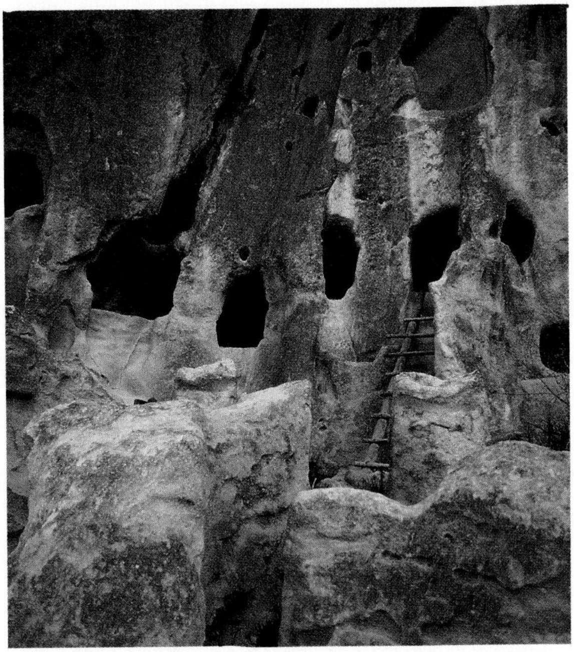

The Anasazi people dug caves in volcanic tuft at the base of Frijoles Canyon. Now under preservation at the Bandelier National Monument in north central New Mexico, the caves were in use from about AD 1200 to 1600.

The Lascaux cave paintings near the town of Montignac, in southwestern France, are perhaps the most extensive cultural remains dating from the late Aurignacian period (c.15,000 BC).

cave fish Most cave fish (fish that live exclusively in caves) are blind or nearly so. The famous blind cave fish from Mexico, *Astyanax mexicanus*, appears to have no eyes; the orbits are vestigial and overgrown with skin. In North America there is a family of five species (Amblyopsidae) named cave fish; all are blind or have extremely small eyes. Amblyopsid cave fish are distributed throughout the limestone cave regions of the central United States, except for *Chologaster cornuta*, the rice fish, which is not found in caves but in dark swamps.

Cave-dwelling species tend to be pale; their bodies lack pigment as a result of living in environments with little or no light. Blind cave-dwelling fish have heightened acuity of the other senses. In some cases extra tactile organs are distributed on the skin. Despite the fact that these fish are rarely if ever seen in open waters, they are very widely distributed, probably through extensive underground channels.

Cavendish, Henry The English chemist and physicist Henry Cavendish, b. Oct. 10, 1731, d. Feb. 24, 1810, was the first to recognize HYDROGEN gas as a distinct substance. Cavendish attended Cambridge University from 1749 to 1753 but left without a degree. After touring Europe with his brother, he lived frugally in London, even after an inheritance made him one of the wealthiest men in England.

Cavendish approached most of his investigations through quantitative measurements. In order to establish that hydrogen gas was a substance entirely different from ordinary air, he calculated their densities as well as the densities of several other gases. He found that common air is made up of four parts nitrogen out of five (4:1 ratio) by volume. He also showed that water is composed of oxygen and hydrogen. Cavendish's measurements of freezing points showed the existence of compositions that yield maximum and minimum freezing points.

Cavendish compared the electrical conductivities of equivalent solutions of electrolytes and expressed a version of OHM'S LAW. His last major work was the first measurement of Sir Isaac NEWTON's gravitational constant, together with the mass and density of the Earth. The accuracy of this experiment was not improved on for nearly a century.

Cavendish, Thomas Thomas Cavendish, b. *c.*1555, d. 1592, was an English navigator whose expedition was the third (after those of Ferdinand Magellan and Sir Francis Drake) to sail around the world. The voyage, which began in July 1586, took him to Patagonia in South America, where he discovered Cape Desire, and through the Straits of Magellan to the Pacific. Cavendish returned to England in September 1588; only one of his three ships completed the journey, however.

Cavendish Laboratory Cambridge University's Cavendish Laboratory for experimental physics was founded in 1871 with funds from Spencer Compton Cavendish, 8th duke of Devonshire. It gained world fame under successive holders of the Cavendish chair: James Clerk Maxwell, Lord Rayleigh, J. J. Thomson, Ernest Rutherford, Lawrence Bragg, and Nevill Mott. Achievements there include discovery of the electron and neutron, development of the cloud chamber, and the first artificial disintegration of an atomic nucleus. All buildings of the Cambridge physics department are now called the Cavendish Laboratories.

caviar Caviar, a gourmet delicacy, is the roe, or eggs, of the sturgeon, which has been pressed into cakes or preserved in brine. Today nearly all genuine caviar comes from Russian or Iranian sturgeon—both in dwindling supply because of overfishing and pollution. Sturgeon eggs vary in color from black to gray, yellow, green, or brown. Less-costly caviar varieties are the red eggs from North Atlantic salmon and the roes of whitefish, lake herring, cod, and carp, which are usually dyed black when processed.

Cavour, Camillo Benso, Conte di [kah-voor,' kah-meel'-oh bayn'-soh, kawn'-tay dee] Camillo Benso di Cavour, b. Aug. 10, 1810, d. June 6, 1861, was a Piedmontese statesman of the RISORGIMENTO who was largely responsible for unifying Italy under the House of SAVOY. The son of a prominent Turin family, Cavour became a page to Prince Charles Albert of Sardinia-Piedmont in 1824. Two years later he was banished from the conservative Turin court because of his liberal tendencies.

Going to Genoa as a military engineer in 1830, Cavour became involved in radical politics. He visited England and France and in 1835 began a career as a financier and industrialist. In 1847 he founded the Turin newspaper *Il Risorgimento*, which championed liberal constitutionalism and a war against Austria. In 1848 he was elected to parliament and two years later was made minister of agriculture, industry, and commerce. In 1852 the new king of Sardinia-Piedmont, VICTOR EMMANUEL II, named him premier.

Cavour's modernization of Sardinia-Piedmont made it a model for the rest of Italy. He won the support of NAPOLEON III of France for the liberation of northern Italy by a joint war against Austria in 1859. Napoleon abruptly halted this conflict soon after Lombardy, but not Venetia, had been won. Although Cavour resigned in protest, he continued to work for the annexation of Romagna, Parma, Modena, and Tuscany. Soon afterward, he returned to office and struck a bargain with Napoleon whereby Piedmont gained these regions in exchange for ceding Savoy and Nice to France.

Cavour's relationship with Giuseppe GARIBALDI during the latter's invasion of Sicily in 1860 is unclear, but he seized this opportunity to weld Italy into one kingdom. On the pretext of preventing Garibaldi from taking Rome, Cavour sent the Piedmontese army across the papal frontier and deprived PIUS IX of most of his territory. In 1861,

Chief minister to King Victor Emmanuel II of Sardinia-Piedmont, the conte di Cavour enlisted French aid to expel Austrian power from Italy and unite the country under Victor Emmanuel's rule. (Francesco Hayez; Pinacoteca di Brera, Milan.)

Cavour became the first premier of the newly proclaimed Kingdom of Italy, and he tried in vain to get the pope to accept "a free church in a free state" policy that would open the way for Rome to be the capital.

cavy [kay'-vee] Cavies are any of several rodents belonging to the order Rodentia. A well-known cavy is the GUINEA PIG, which is often kept as a pet and is used as a laboratory animal, especially in biomedical research. Cavies have stocky bodies and short hind legs and ears; the coat varies from smooth to coarse. The hind feet have three digits and the forefeet four digits, all equipped with sharp claws. There are 5 genera and 23 species of cavies. All are found in South America, where they live in savannas, rocky areas, forest edges, and swamps. The long-legged, rabbitlike mara, or Patagonian cavy, genus *Dolichotis*, inhabits arid regions. It is the largest cavy, weighing up to 16 kg (35 lb) and measuring 76 cm (30 in) in length.

Most cavies dig burrows or use abandoned burrows of other animals. They are gregarious, associating in groups of five to ten. Cavies eat many kinds of plant material, including grass, leaves, buds, and garden plants. Although some species are diurnal, most are nocturnal.

The Patagonian cavy or mara can gallop at speeds of up to 30 km/h (19 mph) and may also move with rabbitlike hops.

Caxton, William William Caxton, b. *c.*1422, d. 1491, was a merchant and writer who established the first printing press in England, in 1476. About 1471, Caxton visited Cologne, where he learned the art of printing; he later founded a press in Bruges, Belgium. In 1477, Caxton's press at Westminster produced *Dictes or Sayenges of the Phylosophers*, the first dated book printed in England. Caxton subsequently published more than 90 editions, including works by Chaucer, Gower, and Malory, as well as his own translations of French and Latin works.

Cayenne [kay-en'] Cayenne is the capital and main port of French Guiana and has a population of 38,135 (1982). It lies off the north central coast of South America on the island of Cayenne. Exports include timber, gold, essence of rosewood, and rum. Founded by the French in 1643, the city was resettled in 1664 after it had been razed by Indians. Cayenne was held twice by the Dutch during the 17th century. Penal colonies, including the infamous DEVIL'S ISLAND, were maintained by the French from about 1885 to 1946.

cayenne pepper see PEPPER (VEGETABLE)

Cayman Islands [kay'-muhn] The Cayman Islands are a British colony in the Caribbean Sea, about 160 km (100 mi) south of Cuba and 240 km (150 mi) northwest of Jamaica. The group is composed of three low-lying coral islands: Grand Cayman, where Georgetown, the capital, and an international airport are located; Little Cayman; and Cayman Brac. The total area is 306 km^2 (118 mi^2). The population (1987 est., 22,000) is divided between British and native islanders, who speak Spanish. Fishing, tourism, and banking are the chief economic activities. Discovered by Christopher Columbus in 1503, the islands were taken over by the British about 1670.

Cayuga [kay-yoo'-guh] The Cayuga, a North American Indian people, were one of the five original members of the IROQUOIS LEAGUE. They traditionally lived in an area extending westward from between the Skaneateles and Owasco lakes to Seneca Lake in central New York. The "people at the landing, or at the mucky land," as they were called, spoke an Iroquoian language which closely resembled that spoken by their Seneca neighbors to the west. They were bordered on the east by the Onondaga. The league's grand council had ten sachems, or chiefs, from the Cayuga tribe. Like the Seneca, Onondaga, Mohawk, and Oneida tribes, the Cayuga lived in bark-covered longhouses and were an agricultural people whose staples were maize, beans, and squash. Women tended gardens and gathered wild plant foods; men cleared fields, hunted, traded, and engaged in warfare. Subsistence activities were symbolically and ritualistically represented in a yearly round of religious ceremonies. Matrilineality dominated the family, social, and political structures. During the American Revolution the Cayuga joined the Seneca and Mohawk tribes in supporting the British. Today, members of the tribe are found at the Cattaraugas, Tonawanda, and Allegany reserves in New York, at the Six Nations Reserve, Ontario, and on reserved land in Oklahoma.

Cayuse [ky-yoos'] The Cayuse are a North American Indian tribe that aboriginally occupied parts of southeastern Washington State and northeastern Oregon. Their language is related to the Sahaptin–Nez Percé branch of the Penutian linguistic family. Traditionally, salmon fishing dominated their subsistence activities. A seminomadic people, they lived in small extended families in semisubterranean houses, with residence determined according to male ancestry. Social and political organization was influenced by the cultures of neighboring Plains Indians. Tribal chiefs and councils ruled, and shamans were both religious and social leaders.

The physician and missionary Marcus WHITMAN established a mission among the Cayuse in 1836. After a period of white encroachment and growing hostilities, a band of Cayuse massacred (1847) Whitman, his family, and several others, blaming them for a measles outbreak among their tribespeople. The settlers subdued the Cayuse and confined them in 1855 to the Umatilla Reservation. In recent years Cayuse tribal members have lived on reservations in Oregon, Washington, and Idaho.

CB radio see CITIZENS BAND RADIO

CBS see RADIO AND TELEVISION BROADCASTING

Ceauşescu, Nicolae [choh-shes'-koo, nee-koh-ly'] As leader of his country's Communist party, Nicolae Ceauşescu, b. Jan. 26, 1918, d. Dec. 25, 1989, dominated Romania from 1965 to 1989. He became prime minister in 1967 and president of the republic in 1974. Always a maverick among Eastern European leaders, in his early years he charted a course independent of the USSR and cultivated friendly relations with the West. At home, however, his regime became increasingly repressive and unpopular. After he brutally tried to crush protests against his rule, he was overthrown and executed with his wife and associate, Elena Ceauşescu.

Cebu (city) [say-boo'] Cebu, a city of 552,200 (1984 est.) people on the east coast of Cebu island, is the capital of Cebu province and the oldest Spanish settlement in the Philippines. Its bustling port, protected by outlying Mactan Island, handles most interisland commodities and is second only to Manila in international trade.

Already a thriving port when Ferdinand Magellan arrived in 1521, it was chosen as the site of the first Spanish colony in the archipelago in 1565. Today, it retains considerable Spanish influence. Occupied by the Japanese during World War II, Cebu was heavily damaged by both U.S. and Japanese forces. The city is a Roman Catholic archbishopric and the seat of the University of San Carlos (1595), the University of the Southern Philippines (1927), the University of the Visayas (1919), and Southwestern University (1946).

Cebu (island) Cebu, one of the Visayan Islands, is a main island of the Philippines, of which it and small nearby islands form a province. Its area is 4,422 km^2 (1,707 mi^2), and its maximum elevation (Mount Cabalasan) is 1,013 m (3,325 ft). The provincial population of 3,301,000 (1989 est.) is of Malayan and Spanish descent. A volcanic island largely overlaid with coral, Cebu has a mountainous interior. On coastal plains, peanuts, maguey, corn, rice, sugarcane, cotton, hemp, and tobacco are grown. The island's exports include copra, sugar, molasses, copper, and pyrites. Coal is mined, and oil deposits have been found. The provincial capital, Cebu, is an important port. Cebu became known to Europeans with the arrival of Ferdinand Magellan in 1521. The Spanish made their first Philippine settlements on Cebu in 1565 and held the island until the Spanish-American War; it came under U.S. administration in 1901.

Cecilia, Saint Saint Cecilia, the patroness of music and musicians, was a 2d- or 3d-century Roman Christian martyr. According to tradition, she refused to worship the Roman gods and was beheaded. Her association with music probably stems from a medieval misreading of a statement in the *Acts*, a 5th-century account of her life. Feast day: Nov. 22.

cedar True cedars are evergreen trees of the genus *Cedrus* in the PINE family, Pinaceae, native to mountainous areas of the Middle East and extending into the Himalayas. The trees, pyramidal when young, often develop massive trunks and tablelike branches as they age, and the grayish bark of the young trees becomes deeply furrowed. The needlelike leaves last for 3 to 6 years; except for terminal shoots, they are borne in tufted masses. The large, short-stalked cones are erect, barrel-shaped, and resinous. The four *Cedrus* species are the Atlas cedar, *C. atlantica*, of northern Africa; the deodar, *C. deodara*, a commercially harvested tree of the Himalayas; the biblical cedar of Lebanon, *C. libani*, now scarce in Lebanon but still found wild in the Taurus Mountains; and *C. brevifola*, native to the island of Cyprus. All four species are used along the Pacific coast and in temperate areas of the eastern United States as landscape plants.

The cedar of Lebanon, a large tree native to the Middle East, supplied the wood used by Solomon, king of ancient Israel, to build his great temple. It grows to about 30 m (100 ft) high.

The fragrant "cedar" woods used to make chests, boxes, closet linings, and other articles of commerce come mainly not from *Cedrus* but from other tree genera. These include *Juniperus* (see JUNIPER), *Cedrela* (see MAHOGANY), and *Thuja* (see ARBORVITAE), along with several other species.

Cedar Rapids Cedar Rapids, a city in east central Iowa on the Cedar River, is the seat of Linn County. It has a population of 108,751 (1990). Located in the middle of the Corn Belt, the city is a rail and distribution center for grain, livestock, and industrial products. Its diversified industries process foods and manufacture farm and road machinery, electronic equipment, paper and plastic products, pharmaceuticals, and gymnastic equipment. Settled in 1838 and named Rapids City, it was renamed Cedar Rapids after incorporation as a town in 1849.

Cela, Camilo José [thay'-lah] Camilo José Cela, b. May 11, 1916, is an important contemporary Spanish writer with a penchant for strong, brutal realism. His first novel, *The Family of Pascual Duarte* (1942; Eng. trans., 1964), is the story of a man who murders his mother. The experimental *The Hive* (1951; Eng. trans., 1953) describes the clash of personalities in impoverished Madrid. *Mrs. Caldwell Speaks to Her Son* (1953; Eng. trans., 1968), which is about incest, again experiments with new narrative forms. In 1989, Cela was awarded the Nobel Prize for literature.

celadon Celadon is the name for stoneware decorated with a gray green or gray blue glaze. The celadon colors result from a process known as the wood-ash glaze technique, perfected by the Chinese during the 3d century AD. Chinese celadons, produced through the Qing period (1644–1911), are valued for their subtlety of color, hard jadelike surface, and high transparency. Celadon wares were also produced in Japan, Korea, and Siam.

Celan, Paul [se-lah'] The poet Paul Celan, b. Paul Antschel in Romania on Nov. 23, 1920, d. May 1, 1970, is considered the most important German-language poet of post–World War II Europe. Celan was a student of languages and a long-time resident of Paris, and his poetry shows obvious surrealist influences. His overriding theme is the Holocaust, and his best-known poem, "Death Fugue," is an evocation of Auschwitz. Celan's second published collection, *Mohn und Gedächtnis* (Poppy and Memory, 1952), established his reputation in Europe, but English translations of his work are few: his own selection, *Speech Grille and Selected Poems* (1957; Eng. trans., 1971), and several volumes of selections made by his translators.

celery Celery, *Apium graveolens*, is a vegetable that is grown for its thickened stalk, which is eaten raw or cooked. It belongs to the parsley family, Umbelliferae. Indigenous to the countries of the Mediterranean and Eurasia, the plant was long valued as a medicinal herb.

Celery is normally a biennial, producing fleshy stalks with pungent leaves the first year and a 1-m (3-ft) flower stalk the second year. Usually grown from transplanted, greenhouse-raised seedlings, it requires a rich, moist soil and a long, cool growing season. A related vegetable, celeriac, is grown for its large, edible root.

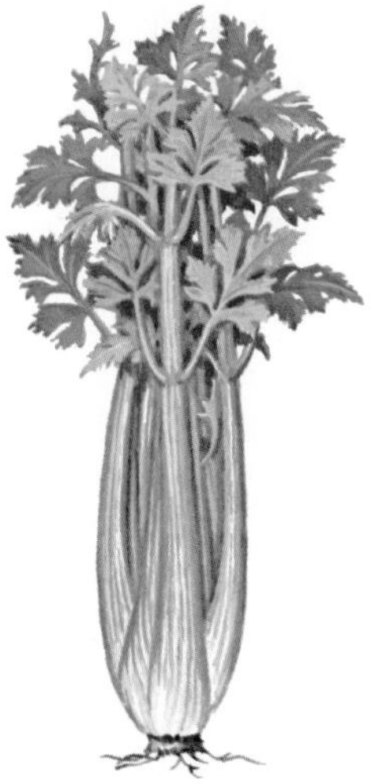

The vegetable celery is not well adapted to home gardens because it requires very rich soil and up to half a year of rather cool temperatures to mature. Older varieties also required blanching, which was accomplished by hilling up earth around the stalks or using boards to exclude the light. The unblanched and self-blanching varieties available today are somewhat easier to grow.

celesta [se-les'-tuh] The celesta, a keyboard percussion instrument that looks like a small piano, has hammers that strike steel bars resting over wooden resonators. It has a range of five octaves and can play chords. Invented by Auguste Mustel in 1886, it was used by Peter Ilich Tchaikovsky in his ballet *The Nutcracker Suite* (1892) and by Richard Strauss in *Der Rosenkavalier* (1911). The celesta is used almost entirely as an orchestral instrument and is frequently a part of opera and ballet orchestras.

The celesta is a small keyboard instrument that produces clear, chiming tones. Invented in 1886, the celesta operates like a piano, with hammers striking steel plates rather than strings.

celestial mechanics Celestial mechanics is a branch of science concerned with the investigation of the movement of bodies in space.

The field originated 300 years ago with Isaac NEWTON, and most of its foundations and calculations are still based on Newtonian MECHANICS and Newton's law of GRAVITATION. In spite of contributions to the subject by mathematicians such as L. EULER, P. S. LAPLACE, J. L. LAGRANGE, K. F. GAUSS, H. POINCARÉ, and G. D. Birkhoff, many unsolved problems remain. Newton solved only the problem of the motion of two bodies, and he generalized KEPLER'S LAWS. If there are more than two bodies, as is the case for nearly all problems posed in nature, no precise solution exists. For such problems the motion can often be considered in terms of small modifications, called PERTURBATIONS, of Keplerian motion.

See also: ASTRONAUTICS; THREE-BODY PROBLEM.

celestial sphere The celestial sphere is an imaginary sphere surrounding the Earth, on which the stars seem to be placed and which seems to rotate from east to west. Ancient astronomers believed this actually to be the case, with the stars as crystal studs, or distant holes through which fire is observed. Usually the Earth is put at its center, forming the so-called geocentric celestial sphere, the basis for the standard COORDINATE SYSTEM in astronomy. The axis of rotation of the Earth extends to meet this sphere in the north and south celestial poles. The celestial equator (or equinoctial) is the great circle midway between the poles. The yearly path of the Sun across the celestial sphere is a great circle called the ECLIPTIC. The points in the ecliptic furthest north and south of the celestial equator are called the summer and winter solstices. The points where the Sun crosses the equator moving north or south are called the vernal or autumnal EQUINOXES. Because of the Earth's rotation, the celestial sphere appears to rotate once every sidereal day. This is about four minutes shorter than the mean solar day because of the Sun's motion.

See also: ORBITAL ELEMENTS.

This imaginary celestial sphere is used as a standard frame of reference by astronomers in plotting geocentric coordinate systems.

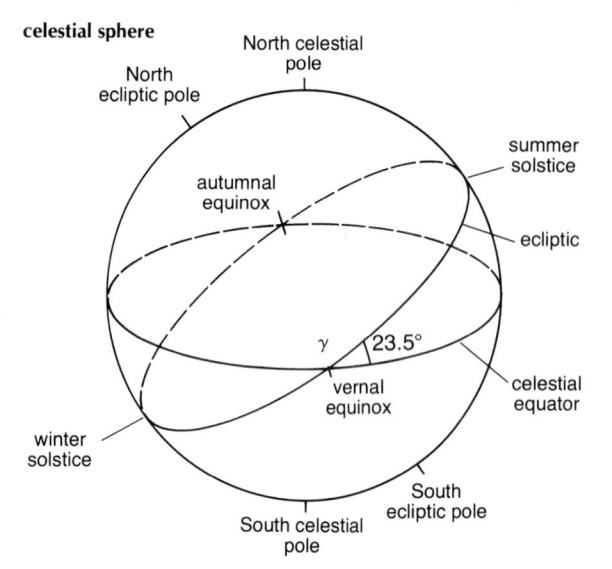

celestial sphere

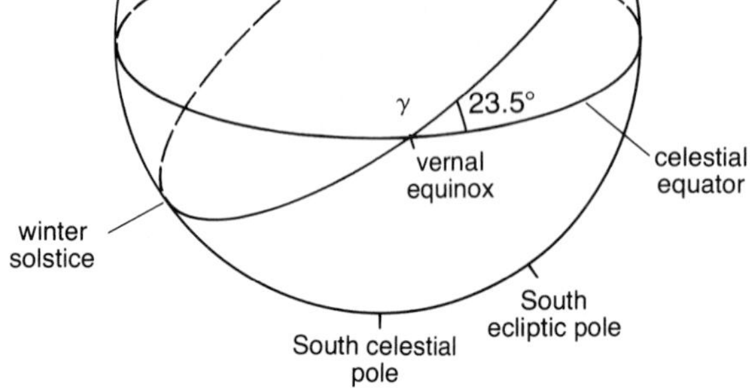

Celestine V, Pope [sel'-es-tyn] Celestine V, b. *c.*1215, d. May 19, 1296, was pope for five months during 1294 and was the founder of the Celestine monastic order, a branch of the BENEDICTINES that lasted until 1785. As a hermit named Pietro del Murrone, he became the center of a celebrated reclusive community. Elected (July 5) pope through the influence of CHARLES II of Naples, he became the first pope to abdicate (December 13). His successor, BONIFACE VIII, abrogated his official acts and had him imprisoned until his death. Celestine was canonized in 1313. Feast day: May 19.

celestite [sel'-es-tyt] Celestite, $SrSO_4$, a SULFATE MINERAL, is the principal ore of strontium. It forms crystals as well as nodules and granular masses. Hardness is 3–3½; streak and color, white; luster, vitreous; and specific gravity, 3.9. Deposits of celestite occur in EVAPORITES, hydrothermal veins, and metallic ORE DEPOSITS.

celibacy Celibacy is the practice of remaining unmarried and abstaining from sexual activity. It is practiced in some form in most religions, usually for reasons of ASCETICISM. Roman Catholic priests, for example, are forbidden by canon law to marry. This requirement is distinct from the vow of chastity taken by monks and nuns, who choose a life of consecrated chastity.

Celibacy is required of priests in the Roman Catholic church, but only of bishops in the Eastern church. It first appeared in church law *c.*306 with the enactments of the Council of Elvira in Spain. Gradually it became part of the common law of the church. Practice frequently did not coincide with the law, however, and clerical concubinage was a problem for many centuries. During the Reformation it was strongly urged that the requirement of celibacy be dropped. This did not happen in the Roman Catholic church, however, although the practice was dropped by Protestants. After the Second Vatican Council (1960–65), the issue of celibacy was again debated vigorously with the hope of making it optional for the clergy. Popes PAUL VI and John Paul II, however, reconfirmed the traditional teaching that celibacy would remain mandatory for the clergy of the Latin church. Reasons generally given are promotion of single-minded dedication to the ministry and the need for freedom for prayer.

Céline, Louis Ferdinand [say-leen'] Louis Ferdinand Céline was the pen name of Louis Ferdinand Destouches, b. May 27, 1894, d. July 1, 1961, a French writer whose innovative novels *Journey to the End of the Night* (1932; Eng. trans., 1943), *Death on the Installment Plan* (1936; Eng. trans., 1938), and *Guignol's Band* (1944; Eng. trans., 1954) provide a chaotic, antiheroic vision of human suffering and are significant expressions of ABSURDISM and ALIENATION. His fiction is pervaded by pessimism, nihilism, and BLACK HUMOR. Céline, who worked as a doctor to the poor for most of his life, also wrote virulently anti-Semitic pamphlets in the late 1930s and, although a pacifist, was accused of Nazi collaboration. He fled (1944) France to live in Germany, at Sigmaringen, and then moved (1945) to Denmark. Condemned (1950) by default to a year of imprisonment, he was exonerated the next year and returned to France. His later works, which mainly trace his exile, include *Castle to Castle* (1957; Eng. trans., 1968), *North* (1960; Eng. trans., 1972), and the posthumous *Rigadoon* (1969; Eng. trans., 1974).

cell The concept that all living material is made of cells is a central, unifying one in modern BIOLOGY. The concept—of the cell as the fundamental, irreducible unit of life—is the basis for an understanding of living organisms as well as the foundation of modern research in the life sciences.

History. The word *cell* was introduced by Robert HOOKE in 1665. In the course of microscopic studies of cork, Hooke noticed that the material under study was made up of many "little boxes." Ten years later, Antoni van LEEUWENHOEK, using a hand-held lens, described several tiny microscopic creatures later found to be bacteria and Protozoa. Over the next 150 years, numerous investigators, using the MICROSCOPE, examined living tissue and developed detailed descriptions of it.

The cell theory of life was developed over a period of many years. The initial statement was formulated by Lorenz Oken in 1805. In 1839, Theodore SCHWANN stated the theory essentially in its present form. Subsequent research led Rudolf Virchow to state (1858) that every cell forms from a preexisting cell. The current theory may be presented as a set of six statements: (1) all living material is made up of cells; (2) all cells are derived from previously existing cells—most cells arise by cell division, but in sexual organisms they may be formed by the fusion of sperm and egg; (3) a cell is the most elementary unit of life; (4) every cell is bounded by a plasma membrane, an extremely thin skin separating it from the environment and from other cells; (5) all cells have strong biochemical similarities; and (6) most cells are small, about 0.001 cm (0.0004 in) in length.

Cell Classes. Two classes of cells exist: the prokaryotes and the eukaryotes. The prokaryotes include bacteria and blue-green algae (kingdom Monera), all single-celled organisms that lack a nucleus and other membrane-bounded cellular substructures. The genetic material responsible for the transmission of characteristics from one generation to another is contained in a single large molecule of circular deoxyribonucleic acid, or DNA. The eukaryotes include plants, animals, protozoans, and fungi. These

(Right) *Prokaryotic cells lack distinct, membrane-bounded nuclei. Genetic information is contained in a molecule of DNA* (1). *Ribosomes* (2) *are the only specialized cellular structures found within the cytoplasm* (4). *Respiratory enzymes found in the interior of eucaryotic cells are located in the mesosomes* (3), *which are inward folds of the procaryotic cell membrane* (5).

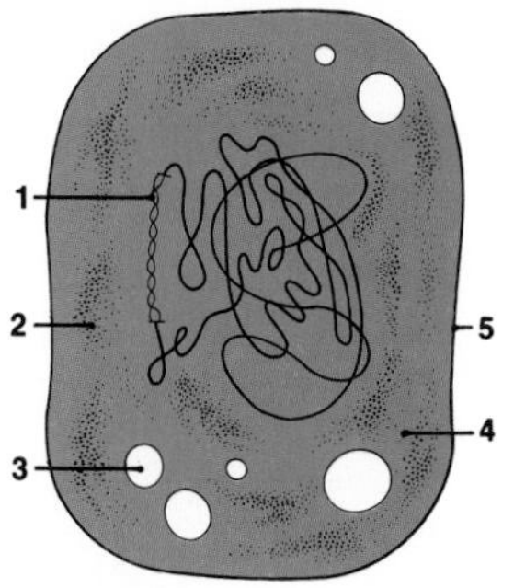

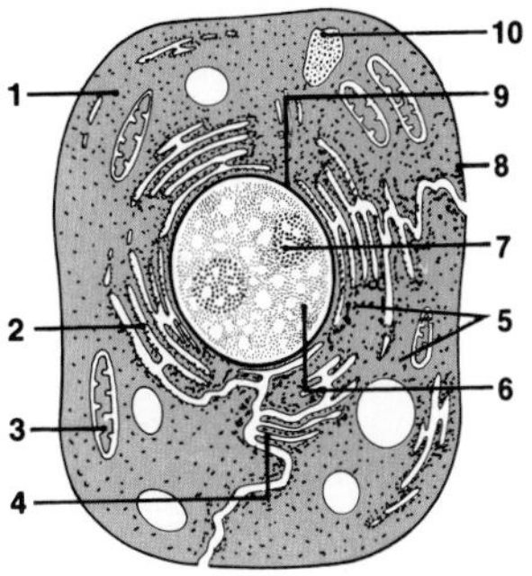

(Left) *Eukaryotic cells have well-defined nuclei. Structures within the cytoplasm* (1) *include the endoplasmic reticulum* (2), *mitochondria* (3), *Golgi apparatus* (4), *ribosomes* (5), *a nucleus* (6) *with one or more nucleoli* (7) *surrounded by a nuclear envelope* (9), *and lysosomes* (10). *Eucaryotes, like procaryotes, are bounded by a semipermeable membrane* (8).

cells contain nuclei and other membrane-bounded cell components, or organelles, such as mitochondria and plastids. The genetic material is organized into chromosomes (see GENETIC CODE).

Methods of Study. The study of cell structure includes the fields of CYTOLOGY (for cells) and HISTOLOGY (for tissues), whereas the function of cells is studied in CELL PHYSIOLOGY, biochemistry, and cytogenetics. The first instrument used in studying cell structure was the light microscope, which remains an important tool today. Electron and scanning electron microscopes have extended the range of observed detail as well as the kinds of cell structures that can be observed.

In examining biological specimens, using microscopic techniques, it is necessary to stain the material and cut it into samples thin enough for a light beam or an electron beam to penetrate them. First, the tissue is treated, to "fix" the structures so they will not be altered by the staining and slicing. Usually this is done by using chemicals. Machines for slicing embedded tissue preparations are called microtomes, and the procedure is known as sectioning.

Stains have been developed that react differently with cell structures, depending on their chemical composition or enzymatic activity. The science of analyzing structures by their chemical reactions is called cytochemistry, and the study of the staining properties of tissues is part of histochemistry. The use of stains containing radioactive atoms, known as autoradiography, may be combined with the study of cell physiology by feeding cells specific compounds with radioactive atoms and then microscopically observing on a photographic emulsion the distribution of radioactive events.

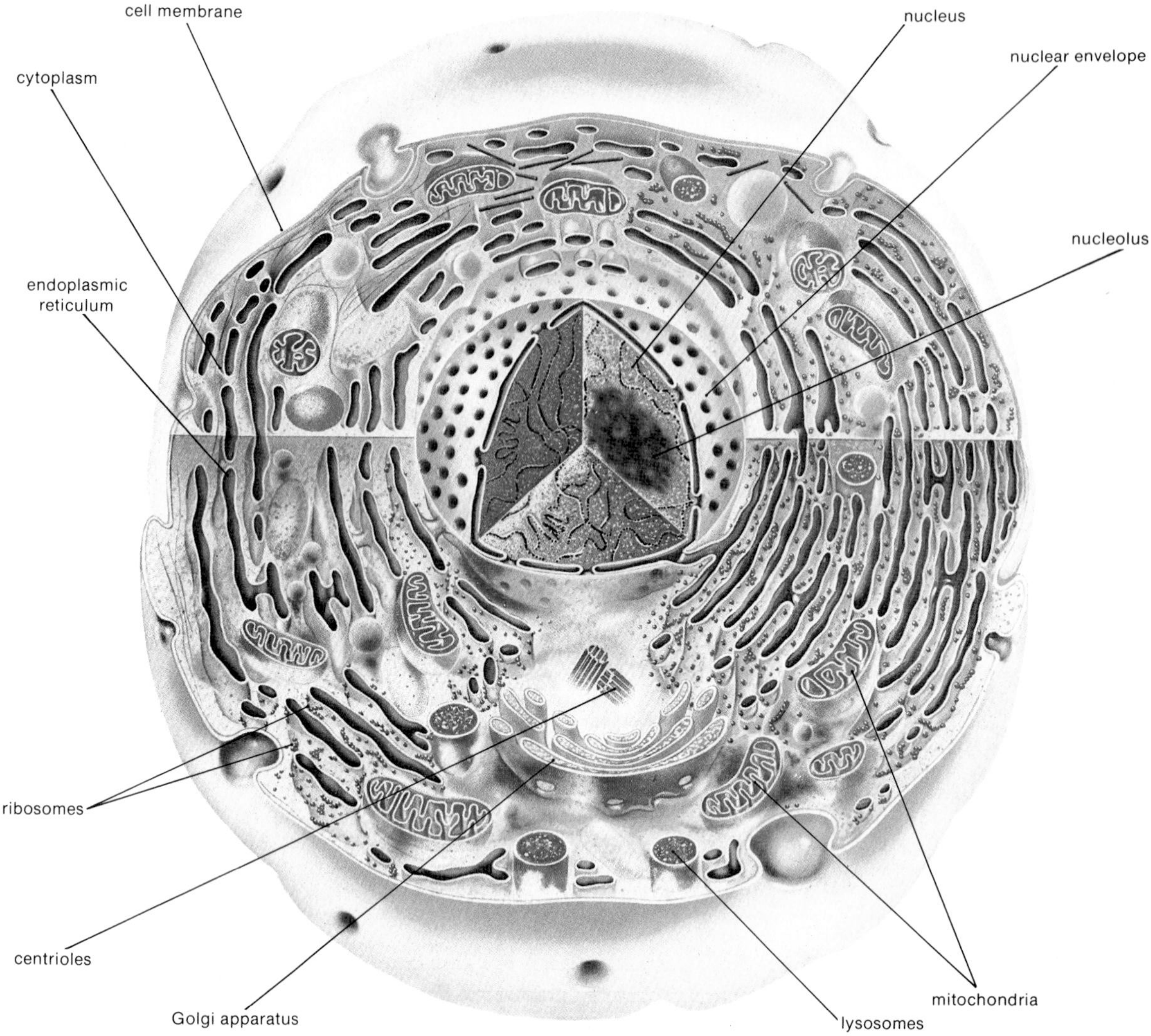

Development of the electron microscope has made possible identification of many of the organelles in the highly structured interior of the cell. The generalized human cell (drawn at a magnification of about 5,000 times) is, like all cells, surrounded by a cell membrane through which all food, wastes, and other substances involved in cell functions must pass. The cytoplasm is the fluid medium in which the organelles are suspended, including the endoplasmic reticulum, a network of sacs and tubules that act as channels for material passing through the cell. Ribosomes are the sites where proteins are assembled from amino acids. Certain molecules synthesized in the cell or absorbed from outside are stored in the Golgi apparatus; enzymes are stored in the lysosomes. The mitochondria are the main source of energy in the cell. Centrioles are hollow cylinders that move to opposite poles of the cell during cell division. The largest structure in the cell is the nucleus, which controls the cell's overall activity. Bounded by a porous membrane called the nuclear envelope, the nucleus contains at least one nucleolus that is involved in formation of the ribosomes. The nucleus also carries DNA, the basic genetic material, in its chromosomes.

The generalized functions of most cells are self-maintenance, synthesis of cell products, and cell division. These require that the cell take in nutrients and excrete waste products. The nutrients are either used as building blocks in synthesizing large molecules, or they are oxidized, producing energy for powering the cell's activities. Because the various activities all require energy, a major chemical activity in nearly all types of cells is the energy-linked conversion of metabolites. Adenosine triphosphate (see ATP) is the universal energy-transfer molecule; it is constantly utilized and regenerated by energy-yielding chemical reactions.

Components of Cells

A cell is bounded by a cell membrane (see MEMBRANE CHEMISTRY). The material known as the CYTOPLASM lies within the membrane and contains several organelles and granules in suspension. Plant and bacteria cells have an additional membrane, or wall, that lies outside the cell membrane and is not essential to the functioning and growth of the cell.

Plasma Membrane. Cells are surrounded by a membrane of lipid (fat) and protein. It controls the transport of molecules in and out of the cell, thus serving as a line of demarcation between the cell and its surroundings. Outside the plasma membrane may be other envelopes such as an outer membrane, the cell wall (in plants), and other extracellular material. Unit membranes also occur in a eukaryotic cell's interior, for example, as part of the endoplasmic reticulum and nuclei. Exterior portions of the cell surfaces determine cell-to-cell interactions and are thus important in the formation and control of tissue. The extracellular material also acts as a glue that holds cells together in tissues.

Nuclei. Most cells have a single NUCLEUS bounded by a nuclear envelope, or membrane, with pores. Pores provide continuity between the nucleus and the cytoplasm. The nucleus contains one or more discrete structures, known as nucleoli, which are sites of ribosomal ribonucleic acid (rRNA) synthesis. Hereditary information is carried in the DNA contained within the chromosomes in the nucleus. This information is transcribed into RNA in the nucleus, which then serves as a messenger. The messenger moves outside the nucleus to the RIBOSOMES, where it guides the synthesis of proteins. Thus, the nucleus directs the activity of the cell.

Ribosomes. Ribosomes are tiny particles within the cell. Made of RNA and protein, they are present in large numbers in most cells and are the site of protein synthesis.

Endoplasmic Reticulum. Within most eukaryotic cells is a complex set of membranous structures. When viewed in the electron microscope, the membranes are either rough (covered with granules or ribosomes) or smooth. Generally, the rough endoplasmic reticulum is highly developed in cells that synthesize large amounts of protein.

Golgi Apparatus. A special type of membrane aggregate, the Golgi apparatus, is often found near the nucleus. In cells that synthesize and secrete products, the Golgi apparatus is the site of the material that is accumulated.

Mitochondria. Mitochondria (see MITOCHONDRION) are composed of an outer membrane and a highly convoluted inner membrane. A series of chemical reactions that occur on the inner membrane convert the energy of oxidation into the chemical energy of ATP. In this process, the predominant energy-transfer molecule is ATP. Almost all of the energy passes through this molecule before being utilized in cell function. Cells that have high rates of metabolism usually have a large number of mitochondria.

Chloroplasts. Plant cells contain chloroplasts, organelles with a membranous outer envelope and a high laminated inner membranous structure. The interior membranes contain chlorophyll and are responsible for photosynthesis.

Centrioles. Most cells have two cylindrical bodies, called centrioles, near the nucleus. The centrioles appear as sets of triple tubules. Centrioles play a part in cell division.

Other Organelles. The material containing the organelles is called ground substance, or cytoplasm. It contains proteins, small molecules, and a group of entities organized as microfilaments and microtubules. Microfilaments are long, thin, contractile rods that appear to be responsible for the movement of cells, both external and internal. Microtubules are hollow, cylindrical aggregates of tubelike structures that help give the cell shape and form; they are also involved in other cell processes.

LYSOSOMES are small bodies in which large numbers of enzymes are stored until needed. Many cells, particularly those of plants, contain large liquid-filled areas known as vacuoles, which appear to be involved in digestion or excretion, or both.

Storage particles comprise a diverse group of structures and contain lipid droplets and glycogen granules whose function is the long-term storage of energy.

Morphogenesis

All large organisms, regardless of their complexity, begin as single cells. By repeated cell growth and mitosis, or division, the organism eventually develops into an adult containing thousands of billions of cells. This process of development is called morphogenesis. Since many different types of cells exist in fully grown plants and animals, morphogenesis involves not only cell growth but differentiation into specialized types of cells. This differentiation is controlled by the genes; the information needed to program and guide the growth is contained within the chromosomes. The size, shape, and chemical activity of the cells are governed to some extent by the function of the tissue in which they are found.

Each cell contains the same total genetic information that was present in the fertilized egg. Because of this, the question arises as to why the cells are not identical. It appears that in different types of cells, groups of genes are controlled (in effect, switched on and off) by various biochemical processes, so that each cell manufactures the proteins and structures needed for it to function, such as hemoglobin in red blood cells, flagella in sperm, and so forth.

The development of a cell is determined by its position in the developing embryo, the chemical products of neighboring cells, and an internal program that is genetically controlled. Ultimately, these are regulated by the DNA in the nucleus and by the transfer of selected portions of the DNA information to the cytoplasm, through the intermediate molecules of messenger RNA. It is estimated that, on average, only about 10 percent of the genes of any cell are functional—which genes, in particular, varying with the type of cell.

Cell Division

Cell division depends on two complementary events—the replication of the DNA molecules that make up the basic genetic material of all cells, and the orderly separation of the products of this replication. In simple prokaryotes, where only a single unit of DNA exists, these two events are intimately coupled with an inward growth of the cell membrane.

In eukaryotes, the process is more complex. Here, the DNA is combined with histone protein and is separated into two or more discrete chromosomes that are enclosed in a distinct nuclear membrane. Division of the nucleus thus precedes division of the cytoplasm, and both are necessary for cell division. During nuclear division, the behavior of the individual chromosomes must be coordinated, both spatially and temporally. This is achieved by the assembly of two temporary sets of microtubules that together form a spindle. The products of chromosome replication are oriented and move within this system as a result of the activity of specialized chromosome regions, called kinetochores, or centromeres.

In most animal cells, two pairs of centrioles are present at one pole of the cell. Where centrioles are present, a radiating system of microtubules (the aster) may form around them. During the initial stages of nuclear division, these astral microtubules proliferate and lengthen. Simultaneously, each centriolar pair moves away from the other pair until they occupy diametrically opposed positions outside the nuclear membrane. This is accompanied by the development of a system of spindle fibers between—but not connected with—the separating centriolar pairs.

The Mitotic Cycle

Mitosis is part of the overall cell cycle that includes a long phase, called interphase, which may be subdivided into three stages—G_1, S, and G_2—on the basis of the synthetic activities occurring within them. The synthesis of DNA occurs only during the S phase, when it coincides with the synthesis of histone protein. As a result of these coupled syntheses, each chromosome now consists of two sister chromosomes, called chromatids, that are identical in their morphological and genetic organization and that are joined at the kinetochore. Chromatids become visible when mitosis sets in; the remainder of the mitotic cycle involves their separation into two offspring nuclei. Mitosis depends on four major events—coiling, orientation, movement, and uncoiling—which, in turn, define four essential stages of the mitotic cycle.

In the mitotic cycle a cell's chromosomes are maneuvered during prophase (1, 2), prometaphase (3), and metaphase (4), until the identical sister chromatids separate and move toward opposite poles in anaphase (5). The cell divides during telophase (6, 7), and two new daughter cells (8) are formed, each identical to the parent cell.

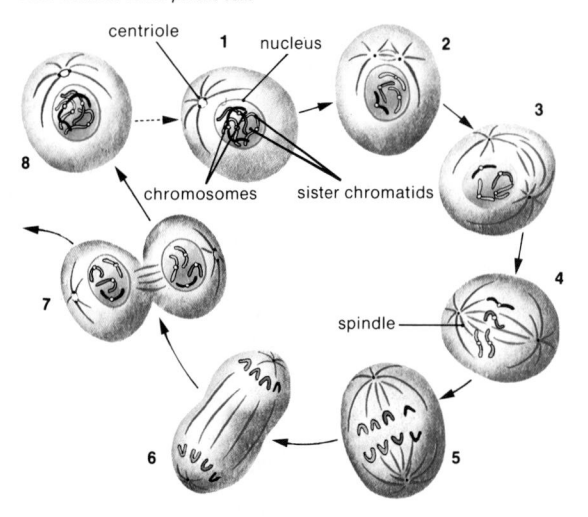

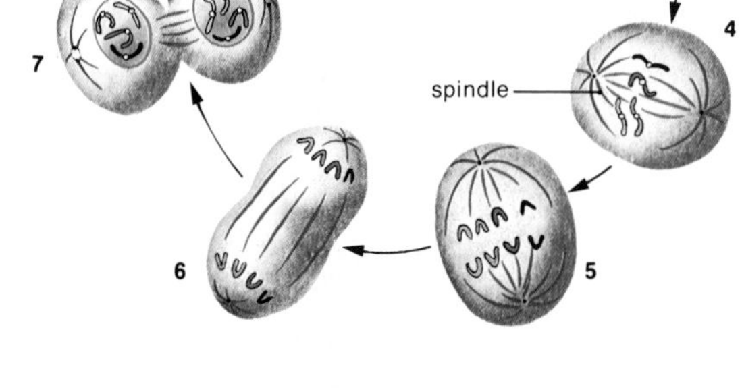

Prophase. Initially, each chromosome is a long double thread consisting of two chromatids. Changes in the internal configuration of the nucleoprotein component of each chromatid cause a cycle of coiling to be initiated in which the chromosomes become shorter and thicker. Toward the end of the prophase, the microtubules forming the spindle proliferate in the cytoplasm just outside the nuclear membrane. The end of prophase is signaled by the disruption of the nuclear membrane. When the relatively condensed chromosomes come in contact with the spindle, their kinetochores accumulate short fibers that establish a connection to the free microtubules.

Metaphase. The manner in which the chromosomes are distributed at the equator following a reorientation mechanism depends on the relative sizes of the members of the chromosome set, as well as on the size of the cell itself. If the cell is large, the spindle is usually hollow, with all the kinetochores arranged on the periphery of a circle or an oval.

Anaphase. The connection between sister chromatids is broken when the kinetochore divides and the component chromatids (now the chromosomes) have separated completely. All sister kinetochores begin their movement toward opposite poles simultaneously, apparently triggered by changes in the disposition of the kinetochore fibers.

Telophase. A new nuclear membrane begins to form at the surface of each of the two separated sets of chromosomes. At the same time, the chromosomes themselves uncoil and return to an extended (and diffuse) interphase state.

Cytokinesis. The completion of cell division requires that the cell cytoplasm be divided following division of the nucleus. The mechanism of cytoplasm division (cytokinesis) differs between animals and plants. In animals, where no rigid cell wall exists, the cytoplasm becomes shaped like a dumbbell as the result of constriction initiated at the cell's surface, which extends inward. In plants, a new cell wall is built across the middle of the cell and gradually extends outward.

The Meiotic Cycle

Whereas mitosis rarely lasts more than two hours, the meiotic cycle may take days or weeks to produce the gametes, or sex cells in animals and spores in plants, since it involves two successive sequences of spindle activity and chromosome movement, namely, two meiotic divisions. The first sequence is preceded by a lengthy prophase during which chromosome pairing and any exchange of chromosome segments take place. This prophase is divided into five substages. DNA synthesis is completed before meiosis starts.

Prophase-I. In the first stage of prophase, called lepto-

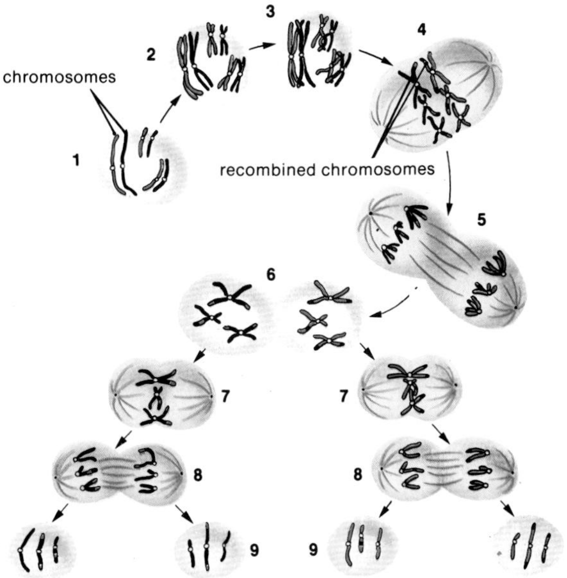

Meiosis, the process by which sex cells are formed, consists of two separate divisions. At the first meiotic division (1–6), genetic recombination may occur. The two resulting cells then undergo the second meiotic division (7, 8). Each of the four resultant daughter cells (9) has half the number of chromosomes of the parent cell.

tene (literally, "thin thread"), the chromosomes become visible but initially remain uncoiled. Localized areas of increased coiling, called chromomeres, then form. Their size and position are constant for homologous (similar) chromosomes.

In the second stage, zygotene ("yolked thread"), in a process called synapsis, the chromosomes shorten and homologous chromosomes associate, or meet. Individual pairs in close apposition are called bivalent chromosomes. This pairing can occur anywhere along their lengths.

The third stage, pachytene ("thick thread"), is a long period in which the bivalent chromosomes shorten and thicken and appear to be rodlike. At this stage there may be an exchange of chromosomal segments, called crossing over, between nonsister chromatids of homologous chromosomes.

The diplotene, or double-thread, stage is characterized by partial separation of the chromosomes into four separate chromatids; they are still held together, however, at one or more points, called chiasmata, along their lengths, which represent points at which crossing over had occurred during the previous pachytene stage. The chromosome pairs resemble a cross if joined at one point, or, if they adhere at two points, a loop. Meanwhile, the chromosomes continue to coil and shorten.

In diakinesis, the last prophase stage, the chromosomes contract further, thereby increasing the tightness of the coiling. They also tend to move to the periphery of the nucleus. The chiasmata sometimes move toward the ends of the chromosomes, in a process known as terminalization. Disruption of the nuclear membrane enables the bivalents to interact with the spindle system formed at this time.

Metaphase-I. When the above arrangement is complete, the bivalents lie in a temporarily stable state in which their kinetochores are equidistant above and below the spindle equator. The shape adopted by a particular bivalent at this time depends on the location of its kinetochore and on the number and position of the chiasmata within the bivalent. Bivalents with a single chiasma appear as open crosses.

The stability of the first metaphase is the result of the tension exerted on the two kinetochore pairs of each bivalent by the kinetochore fibers, as well as on the continued association of sister chromatid pairs.

Anaphase-I. When this association ceases, the chiasmata complete their terminalization, thus freeing the sister kinetochore pairs to move poleward as the kinetochore fibers draw the half-bivalents apart.

Telophase-I. During this stage the nuclear membrane reforms, nucleoli reappear, and cytokinesis occurs, forming two daughter cells.

Interphase. This stage is extremely short. There is no DNA replication between meiosis I and meiosis II.

Second Meiotic Division. In plants, meiosis results in the formation of spores (sporogenesis), and in some species telophase-I, interphase, and prophase-II are virtually eliminated. In most plants and in all animals, however, the second meiotic division consists of the usual four stages of cell division. In prophase-II, a spindle forms and the nuclear membrane disappears. In metaphase-II, half-bivalents are auto-oriented at the equator of the division-II spindle. In anaphase-II, they separate into their component chromatids. Telophase-II involves the formation of the nuclear membrane and cytokinesis.

The combined effects of the two meiotic divisions is to partition the four chromatids of each bivalent into one of each of the four nuclei produced from each cell that entered meiosis. This automatically leads to a halving of the number of chromosomes in each meiotic product as well as compensating for the fertilization that follows meiosis. The two meiotic divisions also lead to a recombination, both of individual chromosomes (reassortment) and of particular parts of the chromosomes (crossing over).

Reassortment occurs because the co-orientation of sister kinetochore pairs in the first division and the auto-orientation of sister half-kinetochores in the second divisions are random events. Crossing over is the exchange of like segments between two nonsister chromatids, which occurs when chiasmata are formed.

Types of Cells

Several major types of animal cells may be distinguished, including absorptive, secretory, nerve, sensory, muscle, and reproductive cells. All must arise during morphogenesis from cells that are less differentiated.

Absorptive Cells. Absorptive cells often occur as continuous sheets on surfaces where material is transported to the cells. For example, the single layer of epithelial cells lining the surface of the small intestine selectively absorbs food molecules from the gut into the bloodstream. These cells have a free surface that faces the digestive tract and a base surface that is in contact with the capillaries. The free surface is covered with many projections called microvilli, which vastly increase the area available for molecular flow. In digestion, the products of the ingested food are transported through the microvilli into the cell. They are then pumped into the capillaries from the other side. Similar cells are found in the kidney. The microvilli are an example of a cell structure precisely fitted to the function of the cell. Because an absorptive cell needs maximum area for transport, the shape of the cell surface is altered to achieve the optimum transfer of molecules.

Secretory Cells. Secretory cells produce products that are subsequently deposited in either the bloodstream or a special duct to an organ, where they are used. The pancreas and pituitary are glands that have large numbers of secretory cells. Proteins and other cell products are synthesized throughout the cytoplasm and transported to the Golgi apparatus, where they are packaged in membrane-bounded vesicles that come to a cell's surface and discharge the secretion outside the cell.

Nerve Cells. A nerve cell consists of a group of cell fibers called dendrites that join the main cell body, which in turn leads to a long thin structure known as an axon. The connections between nerve cells are called synapses. When these structures are combined, they form an electrical network known as the NERVOUS SYSTEM.

Sensory Cells. Sensory cells respond to impulses by emitting electrical signals. An example is the rod cell of the eye, in which the central cell body has two long, thin appendages. One appendage has an outer segment consisting of specialized stacked membranes for the reception of light. At the other end is a long, thin connection to a nerve cell that leads to the optic nerve fiber.

Muscle Cells. Muscles are of three types—skeletal, cardiac, and smooth. All function similarly: the contraction of fibers generates a mechanical force. The skeletal muscle is a multinucleate structure that has an outer envelope known as the sarcolemma. This system does not fit the definition of a cell given above and may be regarded, instead, as a tissue in which the cells have merged. Most of the interior consists of long, thin myofibrils that are actually the contractile elements.

Reproductive Cells. Gametes are formed after completion of the process of meiosis, which halves the number of chromosomes. Male gametes are usually motile, whereas female gametes are usually larger and are stationary; the function of the latter is to store supplies of food for the developing embryo. Fertilization occurs when a sperm is fused with an egg; this stage is followed by mitosis and morphogenesis.

Abnormal Cells. In addition to normal cell types, most organisms may occasionally give rise to abnormal cells. The most significant of these are CANCER cells. Cancer cells possess the organelles of normal cells but are less highly differentiated and seem to lack some control mechanisms that regulate the life cycle of the cell.

Cell Culture

A major proof that the cell is the fundamental unit of life came early in the 20th century, when it was shown that cells can be removed from adult tissue, placed in a nutrient medium, and cultivated. Years passed before it was shown that a single mammalian cell may, under the appropriate conditions, give rise to a clone, a population consisting of the descendants of one cell (see CLONING). The technique of cell culture has become one of the principal tools of modern biology.

The existence of cultures of human cells allows scientists to perform a wide range of experiments that could not otherwise be carried out in humans. Thus, drugs and environmental toxins may be tested and virus growth in human cells studied. Various types of cells can be fused, yielding hybrids that provide information about the GENETIC CODE and GENETIC DISEASES, as well as about the relationship of genes to cell activity.

cell, electric see BATTERY; ELECTROCHEMISTRY

cell physiology Cell physiology, a division of cytology, is the study of processes that occur in living CELLS. Cell physiologists study cell division, PROTEIN synthesis, cell nutrition, the transfer of materials across cell membranes, genetic processes (see GENETICS), cell specialization, and the cellular systems that regulate these functions. Cell physiology is currently one of the most active areas of physiological research.

Cellini, Benvenuto [chel-lee'-nee] Benvenuto Cellini, b. Nov. 3, 1500, d. Feb. 13, 1571, was a versatile artist of the Italian High Renaissance, equally at home as a sculptor, goldsmith, architect, and writer. From late 1540, Cellini worked at Fontainebleau (see FONTAINEBLEAU, CHÂTEAU DE) and in Paris for Francis I, for whom he made the famous *Salt Cellar* in gold and enamel (1543; Kunsthistorisches Museum, Vienna) and began work on silver figures of Jupiter, Juno, Vulcan, and Mars (now lost). He also made his first large-scale sculptural works: the bust of Julius Caesar (1540–41; now lost) and the bronze relief *Nymph of Fountainebleau* (1543–44; Louvre, Paris) for the lunette of the Golden Door at the Château.

Returning to Florence, in 1545 he cast the large, impressive bust of Cosimo I de'Medici (Bargello Museum, Florence) and in 1550 that of Bindo Altoviti (Gardner Museum, Boston), two portraits in which likeness is subordinated to interpretation. His best-known work, the *Perseus,* now gracing the Loggia dei Lanzi in Florence—a larger-than-life study of the Greek hero holding aloft the bloody head of Medusa—was produced between 1545 and 1554. Its casting was a technical triumph.

Contemporaneous works by Cellini include the marble *Apollo and Hyacinth* (1546), *Narcissus* (1547–48), and an antique torso restored as a *Ganymede* (1545–47; all Bargello Museum, Florence). In 1556–62, he carved the

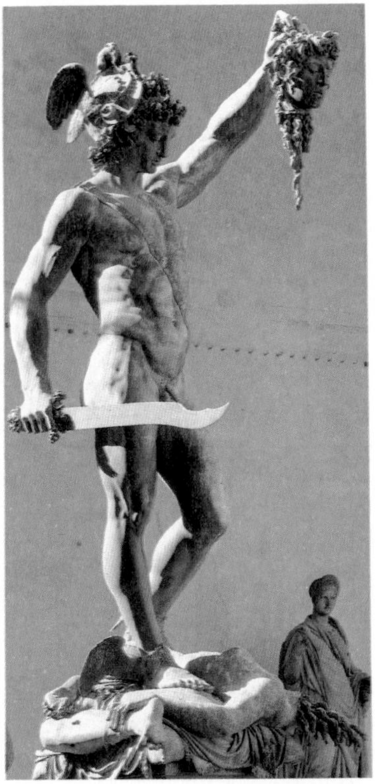

The Italian Mannerist goldsmith and sculptor Benvenuto Cellini finished this famous bronze figure Perseus with the Head of Medusa *in 1554. This elegantly finished work is noted for its casting technique and the virtuosity of its design. (Loggia dei Lanzi, Florence.)*

marble *Crucifix* (Escorial, Spain) later sent by Francesco I de'Medici to Philip II of Spain.

In his art, Cellini well illustrates the stylistic aims of later MANNERISM: complexity, virtuosity, and grace, with a figurative vocabulary strongly derived from the works of antiquity and from MICHELANGELO. Whereas artists such as Bandinelli emphasized anatomical structure, contorted poses, and attenuated proportions, Cellini subordinated his debt to Michelangelo through the Lysippean grace of his designs and a technical finish rivaling that of ancient bronzes and marbles. He strongly influenced the painting and sculpture of the FONTAINEBLEAU SCHOOL and set a high standard of technical accomplishment for his Florentine contemporaries.

cello [chel'-oh] The cello, or violoncello, is the second largest member of the VIOLIN family of musical instruments. It is tuned an octave below the VIOLA and serves as both a melodic and a bass instrument in chamber and orchestral music. The body of the cello is approximately 76 cm (30 in) long and is much deeper than those of the violin and viola. The cellist is seated and supports the instrument between his or her calves, with its lower end raised off the floor by an end pin. The cello emerged in the 16th century and was used primarily in FIGURED-BASS accompaniments for half of the 17th century, after which its warm tone and wide range inspired a wealth of solo and chamber music.

cellophane Cellophane is a transparent packaging film based on the CELLULOSE derived from wood pulp. Films with virtually any degree of permeability can be produced by coating one or both sides of the cellophane with other materials. Cellophane is the only clear film that does not soften with heat. It tears easily when notched, and tear tapes are often supplied for ease in opening the film wrap. However, it grows brittle and shrinks with age. Since the early 1960s and the advent of inexpensive petrochemical films, such as polyvinyl chloride and polypropylene films, the consumption of cellophane has dwindled.

cellular radio Cellular radio is a radiotelephone communications system that began to develop rapidly in the early 1980s. Basically, it is a small-scale, "cellular" version of the communication linkage provided by large radio-broadcasting systems. An area is divided up into smaller units, called cells, that have a radius of about 13 to 19 km (8 to 12 mi); each cell has its own small radio transmitter. If necessary, a cell can be further subdivided into smaller cells. In this way, the honeycomb pattern of cells can repeatedly use the same range of radio frequencies without interfering with one another, so long as neighboring cells do not use precisely the same radio channels. Individuals with mobile phones in their automobiles use the system as if they were making a standard telephone call.

Computerized switching is essential to the operation of cellular radio, so that when mobile-unit calls are switched

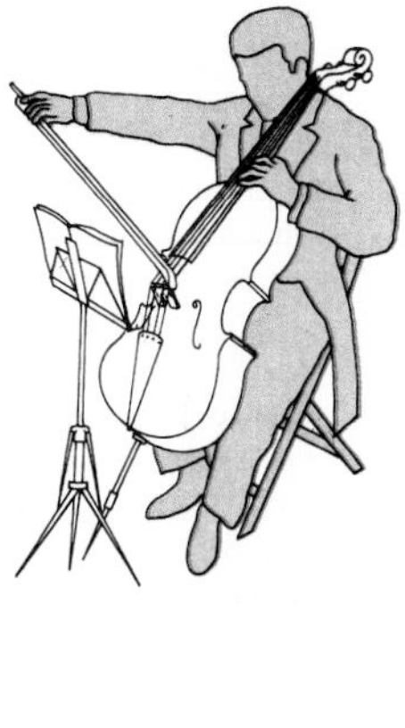

The cello originated during the 16th century as a five-stringed bass violin. First used as a bass accompaniment, it became a solo instrument because of its expressive tone. The cello is played by placing it on the floor—where it is supported by an endpin, or spike—and holding it upright.

from one call to the next, the transfer in channels can take place without interruption or at most a brief delay. The growth of electronic switching systems and the development of microprocessors have made this possible. For each area to be covered by cellular radio, the U.S. Federal Communications Commission (FCC) licenses two types of organization: one must be a telephone company; the other, a business that agrees to construct the necessary radio system.

celluloid The first synthetic plastic material, celluloid was synthesized in 1856 by Alexander Parkes and developed as a commercial product in 1869 by John Wesley Hyatt. It is made from a mixture of cellulose nitrate and camphor. Its strength, toughness, luster, and colorability and its low cost made it a cheap substitute for ivory and other natural materials in such items as billiard balls, shirt-collar stays, dentures, combs, brushes, and photographic film.

cellulose Cellulose is a complex CARBOHYDRATE—a POLYSACCHARIDE—that forms the major part of the cell walls of all plants and is practically pure in the fibers of cotton, flax, jute, and ramie. Upon hydrolysis, it is broken down into glucose and thus serves as a food for grazing animals, whose digestive tract microbes catalyze the reaction (see RUMINANT). Cellulose is insoluble in water and is rather inert chemically, although it may undergo reactions typical of the alcohols because each glucose unit has three hydroxyl (OH) groups. Thus, with nitric and sulfuric acids, nitrate esters such as guncotton are formed. The acetate esters of cellulose are plastics used as films and textiles. Other esters and some of the ethers of cellulose have specialized uses, such as the filling (laminate) used in the manufacture of safety glass.

Cellulose can be dissolved (with some partial hydrolysis) in a mixture of carbon disulfide and sodium hydroxide to form a sodium xanthate, an unstable ester. The solution, called viscose, when forced through fine holes or slits into an acidic solution, regenerates the cellulose in the form of threads or sheets (RAYON or cellophane). Paper is an impure cellulose derived from wood pulp, made by removing the lignin.

Celsius scale The Celsius scale (C) is a temperature standard adopted in 1948 and named in honor of the Swedish astronomer Anders Celsius (1701–44). In the original scale devised by Celsius, the value 0 was assigned to the boiling point of water, 100 to the freezing point. These values were reversed several years later by the Swedish botanist Carolus LINNAEUS. This TEMPERATURE scale was formerly called the Centigrade scale (also abbreviated C). Temperatures on the Celsius scale, *t*, are related to temperatures on the absolute, or KELVIN SCALE, *T*, by this formula: t (Celsius, °C) = T (in Kelvins, K) - 273.15. The formula for conversion to the Fahrenheit scale is: °F = 9/5°C + 32.

Celtic art Celtic art is the highly stylized curvilinear art that originated during the second half of the 1st millennium BC among the Celtic peoples of IRON AGE Europe. The term refers to two separate traditions: LA TÈNE art, which was named for a major Celtic site in Switzerland and was produced by the pre-Christian CELTS from the 5th century BC until the 2d century AD; and Christian Celtic art, which was produced in Britain and Ireland from AD 400 to 1200. The term also sometimes refers to Scottish and Irish works of the 16th century to the present that borrow freely from Celtic Christian art.

La Tène Art

La Tène art grew out of the native art of the HALLSTATT phase (*c.*750–500 BC) of the Celtic Iron Age. It appeared principally on objects of fine metalwork, including bracelets, torcs (neck rings), weaponry, and household and ritual vessels fashioned of bronze, gold, silver, and iron. La Tène sculptures in stone and wood have also been unearthed, the most notable being the 2d century BC stone head of a Celtic warrior found near Prague, Czechoslovakia (now in the National Museum, Prague), and a series of wooden figures (now in the Archaeological Museum, Dijon) from Sources-de-la-Seine in northern France, dated from the 1st century BC.

A typically Celtic spiral motif graces this 2d-century BC limestone head of a warrior. (Narodni Museum, Prague.)

(Left) *This ornamental drinking goblet, decorated in gold leaf and curved like an animal's horn, is typical of metalwork from the Hallstatt phase of the Celtic Iron Age (c.750–500 BC).* (Below, left) *This miniature Celtic war chariot, fashioned of bronze, dates from the 7th century BC. The goddess at the center is taller, symbolizing her status. (Below) This small statue of a man holding a battle axe was found in Bohemia. Dating from the La Tène period of Celtic culture (c.450–50 BC), it was probably made to commemorate a heroic warrior. (Narodni Museum, Prague.)*

During the period of the early La Tène style (early 5th to mid–4th century BC), the Celtic artist experimented with new forms and a great diversity of ornament. Highly influential were Greek and Etruscan motifs; the Celts also became acquainted with a wide array of fantastic animal forms derived from the STEPPE ART of the nomadic SCYTHIANS.

The Waldalgesheim style (mid–4th to late 3d century BC) represents the classic period of La Tène art. It is named for an elaborate Celtic gravesite in the German Rhineland, which yielded a fine gilt-bronze flagon, bronze plaques with human figures, and gold torcs bearing the characteristically curvilinear ornament of the period.

The so-called Plastic style of La Tène art emerged during the 3d to 1st centuries BC. It is distinguished by the use of high-relief ornament and by a delight in complex transformations of form, from abstract to figurative and from plant to animal. The Sword style, which occurred concurrently with the Plastic style, is found, as its name suggests, principally on sword scabbards from sites in Switzerland and is characterized by finely engraved vegetal designs.

In the 2d century BC various regional schools of Celtic art developed in Britain. The full flowering of the insular tradition can be seen in the so-called Mirror style of southern Britain, which flourished in the late 1st century BC and early 1st century AD. Produced for Belgic overlords, Mirror-style products included bronze mirrors and tankards with ornamented handles, and ornamental ironwork. Characterized by symmetry and the use of basketry

This incised and patinated bronze mirror back is from 1st-century BC Desborough, England. The flowing lines and ornamental symmetry of the mirror back, as well as its handle, are typical of the "mirror style" of southern Britain. (British Museum, London.)

patterns, this style is seen at its best on mirror backs, an outstanding example of which is the incised and richly patinated example from Desborough, Northamptonshire (British Museum, London).

Insular art continued to be produced after the Roman conquest of Britain in AD 43. In the 1st century AD two major hoards of ornamental metalwork were deposited in Wales: the Llyn Cerrig Bach (Anglesey) and Tal-y-Llyn (Merioneth) treasures (both in the National Museum of Wales, Cardiff).

Christian Celtic Art

After the 2d century AD Celtic art effectively died out in Britain. It was revived in the 5th century with the production of brooches, hanging bowls, and other objects. The revival represents a separate tradition from that of the La Tène Celts, however, and owes much to late Roman provincial and contemporary Anglo-Saxon designs. It was rapidly transmitted to Ireland, where some La Tène art may have survived, and there reached its greatest heights.

The objects decorated in the new Christian tradition are mainly ecclesiastical and include metal reliquaries, stone crosses and cross-decorated stone slabs, and gospel books produced in the Early Christian monasteries. These ILLUMINATED MANUSCRIPTS were decorated with the graceful interlaced lines and stylized animal heads reminiscent of pagan Celtic art. The BOOK OF KELLS (Trinity College Library, Dublin), an illuminated manuscript believed to date from the 9th century, is generally regarded as one of the finest examples of Christian Celtic art. In northern Scotland the Christian PICTS developed their own tradition, of which the most splendid is the treasure of St. Ninian's Isle, Shetland (National Museum of Antiquities of Scotland, Edinburgh), a rich hoard of silver and metalwork that had been buried in AD *c.*800. Pictish carvings on stone, widespread in early churchyards, are decorated with mysterious inscribed symbols.

In Ireland outstanding examples of Celtic Dark Age metalwork are the Ardagh Chalice and Tara Brooch (both of the 8th century; National Museum of Ireland, Dublin). The VIKINGS revitalized Irish art, and ornamental metalwork in Celtic style continued to be produced until the 12th century AD; notable examples dating from this period are the Cross of Cong and the Lismore Crozier (both in the National Museum of Ireland, Dublin). Celtic Christian art influenced the artistic traditions of the Anglo-Saxon kingdom of Northumbria; it also played a part in the development of Frankish art through the missions of Irish monks to the Continent (see also MEROVINGIAN ART AND ARCHITECTURE).

This ornamental page from the 7th-century Book of Durrow is a splendid example of Christian Celtic art dating from the early Middle Ages. The manuscript illumination forms a highly refined pattern of abstract geometrical shapes and stylized animal motifs. (Trinity College, Dublin.)

The base of the silver-plated Gundestrup cauldron, found in Denmark, is dated c.*100* BC. *At this time, Celtic art was widely disseminated across Europe. (National Museum, Copenhagen.)*

Celtic languages The Celtic languages, members of the family of INDO-EUROPEAN LANGUAGES, disappeared from continental Europe in the late 5th century but are still spoken in the British Isles and in BRITTANY. Continental Celtic, or Gaulish, is preserved mainly in brief inscriptions. Insular Celtic is divided into Goidelic (also called Gaelic), including Irish, Scottish Gaelic, and Manx; and Brythonic (also called British), including Welsh, Cornish, and Breton. Manx and Cornish are extinct.

Among the phonological differences between Goidelic and Brythonic is the treatment of Indo-European k^w: Irish *mac,* "son," contrasts with Welsh *map.* These two branches, sometimes called *q*-Celtic and *p*-Celtic, underwent certain changes but with different results. Stress became fixed on the first syllable in Irish and on the penultimate syllable in Welsh. Indo-European final syllables were lost, leading to the disappearance of a case system in Welsh. Many words were further shortened through loss of certain interior vowels. A system of initial consonant mutations developed; for example, Old Irish *cenn,* "head," becomes *a chenn* in the phrase "his head."

Irish. Old Irish preserves five cases of the noun, three genders, and three numbers. The verbal system has developed new forms for expressing past action, an s-subjunctive, and an f-future for weak verbs. Dual number is lost in Middle Irish (900–1200), along with neuter gender, as in Welsh. The use of pronouns inserted within verbs to serve as verbal objects gives way to the use of independent pronouns in Early Modern Irish (1200–1400). The verbal system is gradually simplified—analytic forms develop, many strong verbs become weak, compound verbs become simple, and verbs conjugated with deponent endings adopt undeponent ones. Taught today in Irish schools, Modern Irish is spoken as a native language mainly on the western and southern coasts.

Scottish Gaelic and Manx. Scottish Gaelic, which diverged significantly from Irish by the 16th century, today has roughly 81,000 speakers, excluding the many Gaelic speakers in Nova Scotia, living mainly in the Highlands and Western Islands of Scotland. In the present tense, a verbal noun construction replaces the old synthetic present, which acquires future meaning as the old future tense disappears. In general, the inflection of both the noun and verb is greatly simplified, as it is in Manx, the extinct language of the Isle of Man, first written down early in the 17th century. Both Manx and Scottish Gaelic have absorbed many Norse loanwords.

Welsh, Cornish, and Breton. In Welsh, with about 656,000 speakers in Wales, the verbal system was greatly simplified by the Middle Welsh period (12th to 15th centuries). As in Scottish Gaelic, present-tense forms are used with future-tense meaning. Cornish, the extinct language of Cornwall, first recorded in the 10th-century *Bodmin Gospels,* differs phonologically from Welsh in several ways, and the structure of the language is closer to Breton, four main dialects of which are still widely spoken in Brittany. Breton differs from Welsh in its use of the subjunctive as a future and its heavy borrowing of words from French.

Celtic literature see IRISH LITERATURE; SCOTTISH LITERATURE; WELSH LITERATURE

Celtic mythology see MYTHOLOGY

Celts Celts was the name applied by ancient Greek writers, from the 5th century BC on, to a group of barbarian peoples who inhabited central and western Europe. From the 2d millennium to the 1st century BC these people, who spoke Indo-European dialects later classified as Celtic languages, spread through much of Europe. From a

This reconstructed scene of a fortified village during the La Tène phase of the Celtic Iron Age shows a victorious warrior returning from a raid. The severed heads of enemy warriors were highly prized by the warlike Celts, who placed great stress on the display of valor and skill in battle. The Celts excelled in metal-working for both weapons and ornamental or utilitarian objects; here, the torcs (neck rings), belts, chariot, harness, shields, helmets, and wine flagon reflect the designs that characterize Celtic art from the La Tène period.

heartland in central Europe, they settled the area of France (GAUL), penetrated northern Spain, and crossed to the British Isles probably in the 8th and 7th centuries BC. Moving south and southwest, they sacked Rome *c*.390 BC and attacked Delphi in 279 BC. One group then crossed into Anatolia and established the state of GALATIA. The modern populations of Ireland, Scotland, Wales, Cornwall, and Brittany retain strong Celtic elements.

Accounts of the ancient Celts come from Roman and Greek writers, notably Julius CAESAR and STRABO, who probably based much of their Celtic ethnography on the now lost writings of POSIDONIUS. These records are corroborated by early IRISH LITERATURE, including the epic tales of the Ulster Cycle.

From these sources inferences may be drawn regarding the structure of Celtic society as well as its customs and beliefs. Recurrent themes include the high-spirited and boastful character of the Celtic warrior, the practice of single combat, and the prizing of the severed heads of defeated foes. DRUIDS and seers feature prominently in the sources, and many of the Celtic traditions are imbued with supernatural aspects.

Archaeologically, the origins of the Celts have sometimes been sought in the Urnfield culture of the 2d millennium BC, but they are more generally associated with the widespread culture of the second Iron Age in Europe, designated LA TÈNE. Especially characteristic of this period is the emergence of a vigorous and exuberant art style in which earlier Celtic influences derived from native HALLSTATT antecedents were mixed with floral and formal classical motifs and even exotic oriental designs. The new distinctive curvilinear style was displayed on metal goods such as gold and silver bracelets and neck torcs, wine flagons, parade armor, and weaponry. Evidence of the La Tène culture of central and western Europe is drawn from fortified sites and burial and cemetery sites. Grave goods indicate a flourishing trade with the Mediterranean world.

Celtic culture was largely extinguished by the onslaught of the Romans from the south and the GERMANIC PEOPLES and other groups from the north and east. Gaul was subjugated by Julius Caesar in the GALLIC WARS (58–51 BC), and the Romans conquered Britain in the 1st century AD. Later the Germanic tribes renewed their drive westward into the former Celtic lands. Only along the Atlantic fringe of Europe did Celtic culture survive in distinct form.

See also: CELTIC ART; MYTHOLOGY.

cement and concrete Cement is a material with adhesive and cohesive properties that make it capable of bonding mineral fragments into a compact whole. The cement most commonly used in civil engineering and building (see BUILDING CONSTRUCTION) is portland cement. Concrete is the compact whole achieved by bonding fine and coarse aggregate particles with cement paste, which is a mixture of cement and water.

The use of cementing materials goes back to the ancient Egyptians and Romans, but the invention of modern portland cement is usually attributed to Joseph Aspdin, a builder in Leeds, England, who obtained a patent for it in

Cement is produced by heating a mixture of limestone and clay in a large, rotating cylindrical furnace, or kiln. The kiln is slightly inclined so that material fed in at the upper, cooler end (right) *travels slowly to the lower, hot discharge end* (left).

1824. Nowadays, the annual world production of portland cement is around 700 million metric tons.

Manufacture of Cement

Portland cement is usually made from a calcareous mate-

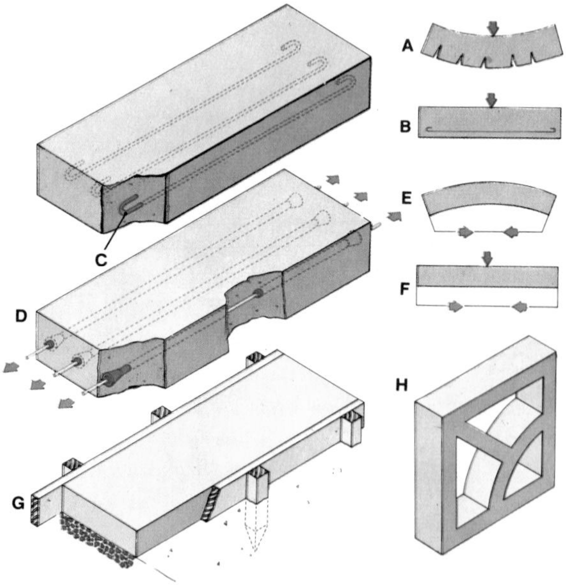

A concrete beam (A) *under load pressure* (red arrow) *may bend and crack. Steel-rod reinforcement* (B) *takes up the pressure, and hook-bends in the rods* (C) *provide better bonding between rod and concrete. Prestressed concrete* (D) *incorporates rods kept under tension* (blue arrows) *in metal sheathing. A beam held under tension* (E) *curves slightly until a load* (F) *is applied. Ordinary concrete* (G) *is cast over a stone base in a form made of wood planks secured by pegs. Precast concrete blocks* (H) *are often used as decorative trim.*

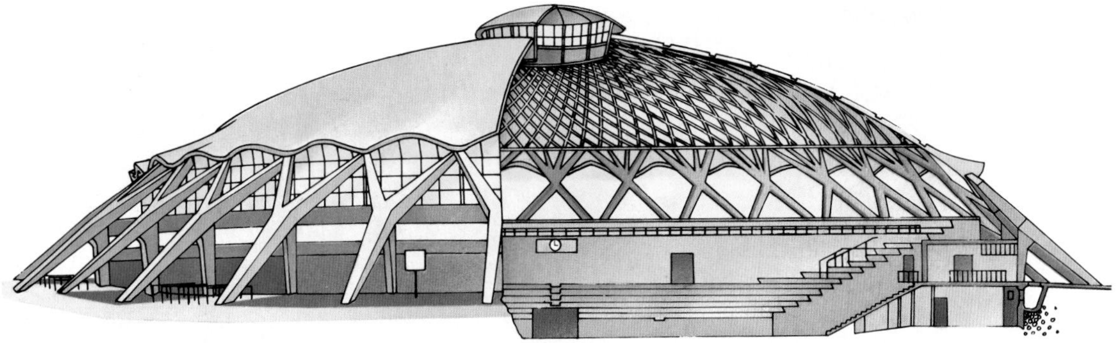

The Pallazzo dello Sport in Rome is a circular concrete structure built for the 1960 Olympic Games. A cutaway reveals some of the 1,620 precast, reinforced concrete panels that constitute its dome, supported by 36 Y-shaped concrete struts.

rial, such as LIMESTONE or CHALK, and from alumina- and silica-bearing material, such as clay or shale. The manufacturing process essentially consists of grinding the raw materials, mixing them intimately in specified proportions, and burning in a large rotary kiln at a temperature of approximately 1350° C (2500° F), when the material sinters and partially fuses into balls known as clinker. The clinker is cooled and ground to a fine powder, and GYPSUM is added to control the speed of setting when the cement is mixed with water.

Composition and Hydration of Cement

The main compounds in portland cement and their typical percentage content are tricalcium silicate (55%), dicalcium silicate (25%), and tricalcium aluminate (10%).

The chemical reaction of the two silicates with water produces calcium silicate hydrates and calcium hydroxide. These HYDRATES make the largest contribution to the strength of the hydrated cement paste. Tricalcium aluminate also forms a hydrate, but it contributes little to the strength of the paste. Moreover, the reaction of hydration of this compound is so rapid that it has to be controlled by gypsum. The presence of tricalcium aluminate is, however, advantageous in the process of burning in the kiln.

Composition and Strength of Concrete

Concrete is produced by intimately mixing cement, water, fine aggregate (sand), and coarse aggregate (gravel). The mixture is then placed in forms, compacted thoroughly, and allowed to harden. Typically, three-quarters of the volume of hardened concrete is occupied by the aggregate, the maximum size depending on the size of the concrete member and on the steel reinforcement in it.

Compaction of the fresh concrete is essential because the strength of hardened concrete depends on the volume of air voids within it as well as on the water-cement ratio of the cement paste.

Reinforced and Prestressed Concrete

The tensile strength of concrete is relatively low, so concrete structures are designed to exploit the good compressive strength properties of the material, and steel reinforcement is placed where it is necessary for structural members to resist tensile forces. This is called reinforced concrete. The steel reinforcement is bonded to the surrounding concrete so that stress is transferred between the two materials.

In a further development the steel is stretched before the development of bond between it and the surrounding concrete. When the force that produces the stretch is released, the concrete becomes precompressed in the part of the structural member that is normally the tensile zone under load. The application of loads when the structure is in service reduces the precompression, but tensile cracking is generally avoided. Such concrete is known as prestressed concrete.

Versatility

Concrete can be formed to obtain any design shape. It can be mixed near the construction site, or it can be mixed at a central plant and then transported by special agitator trucks if the operation can be completed within about 90 minutes. Such concrete is known as ready-mixed.

cemetery A cemetery is a place designated for BURIAL of the dead. Prehistoric burial grounds have been found in Asia, Europe, and other parts of the world; they often provide archaeologists with a rich source of cultural information.

Cemeteries of the Past. The term *necropolis* ("city of the dead") is applied to the often elaborate cemeteries associated with cities of the ancient Egyptians, Greeks and Romans, Etruscans, and others. Famous Egyptian examples along the Nile are the necropolis of Memphis at SAQQARA and the spectacular VALLEY OF THE KINGS, opposite Thebes. The necropolis of Caere in Italy contained richly furnished Etruscan tombs.

The term *cemetery* (from a Greek word for "resting place") was first used to refer to burial grounds by the early Christians, reflecting their belief in resurrection of the dead. Early Christian cemeteries were at first located outside city walls and from the 3d century in CATACOMBS

Cemeteries reflect the values and religious beliefs of the societies that build them. (Left) *Arlington National Cemetery is dedicated to the memory of military veterans and others who have served the United States.* (Above) *The rock tombs of the Toradja, an isolated people of Celebes, Indonesia, are decorated with effigies of dead ancestors, whom the Toradja honor with elaborate burial rites.*

beneath the city. Interment in church crypts or churchyards became prevalent in medieval times. As churchyards in populous towns and urban centers became overcrowded, cemeteries came to be established outside city limits, supplanting parish graveyards.

Cemeteries Today. Modern cemeteries are operated by the government, by churches, or by private corporations. They may be classified as perpetual care or nonperpetual care cemeteries. In perpetual care cemeteries, a certain percentage of the payment for each plot, usually 20 percent, is set aside in an endowment fund. The fund itself remains inviolate, but the accrued interest is used for maintenance and improvement of the cemetery. A nonperpetual care cemetery has no endowment fund and assesses lot owners for cemetery maintenance and improvement.

Most cemeteries are laid out in the form of burial plots for earth interment. Some permit the erection of large family monuments; in so-called park cemeteries, however, only grave markers that are flush with the ground may be installed. More and more large cemeteries have facilities for burial either in-ground or aboveground in a mausoleum. Many also provide a crematory for CREMATION of the deceased and a columbarium where cremated remains in urns may be placed.

Notable cemeteries include Père Lachaise in Paris; Kensal Garden in London; ARLINGTON NATIONAL CEMETERY in Washington, D.C.; and Forest Lawn near Los Angeles, Calif. Pet cemeteries exist in most large U.S. cities.

Cenozoic Era see EARTH, GEOLOGICAL HISTORY OF; GEOLOGIC TIME

censorship *Censorship* is a word of many meanings. In its broadest sense it refers to suppression of information, ideas, or artistic expression by anyone, whether government officials, church authorities, private pressure groups, or speakers, writers, and artists themselves. In its narrower, more legalistic sense, *censorship* means only the prevention by official government action of the circulation of messages already produced. There are almost as many justifications offered for the suppression of communication as there are would-be censors, but at root the motivation is always the same. It is a fear that the expression, if not curtailed, will do harm to individuals in its audience or to society as a whole.

Censorship has been practiced in both the narrower and the broader senses as long as there have been organized cultures. Those societies which have been most confident of their principles and of the loyalty of their members have allowed the greatest freedom from censorship, for they have been the least fearful of the consequences of dissent. In societies whose values have not been fully accepted by their people or whose leadership rests on shaky foundations, the heaviest hand of censorship has fallen. The relative prevalence of censorship is one of the features that has most distinguished autocratic from democratic societies.

Although one may look to Athens as the birthplace of democracy, it produced its share of censorship. Athenian legislators who were suspected of "dishonorable acts" were subjected to the "scrutiny of orators," an inquiry that could lead to a ban on further speaking in the assembly or courts. In Rome, Emperor Nero deported critics and burned manuscripts of which he disapproved. The

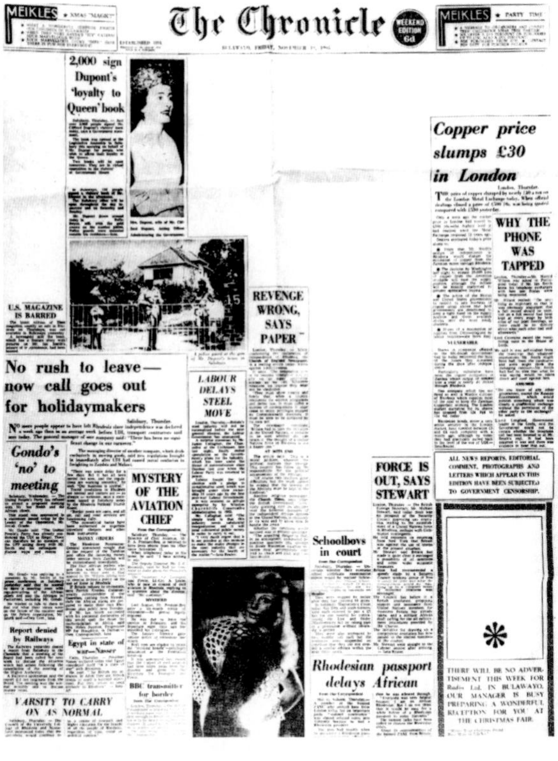
The Chronicle

2,000 sign Dupont's 'loyalty to Queen' book

Copper price slumps £30 in London

WHY THE PHONE WAS TAPPED

U.S. MAGAZINE IS BARRED

REVENGE WRONG, SAYS PAPER

No rush to leave— now call goes out for holidaymakers

LABOUR DELAYS STEEL MOVE

Gondo's 'no' to meeting

MYSTERY OF THE AVIATION CHIEF

FORCE IS OUT, SAYS STEWART

ALL NEWS REPORTS, EDITORIAL COMMENT, PHOTOGRAPHS AND LETTERS WHICH APPEAR IN THIS EDITION HAVE BEEN SUBJECTED TO GOVERNMENT CENSORSHIP.

Schoolboys in court

Report denied by Railways

Egypt in state of war—Nasser

Rhodesian passport delays African

VARSITY TO CARRY ON AS NORMAL

BBC transmitter for border

THERE WILL BE NO ADVERTISEMENT THIS WEEK FOR Radio Ltd. IN BULAWAYO. OUR MANAGER IS BUSY PREPARING A WONDERFUL RECEPTION FOR YOU AT THE CHRISTMAS FAIR.

The front page of this issue of the Bulawayo Chronicle *shows blank spaces where articles were removed by government censors. The deleted articles dealt with Rhodesia's declaration of independence from Great Britain in 1965.*

most notable censorship of the Middle Ages was by church authorities seeking to stamp out heresy. The Fourth Lateran Council in 1215 proscribed the works of Aristotle; the Council of Trent in 1564 established the INDEX of Forbidden Books, which was to last for centuries; and in 1633, Galileo was forced by the Inquisition to disavow his Copernican belief that the Earth was not the center of the universe.

Censorship in Britain

In 1520 a shipment of allegedly heretical books from the Continent to England alarmed the clergy there and led to a proclamation (1529) by Henry VIII against heretical and blasphemous books. Henry then established a licensing system that required the screening of all matter that was to be printed. That system was condemned in John Milton's famous pamphlet *Areopagitica* (published without a license in 1644) and was repealed by Parliament in 1695. Concern over religious heresy gave way in 18th-century England to a preoccupation with attacks on public officials, which were labeled "seditious libel"; in the 19th century obscenity became the chief censorial worry. In 1802 a Society for the Suppression of Vice was founded by Thomas Bowdler, who gave a new term to the English language when he "bowdlerized" (pruned of "indecent" language) an edition of Shakespeare. In 1857, Parliament adopted the Obscene Publications Act, which established procedures for the seizure of obscene material. Starting in the 16th century, the theater in London was also subjected to preproduction review of its plays by the lord chancellor—a practice that was not ended until 1968. Present-day Britain maintains rigid controls over press coverage of pending and ongoing criminal trials, has a strict law against racist rhetoric, and curbs the release of government material through its Official Secrets Act (1911).

Censorship in the United States

Although the legal system in the United States is descended from British law, there have been significant deviations, the most dramatic being the written guarantees of freedom of expression embodied in the 1ST AMENDMENT to the Constitution. Historians continue to debate what the nation's founders meant to include when they wrote that there shall be "no law" abridging the freedom of speech or press, but there is agreement that, at least, they wished to reject the common law of seditious libel, thus making public officials fair game for criticism (see NEW YORK TIMES COMPANY V. SULLIVAN), and to create a barrier against prior restraints by government.

U.S. censorship today is most evident in the areas of government secrecy, public school textbooks and libraries, obscenity and indecency, and restraints (primarily nongovernmental) on the mass media of communication.

Government Secrecy. Information that is produced or collected by government covers a tremendous range. Much of it clearly must be shared with the public if citizens are to make informed judgments about public policy. Some of it just as clearly must be withheld from the public, whether to protect military secrets, investigations of criminal activity, or the privacy of individuals who have been compelled to submit personal data for census or tax purposes. It is the gray area in between that leads to bat-

A photograph taken in prewar Germany shows a band of Nazi party members gathering books allegedly containing "un-German" themes. The offending works were burned at mass rallies.

tles. The government may attempt to suppress material it claims must be kept confidential for national security or other reasons when in fact the principal motive may be to avoid personal or political embarrassment.

Since the administration of George Washington there have been repeated struggles between Congress and the president over information that the legislature wanted to have and that the executive wished to withhold. These contests over what later came to be called EXECUTIVE PRIVILEGE were usually resolved by mutual accommodation. It was not until Richard M. Nixon persisted in his refusal to release particular tape recordings being sought by the WATERGATE special prosecutor that the matter ended up in the U.S. Supreme Court. In *United States* v. *Richard M. Nixon* in 1974 the Court recognized that although there may be some circumstances in which executive privilege might justifiably be claimed, Watergate was not one of them. Twelve days later the incriminating "smoking gun" tape was released, and three days after that Nixon became the first U.S. president to resign from office.

Other examples of the withholding of government information are the sometimes arbitrary classification of material as secret or top secret and thus not to be divulged; the many exemptions from disclosure that were included in the FREEDOM OF INFORMATION ACT of 1966, such as those for internal personnel matters, trade secrets, and matters related to national defense and the conduct of foreign policy; the contracts that Central Intelligence Agency (CIA) employees are required to sign promising for the rest of their lives to submit to the agency for prior review any publication of information learned as a result of their employment; and the exclusion of the press from access to certain events, such as the initial stages of the U.S. invasion of Grenada in 1983 and a wide range of military activities in the Persian Gulf in 1991. With regard to the right of press and public to observe trial proceedings, however, the Supreme Court said in 1980 in *Richmond Newspapers* v. *Virginia* that in the absence of "overriding interest... access to a criminal trial must be open to the public."

Sometimes government efforts to withhold information are thwarted by leaks or by diligent investigative reporting, in which event another tool of censorship is sometimes invoked—a court injunction or restraining order against press dissemination of the material. The Supreme Court in the PENTAGON PAPERS case overturned the temporary restraining order that had been issued by a lower court and held that there is a strong presumption against such prior restraints. The 1st Amendment, said one of the justices, places upon the government the heavy burden of proving that the information, if released, would lead to "direct, immediate and irreparable harm" (see NEW YORK TIMES COMPANY V. UNITED STATES).

As for injunctions against publication of information about pending criminal trials—so-called "gag orders" on the press—the Supreme Court held unanimously in *Nebraska Press Association* v. *Stuart* in 1976 that such orders are permitted only as a last resort, when all other means of securing a fair trial, such as moving its location and sequestering the jury, are inadequate.

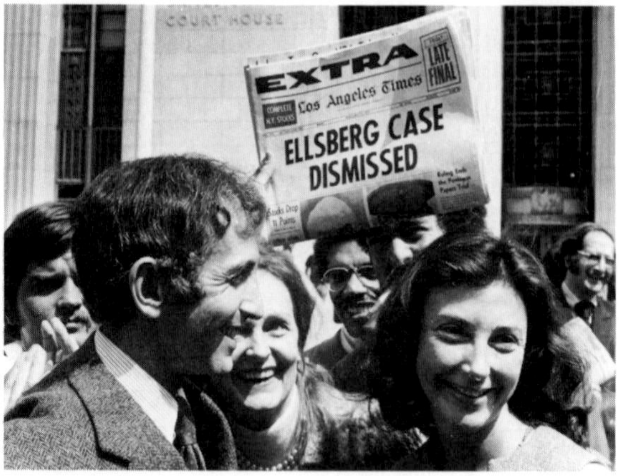

Daniel Ellsberg and his wife celebrate the 1973 court decision to dismiss all charges against him for his unauthorized release of the Pentagon Papers *(1971), classified documents related to U.S. involvement in Indochina between 1945 and 1969.*

Public Schools and Libraries. Another arena that has been rife with controversies over censorship has been the public school system, where students, teachers, parents, administrators, and outside pressure groups often vie over the information and ideas to which students should be exposed. Frequently, the courts are called upon to adjudicate these disputes, not always with consistent results. Generally, it has been held that students may circulate underground newspapers and other literature without censorship by school officials if they do not disrupt the educational process. Regular school newspapers, supported by public funds, may be subjected to the counsel of a faculty advisor, prior review of material, and even to required deletions if those decisions are reasonable and conform to announced criteria. Policies regarding textbook adoptions and removals vary. Some educational authorities have fairly elaborate written procedures to ensure participation by the public, and others operate more informally and even mysteriously. Texas, which has one of the largest school populations in the country, has a Textbook Commission that must approve all books to be used in the state's public schools. A decision by that body can have a restrictive impact on the entire nation (as it had in the treatment of evolution in biology texts), for book publishers do not want their wares to be excluded from one of their largest markets, and they censor their manuscripts accordingly. Furthermore, an inordinate amount of influence by a small but diligent pressure group may be exerted on the decisions of such a commission. The effects of pressure groups are also commonly felt with respect to material in school libraries. All across the country over the years there have been and continue to be incidents in which school officials have ordered the removal from their libraries of everything from J. D. Salinger's *Catcher in the Rye* (1951) and Eldridge Cleaver's *Soul on Ice* (1968) to various works by Judy Blume and Kurt Vonnegut. The grounds have been objectionable language, allegedly unpatriotic or immoral ideologies, or too vivid a portrayal of unpleasant realities. The Supreme Court in 1982 ruled that students and parents are entitled to court review of such decisions but that school boards must have broad discretion. They violate the 1st Amendment only if their motivation is to suppress ideas "in a narrowly partisan or political manner," but not if their criterion is educational suitability.

Obscenity and Indecency. Remarkable changes have occurred in the United States since the days before 1933, when James Joyce's *Ulysses* (1922) was barred from import into the country (see PORNOGRAPHY). Despite the continued position of a slim majority of the Supreme Court that laws against the dissemination of obscene material, even to consenting adults, do not violate the 1st Amendment, as a practical matter, sexually oriented material of a great variety is widely available in "adult" bookstores and movie houses as well as on videotapes. Zoning regulations to control the location of "adult establishments," also upheld by the Supreme Court, are more frequently invoked, as are the Supreme Court-approved laws adopted in many states against child pornography—pictorial material depicting youngsters engaged in sexual activities. The Supreme Court, finally, has upheld the power of the Federal Communications Commission (FCC) to require broadcasters to confine the airing of "indecent" language to time periods when children are not likely to be in the audience.

Restraints on the Mass Media. Aside from restraints on obscenity and indecency, broadcasting in the U.S. has been largely free from government censorship because it has policed itself quite vigorously. One exception has been the portrayal of violence on television, which has aroused the concern of parent groups whose lobbying has been somewhat successful in bringing about change. Occasional libel suits against hard-hitting TV journalism—such as the inconclusive but costly one of Gen. William C. WESTMORELAND against CBS (1984–85) for its treatment of his command during the Vietnam War—may have some inhibiting effect.

As to motion pictures, dramatic changes have occurred during the 20th century. In 1915 the Supreme Court described movies as merely entertainment and thus outside the protections of the 1st Amendment; in 1952, however, the Court rejected that precedent. The prescreening and licensing of movies were still tolerated by the Court, however, and were widely practiced until the mid-1960s. Simultaneously, the movie industry operated under a self-imposed code of standards that was originally very conservative in its provisions but was liberalized over the years. By the mid-1970s governmental movie-censorship boards had been almost universally abolished, and the advisory classification of movies as being for adults or for a general audience had been widely adopted, with some communities invoking the force of law to keep children from adult movies but most relying on the voluntary actions of theater managers. At the same time the content of motion pictures had been thoroughly revolutionized as to the bluntness of the language used, the explicitness of sexual activity portrayed, and the vividness of violence depicted. Movies, as well as the magazines and books sold in the United States today, are virtually free of the hand of the censor.

See also: FREEDOM OF SPEECH; FREEDOM OF THE PRESS.

census A census is an official count at a particular time of people, houses, business firms, or other items of interest. Censuses of some sort have been made throughout human history, beginning in ancient Babylonia, Persia, China, and Egypt. The Romans carried out periodic censuses of the empire for purposes of recruiting and taxation. The U.S. Constitution requires that a census be made every 10 years for the purpose of apportioning representatives in Congress according to population, and the first census in the United States was conducted in 1790. In 1902 the U.S. Bureau of the Census was established.

A census of the U.S. population attempts to count everyone in the country at a specific time. A questionnaire is sent to every household, inquiring how many persons were living there at the designated time and asking for information about sex, age, race, education, previous residences, and number of children living or dead. Some households are asked for additional information as a sample of the total population. To supplement the questionnaire, trained census workers are sent out to interview people directly.

Other census information is obtained by sampling. Computer-assisted statistical procedures make it possible to obtain useful information about many characteristics of the population in general by questioning a selected sample of persons. The census bureau's data-collection activities also include many other kinds of programs: annual surveys of housing and censuses every 5 years of such areas as agriculture, manufacturing, business, and service industries.

Census data are used principally by governments and business firms (especially for market research). Changes in the data are indispensable in forecasting trends in employment, educational requirements, and demand for public services.

Nearly every country now conducts a census of some kind, usually at intervals of 5 or 10 years. The information obtained ranges from basic data on the size, ages, and locations of a country's population to information on migration, family composition, income, and standard of living. Censuses vary in their accuracy. For example, it is known that people tend to exaggerate their amount of education and conceal information about divorces. The U.S. census has been criticized for selective undercounting, particularly of minorities and illegal aliens living in the inner cities. Undercounting affects the level of federal contributions to welfare programs as well as the apportionment of congressional representation.

Centaur [sen'-tawr] Centaur was the first U.S. rocket to employ the high-energy propellants liquid oxygen and liquid hydrogen. The project, originated by the Defense Advanced Research Projects Agency in 1958, was turned over to NASA on July 1, 1959, and developed by its Lewis Research Center. The first launch of the Centaur, as the second stage of a modified Atlas D, took place at Cape Canaveral on May 8, 1962, but the vehicle exploded at 6,100 m (20,000 ft) after the failure of the nose shroud. With the launching of *Surveyor 1* in 1966, the Atlas-Centaur combination became operational.

centaur In Greek mythology a centaur was half man (from head to waist) and half horse and was said to dwell in the mountains. The offspring of IXION, most of the centaurs were crude and savage. CHIRON, however, one of the best-known centaurs, was versed in the arts of hunting, healing, and prophecy.

Centaurus [sen-tohr'-uhs] Centaurus is one of the largest constellations in the Southern Hemisphere. Its brightest star, Alpha Centauri, is the third brightest star in the heavens and a member of a triple star system that includes Proxima Centauri. At a distance of 4.3 light-years, Proxima Centauri is the nearest known star to the Earth, other than the Sun. The constellation also contains the brightest and nearest of the globular clusters, known as Omega Centauri.

Centennial Exposition The Centennial Exposition of 1876, held in Fairmount Park, Philadelphia, to commemorate the 100th anniversary of the signing of the Declaration of Independence, was the first world's fair held in the United States. Nearly 50 foreign countries and 26 states contributed exhibits in technology and the arts and sciences. Many of the almost 10 million visitors were attracted by the display of new machines, including the typewriter, Edison's duplex telegraph, the Westinghouse air brake, the telephone, and the continuous-web printing press. The fair's power was supplied by a steam engine built by the American inventor George Corliss. Originating in a proposal by an association of Philadelphians, the fair was authorized by Congress and then underwritten by the states and by individual and public subscriptions. Memorial Hall is one of the few structures remaining from the exposition.

The torch of the Statue of Liberty (or Liberty Enlightening the World) *was displayed at the Centennial Exposition, held in 1876 in Philadelphia.*

center of gravity The center of gravity of an object is a point at which all of the object's weight may be conceived as being concentrated. The center of gravity of a symmetrical, uniform object lies at the object's geometric center, but it may lie outside the boundaries of irregularly shaped objects. It can be found by suspending an object successively from any two points and finding the intersection of the plumb lines dropped from each point.

The concept of the center of mass is similar to that of the center of gravity, and for objects in a uniform gravitational field the two centers coincide. Where gravity is not uniform or is noneffective (as in free fall or on the atomic level), however, the center of mass is the applicable concept. Thus, the Earth and Moon revolve about a common center of mass located 4,700 km (3,000 mi) from the Earth's center.

The physical laws of the trajectory of a moving object actually apply to the center of mass of the object. Although the object may tumble or spin, the center of mass moves in a smooth curve in accordance with the laws of motion.

Centers for Disease Control The Centers for Disease Control (CDC) is a federal agency that is a part of the United States Public Health Service (see PUBLIC HEALTH). It was originally established (1946) as the Communicable Disease Center and acquired its present title in 1970. Its headquarters and main laboratories are in Atlanta, Ga. The CDC's main components are the Epidemiology Program Office, International Health Program Office, Laboratory Improvement Program Office, Center for Prevention Services, Center for Environmental Health, National Institute for Occupational Safety and Health, Center for Health Promotion and Education, Center for Infectious Diseases, and Center for Professional Development and Training. These divisions conduct disease research, prevention, control, and education programs; train doctors; provide information; develop immunization services; and establish standards for working conditions.

Centigrade scale see CELSIUS SCALE

centipede A centipede is an ARTHROPOD with an elongated, flattened, wormlike body and 15 or more pairs of legs. About 2,800 species are distributed worldwide. These animals typically remain hidden by day and hunt small invertebrates at night. All have poison jaws for paralyzing prey. The smaller centipedes are harmless to humans, but a painful bite can be inflicted by such larger ones as the East Indian *Scolopendra gigantea*, which may be as long as 28 cm (11 in).

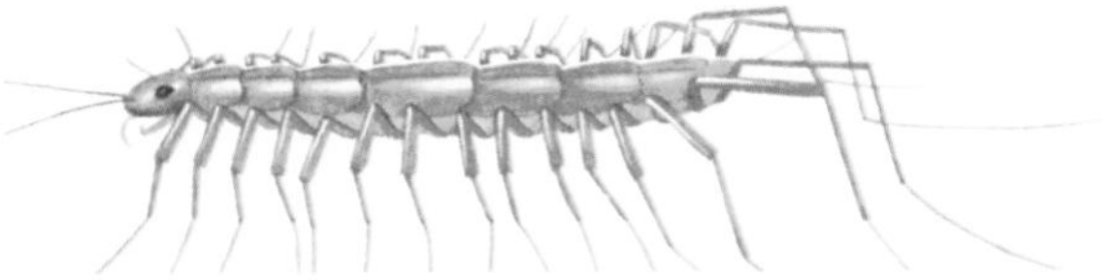

The house centipede is distinguished from other centipedes by its long, spiderlike legs. It lives in damp and dark rooms of houses, where it hunts for insects.

Central Central is an administrative region in the middle of Scotland. Its area is 2,631 km^2 (1,016 mi^2), and it has a population of 271,600 (1988 est.). The River Forth has created a valley in the center of the region, which is otherwise mountainous. The highest point is Ben More in the northern highlands, reaching 1,171 m (3,843 ft). Central was formed in 1975 from parts of the former counties of Perth, Stirling, and West Lothian, and all of Clackmannan.

Central African Republic The Central African Republic (C.A.R.), formerly the Central African Empire (1976–79) and prior to 1960 a French colony, is close to the geographic center of Africa. It is bordered by Chad on the north, Sudan on the east, Zaire and the Congo Republic on the south, and Cameroon on the west.

Land

Most of the C.A.R. is composed of plains between 600 and 900 m (2,000 and 3,000 ft) in elevation. Mount Kayagangire, the highest point in the country, rises to 1,420 m (4,659 ft). The UBANGI RIVER forms the border with Zaire. The climate is tropical, with a rainy season from April to October. Annual precipitation averages 137 cm (54 in), and temperatures range from about 25° C (76° F) during the rainy season to 30° C (85° F) during the dry season. Most of the vegetation is tropical savanna grassland, but rain forests are located in the southwest, and dry savanna grasslands are found in the extreme northeast.

People

While the C.A.R. is a land of many peoples, there are four major ethnic groups: the Baya-Mandja (30% of the population) in the west, the Banda (30%) in the east, and the Nzakara and Azande in the south. Each group has its own language, but most people also speak Sango, a Ubangi language that spread throughout the country during the colonial era. French remains the official language. Most people in the empire still adhere to classical African religions, and the arts—sculpture, oral literature, singing, and dancing—remain closely tied to this traditional milieu. Large areas in the east remain virtually uninhabited, and most of the population is concentrated in the western half of the country. The principal towns are BANGUI, the

AT A GLANCE

CENTRAL AFRICAN REPUBLIC

Land: Area: 622,984 km^2 (240,535 mi^2). Capital and largest city: Bangui (1988 est. pop., 596,776).

People: Population (1990 est.): 2,877,365. Density: 4.6 persons per km^2 (12.0 per mi^2). Distribution (1987): 33% urban, 67% rural. Official language: French. Major religions: traditional religions, Roman Catholicism, Protestantism, Islam.

Government: Type: republic. Legislature: none. Political subdivisions: 14 prefectures, 2 economic prefectures, autonomous commune of Bangui.

Economy: GDP (1988 est.): $1.27 billion; $453 per capita. Labor distribution (1985): agriculture—68%; mining, manufacturing, construction, and public utilities—4%; government and services—8%. Foreign trade (1988 est.): imports—$285 million; exports—$138 million. Currency: 1 C.F.A. franc = 100 centimes.

Education and Health: Literacy (1985): 40% of adult population. Universities (1990): 1. Hospital beds (1984): 3,774. Physicians (1984) 112. Life expectancy (1990): women—48; men—45. Infant mortality (1990): 141 per 1,000 live births.

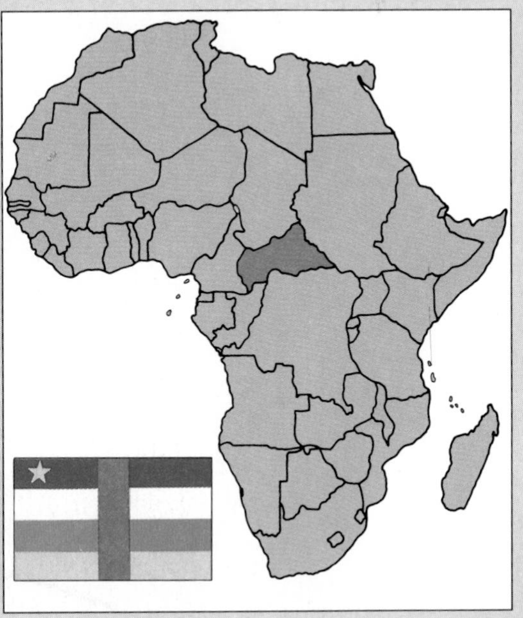

capital, Berbérati, and Bouar. Although eight years of schooling is compulsory, fewer than 60% of school-age children attend.

Economic Activity

The C.A.R. is one of Africa's poorest and most isolated nations. Economic development is slowed by its landlocked location and an inadequate transportation network. The country receives substantial economic aid from France.

The bulk of the population is engaged in subsistence agriculture, and production generally meets domestic food needs. Since independence, however, the government has encouraged the production of cash crops, primarily coffee and cotton. Forestry activities will become increasingly important as transportation facilities are improved.

Diamonds are found in the west, but production declined significantly after the expulsion of foreign mining companies in 1969; uranium deposits near Bakouma are under development, and iron has been found near Bangui. Industrial activities are limited to food processing and light manufacturing.

The C.A.R.'s principal trade route is the river and rail route along the Ubangi and Congo rivers to Brazzaville in the Republic of the Congo, and then by rail to the Congolese port of Pointe-Noire. A road from the western border of C.A.R. to Yaoundé, Cameroon, provides access to the Cameroon port of Douala. The principal imports are machinery, transportation equipment, and textiles. The principal exports are coffee, timber, diamonds, and cotton.

History and Government

Great stone formations near Bouar suggest the existence of an ancient civilization in the northwest, and stone tools found in the east indicate that people lived in this region several thousand years ago. But most of the country's present-day inhabitants are refugees from Muslim slave-raiders in adjacent parts of Africa in the 19th century. The raiders' relentless pursuit resulted in the depopulation of vast regions of the C.A.R. between the 1880s and 1915. About the same time, French military expeditions reached the area, and in the 1890s the region was annexed to the colony of the French Congo; subsequently it became a separate colony in French Equatorial Africa. Internal self-government was granted by the French in 1958. In 1960 the country became independent.

David Dacko became the first president after independence. Dacko was ousted by the military in 1965 and replaced by Jean Bedel BOKASSA, who proclaimed the state an empire in 1976 and crowned himself emperor in a lavish ceremony in 1977. In 1979 he was ousted in a bloodless coup backed by France and led by Dacko, who reestablished the republic and again became president. Dacko was in turn overthrown in a 1981 military coup led by Gen. André Kolingba. A new constitution approved in a

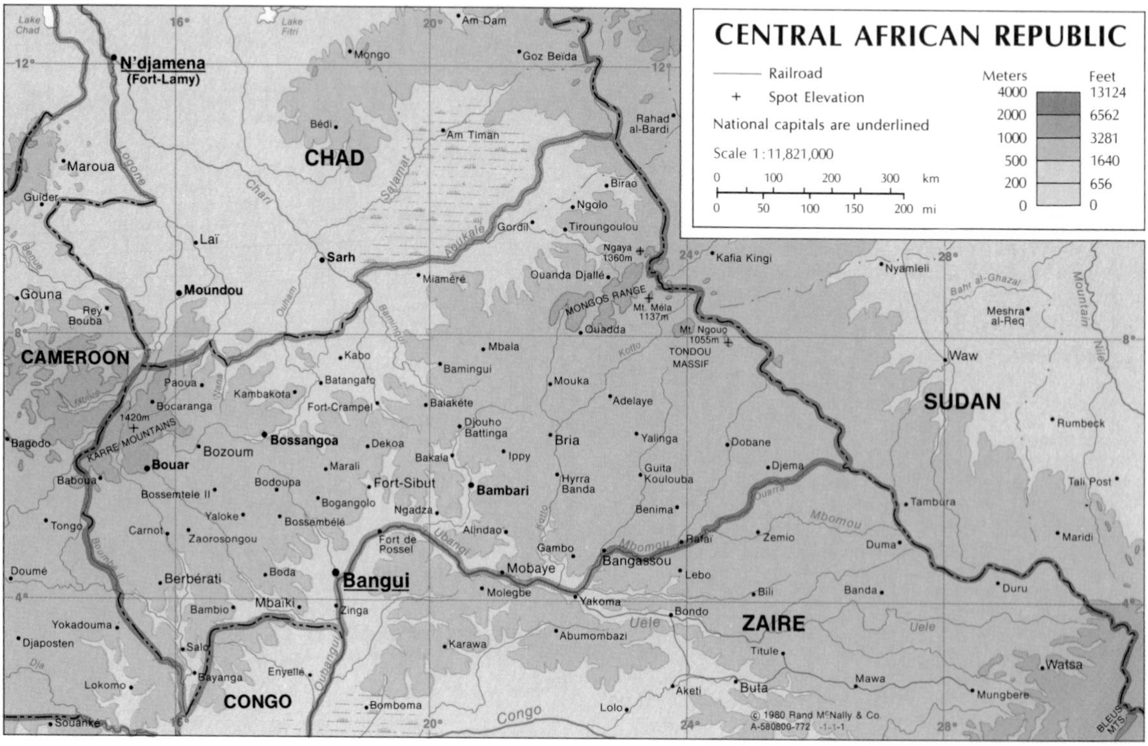

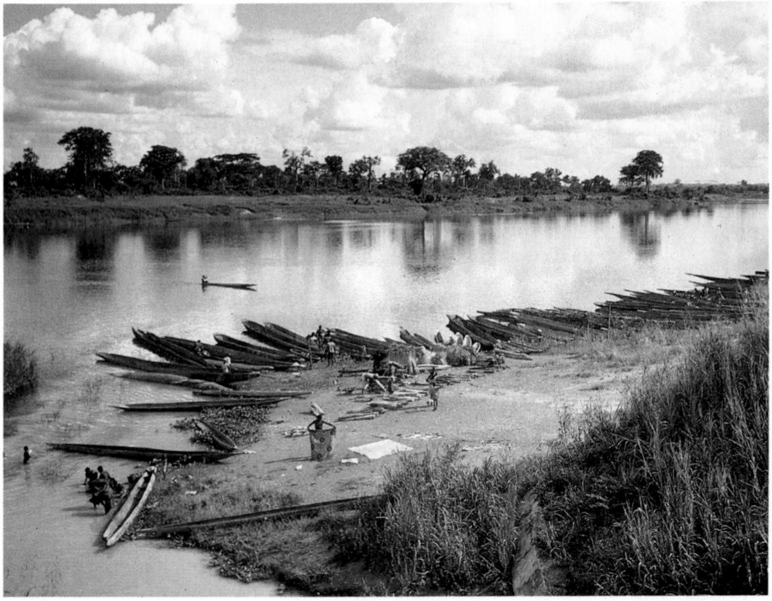

Dugout canoes line the banks of the Ubangi River, a major tributary of the Congo River and a vital artery of the Central African Republic's commercial transport.

1986 referendum made the C.A.R. a one-party state with an elected legislature. In the early 1990s Kolingba, who remained president, faced growing demands for a return to a multiparty system.

Central America

Central America Central America consists of seven small nations: Belize, Guatemala, El Salvador, Honduras, Nicaragua, Costa Rica, and Panama. They are strung along the narrow isthmus that links North America (Mexico) with South America (Colombia), with the Caribbean Sea to the north and east and the Pacific Ocean to the west and south. This strategic location has helped shape the region's history, culture, and economy.

Geography. Central America has an area of about 522,000 km^2 (202,000 mi^2), and its population in 1990 was estimated at about 29 million. Its geography varies from towering volcanoes to some of the world's densest jungles. The volcanoes are the most spectacular feature, forming a nearly 1,300-km-long (800-mi) chain from the Mexican border into central Costa Rica and reaching heights of over 3,650 m (about 12,000 ft). Many of these peaks are still active, contributing to both the richness of the soil and the dangers of life in the area. Central America is also prone to earthquakes.

There is a major break in the chain of volcanoes and mountains in southern Nicaragua, and the chain ends in central Panama. This has made these two areas particularly attractive for trade routes between the Atlantic and Pacific oceans and as possible canal sites.

The coastal lowlands are hot and humid. On the Caribbean side, rainfall may reach 5,080 mm (200 in) a year, and hurricanes often produce major damage. Much of the population live in more temperate, highland areas.

History and Economy. Numerous Indian civilizations rose and fell in Central America before the arrival of the Spaniards. Most notable were the MAYA. Columbus discovered Central America in 1502, and Balboa crossed the isthmus in 1513, but major Spanish conquest and settlement did not take place until the 1520s.

Guatemala was the Spanish colonial capital, but poor communications limited its authority and contributed to local autonomy. Independence came with little fighting in the 1820s. Panama was joined with Colombia, while the rest of the area first united with Mexico, then formed the short-lived CENTRAL AMERICAN FEDERATION, which broke up into five separate nations in 1838. Panama remained part of Colombia until 1903, and Belize finally achieved independence from Great Britain in 1981.

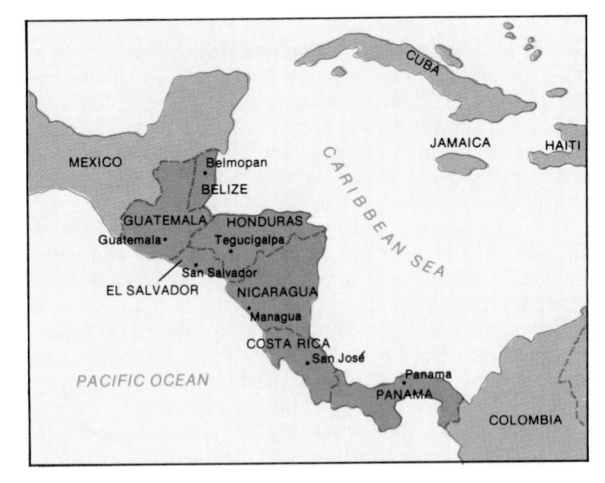

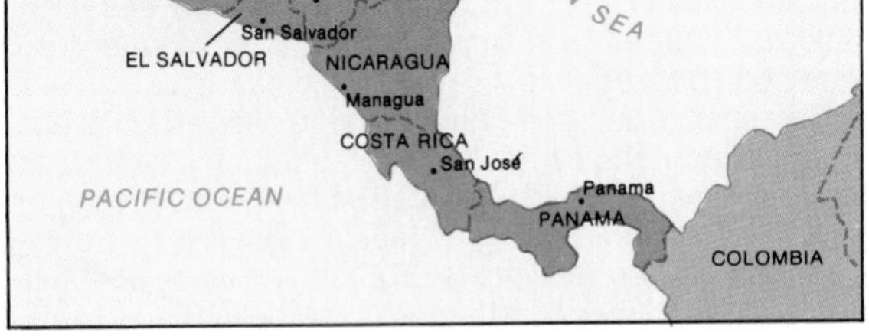

The 19th century was dominated by internal conflicts between liberals and conservatives, by U.S. and British efforts to expand their political influence, and by the introduction of coffee as a major crop. By the end of the century, the coffee business had produced a class of large, wealthy landowners, military dictators had provided some stability, and the United States had become the dominant foreign power. The construction of the PANAMA CANAL and the growth of the U.S.-dominated banana industry further increased U.S. influence in the early 20th century, and frequent landings of U.S. Marines in the region fueled resentment over this influence. Economics and society changed faster than politics. Economic development produced better communications and more education. The growing middle class began to demand more democratic and efficient governments. At the same time, new export crops took the best land away from the rural poor, leading many to move to the cities. As pressures for change mounted, large landowners combined with conservative military leaders to use increasing force to defend their power. In most countries, the path to peaceful change seemed closed, prompting many to support radical-left violence as a means of social and political change. As fighting spread (with the United States, the USSR, and Cuba aiding various groups), tourism and investments declined sharply and debts rose. The Central American Common Market (founded 1960) virtually disintegrated, and high interest rates and low crop prices contributed to near economic collapse.

In 1987, Costa Rica, Guatemala, Honduras, El Salvador, and Nicaragua signed a peace plan that helped bring about elections in Nicaragua in 1990 and the disbanding of U.S.-supported Nicaraguan rebels (contras) based in Honduras. The United States continued to exert its influence, however, intervening militarily in Panama in late 1989. A peaceful transfer of power between elected civilian governments in Guatemala took place in early 1991, and negotiations between the government and rebel forces took place in El Salvador, but an end to regional instability still seemed far away.

Central American Federation The Central American Federation, also called United Provinces of Central America, was a confederation that, from 1823 to 1838, included the present states of El Salvador, Costa Rica, Guatemala, Nicaragua, and Honduras. After winning independence from Spain on Oct. 15, 1821, these provinces were briefly annexed to Mexico. Then, in July 1823, they declared themselves an independent federal republic. Guatemala City was made the capital, and each state was granted local autonomy. In 1825, Manuel José Arce became president.

Dissension between liberals and conservatives broke into civil war. The liberal leader Francisco MORAZÁN took the presidency in 1829 and in 1834 moved the capital to San Salvador. In 1838 the Indian leader José Rafael CARRERA captured Guatemala City, and the union of states was ended. Numerous attempts have been made to restore the union.

Central Asia The term *Central Asia* denotes a huge, generally arid area—much of it actually desert—in the center of the Eurasian land mass. The term has no political meaning, for it refers to portions of the USSR, China, Mongolia, Iran, and Afghanistan. The size of the area may be estimated at 7,500,000 km^2 (2,900,000 mi^2). The population is mostly Turkic and Mongolian, although large-scale movements of Russians and Chinese into their respective territories have changed its composition somewhat.

central bank A central bank is a national institution that functions as the principal controller of the money supply. A central bank has no contact with the general public but acts as a "banker's bank," with the authority to issue currency and to make loans, at interest rates it determines, from its holdings of the cash reserves of commercial banks. It administers foreign-money exchange controls and buys and sells reserves of gold and foreign currencies, thus influencing the value of its country's currency on the international market. Generally, it operates independently of its government, although it often acts as a financial advisor to the administration.

Bank of England. The first bank to assume central banking functions was the BANK OF ENGLAND. From its founding in 1694 it acted as the government's banker, lending it money to fund the NATIONAL DEBT. It soon acquired a practical monopoly of the note issue; eventually other banks began keeping deposits with the Bank of England and using it as a clearinghouse for their transactions with one another. By the 19th century, the Bank of England had acquired another function associated with central banking—that of being the "lender of last resort," to which other banks could turn for aid when they were hard pressed.

During the 19th century the Bank of England developed techniques for regulating interest rates and the amount of credit issued by itself and by the banking system generally. As the leading bank in the world's leading financial center, its actions were considered critical in maintaining the international GOLD STANDARD. By adjusting its discount rate, that is, the interest it charged on loans to commercial borrowers, it was able to affect the international flow of short-term capital. The Bank of England was nationalized in 1946.

Federal Reserve System. The United States had no central bank between 1836, when the second BANK OF THE UNITED STATES ceased to exist, and 1913, when the FEDERAL RESERVE SYSTEM was established. The impetus behind the Federal Reserve was the need for a lender of last resort for the commercial banks, to prevent financial panics. The system was devised after much study of central banks in other countries, particularly of their ability to regulate the supply of credit by adjusting the discount rate. Soon, however, the U.S. banking authorities discovered that they could regulate the supply of money and credit more easily through so-called open-market operations, that is, through buying and selling federal government securities in the open market. When the Federal Reserve sells securities, the reserves of the commercial banks are reduced, and consequently their ability to make loans is decreased. The securities are paid with checks, and checks reduce the reserves of the banks on which they are drawn. When the Federal Reserve buys securities, the opposite effect is achieved: the reserves of the banks are increased, and correspondingly their ability to make loans. One effect of the Depression of the 1930s was to focus attention on central banking as a means of regulating booms and slumps in the economy (see also MONETARY POLICY; MONETARY THEORY).

Other Central Banks. The Banque de France was established in 1800 under Napoleon. It was nationalized in 1945, along with a large number of private commercial banks. French monetary policy is largely under the control of the National Credit Council and the Control Commission.

The BANK OF CANADA, established in 1934 and nationalized in 1938, directs monetary policies through a number of large chartered banks, much as the U.S. Federal Reserve System does through its member banks. Germany's central banking system is similar in many ways to those of the United States and Canada. The Deutsche Bundesbank, owned by the federal government, has branches throughout the German states. It is responsible for maintaining the value of the mark, and it is required to assist the federal government in carrying out economic policies. It is independent, however, in its open-market operations and credit policies.

Central banks play an important role in international negotiations over EXCHANGE RATE problems. The chairs of the European central banks meet regularly at the Bank for International Settlements in Basel, Switzerland, together with representatives from the U.S. Federal Reserve System, to discuss matters of common concern, including the coordination of national monetary policies.

See also: BANKING SYSTEM; MONEY.

Central Europe Central Europe includes the nations of Austria, Czechoslovakia, Hungary, Liechtenstein, Poland, Switzerland, and Germany. The geographic region is bounded by the Alps on the south, the USSR on the east, the Baltic Sea on the north, and the Rhine River valley on the west. The states of Central Europe have dominated much of European history. Because of its central location, the region was settled by ethnically diverse groups. Germanic, Slavic, and Magyar peoples live there.

Central Intelligence Agency The Central Intelligence Agency of the United States (CIA) is one of several organizations responsible for gathering and evaluating foreign intelligence information vital to the security of the United States. It is also charged with coordinating the work of other agencies in the intelligence community—including the NATIONAL SECURITY AGENCY and the Defense Intelligence Agency. It was established by the National Security Act of 1947, replacing the wartime OFFICE OF STRATEGIC SERVICES. Its first director was Adm. Roscoe Hillenkoetter.

The CIA's specific tasks include advising the president and the NATIONAL SECURITY COUNCIL on international developments; conducting research in political, economic, scientific, technical, military, and other fields; carrying on counterintelligence activities outside the United States; monitoring foreign radio and television broadcasts; and engaging in more direct forms of ESPIONAGE and other INTELLIGENCE OPERATIONS.

Throughout its history the CIA has seldom been free from controversy. In the 1950s, at the height of the cold war and under the direction of Allen Welsh DULLES, its activities expanded to include many undercover operations. It subsidized political leaders in other countries; secretly recruited the services of trade-union, church, and youth leaders, along with businesspeople, journalists, academics, and even underworld leaders; and financed cultural organizations and journals.

After the failure of the CIA-sponsored BAY OF PIGS INVASION of Cuba in 1961, the agency was reorganized. In the mid-1970s a Senate Select Committee and a Presidential Commission investigated charges of illegal CIA activities. Among other things, they found that the CIA had tried to assassinate several foreign leaders, including Fidel CASTRO of Cuba. It had tried to prevent Salvador ALLENDE from winning the 1970 elections in Chile and later had worked to topple him from power.

Between 1950 and 1973 the CIA had also carried on extensive mind-control experiments at universities, prisons, and hospitals. In 1977, President Jimmy Carter directed that tighter restrictions be placed on CIA clandestine operations. Controls were later also placed on the use of intrusive surveillance methods against U.S. citizens and resident aliens.

Late in the 1970s, however, fears arose that the restraints had undermined the CIA and compromised U.S. security. In 1981, President Ronald Reagan and CIA director William J. Casey pledged to bolster the CIA's effectiveness. Subsequently, CIA activities furthering the Reagan administration's policy of supporting the "contra" rebels against the Sandinista government of Nicaragua received critical attention. Late in 1986 the IRAN-CONTRA AFFAIR, which involved arms sales to Iran and diversion of some of the profits to the contras, came to light. Casey, who died in May 1987, was succeeded as CIA director by William H. WEBSTER.

central nervous system see NERVOUS SYSTEM

Central Pacific Railroad see TRANSCONTINENTAL RAILROAD

Central Park New York City's Central Park, occupying 340 ha (840 acres) in the center of Manhattan Island, was one of the first public parks laid out by landscape architects. Purchased by the city in 1856, the site was designed by Frederick Law OLMSTED and Calvert VAUX to include walks, lakes, and open fields. The park's attractions include a zoo, the Metropolitan Museum of Art, the Wollman Skating Rink, and the Delacorte Theater, which offers open-air theatrical productions. The park is bordered by expensive apartments and other elegant buildings on three sides—Fifth Avenue, 59th Street, and Central Park West. Its northern edge, at 110th Street, extends into Harlem.

Central Powers Central Powers was the name given to the military alliance of Germany and Austria-Hungary during WORLD WAR I. Until 1914 the two countries had been part of the TRIPLE ALLIANCE with Italy, but in 1915 the latter entered the war on the other side. Germany and Austria-Hungary were joined by the Ottoman Empire in 1914 and Bulgaria in 1915. The Central Powers were defeated in 1918.

central processing unit The central processing unit (CPU) is that part of a digital COMPUTER where the instructions are interpreted and the specified arithmetic operations and data manipulations are carried out. Ordinarily the CPU has connected to it one or more COMPUTER MEMORY units and INPUT-OUTPUT DEVICES, which are usually connected to the CPU via interface terminals and addressed and commanded by the CPU. Thus, in terms of function, the CPU contains both the main calculational workshop and the governing control of the computer system. Accordingly, an entire computer system is usually referred to by the name and type of its CPU.

During the 1960s a CPU usually consisted of at least the arithmetic unit and associated registers, instruction registers, decoders, counters, and enactment controls, and other memory registers and controls. At that time the CPU was usually physically the largest and most complex unit in a computer system and was sometimes also called the mainframe. In the 1970s and 1980s, however, the CPU was reduced substantially in physical size. In modern microcomputers (see COMPUTER, PERSONAL), extremely small silicon chips constitute CPUs.

Central Treaty Organization The Central Treaty Organization (CENTO) was an alliance between Turkey, Iran, Pakistan, and Great Britain for mutual defense. It originated as the Baghdad Pact, signed by Turkey and Iraq on Feb. 24, 1955. Later that year Britain, Pakistan, and Iran joined the alliance. Iraq withdrew after a revolution in 1958, and the headquarters of the alliance was moved to Ankara, Turkey, in October 1958. In 1959 the name was changed from Baghdad Pact to Central Treaty Organization.

The United States was closely associated with CENTO but did not become a full member. It belonged to various committees and sent observers to meetings of the council of ministers, which was the governing body of CENTO.

The council of ministers functioned with a secretariat that was headed by a secretary-general. CENTO had no military staff and no troops. Its main activities were in the fields of economic development and technical cooperation. At the beginning of 1979, Iran and Pakistan withdrew from CENTO, and the remaining members then dissolved the organization.

centrifugal and centripetal forces [sen-trif'uh-gul, sen-trip'-uh-tul] Centripetal ("center-seeking") force is the radial force required to keep an object continually diverted in its path so that it travels in a circle. When a ball on a string is swung in a circle, the string supplies the centripetal force; if the string breaks, the ball will move in a straight line tangential to the original circle. In satellite motion, gravitation between the parent body and the satellite supplies the centripetal force.

Centrifugal ("center-fleeing") force refers to the same phenomenon as centripetal force, but is the force experienced by a circling object as observed from the rotating frame of reference.

Some physicists prefer to think of forces that arise because of acceleration of the reference frame as pseudoforces. A consistent description of resulting motion can be obtained in either the moving or stationary reference frame, however, as long as the two are not confused. It is not appropriate, for instance, to think of the centrifugal force as the equal but opposite reaction to the action of the centripetal force.

The centrifugal force experienced in a rotating system is proportional to mass; therefore, rotating systems can create gravitationlike conditions. In space, for instance, people could live comfortably with normal apparent weight on the inside of rotating structures. For them, "down" would be in the outward radial direction.

See also: MOTION, CIRCULAR.

centrifuge [sen'-tri-fuej] The centrifuge is a mechanical device for separating substances of different relative mass using centrifugal force (see CENTRIFUGAL AND CENTRIPETAL FORCES). A bucket swung in a circle at the end of a rope is a simple example of a centrifuge.

The most common use of the centrifuge is to separate particles suspended in a solution. If the particles are heavier than the solution, they will move to the bottom; if they are lighter, they will float to the top. If particles of different mass are mixed, the particles will be deposited in strata, depending on their relative mass. Centrifuges are widely used in testing laboratories for such tasks as removing the red and white blood cells from serum, obtaining particle-free test solutions, and collecting the sediment from water and sewage samples for examination.

Centrifuges usually have an electric motor to which a rotor, or head, is attached. This rotor is equipped with cups or shields into which the sample tubes to be centrifuged are placed. In manufacturing, continuous-flow centrifuges are sometimes used. A bucket, or drum, spins at high speed as the fluid to be separated flows in. Lighter parts of the mixture come to the top, where they can be drawn off or escape through special ports.

Ultracentrifuges, operating at speeds from 20,000 to

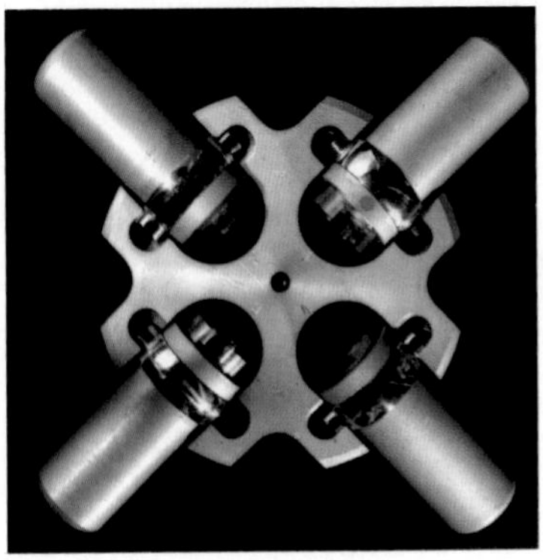

This ultracentrifuge contains four steel cylinders in which solutions and mixtures can be spun at high speeds and subjected to acceleration forces hundreds of thousands of times greater than that of gravity. Such forces can separate large biological molecules from colloidal solutions or liquids from solids of nearly equal density.

5,000,000 revolutions per minute, are made for special applications such as separating and identifying ultrafine particles.

Since centrifugal force accentuates the force of gravity, very large centrifuges are designed to simulate the effect of gravity on other planets or to simulate the force brought to bear in rapid acceleration, such as during a rocket blast-off. Centrifugal force can be calculated using the formula $RCF = 0.00001118 \times r \times N^2$, where RCF is relative centrifugal force (gravities), r is the radius in centimeters, and N is the rotating speed in revolutions per minute.

century plant see AGAVE

cephalic index [se-fal'-ik] The cephalic index is the ratio of the width of the human head to its length. In ANTHROPOMETRY, it is used to measure and compare the head shape of living humans. The index is computed by dividing the maximum width of the head, normally measured just behind and above the ears, by the maximum length, measured from the middle of the brows to the back of the head, and multiplying by 100. This affords a rough means of classifying the head shape as long (dolichocephalic), intermediate (mesocephalic), or broad (brachycephalic).

Cephalochordata [sef'-uh-loh-kor-dah'-tuh] Cephalochordata is one of three subphyla in the phylum Chordata. It and the Urochordata (tunicates) make up the two invertebrate subphyla; the third subphylum, the Vertebrata, contains all the backboned animals. The Cephalochordata includes some 20 to 30 species of widely distributed marine animals, commonly called lancelets, grouped in two genera, *Branchiostoma* and *Asymmetron*. Members of *Branchiostoma* are also called amphioxus, an earlier scientific name.

Lancelets are small, commonly reaching no more than 7.5 cm (3 in) long, and resemble thin, translucent fish. The sexes are separate, and breeding occurs at least once a year. Lancelets spend most of their time buried in the sand, with only their anterior ends protruding. They feed by filtering microscopic organisms from the water.

cephalopod see MOLLUSK

Cepheids see VARIABLE STAR

ceramics Materials made of clay are among the most ancient manufactured articles and have played a vital role in human civilization. Although clay, as a ceramic material, is still widely used, modern ceramics include a wide range of nonorganic, nonmetallic materials whose manufacture requires heating at high temperatures. Important ceramics products include brick (see BRICK AND BRICKLAYING), tile, clay pipe, refractory brick, POTTERY AND PORCELAIN articles and enamels, ferrites in computer memories, barium titanate and alumina in electronics, uranium dioxide as nuclear fuel, and garnets in lasers. GLASS and cement are also major ceramic materials (see CEMENT AND CONCRETE).

The raw materials used to make ceramics are inexpensive and widely available and include clay (see CLAY MINERALS), FELDSPAR, QUARTZ, sand, iron oxides, and alumina. Clay is made up of fine, platelike crystals of hydrated aluminosilicates.

Ceramics Manufacture

Three main steps are involved in making ceramic articles: forming, drying, and firing. Powdered raw materials are mixed with water or other binding liquids, and are formed into articles of the desired shape. Clay articles and re-

This red-figure-style amphora (c.480 BC) presents Athena with her characteristic accoutrements. In red-figure pottery, the decorations were outlined before the entire background was blackened, leaving the figures the natural reddish color of the clay. Details were painted, not incised, allowing a broader range of expression and a more fluid treatment of the subject. Unlike modern ceramic techniques, most of the decoration of Greek pottery took place before the piece had been fired. (Collection Ciba, Basel, Switzerland.)

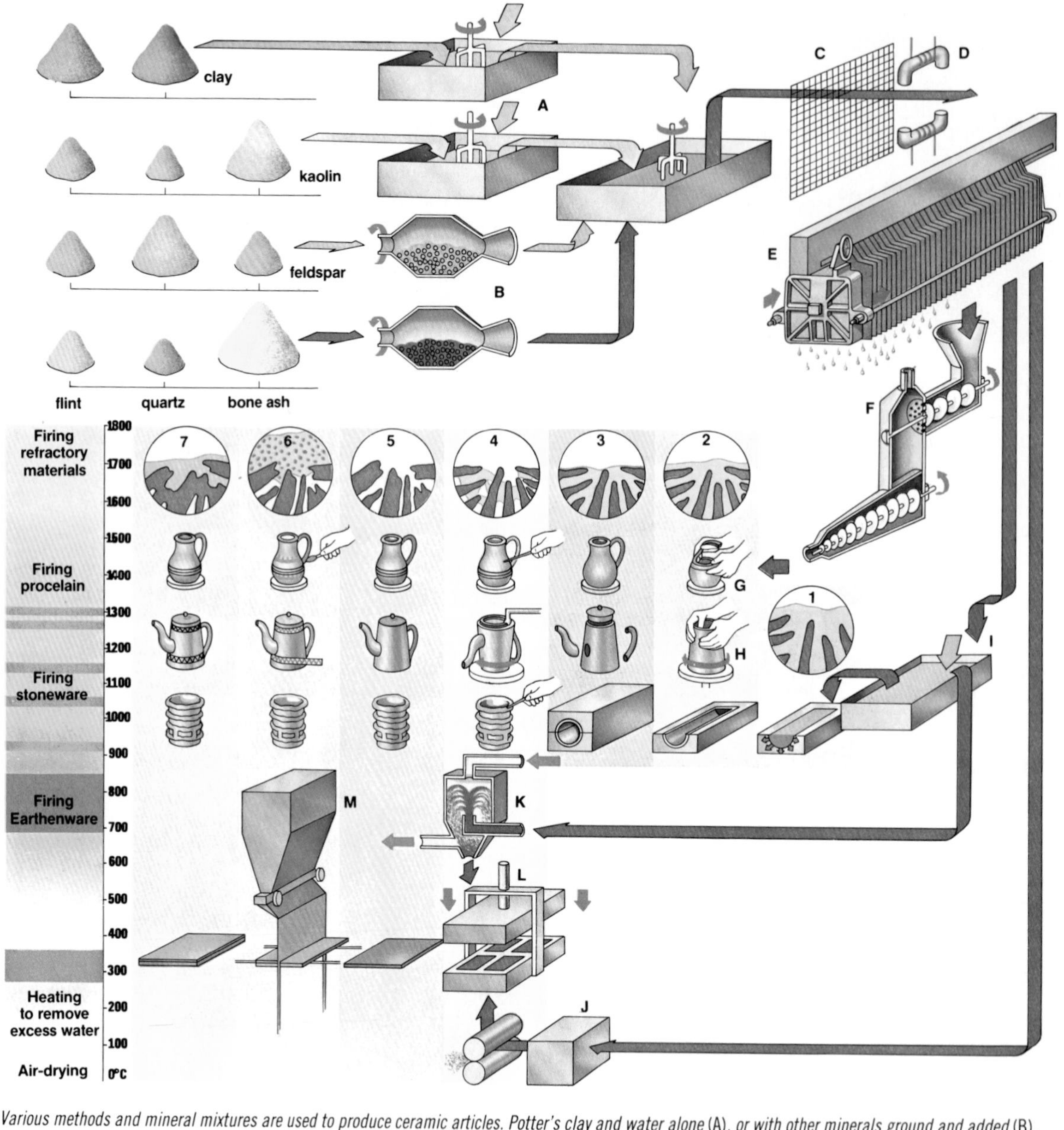

Various methods and mineral mixtures are used to produce ceramic articles. Potter's clay and water alone (A), *or with other minerals ground and added* (B), *are passed through a screen* (C), *freed of iron particles by an electromagnet* (D), *then pressed* (E) *and remixed in a pug mill* (F). *The extruded mix is used for coiling* (G) *or throwing* (H) *pottery; it is mixed with water for slip-casting* (I), *or it is dried and powdered* (J, K) *for pressing* (L). *Glaze is applied* (M) *after the first firing. The numbered circles represent water-suffused, malleable clay* (1); *worked clay, air-dried or heated* (2–4); *the first, or bisque, firing* (5); *glazing* (6); *and glaze firing* (7). *Firing temperatures* (left) *are approximate.*

fractory brick are usually pressed damp, with about 10 percent water, into dies or molds under moderate pressures. Ceramics made of purified powders such as alumina and ferrites are pressed dry at higher pressure with an organic binder. In *isostatic pressing,* the powder is held in a rubber mold, and the pressure is applied with a fluid such as glycerine, which gives uniform pressure throughout the sample with less warping and fewer defects.

In *slip casting,* complex shapes can be made economically. A suspension of ceramic powder is poured into a plaster-of-paris mold, which absorbs water, so that a hard lining on the mold wall is built up; then excess liquid is poured out of the mold.

After forming, the ceramic ware must be carefully

heated for a few hours at about 100°–200° C (about 200°–400° F) to remove excess water or binder. After drying, the article is fired at a high temperature (800°–2000° C/1500°–3500° F) to SINTER the individual crystals of the ceramic powder into a solid, coherent mass.

In *solid-state sintering,* individual particles join together in an increasingly dense mass, as continuous pores are formed, and finally only isolated pores remain. The smaller the particles in the original powder, the more rapid is the sintering.

In *hot pressing,* a sample is heated to the firing temperature and pressed at the same time. This process is expensive because special dies, usually of graphite, are needed.

Important Ceramic Categories

The most common ceramic articles of pottery, porcelain, brick, and pipe form complex mixtures of several different solid phases after firing. Traditional *whitewares* and *porcelains* contain at least three starting materials—clay, feldspar, and silica sand. When a mixture of these materials is heated at high temperatures (above 1200° C/2200° F), the feldspar (potassium-sodium aluminosilicate) melts and coats the clay and sand crystals. As firing proceeds, fine, needlelike crystals of an aluminosilicate called mullite are formed from the clay. In the cooled structure there is a glassy phase from liquid feldspar that binds together sand grains and mullite crystals. This glassy phase may also give the ware a smooth, polished surface.

Firing at an intermediate temperature (about 1100° C/2000° F) produces stoneware, a heavy, opaque ceramic, nonporous and glazed. At lower firing temperatures (less than 1000° C/1832° F), earthenware, a more porous ware with a rough surface, results. Fine, translucent porcelain requires a higher firing temperature (up to 1400° C/2500° F).

New Ceramics Applications

"High technology" ceramics are new types of materials that surpass earlier ceramics in strength, hardness, light weight, or improved heat resistance. For example, ceramic powders can now be made from particles of absolutely uniform size, which produce ceramics that are far less vulnerable to fracture than ordinary ceramics. Added to a matrix of metal, thin ceramic fibers increase the tensile strength of such a composite material.

Ferrites are iron oxides that are magnetic but do not conduct electricity. They are used in electronic devices such as filters and transformers, and in computer memory cores. Other new metallic ceramics are superconductors. At relatively high temperatures (77 kelvins), they conduct electrical current without resistance (see SUPERCONDUCTIVITY).

Barium titanate has a high dielectric constant and consequently is used in CAPACITORS. Because it is also strongly piezoelectric (see PIEZOELECTRICITY), it is used in microphones, phonograph pickups, strain gauges, and ultrasonic devices.

The APATITES are a family of calcium phosphate minerals that have been widely used as phosphors in fluorescent lamps. Hydroxylapatite is a bone mineral, and has recently been developed as a bone and tooth implant material.

Uranium ores are reacted and purified to form the pure metal, which is then sintered into pellets that serve as nuclear fuel.

Ceramics, such as ruby and garnet, have proven to be ideal hosts for the fluorescent ions needed in LASERS.

Amorphous ceramics are produced by firing ceramic material for a short time at low temperatures, to produce substances that lack the usual crystalline ceramic structure. They are used to make complex shapes and thin ceramic films.

Ultrahard ceramic layers are built into the steel in tank bodies, making them better able to withstand incoming projectiles.

For use at high temperatures, ceramics are in many ways superior to metals. An engine made from ceramic material would, for example, be lighter in weight, less subject to corrosion and chemical wear, and could operate at higher temperatures without requiring a water-cooling system. Although ceramics are used today for such mechanical applications as the blades of turbines, a fracture-proof ceramic material for the basic parts of a diesel or gas-turbine engine is still under development.

Cerberus [sur'-bur-uhs] In Greek mythology, Cerberus was the three-headed dog that guarded the entrance to HADES. He had the tail of a snake and had snakes wrapped around his neck. One of the 12 labors of HERCULES was to subdue him.

cereal see GRAIN

cerebral palsy [suh-reeb'-rul] Cerebral palsy is a nonspecific condition in which brain damage before or at birth leads to partial paralysis. The most common cause of the disorder is traumatic delivery due to either small maternal pelvis, large fetal head, forceps compression of the head, umbilical cord strangulation, or the partial separation of the placenta from the uterus before delivery. Other causes include oxygen deprivation in the newborn due to excessive anesthesia, delayed spontaneous respiration, or severe cardiac malformations.

Certain infections during pregnancy may also increase the risk of cerebral palsy. These infections include toxoplasmosis, measles, mumps, cytomegalic inclusion disease, and syphilis, all of which may affect brain tissue. Bacterial meningitis or encephalitis may occur as a result of nonsterile delivery and cause brain damage. Similarly, a fetus subjected to radiation or toxic chemicals, including alcohol, is also a candidate for cerebral palsy.

As a result of the above, the infant may have a small brain, hydrocephalus, or focal lesions in the brain. The child's appearance ranges from the demented and deformed to the bright, alert, and happy, with one wasted and spastic limb. Physical therapy may provide some benefit, but the frequency of cerebral palsy will diminish only with improved prenatal care and delivery techniques.

See also: NERVOUS SYSTEM, DISEASES OF THE.

Ceres (astronomy) [sir'-eez] Ceres, the largest of the minor planets, or ASTEROIDS, was the first to be discovered by Giuseppe Piazzi, on Jan. 1, 1801. Its diameter is about 785 km (488 mi), and it orbits the Sun every 4.6 years at an average distance of 414 million km (257 million mi). Its mass accounts for approximately one-half the combined mass of the asteroids.

Ceres (mythology) Ceres was the Roman goddess of agriculture whose functions and worship were patterned after those of her Greek counterpart, DEMETER. The cult of Ceres was introduced in Rome in order to end a famine. Ceres was invoked as the goddess of grains, particularly corn. The Roman Cerealia, from which the English word *cereal* is derived, was a spring festival in her honor. At the sacrificial altars in her temples, pregnant pigs, the symbols of fecundity, were offered.

Cerf, Bennett Bennett Cerf, b. New York City, May 25, 1898, d. Aug. 27, 1971, was a major figure in U.S. publishing. He was also a television personality who offered puns and wry observations on the show "What's My Line?" from 1952 to 1966. In 1925 he founded the Modern Library, which made inexpensive hardback standard works available to many. He founded Random House in 1927 and was president until 1966. In 1933, after a court battle that resulted in a landmark decision on censorship, Cerf won the right to publish James Joyce's *Ulysses* in the United States. In his syndicated columns and in his books, including *Try and Stop Me* (1944) and *The Laugh's on Me* (1959), he revealed his wide interests and optimism. After his death, a series of interviews with Cerf was compiled to form a sort of autobiography, *At Random* (1977).

cerium [sir'-ee-uhm] Cerium is a chemical element, the most abundant of the LANTHANIDE SERIES. Its symbol is Ce, its atomic number is 58, and its atomic weight is 140.12. It occurs in many minerals, especially monazite and bastnaesite. The element was discovered in 1803 by M. H. Klaproth and independently by J. J. BERZELIUS and W. Hisinger. It was named for Ceres, an asteroid. Finely divided cerium, which may ignite spontaneously, is a constituent of an iron alloy used for lighter flints. Cerium and misch metal, an alloy of 50 percent cerium with several other rare-earth metals, are used to remove oxygen in vacuum tubes.

CERN Laboratory see EUROPEAN ORGANIZATION FOR NUCLEAR RESEARCH

Cerro Tololo Inter-American Observatory [say'-roh toh-loh'-loh] Cerro Tololo Inter-American Observatory is situated on a 2,200-m (7,200-ft) peak in the Andes Mountains, 400 km (250 mi) north of Santiago, Chile. It was dedicated in 1963 by the Association of Universities for Research in Astronomy (AURA) and is closely linked with AURA's other major facility, KITT PEAK NATIONAL OBSERVATORY, in Tucson, Ariz. The clear, stable air at Cerro Tololo makes it an especially fine site for observation. Instruments include a 4-m (158-in), a 1.5-m (60-in), a 102-cm (40-in), a 92-cm (36-in), a 61-cm (24-in), and two 41-cm (16-in) reflecting telescopes. The 4-m instrument is identical to the 4-m Mayall Telescope at Kitt Peak; both took 13 years to build and incorporate significant technological refinements. The observatory is especially important because of its capability of viewing southern-declination celestial objects, particularly the central portion of the Milky Way galaxy.

cerussite [sir'-uh-syt] The CARBONATE MINERAL cerussite ($PbCO_3$) is a widely distributed and common ore of lead. It forms white or tinted crystals with adamantine-to-vitreous luster, hardness of 3 to 3½, and specific gravity of 6.4 to 6.6. Cerussite forms by chemical action in the upper, oxidized zones of ORE DEPOSITS.

Cervantes Saavedra, Miguel de [sair-vahn'-tays, sah-ah-vay'-drah, mee-gel' day] Miguel de Cervantes Saavedra, b. Sept. 29?, 1547, d. Apr. 23, 1616, a Spanish novelist, dramatist, and poet, was the author of the novel DON QUIXOTE (Part 1, 1605; Part 2, 1615), a masterpiece of world literature. Cervantes was born to a poor family in the university town of Alcalá de Henares. Without the means for much formal education, he became a soldier, lost the use of his left hand in the Battle of Lepanto (1571), and was imprisoned (1575–80) in Algiers. On his return to Spain he worked at a series of government jobs that involved extensive travel in Andalucía. Only at the end of his life was he able to devote full attention to his writings.

Cervantes's first literary efforts, as a playwright and as author of a pastoral novel, *Galatea* (1585; Eng. trans., 1867), were unsuccessful. The work best received by his contemporaries was his *Exemplary Novels* (1613; Eng. trans., 1640), a collection of 12 tales in various genres. Cervantes's most theoretically ambitious work was *The Travels of Persiles and Sigismunda,* published by his widow in 1617 (Eng. trans., 1619), in which he tried to create a prose epic in imitation of the recently rediscovered *Ethiopian Story* of Heliodorus.

Cervantes's place in world literature, however, rests on *Don Quixote,* of which the full Spanish title is *El ingenioso hidalgo Don Quijote de la Mancha.* Cervantes declared in the prologue that his intent was to destroy the popularity of the Spanish romances of chivalry, and in much of the book he does parody them. Don Quixote, an old and unattractive man, is the opposite of a knight-errant; his

Miguel de Cervantes Saavedra joined the Spanish army as a young man and lost the use of a hand in battle. On his return, he was kidnapped by pirates and suffered for years in slavery. Many of Cervantes's military experiences formed the basis for adventures featured in Don Quixote de la Mancha, *his classic tale of a misguided knight-errant who lives by a code of chivalry from a bygone age.*

misguided attempts to treat as characters from his reading the everyday people he meets on his travels are hilarious. *Don Quixote* has another purpose besides humor, however: it is a study of reality, or an examination of the value of idealism. The best of the many translations into English of *Don Quixote* is that of Samuel Putnam (1954).

Cervantes's other works include a long poem, *The Trip to Parnassus* (1614; Eng. trans., 1870), and a collection of plays, *The Interludes of Cervantes* (1615; Eng. trans., 1948).

cervicitis Cervicitis is an inflammation of the membrane lining the cervix, the narrow opening to the uterus in the female reproductive system. It is usually characterized by redness; increased numbers of leukocytes, or white blood cells; tenderness; severe pain on movement in the area; urinary disorders; bleeding following coitus (sexual intercourse); and a pus-containing cervical discharge.

Cervicitis occurs most frequently in young women and results mainly from coitus. Infections by streptococci and staphylococci may also cause cervicitis secondary to abortion or to the use of intrauterine devices (IUDs) for birth control. The most common cause of acute cervicitis is gonorrhea, which results in an inflammation of the glands of the most interior portion of the cervix. Diagnosis is made based on a culture of material obtained from the purulent discharge. Since the symptoms may also suggest tumors of the cervix, it is essential to rule them out before treatment for cervicitis begins. Treatment consists of avoiding coitus and IUDs and using specific antibiotics, depending on the organism responsible.

Césaire, Aimé [say-zair', ay-may'] The black poet, playwright, and essayist Aimé Césaire, b. Martinique, June 25, 1913, formulated the concept of Negritude with Senegalese poet Léopold Sédar SENGHOR. That concept encouraged blacks to accept their African heritage and embrace a black culture independent of that imposed by French colonialism. Using the imagery of surrealism to free himself, Césaire voiced his sense of Negritude in the poems of *Return to My Native Land* (1947; Eng. trans., 1968) and *Ferrements* (1960). His increasing black militancy and anticolonialism found expression in such plays as *La tragédie du roi Christophe* (The Tragedy of King Christophe, 1963) and *Une saison au Congo* (A Season in the Congo, 1966).

cesarean section Cesarean section is the surgical delivery of an infant through an abdominal and uterine incision. Conditions indicating that a cesarean section may be preferable to natural birth include a previous section, pelvic tumors, narrow pelvis, hemorrhage resulting from an accident, abnormal position of the fetus in the uterus, fetal distress, or an unusually large child. In the late 1950s, sections were performed in 1 out of 20 deliveries; by the late 1980s, they were performed in 1 out of 4 deliveries. Critics claim that the procedure is often performed unnecessarily (to save time or as "insurance" against malpractice suits) and that it is dangerous to both mother and child.

cesium [see'-zee-uhm] Cesium is a chemical element, a soft, silver-white ALKALI METAL. Its symbol is Cs, its atomic number is 55, and its atomic weight is 132.905. The element was discovered by Robert BUNSEN and Gustav KIRCHHOFF in 1860. The stable isotope ^{133}Cs occurs naturally. Many radioactive isotopes have been produced artificially; ^{137}Cs, with a half-life of 33 years, is used as a source of gamma radiation. Cesium reacts violently with water and may ignite spontaneously on exposure to moist air.

Because of its sensitivity to light, it is used in photoelectric devices. It is used to remove traces of gas in vacuum tubes. The natural frequency of the cesium atom is used as a time standard in the cesium clock, a type of ATOMIC CLOCK.

Céspedes, Carlos Manuel de [says'-pay-days] Carlos Manuel de Céspedes y del Castillo, b. Apr. 18, 1819, d. Feb. 27, 1874, was a revolutionary leader in preindependent Cuba. A skilled guerrilla fighter, he led the armed revolt against Spanish rule that developed into the TEN YEARS' WAR (1868–78). As president of the revolutionary government from 1868, Céspedes campaigned unsuccessfully for U.S. recognition and presided over the constitutional convention that opted for a representative form of government and the abolition of slavery. After being deposed in 1873, he was captured and killed by Spanish forces the following year.

cetacean [see-tay'-shuhn] Cetaceans, of the aquatic mammalian order Cetacea, include DOLPHINS, NARWHALS, PORPOISES, and WHALES, some of which are the largest animals in the world. The blue whale measures up to 30 m (100 ft) long and weighs up to 150 tons. Some dolphins, however, may be less than 1.2 m (4 ft) long and weigh 27 kg (60 lb). A cetacean has its tail flukes in a horizontal position instead of vertical, as in a fish, and it propels itself through the water by up and down movements of its tail. It has a torpedo-shaped body and no gills; the front limbs are modified into flippers. Oily secretions of the tear ducts protect the eyes from salt water. Cetaceans breathe directly into the lungs through single or double blowholes on top of the head. The phrase "Thar she blows!" refers not to a water spout but to a fountain of condensed moisture and mucus from the blowhole. The largest species of whale can submerge for a period that exceeds one hour by expelling air from its lungs and closing its blowhole. Cetaceans live in all oceans and in tropical rivers and lakes. A cetacean dies if it is out of water for a considerable length of time.

Cetewayo, King of the Zulus [set-eh-wah'-yoh] Cetewayo, b. *c.*1825, d. Feb. 8, 1884, was the last king of independent Zululand (1872–79, 1883–84). A nephew of SHAKA, he became effective ruler in 1856, although he did not succeed his father to the throne until 1872. Cetawayo sought alliance with the British to forestall AFRIKANER encroachment on his domains. The British, however, invaded Zululand. Although routed in the Battle of Isandhlwana (1879), the British returned to defeat the Zulu forces and deposed Cetewayo in 1879. Restored to power (1883), he was again deposed by rivals and died a fugitive.

Ceylon see SRI LANKA

Cézanne, Paul [say-zahn'] The French painter Paul Cézanne, b. Jan. 19, 1839, d. Oct. 22, 1906, exhibited little in his lifetime and pursued his interests increasingly in artistic isolation. Today he is regarded as one of the great forerunners of modern painting, both for the way that he evolved of putting down on canvas exactly what his eye saw in nature and for the qualities of pictorial form that he achieved through a unique treatment of space, mass, and color.

In Paris Cézanne met Camille PISSARRO and came to know others of the impressionist group, with whom he exhibited in 1874 and 1877. Cézanne, however, remained an outsider to their circle; from 1864 to 1869 he submitted his work to the official SALON and saw it consistently rejected. His paintings of 1865–70 form what is usually called his early "romantic" period. Extremely personal in character, it deals with bizarre subjects of violence and fantasy in harsh, somber colors and extremely heavy paintwork.

Thereafter, as Cézanne rejected that kind of approach

The Card Players *(1890–92) reveals Cézanne's development of a new, formal system of space and structure, using flat planes in which the spaces between figures are as solidly rendered as the stable, simplified figures. (Musée d'Orsay, Paris.)*

and worked his way out of the obsessions underlying it, his art is conveniently divided into three phases. In the early 1870s, through a mutually helpful association with Pissarro, with whom he painted outside Paris at Auvers, he assimilated the principles of color and lighting of IMPRESSIONISM and loosened up his brushwork; yet he retained his own sense of mass and the interaction of planes, as in *House of the Hanged Man* (1873; Musée d'Orsay, Paris).

In the late 1870s, Cézanne entered the phase known as "constructive," characterized by the grouping of parallel, hatched brushstrokes in formations that build up a sense of mass in themselves. He continued in this style until the early 1890s, when, in his series of paintings titled *Card Players* (1890–92), the upward curvature of the players' backs creates a sense of architectural solidity and thrust, and the intervals between figures and objects have the appearance of live cells of space and atmosphere.

In his late phase, Cézanne concentrated on a few basic subjects: still lifes of studio objects built around such recurring elements as apples, statuary, and tablecloths; studies of bathers, based upon the male model and drawing upon a combination of memory, earlier studies, and sources in the art of the past; and successive views of the Mont Sainte-Victoire, a nearby landmark, painted from his studio looking across the intervening valley. The landscapes of the final years, much affected by Cézanne's contemporaneous practice in watercolor, have a more transparent and unfinished look, while the last figure paintings are at once more somber and spiritual in mood. By the time of his death, Cézanne's art had begun to be shown and seen across Europe, and it became a fundamental influence on virtually all advanced art of the early 20th century (see FAUVISM and CUBISM).

Chabrier, Emmanuel [shah-bree-ay'] Emmanuel Chabrier, b. Jan. 18, 1841, d. Sept. 13, 1894, was a French composer best known for his orchestral rhapsody *España*. In Paris he studied not only piano and composition but law, and had a brief career in government service. A trip to Spain resulted in *España* (1883), which draws heavily from the lyricism, color, and rhythmic vitality of Spanish music. An influence on Claude Debussy and Maurice Ravel, Chabrier, in his personality as well as in his music, reflected dry wit and considerable *joie de vivre*. He also wrote operas, piano pieces, songs, and works for orchestra and voice.

Chaco [chah'–koh] The Chaco (or Gran Chaco) is a huge lowland area of mostly arid plains in south central South America. It covers approximately 725,000 km^2 (280,000 mi^2) in Argentina, Bolivia, and Paraguay. The Chaco is an alluvial region. Soils are sandy, and swamps are common, with the eastern area subject to widespread flooding. Population is sparse, and cattle raising is the main economic activity. The Chaco Boreal, the main portion of the region, was disputed by Bolivia and Paraguay for 86 years. A traditional Bolivian territory, it had been settled by Paraguayans, and was fought over in the CHACO WAR (1932–35). Most of the area was awarded to Paraguay and remains of little economic value.

Chaco Canyon Chaco Canyon, in northwest New Mexico about 70 km (45 mi) south of Bloomfield, is the site of numerous ruins of the prehistoric ANASAZI culture, including the largest and most completely excavated multistoried communal dwelling, Pueblo Bonito. A national monument from 1907, it was renamed Chaco Culture National Historic Park in 1980. The 88-km^2 (34-mi^2) park constitutes, with MESA VERDE, one of the most extensive collections of pueblo ruins in the southwest.

Chaco War The Chaco War was a conflict between Bolivia and Paraguay over ownership of the Chaco Boreal, a 259,000-km^2 (100,000-mi^2) area of the CHACO. The area assumed importance when Bolivia, which had lost its coastal territory to Chile in the War of the Pacific (1879–83), sought a new outlet to the sea through the Río de la Plata system. It began to fortify the Chaco Boreal in 1906, provoking Paraguay to build its own forts. Skirmishing began in 1928, and full-scale war erupted in 1932. Led by the brilliant Col. José Felix Estigarribia, Paraguayan forces drove the Bolivians back and, on Nov. 17, 1934, captured the key Bolivian fort of Balliviáh.

A truce was signed on June 12, 1935. The peace treaty of July 21, 1938, gave Paraguay title to the majority of the disputed land, but Bolivia received a corridor of access to the Paraguay River and a port (Puerto Casado).

chaconne see PASSACAGLIA AND CHACONNE

Chad The Republic of Chad is a landlocked state in north central Africa. The largest country of the former French Equatorial Africa, it is bounded on the north by Libya, on the east by Sudan, on the south by the Central African Republic, on the southwest by Cameroon, and on the west by Nigeria and Niger. The capital is N'DJAMENA (formerly Fort-Lamy).

Land and People

Most of Chad is a large basin bordered by mountains and highlands in the north (where Emi Koussi, the highest point in the country, rises to 3,415 m/11,204 ft), east, and south. A vast inland sea once filled the depression, of which Lake CHAD is a remnant. Neolithic rock paintings exist in the northern mountains, and archaeological evidence around the lake and its main tributaries, the Logone and Shari rivers, suggests the existence of a settled civilization as early as the 9th century.

The country has three climatic zones. The north is arid, and vegetation is limited to scattered oases; the south is tropical, with light woodlands and grasslands. In the semiarid middle region the drier grasslands give way

AT A GLANCE

REPUBLIC OF CHAD

Land: Area: 1,284,000 km^2 (495,755 mi^2). Capital and largest city: N'djamena (1986 est. pop., 511,700).

People: Population (1990 est.): 5,000,000. Density: 3.9 persons per km^2 (10.1 per mi^2). Distribution (1987): 27% urban, 73% rural. Official languages: French, Arabic. Major religions: Islam, traditional religions, Christianity.

Government: Type: military rule. Legislature: National Assembly (suspended 1990). Political subdivisions: 14 prefectures.

Economy: GNP (1988): $850 million; $160 per capita. Labor distribution (1985): agriculture, herding, and fishing—81%; services—14%; industry—5%; Foreign trade (1986): imports—$206.1 million; exports—$98.6 million. Currency: 1 C.F.A. franc = 100 centimes.

Education and Health: Literacy (1985): 25% of adult population. Universities (1990): 1. Hospital beds (1986): 4,284. Physicians (1987) 74. Life expectancy (1990): women—40; men—38. Infant mortality (1990): 136 deaths per 1,000 live births.

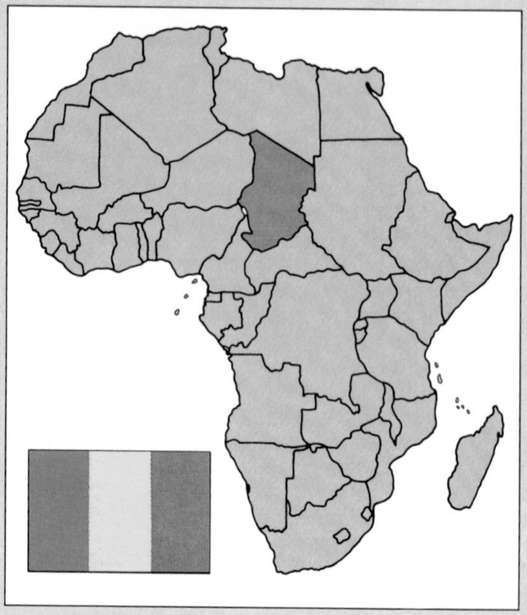

to thornbush. The rainy season lasts from May to October and is somewhat longer in the south, with annual precipitation increasing from 300 to 1,270 mm (12 to 50 in) between the capital and the far south. In the northern Saharan region, rainfall is rare. Temperatures range between 27° and 38° C (80° and 100° F). Animal life is varied, and fish are plentiful.

The many different ethnic groups in Chad include the Sara peoples in the south; the FULANI, Barma, Kanembu, Arabs, and Maba in the middle zone; the nomadic Teda, Daza, and Tubu in the north; and the Kotoko along the rivers. Most of the people in the northern two-thirds of the country, or about half the total population, are Muslims. In the tropical south the population is divided between

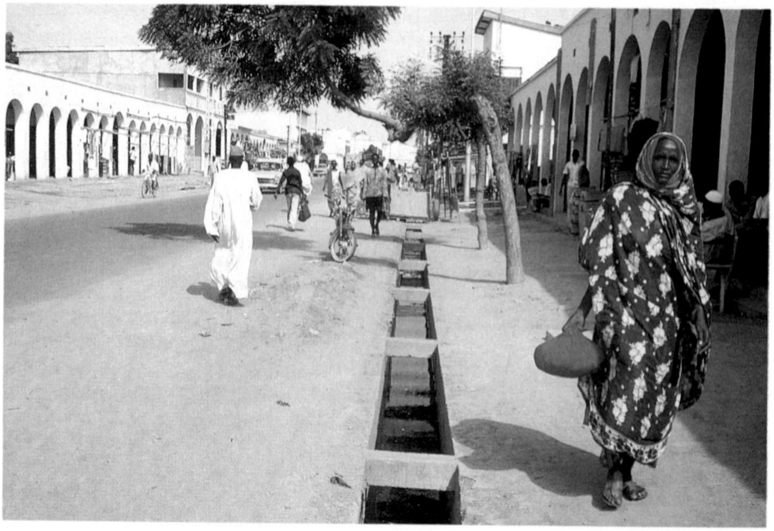

N'djamena, formerly known as Fort-Lamy, is the capital of Chad and the nation's most important economic center. Prominent features of N'djamena's Arabic architecture—massive walls and recessed entrances—closely parallel those of its modern buildings.

adherents of Christianity and traditional African religions. Both Arabic and Sara serve as trade languages, but French is the official language.

The population of Chad is overwhelmingly rural with a very low density, particularly in the northern half. The scattered population and the country's sheer size, along with its poverty, have hindered the development of education and medical care. In addition, animosity exists between northerners and southerners as a result of Muslim slave raiding in the south before the French conquest in the early 20th century. It has been difficult, therefore, to mold a common national identity since independence.

Economy and History

The economy of Chad is based primarily on livestock raising and subsistence agriculture, although the former was severely damaged by drought in the SAHEL region of the north in the 1970s and again in the 1980s. Cotton is the major commercial crop. Although low-profit yield makes cotton an unpopular crop among farmers, the government insists on its cultivation because it is a source of export earnings. The northern edge of Lake Chad is extremely fertile, but civil war, recurrent drought, and inadequate transportation facilities have severely hampered development efforts. A bridge across the Chari River, completed in 1985, improved links to Cameroon. There are few proven mineral resources; some petroleum is extracted, and natron—a sodium carbonate used as a salt—is mined in the lake region. The Aozou strip in the north, thought to be rich in uranium, was occupied by Libya in 1973.

In the precolonial period Muslim states controlled the northern and central parts of the country, but the French conquered them between 1897 and 1908. Chad was made part of French Equatorial Africa in 1910 and a separate colony within it in 1920. It became independent in August 1960 under President N'Garta Tombalbaye. In 1975, Tombalbaye died in a coup d'état, and various factions began competing for power. In early 1979 a coalition government headed by Goukouni Oueddei assumed power. In mid-1982, Oueddei was ousted by former prime minister Hissène HABRÉ. Both Libya (which signed a defense agreement with Oueddei in 1980) and France repeatedly intervened in the ongoing Chadian conflict. Habré gradually consolidated control over southern Chad but did not control the north until early 1987, when Libyan troops there were driven back to the Aozou strip with Oueddi's aid. In December 1989, Habré won a 7-year term under a new constitution. A year later he was overthrown by rebels, and the constitution was suspended. The competing claims to the Aozou strip remained unresolved.

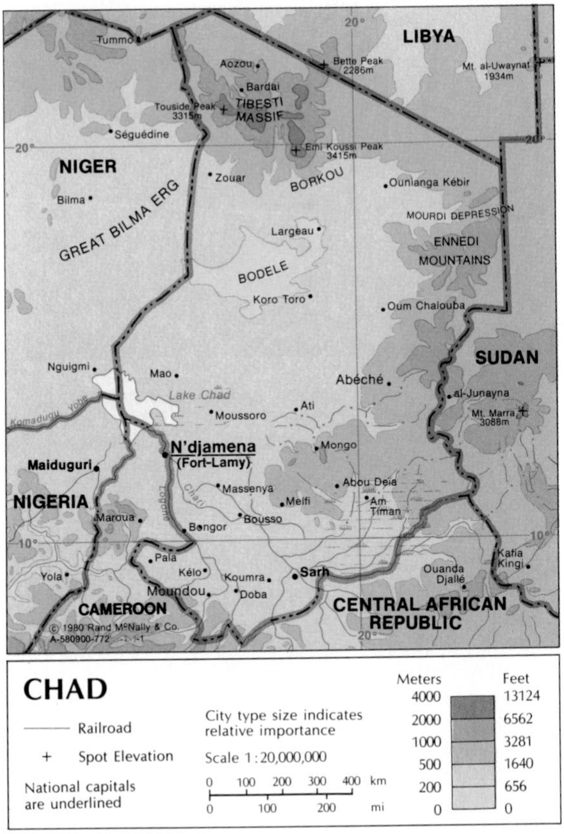

Chad, Lake Lake Chad is a freshwater lake at the junction of Nigeria, Cameroon, Chad, and Niger in northwest central Africa. The lake varies in area from about 10,360 to 25,900 km^2 (4,000 to 10,000 mi^2) and is 4 to 11 m (13 to 36 ft) deep. It is navigable in the south, and it is fished. In the shore areas seasonal flooding irrigates rice and Guinea corn crops. Most west African rivers drain into the Lake Chad-Senegal River-Niger River trough. The lake itself is fed by the Chari River from the south and by many smaller rivers and streams. It has no outlet, although there is underground seepage. Animal life includes crocodiles and hippopotamuses.

Romans traveling from Egypt may have visited Lake Chad. Early African states existed on the shores of the lake, and the first European explorers reached the lake in 1823.

Chadli Benjedid [sha-dlee' ben-zhe-deed'] Chadli Benjedid, b. Apr. 14, 1929, became president of Algeria in February 1979 following the death of Houari Boumedienne. Born to a poor peasant family, he became a soldier in the Algerian liberation movement (FLN) in the 1950s. After Algeria won independence (1962), he served in various military posts, becoming a colonel in 1969. In June 1965 he supported Boumedienne in his overthrow of Ahmed BEN BELLA. He served as minister of defense from November 1978 to February 1979. As president, he stressed agricultural production and consumer goods, increasing the role of the private sector in Algeria's economy. He was reelected in 1984 and 1988. In 1989, in response to popular protests, he introduced a variety of democratic reforms.

Chadwick, Florence Florence Chadwick, b. San Diego, Calif., Nov. 9, 1918, was an American long-distance swimmer who became famous for swimming the English Channel. In 1950 she swam from Cape Gris-Nez, France, to Dover, England, in 13 hours, 23 minutes, breaking Gertrude EDERLE's 24-year women's record. A year later she became the first woman to swim the Channel westward. She held a number of firsts for long-distance swimming and swam the Channel two more times before her retirement in 1960. Chadwick was inducted into the International Swimming Hall of Fame in 1970.

Chadwick, George Whitefield George Whitefield Chadwick, b. Lowell, Mass., Nov. 13, 1854, d. Apr. 4, 1931, was a leading American composer of his time. He studied (1879) in Germany with Josef Rheinberger and later was a church organist in Boston and an influential teacher (director from 1897) at the New England Conservatory. Chadwick's music is generally conservative in style, and in the late romantic tradition. Chadwick was prolific, writing operas (both comic and serious), choral works, symphonies, overtures, chamber music, piano and organ pieces, and songs. His best-known work is probably the symphonic ballad *Tam O'Shanter* (1914–15), inspired by the Robert Burns poem.

Chadwick, Lynn Lynn Chadwick, b. Nov. 24, 1914, has been one of the leading figures in the post–World War II renaissance of British sculpture. He worked in an architecture firm during the 1930s and served as a pilot in the Fleet Air Arm during World War II. He turned from architecture to sculpture after the war and had his first one-man show in 1950. His earliest works were characterized by angular and roughly finished metal forms that suggest menacing presences. This air of tension and threat remained in his subsequent works, and references to animal and human form became clearer. In 1956, Chadwick won the International Sculpture Prize at the Venice Biennale.

Twister II *(1962), a sculpture by the British architect-turned-sculptor Lynn Chadwick, is made of iron and other materials. The configuration of roughly textured, abstract geometric forms suggests a totemic personage, an imagery made popular by surrealism. (Collection of the artist.)*

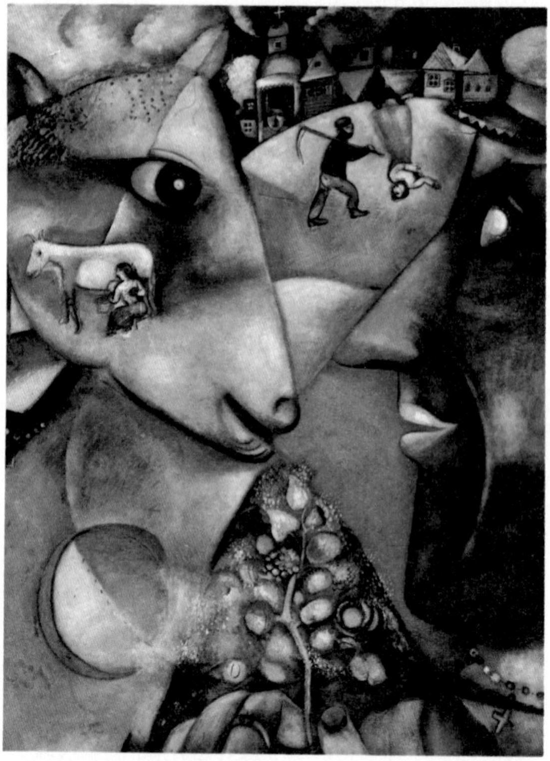

Marc Chagall, a Russian-born Jew, painted I and the Village *in 1911 while living in Paris. Using the faceted planes of cubist structure, Chagall portrayed fantasies based on his memories of Russian and Hebraic folklore and the rural Russia of his childhood. (Museum of Modern Art, New York City.)*

Chagall, Marc [shah-gahl'] The Russian artist Marc Chagall, b. July 7, 1887 (or 1889?), d. Mar. 25, 1985, created a genre virtually his own with his lively, large-scale renderings of Russian village life, as filtered through the prism of Yiddish folklore, and his illustrations of folk tales and Bible stories. Chagall's highly imaginative and very personal style took shape after he moved (1910) to Paris. His dreamlike images had some of the characteristics that were later associated with SURREALISM. *I and the Village* (1911; Museum of Modern Art, New York City) dates from this period. Chagall returned to Russia in 1914, and at first welcomed the Russian Revolution of 1917. He became commissar of fine arts (1918) in his native Vitebsk and director (1919–20) of the local art academy. Disagreements with the suprematist Kasimir MALEVICH, however, resulted in Chagall's departure for Moscow, where he designed sets for the Karmerny State Jewish Theater.

His return to Paris in 1923 inaugurated a second career, not only as a painter with a rich, poetic sense of fantasy and color, but also as a graphic artist of distinction. *The Bride and Groom of the Eiffel Tower* (1939; artist's collection, Saint-Paul, France) is representative of this second period, as are his illustrations for La Fontaine's *Fables* (commissioned 1925, published 1952) and for the Bible (commissioned 1930, published 1957); both projects were commissioned by the renowned Parisian art dealer Ambroise VOLLARD. Chagall spent World War II in the United States, where he designed for the ballet, including Stravinsky's *Firebird* (1945). His later work, infused with strong religious overtones, includes stained-glass windows (1960–61) for the Hadassah-Hebrew University hospital synagogue in Jerusalem and mosaics and tapestries (1966) for the Israeli Knesset. The popular success of his designs for the dome of the Paris Opéra in 1964 led to a commission (1966) for two enormous murals in the foyer of New York's Metropolitan Opera House. In 1977, Chagall became the first living artist to be exhibited at the Louvre.

Chagas' disease see TRYPANOSOMIASIS

Chaikin, Joseph [chay'-kin] The actor and director Joseph Chaikin, b. Brooklyn, N.Y., Sept. 16, 1935, helped found the experimental theater group The Open Theater (1963–73). After working with The Living Theater, Chaikin directed several of The Open Theater's best productions, including *The Serpent* (1969) and *Terminal* (1970). When The Open Theater disbanded, he worked with other experimental groups, directing Jean Claude VAN ITALLIE's *A Fable* (1975) and new adaptations of *The Seagull* (1975) and *The Dybbuk* (1978), and collaborating with Sam SHEPARD on several dramatic monologues.

chain of being The chain of being, or the great chain of being, is a Neoplatonic metaphor for the hierarchical nature, function, and organization of the universe. The concept, created by PLOTINUS (205?–270), was applied to literature, science, and philosophy, and dictated a series of linked stages from God, to Angel, to Man, to Animal, to Plant, to Dust. Popular from the Renaissance to the 19th century, it influenced the literature of Pope, Shakespeare, and Wordsworth, the philosophy of Leibniz and Spinoza, and the scientific views of Newton.

chain reaction A chain reaction is a type of chemical reaction in which the initial products participate in the formation of additional products. This type of reaction has an important role in the plastics industry (see POLYMERIZATION) and is the natural process that occurs during COMBUSTION and the formation of smog. In nuclear fission, a chain reaction is a self-sustaining sequence of fissions (see FISSION, NUCLEAR). The first man-made nuclear chain reaction was achieved on Dec. 2, 1942, as part of the Manhattan Project.

A chain reaction comprises three steps: (1) initiation: production of reactive intermediates by reaction of starting material with an initiator; (2) propagation: production of more reactive intermediates by reaction of initial reactive intermediates with starting material; (3) termination: end of reaction by destruction or consumption of reactive intermediates. Steps 1 and 2 are repeated so long as termination does not take place.

chair The chair may be the oldest of all FURNITURE, although its importance has varied from time to time and from country to country. It appeared in China about 3000 BC. Chairs have been found in Egyptian tombs and were used by both the Greeks and the Romans. They varied in form from simple, backless stools to the sophisticated scissors chair.

Following the collapse of the Roman Empire, most furniture-making skills were lost, and unsettled living conditions militated against permanent furnishings of any

The X-shaped, or scissors, chair, the most common chair of the late Middle Ages and early Renaissance, was one of only two types widely used by the nobility. Based on the ancient Roman curule, the X chair was modified during the Italian Renaissance to include cushioning and decoration. Unlike the oak furniture typical of the Middle Ages, these chairs were frequently carved out of walnut. Shown are the 15th-century Italian "Savonarola" (1), *the "Dantesca"* (2), *and the 17th-century Dutch* (3) *and English* (4) *versions of the X-shaped chair.*

kind. However, with the restoration of stability during the Renaissance, a variety of seating furniture was used. The Italians developed the *casapanca*, a couch derived from the chest; the French introduced fabric-covered furniture; and various other forms, such as the side chair and the armchair, appeared.

As living spaces became specialized with dining rooms, living rooms, and bedrooms, appropriate chairs were created. So thoroughly did the early designers work that, with the exception of the rocking chair and such modern innovations as inflatable and sack chairs, few real advances have taken place in the field since the 18th century.

Seating furniture is by no means universally popular. The Japanese used few chairs before the mid-20th century. In Africa, the Pacific Islands, and the Middle East, the chair was seldom seen until it was introduced by Westerners. In Africa and Polynesia, seats—usually in the form of low, elaborately carved stools—were reserved for chieftains and dignitaries. The nomadic Bedouins of the Middle East, with little need for furniture that could not be packed atop a camel or donkey, preferred to sit on pillows and rugs.

The American Indians did not use chairs, but early settlers brought European types with them. These early styles evolved into distinctly American forms such as the Windsor, a graceful, all-wood chair, and the rocker, which originated when someone decided to put a pair of cradle rockers on the feet of an old armchair. During the later 1800s, craftsmen invented innersprings to add comfort to overstuffed furniture, and they also developed such Victorian standbys as the reclining morris chair and the swivel chair.

Nearly all chairs were handmade until around 1850, when American artisans began to employ steam-driven presses and saws that industrialized the chair-making industry. These techniques soon spread to other parts of the world.

Chaka see SHAKA

Chalcedon, Council of [kal'-sid-ahn] The Council of Chalcedon was the fourth ecumenical council of the Christian church (see COUNCIL, ECUMENICAL). It was convoked in 451 by Marcian, Roman emperor in the East, at the behest of Pope LEO I. In 449 a council meeting in Ephesus without papal approval had upheld MONOPHYSITISM. The Council of Chalcedon formally condemned the Ephesus assembly and promulgated a dogmatic statement called the "Faith of Chalcedon," which described Christ as having two natures, divine and human, "without confusion, without change, without division," perfectly united in a single person.

chalcedony [kal-sed'-uh-nee] Chalcedony is a fine-grained, microcrystalline SILICA MINERAL related to CHERT. Like QUARTZ, its hardness is 7, specific gravity is 2.60–2.64, and composition is silicon dioxide (SiO_2).

Used for centuries as the principal engraved and carved ornamental stone, it is also rounded and polished as a semiprecious gem (see GEM CUTTING). AGATE, BLOODSTONE, carnelian, chrysoprase, plasma, prase, sard, and sardonyx are semiprecious varieties of chalcedony.

chalcopyrite [kal-koh-py'-rite] Chalcopyrite, a copper and iron SULFIDE MINERAL ($CuFeS_2$), is one of the most widely distributed and important ores of copper. It usually forms brittle, metallic, compact masses with a brassy yellow, often tarnished or iridescent color. Chalcopyrite commonly occurs in IGNEOUS ROCKS as the original constituent from which many other copper minerals have been derived by alteration. It also occurs in PEGMATITES, contact metamorphic zones in limestone, and sulfide ore veins.

See also: ORE DEPOSITS.

Chalcopyrite, a copper-iron sulfide, is the most common copper ore and a major source of the metal. Because of its resemblance to regular pyrite, or "fool's gold," it is also called copper pyrite. The mineral usually is found in compact masses or in mixtures with other minerals, as opaque, brass-yellow, tetragonal crystals.

Chaldea [kal-dee'-uh] Chaldea was an ancient name for the marshy sea lands at the head of the Persian Gulf comprising extreme southern Iraq and part of Kuwait. For a brief period after 625 BC, however, the term was extended (as in the Old Testament books of Kings and Chronicles) to include BABYLONIA, mainly because the Babylonian kings from 626 to 539 BC were of Chaldean origin.

In the first millennium BC, Chaldea was populated by Arab tribes that were not politically unified but were willing to follow powerful sheikhs in attacks on Babylonia, then a province of ASSYRIA. The Chaldeans warred with the Assyrian kings SARGON II, SENNACHERIB, ESARHADDON, and ASHURBANIPAL, but when the last of these died in 626 BC the Assyrian governor Nabopolassar, who was a Chaldean, revolted and established the Chaldean dynasty in Babylonia. His son was the famous NEBUCHADNEZZAR II (r. 605–562 BC). The last Chaldean king of Babylonia was Nabonidus (r. 556–539 BC), whose reign was ended by the Persian conquest.

chalet see HOUSE (in Western architecture)

Chaliapin, Fyodor Ivanovich [shuhl-yahp'-in] Fyodor Ivanovich Chaliapin, b. Feb. 13 (Feb. 1, O.S.), 1873, d. Apr. 12, 1938, was one of the greatest Russian opera singers. He appeared at La Scala (1901); the Metropolitan Opera (1907), where he was not appreciated; the Paris Opéra (1908); and Covent Garden (1926). A return engagement (1921) at the Metropolitan as Boris Godunov was an unqualified success. Besides Russian roles, he excelled as Gounod's Méphistophélès, and as Don Basilio, Leporello, and King Philip. A huge man with a dark-timbred basso voice, Chaliapin was one of the first singers to apply psychological techniques to operatic acting.

chalk Chalk is a soft, white variety of fine-grained LIMESTONE that is composed of minute fossil fragments of unicellular organisms (*Foraminifera* or algae) along with some larger organisms (bivalve shells) and crystals of CALCITE. Beds of chalk often contain lumps of CHERT AND FLINT. Because calcite and many of the fragments of the marine organisms are composed of calcium carbonate, chalk usually consists of more than 50 percent of this compound. Chalks were formed when marine organisms died and settled to the bottom of shallow to moderately deep seas, forming a mud that was cemented by precipitating calcite, and then compacted into beds (see SEDIMENT, MARINE).

Famous chalk deposits include the white cliffs of Dover, England, and the fossil beds in western Kansas, in which preserved skeletons of extinct animals such as ICHTHYOSAURUS have been found (see FOSSIL RECORD). Chalk is used in making rubber goods, paint, putty, polishing powders, and portland cement, and as a soil conditioner.

Challenger Expedition see OCEANOGRAPHY

chamber of commerce A chamber of commerce is a nonprofit organization of businesspeople organized to represent the interests of the business community. In the United States, chambers of commerce are found in virtually every urban area and on the state as well as the national levels, where they are represented by the Chamber of Commerce of the United States, which has its headquarters in Washington, D.C.

chamber music Chamber music is composed for small groups of performers, usually two to eight persons. When it was first composed in the late 15th or early 16th centuries, it was intended for performance in small chambers or homes, as opposed to music written for the church or the theater. Since the early 19th century, however, it has become part of the concert repertoire. It is usually considered a branch of instrumental music (although some compositions include parts for voices) and is generally intended for one performer on each part, thus usually requiring no conductor.

Franz Josef Haydn, who composed more than 80 string quartets, helped perfect the classical sonata form that was to dominate instrumental music until the 20th century.

A 16th-century French vocal-ensemble form known as the CHANSON was indirectly a principal source of later forms of chamber music. Composed of several short sections in contrasting texture and meter, the chanson was often arranged for the LUTE or for combinations of instruments; generally, however, its sectional structure was retained. About 1525 the chanson was adopted by Italian composers, who called it a *canzona*, and was further elaborated. Soon, original *canzones* modeled on the pattern of these arrangements were composed for small instrumental ensembles.

Paralleling this development was another that led to the dance suite. Sixteenth-century dances in western Europe were usually performed in pairs: one dance slow, stately, and in duple meter, and the other fast, lively, in triple meter, and related melodically to the first. Various attempts were made to enlarge the dance pair and change it into a suite, and the French version became the most successful. The French suite consisted of four or five movements in contrasting dance rhythms, meters, and tempos (see SUITE).

By the end of the 17th century, the *canzona* had been transformed and had become known generally as the *sonata da chiesa*, or "church SONATA," because it was often used in liturgical services. The expanded dance suite was called the *sonata da camera*, "chamber sonata." The most common performing group for both types included two violins and a continuo which consisted of a keyboard instrument that amplified, or "realized," a bass line supplied with symbols and figures indicating the desired harmonies, plus a cello or a bass (see FIGURED BASS). The types differed in texture and spirit, however: the *sonata da chiesa* contained much COUNTERPOINT and expressed a serious mood; the *sonata da camera* contained dance rhythms and was more sprightly. The *sonata da chiesa* and the *sonata da camera* began to influence each other, and eventually they merged to form the *trio sonata*.

After 1750 the device of the continuo gradually fell out of favor, and all parts were written out in full. The trio of string instruments was augmented by a viola, and the STRING QUARTET (two violins, a viola, and a cello) was born. Simultaneously, the harpsichord (later, the piano), relieved of its task of supplying merely improvised chordal accompaniment, emerged with a chamber-music literature of its own.

Chamber music since about 1750 often takes a four-movement form analogous to that of the SYMPHONY. The typical pattern of the classical period and the 19th century consisted of: a first movement in sonata form, with exposition of two or more contrasting themes, development, and recapitulation; a slow movement often consisting of a set of VARIATIONS; a MINUET (later a scherzo), with trio and recapitulation; and a finale, often another sonata form or a rondo. A notable exception to this pattern is the omission of the minuet or scherzo in many violin sonatas. Equality of all parts is a characteristic of chamber music, especially in string quartets, along with an intimate mood that permits little virtuosic display by individual players.

Chamberlain, Sir Austen The British Conservative political leader Joseph Austen Chamberlain, b. Oct. 16, 1863, d. Mar. 16, 1937, was the son of Joseph Chamberlain and the half-brother of Neville Chamberlain. He entered Parliament in 1892 and subsequently held a variety of high offices, including chancellor of the exchequer (1903–05 and 1919–21), secretary of state for India (1915–17), member of the war cabinet (1918–19) of David LLOYD GEORGE, and foreign secretary (1924–29) under Stanley BALDWIN. In 1921–22, Chamberlain served as Conservative party leader.

As foreign secretary, Chamberlain played a leading role in negotiating the 1925 LOCARNO PACT, a series of treaties intended to settle the disputed borders of Germany. In recognition of his efforts, Chamberlain was awarded (with Charles G. DAWES) the Nobel Peace Prize for 1925. He served in Parliament until his death.

Chamberlain, Houston Stewart The Anglo-German writer and thinker Houston Stewart Chamberlain, b. Sept. 9, 1855, d. Jan. 9, 1927, is remembered for his advocacy of the superiority of the so-called Aryan peoples and his denigration of Jews. In his best-known work, *Die Grundlagen des neunzehnten Jahrhunderts* (The Foundations of the 19th Century, 1891), he postulated that all history is a struggle between races, and that Germans are superior to others. He married Richard Wagner's daughter Eva in 1908 and became a naturalized German in 1916. Chamberlain also wrote works on music, religion, and philosophy. His racist ideas influenced Adolf Hitler and other leading Nazis.

Chamberlain, John John Angus Chamberlain, b. Rochester, Ind., Apr. 16, 1927, is a leading American sculptor. Educated at the Art Institute of Chicago, the University of Illinois, and Black Mountain College, N.C., he moved to New York in 1956. Chamberlain is best known for the sculpture he constructed (1957–63) from crushed automobile body parts. These works provided a 3-dimensional equivalent to the violently gestural ACTION PAINTING then dominant in New York. Subsequently, Chamberlain constructed highly individual forms in various materials, including galvanized metal sheets, crushed aluminum, paper bags, polyurethane, and Plexiglas.

Chamberlain, Joseph The British political leader Joseph Chamberlain, b. July 8, 1836, d. July 2, 1914, was one of the most celebrated radical statesmen of his day. An efficient administrator, accomplished debater, and fine platform speaker, he combined in unusual degree practical and imaginative qualities.

Chamberlain was born into a family of merchants in London, and at the age of 18 he went to Birmingham and took charge of the company's operations there. Moved by a strong social conscience, he entered municipal politics and became mayor of Birmingham (1873–76).

Chamberlain was elected to Parliament as a Liberal in 1876. He served under William GLADSTONE as president of the Board of Trade (1880–85), but in 1886 he opposed Gladstone's HOME RULE BILL for Ireland and broke with the government.

As leader of the Liberal-Unionists, those Liberals who wished to preserve the union with Ireland, Chamberlain entered the Conservative government of the 3d marquess of SALISBURY in 1895. As colonial secretary he helped provoke the SOUTH AFRICAN WAR (1899–1902), but his administrative capacity raised the standing of that office. In 1903, convinced that the day of FREE TRADE was over and that the countries of the BRITISH EMPIRE would be drawn together by a system of preference tariffs, he left

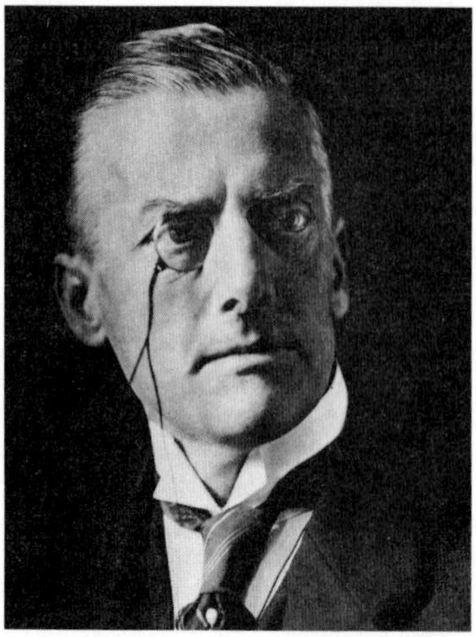

The British statesman Joseph Chamberlain, a member of William Gladstone's cabinet from 1880 to 1885, broke with the Liberal party in 1886 because he opposed home rule for Ireland. As colonial secretary (1895–1903) in the Conservative government, he worked for imperial expansion in Africa and closer ties within the British Empire.

office to campaign on those issues. The ensuing debate led to the defeat of the CONSERVATIVE PARTY in 1906. The victim of a stroke in 1906, Chamberlain then retired from politics.

Chamberlain, Neville Arthur Neville Chamberlain, b. Mar. 18, 1869, d. Nov. 9, 1940, prime minister of Great Britain from 1937 to 1940, pursued a policy of appeasement toward Nazi Germany, which, however, failed to check the expansionist aims of Adolf HITLER. Chamberlain was the son of Joseph Chamberlain and half-brother of Austen Chamberlain. He was lord mayor of Birmingham from 1915 to the end of 1916. Elected to Parliament as a Conservative in 1918, he became chancellor of the exchequer (1923) and minister of health (1923, 1924–29). His links with the Conservative party's organization and the credit that he gained for the rebuilding of the economy while serving again as chancellor (1931–37) made Chamberlain the natural successor to Stanley BALDWIN as prime minister in 1937.

The British prime minister Neville Chamberlain returns to London following the Munich Conference in September 1938. In agreeing to German annexation of the Sudetenland, part of Czechoslovakia, Chamberlain believed that he had secured "peace for our time." World War II began 11 months later.

Gravely handicapped by Britain's military weakness in his dealings with Germany, Italy, and Japan, Chamberlain pursued the policy of appeasement with tenacity and vigor. During the Czechoslovakian crisis of 1938, he returned from the MUNICH CONFERENCE claiming to have secured "peace for our time." The events of the following year dashed that hope, and in September 1939, Chamberlain led a united nation into WORLD WAR II. In May 1940, Chamberlain was forced to turn over the premiership to Winston Churchill. He served as lord president of the council until illness forced his retirement.

Chamberlain, Wilt Wilton Chamberlain, b. Philadelphia, Aug. 21, 1936, was the most prolific offensive player in the history of basketball. Chamberlain, a 7-ft 1-in (216-cm) center, first gained fame at Philadelphia's Overbrook High School, then as an All-American (1957) at Kansas University. He played with the Harlem Globetrotters for a year before joining the National Basketball Association for the rest of his career (Philadelphia Warriors, 1959–65; Philadelphia 76ers, 1965–68; Los Angeles Lakers, 1968–73). Although his career point total (31,419) was eclipsed by Kareem Abdul-Jabbar, Chamberlain holds virtually every other career, season, and single-game scoring and rebounding record. In 1962, for example, he scored 4,029 points (50.4 per game) during the season and 100 in a single game. He led the NBA in field-goal percentage 7 times, in rebounding 11 times, and in scoring for 7 consecutive seasons. He was the NBA's Most Valuable Player 4 times, led his teams to 2 NBA titles (1967, 1972), and was first-team All-NBA 7 times. Chamberlain, a Hall-of-Famer, once amassed 55 rebounds in a game—against his chief rival, Bill Russell.

Chamberlain's Men The Chamberlain's Men, known as the King's Men after 1603, was the leading Elizabethan and Jacobean theatrical company. Ben Jonson occasionally wrote for it, but its chief playwright was William Shakespeare, who, along with Richard and Cuthbert Burbage, Augustine Phillips, Thomas Pope, John Heminge, and the comedian William Kempe, was a part owner. Its greatest actor was Richard BURBAGE, famous initially for his role as Richard III. Formed in 1594, the company performed first in the Theatre, after 1598 in the Globe, and from 1608, in the Blackfriars.

Chambers, Whittaker see HISS, ALGER

chameleon [kuh-meel'-yuhn] Chameleons, family Chamaeleonidae, are Old World lizards that dwell in trees, except for the stump-tailed chameleon, genus *Brookesia*, which lives mainly on the forest floor. Chameleons range from Africa and Madagascar to southern Spain, India,

Jackson's chameleon (top) is a 3-horned species found in Africa. All chameleons are tree dwellers and can change skin color. This species catches insects with its long, sticky tongue.

and Sri Lanka. They are noted for their ability to change color in response to light, heat, and other stimuli. The range of colors is limited to shades of green, yellow, or brown. The males, in particular, often have horns, crests, or flaps on their heads. The lizards range in length from less than 7.5 cm (3 in) for *Brookesia* to more than 60 cm (24 in) for some species of *Chamaeleo*. Chameleons have a long, flattened body and—except for the stump-tailed variety—a prehensile tail that serves as an extra limb. The hind foot has two toes on the inside and three on the outside; the forefoot has the opposite arrangement. The chameleon's protruding eyes are almost completely covered by eyelids, leaving only a narrow opening; the eyes can rotate independently in a complete hemisphere. The tongue, which may be longer than the body, is used to snare food. Most species feed on insects, but a few large species eat birds and small rodents. Chameleons are mostly oviparous, developing and hatching their eggs outside the body, but a few are ovoviviparous, producing living young within the body.

chamois [sham'-ee] The chamois, *Rupicapra rupicapra*, family Bovidae, order Artiodactyla, is a small goatlike antelope found among the mountain crags of Europe and western Asia. Both sexes have slender vertical horns 15 to 20 cm (6 to 8 in) long that hook backward at the top. The chamois is about 122 cm (48 in) long and weighs 23 to 45 kg (50 to 100 lb). It eats lichens and mosses in winter. Hunted for meat and its soft skin, it is now protected in the Swiss National Park in Graubünden.

The agile chamois has padded hooves that make it extremely surefooted in mountainous, snowy regions of Europe.

chamomile [kam'-uh-meel] Chamomile is a common name applied to two genera (*Anthemis*, also called dog fennel, and *Matricaria*) of annual, biennial, or perennial plants belonging to the composite family, Compositae. Both genera commonly have scented leaves and daisylike flowers, usually yellow, or white with yellow centers. Dried *Anthemis* flower heads are used to make chamomile tea; an extracted oil has been used medicinally and as a hair rinse. Certain species of *Anthemis* are sometimes placed in a separate genus, *Chamaemelum*.

Chamorro [chah-mor'-oh] Chamorro, or Guamanians, are the native peoples of Guam in the western Pacific. They make up about one-half of Guam's population of 116,000 (1983 est.). The Chamorro were part of the ancient migrations of Polynesians from the Asian mainland to the Pacific. Although Guam was discovered by Magellan in 1512, the first Spanish mission was not open on the island until 1668. Today most Chamorro are Roman Catholics and speak English. Their major crops are rice, corn, vegetables, and coconuts.

Chamorro, Violeta Barrios de Violeta Barrios de Chamorro, b. Oct. 18, 1929, was elected president of Nicaragua on Feb. 25, 1990, defeating the Sandinista incumbent, Daniel ORTEGA SAAVEDRA. Her election brought an end to the 8-year civil war between the Sandinista government and the U.S.-backed rebels, or "contras." Chamorro first entered public life in 1978 following the assassination of her husband, publisher of the newspaper *La prensa.* She became an important figure in the Sandinista movement and, after the overthrow (1979) of the SOMOZA dictatorship, briefly held a government post. During the 1980s, as publisher of *La prensa*, she became a leading critic of the Sandinistas.

Champa [cham'-puh] The kingdom of Champa, located on the Indochinese peninsula and inhabited by the Chams, a people ethnically related to the present-day peoples of Indonesia, Malaysia, and the Philippines, came into being late in the 2d century AD. Originally based in the province of Quang Nam near Hué, Vietnam, it extended south to Camranh Bay and west into Cambodia and Laos. Chinese accounts of the 3d century mention raids by the Chams against China.

Champa's culture was derived from India and embodied Hindu religious and artistic concepts. In 939, following Chinese recognition of the independence of Annam (in the northern part of modern Vietnam), the Annamese made their first attack on the Chams. Nearly five centuries later, in 1471, a decisive defeat by Annam effectively ended Champa's existence. Today there is a Cham minority in Vietnam.

Champagne Champagne is a historic province in northeastern France. The name derives from the Latin *campania*, meaning "plain." The county of Champagne was incorporated into France in 1314. Champagne now comprises the departments of Ardennes, Marne, Aube, and Haute-Marne and parts of Aisne, Seine-et-Marne, Yonne, and Meuse. Its strategic location has made it a battleground whenever France has been invaded from the east. The Falaise de l'Île-de-France, a limestone ridge,

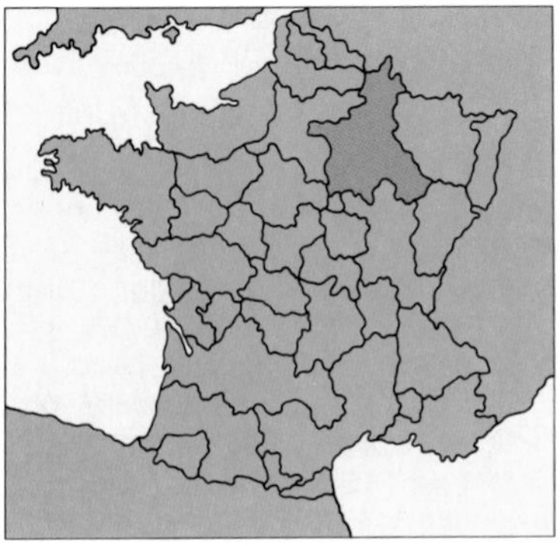

Champagne is located between the Low Countries and Lorraine on the north and east and the île de France on the west. A crossroads of commerce during the Middle Ages, Champagne achieves most of its wealth today from wine grapes grown in the western part of the province.

borders Champagne on the west, separating it from the ÎLE-DE-FRANCE. Grapes grown on the lower slopes of the Falaise are made into the famous sparkling wine in cellars carved out of the chalk under REIMS and Épernay. Both cities are route centers where the AISNE and MARNE rivers breach the Falaise. The kings of France were crowned in Reims Cathedral. Reims also has a flourishing textile industry. An infertile chalk plain constitutes most of the province and is being reforested. To its east are fertile fields and orchards. The principal town is TROYES, the medieval capital of Champagne.

champagne Champagne is a sparkling WINE originating in the Champagne region of France. The French government allows the use of the name only by wines grown in this region, and has often sought to prevent its use by other makers of sparkling wine. The champagne method dates from the 17th century and was discovered by the monk Dom Pérignon, who is said to have been the first to stopper wine bottles with a cork. Wines of this period were bottled while still fermenting; the cork stopper forced the carbon dioxide produced by fermentation back into the wine, creating an effervescent liquid that tasted, as the Dom said, like stars. Modern champagnes are blends of Pinot Noir, Pinot Meunier, and Chardonnay wines, bottled with a small quantity of sugar that fuels a second fermentation. After aging from three to five years, the bottles are uncorked and the sediment disgorged. Recorked and wired, the wine is ready to drink. Its alcohol content ranges between 11 percent and 12 percent. *Brut* indicates a very dry wine; *sec* is medium sweet; *doux* is the sweetest.

Champaign-Urbana Champaign-Urbana is a community composed of adjoining cities in east central Illinois. Champaign has a population of 63,502 (1990), and Urbana, 36,344 (1990). The towns share an economic and cultural focus in the University of Illinois. Agriculture—mainly corn, soybean, and livestock raising—is important in the fertile surrounding area. The cities' industries include railroad and machine shops as well as the manufacture of electronic systems, metal products, and academic apparel. Foods are also processed. Urbana was settled in 1822, and in 1833 it was incorporated and became a county seat. By 1860, Urbana was chartered as a city. Champaign, first called West Urbana, was founded in 1855, when the Illinois Central Railroad came through the area.

Champaigne, Philippe de Philippe de Champaigne, b. May 26, 1602, d. Aug. 12, 1674, known for his sober portraits and religious paintings, represents the rational aspect of French 17th-century painting. In 1628 he became painter to the Queen Mother, Marie de Médicis. Soon thereafter, he also won the favor of Louis XIII and his first minister Richelieu, whose portraits he frequently painted. *Cardinal Richelieu* (1636; Louvre, Paris) is typical of Champaigne's official style. Both the portraits and the religious paintings of this period, such as those executed for the Carmelite convent, owe a good deal to the influence of the Flemings Van Dyck and Rubens. In 1648, Champaigne helped found the Royal Academy of Painting and Sculpture.

In his masterpiece, *Two Nuns of Port Royal* (1662; Louvre, Paris), with its emphasis on devotion and spirituality, superfluous detail is eliminated altogether. The scene depicts Champaigne's daughter, a Jansenist nun, being miraculously cured of paralysis.

Champlain, Lake Lake Champlain forms the boundary between New York and Vermont for 160 km (100 mi) and extends into Quebec, Canada. Its total length is 172 km (107 mi), and its greatest width, 23 km (14 mi). It is named for the French explorer Samuel de Champlain, who discovered it in 1609. Lake Champlain is a link in the Hudson-St. Lawrence Waterway and was vital to armies in the French and Indian War and the American Revolution. The forts of Crown Point and TICONDEROGA stood on its shores. The first naval battle between Americans and British was fought at Valcour Island on Oct. 11, 1776.

Champlain, Samuel de Samuel de Champlain, b. *c.*1570, d. Dec. 25, 1635, was a French cartographer, explorer, and colonizer. He is known as the founder of Quebec, the father of NEW FRANCE, and the discoverer of the Ottawa River and Lakes Champlain, Ontario, and Huron. Champlain traveled to North America 12 times between 1603 and 1633. His objectives were to find a route through the continent to Asia, to promote trade in furs and other commodities, to establish colonies, and to promote Christianity.

On his seven voyages from 1603 to 1616, he significantly increased geographical knowledge, founded settlements, cemented alliances with Algonquin tribes and HURONS against the IROQUOIS LEAGUE, and increased the volume of the French fur trade. From 1604 to 1607,

Samuel de Champlain, a French explorer and the founder of the city of Quebec, first traveled to New France in 1603. During the ensuing 30 years he explored much of the St. Lawrence River and the North Atlantic coast. Champlain became virtual governor of the French colony in 1627.

Champlain accurately mapped the Atlantic coast from the Bay of Fundy to Cape Cod. In a sense the post founded (1605) at Port Royal formed the basis of the future French colony of ACADIA. In 1608 Champlain founded Quebec, a tiny collection of buildings that became the capital of New France.

In 1609, Champlain ascended the St. Lawrence and Richelieu rivers to the lake that now bears his name and routed a party of Iroquois, on behalf of his Algonquin allies. Having gone up the Ottawa River as far as Allumette Island in 1613, Champlain continued (1615) from there to the Huron country south of Georgian Bay via Lake Nipissing and the French River.

Champlain's visits to Canada from 1618 to 1633 emphasized permanent settlement. He was named commandant of New France by Cardinal Richelieu but in 1629 was forced to surrender Quebec to Sir David KIRKE, who held it for the English until 1633. When Champlain died at Quebec in 1635, only 150 settlers lived there. Champlain's fur-trade network, however, had laid solid foundations for the large French North American empire, which lasted for 125 years.

Champollion, Jean François [shahm-pohl-ee-ohn'] Jean François Champollion, b. Dec. 23, 1790, d. Mar. 4, 1832, deciphered the HIEROGLYPHIC script of the ancient Egyptians. He began his oriental studies as a child of 11, becoming professor of ancient history at Grenoble at the age of 18. In 1816 he lost his post through political activities directed against the Napoleonic regime. Six years later, in September 1822, he read his epochal paper to the French Academy outlining his decipherment of Egyptian hieroglyphic script, basing his conclusions largely on the inscriptions of the ROSETTA STONE.

In 1828–29 he led a joint French and Tuscan mission to Egypt to copy inscriptions on monuments lying between Alexandria and the Second Cataract, and to collect antiquities for the Louvre, of which he had been appointed curator in 1826. Most of his work was published posthumously by his brother, Jacques Joseph Champollion-Figeac.

Chan Chan Chan Chan, located in the Moche Valley on the north coast of Peru, was the capital of the pre-Inca CHIMU kingdom. One of the largest cities in pre-Columbian South America, it covered at least 15.5 km^2 (6 mi^2) and was surrounded by extensive farmland. Construction probably began *c.*800, two centuries before the empire arose. Chan Chan declined rapidly after the Inca conquest of the region sometime after 1450.

In spite of its vast area, Chan Chan may not have had a large permanent population. Some archaeologists estimate that the permanent population may have been no more than 25,000. Many of the city's buildings served as

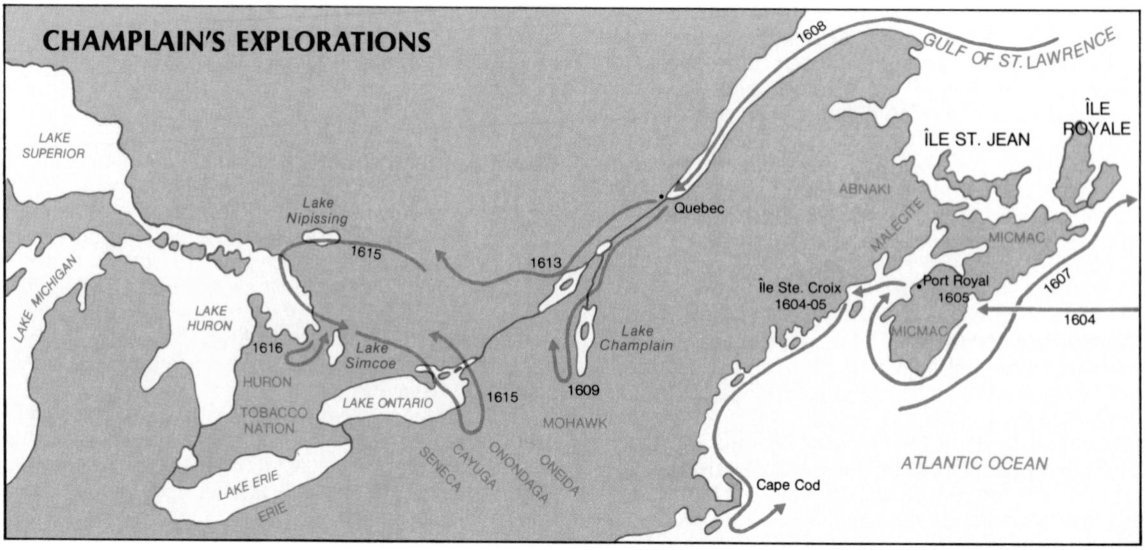

reservoirs and food storehouses, and enormous burial mounds for dead rulers were a prominent architectural feature.

chance see PROBABILITY

chancellor The term *chancellor,* from the Latin *cancellarius* ("secretary"), has been used to denote many high officials in government and education. In Austria and Germany during the 19th and 20th centuries the chancellor (*Kanzler*) has been the head of government or prime minister. In medieval England the lord high chancellor was the king's chief minister; in modern Britain this official heads the judiciary and presides over the House of Lords. The chancellor of the exchequer is the British finance minister. High university officials are also often called chancellors.

Chancellor, John John William Chancellor, b. Chicago, July 14, 1927, was the coanchor of the "NBC Nightly News" from 1970 until 1982, when he assumed the role of commentator. He began his career as a newspaper reporter, joined NBC News in 1950, and was a political correspondent in the 1960s. He also was director of Voice of America (1966–67).

Chancellor, Richard Richard Chancellor, d. Nov. 10, 1556, an English navigator, visited Moscow in 1554, leading to the formation (1555) of the English Muscovy Company for trade with Russia. Setting out (1553) in search of a NORTHEAST PASSAGE, Chancellor reached the White Sea and was there invited to travel overland to Moscow. He was shipwrecked returning from a second journey to Moscow.

Chancellorsville, Battle of The Battle of Chancellorsville in the U.S. CIVIL WAR occurred on May 1–3, 1863, in the wilderness of northern Virginia. A Union army under Joseph HOOKER, planning to capture Richmond, Va., was defeated by Stonewall JACKSON, who was commanding Robert E. Lee's II Corps. Displaying his usual brilliance in flanking operations, Jackson marched beyond the Union's right on May 2 and attacked it from behind. That night, after a smashing success, Jackson rode beyond his lines to reconnoiter. Upon returning, he was mistaken for a Yankee and wounded by his own men; he died eight days later. Jackson's death made Chancellorsville a decisive battle in the war, for the impetus for Confederate victory in the east died with him.

chancery In law, chancery is a court that administers the law of EQUITY. Originally, in England, it was the court of the lord chancellor. Separate courts of chancery exist today only in a few states of the United States. The term is often used to mean the legal procedures of equity.

chandelier [shan-duh-lir'] A chandelier is a lighting fixture suspended from a ceiling; the term *chandelier* comes from the French word for candlestick. Medieval chandeliers were hoops of iron or bronze with protruding spikes that held candles. By the 15th century, Flemish brass chandeliers had evolved into a standard form: S-shaped arms radiating from a central baluster, or column. In the 18th century, elaborate chandeliers were made of silver, porcelain, *bronze doré* (gilded bronze), *tôle* (painted tin), and glass. Crystal chandeliers—lead glass creations with cascades of prisms (called lusters)—appeared in England and Ireland about 1720.

Chandigarh [chuhn'-dee-gahr] Chandigarh, a city in northwestern India with an area of 114 km^2 (44 mi^2) and a population of 451,610 (1981), is located near the foothills of the Himalayas. It was originally designed to serve as the capital of the state of East Punjab. In 1966, when the former East Punjab was further divided into Punjab and Haryana, Chandigarh (a union territory administered by the federal government) became the capital of Punjab and the temporary capital of Haryana.

The city, designed by French architect LE CORBUSIER and begun in 1950, is considered an outstanding example of URBAN PLANNING. A complex of government buildings stands at one end. The town center is surrounded by residential neighborhoods and a system of roads with green buffer zones. Chandigarh is the site of Punjab University.

Chandler, Happy Albert Benjamin "Happy" Chandler, b. Corydon, Ky., July 14, 1898, d. June 15, 1991, was Democratic governor of Kentucky (1935–39 and 1955–59), U.S. senator from Kentucky (1939–45), and commissioner of baseball (1945–51). He was elected to baseball's Hall of Fame in 1982.

Chandler, Raymond T. An American writer of hard-boiled detective novels, Raymond Thornton Chandler, b. Chicago, July 23, 1888, d. Mar. 26, 1959, along with Dashiell Hammett, set the style for American detective fiction. His series hero, Philip Marlowe, is tough-minded, loyal, and incorruptible in his dealings with the seamy side of American life and politics. Chandler wrote such original screenplays as *The Blue Dahlia* (1946) and co-authored *Double Indemnity* (1944) and *Strangers on a Train* (1951). Six of his novels were successfully filmed, including *The Big Sleep* (1939; films, 1946, 1978), *Farewell, My Lovely* (1940; films, 1942, 1944, 1975), and *The Long Goodbye* (1953; film, 1973), which won the 1954 Edgar Allan Poe Award.

Chandler, Zachariah Zachariah Chandler, b. Bedford, N.H., Dec. 10, 1813, d. Nov. 1, 1879, U.S. senator from Michigan (1857–75, 1879), was an early Republican party boss. During the Civil War and RECONSTRUCTION he was a leader of the Radical Republicans and played a prominent role in the impeachment of President Andrew Johnson. At the same time, Chandler used his powerful post as chairman of the Senate Committee on Commerce (1861–75) to secure control of the Michigan Republican organization. Defeated for reelection in 1874, he served as secretary of the interior from 1875 to 1877. In 1879, shortly before his death, Chandler was chosen to fill a Senate vacancy.

Chandragupta Maurya, Emperor of India [chuhn-druh-gup'-tuh] Chandragupta, d. 286 BC, was the founder and first king (r. 321–297 BC) of the MAURYA dynasty of India. Known as Sandracottus to the Greeks, he was said to have met (*c.*326–325 BC) ALEXANDER THE GREAT in the Punjab. In 324–323 BC, Chandragupta organized a revolt to end Greek rule in Punjab. He took (*c.*321) his army to his native kingdom of Magadha (in modern Bihar), killed the Nanda king, and occupied the capital, Pataliputra (Patna).

By 305 BC, Chandragupta had defeated SELEUCUS I Nicator in his attempt to recover Alexander's Indian provinces and had consolidated the Maurya empire across northern India. He abdicated (*c.*297) to his son Bindusara and, according to tradition, either became a Jain monk or went to southern India, where he died. The authoritarian regime he established became the pattern for succeeding Indian kingdoms. Chandragupta was the grandfather of ASOKA.

Chandrasekhar, Subrahmanyan [chuhn-druh-shay'-kur] The Indian-born U.S. theoretical astrophysicist Subrahmanyan Chandrasekhar, b. Oct. 19, 1910, was the cowinner of the 1983 Nobel Prize for physics for his fundamental research on stellar atmospheres and interiors, and on the dynamic properties of star clusters and stellar systems. In 1939, Chandrasekhar published *An Introduction to the Study of Stellar Structure*, a classic work that presented for the first time a broad exposition of the nuclear reactions taking place inside stars. He determined that an evolving star cannot directly become one of the dense stars known as WHITE DWARFS if its mass exceeds the Sun's mass by a factor of more than 1.44, a limit now called the Chandrasekhar limit. If the star does not lose enough mass to drop below this limit, it must end as a NEUTRON STAR or BLACK HOLE.

Chanel, Coco [shah-nel'] Gabrielle "Coco" Chanel, b. Aug. 19, 1883, d. Jan. 10, 1971, was one of the most celebrated Parisian couturiers of the 20th century (see COSTUME). Her versions of the short skirt and the women's tailored suit, of subtle and unmistakable cut and in neutral hues such as beige and gray, became haute couture classics. Her accessories and her perfumes, notably Chanel No. 5, became worldwide synonyms for luxury and chic.

Chanel launched her career with a millinery shop in 1909. By the mid-1920s she was one of the most influential designers in the history of FASHION DESIGN. In 1954, at the age of 70, she successfully countered Christian Dior's romantic "New Look" with classic suits and tweeds consciously reminiscent of her 1920s creations.

Chaney, Lon [chay'-nee] Lon Chaney, b. Alonso Chaney in Colorado Springs, Colo., Apr. 1, 1883, d. Aug. 26, 1930, Hollywood's "man of a thousand faces," was a leading character actor specializing in macabre roles. His ability to mime and his skill with makeup served him well in such films as *The Hunchback of Notre Dame* (1923) and *The Phantom of the Opera* (1925). He also appeared successfully in dramatic roles that required no disguise, as in *Laugh Clown Laugh* (1928).

Lon Chaney, a gifted actor, stuntman, and makeup artist, terrified film audiences in 1925 with his performance as the disfigured musician in The Phantom of the Opera, *a now-classic horror film.*

Chang Chih-tung see ZHANG ZHIDONG

Chang Hsueh-liang see ZHANG XUELIANG

Chang Jiang (Yangtze River) [zhang jee-ang] The Chang Jiang (Yangtze River), in central China, is the longest river in Asia and the third longest river in the world. Rising in northeastern Tibet, the river flows 5,990 km (3,720 mi) to the East China Sea. The drainage basin of the Chang Jiang covers more than 1,827,000 km^2 (705,200 mi^2). The river's mouth discharges 34,000 m^3 (1,200,000 ft^3) per second. The Chang Jiang is commonly referred to in China as "the Long River." The name *Yangtze*, which was long applied to the whole river in the West, is only a local name for the river in Jiangsu (Kiangsu) province.

The Chang Jiang and its tributaries are navigable for a total length of 30,000 km (18,640 mi). The volume of transportation on the Chang Jiang system is greater than the total traffic on all the other rivers and waterways of China combined. The Chang Jiang is ice-free all year. Oceangoing vessels can sail inland as far as Wuhan.

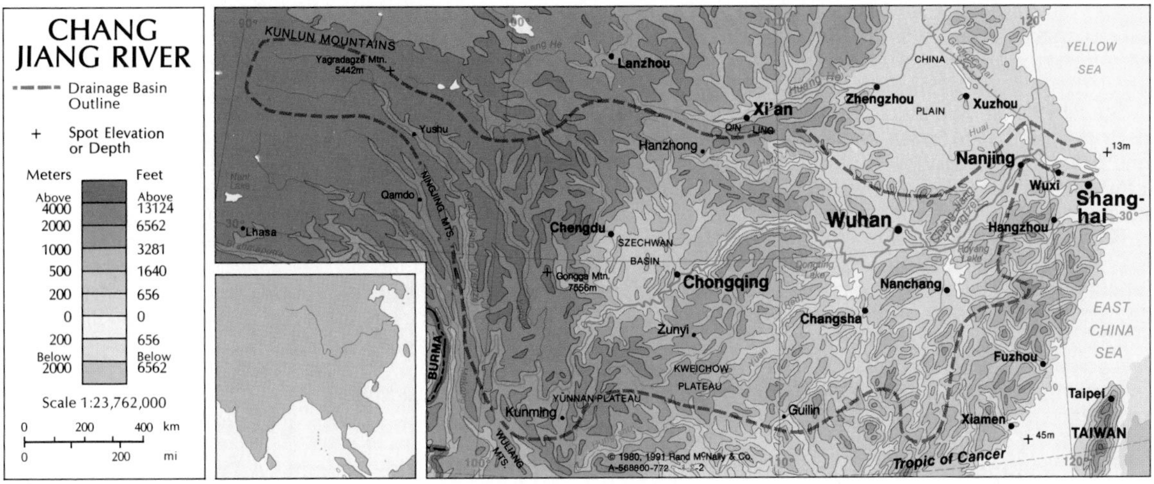

Yichang (Ich'ang) is often considered the head of navigation of the river, and it is accessible to 8,000-ton vessels during the summer. Five of China's largest cities are on or near the river system: Shanghai, Wuhan, Chongqing (Chungking), Chengdu (Cheng'tu), and Nanjing (Nanking). The Chang Jiang has a hydroelectric potential of 220,000,000 kW, or about 40% of China's total, but it is still largely undeveloped. Several multipurpose projects have been built since 1949, including the Jingjiang (Kingkiang) flood-retention center north of Tongting (Tung-t-'ing) Lake and the Gezhouba (Kechoupa) Dam near Yichang. A proposed dam at the nearby Yangtze gorges would be among the world's largest water projects. The depth of the river in the gorges is 152 to 183 m (500 to 600 ft), making it the deepest river in the world.

The Chang Jiang rises in the Jinghai-Tibet Plateau in western China at an elevation of more than 5,400 m (18,000 ft). Eight major tributaries join it as it flows eastward to the East China Sea. They are the Yalong (Yalung), Jialing (Chialing), Han Shui, Wu, Yuan, Xiang (Hsiang), and Gan (Kan). The river carries an average 490.5 million metric tons (540.8 million U.S. tons) of sediments annually into the sea, extending its delta at the rate of 1 km per 40 years (1 mi per 64 years). Where the land is not cultivated, the Chang Jiang Valley is covered by mixed forests. Approximately 70% of China's rice comes from the river basin.

Chang Tso-lin see ZHANG ZUOLIN

Changchun (Ch'ang-ch'un) [chahng-choon] Changchun is a city at the center of an extensive fertile lowland drained by the Songkua (Sungari) and the Liao rivers, in northeast China. Changchun is the capital of Jilin (Kirin) province and has a population of 2,000,000 (1988 est.). The city is the economic and transportation center of the province and is noted for producing machinery and transportation equipment. Other products include cigarettes, footwear, food, carpets, plywood, enamelware, and pharmaceuticals. This 1,000-year-old city was a village until the end of the 18th century. Changchun, renamed Xingjing, was the capital of Manchukuo from 1932 to 1945, when Japan dominated China's northeast.

Channel Islands (California) see SANTA BARBARA ISLANDS

Channel Islands (United Kingdom) The Channel Islands are a group of islands in the English Channel. They form autonomous parts of Britain, although they all lie within 48 km (30 mi) of the French coast and are 121

St. Peter Port, capital of Guernsey, is situated on the island's east coast. The 13th-century Castle Cornet (shown) *stands on a rocky promontory that shelters the town's harbor.*

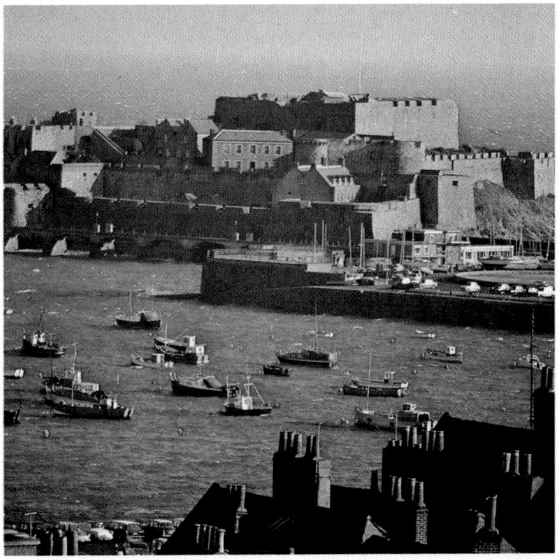

km (75 mi) from the south coast of England. There are four principal islands: JERSEY (117 km^2/45 mi^2), the largest and most southerly; GUERNSEY (62 km^2/24 mi^2); Alderney (8 km^2/3 mi^2); and Sark (5 km^2/2 mi^2).

The islands are made up of hard Paleozoic and igneous rocks, similar to those of nearby France. Relief is gentle, and at no point do the islands much exceed 125 m (400 ft) in elevation. Acute water shortages sometimes occur during the summer.

The population is mostly of French descent, and until recently French was the prevailing language. An influx of settlers from Britain, however, has made English the more common language. Both languages are now official. The total population is 138,100 (1986 est.). The economy rests on cultivation of early vegetables, fruits, and flowers for the British market, and on the tourist industry. Sea and air links with the English and French coasts facilitate tourism. The principal towns are St. Helier (Jersey) and St. Peter Port (Guernsey).

The islands became part of the medieval duchy of Normandy in 933 and were retained by England when Normandy was lost to the French in 1204. The islands were occupied by the Germans from 1940 to 1945. Each island is domestically independent and has its own assembly. The islanders are not represented in the British Parliament.

Channing, William Ellery William Ellery Channing, b. Newport, R.I., Apr. 7, 1780, d. Oct. 2, 1842, was one of the most eloquent preachers and the most prominent spokesman for American UNITARIANISM in the early 19th century. As minister of the Federal Street Church in Boston, he was drawn into the dispute over religious liberalism. He preached a sermon in Baltimore in 1819 that was widely accepted as a manifesto of the liberal party, which thereafter accepted the name Unitarian. In his later preaching he turned increasingly to social reform as an expression of his religious concern for the worth of human personality.

chanson [shawn-sohn'] The term *chanson* applies to any SONG with French text; historically, it was a polyphonic, secular composition in French that flourished from the mid-15th to the mid-16th century. French solo songs were first composed in large numbers by the *trouvères* and troubadours. By the 14th century, supporting instrumental parts appeared, and polyphonic vocal texture became common. Generally, the chanson can be identified by its opening rhythm. The form was sufficiently popular in Italy that it spawned there an instrumental counterpart, *canzona francese,* for keyboard or plucked stringed instruments.

chansons de geste [shawn-sohn' duh zhest'] The chansons de geste ("songs of heroic deeds") are a group of about 80 largely anonymous French epic poems that date from the 12th century and deal with historical and legendary events in the 8th and 9th centuries during the reigns of Charlemagne and his successors. The greatest of these, the anonymous *La Chanson de Roland* (*c.*1100), celebrates the bravery of Charlemagne's perfect Hruodlandus (ROLAND), ambushed in 778 by the Basques—who become Saracens in the poem. Typically heroic, the chansons recount the struggles of noble Christian protagonists with each other and with Islam. Whether they were handed down in oral tradition from Carolingian times or were composed by professional poets centuries later, scholars agree that the poems are unreliable as history. Their stylistic vividness, Christian idealism, and patriotic spirit, however, made them popular in medieval France as texts for wandering *jongleurs.*

chant see PLAINSONG

Chanukah [hah'-nuh-kuh] A Jewish festival that occurs in December (the Hebrew month Kislev), Chanukah, also spelled Hanukkah, marks the reconsecration of the Temple of Jerusalem after its recapture from the Syrian Greeks *c.*165 BC. A miracle recorded in the TALMUD—the burning of a day's supply of pure olive oil for eight days, until fresh jars of clean oil could be brought into the temple—accounts for the eight days during which candles are kindled during Chanukah. The eight-branched candelabrum has become a symbol of the holiday.

Chanukah was instituted by the MACCABEES, leaders of the Jews who fought against the Syrian Greeks. The Maccabees took over as priests of the Temple and as rulers of the Jewish state that they founded. Songs and stories associated with the holiday therefore refer to the Maccabees and to their victory. Chanukah is also called the Festival of Lights, the Feast of Dedication, or the Feast of Maccabees.

Chao Meng-fu see ZHAO MENGFU

Chao Tzu-yang see ZHAO ZIYANG

Chaos [kay'-ahs] In Greek mythology, Chaos was the unorganized state, or void, from which all things arose. Proceeding from time, Chaos eventually formed a huge egg from which there issued Heaven, Earth, and Eros (love). According to Hesiod's *Theogony*, Chaos even preceded the origin of the gods.

chaos theory Chaos theory, a modern development in mathematics and science, provides a framework for understanding irregular or erratic fluctuations in nature. Chaotic systems are found in many fields of science and engineering. Evidence of chaos, for example, has been found in models and experiments describing convection and mixing in fluids, wave motion, oscillating chemical reactions, and electrical currents in semiconductors. It is also found in the dynamics of animal populations and of medical disorders.

A chaotic system is defined as one that shows "sensitivity to initial conditions." That is, any uncertainty in the initial state of the given system will lead to rapidly growing errors in any effort to predict the future behavior. For example, the motion of a dust particle floating on the surface of a pair of oscillating whirlpools can display chaotic behavior. The particle will move in well-defined circles around the centers of the whirlpools, alternating between the two in an irregular manner. An observer who wants to predict the motion of this particle will have to measure its initial location. If the measurement is not infinitely precise, however, the observer will instead obtain the location of an imaginary particle very close by, which will follow a path that diverges from the path of the real particle. This makes any long-term prediction of the trajectory of the real particle impossible.

The possibility of chaos in a natural, or deterministic, system was first envisaged by the French mathematician Henri POINCARÉ in the late 19th century. The modern study of chaotic dynamics, however, did not begin until 1963, when American meteorologist Edward Lorenz demonstrated that a simple, deterministic model of thermal convection in the Earth's atmosphere showed sensitivity to initial conditions—that is, it was a chaotic system.

Following this observation, scientists began to study the progression from order to chaos in various systems, as the parameters of the systems were varied. In 1971 it was predicted that the transition to chaotic turbulence in a moving fluid would take place at a well-defined critical value of the fluid's velocity. This prediction was later confirmed experimentally.

An American physicist, Mitchell Feigenbaum, then predicted that at the critical point when an ordered system begins to break down into chaos, a consistent sequence of period-doubling transitions would be observed. This so-called "period-doubling route to chaos" was thereafter observed experimentally by various investigators.

chaparral [shap-uh-ral'] Chaparral is a major vegetation type composed of woody shrubs that form a dense thicket 1 to 4 m (3 to 13 ft) high. It occurs in extensive but discontinuous stands on hillsides and mountain slopes from south central Oregon southward through the coast ranges of California and the foothills of the Sierra Nevada. Chaparral reaches its fullest development in southern California and northern Baja California, Mexico. It is also found in northwestern Arizona. It is prime watershed protection in mountainous areas.

(Chaparral vegetation and wildlife; see key on overleaf.)

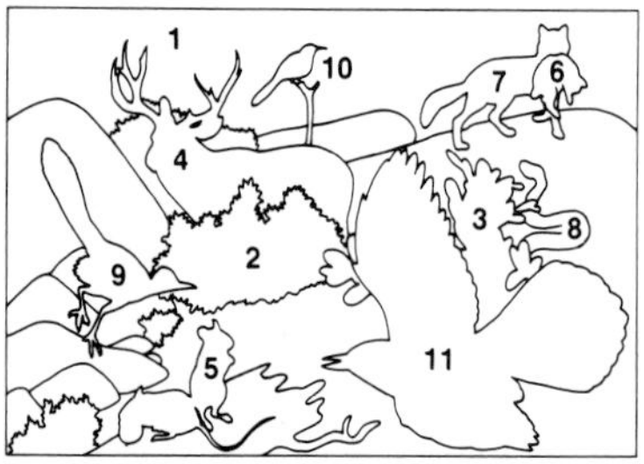

(Page 257) *Chaparral vegetation is dominated by such woody, evergreen shrubs as scrub oak* (1) *and various species of manzanita* (2). *Manzanitas typically bear reddish to brownish berrylike fruit, as shown, in the winter or early spring. Chaparral plants are adapted to hot,dry summers by thick, small leaves and the ability to regenerate quickly after fire. Succulents such as prickly pear cactus* (3) *occur in drier chaparral communities. This environment supports a variety of animals. Herbivores include the mule deer* (4); *California mouse* (5); *and brush rabbit* (6). *Among the carnivores, the gray fox* (7) *preys on rodents and other small animals, such as the brush rabbit; rattlesnakes* (8) *feed primarily on rodents. Both herbivores and carnivores rely on the ability to move quickly in the relatively open woodland. The roadrunner* (9) *consumes insects, scorpions, lizards, and other small animals; it runs quickly but rarely flies. The California thrasher* (10) *is also a ground feeder. The scrub jay* (11) *eats insects and acorns.*

Chaparral is composed of several hundred species of plants, most of which are evergreen shrubs belonging to many plant families such as rose, oak, heath, buckthorn, and sumac. Common shrubs are chamise (*Adenostoma fasciculatum*), scrub oak (*Quercus dumosa*), mountain lilac (*Ceanothus*), manzanita (*Arctostaphylos*), and sumac (*Rhus*). Chaparral supports many resident reptiles, birds, and mammals, such as the alligator lizard and western rattlesnake; roadrunner and scrub jay; and brush rabbit, coyote, and mule deer.

The chaparral environment is harsh. Annual rainfall ranges from 30 to 60 cm (12 to 24 in) with 85 percent falling between November and April. Summers are dry and hot, reaching more than 40° C (104° F). Chaparral edges grasslands and sage scrub along its lower and drier borders, and mixed coniferous forest along its upper and moister borders. Montane chaparral is a cold-adapted form that extends through the coniferous forest zone up to 3,000 m (10,000 ft) high.

Chaparral, a word of Spanish origin, first denoted a thicket of shrubby evergreen oaks common to Mediterranean countries. In time the term was applied in California to dense brushlands in general. The term *chaparral* is also applied to Rocky Mountain foothill vegetation. This vegetation, however, is winter dormant and summer active, whereas California chaparral is winter active and summer dormant.

The leaf is the most distinctive feature of California chaparral shrubs. It is usually small, thick, stiff, waxy, and evergreen. The term *sclerophyll* ("hard-leaved") is applied to chaparral as well as to comparable vegetations in other continents. Wherever a Mediterranean climate (cool, moist winters and hot, dry summers) prevails, sclerophyllous shrublands are found, such as around the Mediterranean Sea (matorral), African Cape (fynbos), southwestern Australia (mallee), Chile and Peru (*espinal*), and California (chaparral). Such plants can capitalize on rainwater minutes after it arrives.

Chaparral is one of the most fire-susceptible vegetations in the world because it is dense, is dry each summer, and contains volatile compounds. Fire denudes vast tracts of chaparral each year. Chaparral plants have adapted to fire in three ways: (1) production of seeds at an early age; (2) production of refractory seeds that retain viability, or the ability to sprout, for decades and are resistant to fire (in some species the heat of fire is required for germination); and (3) sprouting from a root-crown burl (lignotuber).

chapbook *Chapbook*, derived from the Old English word *ceap*, meaning "barter, trade, a business," is a term introduced in the 19th century to describe cheap popular pamphlets sold during the 16th, 17th, and 18th centuries by itinerant peddlers, or "chapmen." They ranged from religious and political tracts to ballads and sensational stories. Although not in themselves significant as literature, chapbooks were valuable sources for playwrights and novelists. Shakespeare's *Titus Andronicus* may have been derived from some early version of an 18th-century chapbook discovered in 1936.

Chapel Hill Chapel Hill (1990 pop., 38,719), a city in north central North Carolina, is the site of the University of North Carolina (1792), the first chartered state university in the United States. It is also the site of Morehead Planetarium, a celestial navigation training center for astronauts.

Chaplin, Charlie Charles Spencer Chaplin, b. London, England, Apr. 16, 1889, d. Dec. 25, 1977, cinema's most celebrated comedian-director, achieved international fame with his portrayals of the mustachioed Little Tramp. As the director, producer, writer, and interpreter of his many movies, he made a major contribution to establishing film comedy as a true art form. Reared in poverty in London's slums, Chaplin, like his parents, became a music hall performer, appearing as a clown in Fred Karno's Mumming Birds company from 1906. While touring the United States in 1913, he was persuaded by Mack SENNETT to join the Keystone studio; Chaplin's first slapstick, *Making a Living* (1914), followed. In *Kid Auto Races at Venice* (1914), he originated the gentleman tramp routine—twirling cane, bowler, tight jacket, and baggy pants—that became his trademark. He also learned to direct his own short films.

During the next four years, Chaplin consolidated his growing international reputation by a prolific output of shorts for Essanay, Mutual, and First National studios. At the same time, he refined his tramp character into a poetic figure that combined comedy and pathos, yet retained his meticulously timed acrobatic skills. His films grew in length and subtlety with *A Dog's Life* and *Shoulder Arms* (both 1918). After cofounding United Artists in 1919, Chaplin began independent production in the 1920s of his best feature-length films: *A Woman of Paris*

(1923), *The Gold Rush* (1925), *The Circus* (1928), *City Lights* (1931), *Modern Times* (1936), and *The Great Dictator* (1940), his first all-talking film, in which he abandoned the tramp to parody Hitler. Among his later films, only the poignant *Limelight* (1952) achieved popularity; the apparent cynicism of *Monsieur Verdoux* (1947) and *A King in New York* (1957) alienated audiences, while his last effort, *A Countess from Hong Kong* (1966), left little impression.

Although loved and appreciated throughout the world as the inimitable Charlot or Charlie, Chaplin's personal life, including his four marriages, a 1944 paternity suit, and his refusal to accept U.S. citizenship, gained him adverse publicity in America. Initially embittered, he returned in triumph in 1972 to receive a special achievement award from the Academy of Motion Picture Arts and Sciences, followed in 1973 by an Academy Award for his score to *Limelight.* In 1975, at age 86, he was knighted by Queen Elizabeth.

Charlie Chaplin, hailed as a genius of motion picture comedy, appears in a scene from the silent film The Gold Rush *(1925).*

Chapman, George George Chapman, b. *c.*1559, d. May 12, 1634, was an English poet and dramatist whose translations of Homer's *Iliad* (1611) and *Odyssey* (1616) inspired Keats's sonnet "On First Looking into Chapman's Homer." His best-known tragedy, *Bussy d'Ambois* (1607), depicts a hero, caught between reason and passion, suffering the whims of fortune. Chapman wrote the comedy *Eastward Ho!* in collaboration with Ben Jonson and John Marston. His other plays included *All Fools* (1605), *The Gentleman Usher* (1606), and *The Widow's Tears* (1612).

Chapman, John John Chapman, b. Massachusetts, Sept. 26, 1774, d. Mar. 10, 1845, is known as Johnny Appleseed in American legend. Around 1800 he arrived in the Ohio River valley, a region he was to wander for the rest of his life. On a rough craft made of two canoes lashed together, and carrying a cargo of apples brought from the orchards of the eastern states, he drifted on the Ohio River, stopping wherever he saw a likely spot to plant a few seeds and establish a tree nursery. The seeds he planted and the saplings he gave to local Indians and new settlers helped build the orchards of the Midwest.

Chapultepec [chah-pool-tay-pek'] Chapultepec is a hill about 60 m (200 ft) high in western Mexico City, Mexico. It was originally the site of the Aztec rulers' residence. After the Spanish conquest (1521), the Spaniards first built (1554) a chapel at Chapultepec, and later, in the 1780s, a summer palace. The latter became the National Military Academy in 1841. During the MEXICAN WAR the hill was stormed (Sept. 12–13, 1847) by U.S. troops, and many of the Mexican cadets were killed in the battle.

In the 1860s the palace was splendidly reconstructed, and it served as the presidential residence until the 1930s. In 1940 it became a museum, and the surrounding area was made a public park. Chapultepec is a major tourist attraction and was the site of the Inter-American Conference on hemispheric security in 1945. The name means "hill of the grasshopper."

char [char] Char are freshwater and saltwater fishes of the genus *Salvilinus*, subfamily Salmoninae of SALMON. They include lake trout and brook trout, which are popular food and game fish in America; the Alpine char of Europe; and the Arctic char, which is commercially important in Siberia and Scandinavia. The splake is a hybrid lake and brook trout widely stocked in Canadian lakes as a sport fish.

Char are distinguished from true trout, genus *Salmo*, primarily by their teeth. They have few teeth at the end of the bone, or vomer, along the middle line of the roof of the mouth, whereas the vomer is studded with teeth in such true trout as rainbow, oceanic, and river trout. Char also have smaller scales than true trout, and light spots on dark skin.

Lake trout attain a length of up to 100 cm (39 in) and weigh 30 to 50 kg (66 to 110 lb). They are popular game fish in the Great Lakes region and in southern Canada, but their numbers have declined as a result of predation by sea lampreys that have spread into their habitats.

Like salmon, the marine char of northern Europe migrate to spawn. During early fall they swim upstream in tributaries of the Arctic Ocean and spawn during the late fall or winter of the following year, usually in lakes. At this time, the belly of the male is a brilliant red.

The brook char, also known as the brook trout, is a much-favored game fish. The clever and elusive fish prefers large, cool mountain streams.

characin [kair'-uh-sin] Characins are freshwater fishes belonging to the family Characidae, order Cypriniformes. They are found in tropical Africa and in South and Central America and are now spreading into North America. They can be distinguished from MINNOWS, which they often resemble, by the presence of an adipose fin and teeth. Because of the extreme diversity of form displayed by this group, they are sometimes divided into 2 families and more than 30 subfamilies. The smallest adult is about 2.5 cm (1 in) in length and the largest more than 1.8 m (6 ft). Their food habits vary from vegetarian to carnivorous.

The ferocious piranha has razor-sharp teeth. The teeth of the upper and lower jaw cut against each other like scissors when the mouth is closed. A school of piranhas can reduce a human to a skeleton in minutes.

The group includes the dangerous PIRANHA of South America; the vicious tiger fish of Africa; the neon tetra of the aquarium trade; and the only known true flying fish, the flying HATCHETFISH. In some species of characins, the mouth is underneath the head; in others, it is located on top of the snout. One species has a terminal mouth and is called a tailstander because of the way it swims tail down; another is called a headstander because it always swims tail up.

charades [shuh-raydz'] Charades is one of the oldest and most popular parlor or party games. The players are divided into two teams. Each team member writes a word, phrase, sentence, book title, movie title, song title, or the like on a separate slip of paper for the opposing team to enact. Then an actor pantomimes the words on the slip in such a way that his or her teammates can guess them. The team with the lowest total time wins the game.

Although the actors may not speak, some prearranged gestures are usually permissible, including beckoning (you're warm); pushing away (you're cold); and finger on nose (that's right).

charcoal Charcoal is a porous, solid product obtained when carbonaceous materials such as cellulose, wood, peat, or bituminous coal are partially burned in the absence of air. Charcoal was the chief fuel used in blast furnaces, as well as in glassmaking, blacksmithing, and metalworking.

Wood charcoal was manufactured by constructing a dome-shaped mound, or "pit," of stripped logs, stacked around a triangular wooden chimney. The mound was sealed with a coating of leaves and charcoal dust, and the chimney filled with kindling and ignited. After two weeks, the pit was raked out and the charcoal removed.

Although charcoal has been replaced by COKE in blast furnaces and by natural gas and other materials as a source of carbon in producing certain chemicals, it is still used as an ingredient in black gunpowder. Highly porous activated wood and cellulose charcoals are used as filtering agents to remove colors, tastes, and odors from gases or liquids. Charcoals are also employed in recovering solvents and other volatile materials, and as catalysts or supports for catalytic agents. The pigment and adsorbent, bone black, is a form of charcoal made from bone.

Charcot, Jean Martin Jean Martin Charcot, b. Nov. 29, 1825, d. Aug. 16, 1893, was the leading neurologist of his time and head of the Saltpêtrière Hospital in Paris. He became a professor of pathological anatomy in 1878 and thereafter made the Saltpêtrière the first postgraduate center for psychiatric education. Outstanding neurologists and psychiatrists, including Sigmund Freud, attended his teaching clinics. Charcot believed, as did most of his contemporaries, that the various forms of psychopathology are caused by degenerative changes in the brain. It was his interest in examining hypnotic phenomena and in studying cases of HYSTERIA, however, that attracted the greatest attention. Charcot held the prevailing view that hysteria is caused by a brain dysfunction. He argued against the opposing view, advanced by the School at Nancy, France, that hysterical symptoms are caused by suggestion. He demonstrated, nevertheless, that pathological ideas can cause hysteria.

Charcot's interest in hypnosis and hysteria was important in stimulating further work on the NEUROSES and in focusing attention on the disorders of nonhospitalized individuals who are not insane.

Jean Martin Charcot, a 19th-century neurologist, leads the discussion at one of his teaching clinics in the Salpêtrière mental hospital in Paris, where Sigmund Freud was among his pupils.

Chardin, Jean Baptiste [shar-dan'] Jean Baptiste Siméon Chardin, b. Nov. 2, 1699, d. Dec. 6, 1779, was one of the greatest 18th-century French masters of still-life and genre painting. Chardin derived the heavy impasto of his mature works from Rembrandt, while displaying

Girl with a Racket and Shuttlecock (1741) is by Jean Baptiste Chardin, a French painter of still lifes and genre scenes. His works capture the mood and beauty in the private domestic moments of ordinary people. (Private collection, Paris.)

an assimilation of the delicate rococo style tonalities of Antoine Watteau and François Boucher.

Chardin achieved his first public success in 1728 when he sent several still lifes to the annual open-air exhibition of young painters in the Place Dauphine. On Sept. 25, 1728, he became a member of the Royal Academy of Painting and Sculpture. Following major exhibitions in 1734 and 1737, Chardin's intimate genre scenes of women at work or children at play enjoyed enormous popularity. Many of these paintings were purchased by royalty in France, Russia, Sweden, and Prussia. This royal patronage was surprising, because Chardin consistently celebrated the dignity of the petite bourgeoisie, and unlike the paintings of his contemporaries, his genre scenes were never sentimentalizing, moralizing, or titillating. Chardin's immense popularity among the general public throughout Europe was due largely to the vast distribution of engravings of his works.

From the 1740s on, Chardin spent much of his time painting copies of earlier works to meet the public demand. Late in life he began to use pastels; as exemplified by *Self-Portrait* (1775; Louvre, Paris), he achieved an unparalleled mastery of technique.

Chardonnet, Hilaire Bernigaud, Comte de see RAYON

charge, electric see COULOMB

charge-coupled device A charge-coupled device, or CCD, is a SEMICONDUCTOR chip designed to capture light images electronically. The most common semiconductor—meaning an element that can be treated to become either an insulator or a conductor—is silicon. A silicon chip becomes photosensitive when it is treated, or doped, to create a series of positively charged regions, or photosites, that act as electron receptors. Photons impinging on the silicon surface liberate electrons from silicon atoms, and these electrons then jump to the receptor regions. The strengths of the incoming light signals are directly related to the numbers of electrons captured. The resulting potentials are then amplified and converted to digital code for storage in a computer memory.

Charge-coupled devices are extremely efficient light gatherers, with some capable of capturing at least 60% of light in the visible spectrum. CCDs also have a powerful dynamic range, capable of recording wide extremes of light intensity within a single image. For such reasons, CCDs are preferred over chemical film in certain applications and have found use in telescopes and cameras. CCDs provide less resolution than chemical film, however, because image density is limited by the number of picture elements that can be constructed.

Charge of the Light Brigade, The "The Charge of the Light Brigade" is a strongly rhythmic, patriotic poem written in 1854 by Alfred, Lord TENNYSON, then poet laureate of England. The poem glorifies an incident in the Battle of BALAKLAVA during the Crimean War in which an English brigade charged the Russian army against hopeless odds and was slaughtered. Although the 673 men understood the foolishness of the command, they did not question it.

chariot A chariot is a fast, open, two- or four-wheeled vehicle pulled by horses and used in ancient times for warfare, hunting, processions, and racing. Built in Mesopotamia as early as 3000 BC (and in China during the 2d millennium BC), chariots spread to Egypt, Greece, Rome, and eventually even to Britain. Chariots were important as instruments of war but also as racing vehicles. Mentioned in Homer's *Iliad* and an event in the Olympic Games and other athletic contests of ancient Greece, chariot racing became enormously popular and widespread in Roman and Byzantine societies.

charismatic movement [kair-iz-mat'-ik] The charismatic movement is an informal international and transdenominational fellowship of Christians who believe that the gifts of the HOLY SPIRIT as described by St. PAUL in I Corinthians 12:4–11 and Galatians 5:22–23 are manifested in these times. Although related to PENTECOSTALISM, the charismatic movement differs in not being denominationally organized and in its refusal to insist upon speaking in tongues as an essential element of authentic Christian experience. Members refer to themselves as charismatic (a term derived from the Greek word for GRACE) or as the new PENTECOST.

Charlemagne, Frankish emperor

Charlemagne, Frankish emperor (Charles the Great) [shar'-luh-mayn] Charlemagne, or Charles the Great, CAROLINGIAN king of the FRANKS, came to rule over most of Europe and assumed (800) the title of Roman emperor. He is sometimes regarded as the founder of the HOLY ROMAN EMPIRE.

Charlemagne was probably born in 742 at Aachen. In 768 he and his brother Carloman inherited the Frankish kingdom from their father, PEPIN THE SHORT. The entire kingdom passed to Charlemagne when Carloman died in 771.

Conquests. Charlemagne doubled the territory under Carolingian control. In 772 he opened his offensive against the SAXONS, and for more than three decades he pursued a ruthless policy aimed at subjugating them and converting them to Christianity. Mass executions—4,500 Saxons were executed on a single day in 782—and deportations were used to discourage the stubborn.

Other peoples were not so resistant. The LOMBARDS were conquered in a single extended campaign (773–74), after which Charlemagne assumed the title "king of the Lombards." In 788 he absorbed the duchy of Bavaria, and then launched an offensive against the Avars, who succumbed within a decade. After one disastrous campaign (778) against the Muslims in Spain, Charlemagne left the southwestern front to his son Louis (later Emperor LOUIS I).

On Christmas Day, 800, Charlemagne was crowned emperor by Pope LEO III, but for several years after he regarded the imperial title as being of little value. He intended to divide his lands among his sons, as was the Frankish custom. At his death on Jan. 28, 814, however, only one son, Louis, survived, and he then assumed control of the empire.

Administration. The internal organization of Charlemagne's empire varied from region to region. In much of what is today France, and especially in the south, the old Roman *civitates* (fortified cities) served as the focus of most important aspects of political, military, religious, and social organization. Both the count of the city, appointed by Charlemagne, and the bishop made their headquarters in the *civitas.*

In those parts of the empire which had not been part of the Roman world, Charlemagne made an effort to impose a similar system. He divided newly conquered lands into *pagi* (districts), which were placed under the jurisdiction of counts. Charlemagne also sought to establish these new *pagi* as dioceses. In frontier areas he often established military districts called marks or marches.

The traditional laws, some unwritten, of each of the various peoples of the Carolingian empire, such as Salian Franks, Ripuarian Franks, Romans, Saxons, Lombards, Bavarians, Thuringians, and Jews, were recognized and codified (or modified if local codes already existed). This judicial autonomy enjoyed by the several peoples of the empire indicates the diversity that flourished under Charlemagne.

The central administration of the empire was rudimentary. A palatine court followed Charlemagne on his

(Right) *Charlemagne, who inherited the Frankish kingdom of Pepin the Short, devoted his reign to the expansion of that realm. His coronation in Rome in 800 is sometimes regarded as the founding of the Holy Roman Empire. (Metropolitan Museum of Art, New York City.)*

(Below) *The map shows the territories included within the European empire founded by Charlemagne. Also indicated are the divisions of the Carolingian Empire among Charlemagne's dynastic successors.*

campaigns; during the later years of his life, when he remained at AACHEN, the court stayed there. Charlemagne also sent *missi dominici*, high-ranking agents of the central government, to see that his orders were enforced. He also sought to standardize weights, measures, and coinage and made an attempt to control and develop trade.

Cultural Development. Charlemagne encouraged a rudimentary educational system based in monasteries, leaving the development and implementation of this system largely to ALCUIN. The latter's work led to what some scholars have called the Carolingian Renaissance. At Charlemagne's court a group of scholars was gathered that included men from England, Spain, and Italy, as well as native Franks and probably Jews.

Evaluation. Charlemagne has been credited with great political and humanitarian vision and a devout religious bent, but in fact he was a gluttonous and superstitious semiliterate with a considerable capacity for brutality. His accomplishments were due mostly to the energy with which he pursued his goals. The main effect of his conquests was to spread Roman Christianity across central Europe.

See also: FRANCE, HISTORY OF; GERMANY, HISTORY OF.

Charleroi [shar-luh-wah'] Charleroi is a town in Hainaut province in south central Belgium on the Sambre River. It has a population of 208,938 (1988 est.). The Charleroi-Brussels Canal (constructed in the 19th century) spurred the growth of industry and manufacturing. Coal mining, metalworks, and glassmaking and ceramic making are the principal industries. Called Charnoy in the Middle Ages, the city was renamed (1666) for Charles II of Spain. In World War I the city was captured (1914) by the Germans after fierce fighting.

Charles, Jacques The French physicist Jacques Alexandre Cesar Charles, b. Nov. 12, 1746, d. Apr. 7, 1823, is best known for his formulation (1787) of one of the basic GAS LAWS, known as Charles's law: at constant pressure, the volume occupied by a fixed weight of gas is directly proportional to the absolute temperature. Charles was better known to his contemporaries for inventing the hydrogen BALLOON. In 1784, the year following the pioneering flights of the Montgolfier brothers using a hot-air balloon, Charles, realizing that hydrogen was lighter than air, constructed the first hydrogen balloon and made several flights up to an altitude of about 1.6 km (1 mi).

Charles, Prince of Wales Prince Charles Philip Arthur George, b. Nov. 14, 1948, eldest son of Queen Elizabeth II of Britain and Prince Philip, is heir to the throne of the United Kingdom. He received his secondary education at Gordonstoun, Scotland, spent a semester at school in Australia, and attended (1967–70) Trinity College, Cambridge. He was named duke of Cornwall in 1952 and Prince of Wales in 1958—he was invested as Prince of Wales in 1969. On July 29, 1981, he married Lady Diana Spencer. Their two children, second and third in line to the throne, are Prince William Arthur Philip Louis, born June 21, 1982, and Prince Henry Charles Albert David, born Sept. 15, 1984.

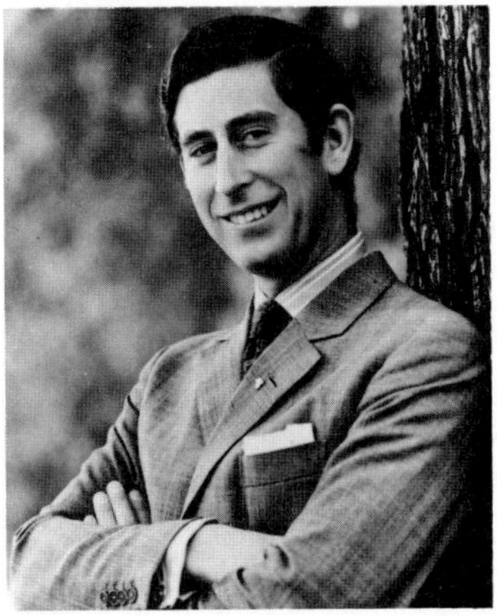

Prince Charles is the heir apparent to the throne of the United Kingdom of Great Britain and Northern Ireland, currently occupied by his mother, Queen Elizabeth II. He has served in both the Royal Air Force and the Royal Navy, and is the first heir to the British crown to earn a university degree.

Charles, Ray The blind singer, pianist, and composer Ray Charles Robinson, b. Albany, Ga., Sept. 23, 1930, has been a major figure in American popular music since the 1950s, when he recorded two of his most influential hits—"I Got a Woman" (1955) and "What'd I Say" (1959). Charles, nicknamed the "Genius" by his peers, was one of the first to blend gospel vocal styles with blues and rock music to create the sound called *soul.* Although in the 1970s and 1980s his music turned increasingly toward both country and western and the sentimental, Charles and his lavish stage productions continued to attract large European as well as U.S. audiences.

Charles the Bold, Duke of Burgundy Charles the Bold, b. Nov. 10, 1433, duke of Burgundy (1467–77), was the last of four Valois dukes whose great accomplishment was to unify the Low Countries. About 1464 he began to take over the government of the family lands from his father, PHILIP THE GOOD. He joined (1465) other French princes in the War of the Public Weal against LOUIS XI, who became his major antagonist. He was able to extort major concessions from Louis in the late 1460s, but he was less successful in the 1470s, when French opposition grew and an English alliance (1468) failed to produce much help.

Charles's ambition was to link the Low Countries to his Burgundian lands and extend his power to the Alps. Although historical tradition has attributed his downfall to the machinations of Louis XI among the Swiss, it was really the hostility of the imperial cities that frustrated Charles in his designs. Not only the Swiss towns but also those of Alsace-Lorraine and the middle Rhine formed a great coalition against him, defeating him at Grandson and Morat (1476) and again at Nancy, where he lost his life on Jan. 5, 1477. The marriage (1477) of his heiress, MARY OF BURGUNDY, to the future Holy Roman emperor Maximilian I, gave the Netherlands to the HABSBURG dynasty.

Charles Martel The Frankish ruler Charles Martel, b. *c.*688, d. Oct. 22, 741, was the first CAROLINGIAN to bring most of what is today France under his control. He was the illegitimate son of Pepin of Heristal, mayor of the palace in Austrasia.

Charles secured his position as mayor in 719, and from then until his death he worked to expand Carolingian domination. In 732 or 733 he stopped the Muslim Arab advance northward from Spain in a celebrated battle between Poitiers and Tours. He conquered (733) Burgundy and fought in the south of France. Although Charles supported the Christian mission of Saint BONIFACE in Germany, he declined to help Pope Gregory III against the LOMBARDS in Italy. Charles was succeeded as mayor of the palace by his sons PEPIN THE SHORT and Carloman.

Charles I, Emperor of Austria-Hungary
Charles I, b. Aug. 17, 1887, d. Apr. 1, 1922, was the last emperor of Austria and (as Charles IV) king of Hungary. He succeeded his granduncle FRANCIS JOSEPH in 1916. Forced to abdicate at the end of World War I (Nov. 11, 1918), he twice tried to recover the Hungarian throne in 1921.

Charles I, King of England, Scotland, and Ireland Charles I, b. Nov. 19, 1600, king of England, Scotland, and Ireland, lost his thrones and life as a result of the ENGLISH CIVIL WAR. The second son of JAMES I, Charles became (1616) prince of Wales after his older brother died.

The 1st duke of BUCKINGHAM and Charles traveled (1623) to Madrid to arrange a marriage between Charles and the Spanish king's sister, but she did not want a Protestant husband. After his accession in 1625, Charles married HENRIETTA MARIA, sister of Louis XIII of France. By then England was involved in a war with Spain, and Charles later declared war on France. Neither war succeeded, and in 1626, Parliament tried to impeach Buckingham. Charles dissolved the body that year but was forced to call it again in 1628. His need for money was now so urgent that he accepted the Petition of Right, a statement of parliamentary grievances. Soon after, Buckingham was assassinated by a Puritan fanatic.

This event altered Charles's life. The queen now won her husband's love, and in 1630 the future Charles II was born. Charles I blamed Buckingham's death on the attacks in Parliament. He decided to rule without a Parliament and did so for 11 years. He also worked to purge Puritan excesses from the Church of England, but the attempts at reform made by his archbishop of Canterbury, William LAUD, aroused considerable resentment.

To obtain funds to suppress the rebellion of the Scottish COVENANTERS (the so-called BISHOPS' WARS), the king called (1640) the Short Parliament, only to find it determined to voice grievances. Charles promptly dissolved it, but his need for money forced him to call another, the so-called LONG PARLIAMENT. Although Charles met some of its demands, notably by signing away the life of his lord lieutenant in Ireland, the earl of STRAFFORD, the Parliament was resolved to transform England into a constitutional monarchy. Civil war ensued on Aug. 22, 1642.

Charles I, king of England, Scotland, and Ireland, appears here in a portrait by Anthony van Dyck. Although a great patron of the arts, Charles was an inept ruler whose conflicts with Parliament led to civil war in 1642. He was deposed and executed in 1649. (Prado, Madrid.)

Charles lost both the first and second civil wars because he was a poor strategist and often broke his promises. Finally defeated by the parliamentarians in 1648, he was tried for treason by a specially created court. He refused to enter a plea at his trial and was convicted. Charles declared on the scaffold that his duty had been to care for his subjects as a loving father, that he had been divinely chosen to govern, and that "a subject and sovereign" were "clear different things." He was beheaded on Jan. 30, 1649.

Charles II, King of England, Scotland, and Ireland Charles II, b. May 29, 1630, d. Feb. 6, 1685, king of England, Scotland, and Ireland (1660-85), was one of the laziest but cleverest of English kings. He was the oldest surviving son of Charles I. After the execution (1649) of his father, Charles was exiled to Holland and France, where he spent 11 years plotting to overthrow the English republic. In 1650 he went to Scotland, where the prevailing party, the COVENANTERS, agreed to recognize him as king of the Scots. In return he promised to uphold the Solemn League and Covenant, which committed him to imposing Presbyterianism on England and Ireland, although he had no intention of doing so. After the Covenanters had been defeated in battle by Oliver CROMWELL, Charles led a Scottish army into England, where he was defeated at Worcester in 1651. Following the death (1658) of Cromwell, many English people favored restoring Charles to the throne. Accordingly, the RESTORATION took place in 1660.

Charles II, who was restored (1660) to the English throne 11 years after the execution of his father, Charles I, learned to manipulate and circumvent Parliament rather than confront it as his father had done. Nonetheless, his pro-French and pro-Catholic sympathies provoked fierce controversy, and he ruled without Parliament during the last 4 years of his reign (1681–85).

The new royalist Parliament restored Anglicanism as the established religion, imposing stiff penalties on NONCONFORMISTS by the so-called CLARENDON CODE (1661–65), and pressed Charles to make war on the Dutch. He did so in 1665 but was forced to agree to a humiliating peace in 1667.

Charles then allied himself with France against the Dutch, but in the ensuing war (1672-74) the Dutch forced him to make a separate peace (see ANGLO-DUTCH WARS). By the Treaty of Dover (1670), Louis XIV of France had secretly promised to pay subsidies to Charles, who in turn promised to convert England to Roman Catholicism, but these payments proved insufficient to sustain another war.

Anti-Catholic hysteria erupted in reaction to the spurious Popish Plot, concocted by Titus OATES, in 1678. Charles resisted efforts led by the 1st earl of SHAFTESBURY to exclude his Catholic brother, the future JAMES II, from the succession, and he dissolved Parliament in 1681 and ruled thereafter without it.

Charles is known as the Merry Monarch, partly because of his numerous mistresses, who included Nell GWYNNE; Louise de Kéroualle, duchess of Portsmouth; and Barbara Villiers, duchess of Cleveland. He also enjoyed horse racing and gambling and was very popular with the common people. His pocketing of bribes and blatant lying to get over difficulties with Parliament, however, did not commend him to his political opponents or to future historians. He was received into the Roman Catholic church just before his death.

Charles I, King of France and Frankish emperor see CHARLEMAGNE

Charles II, Frankish emperor (Charles the Bald) Charles II, or Charles the Bald, b. June 13, 823, d. Oct. 6, 877, was the son of Emperor LOUIS I by his second wife. Resented by three older half-brothers, Charles became a pawn in the court politics of the Frankish empire, but by the Treaty of Verdun (843) he was recognized as king of the West Franks, the first true king of France. Toward the end of his life he was acknowledged (875) as emperor with the pope's support.

Throughout his reign, Charles had to struggle against Viking raiders and disloyal magnates as well as with his own relatives. The French bishops helped him repel his brother LOUIS THE GERMAN in 859, but ten years later Louis prevented Charles from regaining his family's ancient homeland in LOTHARINGIA. The Treaty of Mersen (870), which established the ultimate boundaries of medieval France, deprived him of most of this disputed territory, and by the time of his death the French monarchy was in serious decline.

Charles III, Frankish emperor (Charles the Fat) Charles III, or Charles the Fat, b. 839, d. Jan. 13, 888, Frankish emperor, reunited for the last time the empire of CHARLEMAGNE (except Burgundy). He was the youngest son of LOUIS THE GERMAN, from whom he inherited (876) the kingdom of Swabia. Three years later, on the resignation of his sick brother Carloman, he became king of Italy, and he was crowned emperor by Pope John VIII in 881. His succession to Saxony on the death (882) of his other brother Louis the Younger, made Charles king of all the East Franks (Germany). The deaths of the West Frankish kings Louis III (882) and Carloman (884) gave him France. Charles was deposed in 887 by his nephew Arnulf.

Charles III, King of France (Charles the Simple) Charles III, b. Sept. 17, 879, known as the Simple (meaning "sincere"), was king of France from 898 to 922. The youngest son of Louis II, of France, he was passed over for the throne on the deposition (887) of his cousin, the Frankish emperor Charles III, but succeeded Eudes I in 898. In 911 he accepted the homage of the Viking chief Rollo, who became the first duke of Normandy. He tried to rebuild royal power by establishing his authority in LOTHARINGIA (Lorraine), but this policy irritated the magnates of western France. He was deposed in 922 after the death of his main supporter, Richard of Burgundy, and was murdered in captivity on Oct. 7, 929.

Charles IV, King of France (Charles the Fair) Charles IV, or Charles the Fair, b. 1294, d. Feb. 1, 1328, was king of France from 1322 until his death, and was the last of the direct CAPETIAN line. He intervened maladroitly on behalf of Flemish rebels against their counts, intrigued fruitlessly for nomination as Holy Roman emperor, and invaded (1324) Aquitaine, an English possession. Having aided his sister Isabella to dethrone her husband, EDWARD II of England, he obtained (1327) a peace with England that gave him sections of Aquitaine and a large monetary settlement.

Charles V, King of France (Charles the Wise)
Charles V, or Charles the Wise, b. Jan. 21, 1338, d. Sept. 16, 1380, king of France from 1364 to 1380, was the oldest son of JOHN II of France. Exploited by the opponents of his inept father and forced to head the government during the latter's captivity (1356–60), Charles struggled against domestic brigandage and the peasant revolt called the JACQUERIE. He emerged from this ordeal with increased political maturity and ensured the success of his reign by winning the support of the influential (and previously hostile) northwestern nobles.

The development of France's first regular system of taxation in the 1360s enabled Charles to finance the armies that won the first major French victories in the HUNDRED YEARS' WAR. Charles supported currency reform and patronized artists and intellectuals, but his policies helped bring about (1378) the Great SCHISM in the papacy.

Charles VII's reign (1422–61) brought the Hundred Years' War to a successful conclusion for France. Although Charles initially controlled only a small portion of the country, French hopes were revived by the victories of Joan of Arc. By 1453 the English had been expelled from all of France except Calais. (Louvre, Paris.)

Charles VI, King of France (Charles the Mad or Well-Beloved) Charles VI, b. Dec. 3, 1368, d. Oct. 21, 1422, was the son of Charles V and king of France from 1380 to 1422. Still a child when he succeeded his father, he was dominated by his selfish uncles (notably PHILIP THE BOLD of Burgundy) until they were ousted in 1388 by a coalition of royal officials and northwestern nobles. In the next four years, Charles instituted governmental reforms, but after 1392 he suffered from recurrent insanity. The dukes of Burgundy and ORLÉANS struggled for power, and in the ensuing civil war HENRY V of England successfully invaded France (1415) and forced Charles to disinherit his remaining son and accept Henry as his heir.

See also: HUNDRED YEARS' WAR.

Charles VII, King of France (Charles the Well-Served) Charles VII, b. Feb. 22, 1403, d. July 22, 1461, was king of France from 1422 to 1461. He was the fifth son of Isabella of Bavaria and, presumably, of her husband, Charles VI of France. He became DAUPHIN in 1417, following the deaths of his brothers. In 1419, Charles was involved in the murder of JOHN THE FEARLESS, duke of Burgundy. HENRY V of England, who was conquering northwestern France, concluded a treaty in 1420 with the deranged Charles VI and the duke of Burgundy, PHILIP THE GOOD, disinheriting the dauphin. Therefore, when Charles VI died in 1422, only the southern part of France recognized Charles VII as king.

His cause seemed hopeless until 1429, when a French force inspired by the presence of Saint JOAN OF ARC stopped the English at Orléans. Accompanied by Joan, Charles went to Reims for his coronation as king (July 1429).

Despite the intrigues of competing royal favorites, Charles proved skillful at court politics. He became much stronger after making peace with Burgundy (1435) and recapturing Paris (1436). In the next decade he reestablished regular taxation and instituted (1445) a permanent army. The English were expelled from most of France by 1453.

Charles VIII, King of France Charles VIII, b. June 30, 1470, king of France (1483–98), was the only son of LOUIS XI. Becoming king at the age of 13, he faced an immediate challenge from the princes. Charles's capable sister, Anne, and her husband, Pierre de Beaujeu, retained custody of the young king, reduced taxes, and skillfully pacified opponents at the States General of 1484. Despite a brief rebellion by the princes the next year, Anne and her husband kept intact the power of the monarchy. Charles gradually took over the government and married (1491) ANNE OF BRITTANY. Charles is most famous for laying claim to the throne of Naples and invading Italy in 1494, inaugurating the ITALIAN WARS. After a quick initial victory, which led to his coronation in Naples on May 12, 1495, Charles fought his way out of Italy against a hostile coalition. He was planning a new invasion when he died suddenly on Apr. 7, 1498, following an accidental blow on the head.

Charles X, King of France Charles X, b. Oct. 9, 1757, d. Nov. 6, 1836, was the last BOURBON king of France. Before 1789 he was identified with the most frivolous and reactionary of the nobility at the court of his brother LOUIS XVI, and in the first weeks of the French Revolution he fled France and spent the next 25 years in exile.

During the reign (1814–24) of his second brother, LOUIS XVIII, Charles was the leader of the ultraroyalists. After succeeding to the throne in 1824, he pursued policies favorable to the nobility and the church. For him the monarchy, the church, the dynasty, and society itself were mortally threatened by the liberals in the Chamber of Deputies and by the liberal press. In July 1830, Charles attempted to break the power of the opposition by extralegal changes in the electoral and press laws, but the attempt was met by violent resistance known as the JULY

REVOLUTION. Charles and his son, the duc d'Angoulême, had to abdicate on Aug. 2, 1830. Charles died in exile.

Charles IV, King of Germany and Holy Roman Emperor Charles IV, b. May 14, 1316, d. Nov. 29, 1378, king of the Germans (1346–78) and Holy Roman emperor (1355–78), was also the king of BOHEMIA from 1346. Charles contributed immensely to the evolution of Czech culture. Born in PRAGUE and educated in Paris, he rejected the ebullient chivalry of his father, John of Luxemburg, king of Bohemia (1310–46), and ruled with practical realism and sound political sense. He became German king through the deposition of LOUIS IV. Always preferring diplomacy to war, Charles checked the efforts of Louis's family, the WITTELSBACHS, to regain power and placated the powerful HABSBURGS by the Treaty of Brünn (1364). After a century of fragmentation, Germany needed a new legal framework; this Charles provided by the GOLDEN BULL of 1356. He also strove to maintain good relations with the popes and to curtail their encroachments on German rights. To his Luxemburg patrimony he added Brandenburg and Lusatia, and he procured the election of his own son WENCESLAS to succeed him—the first imperial father-son succession since the HOHENSTAUFEN period. In his Bohemian realm Charles stimulated cultural growth. He founded (1348) in Prague the first university east of the Rhine; built a magnificent castle, cathedral, and bridge; encouraged artists of all kinds; and promoted the writing of historical chronicles. Without ethnic biases, he encouraged Czech national sentiment.

Charles V, Holy Roman Emperor Charles V, Holy Roman emperor (1519–56) and—as Charles I—king of Spain (1516–56), dominated the politics of Europe for 40 years. Charles was born in Ghent, in present-day Belgium, on Feb. 24, 1500, the eldest son of the Habsburg Philip the Handsome (later PHILIP I) and JOAN THE MAD of Castile. From his father, who died in 1506, he inherited the Netherlands (including most of the modern Netherlands and Belgium) and Franche Comté (a French-speaking province that bordered eastern France but belonged to the Holy Roman Empire). After the death (1516) of his maternal grandfather, FERDINAND II of Aragon, Charles became ruler of the kingdoms of Spain and the Spanish dependencies in Italy—the kingdoms of Naples, Sicily, and Sardinia. The HABSBURG possessions of Austria and several south German lordships came to him on the death (1519) of his paternal grandfather, Holy Roman Emperor MAXIMILIAN I, as did hereditary claims to the crowns of Hungary and Bohemia. The latter were made good by his younger brother Ferdinand (later Emperor FERDINAND I) in 1526, after the last independent king of Hungary, LOUIS II, was killed in the Battle of Mohács. Meanwhile, in 1519, Charles had been elected German king and Holy Roman emperor in succession to his grandfather Maximilian.

Ruler of the World. Not since Charlemagne in the early 9th century had any one ruler dominated so much of Europe. Moreover, Charles V's Spanish subjects were conquering vast overseas territories in Central and South America. Hernán Cortés, the conqueror of Mexico, began to refer to his sovereign as "ruler of the world." Charles and his subjects in Europe were certain that God had bestowed so much power on him because he had to defend Christendom from the attacks of the Turks of the OTTOMAN EMPIRE and later from the Protestant heretics. Charles spoke of himself as "God's standard bearer," and his heraldic device bore the legend *plus ultra* ("always further"). For Charles's opponents the problem was more practical: what was he going to do with his power, and how could they preserve their independence?

The 16th century was an age of increasing population, rising prices, growing cities, and expanding trade. Charles could borrow huge sums of money from the wealthy bankers and mine owners such as the German house of FUGGER or from the money market of Antwerp. In return the lenders were given monopoly rights and political protection. Nevertheless, finance was the emperor's greatest problem, and many military campaigns had to be broken off for lack of money.

Control of Spain. In 1517, Charles went to Spain for the first time to claim his maternal inheritance, but his

Charles V, king of Spain (as Charles I) and Holy Roman Emperor, appears here in a portrait by Titian. Charles was forced to defend his Habsburg realm against Valois France, the Ottoman Turks, and the German Protestants. (Prado, Madrid.)

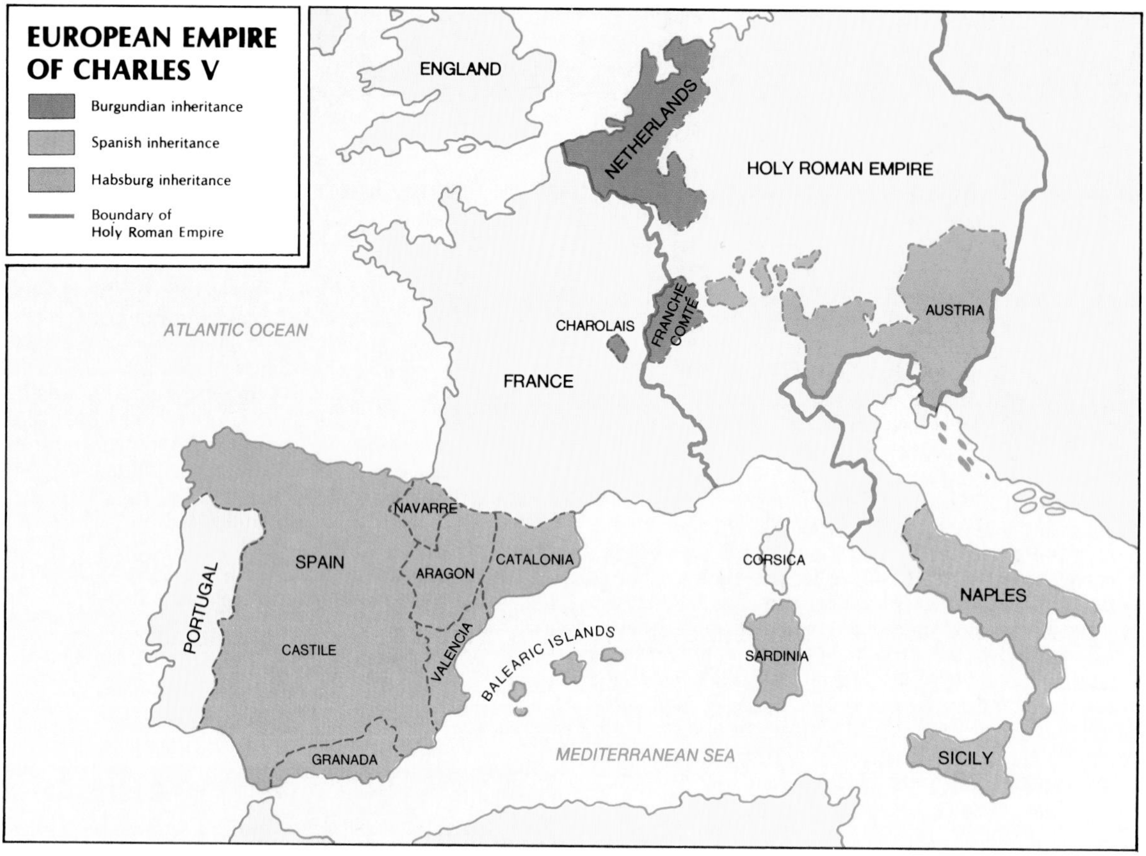

large retinue of Netherlanders made him unpopular. After he left in 1520, the cities of Castile broke into rebellion (1520–21). Only after the nobles defeated the towns was Charles's rule accepted in Spain. His fight against the Turks and the Protestants appealed to the traditions of the Spaniards.

Castile and the Spanish Indies provided an ever-growing proportion of the emperor's revenues. In return Charles appointed more and more Castilians as generals of his armies, governors and viceroys of his provinces, and advisors in his councils. Gradually his international empire turned into a Castilian empire.

Germany and the Reformation. After his visit to Spain, Charles traveled to Germany to be crowned king of that country. In 1521 he presided over the diet (the representative assembly of the German princes and cities) at Worms and witnessed Martin LUTHER's refusal to recant his alleged errors. Charles was not persuaded by Luther, but he recognized the need for a thoroughgoing reform of the Roman Catholic church. It took him until 1545 to persuade a reluctant papacy to summon the Council of TRENT. In the meantime it was necessary to deal with the REFORMATION in Germany. Charles's tactics there varied. When he was otherwise at peace, he tried to enforce the condemnation of the Lutheran doctrines, but when he was at war with France or when the Turks threatened Germany—as they did after the Battle of Mohács and in 1529, when they besieged Vienna—he made considerable concessions to the Protestants. Much to the displeasure of the popes, the emperor's theologians even tried, though without success, to reach a compromise with the Lutheran theologians.

Wars with the Turks and France. The Turks attacked in the Mediterranean, as well as in Hungary. These attacks were supported by the wide-ranging corsairs, or pirates of the BARBARY STATES of North Africa, whose rulers acknowledged themselves vassals to the Turkish sultan. In 1535, Charles commanded his most successful campaign against the Barbary States, conquering Tunis; but in 1541 he failed against Algiers.

Charles's most persistent enemy, however, was France, whose VALOIS kings fought the emperor for the leadership of Europe in general and for the domination of Italy in particular. As early as 1522, Charles made an alliance with HENRY VIII of England to attack and partition France. The plan failed, but the French never forgave Charles or fully trusted him again. In 1525, Charles's army defeated and captured FRANCIS I of France at the

Battle of PAVIA in Italy. But when Francis was released after a compromise peace, the so-called ITALIAN WARS were resumed. The Spaniards finally acquired (1535) Milan and confirmed their domination of Italy.

Schmalkaldic War. In 1546–47, Charles turned against the German Protestant princes, allied against him in the Schmalkaldic League. He captured one of their leaders, John Frederick I, elector of Saxony, at the Battle of Mühlberg (1547), after which the other, PHILIP OF HESSE, surrendered. Other German princes, however, in alliance with France, renewed the war in 1551 and forced the emperor to flee from Germany. Charles's brother, Ferdinand, eventually negotiated the Peace of Augsburg (see AUGSBURG, PEACE OF) in 1555. This gave the German princes, but not their subjects, the right to choose either Catholicism or Lutheranism.

Abdication. In 1555–56, Charles voluntarily abdicated in several stages. He left the Holy Roman Empire to Ferdinand and all his other dominions to his son, PHILIP II of Spain. Many historians have seen Charles's reign as a failure. His contemporaries, however, did not, especially as Philip's marriage (1554) with Queen MARY I of England seemed to open up dazzling new prospects for the house of Habsburg. No one could know that Mary would die young and childless.

Charles retired to a comfortable villa built next to the monastery of San Yuste in Spain. He spent much time in religious devotions but was also surrounded by his fine collection of Renaissance paintings. He listened to music, dismantled and assembled mechanical clocks, ate gluttonously, and continued to meddle in European political affairs. Charles died on Sept. 21, 1558.

Charles VI, Holy Roman Emperor Charles VI, b. Oct. 1, 1685, d. Oct. 20, 1740, Holy Roman emperor (1711–40), was the second son of Emperor LEOPOLD I and younger brother of his immediate predecessor, JOSEPH I. Following the death (1700) of CHARLES II, the last Habsburg king of Spain, Charles was catapulted abruptly into European politics when his father set forth Austrian claims to the Spanish throne on his behalf.

Charles arrived in Spain in 1704 and during the next seven years fought supporters of Louis XIV's grandson, the future PHILIP V of Spain. The unexpected death (1711) of Joseph I made Charles heir to Habsburg possessions in Austria, Bohemia, and Hungary. Elected emperor on Oct. 12, 1711, he reluctantly gave up his Spanish ambitions, since none of the leading European powers would tolerate a union of Austrian and Spanish domains. At the Peace of Rastatt in March 1714 he received territories in Italy and the Netherlands as compensation for the lost Spanish crown.

Because he had no male heir, Charles spent his entire reign trying to gain acceptance of the PRAGMATIC SANCTION, a document designed to protect the succession rights of his daughter MARIA THERESA. His death, however, led immediately to the War of the AUSTRIAN SUCCESSION, a continental conflict that threatened the partition of his lands.

Charles VII, Holy Roman Emperor Charles VII, b. Aug. 6, 1697, German king and Holy Roman emperor, was elected emperor (1742) during the War of the AUSTRIAN SUCCESSION. Also known as Charles Albert, he succeeded (1726) his father as elector of Bavaria and avoided subscribing to the PRAGMATIC SANCTION, by which Emperor Charles VI had made his daughter, MARIA THERESA, heir to the Habsburg Austrian possessions. As emperor, Charles VII was simply a tool of the anti-Austrian coalition. He lost Bavaria to Austrian occupation (1743) and recovered it only shortly before his death on Jan. 20, 1745. He was succeeded as emperor by Maria Theresa's husband, FRANCIS I.

Charles I, King of Hungary (Charles Robert) Charles I, or Charles Robert, b. 1288, d. July 16, 1342, was the first ANGEVIN king of Hungary. Although he claimed the throne immediately after the death (1301) of the last Arpád king, Andrew III, not until 1308 was Charles able to make his claim good. Under his rule, Hungary once more became a significant power in central Europe and was enriched by renewed Western cultural influences from Italy and France. Charles's successful foreign policy, based on strong ties with Poland, resulted in the temporary extension of Hungary's influence into southern Italy and in the short-lived union (1370-82) with Poland under his son, LOUIS I.

Charles I, King of Naples (Charles of Anjou) Charles of Anjou, b. March 1226, d. Jan. 7, 1285, accepted the crown of Naples and Sicily from Pope Urban IV in 1263, culminating more than a decade of papal efforts to find a ruler able and willing to supplant the HOHENSTAUFEN in Sicily. The son of LOUIS VIII and brother of LOUIS IX of France, Charles had devoted his early years to expansion of French interests in Flanders and Provence. After securing the Sicilian crown, he moved to Italy, defeating King Manfred of Sicily at Benevento (Feb. 26, 1266) and Conradin at Tagliacozzo (Aug. 23, 1268). Charles followed in the footsteps of his Norman-Swabian predecessors, but his expansionist policies, particularly in the Balkans, contributed to the SICILIAN VESPERS (1282). He lost Sicily to PETER III of Aragon.

Charles II, King of Naples (Charles the Lame) Charles II, b. 1248, d. May 5, 1309, king of Naples and Sicily, was the son of Charles I (Charles of Anjou). Under his father he played an active role in the military affairs of the kingdom until his capture by the Aragonese in the Gulf of Naples on June 5, 1284. After four years as a prisoner, he was released as a result of the Treaty of Campofranco (Oct. 27, 1288). Thereafter he devoted himself to attempts to reconquer the island of Sicily and to the dynastic interests of his family. He was forced to recognize Aragonese control of Sicily in 1302, but he maintained Angevin control in southern Italy, with Naples as his capital, until his death.

Charles III, King of Naples (Charles of Durazzo) Charles III, b. 1345, d. Feb. 17, 1386, king of Naples, succeeded JOAN I after her deposition by Pope Urban VI in 1380. Charles obtained the pope's support over the claims of LOUIS I of Hungary, whom Joan had named her heir, and succeeded in defeating and capturing Naples in 1381. Charles had Joan strangled on May 22, 1382. Louis's attempt to seize Naples ended with his death in 1384. Charles then promoted his own candidacy for the Hungarian crown, which he obtained (as Charles II) in 1385. Assassinated in 1386, he was succeeded in Naples by his son Ladislas and in Hungary by SIGISMUND, later Holy Roman emperor.

Charles I, King of Portugal Charles I, b. Sept. 28, 1863, was king of Portugal from 1889 until his death in 1908. Although he was a cultured man, an artist, and an oceanographer, Charles was notorious for his extravagance and licentiousness. During his reign, Portugal was torn between rival factions and political parties and embittered by a British ultimatum in 1890 to evacuate south-central Africa. Republicans and radicals attacked the finances of the royal household, and revolts and strikes erupted sporadically. In 1906, Charles appointed João Franco prime minister with dictatorial powers. On Feb. 1, 1908, Charles and his oldest son were assassinated in Lisbon. The Portuguese monarchy survived only two more years under Charles's second son, Manuel II.

Charles I, King of Spain see CHARLES V, HOLY ROMAN EMPEROR

Charles II, King of Spain Charles II, b. Nov. 11, 1661, d. Nov. 1, 1700, was the last HABSBURG king of Spain (1665–1700). The son of PHILIP IV, he was physically and mentally weak, and his strange behavior and convulsive seizures caused him to be labeled the Bewitched. During his reign, Spain reached its political and economic nadir. Charles's inability to conceive heirs led to extensive diplomatic maneuvering among the European powers to secure the succession. Believing that only the French Bourbon candidate, the future PHILIP V, could preserve his empire, Charles named Philip his successor on Oct. 2, 1700. This led, after Charles's death, to the War of the SPANISH SUCCESSION.

Charles III, King of Spain Charles III, b. Jan. 20, 1716, d. Dec. 14, 1788, king of Spain from 1759 to 1788, was one of the most successful enlightened despots of the 18th century. Son of PHILIP V and Isabella of Parma, he ruled the duchy of Parma from 1732 to 1734. In 1734 he became king of Naples, and in 1759 he inherited the throne of Spain from his half brother FERDINAND VI.

Charles III, regarded as the greatest of the Bourbon kings of Spain, ascended the Spanish throne in 1759. He is credited with checking the decline of Spain by instituting economic reforms, curbing the power of the Inquisition, and expelling the powerful Jesuit order.

A moral man of simple tastes, Charles had a talent for choosing good ministers, such as the conde de Aranda and the conde de Floridablanca. His aim was to increase the power of his government in order to achieve the reforms needed to strengthen Spain and preserve its colonial empire. He curbed the power of the INQUISITION and expelled (1766) the JESUITS, whose independence he feared. He reorganized colonial and local administration and established a council of ministers. Charles also removed restrictions on internal and colonial trade, encouraged manufacturing, and strengthened the defense of the empire. His foreign policy was less successful. The Family Compact of 1761, an alliance with France, involved Spain in the last stages of the SEVEN YEARS' WAR. Spain lost Florida in the war but recovered it as a result of supporting the American colonies in the American Revolution.

Charles IV, King of Spain Charles IV, b. Nov. 11, 1748, d. Jan. 20, 1819, king of Spain from 1788 to 1808, was a weak monarch dominated by his wife and chief minister. He inherited the throne from his father, Charles III. A man of little intelligence or willpower, he had the misfortune of ruling during the FRENCH REVOLUTIONARY WARS and NAPOLEONIC WARS, in which Spain was used as a pawn by both France and Britain.

Charles was married to the strong-willed María Luisa of Parma, who persuaded him to appoint her lover, Manuel de GODOY, chief minister in 1792. Neither Charles nor Godoy was able to keep Spain out of an increasingly disastrous series of wars. After the Spanish attack (1793) on France ended in defeat, Spain became first an ally, then a satellite, of France. In 1808 a conspiracy headed by Charles's son, the future FERDINAND VII, attempted to overthrow Godoy. A riot on March 17 of that year forced Charles to abdicate in favor of Ferdinand. NAPOLEON I then lured Charles, Ferdinand, and María Luisa to Bayonne, where he forced Ferdinand to abdicate in favor of his father, and then made Charles turn over the crown to him.

Charles, María Luisa, and Godoy were then exiled to Rome.

Charles IX, King of Sweden Charles IX, b. Oct. 4, 1550, d. Oct. 30, 1611, was the king of Sweden who laid the foundation for the brilliant achievements of GUSTAV II ADOLF. The youngest son of GUSTAV I Vasa, Charles ruled the duchy of Södermanland in central Sweden during the reigns of his brothers, ERIC XIV and John III. When John died in 1592 his son, Sigismund, inherited the crown of Sweden. But the latter was already king of Poland (as SIGISMUND III) and a Roman Catholic, whereas Sweden was Lutheran. Charles, a militant Lutheran, deposed Sigismund in 1599 and then ruled as regent until 1604, when he became king. In 1605 war broke out with Poland, and in 1611, with Denmark. Sweden was thus under attack from two directions when Charles died.

Charles X, King of Sweden Charles X, b. Nov. 8, 1622, d. Feb. 13, 1660, was a great warrior king of Sweden. His maternal grandfather was Charles IX, and he was raised at the Swedish court. Trained as a soldier under Lennart TORSTENSON, Charles succeeded to the throne when CHRISTINA abdicated in 1654. In 1655 he attacked Poland to strengthen Swedish control of the Baltic provinces. Other states allied with Poland, and he shifted his attack to Denmark, destroying the Danish defenses in 1657–58. Later in 1658 he attacked Denmark again, hoping to add it to the Swedish empire. His sudden death left the crown to his son, Charles XI.

Charles XI, King of Sweden Charles XI, b. Nov. 24, 1655, d. Apr. 5, 1697, established an absolute monarchy in 17th-century Sweden. He succeeded his father, Charles X, in 1660. From 1672, Sweden was drawn into a series of difficult conflicts—with the Dutch, Brandenburg, and Denmark. Charles ended (1679) the wars without major losses and established a precarious but lasting peace. In 1680 he repossessed an immense amount of land from the Swedish nobility. This greatly increased royal revenues and allowed him to strengthen the government, army, and navy. In 1693 the parliament granted Charles hereditary, absolute power. He was succeeded by his son, Charles XII.

Charles XII, King of Sweden Charles XII, b. Stockholm, June 17, 1682, king of Sweden, was one of the great military kings of European history. He succeeded his father, Charles XI, in 1697 at the age of 14. Within two years, Denmark, Poland, and Russia attacked his empire, beginning the Great NORTHERN WAR. Charles quickly defeated the Danes and then sailed to Estonia to face the Russians under PETER I. In a blinding snowstorm on Nov. 20, 1700, he personally led the attack that destroyed the whole Russian army. His third foe, AUGUSTUS II of Poland and Saxony, sued for peace, which Charles obtained on his own terms in 1706.

Two years later Charles marched against Russia. Defeated at Poltava on June 28, 1708, he escaped south into the Ottoman Empire and set up camp at Bender in Bessarabia. He succeeded in persuading the Turkish sultan to attack Russia in 1711, but the sultan's patience with him wore thin, and he was arrested (1713) after a battle with Turkish troops.

In 1714, disguised as "Captain Frisk," Charles rode across Europe to Swedish Stralsund. He tried to rebuild the shattered Swedish state, now under attack by Russia, Denmark, Prussia, and Hanover. In 1716 and 1718, he led forays into Norway. On Nov. 30, 1718, before Fredriksten fortress, he was shot through the head. Unmarried and childless, he was succeeded by his sister, Ulrika Eleanora.

A puzzling figure, Charles XII can be regarded either as a great patriot or a bloodthirsty tyrant. Historians differ in judging his role in the Great Northern War.

Charles XIV John, King of Sweden King Charles XIV John of Sweden and Norway b. Jean Baptiste Jules Bernadotte, Jan. 26, 1763, d. Mar. 8, 1844, was the son of a French lawyer. He became an officer in 1792, during the French Revolution, and rose to the rank of prince under Napoleon I.

In Sweden, ruled from 1809 by the childless Charles XIII, Bernadotte seemed a good choice as heir to the throne. In August 1810, therefore, he was elected crown prince as Charles John. Abandoning Finland to Russia, he joined the allies against Napoleon in 1813 and was rewarded in 1814 with the union of the Norwegian and Swedish crowns, though he had to recognize Norway's separate constitution. When Charles XIII died in 1818, Bernadotte became king of Sweden and Norway, ruling with a firm hand until his death. He was succeeded by his son, Oskar.

Charles XVI Gustav, King of Sweden Charles XVI Gustav, b. Apr. 30, 1946, ascended the Swedish throne on Sept. 19, 1973, after the death of his grandfather, King Gustav VI Adolf. He became crown prince in 1947, on the death of his father, Prince Gustav Adolf. As king, Charles XVI Gustav has virtually no official prerogatives, due to a constitutional change in 1971 that allows Swedish monarchs to participate only in ceremonial functions.

Charles's law see GAS LAWS

Charleston (dance) The Charleston, a frenzied combination of swinging arms, kicking legs, and turned-in toes and knees in syncopated 4/4 time, was the ballroom dance sensation of the 1920s. Named for Charleston, S.C., it probably evolved from African dance steps then common in the South, specifically the Jay-Bird and the

Juba. What began as a simple, rhythmic twisting of the feet took on a fast, flapping kick in Harlem. With the opening (1923) in New York of *Runnin' Wild*, an all-black revue that introduced the dance to the public, the Charleston took the United States by storm.

Charleston (South Carolina) Charleston (1990 pop., 80,414) is South Carolina's oldest city and a major Atlantic coast port. On a narrow peninsula at the confluence of the Ashley and Cooper rivers, the city has an excellent sheltered harbor and a mild climate.

Charleston is a transportation center with diversified industry: fertilizers, paper, chemicals, and textiles. It is the headquarters of the 6th U.S. Naval District and the U.S. Air Force Defense Command. The city adopted (1931) the first historic preservation zoning ordinance in the United States. The Citadel (a military college), the College of Charleston, and the Medical University of South Carolina are in the city. The Spoleto Arts Festival, held since 1977, and Charleston's many historic buildings make it an important tourist center.

Founded in 1670 at Albemarle Point, the city, called Charles Towne for Charles II, was moved to its present location in 1680. It rapidly developed a rich trade in rice, deerskins, and indigo and was the state capital until 1790, when the seat of government was moved to Columbia. The firing on FORT SUMTER in Charleston harbor precipitated the Civil War. In 1886 the city was struck by one of the most severe earthquakes ever to occur in the eastern United States. Hurricane Hugo in 1989 badly damaged Charleston and its environs.

Georgian-style residences border Charleston's White Point Gardens, located at the mouth of the Ashley River on the city's harbor. Charleston, the fourth largest city in South Carolina, was founded in 1670 and was named for Britain's King Charles II.

Charleston (West Virginia) Charleston is the capital of West Virginia. Located in the Allegheny Mountains, at the confluence of the Elk and Kanawha rivers, the city has an elevation of 184 m (604 ft). It has a population of 57,287 (1990) for the city alone and 250,454 (1990) for the metropolitan area. The permanent state capital since 1885, it is also the seat of Kanawha County. Settled (1788) around Fort Lee, the town was named Charles Town and renamed Charleston in 1818. An important stop on the migration route to the Ohio Valley, the area attracted as residents such frontiersmen as Daniel BOONE. The implementation of steam engines (1824) to operate the brine wells made Charleston an important salt-producing center. The modern city is the trade center for the industrial Kanawha Valley. The coal, oil and natural gas, and brine make this area one of the largest production centers of chemicals and glass in the United States. West Virginia State College (1891) and Morris Harvey College (1888) are located in the city.

Charlotte Charlotte, the seat of Mecklenburg County, is the largest city in North Carolina. The city proper has a population of 395,934 (1990), and the 3-county metropolitan area, 1,162,093 (1990). Situated in the Piedmont Plateau, Charlotte is noted for retailing and manufacturing. A leading U.S. textile-manufacturing center, the city also has factories producing machinery, metal, and food products. Queens College (1857), Johnson C. Smith University (1867), and a branch of the University of North Carolina (1946) are located there.

Settled in about 1750, the city was named for Princess Charlotte Sophia of Mecklenburg-Strelitz, later the wife of England's George III. The MECKLENBURG DECLARATION OF INDEPENDENCE was signed in Charlotte in May 1775. The Charlotte area was the chief source of gold in the United States until the California gold rush (1849).

Charlotte Amalie [shahr'-luht uh-mahl'-ee] The town of Charlotte Amalie is the capital of the U.S. Virgin Islands. The population is 11,756 (1980). Located on Saint Thomas island, this tourist resort was established as a Danish town in 1672 and named for the Danish queen. The islands came under U.S. jurisdiction in 1917. A naval submarine base is located near Charlotte Amalie.

Charlotte's Web *Charlotte's Web* (1952) is an anthropomorphic children's story by E. B. WHITE. The hero is a pig named Wilbur in danger of being slaughtered. He is rescued by the machinations of a wise spider named Charlotte. In reconciling himself to Charlotte's inevitable death at the end of the year, Wilbur learns to accept the rhythms of life.

Charlottesville The city of Charlottesville (1990 pop., 40,341) is located in the foothills of the Blue Ridge Mountains in the Piedmont Plateau of Virginia. Although it is the seat of Albemarle County, it is politically independent of the county. Settled in the 1730s and established as a town in 1762, the city was named for Queen Charlotte Sophia, consort of George III. The University of Virginia was founded there in 1819 by Thomas Jefferson. Jefferson's home, MONTICELLO, is on a hill overlooking the city, and Ash Lawn, the home of James Monroe, is nearby. The economy of Charlottesville depends primarily on the university and some light industry.

Charlottetown Charlottetown, a deepwater port city with a population of 15,776 (1986), is the seat of Queens County and the capital and commercial center of Prince Edward Island, Canada. Its economy is based on tourism, food processing, and the manufacture of clothing, marine equipment, and building supplies. It is the site of the University of Prince Edward Island. Located on Hillsborough Bay, the city was founded in 1720 by the French and called Port La Joye. The present city was laid out in 1768 and named for Queen Charlotte Sophia, wife of George III. In 1864 the conference leading to the confederation of the Canadian colonies was held there.

charm (amulet) see AMULET

charm (quantum mechanics) see QUARK

Charolais cattle see CATTLE AND CATTLE RAISING

Charon [kair'-uhn] In Greek mythology, Charon is the boatman who ferries the dead across the river STYX to HADES. Although old and gray, Charon is strong and sturdy. Dressed in a short cloak, he chooses his passengers from among the multitudes of the dead that crowd the shore. Only those properly buried in the world above are chosen, and then only if they have the fare—a silver coin placed in the mouth of the corpse before burial.

Charpentier, Gustave [shahr-pahn-teeay'] The French composer Gustave Charpentier, b. June 25, 1860, d. Feb. 18, 1956, studied with Jules Massenet at the Paris Conservatoire and won the Prix de Rome in 1887. His fame is based on a single opera, *Louise,* produced in Paris in 1900. The opera—sentimental, picturesque, and containing such realistic touches as Paris street cries—has remained in the standard operatic repertoire.

Charpentier, Marc Antoine Marc Antoine Charpentier, b. *c.*1634, d. Feb. 24, 1704, a French baroque composer, is credited with having introduced the Latin oratorio into France.

Charpentier, while still a youth, went to Rome to study painting but soon became a pupil of Giacomo Carissimi, who greatly influenced his style. Charpentier collaborated briefly at the Théâtre Français with Molière. He served as music master to the Jesuits in Paris and to their College of Clermont; he taught Philippe of Orléans, later regent of France; and he was music master of the Sainte-Chapelle. His works include operas, masses, oratorios, psalm settings, motets, and other genres.

charter A charter is a document issued by a sovereign government to a local government, university, or private company, bestowing certain rights and privileges. Formerly, charters were issued by kings, for example, the charters granted by the king to English colonies in America. Trading organizations such as the British, French, and Dutch East India companies also operated under royal charters. Such chartered companies were the forerunners of modern corporations, which receive their charters from the state. In a landmark decision of 1819, the U.S. Supreme Court gave constitutional protection to the rights granted in a charter.

Charter Oak Charter Oak was the name of a tree that stood in Hartford, Conn., until 1856. According to tradition, colonists used the tree in 1687 to hide Connecticut's 1662 charter from Sir Edmund ANDROS, who was authorized by King James II to establish a Dominion of New England. Connecticut did submit to the dominion, but it lasted only until 1689.

Charterhouse see CARTHUSIANS

Chartism Chartism was a premature political reform movement by hungry British workers afflicted by the stresses of the Industrial Revolution. Active in the 1830s and 1840s, it attempted to secure a democratic constitution and thereby a more egalitarian society. The movement was inaugurated by the London Working Men's Association, which drew up (1838) a six-point People's Charter calling for universal male suffrage, abolition of property qualifications for members of Parliament, payment of members of Parliament, and other reforms. The movement spread to the provinces, where, after Parliament's rejection of the charter in 1839, riots such as those in Newport, Wales, developed. Chartism attracted only some workers and was incapable of mounting a general strike, as was threatened after Parliament again rejected a Chartist petition in 1842. Nonetheless, the unrest was serious enough to unite the middle and upper classes against the Chartists, especially since the militant leader Feargus O'Connor lumped those classes together as the common enemy in his speeches and his influential newspaper, the *Northern Star.* Chartism waned as economic conditions improved and the CORN LAWS were repealed (1846). The last Chartist demonstration, which took place in London in 1848 (the year of revolutions in Europe), ended in rain, a total fiasco.

Chartres [sharht] Chartres (1982 pop., 37,119) is the capital of Eure-et-Loir department in north central France, situated on the Eure River about 80 km (50 mi) southwest of Paris. It has many light industries and is a market center for the surrounding region but is more famous for its magnificent cathedral.

Chartres Cathedral Notre Dame de Chartres, or the Cathedral of Our Lady of Chartres, considered by many to be the supreme monument of High GOTHIC ART AND ARCHITECTURE, dominates the small town of Chartres, about 90 km (55 mi) southwest of Paris. In no other Gothic church of comparable size are the architecture, sculpture, and stained glass so harmonious and of such quality, owing to the comparatively short (1194–1220) period of construction for the major parts of the edifice. The present church, the sixth on the site, was begun immediately after the fifth church burned in 1194. People of every rank helped rebuild the church, with labor or with lavish benefactions.

The new cathedral, 134 m (428 ft) long, incorporated the transitional Gothic facade and the south tower, both survivors of the fire, preserving the splendid, sculptured bays of the triple Royal Portal (1140–50) and the three stained-glass windows (*c.*1155) above. The rest of the cathedral was directly inspired by Abbé Suger's Abbey of SAINT-DENIS in Paris. Inside, the unearthly radiance of the stained glass, particularly the glowing "Chartres blue," fills the entire church.

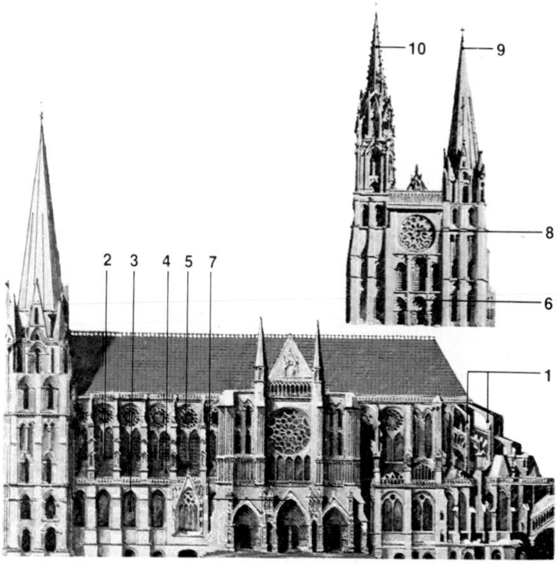

Chartres Cathedral is one of the most impressive High Gothic cathedrals in France. Its nearly 200 windows contain the finest stained glass of the 12th and 13th centuries. The cathedral's soaring elevation is made possible by flying buttresses (1), which strengthen the nave walls (2) and allow greatly heightened side aisles (3). Above the triforium (4) are the clerestory windows, each with two lancets and a rose window (5). The Royal Portal (6) is splendidly sculptured, as are the south (7) and north porches. Above the portals are huge 13th-century rose windows (8). The 12th-century octagonal south spire (9) is simpler and shorter than the 16th-century north tower (10).

Charybdis see SCYLLA AND CHARYBDIS

Chase, Lucia The American ballet director and dancer Lucia Chase, b. Waterbury, Conn., Mar. 24, 1907, d. Jan. 9, 1986, is the name most frequently associated with the history of AMERICAN BALLET THEATRE (ABT). From 1940, when ABT had its inception (as Ballet Theatre), to 1980 she directed the company (at first in an unofficial capacity), in association with Richard Pleasant and then with the scenic designer Oliver Smith and others. She supported ABT substantially from her own funds. Chase created the role of the Eldest Sister in Antony Tudor's *Pillar of Fire* (1942).

Chase, Salmon P. Salmon Portland Chase, b. Cornish, N.H., Jan. 13, 1808, d. May 7, 1873, culminated a distinguished legal and political career by serving as the sixth chief justice of the United States (1864–73). He entered legal practice in 1830 and became known as a defender of fugitive slaves. He was active in the Liberty party (founded 1840) and then the Free-Soil party and served (1849–55) as U.S. senator from Ohio. He was Republican governor of Ohio from 1855 and, after losing the Republican presidential nomination to Abraham Lincoln in 1860, agreed (1861) to serve as secretary of the treasury. He proposed the national banking system that was established in 1863. Policy disagreements, aggravated by Chase's presidential ambitions, led to his resignation from the cabinet in 1864, but he was appointed chief justice soon after and served until his death. He presided with evenhanded firmness over the impeachment trial of President Andrew Johnson in 1868.

Chase, Samuel Samuel Chase, b. Somerset County, Md., Apr. 17, 1741, d. June 19, 1811, was a strong supporter of the American Revolution, a signer of the Declaration of Independence, an ardent Federalist, and the only Supreme Court justice to be impeached. A lawyer by profession, he became chief justice of the General Court of Maryland in 1791 and in 1796 was named to the U.S. Supreme Court by President Washington. In 1804 he was impeached by the House of Representatives for alleged prejudice against the Jeffersonians in treason and sedition trials. But the Senate, in a decision that indicated reluctance to remove judges for purely political reasons, did not convict him, and he remained on the Court until his death.

Chase, William Merritt William Merritt Chase, b. Williamsburgh, Ind., Nov. 1, 1849, d. Oct. 25, 1916, was an eclectic American painter known for his portraits,

William Merritt Chase's studio scene, A Friendly Call *(1895), demonstrates the American painter's attention to detail and fluid brushwork. (National Gallery of Art, Washington, D.C.)*

landscapes, and still lifes. He was also a greatly influential teacher for 36 years. In his portraits and interiors, he was influenced by Dutch and Spanish Renaissance painters and by his contemporaries John Singer SARGENT and James McNeill WHISTLER; Chase's portrait of Whistler (1885; Metropolitan Museum of Art, New York City), painted in Whistler's style, is one of his major works. Also greatly admired were his still-life paintings, such as *Still Life—Fish* (*c.*1890–1908; Museum of Fine Arts, Boston), which recall 17th-century Dutch masterpieces.

Chasidism see HASIDISM

chastity belt A chastity belt, or chastity girdle, was a beltlike article supposed to have been worn by women in the Middle Ages to prevent sexual intercourse or masturbation. The device was designed to cover the external sexual organs without inhibiting elimination. A lock, usually placed on the portion of the belt encircling the hips, secured the apparatus to the wearer.

Evidence suggests that perhaps European Crusaders derived the idea from certain Oriental practices designed by jealous males to prohibit their wives and daughters from illicit intercourse. References to the belts appear in European literature as early as the 12th century, but the earliest surviving examples are from the 16th century.

château [sha-toh'] In French architectural history, the word *château* refers to any large-scale, secular dwelling inhabited by a king, noble, or wealthy bourgeois. The designation *palais*, or palace, was normally applied to a royal château, especially when it served as a seat of government. The château underwent two major phases of development: from the *château-fort*, or fortified CASTLE, of the Middle Ages to the *château de plaisance*, or country house, of the 16th century and later.

During the medieval period, the château was the administrative center of a feudal estate. Erected on high ground and protected by a ditch or moat, it consisted of an easily defended towerlike structure called the *donjon*, or keep, and a large courtyard surrounded by battlemented walls marked at the angles by circular towers.

When the end of feudal strife eliminated its military function, the French château was transformed, especially in response to the taste for Italian RENAISSANCE architecture that developed during the 1500s. In the Château de Chambord, begun in 1519 for Francis I by French and Italian architects, the moat, towers, and wings were retained, but the new Italian influence is evident in the symmetry of the plan and in the grid of classical orders superimposed on the elevations. The architects Pierre Lescot and Philibert de L'Orme endowed the château with a classical correctness, which was best expressed in Marie de Médicis's Luxembourg Palace in Paris, begun by Salomon de BROSSE in 1615.

Simultaneously, de Brosse initiated a significant change of direction with his Château de Blérancourt (1612–19): the wings were eliminated and the château was reduced to a freestanding block comparable to an Italian villa. The high point of this tradition is François MANSART's Château de Maisons (1642–46). Even more influential was Louis LE VAU's Château de Vaux-le-Vicomte (1657–61), in which the geometric vigor of the house (still with a moat) was extended down a continuous spatial axis to the forecourts and to vast formal gardens designed by André LE NÔTRE. The great oval salon, pro-

The early Renaissance Château de Chambord (1519–47), ascribed to the Italian architect Domenico da Cortona, is the largest château in the Loire Valley. The central square block, the donjon (1), *is enclosed on three sides by a fortified wall with massive conical towers* (2). *The facade* (3), *whose horizontal and vertical balance reveals the Italian influence, forms the fourth side of the donjon. A double spiral staircase* (4) *is located at the intersection of the four corridors of the donjon. It leads to the* appartements (5), *the predecessors of modern suites, which are located in the corners on each of the three levels. The staircase is crowned with an elaborate lantern tower.*

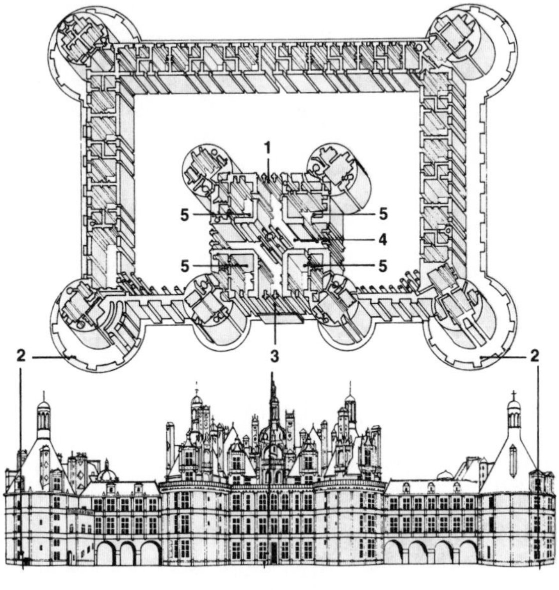

jecting from the garden facade, was imitated in numerous 18th-century châteaux.

See also: FRENCH ART AND ARCHITECTURE.

Chateaubriand, François René, Vicomte de [sha-toh-bree-ahn'] François René de Chateaubriand, b. Sept. 4, 1768, d. July 4, 1848, an early exponent of French romanticism, is best known for his *Mémoires d'outre-tombe* (Memoirs from beyond the Tomb, 1849). Of a noble Breton family, Chateaubriand grew up in the medieval castle of Combourg, and foreign travel, nature, history, and the aesthetic aspects of religion all became refuges from the unpalatable French Revolution. Chateaubriand's first work, *Essai sur les révolutions* (1797), published while he was in exile in England (1793–1800), dealt with that upheaval. He established his reputation with *The Genius of Christianity* (1802; Eng. trans., 1856), written after his conversion from freethinking. A brief trip to the United States in 1791 had meanwhile generated a fascination with the Indians, which found expression in three romantic novels, *Atala* (1800), *René* (1802), and *Les Natchez* (1826), as well as in his nonfictional *Travels in America* (1827; Eng. trans., 1968). *The Martyrs* (1809; Eng. trans., 1812, 1859) and *Itinéraire de Paris à Jérusalem* (1811) show his continued interest in the exotic.

François René de Chateaubriand, one of France's first romantic writers, is known for the rich, emotive descriptions of nature in his novels and memoirs.

Chatham, William Pitt, 1st Earl of see PITT, WILLIAM (the Elder)

Chattahoochee River The Chattahoochee River is formed in northern Georgia by the confluence of several small streams in the Blue Ridge Mountains. It flows southwest and south about 700 km (435 mi), joining the Flint River at Chattahoochee, Fla., to form the Apalachicola, which empties into the Gulf of Mexico. Parts of the Chattahoochee serve as boundaries between Georgia and Alabama and Georgia and Florida. Atlanta and Columbus are the major cities on its banks. Buford Dam created Lake Sidney Lanier, giving Atlanta a water supply and recreational facilities. Walter F. George Dam on the lower river made Lake Eufaula, and Jim Woodruff Dam created Lake Seminole at the Florida border.

Chattanooga Chattanooga is a port on Moccasin Bend of the Tennessee River in southeastern Tennessee. It is the seat of Hamilton County and has a population of 152,466 (1990) within the city and 433,210 (1990) in the metropolitan area. At the junction of river, rail, and roads, it is a transportation hub, a marketing and commercial center, and a major industrial city fueled by power from the Tennessee Valley Authority (TVA), which has its headquarters in the city. Almost completely surrounded by steep mountains, Chattanooga has iron and coal mines and more than 600 major industries. A campus of the University of Tennessee and several other institutions of higher learning are located in the city.

Settled in 1815, the city grew with the arrival of the steamboat in 1835 and the railroads in the 1840s. Chattanooga was the starting point for the forced exodus of the Cherokee Indians in 1838, a journey that is known as the Trail of Tears. The city was an important Confederate communications point during the Civil War and the scene of the decisive battles (1863) of Chickamauga, Lookout Mountain, and Missionary Ridge. Today, Lookout Mountain (729 m/2,392 ft) is ascended by one of the world's steepest railroad inclines. From its summit, it affords a view of seven states. Nearby, Signal Mountain overlooks the "Grand Canyon of the Tennessee," where the Tennessee River cuts a gorge 300 m (1,000 ft) deep.

Chattanooga, Battles of The Battles of Chattanooga, in the U.S. CIVIL WAR, were a series of engagements fought around Chattanooga, Tenn., in September and November 1863. The Confederates were commanded by Braxton BRAGG, and the Union forces were first under William S. ROSECRANS, then George H. THOMAS, and finally Ulysses S. GRANT. Rosecrans maneuvered Bragg from Chattanooga in early September, but his Army of the Cumberland was met by reinforced Confederate forces and defeated in the Battle of CHICKAMAUGA on September 19–20. Bragg threw an incomplete siege around Chattanooga and detached troops to attack Knoxville. Grant, arriving at Chattanooga on October 23, reinforced the Army of the Cumberland (now under Thomas's command), bringing it to 60,000 men. In the confused battles of Lookout Mountain and Missionary Ridge (Nov. 24–25, 1863), Thomas and Grant decisively defeated Bragg's 40,000 men. The result left Tennessee in Union hands.

chattel see PROPERTY

Chatterjee, Bankim Chandra [cha'-tur-jee, bung'-kim chuhn'-druh] Bankim Chandra Chatterjee, b. June 27, 1838, d. Apr. 8, 1894, is considered a pioneer of modern Indian fiction. A patriotic Hindu, Bankim Chandra began publishing his own politically oriented newspaper, *Banga Darshan*, in 1872. His social semihistorical novels treat domestic themes in the romantic manner of Western novelists, particularly Sir Walter Scott. *Ānandamāth* (Abbey of Bliss, 1906) deals with Hindu–Muslim conflict and contains the popular nationalist song "Bande Mātaram ("Hail to Thee, Mother"). Other novels include *Durgesnandini* (The Chieftain's Daughter, 1864), *Kapalakundala* (1866), and *Krishnakanter Uil* (1878; *Krishnakanta's Will*, 1962). A brilliant storyteller and short-story writer, Chatterjee also wrote religious and scientific essays.

Chatterton, Thomas Thomas Chatterton, b. Nov. 20, 1752, d. Aug. 24, 1770, was the author of the so-called Rowley poems, which he attributed to medieval writers. Written when he was only 12, the poems duped such critics as Horace Walpole. Chatterton left his native Bristol for London in 1770 and, failing to achieve success there, committed suicide at the age of 17. His poetry was praised by Wordsworth and imitated by Keats and Shelley.

Chaucer, Geoffrey [chaw'-sur] Geoffrey Chaucer, b. *c.*1340, d. Oct. 25, 1400, is recognized as one of England's greatest poets. In his work there is a range of subtlety surpassing that of all other medieval writers, with the exception of DANTE. He is best remembered for The CANTERBURY TALES.

Early Life. The earliest record of Chaucer's life dates to 1357, when he was placed as a page in the household of Elizabeth de Burgh, wife of Edward III's third son, Lionel. During military service in France in 1359, Chaucer was captured near Rheims but ransomed by the Crown. In the early 1360s he may have studied at the Inns of Chancery and the Inns of Court, and possibly at Oxford. In 1366 he married Philippa de Roet, an aristocratic lady whose sister Katherine was later the mistress and, in 1396, the third wife of John of Gaunt, King Edward's second son. By 1367 Chaucer was a yeoman, or valet (*vallectus*), in Edward III's household; in 1368 he is mentioned as the king's *armiger* (esquire). For the rest of his life Chaucer served the royal court in some capacity—which included giving readings of his poetry—traveled widely on the continent, and maintained a close relationship with John of Gaunt.

Civil Service. The life records that have been assembled show that Chaucer was an exceptionally able and trusted civil servant, a courtier entrusted by three kings with important administrative and diplomatic tasks. His ambassadorial missions frequently took him to France—once, in 1377, to negotiate a marriage between Princess Marie of France and Prince Richard, who was in that year to become Richard II—and at least twice to Italy (1372–73 and 1378). On June 8, 1374, Edward III appointed Chaucer controller of the customs on wool, skins, and hides for the port of London, and in 1382, Richard II made him controller of petty customs. He served in 1385 as justice of peace for Kent, and in 1386 he was elected to Parliament. He was appointed clerk of the king's works in 1389 and continued to receive gifts and annuities, the last of these coming from Henry IV. Chaucer's tomb in Westminster Abbey was the first in what is now known as Poets' Corner.

Geoffrey Chaucer, the greatest of England's medieval poets, described the panoply of 14th-century life in his masterpiece, The Canterbury Tales. *An administrator and diplomat by vocation, Chaucer was keenly observant of human character and used this ability in the vivid portraits of his Canterbury pilgrims.*

Early Literary Works. Chaucer's earliest models were probably French, the culture most familiar to the English court. A surviving copy of a partial translation of *Le Roman de la rose* may be his, and in late 1369 or early 1370 he wrote *The Book of the Duchess,* an elegy cast as a traditional French dream-vision, for Blanche, duchess of Lancaster and John of Gaunt's first wife. These poems and *The House of Fame* are written in eight-syllable lines rhymed in couplets, a form characteristic of French poetry. *The House of Fame* contains some overt parody of Dante's *Divine Comedy* and is usually dated after Chaucer's Italian mission in 1372.

Translation and Later Works. Chaucer translated (*c.*1380) a number of meditative Latin works whose terms are important in his own artistic terminology: Boethius's *Consolation of Philosophy*; Pope Innocent III's *On the Misery of the Human Condition,* which translation survives in part in *The Canterbury Tales* in the "Man of Law's Tale"; and a *Life of Saint Cecilia* from the *Golden Legend.* He may also have translated a condensed French version of part of the *Book of Consolation and Counsel* by Albertanus of Brescia, which appears as the "Tale of Melibeus" in *The Canterbury Tales.*

At about the same time, Chaucer also wrote or began to write a satirical dream-vision *The Parliament of Fowls* (*c.*1382), the *Legend of Good Women*, an unfinished series of nine so-called lives of Cupid's saints like Cleopatra and Dido, and *Troilus and Criseyde.* This last, a penetrating and humane "tragedy" in five books and more than 8,200 lines in rhyme royal stanzas, is often called the finest medieval romance. In it Chaucer transformed BOCCACCIO's stylized *Filostrato* by deeply analyzing common human motives within a Boethian and ultimately Christian overview.

Between 1386 and his death, Chaucer sought to complete *The Canterbury Tales,* an undertaking that, in its final form, would have presented 30 tellers and 120 tales within a unified dramatic and philosophical design. Twenty-four tales, a few of them incomplete, were written, ranging from the lofty to the scurrilous. In them he subtly adapted language and perspectives to individual tellers and thus established a model for Shakespeare and the Elizabethan dramatists.

Chauncy, Charles [chawn'-see] Charles Chauncy, b. Jan. 1, 1705, d. Feb. 10, 1787, was an American Congregational minister and theologian who blended the Puritan tradition with the emphases of the Enlightenment. He criticized the revivalist preaching of the GREAT AWAKENING. For Chauncy, emotion was irrationality; he held that religion was reasonable growth. He rejected views of a wrathful God in favor of a benevolent deity and preached that God intended the happiness of all his creatures.

Chausson, Ernest [shoh-sohn'] Ernest Chausson, b. Jan. 20, 1855, d. June 10, 1899, was a French composer whose works reflect the transition from late romanticism to impressionism. He was greatly influenced by his teacher, César Franck. Independently wealthy, Chausson served for ten years as the secretary of the Société Nationale de Musique, encouraging the efforts of contemporary composers such as Claude Debussy. His music includes the lovely but melancholy Symphony in B-flat Major, the *Poème* for violin and orchestra, as well as chamber music, choral works, operas, and songs. Soon after achieving public recognition, Chausson was killed in a bicycle accident.

Chautauqua [chuh-taw'-kwuh] Originally the name of an adult education program in the United States, the term *Chautauqua*—like LYCEUM—later came to be used for the traveling popular lectures, concerts, and dramatic productions that frequently were given in tents between the 1870s and the 1920s. The original Chautauqua movement began as the Fair Point Sunday School Assembly, founded in 1874 by the clergyman John Heyl VINCENT and the businessman-inventor Lewis Miller near Chautauqua, N.Y. It soon developed a curriculum that ranged from temperance lectures to contemporary science courses. In 1881 it introduced the first successful correspondence education program in America. It founded the Chautauqua Literary and Scientific Circle, a home-reading program in American, English, continental, and classical literature and history. The circle still offers four-year correspondence courses in a variety of fields.

The introduction of a summer school program (1883–97) under the direction of William Rainey HARPER attracted thousands. The Chautauqua center became a university in 1883 but gave up the power to grant degrees in 1898. In 1918 the lectures and other entertainments became commercial, with programs supplied to Chautauqua societies throughout the United States. As much as one third of the U.S. population was participating in some aspect of the Chautauqua movement at its peak in 1924. The movement lost popularity after World War I, perhaps because of the mobility offered by the automobile and the availability of other forms of entertainment.

Chávez, Carlos [chah'-vays] Carlos Chávez, b. June 13, 1899, d. Aug. 2, 1978, is the foremost Mexican composer of the 20th century. He began composing at an early age, developed rapidly, and wrote a symphony when he was 20 years old.

In 1928, Chávez became director of the National Conservatory and conductor of the Orchestra Sinfonica de Mexico. He organized concerts for workers and wrote his *Sinfonia Proletaria*, first performed in 1934. His *Sinfonia India* (1936), an expression of native primitive elements, makes use of Mexican instruments. Chávez's music is characterized by a strong rhythmic drive, derived in part from Mexican folk music. His works include symphonies, chamber music, concertos, choral works, songs, and piano pieces.

Chavez, Cesar [shah'-vez] Cesar Estrada Chavez, b. Yuma, Ariz., Mar. 31, 1927, organized farm workers into the United Farm Workers (UFW). The son of a migrant farm worker, he attended more than 30 elementary schools. He worked with the Community Service Organization founded by Saul Alinsky from 1952 until 1962, when he left to begin organizing farm workers, going on to found the UFW. He organized nationwide boycotts of grapes, wine, and lettuce in an attempt to bring pressure on California growers to sign contracts with the UFW. Membership declined when the Teamsters' union began to organize farm workers in competition with the UFW. The two unions reached an agreement on jurisdiction in March 1977.

The American labor leader Cesar Chavez organized California farm workers into an effective union, the United Farm Workers, an affiliate of the AFL-CIO. From 1966 until 1978 he mobilized nationwide boycotts of produce such as grapes, lettuce, and citrus fruits, thereby gaining negotiating leverage with growers.

Chavín de Huántar [chah-veen' day wahn'-tahr] The archaeological site of Chavín de Huántar is located at the junction of the Mosna and Wacheksa rivers in north-central Peru, at an elevation of 3,350 m (11,000 ft). A major urban and ceremonial center of ancient Andean culture, the site gives its name to Chavín culture, one of the earliest cultures in the New World; its origins may date from 1200 BC or earlier. The associated art style, with its distinctive jaguar designs that appear on ceramics, textiles, stone and bone carvings, and metalwork, flourished in much of northern Peru from about 900 BC to about 200 BC. The Chavín style also influenced the PARACAS style of southern Peru.

The famous stone sculptures and reliefs of Chavín de Huántar represent highly stylized human and animal figures, the most common of which are birds. The images carved into the stone are sometimes interpreted as deities, and the Chavín style is interpreted as a sign of a religious cult that expanded over a large area.

See also: PRE-COLUMBIAN ART AND ARCHITECTURE.

Chayefsky, Paddy [chy-ev'-skee] The American scriptwriter and dramatist Sidney "Paddy" Chayefsky, b. New York City, Jan. 29, 1923, d. Aug. 1, 1981, was instrumental in creating the naturalistic style of television drama during the 1950s and '60s. He established his reputation with the television play *Marty* (1953), which he adapted (1955) into an Academy Award–winning film. His stage plays include *Middle of the Night* (1956; film, 1959) and *The Latent Heterosexual* (1968). He won Academy Awards for the screenplays of *The Hospital* (1971) and *Network* (1976).

check A check is a written order from a checking-account depositor directing his or her bank to make funds available to a specified person or to "cash" (anyone presenting the check for payment). A cashier's check is drawn by a bank against its own funds. Unlike a personal check, it has unquestioned validity. A TRAVELER'S CHECK is a form of cashier's check.

Checks are convenient to carry and use, are less subject to theft than is cash, and serve as receipts after they are processed and returned.

A bank receiving a check drawn on another local bank sends it through a local clearinghouse, which adjusts the bank's accounts. Checks from out-of-town banks are handled through the Federal Reserve System's clearing facilities, and therefore the adjustment usually takes somewhat longer.

checkers Checkers, known in England as draughts, is played by two persons who face each other across a board of 64 squares—8 rows of 8 squares each, alternately light and dark. Play is conducted only on the 32 dark squares.

Each contestant begins with 12 playing pieces, also called *men*, of one color. Whatever the opposing colors may in fact be, they are referred to as white and black. The pieces—disks about 2.5 cm (1 in) in diameter and slightly less than half as thick—are placed on the dark squares in the three horizontal rows nearest each player.

To win, a player must capture all the opponent's men or block them so that no further movement is possible. Black moves first; after that, the players move alternately.

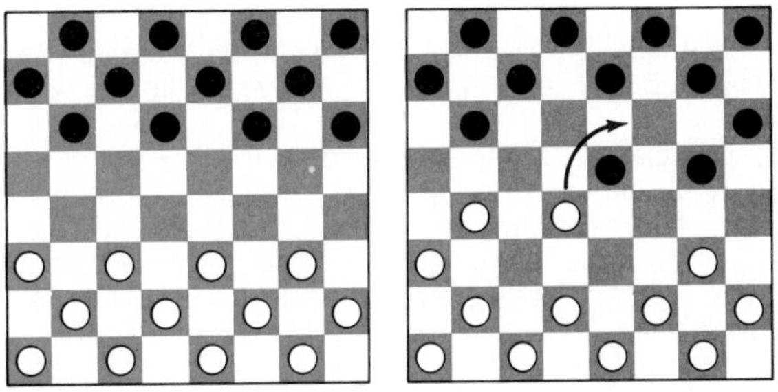

(Left) *The standard layout for checkers shows each player's pieces, or men, arranged on the dark squares of three horizontal rows. Pieces are moved in single-square, diagonal moves, with players alternating turns.* (Right) *A game in progress illustrates the jump used to capture an opponent's man. Successive jumps may be made in a single turn, thus capturing two or more pieces from the board.*

A noncapturing move consists of moving a man diagonally forward to an adjacent unoccupied square. In a capturing move, a checker is jumped over an opponent's man diagonally adjacent and lands on a vacant square behind that man (in the direction of the intended move). The captured enemy piece is removed from the board. In this same manner, one man may capture two or more opposing men in a series of consecutive jumps in any single turn. Multiple captures may be made by jumping diagonally left or right after the initial jump.

When a player's checker reaches any square in the row nearest his opponent, the opponent crowns that piece, making it a king. This is done by placing a second checker of the same color, or a suitable substitute, atop the single man. Although a single man may move forward only, a king may move, and capture, backward as well as forward.

When the game is down to few men of equal number for both opponents, and neither side is able to gain a clear advantage, a draw is declared, especially in tournament play. If one player rejects this decision, that player must establish a decided advantage within 40 moves, or the game is officially a draw.

The earliest modern book on checkers was written by Antonio Torquemada and published in Valencia, Spain, in 1547. Peter Mallet, a French professor of mathematics, made the first scientific study. Published as a manual in 1668, it maintained that checkers was played throughout the world and was probably as old as CHESS.

Although its rules are simple, the game of checkers requires far-sighted planning of moves. The widespread development of checker leagues and of national and international championship tournaments belies the notion that little skill is required.

Cheddar Cheddar, in Somerset county, England, is the site of two important archaeological finds. Gough's Cavern in the Cheddar Gorge yielded (1903) a nearly complete human skeleton that has become known as the Cheddar man. Approximately 10,000 to 12,000 years old, the skeleton was found in a flexed burial position. Extinct animal remains and stone and bone tools of the Magdalenian cultural tradition were found at the same level.

Cheddar is also the site of the palace complex of the ANGLO-SAXON kings of WESSEX. A wooden hall, outbuildings, and an elaborate drainage system were in place prior to 930. After 930 a new hall, stone chapel, and additional outbuildings were constructed. Considerable rebuilding was undertaken in the 11th century.

The area has also lent its name to Cheddar cheese, first manufactured there at least as far back as the 15th century.

cheese Cheese, one of the oldest and most nutritious food products, is formed by the coagulation of milk by enzymes, and the draining off of the liquid whey. Ripening, or curing, is the result of bacterial processes. In temperate climates, milk from cows is commonly used; in mountainous regions, from sheep and goats; in hot countries, from buffalos; and in cold climates, from reindeer, horses, yaks, and other mammals.

It is believed that the first cheese was produced inadvertently, probably through the practice of carrying milk in pouches made from animal stomachs. The bacteria in the milk and the digestive juices from the stomach worked together to form a curd and then a crude cheese. Cheesemaking artifacts dating from 2000 BC have been found. The Romans developed a large cheese industry, and later, cheesemaking became a specialty of monasteries. Many European abbeys developed secret recipes, and particular varieties began to be developed in certain regions of Europe. Today, although mechanization has largely replaced the old hand-techniques, the characteristics of hundreds of individual cheese types have been preserved.

Varieties of Cheese

The following are primarily responsible for the character of a cheese: moisture content, which is controlled by the extent of cutting and draining of the curd; the types of microorganisms added and encouraged to grow; the temperatures and acidities employed in the production process; and the temperature, humidity, and length of maturation, or ripening, time. The percentage of fat in the milk is also important: the higher the fat content, the more mellow and attractive the cheese. Low-fat cheeses are tough and lack flavor.

It is impossible to state the number of named varieties of cheese because new names—usually associated with a town or a region—are constantly being introduced. Cheeses can, however, be classified into major categories, according to several distinguishing characteristics: type of milk used—cow's milk, sheep's milk (Roquefort), or goat's milk (Chèvre); degree of hardness—very hard (Parmesan); hard without eyes (Cheddar) or with eyes (Gruyère); semisoft (Muenster); ripened by interior mold (Gorgonzola); ripened by exterior mold (Camembert). Soft cheeses distinct from all others are the unripened cottage cheese and ricotta types, where the drained, pressed curd is eaten fresh, without undergoing the maturing process. Further differentiations include cheeses that are ripened by surface bacteria (Limburger); cheeses that are made by plasticizing the curd in hot water (Caciocavallo); and cheeses salted by adding salt to the curd (Cheshire) or by

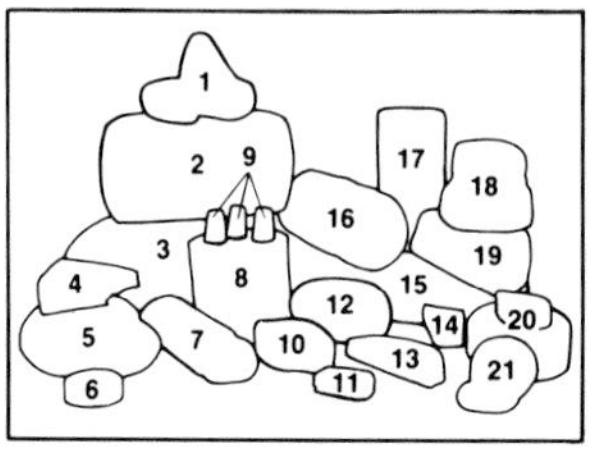

This selection of famous European cheeses includes many that are now also produced in the United States: spiced Pompadour from Holland (1); *Parmesan* (2); *Emmentaler, or "Swiss," cheese* (3); *Cheddar* (4); *Gouda* (5); *Camembert* (6); *chèvre, a goat's milk cheese* (7); *Stilton* (8, 10); *sapsago, a Swiss herbed cheese* (9); *Limburger* (11); *the French Doux des Montagnes* (12); *Brie* (13); *pressed ricotta* (14); *Gruyère* (15); *provolone* (16); *Colby* (17); *Muenster* (18); *Leyden* (19); *Roquefort* (20); *and Edam* (21).

LEADING VARIETIES OF CHEESE

Type	*Country of Origin*	*Characteristics*	*Milk**	*How Eaten*
Very Hard				
Parmesan	Italy	Granular; sharp, piquant	PS	Grated, for seasoning
Sapsago	Switzerland	Granular; light green; mildly sweet	PS and Buttermilk	Grated, for seasoning
Hard				
Pecorino	Italy	Granular; varies from brownish to greenish; slightly peppery	SH or W	Grated or cubed, for seasoning
Emmentaler	Switzerland	Smooth, with large holes; mild, sweet, nutlike	W	As is or in cooked foods
Cheddar	England	Firm, dense; mild to sharp	W	As is or in cooked foods
Provolone	Italy	Smooth, rubbery; mild to sharp; sometimes smoked	W	As is, grated, or in cooked foods
Caciocavallo	Italy	Smooth, rubbery; mild to sharp	W, PS, or G	As is, grated, or in cooked foods
Semihard				
Colby	United States	Firm, dense; mild, Cheddar-like	W	As is or in cooked foods
Edam and Gouda	The Netherlands	Mealy, dense; mild and nutty	W or PS	As is
Monterey Jack	United States	Cheddar-like, similar to Colby; mild	W	As is or in cooked foods
Port Salut	France	Smooth, rich; from fairly mild to strong	W	Dessert cheese, as is
Mozzarella	Italy	Rubbery; mild	W or PS	Used mainly for cooking
Muenster	Germany	Smooth, waxy; mild to mellow	W	As is or in cooked foods
Soft				
Camembert, Brie, Coulommiers	France	Thin crust, creamy interior. Flavor intensifies with aging, as does texture, which becomes softer, more liquid.	W	Dessert cheeses, eaten on bread or crackers
Chèvre	France	Generic name for a variety of goat's milk cheeses; most are soft, white; pungent	G	Dessert cheese
Limburger	Belgium	Strong odor and flavor; slightly runny when fully ripe	W or PS	Dessert cheese
Veined				
Roquefort	France	Crumbly; streaked with blue green mold; sharp, spicy, rich	SH	Dessert cheese
Stilton	England	Flaky; blue-veined; spicy, but milder than Roquefort	W or with cream added	Dessert cheese
Unripened				
Cottage cheese and Ricotta	Italy	Soft curds, sometimes in a creamy sauce; mild, slightly tangy	PS or W	As is or in cooked food
Cream cheese	United States	Soft, buttery; mild	W or with cream added	Dessert cheese or in cooked foods
Neufchâtel	France	Soft, buttery; mild	W or with cream added	Dessert cheese or in cooked foods

* W = whole milk; G = goat's milk; PS = partly skimmed milk; SH = sheep's milk

immersing the cheese in brine (St. Paulin). Herbs, seeds, alcoholic beverages, and vegetable dyes may also be incorporated.

Processed cheese is a mixture of ground cheese (usually hard varieties), emulsifying salts such as phosphates, other ingredients such as milk powder, whey powder, coloring and flavoring materials, and, sometimes, spices.

Modern Cheesemaking

All types of cheese are made in the same basic manner, but production details may differ considerably. Cheddar production, which employs nearly all the basic treatments used in modern cheesemaking, is described here.

In the factory milk is pasteurized, or heat-treated, at about 70° C (158° F) to kill all common pathogenic bacteria. After cooling to about 30° C (86° F), it is pumped into the cheese vat, a closed cylindrical vessel. Here it is mixed with the starter, which is a culture of lactic streptococci and other organisms. These sour the milk by fermenting the lactose, or milk sugar, to lactic acid, in order to create the acid conditions necessary for the rennet to act. Cheddar is sometimes colored red orange by adding vegetable dye to the milk.

Rennet is a brown liquid prepared by extracting the macerated fourth stomach of the calf with salt solution. It is rich in digestive enzymes that clot milk. Coagulating enzymes derived from fungi may be used instead. About 30 minutes after rennet is added to the souring milk, the milk clots and can be cut into tiny cubes by rotating knives. After a short time the temperature is raised slowly, by admitting steam to the outer jacket of the cheese vat, until a temperature of about 40° C (104° F) is reached. At this point the curd is solid enough to be matted into a cohesive mass, which is formed into slabs, salted, drained, and pressed to remove some of the whey. The slabs are placed in cloth-lined metal containers, called hoops, and pressed to form blocks weighing about 18 kg (40 lb). The blocks are either dipped in wax or wrapped in plastic film and left to cure at temperatures of about 10° C (50° F).

Although it is considered mature at 3 months, a well-matured Cheddar should be kept for 12 months or longer.

Nutritional Value

Hard cheese such as Cheddar is one of the most concentrated of common foods: 100 g (about 3.5 oz) supplies about 36 percent of the protein, 80 percent of the calcium, and 34 percent of the fat in the recommended daily allowance. Cheese is also a good source of phosphorus, other minerals, and vitamins. Cheese whey is condensed or dried and used for animal feeds or special dietary human foods.

A major 20th-century American novelist and short-story writer, John Cheever took for his subject the lives, manners, and mores of the American upper-middle class. His final work, Oh What a Paradise It Seems, *was published a few months before his death in 1982.*

cheetah Cheetahs, genus *Acinonyx*, are swift-moving spotted carnivores belonging to the cat family, Felidae, order Carnivora. Exterminated in India in the 1950s, they are still found on the open plains of tropical Africa. Two species exist: *A. jubatus* and the uncommon *A. rex* of east central Zimbabwe (formerly Rhodesia), both endangered. Cheetahs are sometimes called hunting leopards because for thousands of years in Asia they have been successfully trained for hunting. They are the fastest land animals, achieving speeds of 110 km/h (70 mph) for short durations. The head and body of the cheetah may be 150 cm long (5 ft), with a 76-cm (2.5-ft) tail and long, slender legs. The height at the shoulder is 100 cm (39 in), and the maximum weight is 65 kg (140 lb). Closely set black spots dot the tawny fur. The claws are not retractile.

The cheetah has extremely long legs and uses its heavy tail for balance when executing sharp turns. It races after its prey, unlike most other cats, which usually pounce on their victims.

Cheever, John The American writer John Cheever, b. Quincy, Mass., May 27, 1912, d. June 19, 1982, was a master of the sophisticated, satirical short story and the socially critical novel. His early stories, collected in *The Way Some People Live* (1943) and *The Enormous Radio* (1953), are set among the apartment dwellers of New York's fashionable Upper East Side; later collections, notably *The Housebreaker of Shady Hill* (1958), *The Brigadier and the Golf Widow* (1964), and *The World of Apples* (1973), follow this same class to the Westchester, N.Y., and Connecticut suburbs.

As a close observer of the life he described, Cheever had a command of detail that gives his fiction an anthropological appeal. His novels include *The Wapshot Chronicle* (1957), winner of a National Book Award, *The Wapshot Scandal* (1964), *Bullet Park* (1969), *Falconer* (1977), and *Oh What a Paradise It Seems* (1982). The 61 short stories collected in *The Stories of John Cheever* (1978) won a Pulitzer Prize.

Chekhov, Anton Anton Pavlovich Chekhov, b. South Russia, Jan. 29 (N.S.), 1860, d. July 15 (N.S.), 1904, was a master of the short story and one of modern literature's foremost playwrights. In both fiction and drama Chekhov was an innovator, distinguished by a flair for extracting tension, comedy, and pathos from superficially undramatic themes. He skillfully exploited the cunningly contrived anticlimax in works that stress mood and atmosphere rather than plot and action. As a master of hints, half statements, and eloquent silences, he differed from his Russian predecessors Leo Tolstoi and Fyodor Dostoyevsky, whose fiction was longer, more explicit, and less disciplined.

Chekhov's chief contributions to narrative fiction are among the 60 short stories that he published between 1888 and 1904. The longer of these are "The Duel," "Ward Number Six," "An Anonymous Story," "Three Years," and "My Life"; outstanding shorter ones include

Anton Chekhov, a Russian dramatist and writer of short stories, revolutionized the theater in the late 1890s with his use of indirect action and inner dialogues. The universality of Chekhov's writing prompted Leo Tolstoi to remark, "He is understood not only by every Russian, but by all humanity."

"A Dreary Story," "The Butterfly," "Neighbours," "Terror," "The Black Monk," "The Russian Master," "Murder," "Ariadne," "The Artist's Story," "Peasants," "Doctor Startsev," "A Lady with a Dog," and "In the Hollow." His dramatic writings include five outstanding four-act plays: the early *Ivanov*, the transitional *Seagull*, and the fully mature *Uncle Vanya*, *The Three Sisters*, and The CHERRY ORCHARD. He also wrote such popular one-act plays as *The Bear* (1888), *The Marriage Proposal* (1888), and *The Wedding* (1889).

The son of a struggling provincial grocer, Chekhov attended the local high school and graduated (1884) from Moscow University with a degree in medicine. He practiced medicine only sporadically but drew on his clinical experiences for his fiction and plays. A resident of Moscow throughout the 1880s, Chekhov spent most of 1890 on a 24,000-km (15,000-mi) trip to the Russian penal settlement of Sakhalin Island, north of Japan, an episode commemorated in his documentary study *Sakhalin Island* (1893–94). After that he settled down as a doctor, farmer, and author in the village of Melikhovo, south of Moscow. In 1897, however, he was found to be suffering from chronic tuberculosis and was soon forced to move to Yalta, in the Crimea, where he spent his last winters.

Chekhov's major writing for the stage began in 1895 with *The Seagull*. Its premiere (1896) was a disastrous flop in Saint Petersburg, but the play was successfully staged in Konstantin Stanislavsky's MOSCOW ART THEATER in 1898, as was *Uncle Vanya* in 1899. His last two plays, *The Three Sisters* and *The Cherry Orchard*, were written specially for the Art Theater, which eventually adopted the seagull as its emblem, calling itself "the house of Chekhov."

Renowned in his lifetime in his native Russia, Chekhov did not become known to the world at large until the 1920s. Since then his stories have been read in countless editions in all major languages, and his plays have become standard features in the repertoires of theaters worldwide.

Chekiang see ZHEJIANG

chelation [kee-lay'-shuhn] Chelation is a chemical reaction in which a metal ion forms bonds to two or more electron-donating groups such as carboxylate or amino, that are themselves part of a single molecule. The molecules of the resulting compound, called a chelate, contain one or more rings of atoms in which the metal ion is so firmly bound that many of its properties are profoundly modified. For example, the toxicity of lead in the bloodstream is suppressed by undergoing chelation with an injected chelating agent.

Chelsea ware [chel'-see] Chelsea ware, a porcelain made between 1743 and 1784 at a factory in Chelsea, a district of London, is prized for its delicate decoration in ROCOCO STYLE. It was of the porcelain type known as soft paste. The output of the factory is divided into four distinct periods, each defined by a particular distinguishing mark: the triangle (1743–50), the raised anchor (1750–52), the red anchor (1752–56), and the gold anchor (1756–70). Red-anchor pieces are considered the finest for their ideal balance between form and decoration. The best-known Chelsea pieces were delicately modeled figures, often made in pairs or sets. Tureens and dishes modeled in animal and vegetable forms, such as hares, bunches of asparagus, or heads of cauliflower, are highly prized today.

Chelyabinsk [chil-yah'-binsk] Chelyabinsk is the capital of Chelyabinsk oblast in the Russian republic of the USSR. It is situated on the eastern slopes of the Ural Mountains. The city has a population of 1,143,000 (1989). One of the principal cities of the Urals industrial region, Chelyabinsk is also a transport center on the Trans-Siberian Railroad. Its heavy industries include steel, ferroalloys, zinc, and rare-metals smelters; tractors and heavy machinery are also manufactured. The town dates back to 1736, when it became a Russian stronghold against the encroachments of southern nomads. In the 19th century it was primarily an agricultural processing town. It received its first metallurgical processing plant in 1928, and industrial growth was particularly rapid in World War II and in the postwar era.

Chemakum see QUILEUTE-HOH AND CHEMAKUM

chemical and biological warfare Chemical warfare (CW) is the deliberate use of chemical substances to incapacitate or kill plants, animals, or human beings. Biological warfare (BW) is the use of biological organisms or products (BW agents) to produce incapacitating disease or death. Modern chemical warfare traces its origin to World War I, when both sides experimented with a number of chemical warfare agents and methods of delivery. Chlorine gas, released directly from cylinders, and shrapnel fragments coated with irritant powders are examples of early attempts to wage chemical warfare. The

American C-123 Providers trail a fog of defoliants, chemical or biological agents that cause trees to shed their foliage prematurely. Defoliants were used by the U.S. military in the air war over Vietnam to denude jungle tracts that provided cover for the Viet Cong.

unwieldiness of the cylinders and the unpredictable effect of weather and changing winds led to efforts to find better methods for disseminating chemical warfare agents. By the end of World War I, artillery shells filled with phosgene (carbonyl chloride) or mustard gas (2,2'-dichloro-diethyl sulfide) were being delivered on target by bursting artillery charges. The heavy casualties suffered by both sides, totaling about 800,000, convinced the military forces of the effectiveness of toxic chemical agents in warfare. The Russians are believed to have suffered the greatest damage from such attacks, their casualties including nearly 60,000 fatalities. Some historians consider those terrible losses a major factor in the modern Soviet army's strong and continuing interest in chemical warfare.

(Right) *During World War I, Allied troops were routinely outfitted with gas masks after the second Battle of Ypres (April-May 1915), when the Germans used poison gas for the first time on the Western front.*

World War II. Research just before and during World War II led to the development of highly lethal nerve agents. In the late 1930s, Germany developed tabun (dimethylaminoethodycyanophosphine oxide), and during 1942–45 a plant at Dyhernfurth, Germany, produced a large quantity of this compound. The Soviets seized this plant at the end of the war, and the nerve gases then entered their arsenal. However, no major power in the European Theater of World War II used chemical warfare. Historians have speculated that the Germans did not use tabun because they feared massive retaliation, including the possibility of attacks against their cities.

During the war in Vietnam the United States used herbicides and riot-control or incapacitating agents and experimented with advanced delivery systems.

Modern Chemical Warfare Agents. Chemical warfare agents designed to incapacitate by entry through the skin are probably best exemplified by the well-known mustard gas and Lewisite (chlorovinyl dichloroarsine). These agents severely burn or blister the skin and may cause permanent damage to the lungs if they are inhaled. Mustard gas was especially feared during World War I, and large stocks are still held by some countries, including the United States. Harassing agents, such as TEAR GAS, have been developed to produce a more limited and nonlethal effect.

Large numbers of naturally occurring poisons also have been examined to determine their value as chemical warfare agents. These include capsicin (an extract of cayenne pepper and paprika), ricin (a toxic substance found in the castor bean), and saxitoxin (a toxic substance secreted by certain shellfish). Of the many natural toxic materials, none has received more attention than the toxin of the common bacterium *Clostridium botulinum*, which is sometimes ingested from food that has been improperly canned or preserved. An extremely small quantity can produce death. Sprayed in the air or introduced into a water system, it might prove to be a highly effective agent.

The group of toxic substances that has received the greatest attention are the organophosphorous nerve agents. The German product tabun was only the first in a series of these compounds, which now include the U.S. standard nerve agent sarin (methyl-isopropoxy fluorophosphine oxide) and the USSR's soman (methyl pinacolyloxyfluoro phosphine oxide). All these nerve agents produce the same basic physiological effect: they act upon enzymes at the myoneural (muscle-nerve) junction, causing immediate convulsions, paralysis, and death. They are capable of entering the body through either the lungs or the skin and are deadly in very small quantities; treatment following exposure is difficult.

Some chemical agents are designed to permit the selective destruction or defoliation of plants, including food crops. The defoliant Agent Orange was widely used in Vietnam (see also HERBICIDE and POLLUTANTS, CHEMICAL). Compounds that can cause severe psychological disorientation are also available, and research continues on other exotic chemical agents.

Development of Biological Warfare Agents. By the end of World War II at least six countries—the USSR, the United States, the United Kingdom, France, Japan, and Canada—are believed to have worked on the technology for large-scale use of biological warfare agents. Rumors had suggested secret efforts in the USSR even before World War II. Research facilities are known to have been established in England and Canada and in the United States at Fort Detrick, Md.

Biological warfare research has succeeded in producing a full spectrum of agents capable of inducing a range of effects from incapacitation to death. These include the toxin of a *Staphylococcal* species that is the cause of severe food-poisoning symptoms; Venezuelan equine encephalomyelitis (a virus); plague, anthrax, and tularemia (bacteria); coccidioidomycosis (a fungus); and a large number of antianimal and antiplant agents, such as foot-and-mouth disease, fowl plague, potato blight, black stem-rust of cereals, rice blast, and diseases of other economically important crops. There have been no successful large-scale uses of biological warfare agents in modern war.

Delivery Systems. A variety of weapons has been designed to place chemical or biological warfare agents on target, including chemical-filled rocket and missile warheads, aircraft and submarine spray systems, and even a type of shrapnel—tiny poison darts that are released from bursting artillery shells. The most recent development—the binary, or two-part, artillery shell—is designed to improve the safe handling and storage of toxic agents. It holds two relatively nontoxic intermediate forms of a nerve agent in separate compartments. When fired, the components are mixed within the shell, and toxic nerve gas is released when the shell explodes.

Chemical and Biological Warfare Defensive Systems. Many highly technical defense systems against chemical and biological warfare have been developed. Protective gas masks combine particulate filters with substances that absorb gases and can remove a variety of toxic agents. Other protective devices include chemically treated clothing and suits with portable ventilating systems, and sealed and air-conditioned tanks and personnel carriers.

The availability of antitoxins and training of medical-corps personnel to handle casualties are important defensive measures. Most are reasonably effective if some early warning is possible. In the absence of warning, a successful chemical and biological warfare attack would have an immediate impact on military operations. For this reason, military commanders attribute maximum success to the surprise attack.

International Controls. The single most important treaty in the control of chemical and biological warfare agents is probably the Geneva Protocol of 1925, which has now been ratified by about 100 countries. The United States proposed the protocol and signed it on June 17, 1925. It was not ratified by the Senate until 1974, however. The treaty is limited to the use of chemical and biological agents in war, and most signatories reserve the right to use such weapons in retaliation. In effect, the treaty proscribes a "first use" of these agents.

A major step toward achieving the elimination of biological warfare agents occurred in 1969–70 when President Richard M. Nixon declared that the United States unilaterally renounced any use of biological weapons and ordered the destruction of biological warfare stockpiles and the conversion of the research facility at Fort Detrick, Md., to a cancer-research laboratory. (It later became the U.S. Army's Research Institute of Infectious Diseases.) In 1972 the United Nations successfully negotiated the Convention of the Prohibition of Biological and Toxin Weapons, which forbade the production or stockpiling of these weapons, although it allowed "defensive research." The Convention was approved by the U.S. Senate in 1974 and by more than 100 other countries.

In 1988 the U.S. government justified the Department of Defense (DOD) program to develop defenses against biological weapons by claiming that some ten nations were producing weapons using biological agents. DOD defensive research may include the development of new toxins and antidotes through genetic engineering, and the genetic manipulation of existing organisms to make them virulent or easier to produce and store. The department claims that its research is aimed at producing vaccines and curative drugs for such deadly diseases as anthrax.

In April 1987, Soviet leader Mikhail Gorbachev announced that his country had ended its production of chemical weapons. In December 1987, however, the United States resumed the manufacture of nerve gases, now made in binary form, and planned for the production of the 227-kg (500-lb) Bigeye, a binary shell containing materials for a lethal nerve gas.

A treaty banning chemical weapons became a real possibility in 1989 when the United States and the USSR agreed to on-site inspections of their chemical-weapons facilities. It was feared, however, that other nations might not agree to eliminate their own stockpiles. Some 20 countries may have chemical arsenals or possess the capability to make them. Nerve agents resemble some pesticides in chemical composition, and it is possible to convert a pesticide factory into one that produces nerve gas, as Iraq did with three of its plants. Libya, in

1988, built a chemical weapons plant masquerading as a pharmaceuticals factory, using chemicals supplied by a West German firm. Mustard gas is easily produced, and Iraq used it often in its war with Iran (see IRAN-IRAQ WAR), as well as in an ongoing conflict with its Kurdish minority. Iran has also used poison gases, and other countries engaged in smaller wars have been suspected of doing so.

chemical bond A chemical bond is formed when separate atoms are brought together and the sharing or transfer of electrons occurs. Chemical bonds can be weak or strong, depending on the nature of the interactions. The physical and chemical properties of most compounds are due, in large part, to these bonding forces.

Ionic Bonding. When two or more atoms combine, a competition for the available electrons can occur that leads to a nearly complete transfer of one or more electrons. The resulting formation of an ionic bond involves the removal of an electron from one atom, a process known as ionization. The energy required is called the ionization potential of the atom (see ION AND IONIZATION). The other atom gains an electron, and the measure of its ability to do so is known as its electron affinity. An ionic bond results from the strong electrostatic forces of attraction between the negatively charged anions and positively charged cations. When atoms of sodium and chlorine are brought together, for example, table salt (NaCl) is formed; a more proper representation might be Na^+Cl^-.

Ionic bonding is common in inorganic compounds such as salts (see SALT, chemistry), where the charges are easily accommodated on relatively small ions. In more complex solids the ions form three-dimensional arrays in which a basic framework is repeated to generate the observed structures so obvious in CRYSTALS. A single anion might be shared by several adjacent cations, so that the network of packing leads to very simple lattice structures. Because the forces are relatively strong, ionic solids tend to be strong materials, to have definite patterns of cleavage, and to have high melting points.

The formation of an ionic bond is the result of the competition for available electrons. A useful measure of this property is known as the electronegativity of an atom. In general, a more electronegative element will take a larger share of any bonding electrons when forming a chemical bond. If a great disparity exists between the electronegativities of the atoms in a particular compound, the uneven sharing will likely result in a complete transfer of one or more electrons and the formation of an ionic bond.

Covalent Bonding. When the competition for bonding electrons is not as severe as in the case of ionic bonding, a sharing of the available outer electrons of the atoms occurs and a covalent bond is formed. The outer electrons that participate readily are termed VALENCE electrons. For example, two atoms of hydrogen, each with a valence of one, can combine to form diatomic H_2, with two shared electrons forming a single covalent bond. As two atoms approach each other, the electron cloud of one "senses" the attractive force of the positive nucleus of the other atom. This attraction is countered, at short interatomic distances, by the repulsions of the two positive nucleii and the two electron clouds. The preferred separation is achieved where there is maximum stabilization, and this distance corresponds to the equilibrium internuclear distance, or bond distance. In H_2 this separation is 0.74 Å, where one angstrom (Å) equals 10^{-10} m. The difference between the energy of the separated atoms (generally set at zero) and the energy of stabilization of H_2 is the bond energy, 104 kcal/mole (435 kJ/mole). (See MOLE, unit of substance).

The number of covalent bonds an atom can form is determined by its ELECTRON CONFIGURATION. Many stable compounds result from electron sharing between atoms so that two electrons fill *s* orbitals and six electrons fill *p* orbitals, giving eight electrons in a full valence shell. Atoms that bond in this manner obey the so-called octet rule. Fluorine atoms, for example, each have seven valence electrons and by sharing one electron pair in the F_2 molecule follow the octet rule.

Atoms can also share more than one electron pair to give multiple bonds. Carbon atoms often share two of their four valence electrons to give a double bond, as in ethylene, $H_2C{=}CH_2$. In molecular nitrogen, N_2, nitrogen atoms share three pairs of electrons to give a triple bond, $N{\equiv}N$. Multiple bonds are stronger than single bonds, resulting in shorter bond lengths and larger bond energies.

For the heavier elements in the periodic table, the *d* electrons may also participate in bonding; the valence shell then expands past the octet limitation. Thus in sulfur hexafluoride, SF_6, six S—F bonds are present, and the central sulfur atom shares six pairs of electrons. In many cases a single atom may contribute a complete electron pair to a vacant orbital of another atom. Such a bond, called a coordinate covalent bond, is common in the chemistry of transition metal compounds and COORDINATION COMPOUNDS.

Unequal sharing of electron pairs leads to bonding that is intermediate between ionic and covalent. When electronegativities are different, but not so different that an ionic bond forms, electrons stay closer to the more electronegative atom. In hydrogen chloride, HCl, for example, the more electronegative chlorine atom has a partial negative charge and the less electronegative hydrogen atom has a partial positive charge, creating a DIPOLE and giving what is known as a polar bond. Attraction between the oppositely charged ends of polar bonds or molecules is one of the various INTERMOLECULAR FORCES that largely determine the physical properties of covalently bonded compounds.

Metallic Bonding. Due to the relatively low ionization potential of the metallic elements in the periodic table, electrons are easily removed and are mobile in most metallic solids. The resulting positive ions occupy sites in an extended array in three dimensions, but the electrons are delocalized. The mobile electrons are responsible for many of the properties of these materials, such as their high thermal conductivity, strength, high melting points, high densities, color, and electrical conductivity.

Van der Waals Bonding. The forces of attraction between molecules due to the interaction of dipoles are collectively known as van der Waals forces. If, for example, electrons shift for an instant to create a temporary dipole, similar dipoles are induced in nearby molecules, resulting in a momentary attraction between molecules. Van der Waals "bonding" is weak—generally one-thousandth as strong as a covalent bond. The properties at very low temperatures of materials such as liquid nitrogen or helium are due to such weak interactions.

Hydrogen Bonding. Hydrogen atoms bonded to highly electronegative atoms have a relatively large partial positive charge. The attraction between such a hydrogen atom and a center of negative charge in another compound, often an unshared electron pair on nitrogen or oxygen, is known as a HYDROGEN BOND. Though only about 5% as strong as covalent bonds, hydrogen bonds are important to the physical and chemical properties of many compounds. The properties of water and the structure and function of many biochemical molecules, notably DNA, are largely determined by hydrogen bonding.

Molecular Orbital Theory. Although the picture of shared electrons in covalent bonds is useful, a more general approach based on QUANTUM MECHANICS is needed to account for the bonding in many molecules. Molecular orbital theory treats the valence electrons of all atoms in a molecule as contributing to the bonding character of the entire molecule. The electrons are pictured as occupying a series of energy levels that belong to the molecule as a whole. The molecular orbital approach is especially valuable for molecules like benzene, C_6H_6, in which no combination of single or double bonds accounts for the equal lengths and strengths of the six carbon-carbon bonds in the benzene ring.

chemical combination, laws of The laws of chemical combination were formulated in the early part of the 19th century. They are a result of the first use of quantitative measurement in chemistry.

In 1799, Joseph Proust proposed the law of definite proportions (also called the law of constant composition). The law states that compounds contain elements in certain fixed proportions and in no other combinations, regardless of the method of preparation. Thus, chalk, or calcium carbonate, $CaCO_3$, is always 40% calcium, 12% carbon, and 48% oxygen, by weight.

In 1803, John DALTON articulated the law of multiple proportions. This law states that if two elements combine to form more than one compound, then the ratio of the weights of the second element (which combines with a fixed weight of the first element) will be small whole numbers. For example, carbon and oxygen can form two compounds, carbon monoxide and carbon dioxide. In carbon monoxide 12 g of carbon combine with 16 g of oxygen, and in carbon dioxide, the same weight of carbon combines with 32 g of oxygen. Thus, the oxygen weight ratio that combines with 12 g of carbon is (32/16), or 2. The law of combining weights, also proposed by Dalton, states that in every compound, the proportion by weight of each element in the compound may be expressed by the ATOMIC WEIGHT or a multiple of the atomic weight of each element. (This law was discovered before the atomic theory was postulated and was thus worded more generally.) The law of combining weights can be seen to follow directly from the atomic theory. In the case of water, H_2O, each molecule of water is composed of two atoms of hydrogen (atomic weight 1) and one atom of oxygen (atomic weight 16). Thus, all molecules of water consist of 2 parts of hydrogen and 16 parts of oxygen by weight. All other compounds can be analyzed similarly.

These three laws, proposed from the first use of quantitative experimental techniques, resulted (1803) in Dalton's atomic theory (see ATOM).

chemical energy Chemical reactions are accompanied by energy changes that usually are observed as an absorption or emission of heat or light. Germain Henri Hess (1802–50) carefully measured the quantities of heat evolved in chemical reactions and showed that the amount of heat produced or absorbed would be the same for a given set of reactants and products regardless of the intermediates. This generalization is known as HESS'S LAW.

Energy changes are measured in a calorimeter, a reaction chamber usually surrounded by a known quantity of water, the temperature of which is measured before and after the reaction. The HEAT CAPACITIES of the water and the vessel are known, and the amount of energy absorbed (temperature lowered by the reaction) or evolved (temperature raised by the reaction) can be calculated. The reaction is called endothermic if heat is absorbed, exothermic if heat is evolved.

Molecular structure is related to chemical energy through the CHEMICAL BOND. Energy is required to break a chemical bond between two atoms. The reverse process, bond formation, evolves energy. The energy change of a chemical reaction depends on the number and type of chemical bonds broken or formed during the reaction.

Chemical energy is used in many ways, all involving the conversion of chemical energy to a different energy form. Burning fossil fuels such as coal and oil supplies most energy used in industry and for home heating. In the presence of oxygen, the carbon present in fossil fuels burns to produce carbon dioxide and heat energy. All living organisms depend on chemical energy. It is the driving force of all life processes. The chemical energy from energy-releasing reactions is used to fuel the energy-requiring reactions vital to life. This energy transfer is a direct use of chemical energy.

chemical engineering see ENGINEERING

chemical equilibrium see CHEMICAL KINETICS AND EQUILIBRIUM

chemical industry The chemical industry manufactures chemicals either from natural substances or from other chemicals. One of the five leading manufacturing industries in the United States, the chemical industry is

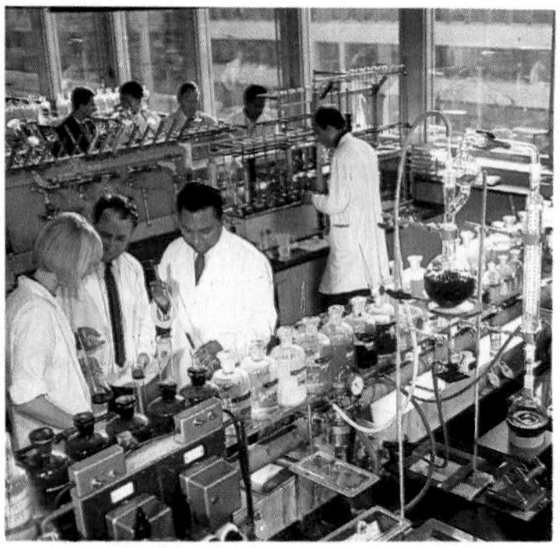

(Above) *Research laboratories are a necessary part of modern chemical manufacturing plants. In order to keep up with competition, better and less expensive methods for producing existing products and developing new ones are continuously being sought.*

(Right) *Conversion of petroleum and natural gas to petrochemicals requires complex specialized equipment, such as distillation towers and reactors. The equipment is kept in continuous operation except for periods of routine maintenance.*

important because chemical production is a basic necessity for industry as a whole. Almost every modern product or process uses manufactured chemicals.

The enormous industrial growth of the past century has depended to a large degree on industrial chemistry, which has devised ways to restructure molecules and control their reactions in order to create synthetic substances—substances not produced in nature. Relying heavily on research, the chemical industry produces about 1,000 new chemicals each year.

Scope of Chemical Production

The products of the chemical industry are so wide-ranging that no single method of classifying them exists. A simple division can be made between organic chemicals (chemicals based on combinations of hydrogen and carbon) and inorganic chemicals. Business analysts commonly speak of heavy chemicals, those produced in great quantities at relatively low prices, and fine chemicals, those produced in small quantities for special end uses. Marketers often classify products by end use: agriculture, automotive, and fiber or glass chemicals, fertilizers, pharmaceuticals, and so forth. Another classification is based on the product's derivation: petrochemicals, derived from petroleum; electrochemicals, manufactured through using electricity; coal and coal-tar chemicals; and chemicals made from wood or other basic substances.

Still another common classification divides the industry's products into three categories: (1) basic chemicals, the relatively simple chemical products used to formulate more complex chemicals; (2) intermediate chemicals, such as plastic materials, fiber chemicals, and other materials used in manufacturing end products—synthetic fibers, for example; and (3), finished ready-to-use chemicals, such as fertilizers, insecticides, paints, and pharmaceuticals.

Development of the Chemical Industry

Since the first civilization, humanity has manipulated natural substances, transmuting them into other, more useful materials. Making glass from sand and ashes, for example, or fermenting grape juice to make wine are chemical processes that were used by the ancient Egyptians and Chinese. A vast store of knowledge about the properties of substances has accumulated over the centuries, primarily in the various crafts. Large-scale production of chemicals became possible, however, only when chemical discoveries were applied to specific manufacturing needs. The beginning of volume ALKALI production in the late 1700s is generally considered the birth of the chemical industry.

Growth of the Alkali Industry. Alkalis—caustic salts of potassium or sodium—were widely used in making soap, glass, and textile bleaches. They had been produced by leaching plant ash with water, a slow process that required large quantities of wood or other plant materials and produced only small amounts of alkali. In 1789, Nicolas Leblanc, a French surgeon, patented a technique for the chemical manufacture of soda ash, or sodium carbonate, in which the initial step involved treating salt with sulfuric acid, a well-known chemical. The product was then calcified using limestone and charcoal. Leblanc's method stimulated demand for sulfuric acid.

Leblanc's process produced large quantities of gaseous hydrochloric acid as a by-product. At first, the gas was released into the air; it was found, however, that the waste gas could be captured and reacted with manganese dioxide to produce CHLORINE, a valuable chemical already well known for its bleaching properties.

The Leblanc process was used for more than a half century until the development in 1861 of the more efficient, less costly Solvay process, which used ammonia to produce alkali. A method for the industrial synthesis of ammonia was perfected in 1913 by Carl Bosch. Basing his process on the research of Fritz HABER, Bosch was the first industrial chemist to successfully use high-pressure technology for large-scale chemical synthesis.

ELECTROLYSIS, the separation of chemical elements by passing an electric current through a chemical compound, was first used in the 1880s in an early process for manufacturing aluminum and, at the turn of the century, in a new technique for the production of alkali from brine. Electrolysis of brine produces equal amounts of alkali and chlorine; the rapidly growing paper, pulp, and textile industries needed ever-increasing quantities of chlorine for bleaching the products. Electrolysis has largely replaced the Solvay process in the manufacture of alkalis.

The Organic-Chemical Industry. Organic chemicals (see ORGANIC CHEMISTRY) are compounds containing carbon and hydrogen. Although many chemicals are produced from natural raw materials, the organic-chemical industry is based almost exclusively on the products of coal and petroleum. Coal carbonization to produce COKE dates back to the early 17th century. The by-products of carbonization are coal gas and coal tar. Coal gas was first used for lighting in the early 1800s. COAL TAR became the subject of intense scientific research, and in 1856 the first DYE derived from it was discovered by Sir William Perkin. Perkin's success led to the development of other coal-tar-based dyes, to the discovery of new synthetic flavorings and PERFUMES (1879), and to the creation (1909) of bakelite, the first synthetic PLASTIC.

Petrochemicals. The most important division of the organic-chemical field, petrochemistry uses chemicals derived from petroleum and natural gas to manufacture a wide range of products: plastics, pharmaceuticals, PAINTS and dyes, synthetic RUBBER, SYNTHETIC FIBERS, fertilizers, and PESTICIDES. The sophisticated processes necessary to extract the petroleum derivatives used in the production of these new synthetic materials were mostly developed after World War II. The PETROCHEMICAL industry is currently the fastest-growing industrial chemical field. Because most of its products are considered hazardous at some stage in their manufacture, the petrochemical industry has been profoundly affected by government environmental regulations (see DISEASES, OCCUPATIONAL; POLLUTANTS, CHEMICAL).

Fertilizers and Explosives. The FERTILIZER industry has been a principal producer of heavy chemicals since the end of the 19th century. The production of nitrogenous fertilizers using ammonia as the nitrogen source is based on the Haber-Bosch process of ammonia synthesis. Nitrogen compounds, essential for fertilizers, are also necessary for producing such explosives as nitroglycerine and TNT.

Pharmaceuticals. Synthetic rather than natural substances have been used as medicinal preparations increasingly since the beginning of the 20th century. Although today many new drugs are made by other means, a large proportion of new pharmaceuticals are the result of chemical synthesis.

The production of nitric acid illustrates the complexity of many of the processes used by the chemical industry. Nitric acid is produced by the oxidizing of ammonia into nitrogen dioxide, which is then combined with water to form the acid. The process begins with liquid ammonia, NH_3 (1), which is heated and vaporized into ammonia gas (2) and filtered (3). Air is heated in a steam jacket (4). In a converter (5), the heated air and gaseous ammonia are mixed and passed over a heated, platinum-rhodium wire-gauze catalyst (6), oxidizing the ammonia to the gas, nitrogen dioxide, NO_2. The heat in the converter is also used to generate steam for powering the compressor (8). The nitrogen dioxide enters a water-spray cooler (7), where a portion is removed as a 1% nitric acid solution, HNO_3, and the remainder, mixed with water, is led to the compressor (8), which heats the gas to 150° C (302° F). Compressed and heated, the gas is cooled again (9), forming a condensate of 20% nitric acid. This condensate enters the absorption tower (10), together with the weaker acid from the first cooler. There, the acid and water are combined as they are led over a series of bubble trays. The end product is a 60% nitric acid solution.

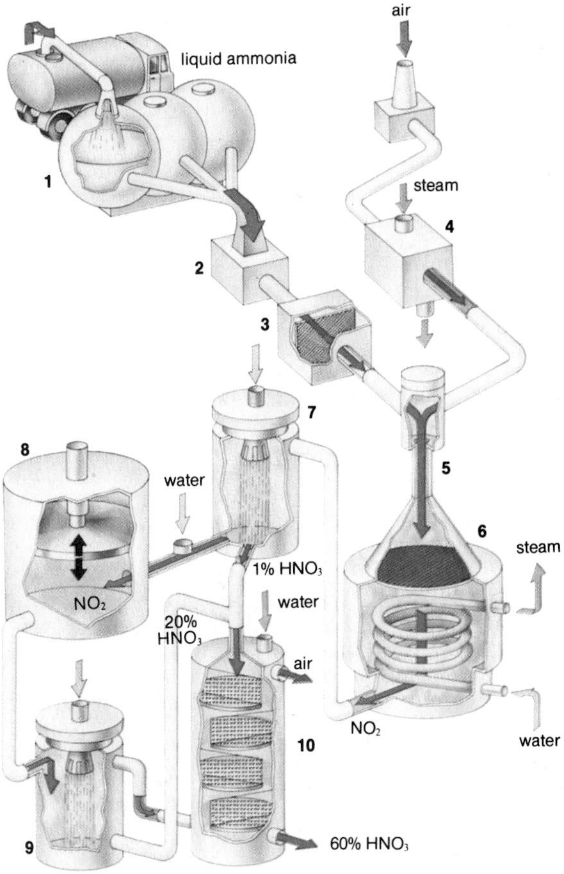

The Modern Chemical Industry

The chemical industry is highly capital-intensive, and the trend has been toward concentration within a small group of giant firms. U.S. chemical firms dominate the world market, in part because the industry from its beginnings has been able to use the vast continental reserves of such raw materials as coal, salt, sulfur, phosphates, petroleum, natural gas, forest and cropland, and water. In the early 20th century, for example, the United States exploited its abundant supplies of petroleum by pioneering in the production of petrochemicals. Huge deposits of sulfur in the Gulf of Mexico region have also helped make the nation the world's largest producer of the most important industrial chemical, sulfuric acid. In addition, the United States has a well-funded research-and-development establishment.

In recent years, however, several factors have combined to reduce the importance of the U.S. industry in world markets. The early 1980s saw the most severe depression in world sales of chemicals since the Great Depression of the 1930s. Large companies had developed new, more efficient production methods, but at the same time rising petroleum prices increased costs, and world demand for basic, "commodity" chemicals shrank. Chemical companies abroad also had enlarged their production facilities, and their competition cut into U.S. sales.

In order to compete more successfully, many chemical firms reduced their production of high-volume, basic chemicals such as chlorine and ethylene, and instead went into the manufacture of "specialty" chemicals, such as gene-spliced agrichemicals, pharmaceuticals made using biotechnological methods, very high purity acids for etching silicon wafers, new catalysts, and thermoplastic products.

These changes have been successful, but again, competition from abroad keeps sales from soaring. Because it has so few natural resources, Japan has concentrated its chemical industry's efforts on specialty products.

In the late 1980s European chemical firms owned nearly $27 billion in U.S. chemical corporations and formed the largest foreign investment group in the United States. These foreign firms are attracted to the U.S. market because it is the world's largest, it buys huge quantities of specialty chemicals, and its industry spends generously on research and development.

Toxic-Waste Production

The discovery of the enormous amounts of toxic wastes released by the chemical industry (the disastrous contamination of Love Canal was found as early as 1971, but the extent of chemical pollution became known only gradually thereafter) increased industry costs for controlling and cleaning up toxic wastes. After the 1986 chemical-plant disaster in Bhopal, India, public demands for tighter industry regulation grew. In 1988 the chemical industry spent $3 billion (about 17% of all industry capital outlays in that year) on environmental and pollution-control systems.

Three-quarters of all hazardous waste produced in the United States originates in chemical companies. In 1986 an amendment to the 1980 Superfund Act set aside federal funds to be used for cleanup and to be repaid by the industry.

chemical kinetics and equilibrium

chemical kinetics and equilibrium The degree to which a chemical reaction proceeds to form a useful product and the time required to complete the conversion are two important aspects of modern chemistry. Chemical kinetics is the study of factors important to the speed at which a reaction forms product molecules. The final distribution of products and unconsumed reactants is often predetermined by the nature of the process and is representative of the chemical equilibrium, or balance, that is achieved.

Chemical Kinetics

Chemical kinetics is the study of the rates of chemical reactions and the factors that control both the yields of product molecules and the consumption of the reacting species. A detailed molecular picture showing the process at the most elementary level is known as a reaction mechanism.

Reaction Rates. A measure of the speed at which a reaction proceeds to form products is given by the reaction rate law, a relation based on experimental measurements. If molecules A and B react to form products C and D, this process may be written as

$$A + B \rightarrow C + D$$

The rate of the reaction expresses the speed at which A or B is lost, or C or D is created, and might be determined as

$$\text{Rate} = k[A][B]$$

where k is a proportionality constant (the rate constant) and the brackets around A and B indicate that their concentrations are to be used in the rate equation. Such a simple rate law is appropriate if the reaction is the result of a collision in which one molecule of A strikes one molecule of B to form the chemical products. This collision would be an example of an elementary process (in this case a bimolecular reaction), and the association with the simple rate is straightforward. The molecularity of the reaction is the number of reactant molecules that participate in the elementary process (in this case, two).

Many reactions involving only two chemical components are more complex and involve unstable species known as chemical intermediates that do not appear in the reaction equation. In such cases the rate expression is more complicated and must be determined by experimental variation of the concentrations of the reaction components.

Because collisions between molecules often control the formation of products or chemical intermediates, a simple model for treating the dynamics of reactions is available, based on the KINETIC THEORY OF MATTER. The effect on the observed reaction rate of increasing the concentrations of the reactants can be viewed in terms of the increased number of collisions. The effect of temperature on the reaction rate, often complex, is related to the higher velocities and energies available to the reactants as the temperature of the reaction mixture is increased. Merely bringing the molecules together is not sufficient if an added amount of energy is necessary to promote the formation of the products. This energy is the activation energy of the reaction. A high activation energy generally inhibits the reaction and results in a slow reaction rate. Raising the temperature and thus the energies of the reactants is one method for accelerating the rate of the reaction.

Catalysts. A catalyst is a material that is added to a reaction mixture to accelerate the process but is itself not consumed. Rates may be increased by several orders of magnitude by trace amounts of these substances. On a microscopic scale the catalyst's role may be complex, but it has the end result of effectively lowering the activation energy of the reaction. In many cases reactions that would normally require high temperatures can be run at room temperature, with substantial savings in the cost of electricity or heating fuel. In biological systems many slow processes are enhanced through the use of highly selective biochemical catalysts called enzymes.

Chemical Equilibrium

In the previous discussion of reaction rates, the general processes noted resulted in the formation of products, with the reactions proceeding from left to right as written. Many processes are reversible and are more properly represented by

$$aA + bB \rightleftharpoons cC + dD$$

where forward and reverse steps are indicated by the double arrow. If a mixture of A and B, C and D, or of three or all four of the components is placed in a reaction chamber at fixed temperature, the reactions will proceed and eventually reach a special state. At this point the rates of the forward and of the reverse reaction are equal. This final state is reached regardless of the original composition of the mixture, and is approached in a spontaneous manner. At this point chemical equilibrium has been achieved, and subsequent probing of the mixture will show that no net change in the concentrations of the chemical components is occurring.

Le Chatelier's Principle. Once a chemical system has reached equilibrium, effects due to changes in the temperature or pressure, or due to the addition or removal of chemical species, can be predicted using simple relations described by Henri Le Chatelier in 1884. A system that is stressed will adjust its character to relieve the stress. For example, ammonia is formed in the gas-phase reaction

$$N_2 + 3H_2 \rightleftharpoons 2NH_3$$

If, at equilibrium, N_2 is added, stress is relieved by driving the reaction to the right, consuming some N_2 (and H_2) and generating ammonia. If ammonia were added, the equilibrium would be displaced to the left. If the external pressure is increased, the reaction can effectively occupy a smaller volume by moving toward product, since two molar volumes of product are generated from four molar volumes of reactants. The reaction is known to release energy in forming products. The effect of increasing the temperature is therefore relieved by generating reactants that consume the added energy.

Types of Chemical Equilibriums. Although the previous discussion of equilibrium systems centered on simple reactions between gases or molecules in solution, many other situations arise. Many ionic solids, such as salt, NaCl, readily dissolve in solution, and ionic equilibrium expressions are applicable. Sodium cations and chlorine anions are in dynamic equilibrium with the solid NaCl. In many industrial processes a reaction is facilitated by the addition of a solid catalyst that does not go into solution (a heterogeneous catalyst), and a suitable equilibrium expression can be applied. Many OXIDATION AND REDUCTION reactions are important in the fields of electrochemistry and metallurgy. In these processes electrons are exchanged between reactants or products, and equilibrium expressions are employed to predict the direction and efficiency of the reactions. An electric battery is a self-contained chemical system in which the energy exchanged in a spontaneous electron transfer is employed to generate a small voltage. Equilibrium expressions can be used to determine the amounts of reactants and products involved in this common chemical process.

chemical nomenclature

chemical nomenclature More than 9 million chemical compounds are known, with the number steadily increasing. Chemical nomenclature is used for assigning to each compound at least one unambiguous name by which chemists will recognize it as distinct from all other compounds. Although some difficulties remain, this task has been largely accomplished. Furthermore, developments are underway that promise to simplify the use of systematic chemical nomenclature.

The underlying principle behind chemical nomenclature is the development of systems that relate the name to a structure. Three events in the development of chemical nomenclature stand out above all others. The first was the presentation in 1787 of a general system for inorganic compounds by a group of early French chemists, including Antoine Laurent LAVOISIER and Claude Louis BERTHOLLET. The second was the Geneva Congress in 1892, which set forth principles for the nomenclature of organic compounds.

The third was the establishment of nomenclature commissions as an important part of the activities of the International Union of Pure and Applied Chemistry (IUPAC). First organized in 1911 as the International Union of Chemistry (IUC), the IUPAC was reestablished in 1920 after World War I. The Organic Nomenclature Commission published a definitive report in 1930, and the Inorganic Nomenclature Commission, in 1940; both have since been extended. Today all developments in chemical nomenclature eventually are considered by the IUPAC nomenclature commissions. In the United States the focal points for nomenclature development are the American Chemical Society (ACS) Divisional Committees on Nomenclature and the Chemical Abstracts Service.

chemical reaction see REACTION, CHEMICAL

chemical symbolism and notation Chemists have developed a unique system of symbols and notation designed to represent chemical substances and their chemical reactions in writing.

Elements and Chemical Compounds. The chemical ELEMENTS are represented by symbols based on their names. A few symbols are the first letters of the names; O thus stands for oxygen, C for carbon, H for hydrogen, and so on. Most are two-letter symbols, for example, Ne for neon, Ni for nickel, Ar for argon. Some elements have symbols based on their Latin names, such as Au for gold (*aurum*), Fe for iron (*ferrum*), and Pb for lead (*plumbum*). Whenever two letters are used for an element, the first letter is capitalized and the second is not.

Chemical compounds are represented by chemical formulas composed of the symbols of the elements combined. Thus CO represents carbon monoxide and NaCl represents sodium chloride, in both of which atoms of the elements are combined in a 1-to-1 ratio. Subscripts are used to indicate the numbers of atoms combined in other ratios, for example, $CaCl_2$ or NH_3. For compounds with covalent bonds, the subscripts show the exact numbers of atoms in one molecule (see CHEMICAL BOND). Thus, H_2O shows that a water molecule has two H atoms and one O atom combined.

Certain combinations of atoms combine in stable groups, called radicals, which form chemical bonds as intact units. To show the presence of more than one of a given radical, parentheses are used. Calcium phosphate, a major constituent of bones and teeth, is written $Ca_3(PO_4)_2$ rather than $Ca_3P_2O_8$ to show that there are two phosphate radicals (PO_4) for every three calcium atoms (Ca).

Ions. An ION is a chemical species—an atom, a group of atoms, or a subatomic particle—that carries an electric charge. Charge is indicated by a superscript plus or minus sign: the hydrogen ion is H^+; the ammonium ion, NH_4^+; and the electron itself, e^-. Each species bears a single charge; multiple charges may be indicated either as CO_3^{--} or CO_3^{2-} (carbonate ion).

Reactions. Chemical reactions, in which substances change identity, are represented by writing chemical equations. The reactants, or starting materials, are written on the left, followed by an arrow pointing to the right where the products, the substances formed, are written. The reaction of hydrogen (H_2) with oxygen (O_2) to give water (H_2O) is thus represented by the equation

$$2H_2 + O_2 \rightarrow 2H_2O$$

Chemical equations are balanced—the same number of atoms of each element appear on both sides. Because formulas cannot be changed to balance an equation, two molecules of H_2 must react with one molecule of O_2 to give two molecules of H_2O.

Sometimes the physical phase of reactants and products is included in an equation. The symbols commonly used are (s), solid; (l), liquid; (g) gas; and (aq), in aqueous (water) solution. Occasionally, formation of a gas is shown by an upwards arrow, $H_2\uparrow$, and formation of a solid (a precipitate) by a downwards arrow, $AgCl\downarrow$. To indicate reactions that come to equilibrium with both reactants and products in the system, the single arrow $\rightarrow$ is replaced by a double arrow, $\rightleftharpoons$.

Isotopes and Nuclear Reactions. The atoms of isotopes of an element contain the same number of protons but different numbers of neutrons, and thus have different mass numbers (neutrons + protons). To indicate an isotope, the mass number is written either as a superscript to the atomic symbol or as a number following the name of the element. For instance, ${}^{235}_{92}U$ and ${}^{238}_{92}U$ are two isotopes of uranium.

In nuclear reactions, the numbers of protons and neutrons in atoms can change. Protons are given the symbol ${}^{1}_{1}p^+$; neutrons, the symbol ${}^{1}_{0}n$; and electrons the symbol ${}^{0}_{-1}e$. Equations for nuclear reactions must be balanced with respect to mass number and proton number, meaning that the subscripts and superscripts on both sides of an equation must add up to the same number, for example:

$${}^{238}_{92}U + {}^{1}_{0}n \rightarrow {}^{239}_{93}Np + {}^{0}_{-1}e$$

Bonding and Molecular Structure. The bonding, location of electrons, and arrangement of atoms in a molecule are vitally important in chemistry. Often covalent bonds and the location of valence electrons are shown with electron-dot notation, or Lewis symbols. Valence electrons are shown by dots surrounding the atomic symbol and covalent bonds by a shared pair of dots.

hydrogen chlorine hydrogen chloride

A less cumbersome method is to omit dots and show single covalent bonds by a dash (H—Cl), double bonds by a double dash ($H_2C{=}CH_2$), and triple bonds by a triple dash ($HC{\equiv}CH$). In a complete structural formula, all bonds are written out. In a condensed structural formula, only bonds significant to the molecular structure are displayed.

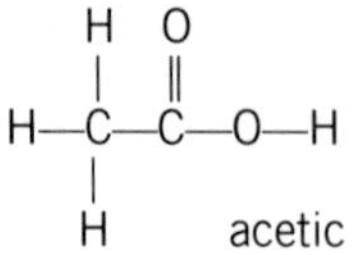

acetic acid

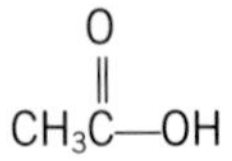

acetic acid

Organic compounds with rings consisting of carbon atoms with attached hydrogen atoms are often drawn without any atomic symbols. A carbon atom and enough hydrogen atoms to complete the carbon valence of four is assumed to be present at each corner. A simple example is cyclohexane, C_6H_6:

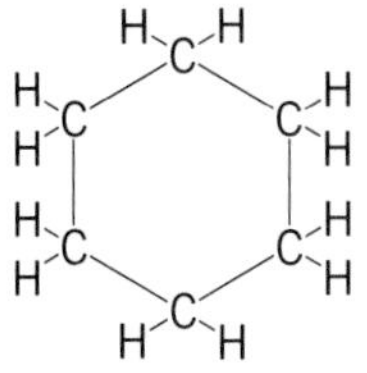

or

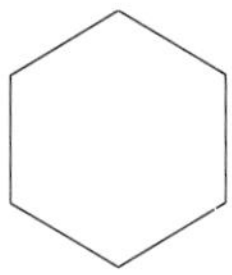

cyclohexane

chemin de fer [shuh-man' duh fair] Long a popular casino card game in Europe and Latin America, chemin de fer is rapidly finding its way into casino operations in the United States. As in the game of baccarat, which it resembles, a chemin de fer table usually has 12 seats, for 11 players and the croupier. The player seated to the right of the croupier is the banker, who determines the amount of the stake. The player to the right has the first chance to bid for the entire stake and in so doing calls "banco." If the banker wins, the stake is doubled; if not, the position of banker passes to the player on the right.

The object of the game is to obtain cards that total 8 or 9, called a natural. Picture cards and the ten have no value. The banker deals two cards face down to himself or herself and to the player who has called "banco." This player may withdraw if the hand is more than 9, or reveal a natural, or ask for another card. Because the rules governing the call for another card are based on the total held, and the banker does not decide whether to draw another card until the opponent's draw card has been seen, the banker has a double advantage.

chemistry Chemistry is the physical science that deals with the composition, structure, and properties of substances and also the transformations that these substances undergo. Because the study of chemistry encompasses the entire material universe, it is central to the understanding of other sciences.

A basic chemical theory has been formulated as the result of centuries of observation and measurement of the various elements and compounds (see CHEMISTRY, HISTORY OF). According to this theory, matter is composed of minute particles called ATOMS. The more than 100 different kinds of atoms that are known are called chemical ELEMENTS. Atoms of the same element or of different elements can combine together to form MOLECULES and compounds (see COMPOUND, CHEMICAL). The atoms are held together by forces, primarily electrostatic, called CHEMICAL BONDS. In a chemical reaction two or more compounds can undergo various changes to form different compounds by means of breaking and making the chemical bonds (see REACTION, CHEMICAL).

Branches of Chemistry

Five subdivisions traditionally are used to classify various aspects of chemistry. The study of ORGANIC CHEMISTRY originally was limited to compounds that were obtained from living organisms, but now the field deals with hydrocarbons (compounds of carbon and hydrogen) and their derivatives. The study of INORGANIC CHEMISTRY includes compounds derived from all of the elements except for hydrocarbons. BIOCHEMISTRY is the subdivision in which the compounds and chemical reactions involved in processes of living systems are studied.

PHYSICAL CHEMISTRY deals with the structure of matter and the energy changes that occur during physical and chemical changes of matter. This field provides a theoretical basis for the chemical observations of the other subdivisions. ANALYTICAL CHEMISTRY is concerned with the identification of chemical substances, the determination of the amounts of substances present in a mixture, and the separation of mixtures into their individual components.

Special subdivisions of chemistry are now recognized that account for knowledge at the interface of chemistry and other physical sciences. For example, recent research has involved the chemical origin of life—reactions between simple molecules at low pressures to form such complex organic molecules as proteins found in living organisms.

Astrochemistry is the interdisciplinary physical science that studies the origin and interaction of the chemical constituents, especially INTERSTELLAR MATTER, in the universe. GEOCHEMISTRY is concerned with the chemical aspects of geology—for instance, the improvement of ore processing, coal utilization, shale oil recovery—and the use of chemicals to extract oil from wells that are considered dry by ordinary standards.

Nuclear chemistry deals with natural and induced transformations of the atomic nucleus. Studies in this field now center on the safe and efficient use of nuclear

Controlling, analyzing, and measuring chemical changes are among the principal jobs of a research chemist.

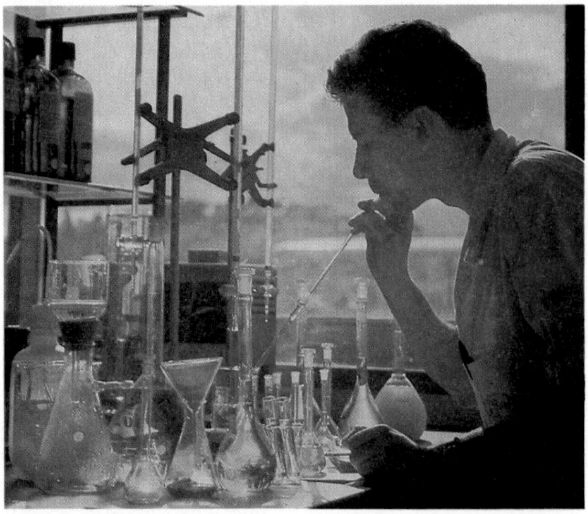

power and the disposal of nuclear wastes. Radiochemistry deals with radioactive ISOTOPES of chemical elements and the utilization of those isotopes to further the understanding of chemical and biochemical systems. Environmental chemistry is a subdivision that has as its subject the impact of various elements and compounds on the ecosphere.

Tools of Chemistry

Chemistry is a precise laboratory science, and the equipment of a chemical laboratory is usually involved with measurement. BALANCES are used to measure mass, pipettes and burettes to measure volume, and THERMOMETERS to measure temperature changes. Advances in electronics and computer technology have enabled the development of scientific instruments that determine the chemical properties, structure, and content of substances accurately and precisely.

Most modern chemical instrumentation has three primary components: a source of energy, a sample compartment within which a substance is subjected to the energy, and some sort of detector to determine the effect of the energy on the sample. An X-ray diffractometer, for instance, enables the chemist to determine the arrangement of atoms, ions, and molecules that constitute crystals by means of scattering X rays. Most modern laboratories contain ultraviolet, visible, and infrared spectrophotometers, which use light of various wavelengths on gaseous or liquid samples. By such a means the chemist can determine the ELECTRON CONFIGURATION and the arrangement of atoms in molecules. A nuclear magnetic resonance spectrometer subjects a sample in a strong magnetic field to radio frequency radiation (see Nuclear Magnetic Resonance Spectroscopy under SPECTROSCOPY). The absorption of this energy by the sample gives the chemist information about the bonding within molecules. Other instruments include mass spectrometers (see MASS SPECTROMETRY), which use electrons as an energy source, and differential thermal analyzers, which use heat.

An entirely different class of instruments are those which use CHROMATOGRAPHY to separate complex mixtures into their components. Chemists are also using extremely short pulses of LASER light to investigate the atomic and molecular processes taking place in chemical reactions at the microsecond level. These and other devices generate so much data that chemists frequently must use computers to help analyze the results.

Impact on Society

Chemistry is closely associated with four basic needs of humans: food, clothing, shelter, and medical services. The applications of chemistry usually bring to mind industries engaged in the production of chemicals. A significant portion of the CHEMICAL INDUSTRY is engaged in the production of inorganic and organic chemicals, which are then used by other industries as reactants for their chemical processes. In the United States the great majority of the leading chemicals being produced are inorganic, and their manufacture is a multibillion dollar industry.

The chemistry of polymers—large molecules made up of simple repeating units linked together by chemical bonds (see POLYMERIZATION)—includes PLASTICS, RESINS, natural and synthetic RUBBER, SYNTHETIC FIBERS, and protective coatings. The growth of this segment of chemistry has been phenomenal since the late 1930s. The fabrication of natural rubber and coatings (paints, varnishes, lacquers, and enamels) derived from natural agricultural products has been a mainstay of the chemical industry for more than 150 years.

The search for new ENERGY sources and the improvement of existing ones are in many ways chemical problems (see FUEL). At the heart of the PETROLEUM INDUSTRY is refining crude hydrocarbons into such products as gasoline and PETROCHEMICALS. The utilization of nuclear power depends heavily on the chemical preparation and reprocessing of fuel, the treatment and disposal of nuclear waste, and the problems of corrosion and heat transfer. The conversion and storage of SOLAR ENERGY as electrical energy is primarily a chemical process, and the development of FUEL CELLS is based on either chemical or electrochemical technology (see ELECTROCHEMISTRY).

Chemical research has been the basis of the pharmaceutical industry's production of DRUGS. The controlled introduction of specific chemicals into the body assists in the diagnosis, treatment, and often the cure of illness. Chemotherapy is a prime treatment in combating CANCER.

Tremendous agricultural gains have been achieved since about 1940 as a result mainly of farmers' use of chemical FERTILIZERS and pesticides (see PESTICIDES AND PEST CONTROL). Other chemical industries include SOAP and DETERGENT production; food processing; and the production of glass, paper, metals, and photographic supplies.

Specialized Uses. Outside the mainstream of what is traditionally considered chemistry is research that supports other professions. Chemistry is used by museums in ART CONSERVATION AND RESTORATION, the dating of objects (see RADIOMETRIC AGE-DATING), and the uncovering of frauds. Forensic chemists work in crime laboratories, carrying out tests to assist law-enforcement agencies (see FORENSIC SCIENCE). Toxicologists study the potentially adverse effects of chemicals on biological systems (see TOXICOLOGY), as do those involved in industrial hygiene. The chemistry involved in sanitary engineering and sewage treatment has come to be of major importance to society as populations increase and environmental concerns intensify.

Problems. Through the use of chemistry and related technology, chemical substances have been produced that either immediately or eventually are harmful to humans, animals, and the environment. Pollution is not a new problem, but the combination of a rapidly growing chemical industry and the use of sophisticated detection devices has brought the extent of pollution to the public's attention (see POLLUTION, ENVIRONMENTAL).

The discharge and disposal of industrial waste products into the atmosphere and water supply have caused grave concern about environmental deterioration (see POLLUTANTS, CHEMICAL). The repeated exposure of workers to some toxic chemicals at their jobs has caused long-range health problems (see DISEASES, OCCUPATIONAL). In addition, the use of some pesticides and herbicides can cause long-term toxicity, the effects of which are still only partially understood. The safe storage and disposal of CHEMICAL AND BIOLOGICAL WARFARE agents and nuclear waste (see NUCLEAR ENERGY) continue to be a serious problem. An advance in chemical technology almost always involves some trade-off with regard to an alteration of the environment.

Challenges and Trends. Much of the future of chemistry will lie in providing answers to such technological problems as the creation of new sources of energy and the eradication of disease, famine, and environmental pollution. The improvement of the safety of existing chemical products, for example, pesticides, is another challenge. Research into the chemical complexities of the human body may reveal new insights into a variety of diseases and dysfunctions. The improvement of industrial processes will serve to minimize the use of energy and raw materials, thereby diminishing negative environmental effects.

chemistry, history of

chemistry, history of Humans began to practice chemistry—the transformation of material things—in prehistoric times, beginning with the use of fire. Primitive humans used fire to produce such chemical transformations as the burning of wood, the cooking of food, and the firing of pottery and bricks, and later to work with such ores as copper, silver, and gold. As civilization developed in China, Mesopotamia, and Egypt, artisans performed further transformations to produce a variety of dyes, drugs, glazes, glasses, perfumes, and metals.

Early theoretical explanations of chemical phenomena were generally magical and mythological in character. The ancient Greeks added little to the chemical practice that they inherited from older and neighboring civilizations, but they did refine the theoretical explanations of transformations observed in the artisans' shops and in the environment.

ARISTOTLE, in the 4th century BC, formulated a theory that dominated scientific thinking for almost 2,000 years. He postulated the existence of four elements: fire (hot and dry), air (hot and wet), earth (cold and dry), and water (cold and wet). All material things were viewed as different combinations of these four elements. LEUCIPPUS and DEMOCRITUS proposed that all matter coalesced out of indivisible atoms moving rapidly and at random in a void.

ALCHEMY, the next major phase of the history of chemistry, developed in Alexandria, Egypt, and combined aspects of Greek philosophy, Oriental artisanship, and religious mysticism. Its main objective was the transformation of base metals into gold. In the 4th and 5th centuries, the emigrant Nestorians brought the craftsmanship of Egyptian artisans to the Arabs in Anatolia. This Arabic alchemy came into Western Europe between the 11th and 16th centuries through Sicily and Spain. The mystical ideas so introduced were accompanied by practical advances in chemical procedures, such as distillation, and by the discovery of new metals and compounds.

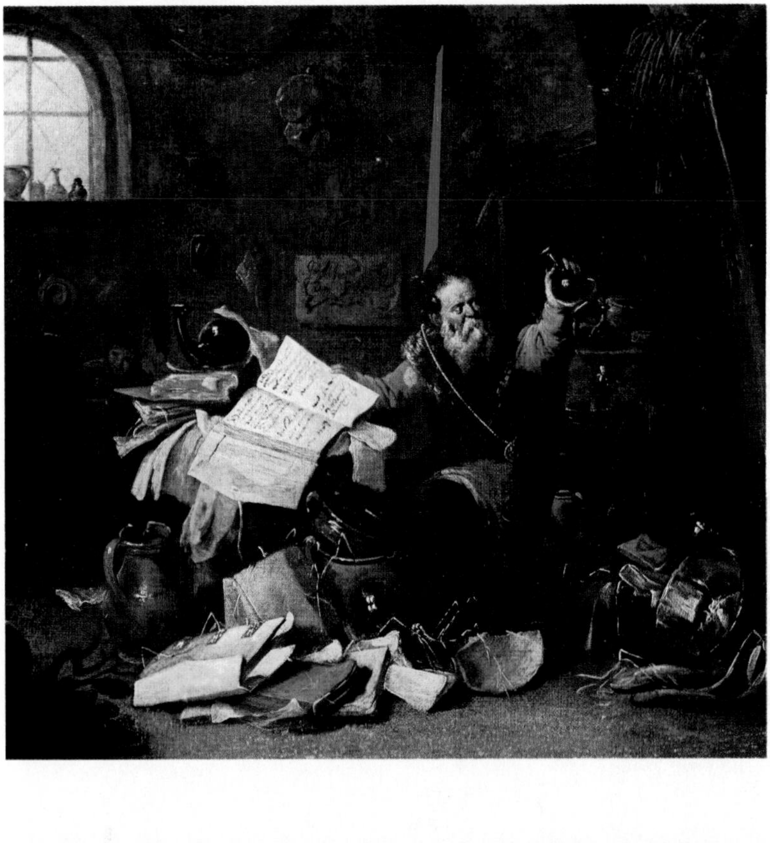

(Left) *Alchemy was the forerunner of chemistry; many of the basic techniques and tools of modern chemistry were developed in the alchemist's workshop. (Galleria Palatina, Florence.)*

(Below) *Antoine Lavoisier, a founder of modern chemistry, explained oxygen's role in combustion (1772). The first to distinguish between elements and compounds, Lavoisier initiated the modern system of chemical nomenclature.*

(Right) *Michael Faraday proposed the basic laws of electrolysis in 1834. In pioneering the field of electrochemistry, Faraday coined many of its terms, including* ion *and* electrode.

(Below) *The English chemist John Dalton developed the atomic theory in the early 1800s. His work led to the discovery of the law of partial pressures, or Dalton's law.*

The art of METALLURGY became more sophisticated, and chemicals were introduced into medical practice by PARACELSUS in the 16th century.

Seventeenth and Eighteenth Centuries

At the beginning of the 17th century chemistry became recognized as a science. During this century many new compounds were prepared by distilling animal and vegetable materials, and the PHLOGISTON THEORY was proposed by Georg Ernst STAHL as a unified explanation of combustion and calcination (rusting): when a substance burned or a metal was converted into calx (rusted), a proposed substance known as phlogiston was lost.

Refined Techniques. The invention of the pneumatic trough and the balance stimulated the development of chemistry in the 18th century. The pneumatic trough, filled with water or mercury and containing an inverted vessel also filled with water or mercury, permitted easy collection, transfer, and study of gases. Joseph Black discovered carbon dioxide (1756), and Karl SCHEELE (1772) and Joseph PRIESTLEY (1774) discovered oxygen, using the pneumatic trough. The balance was used effectively by Antoine LAVOISIER, at the end of the 18th century, to disprove the phlogiston theory and establish the true nature of combustion, calcination, and biological respiration.

Refined Theory. Lavoisier demonstrated that the process of combustion was the reaction of oxygen with carbonaceous material to form carbon dioxide and water, and that respiration was biological combustion. More generally, Lavoisier defined a chemical ELEMENT as a substance that could not be decomposed into simpler substances by heat or chemical reaction. A compound was defined as a combination of two or more elements in a definite proportion by weight. This innovative concept placed chemistry on a quantitative basis.

The atomic theory of John DALTON, at the beginning of the 19th century, further extended Lavoisier's theories. Dalton assumed that each element was composed of very small particles, called ATOMS, which have a characteristic weight, and that chemical reactions resulted from the combination or reshuffling of atoms.

In 1869, Dmitry Mendeleyev formulated the periodic law, which states that the chemical properties of all elements are related to their atomic weights. When Mendeleyev arranged a chart of the elements according to increasing atomic weight, he found that elements with similar properties recur periodically.

Nineteenth and Early Twentieth Century

Discovery of New Elements and Their Systematization. During the first half of the 19th century new elements were discovered at an increasing rate. Michael FARADAY showed that during ELECTROLYSIS the amount of current necessary to liberate an EQUIVALENT WEIGHT (combining weight) of an element was the same for all elements. At the First International Chemical Congress (1860) at Karlsruhe, Germany, Stanislao CANNIZZARO showed how the hypothesis of Amadeo AVOGADRO—that equal volumes of gases at the same temperature and pressure contain the same number of molecules—could be used to determine MOLECULAR WEIGHTS and ATOMIC WEIGHTS. The understanding of atomic weight was extended by the formulation in 1869 by Dmitry MENDELEYEV and in 1871 by Lothar Meyer of the PERIODIC TABLE, which systematized the large number of elements according to their atomic weights and correlated their physical and chemical properties.

Theories of Chemical Bonding. During the first half of the 19th century, new carbon compounds were being isolated, purified, and characterized. The then-accepted theories of chemical bonding were found unable to explain these compounds. The confusion was enhanced by the failure to distinguish among atomic, equivalent (combining), and molecular weights. It became apparent, however, that a given type of atom could bind only a fixed number of other atoms or radicals: hydrogen, one; oxygen, two; and nitrogen, three. Friedrich KEKULE VON STRADONITZ and A. S. Couper (1831–92) proposed that carbon not only could bind four atoms but also could bond with other carbon atoms to form chains and rings. The number of such bonds was called the VALENCE of the element.

Valence theory led to the structural theory of ORGANIC CHEMISTRY expounded by Aleksandr Butlerov. This theory explained the differences between two compounds, such as dimethyl ether and ethyl alcohol, having the same composition, molecular weight, and molecular formula (in this case, C_2H_6O), but markedly different chemical properties, by assigning them different structural formulas (here, CH_3OCH_3 and C_2H_5OH).

In 1897, Joseph John Thomson discovered the electron and suggested that the atoms of all matter contain these subatomic particles. He won the Nobel Prize for physics in 1906 for his work on the conduction of electricity through gases.

Marcelin Berthelot, a founder of thermochemistry, measured the heat produced or absorbed in various chemical reactions and coined the terms exothermic *and* endothermic *to describe the reactions. He also synthesized many compounds, helping to disprove the theory that a special vital force, or life force, was necessary to produce organic substances.*

In 1874, Jacobus VAN'T HOFF (1852–1911) and Joseph Le Bel extended these formulas into three dimensions, opening up the new field of STEREOCHEMISTRY. By the end of the 19th century, organic chemistry had not only acquired a comprehensive theory of structure but had also developed new methods for the synthesis of dyes, perfumes, explosives, and medicines. The starting materials for these syntheses were obtained from the coal-tar industry.

Contributions of Physics. During the 19th century, chemistry developed for the most part independently of physics, where progress was being made in mechanics, electricity, magnetism, thermodynamics, and optics. Nevertheless, there were interactions between the two fields. Electrolysis and chemical batteries involved electricity. Some new elements were detected by spectroscopy, notably by Robert BUNSEN. In 1884 Svante ARRHENIUS formulated the theory of electrolytic dissociation. Thermodynamics was applied to chemistry during the middle of the century in the measurement of heats of reaction by Germain Hess, Marcelin BERTHELOT, and Julius Thomson (1826–1909). J. Willard GIBBS, Jr., developed the thermodynamics of heterogeneous equilibria and formulated (1876) the phase rule. He also formulated the discipline of statistical mechanics.

Chemical Analysis through Spectroscopy. The ability to analyze gases spectroscopically by passing electricity through them proved to be a major new analytical tool. Electrolysis of gases had not been possible until the invention of an efficient vacuum pump to provide low pressure gases in a glass tube. When an electric potential is applied to such a gas it becomes conductive and produces visible radiation that can be analyzed with a spectroscope.

The development of the gas discharge tube was essential to the development of modern physics and chemistry. The electric charge carriers inside the discharge tube were found to include both positive (canal) rays and negative (cathode) rays. The positive rays were composed

In 1895 the German physicist Wilhelm Conrad Roentgen discovered X rays—shortwave, electromagnetic radiation that can pass through matter. This important discovery enabled scientists to extend their study of the structure of the atom. Roentgen received (1901) the first Nobel Prize for physics.

of different ionized atoms when different gases were in the discharge tube, but the cathode rays (see CATHODE-RAY TUBE) were always the same no matter what residual gas was in the tube. The cathode rays were identified as electrons by Sir Joseph John THOMSON in 1897. Using an appropriate arrangement of magnetic and electric fields, Francis ASTON constructed a mass spectroscope, which he used to separate ions of the positive rays according to their atomic weight. In this way, not only were atoms of different species separated from each other, but also some elements were found to consist of atoms with differing weights (ISOTOPES).

Structure of the Atom. In 1913, Niels BOHR proposed his atomic theory for the hydrogen atom. This theory postulated that the hydrogen atom consisted of a positive massive nucleus and an electron traveling in definite discrete orbits around it.

Despite its many virtues, the Bohr theory had several shortcomings, particularly a lack of self-consistency. In 1925, Louis DE BROGLIE proposed that electrons have wave properties; Clinton Davisson and Lester Germer (1896–1972) in the United States and Sir George Thomson in England confirmed this by showing diffraction of electrons by crystals. Erwin SCHRÖDINGER developed this concept into wave mechanics, which was modified by Paul DIRAC, Werner HEISENBERG, and John VON NEUMANN. Other important developments were the formulation of the EXCLUSION PRINCIPLE (1925) by Wolfgang PAULI and the formulation of the UNCERTAINTY PRINCIPLE (1927) by Heisenberg. These developments constituted the new quantum theory.

The gas discharge tube also led to new knowledge about the structure of matter. In 1895, Wilhelm ROENTGEN discovered a penetrating invisible radiation (X RAY) that was emitted from the discharge tube. The characteristics of this radiation were determined by the electrode in the discharge tube. In 1913, Henry Moseley used X-ray spectroscopy to show that each element could be assigned a characteristic integer, the atomic number, which was equal to the positive charge on the nucleus and also corresponded to the element's position in the periodic table.

The first half of the 20th century was marked by far-reaching discoveries concerning the nucleus that began the age of radioactivity. Marie and Pierre CURIE discovered the radioactive elements polonium and radium. Sir Ernest RUTHERFORD formulated the spontaneous nuclear disintegration theory of natural RADIOACTIVITY. In 1919, Rutherford produced the first artificial transmutation of elements, realizing the dream of alchemists. By bombarding nitrogen with alpha particles, he transformed the nitrogen into oxygen and the alpha particles into protons. This opened up the new field of nuclear chemistry. In 1932, Sir James Chadwick discovered the neutron, which in turn led to the discovery of artificial radioactivity by Irène and Frédéric JOLIOT-CURIE, to the synthesis of transuranium elements, and to the realization of nuclear fission. The periodic table was extended to atomic number 103 by Glenn SEABORG.

Recent Advances

Inorganic Chemistry. World War II research spurred important advances in INORGANIC CHEMISTRY. The atomic weapon and nuclear power projects intensified studies of uranium and the transuranium elements, the chemistry of fluorine compounds, and the metallurgy of fuel element components such as zirconium. Rare earths were separated in pure state by CHROMATOGRAPHY and were made available for chemical study. Neil Bartlett (1932–) prepared compounds of inert gases.

With the development of solid state devices, modern electronics has become highly dependent on inorganic chemistry. The growth of ultrapure single crystals of germanium, silicon, and other semiconductors has become an industry, and elegant techniques are used to produce thin films and microelectronic circuits on single-crystal chips.

Marie Curie and her husband, Pierre, investigated the nature of radioactivity in pitchblende. This research led to their discovery of the radioactive elements polonium and radium in 1890. Along with Antoine Becquerel, who discovered the radioactive property of uranium, the Curies were awarded the 1903 Nobel Prize for physics. Marie Curie also won the Nobel Prize for chemistry in 1911.

William Henry Bragg invented (1913) the first X-ray spectrometer, a device that measures X-ray wavelengths, to examine the atomic structure of crystals.

The study of COORDINATION CHEMISTRY has led to extensive investigation of organometallic compounds, which link the chemistry of inorganic and organic materials (see COORDINATION COMPOUNDS). Organometallic compounds have found extensive use as polymers, plastics (silicones), antioxidants, insecticides, herbicides, and catalysts.

Organic Chemistry. Before World War II, organic chemistry was based on the coal-tar industry, but after the war petroleum became the major source of organic compounds. Petrochemicals are now the raw materials for the plastics, synthetic fibers, and solvent industries. Also, numerous valuable new pharmaceuticals have been synthesized, notably vitamin C (1933), the first sulfa drug (prontosil, 1932), and the ANTIBIOTIC penicillin (1957). Outstanding contributions to the field of organic synthesis were made by R. B. Woodward and Sir Alexander Todd. The applications of organic chemistry to BIOCHEMISTRY are profound and have led recently to substantial advances in the latter field.

Physical Chemistry. PHYSICAL CHEMISTRY, a discipline on the border between physics and chemistry, is concerned with the macroproperties of chemical substances and the changes they undergo when subjected to pressure, temperature, light, and electric and magnetic forces. It also investigates changes produced by dissolution in a solvent or chemical reactivity.

Subjects of particular study in the 20th century have included adsorption of gases, by Irving LANGMUIR; catalysis, by Giulio Natta and Karl Ziegler; and the kinetics of chemical reactions, by Sir Cyril Hinshelwood and Nikolai Semenov. The kinetic theory of gases, the liquid state, solution theory, electrochemistry, and thermodynamics were studied by Lars Onsager. Ilya PRIGOGINE researched the areas of phase equilibrium, photochemistry, and the electric and magnetic properties of substances. The low-temperature phenomenon called SUPERCONDUCTIVITY was first observed in 1911; in the 1980s, scientists discovered materials that become superconductive at relatively high temperatures.

Analytical Chemistry and Structure Determination. During the last half of the 20th century, instrumental methods have replaced the standard gravimetric and volumetric procedures in ANALYTICAL CHEMISTRY. As few as a hundred atoms of a substance can be analyzed using neutron activation, mass spectrometry, or fluorescence spectrometry. The separation of complex mixtures has been simplified by a variety of chromatographic methods.

Several techniques have been developed for structure determination and identification. X-ray diffraction, due to the work of Max von Laue and William H. BRAGG, allows determination of the arrangement of atoms in crystals. Study of the structure of organic compounds has been facilitated by ultraviolet, visible, and infrared SPECTROSCOPY; mass spectrometry; and nuclear magnetic resonance spectrometry. Electron paramagnetic resonance has proved valuable in the study of transition metals.

The scanning tunneling microscope, a type of ELECTRON MICROSCOPE, has revolutionized the study of surfaces and made it possible to manipulate matter at the atomic level. To observe the details of rapid chemical reactions, researchers use lasers that emit short pulses of light.

Thus chemistry has become a highly sophisticated branch of science, involving complex apparatuses for experimental work, a highly refined theoretical approach in the interpretation of results, and an impact on every segment of the world economy.

Chemnitz [chem'-nits] Chemnitz, known as Karl-Marx-Stadt from 1953 to 1990, is a city in Saxony, in east central Germany. It lies on the Chemnitz River at the foot of the Erzgebirge (Ore Mountains), about 70 km (43 mi) southeast of Leipzig. The population is 313,238 (1988 est.). Long known for its textiles, the city also manufactures automobiles, machine tools, electrical equipment, and furniture and is a transportation hub.

Originally settled by the Slavic Wends, the city began to flourish as a textile center in the 12th century. Heavily damaged during the Thirty Years' War (1618-48), it recovered its prosperity with the advent of cotton manufacturing. In the 19th century, Chemnitz pioneered in machine construction. Although damage during World War II was severe, a few historic buildings remain or have been reconstructed, including several Gothic churches and the 15th-century town hall. A 12th-century Benedictine monastery houses the city museum.

Cheney, Richard B. [chay'-nee] Richard Bruce Cheney, b. Lincoln, Nebr., Jan. 30, 1941, became U.S. secretary of defense under President George Bush in March 1989. Cheney, a Republican, served (1975–77) as chief of staff to President Gerald Ford. Regarded as a conservative and a pragmatist, he was elected to Congress from Wyoming in 1978 and reelected five times. As secretary of defense, Cheney was instrumental in the formulation of U.S. military policy in the Persian Gulf following the Iraqi invasion and occupation of Kuwait in 1990 and the subsequent successful attack on the Iraqi military by U.S. and coalition military forces.

Cheng-chou see ZHENGZHOU

Cheng Ho see ZHENG HE

Chengdu (Ch'eng-tu) [chuhng-doo] Chengdu, the capital and second largest city (1988 est. pop., 2,690,000) of Sichuan (Szechwan) province, China, is situated in a fertile irrigated lowland. In addition to handicrafts, the city has such modern industries as electronics and precision-machinery manufacturing. Chengdu served as the capital of the Kingdom of Shu in the 3d century BC.

Chénier, André [shay-neeay'] The only substantial French poet of the 18th century, André Marie de Chénier was born on Oct. 30, 1762, in Constantinople, where his father was French consul. Brought up in France, he became an opponent of the extremists of the French Revolution and died on the guillotine on July 25, 1794. At that time only two of his poems had been published. The rest of his work, some of it sketchy or fragmentary, began to appear 25 years later. In the poems that make up his *Idylles, Élégies,* and *Bucoliques*, Chénier revealed himself as a gifted poet who embraced the classical ideal.

chenille plant [shuh-neel'] Chenille plant is the common name of a shrub, *Acalypha hispida,* of the spurge family, Euphorbiaceae, that may have first been native to the Malay Archipelago. It is deciduous and grows up to 4.6 m (15 ft) tall. Flowers are dense; the hanging female spikes are red or purple. The chenille plant is grown in southern U.S. gardens or in greenhouses in the north. Its long red spikes resemble those of the amaranth.

Chennault, Claire L. [shuh-nawlt'] Claire Lee Chennault, b. Commerce, Tex., Sept. 6, 1890, d. July 27, 1958, a general in the U.S. Army Air Force, became famous in World War II as the leader of the Flying Tigers. He served in the Army Air Service (later Army Air Corps) from 1918 to 1937, when he retired to become air advisor to CHIANG KAI-SHEK during the Second SINO-JAPANESE WAR. In 1941 he organized in China the American Voluntary Group, a force of American fighter pilots known as the Flying Tigers. After America's entry into World War II, Chennault was recalled into the U.S. Army Air Corps and headed the air task force in China. He retired as a major general in 1945.

Gen. Claire Lee Chennault, who retired from the U.S. Army in 1937 to organize China's defenses against the invading Japanese, is best remembered as the commander of the Flying Tigers, an air force composed of American volunteers.

Cheops see KHUFU

Chephren see KHAFRE, KING OF EGYPT

Cherbourg [shair-boor'] Cherbourg is a town in Normandy in northwestern France. It is in the department of Manche on the English Channel and has a population of 30,112 (1982). A naval base and seaport, Cherbourg includes coal, timber, and shipbuilding among its industries. England and France vied for control of the city until Charles VII of France secured it in 1450. The harbor opens on a wide bay sheltered naturally on three sides. A fortified breakwater to the north was started by Louis XVI in 1776 and was completed in 1846. Cherbourg's extensive port facilities were badly damaged in World War II, but have been reconstructed.

Cherenkov, Pavel Alekseyevich [chuh-reng'-kawf, pah'-vil ul-yik-syay'-yeh-vich] The Soviet physicist Pavel Alekseyevich Cherenkov, b. July 19 (N.S.), 1904, is known for his discovery of the radiation produced by certain high-energy particles traveling faster than light in a transparent medium. For this discovery he shared the 1958 Nobel Prize for physics with I. M. Frank and I. Y. Tamm, who explained the phenomenon theoretically. Chevenkov first observed the bluish glow associated with fast-moving beta rays decelerated in a transparent medium in 1934.

Cherenkov radiation [chuh-reng'-kawf] Cherenkov radiation is the electromagnetic radiation emitted by a charged particle moving through a medium with a velocity greater than the velocity of light in that medium. If a charged particle is accelerated to a velocity only slightly less than the speed of light in a vacuum and then injected into a DIELECTRIC medium such as a block of glass or plastic, its velocity can exceed the velocity of light in that medium, and Cherenkov radiation is emitted.

The properties of Cherenkov radiation make it useful in detectors for fast-charged particles. These detectors, called Cherenkov counters, consist of a mass of transparent material with a high refractive index, such as glass, plastic, or water. The light flashes are recorded with photomultipliers. The speed of the detected particles can be determined from the emission angle θ.

Chernenko, Konstantin [chair-nyen'-koh] Konstantin Ustinovich Chernenko, b. Sept. 24 (N.S.), 1911, d. Mar. 10, 1985, was general secretary of the Soviet Union's Communist party, and effective head of state, from February 1984 until his death. Born into a Siberian peasant family, Chernenko served in the Red Army and later became active in party affairs, serving in various regional posts and becoming closely associated with future party chief Leonid Brezhnev. In 1956 he was promoted to head of the propaganda department of the party's Central Committee in Moscow, becoming a candidate member of the committee itself in 1965 and a full member in 1971. In 1978 he became a member of the Politburo and was considered likely to succeed Brezhnev when the latter died in 1982; the party leader's post, however, went to Yuri V. ANDROPOV instead.

Chernenko took over when Andropov died two years later. His initial speeches stressed continued efforts to rationalize economic administration and hinted at better relations with the West. No discernible reforms or changes were initiated during his tenure, however. He died after only 13 months in office and was succeeded by Mikhail GORBACHEV.

Chernobyl [chair-naw'-bil] The Soviet Union's Chernobyl nuclear power plant, about 130 km (80 mi) north of Kiev, became the site of the world's worst nuclear-reactor disaster on Apr. 26, 1986, when the plant's No. 4 reactor exploded. The accident occurred while an experiment was being conducted with the graphite-moderated reactor running but its emergency water-cooling system turned off. A series of miscalculations permitted neutron buildup in one area of the core, where the nuclear reaction suddenly went out of control. The power surge shattered the fuel. This and a second, steam-induced explosion blew the lid off the reactor, whose containment structure was not designed for such pressures. A third, chemical explosion followed, and scattered fragments caused further local fires.

The disaster killed 31 persons immediately or shortly thereafter and caused the hospitalization of about 500 others. Over the next few days, persons living within 30 km (18.5 mi) of the site were evacuated. The force of the explosion and fire carried much of the radioactivity away from the site to relatively high altitudes, where it spread across the Northern Hemisphere. The heaviest fallout descended on the western Soviet Union and portions of Europe, where preventive steps were taken by several nations to protect food supplies. Data on worldwide effects of this fallout remain inconclusive.

Reactor No. 4 was entombed in concrete, and the other reactors were placed back in operation. In a 1987 trial, six plant officials were convicted for gross safety violations.

chernozem see SOIL

Cherokee [chair'-uh-kee] The Cherokee are a tribe of North American Indians that formerly inhabited the mountainous region of the western Carolinas, northern Georgia, and eastern Tennessee. An Iroquoian-speaking people, they originally lived near the Great Lakes, but after defeat by Iroquois and DELAWARE tribes (see IROQUOIS LEAGUE), they migrated to the Southeast, eventually becoming the largest and most powerful group in that region. Their traditional culture included maize agriculture, settled villages, and well-developed ceremonialism.

The Cherokee aided the British during the American Revolution and continued their hostilities against the Americans until 1794. Thereafter, influenced by white culture, they adopted plow agriculture, animal husbandry, and cotton and wool industries, as well as slavery. A syllabic alphabet was invented (*c.*1820) by SEQUOYA, and in 1827 the Cherokee established a constitutional form of government.

A series of fraudulent, land-acquiring treaties were imposed on the Cherokee in the 1830s. The Treaty of New Echota (1835), in which a small tribal faction sold 2.83 million ha (7 million acres) of Cherokee land, required their removal westward within 3 years. The vast majority of the Cherokee Nation repudiated this document, but under Gen. Winfield SCOTT, most remaining Cherokee were driven from their land and forcibly marched to Arkansas and Indian Territory (now Oklahoma) in 1838–39. About 4,000 of the more than 15,000 Cherokee involved died of disease and exposure.

In Indian Territory, they joined the CHICKASAW, CHOCTAW, CREEK, and SEMINOLE to form the so-called FIVE CIVILIZED TRIBES. Tribal lands were lost in the 1860s, after the Five Tribes sided with the South during the Civil War, and again in the early 1880s, when tribal ownership of lands was abolished. When Indian Territory became the state of Oklahoma in 1907, all tribal lands were opened for white settlement.

In the 1980s, 43,000 persons of Cherokee descent lived in eastern Oklahoma, and about 6,000 in North Carolina.

Sequoya, a Cherokee Indian, devised (c.1820) a syllabary, a set of 85 or 86 written characters representing each syllable of the spoken Cherokee language, and brought literacy to his people. The giant sequoia tree is named for him.

cherry Cherries are the fruit of certain species of trees belonging to the genus *Prunus* in the rose family, Rosaceae. This genus also includes the plum, peach, apricot, and almond. Cherries are native to Europe, Asia, and North America, and more than 1,000 varieties are grown in the United States alone. They range from the chokecherry and the bitter cherry to the two broad groups that are most widely cultivated: sweet cherries, most of which are sold fresh or canned, and sour cherries, which are processed for pie filling and jams and jellies. Sour cherries are generally hardier than sweet cherries and are self-fertile; most sweet-cherry trees must be cross-pollinated with other varieties in order to bear fruit abundantly. Cherries are globular smooth-skinned fruits with a single pit or stone, and they range from 6 to 25 mm (¼ to 1 in) in diameter. Most cultivated cherries are bright red in color when ripe. Many kinds of cherry trees, particularly the wild black cherry, are highly valued for their beautiful wood. Japanese cherries are grown as ornamentals for their attractive flowers.

The cherry tree is prized for its fragrant blossoms and its fruit, although some trees—such as the Japanese varieties in Washington, D.C.—are grown solely for ornament.

Cherry Orchard, The *The Cherry Orchard* (1904), a four-act play subtitled a comedy by its Russian author Anton CHEKHOV, describes the loss of a family estate sold at auction through the helplessness of its owners. So emotionally shallow are these distressed gentlefolk that the anticipated loss of their home does not seem to affect them deeply. Only secondarily the analysis of a decaying class, the play evokes sympathy and amusement.

chert and flint [churt] Chert is a hard, extremely dense, dull-to-semiglossy SEDIMENTARY ROCK consisting predominantly of silica (QUARTZ), with occasional impurities such as calcite, iron oxides, clay minerals, and the organic remains of marine organisms made of silica, amounting to about 10 percent. Because it is so finely crystalline, a characteristic of chert is its conchoidal fracture; thus, it breaks like glass into smooth, curved flakes. It may be white or one of various shades of gray, green, pink, red, yellow, brown, or black. Chert occurs principally as nodules or CONCRETIONS in limestone, dolomites, and chalk beds. Sometimes, however, it forms a bedded or layered deposit or a thin, wedgelike discontinuous layer; such beds are commonly associated with volcanic deposition.

Flint, a dark-colored form of chert, is a hard, microcrystalline quartz that occurs widely in sedimentary rocks. The substance was used by primitive peoples for tools and weapons, as well as for striking sparks to start their fires.

Some cherts are made up largely of spines and shells of silica secreted by microscopic organisms such as DIATOMS, RADIOLARIANS, and SPONGES, or of their partly dissolved and reprecipitated remains. Other cherts are of inorganic origin. Some precipitated around HOT SPRINGS rich in silica, others formed when silica-bearing solutions replaced wood, limestone, shale, or other materials, and some are associated with volcanism.

Flint is the dark variety of chert that contains organic matter. It was a favored material of prehistoric humans, who used it (and chert in general) to make tools and weapons, because it would chip into sharp edges. Later, they discovered that flint gave off a spark when struck against some hard metals and could be used to start fires. Many geologists and archaeologists suggest that the term flint be discarded or used only to identify artifacts of prehistoric humans.

cherubim and seraphim see ANGEL

Cherubini, Luigi [kay-roo-bee'-nee] Maria Luigi Carlo Zenobio Salvatore Cherubini, b. Sept. 14, 1760, d. Mar. 15, 1842, was an Italian composer, theorist, author, and teacher and a leading conservative influence in a time of great change in music. After 1780 he composed operas, both serious and comic, for many years. In 1784, Cherubini went to London, where for one year he was composer to the king. In 1788 he settled in Paris and gradually developed a new, grander, and more serious operatic style, first in Italian, then in French. Because of disagreements with Napoleon, Cherubini went to Vienna in 1805, but returned to Paris in 1806 after Napoleon captured Vienna. After the political climate in France changed, Cherubini became superintendent of the King's Chapel and professor of composition and then director of the Paris Conservatory. His later compositions consist of church music, orchestral and chamber music, and a few operas. Musical fashions had shifted to the Romantic style, which Cherubini was unable to fully adopt, and most of his more than 400 compositions were forgotten until their rediscovery in the 20th century. *Les Deux Journées* (The Two Days) is considered his finest opera and influenced Beethoven's *Fidelio*.

Chesapeake A U.S. frigate, the *Chesapeake* was involved in an incident with the British man-of-war *Leopard* off Norfolk Roads, Va., on June 22, 1807. The British fired on the *Chesapeake*, boarded it, and seized four men alleged to be deserters. The *Chesapeake* was not fully armed at the time, but its commander, James Barron, was nonetheless court-martialed for not taking preventive action.

The incident sparked demands for war in the United States, but President Thomas Jefferson preferred to use diplomatic methods to secure reparation. British ships continued the practice of impressment (seizing alleged deserters), however, which was a major factor leading to the WAR OF 1812.

Chesapeake Bay Chesapeake Bay, in Maryland and Virginia, is the largest bay on the Atlantic coast of the United States. It is about 320 km (200 mi) long from north to south and from 5 to 40 km (3 to 25 mi) wide. The Susquehanna and the Potomac are the largest of its many tributary rivers and creeks. The bay is a shipping artery, and the bay cities of Norfolk, Va., and Baltimore, Md., are among the nation's leading ports. The Chesapeake and Delaware canal at the north end is part of the Atlantic Coastal Waterway. The Chesapeake Bay Bridge near Annapolis and the Chesapeake Bay Bridge Tunnel near Norfolk provide crossings. Waterfowl, fish, oysters, and crabs, long abundant, have been threatened by pollution in recent years. The Virginia colonist John SMITH explored the bay in 1608.

Chesapeake Bay retriever The Chesapeake Bay retriever is the only retriever and one of only a few breeds to have been developed in the United States. According to legend, an English ship with dogs aboard was shipwrecked on the Maryland shores of the Chesapeake Bay in 1807. The dogs were presented by the ship's crew to their rescuers, who were impressed with the dogs' retrieving abilities. The Chesapeake Bay retriever is almost certainly descended from English curly and flat-coated retrievers. By the end of the 19th century, the breed had been established in its present form—large, brown colored, and heavy coated. A water dog with an oily outercoat that sheds water, the Chesapeake is used primarily to retrieve ducks and geese from icy waters, but it is also used to hunt on land.

The Chesapeake Bay retriever, an American sporting dog, is considered the best cold-water retriever. An oily outercoat and woolly undercoat protect it from icy water.

The Chesapeake stands from 53 to 66 cm (21 to 26 in) high at the shoulder and weighs up to 34 kg (75 lb). A tough, intent dog, it retrieves enthusiastically but requires firm handling.

Cheshire Cheshire is a county in northwestern England between Liverpool and Manchester. It covers 2,330 km^2 (900 mi^2) and has a population of 955,800 (1988 est.). CHESTER is the county town. A rural plains area between the Pennine uplands and the mountains of northern Wales, Cheshire is drained by the rivers MERSEY, Dee, and Weaver. Potatoes and wheat are the main crops, and dairy farming is very important. Textiles are manufactured in several towns, and locomotive works are located at Crewe. Jodrell Bank Experimental Station has one of the world's largest radio telescopes.

The Romans built a fort at Chester in the first century AD. It was later part of the Anglo-Saxon kingdom of Mercia from 830 to the 10th century. The size of Cheshire was greatly reduced following the 1974 redistricting of British counties.

Chesnutt, Charles Waddell Charles Waddell Chesnutt, b. Cleveland, Ohio, June 20, 1858, d. Nov. 15, 1932, considered the first major black novelist in America, is best known for his works portraying the struggle against racial prejudice. In his twenties, Chesnutt was a school principal, and in 1887 was admitted to the Ohio bar. In August of that year, however, his story "The Goophered Grapevine" became the first piece by a black writer to be accepted by the *Atlantic Monthly,* and he decided on a literary career. His principal works are a biography of the abolitionist Frederick Douglass, stories collected in *The Conjure Woman* and *The Wife of His Youth and Other Stories of the Color Line* (both 1899), and the novels *The House Behind the Cedars* (1900), *The Marrow of Tradition* (1901), and *The Colonel's Dream* (1905).

chess Chess is a game for two people played on a square board of eight rows of eight squares each, alternately light and dark in color. The board is placed so that each player has a light square at the nearest right-hand corner. Each player begins with 16 pieces of one color, again either light or dark and referred to as black or white. In descending order of importance, they are one king, one queen, two rooks (or castles), two bishops, two knights, and eight pawns. The queen sits on a square of her own color at the start of the game.

Rules and Play

The object of chess is for one of the players to capture the other's king. When an opposing piece threatens a king, the king is said to be in check. Then the king must do one of the following: (1) capture the attacker; (2) move to safety; or (3) place one of its pieces on a square between the two, thus shielding the king from the attacking piece. When a check cannot be averted, the king is said to be captured, mated, or checkmated, and the game is over.

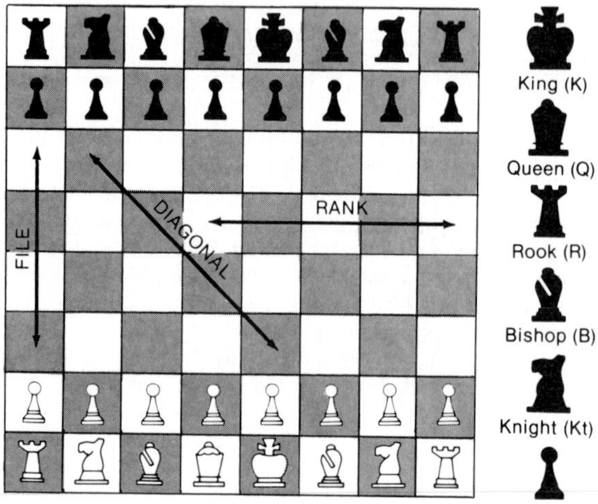

1

(Above and Right) *The chessboard* (1) *shows chess pieces, or chessmen, arranged as at the beginning of a game.* (2) *The queen, the most powerful piece, moves any number of squares on a file, diagonal, or rank.* (3) *The rook moves any number of squares on a file or rank. The bishop moves any number of squares on a diagonal, keeping always to the color square on which it starts. The king, like the queen, may move in any direction but only 1 square at a time, except when castling.* (4) *The knight's move is 2 squares on a file or rank, then 1 square to either side, or vice versa.* (5) *A pawn, on its first move, moves 1 or 2 squares in its file. Subsequent moves are only 1 square at a time and only forward. A pawn may capture only by moving 1 square ahead on a diagonal. Only the knight among the chessmen may jump over another piece or pawn in its path.* (2, 4) *Castling is a defensive move to protect the king, usually by placing it behind a rank of pawns and giving the rook control over a more central file. Castling may be done either to the king's side or the queen's side of the board.* (6) *In standard chess notation, every square on the chessboard has two designations, one for each player. The board must be positioned so that the corner square to each player's right is white. White always moves first.*

Each of the six kinds of pieces moves in a different way. A piece may move to any square if the square is unoccupied by one of its own pieces; if the opponent's piece occupying the square is captured, removed from the board, and replaced by the attacking piece; or if the move does not, except for the moves of a knight, cross a square occupied by one of either player's pieces.

The king can move one square in any direction (sideways, forward, backward, or diagonally), so long as the move does not place it in a square under attack by an enemy piece. The queen is the most powerful piece because it can move in a straight line in any direction for any unobstructed distance. The rook can move any distance, forward, backward, or sideways, provided the line is un-

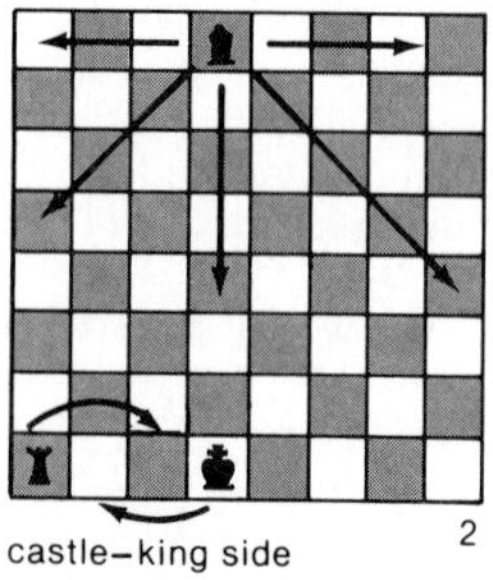

2

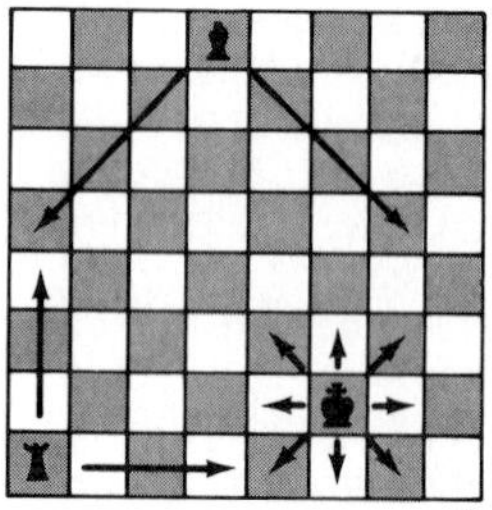

3

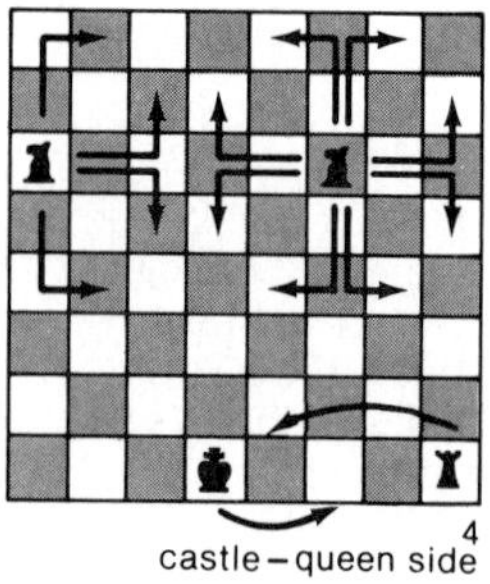

4

5

BLACK

QR1 QR8	QKt1 QKt8	QB1 QB8	Q1 Q8	K1 K8	KB1 KB8	KKt1 KKt8	KR1 KR8
QR2 QR7	QKt2 QKt7	QB2 QB7	Q2 Q7	K2 K7	KB2 KB7	KKt2 KKt7	KR2 KR7
QR3 QR6	QKt3 QKt6	QB3 QB6	Q3 Q6	K3 K6	KB3 KB6	KKt3 KKt6	KR3 KR6
QR4 QR5	QKt4 QKt5	QB4 QB5	Q4 Q5	K4 K5	KB4 KB5	KKt4 KKt5	KR4 KR5
QR5 QR4	QKt5 QKt4	QB5 QB4	Q5 Q4	K5 K4	KB5 KB4	KKt5 KKt4	KR5 KR4
QR6 QR3	QKt6 QKt3	QB6 QB3	Q6 Q3	K6 K3	KB6 KB3	KKt6 KKt3	KR6 KR3
QR7 QR2	QKt7 QKt2	QB7 QB2	Q7 Q2	K7 K2	KB7 KB2	KKt7 KKt2	KR7 KR2
QR8 QR1	QKt8 QKt1	QB8 QB1	Q8 Q1	K8 K1	KB8 KB1	KKt8 KKt1	KR8 KR1

WHITE

6

WORLD CHAMPIONSHIP

Year	Player	Country
Men's unofficial champions		
1843–51	Howard Staunton	England
1851–58	Adolf Anderssen	Germany
1858–62	Paul Morphy	USA
1862–66	Adolf Anderssen	Germany
1866–86	Wilhelm Steinitz	Austria
Men's challenge matches, world champions		
1886–94	Wilhelm Steinitz	Austria
1894–1921	Emanuel Lasker	Germany
1921–27	José Capablanca	Cuba
1927–35	Alexander Alekhine	France
1935–37	Max Euwe	Netherlands
1937–46	Alexander Alekhine	France
1946–48	Vacant	
Men's FIDE* cycles, world champions		
1948–57	Mikhail Botvinnik	USSR
1957–58	Vasily Smyslov	USSR
1958–60	Mikhail Botvinnik	USSR
1960–61	Mikhail Tahl	USSR
1961–63	Mikhail Botvinnik	USSR
1963–69	Tigran Petrosian	USSR
1969–72	Boris Spassky	USSR
1972–75	Robert Fischer	USA
1975–85	Anatoly Karpov	USSR
1985–	Gary Kasparov	USSR
Women's championship tournaments, world champions		
1927–44	Vera Menchik	Czechoslovakia
1944–50	Vacant	
1950–53	Ludmila Rudenko	USSR
Women's FIDE cycles, world champions		
1953–56	Elizaveta Bykova	USSR
1956–58	Olga Rubtsova	USSR
1958–62	Elizaveta Bykova	USSR
1962–78	Nona Gaprindashvili	USSR
1978–	Maya Chiburdandze	USSR

*FIDE: Fédération Internationale des Échecs.

obstructed by any other piece. The bishop moves diagonally (forward or backward) for any unobstructed distance, restricting itself to the diagonal lines of the same color as that on which it originally stood. The knight, in a single move, goes two squares in any direction, forward, backward, or sideways, then one more square at right angles to that, unaffected by intervening pieces. The pawn can move only in a forward line; on its opening move each pawn can move either one or two squares but can move only one square at a time thereafter.

Capturing is always optional, and all pieces except pawns capture other pieces by moving in the same way that they normally move. The pawn, however, instead of capturing in a forward direction, does so diagonally, advancing to either of the two occupied squares diagonally adjacent to and ahead of it and taking the piece on that square. A pawn also can capture another pawn *en passant,* or "in passing"; that is, if a pawn opens with its optional double move, it can be captured by an opposing pawn that could have captured it had it moved only one

The U.S. chess champion Bobby Fischer (right) *meets his Soviet opponent, Boris Spassky, in 1970. Although Fischer lost to Spasky then, he defeated Spassky in 1972 to become the first American to win an official world chess championship.*

square. The *en passant* capture must be executed immediately; it may not be made on any later turn. If a player's pawn reaches a square on the opponent's row of squares farthest from the first player, he or she asks for it to be replaced by a queen, rook, bishop, or knight, at the player's option, and it immediately assumes that piece's power.

Once during a game a player may make a move called castling, the purpose of which is to reposition the king onto a "safe" square and to shift a rook for offensive or defensive purposes. Castling is a simultaneous move of two pieces, the king and a rook; it is permissible only under the following circumstances: when the king and the rook have not moved off their original squares, the king is not in check, and the squares on the row between the king and the rook are vacant and no enemy piece is attacking any of the squares through which the king must move to castle. Castling is accomplished by first moving

UNITED STATES CHAMPIONS

Year	Player	Year	Player
1909–36	Frank Marshall	1978–80	Lubomir Kavalek
1936–44	Samuel Reshevsky	1980–81	Walter Browne; Larry Christiansen; Larry Evans
1944–46	Arnold Denker		
1946–48	Samuel Reshevsky	1981–83	Walter Browne; Yasser Seirawan
1948–51	Herman Steiner		
1951–54	Larry Evans	1983–84	Walter Browne; Larry Christiansen; Roman Dzindzichashvili
1954–57	Arthur Bisguier		
1957–61	Bobby Fischer		
1961–62	Larry Evans	1984–85	Lev Alburt
1963–67	Bobby Fischer	1986–87	Yasser Seirawan
1968–69	Larry Evans	1987–88	Joel Benjamin; Nick de Firmian
1969–72	Samuel Reshevsky		
1972–73	Robert Byrne	1988–90	Michael Wilder
1973–74	Lubomir Kavalek; John Grefe	1990–	Lev Alburt
1974–77	Walter Browne		

the king two squares in the direction of the rook, then placing the rook on the square passed over by the king. At no other time may the king move two squares.

History

Certain similarities exist between modern chess and an Indian game called *chaturanga,* which dates back to about the 6th century AD, and most scholars are of the opinion that chess itself originated in India about the 7th century AD. The modern era of chess, however, may be said to date back to about the 15th century, when the pieces gained their present form. The first serious analyst of the game was Spain's Ruy López de Segura (fl. 16th century), who in 1561 devised an opening that is still used. A new era was heralded with the publication of François Philidor's influential *Analyse du jeu des échecs* (1749), which was translated into several languages.

Adolf Anderssen (1818–79) of Germany defeated a field of outstanding players to win the first modern international tournament, held in London in 1851. The first American chess champion of the world was Paul Morphy, of New Orleans, La., who at the age of 20 won first place at the First Chess Congress, held in New York City from Oct. 5 to Nov. 10, 1857. On October 10 of that year a national organization, the United States Chess Federation, was established.

Many authorities regard the Cuban player José Raúl CAPABLANCA as the greatest in the history of chess. Bobby FISCHER, an American, has been rated by numerous experts, however, as Capablanca's superior.

From 1975 to 1985 the world championship was held by Anatoly KARPOV of the USSR, who was dethroned by his countryman Gary KASPAROV. Kasparov retained the title in subsequent championship matches (1986, 1987, 1990) against Karpov.

Computer Chess

The highly structural nature of chess has attracted the attention of computer scientists. In 1957 the first chess program was written at the Massachusetts Institute of Technology (MIT). It is estimated that before the end of the 20th century a program will be developed that can defeat even the best players in the world.

chest The chest, or thorax, is the upper part of the human body and is situated between the neck and the abdomen. It is formed by 12 vertebrae, 12 pairs of ribs, the sternum (breastbone), and associated muscles and fascia. The thorax is separated from the abdomen by the diaphragm. Present within the thoracic cavity are the chief organs of the respiratory system and certain components of the circulatory and digestive systems. The LUNGS occupy lateral regions of the thoracic cavity, whereas the HEART and ESOPHAGUS are enclosed in a compartment known as the mediastinum. The mediastinum also encloses certain large vessels that arise from the heart, the trachea, the thymus gland, and certain nerves. Thorax functions include protection of the enclosed organs, support for the bones of the shoulder girdle and upper extremities, and expansion and contraction of the thoracic cavity during respiration.

See also: HUMAN BODY.

Chester (England) A railroad junction and major tourist attraction, Chester is situated on a bend of the River Dee in west central England. It is the county town of Cheshire and has a population of 116,600 (1985 est.). Chester is one of England's most picturesque medieval cities, characterized by quaint black and white timbered houses and arcaded shops with projecting second stories. It has a cathedral, a great Norman castle, and numerous Roman remains. It was founded (AD *c.*60) as a Roman camp and became a legionary fortress called Castra Deva.

For many centuries the city was of strategic importance, guarding the avenues to Wales and the sea. It was the last Saxon stronghold to succumb to William the Conqueror in the 11th century. During the Middle Ages, Chester was a thriving river port, but silting of the Dee and the competition of Liverpool caused the decline of its river trade by the 1700s. The famous Chester mystery plays were presented there from the 13th to the 16th century.

Chester (Pennsylvania) Chester, Pa. (1990 pop., 41,856), is an industrial city and important freshwater port on the Delaware River, 22 km (14 mi) south of Philadelphia. It is known for shipbuilding and has one of the largest shipyards in the country. Lining its waterfront and narrow old streets are large steel mills, oil refineries, petrochemical plants, and factories that make a variety of products. One of the oldest cities in Pennsylvania, Chester has many historic houses. It was founded by Swedes in 1644 and named Uppland. William Penn landed there on his first trip to the New World in 1682. He renamed the settlement and convened Pennsylvania's first assembly there. Incorporated as a borough in 1701, it became a city in 1866.

Chesterfield, Philip Dormer Stanhope, 4th Earl of The 4th earl of Chesterfield, b. Sept. 22, 1694, d. Mar. 24, 1773, was an English man of letters who is remembered chiefly for his *Letters to His Son* (1774), which portray the ideal 18th-century gentleman. His public career included service as ambassador to The Hague (1728–32), as lord lieutenant of Ireland (1745–46), and as secretary of state (1746–48). He was a patron of several playwrights and poets.

Chesterton, G. K. Gilbert Keith Chesterton, b. May 29, 1874, d. June 14, 1936, was an iconoclastic English author at home in many genres. He wrote novels (*The Napoleon of Notting Hill,* 1904), criticism (works on Robert Browning, Charles Dickens, and George Bernard Shaw), poetry (*New and Collected Poems,* 1929), biography (*St. Francis of Assisi, St. Thomas Aquinas*), and innumerable essays. He was also a talented artist, as seen in the illustrations of his own works. Among his short stories, the best known are those about the priest-detective Father Brown, who first appeared in *The Innocence of Father Brown* (1911) and continued through five collections.

A doctrinal and social conservative, Chesterton was received into the Roman Catholic church in 1922 by his friend Father John O'Connor (the model for Father Brown), and exercised a considerable influence on later English Catholic writers, notably Evelyn Waugh. In 1936 he published his *Autobiography.*

The British writer G. K. Chesterton began his writing career while studying art; subsequently he illustrated many of his own works. The author of essays, biography, poetry, and fiction, he is best known for his series of detective stories, "Father Brown."

chestnut The chestnuts, or chinquapins, genus *Castanea,* are deciduous hardwood trees belonging to the beech family, Fagaceae. Chestnuts have deciduous serrate leaves. The fruit is characterized by two to four compartmented burrs covered with needle-sharp branched spines.

About ten species are found in southern Europe, northern Africa, southwestern and eastern Asia, and the eastern United States. The nuts of the Chinese chestnut, *C. mollissima,* and the Japanese chestnut, *C. crenata,* are important sources of food in their native countries. Large quantities are also exported to the United States. Oriental chestnuts and the Spanish chestnut, *C. sativa,* are also planted in the United States.

In the early part of the 20th century, more than one-fourth of all hardwood sawtimber in the southern Appalachian Mountains of the United States was cut from the American chestnut, *C. dentata.* It was eliminated as a commercial species, however, by a blight caused by the fungus *Endothia parasitica.* Scientists have since found that inoculation of trees with attenuated strains of *E. parasitica* may protect trees against more virulent strains.

The American chestnut (left) *was once a rich source of timber and nuts. The spiny burr* (bottom) *carries three chestnuts. The leaves are about 15 cm (6 in) long and bear male, staminate flowers, or catkins, and shorter bisexual catkins with pistillate flowers.*

Chetumal [chay-too-mahl'] Chetumal (1982 est. pop., 97,999) is the capital of Quintana Roo state in eastern Mexico, situated on the Bay of Chetumal on the east coast of the Yucatán Peninsula. Founded in 1899 as a military base, it became the territorial capital in 1902, and the city now also serves as the commercial and trade center for forestry products from the nearby rain forests.

Chevalier, Maurice [shuh-vahl'-ee-ay] Maurice Chevalier, b. Sept. 12, 1888, d. Jan. 1, 1972, was a debonair French singer, actor, and dancer who for more than 50 years was a popular international cabaret artist. He had two Hollywood careers: as a romantic lead in such films as *The Love Parade* (1930), *Love Me Tonight* (1932), and *Folies Bergère* (1935), and as an elderly character actor in *Gigi* (1958), *Fanny* (1961), and *In Search of the Castaways* (1962).

Cheverus, Jean Louis Lefebvre de [shev'-uh-ruhs] Jean Lefebvre de Cheverus, b. France, Jan. 28, 1768, d. July 19, 1836, was the first Roman Catholic bishop of Boston. After serving as a missionary among the Indians of Maine and visiting scattered congregations in New England, he was consecrated (1810) bishop of Boston. He returned to France in 1823 and became a cardinal in 1836.

chevrotain [shev'-ruh-tayn] The chevrotain, or mouse deer, is a small ruminant mammal in the mammalian order Artiodactyla of the family Tragulidae. Much larger than a mouse and not really a deer, it is classified in its own family. Two living genera survive from an ancient and once numerous group. Chevrotains are 46–89 cm (18–35 in) long, with a 6.3-cm (2.5-in) tail, and stand 20–33 cm (8–13 in) high at the shoulder. They weigh from 2 to 5 kg (4.5 to 11 lb). Chevrotains differ from deer in having

The Asian chevrotain is among the smallest of hoofed animals. Adult males have well-developed upper canine teeth that protrude downward from the mouth as small tusks.

three stomach divisions and four fully developed toes on each foot. They walk on the tips of their hooves. The coat is brown with some spots and stripes and white underparts. Six species (genus *Tragulus*) live in tropical Asia. The water chevrotain, *Hyemoschus aquaticus,* lives in west central Africa.

chewing gum Chewing gum is a mixture of natural or synthetic gums and resins, sweetened with sugar and corn syrup, with added color and flavor. It is a uniquely U.S. product, discovered during the search for rubber materials in the 1860s. The first manufacturing patent for chewing gum was issued in 1869.

The basic raw material for all chewing gum is the natural gum chicle, obtained from the sapodilla tree indigenous to Central America. Because chicle is relatively expensive and often difficult to procure, other natural gums are also used. Recently, synthetic materials such as polyvinylacetate and similar polymers have come into widespread use.

Bubble gum differs from ordinary gum only in that its base is formulated with rubber latex for greater strength. Sugarcoated gum is made by whirling small cubes of gum in copper pans with sugar syrup, powdered sugar, color, and flavor. This mixture builds the colorful, polished, crystallized sugar shell. Sugarless gums are made by substituting sugar alcohols (xylitol, mannitol, or sorbitol) for ordinary sugar.

Cheyenne (Indian tribe) [shy-an'] The Cheyenne are a North American Indian people who were famous as mounted hunter-warriors on the Great Plains during the 19th century. These Algonquian-speakers originally lived as sedentary farmers in northeastern Minnesota, from which they began migrating westward in the late 1600s; they later settled along the Cheyenne River of North Dakota. Dislodged *c.*1770 by raiding OJIBWA, they gradually moved southwestward; when encountered (1804) by the Lewis and Clark Expedition, they were living as nomadic buffalo-hunters in the Black Hills of South Dakota.

In 1832 the tribe split into two branches, the northern Cheyenne, who inhabited the area around the Platte River, and the southern Cheyenne, who lived near the Arkansas River. The Cheyenne were constantly at war with the KIOWA, APACHE, and COMANCHE until 1840, when an alliance was formed. From 1857 to 1879 they fought white settlers and the U.S. Army, especially after the brutal SAND CREEK MASSACRE of 1864, in which an estimated 150 to 500 Cheyenne were killed. The Cheyenne played an important role in the defeat of Gen. George Custer and the 7th Cavalry at the Battle of the LITTLE BIGHORN (1876).

Today the Cheyenne occupy two reservations, at Tongue River, Mont., and in southwestern Oklahoma. They numbered about 7,300 in 1987.

Wolf Robe, a chief of the southern Cheyenne Indian tribe, appears in a 1909 photograph. During the late 1870s, Wolf Robe's tribe was forced to leave the open plains and relocate on a reservation in Oklahoma.

Cheyenne (city) [shy-an'] Cheyenne is the capital and largest city of Wyoming. It has a population of 50,008 (1990). Situated in the southeastern corner of the state, it is also the seat of Laramie County and a central beef-shipping and trade center.

Cheyenne was named after the Cheyenne tribe of Algonquian-speaking Indians by white squatters who arrived in 1867, just ahead of the Union Pacific Railroad, which had selected the site for a terminal. It was made the capital of Wyoming Territory in 1869 and soon became a shipping point for livestock from the surrounding ranches and a supply center for gold mining in the Black Hills. The town was notoriously lawless for a period until vigilantes imposed some order. The city commemorates its lively past with the annual Frontier Days celebration. Nearby Fort D. A. Russell, established in 1867 and renamed Fort Francis C. Warren in 1930, housed (1960) the first intercontinental ballistic missiles.

Ch'i Pai-shih see QI BAISHI

Chiang Ch'ing see JIANG QING

Chiang Ching-kuo [jee-ahng' jing gwaw] The eldest son of Nationalist Chinese leader Generalissimo Chiang Kai-shek, Chiang Ching-kuo, b. Mar. 18, 1910, d. Jan. 13, 1988, succeeded his father as leader of the Republic of China on Taiwan. He was appointed defense minister in 1965, vice-premier in 1969, and premier in 1972. He became head of the KUOMINTANG when his father died in 1975 and was elected president in 1978 and reelected in 1984. Under Chiang's rule, Taiwan experienced impressive economic growth. He also began cautious political liberalization, tolerating opposition political parties and lifting (1987) martial law. He was succeeded as president by LEE TENG-HUI.

Chiang Kai-shek [jee-ahng' ky-shek] Chiang Kai-shek, b. Oct. 31, 1887, d. Apr. 5, 1975, was a Chinese political and military leader who headed the Nationalist government in China and on the island of Taiwan. Raised by his widowed mother, Chiang early decided on a military career. In 1908 he joined a revolutionary organization devoted to the overthrow of the QING (Manchu) dynasty, an effort that succeeded in 1911–12.

After 1920, Chiang allied himself with SUN YAT-SEN, who built up the KUOMINTANG (Nationalist party) at Guangzhou (Canton) with Soviet aid. He was made commandant (1924) of the party's Huangpo (Whampoa) Military Academy, and his power as a military leader grew rapidly after Sun's death in 1925. In the NORTHERN EXPEDITION of 1926–27, Chiang secured the backing of the Shanghai business community, whereupon he suppressed the labor movement, purged Communist influence, forced out the Russian advisors, and brought numerous warlords into the Nationalist fold. In December 1927, Chiang married Soong Mei-ling of the wealthy Christian SOONG family.

From 1928, Chiang headed a new Nationalist government at Nanjing (Nanking), giving first priority to the elimination of the Chinese Communists; he ineffectually resisted the Japanese occupation of Manchuria in 1931. In 1937, when the Japanese invasion of China launched the Second SINO-JAPANESE WAR, Chiang was compelled to form a united front with the Communists. He led the war from Chongqing (Chungking) in southwest China. Chiang became increasingly dependent on the United States, while the morale of his own forces declined and corruption became rampant. After the Japanese surrender in 1945, Nationalist-Communist hostilities were renewed. The Nationalists lost the civil war (1945–49), and in 1949 remnants of the Kuomintang fled to the island of Taiwan, where Chiang ruled until his death.

Chiang exercised power through various posts—party leader, chairman of the Supreme National Defense Council, and president of the Republic of China. Intellectually, he was a conservative who admired the authoritarian aspects of Confucianism, which he revived as a state cult.

Generalissimo Chiang Kai-shek led the Chinese Nationalist government from 1928 until his death in 1975. Except for the period of the Sino-Japanese War (1937–45), Chiang was engaged in constant warfare with the Communists, who finally defeated him in 1949 and forced him to remove the Nationalist government to Taiwan.

Chiang Mai [jee-ahng' my] Chiang Mai, Thailand's third largest city, is at the terminus of the northern railroad line, about 580 km (360 mi) north of the capital, Bangkok. It has a population of 157,843 (1986 est.). Silver hammering, carving teak statuary, and making decorative umbrellas are important economically.

Founded in its present location in 1296 by King Mengrai, Chiang Mai was once the capital of a Lao kingdom, for whose control the Burmese and Thai frequently fought. This is evidenced by elaborate fortifications. The city has many temples, notably Wat Phra Dhat Doi Suthep.

Chiang Tse-min see JIANG ZEMIN

Chiapas [chee-ah'-pahs] Chiapas is the southernmost state in Mexico and is situated on the Pacific coast. It covers 74,211 km^2 (28,653 mi^2), and its population, primarily Indian, is 2,559,463 (1989 est.). TUXTLA GUTIÉRREZ is the capital. Most of Chiapas is mountainous. The economy is based on stock raising, rubber, cacao, and coffee cultivation, and natural gas and petroleum resources are exploited. Important Maya remains are found at Bonampak and Palenque. In 1824, Chiapas became a Mexican state.

chiaroscuro [kee-ar-uh-skyur'-oh] *Chiaroscuro*, an Italian word meaning "clear and obscure" (or "light and dark"), refers to the technique of painting three-dimensional figures and space through the distribution of light and shadow. The development of chiaroscuro was initiated in the 14th century by artists of the INTERNATIONAL STYLE. Manuscript illustrators introduced shadows adjacent to figures whose contours and volume were still rendered traditionally by line; the contrast between dark and light passages suggested a three-dimensional image. In the Renaissance, artists achieved a three-dimensional effect by modeling both forms and space through the use of light and shadow, integrating figures and objects into an atmospheric, spatial environment.

Chibcha [chib'-chah] Chibcha, a group of Colombian Indian tribes, came to dominate the highlands of east central Colombia as their political power spread throughout the region in the century before the arrival (1536) of the Spaniards. Living at altitudes of up to 3,000 m (10,000 ft), Chibcha were intensive agriculturists, growing maize, manioc, potatoes, and other domesticated plants. The most highly developed of the Colombian tribes, they lived in permanent settlements of up to several thousand people, with their main center at BOGOTÁ. Their society was patrilineally organized, although the succession of chiefs may have been matrilineal. Religious ceremonies, administered by a hereditary class of priests, included human sacrifice.

At the time of the Spanish conquest, Chibcha numbered 500,000 and had a federated government second in complexity only to that of the INCA. They were divided into five large political territories, each one ruled by a powerful chief. These states failed to unite against the Spaniards and were easily defeated by them. Chibcha culture and traditional organization changed rapidly as they were absorbed into the colonial world. Remaining Chibcha-speaking tribes include the CUNA and LENCA of Central America.

Chicago Chicago is a port and transportation center on the southwestern shore of Lake Michigan in the state of Illinois. It has a population of 2,783,726 (1990) and has been the seat of Cook County since 1931.

Long known as the nation's "second city," Chicago dropped to third place among largest U.S. cities during the 1980s as its population declined during the decade by about 7.5%. Its three-state metropolitan area population totaled 8,065,633 (1990 est.). Many of Chicago's people descend from 19th-century European immigrants, attracted to the city by industrial jobs. About 40% (1980) of the population are blacks.

The first steel-framework skyscraper was built (1884) in Chicago, and the city's impressive skyline includes such structures as the SEARS TOWER (443 m/1,454 ft), which is the world's tallest building. Indeed, the city has given its name to the Chicago School of Architecture. The Loop, the downtown area, was so named in the 1890s because of the rectangle formed by the tracks of the elevated trains. Lake Michigan exerts a strong influence on the city's climate, and Chicago has been appropriately nicknamed the Windy City.

Contemporary City. The center of a heavily industrialized area, Chicago leads the country in the manufacture of telephone equipment, radios, television equipment, confectionery products, household products, musical instruments, and frozen and canned foods. Its largest industry is metal fabrication, particularly iron and steel. Several of the largest printers and publishers in the world are in Chicago.

The Federal Reserve Bank was founded (1914) in Chicago, and the city still has a district bank. The Chicago Mercantile Exchange, the Midwest Stock Exchange, and the Chicago Board of Trade, which is the world's largest commodity futures market, are there. Chicago's early importance as a transportation center has continued. Today its major airport, Chicago-O'Hare International, is the busiest in the world. Chicago's harbor, the largest on the Great Lakes, handles mostly grain and iron ore.

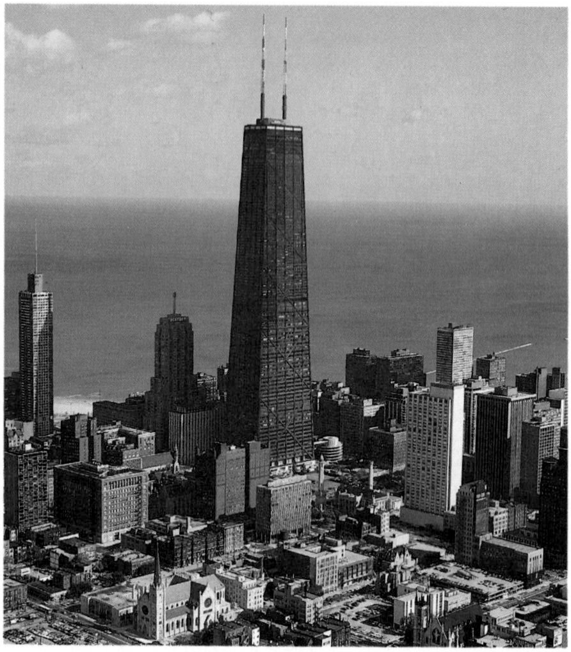

The John Hancock Center, at 344 m (1,127 ft) one of the world's tallest buildings, dominates this view of Chicago's downtown area.

The University of Chicago (1890) is one of the most prestigious private universities in the country. Other institutions include the Illinois Institute of Technology (1892), Northwestern University (1851), and the Roman Catholic-supported Loyola (1870) and DePaul (1898) universities.

The Art Institute of Chicago has a world-famous collection. The Museum of Contemporary Art was founded in 1967. Scientific institutions include the Field Museum of Natural History, the Adler Planetarium, the Shedd Aquarium, and the Museum of Science and Industry. The city is home to the Chicago Civic Opera and the famous CHICAGO SYMPHONY ORCHESTRA.

History. The site of Chicago had long been an important portage point on the water route linking the Great Lakes with the Mississippi River. The United States bought a tract from the Indians in 1795, and the original settlement was a cluster of traders' shacks outside FORT DEARBORN (built 1803). After the opening (1825) of the ERIE CANAL, Chicago became the focal point of the westward movement, and the arrival (1852) of the railroad assured its growth. Industry developed along with transportation, and steel production was a major boost to the city's economy. Lumbering and meat-processing plants

Cartographic Production by Lothar Roth & Associates, 1979.

were also established; the Union Stock Yards opened in 1865 and successfully operated for more than a century. Just as Chicago was emerging as a major city, a devastating fire (Oct. 8–9, 1871) swept through part of the city, leaving almost 100,000 people homeless and causing millions of dollars in damage. The city embarked on a rebuilding program, using stone to replace wooden buildings and creating one of the first modern fire departments in America. Chicago was the site of the WORLD'S COLUMBIAN EXPOSITION OF 1893.

A second major surge of growth occurred toward the turn of the century, when thousands of European immigrants came to the city. As the labor movement emerged, union organizational activities were often marred by violence on both sides—the HAYMARKET RIOT (1886) and the PULLMAN STRIKE (1894) were two notorious examples. At the same time, movement to the suburbs began, and during the 20th century the city's population growth began to slow down. Between 1970 and 1980, Chicago had a population loss of 10.8%. The stock market crash (1929) halted major building construction, which did not resume until the election (1955) of Mayor Richard J. DALEY. Although Daley was influential as the head of one of the last old-time city political machines and stressed urban renewal, downtown Chicago deteriorated as the city dwellers moved to the suburbs. The city made history in 1979, when Jane Byrne became Chicago's first woman mayor. Following her defeat in 1983 Democratic mayoral primaries, Harold WASHINGTON was elected the city's first black mayor. He was reelected in April 1987 but died later in the year. In 1989, Daley's son, Richard M. Daley, was elected mayor.

Chicago, Art Institute of The Art Institute of Chicago evolved from the Chicago Academy of Design established in 1866. It was incorporated as the Chicago Academy of Fine Arts on May 24, 1879, and assumed its present name in 1882. Since 1893 it has been located on Michigan Avenue in a large Renaissance-style structure built by Shepley, Rutan, and Coolidge for the World's Columbian Exposition of 1893. The Institute's collections cover all periods of European and American painting, sculpture, classical art, Near Eastern and Oriental decorative arts, textiles, African, Oceanic, and American Indian arts, period rooms, prints, drawings, and photography. The main strength of the painting collection lies in the very fine holdings of French impressionists and postimpressionists, including Georges Seurat's pointillist *Sunday La Grande Jatte* (1884–86). Twentieth-century and American art are also well represented, especially American artists after 1950. The print collection contains over 50,000 items, ranging from the 15th to the 20th century, including a particularly rich selection by 19th-century French masters. The School of the Art Institute has achieved world renown, and the Goodman Theater, its other teaching branch, is in the top rank of U.S. drama schools.

Chicago, University of The University of Chicago, established in 1890 by the American Baptist Education-al Society, is a private institution, now nondenominational, in Chicago, Ill. Its founding and early growth were made possible by large gifts from John D. Rockefeller and his descendants. It was among the first American institutions modeled after the German universities, emphasizing graduate research, and was the first major university to accept women on an equal basis with men. Among its presidents, William Rainey HARPER and Robert M. HUTCHINS were important influences on American colleges. The university is the center of a noted group of theological institutions.

Chicago school of architecture see SKYSCRAPER

Chicago Symphony Orchestra The Chicago Symphony Orchestra is the third oldest symphony orchestra in the United States. Organized by Theodore Thomas in 1891, it is managed under a permanent endowment by the Orchestral Association of Chicago, founded that year. The association owns Orchestra Hall, the symphony's home, which was built in 1904 (and renovated extensively in 1966 and 1981). In 1905, Frederick Stock succeeded Thomas as conductor and remained with the orchestra until 1942. Distinguished regular conductors since then have included Rafael Kubelik, Artur Rodzinski, Fritz Reiner, Jean Martinon, and, from 1969, Sir Georg SOLTI, who increased the number of tours the orchestra makes in the United States and abroad. The orchestra made the first of several European tours in 1971, and in 1977 it performed in Japan. Daniel BARENBOIM was named to succeed Solti as music director of the Chicago Symphony beginning with the 1991–92 season. Under Solti, who also conducted other orchestras, guest conductors included Carlo Maria GIULINI and Claudio ABBADO. The Chicago Symphony Chorus was formed in 1957, with Margaret Hillis as director.

Chicano [chi-kah'-noh] The term *Chicano,* a shortened version of *Mexicano*, was originally used as a derogatory label for Mexicans who had recently arrived in the United States, but in the 1960s it became accepted as a symbol of self-determination and ethnic pride by militant young Mexican-Americans. *Chicano* has since become a common synonym for the generic ethnic term *Mexican-American* among that ethnic minority.

During the 400 years since the Spanish conquest of the New World, persons of Mexican descent in the United States had been dominated by Americans of European descent. A departure from this pattern began with the creation of organizations to facilitate U.S. citizenship and to foster patriotism among Mexican-Americans. In 1929 these merged into the League of United Latin American Citizens (LULAC), which supported accommodation to middle-class American standards. Following World War II,

Members of the United Farm Workers of America march through Salinas, Calif., during the union's 1979 strike against area fruit and vegetable growers. Formed in 1962, the UFW has been an effective voice in the Chicano movement.

returning Mexican-American soldiers organized the American G.I. Forum. They sought ethnic separation as well as parity with Anglo-American institutions, mainly through legal means.

The Chicano movement (or movements) was born during the turbulent 1950–70 era. Its initial impetus came from the charismatic preacher Reies Lopez Tijerina in northern New Mexico, who fought to regain control of ancestral lands. Within a half-dozen years he was involved in civil rights causes, becoming a cosponsor of the Poor People's March on Washington in 1967. In Denver, another leader, Rodolfo "Corky" Gonzales, proclaimed on Palm Sunday 1969 that the Chicano people of the southwest were *Aztlan*—meaning in need of liberation from the dominant society through sacrifice and isolation. This utopian stand won many supporters at first, but eventually they shrank to a small group of organized militants.

Chicano efforts to gain influence by "working within the system" began in 1958 with organizations such as the Mexican American Political Association (MAPA). Except for isolated successes, however, as in the heavy ethnic voter turnout and resulting election of Mexican-American candidates in Crystal City, Tex., in 1963, the gains were few. Some Chicano youth turned toward more radical means of gaining influence. Even under the able leadership of José Angel Gutiérrez, the Raza Unida political party (1970) won little national and regional support, although it elected Chicano candidates to south Texas school boards and city councils. (In the 1970s and '80s, other Mexican-Americans not identified with the movement served in such high posts as governor.)

The activist but peaceful policies of Cesar CHAVEZ, the leader of the United Farm Workers, were advanced by his organizational ability. His deft weaving of the voluntary efforts of illiterate farm laborers, liberal activists and pacifists, and college students into an effective struggle (*la lucha*) against powerful agribusiness interests was one of the Chicano movement's greatest successes.

See also: HISPANIC AMERICANS.

Chichén Itzá [chee-chayn' eet-sah'] Chichén Itzá, a MAYA city in northern Yucatán, Mexico, was, from AD 900 to 1100, one of the largest cities in MESOAMERICA and the center of a political state. "Chichén" means "at the mouth of the well," and generations venerated the sacred *cenote*, or sinkhole, there. "Itzá" was added when the Maya group of that name went there in the 9th or 10th century.

By 500 BC, Chichén was the site of a village. During Late Classic times (AD 550–900) the site grew rapidly,

The Temple of the Warriors, a major structure of the Maya city of Chichén Itzá, is similar to but much grander than Temple B at faraway Tula, Hidalgo state. The columns at the base and on top of the temple probably supported perishable roofs. The ruler may have directed his realm from the private chambers at top.

and during the Early Postclassic it became an international center similar to TULA, the TOLTEC capital. During the 12th century, Chichén was abandoned and a new capital founded at MAYAPÁN.

The surviving Late Classic architecture is similar to that at Tula, but the Chichén structures are larger and more abundant, built with warrior columns, reclining figures called chacmools, and serpent columns. Carvings of ballplayers sacrificing their defeated enemies flank the interior walls of the Great Ballcourt, the largest such construction in Mesoamerica.

Chichester [chih'-ches-tur] Chichester is the county town of West Sussex (until 1974, along with East Sussex, one of the divisions of Sussex county) in southern England. Located about 26 km (16 mi) northeast of Portsmouth, the city is connected by a canal to Chichester harbor, an inlet of the English Channel. The population is 24,189 (1981). Chichester is a regional trading center and has some light industry. Historical landmarks include a 12th-century Norman cathedral. Chichester Festival Theatre has a notable summer season.

Chichester was originally the Roman city of Regnum, and the ruins of the Roman city wall (dated AD *c.*200) still remain. During the Middle Ages, the city was an important wool and wheat market.

Chichester, Sir Francis Francis Charles Chichester, b. Sept. 17, 1901, d. Aug. 26, 1972, was an English yachtsman who in 1966–67 sailed around the world alone. His journey in the 16.2-m (53-ft) ketch *Gipsy Moth IV* began on Aug. 27, 1966, from Plymouth, England. After a 47-day rest in Australia because of an elbow injury, Chichester landed on May 28, 1967, at Plymouth, welcomed by a crowd estimated at 250,000. His voyage was followed closely by the press and earned worldwide acclaim on its completion. Chichester was knighted in July 1967.

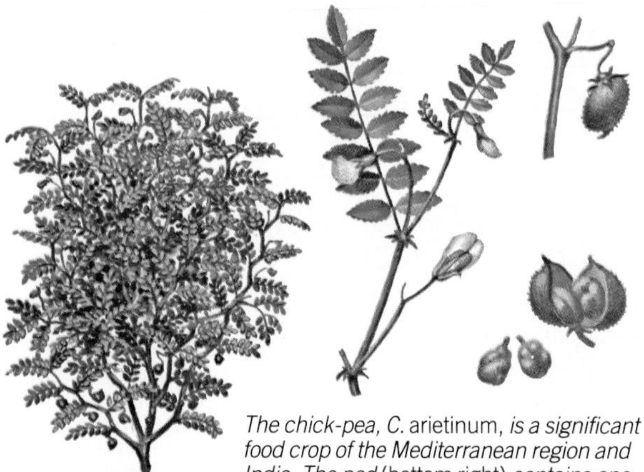

The chick-pea, C. arietinum, *is a significant food crop of the Mediterranean region and India. The pod* (bottom right) *contains one or two seeds (peas), which are frequently dried and roasted or ground into flour.*

chick-pea The chick-pea, *Cicer arietinum,* also known as Egyptian pea, garbanzo, or gram, is cultivated for its edible nutritious seeds. It is, like beans and other peas, a member of the Leguminosae family. Indigenous to the Mediterranean area, it has been cultivated there since ancient times. The plant is a herbaceous, sprawling annual, 50 to 70 cm (20 to 28 in) tall at maturity. The hairy stems have compound leaves with 9 to 17 leaflets, and the small flowers are white or pink. The fruit is a legume, 2 to 3 cm (0.8 to 1.2 in) long and 1 cm (0.4 in) wide, containing one or two rounded, light-colored seeds.

chickadee Chickadee is the common name for seven species of small (13 cm/5 in) North American birds of the titmouse family, Paridae. Chickadees have black bibs, dark caps, white cheeks—one species also has a black stripe—and usually gray backs—chestnut brown in one species. They are active, acrobatic in feeding, and not timid toward humans. The black-capped chickadee, *Parus atricapillus,* is found in the northern United States and Canada. The similar Carolina chickadee, *P. carolinensis,* is found from central New Jersey and southern Kansas southward.

The tiny mountain chickadee is found in the conifer forests of mountain ranges in the western United States at altitudes of 1,800 to 2,600 m (6,000 to 8,500 ft).

Chickamauga, Battle of [chik-uh-maw'-guh] Chickamauga was a major battle of the U.S. CIVIL WAR fought on Sept. 19–20, 1863. The Confederate army of 66,000 men under Gen. Braxton BRAGG attacked a 58,000-strong Union army under Gen. William S. ROSECRANS along Chickamauga Creek in northwestern Georgia. On the second day of battle the Confederates drove much of the Union army from the field in disorder. Only the stubborn stand of the Union left flank under Gen. George H. THOMAS saved Rosecrans's army from destruction. Bragg failed, however, to follow up his victory aggressively. This lessened its impact on the war and contributed to the Confederate defeat at Chattanooga in November (see CHATTANOOGA, BATTLES OF).

Chickasaw The Chickasaw are a North American Indian tribe of the Muskogean linguistic stock who formerly ranged over much of present-day Mississippi, southwestern Kentucky, and western Tennessee. By the late 17th century, their population of about 4,000 was concentrated around the Tombigbee River drainage in northern Mississippi and Alabama. The Chickasaw lived by hunting, fishing, and farming. They were able warriors and fought constantly with their neighbors, the CHEROKEE, CHOCTAW, CREEK, and SHAWNEE. In 1541 they battled and nearly defeated Hernando DE SOTO and his exploration party; in 1729 they supported the NATCHEZ in their wars against the French.

The Chickasaw ceded most of their lands to the United States in treaties signed in the early 1800s. By 1837 they were forced to move west into Indian Territory (present-day Oklahoma), where they became one of the FIVE CIVILIZED TRIBES. The Chickasaw Nation was established in 1856; tribespeople raised crops and livestock, operated grist and lumber mills, and engaged in commerce in their new territory. Their growing prosperity was disrupted by the Civil War and the arrival of large numbers of white settlers. Oklahoma statehood was approved in 1906, whereby the Chickasaw Nation ceased to exist. The Chickasaw numbered 11,780 on or near their reservation in Oklahoma in 1987.

The chicken is the most widespread of all domestic fowl. Popular types are the Cornish (left; hen shown), *a deep-breasted English breed grown for its meat, and the Leghorn* (right; rooster shown), *a Mediterranean breed that is the world's leading egg producer.*

chicken The chicken, *Gallus gallus* or *G. domesticus*, is a domestic fowl, probably the most common bird in the world. It is raised for meat, eggs, and by-products such as feathers; for sport; and as a hobby. Developed chiefly from the red jungle fowl (*G. gallus*) of southeast Asia, the chicken has been fully domesticated for at least 4,000 years. Chickens were kept for their eggs, and when the birds grew too old to lay, they were used for meat. The development of different breeds of chickens either for egg laying or for meat production, the transfer of farming operations indoors where the environment can be controlled, and the use of sophisticated mass-production techniques led to the modernization of the chicken industry.

Most chickens range in weight from 3 to 4.5 kg (7 to 10 lb), with the larger breeds reaching about 6 kg (13 lb) and some bantams only 670 g (1.5 lb). Hens start laying at 22 weeks of age. During the hen's most productive period, an egg may be laid about every other day for most of the year. Eggs hatch in 21 days.

See also: EGG PRODUCTION; POULTRY.

chicken pox Chicken pox, or varicella, a highly contagious disease that strikes many children, is caused by the HERPES zoster virus. Transmitted by the respiratory system, the virus is carried by the bloodstream to all parts of the body; the principal manifestations of infection occur on the skin. Initial symptoms—loss of appetite, fever, and headache—appear about two weeks after exposure. Within about two days a rash appears, mainly on the trunk and face but also on the extremities. The rash soon develops into itching blisters that break in a few days and are covered by scabs. The lesions leave no scars unless they become infected by bacteria as a result of scratching. Usually no more treatment is necessary than medications to relieve the itching. Chicken pox can be serious in infants, however, if the disease is transmitted to them by their mother in the last few days of pregnancy. It can also be life-threatening to children suffering from suppressed-immune conditions. Most adults develop a natural immunity to the disease, but it can be dangerous for those who have not; the same virus can also flare up as SHINGLES in adults. A vaccine became available in the 1970s for persons in high-risk categories, and live attenuated vaccines were being tested in the mid-1980s, with licensing possible in the early 1990s.

chickweed Chickweed, *Stellaria media,* is a widespread herb of the pink family, Caryophyllaceae, that is a serious garden weed throughout North America. Although originally native to southern Europe, it has become naturalized in most parts of the world. The rounded, opposite leaves are usually less than 4 cm (1.6 in) long. The white starlike flowers are 1.3 cm (0.5 in) across. The name chickweed is also given to other species of *Stellaria*, to mouse-ear chickweeds of the pink family genus *Cerastium,* and occasionally to other similar garden pests.

chicory Witloof chicory, *Cichorium intybus*, also known as Belgian or French ENDIVE, is a perennial herb belonging to the family Compositae. Native to the Mediterranean area, it now grows wild in North America.

Chicory is grown mostly for its blanched, elongated head (right), *but the greens* (left) *and root are also edible.*

Creamy white, elongated heads, about 5 cm (2 in) in diameter and from 12 to 18 cm (5 to 7 in) long, are produced from fleshy storage roots by growing them in the dark at 10° to 15° C (50° to 59° F). Highly prized for its unique and delicate flavor, witloof is also grown outdoors for greens. The dried, ground chicory root is sometimes used as a coffee substitute or adulterant.

Chicoutimi [shee-koo-tee-mee'] Chicoutimi, a Canadian city in the southern part of Quebec province, is located at the confluence of the Chicoutimi and Saguenay rivers. The city has a population of 61,083 (1986), and the Chicoutimi-Jonquière metropolitan area, 158,468 (1986). The city was established in 1676 as a Jesuit mission and trading post. After 1850 the area developed as a center of the lumber industry. Hydroelectric development of the Saguenay River has played an important role in the growth of Chicoutimi, which is today a manufacturing and distribution center for paper products and aluminum.

chief A chief, or chieftain, is the political leader of a social and territorial unit in a nonliterate society such as a village, CLAN, TRIBE, or confederation of tribes. The political leader of the socioterritorial unit known as the BAND is commonly referred to as a chief, but is more properly known as a "headman" because the position is loosely defined and does not have as much authority or power as that of a chief.

The principle of selection for a chief is often LINEAGE or territoriality. Commonly, chiefs govern with the aid of councils; more advanced nonliterate peoples often have subordinate chiefs under the authority of a single paramount chief.

Some of the roots of the chief's authority are informal, being based on community consensus, personal respect and popularity, age, and knowledge. The functions of a chief are varied, depending on the political structure and socioeconomic environment of the unit. The office carries some moral authority, sometimes reinforced by ritual responsibilities. Especially in larger units, the chieftaincy as an office may carry formal, coercive authority, with the right to levy tribute or taxes and to hand down fines or punish wrongdoers in other ways. Chiefs retain some duties in many PRIMITIVE SOCIETIES in Africa, Oceania, and South America.

Ch'ien-lung see QIANLONG

chiffon Chiffon is a term used to describe certain light, sheer, plain-weave fabrics. It may be made of silk, wool, or synthetic fibers and is woven in an open weave with tightly twisted yarns. Silk chiffon is made of raw silk yarn that has been twisted some 50 to 80 turns to 0.25 cm (0.1 in). Some chiffon constructions made of fibers other than silk are sized to give them the hand and feel of silk. The word is often used before the names of other fabrics to indicate a lightness of weight, as in "chiffon" taffeta.

Chifley, Joseph Benedict [chif'-lee] Joseph Benedict Chifley, b. Sept. 22, 1885, d. June 13, 1951, was Labor prime minister of Australia (1945–49) and continued to lead his party until his death. A New South Wales trade unionist, he entered Parliament in 1928 and was minister of defense from 1929 until 1931. When Labor returned to power, Chifley became treasurer (1941), then minister of postwar reconstruction (1942) under John CURTIN. He directed Australia's economic effort in World War II. As prime minister, he spurred postwar development through banking reforms, expansion of social services, and general economic growth.

chigger Chiggers, or harvest mites, are the six-legged larvae of trombiculid MITES. They are blood-sucking ectoparasites that have a wide range of hosts, including humans. Their saliva contains allergenic substances to which the host may be sensitive or become sensitized. The delayed reaction causes irritating lumps, in the center of which may often be seen a tiny scarlet mite. The rash is known as scrub itch, or trombidiasis.

Every continent has one or more species of chiggers that attack humans in this way. One is an important parasite of sheep in Australia. In most parts of the world, chiggers do not transmit human diseases, but in Southeast Asia a few species transmit the rickettsias of scrub typhus, or tsutsugamushi fever, a disease endemic among the rodents of that region.

Chiggers inhabit the upper layers of the soil and the detritus that covers it. When seeking food, they crawl up vegetation and attach themselves to passing mammals, responding to carbon dioxide gas in the mammals' breath.

Chihuahua (city) [chee-wah'-wah] Chihuahua (1980 pop., 406,830) is the capital of Chihuahua state in northern Mexico. The area's silver-mining, ranching, and timber operations give the city a frontier atmosphere. Chihuahua University was founded in 1954.

Chihuahua was settled in about 1639 and made a city in 1709. It was the headquarters of Gen. Pancho VILLA and his troops during the Mexican Revolution. His home, La Quinta Luz, is a popular tourist attraction. Other notable buildings include a cathedral (built 1717–89) and the 18th-century Church of San Francisco. West of the city is Cascade Basaseáchic (305 m/1,000 ft), one of the world's highest waterfalls.

Chihuahua (dog) [chi-wah'-wah] The Chihuahua is the smallest breed of dog, ranging in weight from 0.5 to 2.7 kg (1 to 6 lb). The breed is named for the Mexican city and state of the same name. Some authorities speculate that the Aztecs and other pre-Columbian peoples

The chihuahua is the smallest breed of dog recognized by canine associations. Although associated with Mexico, the origins of the dog are obscure. One possible source is China, where miniature dogs have been bred for centuries.

bred the ancestors of the Chihuahua, but no authenticated pre-Columbian dog remains have been discovered. It has also been suggested that the Chihuahua descended from dogs brought by the Spaniards or from China.

The Chihuahua is a tiny breed, standing only about 13 cm (5.1 in) high at the shoulder. It has a well-rounded, apple-shaped skull, with large, round eyes. The ears are large, conspicuous, and erect when the dog is at attention. The two coat types are smooth and long-haired; the coat may be any color or combination of colors, although black with tan or white markings is preferred in Mexico.

Chihuahua (state) [chee-wah'-wah] Chihuahua, the largest state of Mexico, is in the northern part of the country, south of the New Mexico and Texas borders. It covers 244,938 km^2 (94,571 mi^2), and the population is 2,553,975 (1989 est.). Chihuahua city is the state capital. The Mesa del Norde, an arid elevated plateau, covers the northern portion of the state. In the west, a range of the SIERRA MADRE reaches 2,725 m (8,940 ft). The principal economic activity of Chihuahua is mining; iron, lead, zinc, copper, silver, and gold are exploited. Cattle raising and cotton cultivation on irrigated land are also important. Chihuahua was originally inhabited by Apache Indians, whose population is now greatly reduced. In the early 1900s Pancho VILLA made the northern part of the state the center of his activities.

Chikamatsu Monzaemon [chee-kah-maht'-soo mawn'-zah-em-ahn] Chikamatsu Monzaemon is the pen name of Sugimori Nobumori, 1653–1725, commonly considered premodern Japan's finest playwright. He wrote his most important plays for the chanters and near life-size puppets of *joruri* theater. Chikamatsu's first known play, *Yotsugi Soga* (The Soga Heir, 1683), was of this type, but with *Shusse Kagekiyo* (Kagekiyo Victorious, 1686), he departed from the genre. His most popular play was *The Battles of Coxinga* (1715; Eng. trans., 1951), of the type called *jidaimono* (history plays). Chikamatsu also pioneered in writing *sewamono* (domestic dramas), including *The Love Suicides at Sonezaki* (1703; Eng. trans., 1955) and *The Love Suicides at Amijima* (1720; Eng. trans., 1953).

Child, Julia The television personality and author Julia Child, b. Aug. 15, 1912, stimulated American interest in French cuisine with her popular cooking show, "The French Chef," as well as with her cookbooks and magazine articles. In 1948 she enrolled in the Cordon Bleu École de Cuisine in Paris. Later, with Simone Beck and Louisette Bertholle, she opened her own school and wrote *Mastering the Art of French Cooking* (2 vols., 1961, 1970). She inaugurated her first television series on Feb. 11, 1963, launching a long-lasting career.

Child, Lydia Maria Lydia Maria Frances Child, b. Medford, Mass., Feb. 11, 1802, d. Oct. 20, 1880, was a U.S. author and abolitionist. She edited (1826–34) *Juvenile Miscellany,* the first American children's periodical, and wrote *The Frugal Housewife* (1829), a popular guide to household thrift. With her husband, David Lee Child (1794–1874), she published *An Appeal in Favor of That Class of Americans Called Africans* (1833), which helped convert William Ellergy CHANNING, Charles SUMNER, and Thomas Wentworth Higginson to the antislavery cause. She and her husband edited the weekly *National Anti-Slavery Standard* from 1841 to 1849.

child abuse Child abuse is defined in a variety of ways. Some definitions characterize it as "nonaccidental harm" to children by their parents or other caretakers. Others describe child abuse as any "intentional act of commission or omission that prevents or impedes a child's growth and normal development."

Child abuse or child maltreatment consists of different types of harmful acts. In physical abuse children are slapped, hit, kicked, shoved, or have objects thrown at them. Bruises, wounds, broken bones, or other injuries are common. Severe abuse may result in major injury, permanent physical or developmental impairment, even death. Neglect involves the failure to feed or care for a child's basic needs or to adequately supervise the child. Neglected children may be irregularly fed or kept in dirty clothes for long periods of time. Emotional abuse involves humiliation, berating, or other acts carried out over time that terrorize or frighten the child. Sexual abuse consists of a wide range of sexual behavior including fondling, masturbation, and intercourse. Sexual abuse can also involve children in pornography.

Incidence. Estimates about the extent of child maltreatment vary greatly. It is believed that much child abuse goes unreported, although the magnitude of unreported cases is not known. Estimates run from a low of several hundred thousand to 2–3 million children abused each year in the United States. Estimates for sexual abuse also vary. One estimate suggests that one in five girls and one in eleven boys fall victim to sexual abuse before turning 18. Although statistics are important in understanding the magnitude of the problem, they can also impede understanding. Large estimates, even those developed in well-designed research studies, tend to create a sense of disbelief about the magnitude of child abuse. It is difficult to imagine that so many children are intentionally hurt by adults.

Children are abused by adults they know and in many cases by members of their own families. Physical abuse of children is often committed by a child's parent or parent substitute (for example, a boyfriend or girlfriend of the child's parent). In physical-abuse cases, females are more often the perpetrators. This is thought to result from the fact that women spend more time around children, not that females are more inclined to abuse children. Abuse of a child by a male more often results in serious or lethal abuse of a child. Sexual abuse of children is committed by males in 90% of the cases.

Causes. Theories about the causes of child maltreatment vary. Until recently many people believed that abuse of children was the result of defects in the individual adult's personality. Increasing evidence suggests that many types of abuse are related to social and economic conditions. Poverty, unemployment, dilapidated housing, urban crime, drug use, and other stresses are associated with physical abuse and neglect of children. Many abusive parents were themselves raised in abusive, discordant environments where violence was common. These conditions help produce adults who are unable to empathize with other human beings and who are inclined to use violence in interpersonal interactions.

Programs. In 1974 the U.S. government established the National Center on Child Abuse and Neglect (NCCAN), now part of the Department of Health and Human Services. NCCAN funds demonstration and research projects in states across the nation to treat and prevent child maltreatment.

Child maltreatment has many dimensions. It is against the law in every state. Most abused children require medical examinations to detect the presence of injury or disease. Many abused children will suffer short- or long-term psychological or emotional trauma. Abusive adults require a range of mental-health and social services to help them remedy the conditions associated with their behavior. Thus, professional response to child abuse comes from law-enforcement, medical, mental-health, and social agencies.

child development Child development, as an area of study, encompasses four major aspects of human growth from birth to adolescence: maturation, comprising the stage-by-stage development of the body's physical systems; mental development, or the progressive elaboration of intellectual skills; personality development, involving the complex interaction between psychosocial factors and physical maturation; and socialization, the process by which children adjust to the expectations of society. Maturation is primarily studied by medical science, and the mental aspects of child development are primarily the province of DEVELOPMENTAL PSYCHOLOGY. Although the innate, orderly progression of the maturation process is both measurable and demonstrable, many related variables make formulating a comprehensive theory of child development difficult. Nevertheless, the theories of Jean PIAGET and Sigmund FREUD are of key importance.

Maturation

From birth on, the progressive integration of the nervous, muscular, and sensory systems proceeds rapidly. The child moves steadily from undifferentiated, global capacities and activities toward more finely differentiated, specialized ones. (See INFANCY.) Within about the first 3 months of life, the child learns to distinguish himself or herself from other persons and objects, to smile, and to control the head. The motor skills of sitting, grasping, creeping, and standing generally follow in quick succession. By the age of 15 months, allowing for individual variations, most children can walk, use a feeding utensil, and speak several recognizable words denoting objects. By the age of 2 years, the bladder and sphincter muscles are sufficiently under command to allow toilet training. Social responsiveness is manifested in the child's interaction with siblings and parents. A small vocabulary is employed in simple sentences.

Between the ages of 2 and 3, the child masters new motor skills such as running, jumping, and climbing. By the age of 3, language and social skills are elaborated, as is manual dexterity with crayons and paints, scissors, and building blocks; some 3-year-olds may even draw or print. By the age of 4, the child can maintain friendships with peers. At the age of 5, the child is capable of vigorous motor activity such as riding a bicycle, and can also control this energy in structured social and play situations.

No later period in childhood matches the rapid growth pace exhibited during the first 5 to 6 years. From ages 6 to 12, growth is a steady, progressive expansion of the basic physical, intellectual, and psychological skills. The next major event in the maturation process is the advent of puberty, at which time the child enters ADOLESCENCE.

The maintenance of a normal pattern of growth depends on two conditions: (1) that the fundamental biological integrity of the child has not been violated by disease, physical or emotional trauma, malnutrition, or other handicapping factors; and (2) that the child's individual experience has effectively interacted with maturation to produce a healthy intellectual, social, and emotional development.

Mental Development

The highly influential cognitive theory put forth by Jean Piaget hypothesizes that preadolescent intellectual development occurs in three stages: first, the sensorimotor developments from 4 months to the end of the second year; second, developments focused on the uses of symbols, from the age of 2 to the ages of 5 to 6; and third, the development of conceptualization and abstraction extending progressively from the age of 6 to the ages of 10 or 12. This theory assumes a design in cognitive development that will be manifested in specific and unvarying sequences. An important outcome of this approach is the concept of learning readiness, which implies that children cannot be trained to learn just anything at any stage, but must first be ready for it.

In contrast, the environmentalist view suggests that

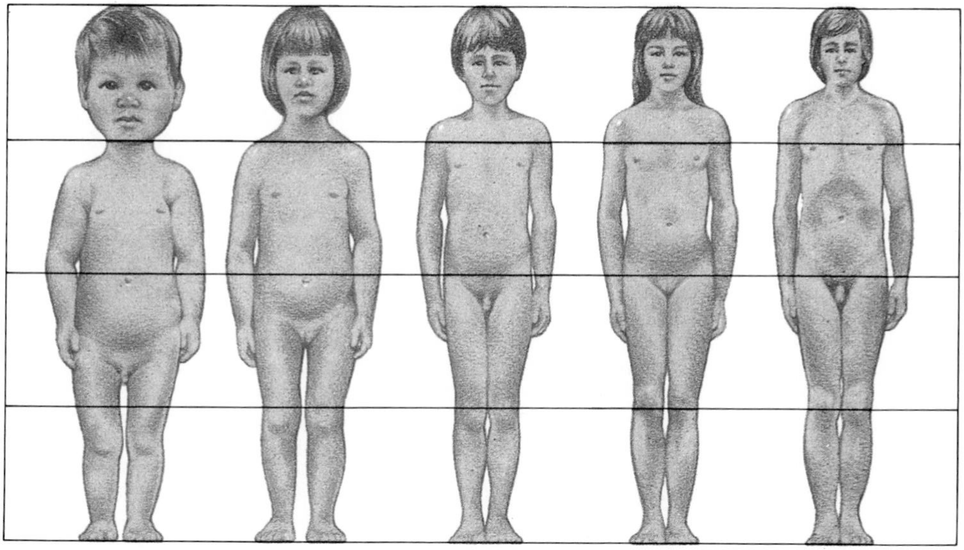

The changing proportions of the human body are illustrated in this diagram showing, alternately and drawn to the same height, the male and the female at 18 months, 3 years, 7 years, 11 years, and 15 years. As a result of rapid prenatal development of the brain, the infant's head is about one-fourth the size of its body. The torso and the limbs develop more rapidly after birth, diminishing the relative size of the head to about one-seventh of body height at puberty.

development may be more continuous, depending on the environmental stimulation. Contemporary research indicates that children whose family and preschool setting provide them with varied opportunities for learning, and with encouragement and praise, will reflect a degree of INTELLIGENCE in the later classroom situation superior to that of understimulated children. According to the environmentalists, intelligence, instead of being innate or dependent on a neurologically programmed readiness, is an outcome of the child's social interaction with the dynamics of maturation. The influence of this theoretical position has resulted in the contemporary emphasis on early childhood experience within the familial setting.

Although learning can account for some types of cognitive skills, it is not clear to what degree it can be applied to the development of conceptualization and abstraction. Nor does the learning model take into account such factors as possible genetic determinants of intelligence, the role played by family setting, or the relationships among emotional development, motivation, and achievement.

In contrast to environmentalists and learning-oriented psychologists, a strictly genetic point of view would maintain that intelligence is hereditary. Such an extreme position has been moderated in recent years as the result of in-depth environmental studies. It is clear that physical characteristics are transmitted genetically; however, there is no equally firm evidence for the application of genetic laws to intelligence and social behavior, except those cases in which sensory pathology or other biological defects have been inherited. It is difficult to determine exactly where biology ends and environmental influences begin. The attitudes of a parent of limited intelligence might adversely affect the intellectual development of a child even if the intelligence level has not been transmitted at birth. The issue involves defining the constituent parts of intelligence. Work in genetic research continues with animals, carrying with it the potential for future application to child-development theory.

None of the approaches outlined above has conclusively answered the question of whether innate limitations on intelligence exist and, if so, to what degree they can be overcome. However, intelligence or intellectual development can be stimulated by appropriate environmental or behavioral intervention.

Personality Development

Students of personality development are primarily concerned with a child's ability to secure satisfaction and to tolerate frustration, with the anxieties relating to dependency and independence, with aggressive and submissive behavior, and with inner conflicts that could produce deviant or problem behavior.

Most of the theory in this field stems from the clinical work of CHILD PSYCHIATRY, which, with modifications and adaptations, is based on PSYCHOANALYSIS. The emotional experiences to which the child is subjected in the first 5 years of life produce the basic adult emotional pattern or personality structure. Significant contributions to the understanding of emotional development have been made by such outstanding theorists and researchers in the field of child psychiatry as Sigmund Freud, Melanie KLEIN, Anna FREUD, Erik ERIKSON, Margaret Mahler, and Stella Chess.

Socialization

Young children, from about the age of 18 months on, must learn to conform to the behavioral requirements of the larger society as these are interpreted by their parents and other significant adults. In so doing, they must learn self-control, cleanliness, repression of anger, and respect for elders and property.

If the child fails to make an adequate transition from self-being to social being, he or she is thought to display aberrant behavior, which will affect intellectual, emotional, and social progress.

Some of the work done by practitioners of child psychiatry has influenced psychology in the form of social learning theory. This approach is concerned with guiding parents away from improper methods of child training such as inconsistency of behavior, threats, harsh punishment, and the withholding or withdrawal of love, that may result in later deviant behavior. Benjamin SPOCK's *Baby and Child Care* (1st ed., 1946) has been particularly influential. An offshoot of this approach is the contemporary concern with role models, based on the belief that children may consciously or unconsciously model their behavior on that of the parent or significant adult in their lives; this again brings to the fore the influence of parenting on child development.

child labor Child labor is the employment of children under the age of physical maturity in jobs requiring long hours. In industrialized countries, few persons under the age of 15 are now permitted to work, except on farms or in family enterprises. The laws are not always effectively enforced, however.

The exploitation of children was one of the scandals of the 19th century. The novelist Charles Dickens and the socialist Karl Marx were among those who helped to arouse public opinion against it. The Industrial Revolution had brought numbers of young children into mines and factories, where they worked long hours in dangerous and filthy conditions. Children had worked hard long before that time, however, in agriculture and in shops where they worked for their parents.

The first laws regulating child labor were passed in Great Britain in 1802. These were not effective because no provisions were made for enforcing them. The Factory Act of 1833 eliminated some of the worst abuses. In France, Germany, and other countries of Western Europe laws regulating child labor began to appear in the first half of the 19th century. Opposition to child labor came from a variety of sources: from labor unions, from social reformers, and even from the Prussian army, which was concerned about the physical fitness of its recruits.

The abuse of child labor emerged as a grave problem during the 19th century as industrialization increased. Children such as these miners were a steady source of cheap labor, often working 12 or more hours a day under dangerous conditions.

In the United States, some states passed laws against child labor in the 19th century, but they were not always enforced. Federal laws prohibiting child labor were twice struck down by the Supreme Court in *Hammer* v. *Dagenhart* (1918) and *Bailey* v. *Drexel Furniture Company* (1922) before the enactment of the Fair Labor Standards Act in 1938. This and the laws of the states now prohibit the employment of children under 16 during school hours. The most extensive use of child labor today is in agriculture, particularly among migrant workers, but even these children are required to attend school.

The problem of child labor has been largely supplanted in the United States by that of unemployment among young people who are no longer in school. The exploitation of child labor remains a major problem in many developing countries.

child psychiatry Child psychiatry, a specialized field of medicine, diagnoses and treats behavioral disorders that occur from infancy through adolescence. Many disturbances often receive psychiatric intervention: compulsive and repetitive motor movements, or hyperactivity; regressive social behavior such as bed-wetting; manifestations of obsessive fears and anxieties; withdrawal or other bizarre behavior, as seen in the autistic or schizophrenic child; learning difficulties; and aggressive and hostile behavior.

Aberrant behavior in children may be caused by neurological impairment, MENTAL RETARDATION, environmental inadequacies, traumatic emotional or physical experiences, or a combination of such factors. Diagnostic procedures in child psychiatry therefore require a variety of special testing and assessment techniques, as well as evaluatory input from other disciplines such as NEUROLOGY and PEDIATRICS. Because the child is still growing, the psychiatrist must be well aware of the stages of CHILD DEVELOPMENT, in order to assess what is in fact problem behavior and what is not. Moreover, because communicating with disturbed children is often difficult, special procedures are required—play therapy, projective techniques such as drawing and painting, and other nonverbal activities. Much of a child's disruptive behavior may be derived from or reinforced by the familial setting, so treatment frequently includes parent counseling.

Currently there are two main approaches to child psychiatry: one is the traditional psychoanalytic approach based on Freudian theory, stressing the behavioral role of unconscious mechanisms that develop as a result of unresolved emotional conflicts with parents; the other is the more recent, neurochemical approach, stressing neurological and sensory factors and relying heavily on the extensive current research in biochemical influences on behavior.

child psychology see DEVELOPMENTAL PSYCHOLOGY

Childe, V. Gordon Vere Gordon Childe, b. Apr. 14, 1892, d. Oct. 19, 1957, an Australian-born British archaeologist and prehistorian, influenced later anthropologists. Studying European prehistory of the 3d and 2d millennia BC and its relation to the Near East, he instilled an international approach in such works as *The Dawn of European Civilisation* (1925).

childhood diseases see DISEASES, CHILDHOOD

Children's Crusade The Children's Crusade was a tragic episode in 1212 after the Fourth CRUSADE. Hundreds of children led by Nicholas, a 12-year-old boy of Cologne, marched from the German Rhineland through the Alps to Italy, hoping to cross the sea dry-shod and to recapture Christ's Sepulcher in Jerusalem. Most of them perished or stayed in Italy. Tradition has confused them with a French children's group, led by young Stephen of Cloyes, which is said to have been promised free passage from Marseille to the Holy Land but was sold into slavery instead. Crusading preachers, mass hysteria, and popular respect for children as God's instruments probably contributed to this phenomenon.

children's language see PSYCHOLINGUISTICS

children's literature Children's literature is the only literary type defined not by any special features of its own, but by its audience. The designation is inaccurate in at least two obvious ways: "children's literature" is read and enjoyed by many who are no longer children, and many books—such as Daniel Defoe's *Robinson Crusoe* (1719), Jonathan Swift's *Gulliver's Travels* (1726), and Mark Twain's *The Adventures of Huckleberry Finn* (1884)—were not written for children, although they have been read and enjoyed by them.

At the very least, to have a literature for children there must be children—not just people younger than a certain age, but people recognized as belonging to their own special phase of life. The category children—that is, a group having identifiable needs in clothing, diet, sleep, education, music, and literature—is a phenomenon created by a middle class, and it came into existence in the West as the middle class grew large and strong enough to know its needs and to create markets to supply them. To judge from pictures of young people in groupings of the Seven Ages of Man, or in portraits of the families of nobility in pre-17th-century Europe, people the age of "children" look like small adults. At the age of about seven, they joined the human community at large. If they worked less hard because they were smaller or not as strong as others, their games, music, and stories were nevertheless the games, music, and stories of everyone. Thus FAIRY TALES, which for two centuries have been thought of as a fundamental part of children's literature, in fact had a long previous existence as an oral communal literature.

Fairy Tales

One book often cited as the first work for children is Charles Perrault's *Histoires ou Contes de temps passé*; (1697; Histories or Stories of Past Times), often known by its subtitle, *Contes de ma mère l'oie*, or *Mother Goose Tales*, as the title read in its first English translation (1729). Many of Perrault's stories were familiar throughout Europe. Some had already appeared in earlier collections, such as those by the Italians Giovanni Straparola and Giambattista Basile.

Perrault's collection included such familiar tales as "Little Red Riding Hood," "Cinderella," "The Sleeping Beauty in the Wood," "Puss in Boots," and "Hop o' My Thumb." What makes his *Contes* a children's book is really only his effort to keep the tales short. Otherwise, their wit and sophistication imply adult listeners. Perrault was in no way a folklorist, as were later collectors of the tales of a nation or region, like the brothers Grimm in Germany or Peter Asbjørnsen and Jørgen Moe in Norway.

Beginnings of a Children's Literature in English

The first concerted effort to create a separate literature for children came in England, beginning about 50 years after Perrault. England had developed a burgeoning and prosperous middle class earlier than other European countries, and these people wanted to educate their young and needed books to help them. The pride of place as the first children's book in England probably goes to Mary Cooper's *Tommy Thumb's Pretty Song Book (for all little Masters and Misses; to be sung to them by their Nurses 'till they can sing themselves...)*, the earliest (1744) known collection of NURSERY RHYMES. The second collection, whose name was taken from the Perrault tales, was *Mother Goose's Melody* (1760), probably published by the bookseller John Newbery.

Newbery, who published many more books for adults than he did for children, understood that there was a whole class of adults who themselves were new to literacy, and for whom poems, stories, histories, and aids to prayer and piety had already been published. These could quite easily be shortened, simplified, and illustrated for children. Newbery's most famous book, *Goody Two-Shoes* (1765), probably written for him by Oliver Goldsmith, is now so little read that many misname it a "moral tale." It is that, but not in a solemn or preaching way; mostly it offers a Goldsmithian view of English country life, its pages filled with such characters as Margery Meanwell, Farmer Graspall, and Sir Timothy Gripe.

The following 100 years—which produced little still read today except *Grimm's Fairy Tales* (1812–15; first Eng. trans., 1823)—are notable mostly for their "moral tales." These were written in part as a reaction against the popularity of fairy-tale collections—which were condemned as simply fanciful or the product of superstitious ignorance—and in part to teach. First written in the 18th century, by the early 1800s they had become the most popular type of children's book in England. As the 19th century wore on, the genre became more heavily didactic. In its use of extreme situations to carry moral lessons (in

Mrs. Sherwood's *Fairchild Family*, 1818, for example, a father delivers his moral to his children by showing them a hanged murderer in a forest), the moral tale came to resemble the somewhat more primitive cautionary tale, a story of gory happenings meant to deliver a warning. Hilaire Belloc parodied that genre in his *Cautionary Tales for Children* (1907), which was about "Matilda, who told Lies, and was Burned to Death," and other unfortunate juveniles.

The Golden Age

It was not until the 1860s that a still-vital children's literature really began, with Charles Kingsley's *Water Babies* (1863), Christina Rossetti's *Goblin Market* (1862), and—most famous of all—Lewis Carroll's *Alice's Adventures in Wonderland* (1865) and *Through the Looking-Glass* (1872).

Wordsworth's great poetic explorations of childhood were written mostly in the first decade of the 19th century, and Charles Dickens wrote *Oliver Twist* in the 1830s. Some of the great heirs to Wordsworth's children, and to Oliver, David Copperfield, Jane Eyre, and Catherine Earnshaw, are to be found decades later in George Macdonald's *At the Back of the North Wind* (1871) and the *Princess* books (1872, 1883), Robert Louis Stevenson's *Treasure Island* (1882) and *Kidnapped* (1886), Rudyard Kipling's *Jungle Books* (1894–95) and *Just-So Stories* (1902), Andrew Lang's fairy-tale collections (1889–1907), E. Nesbit's *Bastable* books (1899–1910), Frances Hodgson Burnett's *The Secret Garden* (1912), Kenneth Grahame's *The Wind in the Willows* (1908), and Beatrix Potter's matchless array of small books about animals (1900–12).

Children's Book Illustrators

The great names of book illustration are Walter Crane, Kate Greenaway, Ralph Caldecott, and Arthur Rackham in England; Maurice Boutet de Bonvel in France; and Ernest Kreidolf in Germany. Other irreplaceable illustrators include John Tenniel for the *Alice* books, Beatrix Potter, W. W. Denslow and John R. Neill for the *Oz* books (1900–20), N. C. Wyeth for Stevenson, Attilio Mussino for C. Collodi's *Pinocchio* (1924), and E. H. Shepard for A. A. Milne's books of Christopher Robin and Winnie-the-Pooh (1924–28) and for *The Wind in the Willows* (1933).

Children's Literature in the 20th Century

Increasingly in the last 50 years, and especially in the United States, the most striking fact about children's books has been the vast increase in their number. In any given year during the period 1975–85, for example, more books—over 2,000 per year—have been offered by the juvenile divisions of American publishers than were published in two decades a century ago. The same flourishing children's-book industry can be found wherever a thriving middle class seeks ways to educate and influence its children.

Perhaps the most positive development accompanying this large output has been the growing awareness on the part of many young readers of the possibilities of life in other countries. Translations from foreign literature accompanied most of the great national collections of fairy and folk tales; Andrew Lang's famed collections (*The Blue Fairy Book*, 1889, and its successors) ranged over the Eurasian continent for their materials, and the Italian *Pinocchio* first appeared in English in 1892. It was when children's books began to be published on a mass scale, however, that English-speaking children could read about *Bambi* (Eng. trans., 1928), by the Austrian Felix Salten; *The Wonderful Adventures of Nils* of Selma Lagerlöf (Eng. trans., 1907) and Astrid Lindgren's *Pippi Longstocking* (Eng. trans., 1950), both Swedish; the Swiss *Heidi*, by Johanna Spyri (Eng. trans., 1884); the Hungarian *Good Master*, written in English in 1935 by Kate Seredy; the Nigerian Chinua Achebe's *Chike* (1966); the Dutch novels of Meindert De Jong (the 1950s and '60s); and, perhaps the greatest of all illustrated books, the *Babar* series by Jean de Brunhoff, translated from the French beginning in 1933.

A more conspicuous accompaniment to the massive number of children's books has been the influence over them exerted by people with a professional expertise concerning children: teachers, librarians, psychologists, and editors of children's books. Inevitably, this influence has established rules for what is "suitable" for children at large as well as for children of particular ages: "suitable" can include a prohibition of what children should not know, as well as an insistence on the presence of what they should know. Another result of this influence has

The original version of Lewis Carroll's Alice in Wonderland *was called* Alice's Adventures Underground. *It was written and illustrated by Carroll in 1862–63 and, bound in green leather, given as a Christmas gift to his young friend, Alice Liddell.*

since her swim in the pool, and her walk along the river-bank with its fringe of rushes and forget-me-nots, and the glass table and the little door had vanished.

Soon the rabbit noticed Alice, as she stood looking curiously about her, and at once said in a quick angry tone, "why, Mary Ann! what are you doing out here? Go home this moment, and look on my dressing-table for my gloves and nosegay, and fetch them here, as quick as you can run, do you hear?" and Alice was so much frightened that she ran off at once, without

(Left) *Beatrix Potter's illustrations, small as they are, always contain a lot to think about. This picture, from* Peter Rabbit *(1901), shows Potter's ability to give human feeling to her animals without giving them human faces.* (Center) *Ernest Shepard's illustrations for* Winnie-the-Pooh *(1926) defined A. A. Milne's characters for generations of readers.* (Right) *Modern children's books often make the text subordinate to the illustration. In many of Maurice Sendak's books—such as* In the Night Kitchen *(1970)—the pictures take over almost entirely from the text.*

been the production of books that gear their vocabulary, illustrations, and narrative density to a precisely calculated, narrow notion of what children of a given age can be expected to know, understand, or be interested in. The recognition that books may have an intellectual, emotional, or imaginative effect on the children who read them—that is, that children's books are, in an important sense, "serious"—has led various adult groups to object to many books because they do not conform to the morality of those groups, which label them "elitist," "racist," "sexist," "communist," "dirty," or sometimes just "stupid."

For at least two generations in the United States, children's literature was strongly characterized by an image of America that was rural and peaceful, innocent even in its wisdom, practical even in its approach to the magical, optimistic and nostalgic. Inevitably, in these books adult writers presumed to understand children and to believe that adult society was a place that children would wish to inhabit when they grew up. An ordinary writer like Lucy Fitch Perkins went so far as to adapt and transpose this America and these values in a series of books ostensibly about children from other countries (*The Dutch Twins*, 1911, and many others). Nevertheless, within this milieu, however unrealistic, many good books appeared: the *Freddy* books of Walter R. Brooks (1930s–1950s); Robert McCloskey's *Make Way for Ducklings* (1941) and *Homer Price* (1943); Laura Ingalls Wilder's realistic saga about her pioneer family, *The Little House* series (1932–43); Virginia Lee Burton's *Mike Mulligan and His Steam Shovel* (1938); E. B. White's *Charlotte's Web* (1952). Small children learned to read from the pages of Dr. Seuss (beginning with *And to Think That I Saw It on Mulberry Street*, 1939), whose whacky verses and pictures are open, easy, hearty, upbeat, and ineffably American.

Similarly, during the same period, English children's literature often seemed dominated by an image equally unrealistic: a large house, a group of brothers and sisters, adults who understand little, and encounters with magic. E. Nesbit's *Bastable* books and Frances Hodgson Burnett's *The Secret Garden* may be said to have inaugurated this tradition, but it has insistently persisted so that—even after such houses have all but disappeared from England—M. L. Travers in her books about *Mary Poppins* (1934–82), and Mary Norton in hers about *The Borrowers* (1952–82), created stories that equal or surpass Nesbit's and Burnett's.

In America, when the reaction against images of safe children in a safe country came, it predictably came very powerfully. In the 1960s and '70s the emphasis turned to grim realism, to "problems," to minorities: children from broken homes, autistic and retarded children, children adventuring into sex and drug addiction. These books often conveyed the sense that childhood was not safe, and that the passage to adulthood must be marked by danger and violence. Yet it would seem once again that however revealing these new emphases are about adult perceptions of children—or about childhood itself—the books written under their influence may not be read after these perceptions change.

The great figures in these years seem almost untouched by any of these concerns. The two major influences have been, on both sides of the Atlantic, J. R. R. Tolkien and the American Maurice Sendak. Tolkien, an English scholar of ancient language and lore, and in temperament quite withdrawn from the 20th century, nonetheless in *The Hobbit* (1938) and *The Lord of the Rings* (1953–55) created possibilities for adventure, for danger, for the relation of the magical to the natural, that have left a generation of addicted readers and an influence on fantasy literature, designed for adults as well as children, as great as any in the century.

The case of Sendak is also unlikely and extraordinary. As has gradually become clear, he is the first great author and illustrator of books for children who is also a great connoisseur about children's literature and, though technically only an amateur, a great knower about children. Unlike Tolkien and unlike most of the writers and illustrators of the Golden Age, Sendak clearly thinks about children, and enjoys being around them and painting and drawing for them. *Where the Wild Things Are* (1965), *In the Night Kitchen* (1970), and *Outside over There* (1981) are Sendak's three great original picture books. *Higglety Pigglety Pop!* (1967) bears a closer resemblance to a book with pictures, as it narrates the adventures of Jennie, the Sealyham terrier who leaves home because "there must be more to life." Sendak is as happy illustrating the works of others as creating his own tales, and his output is therefore immense; yet the Sendak style is so adaptive and changing that his imitators are often hard put to discover which style is truly "his."

See also: separate articles on many of the authors and illustrators mentioned.

children's rights The rights of children, or minors, have traditionally been limited in English-speaking countries because common law has regarded them as the property of their parents. The age at which adulthood is reached varies from country to country and in different legal contexts. Since 1971, when the 26th Amendment to the U.S. Constitution lowered the federal voting age from 21 to 18, most states have similarly lowered the age of adulthood for most purposes.

U.S. courts have long granted children certain rights as citizens, such as the right to claim an inheritance or sue for damages. The U.S. Supreme Court has further held (1967) that minors accused of crimes are entitled to many of the same safeguards as adult defendants (see Juvenile Delinquency). Some adult rights are tailored to fit children's special needs. Children possess rights under the 1st Amendment, for example, but not so far as to allow them free access to pornography. Children may enter into most types of contracts, but few such contracts are held to be binding on the child.

Certain rights are specific to children because of their special dependency on adults for support and protection. Child Abuse and neglect laws define situations in which official intervention in a family on a child's behalf is justified.

Chile [chil'-ee] Chile is a country on the west coast of South America. It stretches in a ribbon more than 4,200 km (2,600 mi) from Peru to the southern tip of the continent at Cape Horn, including the larger part of Tierra del Fuego, an archipelago separated from the mainland by the Strait of Magellan. It has an average width of 177 km (110 mi). Excluding a disputed territory of about 1,251,000 km^2 (483,000 mi^2) in Antarctica, also claimed by Great Britain, Chile is slightly larger than Texas. Outlying territories include Easter Island, the Juan Fernández Islands, and other islands in the Pacific. The

AT A GLANCE

REPUBLIC OF CHILE

Land: Area: 756,945 km^2 (292,258 mi^2). Capital and largest city: Santiago (1987 est pop., 4,858,342).

People: Population (1990 est.): 13,200,000. Density: 17.4 persons per km^2 (45.2 per mi^2). Distribution (1990): 84% urban, 16% rural. Official language: Spanish. Religion: Roman Catholicism.

Government: Type: republic. Legislature: Congress. Political subdivisions: 12 regions, 1 urban district.

Economy: GDP (1989 est.): $25.3 billion; $1,970 per capita. Labor distribution (1988): agriculture—14.8%; manufacturing—16.4%; mining—2.8%; construction—5.8%; public utilities, transportation, and communications—5.7%; trade—14.4%; finance—6.8%; public administration, defense, and services—21.6%; other—11.7%. Foreign trade (1988): imports—$4.9 billion; exports—$7.05 billion. Currency: 1 peso = 100 centavos.

Education and Health: Literacy (1988): 94.3% of adult population. Universities (1989): 23. Hospital beds (1986): 33,136. Physicians (1985): 12,334. Life expectancy (1990): women—77; men—70. Infant mortality (1989): 18 per 1,000 live births.

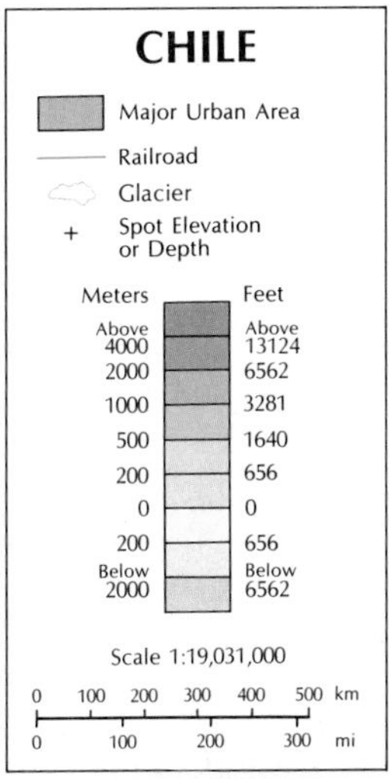

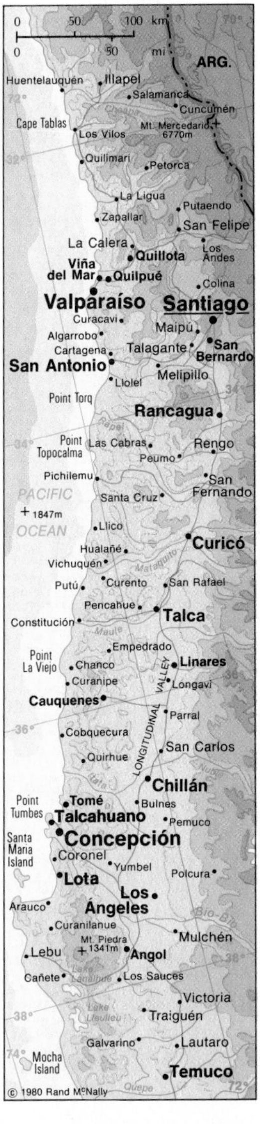

ANDES Mountains, reaching to more than 6,700 m (22,000 ft) above sea level, separate the country from Argentina and Bolivia. The capital and largest city is SANTIAGO, in the central part of the country. Manufacturing and mining make Chile one of the most important industrial nations in Latin America. Chile, from the Indian *Tchili* meaning "the deepest point of the Earth," achieved independence in 1818.

Land

Three principal geologic regions run north and south through Chile: the Andes; the Central Valley, which is divided by mountain spurs; and a coastal escarpment (762 m/2,500 ft high), which ends in steep cliffs along the Pacific coast and includes many islands in the south. The mountain ranges in the central region include volcanoes, such as Tupungato (6,800 m/22,310 ft) and Ojos del Salado (6,863 m/22,516 ft), which is the second highest peak in the Western Hemisphere. The country has suffered frequent destructive earthquakes.

Chile's great length and the cold waters of the Peru Current offshore create three distinct latitudinal climatic regions. About 70% of all Chileans live in the region known as Middle or Mediterranean Chile, which constitutes about 20% of the country's total area. This region extends from La Serena to Osorno and includes the Central Valley and the harbor of VALPARAÍSO. The region south of CONCEPCIÓN has stormy winters and cool summers. The forests, lakes, and snow-capped mountains, which reach 4,267 m (14,000 ft) around Temuco, make up the country's principal vacation area.

The northern region, about 1,127 km (700 mi) long, consists of dry basins, broken by a few rivers, and the ATACAMA DESERT. Perched atop the coastal escarpment are the port cities of ANTOFAGASTA, ARICA, and Iquique. The region occupies about 40% of the country's total area but has only 15% of the population.

About 15% of the population live in the southern one-third of Chile, a narrow strip of forests, lakes, fjords, and islands that extends south from Puerto Montt.

Climate. The Peru Current stabilizes temperatures in both central and northern Chile. In Santiago temperatures average 21° C (69° F) in summer (January) and 9° C (48° F) in winter (July); annual rainfall averages 356 mm (14 in), most of which occurs between May and September. Heavy fog stabilizes temperatures in the northern coastal zone at 21° C (70° F) during the summer and 16° C (60° F) during the winter.

In the south, average annual rainfall varies from 2,200 cm (86 in) at Puerto Montt to only 500 mm (19 in) at PUNTA ARENAS. Winter and summer temperature ranges from 8° to 16° C (46° to 60° F) at Puerto Montt and from 2° to 11° C (36° to 52° F) at Punta Arenas. In the far south, only grasses, mosses, and ferns can survive the windy, cold weather.

Resources. Chile is one of the world's most important suppliers of copper and has large reserves of iron ore, coal, sodium nitrate, iodine, borax, molybdenum, gold, silver, lead, zinc, and sulfur. The hydroelectric potential is large and well distributed, except in the desert north.

(Right) *Santiago, the capital and most populous city of Chile, is located on a broad plain at the base of the Andes. The city was originally named (1541) Santiago del Nuevo Extremo (Santiago of the New Frontier) by its founder, the Spanish conquistador Pedro de Valdivia.*

(Below) *Viña del Mar, a resort city whose name means "vineyard by the sea," is situated on the Pacific coast, northeast of Valparaíso. Viña del Mar's casinos and beach are important to Chile's developing tourist industry.*

People

About two-thirds of Chile's people are mestizos (of mixed Indian and white ancestry). Small numbers of Germans, Swiss, Italians, British, French, and Yugoslavs settled in central and southern Chile during the 19th and 20th centuries. About 150,000 descendants of the original ARAUCANIAN Indians live in the forests south of the Bío-bío River.

Spanish, the official language, is spoken by nearly all the population, but some Indians retain their own languages. About 80% of Chileans are Roman Catholic.

Demography. Since 1920 the urban population has increased by more than 70%. About 37% of all the people live in Santiago province; many migrants have settled in *callampas* (shantytowns) on the outskirts of the city. Another 15% live in 11 provincial capitals.

Education and Health. Since 1966 eight years of primary education have been free and compulsory. Secondary education consists of four years of scientific and humanistic studies for university-bound students or technical and vocational training. The largest institution of higher learning is the University of Chile (1738). The country has one of the highest literacy rates in Latin America. Since 1973 the once extensive state-run social welfare and public health system has been reduced.

Arts. The poets Gabriela Mistral and Pablo NERUDA have both won Nobel prizes. Manuel Rojas has portrayed the grim existence of the poor in his novels, and Eduardo Barrios is a master of the psychological novel (see LATIN AMERICAN LITERATURE). Noted musicians include the pianist Claudio ARRAU, the singer Ramon Vinay, and the composers Gustavo Becerra and Domingo Santa Cruz.

Economic Activity

The Chilean economy is based on manufacturing and services. Mining, which provides about half of all exports, employs a tiny percentage of the labor force. The government has played a major role in economic development since 1939, when the Production Development Corporation (CORFO, from its Spanish name) was created to support substitution of domestic manufactures for imported goods. After seizing power in 1973, the Pinochet government dismantled tariff barriers, and its policies tended to concentrate wealth in fewer hands. Competition from foreign imports, falling prices for mineral exports, and a rising external debt (much of it incurred by the private sector) led to a recession in the 1980s.

Chile surpassed the United States as the world's leading producer of copper in 1982. The large copper mines, nationalized by the Allende government, remain under state control. Molybdenum, iron ore, gold, silver, nitrates, lithium, and other minerals are also exported, and petroleum fields in the south supply about half of all domestic requirements. Major manufactures include automobiles, chemicals, rubber products, cement, and consumer goods. Another export is the well-known Chilean wine.

The colonial system of land tenure survived until the passage of the Agrarian Reform Law in 1967. By 1972 the government had distributed more than 7 million ha (17 million acres) to more than 40,000 families, but the Pinochet government returned some expropriated land to its original owners. Stock raising is the chief activity in most rural areas. Wheat, other grains, and vegetables are grown for food.

Chile's extensive railroad system, largely state owned, connects many cities with the coast and with Argentina, Bolivia, and Peru. A paved highway system runs the length of the country, and port facilities are well developed.

Government

Chile returned to democratic government in 1990 after being governed by a military junta led by Gen. Augusto PINOCHET UGARTE since a 1973 coup d'état. A 1980 plebiscite approved a new constitution, which replaced the 1925 charter suspended in 1973. Under the 1981 constitution (not fully in effect until 1989), executive power rests with a directly elected president; legislative power is vested in a bicameral National Congress.

History

The first European exploration of the region that is now Chile was made in 1535 by Diego de ALMAGRO. Unlike Peru, the land yielded little gold, and the native Araucanian Indians offered fierce resistance. In 1541, Pedro de VALDIVIA established several settlements, including Santiago. In 1553, Valdivia was killed by LAUTARO, an Araucanian who became the hero of the epic poem *La Araucana.* Chilean-born Spaniards (Creoles) declared their autonomy and established a governing junta on Sept. 18, 1810. Although the Spanish crown regained control, its forces were defeated by Chileans and Argentines led by Bernardo O'HIGGINS and José de SAN MARTÍN.

Independence was proclaimed on Feb. 12, 1818, and O'Higgins was elected supreme director. By 1830, O'Higgins was in exile, and conservative landowners and merchants were in control of a centralized government. After defeating Bolivia and Peru in the War of the Pacific (1879-84), victorious Chilean armies finally defeated Araucanian forces to end the Indian wars. A new constitution in 1925 provided for direct popular election of the president, separation of church and state, and compulsory primary education.

In 1964, President Eduardo FREI MONTALVA of the Christian Democrats began buying the U.S. copper companies and expropriating land. In 1970, Salvador ALLENDE, head of a new Popular Unity coalition made up of Socialists, Communists, and leftist Radicals, won an electoral plurality and was confirmed as president. He became the first constitutionally elected Marxist president of an independent state in the hemisphere.

Allende then finished the process of nationalizing the U.S. copper firms, nationalized all private banks, and accelerated land distribution. After three turbulent years, the military seized power in a bloody coup. Subsequently, it was revealed that anti-Allende forces had been financed by the U.S. Central Intelligence Agency (CIA). Censorship and a state of siege were imposed as the right-wing junta dedicated itself to eradicating "the cancer of Marxism." Consequently, the Pinochet government was widely criticized for violating human rights. The new government returned many factories, banks, and expropriated land to private owners. After sustained economic growth in the late 1970s, Chile plunged into a deep recession in 1982–83, which sparked an upsurge of political opposition. In the mid-1980s the economy began a marked upturn. During 1988, Pinochet lifted all states of emergency and gave permission for all remaining political exiles to return. In October, Pinochet was the sole candidate in a plebiscite on whether he should serve an additional eight years in a transition to democracy. The fragmented opposition united to defeat him, but he remained in office until March 1990, when Patricio AYLWIN, elected in 1989, became president. Pinochet continues as army commander in chief.

chili see PEPPER (vegetable)

Chillicothe [chil-i-kahth'-ee] The seat of Ross County, Chillicothe (1990 pop., 21,923) is a city in south central Ohio at the junction of the Scioto River and Paint Creek. Settled in 1796, it was the capital of the Northwest Territory in 1800 and was twice the capital of Ohio. The Mound City Group, a series of ancient Indian burial mounds, is nearby.

Chilpancingo [cheel-pahn-seeng'-goh] Chilpancingo (full name: Chilpancingo de los Bravos) is the capital of Guerrero state in south central Mexico, about 220 km (135 mi) south of Mexico City. The city's population is 98,266 (1980). Chilpancingo is an administrative center and a processing center for agricultural and forest products from the surrounding region. The city was founded by Spaniards in 1591 on a pre-Aztec site. In 1813 the first Mexican congress, which declared the country independent, met there.

chimaera [ki-mair'-uh] Chimaeras are cartilaginous marine fishes related to the sharks. They belong to three families: Chimaeridae, Rhinochimaeridae, and Callo-

The short-nosed chimaera has a venomous spine in front of the first dorsal fin. The clasper on the forehead of the male (below) *is used to hold the female when mating takes place.*

rhinchidae. They are found in the deep water of all temperate oceans. The most representative species is the ratfish, *Hydrolagus colliei*, so named for its long, pointed tail. Chimaeras have large heads with big eyes. Their smooth, scaleless skin is black, gray, or silver, and sometimes striped or spotted. Chimaeras reach up to 2 m (6.5 ft) in length.

Chimaeras resemble sharks in that they have a cartilage skeleton and that the female is fertilized internally, by means of a modified fin ray. They resemble bony fish in possessing a bony covering over the gill slits, and an upper jaw fused to the skull as in the lungfish. In breathing, chimaeras inhale water mainly through the nostrils rather than through the mouth. Chimaeras eat small invertebrates and fish.

Chimborazo [cheem-boh-rah'-soh] Chimborazo is a volcanic peak in the Occidental Andes of west central Ecuador. The highest point in Ecuador at 6,265 m (20,561 ft), it is a difficult climb and was first conquered in 1880 by Edward Whymper. Its crater is buried under a thick ice cap. Tributaries of the Guayas River rise from the western glaciers, and tributaries of the Amazon rise on the east.

Chimera see BELLEROPHON

chimes see BELL

chimney A chimney is a hollow vertical shaft used to remove the products of combustion from a building. Since prehistoric times, humans have had to cope with the venting of smoke from household fires used for warmth and cooking.

Origins. Originally, the term *chimney* referred to the hearth, its surroundings, and the flue, but it is now understood to mean the structure that conducts smoke and gases from the fireplace or other fuel-burning appliance to the atmosphere. Although the Romans heated their baths and public buildings, no Roman fireplaces or chimneys have been found.

In the colder climate of Central Europe, fireplaces with cylindrical masonry chimneys were used as early as the 11th century, and 100 years later the chimney was a fixture in most secular buildings in Europe.

Function of the Flue. The exhaust function of the chimney flue depends on the difference in density between the air column in the shaft and an equal column of outside air. The warmer air in the flue, being less dense, is forced up and out, carrying the smoke and gases from the fire with it.

The size and shape of the flue affect the efficient operation of the fireplace or appliance it services. Lining is recommended for all masonry chimneys serving fireplaces fired by solid fuels, since the rough surfaces of unlined chimneys tend to collect creosote, the highly flammable distillate of the fuel, and create the potential for chimney fires.

Construction. Chimney construction is generally masonry, using brick, load-bearing clay tile, or concrete masonry units. In multiwalled metal chimneys, cool air from the room is introduced in the space between the flue walls at the bottom of the chimney.

Chimney-Related Fires. The accumulation of combustible soot and creosote on interior surfaces can be a hazard in stacks that induce insufficient draft and in flues used infrequently. It is recommended, therefore, that before using a fireplace each season, the lining be inspected and excessive soot removed.

Smokestacks. Smokestacks are tall chimneys built to vent industrial gaseous effluents high into the atmosphere. The U.S. Clean Air Act of 1970 encouraged the building of very tall smokestacks. Smokestacks reduce air pollution in the immediate area of the plant, but particulates may be carried far away by winds (see ACID RAIN). Smoke scrubbers, which remove most of the particulates, can be fitted to smokestacks (see POLLUTION CONTROL).

chimpanzee The chimpanzee, an APE, forms a single species, *Pan troglodytes,* in the family Pongidae of the mammalian order Primates. Chimpanzees, commonly called chimps, inhabit tropical central African rain forests and are the most intelligent and easily educated of the apes. The body is 63–91 cm (25–36 in) long. Standing erect, the chimp is 1–1.7 m (3¼–5½ ft) tall. The powerful arms are about one and a half times as long as the animal's standing height. The chimp has no tail. Males weigh 56–80 kg (123–176 lb); females weigh 45–68 kg (99–149 lb). The chimpanzee coat is usually black with a white patch near the rump. The brow ridge is prominent, and the face is bare skinned and black, mottled, or pale. The hands, feet, ears, and nose are pinkish. A small, or pygmy, form of chimpanzee, *P. paniscus,* lives south of the Congo River. Some mammalogists regard it as a subspecies of *P. troglodytes.*

Chimpanzees are among the noisiest of jungle dwellers. They shriek and scream, slap the ground, and keep

Chimpanzees use twigs stripped of leaves to insert into termite holes and then carry the insects to their mouths. Some anthropologists describe this technique as a very simple tool use.

up an almost constant hooting and muttering. "Nursery groups" of mothers and infants are relatively quiet. All usually fall silent and disappear into the forest when humans intrude. Chimps are equally at home on the ground and in the trees. Aloft, they use hands and feet to move about and sometimes brachiate, or swing from branch to branch with their arms. On the ground, they usually walk on all fours. Chimps also walk upright and are agile runners.

Feeding occupies about seven hours a day. They eat fruits, leaves, and other plant materials and occasionally meat; they are also fond of ants and termites. Chimps are called toolmakers because they shape a stem or a twig to insert into the termite nest, gathering insects to eat. They also pick up clubs and stones to defend themselves against intruders. Chimpanzees usually drink from streams by sucking water between their lips. They also fashion cups from leaves to dip up water. Chimpanzees rest at midday, usually on the ground but sometimes in trees. As night shelters, they build nests in trees.

Chimpanzees greet one another in many ways, from touching their fingertips to embracing. A chimpanzee that wants something from another—a morsel of food or simple friendship—holds out its hand, palm uppermost. Females come into heat at various times of the year. The birth of one, rarely two, young occurs after a gestation period of about 230 days. The baby, at birth weighing about 9 kg (4 lb), is completely dependent on the mother for about 2 years, clinging to her front and later riding on her back. Sexual maturity comes at 12 years. Chimpanzees live about 40 years.

Chimpanzees, widely used in behavioral and medical research, are able to communicate using various signs and symbols (see ANIMAL COMMUNICATION).

Chimu [chee'-moo] Chimu, also called Chimor, was a powerful ancient state on the north coast of present-day Peru. The kingdom stretched from near the present border between Peru and Ecuador to just north of Lima. Alliances were formed with some highland groups, but the empire was limited to the desert coast. It ruled from about AD 1000 until it fell to the INCA around 1450–70.

The Chimu are known for their well-planned adobe cities, of which CHAN CHAN, the capital, was the largest example. A major technological achievement was the elaborate irrigation system that allowed the Chimu to cultivate the rich desert valleys of the area. Their culture is also known for several varieties of black monochrome ceramics, especially effigy vessels decorated in low relief. Chimu crafts reached their height in fine goldwork and silverwork, frequently inset with precious stones.

Little is known about the social and political organization of the Chimu kingdom, because its peoples did not possess writing and its power had been eclipsed by the time the invading Spaniards made their observations. The Chimu were probably similar in many respects to their Inca conquerors, establishing indirect rule over a large area through local leaders and financing the state through a kind of labor tax.

Ch'in see QIN

Chin see JIN

China China, located in East Asia, is the third largest country in the world in terms of area (after the USSR and Canada) and the world's most populous nation, with a population of more than 1 billion, or nearly one-fourth of the world's total population. Its coastline, bordering on the Yellow, East China, and South China seas, is about 12,000 km (7,500 mi) long. China shares a land border of about 21,260 km (13,210 mi) with 11 other countries: North Korea, the USSR, Mongolia, Afghanistan, India, Pakistan, Nepal, Bhutan, Burma, Laos, and Vietnam. Other neighbors include the British Crown Colony of Hong Kong and the Portuguese territory of Macao, scheduled to return to Chinese control in 1997 and 1999. The offshore island of Taiwan is a separate political entity from China, which has continued to demand the return of the island to its political jurisdiction since 1949. China disputes the ownership of the SPRATLY ISLANDS and the Paracel Islands.

The official name of China is the People's Republic of China (Zhonghua Renmin Gongheguo). The republic was established in 1949, but the name China, which is commonly used by foreigners, is probably derived from the Qin (Ch'in) dynasty (221–206 BC), which first unified the nation. The Chinese themselves use the name Zhonggua (Middle Country), which originated with the early Chinese concept that China was in the middle of the world.

China is divided into 23 provinces (including Taiwan) and 5 autonomous border regions, where other ethnic groups constitute a majority of the population. For ease of reference the provinces and autonomous regions are usually grouped into six large administrative regions. These units are as follows: (1) the Northeastern Region, which includes the provinces of Heilongjiang (Heilungkiang), Jilin (Kirin), and Liaoning (see MANCHURIA); (2) the Northern Region, which includes the provinces of HEBEI (Hopei) and SHANXI (Shansi), the Nei Menggu (Inner Mongolia) Autonomous Region (see INNER MONGOLIA), and the centrally controlled municipalities of BEIJING (Peking) and TIANJIN (Tientsin); (3) the Eastern Region, which includes the provinces of SHANDONG (Shantung), JIANGXI (Kiangsi), JIANGSU (Kiangsu), ANHUI (Anhwei), ZHEJIANG (Chekiang), and FUJIAN (Fukien) and the centrally controlled municipality of SHANGHAI; (4) the South Central Region, which includes the provinces of HAINAN, HENAN (Honan), HUBEI (Hupei), HUNAN, and GUANGDONG (Kwangtung) and the Guangxi Zhuang (Kwangsi Chuang) Autonomous Region; (5) the Southwestern Region, which includes the provinces of SICHUAN (Szechuan), GUIZHOU (Kweichow), and YUNNAN and the Xizang (Tibetan) Autonomous Region (see Tibet); (6) the Northwestern Region, which includes the provinces of Shaanxi (Shensi), GANSU (Kansu), and QINGHAI (Tsinghai) and the Xinjiang Uygur (Sinkiang Uighur) Autonomous Region (see XINJIANG).

China's written history began during the SHANG dynasty (*c.*1600–*c.*1027 BC). China was ruled by a series of dynasties until 1912, when a republic was established. In

AT A GLANCE

PEOPLE'S REPUBLIC OF CHINA

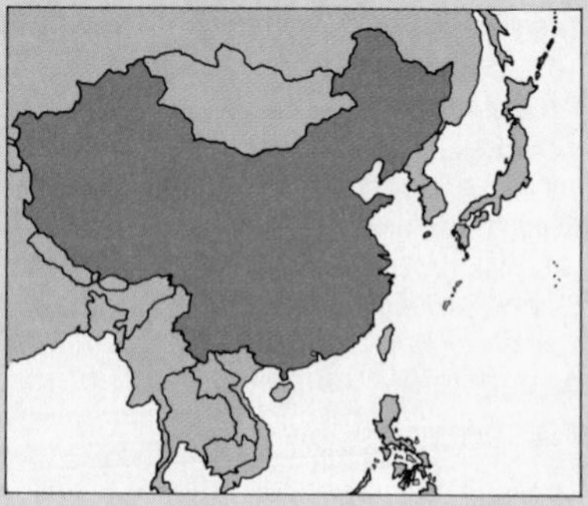

Land: Area: 9,562,904 km^2 (3,692,244 mi^2). Capital: Beijing (1989 est. pop., 6,500,000). Largest City: Shanghai (1989 est. pop., 8,000,000).

People: Population (1990 est.): 1,118,162,727. Density 117 persons per km^2 (303 per mi^2). Distribution (1988): 46.6% urban, 53.4% rural. Official language: Mandarin Chinese. Major religions: Taoism, Buddhism, Islam, folk religions.

Government: Type: single-party Communist state. Legislature: National People's Congress. Political subdivisions: 23 provinces (including Taiwan), 3 municipalities, 5 autonomous regions.

Economy: GNP (1988): $365 million; $340 per capita. Labor distribution (1987): agriculture—61%; industry—18%; commerce and trade—5%, construction—5%; science, education, health, and welfare—4%; transportation and communications—3%, government—2%. Foreign trade (1989): imports—$59.1 billion; exports—$52.5 billion. Currency: 1 Renminbi (yuan) = 100 fen.

Education and Health: Literacy (1988): 77% of adult population. Universities and other higher-education institutes (1987): 1,063. Hospital beds (1988): 2,503,000. Physicians (1988): 1,618,000. Life expectancy (1990): women—69; men—67; Infant mortality (1990): 34 per 1,000 live births.

1921 the Chinese Communist party was founded, and in 1926 the long civil war between the ruling nationalists, or KUOMINTANG, led by CHIANG KAI-SHEK, and the Communists, led by MAO ZEDONG (Mao Tse-tung), began. The Communists took over the mainland in 1949, establishing the People's Republic of China. The Kuomintang retreated to the island of TAIWAN, continuing as the Republic of China.

Land and Resources

The topography of China is often described roughly as forming three levels of elevation, which rise, like steps, from the lowlands along the east coast to the high mountains in the west. Each step, or level, of elevation occupies approximately one-third of the country. The highest level, with altitudes above 2,000 m (6,600 ft), occupies all of Tibet and adjacent areas of southwestern and south central China. The intermediate level, at altitudes from about 1,000 to 2,000 m (3,300 to 6,600 ft), occupies the northern border regions of Inner Mongolia and Xinjiang and extends southwestward across the center of the country to the rugged province of Yunnan. The third and lowest level, at elevations below 1,000 m (3,300 ft), occupies the eastern and most populated section of the country. The three elevation steps are themselves crossed by east-west trending mountain ranges that subdivide the three elevation regions into nine subregions.

Tibetan Highland. At the core of this region is the Tibetan Plateau, with an average elevation of more than 4,000 m (13,000 ft). The plateau is rimmed by mountain ranges with peaks that rise to more than 6,100 m (20,000 ft). Forming the northern edge of the plateau are the KUNLUN MOUNTAINS and the Nan Shan range, which enclose the KOKO NOR (Qing Hai; Ch'ing Hai), a lake. On the southern edge of the plateau are the HIMALAYAS, which rise to the world's highest elevation (8,848 m/29,028 ft) in Mount EVEREST, on the Tibet-Nepal border. The Tibetan Plateau is bordered on the west by the KARAKORAM RANGE and the PAMIRS. The eastern edge of the plateau is cut off from the rest of China by canyons and intervening rugged mountain ranges from which flow China's principal river, the CHANG JIANG (Yangtze), and some of the major rivers of Southeast Asia, including the Yalu Zangbo (Upper Brahmaputra), Salween, and Mekong rivers.

Uplands. The second elevation step consists of five subregions, which are, from north to south: the Xingjiang-Mongolian upland, the Mongolian border upland, the Qin Ling (Tsinling) Mountains, the Sichuan Basin, and the Yunnan-Guizhou Plateau upland. The Xinjiang-Mongolian upland covers most of Inner Mongolia, Gansu, and Xinjiang. A semidesert region, it includes, in the west, the Junggar (Dzunarian) and Tarim basins of Xinjiang, the latter containing the TAKLA MAKAN DESERT. The basins are separated from each oher by the Tian Shan (Tien Shan) range. The eastern portion of the upland lies mainly within the GOBI and Ordos deserts.

The second subregion of the middle elevation step is the Mongolian border upland; it lies between the Gobi and Ordos deserts of Inner Mongolia and the North China plain to the southeast. The main features of this subregion are the Da Hinggan (Greater Khingan) range (Tahsinganling Shanmo) and the Loess Plateau, which occupies most of Shaanxi, Shanxi, Henan, and Gansu provinces.

The third subregion of the middle elevation step is the Qin Ling Mountains, a range that extends east-west from the Kunlun Mountains. The Qin Ling are important as a divide between the HUANG HE (Hwang Ho; Yellow River) and Chang Jiang basins.

The fourth subregion, located south of the Qin Ling Mountains, is known both as the Red Basin, on account of its underlying red sandstones, and the Sichuan Basin, because of its location in Sichuan province. The basin is traversed by the Chang Jiang.

The fifth and most southerly of the five middle elevation subregions is the Yunnan-Guizhou Plateau upland, located in Yunnan and Guizhou provinces. Underlain mainly by limestone, the plateau is known for a spectacularly eroded karst scenery, often depicted in traditional Chinese painting.

Lowlands. The lowest elevation step lies in eastern China. It consists of three subregions: the eastern lowland, the eastern Manchurian upland, and the southeastern upland.

By far the most important subregion is the eastern lowland, which covers only about 10% of China's total area but is where most of China's huge population is concentrated. The principal lowlands of this region are the lowlands of the Manchurian plain, which are drained by the Liao River and upper reaches of the Songhua River; the alluvial North China plain, drained by the Huang He; and the vast plains of the Chang Jiang lowland, drained by the Chang Jiang and the Huai River, in central China.

For centuries, the North China Plain, one of China's most intensively cultivated areas, has been vulnerable to flooding of the Huang He (Yellow River). Flood damage has been reduced since 1955, when the government began an ambitious program of dam construction.

(Left) *The Li Jiang River courses through a spectacular* karst *landscape near the city of Guilin in southeastern China. The conical hills are formed by the erosion of water-soluble limestone. Similar formations are often depicted in the famous* shan shiu *(mountains, water) watercolors by Chinese artists.* (Right) *The Great Wall of China, which extends more than 2,400 km (1,500 mi), was built during the 3d century BC to provide protection from invading nomadic tribes.*

Turgay
Novosibirsk
Krasnoyarsk
Ust-Kut
Tselinograd
Barnaul
Abakan
U.S.S.R.
BAIKAL MTS.
Lake Baikal
YABLONOVY
Karaganda
Semipalatinsk
SAYAN MTS.
Irkutsk
Ulan-Ude
KAZAKH HILLS
Kyzyl
Kzyl-Orda
Balkhash
Ayaguz
Ulaangom
Moron
Khapcheranga
Lake Balkhash
Syr Darya
Chuguchak
ALTAI MTS.
Chovd
Taldy-Kurgan
Fuhai
Chimkent
Druzba
Ulan Bator
Tashkent
Frunze
Alma-Ata
Karamay
MONGOLIA
Yining
Usu
Altaj
Manas
Mandalgov
Osh
TIEN SHAN
Ürümqi
Yanhu
Qitai
Aksu
Kuga
-154m
Turpan
TURFAN DEPRESSION
PAMIRS
Kashi
XINJIANG UYGUR
Korla
Hami
Dalandzadgad
Feyzabad
Khorog
AFG.
TARIM BASIN
Aqitag 1524m
GOBI
Shache
TAKLA MAKAN DESERT
Ejin Qi
Pishan
Lop Nur
KARAKORAM RANGE
K2 8611m
Dunhuang
Anbei
Urad Houqi
Wuyuan
Hohhot
Yumen
Jiayuguan
Jiuquan
Linhe
Islamabad
Hotan
Qiemo
Wuhai
ORDOS DESERT
Yutian
Qilian Mtn. 5547m
Shizuishan
Rawalpindi
KUNLUN MOUNTAINS
Zhangye
NAN SHAN
GANSU
Yinchuan
GREAT WALL
Srinagar
TSAIDAM BASIN
Wuwei
PAKISTAN
Wuzhong
NINGXIA HUI
Zhongwei
Yulin
Bukadaban Mtn. 7720m
Menyuan
SHAANXI
Rutog
Delingha
Golmud
LOESS PLATEAU
Yan'an
Lahore
Amritsar
Xining
Pingliang
Lanzhou
Zhaxigang
PLATEAU OF TIBET
Linxia
Dingxi
Garyarsa
Maqên
Minxian
Tianshui
Baoji
Xi'an
Basatongwula Mtn. 6096m
Burang
Yushu
Taibai Mtn. 3767m
QIN MOUNTAINS
Delhi
New Delhi
Sêrxü
Hanzhong
Amdo
Songpan
Ankang
HIMALAYAS
Jaipur
Burang
Xainza
NINGJING MTS.
Nepalganj
Sadêng
Qamdo
Garzê
Guanxian
Wanxian
Yangtze
Xigazê
Lhasa
Chengdu
SZECHWAN BASIN
Kathmandu
Gyangzê
Gyaca
Batang
Pengshan
Enshi
Kanpur
Lucknow
NEPAL
Mt. Everest 8848m
Mt. Chomo 7413m
Kangding
Neijiang
Chongqing
Birganj
Kanchenjunga 8598m
Paro
Thimbu
Lhünzê
Gongga Mtn. 7590m
Yibin
Luzhou
BHUTAN
Varanasi
Siliguri
Dibrugarh
Tropic of Cancer
Indore
Yongning
Xichang
GUIZHOU
Zunyi
Jabalpur
Ganges
Zhaotong
KWEICHOW PLATEAU
Lijiang
Dukou
Guiyang
Shillong
Guiding
Duyun
BANGLADESH
Myitkyina
Xiaguan
Dongchuan
Anshun
INDIA
Asansol
Imphal
YUNNAN PLATEAU
Qinglong
Guilin
Nagpur
Dhaka (Dacca)
Kunming
Baoshan
Nandan
Yishan
Ruili
Luxi
YUNNAN
Anlong
Liuzhou
Calcutta
WULIANG MTS.
GUANGXI
DECCAN PLATEAU
Chittagong
Lashio
Gejiu
Wenshan
Bose
Litang
SHAN PLATEAU
Jiangcheng
Tiandong
Nanning
Cuttack
Mandalay
Menglian
Laocai
ZHUANGZU
Mt. Victoria 3053m
Fan Si Pan 3143m
Pingxiang
Hyderabad
EASTERN GHATS
Sittwe
BURMA
Mengla
VIETNAM
Beihai
Taunggyi
Hanoi
Vijayawada
Bay of Bengal
Irrawaddy
Luang Prabang
Gulf of Tonkin
62m
Mt. Inthanon 2600m
Chiang Mai
LAOS
Mt. Bia 2820m
HAINAN
Danxian
Dongfang
THAILAND
Vinh
Hainan Island
Yaxian
Vientiane
Mekong
Rangoon
Madras
Moulmein
© 1980, 1991 Rand McNally & Co.

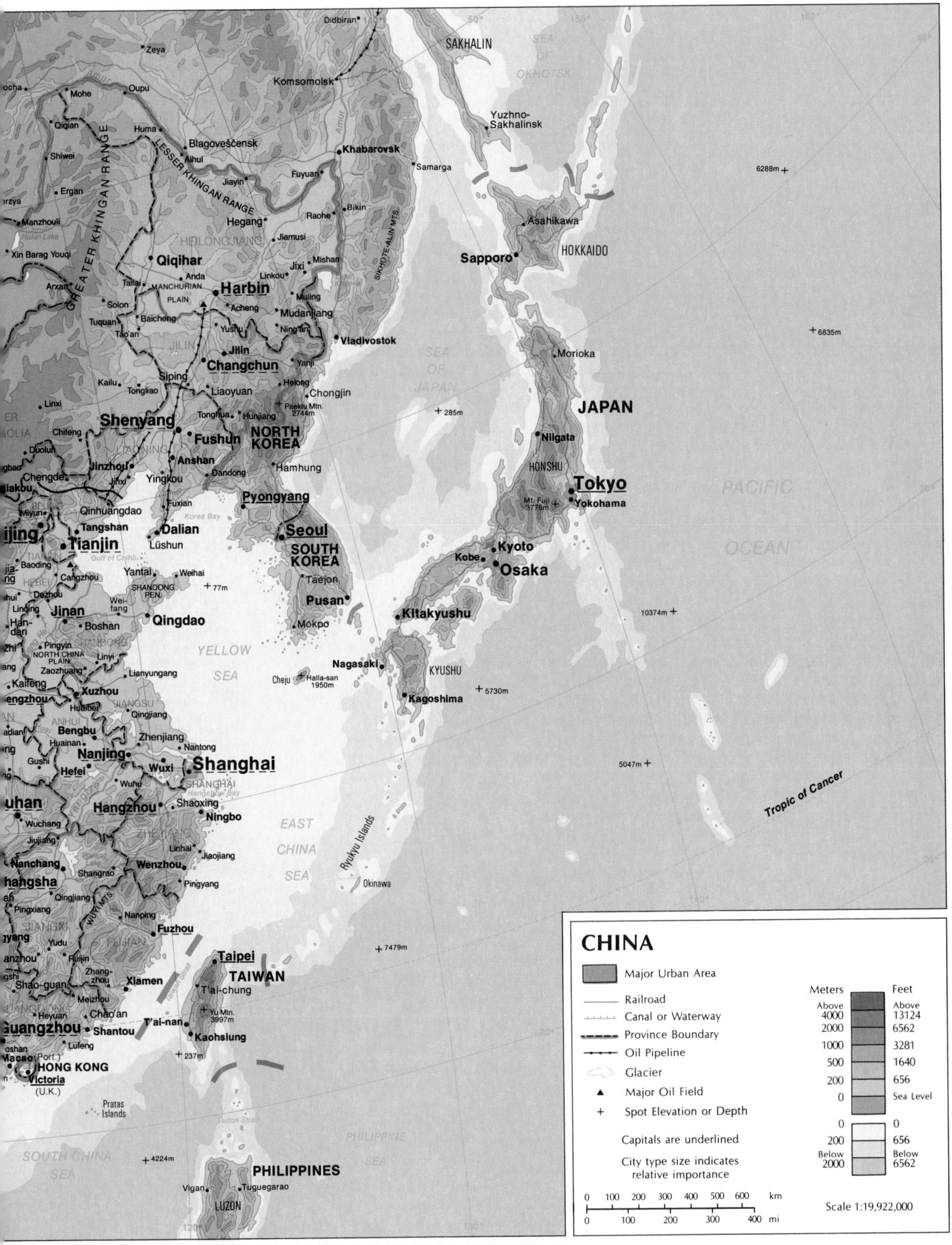

Didbiran
Zeya
SAKHALIN
SEA OF OKHOTSK
Komsomolsk
Mohe
Oupu
Amur
Yuzhno-Sakhalinsk
Qiqian
Huma
Blagoveščensk
Shiwei
Aihui
Khabarovsk
Samarga
GREATER KHINGAN RANGE
LESSER KHINGAN RANGE
Jiayin
Fuyuan
6288m
Ergan
Bikin
Manzhouli
Hulun Lake
Raohe
Hegang
SIKHOTE-ALIN MTS.
Asahikawa
HEILONGJIANG
Jiamusi
Xin Barag Youqi
Qiqihar
Jixi
Mishan
Sapporo
HOKKAIDO
Anda
Linkou
Arxan
Tailai
MANCHURIAN PLAIN
Harbin
Solon
Acheng
Muling
Tuquan
Baicheng
Mudanjiang
Tao'an
Yushu
Ning'an
Vladivostok
6835m
JILIN
Jilin
Changchun
Yanji
SEA OF JAPAN
Morioka
Siping
Kailu
Tongliao
Liaoyuan
Helong
Chongjin
Linxi
Paektu Mtn. 2744m
285m
JAPAN
Shenyang
Tonghua
Hunjiang
Chifeng
Fushun
NORTH KOREA
Niigata
Duolun
LIAONING
Anshan
Jinzhou
Hamhung
HONSHU
Chengde
Yingkou
Dandong
Jinxi
Tokyo
PACIFIC OCEAN
Pyongyang
Fuxian
Mt. Fuji 3776m
Yokohama
Qinhuangdao
Korea Bay
Miyun
Tangshan
Dalian
Seoul
Tianjin
Lüshun
SOUTH KOREA
Kyoto
Gulf of Chihli
Kobe
Osaka
Baoding
Cangzhou
Yantai
Weihai
Taejon
HEBEI
SHANDONG PEN.
77m
Dezhou
Pusan
Linqing
Jinan
Weifang
Handan
Boshan
Qingdao
Mokpo
Kitakyushu
10374m
Pingyin
NORTH CHINA PLAIN
SHANDONG
YELLOW SEA
Linyi
Nagasaki
Zaozhuang
Lianyungang
Cheju
Halla-san 1950m
KYUSHU
Kaifeng
Xuzhou
5730m
Zhengzhou
Huaibei
JIANGSU
Kagoshima
Qingjiang
ANHUI
Bengbu
Zhenjiang
Huainan
Nantong
Gushi
Nanjing
Wuxi
Shanghai
5047m
Hefei
Wuhu
SHANGHAI
Hangzhou Bay
Tropic of Cancer
Wuhan
Hangzhou
Shaoxing
Ningbo
Wuchang
ZHEJIANG
EAST CHINA SEA
Ryukyu Islands
Jiujiang
Linhai
Jiaojiang
Nanchang
Poyang Lake
Wenzhou
Changsha
Shangrao
Okinawa
Pingyang
Qingjiang
WUYI MTS.
Pingxiang
Nanping
JIANGXI
Fuzhou
FUJIAN
Yudu
7479m
Taipei
Ruijin
Zhangzhou
Xiamen
TAIWAN
Shao-guan
T'ai-chung
Taiwan Strait
Meizhou
Heyuan
Chao'an
Yu Mtn. 3997m
T'ai-nan
Guangzhou
Shantou
Kaohsiung
Lufeng
237m
Macao (Port.)
HONG KONG
Victoria (U.K.)
Pratas Islands
Luzon Strait
PHILIPPINE SEA
SOUTH CHINA SEA
4224m
PHILIPPINES
Vigan
Tuguegarao
LUZON
CHINA
Major Urban Area
Railroad
Canal or Waterway
Province Boundary
Oil Pipeline
Glacier
Major Oil Field
Spot Elevation or Depth
Capitals are underlined
City type size indicates relative importance
Meters
Feet
Above 4000
Above 13124
2000
6562
1000
3281
500
1640
200
656
0
Sea Level
0
0
200
656
Below 2000
Below 6562
0 100 200 300 400 500 600 km
0 100 200 300 400 mi
Scale 1:19,922,000

Floral decorations suspended from balloons float above a parade in Beijing (Peking) during October 1st festivities. That date, which marks the anniversary of the founding of the People's Republic of China in 1949, is observed as a national holiday.

The eastern Manchurian upland, located in northeastern China, consists of low hills with elevations of less than 900 m (3,000 ft). The southeastern upland, which occupies all of eastern China south of the Chang Jiang lowland, consists mostly of low mountains. The Guangzhou (Canton) plain is the largest lowland in the southeastern upland.

Soils. Alluvial soils, found mainly in the lowlands of the North China plain, the Chang Jiang valley and delta, the Guangzhou plain, and most other flood-prone valleys, are well-suited to rice and wheat cultivation. The small chernozem belt, excellent for grain cultivation, is located mainly in the northern area of the Manchurian plain and along the southern border of Inner Mongolia. Moderately fertile brown and chestnut-brown soils, found on the drier margins of the chernozem zone, are used mainly for pasture because of the limited rainfall areas where they occur.

Podzols and gray brown forest soils are associated with coniferous forests in northeastern Manchuria, the Qin Ling Mountains, and other central uplands. Gray desert soils, which occur widely in Inner Mongolia and Xinjiang, are used mainly as pasturage. Saline soils are found both in the inland desert basins and along the seacoasts. After removal of the salt, the maritime saline soils are fertile for cotton or rice cultivation. The lateritic red and yellow soils in the subtropical areas of southern China are used for growing rice, tea, and mulberry trees.

Climate. Most of China lies in the temperate mid-latitude climate zone. Southeastern China has a subtropical climate with heavy summer rains. Central and southwestern China have a continental climate with cold, dry winters. A belt of arid mid-latitude climate prevails in the desert lands, and subarctic conditions characterize the uplands of Tibet and northern Manchuria.

June and July mark the beginning of the monsoon rains in central China, after which the rainfall belts shift to northern China. The average annual precipitation decreases markedly from 2,000 mm (80 in) along the southeastern coast to 750 mm (30 in) in central China south of the Qin Ling Mountains. Northern China generally receives less than 500 mm (20 in), and as little as 100 mm (4 in) are recorded in parts of the Takla Makan and Gobi deserts.

Temperatures also vary considerably from north to south and between summer and winter. Average January temperatures are below freezing throughout the north and west, but they rise steadily southward to an average of 5° C (40° F) at Wuhan to 16° C (60° F) at Guangzhou. China's summer temperatures are more uniform. Average July temperatures are above 20° C (70° F) in most of China and decrease toward the western highlands. The annual temperature range increases between summer and winter from 9 C degrees (15 F degrees) in HAINAN, an island province in the extreme south, to more than 44 C degrees (80 F degrees) in northern Manchuria.

Drainage. China's rivers carry about 2,800 km^3 (670 mi^3) of water to the sea every year, amounting to 40% of Asia's total annual runoff. By far the largest system is the Pacific Ocean drainage basin, which covers about 5,400,000 km^2 (2,100,000 mi^2). Five major river systems lie within this basin, the AMUR, Huang He, Huai He, Chang Jiang, and Zhu Jhiang. The Amur has a total length of 4,700 km (2,900 mi) and is joined by the Songhua and the Wusuli rivers. The Huang He is 4,800 km (2,980 mi) long and has a basin area of 772,000 km^2 (298,000 mi^2). It rises from the Tibetan highlands and eventually enters the North China plain, where its bed is enclosed on both sides by dams. The Huai He is 1,100 km (680 mi) long and drains a basin area of 210,000 km^2 (81,000 mi^2). The Chang Jiang, China's principal river, is 5,990 km (3,720 mi) long and drains a basin of 1,800,000 km^2 (700,000 mi^2). The Zhu Jiang, the most southerly of the five rivers in the Pacific drainage basin, is a composite river consisting of Xi Jiang, Bei Jiang, and Tung Jiang, which converge close to the outlet into the sea. The Zhu Jiang drainage basin covers 448,000 km^2 (173,000 mi^2).

The bicycle is the principal means of transportation in China. The rush-hour traffic seen here is crossing a bridge over the Pearl River in Guangzhou (Canton).

Many traditional single-family residences, such as these in Beijing, have been divided into apartments to ease the urban housing shortage. The Chinese government is attempting to alleviate population pressures by encouraging settlement in less-developed regions.

China's three other drainage basins are the Arctic Ocean, Indian Ocean, and inland drainage basins. Of least importance is the Arctic Ocean drainage basin, which covers only 40,000 km^2 (15,000 mi^2) in the northwest. The Indian Ocean drainage basin contains two major rivers, the Yalu Zangbo (Upper Brahmaputra) and the Nu Jiang (Upper Salween), and has an area of 780,000 km^2 (300,000 mi^2). The inland drainage basin, which includes most of the rivers in northern Tibet, Xinjiang, and Inner Mongolia, covers 36% of China's total area. Most rivers are intermittent streams, ending in playas, or salty swamps. The large interior lakes are Koko Nor, Lop Nor, and Nam (Na-mu).

Vegetation. China falls within two major vegetation zones that are separated by a line running diagonally across the country from the Dzungarian Range in the northeast to the Himalayas in the southwest. South and east of this line is the forested vegetation zone, and north and west of the line is the northwestern steppe-desert vegetation zone. Much of the deciduous forests of central China have been depleted, as have much of Manchuria's steppe grasses, in order to plant crops. Recently, reforestation projects have been started as part of flood-control programs. Coniferous forests are found in the mountainous regions and in northern Manchuria. In the less diverse northwest, arid grasslands gradually give way to desert vegetation.

Animal Life. China is rich in vertebrate fauna, with about 3,440 species. In the palearctic region, which covers the Tibetan Plateau, Xinjiang, Inner Mongolia, and northeast and north China, horses, camels, tapirs, river foxes, and forest jerboa are the major native mammals. In the oriental region, which includes southwest, south, and central China, the common mammals are Chinese pangolins, monkeys, apes, gibbons, and tree shrews. Since the late 1960s the government has instituted programs to protect wildlife, of which the giant panda is the most publicized species.

Resources. China is well endowed with mineral resources and has the world's largest reserves of antimony and tungsten. Antimony resources come mainly from southwestern Henan province, and China currently produces almost 20% of the world's output. Tungsten reserves are found mainly in Jiangxi, Henan, and Guangdong provinces, and China produces about 15% of the world's output. China also has considerable reserves of bauxite (from which aluminum is made), iron ore, tin, lead, manganese, mercury, and molybdenum and the world's largest coal reserves. Its potential hydroelectric power is in the range of 500,000,000 to 1,000,000,000 kW but the installed capacity today is only 26,000,000 kW. Southwest, central, and south China have nearly 84% of the country's water power resources. China has proved oil reserves of more than 22 million barrels; by 1987 it had become the world's fourth largest oil producer. Oilfields are spread east-west in a curve from the Manchurian plain through the North China plain, Sichuan, Qinghai, and Gansu to Xinjiang. Another belt runs north-south along the offshore seas from Bo Hai in the Yellow Sea southward along the continental shelf to the South China Sea.

People

China is a multiracial state, whose population includes about 94% Han Chinese and about 6% of some 60 other ethnic groups. National autonomous regions, districts, or counties have been established in areas where these ethnic groups are concentrated.

Chinese students, whose educational opportunities were greatly broadened by reforms during the 1980s, called for further liberalization in the spring of 1989. The demonstrators were massacred by troops, and a period of political retrenchment ensued.

The city of Shenzen in Guangdong province is one of the special economic zones created in 1979 to encourage foreign investment.

Languages. China's languages are classified into four major linguistic families: the INDO-EUROPEAN, SINO-TIBETAN, URAL-ALTAIC, and MON-KHMER. Mandarin dialects, the largest group of the Sino-Tibetan family, are spoken by about two-thirds of China's population. The Mandarin Beijing dialect is now China's national spoken language.

The Ural-Altaic linguistic family includes the Turkic linguistic groups (Kazakh, Kirghiz, Uzbek, Salar, and UIGHUR), Mongolic groups (Meng, Tu, Dongsiang, Baoyin, and Daghurs), and Tungusic groups (Manchu, Evenki, Orochon Gold, and Sibo). The Mon-Khmer linguistic family of Southeast Asia is represented in Yunnan province by the Wa (Kawa), the Puland (Palaung), and the Penglung. The Indo-European linguistic family is represented only by Tadzhik speakers.

Religion. Traditionally, the major religions of China were BUDDHISM and TAOISM. Most Chinese also believed in ANCESTOR WORSHIP and CONFUCIANISM, a system of social and political values. TIBETAN BUDDHISM, or Lamaism, was the religion of the Mongols and the Tibetans. Large Muslim and Christian (primarily Roman Catholic) minorities were also important.

After 1949, under the Communist government, the practice of religion was discouraged, although freedom to believe in religion was guaranteed under the constitution of 1954. During the CULTURAL REVOLUTION of the mid-1960s, religious institutions were destroyed, but since 1978 the government has become more tolerant of religious observance.

Demography. China contains about one-fourth of the world's people; the latest official census, completed in 1982, placed the country's population at more than 1 billion, about half of whom are under the age of 30. During the 1950s the population grew at a rate of 2% per year. The rate of growth slowed to 1.1% by 1984 but then turned upward again after 1985. Current laws obligate couples to practice family planning, and penalties are imposed on families with more than three children. The adoption of a new farming system since 1982, however, has increased the economic value of offspring and made family planning less effective in rural areas.

About 95% of China's people are crowded into the eastern and southeastern sections of the country. Most densely populated are the Chang Jiang plain and the Guangzhou delta.

In 1982 an estimated 21% of China's population were urban, up from 13.3% in 1952. The pace of urbanization accelerated in 1984–86 when many rural counties were incorporated into metropolitan areas, adding 90 million people to the urban population. The largest urban centers are SHANGHAI, BEIJING (Peking), TIANJIN (Tientsin), SHENYANG, WUHAN, GUANGZHOU, HAERBIN (Harbin), CHONGQING (Chungking), NANJING (Nanking), XI'AN (Sian), and CHENGDU (CH'ENG-TU).

Education. In the 1950s and early 1960s educational policy was directed toward producing college and secondary school graduates who were politically reliable and technically qualified. Students were required to spend half of their school hours on academic subjects and the other half learning practical skills in factories and fields. Revolutionary committees ran the schools during the Cultural Revolution, with emphasis on political indoctrination in revolutionary ideology. The traditional university entrance examinations were abolished, and students were selected on the basis of work performance and party loyalty. The educational policies of the Cultural Revolution were abandoned in 1977. Entrance examinations were reintroduced and tuition for higher education was reinstituted in 1985. More than 40,000 bright students were sent to study in colleges and universities in Western Europe, Japan, and the United States, although the government has reduced the number of students sent abroad since 1988. Efforts have been made to extend the years of schooling to 10 in urban areas and 9 in rural areas (5 years at the elementary level and 4 to 5 years of secondary school). In 1986, 96% of school-age children were enrolled in schools.

The first university in China was the Imperial Academy (124 BC). Admission to the academy was by highly competitive examination, and the purpose of the institution

On a wintry day in Jilin (Kirin) City in the Manchurian province of Jilin, shoppers patronize a free market on the street. Such markets proliferated in China during the 1980s.

The Daqing (Taching) oil field in Heilongjiang (Heilungkiang) province is China's oldest oil installation. This Manchurian field began production in the early 1960s and was China's principal source of oil until the end of the 1970s. China has enormous petroleum reserves, however, including extensive offshore deposits.

was to prepare students for the even more rigorous examinations that determined who would serve in the higher-level government bureaucracy. These examinations were concerned exclusively with classical Confucian scholarship into the 19th century, when efforts were made to reform education through the creation of universities on the Western model. Today China has five major types of universities: comprehensive, technological, agricultural, medical, and teacher training. Amongst the largest universities in modern China are Beijing University (1898), the People's University of China (1937), and Qinghua University (1911), all in Beijing; Tianjin University (1895), in Tianjin; Shanghai Riao Dong University (1896) and Futan University (1905), in Shanghai; and Nanjing University (1902), in Nanjing.

Health. Life expectancy has increased greatly since 1949, when it was only about 30 years. General public-health conditions have been significantly improved and major diseases have been brought under control. The number of hospitals and clinics and the number of physicians—both Western-style doctors and doctors of traditional Chinese medicine—have increased dramatically. Health-care and other social-welfare benefits are provided by work units.

The Arts. After 1949, traditional Chinese culture was largely replaced by a new culture, intended to serve the masses and help build socialism. Painting, poetry, fiction, drama, opera, film, and storytelling are all used to implement the government's political programs. (See also CHINESE ART AND ARCHITECTURE; CHINESE LITERATURE; CHINESE MUSIC.)

Economic Activity

Since 1949, China has had a centrally planned economy based on the Stalinist model. From 1953 to 1990, seven five-year plans were implemented to coordinate economic development. The First Five-Year Plan (1953–57) concentrated on the development of heavy industry financed with Soviet assistance. The Second Five-Year Plan (1958–62) was interrupted by Mao Zedong's radical measures of the GREAT LEAP FORWARD and the establishment of rural communes. The new policies caused a great setback for China's economic development. A period of readjustment followed in 1962–65. The Third and Fourth Five-Year plans (1966–70 and 1971–75) were disrupted by the Cultural Revolution. An ambitious Ten-Year Plan (1976–85) calling for modernization in all sectors was inaugurated in 1978 but was soon abandoned in favor of new adjustments and reforms. In September 1982 the government adopted a new program designed to quadruple the gross annual value of the nation's industrial and agricultural output by the year 2000. The Sixth and Seventh Five-Year plans (1981–85 and 1986–90) were designed to attain this long-term strategic goal. During the 1980s the government also pursued a series of reform policies to increase productivity in agriculture and industry through decentralization and to open the door to foreign investment. The reform policies, while increasing industrial and agricultural output substantially, also contributed to inflation, corruption, speculation, and income disparities. Beginning in October 1988 new policies were initiated to reimpose government control and slow down growth to achieve economic stability.

Manufacturing. Since the initiation of economic reforms in 1978, new investment has been concentrated in the textile and consumer durable goods industries. From 1985 to 1988 the output of durable consumer goods showed phenomenal growth, making China one of the world's foremost producers of these products. Industry grew much more vigorously in rural than in urban areas during the 1980s. The astounding growth of rural industry has, however, acted as a disincentive to agriculture. In the coastal areas, four special economic zones offering tax and trade benefits to foreign companies were established. In addition, 14 coastal cities and Hainan island were opened to foreign investment in 1984.

Manufacturing is located in several main industrial regions. The Northeastern Region, with a huge iron and steel complex located at ANSHAN, is China's oldest and most industrialized region. Its diversified resource base

An agricultural worker plows a terraced field along the Huang He. Terraces in this hilly terrain help retain rainwater and are vital in preventing soil erosion. From the late 1950s to the early 1980s, Chinese agriculture was organized under the commune system. With the abolition of the communes, the land was leased or contracted to individual households, which became responsible for their own production. Mechanization is increasing.

supports petroleum refining, coal mining, and iron and steel, chemical, and timber industries. The Northern Region is a relatively new industrial region. About 90% of its industrial projects date from the First and Second Five-Year Plans. It includes the Beijing-Tianjin industrial belt, a coal-mining district producing iron and steel, machinery, chemicals, and textiles. The Eastern Region is an old industrial region centered in Shanghai.

The South Central Region has well-developed food-processing and handicraft industries. Farther north, iron and coal resources support an iron and steel complex at Wuhan as well as other industries. The Northwestern Region is the newest industrial region. Its rapidly growing industrial cities include Xi'an and LANZHOU (Lan-chou) and are supported by petroleum refining and by iron and steel, petrochemical, and cotton textile industries. The Southwestern Region is China's principal producer of nonferrous metals, and its major industrial centers are Chengdu, KUNMING, and Chongqing.

Energy. China's economic development is aided by abundant coal, petroleum, and natural-gas reserves. Coal accounts for 80% of China's energy consumption. In 1988, China produced 970,000,000 metric tons (1,069,240,000 U.S. tons) of coal, making it the number one coal producer in the world. Coal is found in almost every province, and at least one-third of all coal produced is derived from small, locally important coal mines. Crude-oil production has increased dramatically since the early 1960s. In 1988, 137,000,000 metric tons (151,015,000 U.S. tons) were produced.

In 1988, China produced 543,000,000,000 kW h of electricity. About 108,000,000,000 of this was from hydroelectric stations. Most power stations are the traditional large-supply type, but China also leads the world in the use of small power stations that supply local industries. Nuclear power plants near Shanghai and Hong Kong were to be completed by 1993. Plans to build a giant hydroelectric project (17,000 MW capacity) on the Sunmen Gorge of the Chang Jiang were postponed in 1989 for at least 5 years due to concerns over the dam's cost and environmental impact.

Agriculture. Despite the rapid industrialization of recent years, China remains a predominantly agricultural country. Agriculture has undergone major social and technical changes since 1949, however. Due to a land-reform program initiated in 1949, virtually all large landholdings had been redistributed to the peasants by 1952. Peasant households were organized into cooperatives and later into communes. Under rural reforms introduced in 1979, the land was contracted to individual peasant households, giving the peasants more freedom to choose the crops they grew and permitting them to sell any output exceeding assigned levels on the open market. The reforms led to dramatic gains in agricultural production and the emergence of millions of specialized households producing cash crops and engaging in nonagricultural activities.

Of China's total land area, 11% is under cultivation, and an additional 43% is in permanent pasture. Much of China's agricultural land is irrigated, especially in the North China plain, the Chang Jiang lowland, and the Sichuan basin, where some of the irrigation canals date back as far as the 3d century BC. Two crops a year, and in places three, are obtained from irrigated land where winters are mild. New hybrid seed strains and chemical fertilizers further increase the land's productivity.

Food grains constitute the principal crop grown in China, the leading food grains being rice, wheat, corn, millet, and gaoliang (a form of sorghum); legumes (peas and beans) and tubers (potatoes) are also frequently classified as food grains in official Chinese statistics. Production of food grains rose dramatically from 1980 to 1984 but then became stagnant. Output in 1988 totaled 394,010,000 metric tons (434,317,000 U.S. tons). China produced 174,416,000 metric tons (192,240,000 U.S. tons) of rice in 1987 and is the world's leading rice producer. Wheat production in 1987 was 87,768,000 metric tons (96,737,000 U.S. tons) cultivated on 28,812,000 ha (71,145,000 acres) of land, making it the second most important crop in China. Although traditionally cultivated in the cooler north and east, where rice could not be grown, about 80% of all wheat grown today is winter wheat produced as a second crop (after rice) or in rotation with rice and cotton. Gaoliang and millet, most important in the drier areas of the north, northeast, and northwest, are giving way to higher-yielding corn, the third leading food grain. Sweet potatoes are widely grown for food throughout China, as are rapeseed, peanuts, and soybeans, from which oil and other foods are produced. The most important commercial crop is cotton.

The principal livestock raised are pigs and chickens. In 1988, China had about 342,000,000 pigs and an estimated 1,100,000,000 chickens, more than any other country in the world. Efforts are under way to increase production by introducing large-scale, mechanized pig and poultry farms.

Forestry and Fishing. In 1981, China grew about 9% of the world's softwoods and more than 6% of the hardwoods. More than 60% of China's timber comes from the Manchurian mountains, which have China's most extensive forest reserves.

China was the third largest fish producer in the world in 1988, after Japan and the Soviet Union. Fish culture is growing in importance because of the construction of ponds and dams for flood control and for power plants. Marine fishing has also expanded, with most of the powered fleet based at LÜSHUN, QINGDAO (Tsingtao), Hainan, and Shanghai.

Transportation. The backbone of China's transportation is its rail network, which has more than doubled in length since 1949. About 70% of the railroads constructed since 1949 are in the western and northwestern parts of the country.

The length of highways has increased more than elevenfold since 1949. Many new trunk roads have been constructed to open up outlying western regions.

China's domestic air routes radiate mainly from Beijing and Shanghai. International flights serve Beijing, Shanghai, and other cities. The principal seaports are Dalian (Talien), Tianjin, Qingdao, Shanghai, Guangzhou, Zhanjiang (Chanchiang), and Qinhuangdas (Ch'in-huang-tao).

Foreign Trade. From 1949 to 1960, 70% of China's foreign trade was conducted with the USSR and Eastern Europe. After the Sino-Soviet rift, China's trade with Japan and the Western countries increased rapidly. By 1987, trade with the USSR and Eastern Europe accounted for only 5% of total trade. Machinery, industrial raw materials, and consumer goods were the principal imports of the 1980s, and textiles, footwear, and petroleum had become the leading exports by 1988. In 1989, China announced cutbacks of imports in its effort to slow the economy, although it continued to court foreign investors as a source of capital needed for economic modernization.

Government

China is a Communist state, with all authority resting in the Chinese Communist party (CCP). The country has had five constitutions since the Communists reorganized the national government in 1949. The first provisional constitution (1949) was superseded by the 1954 constitution adopted by the First National People's Congress (NPC), by the 1975 constitution adopted by the Fourth NPC, by the 1978 constitution adopted by the Fifth NPC, and by the 1982 constitution adopted by the Sixth NPC. The 1982 constitution restored the post of president, which had been abolished in 1975. In 1983, Li Xiannian (Li Hsien-nien) was appointed president. When he retired in 1988, Yang Shankun was selected as president.

The NPC is the highest organ of state power. It can amend the constitution, elect to or remove from office the highest state dignitaries, and decide on the national economic plan. The NPC elects a Standing Committee, whose chairman is equivalent to the head of state. The NPC is composed of deputies elected to 5-year terms. In 1988 the Seventh NPC selected Wan Li as its chairman.

The highest government administrative organ is the State Council, headed by a premier and several vice-premiers. It consists of more than 30 ministries and committees.

De facto power is held by the CCP, which had 47 million members in 1989. In 1982 the CCP abolished the post of party chairman in favor of a general secretary and named HU YAO-PANG (Hu Yaobang), who had replaced HUA GUOFENG (Hua Kuo-feng) as party chairman in 1981, to the post. Hu resigned in 1987 after student protests and was succeeded by ZHAO ZIYANG (Chao Tzu-yang), who later gave up the premiership to LI PENG. The Thirteenth Party Congress (October 1987) continued a transfer of power to younger leaders begun in 1985 by DENG XIAOPING (Teng Hsiao-p'ing), China's paramount leader. The party leadership was reshuffled in June 1989 after two months of large-scale prodemocracy demonstrations in Beijing and other cities. Deng ordered the demonstrations suppressed by the army on June 4 and dismissed Zhao as general secretary. JIANG ZEMIN (Chiang Tse-min) was named the new party general secretary, but neither hardliners nor reformers appeared to have decisive power.

For local administrative purposes China is divided into 22 provinces (not including Taiwan), 5 autonomous regions, and 3 cities (Beijing, Tianjin, and Shanghai) directly under central government control. The provinces and autonomous regions are broken down into prefectures, cities, counties, and special districts. The counties are further broken down into rural and urban administrative units, communes, and towns. Provinces and autonomous regions are governed by local People's Congresses, and lower levels of government, by local People's Governments.

China, history of

China, history of The human record in China can be traced back at least 1.7 million years with the 1965 discovery in Yunnan province in southwest China of fossils known as Yuanmou man, a closely related ancestor of modern man. Other *Homus erectus* fossils in China include those found at Lantian, Shaanxi province, in 1963, of humans who lived about 600,000 to 700,000 years ago, and the earlier finding (1921) at Zhoukoudian

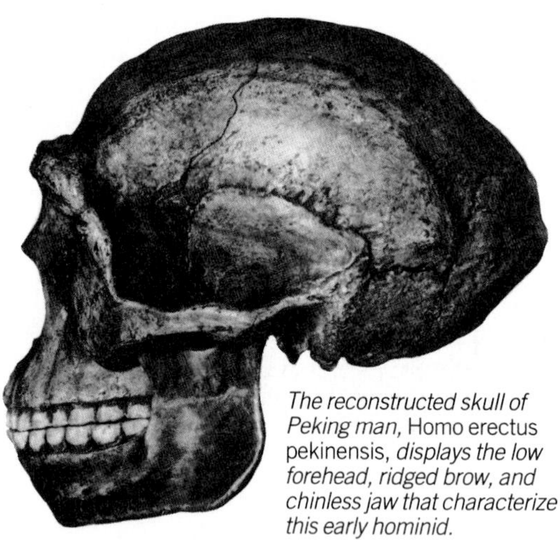

The reconstructed skull of Peking man, Homo erectus pekinensis, *displays the low forehead, ridged brow, and chinless jaw that characterize this early hominid.*

(Chou-k'ou-tien) of the fossils later known as BEIJING (Peking) MAN, who lived approximately 250,000 to 500,000 years ago. By about 25,000 BC, also in the vicinity of Beijing, a fully advanced human, sometimes referred to as Upper Cave man, hunted and fished and made shell and bone artifacts.

Although fossil remains of early humans have been discovered in various other places in China, the North—especially the fertile region watered by the HUANG HE (Hwang Ho; Yellow River)—was the nuclear area of ancient Chinese civilization. There, and also along the southeastern coast, the switch from hunting-gathering methods of food collection to an agricultural way of life first occurred in China sometime during the 6th to the 5th millennium BC, a far-reaching development that scholars have recently come to believe took place independently of the Near Eastern NEOLITHIC revolution.

During the first phase of the Chinese Neolithic period (*c.*5000–2500 BC), called Painted Pottery Neolithic Yangshao, after the first associated site, farmers employed primitive techniques of cultivation, shifted their villages as the soils became exhausted, and lived in semisubterranean houses in the region of modern central Shaanxi (Shensi), southwestern Shanxi (Shansi), and western Henan (Honan) provinces. Their handcrafted, painted pottery occasionally bears a single incised sign that may be a forerunner of Chinese writing.

During the second phase, the Black Pottery or Longshan (Lung-shan), *c.*2500–1000 BC, agriculture became more advanced. Farmers began a wide-spreading cultural expansion into the eastern plains, Manchuria, and Central and South China. Longshan farmers worshipped their ancestors, a Chinese custom that still persists.

Shang Dynasty

The Yangshao and Longshan cultures laid the foundations for the first true Chinese civilization, the SHANG dynasty, which controlled a loose confederation of settlement groups in the Henan region of North China from the 16th century BC to *c.*1027 BC. Shang civilization, known from sites such as ANYANG and ZHENGZHOU, was characterized by an advanced system of writing, a sophisticated bronze metallurgy, the first Chinese calendar, and a genuinely urban way of life. Aided by a priestly class, the Shang kings prayed to their ancestral spirits to intercede on their behalf with the most powerful of the Shang gods, Shangdi, to bring rain for good crops and other blessings. Records of these priestly divinations have survived in the form of ORACLE BONES.

Until recently it was believed that many of the characteristic elements of the Shang, such as bronze making and writing, were importations from the Near East and other places. It now appears that, like the Chinese development of agriculture, these were invented independently and that the emergence of civilization in China was thus largely indigenous.

Zhou (Chou) Dynasty and Warring States

Sometime around 1027 BC the Shang was conquered by the ZHOU, a people living to the west in the region of modern Xi'an (Sian). The early or Western Zhou period (*c.*1027–771 BC) does not represent a sharp break with the immediate past. The Shang supreme deity was still recognized as a powerful god, but now more emphasis was placed on his abode, *tian* ("heaven"). An early Zhou statesman explained the Zhou conquest by saying that the Mandate of Heaven (*Tianming*) had been transferred from the wicked Shang to the virtuous Zhou, thus articulating the Chinese belief that the right to govern was not absolute but dependent on the moral qualities of a dynasty and on heaven's continued favor.

This map shows China toward the end of the Spring and Autumn period (722–481 BC) under the Eastern Zhou. The decline in power of the Zhou kings made it possible for powerful, semiautonomous states to emerge.

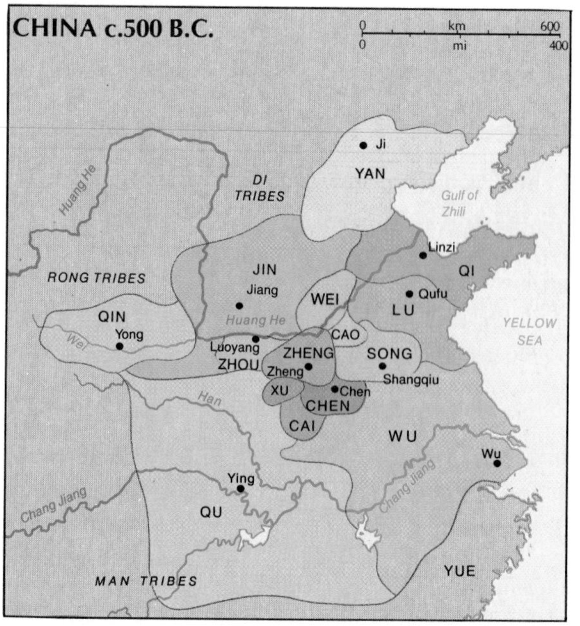

This terra-cotta bust is one of more than 6,000 sculptures in the funerary treasure unearthed in Shaanxi province near the tomb (210 BC) of Emperor Qin Shi Huangdi.

Much like his Shang predecessors, the Zhou king parceled out territories among family members and favored subordinates. The emphasis was on personal loyalties and a chivalric code similar to that of later European feudalism. This code had a parallel in civilian life in the form of complex rules of social etiquette and personal deportment called *li*; those who did not practice *li*, such as the peoples beyond the Zhou domains, were considered barbarians.

Military pressure forced the Zhou to move the capital eastward to Luoyang (modern Henan province) in 771 BC, thus beginning the period of Eastern Zhou (770–256 BC). Beginning in the 5th century BC, warfare among the states became endemic, serving to increase administrative efficiency within individual states.

During this period of the Warring States (403–221 BC) talent, not birth, increasingly became the criterion for employment, and a system of contractual relationships began to emerge. Bureaucrats were given salaries, and peasants were expected to pay taxes on their landholdings. The introduction of the ox-drawn, iron-tipped plow and the development of irrigation improved agricultural productivity and spurred population growth. A steady improvement in communications led to increased trade, and a money economy began to develop. Although the late Zhou was a period of widespread physical destruction, it was also a time of enormous intellectual ferment, producing China's oldest surviving literature, the Classics, and giving rise to China's golden age of philosophy, the most important schools of which were CONFUCIANISM, TAOISM, and Legalism.

Qin (Ch'in) Dynasty

The Legalists were briefly triumphant when the QIN (221–206 BC), a western frontier state whose ruling class had embraced the Legalist authoritarian philosophy, succeeded in conquering all of China. Shi Huangdi (Shih Hwang-ti), or "First Sovereign Emperor," presided over a centralized administrative system that replaced the semi-independent states of late Zhou and inaugurated a series of measures to enhance state power. Weights, measures, and the Chinese writing system were unified, and defenses were strengthened by filling gaps in the northern frontier walls, thereby creating the GREAT WALL OF CHINA. Those doctrines not officially sanctioned were extirpated by the Burning of the Books decree.

Han Dynasty

So much opposition was generated to the Qin's centralization and unification measures and its heavy requisitions for war and public-works projects that it in turn was overthrown by the HAN dynasty (202 BC–AD 220). The Han established a stable and highly centralized government on the Qin model, but it was somewhat more sensitive to the welfare of the peasantry, a perennial Confucian concern. The apogee of Han power was reached under HAN WUDI (r. 140–87 BC), who waged war against the nomadic tribes to the north, moved westward to Central Asia to gain control of the SILK ROAD linking China with the Roman world, and established a Chinese colony in northern Korea.

The map indicates the boundaries of the Chinese Empire as they appeared during the reign of Han Wudi (140–87 BC), the most important of the Han emperors.

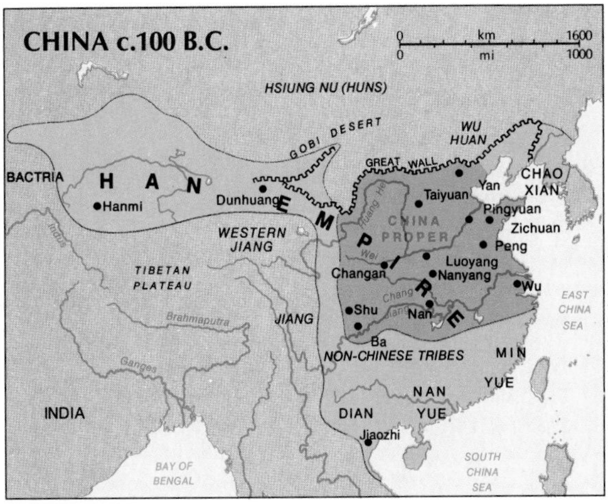

(Left) *Yang-ti, an emperor of the Sui dynasty (581–618), and his entourage proceed through the imperial park in this 18th-century illustration.*

(Right) *This painting on silk depicts two bureaucrats of the Song period (960–1279). By this time, government posts were held by the scholar-gentry class.*

Han dealings with barbarian neighbors were conducted within the tribute system, under which China granted diplomatic recognition and trading privileges only to those states and peoples acknowledging its superiority. Confucian doctrines gained preeminence within the Chinese state. Under the Han, China also began to outstrip other world civilizations in technology, developing the first true paper, a primitive seismograph, and protoporcelain.

Economic hardships and governmental disintegration led to massive peasant rebellion and the dissolution of the Han empire. Then commenced 300 years of political fragmentation known as the Period of Disunion (220–589), during which North China was ruled by a series of semi-Sinicized barbarian peoples and the South was settled by Chinese colonial regimes.

With the breakdown of the Han order came a disillusionment with Confucian emphasis on the selection of morally upright men for office and a return to aristocratic domination of government. Despite its disorder, this period was notable for institutional and cultural developments, especially the transformation of Indian BUDDHISM into a Chinese religion. Technological innovations included the invention of the wheelbarrow and gunpowder.

Sui and Tang Dynasties

Although the Han had been destroyed, the ideal of a centralized empire had never disappeared; it was left to the short-lived, native Chinese dynasty, the SUI (581–618), to fulfill that ideal. But the labor and tax burden of the Sui public-works projects—such as the reconstruction of the Great Wall and the fashioning of a Grand Canal linking the northern capital region with the newly rich agricultural centers of the Chang Jiang (Yangtze River) valley—compounded by ruinous military campaigns against northern Korea, generated popular rebellion and led to the speedy demise of the dynasty.

Yet the Sui laid the foundations for another glorious age, that of the TANG (618–906), which at its height controlled a pan-Asian empire stretching from Korea to the borders of Persia. Chang'an (XI'AN), the Tang capital and the greatest city in all Asia, welcomed tribute envoys, merchants, and devotees of religions from all parts of Asia and farther west. Not only was this the greatest period of Buddhism in Chinese history, but Islam, Manichaeism, Zoroastrianism, Judaism, and Nestorian Christianity all entered China.

At the same time, with the advent of a recentralized empire, the fortunes of Confucianism rose: the civil-service examinations reintroduced by the Sui were significantly expanded and a wide range of Confucian scholarly projects was undertaken under imperial sponsorship. Tang power and prestige reached a zenith during the reign of TANG XUANZONG (T'ang Hsuan-tsung; 712–56). Chinese lyric poetry reached a high point, and the world's first printed book was produced.

Theater, traditionally a private domain of the Chinese intelligentsia, became popular during the Yuan dynasty (1279–1368). This 18th-century illustration shows a satirical play contrasting the Mongol barbarians (left) *with a group of intellectual Chinese bureaucrats* (right). *(Bibliothèque Nationale, Paris.)*

Eventually, however, military victories gave way to defeat, notably at the hands of the Arabs in 751; and in 755 the revolt of An Lushan, a semibarbarian general in the Tang employ, transferred considerable power from the central government to military governors in the provinces, dealing the dynasty a blow from which it never fully recovered. The persecution (841–45) of Buddhists was largely an effort to return revenues from tax-free temple lands to the state.

Song Dynasty

The military governors who brought down the Tang founded five short-lived regimes, which, in turn, were replaced by a new age of prosperity under the SONG (Sung; 960–1279), the beginning of China's early modern age. Although never so militarily powerful as the Han or Tang, the Song is nevertheless notable for establishing political, social, economic, and cultural patterns that remained largely unaltered in China for a millennium. The Sung saw the final demise of the old aristocratic domination of government. Replacing the old aristocrats was a new group, the scholar-gentry class, whose power came from landholding and long years of educational training. Agriculture benefited by the introduction of new, early-ripening strains of rice, and enormous advances were made in commerce. Cities based on trade and industry multiplied rapidly, and Chinese landscape painting reached its full maturity. A new form of Confucianism, a syncretism of Confucian ethics and Buddhist metaphysics called neo-Confucianism, became state orthodoxy, a policy that persisted until the 20th century. Not everyone benefited, however. The peasants fell ever deeper into tenantry, and the status of women declined. The latter was symbolized by the growth of concubinage and the introduction of FOOT-BINDING.

This illustration from the Qing period (1644–1911) depicts Chinese women engaged in silk production. When European powers established maritime commerce during the 16th century, silk became the most popular item of trade.

A European in early 19th-century Hong Kong signs an agreement to purchase tea from a cohong, *a Chinese merchant granted a trade monopoly by the Qing emperor.*

Song military weakness eventually took its toll. Even at the height of Song power, parts of northern and northwestern China were occupied, respectively, by the Khitan and Tanguts. Beginning in 1127, all of North China was conquered by the Jurchen, leaving the Song in control of only a truncated southern regime, with its capital at Hangzhou (Hangchow).

Mongol Rule

A century and a half later, the MONGOLS conquered both the Jurchen and the Song, marking for the first time the occupation and rule of all China by a barbarian. The genius behind Mongol power was GENGHIS KHAN; by the time of his death in 1227 the Mongols possessed an empire stretching from Korea to Russian Turkistan and from Siberia to northern India. But even then China had still not been made part of the Mongol empire. This work was left to Genghis's successors, especially his grandson KUBLAI KHAN, who in 1279 at last succeeded in conquering the Southern Song and founded the Chinese-style YUAN dynasty (1279–1368), with its capital at Beijing.

With the peace that settled over Asia as a result of Mongol rule, access to China became relatively easy, and thus another age of cosmopolitanism and broad foreign contact, particularly with the West, was begun. The Mongols supported foreign mercantile ventures in China, welcomed foreign faiths like Nestorian Christianity and Islam, and patronized Tibetan Buddhism, or Tantrism. They also employed numerous foreigners in the state bureaucracy, such as the Venetian Marco POLO, who journeyed to China with his father and uncle about 1275. The Chinese were systematically discriminated against for government service and suffered numerous legal disabilities. Despite this repression, native arts flourished.

Ming Dynasty

Mongol rule in China was brought to an end after civil war among Mongol princes and increasing conversion to the sedentary Chinese way of life robbed the Mongol military machine of much of its effectiveness. Repeated natural disasters were followed by a massive peasant rebellion that the alien rulers could not quell. The Mandate of Heaven now shifted to one of the peasant leaders, who established the MING dynasty (1368–1644) at Nanjing (Nanking) in the south. The third Ming ruler, the despotic YANGLE (Yung-lo) emperor (r. 1403–24), moved the capital northward to a rebuilt Beijing and launched a series of large-scale maritime expeditions as far as the Indian Ocean, the Persian Gulf, and East Africa. Agricultural productivity increased with the introduction of New World crops, and population rose by the end of the dynasty to somewhere around 160 million to 260 million.

Chinese attention gradually turned inward, however, and overseas trade and contacts were reduced. Even in the realm of philosophy, China turned from the systematic investigation of things to a greater reliance on introspection and intuition, thus hindering many scientific advances and the development of new technologies. A decline in imperial leadership and a debilitating court factionalism between Confucian scholar-officials and eunuchs led to administrative paralysis. Continued defense problems with the Mongols and marauding pirates along the southeastern coast led the state to the brink of bankruptcy. Natural disasters in the early 17th century gave rise to peasant rebellion, signalling the end of the dynasty.

Early Qing (Ching) Dynasty

The successors of the Ming were another foreign people—the Manchus—descendants of the Jurchen. The Manchu homeland lay in the region of Manchuria and Liaodong (Liaotung). Rising to power on the fringe of Chinese culture, the Manchu tribes, like the Mongols before them, learned from China on a selective basis, particularly about how to govern a sedentary Chinese state. NURHACHI (1559–1626) united the Manchu and Jurchen tribes under his personal authority, and he and his successors developed a civil administration on a Chinese model, even adopting Confucianism as the basis of rule. In 1644 the Manchus seized Beijing and proceeded to occupy all of the country. But the alien QING dynasty (1644–1911) that they established represented more a continuation of the Ming than any sharp break.

The high point of Qing was reached under the long reigns of the KANGXI (K'ang-hsi) emperor (r. 1661–1722) and the QIAN-LONG (Ch'ien-lung) emperor (r. 1736–95). During this time Chinese rule in Asia was extended over an area greater than that of any previous dynasty except the Mongol Yüan. The Chinese empire included Outer Mongolia, Chinese Turkistan (modern Xinjiang province), Tibet, and in 1683, for the first time, TAIWAN. But by the end of the 18th century symptoms of dynastic decline had begun to appear. The overwhelming impact of the West thus came at a most disadvantageous time for China.

Qing Decline

The immediate source of conflict between China and the West was trade. The Qing had attempted to conduct diplomatic and commercial relations with the European powers within the traditional framework of the tribute system and to confine foreign trade to the single port of GUANGZHOU (Canton) in the south. The destruction by the

(Left) The Boxer Uprising (1900), the climax of the antiforeign movement in China, was most virulent in the northern provinces, where Western and Japanese commercial influences were strongest. Railroads, a visible sign of foreign encroachment, were often the target of saboteurs. (Right) *In this French cartoon satirizing the disintegration of China's sovereignty during the early years of the 20th century, the imperialist powers dance around a crumbling Chinese giant.*

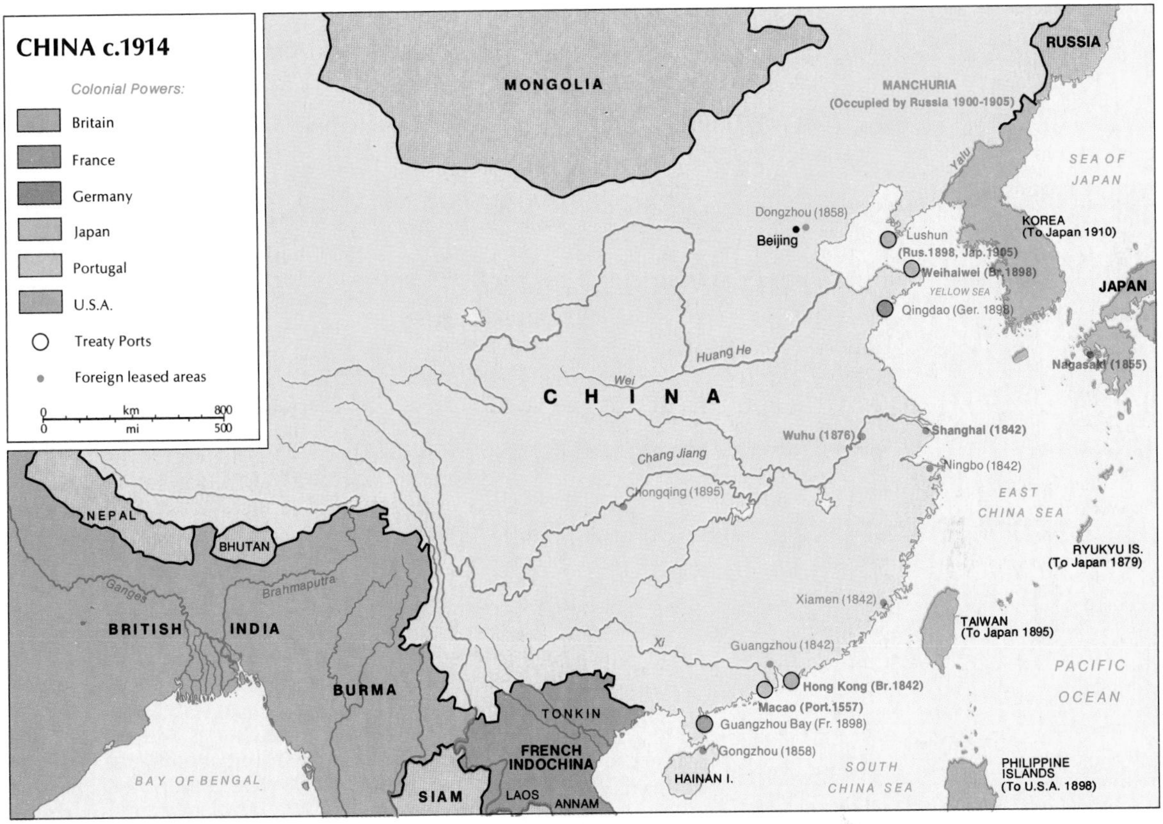

Cartographic Production by Lothar Roth & Associates

This map of China on the eve of World War I shows the internationally operated treaty ports and areas leased by foreign powers. European nations forced the opening of China to the influence of Western powers during the 19th century.

Chinese of all foreign opium at Guangzhou precipitated the OPIUM WAR of 1839–42. At its conclusion the Qing was forced by the Treaty of Nanjing to capitulate to a British naval force, cede Hong Kong to Britain, open several ports to unrestricted trade, and promise henceforth to conduct foreign relations on the basis of equality.

More concessions were wrested from China after the Anglo-French War of 1856–60, which saw the foreign occupation and looting of Beijing and resulted in the opening of all China to Western diplomatic, commercial, and missionary representatives (see TIANJIN, TREATIES OF). This second humiliation to the Qing coincided with a series of internal rebellions sparked by the decline of central authority, the most important of which, during 1851–64, was that of the Taipings, a radical military-religious movement. After achieving initial success, the TAIPING REBELLION was put down by newly created provincial militias loyal to the Qing.

Despite a shift of power in the provinces from Manchus to Chinese and a new period of regionalism in Chinese politics, the provincial leaders allied with the central leadership during the late 19th century in unsuccessfully seeking first to restore the traditional Confucian system as a means of restoring order and later to introduce into China Western technology as part of a self-strengthening movement.

China's continuing helplessness in the face of the foreign threat was revealed most clearly by the SINO-JAPANESE WAR over Korea (1894–95) and yet another defeat for China, which was compelled to recognize Korean independence, to cede Taiwan to Japan, and to allow the European powers and Japan to secure concessions. The defeat sparked the abortive Hundred Days reform movement of 1898, which failed due largely to the corrupt and narrow-minded Dowager Empress CIXI (Tz'u-hsi), who dominated the last three decades of Qing government. But after the BOXER UPRISING of 1900 precipitated yet another foreign occupation, Cixi was compelled to institute genuine reforms.

Nationalist Movement

Ironically, reform paved the way for a more radical political transformation. Revolutionary and nationalistic uprisings gained widespread public support, even among the conservative scholar-gentry. Finally, revolution broke out at Wuchang in Central China on Oct. 10, 1911. On Jan. 1, 1912, SUN YAT-SEN, a longtime activist, was elected provisional president of the Chinese Republic. On Febru-

The map provides a chronology of military operations during China's Communist Revolution (1934–49). The struggle between the Nationalists and the Communists was interrupted to present a common defense against the Japanese during World War II.

ary 12 the last Qing emperor abdicated, ending more than 3,000 years of Chinese monarchy. Although Sun is regarded as the father of the Chinese Republic, he was succeeded just a few months later by YUAN SHIKAI, a late-Qing military strongman who was widely believed to be the only statesman at that time powerful enough to combat not only lingering Manchu reactionism but also foreign aggression.

Yuan soon dissolved parliament and attempted to restore the monarchy. After Yuan's death in 1916 and until 1928, rival groups of militarists with the support of various Western nations contended for power. China had once more entered an age of domination by WARLORDS. Although politically retrogressive, the period (1917–21) witnessed a revolution in Chinese thought and culture collectively known as the May Fourth movement. The result was an intensified nationalism and struggle against imperialism, an enhanced knowledge of Western liberal ideas, a spreading attack on the old Confucian hierarchical social order, and a literary renaissance that created a new vernacular writing style. The period also marked the introduction of Marxism into China and the convening of the first congress of the Chinese Communist party (CCP) in 1921, with MAO ZEDONG (Mao Tse-tung) in attendance.

Internal Struggles

Russian Communists, however, decided to support the numerically superior and more influential Nationalist political party called the KUOMINTANG (KMT), led by Sun Yat-sen. The alliance of convenience between Communists and Nationalists came to a bloody end in April 1927, when KMT troops ravaged the CCP organization and labor movement in Shanghai. The architect of the Shanghai massacre was CHIANG KAI-SHEK, a military advisor of Sun who took over the military command of the KMT after Sun's death in 1925. From July 1926, Chiang led the NORTHERN EXPEDITION to rid China of the warlords.

By the autumn of 1928, Chiang had succeeded in nominally reuniting China for the first time since 1916. But the KMT-controlled government at Nanjing, which survived from 1928 to 1937, was forced to devote almost half its budget to military expenditures and was beset by ineffectual administration, corruption, factionalism, and political repression. Finally, Chiang Kai-shek was less concerned with the social and economic transformation of Chinese society than with the creation of a strong national state. Whatever hopes Chiang may have had of solving the many problems facing his regime were dashed by the full-scale Japanese invasion of China that began in July 1937.

World War II and Communist Victory

The war proved a boon for the CCP. As late as 1934–35, KMT pressure had forced the CCP to embark upon the 8,000-km (5,000-mi) LONG MARCH to the northwestern

Mao Zedong (Mao Tse-Tung), China's leader from 1949 to 1976, has been blamed by the current leadership for the Cultural Revolution (1966–76), which reduced China to near anarchy.

Deng Xiaoping joins in the planting of trees on China's national tree planting day (March 12). Deng remains China's most influential leader.

frontier. It was during the Long March that Mao Zedong achieved unrivaled power in the Communist party. While the KMT bore the brunt of the frontline fighting against the Japanese, Mao seized upon nationalistic fervor and undertook various economic reform programs and peasant mobilization in the less accessible border areas. Although materially supported by the United States and at first far superior to the CCP in numbers, the KMT lacked an inspiring ideology or genuine economic reform program. Defensively entrenched in the cities, it suffered the debilitating effects of wartime inflation and corruption and was increasingly outmaneuvered by the CCP.

By mid-1948 the Communists equaled the Nationalists in numbers. Finally, Mao's armies crossed the Chang Jiang River in 1949 and overwhelmed the Nationalists. KMT military remnants and political leaders fled to Taiwan, where the Nationalists presided over an economic miracle and continued to claim to be the legitimate government of all China.

People's Republic

The history of post-1949 China is the history of the People's Republic, proclaimed by Mao Zedong on Oct. 1, 1949, at its capital, Beijing. This history has been marked by long periods of careful, practical development interspersed with shorter periods of intense ideological mobilization. The first years were ones of thoroughgoing social and economic reorganization on the Russian model, backed by Soviet support. Mobilization of the masses in these reforms may have been facilitated by the patriotism generated by China's involvement in the KOREAN WAR (1950–53).

During the first Five-Year Plan (1953–57) agriculture was collectivized and industrial production expanded. But disappointing agricultural production led to the frenzied GREAT LEAP FORWARD of 1958–60. About the same time, disagreement over the correct methods of achieving socialism led to the great Sino-Soviet split.

By the mid-1960s a feeling by Mao that the revolution was running out of steam led him to launch the CULTURAL REVOLUTION of 1966–69. As stability was restored after this second mass upheaval, China profited from a series of developments in foreign relations, including its admission to the United Nations and the expulsion (1971) from that body of the Nationalist regime on Taiwan.

Mao's Successors

The deaths of China's revered prime minister, ZHOU ENLAI (Chou En-lai), and of Mao himself in 1976 made that a watershed year for the People's Republic. Soon thereafter the radical grouping known as the GANG OF FOUR was removed from power. Under moderate leader DENG XIAOPING (Teng Hsiao-p'ing), China and the United States reestablished diplomatic relations in January 1979. China's leaders officially condemned (1981) the excesses of the Cultural Revolution, and Deng orchestrated a process of economic and political liberalization. An overheated economy and student demands for democracy led to the purges of party leaders HU YAOBANG (Hu Yao-pang) in 1987 and ZHAO ZIYANG (Chao Tzu-yang) in 1989, a slowdown in economic reform, and a military crackdown (June 1989) on the student prodemocracy movement. In foreign affairs, China and Britain reached agreement on the future of Hong Kong in 1984; an accord with Portugal on Macao was reached in 1987. Relations with the USSR improved, but China's leaders appeared deadlocked and divided on how to shape China's future.

China, Republic of see TAIWAN

China Sea, South The South China Sea (Chinese: Nan Hai) is an arm of the Pacific Ocean off the southeast Asian mainland. Bordered by China, Vietnam, and the Malay Peninsula on the west, Borneo to the south, and the Philippines and Taiwan to the east, it is connected to the Indian Ocean by the Strait of Malacca. It contains major shipping lanes and is heavily fished. The Sunda shelf is shallow, but the China Sea Basin reaches a depth of 5,015 m (16,452 ft).

chinaberry The chinaberry, *Melia azedarach,* is a deciduous hardwood tree in the mahogany family, Meliaceae. Native to the Himalayas, it is grown worldwide and is common in the southern United States. It has a stout trunk, spreading branches, and large, alternate leaves that are doubly compound. Its fragrant, violet flowers are borne in loose clusters.

chinaware see POTTERY AND PORCELAIN

chinchilla [chin-chil'-uh] The chinchilla family, Chinchillidae, contains three genera of South American rodents. The chinchilla, *Chinchilla lanigar,* resembles a short-eared, long-tailed rabbit. About 38 cm (15 in) long, with a 15-cm (6-in) tail, it weighs up to 1 kg (2.2 lb) and

The chinchilla is bred in North America and Europe for its highly valuable fur, which can be blue, pearl, or gray, with darker markings and yellow white underparts.

feeds on seeds, fruits, and herbs. Once plentiful in the Andes at elevations of up to 5,500 m (18,000 ft), it has been hunted nearly to extinction for its fur, for which it is now bred on fur farms. The short-tailed chinchilla, *C. chinchilla*, may already be extinct. The three species of mountain viscacha, genus *Lagidum*, also of the high Andes, have very large ears and long tails. These social, rock-dwelling animals are hunted for their long, fine, gray to brown fur and their meat. The plains viscacha, *Lagostomus maximus*, found in Argentina, has a body up to 66 cm (27 in) long and somewhat resembles a marmot, with thick, mottled gray fur. It lives in burrows, the holes of which create hazards for range animals.

Chinese art and architecture During the 2,000 years preceding the revolution of 1912, China evolved a hierarchy of the arts that was but one aspect of the general structure of its society. The literary arts were at the summit (see CHINESE LITERATURE), followed by CALLIGRAPHY, the art of writing with brush and ink. Calligraphy's status was sometimes shared by the art of playing the Chinese lute, or *qin*. These arts were followed by painting, after which came chess and other scholarly pursuits. Manual crafts, including pottery, sculpture, and even architecture, were traditionally considered as products of mere artisans.

Calligraphy

Calligraphy, the noblest of the visual arts, was the most direct expression of that prodigious literacy that marked the elite of China. It was venerated even by the illiterate masses, and its values changed less over 2,000 years than those of any other art. Those who controlled the administration of the Chinese empire, and who therefore wielded the greatest influence over its evolution, cultivated the art of handwriting as an active element in the education of the scholar-gentry class.

The materials of calligraphy are considered essential to proper performance. China's invention and use of paper (around AD 105), preceding its discovery in the West by 11 centuries, profoundly affected the development of calligraphy and eventually of painting. Although calligraphy was often written on silk, its most distinctive qualities emerged out of the reactions between the brush, ink, and paper. The finely pointed brush was usually made from goat or wolf hair. To be perfectly controlled, the brush had to be held essentially upright, so that its tip remained centered over the writing surface. The deep black ink used was mixed when required by rubbing on an ink stone a few drops of water and an ink stick made from pine soot and protein glue. The best paper was made from mulberry bark and imparted a deep glow to the readily absorbed ink. The Chinese honored each of these items as the product of a highly refined craft, and a precise sense of ritual accompanied their use.

The earliest Chinese writing that can be read today dates from around the 13th century BC. Still earlier forms are as yet undeciphered. Two distinct forms are known from the earliest decipherable stage. A vividly pictographic script appears on the magnificent bronze vessels of the SHANG period (*c.*1600–1027 BC), having been engraved into the molds as dedicatory inscriptions. More complex texts in a much more abstract script were engraved by Shang diviners on ox scapulae and turtle plastrons, known as ORACLE BONES.

The QIN (221–206 BC), the first dynasty to unify China under centralized rule, produced a standardized script that came into use throughout the country. Later called small seal script (*xiaojuan*), it had evolved from an increasingly square regularization of the large seal script (*dajuan*) of the ZHOU dynasty (*c.*1027–256 BC), in which the Confucian Classics had originally been written. Bureaucratic requirements during the HAN period (202 BC–AD 220) exerted strong pressure for greater simplification and standardization. The result was a new category of script called simply clerical script (*lishu*). The archaic seal script was often retained for formal titles and was also adapted to the small seals that have been used as signatures from the Han to the present. These small red stamps, often present on documents, letters, books, and paintings, may signify either authorship or ownership. By the 4th century AD, the formal regular script (*garshu*), which is basically the printed script of today, and various abbreviated cursive scripts had evolved. WANG XIZHI, the leading calligrapher of the 4th century, was revered by later generations as the "sage calligrapher" of all time. The TANG dynasty (618–906) was the classic age of regular script; its formality was ideally suited to the aristocratic splendor of that period. The running script (*xingshu*) had many of its greatest practitioners in the SONG dynasty

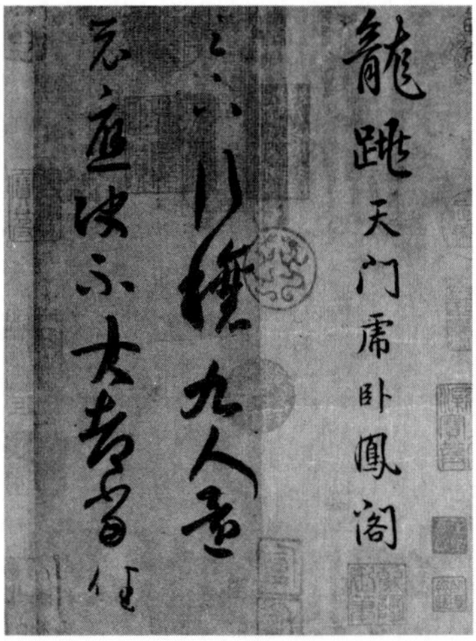

The 4th-century master Wang Xizhi profoundly influenced succeeding generations of Chinese calligraphers. Although none of his works survives today, this early Tang dynasty (608–907) copy of a page of his cursive script is faithful to the original in all details. (Art Museum, Princeton University, Princeton, N.J.)

(Above) *The hand-scroll* Admonitions of the Instructress of the Ladies of the Palace *is executed in fine-lined ink and colors on silk. The earliest scroll painting in existence today, it is attributed to Gu Kaizhi (*c.*345–406?), one of the first recorded painters of China. (British Museum, London).* (Right) Buddhist Temple in Autumn Mountains *is attributed to Li Cheng of the Northern Song period (960–1127). This monumental hanging scroll exemplifies the great tradition of Chinese landscape painting that began during the 10th century. (Nelson Gallery of Art, Kansas City.)*

(960–1279), when calligraphers and other artists explored new modes of self-expression with great originality. Much of the finest cursive script (*caoshu*) was written in the MING dynasty (1368–1644), when great attention was focused on the formal properties of art. In the later QING dynasty (1644–1911) the ancient seal script was revived by calligraphers such as I Pingshou (1754–1815). In this century, when Shang oracle bones were recovered after 3,000 years of obscurity, their archaic script was also translated into a brush-written form.

Painting

The earliest known examples of Chinese painting date from the Han dynasty (202 BC–AD 220), when the walls of temples and official halls were often painted with murals. Almost none of the early mural paintings survive, however, except for some within cave temples and on the walls of tomb chambers. Their style is closely related to the sculptured tomb reliefs of the period.

Through the Tang period (618–906), murals and large screens were probably the painter's main formats. The scroll format evolved concurrently and later became much more important in the history of Chinese painting. The earliest type, the horizontal handscroll, was also the earliest form of the book, in use before a folding format—stitched down one side in a manner similar to the Western book—was developed in the Song (960–1279). To be viewed, the handscroll is placed on a table and the viewer unrolls it, length by length. During the Song, vertical scrolls intended for hanging on a wall also became common.

Scroll painting was traditionally produced for the exclusive enjoyment of a small intellectual elite. Many of the early painters are known by name since they signed their works long before this practice became customary in the West. Names of many other artists are known from their mention in essays on art theory.

Han through Five Dynasties Period. From the Han period through the 8th century, the principal subject matter of painting was the depiction of human figures as edifying exemplars of good character. The earliest surviving scroll painting has been attributed to GU KAIZHI (*c.*345?–406?). In this handscroll, entitled *Admonitions of the Instructress of the Ladies of the Palace* (British Museum, London), the people are embodied by their clothes, rather than by their flesh, and the floating draperies are similar in style to those of 6th-century Buddhist sculpture.

After the 8th century birds and flowers became popular subjects. Bamboo and plum blossom became special categories of painting, sanctioned by the strong symbolic value that these plant forms held for the literate class. Various other themes appeared in painting, but from the 10th to the 20th century, the subject honored above all was landscape. Unlike the Mediterranean world, China had no mythology of anthropomorphic gods. The belief in a self-creating universe led rather to a mythology of landscape itself. Mountains and waters were the grandest of all the cosmic images, supporting each other in a dynamic polarity.

Song and Yuan Periods. The concept that the microcosm of man participates in the macrocosm of landscape is reflected in the tradition of monumental landscape

The silk painting Five-Colored Parakeet on the Branch of a Blossoming Apricot Tree *is attributed to Emperor Huizong (1082–1135). The balanced composition and refined brushwork are typical of the bird-and-flower tradition developed during the Song dynasty. (Museum of Fine Arts, Boston.)*

painting that flourished during the Northern Song period (960–1127). In the enormous hanging scroll *Buddhist Temple in Autumn Mountains* (Nelson Gallery of Art and Atkins Museum, Kansas City, Missouri), attributed to the influential master Li Cheng (919–67), man is portrayed as but one small element within the enormity of nature. In the early 12th century the Song capital moved from Kaifeng, in the Henan region of North China, to Hangzhou, in Zhejiang. Among the marshes of the Chang Jiang delta, Southern Song academy painters such as Xia Gui and Ma Yuan painted scenes depicting a moist climate, where mountains floated elusively over mists, as in Ma Yuan's evocative *Bare Willow and Mountain in Mist* (Museum of Fine Arts, Boston). Another school of Song painting was that of the Chan (Zen) Buddhist masters, who produced boldly outlined works of great simplicity and spontaneity. A notable example is the *Six Persimmons* scroll (Daitoku-ji, Kyoto) by the versatile monk-painter Mu Qi.

A concern with self-expression that had surfaced in other arts during the Song, notably in poetry and calligraphy, began to be explored in the Yuan (1279–1368) through the medium of landscape painting. The pioneer in this development was the calligrapher-painter Zhao Mengfu, active in the late 13th and early 14th centuries. From this date the relationship between calligraphy and landscape painting became even closer. Painters began to talk of "writing" a picture. Outstanding exponents of this new approach to painting were the landscape painters Huang Gongwang, Ni Zan, Wang Meng, and Wu Zhen, collectively known as the Four Great Yuan Masters. The practice of combining painting and calligraphy in a single composition became common.

Ming Period. In the Ming dynasty (1368–1644) the entire process of image making became more calligraphic. The more representational values in pictorial art were often rejected in favor of a greater abstraction of form. Some Ming painters, such as the influential master and art theorist Dong Qichang (1555–1636), declared that ultimately calligraphy and painting were the same *dao* ("way").

Ming artists believed that exemplars from the past could provide aesthetic standards for the present. The Wu school, an important school of Ming landscape painting founded by Shen Zhou, was based on these values.

Dong Qichang's handscroll *Autumn Mountains* (Cleveland Museum of Art, Cleveland, Ohio) is a transformation of two earlier masterpieces, one by the 10th-century artist Dong Yuan, and one by the Yuan artist Huang Gongwang (1269–1354). Dong Qichang turned principally to these two exemplars in establishing an amateur tradition of painting, called the Southern school, that greatly influ-

Walk in the Mountains in Springtime *(c.1200), an ink-and-color study on silk, is by the Southern Song academy painter Ma Yuan. (National Palace Museum, Taiwan.)*

(Above) *This 75-cm (30-in) long bronze tiger,* c.*10th century* BC, *dates from the succeeding Zhou dynasty phase of Bronze Age art. (Freer Gallery of Art, Washington, D.C.)* (Left) *The Shang-dynasty phase of Chinese Bronze Age art (*c.*1600–1027* BC*) produced this bronze food container used in sacrificial rites. (Freer Gallery of Art, Washington, D.C.)*

enced the development of later Chinese painting and orthodox art criticism. This school reflected the values of the scholar-gentry elite. Although they recognized the role of technique in calligraphy, Dong and other literati artists slighted the professional painter's technical skill and the frequently decorative quality of his work. They associated these so-called professional values mainly with two groups of artists: the court academy painters of the Southern Song period, such as Ma Yuan, and the early Ming painters of the imperial court and of Zhejiang province (collectively known as the Zhe school painters).

Qing Period to Present. The first century of Qing rule (1644–1911) was the last period of great creativity in traditional Chinese painting. The orthodox Southern school tradition of Dong Qichang culminated in the styles of the so-called FOUR WANGS. Another large and varied group of artists, who are often grouped by the cities they most frequented, pursued more individualistic aims. The best known of these artists were ZHU DA, Kun Can (1610?–93), and SHITAO. Scholar-artists of the Qing period often tried to maintain a fiction that they never earned money from their paintings. But in the 18th century, with painters such as Jin Nong (1687–1764) and Lo Ping (1733–99), both classed among the "Eight Eccentrics of Yangzhou," this pretense was abandoned as a merchant society of vastly increasing wealth became an important patron.

Although Western techniques of painting were introduced in China in the late 19th century, the prestige of brush painting and brush writing survives. MAO ZEDONG's calligraphy has been much displayed and honored. The calligraphy of Chairman HUA GUOFENG is compared to that of the Tang statesman Yen Chenqing (709–85), who enjoyed great fame as both an administrator and a calligrapher. Twentieth-century masters of Chinese painting in the traditional mode include QI BAISHI, ZAO WOUKI, and LI KERAN.

Technology and Craft: Bronze, Lacquer, Textiles, and Jade

For thousands of years the applied arts in China have revealed a high level of refinement and technical mastery. The Shang dynasty (*c.*1600–1027 BC) established rule over the Central Plains region of the Huang He (Yellow River) about the time that North China entered the Bronze Age. By the time the Shang was defeated by the Zhou dynasty (*c.*1027–256 BC), one of the most remarkable of all Bronze Age arts had been perfected.

Ritual Bronzes. The small but powerful Shang aristocracy required vessels for such rituals as the ancestral sacrifices. Building on a well-developed ceramic technology, craftsmen made clay models and carved them with dense patterns of extraordinary precision; from these models, which often bore inscriptions, section molds of clay were taken and molten alloy was poured into the final assembly of the molds.

The surface decoration of most of the bronzes is formed largely from fragmented zoomorphic motifs combined among densely repeated spirals. Their combination is often dominated by one recurring image, the *taotie* monster mask. By the late Shang a profusion of knoblike protuberances and other exaggerated three-dimensional effects characterized much bronze decor.

Although the manufacture of bronze vessels remained an important craft under the Zhou dynasty, fundamental

This elegantly decorated lacquer bowl dates from the Han dynasty (206 BC–AD *220), when lacquer was a highly developed Chinese art form, used to ornament and preserve a variety of objects. (Seattle Art Museum.)*

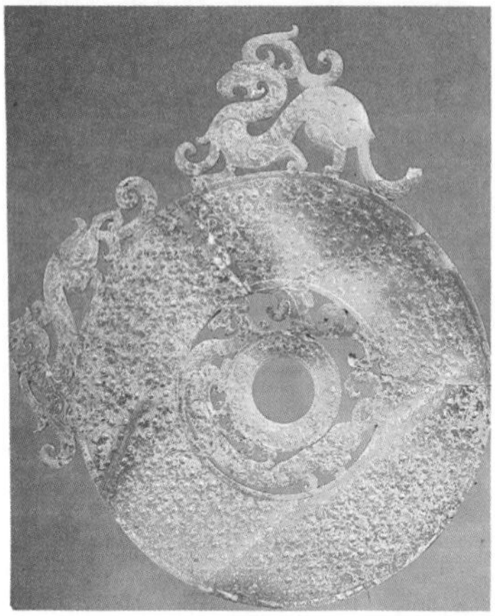

(Above) *This fragment of embroidered silk from the Tang dynasty (618–907) combines abstraction with the Chinese concern for detail. (British Museum, London.)* (Right) *From Jincun comes this nephrite ritual disc of the Late Zhou dynasty (770–256 BC). The tiny jade object is richly ornamented with feline and spiral motifs. (Nelson Gallery of Art, Kansas City.)*

changes took place in the nature of the art. Inscriptions lengthened into major historical documents. In addition, the late Zhou bronzes were sometimes inlaid with gold and silver as were the backs of bronze mirrors, produced from about 600 BC. The decoration of bronze mirrors reached a peak during the Han period, after which the art of bronze casting declined.

Lacquer. The upper and middle reaches of the Chang Jiang were the habitat of the lac tree (*Rhus verniciflua*), the sap of which may have been used for paint as early as the Shang dynasty. By the late Eastern Zhou period (770–256 BC), lacquer was used extensively for preservative and decorative purposes on many articles, such as bowls, musical instruments, and furniture. The kingdom of Qu, on the middle Chang Jiang, was a major early center of this art, the motifs of which were often similar to those used in gold and silver inlay on bronzes. In the Han dynasty (202 BC–AD 220) imperial lacquer factories were set up in the Sichuan region. By the time of the Tang dynasty (618–906), lacquer was also used in modeling life-size, hollow-cored statues. In the 14th century and later, lacquer objects were frequently carved. In this technique the thickness of the lacquer had to be built up from as many as 200 layers. Red and black were the most common colors, sometimes applied in alternating layers. Lacquerware was also produced with representations of landscapes and figures inlaid with mother-of-pearl and precious metals.

Textiles. The weaving of silk was a distinctive craft of China as early as the Shang dynasty. From the Han dynasty the great overland trade routes that linked Mediterranean countries with China, such as the SILK ROAD across Central Asia, brought innumerable merchants and craftsmen from western lands to China. The designs on Tang textiles show extensive influence from Sassanian and other western sources. Also introduced from non-Chinese textile traditions was the process of weft-woven tapestry, in which colors are woven within limited areas instead of from selvage to selvage. The adaptation of tapestry weave, called *kesi,* became the greatest glory of the Chinese weaver's art, perhaps because it proved so suitable for translating paintings and calligraphy into textiles. *Kesi* influenced, in turn, medieval European textile traditions.

Jade. In China jade was traditionally the most valued of all minerals. Jade is so hard that it cannot be cut, only ground away. The earliest abrasive known to have been used was quartz powder, presumably the material used by the Neolithic jade workers. Many jades have been found dating from the Shang dynasty, worked with the same precision as were ritual bronzes. Some of the best known jade forms from Neolithic through late Zhou times functioned as ritual symbols: the pierced disc (*bi*) signified the heavens, the squared tube (*zong*), the earth.

During the Eastern Zhou period (770–256 BC) the working of jades became increasingly elaborate, with finely detailed pierced designs. This fine work probably

The Song dynasty (960–1279) is famous for its classic, exquisitely balanced ceramic wares. A fine example from the Long kilns is this monochrome-glazed Celadon vase. (Fitzwilliam Museum, Cambridge, England.)

The art of glazed ceramic ware, called "blue and white," reached its peak during the Ming dynasty (1368–1644). The underglaze blue decoration on this porcelain Meiping vase shows the highly skilled techniques of painting with cobalt pigment. (Nelson Gallery of Art, Kansas City.)

became possible with the introduction of much more effective rotary tools after cast iron was developed in the 6th to 5th centuries BC. Such pieces are one aspect of the magnificent flowering of decorative arts at that time. From the Han dynasty on, jades were generally much less spectacular. During the Qing dynasty (1644–1911), especially under the emperor Gaozong in the Qianlong era (1736–95), jade carving became an important aspect of an explosive renaissance of craftwork.

Ceramics

Neolithic pottery, which was not discovered until the 1920s, is the earliest form of Chinese art known today.

Early Wares. The wide-bellied, narrow-necked burial jars from Gansu province, their upper halves painted in red and black with powerful spirals, waves, and zigzags, are dated from about 2400 BC, a late phase of the Yangshao culture, which is considered the nuclear origin of Chinese civilization. Dating from the early 2d millennium BC is the Longshan culture, which originated in the coastal region of Shandong. This culture produced a distinctive black ware, its sharply articulated, angular shapes turned to eggshell thinness of body on a fast wheel and burnished to a glossy black. The Bronze Age evolved where the Yangshao and Longshan overlapped in the central Huang He plains.

Although the bronze art of the following millennium largely eclipsed its contemporaneous pottery, during the Shang important technological advances occurred in kiln design, in clay composition (the introduction of pure white kao-lin), and in glazing techniques. In the Han dynasty (202 BC–AD 220) wares with a hard, feldspathic glaze became common, and developed into a high-temperature-fired stoneware by the 6th century AD. Pottery manufacture was widely dispersed over the whole of China by this time.

From the period of the Han dynasty, but especially during the Tang (618–906), lead glazes were used extensively to decorate clay objects made for burials. Combining with various metallic oxides, they make possible a dazzling range of colors. Such glazes fell into disuse soon after the Tang and were forgotten until the modern age.

Classical Wares of Song. The Song dynasty (960–1279) is considered the classic age of Chinese ceramics. The perfection of Song forms arises from their organic balance and dynamic fullness as contrasted with the geometric perfection of classical Greek vases. Most Song bowls and vases are covered with largely monochromatic glazes, with decoration often incised or impressed under the glaze. Famous wares include the ivory-white *Ding* ware, descended from the famous white ware of the Tang; jadelike CELADON, used for official and commercial purposes throughout China; sky-blue *Ru* ware, made for the imperial court of Huizong; its relative, *Jun* ware, with the varying blue of its thick glaze often enlivened by submerged swirls of purple; small, heavily potted *Jian* ware tea bowls, with dark red, brown, and black glazes speckled over coarse clay; slip-painted and sgraffito *Cizhou* wares, with superbly vigorous floral and pictorial decoration.

The technical perfection of Song ceramics was largely based on the Song artisan's mastery of a simple, iron-pigmented, feldspathic glaze. Depending on the firing, it varies from the rich black of saturated oxidation, through deep red, to endlessly subtle green shades of reduction. Not until the Mongol conquest of China and the Yuan dynasty (1279–1368) did the use of other minerals in feldspathic glazes become dominant.

Ming and Qing Wares. The blue-and-white ware resulting from cobalt pigment, originally imported from Iran during the Yuan period, initiated another great era in ceramics production that reached its peak in the Ming dynasty (1368–1644). Many of the Song wares had been stonewares, but most of the important Ming and Qing

Beginning in the 18th century, numerous finely decorated, glazed enamel porcelains were produced for Chinese, European, and Near Eastern markets. This famille rose *(rose pink) porcelain vase, made during the reign of emperor Gaozong (1736–95), is one variety of this famous colored ware. (Avery Brundage Collection, San Francisco.)*

This stone relief, dated 673, is from a series depicting six favorite battle steeds of Taizong, founder of the Tang dynasty (618–906). (University Museum, Philadelphia.)

(1644–1911) wares were porcelain. The potters of blue-and-white ware perfected a method of painting with cobalt under a transparent glaze. Their decorative skills reached the highest refinement and complexity and their products were exported eastward and westward in large quantities, immensely influencing European and Near Eastern wares.

The town of JINGDEZHEN, in Jiangxi province, became the center for imperial Ming kilns. In the Qing dynasty, under the KANGXI emperor (r. 1662–1722), these kilns were reorganized and commenced a final golden age, culminating under the Qianlong emperor, Gaozong (r. 1736–95). Numerous decorative styles were perfected by imperial potters and their provincial cousins during the Ming and Qing dynasties. New monochromes, such as yellow and red, were developed, as were a magnificent range of multicolored, overglaze enamels. From the 18th century on, Qing porcelains decorated in *famille rose* (rose pink), *verte* (pastel green), and *noire* (black) filled the mansions of China and Europe alike. Much of the Chinese porcelain intended for export was decorated with European-inspired motifs and in many cases was made according to European order.

Sculpture

Sculpture of the Shang (*c.*1600–*c.*1027 BC) and Zhou (*c.*1027–256 BC) periods is generally small in scale, carved in marble and other materials, and depicts human or animal forms. Such sculpture was presumably intended for ritual use.

Burial Sculpture. During the Han dynasty (202 BC–AD 8) sculptures associated with the veneration of the dead were produced in great quantities. These burial sculptures were of three types. The first category is the low-relief sculpture used to decorate the walls of the burial chamber, mostly representing scenes of daily life. The second category consists of small fired-clay sculptures that were placed inside the tomb. These objects reproduce in small scale an amazing spectrum of the everyday world of the Han period, from castles and other architectural forms to barnyard pets. This tradition reached its apogee during the Tang (618–906); figures of dancers, polo players, and horses were imbued with an extraordinary sense of life and movement.

The third category of burial sculpture is the monumental carved statuary of animals and guardian figures that line the processional ways leading to important tombs. Recent excavations at the tumulus of the First Emperor of Qin (d. 210 BC), near Xian in Shenxi province, have revealed a vast field of life-size terra-cotta statues depicting soldiers, servants, and horses, estimated to total 6,000 pieces. Their size and style is very different from the mortuary sculpture of the succeeding Han period.

Buddhist Sculpture. By far the largest body of Chinese sculptural art is associated with BUDDHISM, which reached China from India some time in the 3d century AD. From then through the Tang period, Buddhism flourished in China, combining with indigenous traditions in thought and art. Sites such as the cave temples of DUNHUANA vividly preserve in murals, monumental stone sculpture, bronze Buddha images, and even silk banners, the development of Chinese Buddhism between the 5th and 9th centuries.

The first mature phase of Chinese Buddhist sculpture dates from the early 6th century and is characterized by highly spiritualized images of the Buddha, such as the famous gilt-bronze statuette of *Shakyamuni Buddha* (Metropolitan Museum of Art, New York), dated from the Northern Wei dynasty (386–535). In the later 6th and the 7th centuries Chinese sculpture underwent many chronological and regional variations, relating to both external and internal influences. Early in the 8th century these culminated in the flowering of an international style, which spread from India across to China, through Korea

This polychromed wood statue represents the Bodhisattva Kuanyin, deity of compassion. The draped costume and soft appearance typify Buddhist art of the Song (960–1279). (Museum van Aziatishe Kunst, Amsterdam.)

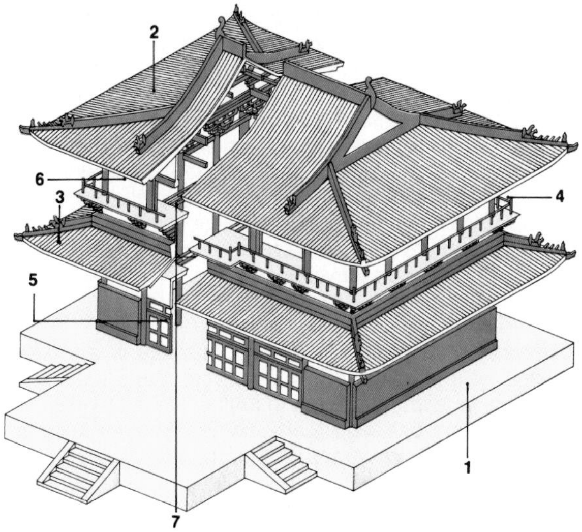

A typical pagoda consists of a stone podium (1); *multistory hall with hipped roof* (2); *shallow overhanging eaves* (3); *brackets supporting eaves and balcony* (4); *three-door entrance* (5); *open bays on upper stories* (6); *and galleries facing the open interior* (7).

and into Japan. In this family of styles, the body is endowed with a tightly structured, muscular presence, articulated with graceful ease, and lightly clothed in garments which may both cling to its form and swirl loosely free. The confident grandeur of the limestone *Seated Buddha* from Tianlongshan (8th century; now in the Fogg Art Museum, Cambridge, Mass.), still imbued with a spiritual idealization, is superbly expressive of the golden age of Tang. In addition to stone, such statues were also made of clay, wood, bronze, and lacquer, although few examples survive. In 845 a nationwide persecution of Buddhism destroyed the majority of Buddhist temples and their contents. Fine Buddhist sculpture was again made in the Song (960–1279), Yuan (1279–1368), and Ming (1368–1644) dynasties.

Architecture

With the exception of the monumental rock-cut cave temples, such as those constructed at Dunhuang, LONGMEN, and YUNGANG, the temples associated with Buddhist sculptures were not built for permanence, and few have survived. Most architecture, both religious and secular, was constructed primarily of wood, on a simple post-and-lintel basis that favored marvelous elaboration. Important exceptions were the celebrated GREAT WALL OF CHINA, built during the Ming dynasty (1368–1644) on the foundations of a 3d-century BC defensive wall, and PAGODAS, tombs, and bridges constructed of stone or brick. The Chinese could build well with these materials; they were particularly advanced in certain forms of arch construction.

Architectural form remained basically the same for well over 2,000 years. Instead of supporting the roof with a rigidly triangulated truss as in the Western timber-frame construction, the Chinese did so with crossbeams in tiers of diminishing length. This was an extremely flexible system, promoting both a great extension of the eaves and

(Below, left) *Known as the Forbidden City, the former Imperial Palace in Beijing was built during the Yuan dynasty (1279–1368) and rebuilt first by Ming and then by Qing rulers. The enormous complex of halls, bridges, steps, and balustraded terraces is highlighted by the double-tiered Tai He Tian (Hall of Supreme Harmony), once the throne room.* (Right) *This view of the Summer Palace in Beijing shows one of the characteristic features of Chinese architectural form: a colored tile overhanging roof arranged in several tiers with gracefully upturned eaves.*

the concave roof line so typical of Chinese architecture. The overhanging eaves were supported by a series of cantilevered brackets. The many elements of this wood frame were often elaborately painted and the roof itself covered with colorfully glazed tiles. The curved roof and complex structural bracket style in architecture reached its peak in the Song dynasty (960–1279). A few temple buildings still survive from that period. In the Ming (1368–1644) and Qing (1644–1911) periods, the roof line tended to straighten.

Little architecture of the Ming period and scarcely any of earlier periods has survived. An important exception is the so-called Forbidden City, the former imperial palace in Beijing. It was built by the Mongol rulers of the Yuan dynasty (1279–1368) in the district where several earlier dynasties had located their capitals. The Ming entirely rebuilt the complex, as did the succeeding Qing rulers to a large extent. The succession of shining, tiled roofs and the hierarchic arrangement of seemingly endless courtyards, corridors, and halls were designed as the representation of a vast cosmic order.

Twentieth-Century Developments

Chinese art, especially painting and calligraphy, showed remarkable vitality and a new spirit of innovation throughout the 19th and well into the 20th century. From the early 1900s, Western influences were openly acknowledged. After the establishment of the Communist state in 1949, however, the authorities refused to tolerate any taint of the West in Chinese art except for SOCIALIST REALISM, imported from the USSR.

The 1980s saw a sporadic softening of official attitudes. Some Chinese avant-garde artists have been allowed to exhibit, and a few Western artists have shown their works in China. Subjects that were once forbidden—nudes, for example, or portraits of the poor—may sometimes be shown without official censure. Artists interested in Western genres experiment in their studios with cubism, surrealism, and abstract art; many are attracted by such realist painters as Andrew Wyeth. Few succeed, however, in giving a Chinese aspect to their borrowings from the West. Since 1980 there has been a significant exodus of artists from China to the West.

Chinese cabbage Cultured for its leaves, which are arranged in a loose head, Chinese, or celery, cabbage, *Brassica rapa pekinensis*, is a member of the Crucifera family. The plant is an annual and is related to the biennial bok choy; both are indigenous to eastern Asia. Chinese cabbage is used raw in salads or cooked as cabbage.

Chinese calendar During the middle years of the Shang dynasty (*c.*1300 BC), the Chinese began using a cyclical system to count days. The system consisted of 2 groups of ideographs, the 12 branches and the 10 stems, which were combined in couples, odd to odd and even to even, to form an endlessly repeating cycle of 60 units. About the time of Christ's birth the system began to be used for reckoning years as well. The Chinese year, which consisted of 12 lunar months, was from time to time adjusted to the solar year by the addition of an intercalary month. The 7-day week was introduced about AD 1200. During the Han dynasty each branch was matched with an animal name, producing the series: rat, ox, tiger, hare, dragon, serpent, horse, sheep, monkey, cock, dog, and pig. In the cyclical round of years, 2000 will be the year of the dragon. The Chinese year begins with the second new moon after the winter solstice, which occurs between January 21 and February 19.

Chinese checkers Chinese checkers is a modern version of the game of Halma (from the Greek word meaning "a leap"), invented in England about 1880. It is usually played by several participants, although there are also Halma solitaire games. In the United States a version called Chinese checkers was marketed successfully before World War II.

Chinese checkers is played on a board in the shape of a six-pointed star, with holes or indentations to hold the playing pieces, either pegs or marbles. Each star point is a different color; each player's set of 15 (sometimes 10) pieces matches the color of the star point that is the player's base. The object is for a player to move all of his or her pieces to the opposite star point before opponents can do so with their pieces. Each player moves one piece in turn; the moves may be a single step or one or more jumps. Players may jump over any other pieces, but steps and jumps may not be combined in a single move. A move can be made in any direction, backward as well as forward, and all moves are made either to advance one's own pieces or to block an opponent's.

Chinese Exclusion Acts The Chinese Exclusion Acts were federal laws passed in 1882, 1892, and 1902 to prevent Chinese immigration to the United States. Large numbers of Chinese came to the West Coast after the discovery (1848) of gold in California and during the construction (1864–69) of the Central Pacific Railroad. The right of Chinese to immigrate to the United States received formal protection under the Burlingame Treaty (1868), but economic competition between Chinese and native white American laborers led to anti-Chinese agitation, which intensified during the depression of the 1870s and culminated (1877) in anti-Chinese riots in San Francisco.

In 1879, Congress passed an act severely restricting Chinese immigration, but the act was vetoed by President Rutherford B. Hayes. The Chinese Exclusion Act of 1882, however, suspended Chinese immigration completely for 10 years. In 1892, Congress extended the exclusion for 10 more years, and in 1902 the prohibition was passed again without a terminal date. These laws were repealed in 1943, when China was a U.S. ally in World War II, but a quota of 105 immigrants a year severely restricted Chinese immigration until the liberalization of the rules under a 1965 amendment to the Immigration and Nationality Act.

Chinese language The Chinese language, one of the SINO-TIBETAN LANGUAGES, is spoken largely in the east and southeast of China, by people referred to ethnically as the Hans, the name of an ancient dynasty that flourished (206 BC–AD 220) in the Huang He basin. Much of north and northwest China falls in the domain of the URAL-ALTAIC LANGUAGES—a far-flung family that includes Mongolian, Japanese, and Korean. Southwest China has many speakers of Tibeto-Karen and Austro-Tai languages.

Varieties of Chinese. The many regional varieties of Chinese are as different from each other as French is from Spanish or as English is from German. Nonetheless, the varieties are called dialects of Chinese, rather than different languages. Two reasons may be given for this. First, a language is usually identified with a nation. Second, all the varieties of Chinese share a common orthography that transcends the differences in the spoken forms. Of more than 50 dialects of Chinese, only 20 existed in written form prior to the Communist period.

Mandarin. Of the seven major Chinese dialects, by far the largest is Mandarin, spoken by 70 percent of the Han people who make up 90 percent of the total population. Mandarin covers a huge sector of China, extending diagonally from the extreme southwest to Manchuria. The chief representative of Mandarin is Pudonghua, or "common speech." Based on the speech of Beijing, it is the official language of China.

Other Dialects. Other major Chinese dialects are Wu—spoken in Shanghai and as far as south of Wenzhou—Min, Kejia, Yue, Gan, and Xiang. Min speakers have inhabited Taiwan for centuries, sharing it with various Austro-Tai-speaking peoples. Yue, also called Cantonese, includes the speech of Hong Kong. Gan and Xiang, inland dialects, are spoken to the west of Min, with Gan centered in the city of Nanzhang and Xiang in Changsha and Shuangfeng. Because of their proximity to the sea, it is the speakers of Min, Kejia, and Yue who have migrated in greatest numbers to other parts of the world, especially Southeast Asia.

Early Chinese. The earliest extant records of Chinese are characters inscribed on ORACLE BONES of the Shang dynasty (*c.*1600–1027 BC). The earliest stage of Chinese for which there is significant evidence about both syntax and phonology dates from the first millennium BC. This stage, called Old Chinese, has been reconstructed from a large number of poems and songs, many of which are anthologized in the famous *Shih Jing* (trans. as *The Book of Songs*, 1927), an anthology of northern Chinese songs compiled *c.*1000–*c.*600 BC.

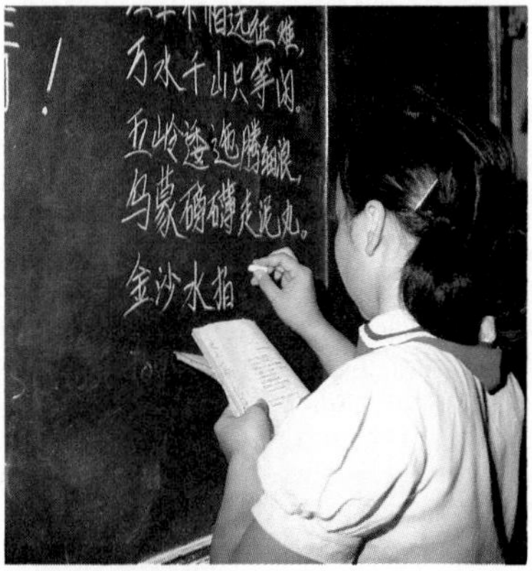

A student in elementary school practices writing Chinese characters. Although phonetic writing systems have been devised for the Chinese language, they have not replaced the traditional characters, which go back to before 2500 BC.

Middle Chinese. The second major stage of Chinese, so-called Middle Chinese, began about 1,400 years ago. Knowledge of it is based primarily on a rhyme dictionary, the *Qie Yun*, compiled by a group of poets at the beginning of the Tang dynasty. This dictionary, presumably reflecting the pronunciation in the area of the Tang capital, situated in the vicinity of present-day Xian, is one of the great cultural treasures of China. The language reconstructed from the *Qie Yun* seems to be close to the ancestral form of almost all the modern dialects of Chinese. The characters in the *Qie Yun* are organized strictly according to phonetic principles. Each character represents one syllable and indicates its tone (of which there were four), its initial consonant, and its rhyme—that is, every sound except the initial consonant.

Lexical Tones. All languages differentiate words by consonants (such as *sea* from *tea*) or by vowels (such as *tea* from *too*). In English, saying a word with different pitch patterns may result in different intonations—for questions, statements, commands—but the basic meaning remains the same. In Chinese, however, giving a certain cluster of consonants and vowels a different tone can result in a different word.

The four tones of Middle Chinese are preserved, with considerable modification, in modern Pudonghua. They are rising tone, falling, level, and dipping—that is, falling then rising. Modern Cantonese, however, has nine tones, all descended from the four of Middle Chinese.

Word Formation. Each Chinese character is pronounced as a single syllable and usually also corresponds to a single morpheme. Word formation in Indo-European languages typically involves the process of conjugation or declension, as in *see, sees, saw, seeing*, or *dog, dogs.* Although Chinese has parts of speech such as nouns, verbs, and adjectives, words are almost never conjugated or declined.

Chinese Characters. Chinese characters date back at least 3,500–4,000 years. Almost every Chinese character is a morpheme, and almost every Chinese morpheme is represented by a single character. Because the character does not reflect internal phonetic structure, it can continue to represent a given morpheme even if the morpheme's pronunciation has changed significantly through the centuries. It is their independence from sound that has made Chinese characters such a cohesive force. In fact, because Japanese is written with about 2,000 Chinese characters, some communication can take place between readers of the two languages, even though their speakers are almost wholly unintelligible to each other.

Although the largest dictionary of Chinese contains more than 50,000 distinct characters, only 3,000–4,000 are needed for day-to-day use; and the task of learning even this smaller number of characters is greatly facilitated by their highly regular and systematic structure. Each character is built up from two basic units: radicals and strokes. There are 214 radicals, but only 20 or 30 different strokes.

The Pinyin System. In order to standardize spelling of Chinese in Western languages, the People's Republic of China devised the Pinyin system of transliteration in 1958. Officially adopted by the Chinese in 1979, Pinyin is replacing the traditional Wade-Giles system used by English speakers. Chinese names are listed in this encyclopedia in their Pinyin form, but the Wade-Giles spelling is also provided parenthetically following the article title.

Chinese lantern plant The Chinese lantern plant, *Physalis alkekengi,* is a perennial herb of the nightshade family, Solanaceae. It is native to southeastern Europe and Asia. The fruit, an edible red berry, is enclosed in a husk formed from modified sepals of the flower. The husk resembles an oriental lantern.

Chinese literature The Chinese literary tradition is remarkable both for its length and for its profuseness. The earliest evidence of Chinese writing on ORACLE BONES dates from 3,500 years ago. Although the shape of the characters has altered considerably over the centuries (see CHINESE ART AND ARCHITECTURE), there has been a remarkable continuity in the written language.

Literacy was an essential qualification for a position in government service. A Confucian official was expected to compose poems and essays with the same facility that he displayed in drawing up a document. An enormous outpouring of literature was the result; more than half of the books published in the world prior to the mid-Qing period were written in Chinese. Before woodblock printing became common during the SONG period most of these literary texts were written with a brush on silk or paper in scroll form. Texts were also inscribed in bronze and stone or recorded on paintings, fans, and screens.

Training in the literary language was long and arduous. A sharp divergence developed between the spoken and literary languages, and only a small elite were able to master the latter. This situation is reflected in the traditional bibliographical classification scheme that comprises the Confucian canon (*qing*), historical and geographical writings (*shi*), philosophy and expository prose (*zi*), and verse and essay collections (*ji*). Fiction and drama were excluded.

The Confucian Canon. Thirteen works constitute the core of Confucian ideology (see CONFUCIANISM and MENCIUS): *Book of Changes* (*I jing*), *Book of Documents,* or *History* (*Shu jing* or *Shang shu*), *Book of Songs* (*Shi jing*), three collections of ritual (*Zhi li, I li,* and *Li ji*), the *Spring and Autumn Annals* together with three commentaries (*Chun qiu, Zuo zhan, Gong yang zhuan,* and *Gu liang zhuan*), *Classic of Filial Piety* (*Xiao qing*), *Analects* (*Lun yu*), *Mencius* (*Mengzi*), and the earliest dictionary (*Er ya*). All of these works are believed to have originated during the late ZHOU period, but they present scholars with enormous textual problems of reconstruction caused by the Burning of the Books carried out at the command of the first QIN emperor.

Historical Writing. One of the finest works of Chinese historiography is *Intrigues of the Warring States. Records of the Grand Historian,* by SIMA QUIAN, the outstanding prose work of the Former Han period, is especially noted for its vivid portrayals of important historical personages. It established the pattern of all subsequent dynastic chronicles. The outcome of a search for new approaches to historiography was the *Comprehensive Mirror for Aid in Government,* by Sima Guang.

Philosophy and Expository Prose. The *Daode jing,* attributed to LAOZI, is well known in the West for its concise, mystical, and poetic statement of Taoist ideals. More important for students of literature is the ZUANGZI, a Taoist anthology that represents the height of imaginative writing before the Tang period. Other works that have a significant place in literary history include the *Xunzi,* the *Huainanzi,* the *Hanfeizi,* and the *Spring and Autumn Annals of Lü Buwei.*

Verse and Essay Collections. Poetry was the supreme literary accomplishment of the Chinese scholar. Apart from the classic *Book of Songs* (*c.*1000–600 BC), a collection of popular songs and ritual odes, the most important early anthology is *The Songs of the South,* comprising the poetry of QU YUAN and his followers. During the Han period elaborate rhyming prose (*fu*) dominated, and Sima Xianru (179–117 BC) was its most able practitioner. Another important type of poetry, the ballad (*yuefu*), reflecting the lives and thoughts of the common people, had a strong impact on such Three Kingdoms poets as Cao Cao (AD 155–220) and his son, CAO ZHI. Two great nature poets, TAO YUANMING and Xie Lingyon (AD 385–433), lived during the Period of Disunion.

Toward the end of the Period of Disunion and under the influence of Indian phonology brought to China by Buddhist monks, new principles for writing poetry were formulated. This led to rules for "regulated verse" (*lüshi*), according to which tonal and syntactical elements were rigorously prescribed. These innovations culminated in the tremendous flowering of Tang poetry. Among the many poets who wrote during the Tang period were the Taoistic LI BO, the Confucian DU FU, the Buddhistic WANG WEI, and the plebeianist BO JU'-YI. In Song times they were followed by such prolific poets as SU DONGPO and Lu Yu (1125–1210). The dominant poetic activity of the Song period was the writing of "lyric meters" (*ci*), verse of irregular line lengths created in response to the massive importation of foreign tunes during the periods of the Tang and the Five Dynasties (AD 907–960). Among the exponents of *ci* were Li Yu, Huang Tingjian (1045–1105), and Li Qingzhao (1094–*c.*1152), China's most famous woman poet. The next major stage in the growth of poetry was the rise of cantos (*sanqu*) during the YUAN period.

A landmark in the history of prose was the return to straightforward, ancient styles of writing (*quwen*) propounded by Han Yu (768–824) and Liu Zongyuan (773–819) in reaction to the ornate, elaborate quality of parallel prose, consisting of alternating phrases of four and six words, that was predominant throughout the Period of Disunion.

Fiction. Before the Tang period, fiction was largely restricted to brief anecdotes about famous people, the elaboration of historical events, and accounts of strange creatures and happenings. Under the influence of Buddhist scriptures known as "transformation texts" (*bianwen*), extended fictional narratives were composed. These formed the basis of such superb novels as the anonymous *Jin Ping* (*c.*1582–96; trans. as *The Golden Lotus*, 1939) and CAO XUEQIN'S's *Honglu meng* (1791; trans. as *The Dream of the Red Chamber*, 1929).

During the Qing period the short story also flourished, well represented in the collections of vernacular tales by Feng Menglong (1574–1646). Fiction in the literary language was also refined. Among the most distinguished examples are the Tang classical tales (*quangqi*) and the intriguing *Liaozhai zhiyi* (*Strange Stories from a Chinese Studio*), by Pu Songling (1640–1716).

Drama. Like fiction, the theater was also influenced by Indian tradition, receiving from it such characteristics as the alternation between sung and spoken parts and certain stock roles. Earlier Chinese theatricals had consisted of mime, jousting, and acrobatics. The theatrical arts slowly evolved toward the magnificent flowering of YUAN DRAMA. Well-known examples include *Mudan ting* (*The Peony Pavilion*), by Tang Xianzu (1550–1616), and *Taohua shan* (*The Peach Blossom Fan*), by Kong Shangren (1684–1718).

Modern Developments. During the 20th century the impact of the West on Chinese writers has been overwhelming. As part of the student movement that began on May 4, 1919, HU SHI and other writers devoted themselves to replacing the classical language (*wenyan*) with modern spoken Mandarin (*baihua*) as the medium of written expression. Experimentation has been particularly intense in poetry, with attempts being made to find new rhythms, ideas, and images. Two of the most accomplished poets of the 20th century were Xu Zhimo (1895–1931) and Wen Yidu (1899–1946).

Short-story and novel writers produced a number of works during the 1920s and '30s, among them *The True Story of Ah Q* (1921; Eng. trans., 1926), by LU XUN; *Midnight* (1933; Eng. trans., 1957), by Mao Dun (1896–1981); and *Rickshaw Boy* (1937; Eng. trans., 1945, 1979), by Lao She (1899–1966).

World War II and the ensuing civil war disrupted literary pursuits, and Mao Zedong's government suppressed writing that did not further socialist aims. With the end of the Cultural Revolution in the mid-1970s, however, restrictions were relaxed. Literary journals proliferated, and poetry on nonpolitical themes flourished once again. After the many years of official insistence on the Chinese version of SOCIALIST REALISM, China's younger writers demonstrated that they were as capable as their Western counterparts of using complex literary techniques and experimental styles. When writers began to question ideology, however—and especially after the student demonstrations of 1986–87—the bureaucracy reimposed strict literary censorship.

Chinese medicine see ACUPUNCTURE; MEDICINE, TRADITIONAL

Chinese music

Chinese music Chinese music has ancient roots. The art flourished in the Shang dynasty after the 14th century BC, and its origins were surely earlier. Though remarkable for its stability, the music of China has not been stagnant and has all the variety and richness expected in the art of a vast, ancient, and populous land.

The importance of Chinese music extends beyond China's national borders. The presence of Chinese musical instruments, as well as repertoire and style characteristics, is conspicuous in Korea, Japan, and throughout Southeast Asia.

Theory

Musical speculation and descriptions of musical performances began to appear in many of the historical, ceremonial, and literary documents written between the 6th and 1st centuries BC. These writings reveal an immensely sophisticated idealism that is the principal musical legacy of ancient China.

Music and musical thought were the expression of an all-embracing worldview. Music, it was believed, was an emanation of the heart and an image of the cosmos. The author Lü Buwei "was able to speak of music only with a man who has grasped the meaning of the world." The influence upon conduct and conviction ascribed to music was accordingly great: it was regarded as the basis of government, of order. This is evident in the sustained attention given to accuracy in musical tuning, which was seen as essential to the harmony of the world: the readjustment of pitch became one of the first acts of a new emperor, and an Imperial Office of Music was established under Han Wudi (r. 140–87 BC).

Chinese melody is ordinarily based on a 5-tone (pentatonic) scale, although additional pitches can be introduced. Expressiveness, however, is often less a function of melodic patterns than of the individual note, which carries cosmological connotations. This emphasis on the single tone raises timbre to a position of enormous importance, and Chinese musicians have employed with immense skill the range of coloristic possibilities afforded by their instruments and voices.

Polyphony is alien to China. Traditional notation involves a separate sign for each degree of the scale, although tablatures are used by zither players, and staff notation has been imported in modern times.

Instruments

Musical instruments are first described in the great classics that document the history of China's kingdoms before the 2d century BC.

The Book of Odes (*Shi Jing*) compiled song texts from periods as early as the 10th century BC. These describe the use of instruments in ritual entertainment. The most frequently mentioned are drums, bells, zithers, flutes, and mouth organs.

(Right) *Instruments such as these are used in the traditional Chinese musical theater. The flat lute,* yueqin (1), *and the unfretted long lute, or* san xian (5), *are used with other stringed instruments for melodic expression. Fiddles such as the* huqin (2) *and the* erhu (9) *lead the melody. Unlike western violins, these instruments have only two strings, which are placed one above another, with the bow drawn between the strings. The* sona (6), *a double-reed instrument that produces a buzzing tone, is occasionally used for military scenes. Rhythm instruments provide contrast and expression, and include the small and large gongs,* xiao luo (3) *and* da luo (4), *the clappers,* ban (7), *and the drum,* gu (8).

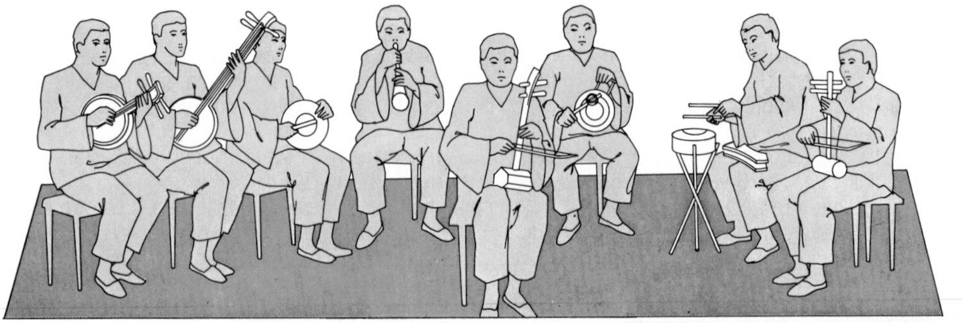

(Left) *The traditional Chinese orchestra consists of seven or eight musicians, although larger groups are used for modern compositions. Because Chinese music emphasizes distinct tones rather than melody or harmony, orchestras include a few diverse instruments.*

Among the percussion instruments, the *qing,* tuned sonorous stone chimes of the Chou era, has been retained today for use in Confucian ceremonies.

Another early instrument is a large barrel-shaped bronze gong, the *tong qu* ("metal drum"), a ritual instrument of southeast Asia that was introduced to China during the Han dynasty's military expeditions. It is remarkable for its metal workmanship and ornamentation. Today, gongs (*luo*) and cymbals (*bo*) in a variety of sizes are used in Taoist ceremonies as well as in opera.

An instrument that is used in the important role of directing the opera is the *ban,* rectangular wood clappers. In Buddhist ceremonies the *muyu;* ("Chinese temple block"), a slit-gong of camphor wood in a symbolic carving of a fish, is used for setting the musical pulse.

The generic term for drum is *gu,* of which diverse types abound. Drums are used in folk music, religious functions, opera, and in a variety of ensembles for entertainment. The skins are generally nailed to the wood shell and are commonly played with sticks.

Of the wind instruments, the flutes made of bamboo have remained as simple in construction as they were in ancient China. The end-blown *xiao* has a gentle quality and is appropriate for small ensembles. The transverse flute *ti* produces a more assertive tone and a wide range of expressive effects. A rice-paper covered hole next to the mouthpiece gives the *ti* a "buzzing" timbre, and performers have developed highly virtuosic techniques.

Of the string instruments, the *shê;* and *qin* are zithers closely associated with the scholars of ancient times, who created a sophisticated repertoire and a highly detailed system of notation. The more brilliant-sounding *zheng,* a 13-string zither, was better suited to entertainment and became widely popular. This instrument was also adopted by adjacent countries; it has been used in Japan since the 7th century and is there called a *koto.*

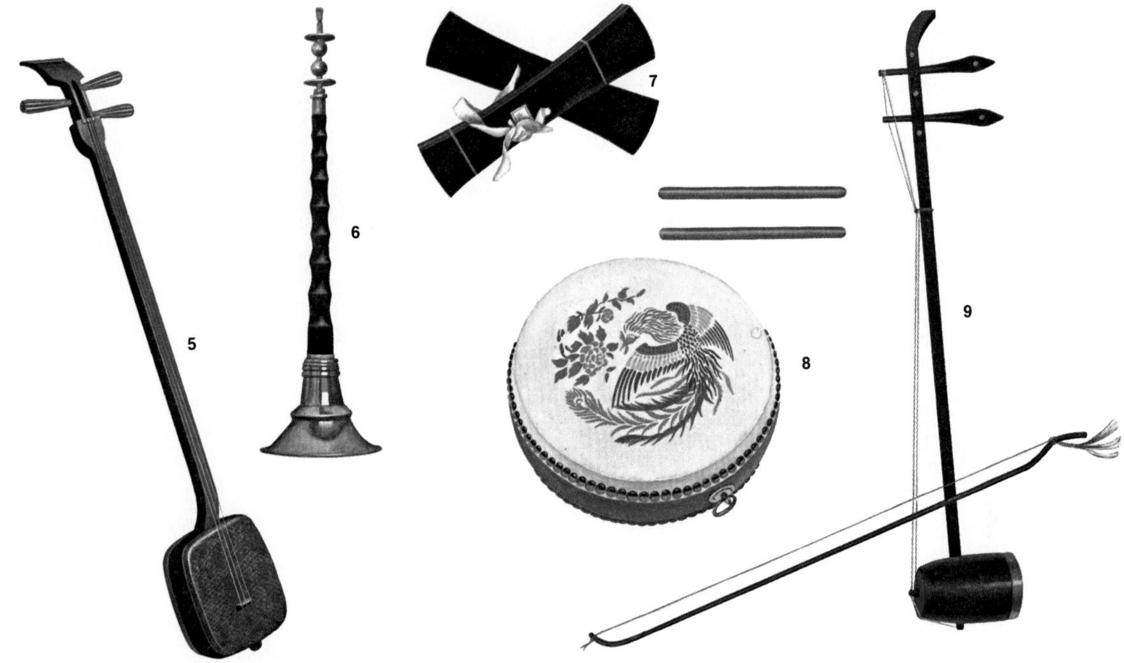

Other plucked string instruments include two short-necked fretted lutes: the *pipa* with a shallow pear-shaped body, and the *yueqin*, called the "moon guitar," with a circular body. A large family of bowed string instruments has evolved since the 9th century. These are generically called *huqin*, while each regional variation is known by a specific term that may differ among regions. They all have a string-bearing neck that projects through a small resonator and a bow, the hair of which passes between the two strings.

Instrumental ensembles in varying sizes have figured in the history of Chinese music. In earlier days, the size of an ensemble reflected the eminence of its owner.

Chinese philosophy see PHILOSOPHY

Chinese Shar-Pei [shahr-pay'] The gray brown Chinese Shar-Pei is one of the most unusual looking dogs in the world. Shaped somewhat like a miniature hippopotamus, it has a blunt muzzle, curved canine teeth, and loose, wrinkled skin covered with sharp, piglike bristles. The breed is nearly extinct in its native China, where it was bred as a fighting dog, but enjoys growing popularity in the United States. In 1988 it was admitted to the miscellaneous class by the American Kennel Club.

Ch'ing see QING (dynasty)

Ch'ing Hai see KOKO NOR

Ching-te-chen see JINGDE ZHEN

chinoiserie [sheen-wah-zuh-ree'] Chinoiserie is a decorative Western art incorporating Oriental motifs in a style simulating that of Chinese art. Characterized by fantastic and elegant asymmetrical patterns dominated by dragons, Chinamen, exotic birds, and landscapes with pagodas, chinoiserie designs appear in quantity in 17th- and 18th-century pottery, porcelains, silks, furniture, tapestries, wallpapers, and bibelots. The taste for an Orientalized art originated in the late 16th century when the various East India companies imported Far Eastern objets d'art. Examples of chinoiserie include furniture by Thomas CHIPPENDALE, featuring Oriental-inspired fretwork that became known as Chinese Chippendale, and the interiors of John NASH's exotic rooms in the Royal Pavilion at Brighton.

Chinook [shih-nuk'] The Chinook were a North American Indian tribe of the Pacific Northwest, occupying the shores of the lower Columbia River in Oregon northward to Shoalwater Bay in Washington. The name was applied to speakers of several dialects of the Chinookan language, the main divisions of which were Upper Chinook, spoken by the Wishram and Wasco, and the now-extinct Lower Chinook of the Clackamas, Chilukitqua, Cathlamet, Clatsop, and Chinook proper. The Chinookan economy was based on salmon fishing and hunting.

Chinookan-speaking groups were numerous and prosperous. Indians from the distant interior congregated at The Dalles on the Lower Columbia to trade furs, mountain-sheep horn, and war captives for salmon, coastal shells, and other goods exchanged by the Chinook. Chinook jargon, a simple aboriginal communications system, was adopted and spread by white traders of the 18th century. The incursion of the Northwest Company and Hudson's Bay Company into the Columbia River region in the early 19th century broke the Chinook trade monopoly and introduced European diseases that decimated the Indians. From an estimated population of about 16,000 in 1805, their numbers were reduced to only about 100 by the 1850s.

chinook [shi-nuk'] A chinook is a warm, dry, westerly wind that occurs on the eastern slopes of the Rocky Mountains in winter and early spring. A type of FOEHN or katabatic wind, the chinook is made up of warm Pacific air that has lost some of its moisture over the western slopes. Further warmed and dried in descending to the plains, chinooks cause temperatures to soar for periods of a day or less several times a year.

See also: MOUNTAIN AND VALLEY WINDS.

chinquapin [ching'-kuh-pin] Evergreen chinquapins, genus *Castanopsis*, are shrubs and trees that grow mainly in eastern Asia, except for two species native to the western United States. One of these, the giant, or golden, chinquapin, *C. chrysophylla*, is a large tree, bearing leaves that are dark green above and have small golden yellow scales below. It grows chiefly on dry, poor soils. Shrubs and trees of the CHESTNUT genus, *Castanea*, are also known as chinquapins. They differ from the chestnut tree in their hairy leaves and smaller, single-seeded burrs. Wood from the common, or Allegheny, chinquapin, *Castanea pumila*, a small tree of the eastern and southern United States, is used for posts.

chintz *Chintz* (from the Hindi word meaning "variegated"), a term originally applied to a printed CALICO from India, now refers to a large group of fabrics characterized by a shiny glaze. Better qualities are made of firmly woven cotton fabric. A nondurable finish is obtained when the fabric is given a wax or starch glaze and then pressed between hot rollers. A durable glaze is produced when the fabric is treated with a resin and then calendered.

chip see INTEGRATED CIRCUIT; MICROELECTRONICS

chipmunk Chipmunks are ground-dwelling RODENTS of the squirrel family, Sciuridae. One species that is common in North America is *Tamias striatus,* the eastern chipmunk. The western chipmunk, found in western North America and central and eastern Asia, belongs to the genus *Eutamias*. The eastern chipmunk is 14–18 cm (5½–7 in) long, not including a 10-cm (4-in) tail. It weighs up to 142 g (5 oz). The western chipmunk is smaller. The fine fur is reddish brown with alternating black, brown, and white stripes. Chipmunks carry food in cheek pouches. They sleep in winter but leave their burrows on warm days.

The Eastern American chipmunk lives in birch and pine forests. Although it climbs trees well, the chipmunk prefers to remain near its underground burrow in case it needs to escape a predator.

Chippendale, Thomas Thomas Chippendale, 1718–79, dominated mid-18th-century English cabinetmaking to such an extent that the name Chippendale became synonymous with all English FURNITURE designs of the 1740s through the 1760s. Although he directed a large and important workshop, Chippendale attained this status primarily with the publication of *The Gentleman and Cabinet Maker's Director* (1754; 2d ed., 1755; 3d ed., 1762). This compilation of contemporaneous designs illustrated the three principal sources of the ROCOCO STYLE in England: the "modern," referring to adaptations of French rococo; the "Gothic," deriving from the intricate and fanciful motifs and patterns of indigenous architecture; and the "Chinese," underscoring the importance of Oriental imports. English ROMANTICISM found one of its most complete expressions in Chippendale's Gothic and Chinese designs. His most notable neoclassical furnishings were produced for Harewood House (1772–75; Yorkshire). Chippendale's influence was maintained by his son, Thomas (*c.*1749–1822), who carried on the studio until the early 19th century.

Chippewa see OJIBWA

Chirac, Jacques [shee-rahk'] Jacques Chirac, b. Nov. 29, 1932, leader of the French Gaullist party (Rassemblement pour la république; RPR), was prime minister of France from 1974 to 1976 and from 1986 to 1988. Elected to the National Assembly in 1967, Chirac held various cabinet posts before becoming prime minister. In his first term he came into conflict with the less conservative president Valéry Giscard d'Estaing and resigned; he became mayor of Paris the following year and ran unsuccessfully for the presidency himself in 1981. In his second premiership under the Socialist president François Mitterrand, Chirac initiated a program of privatization and other measures reversing the policies of his Socialist predecessors. He was defeated in another bid for the presidency in 1988.

Chirico, Giorgio de [kee'-ree-koh] Giorgio de Chirico, b. July 10, 1888, d. Nov. 20, 1978, was a Greek-born Italian painter regarded as an important forerunner of SURREALISM. He first exhibited (1911–15) his enigmatic, dreamlike paintings in Paris, where he came into contact with the symbolist poet Guillaume Apollinaire and the cubists. After his return to Italy in 1915, he collaborated with the former futurist Carlo CARRÀ;. Together the two artists founded the magazine *Pittura metafisica* (Metaphysical Painting) in 1920.

In 1924, de Chirico moved to Paris. His subsequent paintings frequently depict arcaded streets and squares with tall clock towers, often bathed in strong sunlight reminiscent of southern Italy. The idiosyncracies of time and place and the small statuelike figures casting illogical shadows in de Chirico's works are among the most personal of any artist's contributions to the pictorial language of the modernist movement. Like the paintings of René MAGRITTE, which depict a world of dreams, de Chirico's work is often marked by a sinister quality akin to the tone of André BRETON's *Surrealist Manifesto* of 1924.

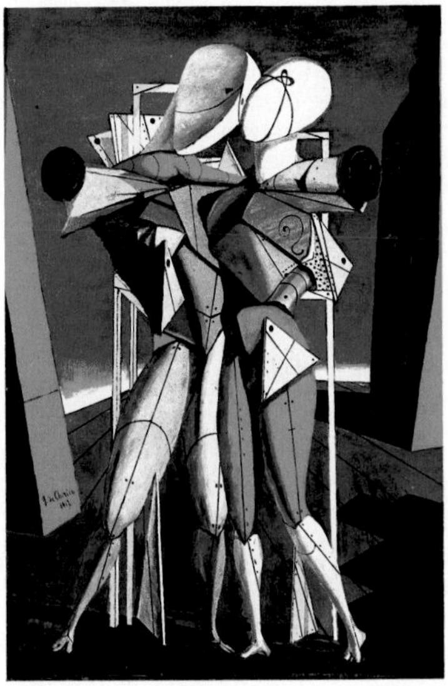

The Italian painter Giorgio de Chirico's Hector and Andromeda *(1917) depicts the mythological figures as strange, mechanical mannequins. This painting is from the period in which de Chirico earned his position as a major precursor of surrealism. (Matteoli Collection, Milan.)*

Chiron (astronomy) [ky'-rahn] The celestial object Chiron drew astronomical attention in 1977 as the first apparently asteroidlike body to be found in the outer solar system. Discovered by Charles T. Kowal on Nov. 1, 1977, the object is only 300–400 km (180–240 mi) in diameter. At its maximum distance of 18.9 astronomical units (AU), it nearly reaches the orbit of Uranus, and at its minimum distance of 8.5 AU it moves inside the orbit of Saturn. Chiron takes 50.7 years to move around the Sun, but its orbit is apparently unstable. The object reaches a maximum visual magnitude of about 14.5 at its closest approach to Earth. In 1989 it was classified as a comet because astronomers detected a cloud of typically cometary materials enveloping the object.

Chiron (mythology) In Greek mythology Chiron was a CENTAUR, variously described as the son of CRONUS and the nymph Philyra or an offspring of IXION. Kindly and wise, unlike other centaurs, he was chosen to teach such legendary heroes as Achilles, Asclepius, Hercules, and Jason. Accidentally given an incurable wound by Hercules, he granted his immortality to Prometheus and was changed by Zeus into the constellation Sagittarius.

chiropractic [ky-roh-prak'-tik] Chiropractic is a healing profession in which the spine, joints, and muscle tissue are manipulated in order to restore the proper function of the nerves. The chiropractor does not use drugs and surgery in treating diseases. In addition, a chiropractor recommends exercise and diet and often uses physical therapy techniques. The name *chiropractic*, derived from Greek, means "practice by hand." It was coined by Daniel David Palmer (1845–1913), an Iowa grocer who developed the theory that spinal manipulation could serve in the maintenance of health. Palmer published his findings and later founded Palmer College of Chiropractic in Davenport, Iowa.

One theory embraced by chiropractic is that the body becomes susceptible to disease when tissue resistance decreases. Interference with healthy tissue function, according to this theory, is caused by subluxation, or the displacement of a spinal vertebra that impinges on a given nerve. When the neural pathway is impaired, the brain cannot regulate activities of body tissue, which becomes predisposed to disease. The chiropractor manipulates the vertebra into its correct position and allows neural impulses to flow properly.

Chiropractors are licensed to practice in all 50 states of the United States, Washington, D.C., Puerto Rico, Canada, and several other countries. Medicare, Medicaid, and workers' compensation cover the costs of chiropractic treatment.

The American Medical Association recognized chiropractic in 1980, after years of questioning the validity of spinal manipulation for treating disease. Although the AMA used to charge that chiropractic was ineffective, it now permits medical doctors to recommend patients to chiropractors—most frequently, patients with back problems.

Recent trends in chiropractic include kinesiology, a diagnostic tool discovered in 1964 by a doctor of chiropractic, George J. Goodheart. He maintained that he could treat a disorder by locating muscular weakness and manipulating the spine in a way that strengthened the muscle. One development in applying kinesiology is the recognition that muscle weakness can be a result of nutritional deficiency or allergy, and therefore can be alleviated by correcting the diet. Since its discovery, kinesiology has been accepted by doctors of chiropractic as well as examined by osteopaths, medical physicians, and physical therapists.

chiropteran see BAT

chirping frog The chirping frogs, genus *Syrrhopus,* family Leptodactylidae, are found primarily in Mexico, but three species range as far north as Texas. These frogs are generally 2–4 cm (¾–1½ in) long and lay their eggs on land. The tadpole stages are completed within the egg. The sound of many of these frogs resembles a cricket's chirp.

Chisholm, Shirley [chiz'-uhm] Shirley Anita Chisholm, b. Brooklyn, N.Y., Nov. 30, 1924, was the first black woman to serve in the U.S. Congress. A teacher and educational consultant, she was elected Democratic representative from the 12th district of New York in 1968. She became widely known for her advocacy of minority and women's rights and served seven terms before retiring in 1983.

Shirley Chisholm, who served 14 years in the U.S. House of Representatives, is a vocal exponent of minority rights and a practiced politician whose major achievements include legislation requiring that domestic workers be covered under federal minimum-wage laws.

Chisholm Trail The Chisholm Trail was the major route along which, after the U.S. Civil War, Texas cattle ranchers drove their herds north through the Indian Territory (Oklahoma) to railroad points in Kansas. Extending from San Antonio, Tex., to Abilene, Kans., the trail was named for Jesse Chisholm, an Indian trader who traveled the route by wagon in 1866. When Abilene became a railroad shipping center the next year, the cattle drovers followed Chisholm's wheel ruts northward. Traffic on the trail peaked in 1871 at 600,000 cattle. Its use subsequently declined as settlement moved west and Dodge City, Kans., became the primary shipping center.

chitin [ky'-tin] Chitin, a POLYSACCHARIDE similar in chemical structure to cellulose, is the major component of the exoskeleton, or shell, of ARTHROPODS such as insects, crabs, and lobsters. The shell gives support to the organism by covering the surface of the body. Although chitin is rigid, it is thin enough in joints and between body segments to allow for movement. Periodically, the shell is shed and a new, larger shell is secreted by the epidermis, allowing room for growth. Chitin is also found in the internal structures of some INVERTEBRATES.

chiton [ky'-tuhn] Chiton is the common, nonscientific name given to members of the subclass Polyplacophora—a separate class, in some systems—in the MOLLUSK class Amphineura. In existence since the Upper Cambrian Period, chitons are living fossils. About 600 species of chiton exist today. Although distributed worldwide, they are more abundant in warm regions. Chitons are bilaterally symmetrical, oval, and flattened. They are usually 5 cm

The chiton, a slow-moving marine animal, has eight overlapping plates (1) *that are made of calcium carbonate and are embedded into mantle flesh* (2). *It has a broad, sticky foot* (3) *that is used to fasten itself onto rocks and shells. If the chiton is pulled from a rock, it rolls into a tight ball. The chiton's head* (4) *has a mouth, but no eyes. Three species shown are:* C. chiton (A), *with many spines edging its mantle;* Lepidochiton cinereus (B), *which has a dull-colored shell and flesh; and* Acanthochiton crinitus (C), *with tufts of bristles lining its mantle.*

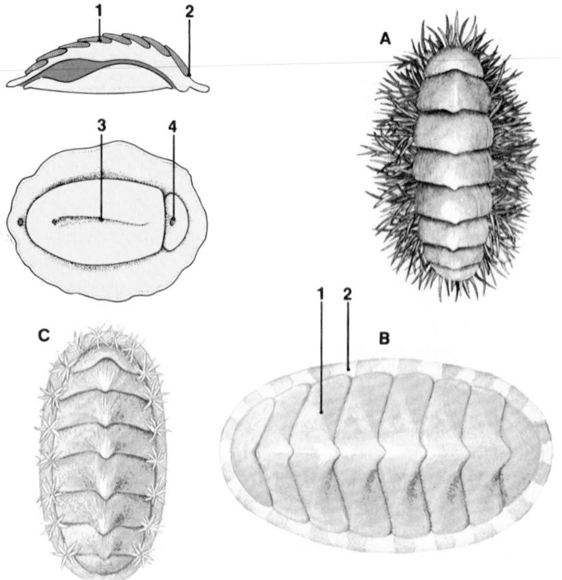

(2 in) in length, are protected dorsally by eight calcareous plates, and have a strong, muscular foot. Most species are nocturnal, foraging for algae, which they scrape from rocks with their rasping tongue, or radula. Chitons have separate sexes. Once fertilized, the eggs develop into free-swimming ciliated larvae, called trochophore larvae, which form an important portion of marine PLANKTON.

Chittagong [chit'-uh-gawng] Chittagong is the chief port of Bangladesh and has extensively developed port facilities for ocean steamers. Situated on the Karnaphuli River about 19 km (12 mi) from its mouth at the Bay of Bengal, Chittagong is the commercial and manufacturing center of the nation, with a population of 1,840,000 (1987 est.). The city's many industries, powered by a hydroelectric plant up the river, use the products of the area—jute, cotton, rice, tea, petroleum (from offshore installations), and bamboo. The bamboo is harvested chiefly from the Chittagong Hill tracts, 13,191 km^2 (5,093 mi^2) of rugged, thickly forested land along the Bay of Bengal that is inhabited by primitive mountain tribes who have opposed recent Bengali settlement in the area. Chittagong's setting is picturesque: it is surrounded by the bay, the river, and hills that culminate in mountains up to 1,200 m (4,000 ft) high.

An ancient city, Chittagong passed from Tippera (Buddhist) dominance to Arakan (Hindu) and then Mogul (Muslim) rule, with periods of reconquest and recontrol. The Portuguese made inroads in the 16th century, and the British gained control in 1760.

Chittenden, Thomas [chit'-en-den] Thomas Chittenden, b. East Guilford, Conn., Jan. 6, 1730, d. Aug. 25, 1797, was a Vermonter who worked for the recognition of his state as a separate entity during and after the American Revolution, when both New York and New Hampshire claimed jurisdiction over it. He served as governor of independent Vermont (1778–89) and then as first governor of the state of Vermont (1791–97).

Chiusi [kee-oo'-zee] Chiusi (Latin: Clusium; Etruscan: Chamars or Clevsin), in central Italy, was a major city of the ancient ETRUSCANS. It was situated on a hill that dominated the fertile valley of the Clanis River, an affluent of the Tiber and an easy route for north-south traffic. Its famous king, LARS PORSENA, besieged Rome about 500 BC. Chiusi later became a Roman colony. According to tradition, the Gauls learned to drink wine at Chiusi.

chivalry [shiv'-ul-ree] Chivalry was a system of ethical ideals developed among the KNIGHTS of medieval Europe. Arising out of the FEUDALISM of the period, it combined military virtues with those of Christianity, as epitomized by the Arthurian legend in England (see ARTHUR AND ARTHURIAN LEGEND) and the CHANSONS DE GESTE of medieval France.

The word *chivalry* is derived from the French *chevalier,* meaning "horseman" or "knight." Chivalry was the code of conduct by which knights were supposedly guided. In addition to military prowess and valor and loyalty to God and the knight's feudal lord, it called for courtesy toward enemies and generosity toward the sick and oppressed, widows, and other disadvantaged people.

Also incorporated in the ideal was COURTLY LOVE—romantic devotion for a sexually unattainable woman, usually another man's wife. Veneration for the Virgin Mary played a part in this concept.

Chivalric ideals influenced the founding of religious military orders during the period of the CRUSADES, among them the TEMPLARS and the HOSPITALERS, the TEUTONIC KNIGHTS, and the Spanish orders of Alcantara, Calatrava, and Santiago. In the late Middle Ages, rulers formed secular orders of chivalry such as the English Order of the Garter (1349) and the Burgundian Order of the Golden Fleece (1429). By this time, however, chivalry had become largely a system of etiquette. Tournaments, in which knights had originally risked their lives in jousting combat before the ladies, became simply elaborate, stylized, and harmless entertainments. Moreover, the expense of this and other trappings of knighthood led many nobles who were eligible for knighthood (having served the customary apprenticeship of seven years as a page at a noble court and another seven as a squire, or attendant, to a knight) not to become knights at all. From chivalry, always larger in literature than in life, comes the modern concept of the gentleman.

chive Chive, *Allium schoenoprasum,* a perennial herb cultured for its mild, onion-flavored leaves, is closely related to ONION, garlic, and leek. Native to Europe and Asia, chive is cultured in herb and vegetable gardens, as an indoor pot plant, and occasionally as a commercial crop, mostly for dehydration.

Propagation is by seed or by division of the underground clump of small bulbs. The showy, lavender-colored flowers are clustered on a stalk. The leaves may be used fresh, or dried or frozen for later use.

Chive, a popular herb, is the smallest plant of the onion family. Its hollow leaves, which grow in clumps, can be snipped for flavoring egg and vegetable dishes. Chives produce globelike clusters of flowers that add color to ornamental borders in gardens.

Chlamydia [kluh-mid'-ee-uh] *Chlamydia* is a genus of parasitic bacteria that live within the cells of their host. *Chlamydia trachomatis* causes the sexually transmitted disease called chlamydia, which in the early 1980s was determined to be the leading venereal disease in the United States. The delay in this finding was caused in part by the frequent occurrence of chlamydia with gonorrhea and the masking of its usually milder symptoms, such as discharges and painful urination, by the effects of that disease. The chlamydia desease is also often symptomless.

In women, cervical infections are common. If untreated, they can cause pelvic inflammatory disease and infertility or ectopic pregnancy (gestation other than in the uterus). Infants born to infected women may develop conjunctivitis or pneumonia. In men, untreated infections of the urethra may spread to the sperm-carrying canals and cause sterility. In less developed countries, chlamydia also often leads to TRACHOMA. Simple tests for chlamydia have now been developed, and antibiotics deal readily with the disease.

chloral hydrate [klor'-ul hy'-drayt] Chloral hydrate is a simple organic chemical, related to both ethyl alcohol and chloroform, that has been used for more than a century as a hypnotic or SEDATIVE. A relatively weak hypnotic, chloral hydrate is often found suitable for older persons; it is usually available in capsules or in solutions. In overdose or with alcohol it can produce coma, and there have been reports of habituation or addiction. Chloral hydrate is used less frequently than barbiturates and newer sedative-hypnotics.

chlordane Chlordane, a chlorinated hydrocarbon, is a pesticide that has been used primarily to control termites. The commercial product is 60% chlordane, with related insecticides such as heptachor also present. Chlordane has also been used for veterinary purposes—to kill fleas, ticks, and lice—and as an agricultural pesticide, but its use was restricted when it was recognized as a carcinogen in the 1970s. In 1987 the U.S. Environmental Protection Agency banned all uses of the pesticide except injection into the ground beneath homes by professional exterminators to kill termites.

Chlorella [kluh-rel'-uh] Chlorella, genus *Chlorella,* is any of a group of one-celled green ALGAE of the phylum Chlorophyta. They float or drift about in ponds, lakes, and other bodies of fresh water; they also live in soil and on the bark of trees. Each chlorella has a single round body with one nucleus and a cup-shaped chloroplast containing chlorophyll, the green pigment needed for photosynthesis. Chlorella produce nonmotile spores. Scientists often use these algae to study photosynthesis and other chemical processes. Researchers are also interested in growing them as a possible source of protein and B vitamins.

chlorine The chemical element chlorine is a greenish yellow gas with a sharp, disagreeable odor. It belongs to the HALOGENS, Group VIIA in the periodic table, which also include the elements BROMINE, FLUORINE, IODINE, and astatine. Its chemical symbol is Cl, its atomic number is 17, and its atomic weight is 35.453. Chlorine is about 2.5 times as dense as air and moderately soluble in water, forming a pale yellowish green solution. The name "chlorine," from a Greek word meaning "greenish yellow," was given to the gas by Sir Humphry DAVY, who proved (1810) it was an element. The gas had been discovered in 1774 by Swedish chemist Carl Wilhelm SCHEELE.

Because chlorine is very reactive, it never occurs free in nature. Chemically bound as an ion, the chloride ion (Cl^-), it constitutes 0.15% of the Earth's crust and 1.9% of seawater. In the human body, chloride and sodium ions are the main ions in extracellular materials.

Toxicity and Precautions. Chlorine was used in World War I as a poison gas. It is very corrosive to moist tissue and has a very irritating effect on the lungs and mucous membranes of the nose and throat. Inhalation of chlorine gas can cause edema of the lungs and respiratory stoppage.

Chlorine is easily liquefied and is usually transported in its liquid state in pressurized drums. In the United States and most European countries, large quantities of chlorine may be transported only by train. The present trend is to limit transport as much as possible by producing and using the element in the same location.

Chemical Properties. Like all halogens, chlorine has a strong tendency to gain one electron and become a chloride ion. Chlorine is less active than fluorine but more so than bromine and iodine. It readily reacts with most elements. A mixture of hydrogen and chlorine gases is stable if kept in a cool, dark place, but if heated or exposed to sunlight it explodes violently.

Chlorine can support combustion; a candle thrust into a vessel of chlorine continues to burn, releasing dense, black clouds of smoke. The chlorine combines with the hydrogen of the paraffin, forming hydrogen chloride, and uncombined carbon is left in the form of soot.

Preparation. By far the most important method for the preparation of chlorine is the electrolysis of a solution of common salt, sodium chloride (NaCl). The chlorine gas is liberated at the positive anode, which is made of graphite since a metal anode would react with chlorine. At the iron cathode, sodium ions are reduced to sodium metal, which reacts immediately with water to form sodium hydroxide (NaOH).

Chlorine Compounds. Chlorine is one of the most important basic chemicals. Numerous chlorine-containing compounds are used as reactants to produce other chemicals.

The bleaching action of chlorine in aqueous solution is due to the formation of hypochlorous acid, HClO, a powerful oxidizing agent (see OXIDATION AND REDUCTION). Liquid bleach is usually an aqueous solution of sodium hypochlorite, NaOCl, and dry powdered bleaches contain chloride of lime (calcium hypochlorite), $Ca(OCl)_2$. Because chlorine destroys silk and wool, commercial hypochlorite bleaches should never be used on these fibers.

The oxidizing ability of chloride of lime enables it to destroy bacteria; therefore large quantities are used to treat municipal water systems. This chemical is also used in swimming pools and for treating sewage.

Many chlorinated organic compounds can be polymerized into useful synthetics (see PLASTICS). Phosgene ($COCl_2$) is used, among other compounds, for the preparation of polyurethanes; VINYL chloride ($CH_2{=}CHI$) is used for PVC; and chloroprene ($CH_2{=}CHCCl{=}CH_2$) is used for a type of synthetic rubber.

Large quantities of chloroform ($CHCl_3$), CARBON TETRACHLORIDE (CCl_4), trichloroethylene ($Cl_2C{=}CHCl$), and perchloroethylene ($Cl_2C{=}CCl_2$) are used as industrial solvents for dissolving and diluting other organic compounds.

Although DDT (see DDT) has come into disrepute because of its adverse ecological impact, it is still used in parts of the world where the emphasis is placed on highest possible crop yields. Dieldrin and other chlorinated compounds are effective in controlling insect pests (see PESTICIDE).

Various other chlorine compounds play an important part in chemistry and the chemical industry, including common salt (NaCl) and a series of other important chlorides (salts that contain the Cl^- ion). The chlorides of most metals are easily soluble in water, which widens their applicability. HYDROCHLORIC ACID, HCl, is one of the most frequently used acids.

chlorite minerals Chlorite is a green, magnesium- and iron-rich member of the MICA family, common in many kinds of rocks, especially soapstone (see TALC). Like other micas, chlorite crystallizes in flat, flakelike crystals, and it has perfect cleavage. Chlorite is so soft that its flakes can be scratched with the fingernail. Most chlorite ranges in color from pale to dark green; it is the only common green mica.

Chlorite is typically a constituent of magnesium- and iron-rich METAMORPHIC ROCKS called greenstones or greenschists because of the color imparted by chlorite and other iron and magnesium SILICATE MINERALS. Chlorite may also be formed by the action of hot water on magnesium-bearing IGNEOUS ROCKS. Chlorite is quite resistant to chemical weathering and is common in SEDIMENTS. It is also formed by the weathering and alteration of other micas.

Chlorites are common soft, sheet-forming, basic silicates. Closely related to the micas, they mainly comprise varying compositions of aluminum, iron and magnesium.

chloroform Chloroform, also called trichloromethane, $CHCl_3$, is a colorless, heavy, sweet-smelling liquid used in the past as an ANESTHETIC but now considered too toxic. Chloroform is produced by the chlorination of ethyl alcohol, acetone, or methane, or by the reduction of carbon tetrachloride. Chloroform is widely used as an extractant and solvent; in these applications its nonflammability is an advantage.

chlorophyll All green PLANTS contain the pigment chlorophyll, which gives them their color. Chlorophyll is essential for PHOTOSYNTHESIS, the process by which plants manufacture food. Chemically, chlorophyll is similar to the red pigment hemoglobin, which is present in blood.

Chlorophyll is found in chloroplasts, which are in small granules in plant cells. Although nearly every part of a plant contains chlorophyll, the leaves are specialized for photosynthesis and are especially rich in the pigment. Chloroplasts also contain yellow, orange, and occasionally red pigments, called carotenoids, which may mask the green chlorophyll and give the characteristic yellow or orange color to many flowers, ripe fruit, and autumn leaves.

Several types of chlorophyll occur in organisms capable of photosynthesis. The most common type is chlorophyll *a*, which is distributed throughout nearly all green plants. Chlorophyll *b* is the second most widely distributed; it is found in all higher plants and some algae. The photosynthetic bacteria contain still other chlorophylls.

Chlorophyll traps the energy of sunlight. When it absorbs a single photon, the smallest energy unit of light, the energy is transferred to one of the highly mobile electrons of the chlorophyll molecule and raises the electron to a higher energy state. The additional energy is used to break down water in the plant into oxygen and hydrogen. Oxygen is released, but hydrogen is used to convert atmospheric carbon dioxide into plant sugars and starches.

chloroplast see PHOTOSYNTHESIS

chlorosis see DISEASES, PLANT

Chmielnicki, Bohdan [kmel-neet'-skee buhk-dahn'] Bohdan Chmielnicki (or Khmelnytsky), b. *c.*1595, d. Aug. 6, 1657, was a leader in the Ukrainian struggle for independence from Poland. As a COSSACK he received certain privileges in return for military service, but after a Polish force raided his estate, kidnapped his wife, and killed his son, he became a rebel leader. Elected hetman, or chief, of the Zaporozhye Cossacks in 1648, he led them in an uprising against the Poles that soon became a struggle for complete Ukrainian independence.

Choate, Joseph Hodges [choht] Joseph Hodges Choate, b. Salem, Mass., Jan. 24, 1832, d. May 14, 1917, was a U.S. trial lawyer and diplomat. He participated in several well-known cases, such as the Standard Oil antitrust case and *Pollock* v. *Farmers' Loan and Trust Co.* (1895), in which he argued against the constitutionality of the 1894 income tax law. Choate also became known for his investigation of graft in New York City finances. From 1899 to 1905, he served as U.S. ambassador to Great Britain. He helped settle the Alaskan-boundary dispute between the United States and Canada and was involved in negotiating the 1901 Hay-Pauncefote Treaty, which opened the way for U.S. construction of the Panama Canal.

chocolate Chocolate is the food made by combining the roasted ground kernel of the CACAO bean with sugar and cocoa butter, the fat released when the bean is ground. Chocolate may also contain natural or artificial flavors, emulsifiers, and—in the case of milk chocolate—milk solids.

Bitter chocolate, or chocolate liquor, is the roasted ground kernel (nib) of the cacao bean; it is commonly known as baker's, or baking, chocolate. A minimum of 15% liquor mixed with sugar and cocoa butter is sweet chocolate. When the amount of liquor is greater than 35%, the product is bittersweet chocolate. A combination of at least 12% dry whole milk solids, sugar, cocoa butter, and at least 10% chocolate liquor produces milk chocolate.

History

The term *chocolate* was originally applied to a drink similar to today's hot chocolate. The explorer Hernán Cortés introduced the drink to Spain upon returning from his Mexican expedition (1519). Gradually spreading through Europe and into England, the chocolate drink became increasingly popular.

In 1828 the Dutch made chocolate powder by squeezing most of the fat from finely ground cacao beans. The cocoa butter from pressing was soon being added to a powder-sugar mixture, and a new product, eating chocolate, was born. In 1876 a Swiss firm added condensed milk to chocolate, producing the world's first milk chocolate.

The United States ranks tenth in the world with a per capita consumption of 4 kg (9.7 lb) annually, far behind the first-place Swiss, who eat 9.5 kg (21 lb) per person annually.

Chocolate Production

With a proper mix of chocolate liquor, sugar, cocoa butter, and milk solids (for milk chocolate), the production of chocolate begins. The ingredients are thoroughly blended, then conveyed to refiners. These heavy machines have large rollers and crush the mixture four times. The particles are reduced to microscopic fineness to produce the smoothness typical of fine eating chocolate. The chocolate is now conched, a process that completely mixes the chocolate at high temperatures while exposing it to a blast of fresh air. During conching, complex chemical changes take place that further develop the chocolate's delicate flavor.

The addition of vanilla or other natural or artificial flavors provides a final flavor note. Lecithin, an emulsifier derived from the soybean, is also added; this establishes the precise viscosity necessary for proper flow in molding or coating.

The chocolate is now ready for use in molded bars, in hollow molded bunnies or eggs, or as the coating around a candy.

Choctaw [chahk'-taw] The Choctaw, a Muskogean-speaking North American Indian people, lived in numerous villages in central and southern Mississippi in the 18th century. They were organized into three regional divisions that met annually. Their economy was based on agriculture and cattle raising. They played a ritual ball game, practiced head deformation, and deposited the bones of their dead in ossuaries.

The Choctaw fought the Spanish, English, CHICKASAW, and CREEK. By the early 19th century, numerous American settlers, eager for land, intruded into Choctaw territory. In the Treaty of Dancing Rabbit Creek (1830), the Choctaw ceded all their land east of the Mississippi River to the United States. By 1834 nearly 13,000 Choctaw had moved to Indian Territory in Oklahoma, where they became one of the FIVE CIVILIZED TRIBES. They farmed the land, built new towns, and established the Choctaw Republic. In 1907 they helped form the state of Oklahoma, where they still live in great numbers.

Chodowiecki, Daniel Nikolaus [kaw-dawr-yet'-skee] Daniel Nikolaus Chodowiecki, b. Oct. 16, 1726, d. Feb. 7, 1801, was the most influential painter and printmaker in Berlin in the late 18th century. As director of the Berlin Academy, he established REALISM as the dominant artistic tendency in Berlin, where it prevailed throughout the 19th century. In 1758 he began to experiment with GRAPHIC ARTS techniques and soon established a reputation as an illustrator. He is best known for his intimate studies of everyday middle-class life, such as *Company at Table* (1758–62; Kunsthalle, Hamburg).

choir see CHORAL MUSIC

Choiseul, Étienne François, Duc de [shwah-zul'] Étienne François, duc de Choiseul, b. June 28, 1719, d. May 8, 1785, was a French army officer, skillful ambassador at Rome and Vienna, and finally leading minister of King LOUIS XV. First appointed minister of foreign affairs in 1758, he added (1761) the ministries of war and the navy. The hardworking Choiseul negotiated (1761) the Family Compact allying Bourbon Spain with Bourbon France, but had to cede French Canada and India to Britain in the humiliating Peace of Paris (1763), which concluded the SEVEN YEARS' WAR. During his ministry France acquired (1766) Lorraine by inheritance and purchased (1768) Corsica. Choiseul fell (1770) from power after siding with the obstructionist PARLEMENTS against his fellow ministers' financial reforms.

Chokwe [chahk'-wee] The Chokwe, or Jokwe, are BANTU speakers of south central Africa. They are celebrated for their plastic art, which presents a range of contrasting styles that is rare in Africa. It is rich both in realistically sculpted ancestor figures and in abstract human, animal, bird, and snake forms.

Chokwe art, which reaches one peak of expression in the mask form, is the achievement of a fiercely politicized society. From colonial times under the Portuguese to the present, Chokwe public life has been dominated by political assassinations, dethronements of chiefs, and extended legal battles between rival lineages. Many Chokwe tribesmen turned themselves into slavers for the Portuguese and wreaked havoc among other central Bantu. Never united among themselves, the Chokwe split repeatedly and now form a vast diaspora, more than a million in number, spread over at least five countries.

cholera [kah'-lur-uh] Cholera is an acute infectious disease in humans caused by the bacterium *Vibrio cholerae.* Infection usually occurs from drinking contaminated water. The first, abrupt symptom is profuse diarrhea, often accompanied by vomiting. This may lead to rapid loss of fluid and salts, causing muscle cramps, severe thirst, and cold, wrinkled skin. Coma and death may follow within 24 hours, but intravenous infusion of large volumes of saline fluid may be life-saving. Treatment with tetracycline may also aid recovery.

Cholera, endemic in India, periodically spreads to other countries. Vaccine prepared from dead cholera bacteria confers limited protection, but the best preventive measure is a supply of pure drinking water.

See also: IMMUNITY (BIOLOGY).

cholesterol [kuh-les'-tur-awl] Cholesterol is the best-known member of the STEROLS, a biologically important group of LIPID alcohols. It is the major sterol in the tissues of all vertebrates and is found, in association with other sterols, throughout the animal kingdom. Cholesterol seldom occurs in significant amounts in higher plants, although these plants contain related sterols (phytosterols).

Function. In higher animals, cholesterol is found in all CELLS, primarily as a structural component of cell membranes. The cholesterol content of a membrane, relative to other lipids, varies with the tissue and with specific membrane function. The ratio of cholesterol to polar lipids (phospholipids and glycolipids) affects the stability, permeability, and protein mobility of a membrane. Membranes with high ratios, such as the myelin membranes that sheath cells of the central nervous system, have high stability and relatively low permeability. Their major function is as a protective barrier. Membranes of intracellular organelles (microsomes, mitochondria) have low cholesterol ratios and are consequently fluid and permeable. They serve primarily in synthetic and degradative reactions and in energy (ATP) production, all functions dependent on high permeability and protein mobility. The outer membranes of most cells have intermediate cholesterol-polar lipid ratios and have both protective and metabolite-transport functions.

In addition to its role in membrane structure, cholesterol has other important functions. Cholesterol is stored in the adrenals, testes, and ovaries, chiefly as the fatty acid ester, and converted to STEROID hormones. These hormones include the male and female SEX HORMONES (androgens and estrogens) as well as the adrenal corticoids (cortisol, corticosterone, aldosterone, and others). In the liver, cholesterol is the precursor of the bile acids, a group of 24 steroid carboxylic acids that, when linked with the amino acids glycine or taurine, form the bile salts. Bile acids are secreted into the intestine to aid in the digestion of food, especially lipids.

Metabolism. Cholesterol is obtained from foods having saturated FATTY ACIDS and is also derived biosynthetically from acetate, primarily in the liver. Normally, the total amount of cholesterol from these two sources remains constant because the rate of cholesterol synthesis in the liver is under feedback control. When the dietary intake is high, liver synthesis is low; when intake is low, synthesis increases.

Dietary cholesterol is transported in the blood from the intestine to the liver by means of large lipoprotein molecules known as chylomicrons. The liver then secretes very-low-density lipoprotein (VLDL)—containing cholesterol and cholesterol ester, among other compounds—into the blood. VLDL is partially converted in adipose tissue (fat) to low-density lipoprotein (LDL). LDL is the major transport protein for cholesterol, supplying both free and esterified cholesterol to the various body tissues. High-density lipoprotein (HDL) appears to be involved in the transport of cholesterol in the opposite direction, that is, from the tissues to the liver.

In the average American adult, the total amount of lipoprotein-bound cholesterol circulating in the blood is about 200 mg per 100 ml of serum. If a person's intake of dietary fat is high, many experts consider that levels of serum cholesterol will also increase, causing greater risk of HEART DISEASE and especially ATHEROSCLEROSIS. Studies

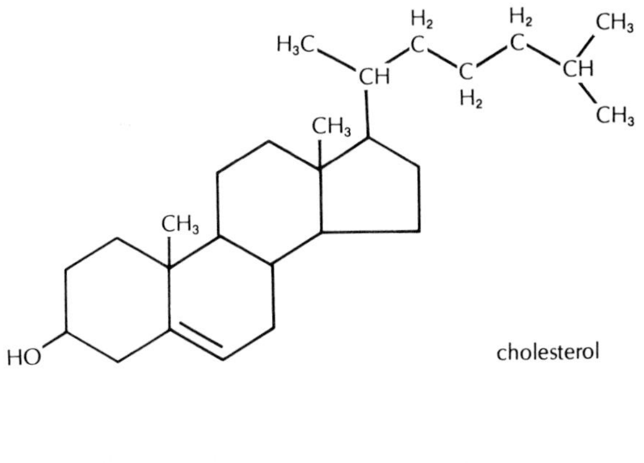

cholesterol

have shown, however, that high levels of HDL cholesterol reduce risk, and high levels of other lipoproteins, particularly LDL, have the opposite effect. A report issued in 1984 seemed clearly to indicate that reduction of LDL ratios would lower the risk of heart disease, and a 1987 report provided evidence that reduction of cholesterol could have a positive effect in some persons with high cholesterol levels. A 1989 report indicated that a third of all American adults had cholesterol levels that placed them at high risk of coronary disease. Various drugs have been developed to lower cholesterol levels.

Cholula [choh-loo'-lah] Cholula, a village and tourist center near Puebla city, is probably the oldest continuously occupied town in Mexico. Shortly after 200 BC, Cholula came within the orbit of TEOTIHUACÁN civilization, and a temple-pyramid was built. The pyramid was enlarged four times, becoming the largest structure of pre-Spanish Mexico, a vast mound about 55 m (180 ft) high, the base of which covered roughly 18 ha (45 acres). Tunneling has revealed the older pyramids nesting within the temple.

About AD 800–900, Cholula, like Teotihuacán, declined, and its pyramid was abandoned forever. By 1300 the city had revived under the influence of the MIXTECS and was famous for its painted pottery. Cholula remained independent of the Aztecs but fell to the Spanish, who described it as a city of more than 2,000 houses and 400 temples.

Chomsky, Noam [chahm'-skee, nohm] Avram Noam Chomsky, b. Philadelphia, Dec. 7, 1928, is a prominent American linguist, social critic, and political activist. His *Syntactic Structures* (1957) initiated a shift in emphasis away from empiricism, which had dominated American linguistics and social science generally, to an investigation into language and universal grammar as a uniquely human mental faculty with its own biologically determined structure and principles. Chomsky's major claims about language include: the ordinary use of language is creative (innovative and stimulus free); there is a fundamental distinction between knowledge and behavior, and the former is the proper focus of scientific study; an adequate description of a speaker's linguistic knowledge requires positing a set of abstract principles; the discovery of such a set of principles suggests a complex biological component in language acquisition; these principles of universal grammar are specific to the language faculty and contribute to a view of the mind as a set of mental organs, language being perhaps the best understood.

Chondrichthyes [kahn-drik'-thee-eez] Chondrichthyes is the class of cartilaginous fishes that includes the RAYS, SHARKS, SKATES, and holocephalans (see CHIMAERA) among living fish. Many other extinct forms are known from Paleozoic rocks; evidence from these fossils provides the basis for assigning the chimaera to this class.

Chondrichthyes fishes have a cartilaginous skeleton (calcified to a degree, but never true bone), scales that are toothlike where present, two nostrils without openings to the mouth, a well-developed lower jaw, bony teeth, and the lack of an air bladder. They differ from the class AGNATHA by having paired limbs, well-developed jaws, and bony teeth, and from the higher fish by the lack of true skeletal bone.

Skates, rays, and sharks have from five to seven gill slits with external openings not covered by a flap, or fold, of skin; claspers developed on the pelvic fins to effect internal fertilization; and a dorsal fin or fins. Holocephalans are distinguished by their upper jaw being fused to the cranium, a single skin cover over gill slits, and the lack of toothlike scales.

chondrite see METEOR AND METEORITE

Chongqing (Chungking) [choong-king] Chongqing, the largest city in Sichuan (Szechwan) province in China, was granted the economic and administrative powers of a province in 1983, although it remains in Sichuan. By 1988 its population was an estimated 12,890,000.

The city is located on hilly uplands at the confluence of the Chang Jiang (Yangtze) and the Jialing (Chia-ling) river, and it is a river port. Cable cars carry passengers to the city from the valleys below, and new bridges link the river banks. The city is a transportation hub for southwestern China. Its manufactures include iron and steel, machinery and machine tools, vehicles, armaments, chemicals, appliances, and textiles. The city is a notable center for trade in medicinal herbs. Chongqing served as the wartime capital of China during the Japanese invasion (1937–45), and many institutions and factories were relocated there.

Chopin, Frédéric [shoh-pan'] Frédéric François Chopin was the most eminent composer who specialized in piano music. There are conflicts about his birth date in the record, but most scholars believe Chopin was born on Mar. 1, 1810, in Zelazowa Wola, near Warsaw, Poland. His father was French, and his mother Polish.

Career. Chopin gave his first public piano recital at the age of eight and began concert tours in 1828. After visits to several German cities and to Vienna with a return to Warsaw in 1829, he gave a concert in Paris in 1832. He then decided to settle in Paris permanently. Chopin excelled as a piano teacher, gave yearly concerts of his own music, and frequently performed in the fashionable Parisian salons; he was renowned for his subtle and refined playing.

In 1837, Franz Liszt introduced Chopin to the writer George SAND. She spent the winter of 1838–39 on the island of Majorca with Chopin, who was suffering from a respiratory ailment. Their relationship continued until 1847, and after they separated, Chopin's ailment was diagnosed as tuberculosis. Exhausted by a concert tour of England and Scotland in 1848, Chopin returned to Paris, where he died on Oct. 17, 1849.

The Polish-born composer Frédéric Chopin created dance and lyric compositions of great virtuosity. Written almost exclusively for piano, his works are filled with romantic intensity and have a classical clarity of expression.

Music. Aside from several songs and pieces for cello and piano, Chopin wrote almost exclusively for the piano. His playing included *rubato,* a flexibility of tempo essential for the proper interpretation of his music.

Among Chopin's shorter works are MAZURKAS, which are based on Polish dances in 3/4 time; preludes, brief pieces inspired by Bach; and etudes, a genre that Chopin raised from the level of a technical exercise to a work of musical merit.

Among the longer forms, the POLONAISES—aristocratic dances of a passionate, Polish character—NOCTURNES, and ballades deserve special mention. Chopin's nocturnes range from melodious salon pieces to deeply pessimistic compositions. The ballades are dramatic and narrative in character.

Of Chopin's large-scale works, the two piano concertos (F minor and E minor) are early compositions; his mature piano sonatas (B-flat minor, which contains the well-known funeral march, and B minor) show great structural and harmonic ingenuity. His F Minor Fantasy influenced Liszt's new concepts of musical form. Chopin's style includes delicate passage work and subtle ornamentation. His harmonic innovations influenced Liszt, Wagner, and Scriabin.

Chopin, Kate O'Flaherty [shoh'-pan] Kate Chopin, b. St. Louis, Mo., Feb. 8, 1851, d. Aug. 22, 1904, was an American writer whose 1899 novel *The Awakening* was not fully appreciated until the 1960s. It is the story of a woman whose needs for sexual and artistic fulfillment prove unresolvable in a society that views extramarital love as pathological. Chopin did not begin writing until several years after her husband's death. She then published a number of accomplished local color sketches set in Louisiana and collected in *Bayou Folk* (1894) and *A Night in Acadie* (1897).

choral music The words *chorus* and *choir*—both derived from the ancient Greek word *choros,* meaning a band of dancers and singers—are commonly understood to mean a large group of singers who combine their voices (with or without instrumental accompaniment) in several "parts," or independent melodic lines. The most common type of choral ensemble today performs music in four parts, each assigned to a different voice range: soprano (high female), alto (low female), tenor (high male), and bass (low male). The abbreviation SATB refers to this type of "mixed" chorus, and to the music composed for it. There are many other common types: women's chorus (two soprano parts and two alto, or SSAA), men's chorus (TTBB), and double chorus (two distinct SATB groups), to name a few. Many choral works are in more or fewer than four parts, from as few as one ("monophonic," all singers singing the same melody) to as many as several dozen (as in the 40-part motet *Spem in alium* by Thomas TALLIS, or certain 20th-century works).

The distinction (unique to English) between *choir* and *chorus* is fairly clear: a choir generally sings sacred or art music of earlier centuries (as in "madrigal choir"), whereas a chorus is associated with concert works, opera, musical theater, and popular entertainment.

Early Choral Music. Many cultures have traditions of group singing, but the two that laid the foundations of Western choral music were the Greek and Jewish cultures of the pre-Christian era. The chorus in Greek drama grew out of groups that sang and danced at religious festivals. (The sense of "dance" survives in such terms as *choreography* and *chorus line.*) The Old Testament contains many references to choral singing on important occasions in Jewish life. Both Greek and Jewish choral music of this period was monophonic and antiphonal—that is, performed responsively between soloists and choirs, or between two choruses.

This painting portrays a medieval church choir accompanied by vielle *(a bowed lute), bells, and psaltery. With the beginning of polyphonic music in the 9th century, instruments were often used to reinforce the vocal parts.*

Soon after the Roman emperor Constantine the Great officially sanctioned Christianity in 313, however, the first *schola cantorum* (literally, "choir school," as well as the performing group from such a school) was founded in Rome by Pope Sylvester I.

In early medieval choirs, a small number of men, or men and boys, sang PLAINSONG, a metrically free, monophonic setting of liturgical text. Gregorian chant, an outgrowth of the liturgical reforms of Pope Gregory I (r. 590–604), became the dominant form of plainsong by the 10th century, and has remained in use ever since.

Part-Singing and the Renaissance. The practice of singing in unison began to give way to POLYPHONY, in which one or more independent parts departed from and decorated the melody.

By this time, the term MOTET had come to mean a polyphonic vocal setting of any sacred Latin text except sections of the Mass. Between about 1450 and 1600, the motet and MASS developed into elaborate compositions with three to six melodic lines, as in the works of John Dunstable, JOSQUIN DES PREZ, and PALESTRINA. Andrea and Giovanni Gabrieli (see GABRIELI family) added to the splendor of Venice with works in eight parts or even more, performed by multiple choirs. In the Church of England, which separated from the Roman church in 1534, a motet on an English text became known as an ANTHEM (which is still the English and American term for a choral piece sung during worship).

The exclusion of women from liturgical roles extended to the choir as well; high-voice parts were sung by boys, falsetto singers, or (in some Roman Catholic countries after about 1570) CASTRATI. In England particularly, the training of boy singers for cathedral choirs became a well-established tradition that continues today.

The Baroque Era. Virtually no secular choral music existed before 1600; the Renaissance MADRIGAL, a polyphonic song, was only rarely performed with more than one singer to a part. The first Italian operas, of which Claudio MONTEVERDI's *Orfeo* is the leading example, represented an attempt to revive classical Greek drama, and so featured the chorus prominently. But when the audience's attention focused on solo virtuosity and spectacle, the chorus lost some of its importance in baroque opera. It thrived, however, in ORATORIO, a form of concert opera that dramatized a story (usually biblical) without the use of costumes or scenery. George Frideric HANDEL's oratorios sometimes put the chorus ahead of the soloists in importance, as in *Israel in Egypt* (1738).

Whether composed for a prince's birthday or a Sunday on the liturgical calendar, the CANTATA for voices and instruments included such operatic elements as arias, recitatives (a kind of sung-spoken narration), and often choruses. The church cantatas of composers such as J. S. Bach and Georg Philipp TELEMANN incorporated German CHORALES (hymn tunes).

Choral Music as Mass Expression. In the political and industrial revolutions of the late 18th and early 19th centuries, a large and prosperous middle class emerged, eager for cultural accomplishments. They founded such choruses as the Berlin Singakademie—a choir comprising both men and women from its inception in 1791. The mania for Handel, continuing for decades after the composer's death, led to ever-larger performances of *The Messiah* (a London concert in 1791 used over 1,000 performers) and to the foundation of choral clubs such as the Sons of Handel (Dublin, 1810) and the Handel and Haydn Society (Boston, 1815). Following Handel's lead, composers glorified the mass of humanity in works for large chorus and orchestra, beginning with Beethoven's Ninth Symphony (1824). The chorus returned to the opera stage in force after dwindling during the classical period.

The strong choral traditions of the United States arrived with European immigrants, spread through music programs in the public schools, and were transformed by Afro-American church music, which contributed rhythmic complexity and a call-and-response style of composition. Professional choruses explore not only older classical repertory but new works that contain every innovation found in new instrumental music: the tone clusters and vocal slides of Krzysztof PENDERECKI, the aleatory (chance) techniques of John CAGE and Lukas FOSS, the minimalist music of Philip GLASS.

chorale [kuh-ral'] The German Protestant hymn, intended for congregational use, is called the chorale (German, *Choral*). Important in itself as a large body of hymnic material that supplemented the spoken word in the Lutheran service, it also served as the basis for a variety of musical forms that quoted the tunes as part of their structure. Hence, chorale cantatas, chorale preludes, chorale fantasias, and the like perpetuated the use of tunes that might otherwise have been confined to hymnals and a folk, rather than an art, tradition. The tunes were borrowed from plainsong and folk song or originally composed. Strong rhythms gave these pieces a vitality lacking in other hymnic traditions, but arrangements surviving from the 18th century have been simplified for congregational participation.

chord see HARMONY

chordate The chordates, or phylum Chordata, a large and important group of animals, include all the vertebrates and two protochordate groups. Chordates are characterized by the possession of a notochord, paired pharyngeal clefts (gill slits), and a dorsal, hollow nerve cord. These structures are present either throughout life or at some stage of the animal's development; in humans, for example, gill slits appear only in the embryo. The notochord is a flexible rodlike support that consists of densely packed cells and lies just beneath the nerve cord. The pharyngeal gill slits are openings through the lateral, or side, walls of the pharynx. Other common features include an elongated, bilaterally symmetrical body composed of an anterior enlargement of the nerve cord (brain) associated with specialized sensory organs, and an internal body cavity (COELOM) lying between an inner tube (the digestive tract) and an outer tube (the body wall).

The most advanced and numerous chordates are the vertebrates—the subphylum Vertebrata, which, according to some authorities, numbers about 40,000 species. The protochordates include two major subphyla, the Urochordata (about 1,500 species) and the Cephalochordata (about 25 species). Some classification systems still include the phylum Hemichordata as an additional subphylum (see HEMICHORDATE).

Vertebrates are so named because, in late embryonic life, a segmented vertebral column develops in addition to the notochord or, more generally, as a replacement of it. Vertebrates possess a well-developed head, with brain, brain case, and paired sense organs. The vertebrates include the classes AGNATHA (for example, HAGFISH, LAMPREYS); CHONDRICHTHYES (RAYS, SHARKS, SKATES); OSTEICHTHYES (bony fish); Amphibia (FROGS, SALAMANDERS, TOADS; see AMPHIBIANS); Reptilia (CROCODILES, LIZARDS, TURTLES, SNAKES; see REPTILE); Aves (BIRDS); and Mammalia (MAMMALS).

A typical cephalochordate (see CEPHALOCHORDATA) is the lancelet, or *Amphioxus*, a fishlike animal about 5 cm (2 in) long that retains the notochord in the adult but lacks an anterior brain and associated sensory organs. Among the urochordates, such as the TUNICATES, only the larvae exhibit chordate features; during metamorphosis the notochord disappears and the nervous system collapses to become a single cluster of nerve cells (a ganglion).

See also: CLASSIFICATION, BIOLOGICAL; EVOLUTION.

choreography [kohr-ee-ah'-gruh-fee] Choreography is the arrangement of DANCE movements, usually by one person, the choreographer, in visually pleasing patterns that may be decorative, narrative, interpretive (either of music, mood, or emotion), or purely inventive (stylistic exercises that display the dancers' technical virtuosity). The term derives from the Greek words *choria* ("dancing") and *graphia* ("writing"). In its earliest usage (*c.*1700), it stood simply for the notation or written record of dance steps. As the dance vocabulary grew, however, and the choreographer invented fresh ways to use it, choreography came to stand for the final result of his or her efforts. To this day, it applies only to theatrical dance forms, for which dancers are rigidly schooled in a particular vocabulary of movement (see glossary under BALLET).

Mikhail Fokine (right), *one of the most celebrated choreographers of the 20th century, appears in the Ballets Russes production of* Schéhérazade.

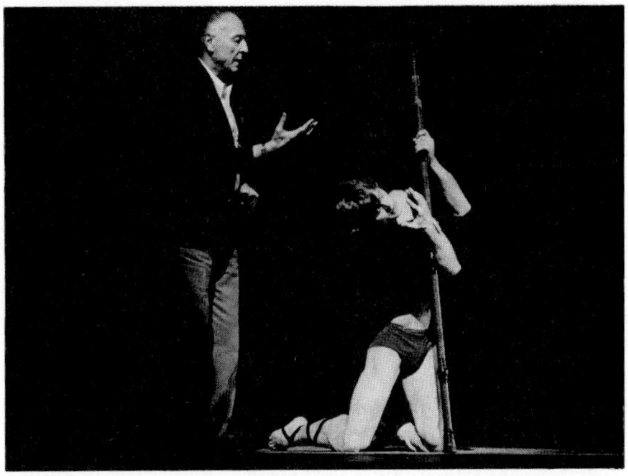

Choreographer George Balanchine (left) *directs Mikhail Baryshnikov during a rehearsal of* The Prodigal Son. *Under Balanchine the New York City Ballet became one of the world's most respected dance companies.*

Throughout its 400-year history, choreography in classical ballet has evolved naturally within an ever-changing context of artistic trends and social customs. The court dances of the 16th century, from which ballet emerged, were linear in structure, and designed for an audience watching from a raised gallery on three sides of the floor. The permanent adoption of the framing proscenium (*c.*1640) established a head-on view of dancing, thus changing the shape of choreography forever.

The great 18th-century French choreographer and teacher Jean Georges NOVERRE worked to free dance from the thematic restrictions of spectacle and opera. His dramatic ballets blossomed with the asymmetrical curves of the period's baroque music and art.

Basic conventions of MIME AND PANTOMIME, with gestures taken from nature, were fixed by 1750 and used with increasing frequency as explanatory links in narrative dance action, like built-in subtitles. When courtly life declined, trained dancers replaced courtiers as performers; with them, virtuosity, speed, and variety of movement replaced static posturing.

Given such able personnel, the Italian choreographer Salvatore VIGANÒ;, in the late 18th and early 19th centuries, combined the formal vocabulary of the *danse d'école* and the dramatic principles of Noverre's *ballet d'action* in *choreodrammi*, in which even the corps de ballet dancers moved individually and expressively.

By the early 19th century, the development of the stiffened toe shoe, on which women seemed to float above the ground, enabled choreography to express the most ethereal romantic concepts with perfect fidelity. Toe shoes survived into the 20th century, but romanticism did not. The American Isadora DUNCAN danced barefoot and uncorseted, inspired by the shapes and rhythms of nature. Inspired in turn by Duncan, the Russian Mikhail FOKINE rebelled against the standard use of ready-made combinations of ballet steps by unifying movement, mime, and music stylistically to suit each ballet he choreographed.

The earliest known dance notation appeared in Egyptian hieroglyphs. Various other systems, employing stick figures, musical notes, numbers, or abstract symbols to represent the parts of the body and the arrangement of movements, have been devised over the years. In the 20th century, those developed by Rudolf von LABAN in 1928, by Rudolf Benesh in 1956, and by Noa Eshkol and Abraham Wachmann in 1958 have been the most widely adopted.

Choreography continues to evolve with the passage of time. George BALANCHINE streamlined the classical ballet vocabulary to fuse it seamlessly with contemporary music. Antony TUDOR informed dance with psychological motivation; the characters in his ballets express their thoughts in movement as clearly as their actions. Whatever its evolutionary form, choreography remains the organized pattern of movement performed by dancers for an audience to follow with its eyes, memories, and intellects.

chorus (drama) see DRAMA

chorus (music) see CHORAL MUSIC

Chou see ZHOU (dynasty)

Chou En-lai see ZHOU ENLAI

Chouteau (family) [shoo-toh'] The Chouteaus were an American family of frontierspeople and traders. **René Auguste Chouteau**, b. September 1749, d. Feb. 24, 1829, joined Pierre Laclède's expedition (1763) to open up the fur trade west of the Mississippi, and in 1764 he set up a trading post that later became St. Louis.

He and his half brother, **Jean Pierre**, b. Oct. 10, 1758, d. July 10, 1849, built up an extensive business and acquired a virtual monopoly of trade with the Osage Indians along the Missouri River and its tributaries. When the Spaniards, then in control of the territory, took away their monopoly in 1795, Jean Pierre moved southwest. He established the first white settlement in what is now Salina, Okla., and persuaded many of the Osages to move with him. The brothers had great influence on the Indians and because of this were frequently used as negotiators; Jean Pierre was the first Osage Indian agent.

His sons extended the family business. One son, **Pierre**, b. Jan. 19, 1789, d. Sept. 6, 1865, was a trader and financier. Another son, **Auguste Pierre**, b. May 9, 1786, d. Dec. 25, 1838, built new trading posts and took command of trading expeditions along the Missouri River. He served as a commissioner, negotiating with the Wichita and other Indian tribes.

chow chow The chow chow is a medium-sized dog. One of the "northern" or spitz breeds, it has been established to be more than 2,000 years old. The chow's coat may be black, red, brown, or cream, and a lionlike mane sets off a large head with a squared-off muzzle, deep-set eyes, and prick ears. The chow must have a blue black tongue to qualify for the show ring and is credited with great scenting power and hunting prowess.

The chow chow, the only breed of dog with a blue tongue, was used for centuries in China to hunt game. It became popular in the U.S. during the 1920s when President Calvin Coolidge, a chow owner, held office.

Chows did not appear in the West until about 1880. Queen Victoria acquired specimens of the breed, which no doubt provided a major impetus for its population. The first chow shown in the United States was exhibited at the 1890 Westminster Kennel Club show.

Chrétien, Jean Joseph Jacques Jean Chrétien, b. Shawinigan, Quebec, Jan. 11, 1934, became the 10th leader of the Liberal party of Canada in June 1990. Educated at Quebec's Laval University, he is a lawyer and politician. As a member of Parliament (1963–86), he served in various government offices, including that of Canada's attorney general and minister of state for social development (1980–82). He indicates that as party leader he will not immediately seek reelection, but will devote his early efforts to rebuilding and unifying his divided party.

Chrétien de Troyes [kray-tee-an' duh twah'] The French poet Chrétien de Troyes, fl. *c.*1160–80, created an episodic verse genre that illustrated a code of COURTLY LOVE inspired by Ovid. His widely translated and imitated works influenced the development of future narrative forms and added substantially to the tales of ARTHUR AND ARTHURIAN LEGEND. Chrétien drew upon historical figures and events of the Middle Ages for the subject matter of his romances *Erec et Enide* (*c.*1160–64), *Cligès* (*c.*1160–64), *Lancelot, ou le chevalier de la charette* (*c.*1164–72), *Yvain, ou le chevalier au lion* (*c.*1164–72), and *Perceval, ou le conte du Graal* (*c.*1180–90), which was left incomplete at his death. A frequent visitor to the court of Marie de Champagne, daughter of Louis VII and Eleanor of Aquitaine, Chrétien found inspiration there for *Le Chevalier de la charette,* a tale concerning the project to liberate Queen Guinevere and prove her innocent of adultery. He also enjoyed the patronage of Philip, count of Flanders, who asked him to versify a book that served as a basis for *Le Conte du Graal.*

Christ see JESUS CHRIST; MESSIAH

Christadelphians [kris-tuh-del'-fee-uhnz] A small Christian sect founded in the United States *c.*1845, the Christadelphians were originally called Thomasites for their founder, John Thomas (1805-71). Rejecting all doctrinal development, they claim to return to biblical belief and practice. They do not believe in the TRINITY, but await the SECOND COMING OF CHRIST and his establishment of a theocracy centered in Jerusalem; only those who believe in the gospel will become immortal.

Christchurch Christchurch is a city on the east central coast of South Island, New Zealand. Located on the Avon River about 240 km (150 mi) southwest of Wellington, it is the largest city on South Island and has a population of 167,700 (1988 est.), with 300,700 (1988 est.) in the metropolitan area. It is both a commercial and cultural center, with light industries processing local products (wheat and wool). Transportation equipment and rubber are also produced. The city is connected to its port, Lyttelton, 13 km (8 mi) to the southeast, by rail and tunnel. Founded in 1850 by Anglican churchmen, Christchurch is the seat of the University of Canterbury (1873) and Christ's College (1850).

christening see BAPTISM

Christian, Charlie The jazz guitarist Charlie Christian, b. Dallas, Tex., *c.*1919, d. Mar. 2, 1942, the first important musician to play the electric guitar, was one of the creators of the jazz style known as bebop. Christian joined Benny Goodman's band in 1939 and was a member of the famed Goodman sextet. There he was teamed with such notables as Gene Krupa, Teddy Wilson, and Lionel Hampton. After hours, he played at Minton's in Harlem, a nightclub where the first experiments in bebop were heard. Christian died at 23 from tuberculosis.

Christian art and architecture, Early see EARLY CHRISTIAN ART AND ARCHITECTURE

Christian Brothers see JOHN BAPTIST DE LA SALLE, SAINT

Christian Church for the Protestant denomination of this name, see DISCIPLES OF CHRIST

Christian Churches and Churches of Christ
Christian Churches and Churches of Christ comprise an undenominational fellowship of Protestant Christians dedicated to the "restoration of New Testament Christianity, its doctrine, its ordinances, and its life." Congregations are self-governing. The movement began in the eastern United States about 1800. Prominent early leaders included Thomas Campbell (1763–1854), Alexander CAMPBELL, and Barton W. STONE. Until 1906 its history was shared with those CHURCHES OF CHRIST which avoid the use of instrumental music in worship; and until 1968 it shared a common history with the then-restructured DISCIPLES OF CHRIST (Christian Church). For their creed and moral code, the Christian Churches and Churches of Christ depend on direct quotations from the Bible. Baptism is by immersion; communion is central to each Sunday's worship.

Christian Endeavor Christian Endeavor is a Protestant youth movement founded in 1881 by the American Congregationalist Francis Edward CLARK. Its purposes are to instruct young people in the fundamentals of Christianity, provide occasions for fellowship, and promote social activities. The movement arose at a time when rapid social changes were upsetting the traditional lives of the churches.

Christian Science Christian Science is a religion emphasizing divine healing as practiced by Jesus Christ; its tenets were formulated by Mary Baker EDDY. In 1879, Eddy founded the Church of Christ, Scientist, with headquarters in Boston. While its branches are democratic in government, they all conform to the rules of the *Manual of The Mother Church* (1895) by Eddy.

Sunday services consist mainly of readings from the Bible and *Science and Health with Key to the Scriptures* (1906), the textbook of Christian Science written by Eddy. Wednesday meetings include testimonies of healing from the congregation. The church has no ordained clergy. Readers, both men and women, are elected from the membership to conduct the services. Practitioners, also both men and women, devote full time to the work of spiritual healing.

Christian Science teaches that God and his spiritual creation are the only realities. God is regarded as infinite Life, Truth, Spirit, Mind, and Principle. The material world, with all its suffering, strife, and death, is considered to be a misconception or distorted view of the divine universe. Christian Science claims to prove through the healing of disease and other difficulties that the understanding of God and his spiritual creation is as effective now as it was in Jesus' time. Its adherents therefore rely on divine law in times of sickness instead of resorting to medical and other material means; the right of Christian Science parents to withhold medical treatment from their children has been challenged in court.

Publications of the Christian Science Publishing Society include the *Christian Science Quarterly*, containing Bible lessons for daily study; *The Christian Science Journal*, a monthly magazine; *Christian Science Sentinel*, a weekly magazine; *The Christian Science Monitor*, a daily newspaper; and *The Herald of Christian Science* in 12 languages and in braille. In the 1980s the group expanded into other media, producing both radio and television news programming.

Christian Socialism The term *Christian Socialism* was devised by the English social reformer F. D. MAURICE in 1848 to indicate that socialism was the logical outcome of Christianity. John Malcolm Ludlow, a young lawyer influenced by French socialism, was its organizer; Maurice, chaplain at Lincoln's Inn, London, was its theorist; and Charles KINGSLEY, an author and clergyman, was its publicist. Dedicated to the principle of cooperation instead of competition, Ludlow and others organized associations of tailors, builders, shoemakers, and the like. The movement died out in the mid-1850s. In the United States, Christian Socialism was associated with proponents of the SOCIAL GOSPEL and with the Society of Christian Socialists (1889).

Christian III, King of Denmark Christian III, b. Aug. 12, 1503, d. Jan. 1, 1559, was king of Denmark and Norway from 1534 to 1559. A zealous Protestant, he had to overcome opposition in the so-called Count's War (1533–36) to succeed his father, Frederick I, to the throne. His Diet of Copenhagen (1536) established a state Lutheran church. In a dynastic struggle with Holy Roman Emperor CHARLES V, who supported the claims of the daughters of deposed Christian II, Christian III barred the Habsburg Netherlands' shipping from the Baltic Sea, and Charles made peace with him in 1544. He left Denmark a well-administered state.

Christian IV, King of Denmark Christian IV, b. Apr. 12, 1577, d. Feb. 28, 1648, was one of the most popular kings to rule Denmark and Norway. Succeeding his father, Frederick II, at the age of 11 in 1588, Christian came of age in 1596 and soon asserted his independence of aristocratic councilors. Claiming dominion over the Baltic and Norwegian seas, he fought a war with Sweden in 1611–13. Continued rivalry with Sweden and his attempt to dominate northern Germany led to a disastrous intervention (1625–29) in the THIRTY YEARS' WAR and to defeat by Sweden in the war of 1643–45. He founded many cities, including Glückstadt in Holstein and Christiania (now Oslo) in Norway. He also improved Copenhagen, where many of his buildings survive. He was succeeded by his son FREDERICK III.

Christian IX, King of Denmark Christian IX, b. Apr. 8, 1818, d. Jan. 29, 1906, became king of Denmark in 1863, touching off a war that began the unification of Germany. The duke of Glücksburg, he was named successor to the childless King FREDERICK VII by the Treaty of London of 1852. When Christian became king, Prussia challenged his right to rule in SCHLESWIG-HOLSTEIN and Lauenburg. A brief war in 1864 left these three duchies in German hands. In Denmark, Christian's long reign was a period of social change and industrial growth.

Christian X, King of Denmark Christian X, b. Sept. 26, 1870, d. Apr. 20, 1947, king of Denmark (1912–47), was the son and successor of Frederick VIII (r. 1906–12). By an act of 1918, Christian also became king of Iceland, thitherto an integral part of the Danish kingdom. In 1944, however, Iceland became totally independent. During World War II, Christian was imprisoned (1943–45) by the German occupation authorities.

Christianity Christianity is the religion whose belief system centers on the person and teachings of JESUS CHRIST. To Christians, Jesus of Nazareth was and is the MESSIAH promised by God in the prophecies of the Old Testament (the Hebrew BIBLE); by his life, death, and RESURRECTION he freed those who believe in him from their sinful state and made them recipients of God's saving GRACE. Many also await the SECOND COMING OF CHRIST, which they believe will complete God's plan of salvation. The Christian Bible, or Holy Scripture, includes the Old Testament and also the New Testament, a collection of early Christian writings proclaiming Jesus as lord and savior. Arising in the Jewish milieu of 1st-century Palestine, Christianity quickly spread through the Mediterranean world and in the 4th century became the official religion of the Roman Empire.

Christians have tended to separate into rival groups, but the main body of the Christian CHURCH was united under the Roman emperors. During the Middle Ages, when all of Europe became Christianized, this main church was divided into a Latin (Western European) and a Greek (Byzantine or Orthodox) branch. The Western church was in turn divided by the REFORMATION of the 16th century into the Roman Catholic church and a large number of smaller Protestant churches: Lutheran, Reformed (Calvinist), Anglican, and sectarian. These divisions have continued and multiplied, but in the 20th century many Christians joined in the ECUMENICAL MOVEMENT to work for church unity. This resulted in the formation of the WORLD COUNCIL OF CHURCHES. Christianity, a strongly proselytizing religion, exists in all parts of the world.

Beliefs. Certain basic doctrines drawn from Scripture (especially from the Gospels and the letters of Saint PAUL), interpreted by the FATHERS OF THE CHURCH and the first four ecumenical councils, historically have been accepted by all three of the major traditions. According to this body of teaching, the original human beings rebelled against God, and from that time until the coming of Christ the world was ruled by SIN. The hope of a final reconciliation was kept alive by God's COVENANT with the Jews, the chosen people from whom the savior sprang. This savior,

CHRISTIANITY

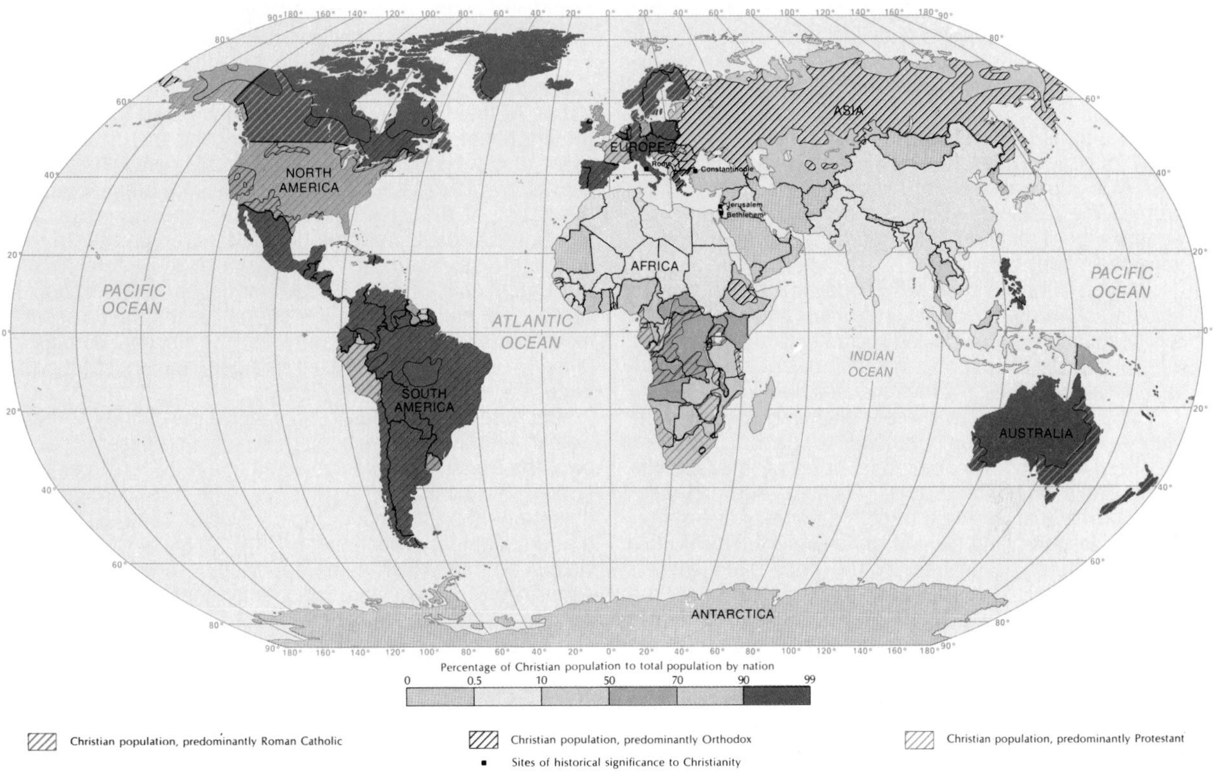

Jesus Christ, partly vanquished sin and Satan. Jesus, born of the Virgin MARY by the power of the HOLY SPIRIT, preached the coming of God's Kingdom but was rejected by the Jewish leaders, who delivered him to the Romans who crucified him. On the third day after his death God raised him up again. He appeared to his disciples, commanding them to spread the good news of salvation from sin and death to all people. This, according to Christian belief, is the mission of Christ's church.

Christians are monotheists (believers in one God). The early church, however, developed the characteristic Christian doctrine of the TRINITY, in which God is thought of as Creator (Father), Redeemer (Son), and Sustainer (Holy Spirit), but one God in essence.

Christianity inherited and modified the Jewish belief that the world would be transformed by the coming of the Reign of God. The Christians held that the bodies of those who had died would rise again, reanimated, and that the righteous would be triumphant, the wicked punished. This belief, along with Jesus' promise of "eternal life," developed into a doctrine of eternal rewards (heaven) and punishments (hell) after death. A source of doctrinal uncertainty was whether salvation depended on God's election in advance of a believer's faith, or even in a decision of God before the disobedience and fall of the first man and woman (see PREDESTINATION).

Although Christians today tend to emphasize what unites them rather than what divides them, substantial differences in faith exist among the various churches. Those in the Protestant tradition insist on Scripture as the sole source of God's REVELATION. The Roman Catholics and Orthodox give greater importance to the tradition of the church in defining the content of faith, believing it to be divinely guided in its understanding of scriptural revelation. They stress the role of ecumenical councils in the formulation of doctrine, and in Roman Catholicism the pope, or bishop of Rome, is regarded as the final authority in matters of belief.

Practice. Christian societies have exhibited great variety in ethos, from mutual love, acceptance, and pacifism to strict authoritarianism and forcible repression of dissent. Justification for all of these has been found in various passages in the Bible. A prominent feature of the Roman Catholic and Orthodox churches is MONASTICISM.

Christians also vary widely in worship. Early Christian worship centered on two principal rites or SACRAMENTS: BAPTISM, a ceremonial washing that initiated converts into the church; and the EUCHARIST, a sacred meal preceded by prayers, chants, and Scripture readings, in which the participants were mysteriously united with Christ. As time went on, the Eucharist, or MASS, became surrounded by an increasingly elaborate ritual in the Latin, the Greek, and other Eastern churches, and in the Middle Ages Christians came to venerate saints—especially the Virgin

Mary—and holy images. In the West seven sacraments were recognized. The Protestant reformers retained two sacraments—baptism and the Eucharist—rejecting the others, along with devotion to saints and images, as unscriptural. They simplified worship and emphasized preaching. Since the 19th century there has been a certain amount of reconvergence in worship among ecumenically minded Protestants and Roman Catholics, with each side adopting some of the other's practices. For example, the Catholic Mass is now in the vernacular. Among other groups in both traditions, however, the divergence remains great.

In most Christian churches Sunday, the day of Christ's resurrection, is observed as a time of rest and worship. The resurrection is more particularly commemorated at EASTER, a festival in the early spring. Another major Christian festival is CHRISTMAS, which commemorates the birth of Jesus.

Polity. Most churches make a distinction between the clergy—those specially ordained to perform spiritual functions—and ordinary believers, or lay people (see MINISTRY, CHRISTIAN). The Roman Catholic and Orthodox churches have an all-male threefold ministry of bishops, priests, deacons, and several minor orders. The Roman Catholic church is headed by the pope, who governs through a centralized bureaucracy (the PAPACY) in consultation with his fellow bishops. In the Orthodox churches and those of the ANGLICAN COMMUNION (which retain the threefold ministry) lay influence is somewhat greater; major decisions are made by the bishops acting as a group with lay consultation, sometimes with votes. Church government among Lutherans, Reformed, and other Protestants generally involves the laity even more fully, policy being determined either by local congregations or by regional assemblies composed of both clergy and lay people. Most Protestant churches, including some provinces of the Anglican Communion, now permit the ordination of women.

During its early history the Christian church remained independent of any political regime. From the 4th century to the 18th century, however, churches accepted the protection of emperors, kings, and princes and became closely allied with secular governments. In some cases monarchs became the leaders of their own national churches. In the 19th and 20th centuries the trend has once again been in the direction of separation of church and state, sometimes amicably achieved, sometimes otherwise.

History of the Early Church. After Jesus was crucified, his followers, strengthened by the conviction that he had risen from the dead and that they were filled with the power of the Holy Spirit, formed the first Christian community in Jerusalem. By the middle of the 1st century, missionaries were spreading the new religion among the peoples of Egypt, Syria, Anatolia, Greece, and Italy. Chief among these was Saint Paul, who laid the foundations of Christian theology and played a key role in the transformation of Christianity from a Jewish sect to a world religion. The original Christians, being Jews, observed the dietary and ritualistic laws of the TORAH and required non-Jewish converts to do the same. Paul and others favored eliminating obligation, thus making Christianity more attractive to Gentiles. The separation from Judaism was completed by the destruction of the church of Jerusalem by the Romans during the Jewish Revolt of AD 66–70.

After that Christianity took on a predominantly Gentile character and began to develop in a number of different forms. At first the Christian community looked forward to the imminent return of Christ in glory and the establishment of the Kingdom. This hope carried on in the 2d century by MONTANISM, an ascetic movement emphasizing the action of the Holy Spirit. GNOSTICISM, which rose to prominence about the same time, also stressed the Spirit, but it disparaged the Old Testament and interpreted the crucifixion and resurrection of Jesus in a spiritual sense. The main body of the church condemned these movements as heretical and, when the Second Coming failed to occur, organized itself as a permanent institution under the leadership of its bishops.

Because of their refusal to recognize the divinity of the Roman emperor or pay homage to any god except their own, the Christians were subjected to a number of persecutions by the Roman authorities. The most savage of these were the one under Emperor Decius (249–51) and that instigated by Diocletian (303–13). Many Christians welcomed martyrdom as an opportunity to share in the sufferings of Christ, and Christianity continued to grow despite all attempts to suppress it.

The principal theme of early Christian theological development was the interpretation of the faith in terms of concepts drawn from Greek philosophical thought. This process was begun by Saint JUSTIN MARTYR, TERTULLIAN, ORIGEN, and other apologists of the 2d and 3d centuries. Following the recognition of Christianity by Emperor Constantine I in the early 4th century, it was continued in a lengthy controversy about the person of Christ. The problem was to define the Trinity in a way that preserved monotheism. The councils of Nicaea (325), Constantinople (381), Ephesus (431), and Chalcedon (451) repudiated among them the alternatives of Monarchianism, Modalism, ARIANISM, NESTORIANISM, and MONOPHYSITISM.

The condemnation of Monophysitism alienated the churches of Egypt, Syria, Mesopotamia, and Armenia, creating dissention in the Eastern Roman (Byzantine) Empire and lessening its ability to withstand the Islamic invasion in the 7th century. For the later history of Christianity, see MIDDLE AGES; MISSIONS, CHRISTIAN; ORTHODOX CHURCH; PAPACY; PROTESTANTISM; REFORMATION; and ROMAN CATHOLIC CHURCH.

Christie, Dame Agatha

Christie, Dame Agatha Dame Agatha Christie, b. Sept. 15, 1890, d. Jan. 12, 1976, was for more than half a century the foremost British writer of mystery novels. Her books have been translated into every major language, and her two most famous creations, the Belgian detective Hercule Poirot and the village-wise Miss Jane Marple, solved dozens of murders after the appearance of her first Poirot book, *The Mysterious Affair at Styles*, in 1920.

Educated at home, she married Archibald Christie in 1914, retaining his surname for professional reasons after their 1928 divorce.

The prolific English mystery writer Agatha Christie was married to the archaeologist Max Mallowan, and she used Middle Eastern archaeological settings in several of her books, including Death on the Nile (1937). *In recognition of her success as a novelist and playwright, she was made a Dame Commander, Order of the British Empire, in 1971.*

Christie's first real success after the Styles book was *The Murder of Roger Ackroyd* (1926), which created controversy among mystery fans because of its unorthodox dénouement. From then until her death, she produced nearly 100 novels, notably *Murder at the Vicarage* (1930), which introduced Miss Marple in a starring role; *Murder on the Orient Express* (1934; film, 1974); *Ten Little Indians* (1939; films, 1945, 1965, 1975); and *Curtain* (1975).

Christie also enjoyed success as a playwright. Her *Witness for the Prosecution* (1954) was made into a popular film in 1958, and *The Mousetrap* (1952) ran almost continuously in London for more than 30 years. Christie's autobiography was published posthumously in 1977.

Christina, Queen of Sweden Christina, b. Dec. 8, 1626, d. Apr. 9, 1689, was the ruler of Sweden who gave up her crown to become a Roman Catholic. The daughter of GUSTAV II ADOLF, she became queen when her father was killed in 1632. She learned to speak seven languages, was thoroughly familiar with theology and philosophy, and learned her politics from Count OXENSTIERNA.

Christina's personal reign as queen of Sweden (1644–54) was distinguished by considerable political skill, but her chief interest was philosophy, which she studied under Descartes. She abdicated (1654) to become a Roman Catholic and pursue her intellectual interests in Rome.

At 18, Christina began to rule and soon established her own independent policies. In 1650 she won the recognition of her cousin, later CHARLES X, as heir apparent. Thereafter, she turned to philosophy, summoning René DESCARTES to her court, and to religion.

In 1654, Christina abdicated to become a Roman Catholic. She went to Rome and spent the rest of her life as a patron of arts and learning.

Christmas Christmas is the feast of the birth of JESUS CHRIST, celebrated on December 25. Despite the Christian birth stories, the church did not observe a festival for the celebration of the event until the 4th century. The date was chosen to counter the pagan festivities connected with the winter solstice; since 274, under the emperor Aurelian, Rome had celebrated the feast of the "Invincible Sun" on December 25. In the Eastern Church, January 6, a day also associated with the winter solstice, was initially preferred. In course of time, however, the West added the Eastern date as the feast of the EPIPHANY, and the East added the Western date of Christmas.

In medieval Europe, folk customs connected with the winter solstice were perpetuated together with the church celebration. The Puritans in England and in New England tried to abolish Christmas, but that move was unpopular, and Christmas survived and has been developed commercially since the Industrial Revolution. This has had the effect of pushing back the Christmas festivities to the period before Christmas; in the traditional church calendar the pre-Christmas season of ADVENT was one of quiet preparation, the festivities belonging to the Twelve Days (December 25–January 6).

Christmas Carol, A *A Christmas Carol* (1843), Charles DICKENS's popular tale of a miser's conversion through the agencies of love and fear, combines elements of the fairy tale, the allegorical dream vision, and the social tract. The story's most memorable elements are of cheer (Christmas food shops, Fezziwig's ball, the Cratchits' goose dinner, the game of forfeits at Scrooge's nephew's) and of pathos (the uncertain fate of crippled Tiny Tim). But Dickens also conveys his morbid concern with personal annihilation and his social indignation through the portrayal of the Ghost of the Future and the figures of Ignorance and Want attending the Ghost of Christmas Present.

Christmas Island (Indian Ocean) Christmas Island is in the Indian Ocean and lies about 1,370 km (850 mi) south of Singapore, between Australia and Indonesia. The area is 155 km^2 (60 mi^2). Volcanic in origin, the hilly island has phosphate of lime deposits that are worked by many of the 3,214 (1983 est.) inhabitants, who are of Malayan and Chinese descent. Annexed by Britain in 1888, it was governed from Singapore (1900–58) and then by Australia. In 1984 it became part of Australia's Northern Territory.

Christmas Island (Pacific Ocean) Christmas Island (1983 est. pop., 1,400), in the Pacific Ocean south of Hawaii, is one of the Line Islands. It is part of KIRIBATI (formerly the British colony of the Gilbert Islands). Its area of 518 km^2 (200 mi^2) makes it the Pacific's largest coral atoll. The island produces copra and has been used by Britain (1957–58) and the United States (1962) for nuclear tests. Capt. James COOK sighted the island on Christmas Eve 1777.

Christo [kris'-toh] Christo Javacheff, called Christo, b. June 13, 1935, is a Bulgarian artist-engineer. He began his career in Paris in 1958 by wrapping small objects, such as bottles, cans, and furniture, in plastic, a technique he calls *empaquetage*. In 1969, Christo produced his first monumental outdoor piece by wrapping 1.6 km (1 mi) of Australia's coastline in 90,000 m^2 (1 million ft^2) of polypropylene sheeting. These packages led to a series of curtain-fence works, initiated in 1972 by *Valley Curtain*, a 22,500-m^2 (250,000-ft^2) drape stretched 37,500 cm (1,250 ft) across a mountain valley at Rifle, Colo. In 1976, Christo expanded the scale in *Running Fence* to a 5.4-m (6-yd) curtain spanning 38.4 km (24 mi) across Sonoma and Marin counties, Calif. In 1983, for *Surrounded Islands*, he skirted 11 islands in Biscayne Bay, Miami, with sheets of flamingo-pink plastic. Because of the nature of Christo's projects, drawings, maps, photographs, and films are the only lasting records.

Christo Javacheff's 1976 spectacle, Running Fence, *a 38.4-km (24-mi) curtain spanning Sonoma and Marin counties in California, is one of the artist's many packagings, or* empaquetages.

Christoff, Boris [kris'-tawf] Boris Christoff, b. May 18, 1919, is a Bulgarian bass singer best known for his operatic performances. He made his operatic debut in 1946 in Puccini's *La Bohème* and in 1948, at La Scala, in Mussorgsky's *Khovanshchina*. He sang the title role in Mussorgsky's *Boris Godunov* in San Francisco in 1956. His repertoire includes some 40 roles in six languages. He is particularly admired for his work in *Boris Godunov* and in Verdi's *Don Carlos* and *Simon Boccanegra*.

Henri Christophe, the revolutionary leader who ruled northern Haiti as president (1806–11) and king (1811–20), appears in this painting by Richard Evans. A capable but autocratic ruler, Christophe built the citadel of La Ferrière and the palace of Sans Souci at Cap-Haïtien.

Christophe, Henri [kree-stawf'] Henri Christophe was a revolutionary leader who became king of Haiti. Born on Oct. 6, 1767, a black slave in the Windward Islands, he fought under TOUSSAINT L'OUVERTURE against the French in 1791 and led the rebel army in the successful uprising (1803–04) of Jean Jacques DESSALINES. Haiti became independent in 1804, and after Dessalines was murdered in 1806, Christophe succeeded him in the north. In 1811 he proclaimed himself king of all Haiti, but he never wrested control of the south from Alexandre PÉTION. Crowned in 1812, Christophe patterned his rule after the absolute monarchies of Europe, and although uneducated, he was an able ruler. On Oct. 8, 1820, paralyzed by a stroke and abandoned by his followers, he shot himself with a silver bullet.

Christopher, Saint Christopher, a 3d-century Christian martyr of Anatolia known only through legend, carried travelers across a river. One day he was carrying a child who became unusually heavy. The reason, he discovered, was that the child was Christ bearing the weight of the world. Christopher (the name means *Christ bearer*) is patron of travelers. Feast day: July 25 (on local calendars).

Christy, Edwin P. Edwin P. Christy, b. Philadelphia, 1815, d. May 21, 1862, helped create the first purely American entertainment form—the minstrel show, a variety show performed by white men masquerading as blacks. His Christy Minstrels, which played in New York from 1846 to 1854, popularized Stephen FOSTER's songs and established the minstrel show's format, including the role of master of ceremonies (interlocutor), which Christy himself perfected. He retired a rich man in 1854.

chromatic aberration see ABERRATION, OPTICAL

chromatography Chromatography, from the Greek for "color writing," is a method used in analytical chemistry to separate and identify the components of mixtures. The name now has no relation to the underlying principles but derives from the earliest techniques, which were applied to the separation of colored substances.

The Russian botanist Mikhail S. Tswett (1872–1919) was the first (1903) to employ a general chromatographic technique. This technique remained a curiosity until the 1930s, when a systematic investigation of its possibilities was begun under the leadership of the German chemist Richard Kuhn (1900–67). Partition chromatography was introduced in 1941, paper chromatography in 1944, and gas chromatography in 1952; the method of thin-layer chromatography was developed for general use in 1958. Since then, many chromatographic techniques have been developed that provide for specific needs. Among others, they include high-performance (or pressure) liquid chromatography, gel-permeation chromatography, ion chromatography, and countercurrent chromatography. Modern methods emphasize both sensitivity and speed.

Column Chromatography. In the simplest application of a chromatographic process, a vertical tube is filled with a finely divided solid known as the stationary phase. The mixture of materials to be separated is placed at the top of the tube and is slowly washed down with a suitable liquid, or eluent, known as the mobile phase.

The mixture first dissolves; each molecule is transported in the flowing liquid, and then becomes attached, or adsorbed, to the stationary solid. Each type of molecule will spend a different amount of time in the liquid phase, depending on its tendency to be adsorbed, so each compound will descend through the tube at a different rate, thus separating from every other compound.

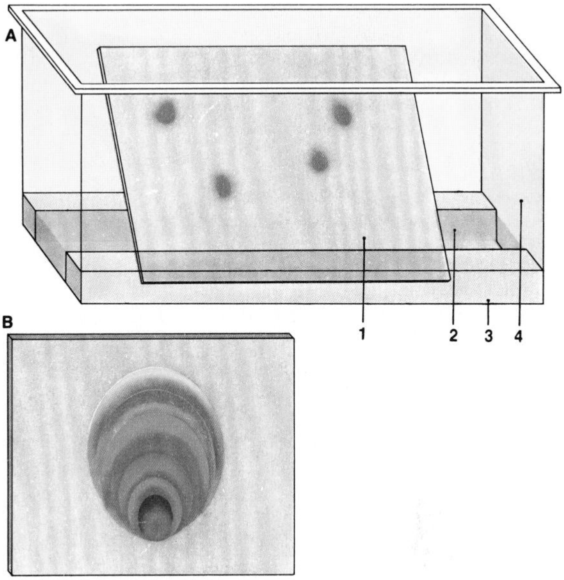

In thin-layer chromatography (A), *a spot of sample solution is placed near one edge of a specially prepared, thinly coated glass plate* (1). *When the sample dries, the plate is dipped in a small amount of solvent* (2) *at the bottom of an airtight development tank* (3). *A sheet of paper* (4) *impregnated with solvent and placed around three sides of the tank ensures a uniform, vapor-saturated atmosphere. As the solvent rises because of capillary action, the components of the original sample separate into a series of characteristic layers* (B).

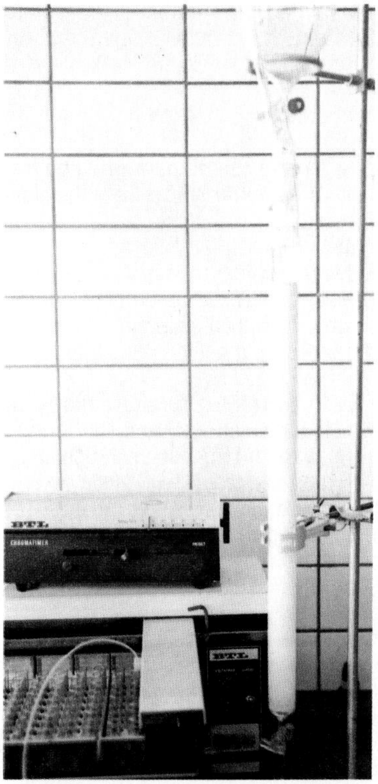
A simple chromatography apparatus consists of a glass tube packed with a finely divided supporting medium that can adsorb a sample added at the top. A solvent or series of solvents is run through the column, and the various constituents of the sample emerge at different times. A fraction collector automatically feeds the outflow into a series of test tubes.

Mobile phases may be gases or liquids, whereas stationary phases are either liquids adsorbed on solid carriers, or solids. When a liquid stationary phase is used, the process is termed partition chromatography, since the mixture to be analyzed will be partitioned, or distributed, between the stationary liquid and a separate liquid mobile phase; if the stationary phase is solid, the process is known as adsorption chromatography.

In the simplest form of chromatography, common adsorbents are silica gel, SiO_2, and alumina, Al_2O_3, which, for optimal flow, are powdered into particles between 0.05 and 0.2 mm (0.002 to 0.08 in) in diameter. If a suitable adsorbent is chosen, and the powder is impregnated with a liquid, stationary phases with very different properties can be obtained, and many different mixtures can be separated. Another technique in column chromatography, called stepwise, or fractional, elution, involves eluting with liquids of increasing or decreasing polarities. The emerging liquid (eluate) may be collected automatically in small portions by a fraction collector, and each fraction can then be analyzed separately. The eluate may then be passed through a spectrophotometer, which indicates, by measuring the light absorption, when a specific substance leaves a column. For the analysis of substanc-

In gas-liquid chromatography, a sample introduced into a heated chamber (7) is vaporized and carried through a coiled column (6) by means of a carrier gas (1). The column, which usually contains a porous solid coated with a thin film of a high-boiling liquid, is enclosed in an oven (3). Because the various constituents of the sample are adsorbed at different rates in the column, they are separated and leave the column at different times. Each component crosses the detector (4), which measures a change in conductivity relative to a reference detector (2). These changes are monitored by a Wheatstone bridge (8), which sends an electric signal to a recorder (9). A characteristic curve is traced out on a recording chart for each component.

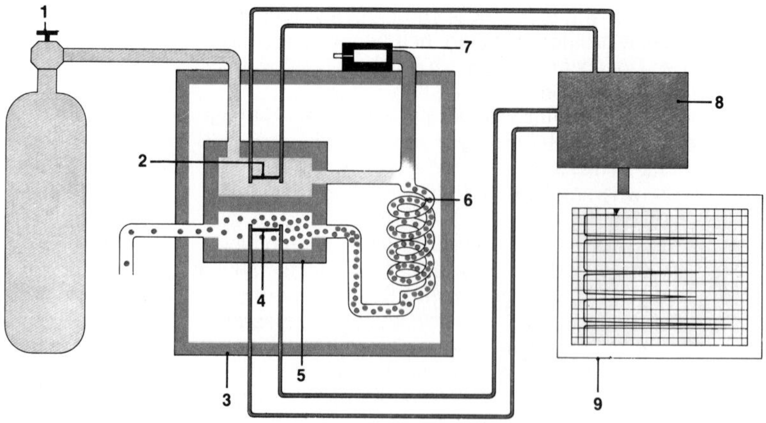

es still in the column, the solid can be carefully pushed out of the column, cut into small sections, and treated.

Other Types. Thin-layer chromatography (TLC) is a related technique, distinguished from the column method in that the stationary phase is a thin layer on a glass plate or plastic film. The term *gas chromatography* usually signifies gas-liquid chromatography (GLC), since the very similar gas-solid (GSC) method is rarely employed. This method can detect as little as 10^{-13} grams of material, and with this capability chromatography has become an essential analytical tool in any chemical laboratory.

High performance liquid chromatography, or high pressure liquid chromatography (HPLC), is a refinement of standard column chromatography and has become, along with GLC, one of the two most commonly used separative techniques.

Gel-permeation chromatography is based on the filtering or sieving action of the stationary phase. This technique is used to separate and measure the molecular weight of polymers, proteins, and other biological substances of high molecular weight.

chromite The only ore mineral of CHROMIUM is the mineral chromite, a chromium and iron oxide, $FeCr_2O_4$, in the SPINEL group of minerals. Metallic black chromite generally is associated with serpentinites, PERIDOTITES, and related rocks. It forms large, irregular, compact masses in ORE DEPOSITS and occurs in stony iron meteorites (see METEOR AND METEORITE). The mineral is also used to make refractory brick for furnace linings.

chromium The chemical element chromium is a lustrous metal of the transition series (see TRANSITION ELEMENTS). Its chemical symbol is Cr, its atomic number is 24, and its atomic weight is 51.996. It is a member of Group VIB in the periodic table. Chromium was discovered in 1798 by N. L. Vauquelin. Its name is derived from the Greek word for color, since most chromium compounds are brightly colored. Chromium, which does not occur free in nature, makes up 0.1–0.3 parts per million of the Earth's crust. The only important ore is CHROMITE. The red color of rubies and the green of emeralds, serpentine, and chrome mica are caused by chromium compounds. Chromium is an essential trace element in human nutrition. It is involved in the metabolism of the sugar glucose.

Preparation. Chromium metal is prepared by reducing the ore in a blast furnace with carbon (coke) or silicon to form an alloy of chromium and iron called ferrochrome, which is used as the starting material for the many iron-containing alloys that use chromium. Chromium to be used in iron-free alloys is obtained by reduction or electrolysis of chromium compounds. Chromium is difficult to work in the pure metal form; it is brittle at low temperatures, and its high melting point (1,900° C) makes it difficult to cast.

Uses. The most important use of chromium is in chrome plating, which creates a hard, wear-resistant, attractive surface. Chrome plating can be performed by immersion or by electrolysis. The latter allows very thin layers to be deposited, but the cathode current efficiency is only 10–15 percent.

Chromium is alloyed with iron to improve its resistance to corrosion, its hardness, and its workability. Genuine stainless steel always contains nickel and chromium. Super corrosion-resistant types of steel contain about 30 percent chromium.

Important nonferrous (iron-free) chromium alloys include stellite, which contains cobalt and tungsten and is used in cutting, lathing, and milling tools; and nickel-chromium (nichrome), which is used in resistance wire in electrical heaters, irons, and toasters.

Compounds. The most important valences of chromium are 3 and 6, although chromium with valences of 1, 2, 4, and 5 has also been shown to exist in a number of compounds. Chromium compounds often have a green color, but yellow, blue, red, and violet compounds also exist. The most important one is chromic oxide, Cr_2O_3, which is used as a pigment (chromic oxide green). A number of other chromium salts are also used in the textile industry as mordants. Chromium compounds with a valence of 6 are called chromates; most have a yellow color and all are toxic. When absorbed into the body they severely irritate the gastrointestinal tract, leading to circulatory shock and renal damage. Chromate yellow, $PbCrO_4$, one of the most important yellow pigments, is highly toxic because it contains both chromium and lead. Chromates are used as anticorrodents in water-cooling systems. Unfortunately, because they are toxic, their runoff has severe effects on river flora. It is desirable, therefore, to remove chromates before wastewater is released. Dichromates, such as sodium dichromate, $Na_2Cr_2O_7$, are orange red compounds that are widely used as oxidizing agents.

chromosome see GENE

chromosphere see SUN

chronic fatigue syndrome *Chronic fatigue syndrome* is the medical term for a grouping of symptoms that has also become known as the "yuppie plague," because it was first identified most commonly among young professional persons. Patients with the syndrome experience symptoms including severe fatigue, weakness, fever, sore throat and lymph nodes, confusion, depression, and a reduced ability to concentrate. First reports of the syndrome appeared in the medical literature in the mid-1980s. The Epstein-Barr herpesvirus was also often present in persons displaying these symptoms, but medical officials have ruled out this virus as the cause, which remains unknown. Treatment thus far has mainly been directed toward relief of symptoms. Research suggests that a drug called nifedipine, normally used to treat migraine and hypertension, may improve a patient's mental functioning.

Chronicles, Books of The two Books of Chronicles are the 13th and 14th books of the Old Testament in the Authorized Version of the Bible. The name Chronicles is a free rendering of the Hebrew title "events of past times." The author, known as the chronicler, is sometimes identified with Ezra. Those scholars who believe that Chronicles and EZRA AND NEHEMIAH were written by a single author date the work in the period 400–250 BC; others date Chronicles as early as 515–500 BC. Chronicles recounts biblical history from Adam to Cyrus the Great (d. 529 BC), paralleling and often directly excerpting from GENESIS through KINGS, but with additional sources, frequent omissions, and different emphases. Extracts from SAMUEL and Kings, historical and legendary materials, sermons, oracles, and prayers are included in a genealogical framework.

The work focuses on DAVID and SOLOMON as founders of the Temple and its priestly and musical orders. The departure of the northern kingdom of ISRAEL from the Davidic dynasty is deplored, and the history of the southern kingdom of JUDAH is told with the intent of reuniting all Palestinian Jews in the purified temple worship at Jerusalem in postexilic times (after 537 BC). Chronicles gives a more flattering view of Judah's kings than do the books of Samuel and Kings, and it emphasizes the element of miraculous divine intervention in biblical history.

chronology Chronology is the measurement of time and the arrangement of events in their order of occurrence. This includes both scientific chronology, which seeks to measure time in precise units and divide it by regular intervals, and historical chronology, which attempts to find a common denominator between the dating systems of many different peoples.

Only 300 years ago most educated Europeans held a relatively simple conception of chronology. The 17th-century Irish bishop James USSHER made perhaps the most famous attempt to calculate both human origin and the age of the Earth. He assumed, as did most of his contemporaries, that the Earth and the heavens were the result of one act of creation. Bishop Ussher carefully studied the genealogical tables and the lists of kings and judges of the Old Testament and arrived at the year 4004 BC as the date of creation.

Scientific Chronology. The development of the natural sciences eroded confidence in these earlier views. In 1788, James HUTTON, in his paper "Theory of the Earth," rejected such theological dating systems and propounded a modern theory of geology. Revisers of geological chronology introduced a new time scale that required millions of years to explain the slow development of the planet (see GEOLOGIC TIME). Similar developments in astronomy also seemed to imply that millions of years would be a more realistic unit of measurement for the solar system. Evolutionary biology also fit into this new scientific chronology, which dwarfed man's brief existence. New fields of study such as PALEONTOLOGY required new techniques for dating fossil remains. DENDROCHRONOLOGY, for example, dates variations in the environment through the study of tree rings.

Historical Chronology. Many ancient peoples devised their own chronological systems. Both the Chinese and the Egyptians traced their dynasties for thousands of years with elaborate annals or lists of kings. The Romans dated their history from the legendary founding of the city of Rome and recorded major events by reference to the dates in office of their consuls and, later, by imperial reigns. This method, however, does not easily permit accurate comparisons with the chronologies of other nations. A common or uniform system of chronology is essential to demonstrate the interconnectedness of human history.

In modern times historians have successfully imposed the Christian dating scheme. This arrangement focuses on the birth of Christ, set (somewhat inaccurately) in AD 1, and expresses dates before and after that fixed point. Using dates in the Christian Era as reference points, historians and archaeologists must still search for corresponding dates in the chronologies of the ancients. Fortunately, these rival chronologies occasionally record the same event, simplifying the task. The development of radiocarbon dating (see RADIOMETRIC AGE-DATING) has made it possible to assign approximate dates to documents and artifacts even when other accurate records do not exist.

chronometer A chronometer is an extremely accurate CLOCK or watch. The term is today most commonly applied to a device used to determine longitude at sea. First devised by Christiaan HUYGENS about 1659 in the form of a pendulum clock, the instrument was perfected (1764) by John Harrison of England after years of experimentation. To overcome the effects of temperature changes throughout the world, he incorporated an auxiliary clockwork drive system to maintain a constant driving force. He also used bimetallic strips, which had different rates of expansion, to act upon the balance spring.

The overall error of Harrison's number 4 chronometer, after 156 days of trials at sea, was less than 0.1 second per day. This instrument, which was 13 cm (5 in) in diameter, was the forerunner of accurate pocket watches. Maritime chronometers are normally set at Greenwich Mean Time, the recognized international time standard.

chrysalis see PUPA

chrysanthemum [kri-san'-thuh-muhm] Chrysanthemums, or "mums," are any of several annual and perennial herbs in a large genus, *Chrysanthemum*, of the daisy family, Compositae. Chrysanthemums are widely grown commercially for their showy red, white, or yellow blossoms, which are produced in late summer and fall. The blossoms range from daisylike in appearance to very shaggy. Although most of the popular varieties are new hybrids, chrysanthemums originally came from China, India, Japan, and Korea; they are the floral emblem of the Japanese imperial family. The Chinese and Japanese varieties are the tallest, reaching heights of 1.2 m (4 ft) or more. Indian varieties have the smallest flowers; Japanese varieties, the largest. Chrysanthemums should be planted in sunny locations, as they become spindly if grown in the shade.

Chrysanthemums are highly popular, late-blooming ornamental flowers. Seen here are (clockwise from top left) *the painted daisy; Shasta daisy;* C. zawadskii *var.* latilobum; *tricolor; and the pompon and the spoon, two classes of the florists' or garden chrysanthemum, a hybrid.*

Chrysler, Walter Percy Walter Percy Chrysler, b. Wamego, Kans., Apr. 2, 1875, d. Aug. 18, 1940, founded a company that became the second largest automobile producer in the United States. Originally a machinist, he had risen to works manager for the American Locomotive Company when, in 1912, he switched to the automobile industry. By 1916 he had become president of the Buick Motor Company, a division of General Motors. In 1921 he joined the Maxwell Motor Company, which in 1925 became the Chrysler Corporation. It absorbed Dodge Brothers in 1928 and later added Plymouth and De Soto to its product lines.

Chrysler Building The Chrysler Building, a landmark of the New York City skyline and one of the most admired SKYSCRAPERS in the ART DECO style, was designed by William Van Alen and completed in 1930. For a few months the 319-m-high (1,048-ft) office tower was the world's tallest building, until the completion of the rival 381-m-high (1,250-ft) EMPIRE STATE BUILDING in the next year. The Chrysler Building, a stepped tower rising from a massive base, is marked at each of its two major setbacks with wide decorative bands and colossal stainless steel gargoyles resembling car hood ornaments. The slender tower is crowned with a pyramid of stainless steel arched forms diminishing to a sharp needle point. The ground-floor lobby is a dazzling period piece in red African marble and patterned chrome steel.

chrysoberyl [kris'-uh-bair-ul] The rare mineral chrysoberyl, a beryllium aluminum oxide, $BeAl_2O_4$, occurs as a variety of CAT'S-EYE and as the red and green gemstone alexandrite. Its tabular crystals are transparent to translucent and usually yellowish green to green or brown. Common chrysoberyl forms crystals or loose, rounded grains in granitic PEGMATITES, and in METAMORPHIC ROCKS such as schist and gneiss.

Chrysostom, Saint John [kris'-uhs-tuhm] John Chrysostom, *c.*346–407, was patriarch of Constantinople and one of the four great Eastern FATHERS OF THE CHURCH. The son of Christian parents, John was educated in rhetoric and later in theology by Diodore of Tarsus. Feeling a call to the monastic life, he practiced a strict asceticism at home and later retreated to a mountainous area, after suffering damage to his health. On his return to Antioch, he was ordained deacon (381) and priest (386).

In 398, John was consecrated as patriarch of Constantinople. An ascetic in an age of luxury, John was unable to be subservient to the emperor ARCADIUS and his wife, Eudoxia. His tactlessness and idealism united the opposition, and he was condemned and deposed at the illegal Synod of the Oaks in 403. After a brief return to Constantinople, he angered the empress again and was forced to leave the city in 404. He died on an enforced journey to Pontus. Feast day: Nov. 13 (Eastern); Sept. 13 (Western).

A writer of pure, almost Attic style, John is one of the most attractive of the Greek preachers, and his eloquence gained him the name of Chrysostom (Golden Mouth). Most of his writings are in sermon form.

chrysotile see SERPENTINE

Chu Hsi see ZHU XI

Chu Ta see ZHU DA

Chu Teh see ZHU DE

Chuang-tzu see ZHUANGZI

Kyphosus sectatrix (top), *a sea chub, is unrelated to the freshwater chubs, such as* Leuciscus cephalus (bottom). *The latter is a game fish prized more for its spirit than for its palatability.*

chub Chub is a common name for several different species of the MINNOW, or CARP, family (Cyprinidae) found in streams and ponds of Eurasia and North America. They are similar to minnows in appearance and taste and, like minnows, are numerous. Hence, with other minnows, they play a significant role in freshwater ecology, preying on small aquatic life and being preyed on by other fish—or used as bait by humans. If any one species were to be designated the "true" chub, it would perhaps be the European chub, *Leuciscus cephalus,* which usually weighs about 1.3 kg (3 lb) but may weigh up to 5.4 kg (12 lb). It is considered a game fish and is also fished commercially in the USSR. Among North American chubs are minnows of the genera *Hybopsis, Nocomis,* and *Notropis*; the creek chub, *Semotilus atromaculatus*; and the lake chub, *Couesius plumbeus.*

Unrelated marine fish of the family Kyphosidae are variously known as sea chubs, rudderfishes, nibblers, and half-moons. Spiny-rayed fish that weigh about 9 kg (20 lb), they are found in tropical and temperate oceans.

Chulalongkorn, King of Siam [choo-lahlawng'-kohrn] Chulalongkorn, b. Sept. 20, 1853, d. Oct. 23, 1910, who ascended the throne of Siam (now Thailand) in 1868, is generally regarded as Thailand's greatest ruler. He was the son of Mongkut, Siam's first great modernizing monarch. Besides abolishing slavery, Chulalongkorn introduced major economic, administrative, and educational reforms. Although he ceded territory to France and Britain, he maintained Siam's independence in a period in which no other Southeast Asian country escaped colonization. He was succeeded by his son Vajiravudh.

Chun Doo Hwan [chuhn doo hwahn] Chun Doo Hwan, b. Jan. 18, 1931, became president of South Korea in August 1980. A career soldier, Chun had risen to the post of head of army intelligence by March 1979, and after the assassination of President Park Chung Hee in October 1979, he used his position to seize power. After the National Assembly was suspended in May 1980 he became head of a Special Committee for National Security Measures. In August he resigned from the army to stand as the sole candidate for president. Initially Chun used martial law to suppress all opposition, most notably in Kwangju. In 1981, however, he lifted martial law and was indirectly reelected to a 7-year term. Chun improved the economy and by 1987 agreed to institute democratic reforms, including direct presidential elections. In February 1988, he was succeeded as president by ROH TAE WOO. Later that year he resigned his official posts, apologized to the nation, and exiled himself to a monastery. In 1990 he testified concerning abuses during his regime.

Chungking see CHONGQING

church In Christian theology, the church is defined as the community of those who are called to acknowledge the lordship of Jesus Christ and to collaborate in his historic mission for the coming of the kingdom, or reign, of God. The word *church* is derived from Greek words meaning "belonging to the Lord," and "an assembly called forth."

In addition to designating the entire body of Christians, *church* is used to denote the individual Christian denominations, as well as the building used for Christian worship (see CATHEDRALS AND CHURCHES).

Church, Frederick Edwin Frederick Edwin Church, b. Hartford, Conn., May 4, 1826, d. Apr. 7, 1900, was a member of the HUDSON RIVER SCHOOL and one of the most celebrated 19th-century American landscape painters. He was the only formal pupil of Thomas COLE, with whom he studied (1844–48) in Catskill, N.Y. Unlike other members of the Hudson River school, Church was as much a scientist as an artist. He employed multiple perspectives in his panoramic views, which in scope recall some of Cole's allegorical works, although lacking their

Twilight in the Wilderness *(1860) exemplifies Frederick Edwin Church's contemplative, panoramic scenes that evoke the spiritual and physical grandeur of the American landscape. Church, a painter of the Hudson River school, dramatically portrays the glowing light effects identified with the trend now called Luminism. (Cleveland Museum of Art.)*

literary content. His paintings, such as *Niagara* (1857; Corcoran Gallery of Art, Washington, D.C.), were enormous, each rendered with meticulous detail and flooded with light.

In 1853, Church accompanied Cyrus Field on an expedition to Colombia and Ecuador, where the artist saw trackless jungles, great waterfalls, and Andean volcanoes. This trip, and a second trip in 1857, provided Church with dramatic and exotic scenic material. The vast tropical scene of *Heart of the Andes* (1859; Metropolitan Museum of Art, New York City) was so detailed that viewers were urged to look at it with field glasses to heighten the illusion. His *Cotopaxi* (1862; Reading Public Museum and Art Gallery, Reading, Pa.) is smaller but rivals even the sublime volcanic dramas of the English landscapist John Martin.

In 1867, Church visited Europe and the Near East; his sketches and paintings of ruins and Mediterranean landscapes are impressive without being theatrical.

Church of Christ, Scientist see CHRISTIAN SCIENCE

Church of England see ENGLAND, CHURCH OF

church music Music that is used as a functional part of corporate Christian worship can properly be called church music. By far the largest amount and the highest artistic level of church music may be found for the choir, that is, in CHORAL MUSIC. The traditional choral forms of the church—MASS, MOTET, ANTHEM, and CANTATA—were developed to fill the needs of the liturgies from which they sprang.

The music of the early church was intended for unison chorus (PLAINSONG), but the general acceptance of POLYPHONY in the Middle Ages moved the performance of part-music into the choir, which further benefited by the addition of instruments to the performing combination. In later years, such widely different sects as the Russian Orthodox and the Disciples of Christ have stressed choral music but have forbidden the use of instruments in their worship. Most denominations however, now use the ORGAN as an effective and affordable accompaniment for both choral and congregational singing.

Pieter Lastman's Altar Scene *portrays an early baroque ensemble performing sacred music of the period. Throughout the 17th century, the developing homophonic style of the baroque competed with Renaissance polyphony for acceptance as the appropriate music for use in church.*

There has been a centuries-long debate on the propriety of the popular idiom in church. Using secular music to "intoxicate the ear" was deplored in the 14th century by Pope John XXII. The CANTUS FIRMUS of the Renaissance was often taken from a CHANSON. Luther adapted secular tunes for his CHORALES, and, since the middle of the 20th century, folk and popular idioms have again been incorporated into the music of the church.

Church of the Nazarene The Church of the Nazarene is a Protestant denomination that arose out of the late 19th-century movement emphasizing scriptural holiness as taught by John WESLEY. Established in its present form at Pilot Point, Tex., in 1908, it resulted from the merger of three independent groups: the Church of the Nazarene, founded (1895) by Phineas F. Bresee (1838–1915) in Los Angeles, Calif.; the Association of Pentecostal Churches in America, formed (1896) in Brooklyn, N.Y.; and the Holiness Church of Christ, founded (1905) in Pilot Point, Tex. From 1908 to 1919 it was known as the Pentecostal Church of the Nazarene. Primary doctrinal emphasis is on entire sanctification, by which believers are freed from original sin and brought into "a state of entire devotement to God." The church's government is representative.

Churches of Christ Churches of Christ are independent congregations in the United States that operate without interlinking organization or headquarters; they are united by the direct adherence of each to the Bible alone as the sufficient rule of faith and practice.

The group operates colleges and universities, orphanages, and schools of preaching and has missionaries in international fields. Publications play a strong role in the life of the church. Faith in the verbal inspiration of the Bible, the divinity of Jesus, the necessity of compliance with biblical teachings, and a firm hope of everlasting life is characteristic of the group.

Churchill, Lord Randolph Lord Randolph Henry Spencer Churchill, b. Feb. 13, 1849, d. Jan. 24, 1895, was a leading member of the British Conservative party, who tried to increase its contact with the working class. A younger son of the 7th duke of Marlborough, he entered Parliament in 1874. In the same year he married Jennie Jerome of New York; their elder son was Sir Winston Churchill. Lord Randolph became secretary for India (1885) and then chancellor of the exchequer and leader of the House of Commons (July–December 1886), but he had to resign when the prime minister, the marquess of SALISBURY, rejected his budget proposals. His premature death curtailed a career of great promise.

Churchill, Sir Winston (statesman) Sir Winston Leonard Spencer Churchill, b. Nov. 30, 1874, d. Jan. 24, 1965, held most of the high offices of state in Great Britain, was a member of Parliament for more than 60 years, and served twice as prime minister. As Britain's leader through most of World War II, he personified resistance to tyranny.

Early Life. Winston Churchill was born at Blenheim Palace. His father was Lord Randolph Churchill, and his mother was Jennie Jerome, an American. Young Churchill loved to read history and poetry and was fascinated by soldiers and battles. From childhood he had an extraordinary memory.

In 1894, Churchill graduated from the Royal Military College at Sandhurst and was commissioned in the 4th Hussars. After service in Cuba and India, he took part in the Battle of Omdurman (1898) in the Sudan and then was sent to cover the SOUTH AFRICAN WAR for the *Morning Post.* He was captured by the Boers in 1899, and his daring escape made him an overnight celebrity.

Liberal Statesman. Churchill was elected to Parliament as a Conservative in 1900 and, although he found speaking an ordeal, quickly made his mark. His political sympathies began to change, however, and he abandoned the Conservative party for the Liberals in 1904.

When the Liberals came to power in 1905, Churchill entered the government as under secretary of state for the colonies. In 1908, the year of his marriage to Clementine Hosier, he became a member of Herbert ASQUITH's cabinet as president of the Board of Trade; in 1910 he was appointed home secretary and in the following year first lord of the Admiralty. Working closely with Admiral Lord FISHER OF KILVERSTONE, Churchill completed British naval preparations for war.

After World War I began, he attempted to exploit the navy's mobility in forcing (1915) the Dardanelles (see GALLIPOLLI CAMPAIGN). This audacious assault failed, and when the Conservatives, many of whom now detested him, joined the government in 1915, Churchill was removed from the Admiralty. After a period of active military service in France, he became (1917) minister of munitions under David LLOYD GEORGE. He subsequently served as secretary of state for war and air (1918–21) and for the colonies (1921–22) and helped negotiate the treaty (1921) that created the Irish Free State. But he lost both his office and his seat in Parliament when Lloyd George's coalition government fell in 1922.

Conservative Chancellor and Critic. Over the next year or two, Churchill moved back into alliance with the Conservatives. Returned to Parliament in 1924, he became chancellor of the exchequer in Stanley BALDWIN's Conservative government (1924–29). The measure with which he is chiefly identified was the return to the gold standard, giving the pound a fixed value against other currencies, in 1925. Churchill took this step with many misgivings, and it proved a mistake. During the General Strike of 1926, Churchill vehemently condemned the strikers. Afterward he tried to heal the breach with labor, but he was never entirely successful.

Between 1929 and 1939, Churchill did not hold office. He disapproved violently of Baldwin's Indian policy, which pointed toward eventual self-government. At the same time he warned against the ambitions of Nazi Germany and urged that Britain should match Germany in air power.

Sir Winston Churchill's expression in this famous 1941 portrait by Yousuf Karsh suggests the determination with which the wartime leader pledged his "blood, toil, tears, and sweat" to the task of defeating Nazi Germany.

When general war broke out in September 1939, Churchill was offered his old post of first lord of the Admiralty by Prime Minister Neville CHAMBERLAIN, and after the latter's resignation he replaced him as prime minister on May 10, 1940, just as Germany invaded the Low Countries.

War Leader. Churchill established personal relations with U.S. President Franklin D. ROOSEVELT, who began to supply arms to Britain immediately after the British army lost most of its equipment at DUNKERQUE (June 1940). In the late summer of 1940, as the Battle of Britain (see BRITAIN, BATTLE OF) raged overhead, Churchill daringly diverted an armored division—one of only two in Britain—to the Middle East. Although no one had been a more convinced opponent of the USSR, he decided immediately to give help to the USSR when it was invaded by Germany in the summer of 1941. The entry of the United States into the war at the end of the same year gave the Allies the advantage in greater resources.

Churchill, was determined that the slaughter he had seen in World War I should not be repeated. Accordingly, he refused to attempt an invasion of mainland Europe until North Africa and the Mediterranean had been cleared of the enemy. The Allied invasion of Sicily and Italy finally began in the summer of 1943, to be followed a year later by the Normandy invasion.

By this time, however, Churchill carried less weight in the general formation of war strategy. For example, in the final stages of the war he favored a fast Western Allied drive on Berlin to forestall Soviet occupation but was overruled by the Allied commander in chief, Dwight EISENHOWER, who wanted to crush the last German resistance in the West. At the time of the YALTA CONFERENCE (February 1945), when substantial concessions were made to the USSR, Churchill spoke in terms of high confidence about Soviet intentions. He soon came to a different opinion, and in 1946, in a speech delivered in Fulton, Mo., he spoke of the "iron curtain" that had descended across Europe.

A general election was called in Britain in July 1945, and the British electorate voted the Conservatives out. When the first results were received, showing a substantial swing to the Labour party, Churchill was taking a bath. He remarked: "There may well be a landslide and they have a perfect right to kick us out. That is democracy. That is what we have been fighting for. Hand me my towel."

Later Years. Nevertheless, Churchill felt deeply this rejection by the electorate and determined to reverse it. By the end of 1951 he was back in power, with a small majority. His energy in the first two years remained astonishing, but in July 1953, soon after his knighthood, he suffered a stroke. Sir Anthony EDEN, whom Churchill preferred as his successor, was himself ill at the time, and part of Churchill's motive in remaining in office was to ensure that Eden would succeed him. Churchill finally left office in April 1955.

Sir Winston's last ten years, marked by increasing health problems, were occupied by occasional travel, a little painting, and the publication of his *History of the English Speaking Peoples* (4 vols., 1956–58). This was the last of his many notable writings, which included *Lord Randolph Churchill* (1906), *Marlborough* (4 vols., 1933–38), and *The Second World War* (6 vols., 1948–54). Churchill occupies a special place in the affections of the British people, symbolizing a magnificent national performance in heroic days.

Churchill River (Newfoundland) The Churchill River in Labrador, Newfoundland Province, Canada, flows east 966 km (600 mi) and enters the Atlantic Ocean through Lake Melville. Near the middle of its course, the river falls 316 m (1,038 ft) in 26 km (16 mi); Churchill Falls is located on the river. The power potential is enormous and is exploited by a hydroelectric power plant. Before 1965, the river was called Hamilton, and the falls were known as Grand Falls; they were renamed for Sir Winston Churchill.

Churchill River (Saskatchewan-Manitoba) The Churchill River, in Saskatchewan and Manitoba, Canada, flows east through a series of lakes to Hudson Bay at Churchill, a deepwater port and railhead. It is about 1,600 km (1,000 mi) long and powers several hydroelectric plants. Its mouth was found by Jens Munck in 1619; trappers and traders used the river for shipping furs.

churn A container for turning milk into BUTTER, the churn has taken many forms through the centuries. The churning process was probably discovered accidentally when skins of milk were carried long distances and the jolting separated butterfat globules from the milk liquid, creating the thick aggregate, butter. Early churns were simply pottery jars for shaking the milk. The classic American wood-barreled dash churn had a long-handled paddle. Box churns, revolving drums, and rocking churns were all used until butter making was mechanized in the latter part of the 19th century.

Churriguera (family) [choo-ree-gay'-rah] The Churriguera family of Spanish architects and sculptors was active in Madrid, Salamanca, and elsewhere in Castile in the late 17th and 18th centuries. **José Simón** (d. 1679), its founding member, worked in Barcelona as a maker of altarpieces. **José Benito**, 1665–1725, and **Joaquín**, 1674–1724, are generally considered the creators of the so-called Churrigueresque style. This term is applied to lavish, highly ornate architectural decoration of the late 17th and 18th centuries in Spain. José's best-known work is the altarpiece in the Church of San Esteban in Salamanca (1693–1700), a three-storied structure of gilt wood is richly elaborated with spiral columns and foliated surfaces. As an architect, he designed (1709–13) the new town of Nuevo Baztán.

Notable buildings in Salamanca by Joaquín include the patio of the Colegio de Anaya, the Colegio de Calatrava (begun 1717), and the cupola and crossing of the new cathedral (1714–24; dismantled after 1755), his most intense revival of Plateresque (Spanish Renaissance) elements.

Alberto Churriguera, 1676–1750, another brother and the last important architect in the family, is remembered principally for the Plaza Mayor in Salamanca (1729–55) and for the lavish church at Rueda (1738–47).

Ciano, Galeazzo, Conte di Cortellazzo [chah'-noh, gah-lay-aht'-soh, kon'-te dee kor'-te-lya-tso] Galeazzo Ciano, b. Mar. 18, 1903, d. Jan. 11, 1944, was an Italian Fascist diplomat whose marriage (1930) to Edda, daughter of Benito MUSSOLINI, helped his political career. He was foreign minister from 1936 to 1943. Although he negotiated the Axis pact with Nazi Germany in 1936, Ciano became distrustful of Adolf HITLER when Germany went to war in 1939 without consulting Italy. Nevertheless, he urged Italian entry into the war in June 1940. When the war went badly, he joined the conspiracy that unseated Mussolini on July 25, 1943. Ciano was executed after Hitler reinstated Mussolini.

Ciardi, John [chee-ahr'-dee] The American poet, teacher, critic, and translator John Anthony Ciardi, b. Boston, June 24, 1916, d. Mar. 30, 1986, achieved lasting distinction in each of his disciplines. Ciardi's prize-winning, often ironic verse—beginning with *Homeward to America* (1940) and well represented in *Selected Poems* (1984)—sought to reaffirm in straightforward language central humanistic values of balance and good humor. After World War II army service he taught at Harvard (1946–53), then Rutgers (1953–61), also bringing his skills as educator to the Bread Loaf Writers Conference for nearly 30 years, half that time as director. Ciardi also served (1956–72) as poetry editor of the *Saturday Review*, forcefully enunciating his views on poetry and art in general. His introduction to poetry, *How Does a Poem Mean?* (1960), remains among the best of its kind. Ciardi's verse translation (1954–70) of Dante's *Divine Comedy*, however, is regarded as his greatest achievement.

Cibber, Colley [sib'-ur or kib'-ur] Colley Cibber, b. Nov. 6, 1671, d. Dec. 11, 1757, was an English dramatist, actor, and theater manager who excelled in writing light sentimental comedies, notably *Love's Last Shift* (1696) and *The Careless Husband* (1704). He also wrote many adaptations of Shakespeare. A colorful figure, Cibber was at the center of the theatrical events of his time; he managed Drury Lane Theatre from 1710 to 1740. His autobiography, *An Apology for the Life of Mr. Colley Cibber Comedian* (1740), is amusing and a valuable document of his times.

Cibola, Seven Golden Cities of [see-boh'-lah] The Seven Golden Cities of Cibola were ZUÑI Indian villages in present-day New Mexico that were rumored in the early 16th century to possess great wealth. CABEZA DE VACA and the other survivors of the disastrous Narváez expedition of 1528 brought back tales of apparently rich Indian pueblos. In 1539 one of the survivors, a black slave called Estevan, accompanied an expedition led by Marcos de Niza (*c.*1495–1558) to locate the riches. Estevan was killed by the Zuñi at the pueblo of Hawikuh, but Marcos returned to Mexico, where he gave a vivid account of the treasures in the pueblo, which he had not even entered. Francisco Vazquez de CORONADO led a better-organized expedition in 1540, took Hawikuh by storm, and found no riches there or in other Zuñi villages.

cicada [si-kay'-duh] The cicada is a blunt-headed, stout-bodied, winged insect of the family Cicadidae, order HOMOPTERA, which also includes aphids and other feeders on plant saps. In North America, where cicadas are also called harvest flies and locusts, the typical loud buzzings or whistles of the male insects may be heard in trees from June through September.

The cicada sound is made by specialized structures on the abdomen and apparently serves to attract females (and predators). After mating, females deposit eggs in slits they cut into twigs and thereby sometimes damage orchard and ornamental trees. Eggs hatch into nymphs,

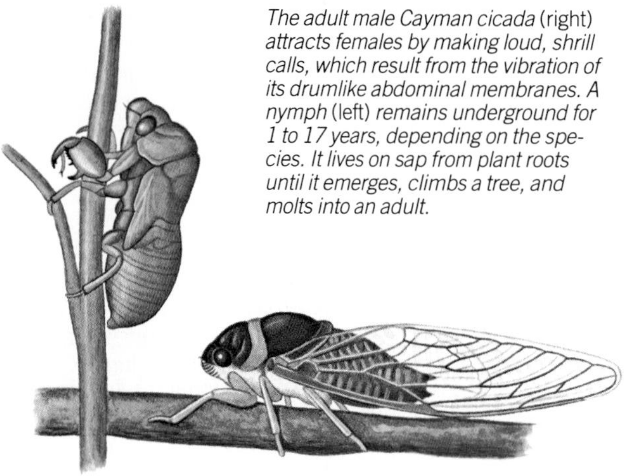

The adult male Cayman cicada (right) *attracts females by making loud, shrill calls, which result from the vibration of its drumlike abdominal membranes. A nymph* (left) *remains underground for 1 to 17 years, depending on the species. It lives on sap from plant roots until it emerges, climbs a tree, and molts into an adult.*

which drop to the ground and burrow into the soil, where they obtain juices from roots of trees and shrubs with their sucking mouthparts. Depending on the species, cicada nymphs remain underground from 1 to 17 years, then emerge.

Cicero, Marcus Tullius [sis'-ur-oh, mar'-kuhs tuhl'-ee-uhs] Famed for his oratory, Marcus Tullius Cicero was a political leader in ancient Rome. He was born at Arpinum on Jan. 3, 106 BC, to a locally prominent family connected with Gaius MARIUS. After a quaestorship spent (75) in Sicily, Cicero advanced his career through the courts and by promoting the interests of POMPEY THE GREAT, especially in the prosecution (70) of Verres and by his speech *Pro lege Manilia* (66). After holding the aedileship (69) and the praetorship (66), Cicero achieved his life's ambition, the consulship, in 63 BC.

As consul, Cicero suppressed the conspiracy of CATILINE, whom he excoriated in four famous orations (*In Catilinam*), and had several conspirators summarily executed. Pompey, who had become jealous of Cicero's prominence, later refused to help prevent Publius CLODIUS from forcing Cicero into exile (58) for these executions. Julius CAESAR offered to protect Cicero in return for cooperation with the so-called First Triumvirate, but Cicero honorably refused.

Recalled in 57 BC, Cicero tried to maneuver Pompey away from Caesar, but after the conference of Luca (April 56) he was forced to support the Triumvirate. Humiliated, Cicero turned to writing philosophical and rhetorical treatises—*De oratore* (55) and *De re publica* (54–51). After governing Cilicia (51–50), he returned to Rome on the eve of civil war between Caesar and Pompey. He finally joined Pompey and the republicans in Greece but took no part in the Battle of Pharsalus (48), where Pompey was defeated. Cicero then returned to Italy, was pardoned by Caesar, and again retired from public life.

After Caesar's assassination (44), in which he was not involved, Cicero returned to politics with renewed vigor. He boldly attacked Mark ANTONY but unwisely allied himself with Octavian (later Emperor AUGUSTUS), who played him false by joining Antony and Marcus Aemilius LEPIDUS in the Second Triumvirate (43). Proscribed at Antony's insistence, Cicero was killed on Dec. 7, 43 BC.

Although a champion of the republic, Cicero held a broader vision than did the narrow-minded oligarchs, such as CATO the Younger, who dominated it. Unlike most men of his time, including Caesar, he looked beyond his own self-interest. In his works on ethics—notably *De amicitia, De officiis, De finibus, De senectute, Tusculanae Disputationes*, and *De natura deorum*—he borrowed heavily from STOICISM and condemned EPICUREANISM. Cicero's political thought greatly influenced 19th-century liberalism, and his speeches and essays have had an unsurpassed stylistic influence in the West.

Cicero, a Roman orator and philosopher, was closely allied with the republican cause of ancient Rome. One of the greatest orators in history, Cicero bequeathed a body of rhetoric and prose noted for clarity of expression and thought. (Museo Capitolino, Rome.)

cichlid [sik'-lid] Cichlids (family Cichlidae) are perch-like freshwater fishes found in South America, Africa, Sri Lanka, and India, with more than 200 species in Lake Malawi (Africa) alone. The dwarf cichlid (*Nannacara anomala*) and the blue acara (*Pelmatochromis pulcher*) are popular aquarium fish, and *Tilapia* cichlids (ranging in

Jack Dempsey cichlid (for the boxing champion of the same name), found from Guatemala south to the Amazon basin, is a favorite aquarium fish. It grows up to 20 cm (8 in) long.

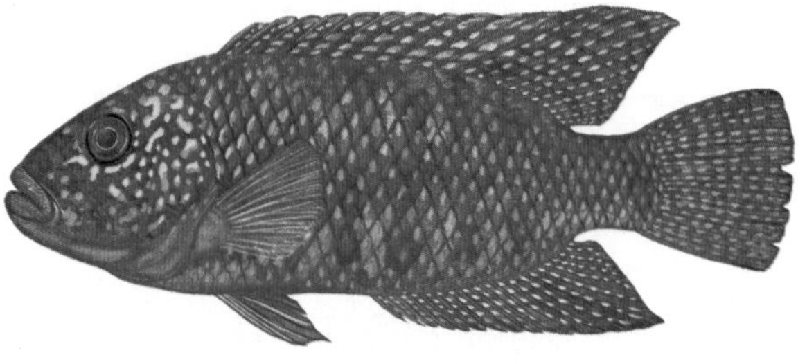

length up to 50 cm/20 in) are important commercial fish.

Some *Tilapia* cichilds exhibit mouth brooding. The eggs are fertilized either in the spawning pit or in the mother's mouth, where the brood then remains until hatched. (First the female lays the eggs in a spawning pit dug by the male, and then she picks them up with her mouth; authorities disagree as to whether she takes up the sperm released by the male into the pit or picks up the eggs after they have been fertilized.) After hatching, the young remain in the mother's mouth until they can swim independently. The young stay close to the mother, fleeing back into her mouth when danger threatens. Eventually the mother resists receiving the young into her mouth, and the offspring are forced to fend for themselves.

Cid, El see EL CID

Cid, The *The Cid* (1637) is a romantic tragedy by Pierre CORNEILLE in which the heroine, Chimène, must choose between her love for Spain's 11th-century soldier-hero Rodrigue and the obligation to avenge her father's death by his hand. Because of the lovers' family feud, the play has often been compared with *Romeo and Juliet.* Its theme of love versus honor was central to French neoclassical drama (see NEOCLASSICISM). Corneille based his play on two others dealing with the same subject (1618) by the Spanish dramatist Guillén de Castro y Bellvís.

cider Cider is a beverage made from the juice of apples. The apples are first washed and then ground into a fine pulp called pomace. The pomace is placed in a series of cloth- or straw-wrapped layers in a cider press, and the juice is extracted by pressure. Much of the best cider is produced by a careful blending of the juices from a variety of apples.

European cider is typically allowed to ferment; the sugar in the juice is converted into alcohol and carbon dioxide gas, and the cider has a yeasty, bubbly quality. In the United States, most cider is unfermented, often pasteurized, with preservatives added. Only a small proportion of the U.S. cider output is allowed to ferment, producing either hard cider or the apple brandy called applejack.

Cienfuegos [syen-fway'-gohs] Cienfuegos (1987 est. pop., 112,225) is a port city in central Cuba on the sheltered Cienfuegos Bay of the Caribbean Sea. Sugarcane, coffee, rice, and tobacco are grown in the area and then sent to Cienfuegos for processing and distribution. Visited by Christopher Columbus in 1494, the site was settled by French colonists in 1819. It was destroyed by a storm and then rebuilt and given its present name in 1825.

cigar and cigarette see SMOKING; TOBACCO

Cilèa, Francesco [chee-lay'-ah] Francesco Cilèa, b. July 26, 1866, d. Nov. 20, 1950, was an Italian opera composer and teacher. His first work, *Gina* (1889), was written while he was still a student in Naples. From 1896 to 1904 he taught at Florence and produced his most popular works: *L'Arlesiana* (1897) and *Adriana Lecouvreur* (1902). Cilèa's last opera, *Gloria*, was written in 1907.

cilia see FLAGELLA

Ciliata Ciliata is a class of unicellular aquatic organisms, the ciliates, belonging to the subphylum Ciliophora, kingdom PROTISTA. They are named for the many hairlike cilia projecting from their bodies, which beat rhythmically and drive the cell through water. The ciliates are the largest and most complex of the PROTOZOA, and some biologists believe they represent the zenith of evolution among unicellular organisms. They are also unique among all organisms in possessing two kinds of NUCLEI—macronuclei and micronuclei. Ciliates feed on bacteria and small protozoans and are animallike in their nutrition. Among the best known are the slipper-shaped PARAMECIUM, the bell-shaped VORTICELLA, and the trumpet-shaped Stentor. The only ciliate parasitic in humans is *Balantidium coli*, which may cause balantidiasis, a disease of the intestine.

Most ciliates have an oral groove and fixed mouth, or gullet, for food ingestion. Food vacuoles circulate within the organism while it is carrying on digestion, and waste products are discharged via an anal pore. In the subclass Spirotrichia (for example, *Euplotes*), a simple body ciliation is replaced by the equivalent of legs. Fused cilia, called cirri, move in steplike fashion and permit the organism to walk over surfaces. Ciliates of the order Entodiniomorphida, which occupy the alimentary tracts of herbivorous mammals, have a skeletonlike cell interior and an animallike mouth, esophagus, and anus.

Cilicia Cilicia was a historical region of southern Anatolia comprising two subregions: Cilicia Tracheia (or Aspera), a broken plateau district of the central Taurus Mountains; and Cilicia Pedias (or Campestris), the coastal plain between the Taurus and the Amanus mountains.

The former was an inhospitable region, which sheltered pirates in all ages. The latter was a richly fertile plain that has served as a strategic passageway throughout history. TARSUS, its capital, was the birthplace of Saint Paul.

Cilician history includes periods of interaction with the Hittites and submission to the Assyrians and Persians. In the Hellenistic period, Seleucids and Ptolemies of Egypt fought over Cilicia, the latter ruling it from 246 to 197 BC. From 67 to 66 BC, it was a Roman province. In the Middle Ages exiles from ARMENIA established (AD 1198) in Cilicia the Kingdom of Lesser, or Little, Armenia, which survived until conquered by the MAMELUKES in 1375.

Cimabue [chee-mah-boo'-ay] The Florentine painter Cenni di Pepi, 1240–1302, commonly known as Cimabue, was a major figure in the transformation of Italian painting from its Byzantine roots to a new assertiveness.

The solemn, monumental figures in Cimabue's Madonna with Angels *(c.1290) represent the culmination of the Byzantine style in Italy. (Louvre, Paris.)*

By exploring real appearances and human feelings in his works, he helped establish the predominant tradition in Western painting.

In the late 1280s and early 1290s, he frescoed parts of the Basilica of San Francesco in Assisi with depictions of the Virgin, Christ, angels, the evangelists, and the Apocalypse. On an exceptionally large wooden panel (347.5 cm × 220 cm/11 ft 7 in × 7 ft 4 in) intended to be viewed from a considerable distance, now in the Uffizi Gallery, Florence, Cimabue also painted *Madonna and Christ Child Enthroned* (*c.*1285), mother and child flanked by eight large angels. The panel illustrates the dual nature of Cimabue's style: the symmetry, gold background, and stylized gold hatching recall the old, Byzantine manner; the solid appearance of the throne and of the angels looks forward to the new style.

The only surviving documented work by Cimabue is the figure of St. John (1301–02) in the mosaic decoration of the apse of the Cathedral of Pisa. It is the sole basis for judging attributions made to him.

Cimarosa, Domenico [chee-mah-roh'-zah] The Italian composer Domenico Cimarosa, b. near Naples, Dec. 17, 1749, d. Venice, Jan. 11, 1801, is one of the fathers of comic opera. Cimarosa wrote his first opera in 1772, and during the next 15 years he created more than 40 stage works in Rome and Naples. He was court composer to Catherine II of Russia from 1787 to 1790, and then succeeded Antonio Salieri as music director of the Austrian court. In 1792 that he produced his most famous opera, *Il Matrimonio segreto* (The Secret Marriage), which is still frequently performed.

In 1793, Cimarosa returned to Naples, where he was received with honors and appointed court music director. His more than 60 sparkling operas are characterized by simple but memorable melodies.

Cimon [sy'-muhn] Cimon, d. 449 BC, was an Athenian statesman and general. The son of Miltiades, he was co-commander with ARISTIDES of the fleet that expelled the Persians from the coast of Thrace. Together with Aristides he formed (478–477) the DELIAN LEAGUE. Cimon liberated the Greek cities of Anatolia and destroyed (*c.*468) the Persian fleet and army at the Eurymedon River. A leader of the aristocratic party, he sought to assist Sparta against the revolt of the helots. He was sent home by the Spartans, however, and then ostracized (461) by the Athenians. Later recalled, he negotiated a truce with Sparta *c.*450 BC. He died in Cyprus on another campaign against the Persians.

Cincinnati Cincinnati, a city in southwestern Ohio on the banks of the Ohio River, is the seat of Hamilton County. With a population of 364,040 (1990), Cincinnati is one of Ohio's largest cities. The 7-county metropolitan area, in Indiana, Kentucky, and Ohio, is rising slightly in population and had 1,744,124 residents in 1990. Cincinnati rises from the Ohio River to a valley, known as the Basin, which is surrounded by hills.

Cincinnati is the most important industrial city in southern Ohio, and much of the population is employed in the manufacture of soaps and detergents, machine tools, and playing cards. The port of Cincinnati is busy; much of the cargo it ships is bituminous (soft) coal.

The University of Cincinnati (1819) is one of the oldest municipal universities in the country. Xavier University (1831), a Roman Catholic institution, and Hebrew Union College (1875), the oldest U.S. Jewish theological school, are also located in the city. It has a noted symphony orchestra, and the Cincinnati Art Museum and the Historical Society are excellent. The Cincinnati Zoological Garden is a progressive zoo. Riverfront Stadium, located on the Ohio River bank, accommodates professional football and baseball teams. An ambitious rehabilitation program has transformed the riverfront and the business district in the flat "basin" area to the north of the river. One of the projects involved the expansion of the city's convention center, which was completed in 1986.

Riverfront Stadium, a sports complex erected in 1970 along the Ohio River, is the home field of the Cincinnati Reds, history's first professional baseballl team (1869). The Basin, Cincinnati's downtown business district, appears in the background.

Cincinnati was founded in 1788 as Losantiville and renamed Cincinnati in 1790. The town grew rapidly during the following decade and became a thriving river port in the 1800s. With the influx of German immigrants beginning about 1840, the city became a center of grape culture and a wine market. A major UNDERGROUND RAILROAD station, the city remained loyal to the Union during the Civil War. It was long one of the largest and most influential cities west of the Alleghenies and was nicknamed "Queen City of the West."

Cincinnatus, Lucius Quinctius Lucius Quinctius Cincinnatus was a Roman patriot of the 5th century BC. He left his farm when named dictator in 458 in order to defend Rome against the Aequi and the Volscians. The invaders defeated, he returned to his farm after 16 days as dictator. Details of his life are uncertain and derived mainly from poetry. According to one account, he was dictator again in 439, when he suppressed a plebeian uprising.

Cinderella The story of Cinderella (literally, "little cinder girl") is a folktale of uncertain origin. The most familiar version appeared in Charles Perrault's *Histories, or Tales of Past Times* (1697; Eng. trans., 1729): a young woman is abused by her stepmother and stepsisters, is magically transported to a ball, and there meets a prince who falls in love with her.

cinema see FILM, HISTORY OF

cinéma-vérité see DOCUMENTARY

cinematography [sin-uh-muh-tahg'-ruh-fee] Cinematography, the act of directing the camera in cinema and television, is a creative art. It is also a field that requires a widely varied knowledge of the technical possibilities inherent in different types of cameras and lenses, photographic film, videotape, lighting, and special effects—both those made with the use of photographic elements and those devised with the help of computers.

In most films (and in many video productions) that have pretensions to quality, the cinematographer is involved in every stage of the film's creation, with the possible exception of the initial script. The director—who, in the early days of FILM PRODUCTION was also the cinematographer—has final control over every aspect of the picture, and the cinematographer may act simply as the director's assistant. Often, however, the director-cinematographer relationship is a collaboration, in which both determine the design elements of the film, its costumes, and locations. The cinematographer alone may decide on the type of film that will be used, the type of shots that will be most effective, the kind of lighting, how special effects will be achieved, and so forth.

The Technical Foundations of Cinematography

The cinematographer must be familiar with the many technical aspects of filmmaking, both on photographic film and on videotape.

Film and Video. Motion pictures can be recorded on light-sensitive silver halide–based photographic film, on magnetically sensitive VIDEOTAPE, or on VIDEODISC. Both film and video can be used to shoot within the studio or on location, to record movies with sound, color, and—within limitations—in three dimensions (3-D). All the requirements of image formation, with lenses of varying focal length, apply to both film and video production. Motion-picture film offers high image quality but requires laboratory processing. Video recording offers instant playback capability and can be transmitted via television but as yet lacks the high resolution of film. Movies on flexible photographic film are transported in cameras at speed (24 frames per second in the United States, 25 frames per second in Europe, for sound film recording) past a film plane, or gate. In the gate, the image is exposed briefly in fixed position as the camera shutter opens and closes. In video, an electronic signal containing both video and audio is magnetically recorded on tape (see VIDEO RECORDING).

Film and Video Formats. Format standards regulate equipment, film, and videotape manufacture, ensuring that movies can be played back successfully from machine to machine. Despite this standardization, there are more than 20 film and videotape formats in use. At the apex of this group in quality and cost is 35-mm motion picture film, a 25- × 19-mm image in a film 35 mm wide. Professional video formats range from 2.54-cm (1-in) to 1.27-cm (½-in) videotape cassettes. Films originally made for television have been shown in movie theaters in photographic form.

Sound. About 1930, when sound first became common in films, its effect was to transform the motion pictures into what was essentially a series of still shots in order for dialogue to reach the immobile microphones.

Walt Disney Company's Tron *(1982) was the first full-length movie to use computer animation. Half of the film is the product of computer devices that create special effects that would be impossible using conventional animation.*

Since all sound had to be recorded simultaneously with the photography, early sound cameras and their operators were enclosed in soundproof booths. Sound, it was soon realized, did not have to be recorded synchronously with the picture and could itself even be used to create illusion, in the absence of an image. Soon, the camera was freed to move in any way the cinematographer chose. Sound could be recorded simultaneously with the shot, using cameras whose motor noise was suppressed, or it could be "post-synched" in a sound lab.

Eventually, many different soundtracks were recorded into one master track, each with a different type of sound: close-up dialogue, distant dialogue, sound effects, and stereo music. With magnetic sound recording, any number of separate tracks can be recorded on up to six master tracks.

Aspect Ratio. The dimensional ratio of width to height that a picture appears to have when it is projected in a theater or shown on a TV screen is called the aspect ratio. The ratio for the vast majority of movies produced from 1895 to 1955 was 1.33 to 1—which also happens to be the basic shape of a television screen. In 1953, however, a new and almost instantly popular aspect ratio appeared: Cinemascope, a system based on the "anamorphic" lens, which could photograph a wide image and then "squeeze," or condense, it to fit standard 35-mm film. A lens in the movie projector restored the ratio to its original wide field, producing a projection aspect ratio of 2.35:1. Other wide-screen technologies of the time included a process called Todd-AO, which used 70-mm film, and Cinerama, in which three synchronized 35-mm cameras were used to photograph three contiguous images, which were transformed in the theater by three linked projectors into an image almost six times standard size.

In addition to requiring new ways of composing shots, however, wide-screen aspect ratios were not adaptable to the standard TV screen, so that the important action in any scene had to be confined to the center portion of the frame.

Two recent large-screen formats, IMAX/OMNIMAX and Disney's 70-mm 3D system, have inherited the niche once filled by Cinerama and Todd-AO.

Lighting. Lighting can alter the look and mood of a scene perhaps more than any other factor, and for many years the cinematographer devoted most of his or her time to designing lighting setups. Today, the increase in location filming and the use of films that are supersensitive to low light levels have changed the need for lighting as a basic photographic requirement, even for color film.

Special Effects. Beyond the reproduction of nature as it appears in reality, it was apparent from the beginning of the motion-picture art that the cinema could also deliver "magic," an illusion of reality. In addition to a growing vocabulary of narrative devices used by innovative cinematographers and directors, movies developed unique enhancements. The camera made people and things disappear. The simple opening and closing of the movie-camera shutter or a fade in and out could establish or end a scene. Undercranking and overcranking the camera produced fast and slow motion. Creative masking of the image area, or frame, produced a variety of image shapes and sizes. The glass shot, back projection, and the matte shot were developed. These are techniques of superimposing action and people on fake backgrounds, techniques that required complex in-camera shutters and high levels of precision in registration to ensure accurate reexposure in the camera. Such effects as fades, wipes, and divisions of the frame—which were at first accomplished by the camera—were eventually created by optical printers outside the camera, increasing laboratory control of special effects.

By about 1970 television-special-effects technology reached and then supassed motion-picture-effects tech-

A camera moving on a dolly track and a hand-held boom mike record a battle scene in Apocalypse Now *(1979), Francis Ford Coppola's nightmare vision of the Vietnam War.*

nology. Today, using combinations of electronic and photographic devices, the cinematographer and the director can specify a vast range of effects. Beginning with George Lucas's *Star Wars* (1977), whole new generations of special-effects equipment have become available. Model making has reached a new level of skill. Using computers and robotics, new camera systems ensure exact repeatability from scene to scene.

In the 1980s, Ampex in America and Quantel in England introduced new video devices that combine the elements of a conventional motion-picture optical printer, animation camera, and video shape and character generator with features that were once the province of the animator (see PAINTBOX). These new devices add color, form, and geometric movement by placing analog video in the digital domain and manipulating the image using computers. (See COMPUTER GRAPHICS.)

Three-dimensional motion pictures are among the oldest of cinematic special effects. The 3-D films shown at Walt Disney's Epcot Center offer remarkable quality. The system uses two interlocked stereo cameras and projectors for taking and viewing that utilize a unique 70-mm format and aspect ratio. The films must be watched in a special theater, and viewers wear Polaroid glasses.

Industrial and Commercial Cinematography

Areas of applied, nontheatrical cinematography include medical cinematography and motion study for use in engineering, like the photographing of automobile crash testing. High-speed cinematography has been used to study the operation of complex electrical and mechanical devices. Interactive videodisc and videotape have become staple training devices of corporate America and the armed forces.

The combination of rock-concert excerpts and avant-garde imagery produced a genre called music video (see VIDEO, MUSIC), first popularized on MTV, an all-music channel.

cineraria [sin-uh-rair'-ee-uh] Cinerarias are daisylike flowers that are grown by florists as greenhouse ornamentals; they can be planted outdoors in warm climates. They are hybrids of various groundsels, one species of which is thought to be *Senecio cruentus*, native to the Canary Islands. Cinerarias are perennial plants but are cultivated as annuals, being discarded after the blooming period is over. Their leaves are broad, heavily veined, and shiny; the top side of each leaf is green, and the underside is purple. The leaves and stems are covered with fine, woolly hairs. The flowers bloom profusely in dense clusters and exhibit a wide range of colors, including pink, blue, violet, or light red; some varieties have two or more colors. Cinerarias bloom in spring but can be forced to flower in winter.

The cineraria is grown as a houseplant for its richly colored, abundant flowers and velvety leaves. It is one of the more ornamental members of the groundsels and is related to the daisy and the sunflower.

Cinna, Lucius Cornelius [sin'-uh] Lucius Cinna, *c.*130–84 BC, was a Roman political leader and rival of Lucius Cornelius SULLA. Elected consul (87), he promised to retain Sulla's reforms when Sulla departed from Rome for war with Mithradates VI of Pontus. Instead he repealed Sulla's laws and was exiled from the city by the conservatives. He then allied himself with Gaius MARIUS, raised an army, and returned to Rome, where their combined strength destroyed Sulla's following. Cinna and Marius ruled as co-consuls until Marius's death (86). Then Cinna ruled alone, restoring order, extending citizenship to all Italians, and introducing financial reforms. He was killed in an uprising of his troops at Brundisium.

cinnabar [sin'-uh-bar] The only common ore of mercury is the mineral cinnabar, a mercuric sulfide, HgS. It occurs as bright-red crusts, granular masses, or earthy coatings that yield a scarlet streak. Cinnabar is found in areas of recent volcanic activity, where it was probably precipitated from alkaline solutions in veins, HOT-SPRING deposits, and porous volcanic rocks. It has been mined for more than 2,500 years at Almadén, Spain, which has the world's most important deposit.

cinnamon The spice cinnamon is the dried inner bark of trees belonging to several species of the genus *Cinnamon* of the laurel family, Lauraceae. The cinnamon tree, *C. zeylanicum*, the source of true cinnamon, is native to India and Sri Lanka and is cultivated in Sri Lanka and elsewhere in the tropics. Cassia, or Chinese cinnamon, *C. cassia*, is sometimes used as a substitute for cinnamon. This tree is cultivated in China, where it is native, and also in Indonesia.

Wild cinnamon trees reach heights of 9 m (30 ft), but the cultivated tree is kept pruned to shrub height. It puts out many slender shoots that are cut and stripped of their bark. The inner bark, which is the aromatic part, is separated and, in drying, curls to form rolled quills, or cinnamon sticks. Broken quills are used in making ground cinnamon.

cinquefoil [sink'-foyl] Cinquefoil, genus *Potentilla*, comprises about 500 species of creeping herbs and low shrubs that belong to the rose family, Rosaceae. They have leaves separated into five, sometimes seven, parts

Creeping cinquefoil grows in cool climates as a spreading ground cover. It has small, yellow flowers and stems that extend roots along their lengths. Native to Eurasia, this species has become naturalized in North America. Cinquefoil means "five leaves" in French.

and simple yellow, white, or reddish flowers. Shrubby cinquefoil, *P. fruticosa*, is native to the northern parts of North America, Europe, and western Asia. Reaching up to 1.2 m (4 ft) in height, several varieties of this shrub have been cultivated for landscaping.

CIO see AMERICAN FEDERATION OF LABOR AND CONGRESS OF INDUSTRIAL ORGANIZATIONS

cipher see CRYPTOLOGY

circadian rhythm see BIOLOGICAL CLOCK

Circassians [sur-kash'-ee-uhnz] The Circassians (Russian: Cherkess) are a people who inhabit the mountainous northwestern region of the CAUCASUS near the Black Sea, now largely a part of the Russian republic of the USSR. Their language, Adyge, which is also the name by which they call themselves, has two dialects, Kabardian and Circassian. The Circassians number an estimated 500,000 in the USSR and 150,000 in Turkey. Their economy is essentially agrarian.

Christianized in the 6th century, the Circassians converted to Islam in the 17th century when their territory, Circassia, was conquered by the Ottoman Turks. In 1829 the Ottoman Empire was forced to cede Circassia to the Russians; up to 500,000 Circassians migrated to Turkey, Bulgaria, and Yugoslavia.

Circe [sur'-see] In Greek mythology, Circe was a sorceress who could transform people into lions, wolves, and swine. When ODYSSEUS reached her island, Circe changed his companions into swine. Aided by Hermes, who gave him the moly plant as a charm against Circe's spells, Odysseus forced Circe to restore his companions to human form.

circle A circle is the set of points in a plane at a given distance from a fixed point in the plane. It is a CURVE having constant CURVATURE. The accompanying diagram illustrates some of the terms concerning a circle. The fixed point *O* is called the center, and the given distance *OS* is the radius. The word *radius* may also refer to any line segment between a point of the circle and the center. A chord, such as *RS*, is a segment whose two end points lie on the circle. A chord that passes through the center of the circle is called a diameter (*RT*, for example). The diameter is twice the length of the radius, and the word *diameter* may refer to the segment or to its measure. An ARC is either of the two pieces of a circle determined by any two points of the circle. For example, the two arcs *STV* and *SRV* are determined by the points S and V. A (straight) line (*TU*, for example) is TANGENT to a circle if it contains exactly one point of the circle; the tangent line will be perpendicular to the radius at that point. A SECANT is any line that intersects a circle at exactly two points.

The circumference of a circle is its perimeter. The ratio of the circumference to the diameter is the same for all circles. This ratio is denoted by the irrational number π (see PI). Thus, the circumference of a circle of diameter d is πd. The area of the region enclosed by a circle (usually called simply the area of the circle) is πr^2, where r is the radius.

Angles often associated with a circle are central angles, which are formed by two radii (angle *SOT*, for example); inscribed angles, which are formed by two chords with a common end point (angle *SRT*, for example); and circumscribed angles, which are formed by two tangents intersecting outside the circle (angle *TUV*, for example). A POLYGON is said to be inscribed in, or circumscribed about, a circle if each of its angles is an inscribed or circumscribed angle of the circle, respectively. The circle may also be said to be circumscribed about, or inscribed in, the polygon. The circle may also be described as one of the CONIC SECTIONS.

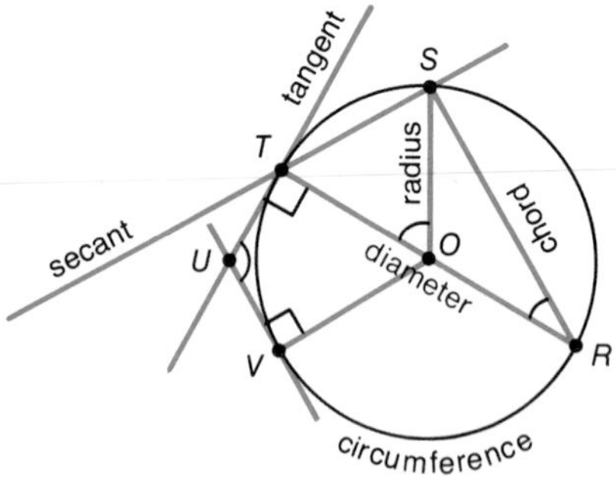

circuit, electric An electric circuit comprises interconnected electrical components forming a path for an electric current, which is a flow of electric charge. The ELECTRICITY often is used to produce a different form of energy, such as light, heat, or sound.

Parts of a Circuit

Most electric circuits have four main parts: (1) a source of electric energy such as a chemical BATTERY, GENERATOR, or SOLAR CELL; (2) a load, or output device, such as a lamp, motor, or loudspeaker; (3) conductors, such as copper or aluminum wire, to transport the electrical energy from the source to the load; and (4) a control device, such as a RELAY, switch, or thermostat, to control the flow of energy to the load (see SWITCH, ELECTRIC).

The source, which may be either DC (direct current, which does not vary in direction) or AC (ALTERNATING CURRENT, which periodically reverses its direction), applies an ELECTROMOTIVE FORCE (emf) to the circuit. This emf is measured in units of VOLTS (V) and is analogous to pressure. It determines how much current (measured in AMPERES) will flow in a given circuit. The typical supply voltage in the United States and Canada is 120 or 240 V at a frequency of 60 hertz (1 Hz = 1 cycle/sec).

Circuits may be broadly divided into four types: series, parallel, series-parallel, and complex circuits. They may be supplied from a DC or an AC source.

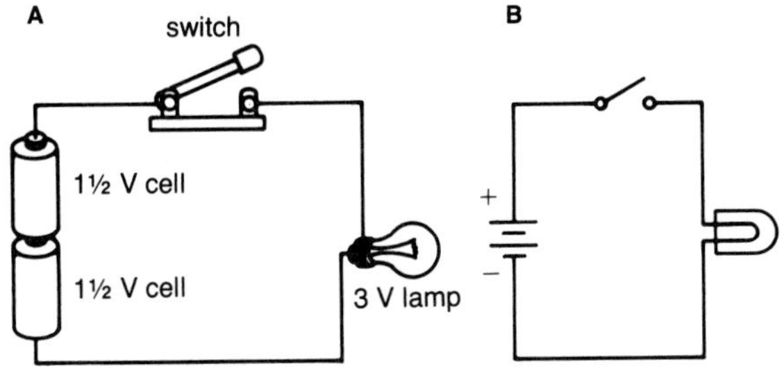

A simple electric circuit may be represented by a pictorial diagram (A), *which involves drawings of the electrical components, or by a schematic diagram* (B), *which consists of interconnected standard symbols used by electricians to depict specific components.*

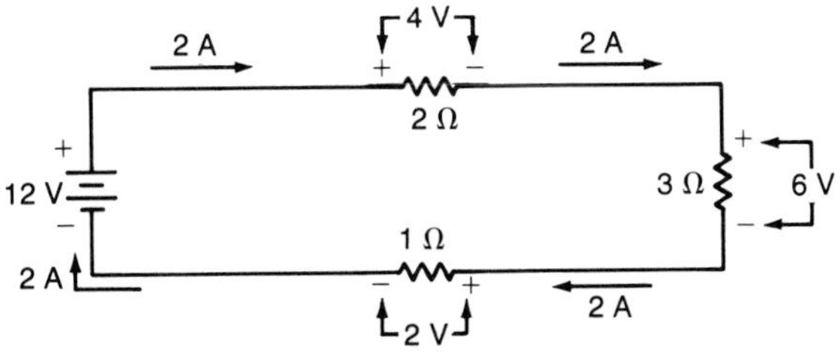

In a direct-current series circuit, such as a string of Christmas lights, all resistors (zigzag lines), *or lights, are connected in sequence. The voltage drop across each light depends on its resistance to the flow of electricity. Because the same current flows through all lights, the current flowing to other lights will be stopped if one burns out.*

DC Circuits

Series Circuit. A series circuit is one in which the current has only one path to take—from one side of the source, through the load, and back to the other side of the source. In a circuit with metallic conductors, this current comprises the very slow drift of ELECTRONS moving from the negative side of the source toward the positive side of the source. In some SEMICONDUCTOR devices—for example, transistors and semiconductor diodes—positive CHARGES also move in the opposite direction. This coincides with what is known as the conventional current, which is a current that is assumed to flow from positive to negative.

A flashlight is an example of a simple DC series circuit. In order to represent such a circuit, a pictorial diagram, which involves drawings that are similar to the physical appearance of the components, may be used. A method that is preferred by electricians and technicians is to use a schematic diagram comprising interconnected symbols, with each symbol representing an electrical component.

The source in a flashlight is generally two series-connected dry cells, each having an emf of 1.5 V, to supply 3 V to the circuit. A 3-V bulb is the load, and a slide switch is connected between source and load. The conducting path in this case is supplied by the metallic case of the tube holding the dry cells, or batteries. When the switch is open, no current flows and the lamp is off. When the switch is closed, a complete path exists and current flows through the circuit, lighting the lamp. The current heats the filament of the lamp to a white-hot incandescence, and in this state the lamp emits light in addition to heat.

If the current flowing in such a circuit is measured by connecting an ammeter in series with the lamp, the resistance (see RESISTANCE, ELECTRICAL) of the hot filament can be calculated by using OHM'S LAW. This law is an equation that relates the three quantities in a DC electric circuit: voltage (E in volts, V), current (I in amperes, A), and resistance (R in ohms, Ω).

Ohm's law may be written in the three equivalent forms: $E = IR$, $I = E/R$, or $R = E/I$. For example, if the flashlight current is 0.1 A from a source of 3 V, the resistance of the lamp R will be 30 Ω. The voltage could be measured by a VOLTMETER connected across the two cells.

Another common example of a series circuit is the series string of Christmas-tree lights. The disadvantage of such an arrangement is that if one lamp burns out, the electrical path is broken and all the other lights go out. When Ohm's law is applied to a series circuit, R is the total resistance of all the series RESISTORS. The total power consumed in such a circuit is the sum of the individual powers expended in each lamp.

Parallel Circuit. A parallel circuit is characterized by all the loads working at the same voltage as the source and independently of one another. That is, if one load is switched off, the remainder are unaffected. The electrical

In a direct-current parallel circuit, such as an automobile electrical system, all the resistors, or loads, are connected to a common power source in parallel branches. Each load is at the same voltage but draws a different amount of current, depending on its resistance.

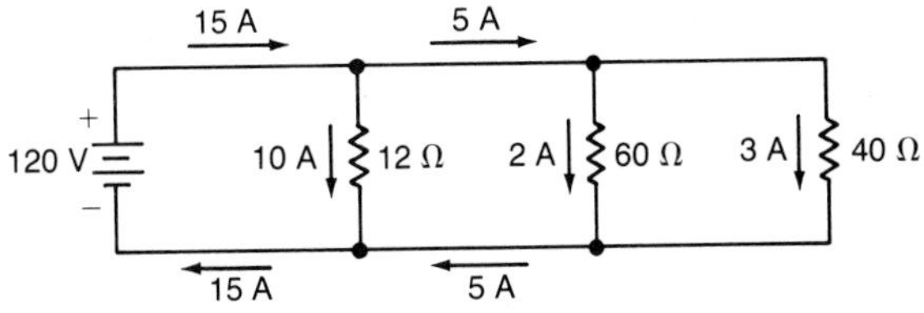

system in an automobile is an example of a DC parallel circuit in which the 12-V voltage from the battery simultaneously supplies electrical energy for the ignition system, headlights, taillights, radio, and air conditioner.

If another load is added in a parallel system, it supplies another path for the current, so that the total current from the source increases. This is an application of Kirchhoff's current law, which states that the sum of the currents entering any point in a circuit equals the sum of the currents leaving that point. The combined resistance of the parallel circuit effectively decreases whenever another resistor is added in parallel. Just as in a series circuit, in a parallel circuit the total power is the sum of the individual powers.

Series-Parallel Circuit. Series-parallel circuits are those that can be identified as having some components in parallel with each other, where the parallel combinations are in series with other components.

Complex Circuits. A complex circuit is one that cannot be broken down into sections of pure series or pure parallel combinations. A Wheatstone bridge, a circuit useful in measuring a resistance, is a good example (see BRIDGE CIRCUIT).

AC Circuits

Communications equipment, such as receivers and transmitters for radio and television, relies on the behavior of series and parallel circuits that have resistance (*R*), INDUCTANCE (*L*), and capacitance (*C*), when connected to AC. A circuit containing *R*, *L*, and *C* is called an *RLC* circuit.

A series *RLC* circuit will have the same current flowing through all the components. If the voltage across the resistor is observed on an OSCILLOSCOPE, a measuring instrument that shows a picture on a screen of how the voltage is varying, it will be found to have the same shape and time relationship as the current; that is, both the current and the voltage will reach a peak at the same instant and will be zero at the same instant. For such a case, they are said to be in phase with each other. The voltage across the INDUCTOR, however, is a quarter of a cycle ahead of the current and is said to lead the current by a phase angle of 90°. This is because the voltage depends on the way the current through the inductor is changing. The opposition to current flow supplied by an inductor is called its inductive reactance and is given by the formula $X_L = 2\pi fL$, where X_L is in ohms if *f*, the frequency, is in hertz and *L*, the inductance, is in henrys.

Conversely, the voltage across the CAPACITOR lags behind the current by 90°, because current flows into or out of a capacitor only when the voltage across the capacitor is changing. The opposition to current flow offered by the capacitor is given by the formula $X_C = 1/(2\pi fC)$, where X_C is the capacitive reactance, which will be in ohms if *f* is in hertz and *C* is the capacitance in farads.

The voltages across the inductor and capacitor are 180° out of phase, which means that one is at its maximum positive value when the other is at its maximum negative value. If the AC source, which may be an incoming radio signal, has a frequency of the correct value, then the inductor and capacitor voltages can be equal and cancel each other. This means that their oppositions to current flow also cancel and the IMPEDANCE of the circuit (the total opposition to current), which in this case is given by $z = \sqrt{R^2 + (X_L - X_C)^2}$ is a minimum and equal to *R*. As a result, a large current can flow in this circuit because only the resistance is opposing current. This condition is called series resonance and occurs at a frequency given by

$$f = \frac{1}{2\pi\sqrt{LC}}$$

where *f* is in hertz if *L* is in henrys and *C* in farads. This is very important because at this frequency a very large voltage can occur across both capacitor and inductor. It is this voltage that is amplified and used to generate the sound or picture. The circuit will respond to a range of frequencies, called its bandwidth, which must be wide enough to receive all the information being transmitted. Frequencies beyond this range, however, from adjacent stations, will not be picked up. Thus the series *RLC* circuit is said to be selective to a certain band of frequencies. By making either the inductor or capacitor variable it is possible to tune the circuit to any desired resonant frequency and receive a particular station.

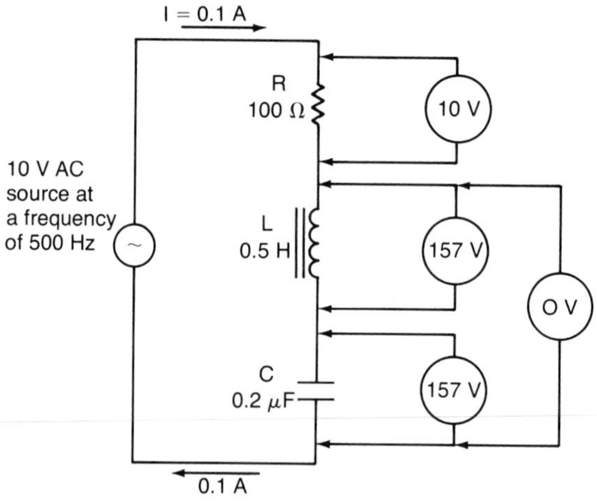

Alternating-current RLC circuits, used in communications equipment, contain a resistance (R), *an inductance* (L), *and a capacitance* (C) *in series. Maximum current flow results when the impedance is a pure resistance. Large voltage drops then occur across both the inductor and the capacitor and can be amplified for use in television circuits.*

A condition of resonance may also be produced in a parallel *RLC* circuit in which all the components have the same voltage across them but each has its own current. At a frequency given by the same equation as that for series resonance, a large current can circulate between the capacitor and inductor in what is called a tank circuit. This can make the circuit sensitive to only a certain band of frequencies, so that the circuit can be used in tuned amplifiers in radio and television receivers.

Parallel AC circuits are found in the home, where the loads are primarily resistive; that is, the loads behave as

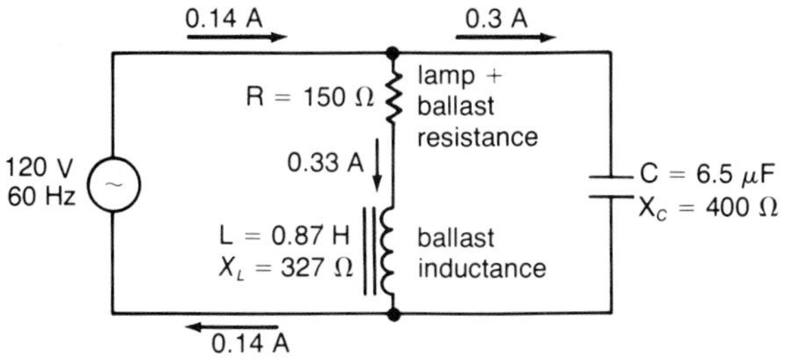

An alternating-current parallel circuit for a 12-watt fluorescent lamp uses a capacitor (C) *to reduce the source current needed to operate the lamp. Transfer of energy between the capacitor and the inductor supplies extra power that would otherwise be drawn from the source.*

resistors (for example, lamps, stove elements, toasters, and irons). Such loads as fluorescent lamps and motors in refrigerators and in furnaces are a combination of resistance and inductance. In industry, the load will most likely be predominantly inductive because of the large number of induction motors used. This can cause a problem to the power company because the current will be out of phase with the voltage, causing what is called a lagging power factor. This lagging power factor can be corrected by connecting large banks of capacitors in parallel with the inductive load at the factory.

circuit breaker see ELECTRICAL WIRING; SWITCH, ELECTRIC

circuit rider The circuit rider, or itinerant preacher, was the mainstay of the Methodist church during its early years in England and the United States. John WESLEY, the founder of METHODISM, pioneered in itinerant preaching. Francis ASBURY, an early leader of America's Methodists, was no less arduous in his travels. Before they died, Wesley had covered an estimated 480,000 km (300,000 mi) and Asbury about 440,000 km (275,000 mi)—mostly on horseback.

Under the supervision of bishops in the American church, circuit riders were the crucial link between Methodist classes (12 to 15 individuals) and societies (larger groups in a locality). Their duties were to visit each class and society at least once a month, quiz members on their growth in the Christian faith, study diligently, and preach the gospel. They brought order and a semblance of civilization to an unruly frontier population.

circulatory system The circulatory system of animals enables dissolved materials—oxygen, carbon dioxide, nutrients, and waste—to be transported throughout the body. The simpler the animal, the simpler the circulatory system. Conversely, the evolution of this system has made possible the development of complex organisms. This system is vital to the METABOLISM of all animal life, for it enables dissolved materials to pass from one area to another by means of DIFFUSION. Even in a single-celled animal, however, diffusion may not meet the body's metabolic requirements. Diffusion, therefore, may be aided by active transport of materials across the CELL membrane.

In animals that are several cell thicknesses in size, the central cavity, or COELOM, is often adapted to continually move the water in which the animal lives into, through, and out of the body. Larger and more complex animals have developed a specialized system of tubes through which a fluid circulates. This fluid is adapted, even in many invertebrates, to transport oxygen and other materials. In more advanced animals this fluid is known as BLOOD and contains hemoglobin cells. In primitive animals the motion of the fluid may be produced by the peristaltic action of the vessels containing the fluid; in more advanced animals muscular HEARTS pump the fluid.

In higher vertebrates the circulatory system is quite complex, with two twin-chambered pumps combined into a single heart of four chambers. One side pumps blood through the pulmonary arteries and veins of the RESPIRATORY SYSTEM, where blood is exposed to gaseous exchange with the environment. The other side pumps blood through the rest of the body to provide oxygen and nutrients to tissues.

Circulatory Systems in Invertebrates

The circulation in more primitive animals is characterized by that in the sponges and some coelenterates. In these animals the water in which they live is drawn into a central cavity through pores in the body wall. The water is kept flowing by the beating action of cilia, which are tiny hairs, and it circulates upward through an opening (the osculum). This circulation continually replenishes the fluid in which the body cells are bathed so that oxygen and nutrients are not depleted.

In animals such as bryozoans, nematodes, and ROTIFERS, fluids are moved through a primitive body cavity (the pseudocoelom) largely by body movements. In some primitive MOLLUSKS, the coelom is specialized to function as a pericardial cavity, the forerunner of a true heart. This cavity is connected by channels to the gonads and kidneys.

Most ARTHROPODS, ascidians, and many mollusks have a defined heart that pumps hemolymph (a primitive blood) through actual vessels and through a hemocoel, which is a specialized circulatory organ. In these animals, the hemolymph passes into the tissue spaces and then returns through sinuses to the heart.

The final stage in this type of development is a closed circulatory system, which is seen in some ECHINODERMS, LEECHES, oligochaetes, some polychaetes, and some mollusks. In closed circulatory systems, the transport medium, such as hemolymph in the INVERTEBRATES, is confined to specialized vessels, which constitute a complete circuit.

The hearts of invertebrates vary from simple vessels, which act by peristaltic contractions, to true hearts, which have muscle that contracts, creating pressure in their cavities. Even the invertebrates have considerable control over their circulatory systems, and measurements of pressure and fluid flow in those systems reveal considerable adaptation to movement, environmental temperature, and other influences.

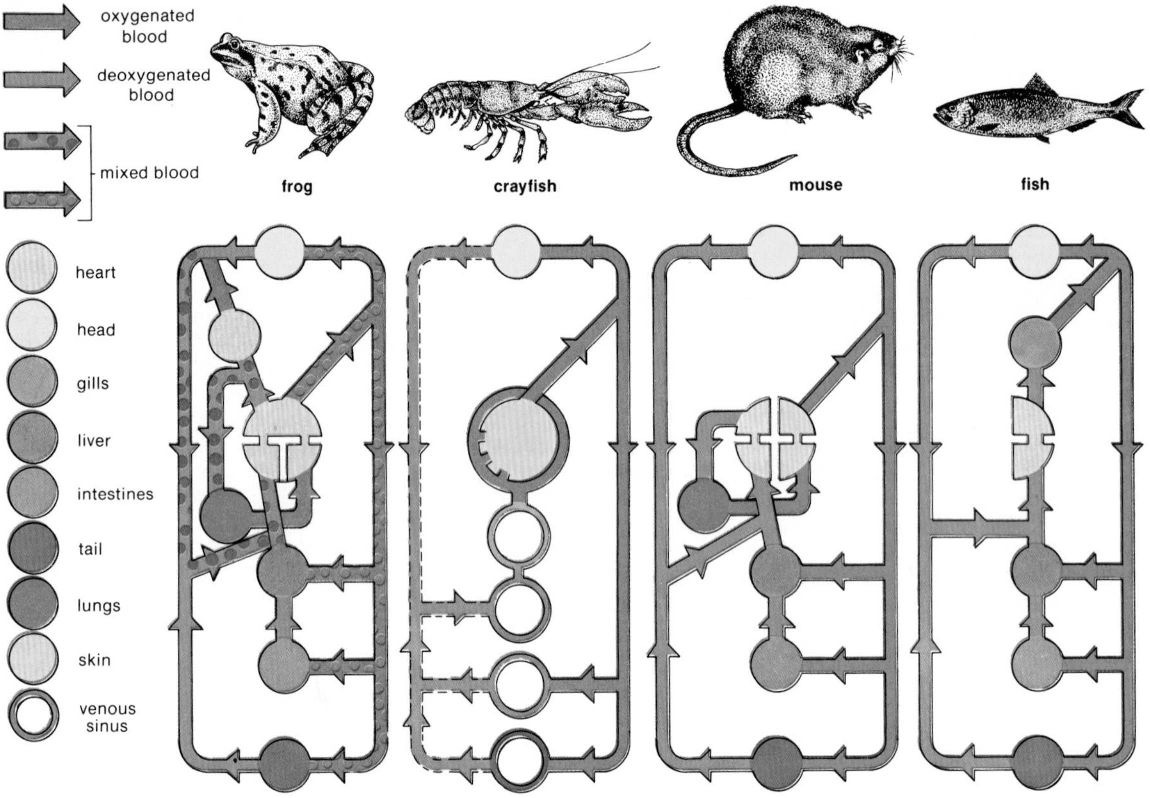

Diagrams reveal the differences in blood circulation systems of four animals. A frog has two systems—pulmonary and systemic—with blood passing from the vessels to the organs by means of capillaries. Oxygen-rich and unoxygenated blood mix in the heart, which does not have completely divided chambers. A crayfish has one system for the whole body, and blood flows from venous sinuses, which are open spaces, to the organs. Like the frog, a mouse has capillaries, two systems and a heart with completely divided chambers. A fish has capillaries and one circulatory system.

Circulatory Systems in Vertebrates

Vertebrates have closed circulatory systems. The most highly developed are in the higher primates, typified by humans. The systems vary considerably. In some the respiratory organs and the general body tissues are combined in a single circuit. In the more advanced vertebrates the blood makes a double transit through the heart; one system carries the blood through the respiratory organs (gills or lungs), and the other takes the blood to the other body tissues.

Most invertebrates have circulatory fluid that contains chlorocruorin (an iron-based pigment in combination with a porphyrin), hemerythrins (iron-based, but not with porphyrin), or hemocyanin (a copper-based respiratory pigment). All these pigments increase the fluid's ability to carry oxygen. Vertebrates, with rare exceptions, have blood that contains HEMOGLOBIN, a highly efficient oxygen transport medium that consists of an iron-porphyrin (heme) combined with a protein (globin). Some invertebrates also have hemoglobin, but it is usually dissolved in the circulating, or coelomic, fluid. In higher invertebrates (echinoderms and higher) the hemoglobin is confined to special blood cells. Vertebrates characteristically have the hemoglobin confined to such cells.

In cyclostomes and FISH, the heart drives blood through the gills, then distributes it by means of the dorsal aorta to the rest of the body tissues. Even in these primitive animals, there is relatively advanced control of the major blood vessels, and blood pressure and heart output are regulated to the needs imposed by exercise. In some primitive vertebrates (elasmobranchs and cyclostomes) a negative pressure is developed in the heart, which helps it to fill; TELEOSTS do not possess such a filling aid. Some cyclostomes have accessory hearts that serve important functions in moving fluid through low-pressure areas with semiopen sinuses.

AMPHIBIANS and REPTILES characteristically have three-chambered hearts (two atria and one ventricle), but the flow pattern in such hearts permits effective function of the heart as two separate heart pumps. In *Amphiuma*, alligators, iguanas, and other animals, left-to-right shunting of blood in the heart serves a useful function in adapting the animal to diving, excessive heat, and so on.

The Human Circulatory System

The human heart begins beating early in fetal life and continues regular beating after birth and throughout the life span of the individual, stopping only at the time of death. If the heart stops beating for more than three to four minutes, permanent brain damage may occur. Blood flow to the heart muscle itself also depends on the continued beating of the heart, and if this flow is stopped for more than a few minutes, the heart muscle is so damaged that it may be irreversibly stopped.

The human circulatory system is organized into two major circulations. Each has its own pump, both pumps being incorporated into a single organ, the heart. The right side of the heart pumps blood through the pulmonary circulation; the left side pumps blood through the systemic circulation.

Blood returning from the body tissues enters the right atrium, which is the upper chamber of the right side of the heart. When the muscles of this chamber contract, they force the blood into the right ventricle, which is the major pump chamber of the right side of the heart. When the ventricle muscle contracts, it forces blood out through the pulmonary artery and through the small blood vessels of the lungs. In these small lung vessels, the blood is separated from air by very thin membranes, and oxygen enters the blood and carbon dioxide leaves the blood by diffusion. This cleaned and refreshed blood then passes into the left atrium.

From the left atrium, the blood passes into the left ventricle. The muscular wall of the left ventricle is powerful, and when it contracts, it pushes the blood, under considerable pressure, into the systemic circulation by means of a large artery called the AORTA. The pressure developed in the aorta by the contractile forces of the left ventricle is great enough to drive the blood to all the tissues of the body in sufficient quantity to supply their needs.

The aorta has many branches, which carry the blood to various parts of the body. Each of these branches in turn has branches, and these branches divide, and so on until there are literally millions of small blood vessels. The smallest of these on the arterial side of the circulation are called arterioles. They contain a great deal of smooth muscle, and because of their ability to constrict or dilate, they play a major role in regulating blood flow through the tissues.

The blood passing through the arterioles passes through a bed of minute vessels called capillaries, which are a single-cell thick, so the exchange of nutrients and waste products takes place easily between the capillary blood and the tissue fluids. Thus, the arterialized blood that enters the capillaries becomes venous blood as it passes through them.

The capillaries empty the venous blood into collecting tubes called venules, and these in turn empty into small veins, which empty into larger veins, and so on until finally all the blood returns to the heart through two large veins, the superior and inferior vena cavae. These terminate in the right atrium, and the systemic circulation is complete.

A one-way flow of blood in this system is maintained by valves located in the heart and veins. Between the right atrium and the right ventricle is the tricuspid valve, which prevents blood from flowing from the ventricle back into the atrium. At the opening of the pulmonary valve is a set of semilunar valves, which prevent blood from flowing back into the right ventricle. Similarly, on the left side of the heart, the bicuspid valves prevent backward flow between the left ventricle and the left atrium, and another set of semilunar valves, the aortic valves, prevent blood from flowing from the aorta back into the left ventricle. Some veins also have semilunar valves, and the pressure of contracting muscles against the veins works with the action of these valves to increase the venous return to the heart.

All the energy required to produce the flow of blood is imparted to the blood by the contraction of the heart muscle. The movement of blood follows the physical principles of fluid flow. Hence, blood always flows from a region of higher pressure to a region of lower pressure.

The Heart. The heart is made up of two muscle masses. One of these forms the two atria (the upper chambers) of the heart, and the other forms the two ventricles (the lower chambers). These muscles are peculiar in that their cells are interconnected by protoplasmic bridges. As a result, each muscle mass acts as a single contractile unit, and activity beginning in one part of either cardiac muscle mass spreads automatically to the rest of that muscle mass. Thus, both atria contract or relax at the same time, as do both ventricles.

The two sides of the heart are separated by septa; in the adult human heart the interatrial septum and the interventricular septum are complete, so that the two sides are anatomically and functionally separate pumping units. Normally, an electrical impulse called an action potential is generated at regular intervals in a specialized region of the right atrium, called the sinoauricular (or sinoatrial) node. Since the two atria effectively form a single muscular unit, the action potential will spread over the atria; a short time later, the atrial muscle contracts, triggered by the action potential.

The ventricles also form a single muscle mass—separate, however, from the atria. When the atrial action potential reaches the juncture of the atria and the ventricles, the atrioventricular node (another specialized region for conduction) conducts the impulse. After a slight delay, the impulse is passed by way of yet another bundle of muscle fibers (the bundle of His and the Purkinje system) specialized for conduction to the muscle of the ventricles. Again, contraction of the ventricles quickly follows the onset of its action potential. From this pattern, it is apparent that both atria will contract simultaneously and that both ventricles will contract simultaneously, with a brief delay between the contraction of the two parts of the heart.

Before the contraction of the atria occurs, blood fills the ventricles, mostly by passive means. Thus, atrial contraction plays a minor role in the pumping action of the heart; it merely completes the filling of the ventricles, and the heart can continue to function quite well even when the atria are not contracting. A property of the heart muscle is its automaticity. This means that any part of the

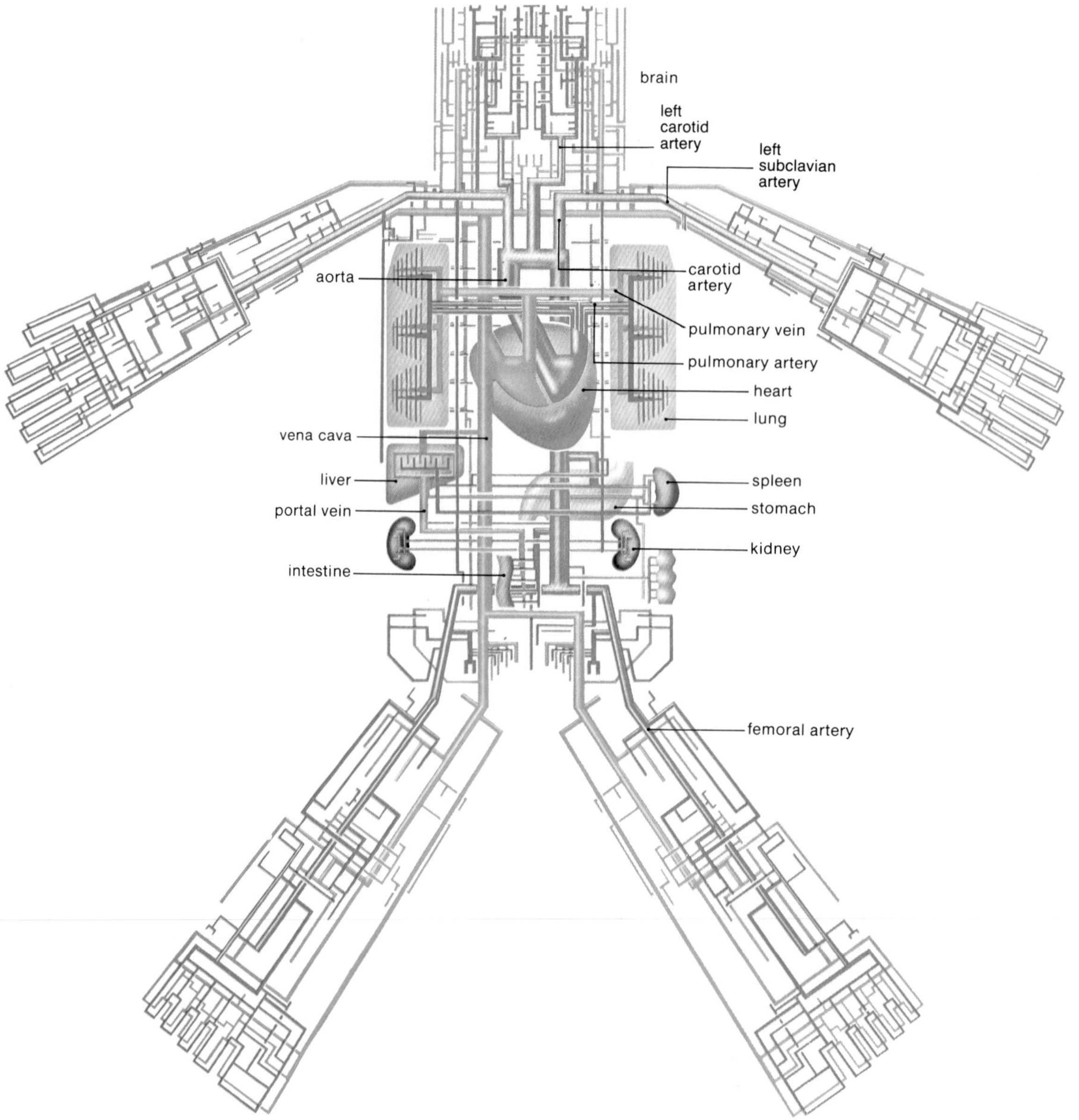

The human circulatory system, comprising the heart, arteries, and veins, is divided into the pulmonary and the systemic systems. The pulmonary system starts with pulmonary arteries that circulate oxygen-poor blood (blue) *from the heart to the lungs, where carbon dioxide is released as a waste product. Oxygen is absorbed from the lungs, and pulmonary veins carry oxygen-rich blood* (red) *back to the heart. The systemic system carries blood to all parts of the body. Oxygen-rich blood travels from the heart to parts of the body through the aorta, which is the largest artery. The blood travels through smaller arteries to capillaries from which oxygen and nutrients pass from the blood to the body tissues. Cellular waste products and carbon dioxide are picked up by capillary blood, which flows into veins. The vena cava, the largest vein of the body, carries the blood back to the heart. Blood vessels absorb nutrients from the stomach and intestines, and the liver and spleen act as blood reservoirs and filtering systems. The kidneys maintain the salt and water balance in the body and filter toxic wastes from the blood. The heart, brain, and lungs receive a large blood supply in order to maintain their vital functions. The carotid artery carries blood to the brain.*

heart can generate an action potential that can trigger the beat of the heart.

The amount of blood ejected by the left ventricle in each beat is called the stroke volume (SV), which is determined by a number of factors, the most important being the amount of blood in the ventricle before contraction. Thus, the rapid filling of the heart results in a larger stroke volume, as does a longer filling time (slow heart rate). The heart rate (HR) is the number of times the heart beats a minute. A normal resting heart rate is about 72 beats a minute. The cardiac output (CO) is the amount of blood pumped by the heart each minute. This is equal to the stroke volume (SV) times the heart rate (HR). Therefore, if the SV is 70 ml a minute and the HR is normal, the cardiac output would be 5,040 ml a minute. Since the total volume of blood for the average adult is about 5,000 ml, this equation (CO = HR × SV) would indicate that the total volume of the blood in the body is circulated every minute.

The cardiac output can be adjusted by altering both the stroke volume and the heart rate. The heart rate of a trained athlete may be increased during EXERCISE to as much as 150 beats a minute, and the venous return of blood to the heart is increased so that the stroke volume may be as much as 170 ml. Thus, the cardiac output under such conditions is 25,500 ml, an increase over the resting value of more than 400 percent. Strenuous activity is made possible by the adaptability of the pumping action.

The pressure in the aorta averages about 100 torr (0.14 kg/cm^2; 2 lb/in^2). The pressure of ejected blood must be greater than this in order to move the blood into the aorta. The pressure energy (equal to pressure times the volume) imparted to the blood by the contraction of the left ventricle is the primary source of energy for the work done by the heart. The right ventricle does about one-sixth as much work as the left ventricle, because the pressure in the pulmonary artery is only about one-sixth that in the aorta. Last, the heart must use energy in imparting motion to the blood. Thus, the total work of the heart is given by the equation $W = 7/6\ PV + mv^2$ in which W is the work per minute, P is the aortic pressure, V is the cardiac output, m is the mass of blood pumped per minute (nearly equal to the cardiac output), and v is the mean velocity of the blood as it passes through the valve openings. At rest, the work of the heart amounts to about 5 percent of the total energy expenditure of the body. The cardiac reserve represents the amount of work the heart can do over and above the requirements at rest. In a diseased heart, the cardiac reservé may be considerably reduced. Exercise and excitement, for example, may call for a cardiac output greater than the cardiac reserve can supply. The result may be heart failure. One complete heartbeat is called a cardiac cycle.

Heart sounds are characteristic of the cardiac cycle and are important in assessing the functioning of the heart. These sounds are associated with the closing of the valves of the heart. There are two major sounds, the first generated by the closing of the atrioventricular valves, and the second by the closing of the semilunar valves of the pulmonary artery and aorta. The sound vibrations are

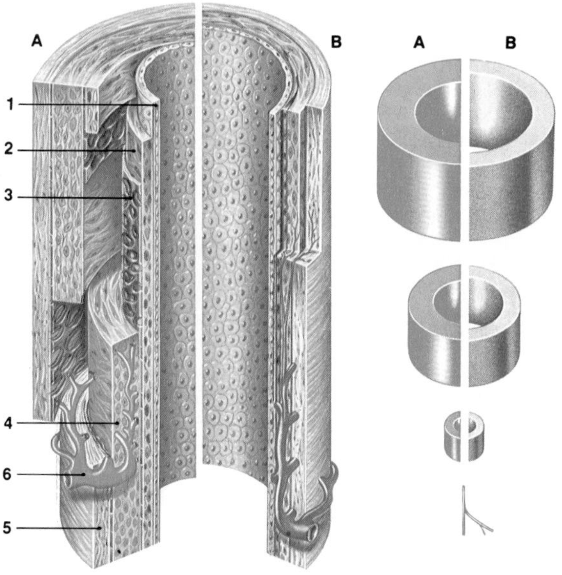

Arteries (A) *and veins* (B), *which are vessels that circulate blood throughout the body, have similar structures, although the arteries have thicker walls* (indicated at right) *in order to withstand the pressure of blood being pumped from the heart. The inner layer of a blood vessel consists of a lining of epithelial cells* (1), *connective tissue* (2), *and elastic tissue* (3). *The middle layer* (4) *is composed of smooth muscle, and the outer layer* (5) *is made of connective tissue and is supplied with blood by minute capillaries* (6).

caused by the stretching of the elastic parts of these valves. The physician, listening to these sounds with a STETHOSCOPE, can tell a great deal about the condition of the heart, and especially the valves.

Blood Vessels. The largest blood vessel in the body is the aorta. Its walls are thick and made of a strong elastic material. Its primary functions are to act as a reservoir for the temporary storage of blood and the distribution of the blood to the systemic circulation. The aorta curves up and back, then down along the spinal column into the abdominal cavity, ending in the lower extremities. All along its course, the aorta branches into the major vessels called ARTERIES. Each branching produces smaller arteries, but the total cross-sectional area of the arterial bed grows larger as this continues. Smaller arteries, the arterioles, contain less elastic tissue and more muscle tissue. This is important for the control of blood flow.

The arterioles supply a bed of capillaries, which are in intimate contact with the tissues. Many of these capillaries are so small that a red blood cell (diameter about 7 microns/0.0003 in) can barely squeeze through. Pores in the capillary wall are large enough to allow the water, sugar, dissolved gases, and other small molecules to pass through them, but small enough to hold back the larger protein molecules.

VEINS are quite thin-walled and are subject to low pressures. Some large veins have valves that serve, with the aid of outside pressure from contracting muscles, to increase the venous return of blood to the heart.

The ability of the aorta and large arteries to act as an elastic reservoir for blood serves to reduce the amount of pressure produced by the ejection of blood into them by the heart. The pressure swing, or pulse pressure, is about 40 torr (0.056 kg/cm^2; 0.8 lb/in^2) at rest. The maximum pressure (systolic pressure) is about 120 torr (0.168 kg/cm^2; 2.4 lb/in^2). The minimum pressure (diastolic pressure), reached as blood drains out of the central reservoir before the next cardiac ejection, is about 80 torr (0.112 kg/cm^2; 1.6 lb/in^2). The mean arterial pressure, as stated, is about 100 torr. For practical purposes, this is the effective pressure producing blood flow. The mean pressure falls gradually in large arteries and more rapidly in small arteries. There is a marked drop in pressure across arterioles, and a modest decrease in capillaries.

The difference in pressures at the arterial and venous ends of the capillaries results in the movement of fluid into the tissue spaces at the arterial end, and from the tissue spaces into the capillaries at the venous end.

Blood Flow in the System. In general, the flow of blood follows the laws of fluid flow. The basic law is expressed by the equation: flow = pressure ÷ resistance. In cardiovascular physiology, the flow considered is usually cardiac output; the pressure is the mean arterial pressure; and the resistance is the resistance to flow of the small blood vessels, especially in the arterioles. Taken in greater detail, this law, as applied to the flow of viscous fluids through rigid tubes, is known as Poiseuille's equation, by which the flow of blood can be roughly described. That equation assumes, however, that the fluid is truly Newtonian, and blood is not; it also assumes that the tubes are rigid, and the blood vessels are not; and it assumes that the fluid is of constant viscosity, and the viscosity of blood is not. As an approximation and for some understanding about the control of blood flow, however, Poiseuille's equation is useful.

The flow of blood in the large and medium arteries is marked by pulsation, which is damped and barely discernible at the arterial end of the capillaries.

Control of Circulation. The pressure-flow relationships are basic to the control of circulation. All circulatory control is by the action of the heart muscle or arteriolar smooth muscle. Cardiac output is controlled primarily by the heart rate; arterial pressure by cardiac output and peripheral resistance; and the flow of blood through local tissue beds by arteriolar constriction or dilation.

The heart muscle and smooth muscle of the circulatory system are controlled by nerves that originate in the medulla oblongata of the brain. These in turn are influenced by nerve impulses from receptors in many parts of the body.

circumcision Circumcision is an operation in which all or part of the prepuce, or foreskin, of the penis is amputated. In many primitive societies it serves as a major part of boys' initiation rites into manhood, and among certain religious groups it is a practice of great religious significance. Circumcision is known to have been practiced in ancient Egypt even before it was introduced to the Jews as part of God's covenant with Abraham, as recorded in Genesis 17:12-13.

For Muslims the authority for circumcision came not from the Koran but from the example of the Prophet Muhammad, who was believed to have been descended from Kedar, a son of Abraham's eldest son Ishmael. The more orthodox Jews and Muslims insist that converts also be circumcised.

Among most Christians, circumcision is not viewed as a rite of any religious significance, but neither is it forbidden. The one exception is the Coptic sect of Egypt and Ethiopia, whose members circumcise their male children before baptism. In many tribal cultures, notably in sub-Saharan Africa, circumcision is part of the rites of PASSAGE of puberty and serves a dual purpose, as a test of courage and endurance, and as a visible sign that a child has entered manhood. In some tribal societies, female circumcision—the removal of the clitoris and the labia minora—is also practiced as an initiation rite.

In modern times circumcision is often performed on newborn males, but physicians disagree on whether or not the procedure is medically advisable (other than in cases of malformation). On one side, urologists claim that circumcised males have far fewer urinary tract infections and are less at risk for catching sexually transmitted diseases than are uncircumcised males. On the other side, pediatricians say that the medical risks attendant upon the surgery far outweigh the possible future consequences of foregoing the operation.

circus The majority of circus acts—including trick riding, juggling, tumbling, and even the exhibiting of wild animals—can be traced to antiquity. The distinct form of entertainment called a circus was not created until 1768, however, when Philip Astley brought these separate features together and displayed them in a ring near London.

A 1910 poster for the Ringling Brothers circus advertises a popular equestrian act. The circus, a historic form of family entertainment, developed in England and later was exported to America.

The circus clown amuses the audience and eases the tension produced by the perilous feats of high-wire, trapeze, and equestrian performers. These clowns assume bizarre garb and character roles to win attention. (Ringling Bros. and Barnum & Bailey Circus.)

The Early Circus

Early circus programs were devoted largely to trick horsemanship in which the riders had to keep within view of the spectators. A circular performance area, or ring, was used. Bestriding two galloping horses, riding with one foot on the saddle and the other on the horse's head, and balancing head downward on a pint bottle placed on the saddle while firing a pistol at some distant target—these were just a few of the sensational feats exhibited by Astley and his competitors in the second half of the 18th century. In the 19th century such acts became more sophisticated. Costumed riders such as Andrew Ducrow performed pantomimes on horseback and graceful *pas de deux* with attractive partners. Others engaged in a more acrobatic style of equestrianism that included somersaults from one horse to another. Some formed human pyramids while riding several horses. The romantic period was also the great age of female trick riders, who leaped over broad bands of cloth (banners) and through paper-covered hoops (balloons), firing the imagination of the audience. Another type of acrobatic trick riding known as voltige, in which the rider leaps on and off a moving horse, was also popular from earliest times. In all these acts the "clown to the ring" played a prominent role, interrupting the performance with acrobatic comedy and wisecracks with the ringmaster, and thereby providing the riders and their mounts needed rest.

Indoor Circuses

Early circuses such as Astley's in London, the Cirque Olympique in Paris, and the amphitheaters of John Bill Ricketts in the United States were permanent, roofed structures. By the 19th century many of these buildings possessed, in addition to the ring, a large scenic stage for presenting spectacular dramas incorporating horses and any other animals belonging to the establishment. Although Astley's retained its stage until it was demolished in 1893, other circuses eventually dissociated themselves from the dramatic element and eliminated their stages, leading to the type of structure seen today at the Cirque d'Hiver in Paris (opened in 1852) and the modern Circus Krone in Munich.

The spectacular pageantry of trained elephants has awed circus audiences since 1874, when elephants first appeared in Howe's Great London Circus in England. Today, these Ringling Bros. and Barnum & Bailey elephants are ridden or accompanied by brilliantly plumaged performers.

Tent Circuses

Tenting circuses began around 1830 and culminated in the great traveling shows of Barnum & Bailey in the United States and "Lord" George Sanger in England. The first of these, at the time of P. T. BARNUM's purchase (1882) of the elephant JUMBO, accommodated 20,000 spectators. It featured the typical American format of three rings, in which individual acts played simultaneously; platforms were between the rings and at the sides for additional displays; and a large hippodrome track surrounded the rings for parades, races, and pageants. In the United States the combined Ringling Bros. and Barnum & Bailey Circus and a number of lesser circuses still follow this format, but it has never gained wide acceptance in Europe, where the single-ring circus is still preferred. Some circuses have had two and as many as seven rings.

Circus Acts

In the second half of the 19th century, a number of new acts were introduced to the circus. Among them was the flying trapeze, invented by the French gymnast Léotard (who gave his name to the one-piece garment worn by many circus artists and dancers today) and first exhibited (1859) by him at the Cirque d'Hiver. The character of Auguste appeared as partner to the traditional white-faced CLOWN, leading to the comic routines or "entrées" still popular in European one-ring circuses. Wild animal acts also became common around this time, especially after the "big cage" was introduced (1888) by the Hagenbecks. Before this, a number of trainers called "lion kings," and some "queens," had performed with caged animals in menageries and circuses, but such acts had suffered from space limitations and could not be seen easily in the ring.

A popular feature of traveling circuses in the second half of the 19th and early 20th century was the spectacular street parade, composed of richly carved and gilded wagons, one or more brass bands, "herds" of elephants, costumed artists mounted on horses or riding in chariots, and a raucous steam musical instrument called the CALLIOPE bringing up the rear.

The Modern Circus

Equestrianism, with which the circus began, has been relegated to a subordinate position in the circus today. The three-and-one-half somersault from a trapeze is now performed by many expert aerialists. The forward somersault has become routine for high-wire walkers. Jugglers perform on the backs of galloping horses, swaying on tightropes, or balancing on moving balls. Animal acts are more daring than ever, and unusual acts—a tiger riding a rhinoceros, a trained giraffe or hippopotamus—can be seen occasionally.

Abandoning its big top in 1956 to play in roofed, air-conditioned arenas, Ringling Bros. and Barnum & Bailey expanded to two complete circuses (the so-called Red and Blue Units) and opened a "clown college" at its winter quarters in Venice, Fla. There are, in addition, dozens of smaller circuses that appear throughout the United States every year. In the Soviet Union nearly every city has a permanent circus building, and thousands of performers belong to the government-subsidized organization of circus artists. Throughout Europe, and around the world, the circus maintains its vitality.

cirque [surk] A cirque is a steep-walled, rock-bound basin, shaped like half an amphitheater, that forms at the head of glaciated valleys. The floor is relatively flat and may contain a small lake. Both the floor and the head wall seem to be closely connected with a large, deep ice fissure, or crevasse, that forms between the back bedrock wall and the moving GLACIER. The crevasse is open in the summer when FROST ACTION tends to cause rapid disintegration of the bedrock wall. The debris from this process avalanches down into the bottom of the crevasse, is incorporated into the glacier, and scours the bedrock floor.

cirrhosis [suh-roh'-sis] Cirrhosis is a disease of the human LIVER characterized by destruction of liver cells and degeneration of liver function. The damage to liver cells is associated with disorders that block blood flow to the liver and may thereby cause portal HYPERTENSION, or excessive blood pressure in the portal vein; JAUNDICE, or the overflow of bile into the bloodstream; or ascites, an accumulation of serous fluid in the peritoneal cavity.

Cirrhosis may be caused by infections such as HEPATITIS or liver fluke, by toxic drugs, or by chronic ALCOHOLISM. The manifestations of the disease are caused by alteration of the liver structure, impairment of blood circulation, and death of liver cells. The liver has an unusual portal (venous) circulation that has two sets of capillaries instead of one. Veins draining the upper intestinal tract unite to form a large vein that divides again to form capillarylike structures, called sinusoids, in the liver; these reunite to form large veins that return blood to the heart. As liver cells die, the fibrous tissue is deposited around the sinusoids, disturbing portal circulation. Destruction of liver cells impairs the liver's ability to store nutrients and to detoxify chemicals.

cirrus clouds Cirrus clouds form whenever the air in the upper TROPOSPHERE rises sufficiently to cause ice crystals to form. Because many of the crystals become large enough to fall with a considerable speed, cirrus clouds often attain an appreciable vertical extent and thus appear as long, narrow filaments, or patches, of white cloud. Vertical changes in horizontal wind speed in the upper troposphere, as well as differences in the speed at which the crystals fall due to variations in their size, often cause the fibrous filaments to seem slanted or irregularly curved. Cirrus clouds that appear as a whitish, fairly uniform veil in the sky are called cirrostratus. Fairly uniform, small patches or ripples of cirrus cloud are known as cirrocumulus clouds.

Cirrus clouds, normally the highest of the high clouds, form at elevations of 6,100 to 12,200 m (20,000 to 40,000 ft). Comprised of ice crystals, cirrus feature elongate, feathered strands formed by rapidly moving horizontal winds.

Cirrus clouds that become thicker over time may be the harbinger of such meteorological phenomena as a warm FRONT, a hurricane, (see HURRICANE AND TYPHOON), or a THUNDERSTORM. In addition, long bands of cirrus clouds occasionally form from the moisture in the exhaust, or contrails, of jet aircraft.

Cistercians [sis-tur'-shuhnz] Cistercians are members of a Roman Catholic RELIGIOUS ORDER founded in 1098 by St. Robert, abbot of Molesme. He and a handful of monks left the Benedictine abbey of Molesme for a secluded area called Cîteaux, not far from Dijon in Burgundy, where they began an austere monastic life. From Cîteaux other monasteries were founded. In 1112 or 1113, St. BERNARD OF CLAIRVAUX entered Cîteaux. His forceful personality and holiness encouraged recruits, and he became the spokesman for this reform movement throughout Europe. By 1151 over 300 monasteries stood, with more than 11,000 Cistercian monks and nuns.

From the beginning, the Cistercians stressed a literal observance of the Rule of St. BENEDICT, withdrawal from feudal entanglements and responsibility, and a return to the simplicity and austerity of the early desert monks. They succeeded by uniting their monasteries through a constitution, called the Charter of Charity, that set forth a uniform type of life, checks and balances in monastic government, centralized authority under the abbot of Cîteaux, and an annual meeting of all the abbots in a general chapter.

The Cistercians wear white habits with a black scapular. During the Middle Ages, they were called the white monks. A reformed group of Cistercians was begun in the 17th century; they are known as TRAPPISTS. The original Cistercian monks are called Cistercians of the Common Observance.

cithara see KITHARA

citizens band radio Citizens band (CB) radio is a two-way radio system that functions as a wireless party-line telephone system for short distances. It permits two or more radio operators to communicate over a range of several kilometers.

Types. CB radios are commonly installed in automobiles and trucks so that the driver can obtain road and weather conditions and other information from operators in nearby vehicles or seek help in an emergency. Such CB radios are called mobile rigs. Hand-held, battery-powered CB radios, which use a compact antenna such as a telescoping type, are called walkie-talkies and have limited range. The maximum possible communicating range is obtained with a base station, a fixed unit with a large, outdoor antenna. Less-expensive units that receive but do not transmit are called receivers. Most units, however, can both transmit and receive and are called transceivers.

History. The Citizens' Radio Service was created in 1948 to provide two-way radio service for business and personal use. In 1958 the FEDERAL COMMUNICATIONS COMMISSION (FCC) acted to create a new Class D, with a band at lower frequencies (in the vicinity of 27 MHz). In 1976, it added 17 more channels to the former 23 in this band, making a total of 40 channels. CB radio in the United States was closely regulated by the FCC for several years, but the fad declined after 1977 and the FCC ceased issuing new licenses in 1983.

CB Language. CB operators have developed a special vocabulary to clarify and speed up the exchange of information over the air. This is especially important when atmospheric conditions interfere with clear transmissions. The 10-code, adopted by the Associated Public Safety Communication Officers (APCO), is perhaps the best-known system.

citizenship A citizen is a member of a legally constituted state, possessing certain rights and privileges and subject to corresponding duties. A citizen of the United States has the right to hold and transfer all types of property, to vote, to seek elective office, to hold governmental positions, to receive welfare and social security benefits, and to enjoy the protection of the Constitution and the laws. Some of these rights are denied to ALIENS, even though they may have been in the United States most of their lives. A U.S. citizen has the corresponding duties of paying taxes, obeying the laws of the United States, and defending it against enemies.

In most monarchies, including the United Kingdom, citizens are usually referred to as *subjects,* meaning that they owe allegiance to the sovereign. The term *national* is used, particularly in international agreements, to mean all those who owe allegiance to a state; in most states nearly

CONDITIONS FOR ACQUIRING U.S. CITIZENSHIP AT BIRTH OUTSIDE THE UNITED STATES AND ITS OUTLYING POSSESSIONS: LEGITIMATE CHILDREN

Date of Birth	*Citizenship Status and Residence Required of Parent(s)*	*Residence Required of Child to Retain Citizenship*
Before May 24, 1934	Father must have been a citizen and resided in U.S. before birth of the child.	None
On or after May 24, 1934, and before Jan. 13, 1941	Both parents must have been citizens; one must have resided in U.S. before birth of the child. One parent must have been a citizen and resided in the U.S. before birth of child.	None Child must have lived two years in the United States, between the ages of 14 and 28.
On or after Jan. 13, 1941, and before Dec. 24, 1952	Both parents must have been citizens; one must have resided in U.S. or an outlying possession before birth of child. One parent must have been a citizen and resided in U.S. or in an outlying possession 10 years, 5 of which were after the age of 16 years. If the citizen parent served honorably in the U.S. armed forces between Dec. 7, 1941, and Dec. 31, 1946, 5 of the 10 years of residence may be after age 12.	None Child must have lived two years in the United States or in an outlying possession, between the ages of 14 and 28, unless the parent was employed abroad by an American organization.
On or After Dec. 24, 1952	Both parents must have been citizens; one must have resided in U.S. or outlying possession before birth of child. One parent must have been a citizen, physically present in U.S. or a possession 10 years, 5 after age 14. Honorable service in U.S. armed forces counts as physical presence.	None Child must have been physically present in the United States for two continuous years, between the ages of 14 and 28.

SOURCE: Immigration and Naturalization Service.

all nationals are citizens, the main exceptions being inhabitants of some colonies who are nationals but not citizens.

In the ancient Greek city-states, citizenship was restricted to a small minority of the population. Athenian democracy did not extend political rights to women, slaves, and foreigners. In Rome, by contrast, citizenship was extended to large numbers of people in distant parts of the empire. In medieval Europe, the notion of citizenship disappeared except among the merchants living in cities and towns. The awakening of a sense of membership in a nation came with the American and French revolutions, when the word *citizen* signified the equal participation of everyone in the SOCIAL CONTRACT. In the United States, however, citizenship was not extended to blacks until the 14TH AMENDMENT to the Constitution (1868).

Citizenship by Birth. Today, all persons born in the United States and subject to its jurisdiction are citizens of the United States and of the state in which they reside. (Children of foreign diplomats are not subject to the country's jurisdiction and therefore are not citizens even if born in the United States.) This rule is called in international law *jus soli* (right of place of birth) and is followed by most English-speaking countries and most Latin American states. The rest of the world, including most European countries, recognizes *jus sanguines* (right of blood or descent) and allows citizenship to be transmitted from father to child regardless of where the child is born. These concepts frequently result in citizenship being conferred upon a person by two countries. Some countries require that a child with dual nationality choose one nationality upon reaching maturity.

Acquisition and Loss of Citizenship. Although the United States recognizes *jus soli*, persons born abroad may be citizens of the United States at birth if they meet certain conditions. Citizenship may also be acquired by NATURALIZATION, a process particularly important in the United States, which has received many immigrants.

Citizenship may be lost through expatriation. In the United States, expatriation must be a voluntary act, carried out by becoming a citizen of another country or by taking a foreign oath of allegiance. These are the only grounds for expatriation allowed under the Constitution as interpreted by the Supreme Court. Other countries, however, may take away a person's citizenship against his or her wish. In some countries a person may be deprived of citizenship for political or other reasons, by executive or legislative decree, or without advance notice or right to a hearing. In other countries a person may lose citizenship by serving in a foreign army, by evading military service, or by residing abroad for a certain period of time.

citric acid Citric acid, $C_3H_4OH(COOH)_3$, a solid, white, organic acid found in the cells of animals and plants and particularly in juices of citrus fruits, is a major intermediate product of METABOLISM. First isolated by the

Swedish chemist Carl Wilhelm Scheele in 1785, citric acid is produced industrially by fermentation for use in medicine, for flavoring food, in electroplating, plastics production, and textile printing, and as a metal-polishing agent. Slightly more acidic than acetic acid, it melts at 153° C (307° F).

citric acid cycle see KREBS CYCLE

citrine see QUARTZ

citron [sit'-ruhn] The citron is an egg-shaped fruit, the largest in the citrus family (see CITRUS FRUITS). The citron tree, *Citrus medica*, is cultivated in the Mediterranean region and in the West Indies, California, and Florida. Its white or purple flowers produce a greenish yellow fruit 15 to 25 cm (6 to 10 in) long, with a greenish pulp and a thick, aromatic rind. The rind, from which essential oils are derived, is used in pastries and candy.

citronella [sit-ruh-nel'-uh] The tropical plant citronella, or lemon-oil grass (*Cymbopogon citratus* and *C. nardus*), is cultivated in Java and Ceylon for the citronella oil that is extracted from its leaves. The fragrant, pale yellow oil is inexpensive and used widely in cheap perfume and soap, although it is better known as an insect repellent. Citronella oil contains a mixture of TERPENES, a type of organic compound common in nature.

citrus fruits Citrus fruits are the edible fruits of plants belonging to the genus *Citrus* and the closely related genus *Fortunella*, both of the family Rutaceae. The plants are spiny evergreen shrubs or trees bearing white or purplish flowers. The fruits, classed botanically as a type of berry called a hesperidium, are leathery-skinned with a fleshy interior divided into sections (locules) by parchmentlike partitions.

Citrus are native to Southeast Asia and the East Indies and have been cultivated in those areas for millennia. Most were introduced into Europe in the 12th century and are now grown in tropical and subtropical areas throughout the world, particularly in North and South America, the Mediterranean region, Australia, and South Africa.

Important Citrus Species

Commercially grown fruits belong to one of eight major citrus species. The most important is the sweet ORANGE, *C. sinensis*, which includes the popular Valencia and navel in the United States, the "blood" (red-pigmented) oranges of the Mediterranean, and the Shamouti, or Jaffa, orange of Israel.

Sour, or Seville, oranges, *C. aurantium*, are grown principally in the Seville region of Spain and are widely used in making marmalade. A sour orange variety, BERGAMOT, is grown in Italy for its aromatic rind.

Mandarins, or TANGERINES, *C. reticulata*, have a smaller fruit and a looser peel than do orange varieties.

LEMONS, *C. limon*, are grown commercially in many varieties. Because the lemon is less hardy than the orange, it is cultivated mainly in regions of low frost hazard.

LIMES, *C. aurantiifolia*, comprise two major groups: the small-fruited West Indian, or Key, lime, and the larger Persian, or Tahiti, lime. The lime is the most frost-tender of the citrus group and is cultivated primarily in tropical areas.

CITRONS, *C. medica*, are grown for their peel, primarily in Italy, Corsica, and Israel.

Pomelos, or shaddocks, *C. maxima*, are large, grapefruitlike fruit grown mostly in tropical Southeast Asia, although two new subtropical varieties have been developed in California.

GRAPEFRUIT, *C. paradisi*, are thought to be a hybrid of the pomelo. In the United States they are most widely grown as a white, seedless fruit or as a red-pigmented mutation.

Several other genera within the Rutaceae family produce fruit that is usually classed as citrus. The small, bitter KUMQUAT, *Fortunella japonica*, is widely grown for its fruit and as an ornamental plant. The trifoliate orange, *Poncirus trifoliata*, is a fairly cold-hardy deciduous plant with inedible fruit. It is used as a rootstock in commercial citrus culture.

Affinities among different species of citrus and some of their near relatives have produced many hybrids. Among the most important are the tangelos (tangerine and grapefruit); the citranges (trifoliate orange and sweet orange); and the tangors, such as king orange and temple orange, which are hybrids of sweet orange and tangerine. The products of kumquat hybridization include the limequats and citrangequats.

Propagation and Cultivation

Most modern commercial citrus orchards grow composite trees, whose rootstocks differ genetically from the tops, or scions. Rootstocks are selected for tolerance to various pests, diseases, or adverse soil conditions. The scion, chosen for its superior fruit or other desirable qualities, is grafted onto a compatible rootstock, which may be trifoliate orange, sour orange, or citrange, among many others.

Citrus fruits are the most important tropical and subtropical fruits grown commercially. Pictured (clockwise from top) *are the lemon, the grapefruit, the orange, and the ugli, a hybrid related to the tangelo.*

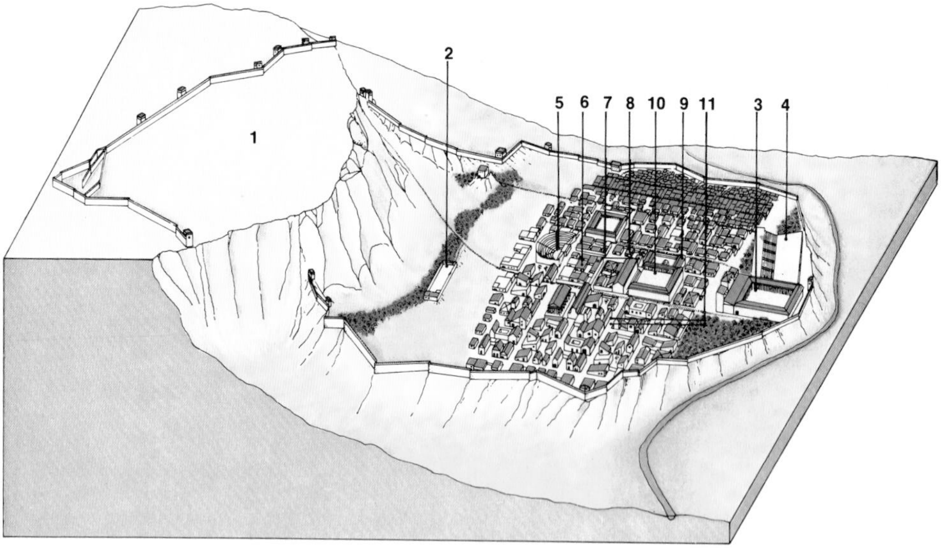

The ancient Greek city of Priene was rebuilt (c.350 BC) at the foot of Mt. Mycale. The acropolis (1) lay within the city walls, which enclosed a rectangular grid of streets. The sanctuary of Demeter (2) was on the perimeter of the city, as were the lower gymnasium (3) and the stadium (4). The theater (5) extended over two insulae (6), or blocks of the residential area. The bouleuterion (7), prytaneum (8), and sanctuary of Zeus (9) surrounded the agora (10), which was centrally located near the main street (11).

Sophisticated systems of production technology have been developed for most types of citrus. A major portion of intensive commercial citrus plantings depends on irrigation; only a minor portion is entirely rain-fed. Intensive culture usually requires several applications of pesticides and fungicides each year, use of herbicides for weed control, frequent irrigation, and ample use of nitrogen and other fertilizer elements. In the colder subtropical regions, orchard heating is necessary to lessen frost damage.

Citrus Use and World Production

Citrus is used not only as a fresh table fruit but also as an important raw material for the food industry, which processes fresh fruit into frozen-concentrated, canned, or refrigerated juice; canned segments; marmalades; cattle food made from the peel; and other by-products such as ESSENTIAL OILS, PECTIN, and chemicals.

The United States is the largest producer of citrus in the world; with about 324,000 ha (800,000 acres) of citrus groves, Florida is the leading citrus region. World production in 1981 was close to 55 million metric tons (60.6 million U.S. tons).

cittern [sit'-urn] The cittern is a plucked string instrument that flourished from the 16th through the 18th century. In its most characteristic form, the cittern's pear-shaped, flat-backed body widens at the bottom. Four or more courses of two to three metal strings stretch over a bridge and fretted neck, and are fastened by pegs.

Probably derived from the medieval citole, which in turn was adapted from the plucked fiddle, the cittern eventually evolved in various sizes. Used mostly for popular music, in England and France it was often found played in barbershops. Many collections of music were published for it in the 16th and 17th centuries.

city In general usage the term *city* is applied to any large and relatively dense concentration of population where the inhabitants are engaged primarily in nonagricultural occupations. Legal definitions are more specific. In the United States a city is an incorporated municipality; the city's boundaries and powers of self-government are set forth in a charter from the state in which it is located. In Great Britain a city is usually a town or borough with a royal charter and one that has been, or still is, the see of a bishop.

History and Development of Cities

In the 20th century the world has become more and more urbanized. Large numbers of people have left the countryside; in the United States and some countries of Western Europe, more than 75% of the population live in urban areas. Throughout most of history, however, the world was predominantly rural. People lived on the land and depended on it for food and shelter.

Ancient Cities. Cities did not become possible until humans were able to produce more than they consumed and had found ways of storing the surplus to provision large numbers of people living away from the fields. The earliest permanent settlements were in the alluvial plains of the Nile in Egypt, the Tigris and Euphrates in Mesopotamia, the Indus in India, and the Chang Jiang (Yangtze) and Huang He (Hwang Ho) in China.

Agricultural surpluses allowed individuals to specialize. The earliest cities were inhabited by officials and priests, who administered empires and invoked the gods. Around them in the city lived the lower classes—craftspersons, artisans, and laborers. The inhabitants of the city were supported by the labor of those outside it who worked on the land.

Another reason for the development of the city was defense. In ancient Greece, the typical CITY-STATE was built on a height called an acropolis, surrounded by fortifications. Since it depended on the hinterland for supplies, the city had to be strong enough to dominate and defend this area against enemies. From its walled safety the city sent out soldiers, who kept order in the hinterland and defended it from roving marauders and from incursions by other city-states.

Cities grew up at the intersections of trade routes, at harbors, and at the mouths of rivers with easy access to the sea. ATHENS, ROME, ALEXANDRIA, and CARTHAGE were near the sea. MECCA, DAMASCUS, and SAMARKAND were inland cities located on caravan routes. The trading function has been important for cities throughout history. All the major cities of the United States, including the cities of the Great Lakes and the Gulf of Mexico, began as centers of trade. The same is true of LONDON, VIENNA, STOCKHOLM, ISTANBUL, BOMBAY, HONG KONG, and SINGAPORE.

Medieval Cities. In the early Middle Ages, Europe's towns almost ceased to exist. The Muslim conquest of North Africa and Spain deprived Europe of most of the commerce that had gone through Mediterranean ports. When commerce began to revive after the 10th century, the towns grew into trading and manufacturing centers. The typical medieval town formed around a castle or walled settlement. The newer inhabitants, mainly merchants and artisans, established their quarters outside the walls and eventually came to dominate the town. The townspeople then erected new walls and fortifications, sometimes a succession of them as the town grew. Fortifications were needed when roving bands pillaged the countryside; plunder was then the primary goal of war. The city gates were closed at night and guarded. Citizens who returned late did so at their peril, and no one who did not belong was allowed in. These fortifications can still be seen in some European cities: Carcassonne in France, for example, and the Italian cities of SIENA, LUCCA, and San Gimignano.

The economic hub of the city was the marketplace, which often faced the cathedral or major church. Most medieval cities were dominated by the spires of a Gothic church, many of which remain today. The church, symbolizing the religious function of the city, also served as physical organizer of its form and as the center of the city's life. The later medieval city was also a cultural and educational center. BOLOGNA, PADUA, PARIS, and MONTPELLIER were noted for their universities.

This 19th-century engraving of Leeds, England, reveals the congestion, squalor, and pollution caused by industrialization. Poor transportation systems forced workers to live near factories. Conditions of poverty and inadequate sanitation led to epidemics.

The medieval city was not large, by either ancient or modern standards. Rome at its height under the empire probably had 800,000 inhabitants, and Carthage up to 300,000. Medieval cities rarely attained populations as large as 50,000. Among the exceptions were the larger Italian cities such as VENICE, FLORENCE, MILAN, NAPLES, and GENOA. Paris may have had 200,000 inhabitants in the 14th century, but FRANKFURT AM MAIN and BASEL in 1450 had only about 8,000, NUREMBERG 20,000, Louvain 25,000, and BRUSSELS 40,000. It was usually a half-hour walk from the center to the outskirts of a typical city. Because transportation was limited to horses or horse-drawn carts, cities had to be small and compact. To accommodate the growing populations, houses were built close together in rows, two or three stories high. The

Coastal ports, such as Naples, continued as cultural and commercial centers during and after the decline of continental cities in the early Middle Ages.

THE GROWTH OF NEW YORK CITY

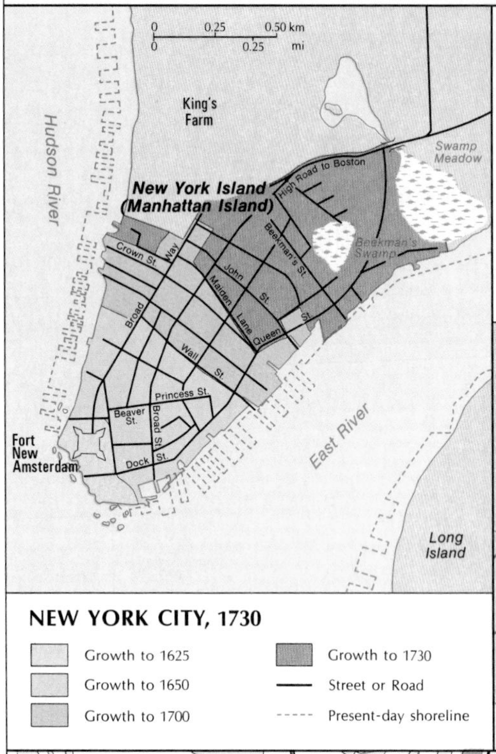

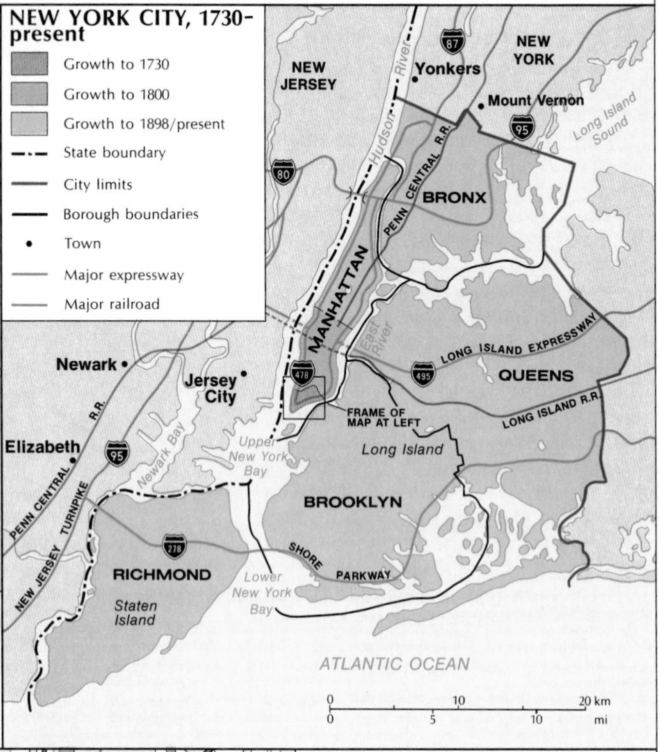

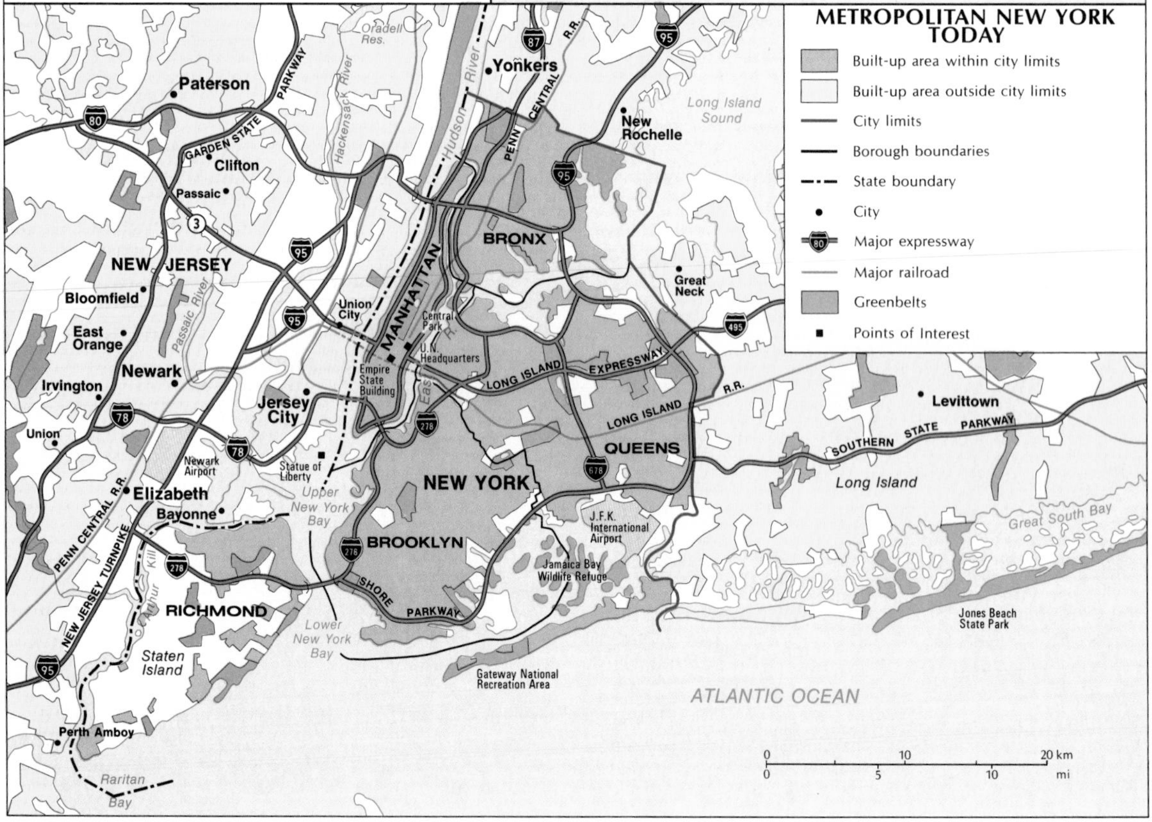

streets, rarely paved, turned to mud in bad weather.

The Industrial City. The INDUSTRIAL REVOLUTION transformed the city. With its concentration of workers and its access to trade, the city was the natural place to locate factories. Some villages turned into towns, however, and towns multiplied in size. In Britain, where the Industrial Revolution began in the latter part of the 18th century, the number of towns of 5,000 inhabitants or more increased from 106 in 1801 to 265 in 1851, and to 622 by 1891. Nearly 20 million people lived in urban districts of 5,000 or more by 1891. People came in large numbers from the countryside to work in the factories and to live in the cheap, jerry-built housing that was constructed near the new industrial sites. The sanitary conditions and water supplies of these industrial towns were dismally inadequate, and epidemics of typhoid, cholera, and dysentery were frequent. Tuberculosis was a common cause of death.

In the United States, by 1890, one-third of the population lived in towns. From 1880 to 1890, the number of U.S. cities of 45,000–75,000 increased from 23 to 39. CHICAGO doubled in size during that decade; DETROIT, MILWAUKEE, COLUMBUS, and CLEVELAND grew by 80%. Industrialization in the United States coincided with heavy immigration from Europe, and by 1890 one-fifth of the inhabitants of the cities were foreign-born. In the Northeast more than half the population lived in towns of more than 4,000 people. Although industrialization transformed the cities of Europe, it furnished the very basis of urban development in America.

The expansion of the city in the industrial era was made possible by improvements in transportation. The building of canals, followed by the great railroad boom in the latter part of the 19th century, enabled the industrial towns to draw their materials from great distances. In the early cities, workers had to live within walking distance of their place of employment, and the city itself was limited in size to the distance a person could cover on foot. In the 19th century, public transportation enabled a somewhat greater dispersion of the population away from the center, although in most industrial towns workers still lived close to the factories. Trolley lines had been established in 300 U.S. cities by 1886. Cities began to spread in star-shaped patterns along streetcar lines and suburban railroads. The major effect of industrialization on the city in the 19th century, however, was the destruction of the physical form inherited from the past. In place of the old, narrow, winding streets, the industrial city was characterized by more or less uniform rectangular blocks that could be laid out wherever there was an open space. The factory and the slum became the most conspicuous features.

By the end of the 19th century, many U.S. cities had paved main streets. Since most of these cities were located on rivers or harbors, it was necessary to build bridges as the cities grew. The BROOKLYN BRIDGE, completed in 1883, was an engineering achievement that ushered in a period of municipal bridge building. But traffic congestion continued to be a major problem. Elevated railroads were built in NEW YORK, Chicago, KANSAS CITY, BOSTON, and other cities and were later followed by subways.

(Opposite page) *Three maps indicate the chronological expansion of New York City.* (Top left) *The site of the original Dutch settlement is illustrated by shaded portions of the map.* (Bottom) *The metropolitan area exceeds the city limits, encompassing portions of Long Island and New Jersey.*

New York is the largest city in the United States and one of the world's leading financial centers. Because Manhattan's physical expansion is circumscribed by its topography, massive skyscrapers have been built.

By 1880, 138 telephone exchanges were operating in U.S. cities. Electric lighting began to replace kerosene and gas. The development of plumbing and municipal sewage systems made the cities more habitable, although the congestion, pollution, and noise continued to increase.

The Contemporary City

The contemporary U.S. city differs greatly from both the old industrial city and the traditional city of Europe. In the United States the widespread use of the automobile has acted as a centrifugal force, dispersing population from the central city outward into the suburbs and even beyond. Another form of transportation, the elevator, has had the opposite effect of concentrating workers in skyscraper office buildings in the heart of the city. Consequently there is a great tidal surge of humanity into the city in the morning and out again at night.

The expansion of the suburbs was also fostered by governmental policies that had consequences not foreseen by their initiators. The federal income tax was used as a lever to encourage home ownership by permitting homeowners to deduct the interest on mortgage loans from their taxable incomes. Other laws enabled middle-income families to obtain mortgages on relatively easy terms. Families moved outward into a world of lawns, privacy, open space, and new schools. By the 1970s most cities were surrounded by residential satellites over which they had no political control. While the suburbs depended in many ways on the city for their existence, they had little interest in the city's problems.

The former city residents were replaced by lower-income people who migrated from the countryside, particularly from the South. The city increasingly became the home of the very poor, many of them drawn there because of its public welfare institutions. Thus, the tax revenues of cities decreased while their expenditures increased.

The difficulties of the cities were aggravated by the departure of industry and big business. No longer tied to rail and water transportation, and drawn by lower rentals and often cheaper labor costs, light industry could move out to the suburbs and even into the countryside.

The Rise of Megalopolis

The dispersal of urban areas led to a new type of social entity that was not circumscribed by the political boundaries of the city. In the United States it was called the metropolitan area and consisted of a city and its adjacent suburbs, some lying 32 km (20 mi) outside the city proper. A few metropolitan areas constitute one continuous urban belt, such as the one extending from Boston to Washington, D.C., more than 960 km (about 600 mi) long and about 50 to 160 km (30 to 100 mi) wide. About 40 million people live in this "Boswash" area. Similar areas have emerged in California, around the Great Lakes in Illinois and Indiana, in England (London and the Midlands), in the Ruhr basin of Germany, and in the highly congested Tokyo and Osaka region of Japan.

European cities have grown more gradually than those of the United States, and no wholesale flight to the suburbs has occurred. But they too suffer from the traffic congestion that is endemic in other large cities of the world.

Some cities in Asia and Latin America have grown to enormous size even though the countries as a whole are still largely rural. In fact, the urban population of poor countries now equals or exceeds that of the industrialized countries. Mexico City has a metropolitan-area population of about 20 million people, and Shanghai about 12 million. Other large cities such as Bombay, Cairo, Calcutta, Jakarta, Manila, and São Paulo are growing at explosive rates. These cities tend to grow from the outside rather than the inside; that is, the migrants from rural areas settle on the periphery rather than in the central cities. Shantytowns, built out of oil drums and corrugated metal sheets, surround many cities in developing countries.

Urban Renewal in the United States

The vast and unplanned growth of many cities has created problems that are beyond the capacity of the cities themselves to handle. In the larger U.S. cities, one often finds an inner city of poverty, inhabited by masses of people who are supported by public welfare and who suffer from unemployment, inadequate housing, poor schools, drug problems, and a high incidence of crime. Escape from the inner city to the suburbs is difficult because low-income housing is generally lacking there.

The Need for Metropolitan Government. Some urban areas, such as those of Miami, Fla., and Minneapolis–Saint Paul, Minn., have developed governmental bodies that are capable of dealing with some of the problems confronting the cities and their satellite towns. But in most urban areas an effective approach is hampered by the lack of an overall metropolitan authority. For example, New York City's metropolitan area lies in the states of New York, Connecticut, and New Jersey. Chicago's lies in Illinois and Indiana, and Detroit's covers parts of two counties. The metropolitan area of Boston is made up of 78 cities and towns, each with its own administration.

Federal Efforts. The U.S. government has made a number of attempts to help the cities address their problems. The Housing Acts of 1949 and 1954 were directed toward the replanning and rebuilding of blighted areas in central cities. Under them federal money was allotted to cities that created renewal agencies and made their own plans. The money was used to buy and assemble tracts of land and demolish the old buildings on them. These tracts were then resold to developers who entered competitive bids. Among the cities that embarked on large projects, Philadelphia and Boston had considerable suc-

Los Angeles continues to grow and expand, absorbing the smaller communities around it. Whereas the proliferating suburbs contribute to the city's horizontal growth, the construction of skyscrapers introduces vertical expansion. Suburbs and city are connected by labyrinthine systems of freeways.

(Above) *Tokyo's subways, used by millions of workers every day, employ "pushers" to crowd commuters into the trains. Tokyo's freeway and public transportation systems are continually clogged by its vast population.*

(Left) *Tokyo has the same transportation, pollution, and housing problems faced by most of the world's major cities. A thriving economy, superior social services, and a homogenous population, however, have mitigated the urban difficulties.*

cess in renewing their central city areas. The urban renewal agencies often created consternation, however, by acquiring land and buildings through their power of eminent domain from people who did not want to move, and charges were made that the agencies simply removed slum dwellers and replaced them with middle-income people.

Other federal programs followed, aimed at improving conditions in the cities. The extent to which they fell short was demonstrated by the RACE RIOTS and incidents of large-scale arson and looting that erupted in the slums of many major cities in the late 1960s. Since then, additional decay has occurred in areas such as the South Bronx in New York City, which by the 1990s had become a national symbol of urban blight.

New Towns

Advocates of city planning, faced with the insuperable problems of existing cities, have often turned to designing NEW TOWNS. They have had their greatest success in England, where Sir Ebenezer Howard began the GARDEN CITY movement at the turn of the century. After World War II the British built 28 new towns, many having their own industries and all carefully planned. These new towns were able to house millions of people near Greater London, MANCHESTER, BIRMINGHAM, and other urban-industrial areas. France, too, in the 1950s and 1960s, developed half a dozen new towns in the areas around Paris, GRENOBLE, and ROUEN.

City of God, The *The City of God* (Latin: *De civitate Dei*), written between AD 413 and 426, was Saint AUGUSTINE's answer to the pagan philosopher Volusanius's contention that the adoption of Christianity by Constantine had led to the Visigoths' sack of Rome in 410. In his treatise Augustine dismisses the pagan position and interprets history in terms of Christian revelation: there are "two cities," the Christian city devoted to God and the earthly pagan city (Babylon) devoted to the devil, prey to moral confusion and strife, and slated for destruction.

city government see MUNICIPAL GOVERNMENT

city planning see URBAN PLANNING

city-state The city-state is a unit of government in which sovereignty is exercised by an independent city. The term is used most often to refer to the polis, the autonomous city of ancient GREECE.

The Greek city-states, of which ATHENS and SPARTA were the most important, originally numbered several hundred. Their sovereignty extended to the countryside around them and embraced both political and social life. Although democracy as practiced in Athens in its heyday is frequently associated with the city-state, many forms of government were represented, including absolute monarchy, military dictatorship, and aristocracy. Even in those city-states with democratic governments, participation was limited to citizens—a category that excluded slaves, women, and others.

The Italian cities of the Renaissance are other examples of autonomous cities. Florence, Genoa, Milan, and Venice were all at various times among the Italian free COMMUNES, or corporate entities. In the 12th century several German trading cities on the Baltic coast, including Bremen, Hamburg, and Lübeck, emerged as independent states. They formed the HANSEATIC LEAGUE in the 13th century.

ILLUSTRATION CREDITS

The following list credits or acknowledges, by page, the source of illustrations used in this volume. When two or more illustrations appear on one page, they are credited individually left to right, top to bottom; their credits are separated by semicolons. When both the photographer or artist and an agency or other source are given for an illustration, they are usually separated by a slash. Those illustrations not cited below are credited on the page on which they appear, either in the caption or alongside the illustration itself.

6 Bell Laboratories; The Bettmann Archive
7 St. Francis Xavier Chapel, NY
9 Photo Researchers/Robert Ashworth; Photo Researchers/Charlie Ott; Photo Researchers/Arthur Markowitz; Photo Researchers/Charlie Ott; Photo Researchers/Kjell B. Sandved
12 Scala, Florence
13 Lothar Roth and Associates
15 The Hark Group Ltd./Slidemakers
16 Sygma/Tom Zimberoff
18 Photo Researchers/Van Bucher
19 Photo Researchers/C. R. Belinky; The Bettmann Archive
21 Photo Researchers/C. A. Peterson
23 Photo Trends
24 Archivo di Stato, Siena
25 Photographie Giraudon
26 The Bettmann Archive
28 Rand McNally & Company
29 The Image Bank/Larry Lee
30 The Image Bank/Richard Steedman; Photo Researchers/Van Bucher
31 Photo Researchers; The Image Bank/ Harald Sund
32 Photo Researchers/Porterfield-Chickering; Photo Researchers/Van Bucher
33 The Image Bank/G. L. C. Kenny; Photo Researchers/Bradley Smith
34 Photo Researchers/Georg Gerster; Photo Researchers/Tom McHugh
37 UPI/Bettmann Newsphotos; UPI/ Bettmann Newsphotos
38 Universiteits-Bibliotheek van Amersterdam; Bibliothèque Nationale, Paris
40 Courtesy of Donald M. Anderson; Victoria and Albert Museum
41 Paul C. Pet
42 Bibliothèque Nationale, Paris
44 Photographie Giraudon
47 Rand McNally & Company
48 Photo Researchers/Paolo Koch; Gamma-Liaison/J. C. Labbe
52 Art Resource
58 AGE/World Photo Service
59 Rand McNally & Company
61 The Bettmann Archive
63 The Bettmann Archive
65 Photo Researchers/Paolo Koch
66–67 Rand McNally & Company
68 Photo Researchers/Björn Bölstad; Photo Researchers/Björn Bölstad
69 Camera Press/P. Hunter
70 Josef Muench; Photo Researchers/ Paolo Koch
71 Canapress Photo Service
72 Photo Researchers/Joe Munroe; Photo Researchers/Michael Philip Manheim
73 Camera Press/Richard Harrington
74 AGE/World Photo Service
75 Photo Researchers/Russ Kinne
77 Courtesy The Huntington Library
78 The National Gallery of Canada
79 The Bettmann Archive
80 Public Archives of Canada
81 Confederation Life Collection
82 Public Archives of Canada; Public Archives of Canada
85 Public Archives of Canada
86 Photo Researchers/James Hanley
88 Photo Researchers/Don Morgan
89 Nakash/Montreal
92 The Bettmann Archive; Mirèille Vautier; Zentrale Farbbild Agentur Zefa/UWS
96 All pictures—Courtesy Skin Cancer Foundation
100 Medical Images/Janet Hayes
102 Photo Researchers/Michael Philip Manheim
103 © 1987 Discover Publications: Paola Villa
104 Mas Ampliaciones y Reproducciones
108 Barnaby's Picture Library
109 Photographie Giraudon
110 The Bettmann Archive
114 Explorer; Rand McNally & Company
119 Woodfin Camp and Associates/ Timothy Eagan
120 Culver Pictures
121 The Bettmann Archive
123 Photo Researchers/Gianni Tortoli
143 Stock Boston/Bill Gillette
147 Foto-archief Spaarnestad
149 Photographie Giraudon
151 The Bettmann Archive
152 Scala, Florence
154 The Bettmann Archive
155 The Bettmann Archive
157 White House Historical Society
158 AGE/F. Penzel
159 Aldus Archives
160 The Bettmann Archive; Magnum Photos/Henri Cartier-Bresson
161 Aretê Archives; Aretê Archives
162 The Bettmann Archive; Bill Mauldin and Wil-Jo Associates, Inc. © 1944 (Reprinted by permission.)
163 Los Angeles Times syndicate; The Bettmann Archive
164 Photo Researchers/Carl Frank
171 Photo Researchers/Stephanie Dinkins; Photo Researchers/Paolo Koch
175 The Bettmann Archive
177 Photographie Giraudon
181 Art Resource/SCALA
184 Culver Pictures
187 Sem Presser
188 Scala, Florence
190 Photographie Giraudon
191 Brown Brothers
192 Photographie Giraudon; Photographie Giraudon
197 Photo Researchers/Joe Monroe; Travel Bureau of Lansing, Michigan
199 Rand McNally & Company
205 The Image Bank/Marc Romanelli
206 Scala, Florence
218 Scala, Florence
219 Holle Bildarchiv; Magnum Photos/Eric Lessing; Holle Bildarchiv
222 F. L. Smidth and Company
224 Photo Researchers/Paolo Koch; Paul C. Pet
225 UPI/Bettmann Newsphotos; Culver Pictures
226 UPI/Bettmann Newsphotos
228 The Bettmann Archive
230 Rand McNally & Company
231 Photo Researchers/Victor Englebert
235 Het Spectrum
239 Culver Pictures
240 Scala, Florence
242 Photo Researchers/Victor Englebert
243 Rand McNally & Company
244 Scala, Florence
246 Photo Researchers/Russ Kinne
247 The Bettmann Archive
248 The Bettmann Archive
249 Ullstein Bilderdienst
252 The Bettmann Archive
254 The Hark Group Ltd./Slidemakers
255 Rand McNally & Company; Vandaag BV
259 The Hark Group Ltd./Slidemakers
260 Institut für die Geschichte der Medizin Universität Wien
262 The Bettmann Archive
263 UPI/Bettmann Newsphotos
264 Scala, Florence
265 National Portrait Gallery, London
266 Photographie Giraudon
267 Photographie Giraudon
270 Photographie Giraudon
272 Photo Researchers/Fred J. Maroon
276 Photographie Giraudon
277 National Portrait Gallery, London
278 UPI/Bettmann Newsphotos
282 Black Star/Brownie Harris
283 The Bettmann Archive
284 Daily Telegraph Color Library; The Bettmann Archive
288 Photo Researchers/E. A. Heiniger; Photo Researchers/Sam C. Pierson, Jr.
293 Superstock/Shostal/Forbert
295 Scala, Florence; The Bettmann Archive
296 The Bettmann Archive; Cooper Bridgman Library; The Bettmann Archive
297 The Bettmann Archive; The Bettmann Archive
298 The Bettmann Archive; The Bettmann Archive
299 The Bettmann Archive
300 The Bettmann Archive
301 Library of Congress
302 Photo Researchers/Russ Kinne
305 UPI/Bettmann Newsphotos
307 The Bettmann Archive
308 Smithsonian Institution/Washington, D.C. National Anthropological Archives, Bureau of American Ethnology Collection
309 UPI/Bettmann Newsphotos
310 Hedrich Blessing
311 Lothar Roth and Associates
313 UPI/Bettmann Newsphotos; Mirèille Vautier
320 The Bettmann Archive
322 Scala, Florence
323 Frederick Warne & Sons. Reprinted by permission.; From *The Pooh Story Book* by A. A. Milne. Compilation and new illustrations © 1965 by E. P. Dutton & Co., Inc. Reprinted by permission.; Courtesy Harper & Row © 1970. Reprinted by permission.
325 Rand McNally & Company
326 Photo Researchers/Tom McHugh; Photo Researchers/Carl Frank
331 Vandaag BV; Magnum Photos; Photo Researchers/Brian Brake
332–333 Rand McNally & Company
334 Photo Researchers/Brian Brake; Sipa Press/Chine Nouvelle
335 Scala, Florence; Magnum Photos/ Rene Burri
336 Black Star/Peter Turnley
337 TSW/Click Chicago/Peter Carmichael
338 Magnum Photos/Marc Riboud
340 The British Museum; Lothar Roth & Associates
341 Audrey Topping; Lothar Roth & Associates
342 Bibliothèque Nationale, Paris; Photographie Giraudon; Bibliothèque Nationale, Paris
343 Photographie Giraudon; Scala, Florence
344 Mary Evans Picture Library; Polyvisie bv
345 Lothar Roth & Associates
346 Lothar Roth & Associates; Foreign Language Press
347 Sovfoto/Eastfoto
354 Robert Harding Associates
355 Agence De Presse Photografique Rapho; Scala, Florence
357 Superstock/Shostal/Scholz
364 UPI/Bettmann Newsphotos
367 Photo Researchers/George Whitely
371 The Bettmann Archive; The Bettmann Archive
373 The Bettmann Archive; Martha Swope Associates
379 Universal Pictorial Press and Agency Ltd.; The Bettmann Archive
380 The Bettmann Archive
381 Het Spectrum
386 The Bettmann Archive
388 © Karsh, Ottawa
390 The Bettmann Archive
393 Photo Researchers/Russ Kinne
394 The Walt Disney Company; Sygma/ Nancy Moran
404 Picture Archives
405 Howard Brainen/Visualeyes; Howard Brainen/Visualeyes
407 Photo Researchers/Russ Kinne
411 Art Resource; BBC Hulton Picture Library
413 Photo Researchers/George Holton
414 Photo Researchers/Tom McHugh
415 Photo Researchers/Georg Gerster; Photo Researchers/Brian Brake